Handbook of Parenting

Volume 3
Status and Social Conditions of Parenting

Handbook of Parenting

Volume 3
Status and Social Conditions of Parenting

Edited by
Marc H. Bornstein
National Institute of Child Health and Human Development

LEA LAWRENCE ERLBAUM ASSOCIATES, PUBLISHERS
1995 Mahwah, New Jersey   Hove, UK

Copyright © 1995 by Lawrence Erlbaum Associates, Inc.
 All rights reserved. No part of this book may be reproduced in any form, by photostat, microfilm, retrieval system, or any other means, without the prior written permission of the publisher.

Lawrence Erlbaum Associates, Inc., Publishers
10 Industrial Avenue
Mahwah, New Jersey 07430

Library of Congress Cataloging-in-Publication Data

Handbook of parenting / edited by Marc H. Bornstein.
     p. cm.
    Includes bibliographical references and indexes.
    Contents: v. 1. Children and parenting — v. 2. Biology and ecology of parenting — v. 3. Status and social conditions of parenting — v. 4. Applied and practical parenting.
    ISBN 0-8058-1085-4 (cloth : set : alk. paper). — ISBN 0-8058-1892-8 (cloth : v. 1 : alk. paper). — ISBN 0-8058-1893-6 (cloth : v. 2 : alk. paper). — ISBN 0-8058-1894-4 (cloth : v. 3 : alk. paper). — ISBN 0-8058-1895-2 (cloth: v. 4 : alk. paper).
    1. Parenting. 2. Parents. I. Bornstein, Marc H.
HQ755.8.H357 1995
649'.1--dc20   95-30114
                                                               CIP

Books published by Lawrence Erlbaum Associates are printed on acid-free paper, and their bindings are chosen for strength and durability.

Printed in the United States of America
10 9 8 7 6 5 4 3 2

For *Marian* and *Harold Sackrowitz*

Contents of Volume 3: Status and Social Conditions of Parenting

PART I: WHO IS THE PARENT

PART II: SOCIAL CONDITIONS OF PARENTING

Foreword

Edward Zigler
Yale University

Parenting has been described as the most challenging and complex of all the tasks of adulthood. It can also be argued that there is no undertaking that is more important to the life of the human community. Yet that community rarely offers adequate guidance, support, or preparation for parenthood; with today's mobile life style and changing family structure, even the cross-generational passing down of parental wisdom that once occurred is no longer common. Our understanding of what it means to be a parent has undergone considerable revision and has taken on many new dimensions.

Today's parents face what may be unprecedented levels of social and economic stress. The growing incidence of such major social problems as poverty, homelessness, violence, crime, and substance abuse makes it difficult for parents to create a decent life for themselves, much less protect their offspring from harm and plan for their children's future. Such stress is most deeply felt by economically disadvantaged and single parents, most of whom are women. In many cases the double disadvantage of poverty and single parenting is combined with extreme youth: The number of teen births continues to rise, making the future precarious for both the child and her young mother.

Among two-parent families in the U.S., both parents typically work outside the home to make ends meet. Although about 44 percent of single mothers with children under 3 work outside the home, an even larger number (57 percent) of under-3s in two-parent families have mothers in the labor force. Thus, there is a special stress even among parents fortunate enough to have employment: the stress of having too little time to spend with one's child. The typical child spent about 30 hours per week with a parent in 1965; by the 1980s, this interaction time had declined to about 17 hours.

These are truly hard times for parents. And to make matters worse, a large number of adults in the so-called "sandwich" generation are called on to assume care of their own elderly parents, even as they struggle to nurture their young children. What's more, parents living in the UnitedStates must tackle all of these challenges largely without the considerable social supports offered by other industrialized nations. Such supports include paid parental leaves, government-subsidized child care, health care, parent education, and other services for families. Although there has been an increased interest in supportive programming and some improvement in meeting family needs, such as the passage of an unpaid parental leave in the form of the Family and Medical Leave Act, parents in most communities, and the practitioners who serve them, are themselves in need of both nurturance and guidance.

The *Handbook of Parenting* should prove invaluable in meeting this need for expert guidance, and the knowledge imparted by the four volumes of the *Handbook* may also help to meet the critical need for increased family supports by enlightening policymakers. At minimum, the stellar contributors assembled for the *Handbook of Parenting* succeed admirably in their attempt to capture and describe the myriad aspects of parenting today.

This is not a handbook in the sense of a manual, although the chapters describing what it is like, for example, to parent a child born prematurely or how to foster sound moral development in one's offspring offer valuable insights that will guide parents. Rather, the volumes that make up the *Handbook* offer a comprehensive account of the state of our scientific and social knowledge regarding virtually every facet of parenting, from a social history of the topic to its psychological, educational, medical, legal, and even its public policy aspects.

These volumes have an extraordinary scope in that the authors share with us an impressive breadth, as well as depth, of experience and learning. The writers are acknowledged experts in their individual fields, and they represent a remarkable diversity of perspective. But this comprehensive approach is essential to reveal the social ecology of parenthood. Just as we have learned that the child does not develop in isolation from the environments of the family, home, school, and child-care setting, parenting also does not take place in a social vacuum.

All of the forces that make up the larger sociopolitical world create the context in which parents must nurture, educate, and struggle to understand their children, and themselves as parents. The *Handbook of Parenting* offers us a detailed roadmap to that context and it tells us a good deal about the needs, beliefs, troubles, wishes, and triumphs of the parents who inhabit our increasingly complex society. The contributors to this excellent compendium have provided a great resource for parents and for the clinicians, educators, and other professionals who attempt to assist parents in carrying on their important work as guardians of the next generation.

Foreword

Robert A. Hinde
St. John's College, Cambridge

It is easy to forget how rapidly ideas about parenting have changed. I was brought up as a Truby King baby. Influenced by this New Zealand pediatrician, my father, also a physician, believed that babies should be fed on a strict 6-hour schedule. Whenever we visited my father after our first child was born, at 6 p.m. he would start to fidget in his chair and say, "Isn't it time he was nursed?" But by then I was much influenced by Niko Tinbergen, the Nobel Prize winning ethologist and my mentor, who used to say "When the baby cries, it is a sign stimulus to the mother requiring attention, and she in turn is predisposed to respond with caregiving behavior." The parenting books that I remember from that time were mostly concerned with caring for the physical needs of the baby, but there was the early Spock, letting the child express himself or herself, and all that. With John Bowlby, psychological issues came right to the fore, with emphasis on the importance of the parent–child relationship and the nature of the child's attachment to the parent.

Now that we recognize that parenting depends on the baby as well as the parent, now that we see the importance of sensitive parenting, of gentle control and setting limits, of scaffolding and the furthering of exploration, we feel we have gotten it right. Have we? An historical eye should tell us there is no reason to think that the changes we have seen will just stop here. Quite apart from the possibility of new insights, the world is changing, and parenting practice is inevitably influenced by the world outside. That is clearly shown by the dilemma that Bowlby bequeathed—babies need a sensitive caregiver, but post-World War II cultural norms led mothers to want something outside the home—a frustrated mother is not a happy mother, and a mother who is not happy is unlikely to be a sensitive caregiver. So we must beware of thinking we have final solutions.

We may not have a final solution, we may not be right on all counts, but at least we know now that we cannot rely on ubiquitously applicable firm dicta about "what parents should do." Parenting practices must fit the child, the parents, and the culture. And if we are to move toward that goal we must have, not generalizations and precepts, but knowledge of process, of the dynamics of parent–child interaction and its consequences for the child and for the parent.

That is why these volumes will without doubt be a pediatric landmark. They synthesize what we now know about parenting practices, about the dynamics of parent–child relationships, about the family context in which parenting occurs, and about the role of cultural norms. And they do so not by making broad generalizations but by bringing together different views, different aspects, and different problems that arise. For example, most of the research on parenting has been done in Europe and North America, and it is easy to slip into assuming that a generalization about parenting in the United States is a generalization about parenting. One of the most refreshing things about these volumes is that so many of the authors recognize the limits of their generalizations, and point to the need for more cross-cultural data. They leave no room for thinking that the dynamics of the mother–daughter relationship, for example, is just the same in Burundi and Boston, or even in Cambridge, England and Cambridge, Massachusetts. The way the volumes are organized shows not only that mothers in general are different from fathers (which is not to say that the one cannot take on the other's role), but that parents are not the only ones who parent, and that children of different ages and with different problems need different sorts of treatment. It implies that parenting has multiple determinants—hormonal, psychological, social, sociological, cultural, historical, and ecological.

The diversity of approaches in these volumes will elicit different responses, but I would emphasize three issues. First, parenting practices must fit the child. Parent–child interaction differs with gender of parent and gender of child, and perhaps should so differ. The issues for infants differ from those of middle and later childhood and adolescence; and they differ for healthy children and children with handicaps. Second, it is the parent–child *relationship* that matters. And, as many of the authors emphasize, this is not something that is imposed by the parent, but something that is co-constructed by parent and child. They are in it together, for better or worse. That means that in real life, one is always dealing with a particular parent and a particular child co-constructing a particular relationship: Parental sensitivity means sensitivity to this child and not necessarily to that one.

Third, because parenting has multiple determinants, there are multiple ways in which parents can be helped. Parents' attitudes and beliefs are important, and most parents are eager for advice. But beyond that, in many parts of the world, there is much that can be done to smooth their way, to increase the chances that they will be able to provide a secure base for their children to lead full and happy lives. And that raises another issue, of how parents' lives are changed materially, socially, and psychologically by what they have become. However, this book is about parenting and not about parents.

I'm sure this book will be a landmark, and I am sure that many will be profoundly grateful to Marc Bornstein and all who have taken part in this challenging and timely enterprise.

Preface

Does parenting come naturally, or must we learn how to parent? What does it mean to be the parent of a preterm baby, of twins, or of a child with a disability? To be an older parent, or one who is divorced, disabled, or abusing drugs? How do personality, knowledge, and world view affect parenting skills? What roles do history, social class, and culture play in shaping parenthood? How should parents relate to schools, daycare, pediatricians, and other everyday nonfamilial influences on their children? These are just a few of the many questions addressed in the *Handbook of Parenting*. This is not a book on how to parent, but rather one on *what being a parent is all about*.

Put succinctly, parents create people. It is the particular and continuing task of parents to prepare the next generation for the physical, economic, and psychosocial situations in which it is to survive and thrive. Whatever other influences on child development there may be, parents are the "final common pathway" to childhood oversight and caregiving, development and stature. Human social inquiry—at least since the Athenians expressed interest in Spartan childrearing practices—has almost always, as a matter of course, included reports of parenting.

Despite the fact that most people become parents and everyone who ever lived has had parents, parenting remains a mystifying subject about which almost everyone has opinions, but about which few people agree. Freud once listed bringing up children as one of the three "impossible professions"—the other two being governing nations and psychoanalysis. One would probably encounter as many views as the number of people one cares to ask about the relative merits of being an at-home or working mother, about whether daycare, family care, or parent care is best for a child, about whether parenting depends on intuition or technique. Moreover, we are witnessing the emergence of striking permutations on the theme of parenting: single parenthood, blended families, lesbian and gay parents, teen versus 50s first-time moms and dads.

The *Handbook of Parenting* is concerned with different types of parents—mothers and fathers, single, adolescent, and adoptive parents—with basic characteristics of parenting—behaviors, knowledge, beliefs, and expectations about parenting—with forces that shape parenting—how employment, social class, culture, and environment contribute to parenthood—with problems faced by parents— the special circumstances of handicap, unhappy marriage, or drug addiction—and with practical concerns of parenting—how to talk to pediatricians, promote children's health, foster social adjustment and cognitive competence, interact with schools, and mediate with children's peers. Contributors to the *Handbook of Parenting* have worked in different ways toward understanding all these diverse aspects of parenting, and all look to the most recent research and thinking in the field to shed light on many topics every parent has wondered about at one time or another.

The *Handbook of Parenting* is divided into four volumes, each with two parts:

Volume 1 concerns children and parenting. Human development is too subtle, dynamic, and intricate to admit that parental caregiving alone determines the course and outcome of ontogeny. Volume 1 of the *Handbook of Parenting* begins intentionally with essays concerned with how children influence parenting. The chapters in Part I, "Parenting Children and the Elderly," discuss the special demands and unique rewards of parenting infants, toddlers, youngsters in middle childhood, and adolescents as well as the modern notion of parenting the elderly. The chapters in Part II, "Parenting Various Kinds of Children," discuss such common matters as parenting siblings and girls versus boys as well as more unique situations of parenting twins, children born preterm, and those with special needs, such as Down syndrome, aggressive and withdrawn disorders, and notable talent.

Volume 2 concerns the biology and ecology of parenting. To be understood as a whole, the psychophysiological and sociological determinants of parenting need to be brought into the picture. Volume 2 relates parenting to its biological roots and sets parenting in its ecological framework. The chapters in Part I, "Biology of Parenting," examine hormonal and psychobiological determinants of parenting in nonhumans and in human beings, parenting in other species, and biological universals in human parenting. The chapters in Part II, "Ecology of Parenting," examine maternal and dual-earner employment status and parenting, socioeconomic, ethnic, cultural, environmental, and historical issues associated with parenting, and also provide a developmental contextual perspective on parenting.

Volume 3 concerns the status and social conditions of parenting. Someone must parent children, and the different someones who do each have their own habits. Volume 3 distinguishes among the cast of characters responsible for parenting and is revealing of the psychological make-ups and social interests of those individuals. Chapters in Part I, "Who Is the Parent," consider successively mothering, fathers and families, single parenthood, grandparenthood, adolescent parenthood, non-parental caregiving, sibling caregivers, parenting adopted children, parenting in divorced and remarried families, and lesbian and gay parenthood. The chapters in Part II, "Social Conditions of Parenting," consider determinants of the transition to parenting, parents' knowledge, expectations, beliefs, and attitudes toward childrearing, as well as parenting in relation to social networks, public policy, and the law.

Volume 4 concerns applied and practical parenting. Parenting is not easy, nor does it go well all of the time. Volume 4 describes problems of parenting and how they are (sometimes) overcome as well as the promotion of positive parenting practices. The chapters in Part I, "Applied Issues in Parenting," explore maternal deprivation, marital interaction and parenting, parenting with a sensory or physical disability, psychologically depressed and substance abusing parents, and parental dysfunction in child maltreatment. The chapters in Part II, "Practical Considerations in Parenting," explore parents and their children's doctors, health promotion, and discipline and child compliance, parenting vis-à-vis children's moral development and cognitive competence, everyday stresses and parenting, the roles which child temperament, television, and play have in parenting, and parents and their children's associations with peers, child care, and schools.

Each chapter in the *Handbook of Parenting* addresses a different but central topic in parenting; each is rooted in current thinking and theory as well as classical and modern research in that topic; each has been written to be read and absorbed in a single sitting. Each chapter follows (more or less) closely a standard organization, including an introduction to the chapter as a whole, followed by historical considerations of the topic, a discussion of central issues and theory, a review of classical and modern research, forecasts of future directions of theory and research, and a conclusion section. Of course, each chapter considers contributors' own convictions and research, but contributors to the *Handbook of Parenting* present all major points of view and central lines of inquiry and interpret them broadly. The *Handbook of Parenting* is intended to be comprehensive and state-of-the-art. To state that parenting is complex is to understate the obvious. As the scope of the *Handbook of Parenting* shows, parenting is naturally and closely allied with many other fields.

The *Handbook of Parenting* is concerned less with child outcomes of parenting, and more with the nature and dimensions of variations in parenting per se. Beyond an impressive range of information, readers will find passim typologies of parenting (e.g., authoritarian–autocratic, indulgent–permissive, indifferent–uninvolved, authoritative–reciprocal), theories of parenting (e.g., psychoanalytic, etho-logical, behavioral, sociobiological), conditions of parenting (e.g., mother versus father, cross-cultural, situation-by-age-by-style), recurrent themes in parenting studies (e.g., attachment, transaction, ecological systems), and even aphorisms (e.g., "A child should have strict discipline in order to develop a fine, strong character," "The child is father to the man"). Patterns of parenting may converge, reflecting inherent truisms, or the historical intersection of styles, or the increasing prevalence of a single pattern through migration or dissemination via mass media. In the end, parents wish to promote general competencies in their offspring, and some do so in manifestly similar ways. Others do so in different ways, and of course specific patterns of parenting are adapted to specific settings and needs. Therefore, variation in parenting philosophies, values, beliefs, ideas, and practices are widespread.

In the course of editing this *Handbook,* I wrote extensive notes abstracting central messages and critical points of view expressed in each chapter fully intending to construct a comprehensive introduction to these volumes. In the end, I took away two significant impressions from my own efforts and the texts of my collaborators in this work. First, my notes cumulated to a near-monograph on parenting ... clearly inappropriate for an introduction. Second, when all was written and done, I found the chorus of contributors to the *Handbook* more eloquent and compelling than my own lone voice could ever be. Each chapter in the *Handbook* begins with an introduction that lays out, in a clarity, expressiveness, and force I could only envy, the meanings and implications of that contribution and that perspective to the parenting whole. In lieu of one introduction, readers are urged to browse the many introductions that lead the way into the *Handbook of Parenting.*

The *Handbook of Parenting* appears at an altogether critical time in the history of parenting. The family generally, and parenting specifically, are today in a greater state of flux and re-definition than perhaps at any other time. One cannot but be impressed on the biological front that artificial insemination now renders postmenopausal women capable of childbearing and with the possibility of designing babies. Similarly on the sociological front, single parenthood is a modern day fact of life, adult child dependency is on the rise, and parents are ever less certain of their roles, even in the face of rising environmental and institutional demands that they take increasing responsibility for their charges, as well as the future.

Once upon a time, parenting was a seemingly simple thing: Mothers mothered. Fathers fathered. Today, parenting has many motives, many meanings, and many manifestations. Parenting is now viewed as immensely time consuming and effortful. The perfect mother or father or family is now firmly a figment of the imagination. Society recognizes "subdivisions" of the call: genetic mother, gestational mother, biological mother, birth mother, social mother. For some, altruistic individual sacrifices that mark parenting are actually directed at offspring for the sole and selfish purpose of passing ones's genes onto succeeding generations. Is this the motive a mother has for planning a second child when her adolescent first, stricken with leukemia, desperately needs matching bone marrow for transplant? Others still wonder aghast at how a mother could stand before a sympathetic nation when she know full well that she has condemned her two babies to a fearful passing. A multitude of factors influence the unrelenting onrush of decisions that surround parenting—biopsychological, dyadic, contextual. Recognizing this complexity is important to informing people's thinking about parenting, especially information-hungry parents themselves. The *Handbook of Parenting* embraces, expresses, and explores the myriad motives, meanings, and manifestations of parenting.

Parenting has never come with a handbook ... until now.

ACKNOWLEDGMENTS

I would like to express my deep gratitude to the staff at Lawrence Erlbaum Associates who made the *Handbook of Parenting* more than I ever could: Judith Amsel, Lawrence Erlbaum, Sharon Levy, Arthur M. Lizza, Anne Patricia Monaghan, Joseph Petrowski, and Robin Marks Weisberg.

—*Marc H. Bornstein*

Contents of Volume 1:
Children and Parenting

Contents of Volume 2:
Biology and Ecology of Parenting

Contents of Volume 4:
Applied and Practical Parenting

Introduction to
Handbook of Parenting
Volume 3
Status and Social Conditions of Parenting

Many people parent children, and they bring with them, as part of the psychological make-up of being the parent, specific as well as common characteristics. Volume 3 of the *Handbook of Parenting* draws portraits of those individuals and highlights unique and shared points of comparison among them. Chapters in Part I, "Who Is the Parent", explore the variation among parent types comprehensively. Kathryn Barnard and Louise Martell and Ross Parke, respectively, address the most common parents in "Mothering" and "Fathers and Families." Many children today grow up in nonnuclear, nontraditional families, such as those discussed in Marsha Weinraub and Marcy Gringlas' chapter on single parenthood, and in "Grandparenthood," Peter Smith brings in a parent often parenting in lieu of mom and dad. Today, too, adolescent parenthood is not uncommon, and Jeanne Brooks-Gunn and Lindsay Chase-Lansdale evaluate the issues it raises. Likewise, nonparental caregiving is increasingly common; Alison Clarke-Stewart, Virginia Allhusen, and Darlene Clements present day care. Around the world sibling caregivers are conventional, and Patricia Zukow reviews that relationship. David Brodzinsky, Robin Lang, and Daniel Smith discuss parenting adopted children, and in a companion piece Mavis Hetherington and Margaret Stanley-Hagan review parenting in divorced and remarried families. Somewhat novel even today is lesbian and gay parenthood; Charlotte Patterson assesses the parenting roles of those life styles.

Chapters in Part II, "Social Conditions of Parenting," take up internal as well as external issues related to parenting, beginning with "Determinants of the Transition to Parenting" by Christoph Heinicke. Parents' cognitions about parenting are recognized to play a significant role in defining the nature of parenting as well as in influencing its effects. In three related chapters, Jacqueline Goodnow discusses parents' knowledge and expectations; Ann McGillicuddy-De Lisi and Irving Sigel, parental beliefs; and George Holden, parental attitudes toward childrearing. Parents' relations to the larger society are elaborated in three additional connected chapters by Moncrieff Cochran and Starr Niego, "Parenting and Social Networks"; James Garbarino and Kathleen Kostelny, "Parenting and Public Policy"; and Pauline Pagliocca, Gary Melton, Victoria Weisz, and Phillip Lyons, "Parenting and the Law."

Chapters in Volume 3 of the *Handbook of Parenting* on the status and social conditions of parenting are complemented by those in Volumes 1, 2, and 4. Volume 1 concerns children and parenting: Development is too subtle, dynamic, and intricate to admit that parental caregiving alone determines the course and outcome of ontogeny, and Volume 1 begins the *Handbook of Parenting* with essays concerned with how children influence parenting. Volume 2 concerns the biology and ecology of parenting: To be understood as a whole, the psychophysiological and sociological determinants of parenting need to be brought into the picture, and Volume 2 relates parenting to its biological roots and sets parenting in its ecological context. Volume 4 concerns applied and practical parenting: Parenting is not easy, nor does it go well all of the time, and Volume 4 describes problems of parenting and how they are (sometimes) overcome as well as steps toward the promotion of positive parenting practices.

PART I

WHO IS THE PARENT

1

Mothering

Kathryn E. Barnard
University of Washington
Louise K. Martell
University of Washington

INTRODUCTION

Mothering is a topic almost everyone has experience with and therefore opinions about. What it is and what it could be or should be; however, surprisingly few scholars have dedicated themselves to the topic. Cultures see mothering as important because the mother is largely responsible for the day-to-day teaching of the culture. Because mothering occurs within the privacy of the family there has been limited opportunity for viewing the role. This chapter reviews what we know about the phenomenon of mothering from the standpoint of how women prepare for and define the role. Emphasis falls on two selected mothering roles. These roles are monitoring and being a responsive partner. Simultaneous to choosing two specific roles we recognized others in the complete mothering repertoire, such as caregiving techniques, and specific roles such as comforter, manager; but these either are less researched or have not been found to influence children's outcomes. In fact as Radke-Yarrrow (1991) stated parental behavior has been studied one dimension at a time and rarely are the multiple roles or the multiple contexts in which the dimensions of mothering are embedded together studied in the same research question.

Although mothering is discussed as a specific role, it is recognized that the role develops in relation to the family system wherein roles of father, siblings, and other extended family members are enacted as well. It is a network of roles. Each person's role is connected with all others in the family system and because that is true there are always variations within cultures because of this calibration of roles between the couple and within the larger family system. It is further recognized that the role of mothering is undergoing rapid change as women assume more of a career orientation. The roles attributed to mothers as women have been a result of their position within the family and larger social system. As the position of women changes, aspects of the mothering role will be assumed by others in the family or in the society. The child's needs for mothering will not change.

For this chapter we sought to highlight the role preparation done during pregnancy and the first year of life (Bornstein, in this *Handbook*). We view this period as the most influential in determining role dimensions because of the traditional view that mothers bear children and are primarily responsible for their care and well-being during the years of the infant's greatest physical and emotional dependency. The chapter begins by defining the characteristics of mothering and then moves on to explore the literature on how women prepare for this role during their pregnancy and how the role attainment proceeds in the first year of life. The second major section of the chapter presents information about early mothering behavior. There is an emphasis on the mother's role as a context for the developing infant with a detailed review of the specific behaviors of monitoring and responding to the child's behaviors. The Barnard model of parent–child interaction is presented; maternal and child behaviors associated with this model of parent–child interaction are discussed. The relation of maternal and infant characteristics to these behavioral dimensions are noted. The chapter concludes with raising challenges for further research about mothering. The study of mothering is evolving now that some measurement techniques are available to the field. There are many new questions to be addressed in relation to early mothering and who does the caregiving; what the dominate values are for child outcomes; and how high-risk factors affect development of maternal identity and how they are each related to maternal role performance.

CHARACTERISTICS OF MOTHERING

At a basic level mothering involves an asymmetrical relationship with a child or dependent individual (Parke, in this *Handbook*). This relationship is characterized by a strong emotional attachment driving a complex of behaviors that promote the survival and well-being of the dependent person in the relationship. Historically, mothering has been linked with the female gender because women in the majority of cultures care for children and dependent members of the group (Harkness & Super, in this *Handbook*). In fact, it is of relevance to analyze the composition of the words *woman, mother, man,* and *father* in the Japanese language. The character for woman is a stick figure with a protruberance, resembling a pregnant abdomen, whereas the character for mother resembles the chest with two breasts. The symbol for man, on the other hand, is the rice field illustrating work. The character for father is a stone axe symbolizing power. The separate character for parenting resembles a monitoring tower and a growing tree. These Japanese characters originated from Chinese, representing both intergenerational and ethnic transmission of thoughts about these important roles within the societies. The character distinction in the Japanese language raises another issue, the comparison of the concept of mothering, fathering, and parenting—are these distinct roles? Do mothers hold a unique role in the birthing and nurturance of children whereas fathers provide the support and control of the family (French, in this *Handbook*)? Is parenting something quite different than mothering or fathering? The Japanese character for parenting, that of watching the growing child, portrays parenting as an important task necessary for the successful raising of children. Is this parental task shared by both parents and by other family members? We return to this question at the end of the chapter.

Rubin (1984) reported on qualitative studies she did in the 1960s and 1970s of many women during the process of childbearing. Her book *Maternal Identity and Maternal Experience* challenges the attribution that mothering is instinctual. She noted, "There is nothing particularly mysterious or exotically sex-linked in the activities of feeding, bathing, protecting or teaching the young. ... Enduring love, altruistic self-denial, and empathy are not exclusive to the maternal woman or to the mother–child relationship. And yet, together these actions within the matrix of affiliate bonds comprise the characteristics of maternal behavior which are seen as the bottom line" (p. 2).

Rubin goes on to claim there is nothing preprogrammed in maternal behavior; it is the product of an interaction between the mother's past and interaction with the developing child (see also Fleming & Corter, in this *Handbook;* Papoušek & Papoušek, in this *Handbook*).

Maternal attitudes and behaviors change in relation to the age, condition, and situation of the child. The literature varies in how completely the concept of mothering is described. In a study of grandmother functions performed in multigenerational families, Flaherty (1988) described seven functions she found in African-American grandmothers. These functions were managing, caretaking, coaching, assessing, nurturing, assigning, and patrolling. Some of the role functions pertain specifically to the grandmothering role, but at least three also describe a mother's role. These include *managing,* which involves "arranging of resources and activities so that they synchronize with each family member and meet family needs" (p. 194). Most mothers will heartily agree with the importance and frequency with which they serve as manager of the child and family. Another role, *caretaking,* deals with providing direct care for the child or dependent members. The third role is *nurturing,* which the author denoted as providing "emotional support and love to the child and other family members" (p. 195; see also Smith, in this *Handbook*).

Dorr and Friedenberg (1983) reviewed the literature from the 1950s until the mid-1970s and concluded that, although direct caregiving techniques of mothers had been studied, none was associated with significant developmental outcomes of the child. Only as investigators began looking at the interaction of the mother and child was a linkage discerned. For the child to develop a sense of secure attachment or trust there needs to be a "loving availability" of the mother toward the child. From a pyschoanalytical perspective, object relations theory informs thinking about the importance of the developmental process whereby the infant/child begins the process of internalizing representations of self and others. These internalized representations start with the mother's own internalized views of herself, others, and her child. It is the mother's perspectives on others, whether she sees others in a positive or distrusting manner, that she communicates to her child. The mother's interactions with her child set the stage for how the child learns to relate with others, and these relationships affect the child's developing representations. When the mother has the capacity to be "lovingly available," the child will likely experience conditions leading to a sense of trust in the environment and enduring self-confidence. These findings confirm the importance of the relationship and interaction aspects of the mothering role.

PREPARING FOR TAKING ON THE ROLE OF THE MOTHER

Through their intimate involvement with women's childbearing experiences, nurses have been witnesses to women becoming mothers from physical, psychological, and social perspectives. Over the past four decades, nurses, especially Rubin (1967a, 1967b, 1977, 1984) and Mercer (1981, 1985), have captured the development of mothering through empirical studies. The processes involved are developing the capacity for mothering and attaining the maternal role, which includes the development of maternal identity and role competency.

Capacity for Mothering

Pregnancy is a time when the transition to the mothering role begins (Heinicke, in this *Handbook*), not only for the first child, but also for each subsequent child because mothering can only be defined in relation to the child, just as the infant can only be defined in relationship to the mother or caregiver. Rubin (1984) described the development of the capacity for mothering during pregnancy. In her model there are four major tasks: (1) seeking safe passage for herself and her child through pregnancy, labor, and delivery; (2) ensuring the acceptance by significant persons in her family of the child she bears; (3) *binding-in* to her unknown child; and (4) learning to give of herself. Characteristics of each task are summarized from Rubin's work.

In seeking safe passage, Rubin (1984) found that a woman begins in the first trimester to concentrate on her well-being and is concerned with what she eats and will often stop using alcohol or drugs. By the second trimester, the pregnant woman develops fears about the baby and the delivery.

She is susceptible to traditional fears, old wives' tales, and stories about behaviors potentially bringing harm to the baby. As the fetus moves and she is aware of her baby, the need to protect herself and her baby is ever present in her mind.

Sensory awareness of the fetus may come prior to feeling fetal movement for contemporary women. With ultrasound, a present-day mother can see the fetus prior to feeling movement. She becomes more cautious in her daily activities and avoids anything that could threaten her abdomen. Because of growing awareness and attachment to the maturing fetus many mothers are motivated to seek prenatal care, knowledge, and help from any form available. By the third trimester with her increasing body size, she is less agile and the pregnancy becomes an uncomfortable experience. Psychologically she feels ugly and normal events become dangerous to her. She avoids crowds, yet may dread being alone. By the 8th month of pregnancy she views delivery as a relief. She is hopeful the physician or midwife will think she is about to deliver or will suggest she go to the hospital. False labor pains generally are felt in the 8th month of pregnancy, so she has continuous reminders about her transitional state.

Rubin (1984) saw the task of ensuring the acceptance of the child by others as one of the most critical. Essentially this involves the mother developing a place both physically and psychologically for the child within the family, the most difficult of the two being the emotional fit. It is necessary for the mother and other family members to adjust their relationships; bonds between existing family members have to be loosened and redefined. This work generally begins as the mother becomes aware of the growing child within and begins sharing with other family members and friends her thoughts and aspirations about the child. Fantasies about the unborn child are ideally shared between family members as a way of envisioning the reality of a new family member. The mother's objective is to gain unconditional acceptance; therefore any conditional acceptances based on sex of the child or normalcy pose a deep worry to the mother because of her fear of the child being rejected if the condition is not met. The mother herself must reformulate her own identity and incorporate this new relationship into her life and her relationship network.

Binding-in is a process that begins in pregnancy and generally results in a state at birth where there already exists a bond between mother and infant. During the first trimester the binding-in begins with the acceptance and rejection process of the pregnancy. At first, even in planned pregnancies, there is the conscious processing of whether the mother really wants this child. We speculate that a woman does not seek confirmation of the pregnancy or prenatal care until she has come to an acceptance of the pregnancy. During the second trimester, the event of fetal movement evokes a special, private experience. Once again, use of technology may modify the expectant mother's psychological development. With the fetal image projected onto a video monitor and with ultrasound and fetal heart tones made audible with Doppler, the pregnancy becomes a more public event. Love and acceptance of the unborn child are very high during the second trimester.

Physical changes associated with pregnancy, the growing fetus's activity, and the sense of "life within her" make the mother especially aware of the child. For the mother this child *is!* Others must await the birth. During the third trimester increasing conflict arises of wanting the child, but hating the pregnancy. This entrapment makes the mother miserable. She wants the birth but still has fear about her and the baby's safety.

Learning to give of oneself begins in the first trimester as the women begins to weigh the demands that pregnancy entails. The changes in body appearance, function, integrity, relationships, lifestyle, and life space represent both loss and change. The basic principle of what she needs to give up and what she will be gaining is evaluated during this time. During the second trimester her identification shifts to the child. Others bring significant gifts to the mother for the baby. The third trimester brings to the surface the realization of the commitment required in giving birth, time, interest, companionship, and concern. The danger of the delivery, the fears that the giving of self will be overwhelming, and that her capacity to give to the baby will not be enough are all commitments she is pondering.

Rubin (1984) saw these tasks of pregnancy as preparing the woman for her continuing maternal role as she develops classical maternal concerns and worries on behalf of her child. This maternal role is characterized by the long-term giving of one's time and interest in the form of enduring love, altrustic self, self-denial, and empathy.

The Process of Attaining the Maternal Role

Mercer (1985) defined maternal role attainment as "a process in which the mother achieves competence in the role and integrates the mothering behaviors into her established role set, so that she is comfortable with her identity as a mother" (p. 98). Other researchers (e.g., Walker, Crain, & Thompson, 1985) define maternal role attainment as confident enactment of culturally defined behavior associated with the role mediated by psychological understanding and interpretation. Coincidental with developing competence in the maternal role, the mother develops a maternal identity that has both cognitive and affective components. The cognitive components include the how, what, and why of child care and the affective components include commitment, empathy, and positive regard for the child. The constructs of maternal role attainment and maternal identity are closely linked and are difficult to describe separately. Whether contemporary women have more or less conflict on attaining their maternal role is an interesting question. For most women integrating the maternal and career roles is difficult because of the opposing priorities.

The process of maternal role attainment as previously discussed begins in pregnancy and continues into the year following birth. Rubin's (1967a, 1967b) work focused on the process during pregnancy and Mercer's (1985) work covered the first year of life. The prominent behaviors women use in maternal role attainment during pregnancy are mimicry, role play, fantasy, introjection-projection-rejection, identity, and grief work. *Mimicry* is the adoption of the behaviors associated with mothers or with what mothers are like. In mimicry, women take on the outward manifestations of the cultural stereotype of mothers such as clothing and actions. She may use her own mother and her peers as models. In mimicry a woman does not have the sense of mothering occurring within a relationship. Through *role play* women act out the role of mother for short, situation-specific periods of time. She may search out subjects for trying on the role such as baby-sitting friends' children or acquiring a pet. "How will family and friends perceive me?" is the underlying theme of *fantasy.* It is a self-oriented process. Dreaming, a form of fantasy, is one powerful mechanism most pregnant women report using. Fantasies of herself as a mother range from romanticized images to fears. Through fantasy, she broadens her repertoire of possibilities for enactment of the maternal role. Through *introjection-projection-rejection,* a woman determines if the models of mothers to which she has been exposed fit her. If a model is not satisfactory, she rejects the model. This process differs from mimicry because it involves a woman's evaluation of models of motherhood. *Identity* means that a woman has a sense of comfort in the role of mother. She sees herself as a mother rather than being "like" a mother. She does not need a reference model because of her own identification as a mother. With the taking on of the maternal role, a woman undergoes grief work. She progressively obliterates her former identity in roles that are not compatible with her new role. This *grief work* is finalized only when her new identity as a mother is fairly well established.

The process of maternal role attainment is not linear and tends to be cyclic. It occurs during pregnancy, birth, and the postpartum period with some tasks being more salient at different times of the childbearing cycle. Mimicry is associated with early to the middle of pregnancy and introjection-projection-rejection with late pregnancy. None of these operations is independent of the others.

As with binding-in during pregnancy, contemporary technology may influence the postbirth process of becoming a mother. Through amniocentesis and ultrasound, the mother has empirical data about her baby that may alter her maternal behavior and attitudes earlier than in Rubin's time. For example, through knowing the sex of the fetus, the mother may identify herself as a mother of a boy or the mother of a girl prior to birth. In fact, because of knowing the sex of the baby many parents chose the baby's name and speak of the infant as if she or he is a real member of their family.

Several factors that could affect women's maternal role attainment were not considered in Rubin's (1967a, 1967b) work. The context of the 1960s undoubtedly influenced Rubin's thinking about mothering. First, the general assumption at that time was that, after the birth of their first babies, women would cease employment or other activities outside the home, which would account for grief work over giving up identities of former roles. Today, women may be expected to be "mother and ..." rather than "mother instead of ..." (Gottfried, Gottfried, & Bathurst, in this *Handbook*). It is now a social norm that women maintain their former roles while taking on the maternal role to the point that many contemporary women endure role strain rather than role conflict. Second, Rubin did not examine the influence of maternal age on maternal role attainment. In Rubin's time the typical age range for childbearing was narrower than today. Contemporary childbearing women include more women in their teens and past 30 years than in Rubin's time. Third, the impact of obstetrical management of birth was not taken into consideration as influencing maternal behavior. With heavy sedation during labor, anesthesia for childbirth, and separation from her baby immediately after birth, a woman of the 1960s probably had more difficulty comprehending the reality of her baby than a contemporary woman who is awake throughout childbirth with her infant constantly close by her. Finally, infants were not seen as active partners in developing the maternal role but as objects to which mothers reacted. During Rubin's time the prevalent conceptualization of infants was *tabula rasa*. More contemporary research on infant temperament indicates that infants actively affect maternal role enactment.

Mercer (1981, 1985, 1986) later explored the relations of women's personal factors and contextual-situational influences with this ease of attaining the maternal role. She asserted that, "A woman defines maternal role performance in interaction with her infant and responds according to the situational context, her perceptions of her past and present experience and her values" (p. 178). Personal factors include physical health, self-esteem, birth experience, level of commitment, and competence. Contextual-situational influences include anticipatory socialization, separation from the infant, social support, and societal value of the maternal role. Age of a mother is seen to be a crucial factor in ease or hindrance of maternal role attainment.

Mercer's (1981, 1985) work on maternal role attainment extended beyond Rubin's (1967a, 1967b) primary focus on pregnancy. Additionally Mercer's work was not as grounded in the physical experience of pregnancy as Rubin's. Therefore, Mercer's work may help to explain the process of maternal role attainment for mothers adopting infants. Mercer studied first-time mothers during the early postpartum period and at 1, 4, 8, and 12 months after birth. The endpoint of maternal role attainment was seen as maternal identity that encompassed confidence and competency in role performance.

Mercer (1981, 1985) applied more rigorous, quantitatively oriented research methods. She compared the process of maternal role attainment in three age cohorts over time. Each of the age cohorts represented clusters of personal and contextual factors that could enhance or hinder maternal role attainment. In the contemporary Euro-American culture, motherhood is considered to be psychosocially inappropriate for teenage women (13- to 19-year-old group); adolescents have demonstrated a more limited repertoire of skills for parenthood and are psychologically unable to focus on the care of another individual as they are struggling with their own identity (Brooks-Gunn & Chase-Lansdale, in this *Handbook*). Women in their 20s (20- to 29-year-old group) are considered to be at an ideal age, both physiologically and socially, for having first babies. Older first-time mothers (30-to 39-year-old group) tend to have maturity, financial and social stability, and life skills for being competent mothers; however they may have more career/mothering role conflict and less physical energy. Maternal role attainment was operationalized by Mercer, as attachment, competency, and pleasure and gratification in the role. The instrument used to measure attachment was *Feelings about Baby* (FAB; Leifer, 1977). The FAB is a 10-item scale asking the mother to rate feelings about the baby, such as "I feel tenderly toward the baby." Pleasure and gratification were measured with the *Gratification in the Mothering Role* (GRAT; Russell, 1974). The GRAT is a 14-item checklist in which the mother is asked to rate her source of satisfaction from the role such as pride in baby's development and closeness with the spouse. The *Maternal Behavior* (MABE; Blank, 1964) is an interview schedule that includes 14 items to rate mother's satisfaction with the baby's development, attentiveness, anxiety, and flexibility. The *Ways of Handling Irritating Child Behaviors* (WHIB; Disbrow, Doerr, & Caulfield, 1977) was used to measure competency, evaluated by the mother's responses to handling 11 child behaviors, such as the child not cooperating.

Mercer (1985, 1986) found differences in these aspects of maternal role attainment across the age groups at different times of measurement. Feelings about the baby in all three maternal age groups peaked at the 4-month measure, coinciding with the height of infant social responsiveness. Gratification in the mothering role was initially highest for adolescent mothers and lowest for older mothers. Adolescent mothers reported a drop in gratification at 8 months, which continued to drop at 12 months. These drops coincided with challenging infant behavior such as separation anxiety at 8 months and increased mobility at 11 months. The older women (30–39 years) reported less gratification from the maternal role at each time point. Just the reverse was true for the mother's competency that was observed during the interviews. The teenage mothers demonstrated the least competency in role at all age periods and the older mothers the greatest competency. This was also true for the WHIB; the least positive ways occurred with greater frequency in the adolescent mothers. However age alone probably does not account for differences in maternal role attainment among groups. It is difficult to differentiate age because of factors associated with age, such as level of education, stability in family life and other relationships, experience with competence in other roles, and socioeconomic status.

Mercer (1985, 1986) also measured views and feelings about maternal role attainment during the first year of the child's life. For example, to measure self-image they were asked to list characteristics of the "ideal mother." Description of the ideal mother by the total sample included: providing an appropriate environment (81 percent), being a loving and giving individual who enjoys mothering (71 percent), teaching the infant (61 percent), playing with the baby (48 percent), comforting and nurturing the baby (48 percent), providing developmental stimulation (47 percent), feeding (35 percent), keeping the baby clean (21 percent). The mothers were also asked to describe their perception of the ideal mother with whom they compared themselves. In listing their major role model 52 percent gave their own mother as the source, 25 percent listed another woman, and 23 percent claimed to have no role model.

In defining their comfort with the maternal role, 3 percent claimed to have internalized the role by pregnancy, 49 percent by 2 months after birth, and 95 percent by 12 months. There was no significant difference in the age cohorts reporting achievement of comfort in the maternal role. In other words, maternal role identity develops broadly throughout the first year after birth. A few women do not have maternal identity at the end of the first year.

Finally a measure of role strain (Burr, 1979) was constructed through content analysis of the interview. The challenges the mothers reported were loss of personal time, gaining role skills, nighttime care/sleep deprivation, total responsibility, and infant's changing behavior. The degree of role strain did not decrease over the first year; as some of the early challenges were mastered the changes in the infant's behavior seemed to replace the necessary earlier adjustments.

Mercer's (1985, 1986) work on maternal role attainment represents a growing body of research concerning how various factors help or hinder maternal role attainment. Koniak-Griffin (1993) discussed maternal factors that help role attainment, including multiparity, good self-esteem, and a positive relationship with their partner. Good feelings about self are associated with mothers' positive regard for their babies. Hindrance includes maternal depression and role conflict/strain. Besides developmental stage, infant variables influencing the mother's attainment of her role include infant temperament and physical health. The environmental factor of social support enhances maternal role attainment whereas stress tends to hinder it.

STUDIES OF THE PREPARATION FOR MOTHERHOOD

Others have also studied development of the capacity for mothering. Lederman (1984) studied the paradigm shift she claims a woman must make from her perception as woman without child to woman with child. Lederman's (Lederman, Lederman, Work, & McCann, 1978) original study of women in labor prompted her to do further work on women's adaptation during pregnancy. Finding that there were woman who demonstrated behavioral and physiological correlates of stress during labor that prolonged stage two of labor, Lederman was eager to study more fully what prenatal psychological factors predicted this difficulty of progressing in labor. She saw the woman as needing to make a paradigm shift from her former lifestyle and behaviors to attain this capacity to give to the child. Lederman proposed that the woman needs to be willing to give up her former self and learn to achieve satisfaction from giving in her relationship with the child.

If the woman has not resolved this paradigm shift during the pregnancy, as labor and delivery approach, she becomes more anxious. Lederman studied the relation between the outcome of labor and the pregnant woman's perceptions regarding this paradigm. The prenatal variables obtained through client interviews were acceptance of the pregnancy, identification of a motherhood role, relationship with own mother, and fears about pregnancy. The variables of acceptance of pregnancy and identification of the motherhood role had the most consistent correlations with progress during labor, including measures of uterine activity, plasma epinephrine, state anxiety, and duration of labor. These findings provide support for Rubin's (1967a, 1967b) assertion that acceptance of the pregnancy and child is an important maternal role attainment task.

Josten (1982) developed a method for prenatal assessment of mothering potential. The method involved review of individual women's prenatal clinic charts for the positive or negative evidence of the following aspects: (1) perception of the complexities of mothering, (2) attachment, (3) acceptance of child by significant others, (4) ensuring physical well-being, and (5) evidence of problem areas such as history of parenting difficulties, lack of knowledge about children, inadequate cognitive function, inadequate support, spouse abuse, mental illness, substance abuse, major stress, rejection of child, or inappropriate use of services.

Prenatal clinic charts were rated using the *Parental Assessment Guide.* A score of positive, negative, or neutral was assigned to each woman for each type of evidence defined. Josten (1982) studied 52 mothers, all part of a larger study at the University of Minnesota. In the larger study, the quality of care had been rated by independent observers. Excellent care was defined as meeting the physical and psychological needs of the infant with sensitivity and cooperative handling by the mother, whereas inadequate care was defined as failure to take action to provide the basic physical or psychosocial care that when absent caused physical or psychological harm to the infant. Josten compared 27 mothers rated as providing excellent mothering with 25 mothers rated as providing inadequate care. From the prenatal chart reviews, the inadequate mothers had more negative scores on their perception of the complexities of the mothering role, acceptance of the child by significant others, and physical well-being during pregnancy. The majority of the inadequate mothers had therefore not prepared for pregnancy including dealing with the emotional tasks of pregnancy. It is apparent that high-risk women have little opportunity to do the psychological work to prepare for mothering. It seems prudent to suggest that in the future demonstration projects or experimental studies be done with high-risk women to help them prepare for the mothering role. To date almost no experimental work has focused on the specific task of preparing women psychologically for mothering. Instead, professionals have been preoccupied with preparing women primarily for the actual labor and delivery experience.

Another investigation of prenatal assessment of the capacity for parenting was conducted by Heinicke (1984). An interview schedule developed by Shereshefsky and Yarrow (1973) to evaluate the parent's self-concept, self-esteem, and their confidence and clarity in visualizing the parental role was used. The investigation found that variables such as maternal adaptation competence, active style of emotional expression, IQ, the capacity for forming relationships, and such self-characteristics as confidence in visualizing self as mother were efficient predictors in anticipating parent–child and child outcomes.

Thus, the capacity of the woman to visualize herself as a mother, as well as her past history of relationships seem to be confirmed as the psychological work a woman must do to prepare herself, not only for ensuring safe passage of the child but also for readying herself for the giving of self to the newly born infant. How does this work get done? It is accomplished through the processes previously described as associated with attaining the maternal role.

A simple self-report measure of the transition to motherhood has been reported. Ruble et al. (1990) constructed a questionnaire and completed preliminary psychometric testing on *The Childbearing Attitude Questionnaire* (CAQ). This scale contains 16 factors: maternal worries, maternal self-confidence, relationship with husband, relationship with mother, body image, identification with pregnancy, feelings about children, negative self-image, attitude toward breastfeeding, pain tolerance, interest in sex, denial, negative aspects of caretaking, feelings of dependency, social boredom, and information seeking. The questionnaire was given at three time points—prepregnant, pregnant, and postpartum—to 51 women recruited in three different cities—Toronto, Seattle, and New York—over the 2-year period from 1981 to 1983. The women were predominately middle-class, college graduates, and White. Between pregnancy and the first 3 months postpartum most of the scales were positively correlated with each other. All scales were positively correlated between 1 and 3 months. This consistency in perceptions of self and others across the transition to motherhood speaks to the lifelong developmental impact of one's self-confidence, social orientation, identification with motherhood, and attitude toward giving birth. This sample of women showed little change in attitudes toward motherhood in going through the transition. These scales need testing in populations of less educated women and in other cultural groups to see whether and how the patterns of stability would differ.

It would be helpful if we could identify preconceptually or prenatally women who will have difficulty with attaining a positive maternal identity and role. We know very little about high-risk samples. The majority of studies previously cited have all studied primarily Euro-American cultures of high achievement. On the other hand there are reports in the literature that make us realize life is difficult for some women. For example, Campbell, Poland, Waller, and Ager (1992) described the problem of physical abuse during pregnancy. What influence does interpersonal violence have on evolving maternal identity? In a Detroit-based maternity clinic sample, Campbell and her colleagues reported an 8 percent battering incidence during pregnancy in a predominatly African-American sample. In extending the study of maternal role attainment to other groups factors such as interpersonal violence will need to examined. There is no sure set of predictive variables, however some of the strongest seem to be personal history of a poor childhood, history of, or current psychopathology, or ambivalence about the prengancy, lack of evidence of forming a positive relationship with the newborn, and lack of capacity for self-care (Gabinet, 1986). In one study (Webster-Stratton, 1985) of families of conduct-disordered children, mother's report of having been abused as a child and low family income were the most potent variables differentiating abusive and nonabusive families.

Frequently a case study integrates the circumstances better than the empirical evidence from groups or theories. The pregnancy of Nell is recounted to illustrate the obstacles and course of maternal role attainment:

Nell was a 17-year-old, unmarried girl, pregnant for the first time. She was a chronic bulemic anorexic who had been binging and purging for 3 years. She had mixed feelings about her unplanned pregnancy. Nell attempted suicide when she found out she was pregnant. Because it was important to Nell to have a thin figure, she continued to binge and purge until she went to a special therapeutic program for adolescents, where they advised her to delay her purging until at least ½ hour after eating, which allowed her body time to absorb as many nutrients as possible. She gradually decreased her bulemic practices, however continued to drink alcohol and smoke both cigarettes and marijuana. Nell was uncertain who the father of her unborn baby was. Her current boyfriend had no occupation other than drug dealing. This boyfriend was unsupportive of the pregnancy. She was not in contact with her mother and rarely saw her father. Nell decided to keep her baby in spite of the lack of support from her partner, friends, or family members. *Acceptance by mother and others in the family is one of the most important tasks during pregnancy. Nell shows some evidence of accepting the pregnancy when she complied with the advice to delay purging with each meal, thus giving the fetus a chance to have appropriate nutrients. Her continuing ambivalence is demonstrated in continuing to smoke. There were no signs of acceptance of the baby by her network of relationships.*

Nell herself had been abandoned by her mother at the age of 2 years due to an illness where the mother was hospitalized for "mental problems." Nell decided to keep her baby during the second trimester and after that time became more cheerful. *Such a history of abandonment bodes poorly for her ability to successfully attain the maternal role.* Although she did not have a good self-image, she began to involve herself in work and designed notecards and a calendar to keep track of prenatal clinic visits. In the third trimester, Nell seemed to gain more confidence as she prepared for motherhood. She asked questions of the public health nurse and kept records of her observations of fetal activity. She was feeling positive about taking care of her baby. She delivered a healthy baby girl whom the nurses made sure she saw and handled immediately. She continued to live with her same boyfriend after the baby was born. He continued to be uninvolved with the baby. Nell continued to rely on him for her primary support. Nell breastfed the baby from birth to 11 months of age. The mother–infant interactions during early feedings were fairly positive; however by 6 weeks the nurse noted that Nell provided little social responsiveness or cognitive stimulation to the baby. Nell perceived her baby as easy and was interested in the baby's development. *The mother's success with taking on the maternal role was mixed. Certainly the commitment to breastfeeding was impressive based on her history of an eating disorder and the discipline that she had to impose on her own eating behavior to successfully breastfeed. Although her family or friends were not supportive, the public health nurse and adolescent clinic she attended during her pregnancy provided support and structure, which helped her with attaining such a positive maternal role in spite of signifant risk factors.* As the first year went on Nell seemed less satisfied with her mothering role and resumed more binging and purging and increased her intake of alcohol and other drugs. *Adolescents tend to show more satisfaction with mothering before 6 months than after that time.*

Maternal role attainment along with maternal identity continue to be provocative aspects of mothering. The current state of knowledge highlights that maternal role attainment is complex and needs more refined, in-depth definition. The time for maternal role attainment to occur is varied ranging from pregnancy to beyond the child's first year. Maternal role attainment must be considered within the context of maternal, infant, and environmental factors. The developing infant is an especially important help or hindrance in maternal role attainment. Studies of infant temperament are begining to show the potentially strong affect that infant temperament can have on the parenting self-efficacy (Cutrona & Troutman, 1986; see also Sanson & Rothbart, in this *Handbook*).

MOTHERING AS A "HOLDING ENVIRONMENT" FOR THE CHILD

To this point we have dealt with attainment of maternal role during pregnancy and the first year of life. Mercer's (1985, 1986) work embraces the first year of the child's life, yet it deals primarily with the mother's own perception of her role and how well she fulfills it and how satisfying it is to her. The next step is to explore what it is that mothers actually do with children. In caring for children are there acts that only mothers can do, versus the child's father or other caregivers? We are of the opinion that few acts of mothering exclusively belong to the mother. The biological holding of the embryo and fetus is at present confined to the capacity of the women as is the intense commitment the mother has to the young, helpless infant. However, there is little empirical evidence about what tasks of mothering are gender specific in that the majority of studies of child care have been focused primarily on the mother of the child. In the vast majority of cultures around the world, the mother remains the primary caregiver of the young child. It is true in many cultures that the extended female family members such as mothers, mothers-in-law, sisters, and aunts are integrated into the caring role, either directly caring for the children or indirectly by caring for the mother and her household responsibilities (Cochran & Niego, in this *Handbook;* Smith, in this *Handbook;* Zukow-Goldring, in this *Handbook*)

Winnicott (1990) described the mothering role to be one of "holding" (p. 49). He defined holding for infants as involving: (1) protecting from physiological insult; (2) taking account of the infant's skin sensitivity, temperature, auditory sensitivity, visual sensitivity, sensitivity to falling, and lack of knowledge of existence of anything other than the self; (3) routine of care through the entire day and night following the minute day-to-day changes belonging to the infant's growth and development, both physical and psychological; and (4) physical holding of the infant, which is a form of love.

Taken in its totality, providing a holding environment for a child is a very demanding role. Winnicott's (1990) formulation can be applied to any age; characteristics of the child form the changing nature of the child's needs for a holding environment. Providing a holding environment requires that the caregiver has the physical and psychological resources to be on alert to the child and respond in a manner that satisfies not only the child's need but also in a way that facilities the child's ongoing development (Bradley, in this *Handbook*).

There are two aspects of the mothering role embedded in Winnicott's (1990) notation of the holding environment that are important to examine in relation to actual behavioral observation of maternal role performance. These aspects are: (1) the monitoring/surveillance function, and (2) responsive caregiving. The major emphasis is on responsive caregiving as observed in the mother–child interaction. Empirical work suggests this aspect of the role has the greatest impact on the child's subsequent development. Considerable research over the last two decades has demonstrated important links between qualities of mother–child interactions and child development outcomes (Barnard, 1994; Barnard, Booth, Mitchell, & Telzrow, 1988; Barnard & Kelly, 1989; Beckwith & Cohen, 1984; Bee et al., 1982; Bell & Ainsworth, 1972; Belsky, Rovine, & Taylor, 1984; Bornstein, 1989a; Bornstein, & Tamis-LeMonda, 1989; Clarke-Stewart, 1973; Coates & Lewis, 1984; Elardo, Bradley, & Caldwell, 1975; Hammond, Bee, Barnard, & Eyres, 1983; Morisset, 1994; Nelson, 1973; Olson, Bates, & Bayles, 1984; Papousek & Bornstein, 1992; Ramey, Farran, & Campbell, 1979; Wachs, U giris, & Hunt, 1971; Yarrow, Rubenstein, & Pedersen, 1975; see also Sternberg & Williams, in this *Handbook*). Researchers have established strong relations between specific elements of early mother–child interactions and later skills or qualities in the child. Overall, positive quality interactions during the first years of life tend to be positively linked to the child's subsequent intellectual and language capacities and to more secure attachments to major caregivers.

Factors related to a person's capacity for mothering are not entirely clear (Goodnow, in this *Handbook;* Holden, in this *Handbook;* McGillicuddy-De Lisi & Sigel, in this *Handbook*). There are studies that indicate the following are associated with poor role performance: (1) mother not having experienced adequate caring herself (Rutter, in this *Handbook*), (2) lacking general knowledge, (3) unmanageable stress, or (4) psychological dysfunction. Kang (1985), in testing a model of parental competence, found that the mother's cognitive structure was important in explaining the parenting competence. She found that actual knowledge of child development was related to what kind of home environment the mother provided, whereas her capacity to form a world view rather than an egocentric orientation was related to how she interacted as a social partner with her child (Bradley, in this *Handbook*).

Monitoring/Surveillance

When talking with a mother of a young infant, one soon becomes aware that the mother's attention is riveted to the infant. Even though she may be engaged in a social exchange with other persons, she visually checks in on the infant's well-being about every 20 seconds. Mothers report that they develop a special sense for the infant's breathing and movement patterns that they monitor during the infant's sleep and that they arouse from their own sleep if they detect an unusual change in those patterns. Winnicott (1988) called this "maternal preoccupation" with the infant. Infants are beginning to develop ability to control their behavior, when they sleep, when they eat, how stressed they get. It is the parent's role to assist the child in developing self-regulatory behavior beginning in infancy. In observing parenting practices in relation to sleep, it has been established that in the first 3 months most infants are not put down to sleep until they are fully asleep, reflecting the belief that infants need help in getting to sleep (Johnson, 1991). By 3 months, parents begin putting the infant down for sleep while infants are still awake, giving the infant a chance to regulate this basic process of putting one's self to sleep. Infants provided with the opportunity to self-soothe learn to get to sleep and stay asleep versus the infant who is always put to sleep by the parents. Infants who are put to bed awake also are encouraged by parents to use objects such as pacifiers and blanket ends to soothe or regulate their distress or arousal. Even after infancy when this intensive monitoring is justified, relative to the infant's lack of physiological homeostasis and general helplessness, the monitoring of the child's behavior and development is a vital role for the parent. There is evidence of this function in most homes, charts where the infant's weight and length are recorded, records of sleep and feeding patterns, marks on the kitchen door frame marking height of each child, video tapes, and albums of pictures. As the child matures, the monitoring extends beyond the family when the child plays with peers. Mothers speculate how their child is doing in relation to others. She may compare motor coordination. Throughout childhood, monitoring the child's activity and knowing when it is appropriate or a signal of time for change, rest, or parental control is vital to the child's own developing self regulation. As a child matures, the child can manage more and more behavior; knowing the child's capacity for self-regulation is the dynamic part of maternal surveillance.

The mother–child relationship is initially embedded in acts of caregiving such as feeding, bathing, playing, and responding to the baby's signs of distress. A particularly challenging part of relating to the infant is learning how to monitor and read the nonverbal language of the infant. The baby has an organized set of nonverbal symbols that communicate the basic message of continue or stop this action. The engagement and disengagement cues of infants have been identified as present right at birth (Barnard, 1976; Sumner & Spietz, 1994). Examples of potent engagement cues are mutual gaze, reaching toward the caregiver, smiling, and turning the head to the caregiver. Potent disengagement cues are more numerous and include back arching, crawling away, halt hand, overhand beating movement of arms, pulling away, spitting up, tray pounding, and withdrawing from an alert to a sleep state. There are also sutble engagement and disengagement cues. Each of these subtle cues in isolation has little meaning; however, when several subtle disengagement cues occur in rapid sequence, such as look away, tongue show, and hand behind ear, this signals distress in the baby; when the mother sees this activity and responds by slowing her pace, stopping, or changing the activity she succeeds in responding to the child's communication about his or her distress. Note the signs of engagement and disengagement in the following description of a newborn feeding at her mother's breast:

> Susie, 1 month, has just attached to her mother's nipple, her arms begin to relax from being held tightly over the center of her body to a more comfortable position at her sides. She is now sucking in a regular rhythm, about 8–10 sucks followed by a pause. She continues in this manner for the next 3–4 minutes with very little body activity and this regular sucking and swallowing pattern. She then opens her eyes, looks toward her mother's face, and quickly looks away. She then brings her arm up to side of her face in a wing-palm position and then grabs her ear. *After several minutes of productive sucking and behavioral engagement, Susie begins to demonstrate some disengagement cues—the turning away from her mother's face, the wing palm hand position, and grabbing her ear. These are cues the mother can use to tell that Susie is possibly wanting a break in the feeding, maybe just a pause or time out, or maybe a chance to change position and burp. Mothers who sensitively monitor these cues seem to have babies who give off less potent disengagement cues such as crying.*

The activity of monitoring is a basic foundation for responsive caregiving. Naturally, as the child matures during the first year language develops, and after the first words and sentences appear it is easier for the parent to clearly know the child's meaning. Nonverbal cues continue to be salient in responsive caregiving after the first year. Examples are the kicking and arm flailing of temper tantrums and glazed-over eyes when the child is sleepy. Parental monitoring becomes less intense as children grow older. An ongoing challenge to mothers is how much freedom should they give their children to investigate their environment. Too close monitoring may stifle growing independence whereas too little monitoring or supervision may lead to childhood behavior problems.

One of the parental behaviors that continues to be important all during childhood is this periodic monitoring of the child's growth, development, and behavior. Often through simple interview questions, a rich clinical picture emerges of how the parent carries out this function. The mother who is able to tell every detail of the infant's sleep behavior has been intensively watching the infant; the detail of her observations also reveal her possible concerns about the infant's survival.

When the child is left to deal with life outside the family boundary in a manner that does not provide the parental feedback based on knowing what the child is experiencing and how they are responding, this can lead to later problem behavior. As an African-American grandmother in talking about mothering said, it was important to watch what children brought home. If they brought home items that they should not have, or that had been stolen, then it was the mother's job to talk to the child about that and make sure that they did not do that again (H. Kitzman, personal communication, June 30, 1994).

Responsive Caregiving/Social Partner Role

In any social interaction there is an exchange. In most partnerships this exchange is an equal one. Exchanged are feelings, emotions, and information. In the mother–child interaction, the rules are altered slightly in that the mother takes on more responsibility for the social exchange, depending on the child's capacity or developmental level. In parent–child exchanges, the parent/mother provides more feedback of an instructional nature during the exchange. Bornstein (1989a) labeled this type of instructional feedback as didactic exchanges.

In a responsive caregiver–child interaction, there are certain behaviors that are cardinal to fulfilling the role. A fundamental aspect of responsiveness is contingency. The ability to monitor, interpret, and respond to the child's behavior in an immediate and appropriate manner is key to the child's developing a sense of the trustworthiness of his environment and that his behavior has an influence on others. The temporal nature of contingency is important. Often in situations where the mother is preoccupied, the ability to be contingent is compromised. She may respond to the child but with a latency that does not allow the child to connect her behavior with her response. Often in families of lower education it is observed that mothers are not responsive to the immediate behavior of the child. It is not uncommon for the parent to punish a child much later for a prior behavior. The lack of concordance between behavior and mother's response makes it difficult for the child to realize cause–effect relations. Successful child behavior management programs aim to help parents improve the concordance between the child's behavior and its consequences (Webster-Stratton, 1992; see also Chamberlain & Patterson, in this *Handbook*).

The primary focus of parenting in the early months of an infant's life is to establish routines, patterns of interaction, and patterns of communication. Theories that attempt to explain the consolidation of mother–infant relationship over time often reflect even larger endeavors to explain all of human relationships. A commonly held view, and basic tenet of "general systems theory," is that parents and children mutually influence and provide feedback to one another. Indeed, just a few moments observing mothers and their young children illustrates how each is affected by the other. And, although the circumstances and goals of interaction change with time, the style and nature of the partnership remains fairly consistent. It is within this framework, built from thousands of repeated interactions between mothers and children, that children's emotional, intellectual, and physical needs are met or not. Although most developmental research has focused on interactions between mothers and young children, studies of fathers and children clearly show the same bidirectional influences. Both mothers and fathers and their children mutually regulate each other's behavior in the course of interaction.

Research has demonstrated that maternal verbal and physical responsiveness relates positively to Cattell scores in adopted middle-class infants, whereas maternal restriction of exploration was correlated negatively with developmental status (Beckwith, 1971). Ainsworth (1973) reported that infants acquire a sense of security through the many interactions they have with their mothers during the first year. When mothers demonstrate sensitive responsiveness to infants in the first months of life, the infants demonstrate secure attachments later and use the mother as a secure base for exploration and as a source of comfort in time of stress. Ainsworth and Bell (1974) found that mothers who were sensitive in responding to their infants and allowed them freedom to explore had infants who were accelerated in development as measured on the Griffiths Scale. Women who had securely attached infants at 13 months had significantly higher 3-month mother–child interaction than those with insecurely attached infants (Spieker & Booth, 1988).

More recently, researchers have examined the relation between attachment security and developing conversational skill among low-socioeconomic status, maltreated and nonmaltreated toddlers, and high-risk samples (Coster, Gersten, Beeghly, & Cicchetti, 1989; Morisset, Barnard, Greenberg, Booth, & Spieker, 1990). Mothers' tendency to provide stimulating and positive interactive experiences was related to children's mental and linguistic abilities at both 24 and 36 months of age (Morisset et al., 1990). It was speculated that secure attachment may operate as a protective factor among the more extreme cases in high-risk populations (Rogosch, Cicchetti, Shields, & Toth, in this *Handbook*).

The socioemotional environment relative to the mother–infant interactive system is established through reciprocal behaviors on the part of both infant and mother (Brazelton, Koslowski, & Main, 1974). During interaction both mother and infant reciprocally influence the behavior of the other in a way that is potentially rewarding for both of them. Through a process of social interaction and bidirectional influences, the mother and infant learn to adapt, modify, and change their behaviors in response to the other. The achievement of heightened positive affect, increased alertness, and extended episodes of mutual attention provide the infant with a framework on which to build future social experience.

Especially for the infant there is a degree of dependency on a mother that makes survival questionable without the commitment of a caregiver. The infant cannot nourish himself with food, nor can the young infant manage to make the environment change or be predictable. The infant requires that an adult bring objects into reach, and both provide and also eliminate auditory stimulation in the environment. Papoušek and Bornstein (1992) described two different forms of caregiving, responsive and didactic, which in turn have been related to different child outcomes. Responsive caregiving involves the social interaction between the partners, whereas didactic caregiving involves the transmission of information between mother and child. Mothers who engaged in more social interaction had infants doing more social orienting, whereas mothers who concentrated more on orienting the infant to the environment had infants who explored objects more and who later had higher verbal intelligence. As the infant develops, the adult is mediating the environment for the child. Only when the child begins to locomote and finally walks and talks does the child begin to have more control over how much stimulation she gets and what activities she engages in. Scarr and McCartney (1983) stated that it is before the age of 3 years that the environment the child is provided most influences on the child's development. After age 3 the child has the ability to seek the environment and activities independently. In studies of children coming from high-risk environments, we have discovered the amount of caregiving and stimulation increases for children after the onset of walking and talking (Barnard et al., 1985).

Because the infant has a limited capacity to accommodate, the quality of the socioemotional environment in the early infancy period is highly dependent on the social competence of the mother. Goldberg (1977) highlighted three areas of infant social competence that contribute optimally to interactions with their caregivers: predictability of behavior (which includes regularity of biological rhythms), social responsiveness, and readability of cues. High-risk or handicapped infants may be compromised in these areas of social competence. These infants may be frequently irritable, be difficult to soothe, be difficult to feed, reject holding or cuddling, and be unresponsive. The ability of the mother to interpret infant behavior and respond contingently, as well as the infant's ability to give clear behavioral cues, influence the quality of mother–infant interactions.

Critical to the success of any interaction is the ability of the mother and child to adapt to one another. Sander (1962, 1964) suggested that initial mother–infant adaptation involves the fitting together of the "active tendencies" of each partner. Parent–infant synchrony is facilitated by a sense of rhythmicity, which is proposed to be an underlying pattern in the flow of interactive behavior (Censullo, Bowler, Lester, & Brazelton, 1987; Censullo, Lester, & Hoffman, 1985; Lester, Hoffman,

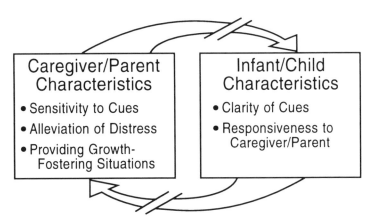

FIGURE 1.1 Barnard model of parent–child interaction.

& Brazelton, 1985). When partners in an interaction are only passively involved, the interaction becomes less adaptive, less positive (Field, in this *Handbook*). These aspects of the mother and infant behavior are depicted in the Barnard model (see Figure 1.1). This model is based on the assumption that mothers and infants have certain responsibilities to keep the interaction going. The infant is responsible for producing clear cues and being responsive to the mother. The mother has the responsibility of responding to the infant's cues, alleviating the infant's distress, and providing opportunities for growth and learning. As a result, each responds and reacts to the other, adapting their behavior to accommodate or modify the other's behavior. This adaptation is shown by the arrows moving from the caregiver to the infant, and from infant to caregiver. When adaptation occurs, it is seen as a smooth, positive interaction.

The break in the arrows represent interference, an interruption in the adaptive process that causes the interactive system to be compromised. This interference can originate in the mother, the infant, or the environment. A mother's lack of knowledge of infant behavior, her illness, or a crisis in the environment are examples of conditions that generally cause interference. Such conditions may cause the mother to become less sensitive to the infant's cues, unable to alleviate the infant's distress, or unable to provide growth-fostering situations for the infant. Likewise mother's education, ethnicity, and stress level influence her performance in the interaction, but these same maternal characteristics seldom are correlated with the child's performance as a social partner (Barnard, 1994; Barnard et al., 1988; Booth, Mitchell, Barnard, & Spieker, 1989; Morisset, 1994; see also Hoff-Ginsberg & Tardif, in this *Handbook*). Mothers of later born children have higher scores on contingency items and cognitive growth fostering (Morisset, 1994). An infant's inability to give clear cues or respond to the mother may also cause interference in the adaptive process. Some examples in which this occurs involve preterm infants (Barnard, Bee, & Hammond, 1984; Lyons, 1981; Slater, Naqvi, Andrew, & Haynes, 1987), drug-exposed infants (Blackwell & Kaiser, 1994; Mayes, in this *Handbook*), or infants born with physical conditions that affect them detrimentally (Lobo, 1992; Lobo, Barnard, & Coombs, 1992; Shonkoff, Hansen-Cram, Krauss, & Upshur, 1992; Meadow-Orlans, in this *Handbook*). Such conditions in either the mother or child contribute to a lack of signaling or contingent behavior and/or low energy levels for one of the partners and, therefore, less adaptive interactions. Anderson and Anderson (1989) reported that both mothers and twins are less optimal social partners; in fact, when the mother feeds both twins at the same time her interaction with either of them is less optimal than when fed alone. The twins during the last few months of their first year also begin communicating more with each other and less with their mothers. These twinship data suggest that amount of attention available within the dyad is a condition for optimal social interaction. The overall score for mother and child is lower when the infant is not in an alert state (Kushner, 1987); when there is diagnosis of nonorganic failure to thrive (Lobo et al., 1992); or when the mother has low education and/or is an adolescent (Barnard, 1994; Morisset, 1994; Ruff, 1987, 1990; vonWindeguth & Urbano, 1989).

Barnard et al. (1989) described the mother–infant interaction system as a dialogue or a mutually adaptive "waltz" between partners. For the waltz to flow smoothly, and for the infant to receive the quantity and quality of stimulation needed for optimum development, both the dance partners and the dialogue must have certain features:

(1) First, the partners in the dialogue must have a sufficient repertoire of behaviors so that interlocking sequences are possible and a smooth-flowing interactive system develops. Low-education mothers and preterm infants who are typically less responsive than term infants are both examples of partners with diminished interactive behaviors (Barnard, 1994; Morisset, 1994).

(2) Second, the partners' responses must be contingent on one another; as the child matures, the mother must remain both consistent and contingent in responding to the child. Low-education mothers are less contingent (Barnard, 1994; Morisset, 1994).

(3) The third element relates to the richness of the interactive content in terms of positive affect, verbal stimulation, and range of play materials provided.

(4) The fourth element is adaptive patterns between mother and child that change over time relative to the emerging developmental capacities of the child.

The mutual mother–infant "dance" has been described by others with terms such as contingency (Greenspan & Lieberman, 1980), attunement (Stern, 1985), emotional availability, reciprocity, or mutuality (Brazelton, Tronick, Adamson, Als, & Wise, 1975), and synchrony (Censullo et al., 1987).

Maternal Responsibilities During Interaction

Sensitivity to cues.   The mother's ability to recognize and respond to the child's cues is demonstrated through her positioning, the kinds of stimulation she provides, and the timing of the stimulation. During an interaction mothers display sensitivity by holding the infant safely and securely so they can see the infant's face and eyes, and feel the baby's body movements. Such positioning facilitates the mother's ability to accurately read and respond to their infant's cues. Mothers stimulate their infants in a variety of ways—through touching, moving, talking to, and looking at their baby. Sensitive mothers time these forms of stimulation so they are contingent to the infant's behavior. Contingent responses follow in time and are appropriate to the infant's behavior. Newborn infants are known to have a memory span of approximately 3–5 seconds. When infants are responded to within this time period following demonstration of a cue, they learn their behaviors are important and that they affect the people and things in their environment. The type of stimulation and its timing, force, rhythm, and duration are powerful qualities in setting the tone of the interaction (Brazelton et al., 1974).

Both breastfeeding and "wearing" the baby on the mother's body seem to provide a holding environment that promotes opportunities for the mother to be more immediately aware of the baby's nonverbal cues (Summer & Spietz, 1994; Virden, 1988). This proximity in turn provides the conditions for mothers to be optimally responsive. On the other hand, physical proximity during the ages when the human infant is essentially helpless provides a context where the likelihood is greater that the infant can have behaviors responded to and thereby develop a sense of trust in the environment.

Alleviation of distress.   The mother's ability to soothe or quiet a distressed infant is an important aspect of mothering. Distress is any potent disengagement cue. The effectiveness of mothers in alleviating distress of their infants depends on several factors. First, the mother needs to recognize the child's cue as distress. Second, the mother needs to know the appropriate action that will alleviate the distress such as rocking, talking to, or holding the baby close. Third, mothers need to be available to put their knowledge into action. Two factors that influence the alleviation of distress are the timing of the mother's response and the success of the mother's intervention. Parents who respond to their infant's distress quickly generally have infants who are readily quieted or soothed. Contrary to popular belief, responding in this way does not result in a demanding, "spoiled" child. Contingent responsiveness communicates to babies that they are important and they can effect their environment. The success of the mother's management is also important. Mothers who succeed in quieting a distressed infant gain confidence and competence in their ability to recognize and appropriately end the distress. Spieker (1989) reported that infants of adolescents, who still lived in their own families of origin, were demonstrating more distress and the infants' distress was negatively correlated with the mother's performance as a social partner. It is likely that in these instances the infant had primary caretaking from someone other than the mother, so that the infant was less familiar with the mother and vice versa. The mother's ability to respond and modify her behavior to meet the infant's needs results in a positive interaction experience. This capacity to be appropriately responsive to an infant depends on having time with the infant so that in experiencing one another they learn each other's ways. If the mother does not have the opportunity to practice this waltz with the baby, she will have difficulty responding to distress, and the infant is also likely to show distress more often because of the mother's lack of recogition and response to the subtle cues. Mother's modification of her behavior to promote a positive or negative interaction with her child persists as the child grows and develops. As with maternal role attainment, the child's development continues to challenge a mother in her interactions with her child.

Provision of growth-fostering situations. This refers to the mother's ability to provide experiences and stimulation that facilitate the infant's growth and development. Mothers provide growth fostering situations in the social-emotional and cognitive areas (Bornstein, 1989a; see also Eisenberg & Murphy, in this *Handbook;* Sternberg & Williams, in this *Handbook*) In order for mothers to be effective in providing these activities they need to have a global view of what is needed by their child. First, the mother needs to have an understanding of the importance of social, emotional, and cognitive stimulation for their child. Second, she needs to have knowledge about her child's current level of functioning and how she can support and facilitate his or her development. Third, she needs to be available to put her knowledge into action.

Social-emotional growth fostering. This relates to the affective domain and communicates a positive feeling tone. During an interaction warmth is reflected in the mother's tone and pitch of voice, facial expressions, types of touch, social forms of interaction, types of statements made to and about the baby, and the positioning of the baby. Mothers who facilitate social-emotional growth during an interaction vary the pitch and tone of their voices, perhaps singing or humming to their baby. They talk to their babies about what they are doing or about some aspect of the infant's personality they like. They use gentle types of touch like stroking or patting and engage their babies in games such as finger play. Voice, touch, and movement primarily serve the purpose of soothing, orienting, and/or alerting the infant and create a warm, supportive atmosphere. Mothers also position their babies so they can see their eyes and face (*en face*) to foster the social exchange of eye-to-eye and face-to-face contact. Vision is a powerful mode for orienting the infant to the mother and for reinforcing the mother's responsiveness to the infant. The visual mode provides the early motivation for the social smile and language development. More specifically, the infant's capacity for eye contact is identified as a source of intense pleasure for the mother and an innate releaser of the caregivng response (Robson, 1967). As babies become more verbal this mode becomes an important stimulus for maternal responsiveness.

Cognitive growth fostering. This involves the type of learning experiences the mother makes available to the child. Mothers do this by introducing babies to different sights, sounds, and experiences. This is seen during interaction in both the quality and quantity of the mother's verbalizations to the child, and the types of exploratory behavior they encourage. A mother's verbalizations to the child are a rich source of stimulation. The very young infant is more responsive to auditory than visual stimuli. In the early months of life mothers tend to talk to their infants for long periods of time in contrast to their infant's short periods of verbalizations (Mario, 1976). Parents who talk more to their infants and in a style that encourages reciprocal communication promote language development (Morisset, 1988).

One of the earliest forms of infant communication occurs during feeding. Babies naturally establish a rhythm of sucking. They suck approximately 8–10 seconds and then pause for 3–5 seconds. During the pauses most mothers will do something, like jiggle, talk, or pat the baby. Although mothers claim these activities are to get the baby to suck again, research has shown that the baby will begin sucking again even if the mother does nothing (Kaye, 1977). This interaction around sucking is the first repeated experience the infant has with establishing a pattern of behavior and responding to that behavior. When mothers do something during the pause, they usually do it at the 3–5 second interval (Kaye, 1977; Shigekawa, 1976). Because the infant's memory is only a few seconds long, it is likely that this is one way infants learn that something will happen to them when they do something, like pause. Over time, the more the mother does during the pause the more the baby pauses. This "suck-pause" is a form of early communication. Nonnutritive sucking has been observed by several researchers to enhance alertness and visual attentiveness to stimuli (Anderson & Vidyasagar, 1979; Gill, Behnke, Conlon, McNeely, & Anderson, 1988; Neeley, 1979). Both nutritive and nonnutritive sucking are inherent to the infant's self-regulation and adaptive interaction with the environment (Kimble, 1992).

Mothers who provide cognitive types of experiences during an interaction also encourage and allow the infant to explore their surroundings. This includes exploring the mother, the bottle, or some part of the environment with the infant's hands, mouth, or eyes. During the early months of life infants learn primarily through touching, looking at, and mouthing various objects in their environment.

There needs to be the opportunity for physical proximity, as well. In addition, the mother must be psychologically available to the child, free from stress and pressure. Anisfield, Casper, Nozyce, and Cunningham (1990) demonstrated that in high-risk mothers the use of a baby carrier like a Snugli to promote mother–infant physical proximity resulted in better social interaction between the mother and infant at 3 months and in more secure attachment at 1 year. Likewise, Gottfried (1984) reported that physical proximity and contact during the first 6 months was one of the important predictors of later IQ.

Infants' Responsibilities During Interaction

Clarity of cues.   This refers to the infant's ability to send clear cues to the mother. The skill and clarity with which infant cues are sent make it either easy or difficult for mothers to "read" the cues and make the appropriate changes in their behavior. Ambiguous or confusing cues interrupt the mother's adaptive abilities and affect the quality of the interaction. During the feeding infants communicate cues of hunger, distress, satiation, interaction, and rest. Infants who demonstrate clarity of cues signal their readiness to eat by displaying some tension at the beginning of the feeding followed by a decrease in tension once the feeding has begun. Infants who give clear cues have periods of alertness during feeding. Babies who are in the awake state prior to feeding and start feeding in the awake state are found to eat better and take less time eating (Fuhrmann, 1984; Kushner, 1987; Page, 1992). Most newborns begin feeding in the active alert or crying state. Infants who are alert during the feeding are more likely to cue their mother for interaction through vocalizations and smiles, as well as cue the mother for a break or rest.

Responsiveness to mother.   Here we refer to the infant's ability to respond to the mother's attempts to communicate and interact. Just as the child sends cues so that mothers can modify their behavior, the child also "reads" and responds to the mother's behavior. During the feeding there are many examples of an infant's responsiveness. Responsiveness to mother is seen when infants stop crying following the mother's attempts to soothe, look in the direction of the mother's face when the mother talks, mold into the contours of the mother's body when held, suck and make feeding sounds following feeding attempts by the mother, and vocalize or smile after the mother's vocalization or smiles. These behaviors are highly reinforcing to the continuation of positive mothering behaviors and adaptive mother–infant interactions.

Although both mother and infant have responsibilities in keeping the interaction going, during early infancy the mother has the major responsibility to manage the interaction. In cases where the infant is unable to give clear cues or respond to the mother, the infant is not in a position to change. It becomes the mother's responsibility to recognize this and adapt her behaviors so that the interaction becomes positive and flows smoothly. Mothers often need additional information and support as they are shown ways to adapt their behavior to meet the needs of their infant (Barnard, Morriset, & Spieker, 1993).

It is believed that most mothers have the skills and desire to do what is best for their infant. The skills mothers need to bring to the interaction include the ability to read their infant's cues, to respond in a contingent manner, to stimulate the baby through touch, movement, talking, and looking at, and to delay stimulating or responding until the infant signals readiness. Among the crucial skills infants need to bring to the interaction are perceptual abilities, such as hearing and seeing, the capacity to look at another for a period of time, and the ability to smile, be consoled, adapt their body to holding or movement, and be regular and predictable in responding. Research demonstrates that the absence of these skills by either partner has a major impact on the nature of the mother–infant interaction pattern and later development (Barnard, Hammond, Booth, Mitchell, & Spieker, 1989).

The Barnard model has been used as a framework to evaluate behaviors of both the mother and the infant that the literature and experience documented as important for fostering the relationship and the child's development. A set of item descriptors were developed for each dimension of the model, tailoring the model's categories to create subscales for observing and rating the dyads' behaviors in the feeding and teaching context. The items are all binary in format; either the behavior occurred or did not occur. In the Nursing Child Assessment Feeding Scale (NCAFS) there are 76 items and for the Nursing Child Assessment Teaching Scale (NCATS) there are 73 items. The psychometrics of the scales are fully reported in manuals that accompany the training video tapes used for instruction in relibility training (Barnard, 1994; Barnard et al., 1989; Morisett, 1994). The total and mothers' scores on both scales are correlated with child verbal intelligence as early as 2 years; the correlations with 1- and 2-year interaction are even stronger with 5 years' IQ scores (Morisset, 1994). This stronger correlation at later ages is counterintutitive and emphasizes the influence of early mother–child interaction on subsequent mother–child relationships and on later development.

CONCLUSIONS

In reviewing the literature for this chapter, the absence of studies linking the transitional process of maternal role attainment with role performance was striking. Upon reflection this is not surprising because the measurement of maternal role attainment and role performance have lacked a history of methodological development to study these processes. Only since the 1960s have we gone beyond speculating about the the dimensions of mothering. Mothering has historically been hidden within the boundaries set by families. Now that more measures are developing and there is expansion of caregiving of the young child to others, we can expect empirical work to proceed.

Within the next decade we need to examine the appropriateness of current measures to our rapidly changing ideas of who is involved in early caregiving. Part of this changing norm is fed by our demographics. The proportion of different ethnic groups in our American culture will bring new dimensions to the role definition of mother. In Asian cultures the extended family is very involved with childrearing. In mainland China the mother's mother typically handles the daily care of the young infant. In African-American families the aunts, uncles, grandmothers, and siblings are very involved in looking after the youngest children. In fact White North Americans may be one of the few cultures in the world that have recently relied so much on mothers to raise children without help from other family members or trained alternative mothers.

In the future, research needs to focus on studying the link between self-concept, knowledge, attitudes, and past experience toward motherhood with both maternal role attainment, identification, and performance. Josten (1982), as reported in this chapter, is one of the few investigators to have done so. If there are strong links, this suggests we need to understand at a deeper level the processes involved. Until this knowledge is available we have little evidence or theory to aid us in designing preventive interventions (Barnard et al., 1988, 1993).

We have little knowledge about whether successfully completing the psychological tasks of pregnancy will lead to more optimal role attainment and hence more optimal mothering. We need to know this before recommending preventive interventions. At the same time we need more cross-cultural work, both to enrich our notions of the mothering role, and to avoid using a limited conceptual schema of the maternal role. America as a culture values achievement and independence. Mothering has been anchored in this ethic of independence. By more cross-cultural knowledge we can add richness and diversity to our concept of mothering.

This chapter has focused on mothering as it emerges during the pregnancy and the earliest period of life. We have not dealt with mothering issues with children beyond infancy. We speculate the processes of monitoring and responsiveness are common to later periods of childhood. The role of the mother as a social partner was highlighted in this chapter. Detailed accounting of mother and infant social responsiveness was given. The data cited support that the mother–child interaction is a reciprocal process and that characteristics of the mother such as her educational level and psychological state influence her role performance in interaction with the child; aspects of the infant such as state, breast or bottle feeding, developmental status, and temperament influence the infant's contribution.

Role strain for women is evolving as they both deal with caring for their children and devote major effort to work. The data reported by Mercer (1985, 1986) suggest that the burden of mothering during the first year does not change; new stages of development present new challenges. How does the mother deal with the demands of child care, work, and time for her own physical and emotional well-being? What is the trade-off of having others perform the mothering role with young children? The evidence suggests that the child needs a holding environment where someone is watching and responding and mediating the environment. Infants without devoted mothering in the first months of life do not thrive and are less likely to develop a sense of security. Mothering is an important role in relation to the growth and development of young children and children with developmental disabilities and chronic health problems; whenever an individual needs a "holding" environment mothering is the role required. Mothering is learned in the process of interaction with the individual mothered. The role demands the capacity to be emotionally available, alert to needs, and responsive to behavior. We provided a review of the role, how women prepare to take the role on, and the measurement and meaning of this role in infancy.

REFERENCES

Ainsworth, M. D. S., (1973). The development of infant–mother attachment. In B. M. Caldwell & H. N. Riccuiti (Eds.), *Review of child development research* (Vol. 3, pp. 1–94). Chicago: University of Chicago Press.

Ainsworth, M. D. S., & Bell, S. M. (1974). Mother–infant interaction and the development of competence. In K. J. Connolly & J. Bruner (Eds.), *The growth of competence* (pp. 97–117). New York: Academic Press.

Anderson, B., & Anderson, A. (1989). *Longitudinal comparative analysis of maternal interaction with singleton and twins.* Unpublished manuscript, University of Alberta, Edmonton, Canada.

Anderson, G. C., & Vidyasagar, D. (1979). Development of sucking in premature infants from 1 to 7 days post birth. In G. C. Anderson, B. Raft, M. Duxbury, & P. Carroll (Eds.), *Newborn behavioral organization: Nursing research and implications* (Vol. 15, pp. 145–171). New York: Liss.

Anisfeld, E., Casper, V., Nozyce, M., & Cunningham, N. (1990). Does infant carrying promote attachment?: An experimental study of the effects of increased physical contact on the development of attachment. *Child Development, 61,* 1617–1627.

Barnard, K. E. (1976). *NCAST II learners resource manual.* Seattle: NCAST Publications.

Barnard, K. E. (1994). What the feeding scale measures. In G. Sumner & A. Spietz (Eds.), *NCAST feeding manual* (pp. 98–121). Seattle: NCAST Publications. (Available only with training, 206-543-8528)

Barnard, K. E., Bee, H. L., & Hammond, M. A. (1984). Developmental changes in maternal interactions with term and preterm infants. *Infant Behavior and Development, 7,* 101–113.

Barnard, K. E., Hammond, M. A., Booth, C. L., Mitchell, S. K., & Spieker, S. J. (1989). Measurement and meaning of parent–child interaction. In F. J. Morrison, C. E. Lord, & D. P. Keating (Eds.), *Applied development psychology* (Vol. 3, pp. 39–80). New York: Academic Press.

Barnard, K. E., Hammond, M., Mitchell, S. K., et al. (1985). Caring for high-risk infants and their families. In M. Green (Ed.), *The psychological aspects of the family* (pp. 245–259). Lexington, MA: Lexington.

Barnard, K. E., & Kelly, J. F. (1989). Assessment of parent–child interaction. In S. J. Meisels & J. P. Shonkoff (Eds.), *Handbook of early childhood intervention* (pp. 278–302). New York: Cambridge University Press.

Barnard, K. E., Morisset, C. E., & Spieker, S. J. (1993) Preventive interventions: Enhancing parent–infant relationship. In C. Zeanah (Ed.), *Handbook on infant mental health* (pp. 386–401). New York: Guilford Press.

Beckwith, L. (1971). Relationships between attributes of mothers and their infants' IQ scores. *Child Development, 42,* 1083–1097.

Beckwith, L., & Cohen, S. E. (1984). Home environment and cognitive competence in preterm children during the first 5 years. In A. W. Gottfried (Ed.), *Home environment and early cognitive development* (pp. 235–271). New York: Academic Press.

Bee, H. L., Barnard, K. E., Eyres, S. J., Gray, C. A., Hammond, M. A., Spietz, A. L., Snyder, C., & Clark, B. (1982). Prediction of IQ and language skill from perinatal status, child performance, family characteristics, and mother–infant interaction. *Child Development, 53,* 1134–1156.

Bell, S. M., & Ainsworth, M. D. S. (1972) Infant crying and maternal responsiveness. *Child Development, 43*(4), 1171–1190.

Belsky, J., Rovine, M., & Taylor, D. G. (1984). The Pennsylvania infant and family development project, III: The origins of individual differences in infant–mother attachment: Maternal and infant contributions. *Child Development, 55,* 718–728.

Blackwell, P., & Kaiser, M. (1994). *The collaborative approach to nurturing: Mother–infant interaction in cocaine affected dyads.* Unpublished manuscript, Tulane University, New Orleans.

Blank, M. (1964). Some maternal influences on infants' rate of sensorimotor development. *Journal of American Academy of Child Psychiatry, 3,* 668–687.

Booth, C. L., Mitchell, S. K., Barnard, K. E., & Spieker, S. J. (1989). Development of maternal social skills in multiproblem families: Effects on the mother–child relationship. *Developmental Psychology, 25,* 403–412.

Bornstein, M. H. (1989a). Between caretakers and their young: Two modes of interaction and their consequences for cognitive growth. In M. H. Bornstein & J. S. Bruner (Eds.), *Interaction in human development* (pp. 197–214). Hillsdale, NJ: Lawrence Erlbaum Associates.

Bornstein, M. H. (1989b). Cross-cultural developmental comparisons: The case of Japanese-American infant and mother activities and interactions, what we know, what we need to know, and why we need to know. *Developmental Review, 9,* 171–204.

Bornstein, M. H., & Tamis-LeMonda, C. S. (1989). Maternal responsiveness and cognitive development in children. In M. H. Bornstein (Ed.), *Maternal responsiveness: Characteristics and consequences. New directions for child development* (Vol. 43, pp. 49–61). San Francisco: Jossey-Bass.

Brazelton, T., Koslowski, B., & Main, M. (1974). The origins of reciprocity: The early mother–infant interaction. In M. Lewis & L. Rosenblum (Eds.), *The effect of the infant on its caregiver.* New York: Wiley.

Brazelton, T. B., Tronick, E., Adamson, L., Als, H., & Wise, S. (1975). Early mother–infant reciprocity. In *Parent–Infant Interaction* (Symposium of the CIBA Foundation) (pp. 137–153). Amsterdam: Elsevier.

Burr, W. R. (1972). Role transitions. A reformulation of theory. *Journal of Marriage and the Family, 34,* 407–416.

Campbell, J. C., Poland, M. L., Waller, J. B., & Ager, J. (1992). Correlates of battering during pregnancy. *Research in Nursing and Health, 15,* 219–226.

Censullo, M., Bowler, R., Lester, B., & Brazelton, T. B. (1987). An instrument for the measurement of infant–adult synchrony. *Nursing Research, 36,* 342–346.

Censullo, M., Lester, B., & Hoffman, J. (1985). Rhythmic patterning in mother–newborn interaction. *Nursing Research, 34,* 342–346.

Clarke-Stewart, K. A. (1973). Interactions between mothers and their young children: Characteristics and consequences. *Monographs of the Society for Research in Child Development, 38*(153, Serial No. 38).

Coates, D. L., & Lewis, M. (1984). Early mother–infant interaction and infant cognitive status as predictors of school performance and cognitive behavior in six-year-olds. *Child Development, 55,* 1219–1230.

Coster, W. J., Gersten, M. S., Beeghly, M., & Cicchetti, D. (1989). Communicative functioning in maltreated toddlers. *Developmental Psychology, 25,* 1020–1029.

Cutrona, C. E., & Troutman, B. R. (1986). Social support, infant temperament, and parent self-efficacy: A mediational model of post-partum depression. *Child Development, 57,* 1507–1518.

Disbrow, M. A., Doerr, H. O., & Caulfield, C. (1977). Measuring the components of potential for child abuse and neglect. *Journal of Child Abuse and Neglect: An International Journal, 1,* 279–296.

Dorr, D., & Friedenberg, L. (1983). Mothering and the young child [Special issue: Social and psychological problems of women: Prevention and crisis intervention]. *Issues in Mental Health Nursing, 5*(1–4), 45–60.

Elardo, R., Bradley, R., & Caldwell, B. (1975). The relation of infants' home environment to mental test performance from six to thirty-six months: A longitudinal analysis. *Child Development, 46,* 71–76.

Flaherty, M. J. (1988). Seven caring functions of Black grandmothers in adolescent mothering. *Maternal–Child Nursing Journal, 17*(3), 191–207.

Fuhrmann, P. J. (1984). *The effect of preterm infant state regulation on parent–child interaction.* Unpublished master's thesis, University of Washington, Seattle.

Gabinet, L. (1986). A protocol for assessing competence to parent a newborn. *General Hospital Psychiatry, 8,* 263–272.

Gill, N. E., Behnke, M., Conlon, M., McNeely, J. B. & Anderson, G. C. (1988). Effect of non-nutritive sucking on behavioral state in premature infants before feeding. *Nursing Research, 37,* 347–350.

Goldberg, S. (1977). Social competence in infancy: A model of parent–infant interaction. *Merrill-Palmer Quarterly, 23,* 163–177.

Gottfried, A. (Ed.). (1984). *Home environment and early cognitive development.* New York: Academic Press.

Greenberg, M. T., & Crnic, K. A. (1988). Longitudinal predictors of developmental status and social interaction in premature and full-term infants at age two. *Child Development, 59,* 554–570.

Greenspan, S. I., & Lieberman, A. F. (1980). Infants, mothers and their interaction: A qualitative clinical approach to developmental assessment. In S. Greenspan & G. H. Pollock (Eds.), *The course of life* (Vol. I, pp. 271–312). (DHHS Publication No. 80-786). Washington, DC: National Institute of Mental Health.

Hammond, M. A., Bee, H. L., Barnard, D. E., & Eyres, S. J. (1983). *Child health assessment: Part IV. Follow-up at second grade.* (Grant RO 1-NU-00816, Final Report of Division of Nursing, Bureau of Health Professions, Health Resources and Services Administration, U.S. Public Health Service). Seattle: NCAST Publications, University of Washington.

Heinicke, C. (1984). Impact of prebirth parent personality and marital functioning on family development: A framework and suggestions for further study. *Developmental Psychology, 20*(6), 1044–1053.

Johnson, M. C. (1991). Infant and toddler sleep: A telephone survey of parents in one community. *Journal of Developmental and Behavioral Pediatrics, 12*(2), 108–114.

Josten, L. (1982). Contrast in prenatal preparation for mothering. *Maternal-Child Nursing Journal, 11*(2), 65–73.

Kang, R. R. (1985). *A model of parental competence.* Unpublished doctoral dissertation, University of Washington, Seattle.

Kaye, K. (1977). Toward the origin of dialogue. In H. R. Schaffer (Ed.), *Studies in mother–infant interaction* (pp. 89–117). London: Academic Press.

Kimble, C. (1992). Non-nutritive sucking: Adaptation and health for the neonate. *Neonatal Network, 11,* 29–33.

Koniak-Griffin, D. (1993). Maternal role attainment. *Image, 25,* 257–261.

Kushner, K. (1987). *The effect of infant state modulation on parent–infant reciprocity: Impact of a nursing program.* Unpublished master's thesis, University of Washington, School of Nursing, Seattle.

Lederman, R. P. (1984). *Psychosocial adaptation in pregnancy.* Englewood Cliffs, NJ: Prentice-Hall.

Lederman., R., Lederman, E., Workk, B. A., & McCann, D. S., (1978). The relationship of maternal anxiety, plasma catecholamines and plasma control to progress in Labor. *American Journal of Obstetrics and Gynecology, 132,* 495–500.

Leifer, M. (1977). Psychological changes accompanying pregnancy and motherhood. *Genetic Psychology Monographs, 95,* 55–96.

Lester, B. M., Hoffman, J., & Brazelton, T. B. (1985). The rhythmic structure of mother–infant interaction in term and preterm infants. *Child Development, 56,* 15–27.

Lobo, M. L. (1992). Parent–infant interaction during feeding when the infant has congenital heart disease. *Journal of Pediatric Nursing, 7,* 97–105.

Lobo, M. L., Barnard, K. E., & Coombs, J. B. (1992). Failure to thrive: A parent–infant interaction perspective. *Journal of Pediatric Nursing, 7,* 251–261.

Lyons, N. (1981). *Behavioral differences in premature and fullterm mother–infant pairs during a feeding interaction.* Unpublished master's thesis, University of Washington, School of Nursing, Seattle.

Mario, M. (1976). *An investigation of verbal behavior of maternal–infant pairs during feeding at one, four, eight, and twelve months of age.* Unpublished master's thesis, University of Washington, Seattle.

Mercer, R. T. (1981). A theoretical framework for studying factors that impact on the maternal role. *Nursing Research, 30,* 73–77.

Mercer, R. T. (1985). The process of maternal role attainment over the first year. *Nursing Research, 34,* 198–204

Mercer, R. T. (1986). *First-time motherhood: Experiences from the teens to forties.* New York: Springer.

Morisset, C. E. (1988). *It takes two to communicate: The role of interpersonal experience in child language acquistion.* Unpublished paper submitted in partial fulfillment of General Examination requirements, University of Washington, Seattle.

Morisset, C. E. (1994). What the teaching scale measures. In G. Sumner & A. Spietz (Eds.), *NCAST Teaching Manual* (pp. 100–127). Seattle: NCAST Publications. (Available only through training, 206-543-8528)

Morisset, C. E., Barnard, K. E., Greenberg, M. T., Booth, C. L., & Spieker, S. J. (1990). Environmental influences on early language development: The context of social risk. *Development and Psychopathology, 2,* 127–149.

Neeley, C. A. (1979). Effects of non-nutritive sucking upon the behavioral arousal of the newborn. In G. C. Anderson, B. Raff, M. Duxbury, & P. Carroll (Eds.), *Newborn behavioral organization: Nursing research and implications* (Vol. 15, pp. 173–200). New York: Liss.

Nelson, K. (1973). Structure and strategy in learning to talk. *Monographs of the Society for Research in Child Development, 38*(1–2, Serial No. 149).

Olson, S. L., Bates, J. E., & Bayles, K. (1984). Mother–infant interaction and the development of individual differences in children's cognitive competence. *Developmental Psychology, 20,* 166–179.

Page, P. (1992). Promoting synchrony in maternal-preterm infant interactions through state modulation. *NCAST National News, 8*(4), 1–3, 9–10.

Papoušek, H., & Bornstein, M. H. (1992) Didactic interactions: Intuitive parental support of vocal and verbal development in human infants. In H. Papoušek, U. Jurgens, & M. Papoušek (Eds.), *Nonverbal vocal communication: Comparative and developmental approaches* (pp. 209–229). Cambridge, England: Cambridge University Press.

Radke-Yarrow, M. (1991). The individual and the environment in human behavioral development. In P. Bateson (Ed.), *The development and integration of behavior. Essays in honour of Robert Hinde* (pp. 389–410). Cambridge, England: Cambridge University Press.

Ramey, C. T., Farran, D. C., & Campbell, F. A. (1979). Predicting IQ from mother–infant interactions. *Child Development, 50,* 804–814.

Robson, K. S. (1967). The role of eye to eye contact in maternal–infant attachment. *Journal of Child Psychology and Psychiatry, 8,* 13–25.

Rubin, R. (1967a). Attainment of the maternal role: Models and referrants. *Nursing Research, 16,* 342–346.

Rubin, R. (1967b). Attainment of the maternal role: Processes. *Nursing Research, 16,* 237–245.

Rubin, R. (1977). Binding-in the postpartum period. *Maternal-Child Nursing Journal, 6,* 67–75.

Rubin, R. (1984). *Maternal identity and maternal experience.* New York: Springer.

Ruble, D. N., Fleming, A. S., Stangor, C., Brooks-Gunn, J., Fizmaurice, G., & Deutsch, F. (1990). Transition to motherhood and the self: Measurement, stability, and change. *Journal of Personality and Social Psychology, 58*(3), 450–463.

Ruddy, M., & Bornstein, M. (1982). Cognitive correlates of infant attention and maternal stimulation over the first year of life. *Child Development, 53,* 183–188.

Ruff, C. C. (1987). How well do adolescents mother? *Maternal Child Nursing, 12,* 249–253.

Ruff, C. C. (1990). Adolescent mothering: Assessing their parenting capabilities and their health education needs. *Journal of the National Black Nurses Association, 4,* 55–62.

Russell, C. S. (1974). Transition to parenthood: Problems and gratifications. *Journal of Marriage and the Family, 36,* 294–301.

Sander, L. W. (1962). Issues in early mother child interaction. *Journal of American Academy of Child Psychiatry, 1,* 141–166.

Sander, L. W. (1964). Adaptive relationships in early mother–child interaction. *Journal of the American Academy of Child Psychiatry, 3,* 231–264.

Scarr, S., & McCartney, K. (1983). How people make their own environments: A theory of genotype to environment effects. *Child Development, 54,* 424–435.

Shereshefsky, R. M., & Yarrow, L. J. (1973). *Psychological aspects of a first pregnancy and early postnatal adaptation.* New York: Raven.

Shigekawa, J. (1976). *An investigation of the burst-pause pattern of sucking as a contingency for maternal infant interaction.* Unpublished master's thesis, University of Washington, Seattle.

Shonkoff, J. P., Hansen-Cram, P., Krauss, M. W., & Upshur, C. C. (1992). Development of infants with disabilities and their families. *Monographs of the Society for Research in Child Development, 57*(6, Serial No. 230).

Slater, M. A., Naqvi, M., Andrew, L., & Haynes, K. (1987). Neurodevelopment of monitored versus non-monitored very low birth weight infants: The importance of family influences. *Developmental and Behavioral Pediatrics, 8,* 278–285.

Spieker, S. (1989). Adolescent mothers: Parenting skills measured using the NCATS and the HOME. *NCAST National News, 5*(4), 3, 4–8.

Spieker, S. J., & Booth, C. L. (1988). Maternal antecedents of attachment quality. In J. Belsky & T. Nezworski (Eds.), *Clinical implications of attachment* (pp. 95–131). Hillsdale, NJ: Lawrence Erlbaum Associates.

Stern, D. N. (1985). Selective attunement. In D. N. Stern (Ed.), *The interpersonal world of the infant* (pp. 297–311). New York: Basic Books.

Sumner, G., & Spietz, A. (Eds.). (1994). *NCAST: Feeding manual.* Seattle, WA: NCAST.

Virden, S. F. (1988). The relationship between infant feeding method and maternal role adjustment. *Journal of Nurse-Midwifery. 33*(1), 31–35.

vonWindeguth, B. J., & Urbano, R. C. (1989). Teenagers and the mothering experience. *Pediatric Nursing, 15,* 517–520.

Wachs, T. D., U giris, I. C., & Hunt, J. (1971). Cognitive development in infants of different age levels and from different environmental backgrounds: An explanatory investigation. *Merrill–Palmer Quarterly, 17,* 283–317.

Walker, L. O., Crain, H., & Thompson, E. (1985). Maternal role attainment and identity in the postpartum period: Stability and change. *Nursing Research, 35,* 68–71.

Webster-Stratton, C. (1985). Comparison of abusive and nonabusive families with conduct-disordered children. *American Journal of Orthopsychiatry, 55*(1), 59–69.

Webster-Stratton, C. (1992). *The incredible years.* Toronto: Umbrella Press.

Winnicott, D. W. (1988). *Babies and their mothers.* Exeter, Great Britain: Short Run Press Ltd.

Winnicott, D. W. (1990). *The maturational process and the facilitating environment.* Exeter, Great Britian: BPCC Wheatons, Ltd.

Yarrow, L. J., Rubenstein, J. L., & Pedersen, F. A. (1975). *Infant and environment: Early cognitive and motivational development.* Washington, DC: Hemisphere.

2

Fathers and Families

Ross D. Parke
University of California, Riverside

INTRODUCTION

Theoretical assumptions that guide research in this area both explain the choice of topics and provide an organizational structure for the chapter. First, to understand fully the nature of father–child relationships, it is necessary to recognize the interdependence among the roles and functions of all family members. Families are best viewed as social systems. Consequently, to understand the behavior of one member of a family, the complementary behaviors of other members also need to be recognized and assessed. For example, as men's roles in families shift, changes in women's roles in families must also be monitored. Second, family members—mothers, fathers, and children—influence each other both directly and indirectly (Lewis & Feiring, 1981; Parke, Power, & Gottman, 1979; Parke & Tinsley, 1987). Examples of fathers' indirect impact include various ways in which fathers modify and mediate mother–child relationships. In turn, women affect their children indirectly through their husbands by modifying both the quantity and the quality of father–child interactions. Children may indirectly influence the husband–wife relationship by altering the behavior of either parent that consequently changes the interaction between spouses. Third, different levels of analysis are necessary in order to understand fathers. The individual level—child, mother, and father—remains a useful and necessary level of analysis, but recognition of relationships among family members as levels or units of analysis is also necessary. The marital, the mother–child, and the father–child relationships require separate analyses. The family as a unit that is independent of the individual or dyads within the family requires recognition.

Fourth, families are embedded within a variety of other social systems, including both formal and informal support systems as well as the cultures in which they exist (Bronfenbrenner, 1989; Cochran & Brassard, 1979; Parke & Tinsley, 1987; Tinsley & Parke, 1984, 1988a). These include a wide range of extrafamilial influences such as extended families, informal community ties such as friends and neighbors, work sites, and social, educational, and medical institutions (Bronfenbrenner & Crouter, 1982; Hoffman, 1984; Repetti, 1993; Tinsley & Parke, 1984).

A fifth assumption concerns the importance of considering father–child relationships from a variety of developmental perspectives. Developmental changes in child perceptual-cognitive and social-emotional capacities represent the most commonly investigated type of development. In addition, a life-span perspective (Elder, 1974, 1984; Elder, Modell, & Parke, 1993; Parke, 1988; Parke

27

& Tinsley, 1984) suggests the importance of examining developmental changes in the adult because parents continue to change and develop during adult years. For example, age at the time of the onset of parenthood can have important implications for how women and men manage their maternal and paternal roles. This involves an exploration of the tasks faced by adults such as self-identity, education, and career and examination of relations between these tasks and the demands of parenting.

Another assumption involves recognition of the impact of secular shifts on families. In recent years, a variety of social changes in America has had a profound impact on families. These include the decline in fertility and family size, changes in the timing of the onset of parenthood, increased participation of women in the work force, rise in rates of divorce, and subsequent increase in the number of single-parent families (Parke & Stearns, 1993; Parke & Tinsley, 1984). The ways in which these society-wide changes impact on interaction patterns between parents and children merit examination.

Another closely related assumption involves the recognition of the importance of the historical time period in which the family interaction is taking place. Historical time periods provide the social conditions for individual and family transitions: Examples include the 1930s (the Great Depression), the 1960s (the Vietnam War era), or the 1980s (Farm Belt Depression). Across these historical time periods, family interactions may be quite different due to the peculiar conditions of the particular era (Elder et al., 1993).

These distinctions among different developmental trajectories, as well as social change and historical period effects, are important because these different forms of change do not always harmonize (Elder & Hareven, 1993; Parke, 1988; Parke & Tinsley, 1984). For example, a family event such as the birth of a child—the transition to parenthood—may have very profound effects on a man who has just begun a career in contrast to the effects on one who has advanced to a stable occupational position. Moreover, individual and family developmental trajectories are embedded within both the social conditions and the values of the historical time in which they exist (Elder & Hareven, 1993). The role of parents, as is the case with any social role, is responsive to such fluctuations.

A final assumption concerns the role of cognitive factors in understanding father–child relationships. Specifically, we assume that the ways in which parents perceive, organize, and understand both their children and their roles as parents will affect the nature of father–child interaction (Goodnow & Collins, 1990; Sameroff, 1983).

In order to understand the nature of father–child relationships within families, a multilevel and dynamic approach is required. Multiple levels of analysis are necessary in order to capture the individual, dyadic, and family unit aspects of operation within the family itself as well as to reflect the embeddedness of families within a variety of extrafamilial social systems. The dynamic quality reflects the multiple developmental trajectories that warrant consideration in understanding the nature of families in infancy, childhood, and adolescence.

The substantive portion of the chapter begins with a discussion of the nature of the father–child relationships and how these shift across development of the child. Next the chapter moves to an examination of the determinants of father involvement to examine the impact of the marital relationship on the parent–infant relationship. Finally, the effect of recent historical changes, namely, shifts in work patterns of family members and changes in the timing of the onset of parenthood on father–child relationships are reviewed. Finally, the implications of fathering for men themselves, their wives, and their children are examined.

A CAUTIONARY HISTORICAL NOTE

This chapter is a review of recent work on fatherhood and devotes less attention to the historical aspects of the topic. However, several recent reviews caution against any simple and linear set of historical trends that lead clearly from the past to the present (Parke & Stearns, 1993; Rotundo, 1985, 1993; Stearns, 1991). Perhaps most striking is the continued tension and variability in fathering behavior—a set of characteristics that have long marked definitions of fatherhood. There have always been counteracting forces that have both promoted and limited father involvement with their children and families. There have been "good dads and bad dads" (Furstenberg, 1988) throughout the course of the history of fatherhood. Even the venerable play orientation of fathers has its origins, only recently in the past century (Parke & Stearns, 1993; Stearns, 1991). Stearns recently characterized the shifts over the last century as follows:

> ... most pressing context for fatherhood over the past century has been the change in work–family relationship. ... An 18th Century father would not recognize the distance contemporary men face between work and home or the importance of sports in father–child relations or the parental leadership granted to mothers or indeed the number of bad fathers. An 18th Century father would, however, recognize certain contemporary tensions such as a balance between seeking and giving love on the one hand and defining proper authority and he might feel kinship to present-day fathers who sense some tension between responses they regard as male and special restraints required for proper family life. (p. 50)

In sum, many of the themes that characterize contemporary thinking about fatherhood have clearer antecedents over the last century than we often assume. There has been a tendency to confuse the resurgence of interest in fathering as research topic with the assumption that the changes in fathering activities have been only recent as well.

PATERNAL VERSUS MATERNAL INVOLVEMENT WITH CHILDREN

In this section we address the issue of the degree to which mothers and fathers are involved with their children. There are overall differences in the quantity of involvement for mothers and fathers, but there are important stylistic or qualitative differences as well.

Not all forms of father involvement are conceptually equivalent. Several researchers have distinguished various types of father involvement (Barnett & Baruch, 1987; Lamb, Pleck, & Levine, 1985; Radin, 1993). The most influential scheme was offered by Lamb and his colleagues (Lamb, 1987; Lamb et al., 1985) who suggested three components: interaction, availability, and responsibility:

> Interaction refers to the father's direct contact with his child through caregiving and shared activities. Availability is a related concept concerning the child's potential availability for interaction, by virtue of being present or accessible to the child whether or not direct interaction is occurring. Responsibility refers to the role the father takes in ascertaining that the child is taken care of and arranging for resources to be available for the child. (Lamb et al., 1987, p. 125)

Several further distinctions have been offered (Radin, 1993). Specifically, it is important to distinguish involvement in child-care activities and involvement in play, leisure, or affiliative activities with the child. There are different determinants of these two types of father involvement (Beitel & Parke, 1993; Grossman, Pollack, & Golding, 1988; Levy-Shiff & Israelashvili, 1988). Radin (1993) also suggested that absolute and relative involvement need to be distinguished because prior work (e.g., Pleck, 1981) suggests that these two indices are independent and may affect both children's and adults' views of role distributions in different ways.

Parent as Manager Versus Direct Interactive Partner

The focus of research on fathers has been primarily on face-to-face parent–child interaction. To a large degree this emphasis reflects the common assumption that parental influence takes place directly through face-to-face contact or indirectly through the impact of the interaction on another family member. Only recently have researchers and theorists begun to recognize the *managerial* function of parents and to appreciate the impact of variations in how this managerial function influences child development (Hartup, 1979; Parke, 1978; Parke, Burks, Carson, Neville, & Boyum, 1994). By managerial, we refer to the ways in which parents organize and arrange the child's home environment and set limits on the range of the home setting to which the child has access and the opportunities for social contact with playmates and socializing agents outside the family. The managerial role may be just as important as the parent's role as stimulator, because the amount of time that children spend interacting with the inanimate environment far exceeds their social interaction time (White, Kaban, Shapiro, & Attonucci, 1976).

Mothers and fathers differ in their degree of responsibility for management of family tasks. From infancy through middle childhood, mothers are more likely to assume the managerial role than are fathers. In infancy, this means setting boundaries for play (Power & Parke, 1982), taking the child to the doctor, or arranging day care. Mothers are higher in all of these domains than fathers. In middle childhood, Russell and Russell (1987) found that mothers continue to assume more managerial responsibility (e.g., directing the child to have a bath, to eat a meal, or to put away toys).

Nor is the managerial role restricted to family activities but includes initiating and arranging children's access to peers and playmates (Ladd, Profilet, & Hart, 1992; Parke & Bhavnagri, 1989). In addition, parents function as supervisors or overseers of children's interactions with age mates especially with younger children. Although both mothers and fathers are equally capable of this type of supervisory behavior as shown in laboratory studies (Bhavnagri & Parke, 1985, 1991), in home contexts, fathers are less likely than mothers to perform this supervisory role (Bhavnagri & Parke, 1991; Ladd et al., 1992).

Even in the 1990s and even in the case of families where husbands and wives share roles, fathers are less likely to engage in management of the household and child care. As Coltrane (1995) noted: "In most families, husbands notice less about what needs to be done, wait to be asked to do various chores and require explicit directions if they are to complete the tasks successfully ... most couples continue to characterize husbands contributions to housework or child care as 'helping' their wives" (p. 175).

Quantitative Assessments of Father Involvement in Intact Families

Two approaches to the issue of father involvement merit distinction. The extent to which fathers in intact families participate in child care needs to be distinguished from the level of involvement of fathers who are not coresident with their children for a variety of reasons including divorce or out-of-wedlock births. In fact, this conceptual distinction reflects the contradictory trends in the fathering literature that Furstenberg (1988) characterized as the "two faces of fatherhood" (p. 193). On the one hand, fathers seem to be increasing their involvement and moving slowly toward more equal participation with their wives in the care and rearing of children. On the other hand, increases in father absence, nonpayment of child support, and denial of paternity suggests that a less desirable side of fatherhood is evident as well. As in prior decades, the movement is not linear and straightforward but is contradictory and inconsistent. In this section, we focus on the former aspect of the issue and in later sections, on adolescent fatherhood and father visitation, we address the issue of nonresidential fatherhood.

In spite of current shifts in cultural attitudes concerning the appropriateness and desirability of shared roles and equal levels of participation in routine caregiving and interaction for mothers and fathers, the shifts are more apparent than real in the majority of intact families. Although more mothers are entering the work force, current occupational arrangements still mean the vast majority of fathers have less opportunity for interaction with their infants and children than mothers (Coltrane, 1995; Lamb, 1987). A number of studies indicate that fathers are less available during babies' awake periods (Pedersen & Robson, 1969) and are present for less time with their infants than are mothers (Kotelchuck, 1976). This pattern is present not only in U.S. samples but in other countries such as Great Britain (Jackson, 1987), Australia (Russell, 1983), and France and Belgium (delaisi de Parseval & Hurtsel, 1987; Szalai, 1972). Mothers and fathers differ in the amount of time that they spend in actual interaction with their children. In a longitudinal study of middle- and working-class families in which mothers, fathers, and their infants were observed when their infants were 1, 3, and 9 months of age, mothers were found to respond to, stimulate, express positive affection toward, and provide more basic care for their infants at all time points. Fathers exceeded mothers in the extent to which they engaged in reading and television viewing (Belsky, Gilstrap, & Rovine, 1984; Belsky & Volling, 1986).

Studies in other cultures confirm these findings. In Israel, Greenbaum and Landau (1982) carried out a cross-sectional study in which they observed middle- and lower class families under naturalistic conditions when their babies were 2, 4, 7, and 11 months. At every age point, mothers greatly exceeded fathers in verbal interactions—regardless of social class. However, the focus on verbal stimulation may have overestimated the nature of the mother–father differences in light of fathers' propensity to interact in a physical mode (Parke, 1979, 1981; Parke & Tinsley, 1981; Power & Parke, 1982). Even more impressive evidence of mother–father differences in involvement comes from the longitudinal study of traditional and nontraditional families in Sweden executed by Lamb and his colleagues (Lamb, Frodi, Hwang, & Frodi, 1982; Lamb, Frodi, Hwang, Frodi, & Steinberg, 1982). Families in which the father elected to stay home as primary caregiver for 1 month or more (nontraditional) were compared with families in which the father elected to be a secondary caregiver (traditional). In an analysis of home observations when babies were 8 and 16 months, mothers surpassed fathers in holding and affectional behavior regardless of family type.

Further support for this pattern of sex-of-parent differences comes from a study of kibbutz families (Sagi, Lamb, Shoham, Dvir, & Lewkowicz, 1985). Kibbutz-reared infants and their parents were observed in the parents' living quarters when the infants were 8 and 16 months of age. Although child care was the primary responsibility of nonparental caregivers (*metapelot*) rather than either parent, sex differences in parental behavior similar to those observed in the United States and Sweden were found. Kibbutz mothers were more likely to vocalize, laugh, display affection, hold, and engage in caregiving than were fathers. Because mothers and fathers on Israeli kibbutzim both work full-time and have their children cared for by other caregivers, the findings suggest that "more sex-role expectations (which certainly exist on the kibbutzim) and/or biological predispositions—rather than immediate competing role demands—appear to account for the widely observed differences between maternal and paternal behavior" (Sagi et al., 1985, p. 282).

These findings are consistent with the more general proposition that pregnancy and birth of a first child, in particular, are occasions for a shift toward a more traditional division of roles (Arbeit, 1975; Cowan & Cowan, 1992; Shereshefsky & Yarrow, 1973). Of particular interest is the fact that this pattern held regardless of whether the initial role division between husbands and wives was traditional or equalitarian (Cowan & Cowan, 1985, 1992). "Despite the current rhetoric and ideology concerning equality of roles for men and women, it seems that couples tend to adopt traditionally defined roles during times of stressful transition such as around the birth of a first child" (Cowan, Coie, & Coie, 1978, p. 20).

The overall pattern of contact time between mothers and fathers with their children that is evident in infancy continues into middle childhood and adolescence (Collins & Russell, 1991). In a study of middle childhood (6- to 7-year-olds), Russell and Russell (1987) found that Australian mothers were available to children 54.7 hours per week compared to 34.6 hours per week for fathers. Mothers also spent more time alone with children (22.6 hours per week) than did fathers (2.4 hours per week). However, when both parents and child were together, mothers and fathers initiated interactions with children with equal frequency and children's initiations toward each parent were similar. Montemeyor (1982), in a study of 15- to 16-year-olds, reported that more than twice as much time was spent with mother alone than with father alone each day. Similar findings were reported for 14- to 18-year-olds by Montemeyor and Brownlee (1987). In summary, mothers and fathers clearly differ in terms of their degree of involvement with their offspring from infancy through adolescence.

Competence Versus Performance

The lower level of father involvement in caregiving and other forms of interaction does not imply that fathers are less competent than mothers to care for infants and children. Competence can be measured in a variety of ways; one approach is to measure the parent's sensitivity to infant cues in the feeding context. Success in caregiving, to a large degree, depends on the parent's ability to correctly "read" or interpret the infant's behavior so that the parent's own behavior can be regulated to respond appropriately. One approach to the competence question involves an examination of the degree to which the caregiver modifies his or her behavior in response to infant cues. Parke and Sawin (1975, 1976) found that fathers' sensitivity to a variety of cues—auditory distress signals during feeding (sneeze, spit-up, cough), vocalizations, mouth movements—was just as marked as mothers' responsitivity to these cues. Both fathers and mothers adjusted their behavior (e.g., looking more closely, vocalizing, etc.) in response to these infant cues. In a later study (Parke & Sawin, 1980) it was shown that parent vocalizations can modify newborn infant behavior such as infant vocalizations. Interaction between fathers and infants—even in the newborn period—is clearly bidirectional in quality; parents and infants mutually regulate each other's behavior in the course of interaction. In spite of the fact that they may spend less time overall in caregiving activities, fathers are as sensitive as mothers to infant cues and as responsive to them in the feeding context. Moreover, the amount of milk consumed by infants with their mothers and fathers in this study was very similar, which suggests that fathers and mothers are not only comparable in their sensitivity but equally successful in feeding the infant based on the amount of milk consumed by the infant. Invoking a competence/performance distinction, fathers may not necessarily be as frequent contributors to infant feeding, but when called upon they have the competence to execute these tasks effectively.

Fathers' ability to perform caregiving tasks does not appear to be different from mothers' in middle childhood. As Russell and Russell (1987) found, both parents reported that they were involved on a regular basis in a variety of caregiving activities even though mothers were higher in their frequencies. For example, both mothers and fathers report "having a cuddle" very nearly every day and that fathers as well as mothers "go over their child's day" and "sit and have a talk" almost every day. Moreover, the degree of warmth expressed by mothers and fathers to their children is similar, although the behavioral manifestations of how warmth is expressed varies as a function of both sex of parent and sex of child (Russell & Russell, 1989). Finally, as noted earlier, fathers can function effectively as managers and supervisors of their children's activities, but do so less than mothers on a routine basis (Bhavnagri & Parke, 1991; Ladd et al., 1992). Again it appears that fathers are capable of this type of caregiving function but execute this function less regularly than mothers. On balance, however, the evidence suggests that fathers are competent caregiving agents.

Qualitative Effects: Stylistic Differences in Mother and Father Interaction

Fathers participate less than mothers in caregiving but spend a greater percentage of the time available for interaction in play activities than mothers do. In the United States, Kotelchuck (1976) found that fathers spent a greater percentage of their time with their infants in play (37.5 percent) than mother did (25.8 percent), although in absolute terms mothers spent more time than fathers in play with their children. Similar findings have been reported from a longitudinal investigation of parent–infant interaction in England (Richards, Dunn, & Antonis, 1977). At both 30 and 60 weeks of age, playing with their infants was the most common activity of fathers, and over 90 percent of the fathers played regularly with their infants. Lamb (1977a) observed interactions among mother, father, and infant in their homes at 7–8 months and again at 12–13 months. Marked differences emerged in the reasons that fathers and mothers pick up infants: Fathers were more likely to hold the babies simply to play with them, whereas mothers were far more likely to hold them for caregiving purposes.

It is not only the quantity of time in play that discriminates between mother and father involvement in infancy; the quality of play activity does so as well. Yogman (1983) studied the interaction patterns of mothers, fathers, and strangers with infants from 2 weeks to 6 months. Limb movement games, which were associated with increases in infant arousal, represented 70 percent of all father–infant games and only 4 percent of mother–infant games. In contrast to this type of physically arousing game used by fathers, mothers played physically by utilizing more conventional motor games such as "pat-a-cake," "peekaboo," or waving.

Stylistic differences in mothers' and fathers' play are not restricted to very young infants and are evident in both lab- and home-based studies. Power and Parke (1982) observed mothers and fathers interacting with their 8-month-old infants in a laboratory playroom. Fathers played more bouncing and lifting games, especially with boys, than did mothers. In contrast, mothers played more watching games in which a toy is presented and made salient by moving or shaking it.

Observations of father– and mother–infant interaction in unstructured home contexts with older infants reveals similar mother–father differences in play style (Power & Parke, 1982). Lamb (1977b), in a study of infants from 7 to 24 months of age, found that fathers engage in more physical (i.e., rough and tumble), parallel play with their infants and unusual play activities than do mothers. Mothers, in contrast, engaged in more conventional play activities (e.g., peekaboo, pat-a-cake), stimulus toy play (where a toy was jiggled or operated to stimulate the child directly), and reading. Similar differences in the style of play patterns were found by Clarke-Stewart (1980) in a study of infants 15–30 months old and their parents: "Fathers' play was relatively more likely to be physical and arousing rather than intellectual, didactic, or mediated by objects—as in the case of mothers" (p. 37).

Nor are these effects evident only in infancy. MacDonald and Parke (1984), in an observational study of the play interaction patterns between mothers and fathers and 3- and 4-year-olds, found that fathers engaged in more physical play with their children than did mothers, whereas, mothers engaged in more object-mediated play than did fathers. According to a recent survey (MacDonald & Parke, 1986), the fathers' distinctive role as a physical play partner changes with age, however. Physical play was highest between fathers and 2-year-olds, and between 2 and 10 years of age there is a decreased likelihood that fathers engage their children physically.

In spite of the decline in physical play across age, fathers are still more often physical play partners than mothers. In an Australian study of parents and their 6- to 7-year-old children (Russell & Russell, 1987), fathers were more involved in physical/outdoor play interactions and fixing things around the house and garden than were mothers. In contrast, mothers were more actively involved in caregiving and household tasks and in school work. Mothers were also involved in more reading, playing with toys, and helping with arts and crafts.

In all studies reviewed, a reasonably consistent pattern emerges: Fathers are tactile and physical, and mothers tend to be verbal, didactic, and toy mediated in their play. Clearly, infants and young children experience not only more stimulation from their fathers, but a qualitatively different stimulatory pattern. Cross-cultural study supports the generality of this pattern of mother–father differences in play style. Parents in England show similar sex differences (Smith & Daglish, 1977); fathers in New Delhi, India, show more rough physical play (tossing, roughhousing) and minor physical play (tickling, bouncing on lap) with infants than do mothers, although rough and minor physical play forms were relatively infrequent (Roopnarine, Hooper, Ahmeduzzaman, & Pollack, 1993; Roopnarine, Talukder, Jain, Joshi, & Srivastav, 1990). However, other evidence suggests that this pattern of mother–father differences in play style may be in part culture-bound. Specifically, neither in Sweden (Lamb et al., 1982) nor among Israeli kibbutz families (Sagi et al., 1985) were there clear sex-of-parent differences in the tendency to engage in play or in the types of play initiated:

> Perhaps this reflects the more egalitarian arrangements effective (at least during observation period) in Sweden and Israel than in the United States. This would suggest that, at least in regard to Sweden and Israel, sex differences in maternal and paternal behavior, are influenced by the concrete competing demands on the parents' time, as well as by their socialization and biogenetic tendencies. (Sagi et al., 1985, p. 283)

DETERMINANTS OF FATHER INVOLVEMENT

The importance of examining the determinants of father involvement stems from the view that the paternal role is less culturally scripted and determined than the maternal role and few clear role models for defining fatherhood exist (Daly, 1993; Marsiglio, 1993). It is assumed that a multifactor approach to father involvement is necessary because a variety of factors determines the degree of father involvement with children. It is useful to distinguish individual, familial, and societal levels of analysis in assessing the determinants of father involvement with children.

Individual Factors

Men's own psychological and family background, attitudes toward the fathering role, motivation to become involved, and child-care and childrearing knowledge and skills all play a role in determining men's level of involvement with their children.

Men's relationships with their family of origin.   The quality of relationship that fathers develop with their own mothers and fathers has been viewed as a possible determinant of fathers' involvement with their own children. However, evidence in support of this proposition is complex and by no means clear-cut. Two views have guided this inquiry (Russell, 1986; Snarey, 1993). First, from social-learning theory (Bandura, 1989) comes a modeling hypothesis that suggests that men model themselves after their fathers, and this modeling process will be enhanced if their fathers were nurturant and accessible. In short, men learn their fathering skills and attitudes from their own fathers. Second, a compensatory or reworking hypothesis argues that fathers tend to compensate or make up for deficiencies in their childhood relationships with their own fathers by becoming better and more involved when they themselves assume this role. There is support for both views. In support of the modeling hypothesis, a number of studies suggest that positive relationships with fathers in childhood are related to higher levels of later father involvement (Cowan & Cowan, 1987, 1992; Sagi, 1982). Support for the second hypothesis is also evident in both classic studies (Biller, 1971; Hetherington, 1967; Hetherington & Frankie, 1967) and more recent reports (Baruch & Barnett, 1986; Russell, 1986). Baruch and Barnett found that men who viewed their own relationships with their fathers as negative tended to be more involved with their 5- and 9-year-old children. As several researchers have noted (Belsky, 1991; Snarey, 1993), the predictive power of earlier familial relationships is especially evident in single-earner families in which wives are not employed. In these instances, fathers have more discretion in determining their level of involvement with their children. Sagi (1982) argued that these two hypotheses "are not mutually exclusive since either process is possible depending on the circumstances" (p. 214). Unfortunately, the specification of the "circumstances" that would lead to the heightened influence of one or the other of these influence patterns remains elusive.

Men's attitudes, motivation, and skills.   Paternal attitudes, motivation, and skills are important determinants of father involvement (Lamb, 1987; Lamb, Pleck, Charnov, & Levine, 1987). There has been a considerable body of research concerning the relation between sex-role attitudes and paternal involvement. Sex-role attitudes are usually indexed by scales measuring masculinity, femininity, and androgyny. In spite of the early promise of laboratory studies, which showed a link between men's higher scores on the traditional femininity scale of the Bem (1974) *Sex Role Inventory* and their tendencies to engage in parenting behavior (e.g., interact with a baby), there has been less support for this position in studies of fathers' involvement with their own children. Russell (1983), in his work on shared-caregiving families in Australia, found that these fathers in comparison with fathers in traditional families were higher on femininity. Moreover, compared to traditional families more fathers (and mothers) in the shared-caregiving families were androgynous, fewer mothers were feminine, and fewer fathers were masculine. However, in traditional families, Russell found no significant link between scores on the Bem *Sex Role Inventory* and level of father involvement. Others have also failed to find links between sex-role attitudes and fathering behavior (De Frain, 1979; Lamb et al., 1982). Moreover, the direction of effect is not clear; prior experience may shape sex-role attitudes rather than vice-versa.

When the focus is more specifically oriented toward beliefs about parental roles, clearer links between are evident. Several studies have found that men who reject the notion of maternal instinct are more highly participant in child-care tasks with their 3- to 6-year-old children (Russell, 1983). However, this view was unrelated to fathers' level of involvement in play. Moreover, several other measures (e.g., attitudes toward mother and father caregiving abilities; views about whether mother's place is in the home) were unrelated to father involvement in either caregiving or play.

Other paternal attitudes relate to measures of father involvement with their 3-month-old infants (Beitel & Parke, 1993). Specifically, fathers' belief in the biological basis of sex differences, their perception of their caregiving skills, and the extent to which they valued the father's role were predictors of fathers' involvement. These attitudinal factors predict when either mothers or fathers were reporters of the level of father involvement. When father reports of their own involvement are used, assessment of their own motivation emerges as a significant predictor as well. Finally, a variety of types of involvement are related to paternal attitudes including play, caregiving, and indirect care (e.g., packs diaper bag, changes crib linen).

In spite of the fact that men are competent caregivers (e.g., Parke & O'Leary, 1976; Parke & Sawin, 1976, 1980), there are wide individual differences among men in their either perceived or actual level of skill in caregiving. In turn, these variations in skill may be related to level of father involvement. Some of the most convincing evidence comes from intervention studies that show that skill-oriented training increases level of father involvement. These studies show that fathers who receive training in caregiving and/or play that presumably increased their skill engage in higher levels of involvement with their infants (Dickie & Carnahan, 1980; Parke, Hymel, Power, & Tinsley, 1980; Zelazo, Kotelchuck, Barber, & David, 1977; see Parke & Beitel, 1986, for a review).

Family Factors

Maternal attitudes: Mother as gatekeeper.   Just as variations in men's attitudes relate to levels of paternal involvement, maternal attitudes need to be considered as a determinant of paternal participation. In role-sharing families women were more androgynous and more masculine in their sex-role orientations (Bem scores) than were women in traditional families (Russell, 1983), which may have facilitated the higher levels of father participation. However, maternal employment status may be important; Barnett and Baruch (1987) found that in dual-earner families mothers with nontraditional sex-role attitudes predicted the proportion of time fathers spent interacting with their children, whereas in single-earner families (non-employed mothers) nontraditional maternal attitudes were associated with higher levels of total interaction time. However, other studies (e.g., Radin, 1982) did not find differences in mothers' sex-role scores across mother primary caregiver, intermediate, and father primary caregiver family types.

Clearer evidence of the role of maternal attitudes comes from studies that focus specifically on maternal attitudes concerning father involvement. The importance of understanding maternal attitudes is underscored by the survey that indicated that 60 to 80 percent of women do not want their husbands to be more involved than they currently are (Pleck, 1982; Quinn & Staines, 1979). At the same time, these same surveys suggest that 40 percent of fathers would like to spend more time with their children than they currently are able to do. As Lamb (1986) noted, mothers may play a gatekeeping role either supporting or inhibiting fathers' involvement with their infants. Although the attitudinal dimensions that define such a gatekeeping role are poorly understood, general support for the proposition that maternal attitudes toward their own caregiver role and the father's caregiver role is evident for both infants and children. Father involvement was positively related to wives' views of their competence as caregivers (Cowan & Cowan, 1987; Natravil-Kline, 1984). In both cases, mothers who view their male partners as competent may facilitate father involvement; alternatively, competent men may be more involved with children which, in turn, shapes their wives' attitudes about their competence.

Beitel and Parke (1993) examined the relation between maternal attitudes and father involvement with 3- to 5-month-old infants. A variety of maternal attitudes concerning father involvement with infants related to the level of father involvement in a sample of over 300 first-time parents. Mothers' judgments about their husbands' motivation and interest to participate in child-care activities, maternal perception of their husbands' child-care skills, and the value that they place on father involvement all predicted father involvement. Mothers' belief in innate sex differences in female and male ability to nurture infants and the extent to which mothers viewed themselves as critical or judgmental of the quality of their husbands' caregiving were negatively related to father involvement. As these results suggest, maternal attitudes play a significant role in understanding father involvement, but the type of involvement needs to be considered, because different attitudes related to different types of involvement (e.g., play, role responsibility, indirect care). Moreover, maternal attitudes predicted level of father involvement even after controlling for a variety of factors including amount of maternal outside employment, type of feeding (bottle vs. breast), father involvement in birth preparation classes, and family history (parents' recollection of their relationship with their own parent). The general pattern was evident whether maternal or paternal reports of father involvement were used.

Marital relationships and father–child relationships.   Models that limit examination of the effects of interaction patterns to only the father–child and mother–child dyads and the direct effects of one individual on another are inadequate for understanding the impact of social interaction patterns in families (Belsky, 1981, 1984; Lewis & Feiring, 1981; Parke, 1988; Parke et al., 1979). The full family group must be considered. Parents influence their children indirectly as well. A parent may influence a child through the mediation of another family member's impact (e.g., a father may contribute to the mother's positive affect toward her child by praising her caregiving ability). As noted earlier, maternal attitudes concerning fathers' skills, abilities, and motivation can potentially impact the father's level of participation. Another way in which one parent may indirectly influence the child's treatment by other agents is by modifying the infant's behavior. Child behavior patterns that develop as a result of parent–child interaction may, in turn, affect the child's treatment by other social agents. For example, irritable infant patterns induced by an insensitive and impatient mother may in turn make the infant more difficult for the father to handle and pacify. Thus, patterns developed in interaction with one parent may alter interaction patterns with another. In larger families, siblings can play a similar mediating role.

Parents have been shown to behave differently when alone with their infant than when interacting with the infant in the presence of the other parent. A sizable body of research indicates that rates of parent–infant interactive behavior decrease in a triadic in comparison to a dyadic context in both the laboratory (Lamb, 1979) and the home (Belsky, 1979; Clarke-Stewart, 1978; Pedersen, Anderson, & Cain, 1980) with children of varying ages. This difference in quantity of stimulation in a triadic context stems in part from the fact that the child has two social agents who each provide less input than either would if alone with the child. Moreover, as Pedersen, Zaslow, Cain, and Anderson (1981) documented, when the parents are together they have the opportunity to interact with one another, a further condition that generally reduces the levels of focused behavior directed toward the infant.

However there are significant exceptions (see Schaffer, 1984, for a review). For example, Parke and his colleagues (Parke, Grossman, & Tinsley, 1981; Parke & O'Leary, 1976) found that certain behaviors, such as positive affect and exploratory behavior, increase rather than decrease from dyadic to triadic situations. Parents verbally stimulate each other by focusing the partner's attention on aspects of the baby's behavior, perhaps stimulating affectionate or exploratory behavior in the partner. It is clear that greater attention should be given to the specification of conditions that are likely to increase as well as decrease parental behavior in the presence of a third person (Parke & Tinsley, 1981; Schaffer, 1984).

Several studies in both the United States (Dickie & Matheson, 1984; Pedersen, 1975) and other cultures (e.g., Japan; Durrett, Otaki, & Richards, 1984) support the conclusion that the degree of emotional/social support that fathers provide mothers is related to both indices of maternal caregiving competence as well as measures of the quality infant–parent attachment.

In another study by Pedersen, Anderson, and Cain (1977), 5-month-old infants were observed individually with their fathers and mothers as well as in a triadic situation in their homes. Although no relations were found between positive affect between the parents and positive affect directed toward the infant, a positive correlation obtained between the amounts of negative affect between the parents and that directed toward the infant.

Other evidence suggests that the quality of the marital relationship is related to father–infant interaction patterns. Moreover, the evidence suggests that the father–child relationship is altered more than the mother–child relationship by the quality of the marriage. For example, Belsky et al. (1984) found that fathers' overall engagement of the infant was reliably and positively related to overall marital engagement at 1, 3, and 9 months, whereas maternal engagement was related to the marital relationship only at 1 month of age. In a second study, mother–infant, father–infant, and husband–wife interaction was observed during three separate naturalistic home observations when infants were 1, 3, and 9 months old (Belsky & Volling, 1986). As in the previous study, there was a greater degree of relation between fathering and marital interaction than between mothering and marital interaction.

Other evidence is consistent with the finding that spousal support is a stronger correlate of competence in fathers than in mothers (Dickie & Matheson, 1984). The level of emotional and cognitive support successfully discriminated high- and low-competent fathers but failed to do so in the case of mothers. This suggests that spousal support is more critical for adequate parenting on the part of fathers than mothers. In a short-term longitudinal study of the antecedents of father involvement, Feldman, Nash, and Aschenbrenner (1983) measured a variety of factors, including the marital relationship during the third trimester of the wives' pregnancies and again at 6 months postpartum. Marital relations predicted father involvement in caregiving, playfulness, and satisfaction with fatherhood. As Feldman and colleagues noted, "In our upper to middle class, highly educated sample, the quality of the marital dyad, whether reported by the husband or wife, is the most consistently powerful predictor of paternal involvement and satisfaction" (p. 1634). Lamb and Elster (1985) addressed a similar question in a sample of adolescent mothers and their male partners. Using an observational scheme similar to that of Belsky and colleagues (1984), they observed mother, father, and infant at home in an unstructured context. Father–infant interaction positively related to the level of mother–father engagement. By contrast, mother–infant interaction was unrelated to measures of mother–father engagement.

Together these findings suggest that successful paternal parenting is more dependent on a supportive marital relationship than maternal parenting. A number of factors may aid in explaining this relation. First, there is prior evidence that the father's level of participation is, in part, determined by the extent to which the mother permits participation (Dickie & Carnahan, 1980; Redican, 1976). Second, because the paternal role is less well articulated and defined than the maternal role, spousal support may serve to help crystallize the boundaries of appropriate role behavior. Third, men have fewer opportunities to acquire and practice skills that are central to caregiving activities during socialization and therefore may benefit more than mothers from informational (i.e., cognitive) support.

Changing Societal Conditions as Determinants of Father–Child Relationships

A number of society-wide changes have produced a variety of shifts in the nature of early family relationships. Fertility rates and family size have decreased, the percentage of women in the work force has increased, the timing of onset of parenthood has shifted, divorce rates have risen, and the number of single-parent families has increased (for reviews see Furstenberg & Cherlin, 1991; Hernandez, 1993). In this section, the effects of two of these changes—timing of parenthood and recent shifts in family employment patterns—are explored in order to illustrate the impact of social change on father–child and family relationships. Exploration of these shifts serves to underscore a second theme, namely, the importance of considering the historical period or era in which social change occurs.

Timing of parenthood and the father's role.   Patterns of the timing of the onset of parenting are changing, although those changes are not evident from an examination of the median age of parents at the time of the birth of their first child. In the first half of the 1950s the median age of women at the birth of their first child was the early 20s, whereas in the 1980s it was approximately the same. This apparent pattern of stability, however, masks the impressive expansion of the range of the timing of first births during the recent decades. During this period, women were having babies earlier *and* later than in previous decades. Two particular patterns can be identified. First, there was a dramatic increase in the number of adolescent pregnancies and, second, there was an increase in the number of women who were postponing childbearing until their 30s. What are the consequences of this divergent pattern of childbearing?

A number of factors need to be considered in order to understand the impact on parenting of childbearing at different ages. First, the *life-course context,* which is broadly defined as the point at which the individual has arrived in his or her social, educational, and occupational timetable, is an important determinant. Second, the *historical context,* namely the societal and economic conditions that prevail at the time of the onset of parenting, interacts with the first factor in determining the effects of variations in timing. Let us consider early and delayed childbirth in light of these issues.

The most significant aspect of *early entry into parenthood* is that it is a nonnormative event. Achieving parenthood during adolescence can be viewed as an accelerated role transition. As McCluskey, Killarney, and Papini (1983) noted, "School age parenting may produce heightened stress when it is out of synchrony with a normative life course. Adolescents may be entering parenting at an age when they are not financially, educationally, and emotionally ready to deal with it effectively" (p. 49).

In addition, adolescent childbearers are at higher medical risk due to poorer diets, malnutrition, and less intensive and consistent prenatal care (Brooks-Gunn & Furstenberg, 1986; Hoffreth, 1986). Teenage childbearing is less likely to be planned and is strongly associated with higher levels of completed fertility, closer spacing of births (Furstenberg, Brooks-Gunn, & Chase-Lansdale, 1989; Hayes, 1987), lower educational attainment—especially for females—and diminished income and assets as well as poverty, relative to individuals who delay childbearing (Card & Wise, 1978). Again, the effect is particularly severe for women. In turn, this has long-term occupational consequences, with early childbearers overrepresented in blue-collar jobs and underrepresented in the professions. Finally, teenage marriages tend to be highly unstable; separation and/or divorce is two to three times as likely among adolescents as among women who are 20 years or older (Baldwin & Cain, 1980; Furstenberg et al., 1989).

In part, this pattern is due to the fact that the fathers also are often adolescents, and, as in the case of teenage mothers, are often unprepared financially and emotionally to undertake the responsibilities of parenthood (Lerman & Ooms, 1993; Parke & Neville, 1987). As Lerman (1993) noted, "young unwed fathers were generally less well educated, had lower academic abilities, started sex at earlier ages and engaged in more crime than did other young men" (p. 47). Low family income and having lived in a welfare household increases the likelihood of entry into young unwed fatherhood. This profile was especially evident for White unwed fathers. In spite of the fact that African-American men are four times as likely to be an unwed father as are White men, African-American unwed fatherhood is less likely to be linked with adverse circumstances but is a more mainstream issue. Several factors reduce the likelihood of becoming a teenage father including church attendance, military service, and higher reading scores. In view of the low rates of marriage and high rates of separation and divorce for adolescents, adolescent fathers, in contrast to "on-schedule" fathers, have less contact with their offspring. However, contact is not absent; in fact, studies of unmarried adolescent fathers indicate a surprising amount of paternal involvement for extended periods following the birth. Recent data (Lerman, 1993) based on a national representative sample of over

600 young unwed fathers indicated that three fourths of young fathers who lived away from their children at birth never lived in the same household with them. However, many unwed fathers remain in close contact with their children, with nearly half visiting their youngest child at least once a week and nearly a fourth almost daily. Only 13 percent never visited and 7 percent visited only yearly. Although these estimates were based on father's own reports, other work (Mott, 1993) that relies on maternal reports yield lower contact estimates. Mott found about 40 percent visited once a week and a third never visited and only contacted yearly.

Several studied report declines in contact as the child develops (Lerman, 1993; Lorenzi, Klerman, & Jekel, 1977). According to Lerman's analysis of the national survey data, 57 percent visited once a week when the child was 2 or under, 40 percent for ages 2 to 4½ years, 27 percent for ages 4½ to 7½ and 22 percent for 7½ and older. Nearly one third of the fathers of the oldest group never visited their offspring.

These declines in father participation appear to continue across childhood and adolescence. In a recent follow-up, Furstenberg and Harris (1993) reported the pattern of contact between adolescent fathers and their offspring from birth through late adolescence. Under half of the children lived at least some time with their biological father at some time during their first 18 years, but only 9 percent lived with their father during the entire period. Instead, children spent about one third of their childhood with their fathers, and this was more likely to occur in early childhood. During the preschool period, nearly half of the children were either living with their father or saw him on a weekly basis. By late adolescence, 14 percent were living with him, and only 15 percent were seeing him as often as once a week; 46 percent had no contact, but 25 percent saw him occasionally in the preceding year.

Fathers who rarely or never visit are less likely to pay child support (Lerman, 1993) which, in turn, adds to the mothers' financial burden and may indirectly have negative effects on the children. Finally, White (30 percent) and Hispanic-American (37 percent) are more likely to have no contact with their offspring than African-American fathers (12 percent).

How have increases in the rate of adolescent childbirth altered the father's role? Or, to pose the question differently, how was being an adolescent father different in a historical period when adolescent childbearing was relatively rare as compared to a period when the rate is significantly higher? First, as rates of adolescent childbearing rise and the event becomes less nonnormative or deviant, the social stigma associated with the event may decrease. In combination with increased recognition that adolescent fathers have a legitimate and potentially beneficial role to play, adolescent fathers' opportunities for participation have probably expanded. Second, the increased availability of social support systems such as day care may make it easier for adolescent fathers (and mothers) simultaneously to balance educational and occupational demands with parenting demands. Clearly, longitudinal studies of the long-term impact of achieving parenthood during adolescence are necessary, as well as more investigation of the impact of adolescent parenthood during different historical periods (see Parke & Neville, 1987).

Finally, there is a variety of deleterious effects of early childbearing for the offspring. First, there is a greater risk of lower IQ (Broman, 1981; Brooks-Gunn & Furstenberg, 1986). It also affects academic achievement and retention in grade (Furstenberg et al., 1989; Kinard & Klerman, 1983). Nor are the effects short-lived; they tend to persist throughout the school years (Hoffreth, 1987). Social behavior is affected as well, with several studies showing that children of teenage parents are at greater risk of social impairment (e.g., under control of anger, feelings of inferiority, fearfulness) and mild behavior disorders (e.g., aggressiveness, rebelliousness, impulsivity) (Brooks-Gunn & Furstenberg, 1986).

In contrast to adolescent childbearing, when *childbearing is delayed,* considerable progress in occupational and educational spheres has potentially already taken place. Education is generally completed and career development is well underway for both men and women. Men who have their children early have more energy for certain types of activities that are central to the father role, such as physical play (Parke & Neville, 1987). Similarly, the economic strain that occurs early is offset by avoiding financial problems in retirement due to the fact that children are grown up and independent earlier. In turn, early fathering generally means beginning grandfathering at a younger age, which in turn permits the early-timed father to be a more active grandparent (for a discussion of these issues, see Tinsley & Parke, 1984, 1988b). In spite of these advantages, when men become fathers early, there are two main disadvantages: financial strain and time strain, due to the competing demands imposed by trying simultaneously to establish a career as well as a family. In contrast, the late-timed father avoids these problems. The late-timed father's career is more settled permitting more flexibility and freedom in balancing the demands of work and family. Further, patterns of preparental collaboration between the parents may already be established and persist into the parenthood period. To appreciate fully the context in which late-timed fatherhood takes place, we briefly examine the work relationships of late-timed fathers.

Delayed fathers have described themselves to be in more stable work situations than early-timing fathers, to be more experienced workers, and have their jobs and careers more firmly established than early-timing peers (Daniels & Weingarten, 1982). Although they are expected to be more satisfied with their jobs, as job satisfaction has been found to be positively associated with age until midlife (Kalleberg & Loscocco, 1983), and less likely to experience the "life-cycle squeeze," during which one's ability to generate income has not yet progressed as fast as the need for income with the introduction of children (Rodman & Safilios-Rothschild, 1983), support for this view is limited. Neville and Parke (1993) in a study of early- (under 25 years of age at first birth) and late- (over 30 years of age) timed fathers found that delayed fathers were more satisfied with their jobs, but the effect was due to socioeconomic status (SES) and salary differences between the groups rather than timing of birth, per se.

The financial strains associated with early career status, therefore, may be more likely to create conflict between the work and family demands of early/normal-timing fathers than delayed-timing fathers. Neville and Parke (1993) found some support for this proposition, but qualified by the sex of the child. Specifically, younger fathers of girls and older fathers of boys reported more interference by work in family life than did older fathers of girls and younger fathers of boys.

What are the effects of late-timed parenthood for the father–child relationship? Are fathers who delay parenthood more or less involved with their offspring? Are their styles of interaction different from early or on-time fathers? What are the consequences of late-timed parenthood for father–child relationships?

Retrospective accounts by adults who were the firstborn children of older parents report that having older parents was an important influence in their lives. Many reported having felt especially appreciated by their parents (Yarrow, 1991) and described fathers who were between the ages 30 and 39 when the respondent was born as more accepting than fathers who were younger or older (Finley, Janovetz, & Rogers, 1990). Parents' retrospective accounts of parenting have also been found to vary with timing. Nydegger (1973) found that late fathers expressed greater self-confidence in the parental role, as well as greater ease and composure in discussing the role than early-timed fathers. Both mothers and fathers have reported that delayed fathers are more interested than younger first-time fathers in parenting, and they are more likely to engage in caregiving (Bloom-Feshbach, 1979). Daniels and Weingarten (1982) found early-timed fathers are less involved in the daily care of a preschool child: Three times as many late-timed fathers, in contrast to their early-timed counterparts, had regular responsibility for some part of the daily care of a preschool child. Possibly, the increase in paternal responsibility assumed by fathers in late-timed families may account for the more optimal mother–infant interaction patterns observed by Ragozin, Bashan, Crnic, Greenberg, and Robinson (1982). Cooney, Pedersen, Indelicato, and Palkovitz (1993) found in a nationally representative sample that late-timed fathers were more likely to be classified as being highly involved and experiencing positive affect associated with the paternal role than on-time fathers. Delayed mothers have also reported being more psychologically ready to take on the responsibility for rearing a child and attaining more satisfaction with parenting (Daniels & Weingarten, 1982; Ragozin et al., 1982; Walter, 1986).

The timing of the onset of parenthood is a powerful organizer of both maternal and paternal roles. In the future, investigators need to examine not only both maternal and paternal interaction patterns with each other and their children, but within the context of careers as well. More detailed attention to cohort issues is warranted as indicated by the suggestive findings of Daniels and Weingarten (1982), who found that women who had children in the 1950s and the 1970s were more likely to follow different patterns of balancing work and family life. Late-timed women in the 1950s were more likely to follow a sequential pattern in which outside employment and parenthood follow one another. By the 1970s women were more likely to follow a simultaneous pattern in which outside work and parenting coexist in parents' lives. Presumably, the decision to delay the onset of parenthood was easier in the 1970s than in earlier decades due to increased acceptance of maternal employment, less rigid role definitions for men and women, and the greater availability of support services such as day care, which permit simultaneous family–career options. It is likely that this shift toward a simultaneous pattern of work and childrearing helps account for the increased levels of father involvement in late-timed families.

There are qualitative differences in styles of interaction for on-time versus late-timed fathers. In a self-report study, MacDonald and Parke (1986) found that age of parent is negatively related to the frequency of physical play. Even after controlling for the age of the child, the size of the relation is reduced but generally reveals the same pattern. However, this relation appears stronger for some categories of play than for others. Some physical activities, such as bounce, tickle, chase, and piggyback, that tend to require more physical energy on the part of the play partner, show strong negative relation with the age of parent. The negative correlation between age of parent and physical play may be ascribable to either the unwillingness or inability of older parents to engage in high-energy affectively arousing activities, such as physical play, or to the fact that children may elicit less physical activity from older parents. Moreover, Neville and Parke (1987) found older parents likely to engage in more cognitively advanced activities with children and to report holding their children more than younger fathers. These and other studies (Zaslow, Pedersen, Suwalsky, Rabinovich, & Cain, 1985) suggest that older fathers may be less tied to stereotypic paternal behavior, adopting styles more similar to those that have been considered traditionally maternal.

Recent observational studies of father–child interaction confirm these early self-report investigations. Volling and Belsky (1991) who studied fathers interacting with their infants at 3 and 9 months found that older fathers were more responsive, stimulating, and affectionate at both 3 and 9 months. In another observational study, Neville and Parke (1993; see also Parke & Neville, in press) examined the play patterns of early- and late-timed fathers interacting with their preschool-age children. Early and delayed fathers' play styles differed; the early fathers relied on physical arousal to engage their children, whereas the delayed fathers relied on more cognitive mechanisms to remain engaged.

Timing effects are important not just for fathers, but for grandfathers as well. Moreover, not only is age per se important but the timing of entry into familial roles may be a determinant of interactional style as well. In their study of grandfathers interacting with their 7-month-old infants, Tinsley and Parke (1988b) found that grandfather age related to the level of stimulating play. Grandfathers were divided into three categories: younger (36–49 years), middle (50–56), and older (57–68). Grandfathers in the middle-age group were rated significantly higher on competence (e.g., confident, smooth, accepting), affect (e.g., warm, interested, affectionate, attentive), and play style (e.g., playful, responsive, stimulatory). From a life-span developmental perspective, the middle group of grandfathers could be viewed as being optimally ready for grandparenthood, both physically and psychologically. Unlike the oldest group of grandfathers, they were less likely to be chronically tired or to have been ill with age-linked diseases. And, unlike the youngest grandfathers, they have completed the career-building position of their lives and were prepared to devote more of their time to family-related endeavors. Moreover, the age of the middle group of grandfathers fits the normative age at which grandparenthood is most often achieved; thus, for these men, the role of grandfather was more age-appropriate than it was for the youngest and oldest groups of grandfathers.

Women's and men's employment patterns and the parental roles in the family.   The relations between employment patterns of both women and men and their family roles are increasingly
being recognized (Crouter, 1993; Hoffman, 1984). In this section, a variety of issues concerning the
links between the worlds of work and family are considered in order to illustrate the impact of recent
shifts in work patterns on both men's and women's family roles. The impact of changes in the rate of
maternal employment on both quantitative and qualitative aspects of father participation is examined,
as well as the influence of variations in family work schedules.

Since the mid-1950s, there has been a dramatic shift in the participation rate of women in the labor
force. The rise has been particularly dramatic for married women with children. Between 1950 and
1990, the employment rate for married mothers of children has increased dramatically to over 70
percent (Hernandez, 1993). How have these shifts affected the quantity and quality of the father's
contribution to family tasks such as housework and child care?

Problems arise in interpreting the main data source—time-use studies—because these studies often
fail to control for the family size and the age of children. As Hoffman (1984) noted, "Since
employed-mother families include fewer children, in general, and fewer preschoolers and infants, in
particular, there are fewer child care tasks to perform" (p. 439). Therefore, the differences between
families with employed and nonemployed mothers may, in fact, be underestimated. A second problem
is that, as noted earlier, the differentiation of tasks performed by fathers is often very crude, and in
some studies it is impossible to determine what specific aspects of the father's family work—such as
primary child care, non-care-related child contact, or housework—are affected. In spite of these
limitations, some trends are clear.

One recent estimate (Coltrane, 1995) suggests that "men's average contributions to inside
housework have roughly doubled since about 1970, whereas women's contributions have decreased
by a third ... the late 1980's men were doing about 5 hours per week or about 20–25% of the inside
chores" (pp. 173–174). These trends are slightly higher in the case of dual-career families. These
trends do not negate the fact that the majority of household tasks are still performed by women,
(Ferree, 1991; Robinson, 1988; Shelton, 1992; Thompson & Walker, 1989), including child care
(Biernat & Wortman, 1991). Moreover, this increase often emerges as a result of wives reducing the
amount of time they devote to housework and child care rather than as a result of increases in the
absolute amount of time men devote to these tasks. In a time-diary study of housework and child care,
Walker and Woods (1976) found that husbands' proportion of all family work (i.e., combining that
performed by both husband and wife) rose from 16 percent (1.6 of 9.7 hours) to 25 percent (1.6 of
6.4 hours) when wives were employed. Other studies confirm the general finding that fathers'
proportional share increases, in part, because they are contributing more absolute time and because
mothers are spending less time on home tasks (Pleck, 1983; Robinson, 1988; Shelton, 1992). These
findings are not without significance for children's development because the impact of the mother
and the father on children is likely to be different in families in which the father and the mother are
more equal in their household participation.

Moreover, there is some evidence for absolute increases in fathers' contributions to family work
when wives are employed, especially in father–child contact. Robinson (1977), in a diary study of a
national sample, found a modest increase of 19 minutes a day in men's total child contact time (or
16.5 percent) when women were employed outside the home. Similarly, Pleck (1981), in an analysis
of a survey using respondents' summary estimates, found that fathers with employed wives performed
about half hour per day more family work that includes housework, child care, and parent–child
contact. Although the proportion of time fathers in the Pleck study spent in child-centered activity
and housework was not determined, other evidence indicates that child care is more likely to increase
than housework (Coltrane, 1995; Hoffman, 1984). In fact, child care by fathers has shown the most
dramatic increase in the last decade than other areas of household work (Coltrane, 1995). The level
of paternal child care has shifted since the mid-1980s, and men contribute nearly one third to this
activity in dual-earner couples. In fact, a recent survey (Census Bureau, 1993) found that the
percentage of children whose fathers cared for them during their mothers' work hours rose to 20

percent in 1991, after a steady level of around 15 percent since 1977. These modest absolute increases assume greater importance because they directly affect the nature of the father–child relationship.

Other evidence is consistent with this hypothesis that fathers' involvement with children will be especially likely to increase when mothers are employed. Child variables, such as age, appear to determine whether or not fathers' family work shifts with maternal employment. Walker and Woods (1976) found an increase in fathers' family work with maternal employment when the youngest child was 1 year of age or younger or the couple had five or more children. Similarly, Russell (1982) in a study of the impact of maternal employment on Australian fathers found that maternal employment altered fathers' involvement in family work only when there were children under 3 years of age. Fathers in this case were slightly more involved when mothers were employed (4.4 hours vs. 3.15 hours for employed vs. nonemployed, respectively). Moreover, Russell found that when mothers are employed, the quality of responsibility that fathers assume shifts: Fathers with employed wives spent time taking sole responsibility for their children, compared to fathers with nonemployed wives (4.7 hours vs. 1.0 hours). Other studies confirm that fathers in families where mothers work outside the home are more involved in solo child care with their infants ($M = 12.7$ months) than fathers whose wives were homemakers but the two groups did not differ in their level of leisure involvement with their children (Crouter, Perry-Jenkins, Huston, & McHale, 1987).

It is clear that there is an increase in father participation when mothers work outside the home, but the data fit well Rappaport's concept for a *psychosocial lag* (Rappaport, Rappaport, & Strelitz, 1977). According to this concept, men's roles in the family change at a slower rate than shifts in women's roles in paid employment. Part of the explanation for the relatively modest size of the shift in men's family work when women enter the job market may be that there has been a "value shift in our culture toward greater family involvement by husbands ... which has effects even on those husbands whose wives are not employed" (Pleck, 1983, p. 47). A similar trend is found in the reduction in time devoted to household tasks by nonemployed women as well as employed women (Hoffman, 1984; Robinson, 1988).

Unfortunately, a number of problems limit the value of these findings to our understanding of historical trends in fathering. Most of the available data come from cross-sectional comparisons of families in which wives are either employed outside the home or not. Although it is assumed that these concurrent data can be extrapolated backward to provide a picture of how men's participation in family activities has shifted across time as a result of the historically documented increases in women's presence in the work force, longitudinal studies of the same families as well as repeated cross-sectional comparisons across time are necessary to place this issue on a firmer empirical basis.

In current literature, cohort, time of testing, and age of children are often confounded. For example, in the studies that show that the fathers' participation is higher when infants and young children are involved, it is not clear whether this is due only to the age of the children or to the difference in the cohorts whose children are younger at the time of evaluation. Value shifts may elicit greater involvement in the current cohort of new parents that may not have affected more seasoned parents. Moreover, once a pattern of father participation has been established, possibly these families will continue to participate more equally in childrearing. If this analysis is correct, future surveys may indicate that father participation extends into later childhood age periods. Alternatively, fathers who are involved early may feel that they have contributed and do less at later ages. The importance of considering the timing of the mother's employment as a determinant of the degree of father involvement is clear. Age of the child is not the only variable, however; other factors such as employment onset in relationship to the family's developmental cycle as well as the reason for employment need to be considered. Both the age of the parents and their point in the occupation cycle will affect paternal involvement and may interact with maternal employment.

Examination of the quantitative shifts in father behavior as a consequence of maternal employment is only one aspect of the problem; it is also necessary to examine the impact of this shift on the quality of the father–child relationship. Some evidence from interviews of a sample of fathers of infants 7–14 months old suggests that maternal employment is related mainly to the level of fathers' instrumental involvement in child care and not to fathers' nurturant expressive behavior (Bloom-Feshbach, 1979).

However, other evidence suggests that shifts in style of father–infant interaction may occur as a function of maternal employment. In one study, Pedersen and colleagues (1980) assessed the impact of dual-wage-earner families on mother and father interaction patterns with their 5-month-old infants. Fathers in single-wage-earner families tended to play with their infants more than mothers did, but in the two-wage-earner families, the mothers' rate of social play was higher than the fathers' rate of play. In fact, the fathers in these dual-wage-earner families played at a lower rate than even the mothers in the single-wage-earner families. Because the observations took place in the evenings after both parents returned from their jobs, Pedersen and colleagues suggested that the mother used increased play as a way of reestablishing contact with her infant after being away from home for the day. "It is possible that the working mother's special need to interact with the infant inhibited or crowded out the father in his specialty" (Pedersen et al., 1980, p. 10). This behavior of the mother is consistent with studies of maternal employment and infant attachment that found no relation between employment status and the quality of infant–mother attachment (Chase-Lansdale, 1981; Hock, 1980) but found evidence of insecure infant–father attachment in dual-career families, although only for sons and not daughters (Chase-Lansdale, 1981, cited by Hoffman, 1984).

In an even more stringent test of the modifiability of play styles as a function of family organization, Field (1978) compared fathers who act as primary caregivers with fathers who are secondary caregivers. In these reversed role families, Field found that primary caregiver fathers retained the physical component in their interaction styles just as secondary fathers did. However, in other subtle ways the play styles of primary caregiving fathers were similar to the play styles of mothers. Primary caregivers—both mother and fathers—exhibited less laughing and more smiling, imitative grimaces, and high-pitched vocalizations than secondary caregiver fathers did. However, both primary caregiving and secondary caregiving fathers engaged in less holding of the infants' limbs and in more game playing and poking than mothers. Together with Pedersen et al. (1980) study, these data suggest that both mothers and fathers may exhibit distinctive play styles, even when family role arrangements modify the quantity of their interaction.

Finally, McHale, Crouter, and Bartko (1991), in a sample of fourth- and fifth-grade children, found that both work status of spouses and role arrangements in families (traditional vs. egalitarian) may, in fact, be independent. To understand the effects of father participation on children, it is important to understand both work status of parents and family type (traditional vs. egalitarian). McHale et al. found that an inequitable division of parents' work and family roles relate to poorer socioemotional adjustment of children. Children from traditional dual-earner families were more anxious and depressed and rated themselves lower in terms of both peer social acceptance and school competence than did children from families characterized by an equitable division in parents' work and family role (e.g., traditional single-earner and egalitarian dual-earner families).

Work quality and father interaction patterns.   Instead of examining whether or not one or both parents are employed, researchers have begun to address the issue of the impact of the quality and nature of work on parenting of both mother and father behavior. As Crouter (1994) recently noted, there are two types of linkage. One type of research focuses on work as an "emotional climate" (Kanter, 1977) which, in turn, may have carryover effects to the enactment of roles in home settings. The focus is generally on short-term or transitory effects. A second type of linkage focuses on the type of skills, attitudes, and perspectives that adults acquire in their work-based socialization as adults and how these variations in job experience alter their behavior in family contexts. In contrast to the short-term perspective of the spillover of emotional climate research, this type of endeavor involves more enduring and long-lasting effects of work on family life.

Work in the first tradition has been conducted by Repetti (1989, 1994) who studied the impact of working in a high-stress job (air-traffic controller) on subsequent family interaction patterns. She found that the male air traffic controllers were more withdrawn and less angry in marital interactions after high-stress shifts and tended to be behaviorally and emotionally withdrawn during interactions with their children as well. Although high workload is associated with withdrawal, negative social experiences in the workplace have a different effect. In addition, distressing social experiences at work were associated with higher expressions of anger and greater use of discipline during interaction with the child later in the day. Repetti viewed this as a "spillover effect" in which there is transfer of negative feelings across settings. Consistent with these findings is the work of Bolger, DeLongis, Kessler, and Wethington (1989), who found that work-related stress (e.g., arguments, heavy work-loads) was associated with more negative marital interactions and less household work.

Other research suggests that positive work experiences can enhance the quality of fathering. Grossman et al. (1988) found that high job satisfaction was associated with higher levels of support for their 5-year-old's autonomy and affiliation in spite of the fact that positive feelings about work were negatively related to the quantity of time spent interacting with their child. This finding underscores the importance of distinguishing quantity and quality of involvement.

One caveat: In contrast to the Repetti studies, the Grossman et al. (1988) study focused on general job satisfaction and demandingness rather than daily fluctuations in the level of positivity or negativity experienced in the work setting. Future studies need to assess these two aspects of job-related affect and involvement separately. Work patterns have long-term links with fathering as well. Fathers on air-traffic controller teams with a poor social climate had less positive and more negative emotional tone in their interactions with their children.

This line of research underscores the importance of distinguishing between different types of work-related stress on subsequent father–child interactions and of considering the direct short-term carryover effects versus long-term effects of work on fathering. In fact, relatively little attention has been paid to the types of local events that account for daily fluctuations in fathering behavior.

Research in the second tradition of family-work linkage, namely the effects of the nature of men's occupational roles on their fathering behavior, dates back to the classic work of Kohn and Schooler (1983) and Miller and Swanson (1958). Men who experience a high degree of occupational autonomy value independence in their children, consider children's intentions when considering discipline, and use reasoning and withdrawal of rewards instead of physical punishment. In contrast, men who are in highly supervised jobs with little autonomy value conformity and obedience, focus on conse-quences rather than intentions, and use more physical forms of discipline. In short, they repeat their job-based experiences in their parenting roles.

Greenberger and O'Neil (1991) extended Kohn's original work by focusing on the implications of job characteristics not only for the parenting behavior of both mothers and fathers but, in turn, the effects of these variations in parenting for children's development. Fathers with more complex jobs (i.e., characterized by mentoring others vs. taking instruction or serving others) spend more time alone with sons and more time developing their sons' skills (e.g., academic, athletic, mechanical, interper-sonal), but this is not the case for daughters. In fact, they spend more time in work and work-related activities if they have daughters. In addition, these fathers tend to behave more warmly and responsively to sons and use less harsh and less lax control with sons, but report more firm but flexible control with daughters. Fathers who have jobs characterized by a high level of challenge (e.g., expected to solve problems; high level of decision making) devote more time to developing sons' skills, give higher quality explanations to their sons, and use less harsh and more firm but flexible control in their interactions with their boys. Finally, fathers with time-urgent jobs (work fast most of the day; it's hard to take a break) spend more time on work activities, less time interacting, and use less lax control if they have daughters. To summarize, when fathers have complex, stimulating, and challenging jobs, boys seem to benefit much more than girls.

In contrast, mothers' job characteristics are, in general, less predictive of their parenting than fathers' job attributes, but again when there is a link, boys seem to benefit (higher quality explanations, warmth, and responsivity) more than girls. Mothers show fewer relationships in part due to the more heavily culturally scripted nature of maternal roles. According to these researchers, different processes may account for the work–home linkages due to stimulating or challenging jobs and complexity of occupation. Greenberger and O'Neil (1991) argued that "spillover of positive mood" may account for the relationships between stimulating/challenging jobs and good fathering, whereas "complexity of work with people may increase fathers' intellectual and emotional flexibility in dealing with their sons" (p. 13). (See also Greenberger, O'Neil, & Nagel, 1994).

CONSEQUENCES OF FATHER–CHILD RELATIONSHIPS

Variations in father involvement have implications for men themselves, and their families as well as for their children.

Consequences of Fatherhood for Men Themselves

Becoming a father impacts on a man's own psychological development and well-being. As Parke (1981) noted, "the father–child relationship is a two-way process and children influence their fathers just as fathers alter their children's development" (p. 9). Three aspects of this issue have been examined, namely (1) marital relationships, (2) work and occupational issues, and (3) "societal generativity" (to borrow Snarey's, 1993, phrase).

Impact on marital relationships.   Perhaps most attention has been devoted to the impact of the transition to parenthood on marriage. The general finding from a large number of studies is that there is a decline in marital satisfaction, especially on the part of men, as a consequence of the birth of a child (see Belsky & Pensky, 1988, for a review). The psychological adjustments associated with the transition to fatherhood are clearly evident in the Cowan and Cowan (1985, 1992) longitudinal study. Their project followed families from pregnancy until the children were 5 years of age. These investigators found that father's marital satisfaction showed a modest decrease from pregnancy to 6 months, but a sharp decline between 6 and 18 months. In contrast, mothers show a much more linear decline beginning in the postpartum period and continuing across the first 2 years. In this same period of 18 months, 12.5 percent of the couples separated or divorced; by 5 years of age, this figure was up to 20 percent.

In spite of the dip in marital satisfaction, two caveats should be noted. First, even though marital satisfaction decreases for men (and women) after the onset of parenthood, marital stability (i.e., the likelihood of staying in the marriage) increases relative to childless couples, where the national average is 50 percent (Cowan & Cowan, 1992). As the Cowans noted, "the marital stability of couples who have preschool children is protected. Although new parents may be experiencing increased tension or dissatisfaction as couples, their joint involvement with managing the baby's and the family's needs may lead them to put off, or possibly work harder on, the problems in their marriage—at least while the children are young" (p. 110).

Not all of the couples showed a decline in marital satisfaction; 18 percent of couples showed increased satisfaction with their marital relationship. This figure rose to 38 percent for couples that participated in a supportive intervention program during the transition to parenthood (C. Cowan, 1988; Cowan & Cowan, 1992). Similar diversity in the pattern of change in father's marital satisfaction is evident in Belsky's longitudinal study (Belsky et al., 1984; Belsky, Rovine, & Fish, 1989). During the transition to parenthood, marital quality declined in about 30 percent of the families, improved in another 30 percent, and in nearly 40 percent of the families showed no change.

A variety of reasons has been suggested for this decline in men's marital satisfaction, including (1) physical strain of child care, (2) increased financial responsibilities, (3) emotional demands of new familial responsibilities, (4) the restrictions of parenthood, and (5) the redefinition of roles and role arrangements (Belsky & Isabella, 1985; Cowan & Cowan, 1992; Snarey, 1993). However, as Cowan and Cowan found, there is little support for the hypothesis that, as the number of negative changes increase, marital satisfaction declines. In their study, they found little relation between declining marital satisfaction and any single negative change. Perhaps, a cumulative negative events model (Rutter, 1987) holds: That is an increase in the number—regardless of quality—of negative shifts is associated with shifts in marital satisfaction. However, several lines of evidence suggest that discrepancies in expectations on the part of mothers and fathers concerning the relative roles that each will play may be an important determinant of postpartum marital satisfaction. The Cowans (1987, 1992) found that, when there was a larger discrepancy between the wives' expectations of their husbands' involvement in infant care and his level of actual participation, there was a greater decline in wives' marital satisfaction between late pregnancy and 18 months. Belsky, Ward, and Levine (1986) found a similar decrease in marital satisfaction when mothers' expectations about father involvement were not met. Men show a similar effect of a discrepancy between attitudes and behavior. McDermid, Huston, and McHale (1990) found greater negative impact of the onset of parenthood when there was a discrepancy between spouses' sex role attitudes and the division of household and child-care labor, whereas McBride (1989) found that traditional fathers who held conservative sex role attitudes but were nonetheless involved in child care reported lower levels of dissatisfaction. Finally, Hock, Demeis, and McBride (1988) found similar results for mothers who wanted to work outside the home, but did not; they were more depressed than mothers whose attitudes and roles were congruent.

On the positive side, when expectations and behaviors match, some evidence suggests that marital satisfaction is correspondingly high. Osofsky and Culp (1989) reported that in a 3-year longitudinal study of transitions to fatherhood, when fathers were satisfied with the division of family tasks and decisions, marital and sexual adjustment was satisfactory.

In summary, research suggests that discrepancies in parental expectations about roles, rather than the level of change per se, may be a key correlate of men's marital satisfaction after the onset of fatherhood.

One of the limitations of much of the literature is the focus on infancy. Less is known about the impact of being a father on marital satisfaction after infancy. An exception is the longitudinal study by Heath (1976) and Heath and Heath (1991) that followed a cohort of college men born in the 1930s into their 30s and mid-40s. Competent fathers were in satisfying marriages. However, these two indices also related to psychological maturity, leaving open the possibility that fathering activities lead to marital satisfaction and maturity or that maturity is the common correlate of being both a competent father and husband. Due to limitations in sample size, reliance on qualitative indices, and the lack of adequate statistical analysis, these results remain suggestive rather than definitive. However, Snarey (1993) found support for the relation between paternal involvement in childhood or adolescence on marital satisfaction. In a follow-up longitudinal study of men originally studied in the 1940s and 1950s by Glueck and Glueck (1950), Snarey assessed the marital success of these men at midlife (age 47). "Fathers who provided high levels of social-emotional support for their offspring during the childhood decade (0–10 years) and high levels of intellectual, academic and social emotional support during the adolescent decade (11–21 years) were themselves as men at mid-life, more likely to be happily married" (p. 111).

Impact on occupational success.   Occupational mobility is also affected by father involvement. In his longitudinal study, Snarey (1993) found that fathers' childrearing involvement across the first two decades of the child's life moderately predicted fathers' occupational mobility (at age 47) above and beyond other background variables (e.g., parent's occupation, his IQ, current maternal employment).

Fatherhood and men's self-identity.   Men's sense of themselves shifts as a function of the transition to fatherhood. A variety of dimensions has been explored in prior research, including their role definitions, their self-esteem, and their sense of generativity. Roles change for both men and women after the onset of parenthood. The Cowans (1987, 1992) assessed role shifts during the transition to fatherhood and found that men who become fathers decreased the "partner/lover" aspect of their self and increased the "parent" percentage of their self-definition. In contrast, men who remained childless significantly increased the "partner/lover" aspect of their relationship over the 21-month assessment period. Self-esteem, however, was not affected by the transition to parenthood for either fathers (or mothers) in the Cowans' project. Grossman (1987), who studied men's transition to parenthood, found that first-time fathers who were both more affiliative (i.e., importantly connected to others, enjoying empathetic relationships ... and more autonomous, viewing themselves as separate and distinct from others) had significantly higher life adaptation scores. Fathers of firstborns who were more affiliative at 1 year also reported being higher in emotional well-being. These findings suggest that "separateness and individuation are not sufficient for men's well being; they need connections as well" (Grossman, 1987, p. 107). Does fatherhood have a longer term impact on men's psychological development? Heath (1977), in a longitudinal study of college men, found that fatherhood related to men's ability to understand themselves, to understand others sympathetically, and to integrate their own feelings.

Finally, does fatherhood affect *generativity,* a concept derived from Erikson's (1975, 1982) theoretical writings? Snarey (1993) provided a succinct summary:

> The psychosocial task of middle adulthood, Stage 7 [in Erikson's Stage theory] is the attainment of a favorable balance of generativity over stagnation and self-absorption. ... Most broadly, Erikson (1975) considers generativity to mean any caring activity that contributes to the spirit of future generations, such as the generation of new or more mature persons, products, ideas, or works of art. ... Generativity's psychosocial challenge to adults is to create, care for, and promote the development of others from nurturing the growth of another person to shepherding the development of a broader community. (pp. 18–19)

Subsequent theorists have distinguished among different types of generativity (Kotre, 1984; Kotre & Hall, 1990). Snarey described three types that apply to fathers, namely (1) biological generativity (indicated by the birth of a child), (2) parental generativity (indicated by childrearing activities), and (3) societal generativity (indicated by caring for other younger adults: serving as a mentor, providing leadership, and contributing to generational continuity). Although, serious questions have been raised about the utility of Erikson's stage notions, especially the inevitability of the ordering of the stages and their universal applicability (P. Cowan, 1988), the concept of generativity is nonetheless a useful marker for assessing the long-term relation between fathering behavior and other aspects of mature men's lives.

A series of studies has examined the relations between fatherhood, especially paternal competence and involvement and social generativity. Heath and Heath (1991) noted a link between fatherhood satisfaction and community participation; fathers who were higher in reported parenting satisfaction were more likely to be active participants in community organizations or professions in the prior decade. Similarly, Valliant (1977) found a positive relation between societal generativity and social adjustment and paternal competence. Men who held positions of responsibility for other adults and who were well adjusted socially were rated higher in terms of their psychological closeness to their children. Is men's societal generativity at midlife related to the level of care and support they provide their children? Snarey (1993) rated father's social generativity on a 3- point scale and tapped whether "he demonstrated a clear capacity for establishing, guiding and caring for the next generation through sustained responsibility for the growth, well-being or leadership of younger adults or the larger society ... beyond the sphere of the nuclear family" (p. 98). Snarey found that men who nurtured their children's social-emotional development during childhood (0–10 years) and who also contributed to both social-emotional and intellectual-academic development during the second decade (11–21 years) were at midlife more likely to become generative in areas outside their family. Again this contribution of fathering participation to societal generativity was evident after controlling for a variety of background variables. Snarey offered several interpretations of these findings. First, a disequilibrium explanation suggests that parental childrearing responsibility results in demands that are difficult to meet, and that, in turn, promote "increased complexity in the fathers' cognitive emotional and behavioral repertoire. ... This commitment beyond the self, in turn, prepares the way for societal generativity which involves a commitment beyond the family" (Snarey, 1993, pp. 117–118). Second, perhaps a nurturing predisposition may underlie both parenting and societal generativity and account for the continuity across time. Third, the arrival of children often leads to increases in men's participation in neighborhood and community organizations on behalf of children, which, in turn, may continue into the midlife years. In summary, although the processes are not yet well understood, it is clear that involved fathering relates in positive ways to other aspects of men's lives. As Snarey noted, "men who are parentally generative during early adulthood usually turn out to be good spouses, workers and citizens at mid life" (p. 119).

Implications of Father Involvement for Children's Development

Three types of approaches to the issue of the impact of father involvement on children's social, emotional, and cognitive development can be distinguished. First, in a modern variant of the earlier father-absence theme, sociologists, in particular, have recently examined the impact of nonresident fathers' frequency and quality of contact on children's development. In contrast to this paternal deprivation approach, a second strategy examines the impact of paternal enhancement. This approach asks about the lessons learned from focusing on unusually highly involved fathers, such as occurs in role-sharing and reversed-role families. The third or normative approach focuses on the consequences of the quality and quantity of father–child interaction on children's development in intact families.

Contact between nonresident fathers and their children. Research in the sociological tradition has focused on large national samples of fathers and children, such as the National Longitudinal Study of Youth (NLSY), the National Survey of Children (NSC), and the National Survey of Families and Households (NSFH). These surveys reveal a high level of disengagement on the part of nonresident fathers, but at the same time sufficient variability to permit an examination of the issue of the impact of contact on children's development. Several findings have emerged (Marsiglio, 1993, provided a recent review). First, several studies report few effects of father contact and level of closeness on 11- to 16-year-old child's well-being (Furstenberg, Morgan, & Allison, 1987). Similarly, King (1994) using NLSY data on a sample of 5- to 9-year-olds found no relation between nonresident fathers' contact and their children's social and cognitive development. On the other hand, Crockett, Eggebeen, and Hawkins (1993) found that father presence during the first 3 years was positively related to child cognitive and behavioral outcomes at ages 4–6. Perhaps, the presence of fathers early in life may be more critical for children's development than later contact. Earlier evidence (Hetherington & Deur, 1972) suggested that loss of paternal presence prior to age 5 was more critical for children's social adaptation than later paternal loss. Finally, Mott (1993) found evidence that emotional development is more affected than cognitive development by father presence. This finding is consistent with the father's role as a play partner and the assumption that emotion regulation may be one of the lessons derived from this type of interchange (Parke et al., 1994). However, quality, not presence/absence alone, is important in assessing the impact of fathers. In a follow-up study of 18- to 21-year-old children of African-American adolescent mothers, Furstenberg and Harris (1993) found little impact of contact alone on young adults' outcomes but clear beneficial effects if the *quality* of the relationship were taken into account. Those who reported a strong bond or attachment with their father during adolescence had higher educational attainment, were less likely to be imprisoned, and were less depressed. These effects were especially evident in the case of children living with the father and were only marginally evident for nonresident biological fathers. The data suggest that both presence and quality matter; but quality is especially important because fathers' presence is unrelated to outcomes when quality (degree of attachment to father) is controlled. This work reflects earlier and recurring themes in the parent–child literature, namely that quality is the critical factor (Parke, 1979; Wachs, 1992).

Impact of increased fathers' involvement. In recent years, a small minority of families have explicitly explored alternative family arrangements such as role sharing and reversing family roles. In spite of their rarity, these alternative family arrangements can inform us about the possible ways in which families can reorganize themselves to provide flexibility for mothers, fathers, and children (see Radin, 1993, for a recent review).

Russell (1983, 1986) examined Australian families in which fathers took major or equal responsibility for child care (12 hours a week for mothers, 9 hours for fathers for the full range of child-care tasks such as feeding, diapering, bathing, and dressing). In traditional families, by comparison, fathers performed these tasks only about 2 hours a week. A similar pattern emerges for play and for other significant interactions, such as the parent helping with homework, child helping parent prepare a meal, and so forth. Fathers and mothers were again approximately equal in their division of playful interactions (18 hours for fathers and 16 hours for mothers), whereas in traditional families fathers spend an average of 10 hours and mothers 23 hours a week. The two types of families were comparable for the absolute amount of time spent by both parents combined (53 hours a week in shared-caregiving families and 56 hours a week in traditional families). Types of play activity varied across these two kinds of families. Although Russell found the usual pattern among traditional families with mothers more involved in indoor, conventional, cognitive, and type-oriented activities than fathers, and fathers more involved in outdoor and physical play than mothers, there were no differences in the types of play activities between mother and fathers in the shared-caregiving families. Nontraditional role-sharing families hold different attitudes toward gender roles than conventional families too. Not surprisingly, fewer of the role-sharing fathers felt that a mother's place is in the home. Parents in nontraditional families had greater faith in the father's ability to care for children. More than 80 percent of the fathers and 90 percent of the mothers in nontraditional families believed that fathers could be capable caregivers—although some felt that fathers were still not as good as mothers. In contrast, only 49 percent of the fathers and 65 percent of the mothers in traditional families felt that fathers were capable of taking care of children.

There are distinct consequences for mothers, fathers, and children from parents' role sharing. Most commonly, mothers experience difficulties associated with the physical and time demands of a dual role; in Russell's (1983, 1986) sample, 60 percent of the mothers reported this strain. On the positive side, mothers reported increased stimulation as a result of outside employment, greater independence, and increased self-esteem. Fathers have mixed reactions as well, with 48 percent reporting difficulties associated with the demands—the constancy and boredom—associated with their full-time caregiving role. On the positive side, 70 percent of fathers reported that their relationship with their children improved. Other advantages include: greater understanding of children, greater awareness of mother-housewife roles, and freedom from career pressures. Although about one third of role-sharing parents felt that children improved their relationships with both parents, over one fourth of both parents viewed the mother–child relationship as less strong. In a 2-year follow-up (Russell, 1986), about a third of the original families were reinterviewed. Nearly two thirds of both parents continued to view improved father–child relationships as the major advantage of this sharing arrangement. There was an increase in tension and conflict in the father–child relationship as well-a not surprising finding in light of the father's increased caregiver role.

An Israeli study of primary caregiver fathers and their 3- to 6-year-old children (Sagi, 1982; Sagi, Koren, & Weinberg, 1987) found that this arrangement had clear benefits for the children. Over half of the fathers were either equally or more involved in child care than were mothers. In addition to finding that children of fathers with intermediate and high involvement exhibited more internal locus of control than children of fathers with low involvement, the intermediate- and high-involvement fathers had higher expectations for independence and achievement and offered more encouragement than did low-involvement fathers. Empathy varied positively with involvement as well, with the children of the high-involved fathers showing the highest empathy scores. Finally, there was evidence of more androgynous sex-role orientation on the part of girls—probably as a result of being reared by more nurturant, involved fathers who were not sex stereotyped themselves and who did not respond to girls in a sex-stereotyped fashion (Radin & Sagi, 1982).

Confirmatory evidence of the impact of high levels of father participation on children's development come from a U.S. study. Radin (1982, 1988) studied 3- to 6-year-old children from families in which fathers were the primary caregivers. Children in these families showed higher levels of internality—a belief in their own ability to control events—than children in traditional families. In addition, children in the role-sharing families scored higher on verbal ability, and their fathers set higher educational standards and career expectations for their children than fathers in traditional families. However, sex-role orientations of the children were not different across the father and mother primary caregiver families.

As Russell (1986) found, the primary caregiver fathers in the Radin (1982, 1988) study viewed improved father–child relationships as a major benefit of this arrangement. However, 40 percent felt that the arrangement interfered with their jobs. Mothers cited reductions in stress and guilt as a result of this shift, but 60 percent felt that they did not have enough time with their children. An 11-year follow-up, when the children were adolescents, assessed the long-term consequences for children as a result of childrearing patterns assessed when the children were preschoolers and when they were 7–9 years old. Williams, Radin, and Allegro (1992) found that a greater amount of paternal involvement in the teen's preschool years was predictive of adolescent support for a nontraditional employment arrangement. This included greater approval of both spouses working full time and sharing child care and less approval of the husbands working full time with this spouse not working and caring for the children on a full-time basis. Second, children who experienced high paternal involvement at 7–9 years were supportive of more nontraditional childrearing arrangements (i.e., high father involvement or shared child care). In summary "norm-violating parental socialization practices do appear to have an impact on children's gender-related attitudes although it may take a decade to become evident" (Radin, 1993, p. 34). In a related report, Williams and Radin (1992) found no long-term impact of father involvement in childrearing on academic grades or expectations for higher education. Perhaps, the models of involved fathers as nonachievement oriented may have diluted their impact on their children's achievement aspirations. In summary, sex roles, but not academic or achievement attitudes and performance, seem to be altered by increased father caregiving participation.

Finally, Pruett (1983, 1985, 1992) in a study of families of primary father families found that infants and children benefit from this arrangement. Infants scored higher than average on standardized tests of development including problem-solving skills as personal and social skills during the first 2 years of life. Follow-up measures 2 and 4 years later revealed no negative impact on sex identity and clear evidence of a heightened appetite for novel experience and stimuli. Pruett suggested that the robust and stimulating style of father–child interaction may contribute to this outcome. In short, men as caregivers seem to do an adequate job of rearing children.

However, caution is necessary because parents who reverse roles are still rare, and evidence suggesting that children from these families fare better is not conclusive. Such parents may be different in other ways from parents who maintain traditional roles and might have influenced their children differently than traditional parents, no matter which parent stayed home. Moreover, the effect of shared caregiving is usually confounded with the effects of related family characteristics such as maternal employment outside the home. However, it is likely that parents who reverse roles are significantly affected by their choice and that, therefore, the nontraditional environment is at least partially responsible for differences between children from traditional and nontraditional families. As new family role arrangements become more common and more intensively studied, the effects of role reversal and other innovations will be better understood.

In spite of this evidence, other data suggest that mother–father roles may be less amendable to social change than these studies indicate. Lamb, Frodi, Hwang, and Frodi (1982) took advantage of a unique national family policy adopted by the Swedish government to offer the equivalent of paid sick leave (up to 90 percent of the individual's regular salary) for 9 months for any parent who wished to stay home to care for a new infant. Although between 1974 and 1979 fewer than 15 percent of new fathers in Sweden took advantage of this opportunity, Lamb and co-workers studied the growing minority of men who took parental level for more than 1 month, during which time they had primary responsibility for their infant's care. These nontraditional families were compared with traditional families in which mothers served as primary caregiver. Based on home observations at 3, 8, and 16 months, some surprising findings emerged. Mothers and fathers—regardless of relative involvement in caregiving—differed in characteristic ways: In general, mothers smiled, touched, and vocalized more than fathers, with only a few exceptions. This pattern is, of course, similar to prior observations of parents in traditional families. Regardless of their family type, mothers and fathers behaved in characteristically different ways:

> Differences between maternal and paternal behavior are remarkably robust, remaining stable inter- and intra-culturally despite variations in the relative involvement of mothers and fathers in childcare. This suggests either that behavioral differences are biologically-based or that they are deeply internalized during years of socialization. We will not be able to evaluate these alternative explanations until we are able to study parents who are themselves reared in a nonsex-typed fashion and allocate family responsibilities in a nontraditional fashion. (Lamb, Frodi, Hwang, & Frodi, 1982, p. 135)

One source of the discrepancy between the Russell (1983, 1986) and Lamb, Frodi, Hwang, and Frodi (1982) findings, in addition to methodological, cultural, and age of children issues, concerns the relative degree of societal support available for this role shift. Social psychologists have shown that attitude change is more likely to occur when effort has to be expended, whereas if less effort is necessary, less shift in attitude will follow (Kelley, 1972). In Russell's case, role sharing was a nonnormative activity, whereas in the case of the Swedish experiment, the participants had extensive societal support for their role shifts. Moreover, as Russell (1986) found in a sobering follow-up of his role-sharing families, only about one fourth of families continued the arrangement after 2 years. A number of factors may account for the small number of families that choose these alternatives and persist in them. For example, in general, men are still paid more than women, so that most families may find that it makes better economic sense for the father to be the breadwinner. Men may also be reluctant even to request leaves of absence that may jeopardize their job security—particularly in times of scarce jobs and inflation. In some cases, such as when the mother is breastfeeding a child, role reversals may be difficult to implement. The basic problem, however, may still be one of attitude; as Levine (1976) pointed out: "There is still the widespread belief that a man does not belong at home taking care of children" (p. 153). Until there is some change in this traditional view about the roles that men and women can or should play in rearing children, few families will either try alternative patterns or persist in them for extended periods.

Impact of normal variations in intact families on children's development. A voluminous literature has emerged over the last three decades that clearly demonstrates relations between quality of paternal involvement and children's social, emotional, and cognitive development (Biller, 1993; Lamb et al., 1985; Parke, 1979, 1981). At the same time, considerable evidence shows a good deal of overlap and redundancy between fathers' and mothers' impact on children. There is less evidence that fathers make a unique contribution to children's development.

Recent work that has focused on fathers' special style of interacting, namely play, has suggested that fathers may contribute in unique ways to children's social adjustment. Parke and his colleagues, for example, examined the relation between father–toddler play and children's adaptation to peers. In one study (MacDonald & Parke, 1984), fathers and their 3- and 4-year-old boys and girls were observed in 20 minutes of structured play in their homes. Teachers ranked these sample children in terms of their popularity among their preschool classmates. For both boys and girls, fathers who were rated as exhibiting high levels of physical play with their children, and eliciting high levels of positive affect in their children during the play sessions, had children who received the highest peer popularity ratings. For boys, however, this pattern was qualified by the fathers' level of directiveness. Boys whose fathers were both highly physical and low in directiveness received the highest popularity ratings, and the boys whose fathers were highly directive received lower popularity scores. Possibly, children who interact with a physically playful father and at the same time have an opportunity to regulate the pace and tempo of the interaction, a characteristic of low-directive fathers, learn how to recognize and send emotional signals during social interactions. Later studies confirmed these findings and showed a link between children's emotional encoding and decoding abilities that are presumably acquired, in part, in these playful interchanges and children's social adaptation to peers (Parke et al., 1987, 1993, 1994). In addition, fathers' affect displays, especially father anger, seem to be a potent correlate of children's social acceptance. In studies in both the laboratory (Carson & Parke, 1992) and the home (Boyum and Parke, in press), fathers' negative affect is inversely related to preschool and kindergarten children's sociometric status. Moreover, Isley, O'Neil, and Parke (1994) found that father's level of affect and control predicts children's social adaptation with peers both concurrently and 1 year later after controlling for maternal effects. Although there is overlap between mothers and fathers, evidence is emerging that fathers make a unique and independent contribution to their children's social development.

Although father involvement in infancy and childhood is quantitatively less than mother involvement, the data suggest that fathers nevertheless do not have an important impact on their offspring's development. Just as earlier research indicated that quality rather than quantity of mother–child interaction was the important predictor of cognitive and social development (e.g., Wachs, 1992; Wachs & Gruen, 1982), a similar assumption appears to hold for fathers as well.

REMAINING ISSUES AND FUTURE TRENDS

A number of issues remain to be examined in future research if we are to describe fully the complexities, specify the determinants and processes, and outline the consequences of father–child relationships. These include the choice of the unit of analysis, the effects of family variation, the types of developmental change, the role of historical change, methodological and contextual issues.

Unit of Analysis

Current work is clearly recognizing the importance of considering fathers from a family systems perspective. However, our conceptual analysis of dyadic and triadic units of analysis is still limited (Barrett & Hinde, 1988; Parke, 1988; Schaffer, 1984). Considerable progress has been made in describing the behavior of individual interactants (e.g., mother, father, child) within dyadic and to a lesser extent triadic settings, but less progress has been achieved in developing a language for describing interaction in dyadic and triadic terms. Even if such terms as *reciprocal* or *synchronous* hold promise, there remains little real advance in this regard. In addition, greater attention needs to be paid to the family as a unit of analysis. A number of researchers have offered differing taxonomies of family types or typologies that move us to this level of analysis (Boss, 1980; Kreppner, 1989; Reiss, 1981), but to date little effort has been made to apply these notions systematically to family relationships in childhood.

Fathers and Family Variation

One of the clear advances of the last decade is recognition of the importance of individual differences in children; one of the next advances will be the recognition of individual differences among families. Recognition of individual variability across families implies the necessity of expanding sampling procedures. In spite of demands for a greater awareness of family diversity, the range of family types that are studied is still relatively narrow. Although progress has been made in describing interaction patterns of fathers and children in different cultures (Bornstein, 1991; Lamb, 1987; Roopnarine & Carter, 1992) and in different ethnic groups in the United States (Harrison, Serafica, & McAdoo, 1984; McLoyd, 1990), this work represents only a beginning. Another form of diversity that warrants more attention is structural variation. In view of the high rates of single mothers and divorced families, caution is necessary in generalizing from intact families to single-parent households. Although, the amount of observationally based interactional work of fathers in families of different structure remains limited, recent work (e.g., Hetherington & Clingempeel, 1992) is beginning to correct this situation.

Types of Developmental Change

Developmental issues need to be addressed more fully to include children at a wider range of ages. Moreover, we need to move beyond childhood and examine more closely father relationships with their adult children—if we are to achieve a life-span view of fathering. Although development traditionally has marked change in the individual child, it is evident from this review that this perspective is too limited and fathers as well as children continue to develop across time (Parke, 1988, 1990). Fathers management of a variety of life course tasks, such as marriage, work, and personal identity, will clearly determine how they will execute parental tasks; in turn, these differences may find expression in measures of father–child interaction. Because developmental shifts in children's perceptual, cognitive, and social development in turn may alter parental attitudes and behaviors and/or the nature of the adults' own developmentally relevant choices, such as work or career commitment, this clearly argues for the recognition of two developmental trajectories—a child developmental course and an adult developmental sequence. The description of the interplay between these two types of developmental curves is necessary to capture adequately the nature of developmental changes in a father's role in the family (Parke, 1988, 1990).

Monitoring Secular Trends

There is a continuing need to monitor secular trends and to describe their impact on father–child interaction patterns (see Parke & Stearns, 1993). Secular change is complex and clearly does not affect all individuals equally or on all behavior patterns to the same extent. In fact, it is a serious oversimplification to assume that general societal trends can isomorphically be applied across all individual fathers and families. Moreover, better guidelines are necessary to illuminate which aspects of processes within families are most likely to be altered by historical events and which processes are less amenable to change. For example, the structural dynamics of early interaction (Stern, 1977) as well as some qualitative aspects of early parent–infant interactive style may be insulated from the influence of secular shifts. Are fathers biologically prepared to interact in a more physical way, and mothers in a more verbal mode? If this assumption about differences in parental play style is, in fact, true, rates of interactions would be more likely to change than would style when employment opportunities for man and women become more equal. Alternatively, the restraints may be more solely environmental, and as opportunities for adult male and female participation in child care and childrearing equalize, some maternal–paternal stylistic differences may diminish.

To date, historical events, such as shifts in the timing of parenting or work participation, have been treated relatively independently, but, in fact, these events co-occur rather than operate in any singular fashion (Parke & Tinsley, 1984). Moreover, the impact of any historical change may be different as a result of its occurrence in the same period as another change or changes. For example, women's increased presence in the workplace and delay in the onset of parenthood vary, and probably each event has different meaning without the other change. This implies the research need for multivariate designs to capture the simultaneous impact of multiple events on fathering activities.

Methodological Issues

It is likely that no single methodological strategy will suffice to understand the development of the father's role in the family. Instead, a wide range of designs and data collection and data analysis strategies is necessary. To date, there is still a paucity of information concerning interrelations across molar and molecular levels of analysis. However, it is becoming increasingly clear that a microanalytic strategy is not always more profitable in terms of describing relationships among interactive partners; in fact, in some cases, ratings may be a more useful approach. A set of guidelines concerning the appropriate level of analysis for different questions would be helpful.

Men's own reports have been underutilized in most research. Self-reports are not a substitute for observational data but can provide important information that can aid in interpretation of observed patterns (Goodnow & Collins, 1990; Parke, 1978). Moreover, recent work on the cultural images of fatherhood that are shared by both fathers themselves and by the wider society have profited from reliance on men's own reports (Marsigilio, 1993).

Reliance on nonexperimental strategies may be insufficient to address the important issue of direction of effects in work on the impact of fathers on children and families. Experimental strategies have been underutilized in studies of fathers. By experimentally modifying either the type of paternal behavior or level of father involvement, firmer conclusions concerning the direct causative role that fathers play in modifying their children's and their wives development will be possible. Intervention studies (e.g., Dickie, & Carnahan, 1980; Parke et al., 1980) aimed at modifying fathering behavior provide models for this type of work and, by extending these studies to include measures of both child and mother and father development, they could provide evidence of the impact of changes in fathering behavior on developmental outcomes. Moreover, these experimentally based interventions have clear policy implications by exploring the degree of plasticity of fathering behavior. Finally, these interventions can serve as a vehicle for evaluation of alternative theoretical views of fatherhood.

Contextual issues. Greater attention needs to be paid to the role of context in determining father–child relationships. How do father–child interaction patterns shift between home and lab settings and across different types of interaction contexts such as play, teaching, and caregiving? Moreover, it is important to consider the social a well as the physical context. Recognition of the embeddedness of fathers in family contexts is critical, and, in turn, conceptualizing families as embedded in a variety of extrafamilial social settings is important for understanding variation in father functioning. In this regard, it is necessary to recognize that variations in family structure and in ethnicity and social class will modify significantly the ways in which social networks are organized and utilized. For example, the role of the extended family is much more prominent in some groups, such as African Americans, than in other groups (Wilson, 1986). Similarly, single-parent families may be more directly embedded in community-based social networks than two-parent families. Descriptions of these variations are necessary for an adequate understanding of the role of extrafamilial networks on father and family functioning.

CONCLUSIONS

In spite of a relatively brief recent history of serious research devoted to fatherhood, considerable progress has been achieved in our understanding of the paternal role and the impact of fathers on themselves and others. Several conclusions are warranted. First, some modest increases over the past several decades have occurred in the level of father involvement with children. However, not all types of involvement shown have been equally affected and managerial aspects of family life remain largely a maternal responsibility. Second, fathers are clearly competent caregivers and playmates in spite of their limited involvement. Third, stylistic differences in interaction with children between mothers and fathers continue to be evident in spite of recent shifts toward greater involvement, although some cross-cultural evidence suggests that the paternal physical play style may not be as universal as previously assumed. Fourth, the father role appears less scripted and less determined than the mother role, which may account for the variability that characterizes the enactment of fathering. Fathering is multidetermined with individual, family, institutional, and cultural factors all influencing this role. Fifth, the focus of the effects of fathers continues to be on children's development and evidence continues to suggest that fathers do impact children's social, emotional, and cognitive development. However, quality of fathering remains an important determinant of paternal influence on children's development, and the independent contribution of fathers relative to mothers remains only weakly documented. Sixth, recent evidence suggests that fathering activities alter men's marital relationships as well as men's own sense of self and their societal generativity.

The study of father–child relationships has matured in the last two decades and is now a more fully contextualized issue. Fathers in the context of their social relationships both within and beyond the family are increasingly the appropriate point of entry for understanding the issue of both paternal roles and their impact on themselves and others. Our conceptual paradigms continue to outstrip our empirical understanding. To reduce this gap is the challenge of the next decade of research. Children, fathers, and families will benefit from this increased understanding.

ACKNOWLEDGMENTS

Preparation of this chapter was supported in part by National Science Foundation Grant SBR 9308941 and National Institute of Child Health and Human Development Grant R01 HD32391 to Parke. Thanks to Marc Bornstein for his comments and to Karin Horspool for her typing of the manuscript.

REFERENCES

Arbeit, S. A. (1975). *A study of women during their first pregnancy.* Unpublished doctoral dissertation, Yale University, New Haven, CT.

Baldwin, W., & Cain, V. (1980). The children of teenage parents. *Family Planning Perspectives, 12,* 34–43.

Baldwin, W. H., & Nord, C. W. (1984). Delayed childbearing in the U.S.: Facts and fictions. *Population Bulletin, 39,* 1–37.

Bandura, A. (1989). Cognitive social learning theory. In R. Vasta (Ed.), *Six theories of child development* (pp. 1–60). Greenwich, CT: JAI.

Barnett, R. C., & Baruch, G. K. (1987). Determinants of fathers' participation in family work. *Journal of Marriage and the Family, 49,* 29–40.

Barrett, J., & Hinde, R. A. (1988). Triadic interactions: Mother–first born–second born. In R. A. Hinde & J. Stevenson-Hinde (Eds.), *Towards understanding families* (pp. 181–190). Oxford, England: Oxford University Press.

Baruch, G. K., & Barnett, R. C. (1986). Fathers' participation in family work and children's sex-role attitudes. *Child Development, 57,* 1210–1223.

Beitel, A., & Parke, R. D. (1993). *Maternal attitudes as a determinant of father involvement.* Unpublished manuscript, University of Illinois, Urbana.

Belsky, J. (1979). Mother–father–infant interaction: A naturalistic observational study. *Developmental Psychology, 15,* 601–607.

Belsky, J. (1981). Early human experience: A family perspective. *Developmental Psychology, 17,* 3–23.

Belsky, J. (1984). Determinants of parenting: A process model. *Child Development, 55,* 83–96.

Belsky, J. (1991). Parental and nonparental child care and children's socioemotional development. In A. Booth (Ed.), *Contemporary families: Looking forward, looking back* (pp. 122–140). Minneapolis: National Council on Family Relations.

Belsky, J., Gilstrap, B., & Rovine, M. (1984). The Pennsylvania infant & family development project, I: Stability & change in mother–infant and father–infant interaction in a family setting at one, three & nine months. *Child Development, 55,* 692–705.

Belsky, J., & Isabella, R. (1985). Marital and parent–child relationships in family of origin and marital change following the birth of a baby: A retrospective analysis. *Child Development, 56,* 342–349.

Belsky, J., & Pensky, E. (1988). Marital change across the transition to parenthood. In R. Palkowitz & M. B. Sussman (Eds.), *Transitions to parenthood* (pp. 133–156). New York: Haworth.

Belsky, J., Rovine, M., & Fish, M. (1989). The developing family system. In M. Gunnar & E. Thelen (Eds.), *Systems and development* (Vol. 22, pp. 119–166). Hillsdale, NJ: Lawrence Erlbaum Associates.

Belsky, J., & Volling, B. L. (1986). Mothering, fathering & marital interaction in the family triad: Exploring family systems processes. In P. Berman & F. Pedersen (Eds.), *Men's transition to parenthood: Longitudinal studies of early family experience* (pp. 37–64). Hillsdale, NJ: Lawrence Erlbaum Associates.

Belsky, J., Ward, H. J., & Levine, M. (1986). Prenatal expectations, postnatal experiences and the transition to parenthood. In R. Ashmore & D. Brodinsky (Eds.), *Perspectives on the family* (pp. 111–146). Hillsdale, NJ: Lawrence Erlbaum Associates.

Bem, S. L. (1974). The measurement of psychological androgyny. *Journal of Consulting and Clinical Psychology, 42,* 155–162.

Bhavnagri, N., & Parke, R. D. (1985, April). *Parents as facilitators of peer-peer interaction.* Paper presented at the biennial meeting of the Society for Research in Child Development, Toronto.

Bhavnagri, N., & Parke, R. D. (1991). Parents as direct facilitators of children's peer relationships: Effects of age of child and sex of parent. *Journal of Social and Personal Relationships, 8*, 423–440.

Biernat, M., & Wortman, C. (1991). Sharing of home responsibilities between professionally employed women and their husbands. *Journal of Personality and Social Psychology, 60*, 844–860.

Biller, H. B. (1971). The mother–child relationship and the father-absent boy's personality development. *Merrill–Palmer Quarterly, 17*, 227–241.

Biller, H. B. (1993). *Fathers and families*. Westport, CT: Auburn House.

Bloom-Feshbach, J. (1979). *The beginnings of fatherhood*. Unpublished doctoral dissertation, Yale University, New Haven, CT.

Bolger, N., DeLongis, A., Kessler, R. C., & Wethington, E. (1989). The contagion of stress across multiple roles. *Journal of Marriage and the Family, 51*, 175–183.

Bornstein, M. H. (Ed.). (1991). *Cultural approaches to parenting*. Hillsdale, NJ: Lawrence Erlbaum Associates.

Boss, P. (1980). Normative family stress: Family boundary changes across the life span. *Family Relations, 29*, 445–450.

Boyum, L., & Parke, R. D. (in press). The role of family emotional expressiveness in the development of children's social competence. *Journal of Marriage and the Family*.

Broman, S. H. (1981). Long term development of children born to teenagers. In K. Scott, T. Field, & E. Robertson (Eds.), *Teenage parents and their offspring*. New York: Grune & Stratton.

Bronfenbrenner, U. (1989). Ecological systems theory. In R. Vasta (Ed.), *Six theories of child development* (Vol. 6, pp. 187–250). Greenwich, CT: JAI.

Bronfenbrenner, U., & Crouter, A. (1982). Work and family through time and space. In S. B. Kamerman & C. D. Hayes (Eds.), *Families that work: Children in a changing world* (pp. 39–83). Washington, DC: National Academy Press.

Brooks-Gunn, J., & Furstenberg, F. F. (1986). The children of adolescent mothers: Physical, academic and psychological outcomes. *Developmental Review, 6*, 224–251.

Card, J., & Wise, L. (1978). Teenage mothers and teenage fathers: The impact of early child-bearing on the parents' personal and professional lives. *Family Planning Perspectives, 10*, 199–205.

Carson, J., & Parke, R. D. (1992, March). *Sociometric status differences in affect sequences in preschool children's play with parents*. Poster presented at the biennial meeting of the Society for Research in Child Development, Seattle.

Chase-Lansdale, P. L. (1981). *Effects of maternal employment on mother-infant and father-infant attachment*. Unpublished doctoral dissertation, University of Michigan, Ann Arbor.

Clarke-Stewart, K. A. (1978). And daddy makes three: The father's impact on mother and young child. *Child Development, 49*, 466–478.

Clarke-Stewart, K. A. (1980). The father's contribution to children's cognitive and social development in early childhood. In F. Pedersen (Ed.), *The father–infant relationship*. New York: Praeger.

Cochran, M. M., & Brassard, J. A. (1979). Child development and personal social networks. *Child Development, 50*, 601–616.

Collins, W. A., & Russell, G. (1991). Mother–child and father–child relationships in middle childhood and adolescence: A developmental analysis. *Developmental Review, 11*, 91–136.

Coltrane, S. (in press). *Family man*. New York: Oxford.

Cooney, T. M., Pedersen, F. A., Indelicato, S., & Palkovitz, R. (1993). Timing of fatherhood: Is "on-time" optimal? *Journal of Marriage and the Family, 55*, 205–215.

Cowan, C. P. (1988). Working with men becoming fathers: The impact of couples group intervention. In P. Bronstein & C. P. Cowan (Eds.), *Fatherhood today* (pp. 276–298). New York: Wiley.

Cowan, C. P., & Cowan, P. A. (1985, March). *Parents' work patterns, marital and parent–child relationships, and early child development*. Paper presented at the meetings of the Society for Research in Child Development, Toronto.

Cowan, C. P., & Cowan, P. A. (1987). Men's involvement in parenthood. In P. W. Berman & F. A. Pedersen (Eds.), *Men's transition to parenthood* (pp. 145–174). Hillsdale, NJ: Lawrence Erlbaum Associates.

Cowan, C. P., & Cowan, P. (1992). *When partners become parents*. New York: Basic Books.

Cowan, C. P., Cowan, P. A., Coie, L., & Coie, J. D. (1978). Becoming a family: The impact of a first child's birth on the couple's relationship. In W. B. Miller & L. F. Newman (Eds.), *The first child and family formation* (pp. 296–324). Chapel Hill: Carolina Population Center.

Cowan, P. (1988). Becoming a father: A time of change, an opportunity for development. In P. Bronstein & C. P. Cowan (Eds.), *Fatherhood today* (pp. 13–35). New York: Wiley.

Crockett, L. J., Eggebeen, D. J., & Hawkins, A. J. (1993). Fathers' presence and young children's behavioral and cognitive adjustment. *Journal of Family Issues, 14*, 355–377.

Crouter, A. C. (1994). Processes linking families and work: Implications for behavior and development in both settings. In R. D. Parke & S. Kellam (Eds.), *Family relationships with other social systems* (pp. 9–28). Hillsdale, NJ: Lawrence Erlbaum Associates.

Crouter, A. C., Perry-Jenkins, M., Huston, T. L., & McHale, S. M. (1987). Processes underlying father involvement in dual-earner and single-earner families. *Developmental Psychology, 23*, 431–440.

Daly, K. (1993). Reshaping fatherhood: Finding the models. *Journal of Family Issues, 14*, 510–530.

Daniels, P., & Weingarten, K. (1982). *Sooner or later: The timing of parenthood in adult lives*. New York: Norton.

De Frain, J. (1979). Androgynous parents tell who they are and what they need. *The Family Coordinator, 28,* 237–243.

delaisi de Parseval, G., & Hurstel, F. (1987). Paternity "a la Francaise." In M. E. Lamb (Ed.), *The father's role: Cross-cultural perspectives* (pp. 59–87). Hillsdale, NJ: Lawrence Erlbaum Associates.

Dickie, J., & Carnahan, S. (1980). Training in social competence: The effect on mothers, fathers and infants. *Child Development, 51,* 1248–1251.

Dickie, J. R., & Matheson, P. (1984, August). *Mother-father-infant: Who needs support?* Paper presented at the meeting of the American Psychological Association, Toronto.

Durrett, M. E., Otaki, M., & Richards, P. (1984). Attachment and the mother's perception of support from the father. *International Journal of Behavioral Development, 7,* 167–176.

Elder, G. H. (1974). *Children of the great depression.* Chicago: University of Chicago Press.

Elder, G. H. (1984). Families, kin and the life course: A sociological perspective. In R. D. Parke, R. N. Emde, H. P. McAdoo, & G. P. Sackett (Eds.), *Review of child development research: Vol. 7. The family* (pp. 80–136). Chicago: University of Chicago Press.

Elder, G. H., & Hareven, T. K. (1993). Rising above life's disadvantage: From the Great Depression to war. In G. H. Elder, J. Modell, & R. D. Parke (Eds.), *Children in time and place* (pp. 47–72). New York: Cambridge University Press.

Elder, G. H., Modell, J., & Parke, R. D. (Eds.). (1993). *Children in time and place.* New York: Cambridge University Press.

Erikson, E. (1975). *Life history and the historical moment.* New York: Norton.

Erikson, E. (1982). *The life cycle completed.* New York: Norton.

Feldman, S. S., Nash, S. C., & Aschenbrenner, B. G. (1983). Antecedents of fathering. *Child Development, 54,* 1628–1636.

Ferree, M. M. (1991). The gender division of labor in two earner marriages: Dimensions of variability and change. *Journal of Family Issues, 12,* 158–180.

Field, T. M. (1978). Interaction behaviors of primary versus secondary caretaker fathers. *Developmental Psychology, 14,* 183–185.

Finley, G. E., Janovetz, V. A., & Rogers, B. (1990). *University students' perceptions of parental acceptance-rejection as a function of parental ages.* Poster presented at the Conference on Human Development, Richmond.

Furstenberg, F. F., Jr. (1988). Good dads—bad dads: Two faces of fatherhood. In A. J. Cherlin (Ed.), *The changing American family and public policy* (pp. 193–218). Washington, DC: Urban Institute Press.

Furstenberg, F. F., Jr., Brooks-Gunn, J., & Chase-Lansdale, L. (1989). Teenaged pregnancy and child bearing. *American Psychologist, 44,* 313–320.

Furstenberg, F. F., & Cherlin, A. J. (1991). *Divided families.* Cambridge, MA: Harvard University Press.

Furstenberg, F. F., & Harris, K. M. (1993). When and why fathers matter: Impacts of father involvement on children of adolescent mothers. In R. I. Lerman & T. J. Ooms (Eds.), *Young unwed fathers* (pp. 117–138). Philadelphia: Temple University Press.

Furstenberg, F. F., Morgan, S. P., & Allison, P. D. (1987). Paternal participation and children's well-being after marital dissolution. *American Sociological Review, 52,* 695–701.

Glueck, S., & Glueck, E. (1950). *Unraveling juvenile delinquency.* New York: Commonwealth Fund.

Goodnow, J. J., & Collins, W. A. (1990). *Development according to parents: The nature, sources and consequences of parents' ideas.* Hillsdale, NJ: Lawrence Erlbaum Associates.

Greenbaum, C. W., & Landau, R. (1982). The infant's exposure to talk by familiar people: Mothers, fathers and siblings different environments. In M. Lewis & L. Rosenblum (Eds.), *The social network of the developing infant* (pp. 229–247). New York: Plenum.

Greenberger, E., & O'Neil, R. (1991, April). *Characteristics of fathers' and mothers' jobs: Implications for parenting and social development.* Paper presented at the biennial meeting of the Society for Research in Child Development, Seattle.

Greenberger, E., & O'Neil, R., & Nagel, S. K. (1994). Linking workplace and homeplace: Relations between the nature of adults' work and their parenting behaviors. *Developmental Psychology, 30,* 990–1002.

Grossman, F. K. (1987). Separate and together: Men's autonomy and affiliation in the transition to parenthood. In P. W. Berman & F. A. Pedersen (Eds.), *Men's transition to parenthood* (pp. 89–112). Hillsdale, NJ: Lawrence Erlbaum Associates.

Grossman, F. K., Pollack, W. S., & Golding, E. (1988). Fathers and children: Predicting the quality and quantity of fathers. *Developmental Psychology, 24,* 82–91.

Harrison, A., Serafica, F., & McAdoo, H. (1984). Ethnic families of color. In R. D. Parke, R. N. Emde, H. P. McAdoo, & G. P. Sackett (Eds.), *Review of child development research: Vol. 7. The family* (pp. 329–371). Chicago: University of Chicago Press.

Hartup, W. W. (1979). The social worlds of childhood. *American Psychologist, 34,* 944–950.

Hayes, C. D. (1987). *Risking the future.* Washington, DC: National Academy Press.

Heath, D. B. (1977). Some possible effects of occupation on the maturing professional man. *Journal of Vocational Behavior, 11,* 263–281.

Heath, D. H. (1976). Competent fathers: Their personalities and marriages. *Human Development, 19,* 26–39.

Heath, D. H., & Heath, H. E. (1991). *Fulfilling lives: Paths to maturity and success.* San Francisco: Jossey-Bass.

Hernandez, D. J. (1993). *America's children.* New York: Russell Sage.

Hetherington, E. M. (1967). The effects of familial variables on sex typing, on parent–child similarity and on imitation in children. In J. P. Hill (Ed.), *Minnesota symposia on child psychology* (Vol. 1, pp. 82–107). Minneapolis: University of Minnesota Press.

Hetherington, E. M., & Clingempeel, W. G. (1992). Coping with marital transitions. *Monographs of the Society for Research in Child Development, 57,* Serial No. 227.

Hetherington, E. M., & Deur, J. (1971). The effects of father's absence. *Young Children, 26,* 233–248.

Hetherington, E. M., & Frankie, G. (1967). Effects of parental dominance, warmth, and conflict on imitation in children. *Journal of Personality and Social Psychology, 6,* 119–125.

Hock, E. (1980). Working and nonworking mothers and their infants: A comparative study of maternal caregiving characteristics and infant social behavior. *Merrill–Palmer Quarterly, 26,* 79–101.

Hock, E., DeMeis, D., & McBride, S. (1988). Maternal separation anxiety: Its role in the balance of employment and motherhood in mothers of infants. In A. E. Gottfried & A. W. Gottfried (Eds.), *Maternal employment and children's development* (pp. 191–229). New York: Plenum.

Hoffman, L. W. (1984). Work, family and the socialization of the child. In R. D. Parke, R. Emde, H. McAdoo, & G. P. Sackett (Eds.), *Review of child development research: The family* (Vol. 7, pp. 223–282). Chicago: University of Chicago Press.

Hoffreth, S. (1987). The children of teen childbearers. In S. L. Hoffreth & C. D. Hayes (Eds.), *Risking the future* (Vol. 2, pp. 174–206). Washington, DC: National Academy Press.

Hoffreth, S. L. (1987). Social and economic consequences of teenage parenthood. In S. L. Hoffreth & C. D. Hayes (Eds.), *Risking the future* (Vol. 2, pp. 123–144). Washington, DC: National Academy Press.

Isley, S., O'Neil, R., & Parke, R. D. (1994, August). *Father–child interaction and children's peer relationships: A longitudinal examination.* Paper presented at the American Psychological Association meeting, Los Angeles.

Jackson, S. (1987). Great Britain. In M. E. Lamb (Ed.), *The father's role: Cross-cultural perspectives* (pp. 29–57). Hillsdale, NJ: Lawrence Erlbaum Associates.

Kalleberg, A. L., & Loscocco, K. A. (1983). Aging, values, and rewards: Explaining age differences in job satisfaction. *American Sociological Review, 48,* 78–90.

Kanter, R. M. (1977). *Work and family in the United States: A critical review of research and policy.* New York: Sage.

Kelley, H. H. (1972). Attribution in social interaction. In E. E. Jones, D. E. Kanouse, H. H. Kelley, R. E. Nisbett, S. Valins, & B. Weiner (Eds.), *Attribution: Perceiving the causes of behavior.* Morristown, NJ: General Learning Press.

Kinard, E. M., & Klerman, L. (1983). Effects of early parenthood in the cognitive development of children. In E. McAnarney (Ed.), *Premature adolescent pregnancy and parenthood.* New York: Grune & Stratton.

King, V. (1994). Nonresidential father involvement and child well being: Can dads make a difference? *Journal of Family Issues, 15,* xx–xx.

Kohn, M. L., & Schooler, C. (1983). *Work and personality: An inquiry into the impact of social stratification.* Norwood, NJ: Ablex.

Kotelchuck, M. (1976). The infant's relationship to the father: Experimental evidence. In M. E. Lamb (Ed.), *The role of the father in child development* (pp. 123–157). New York: Wiley.

Kotre, J. (1984). *Outlining the self: Generativity and the interpretation of lives.* Baltimore: Johns Hopkins University Press.

Kotre, J., & Hall, E. (1990). *Seasons of life: Our dramatic journey from birth to death.* Boston: Little, Brown.

Kreppner, K. (1989). Linking infant development in context research to the investigation of life-span family development. In K. Kreppner & R. M. Lerner (Eds.), *Family systems and life-span development* (pp. 33–64). Hillsdale, NJ: Lawrence Erlbaum Associates.

Ladd, G. W., Profilet, S. M., & Hart, C. H. (1992). Parents' management of children's peer relations: Facilitating and supervising children's activities in the peer culture. In R. D. Parke & G. W. Ladd (Eds.), *Family-peer relationships: Modes of linkage* (pp. 215–254). Hillsdale, NJ: Lawrence Erlbaum Associates.

Lamb, M. E. (1977a). The development of mother–infant and father–infant attachments in the second year of life. *Developmental Psychology, 13,* 639–649.

Lamb, M. E. (1977b). Father–infant and mother–infant interaction in the first year of life. *Child Development, 48,* 167–181.

Lamb, M. E. (1979). The effects of social context on dyadic social interaction. In M. E. Lamb, S. T. Suomi, & G. R. Stephenson (Eds.), *Social interaction analysis: Methodological issues* (pp. 253–268). Madison: University of Wisconsin Press.

Lamb, M. E. (1986). The changing roles of fathers. In M. E. Lamb (Ed.), *The father's role: Applied perspectives* (pp. 3–27). New York: Wiley-Interscience.

Lamb, M. E. (Ed.). (1987). *The father's role: Cross-cultural perspectives.* Hillsdale, NJ: Lawrence Erlbaum Associates.

Lamb, M. E., & Elster, A. B. (1985). Adolescent mother–infant–father relationships. *Developmental Psychology, 21,* 768–773.

Lamb, M. E., Frodi, A. M., Hwang, C. P., & Frodi, M. (1982). Varying degrees of paternal involvement in infant care: Attitudinal and behavioral correlates. In M. E. Lamb (Ed.), *Nontraditional families* (pp. 117–138). Hillsdale, NJ: Lawrence Erlbaum Associates.

Lamb, M. E., Frodi, A. M., Hwang, C. P., Frodi, M., & Steinberg, J. (1982). Effects of gender and caretaking role on parent–infant interaction. In R. M. Emde & R. J. Harmon (Eds.), *Attachment and affiliative systems.* New York: Plenum.

Lamb, M. E., Pleck, J., Charnov, E. L., & Levine, J. A. (1987). A biosocial perspective on paternal behavior and involvement. In J. B. Lancaster, J. Altmann, A. Rossi, & L. R. Sherrod (Eds.), *Parenting across the life span: Biosocial perspectives* (pp. 111–142). Chicago: Aldine.

Lamb, M. E., Pleck, J. H., & Levine, J. A. (1985). The role of the father in child development: The effects of increased paternal involvement. In B. Lahey & E. E. Kazdin (Eds.), *Advances in clinical child psychology* (Vol. 8). New York: Plenum.

Lerman, R. I. (1993). A national profile of young unwed fathers. In R. I. Lerman & T. J. Ooms (Eds.), *Young unwed fathers* (pp. 27–51). Philadelphia: Temple University Press.

Lerman, R. L., & Ooms, T. J. (1993). *Young unwed fathers.* Philadelphia: Temple University Press.

Levine, J. A. (1976). *Who will raise the children: New options for fathers (and mothers).* New York: Lippincott.

Levy-Shiff, R., & Israelashvili, R. (1988). Antecedents of fathering: Some further exploration. *Developmental Psychology, 24,* 434–440.

Lewis, M., & Feiring, C. (1981). Direct and indirect interactions in social relationships. In L. P. Lipsitt (Ed.), *Advances in infancy research* (Vol. 1). Norwood, NJ: Ablex.

Lorenzi, M. E., Klerman, L. V., & Jekel, J. F. (1977). School-age parents: How permanent a relationship. *Adolescent, 45,* 13–22.

MacDonald, K., & Parke, R. D. (1984). Bridging the gap: Parent–child play interaction and peer interactive competence. *Child Development, 55,* 1265–1277.

MacDonald, K., & Parke, R. D. (1986). Parent–child physical play: The effects of sex and age of children and parents. *Sex Roles, 7–8,* 367–379.

Marsiglio, W. (1993). Contemporary scholarship on fatherhood: Culture, identity and conduct. *Journal of Family Issues, 14,* 484–509.

McBride, B. A. (1989). Stress and fathers' parental competence: Implications for family life and parent educators. *Family Relations, 38,* 385–389.

McCluskey, K. A., Killarney, J., & Papini, D. R. (1983). Adolescent pregnancy and parenthood: Implications for development. In E. C. Callahan & K. A. McCluskey (Eds.), *Life-span developmental psychology: Non-normative life events.* New York: Academic Press.

McDermid, S. M., Huston, T., & McHale, S. (1990). Changes in marriage associated with the transition to parenthood: Individual differences as a function of sex-role attitudes and changes in the division of household labor. *Journal of Marriage and the Family, 52,* 475–486.

McHale, S. M., Crouter, A. C., & Bartko, W. T. (1991). Traditional and egalitarian patterns of parental involvement: Antecedents, consequences and temporal rhythms. In R. Lerner & D. Featherman (Eds.), *Advances in life-span development* (Vol. 9). Hillsdale, NJ: Lawrence Erlbaum Associates.

McLoyd, V. (1990). The impact of economic hardship on Black families and children: Psychological distress, parenting, and socioemotional development. *Child Development, 61,* 311–346.

Miller, D. R., & Swanson, G. E. (1958). *The changing American parent.* New York: Wiley.

Montemayor, R. (1982). The relationship between parent–adolescent conflict and the amount of time adolescents spend alone with parents and peers. *Child Development, 53,* 1512–1519.

Montemayor, R., & Brownlee, J. (1987). Fathers, mothers and adolescents: Gender based differences in parental roles during adolescence. *Journal of Youth and Adolescence, 16,* 281–291.

Mott, F. (1993). Absent fathers and child development: *Emotional and cognitive effects at ages five to nine.* Unpublished manuscript, Ohio State University, Columbus.

Natravil-Kline, E. (1984). *Fathers and infants: Selected factors which predict father participation in infant care.* Unpublished doctoral dissertation. Boston University, Boston, MA.

Neville, B., & Parke, R. D. (1987). *Parental age and gender effects on parent-child play.* Unpublished manuscript, University of Illinois, Urbana-Champaign.

Neville, B., & Parke, R. D. (1993). *Waiting for paternity: Interpersonal and contextual implications of the timing of fatherhood.* Unpublished manuscript, University of Washington, Seattle.

Nydegger, C. N. (1973). *Timing of fatherhood: Role perception and socialization.* Unpublished doctoral dissertation, Pennsylvania State University, University Park.

Osofsky, H., & Culp, R. (1989). Risk factors in the transition to fatherhood. In S. Cath, A. R. Gurwitt, & L. Gunsberg (Eds.), *Fathers and their families* (pp. 145–165). Hillsdale, NJ: The Analytic Press.

Parke, R. D. (1978). Parent–infant interaction: Progress, paradigms and problems. In G. P. Sackett (Ed.), *Observing behavior: Vol. 1. Theory and applications in mental retardation* (pp. 69–75). Baltimore: University Park Press.

Parke, R. D. (1979). Perspectives of father–infant interaction. In J. Osofsky (Ed.), *A handbook of infant development* (pp. 549–590). New York: Wiley.

Parke, R. D. (1981). *Fathers.* Cambridge, MA: Harvard University Press.

Parke, R. D. (1988). Families in life-span perspective: A multilevel developmental approach. In E. M. Hetherington, R. M. Lerner, & M. Perlmutter (Eds.), *Child development in life-span perspective* (pp. 159–190). Hillsdale, NJ: Lawrence Erlbaum Associates.

Parke, R. D. (1990). In search of fathers: A narrative of an empirical journey. In I. E. Sigel & G. H. Brody (Eds.), *Methods of family research* (Vol. 1, pp. 153–188). Hillsdale, NJ: Lawrence Erlbaum Associates.

Parke, R. D., & Beitel, A. (1986). Hospital based interventions for fathers. In M. E. Lamb (Ed.), *Fatherhood: Applied perspectives* (pp. 293–323). New York: Wiley.

Parke, R. D., & Bhavnagri, N. (1989). Parents as managers of children's peer relationships. In D. Belle (Ed.), *Children's social networks and social supports* (pp. 241–259). New York: Wiley.

Parke, R. D., Burks, V., Carson, J., Neville, B., & Boyum, L. (1994). Family-peer relationships: A tripartite model. In R. D. Parke & S. Kellam (Eds.), *Advances in family research: Vol. 4. Family relationships with other social systems* (pp. 115–145). Hillsdale, NJ: Lawrence Erlbaum Associates.

Parke, R. D., Grossman, D., & Tinsley, B. R. (1981). Father–mother–infant interaction in the newborn period: A German–American comparison. In T. M. Field, A. M. Sostek, P. Vietze, & P. H. Leiderman (Eds.), *Culture and early interactions* (pp. 95–113). Hillsdale, NJ: Lawrence Erlbaum Associates.

Parke, R. D., Hymel, S., Power, T. G., & Tinsley, B. R. (1980). Fathers and risk: A hospital based model of intervention. In D. B. Sawin, R. C. Hawkins, L. O. Walker, & J. H. Penticuff (Eds.), *Psychosocial risks in infant-environment transactions* (pp. 174–189). New York: Brunner/Mazel.

Parke, R. D., MacDonald, K., Beitel, A., & Bhavnagri, N. (1988). The inter-relationships among families, fathers and peers. In R. D. Peters (Ed.), *New approaches to family research* (pp. 17–44). New York: Brunner/Mazel.

Parke, R. D., & Neville, B. (1987). The male adolescent's role in adolescent pregnancy and childrearing. In S. L. Hoffreth & C. Hayes (Eds.), *Risking the future* (pp. 145–173). Washington, DC: National Academy Press.

Parke, R. D., & Neville, B. (in press). Late-timed fatherhood: Determinants and consequences for children and families. In J. Shapiro, M. Diamond, & M. Greenberg (Eds.), *Becoming a father: Social, emotional and psychological perspectives.* New York: Springer.

Parke, R. D., & O'Leary, S. (1976). Family interaction in the newborn period: Some findings, some observations, and some unresolved issues. In K. Riegel & J. Meacham (Eds.), *The developing individual in a changing world: Vol. 2. Social and environmental issues* (pp. 653–663). The Hague, Netherlands: Mouton.

Parke, R. D., Power, T. G., & Gottman, J. M. (1979). Conceptualization and quantifying influence patterns in the family triad. In M. E. Lamb, S. J. Suomi, & G. R. Stephenson (Eds.), *Social interaction analysis: Methodological issues* (pp. 231–253). Madison: University of Wisconsin Press.

Parke, R. D., & Sawin, D. B. (1975, April). *Infant characteristics and behavior as elicitors of maternal and paternal responsibility in the newborn period.* Paper presented at the biennial meeting of the Society for Research in Child Development, Denver.

Parke, R. D., & Sawin, D. B. (1976). The father's role in infancy: A reevaluation. *The Family Coordinator* [Invited article for special issue on fatherhood], *25,* 365–371.

Parke, R. D., & Sawin, D. B. (1980). The family in early infancy: Social interactional and attitudinal analyses. In F. A. Pedersen (Ed.), *The father–infant relationship: Observational studies in the family setting* (pp. 44–70). New York: Praeger.

Parke, R. D., & Stearns, P. N. (1993). Fathers and child rearing. In G. H. Elder, J. Modell, & R. D. Parke (Eds.), *Children in time and place* (pp. 147–170). New York: Cambridge University Press.

Parke, R. D., & Tinsley, B. R. (1981). The father's role in infancy: Determinants of involvement in caregiving and play. In M. E. Lamb (Ed.), *The role of the father in child development* (2nd ed., pp. 429–457). New York: Wiley.

Parke, R. D., & Tinsley, B. R. (1984). Fatherhood: Historical and contemporary perspectives. In K. McCluskey & H. Reese (Eds.), *Life span development: Historical and generational effects* (pp. 203–248). New York: Academic Press.

Parke, R. D., & Tinsley, B. J. (1987). Family interaction in infancy. In J. Osofsky (Ed.), *Handbook of infancy* (pp. 579–641). New York: Wiley.

Pedersen, F. A. (1975, September). *Mother, father and infant as an interactive system.* Paper presented at the annual convention of the American Psychological Association, Chicago.

Pedersen, F. A., Anderson, B. J., & Cain, R. L. (1977). *An approach to understanding linkages between the parent-infant and spouse relationships.* Paper presented at the meeting of the Society for Research in Child Development, New Orleans.

Pedersen, F. A., Anderson, B. J., & Cain, R. L., Jr. (1980). Parent–infant and husband–wife interactions observed at age five months. In F. A. Pedersen (Ed.), *The father–infant relationship* (pp. xx–xx). New York: Praeger.

Pedersen, F. A., & Robson, K. S. (1969). Father participation in infancy. *American Journal of Orthopsychiatry, 39,* 466–472.

Pedersen, F. A., Zaslow, M. J., Cain, R. L., & Anderson, B. J. (1981). Caesarean childbirth: Psychological implications for mothers and fathers. *Infant Mental Health Journal, 2,* 257–263.

Pleck, J. H. (1981). *Wives' employment, role demands and adjustment* (final report). Unpublished manuscript, Wellesley College, Center for Research on Women, Wellesley, MA.

Pleck, J. H. (1982). *Husbands and wives paid work, family work and adjustment.* Wellesley, MA: Wellesley College, Center for Research on Women.

Pleck, J. H. (1983). Husbands' paid work and family roles: Current research issues. In H. Z. Lopata & J. H. Pleck (Eds.), *Research on the interweave of social roles: Vol 3. Families and jobs.* Greenwich, CT: JAI.

Power, T. G., & Parke, R. D. (1982). Play as a context for early learning: Lab and home analyses. In I. E. Sigel & L. M. Laosa (Eds.), *The family as a learning environment* (pp. 147–178). New York: Plenum.

Pruett, K. D. (1983). Infants of primary nurturing fathers. *Psychoanalytic Study of the Child, 38,* 257–277.

Pruett, K. D. (1985). Oedipal configurations in young father-raised children. *The Psychoanalytic Study of the Child, 40,* 435–460.

Pruett, K. D. (1992). Latency development in children of primary nurturing fathers: Eight-year follow-up. *The Psychoanalytic Study of the Child, 47,* 85–101.

Quinn, R. P., & Staines, G. L. (1979). *The 1977 quality of employment survey.* Ann Arbor, MI: Survey Research Center.

Radin, N. (1982). Primary caregiver and role sharing fathers. In M. E. Lamb (Ed.), *Nontraditional families* (pp. 173–204). Hillsdale, NJ: Lawrence Erlbaum Associates.

Radin, N. (1988). Primary caregiving fathers of long duration. In P. Bronstein & C. P. Cowan (Eds.), *Fatherhood today* (pp. 127–143). New York: Wiley.

Radin, N. (1993). Primary caregiving fathers in intact families. In A. Gottfried & A. Gottfried (Eds.), *Redefining families* (pp. 11–54). New York: Plenum.

Radin, N., & Sagi, A. (1982). Childrearing fathers in intact families in Israel and the U.S.A. *Merrill–Palmer Quarterly, 28,* 111–136.

Ragozin, A. S., Bashan, R. B., Crnic, K. A., Greenberg, M. T., & Robinson, N. M. (1982). Effects of maternal age on parenting role. *Developmental Psychology, 18,* 627–634.

Rappaport, R., Rappaport, R. N., & Strelitz, Z. (1977). *Fathers, mothers and society.* New York: Basic Books.

Redican, W. K. (1976). Adult male–infant interactions in non-human primates. In M. E. Lamb (Ed.), *The role of the father in child development* . New York: Wiley.

Reiss, D. (1981). *The family's construction of reality.* Cambridge, MA: Harvard University Press.

Repetti, R. L. (1989). Effects of daily workload on subsequent behavior during marital interaction: The roles of social withdrawal and spouse support. *Journal of Personality and Social Psychology, 57*(4), 651–659.

Repetti, R. L. (1993). Short-term and long-term processes linking job stressors to father–child interaction. *Social Development, 3,* 1–15.

Richards, M. P. M., Dunn, J. F., & Antonis, B. (1977). Caretaking in the first year of life: The role of fathers' and mothers' social isolation. *Child: Care, Health & Development, 3,* 23–26.

Robinson, J. P. (1977). *How Americans use time.* New York: Praeger.

Robinson, J. (1988). Who's doing the housework? *American Demographics, 10,* 24–28.

Rodman, H., & Safilios-Rothschild, C. (1983). Weak links in men's worker-earner roles: A descriptive model. In H. Z. Lopata & J. H. Pleck (Eds.), *Research in the interweave of social roles: Vol. 3. Jobs and families* (pp. 239–250). Greenwich, CT: JAI Press.

Roopnarine, J. C., & Carter, D. B. (Eds.). (1992). *Parent–child socialization in diverse cultures.* Norwood, NJ: Ablex.

Roopnarine, J. C., Hooper, F. H., Ahmeduzzaman, M., & Pollack, B. (1993). Gentle play partners: Mother–child, father–child play in New Delhi, India. In K. MacDonald (Ed.), *Parent–child play* (pp. 287–304). Albany: State University of New York Press.

Roopnarine, J. C., Talukder, E., Jain, D., Joshi, P., & Srivastav, P. (1990). Characteristics of holding patterns of play and social behaviors between parents and infants in New Delhi, India. *Developmental Psychology, 26,* 867–873.

Rotundo, E. A. (1985). American fatherhood: A historical perspective. *American Behavioral Scientist, 29,* 7–25.

Rotundo, E. A. (1993). *American manhood.* New York: Basic Books.

Russell, G. (1982). Shared-caregiving families: An Australian study. In M. E. Lamb (Ed.), *Nontraditional families* (pp. 139–172). Hillsdale, NJ: Lawrence Erlbaum Associates.

Russell, G. (1983). *The changing role of fathers.* St. Lucia, Australia: Queensland University Press.

Russell, G. (1986). Primary caretaking and role-sharing fathers. In M. E. Lamb (Ed.), *The father's role: Applied perspectives* (pp. 29–57). New York: Wiley.

Russell, G., & Russell, A. (1987). Mother–child and father–child relationships in middle childhood. *Child Development, 58,* 1573–1585.

Russell, A., & Russell, G. (1989). Warmth in mother–child and father–child relationships in middle childhood. *British Journal of Developmental Psychology, 7,* 219–235.

Rutter, M. (1987). Psychosocial resilience and protective mechanisms. *American Journal of Orthopsychiatry, 51,* 316–331.

Sagi, A. (1982). Antecedents and consequences of various degrees of paternal involvement in childrearing: The Israeli project. In M. E. Lamb (Ed.), *Nontraditional families: Parenting and child development* (pp. 205–232). Hillsdale, NJ: Lawrence Erlbaum Associates.

Sagi, A., Koren, N., & Weinberg, M. (1987). Fathers in Israel. In M. E. Lamb (Ed.), *The father's role: Cross-cultural perspectives* (pp. 197–226). Hillsdale, NJ: Lawrence Erlbaum Associates.

Sagi, A., Lamb, M. E., Shoham, R., Dvir, R., & Lewkowicz, K. S. (1985). Parent–infant interaction in families on Israeli kibbutzim. *International Journal of Behavioral Development, 8,* 273–284.

Sameroff, A. J. (1983). Developmental systems: Contexts and evolution. In W. Kessen (Ed.), *Handbook of child psychology* (Vol. 1, pp. 237–294). New York: Wiley.

Schaffer, H. R. (1984). *The child's entry into a social world.* New York: Academic Press.

Shelton, B. A. (1992). *Women, men and time: Gender differences in paid work, housework and leisure.* New York: Greenwood.

Shereshefsky, P. M., & Yarrow, L. J. (1973). *Psychological aspects of a first pregnancy and early postnatal adaption.* New York: Raven.

Smith, P. K., & Daglish, L. (1977). Sex differences in parent and infant behavior in the home. *Child Development, 48,* 1250–1254.

Snarey, J. (1993). *How fathers care for the next generation.* Cambridge, MA: Harvard University Press.

Stearns, P. (1991). Fatherhood in historical perspective: The role of social change. In F. W. Bozett & S. M. H. Hanson (Eds.), *Fatherhood and families in cultural context* (pp. 28–52). New York: Springer.

Stern, D. N. (1977). *The first relationship.* Cambridge, MA: Harvard University Press.

Szalai, A. (Ed.). (1972). *The use of time: Daily activities of urban and suburban populations in twelve countries.* The Hague, Netherlands: Mouton.

Thompson, L., & Walker, A. J. (1989). Gender in families. *Journal of Marriage and Family, 51,* 845–871.

Tinsley, B. J., & Parke, R. D. (1984). The contemporary impact of the extended family on the nuclear family: Grandparents as support and socialization agents. In M. Lewis (Ed.), *Beyond the dyad* (pp. 161–194). New York: Plenum.

Tinsley, B. J., & Parke, R. D. (1988a). Grandparents as interactive and social support agents for families with young infants. *International Journal of Aging & Human Development, 25,* 261–279.

Tinsley, B. J., & Parke, R. D. (1988b). The role of grandfathers in the context of the family. In P. Bronstein & C. P. Cowan (Eds.), *Fatherhood today* (pp. 236–250). New York: Wiley.

U.S. Census Bureau. (1993, April). *U.S. Census Bureau Report.* Washington, DC: Author.

Valliant, G. (1977). *Adaptation to life.* Boston: Little, Brown.

Volling, B. L., & Belsky, J. (1991). Multiple determinants of father involvement during infancy in dual-earner and single-earner families. *Journal of Marriage and the Family, 53,* 461–474.

Wachs, T. D. (1992). *The nature of nurture.* Newbury Park, CA: Sage.

Wachs, T. D., & Gruen, G. E. (1982). *Early experiences and human development.* New York: Plenum.

Walker, K., & Woods, M. (1976). *Time use: A measure of household production of family goods and services.* Washington, DC: American Home Economics Association.

Walter, C. A. (1986). *The timing of motherhood.* Lexington, MA: Lexington Books.

White, B. L., Kaban, B., Shapiro, B., & Attonucci, J. (1976). Competence and experience. In I. C. Uzgiris & F. Weizmann (Eds.), *The structuring of experience* (pp. 115–152). New York: Plenum.

Williams, E., & Radin, N. (1992, May). *Predictors of adolescent achievement and expectations: An 11 year follow-up.* Paper presented at the meeting of the American Orthopsychiatric Association, New York.

Williams, E., Radin, N., & Allegro, T. (1992). Highly involved fathers' children: An 11 year follow-up focused on sex-role attitudes. *Merrill-Palmer Quarterly, 38,* 457–476.

Wilson, M. N. (1986). The Black's extended family: An analytic consideration. *Developmental Psychology, 2,* 246–258.

Yarrow, A. L. (1991). *Latecomers: Children of parents over 35.* New York: The Free Press.

Yogman, M. W. (1983). Development of the father–infant relationship. In H. Fitzgerald, B. Lester, & M. W. Yogman (Eds.), *Theory and research in behavioral pediatrics* (Vol. 1). New York: Plenum.

Zaslow, M., Pedersen, F., Suwalsky, J., Rabinovich, B., & Cain, R. (1985, April). *Fathering during the infancy period: The implications of the mother's employment role.* Paper presented at the meetings of the Society for Research in Child Development, Toronto.

Zelazo, P. R., Kotelchuck, M., Barber, L., & David, J. (1977, March). *Fathers and sons: An experimental facilitation of attachment behaviors.* Paper presented at the biennial meeting of the Society for Research in Child Development, New Orleans.

3

Single Parenthood

Marsha Weinraub
Temple University
Marcy B. Gringlas
The Thomas Jefferson University Hospital

If the two-parent family were a bird, it would be considered an endangered species.

—Cohen, 1993

INTRODUCTION

The proportion of children living in single-parent families has increased markedly around the world since 1960, and this increase has been especially significant in the United States (Burns, 1992; Hobbs & Lippman, 1990). The United States has a higher proportion of single-parent households than any other developed country. The proportion of children in the United States living with only one parent increased from 9.1 percent in 1960 to 24.7 percent in 1990 (U.S. Bureau of the Census, 1992). Although there are differences in the prevalence of single-parent families across ethnic groups, with nearly 55 percent of African-American children living in single-parent families, this increase has affected all groups of Americans. Given current divorce and remarriage trends, demographers predict that about half of all America's children will spend some part of their childhood in a single-parent family (Ahlburg & DeVita, 1992).

For many observers of the national scene, this changing family pattern is particularly alarming. Sometimes considered a prime symptom of the erosion of American culture, single-parent families are often reputed to be responsible for society's declining values and the breakdown of the social fabric. In an *Atlantic* magazine article entitled "Dan Quayle Was Right," Whitehead (1993) characterized the family disruption associated with the rise in single-parent families as "a central cause of many of our most vexing social problems" (p. 77). Indeed, the term *single-parent family* has become "almost a euphemism" for family breakdown, a kind of social pathology, and a major contributor to all that is wrong with our society (Kamerman & Kahn, 1988, p. 1).

To some extent, this alarmist view is accurate. A wide range of research from sociologists and psychologists has shown that children of single-parent families are more likely to have difficulties with emotional and psychological adjustment, with school performance and educational attainment, and they are more likely to have behavioral adjustment problems, later marriage and earlier childbearing, than children of two-parent families. Because single-parent children appear more vulnerable to a wide variety of societal problems, these children are now routinely referred to as "at risk" for developmental difficulties.

However, to say that a child is at risk is a statistical statement, indicating that probablistically speaking, children in single-parent families are more likely to have developmental difficulties than other children. One of the reasons children from single-parent families may be at risk is that these families are also disproportionately poor. Half of all single parents live in poverty. According to Garfinkel and McLanahan (1986), no other major demographic group is so poor, and no other group stays poor for so long. International studies show that poverty rates are higher among children in single-parent families than those in all other family types in every country studied (Hobbs & Lippman, 1990). As a consequence of poverty alone, many children of single parents grow up in deteriorated and dangerous neighborhoods, often with inferior housing and educational systems. These characteristics in and of themselves could be responsible for the at-risk status of these children. How much of the risk status is a result of poverty, and how much is due to other factors characteristic of single-parent families is a question with important psychological and social policy implications.

To unravel the multiple factors that may be responsible for children of single-parent families being at risk, is it necessary to identify the many similar and divergent characteristics of single-parent families. One of the most important characteristics of single-parent families and their children is their heterogeneity. Although half of all children growing up in single-parent families live in poverty, half do not. Similarly, contrary to stereotypical views and journalistic ravings, not all single-mother families are on welfare. Although many single mothers draw funds from public assistance, more than half do not (Kamerman & Kahn, 1988).

The phenomenological experience of growing up in a single-parent family varies depending on the nature of the family, the experiences of the parent, and the family context. Single parents may be divorced, widowed, or unmarried; they may be teenaged or older; they may have been previously married or not. Although the preponderance of single parents are women, the number of male single parents is increasing. Although legally single, some parents classified by census statisticians and researchers as single may be living in a committed, partnered relationship not legally acknowledged. (See Patterson, in this *Handbook,* for information about lesbian and gay parenting. These statistically "single" parents are often rearing their children in the context of a committed, partnered relationship.) For some single parents, becoming a single parent may have been a planned and conscious decision; for others it was not. Some single parents may have chosen to have and to rear their children with another adult parent; they became single parents when this partnership did not work out either because of divorce, separation, or widowhood. Other single parents may have decided to become parents knowing that they would be without partners. The commonality across these varied types of single parents is that the parent does not have a legally married partner in the home. How these individuals came to be parents, the choices they made, and the experiences that were thrust upon them, all have differential implications for their family's life circumstances.

Differences in how the parents came to be single parents affect their employment, their financial circumstances, their relationships with other adults, their involvement with their child, and their competence as parents. The etiology of the parent's single parenthood also has implications for the child's perceptions and experiences growing up. For example, imagine that 10 children from different types of single-parent families are brought together to discuss their experiences. They would describe many common experiences, such as not having enough money, missing their fathers, and problems getting along with their mothers. These concerns, however, do not differ from those of children living in *all* families. Those issues that are *unique* to single-parent families are issues on which there are large individual differences across single-parent families. Depending on their age, children from recently divorced single-parent families might talk of anger at their parents' separation, of fights between mom and dad over custody and child support, and about what happens on dad's day for visitation. Some children of divorce may wonder why dad and mom are not living together anymore;

others may be relieved to be free finally from the marital discord. Children of widowed single parents may be mourning their parent's loss, whereas children of adolescent single mothers may have difficulty with mom's inexperienced and immature ways, and wonder when mom will ever finish going to school. Children of never-married mothers may wonder about their father, who he is, and what he is like. Some children may be confused about who their fathers are, and why they are not around, whereas other children, albeit a minority, may be learning to live without a mother. Some children may feel isolated and alone, whereas others are living in cramped households, with not too much in the way of material goods but plenty of people to be with and love. Researchers need to unravel these various psychological experiences to understand what it is about the single-parent family that may place children at risk.

These issues are the foci of this chapter: to describe the changing demographics of single-parent families, to describe similarities and differences across parenting situations in single-parent families, and to explore some of the parenting factors that might be responsible for the at-risk status of children growing up in single-parent families. In the first section, we consider the changing demographics of single-parent families over the last several decades. We show that not only is the number of single-parent families increasing, but the circumstances that are responsible for the formation of single-parent families—divorce and separation, widowhood, and out-of-marriage births—are changing too. In the next section, we summarize the literature on parenting in common types of single-parent families—divorced parents, adolescent parents, and "not married" mothers—with the intent of identifying parenting features both unique to these specific single family types and common to single parents as a group. We suggest that single-parent families that arise from different circumstances differ in a number of important ways, and these differences need to be considered before any understanding of the more general effects of rearing children in a single-parent family are understood. In the third section, we consider directions for further research.

Because so much critical attention has been focused on the effects on child development of growing up in a single-parent family (examples of excellent reviews include the now classic but still relevant Herzog & Sudia, 1973; as well as Amato, 1988; Amato & Keith, 1991a, 1991b; Cashion, 1982; McLanahan & Bumpass, 1988), we direct our attention in this chapter to describing and understanding the situations single parents face during the time of their single parenthood, and how these situations may influence their behavior toward their children.

DEMOGRAPHIC CHANGES IN SINGLE-PARENT FAMILY FORMATION

Not only has the prevalence of single-parent families changed over the last four decades, but so have the conditions that have led to the formation of single-parent families (U.S. Bureau of the Census, 1992). As Figure 3.1 shows, most children are in single-parent families created by divorce or separation. However, the proportion of single-parent children living in a family created by divorce or separation declined from 73 percent in 1970 to 62 percent in 1990. Also declining, from 20 percent to 7 percent, was the proportion of children living in single-parent families created by widowhood. Most significant is the increase in children in single-parent families headed by a never-married mother. This group increased from 6.8 percent in 1970 to 30.6 percent in 1990. This increase reflects increases in births to unmarried individuals and single-parent adoptions.

More and more women are having children outside of marriage. In the early 1960s, there were about 700,000 births outside marriage. This number increased to about 2.2 million by the late 1980s. Although premarital births have been more common among African-American women since at least the early 1960s, responsibility for the increase in premarital birth ratios is shared across racial groups. For Whites, the increase in percentage of premarital births to total births for women between the ages of 15 and 44 more than doubled during the period from 1960 to 1989, going from 9 percent to 22 percent. For Hispanic Americans, the increase also doubled, from 19 percent to 38 percent. For African Americans, the increase went from 42 percent to 70 percent (U.S. Bureau of the Census, 1992).

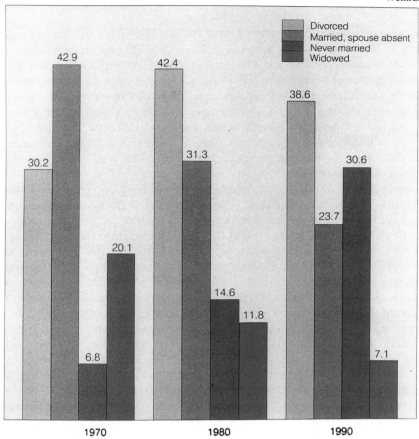

FIGURE 3.1. Children under 18 living with one parent, by marital status of parent: 1970, 1980, and 1990 (in percentages). From U.S. Bureau of the Census (1992).

More interesting is the changing character of the women having out-of-marriage births. Recent reports (Bachu, 1993) show that the largest percentage increase in births outside of marriages are in White employed, and college-educated women. For a number of reasons—increased employment, delayed marriage, reduced likelihood of marriage, and delayed childbearing—single motherhood has been increasing dramatically among affluent and well-educated women as well as among uneducated women. It is true that the rate for women who did not finish high school increased from 35.2 percent in 1982 to 48.4 percent in 1992. However, in that same period, the rates for women with 1 or more years of college doubled from 5.5 percent to 11.3 percent. The percentage of employed women having a child out of marriage went from 11.1 percent in 1982 to 15.5 percent in 1992; among unemployed women, these figures dropped from 29.4 percent in 1982 to 26.2 percent in 1992. This trend for births outside of marriage was particularly dramatic among mothers in managerial and professional occupations, where the percentages more than doubled from 3.1 percent in 1980 to 8.2 percent in 1990. As Figure 3.2 shows, the percent increase in women having children out of marriage is particularly large for older women, especially women in their 30s.

Also, the number of single parents, both male and female, adopting children increased dramatically in the 1980s (Groze, 1991). The majority of adoptions are by women. Estimating the exact increase in single-parent adoptions is not possible because of differences in sampling strategies across studies, and the number of single-parent families adopting children is still low compared to the number of single-parent households in the general population (Groze, 1991). Some studies show that single parents are more likely to adopt older children, particularly boys, and less likely to adopt siblings (Barth & Berry, 1988); Shireman and Johnson (1976) and Feigelman and Silverman (1977) suggested

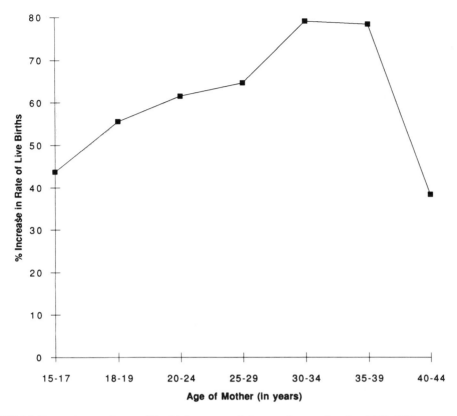

FIGURE 3.2. Percent increase in rate of live births to unmarried women by age of mother: 1980–1990.

that single parents tend to adopt children the same gender as themselves. Perhaps as a consequence of the fact that most single adoptive parents are women, single-parent adoptive families tend to have lower incomes than dual-parent adoptive families (Groze, 1991; Shireman & Johnson, 1976).

Finally, single parenthood is not a permanent, but a transitional status for many parents. Garfinkel and McLanahan (1986) estimated that the median length of time children spend in a mother-only family is about 6 years, about one third of the time most children remain in the household. Whether this single-parent experience begins early in the child's life or late may lead to very different experiences, with different consequences for parents and their children.

African-American Families

Although the dramatic increase in single-parent families pervades all social classes and ethnic groups (Garcia Coll, Meyer, & Brillon, in this *Handbook*), the preponderance of single-parent families in African-American families deserves special note. According to Cherlin (1992), the fact that a far higher proportion of African-American children are born to young unmarried mothers than is the case for other American families reflects historical trends concerning marriage and childbearing rather than a result of increased sexual activity among young African-American, unmarried women. Unmarried African-American teens and young African-American women between 20 and 24 years were no more likely to give birth in the late 1980s than they were in the 1960s. What has happened is that births to married African-American women dropped precipitously, along with declines in childbearing across all groups from 1960 to 1970, and then births to married women leveled off. Meanwhile, fewer and fewer African-American women married during the decades from 1960 to 1980, resulting in a greater proportion of births to African Americans being to unmarried women.

The declining marriage rate among African Americans, said Cherlin (1992), is partially a response to demographic and economic factors. Chronic male unemployment, recent increases in male unemployment, and the increasingly low ratio of male to female wages have made African-American women less likely to marry and less tolerant of unsatisfactory relationships. In addition, longstanding cultural traditions stemming from African styles of family life, specifically the greater emphasis on ties to a network of kin that extend across households (Garcia Coll, Meyers, & Brillon, in this *Handbook*) have contributed to a reduced emphasis on marriage as the foundation of family life. Contrary to popular stereotypes, then, the dramatic increase in the number of African-American single-parent families appears to be largely a response to the health of the American economy rather than a contribution to our nation's social or economic problems. Although economic problems contribute to higher rates of single-parent families in the African-American community, the processes by which these economic factors influence parenting behavior within single-parent African-American (McLoyd, Jayaratne, Ceballo, & Borquez, 1994) and two-parent White (Conger, Ge, Elder, Lorenz, & Simons, 1994) families appears to be similar.

Single-Father Families

One group of single-parent families that has shown tremendous and well-documented increases, especially in the last decade, are single-father families. Approximately 12 percent of all single-parent families in 1990 were headed by fathers. Figures compiled directly from the 1990 census suggest that fathers comprise nearly 14 percent of all single-parent families, up from the 1980s estimates of 10 percent, and three times the number of single-father families in 1970 (U.S. Bureau of the Census, 1991, 1992). Compared to single-parent families headed by mothers, single-parent father families are more often created by circumstances of divorce, more likely to be employed, and less likely to be economically disadvantaged. Evidence also suggests that single-parent fathers are more likely to have custody of older children and boys, and are proportionally more likely to be of European-American background (U.S. Bureau of the Census, 1991) than single-parent mothers. Similarly, telephone interviews with a subsample of single-parent families culled from the Survey of Children and Parents, a nationally representative sample of 1,738 parents and 929 children ages 10 to 17, led Smith (1993) to report that single fathers were more likely to have been created by circumstances of divorce, had higher annual incomes, were more likely to be employed full-time and less likely to be nonemployed, and less likely to be living in poverty than single-parent mothers.

Summary

There is great heterogeneity across single-parent families with regard to the conditions that lead to their formation, and these conditions have been growing more variable over the last decade. Whereas 10 years ago, the preponderance of single-parent families had been created from situations of divorce and widowhood, now a larger proportion of single mothers are women who are not married when they become parents. These nonmarried mothers are more likely to be older and better educated than previous single-parent mothers. And increasingly, fathers are becoming primary custodial parents.

In the next section, unique features of each of these single-parent family types are examined to better understand the heterogeneity of single-parent families and to understand why it may be highly misleading to generalize across single-parent families when describing parent circumstances and parenting behaviors.

PARENTING FEATURES UNIQUE TO SPECIFIC
SINGLE-PARENT FAMILY TYPES

In this section we summarize the literature on four specific types of single parents: single fathers and single mothers, divorced parents with custody, adolescent parents, and a more diverse group of mothers often referred to as "unmarried." Within the divorced parent section, we compare divorced fathers and divorced mothers, showing that although divorced parents have problems unique from other single-parent groups, the experiences of divorced fathers and mothers are more often similar than different. We do not review the literature regarding widowed or adoptive single parents because the research describing these parents is too sparse for generalizations at this time.

Single Fathers and Mothers

Are single-parent fathers a group of single parents unique from single-parent mothers? The literature suggests that, to some extent, they are. First, most single-parent fathers are divorced; it is rare for never-married fathers to live with children, and adoptions by men are uncommon (Groze, 1991). Furthermore, widowhood has declined substantially concomitant with declining maternal mortality rates during childbirth since the turn of the century (Burns & Scott, 1994). The increasing divorce rates along with changing views of gender roles since the 1970s have meant that fathers' opportunities for winning custody in the courts have increased, and fathers have been more interested and willing to take custody of their children. Nevertheless, although the number of single-parent father families has increased threefold from 1979 to 1992 (U.S. Bureau of the Census, 1992), single-parent fathers still comprise only about 12 percent of single-parent families.

As noted earlier, single-parent fathers are more likely to live with older children, and their children are more likely to be males. Single-parent fathers are more likely to be of White background, and they are less likely to be economically disadvantaged (U.S. Bureau of the Census, 1991).

Most of what is known about single-parent fathers comes from small, select samples of volunteers, sometimes, but not always, with comparable samples of single mothers (e.g., DeFrain & Eirick, 1981; Dornbusch & Gray, 1988; Greif, 1985; regarding lesbian and gay single parents, see Turner, Scadden, & Harris, 1990; Patterson, in this *Handbook*). Studies suggest that, prior to divorce, single divorced fathers were not different from other married fathers. Predivorce, these fathers were often not unusually involved in childrearing or household chores, at least, not until their marriage began to deteriorate (Gersick, 1979; Greif, 1985). They became custodial parents, either because the mother did not want custody when the marriage ended or because the father did not want to leave the family home. According to what fathers told Greif, fathers received custody generally because they were open to the possibility of being a single parent, and because either the mother did not want to continue in her custodial role or because the mother was perceived to be incompetent. In some cases, fathers assumed custody because the children wanted to remain in the home with their father. It is rare for fathers to gain custody as a result of contested custodial court trials (Greif, 1985). However, as the next section demonstrates, within divorced families, custodial fathers and mothers face similar challenges.

Divorced Parents With Custody

When marriages end in divorce, newly single parents have to come to terms with the loss of their marriage, and often, with the failure of their marital hopes and expectations. The single parent's partner may have served as an attachment figure, or even a best friend, and these emotional losses can be devastating (Weiss, 1979). Resolving these emotional experiences can take months and in many cases, years. During this time, these emotional experiences may affect the parent's adjustment, well-being, relationships with other adults, and interactions with their children.

During the time of separation and divorce, household routines are being reorganized, and children are often more angry, aggressive, and resentful (Bolton & MacEachron, 1986). These conditions pose significant challenges for competent parenting. Also during this time, many families experience dramatic changes in financial status (Cherlin, 1992). In some families, employment and housing arrangements change, creating adjustment difficulties for parents as well as children (Jones, 1984; Richard, 1982). Common parental responses to divorce are anger, anxiety, and depression, with possible impulsive and antisocial behavior and excessive swings of mood and self-confidence

(Hetherington, 1993). Reoccurring health problems and difficulties with the immune system are not uncommon (Richard, 1982; see also Hetherington & Stanley-Hagan, in this *Handbook*).

Given what is known about how economic and psychosocial stress may affect parents (McLoyd, 1990; McLoyd et al., 1994), it is not surprising that during the first months and years after divorce, divorced parents are more irritable and unresponsive in their interactions with their children (Thiriot & Buckner, 1991). They show poor supervision and erratic and sometimes punitive discipline (Camara & Resnick, 1988; Hetherington, Cox, & Cox, 1982; Wallerstein, Corbin, & Lewis, 1988). As Hetherington and Stanley-Hagan note (in this *Handbook*), many of these symptoms subside as families attain a new homeostasis, usually within 2 years. "Divorced adults may continue to feel more depressed and more anxious than their nondivorced counterparts, and some custodial parents may continue to find single parenting stressful. In spite of this, most restabilized single-parent families function reasonably well provided they are not faced with sustained or new adversities" (Hetherington & Stanley-Hagan, in this *Handbook*).

Financial security, employment stability and satisfaction, "neutral if not positive relationships" with their exspouses, confidence in parenting skills, and the formation of a new intimate support relationship are factors that affect the well-being and parenting skills of the custodial parent (Richard, 1982; Thiriot & Buckner, 1991). As Hetherington and Stanley-Hagan (in this *Handbook*) report, loneliness, task overload, and increased childrearing stress are common experiences of divorced custodial parents. Nevertheless, within 2 years:

> ... three fourths of divorced women report that they are happier in their new situation than in the last year of their marriage, and most, in spite of the stresses, find rearing children alone easier than with a disengaged, undermining, or acrimonious spouse. Furthermore, in addition to perceiving themselves as more able parents than mothers in conflictual, unsatisfying marriages, divorced women on the average are less depressed, show less stable anxiety, drink less, and have fewer health problems than those in unhappy, acrimonious, or emotionally disengaged marriages.

Thus, the prime characteristics of divorced parents and concomitant diminished parenting of divorced parents result from the disorganization and change subsequent to the dissolution of the marriage. As these stresses subside, and as relations with the noncustodial spouse reach equilibrium, the stresses these families experience become increasingly related to the difficulties of having only one adult parent who frequently must combine parenting and financial responsibilities, and who, as a single wage earner, may be limited in earning power and opportunity for workplace advancement.

Divorced fathers and mothers.   Custodial fathers have somewhat different circumstances from those of custodial mothers. Custodial fathers are often older, better educated, and earning better incomes (DeFrain & Eirick, 1981; Dornbusch & Gray, 1988; Greif, 1985). After the divorce, they are less likely to move to either an apartment or a relative's home and more likely to be living in their predivorce homes than divorced mothers. In comparison to mothers who must return to work (Jones, 1984), newly divorced fathers rarely need to find new employment, most continue in their same jobs, and income levels rarely plummet as they do for newly divorced mothers. Many fathers report cutting back on employment so that they can devote more time to household and childrearing duties. Fathers report that because employers are unsympathetic to their situation of having to combine childrearing and employment, full-time employment is sometimes difficult to maintain.

Divorced fathers receive more offers of support from their relatives and community, but they are less likely to take them. Sometimes, their lack of experience with housekeeping, household chores, childrearing, arranging child care and activity schedules make the transition more difficult for fathers than mothers, but most fathers adjust quite quickly, soliciting help from their children, particularly older children, most particularly daughters (Greif, 1985; Kissman & Allen, 1993). Although it is generally assumed that fathers are more likely to hire housekeepers, Greif did not find this to be the case in his 1982 survey of 1,136 custodial fathers, except for widowers.

At the time of divorce, fathers, like mothers, undergo considerable interpersonal stress, with increases in anger, loss, loneliness, lack of self-esteem, and lowered self-confidence (Pichitino, 1983). In contrast, men are less likely than women to have friendships and close emotional relationships outside their marriage, and they may be more likely than women to turn feelings of grief into anger (Kissman & Allen, 1993; Nieto, 1990; Pasick, 1990). Often, they are less likely to seek therapy, and they often feel less comfortable with it (Kissman & Allen, 1993).

However, as time goes on, both divorced fathers and mothers develop a household and social routine adequate to their family needs. DeFrain and Eirick (1981) questioned 33 divorced single-parent fathers and 38 comparable single-parent mothers on a wide variety of topics, and found substantial similarities between fathers and mothers. Both reported that their marriages prior to the divorce were "more bad than good," with lack of communication, extramarital affairs, sexual problems, and loss of interest given as reasons for the breakup. Both mothers and fathers rated divorce as a medium-high to highly stressful event. Both men and women reported that their moods had improved since the divorce, and many of their initial fears had subsided, with the majority of both groups feeling that they were doing "reasonably well." The minority of parents who reported yelling and/or hitting their children after the divorce said that these behaviors had decreased over time, and they found it much easier to control their children since the divorce. Both men and women reported they did not get to spend as much time with their children as they would have preferred. Nevertheless, fathers reported feeling quite satisfied with themselves for coping as well as they did as single parents.

Other investigators have reported similarities and differences in fathers' and mothers' childrearing behavior. Dornbusch and Gray (1988) reported that, like single mothers, single fathers tend to be more permissive than their married counterparts. Contrary to expectations, both fathers and mothers report having an easier time with younger than older children (Greif, 1985). Both mothers and fathers report more difficulties with sons than daughters, but single-parent fathers experience more childrearing problems with daughters than do single-parent mothers (Greif, 1985; Santrock, Warshak, & Elliot, 1982). Compared to age-mates, boys in single-parent father homes appear equally sociable and mature, and daughters in single-parent father families are less sociable, less independent, and more demanding (Santrock et al., 1982). Many fathers in Greif's study reported difficulties understanding and meeting their daughters' emotional needs, and they sometimes called upon their daughters to shoulder child care and household chores disproportionately. Puberty seems especially difficult for fathers and their daughters, with fathers uncomfortable talking about maturation and sexual matters.

Socially, divorced men and women are both equally interested in dating, with nearly four out of five of the parents in Greif's (1985) study reporting that they were currently dating. However, the single father's greater financial resources often makes finding substitute child care easier (Kissman & Allen, 1993). Although no overall differences in dating patterns have been documented, the remarriage rate is higher for divorced men than divorced women. This may be because some men feel that they can best fulfill their childrearing responsibilities by remarrying (Kissman & Allen, 1993).

One of the greatest stresses reported by divorced custodial fathers is combining work and childrearing (Greif, 1985; Kissman & Allen, 1993). Nearly four out of five fathers in Greif's sample reported that combining employment with childrearing was difficult. Compared to their experiences prior to divorce, men reported more interruptions in their daily work schedules and fewer opportunities to take on additional hours and projects, inhibiting their hope for career progress and higher incomes. Of the 1,136 fathers, 66 men had to quit their job because of conflicts with childrearing responsibilities, and 43 men reported being fired. They also experienced problems with having to arrive at work late or leave early, missing work days, or not being able to engage in work-related travel. Only 27 percent of the men interviewed reported no work-related changes were necessary.

As stressful as these childrearing/employment conflicts are for single-parent fathers, they are often even more stressful for single-parent mothers. In Greif's (1985) comparison of single divorced mothers who were asked the same questions as men, women reported greater employment/childrearing conflicts than men. Only 10 percent of the women said that work had *not* been difficult; and more mothers than fathers were fired from or had to quit their jobs. Although the difficulties that fathers and mothers have juggling employment and family conflicts may be similar in some respects, these experiences may be different for men and women because of early socialization differences. Men may not be as prepared for coping with these conflicts as women, and they may not understand these conflicts as well. They may continue to evaluate themselves against standards that they had used previously when they had a wife who performed child care and household tasks for the entire family. As Greif described it, a man "has to change the way he feels about himself as a *MAN*" (p. 70). In contrast, women's difficulties with employment/childrearing conflicts may stem from problems associated with less education, less employment experience, lower occupational prestige, and a lower paying job along with reduced flexibility for juggling child care and employment demands.

Finally, the dynamics of the single-parent mother and single-parent father families, relative to relationships predivorce, may be different. Anecdotal reports indicate that noncustodial mothers may be more active parents in their children's lives after the divorce than are noncustodial fathers (Greif, 1985; Kissman & Allen, 1993). Although divorce in the custodial mother family may cause both mothers and fathers to move away from close supervision of their children and involvement in their lives, in the single-father family, fathers are often drawn into closer contact with their children and have more involvement in their children's lives after than before the divorce. In contrast, after the divorce custodial mothers often may have a somewhat reduced involvement in their parenting role, due to increased financial responsibilities than prior to divorce. The custodial father's higher involvement with his children and his more frequent performance of traditionally female tasks, compared to other nondivorced fathers, may lead children of single-father families to develop more flexible notions of childrearing and gender roles than children in custodial mother or married, two-parent settings (Lamb, Pleck, & Levine, 1986).

Adolescent Single Parents

There is a great deal of overlap between the groups of single parents and adolescent mothers. Although adolescent mothers made up a smaller percentage of births to all nonmarried women in the mid-1980s than they did in 1970, approximately one third of all births to single mothers today are to teen mothers (Bachu, 1993; Kamerman & Kahn, 1988; see also Figure 3.2). The relation between adolescent parenting and single parenting can be presented in another way: Of the group of all adolescent mothers, 68 percent are not married at the time of the child's birth (The State of America's Children, 1994). Considerable ethnic differences exist in the proportion of adolescent mothers who are single. Within the African-American community, most adolescent mothers are single (90 percent to 92 percent); this is less true for Hispanic Americans and Whites, where the incidence of single parenthood is lower (42 percent to 55 percent and 54 percent respectively; Child Trends, 1992; Kamerman & Kahn, 1988).

To what extent is the *adolescent* experience of being a single parent unique from the experiences of other single parents? The evidence suggests that adolescent single mothers do have unique experiences from those of other single parents. According to Astone (1993), adolescent parenting contributes additional information needed to predict parental income 5 years after childbirth than that which can be predicted by single parenthood alone. As Brooks-Gunn and Chase-Lansdale (in this *Handbook*) demonstrate, researchers are beginning to take more sophisticated approaches to the study of adolescent parenting than ever before, teasing out preexisting differences in young women who become adolescent mothers from those who delay childbearing, and exploring developmental and contextual pathways in the lives of young mothers as they affect the childrearing process. This information enables us to understand the uniqueness of adolescent mothers as a subsample of single parents.

Adolescent single parents are perhaps the most disadvantaged of single parents. They come from poor families with parents of low educational backgrounds. They are likely to be from impoverished neighborhoods, they have attended poor-quality schools, and they have suffered school failure and low educational aspirations (Furstenberg, Brooks-Gunn, & Chase-Lansdale, 1989; Hayes, 1987; Miller & Moore, 1990; Scott-Jones, 1991). As Furstenberg et al. pointed out, these conditions do not disappear with the birth of the child, but continue to limit the young mother's movement toward self-sufficiency. Compared to other teens, teenage mothers are more likely to drop out of school, but the causal relation between pregnancy and school dropout rate has not yet been fully explicated and may differ by ethnic group (Scott-Jones, 1991). Teen mothers who drop out of school come from poorer backgrounds than women who do not drop out of school. However, even when teen mothers have graduated from high school, they are less likely than other women to go on for post-secondary schooling.

Commonly, adolescent single mothers and their children live with their family of origin. Brooks-Gunn and Chase-Lansdale (in this *Handbook*) report that coresidence is about twice as likely among African-American as White single mothers. There are benefits and drawbacks to coresidential living, and the effects of these family-of-origin arrangements may depend on the age of the mother, with more positive effects on the young teen mother and her child than on older teen mothers.

Other aspects of their life course are also different. Compared to other mothers, teen mothers are less likely to be employed, less likely to have a stable job, and less likely to earn more than minimum wage on the job (Brooks-Gunn & Chase-Lansdale, in this *Handbook*). They are more likely to collect welfare and less likely to go on to marry than teens who are not mothers. When teen mothers do marry later on, their divorce rates are higher than for the general population. Like other mothers, teen mothers have the predictable difficulties of balancing child care, education, work, and leisure. However, in light of their lower education, poorer earning power, and reliance on neighbors and family members for support, these balancing difficulties are often more severe for the adolescent parent. Child care is more likely to be provided by other family members and more often comprised of makeshift arrangements (Cherlin, in press). Though no more likely to have more children than women who delay childbearing, they are more likely to have children closely spaced (Furstenberg, Brooks-Gunn, & Morgan, 1987).

After childbirth, teenage mothers continue to have low levels of employment and educational attainment compared to other women their age. However, the Baltimore study (Furstenberg et al., 1987) and the New Haven study (Horwitz, Klerman, Kuo, & Jekel, 1991) show surprising diversity in outcomes among these parents' situations, with striking individual differences in educational attainment, employment success, and subsequent births. For example, in the Baltimore study, by 17 years after the initial contact, many of the women had continued their schooling, and nearly three fourths were employed. Although the majority of marriages they entered had ended, only one fourth of the mothers were on welfare. Information about the life course for single rural women who started their families as adolescents is much less available.

Less is known too about the psychological adjustment and coping skills of single teenage mothers over time. There is some evidence that adolescent parents are more depressed than older mothers (Carter, Osofsky, & Hann, 1991; Osofsky, Eberhart-Wright, Ware, & Hann, 1992; Wasserman, Rauh, Brunelli, Garcia-Castro, & Necos, 1990). Because many adolescent mothers live with their mothers, separation and autonomy become important issues to negotiate. Many adolescent mothers depend on their own mothers not only for financial support and living arrangements, but also for child care, guidance, parental supports, and information about parenting (Brooks-Gunn & Chase-Lansdale, in this *Handbook*). As Brooks-Gunn and Chase-Lansdale suggest, developing their identity as mothers at the same time as they are developing their identity as young women may pose a more challenging task than the identity issues facing adolescents who are not parents. Difficulties developing an identity as a competent parent may be further challenged by the increased likelihood of having a premature, low-birthweight, or sick child, circumstances that often co-occur with adolescent pregnancy. Finally, combining these changes with the many life changes that may accompany the young women's changing status from teenager to mother—changes in school, employment, family, and social status—may pose cumulative risks that further inhibit the adolescent mother's adjustment and coping.

Researchers have reported that adolescent parents have more unrealistic expectations for their children, are more restrictive, and provide a less stimulating, responsive, and well-regulated affective and intellectual environment for their children than comparison groups of adult mothers (Brooks-

Gunn & Furstenberg, 1986; Osofsky, Hann, & Peebles, 1994). However, as Brooks-Gunn and Chase-Lansdale (in this *Handbook*) point out, the comparison groups that researchers include in studies of adolescent parents are often not appropriate comparison groups for the adolescent mothers under observation. Most studies confound age and marital status; more serious confounds include differences in education, employment, verbal ability, and poverty status. When these variables are controlled, as in a study by Chase-Lansdale, Brooks-Gunn, and Zamsky (1994), parental age does not seem to be related to parental affect, disciplinary style, or problem-solving style. Interestingly, interventions aimed at improving the parenting skills of teen parents have not been successful (Brooks-Gunn, 1990), perhaps because these programs have generally been of limited intensity (Roosa, 1986). When parenting intervention programs are more intensive—combining child care and parental training with parental supports and training in decision-making and job-related skills—these programs may be more likely to effect changes in parenting behavior (Kissman & Allen, 1993; Mullis & Mullis, 1985). More effective than parenting intervention programs in improving home environment measures and child outcome in teen mother families have been programs aimed at educating and employing adolescent parents. Such programs may have indirect effects on parenting by increasing the family's financial status and the mothers' decision-making ability, self-efficacy, and psychological well-being (Brooks-Gunn & Chase-Lansdale, in this *Handbook;* Kissman & Allen, 1993).

Other Single Mothers

The fastest growing group of single parents is that of the nonadolescent, nonmarried woman. Some of these mothers may be living in a partnered relationships, some are not. Observers have noted several cultural changes that have contributed to this international trend for women to have and rear children outside of traditional marital relationships. These include later age of marriage for men and women, increased infertility and childlessness of later marrying women, increasing divorce rates, and changing social attitudes (Burns & Scott, 1994; Kamerman & Kahn, 1988). The social stigma attached to having a child out of marriage has been declining since the 1960s, as witnessed by the increasing acceptance of unmarried mothers as public figures and as characters in popular films and television programs. Even the politicized labels that have been used to describe unmarried mothers and their children—"unwed mothers" with "illegitimate children"—have been replaced in the popular literature by more morally neutral terms. Some observers have attributed the increasing number of women having children outside the traditional two-parent family structure to the decreasing "complementarity" of men's and women's gender roles in today's culture (Burns & Scott, 1994).

Within the group of nonmarried single-parent families, there is great diversity, and this diversity has important implications for understanding the parents, the parents' circumstances, and the possible effects of these differences on parenting and subsequent child outcomes. In this next section, three groups of these single parents are considered: unmarried single parents who are living with partners, "single mothers by choice," and a third, more inclusive group, whom we call "solo mothers." Each are described in turn.

Unmarried Couples by Choice

Women included in the statistical reports of women unmarried at childbirth include those who are unmarried, but who may be living with a partner in an extralegal relationship. Though many of these couples are composed of a man and woman, some may also be same-gender pairs (see Patterson, in this *Handbook,* for a description of parenting in lesbian and gay couples). Estimating the true proportion of these families is difficult, as statistics on these families are not registered anywhere. It is possible that when the numbers of unmarried mothers living in committed relationships and rearing children with a partner is taken into consideration, the number of single parents is lower than generally thought.

Eiduson and Weisner (1978) and Weisner and Garnier (1992) included these "social contract" or "unmarried couples by choice" in their larger study of nonconventional family lifestyles. Generally, these are women and men who are experimenting with living together and who may or may not later marry. In many ways, the circumstances of unmarried mothers living with male partners are similar to those of married women (Eiduson, 1983), except that their partnerships tend to be more unstable and the values and beliefs about childrearing authority relationships and morality may be less traditional. In comparison to married couples, these mothers and their children may experience relatively frequent changes in their household composition, may live on lower and more unpredictable incomes, and often face various social stigmas, such as lower teacher expectations (Weisner & Garnier, 1992). Regardless of these potential risks, Weisner and Garnier noted that when parents from nonconventional lifestyles have a strong commitment to their chosen family style, their children do not differ from children living in more traditional families on measures of adjustment and school performance.

Single Mothers by Choice

A second group of unmarried mothers has been described as *single mothers by choice* (SMC) by a national support and informational group founded in New York City in 1981. This organization, Single Mothers by Choice, defines a single mother by choice as a woman who starts out rearing her child without a partner. She may have decided to have or adopt a child, knowing she will be her child's sole parent, at least at the outset (Mattes, 1994).

Little information is available about the incidence of single mothers by choice, their living circumstances, their parenting experiences, or effects on children growing up in these homes. Existing information comes from only a few sources: membership surveys of the SMC organization and various adoption agencies, longitudinal observations of a group of single nonpartnered women in Eiduson and Weisner's (1978) study of nonconventional families in California during the 1960s, and anecdotal descriptions in newspaper and magazine articles. Goldsmith (1976) also described a small group of these mothers and compared them to other single mothers who did not deliberately choose to become pregnant and rear a child. More recently, a 10-year study of approximately 200 SMC families to be completed in the year 2000 (Kamerman & Kahn, 1988; Mattes, 1994) has also yielded information.

From these sources, single mothers by choice appear to be in their mid-30s, primarily White, and upper-middle-class. They are financially secure, well educated, and employed in well-paying professional jobs. Many are self-employed and own their own businesses. A number of the women have been previously married and divorced. Some of the women became pregnant accidentally and found themselves delighted at the possibility of having children even though they were not married. Others gave very serious attention and planning to either becoming pregnant or adopting a child. Whereas the mothers of the 1960s appear to have chosen their lifestyles as a result of feminist concerns and the desire to live independent of traditional family styles, concerns with the "ticking of the biological clock" were often the impetus to become a mother by choice for women of the 1980s. Methods of becoming pregnant include having sexual relations with a friend or acquaintance or having artificial insemination. In many cases, SMCs have given serious consideration to the moral, ethical, and legal aspects of the biological father's role (Mattes, 1994; Potter & Knaub, 1988), but very little is known about the biological father's experiences or the effect of his involvement or lack of involvement on the parent or the child.

For many of these women, the decision to become a single parent is a long and difficult one (Kamerman & Kahn, 1988). Because they see their choice as not whether to have a child within a marital relationship or outside such a relationship, but whether or not to have a child during their lifetime, many have chosen single parenthood even though they understand that parenting alone can be a lonely and difficult experience. Most of the women see themselves as capable of becoming "responsible, caring, and nurturing mothers," and so they decide to make a number of life changes to meet their single-parent challenge. Many have bought houses in neighborhoods conducive to single parenting, changed jobs or careers, and saved money in anticipation of parenthood. And many seek social, informational, and practical support, at least in the early part of their parenthood, from formal groups such as the SMC organization (Kamerman & Kahn, 1988).

Observations of single parents by choice who adopt children suggest that those who adopt have a high level of emotional maturity, have a high capacity for frustration tolerance, and are not overly influenced by others' opinions (Branham, 1970; Groze, 1991). These parents are oriented toward children and derive great personal fulfillment from their interactions with them (Jordan & Little, 1966; Shireman & Johnson, 1976). Groze (1991) noted that these parents "had an ability to give of themselves, were not possessive of their children, and were capable of developing a healthy relationship with their children" (p. 326).

Many of the problems with parenting that have been noted with single mothers by choice are not those of inadequate parenting but inadequate supports in their personal, emotional, and parenting roles:

> The help they seek—child care, help when a child is ill, more sensitivity to parenting at the workplace, occasional personal help and support—are the concerns of any working mother, exacerbated only because these are single parents raising their children alone. Whether this type of single-parent family will continue—and grow—remains to be seen; those who choose their life-style make the choice in full knowledge that it will not be easy. They appear very much attuned to the well-being of their wanted children. (Kamerman & Kahn, 1988, p. 137)

Some observers have questioned whether this classification of mothers as single by choice is useful from a scientific point of view. Clearly, these mothers do not have to contend with the effects of divorce and separation or contested custody or child support payments, and they are older than adolescent mothers. However, to what extent is this SMC category of mothers a socioeconomic, sociopolitical distinction, based solely on a mother's access to resources and an attempt to distance these mothers from previous stereotypes of poor and adolescent single mothers? Could not a teen mother who has dropped out of school and decided to raise her child without the presence of a male partner also be considered a SMC? Additionally, some women may not be able to admit openly to themselves or to others that they are acting to become mothers, and so they ascribe their experience to accident or to a "relationship that didn't work." In our research, a mother was asked whether she deliberately chose to become pregnant. She answered that at the time, she did not consciously choose to become pregnant, but now, looking back on the circumstances surrounding her pregnancy, she thinks it was more deliberate than she was able to admit to herself at the time. These concerns raise questions about the usefulness of the SMC categorization of mothers from a developmental research perspective.

Another approach to these questions is to consider nonadolescent single mothers who rear their child without another parenting figure present in the home as "solo mothers." Whether there are effects on the mother or child of deliberate and conscious choice could be tested with large enough samples.

Solo Mothers

In a series of reports, Weinraub and Wolf (1983, 1987), Gringlas and Weinraub (1995), Weinraub (1986), and Wolf (1987) considered *solo mothers,* adult women rearing their children from birth without a male partner. This group of single-parent mothers includes SMC as well as other mothers who may not have chosen to have been single as they reared their children. As a result of circumstances not always under their control, they reared their children from birth or shortly thereafter without a male father figure in the home. Children of solo mothers are those who have had, at least in their memory, no experience living with a father figure in the home, and more important, no experience of family dissolution, marital discord, and/or family realignment. Since early in life, or at least before the onset of language, these children were reared by their mothers, within either a single-parent household or an extended household. Some mothers made a conscious and deliberate choice to become single mothers; others did not.

Weinraub and her colleagues have studied this group of nonrepresentative single-parent families in order to understand the effects on the young child of growing up in a family without the full-time presence of a father, when these effects are not confounded by poverty, immature parenting, or the trauma of separation or divorce. Because this group of single parents is another group of single parents with unique circumstances that help us to understand the heterogeneity of single-parent families, and because this is the only longitudinal, observational study focusing on these single-parent families that has taken into consideration the parent's characteristics, circumstances, parenting behavior, and child outcome, this research is described in some detail.

Weinraub and Wolf identified single-parent and two-parent families matched on a variety of characteristics, including maternal age, education, race, per capita income, neighborhood, child age, and child gender. The solo mothers were a varied group. Some mothers were not married or had already been divorced when they unintentionally conceived, some were married and then separated from their husbands soon after conception or pregnancy, and some mothers deliberately became pregnant with full understanding that there would be no father in their young child's life. Some of these mothers could be classified as single mothers by choice, some could be seen as divorced mothers. In this small sample, no differences between these two groups could be discerned.

Observational measures of maternal and child behavior were taken in the laboratory when the children were between 27 and 55 months of age, and parents completed questionnaires and in-depth interviews in their homes. Seventy percent of the families returned for observation and interviews, when children were between 8 and 13 years of age. For the older children, child measures included a self-perception profile and maternal and teacher reports of behavior problems, social competence, and academic performance. Maternal measures included maternal and child reports of parenting practices, social supports, and stress.

Most of the mothers were college educated and had professional employment. Of the 19 solo mothers, 14 (9 who were never married and 5 who had been married before) had made a conscious decision to rear their children on their own prior to the child's birth; 4 of these mothers had made a deliberate and conscious choice to become pregnant. Five mothers were married at the time of conception and were hoping to rear the child in cooperation with the child's father, but circumstances changed prior to the child's birth, and the mothers divorced or separated from their husbands before the child was born or shortly thereafter. In two of these divorced families, the father had been present for only a few months, so that by the time the children were seen in the study, they had lived in a solo-parent household for the majority of their young lives (at least 3 out of 4 years). All had been divorced for at least 2 years.

Comparisons between solo-parent mothers and comparable married mothers highlight some of the important ways in which even the most stable of single-parent families appear to differ from married-parent families. First, despite careful attempts to match single- and two-parent mothers on employment status, single parents worked longer hours both when their children were in preschool and at preadolescence. When their children were in preschool, single parents reported more difficulties coping with finances, more daily hassles, and slightly more stresses relating to employment. Single mothers of sons reported more stressful life events relating to interpersonal areas of their lives. The largest difference between the mothers concerned social supports. During the preschool period, single parents received fewer emotional and parenting supports. During the preadolescent period, only single-parent mothers of sons reported lower satisfaction with their emotional supports. Their friends and relatives either did not understand or did not address their emotional and parenting needs as well as those of solo mothers of daughters or two-parent mothers.

When the children were in their preschool years, observational measures of parents administering a teaching task to the children revealed few overall differences in mothers' or children's behavior, but differences emerged in maternal behavior as a function of the child's gender. Although no differences in maternal communications and degrees of maternal nurturance were observed, single mothers had difficulties in exercising control and setting appropriate maternal demands with their sons. Not surprisingly, preschool boys in single-parent homes were less compliant with their mothers' requests than boys from two-parent homes, and by preadolescence, teachers reported that children of solo mothers had more behavior problems, lower social competence, and poorer school performance than children of married mothers.

Within each group, maternal social support predicted parenting and child outcomes. During the preschool period, maternal social supports contributed to more optimal parent–child interaction for both single- and two-parent families. The more mothers received support in their role as parents, the more optimal was their behavior in interaction with their preschool child. During preadolescence, only for solo parents was social support predictive of children's academic performance.

Maternal stress, however, had different effects in the solo- and two-parent families. At both assessment periods, more stressful life events predicted less optimal outcomes in solo-parent families. During the preschool period, solo mothers with frequent stressful life events had less optimal interactions with their children in a teaching task, had children who were perceived as more moody, and who had lower intelligence and readiness to learn scores. More frequent stressful life events were associated with reduced parental effectiveness, poorer communication, and less nurturance in solo-parent families. The effects of stress in the preschool period not only indirectly affected child outcome via maternal parenting behavior, but also had direct effects on child outcome independent of the mother's parenting behavior. During preadolescence, children from solo-parent families with high levels of maternal stress were described by teachers and mothers as having the most behavior problems. However, children from low-stress solo-parent families were indistinguishable from children from two-parent families.

These results are similar to other findings documenting the psychological vulnerability of women rearing their children alone (Burden, 1986; Compas & Williams, 1990; Elder, Eccles, Ardelt, & Lord, 1993; Hastings-Storer, 1991; McLanahan, 1983). This vulnerability seems to affect children of single-parent families not only indirectly through parenting behavior, but possibly directly as well. These findings suggest that reduced social supports and increased stresses may be more common for solo parents, even when there is no separation, divorce, and custody difficulties and even when the mothers are mature, well educated, and from secure financial circumstances. Differences in social support and stress can affect parent behavior and child outcome, especially in solo-parent families. Most important, stress may be the main factor placing solo-parent children at risk; children from solo-parent families with low stress may not be at risk. Because Weinraub's sample of solo mothers is small and unrepresentative, more systematic research with broader samples of single mothers from varied circumstances is needed to identify the conditions of maternal stress and sources of social support that may mediate and moderate parental behavior and subsequent child outcome.

Summary.   The group of mothers commonly identified as "unmarried mothers" is actually varied and diverse. Some of these parents may not be truly "single" parents; they may be unmarried but living in homes with a committed partner. As the research of Eiduson and Weisner (1978) and Patterson (in this *Handbook*) has shown, when nonmarried parents are committed to their chosen lifestyle, their children do not differ from children of more traditional household unions on measures of psychological adjustment and school performance. Other mothers rearing their children alone may be single or divorced, but their children are being reared in homes that are truly single-parent homes. Family circumstances vary widely among single-parent homes, with important variations in maternal stress and social supports. As the research of Weinraub and her colleagues shows, variations in these stressful life events and social supports may influence the quality of the mother's interactions with her child. These social context differences may be ultimately the most important differences separating single-parent from two-parent families.

may all contribute to placing children at risk, and these factors often co-occur. Statistical manipulations using data from large archival data sets, such as the National Survey of Families and Households (NSFH) and the National Survey of Family Growth (see Brooks-Gunn, Phelps, & Elder, 1991, for a wider discussion of archival data sets), make it possible to separate the influence of co-occurring factors, identifying critical factors that require social policy and intervention efforts. McLanahan and Bumpass' (1988) study of the intergenerational consequences of family disruptions applied proportional hazard models to the National Survey of Family Growth to test several competing experiences for intergenerational consequences of growing up in a single-parent family on young women. Testing the economical deprivation hypothesis, the social hypothesis, and the stress hypothesis, they found results consistent with the argument that parental role models and parental supervision are the major factors in determining offspring's future family formation behavior. Likewise, Duncan, Brooks-Gunn, and Klebanov (1994) found that income and poverty status account almost entirely for differential intelligence scores found in single- and two-parent families. In contrast, adjustment scores were predicted by family structure effects, despite controls for income and poverty. Studies such as these applied to a wide variety of child outcomes would illuminate the possible different processes that simultaneously influence various aspects of child and later adult development.

An area of research often overlooked concerns developmental outcomes for men. McLanahan and Bumpass (1988) focused on predictors of family formation in young adult women, and Furstenberg et al. (1987) examined the influences of growing up in adolescent mother families on young women's negotiation of identity. Equally important is understanding those variables that influence adult family-related behavior in young men. In a television documentary, Williams (1992) described his search for his father and his attempt to derive a sense of personal identity and destiny from knowledge of his father. His mother's brief liaison more than 21 years earlier had resulted in his birth. Although reared sensitively and lovingly by his mother and other female relatives, Williams seeks his father to answer questions of what kind of a father he will be. Will he ever get married? What will be his own role in nurturing his own children? Research on fatherhood has begun to tell us much about the further life consequences of early fathering experiences (Snarey, 1993). Similar longitudinal studies of young men from less economically advantaged and more ethnically diverse situations may yield useful information on the impact of growing up without a father's presence on life-course choices and developmental pathways for men as well as for women.

The main thrust of this chapter has been the argument that different types of single-parent families exist, and that differing circumstances characterize each family type. However, the contribution of ethnicity and social class has yet to be investigated. Are these differences among single-parent families equally valid for families of all economic and education levels, all ethnic backgrounds, and for rural as well as urban families? Or are some of these differentiations more meaningful for some groups than for others? Not only is single-parent status a transitory status, but none of these particular single-parent types is mutually exclusive, and overlapping single-parent categorizations are possible. At the time that we study them, adolescent mothers may be divorced, and they may also be living in a committed partner relationship. The possibility that the effects of single-parent status may differ for parents of different backgrounds and that parents may have multiple single-parent status classifications suggests that describing families in terms of their family structure may be less meaningful than looking at specific process-oriented features of their experiences.

Studies of the contribution of family structure may need to yield to the studies that focus on understanding family processes. Minturn and Lambert (1964) studied families in six different cultures and concluded that, more important than specific childrearing technologies, were household composition, family size, and parental work load, because these variables influence the time and energy that mothers have available to care for their children. Researchers should direct their energies toward studying, not household composition, family size, and parental work load, so much as the time and energy that single parents have available to care for their children and how they provide for their children when they themselves are not available. Family structure may serve only as a "social address" for locating these more important, process-oriented variables.

Eiduson and Weisner's longitudinal study of nontraditional families of the 1960s (Eiduson, 1983; Eiduson & Weisner, 1978) suggests that the goals and values of the parents may transcend the importance of family structure, with nonmarried parents whose goals were literacy, pronaturalism, or nonconventional achievement having children who were as successful on adjustment and school performance measures as other, more conventional families. Parents' involvement in their children's schooling and parents' commitment to coherent activities and values were more important than family structure in predicting successful child outcome. As Weisner and Garnier (1992) argued, "the categories used to group families, such as single parents, unwed mothers, divorced unmarried couples or married couples, are not capturing important differences in values, commitment, and stability, which influence children living in these kinds of families" (p. 628). As important as differences across different types of single-parent family structure may be, ultimately we need to focus on more proximal characteristics within families that directly affect parenting behavior. Researchers may need to look beyond demographics and family structural variables in order to understand the true role of family structure in affecting child development.

CONCLUSIONS

Understanding the diverse etiology and nature of single-parent families requires us to consider specific contextual issues and factors confronting these families that pose significant risks and benefits to the successful socialization and parenting of children. Single-parent families are a heterogenous group, and knowing that a parent is single may not be as helpful as knowing how he or she became a single parent and the parent's specific life circumstances.

Single parenting is a difficult process. Single parents who face the challenges of parenting without the supportive assistance of or collaboration with other concerned and involved adults may find their parenting abilities strained beyond limit. Economic disadvantage, employment, minimal social supports, and exhaustion can exact a toll on a single parent's parenting abilities and resources. Similarly, poor parental psychological well-being hinders the parent's ability to develop and maintain child-directed energy, optimism, and commitment (Gringlas, 1994). Primary risks to the development of children living in single-parent homes generally derive from an ongoing pattern of stress, exhaustion, depression, and isolation experienced by the family (Sargent, 1992). If a single parent is frequently unavailable because he or she is exhausted or depressed, young children are at risk for social withdrawal and depression, and the disciplining of older children may be erratic and inconsistently enforced. Additionally, chronic illness and intellectual, academic, or emotional child difficulties place increased stress and demands on single-parent families.

Given this myriad of potential difficulties, it is critical to remember that single-parent families can and often do rear their children successfully. In a chapter on family variations, Sargent (1992) described what he believed to be central features that lead to effective childrearing in single-parent families. He cited emotional support from a social network, secure financial status, quality of alternate sources of child care, capacity to maintain appropriate discipline, capacity to parent when exhausted or overwhelmed, ability to develop own rewarding social life and relationships, and capacity to collaborate effectively in childrearing with other involved adults. These parenting variables, and not family structure alone, may be critical to understand and predict successful child outcomes.

ACKNOWLEDGMENTS

This chapter was written while the first author was supported by the NICHD Study of Early Child Care (U10-HD25455). We are indebted to Ronald Taylor, Elizabeth Jaeger, and Laurence Steinberg for suggestions and comments on early drafts of this manuscript and to Jennifer Tweed for her enthusiastic editorial and bibliographic help.

REFERENCES

Acock, A. C., & Demo, D. H. (1994). *Family diversity and well-being.* Thousand Oaks, CA: Sage.

Ahlburg, D. A., & DeVita, C. J. (1992). New realities of the American family. In *Population Bulletin* (Vol. 47, No. 2). Washington, DC: Population Reference Bureau, Inc.

Amato, P. R. (1988). Long-term implications of parental divorce for adult self-concept. *Journal of Family Issues, 9,* 201–213.

Amato, P. R., & Keith, B. (1991a). Parental divorce and adult well-being: A meta-analysis. *Journal of Marriage and the Family, 53,* 43–58.

Amato, P. R., & Keith, B. (1991b). Parental divorce and the well-being of children: A meta-analysis. *Psychological Bulletin, 110,* 26–46.

Astone, N. M. (1993). Are adolescent mothers just single mothers? *Journal of Research on Adolescence, 3,* 353–373.

Bachu, A. (1993). Fertility of American women: June 1992. In *Current Population Reports,* Series P20, No. 470. Washington, DC: U.S. Government Printing Office.

Barth, R. P., & Berry, M. (1988). *Adoption and disruption: Roles, risks, and responses.* New York: Adline de Gruyter.

Bolton, F. G., & MacEachron, A. (1986). Assessing child maltreatment risk in the recently divorced parent–child relationship. *Journal of Family Violence, 1,* 259–275.

Branham, E. (1970). One parent adoptions. *Children, 17,* 103–107.

Brooks-Gunn, J. (1990). Promoting healthy development in young children: What educational interventions work? In D. E. Rogers & E. Ginzberg (Eds.), *Improving the life chances of children at risk* (pp. 125–145). Boulder, CO: Westview Press.

Brooks-Gunn, J., & Furstenberg, F. F., Jr. (1986). Antecedents and consequences of parenting: The case of adolescent motherhood. In A. Fogel & G. Melson (Eds.), *Origins of nurturance: Developmental, biological and cultural perspectives on caregiving* (pp. 233–258). Hillsdale, NJ: Lawrence Erlbaum Associates.

Brooks-Gunn, J., Phelps, E., & Elder, G. H., Jr. (1991). Studying lives through time: Secondary data analysis in developmental psychology. *Developmental Psychology, 27,* 899–910.

Burden, D. S. (1986). Single parents and the work setting: The impact of multiple job and homelife responsibilities. *Family Relations Journal of Applied Family and Child Studies, 35,* 37–43.

Burns, A. (1992). Mother-headed families: An international perspective and the case of Australia. *Social Policy Report, 6,* 8–17.

Burns, A., & Scott, C. (1994). *Mother-headed families and why they have increased.* Hillsdale, NJ: Lawrence Erlbaum Associates.

Camara, K. A., & Resnick, G. (1988). Interparental conflict and cooperation: Factor moderating children's post-divorce adjustment. In E. M. Hetherington & J. D. Arasteh (Eds.), *Impact of divorce, single-parenting, and stepparenting on children* (pp. 169–195). Hillsdale, NJ: Lawrence Erlbaum Associates.

Carter, S. L., Osofsky, J. D., & Hann, D. M. (1991). Speaking for the baby: A therapeutic intervention with adolescent mothers and their infants. *Infant Mental Health Journal, 12,* 291–301.

Cashion, B. G. (1982). Female-headed families: Effects on children and clinical implications. *Journal of Marital and Family Therapy, 8,* 77–86.

Chase-Lansdale, P. L., Brooks-Gunn, J., & Zamsky, E. S. (1994). Young African American multigenerational families: Quality of mothering and grandmothering. *Child Development, 65,* 373–393.

Cherlin, A. J. (1992). *Marriage, divorce, remarriage* (2nd ed.). Cambridge, MA: Harvard University Press.

Cherlin, A. J. (in press). Child care for poor children: Policy issues. In P. L. Chase-Lansdale & J. Brooks-Gunn (Eds.), *Escape from poverty: What makes a difference for poor children?* New York: Cambridge University Press.

Child trends. (1990, November). *Facts at a Glance.*

Cohen, R. (1993, July). Values are important, but the radical transformation of the family may be the key. *The Philadelphia Inquirer,* p. A08.

Compas, B. E., & Williams, R. A. (1990). Stress, coping, and adjustment in mothers and young adolescents in single- and two-parent families. *American Journal of Community Psychology, 18,* 525–545.

Conger, R. D., Ge, X., Elder, G. H., Jr., Lorenz, F. O., & Simons, R. L. (1994). Economic stress, coercive family process, and developmental problems of adolescents. *Child Development, 65,* 541–561.

DeFrain, J., & Eirick, R. (1981). Coping as divorced single parents: A comparative study of fathers and mothers. *Family Relations, 30,* 265–273.

Dornbusch, S. M., & Gray, K. D. (1988). Single-parent families. In S. M. Dornbusch & M. H. Strober (Eds.), *Feminism, children, and the new families* (pp. 274–296). New York: Guilford Press.

Duncan, G. J., Brooks-Gunn, J., & Klebanov, P. K. (1994). Economic deprivation and early childhood development. *Child Development, 65,* 296–318.

Eiduson, B. T. (1983). Conflict and stress in nontraditional families: Impact on children. *American Journal of Orthopsychiatry, 53,* 426–435.

Eiduson, B. T., & Weisner, T. S. (1978). Alternative family styles: Effects on young children. In J. H. Stevens, Jr. & M. Matthews (Eds.), *Mother/child father/child relationships* (pp. 197–221). Washington, DC: National Association for the Education of Young Children.

Elder, G. H., Jr., Eccles, J. S., Ardelt, M., & Lord, S. (1993, March). *Inner city parents under economic pressure: Perspectives on the strategies of parenting.* Paper presented at the Society for Research on Child Development, New Orleans, LA.

Feigelman, W., & Silverman, A. R. (1977). Single parent adoptions. *Social Casework, 58,* 418–425.

Furstenberg, F. F., Jr., Brooks-Gunn, J., & Chase-Lansdale, L. (1989). Adolescent fertility and public policy. *American Psychologist, 44,* 313–320.

Furstenberg, F. F., Jr., Brooks-Gunn, J., & Morgan, P. (1987). *Adolescent mothers in later life.* New York: Cambridge University Press.

Garfinkel, I., & McLanahan, S. S. (1986). *Single mothers and their children: New American dilemma.* Washington, DC: The Urban Institute Press.

Gersick, K. (1979). Fathers by choice: Divorced men who receive custody of their children. In G. Levinger & D. C. Moles (Eds.), *Divorce and separation* (pp. 307–323). New York: Basic Books.

Goldsmith, J. (1976). A child of one's own: Unmarried women who choose motherhood (Doctoral dissertation, California School of Professional Psychology, 1975). *Dissertation Abstracts International, 36,* 3602–3603B.

Greif, G. L. (1985). *Single fathers.* Lexington, MA: Heath.

Gringlas, M. (1994). *Maternal psychological well-being: Determinants of a mother's parenting behavior.* Unpublished doctoral dissertation, Temple University, Philadelphia.

Gringlas, M., & Weinraub, M. (1995). The more things change: Single parenting revisited. *Journal of Family Issues, 16,* 29–52.

Groze, V. (1991). Adoption and single parents: A review. *Child Welfare, 70,* 321–332.

Hastings-Storer, J. (1991). Parenting stress in rural, low-income African American mothers of young children (Doctoral dissertation, University of Missouri-Columbia, 1991). *Dissertation Abstracts International, 52,* 3318B.

Hayes, C. D. (Ed.). (1987). *Risking the future: Adolescent sexuality, pregnancy, and childbearing* (Vol. 1). Washington, DC: National Academy of Science Press.

Herzog, E., & Sudia, C. (1973). Children in fatherless families. In B. M. Caldwell & H. N. Ricciuti (Eds.), *Review of child development research* (Vol. 3, pp. 141–232). Chicago: University of Chicago Press.

Hetherington, E. M. (1993). An overview of the Virginia longitudinal study of divorce and remarriage: A focus on early adolescence. *Journal of Family Psychology, 7,* 39–56.

Hetherington, E. M., Cox, M., & Cox, R. (1982). Effects of divorce on parents and children. In M. E. Lamb (Ed.), *Nontraditional families* (pp. 233–288). Hillsdale, NJ: Lawrence Erlbaum Associates.

Hobbs, F., & Lippman, L. (1990). Children's well-being: An international comparison. *International Population Reports Series* (Series P95, No. 80). Washington, DC: U.S. Government Printing Office.

Horwitz, S. M., Klerman, L. V., Kuo, H. S., & Jekel, J. F. (1991). School-age mothers: Predictors of long-term educational and economic outcomes. *Pediatrics, 87,* 862–867.

Jones, S. C. (1984). Going to work: A challenging time for single mothers. *Journal of Employment Counseling, 21,* 7–12.

Jordan, V., & Little, W. (1966). Early comments on single-parent adoptive homes. *Child Welfare, 45,* 536–538.

Kamerman, S. B., & Kahn, A. J. (1988). *Mothers alone: Strategies for a time of change.* Dover, MA: Auburn House.

Kellam, S. G., Ensminger, M. E., & Turner, R. J. (1977). Family structure and the mental health of children. *Archives of General Psychiatry, 34,* 1012–1022.

Kissman, K., & Allen, J. A. (1993). *Single-parent families.* Newbury Park, CA: Sage.

Lamb, M. E., Pleck, J. H., & Levine, J. (1986). The role of the father in child development. In A. Kazdin (Ed.), *Advances in clinical child psychology* (Vol. 8, pp. 229–266). New York: Plenum.

Mattes, J. (1994). *Single mothers by choice: A guidebook for single women who are considering or have chosen motherhood.* New York: Times Books.

McLanahan, S. S. (1983). Family structure and stress: A longitudinal comparison of two-parent and female-headed families. *Journal of Marriage and the Family, 45,* 347–357.

McLanahan, S. S., & Bumpass, L. L. (1988). Intergenerational consequences of family disruption. *American Journal of Sociology, 94,* 130–152.

McLoyd, V. C. (1990). The impact of economic hardship on Black families and children: Psychological distress, parenting, socioemotional development. *Child Development, 61,* 311–346.

McLoyd, V. C., Jayaratne, T. E., Ceballo, R., & Borquez, J. (1994). Unemployment and work interruption among African American single mothers: Effects on parenting and adolescent socioemotional functioning. *Child Development, 65,* 562–589.

Miller, B. C., & Moore, K. A. (1990). Adolescent sexual behavior, pregnancy, and parenting: Research through the 1980s. *Journal of Marriage and the Family, 52,* 1025–1044.

Minturn, L., & Lambert, W. W. (1964). *Mothers of six cultures.* New York: Wiley.

Mullis, R. L., & Mullis, A. K. (1985). Parenting education for single-parent families: Focusing community resources. *Journal of Child Care, 2,* 29–36.

Nieto, D. S. (1990). The custodial single father: Who does he think he is? *Journal of Divorce and Remarriage, 13*, 27–43.

Osofsky, J. D., Eberhart-Wright, A., Ware, L. M., & Hann, D. M. (1992). Children of adolescent mothers: A group at risk for psychopathology. *Infant Mental Health Journal, 13*, 119–131.

Osofsky, J. D., Hann, D. M., & Peebles, C. (1994). Adolescent parenthood: Risks and opportunities for parents and infants. In C. Zeanah (Ed.), *Handbook of infant mental health*. New York: Guilford.

Pasick, R. (1990). Friendship between men. In R. C. Meth & R. S. Pasick (Eds.), *Men in therapy: The challange of change.* New York: Guilford.

Patterson, C. J. (1992). Children of lesbian and gay parents. *Child Development, 63*, 1025–1042.

Pichitino, J. P. (1983). Profile of the single father: A thematic integration of the literature. *Personnel and Guidance Journal, 9*, 295–299.

Potter, A. E., & Knaub, P. K. (1988). Single motherhood by choice: A parenting alternative. *Family and Economic Issues, 9*, 240–249.

Richard, J. V. (1982). Addressing stress factors in single-parent women-headed households. *Women and Therapy, 1*, 15–27.

Roosa, M. W. (1986). Adolescent mothers, school drop-outs, and school-based intervention programs. *Family Relations, 35*, 313–317.

Santrock, J. W., Warshak, R. A., & Elliot, G. L. (1982). Social development and parent–child interaction in father custody and stepmother families. In M. E. Lamb (Ed.), *Nontraditional families* (pp. 289–314). Hillsdale, NJ: Lawrence Erlbaum Associates.

Sargent, J. (1992). Family variations. In M. D. Levine, W. B. Carey, & A. C. Crocker (Eds.), *Developmental-behavioral pediatrics*. Philadelphia: Saunders.

Scott-Jones, D. (1991). Adolescent childbearing: Risks and resilience. *Education and Urban Society, 24*, 53–64.

Shireman, J., & Johnson, P. (1976). Single parents as adoptive parents. *Social Service Review, 50*, 103–116.

Smith, E. W. (1993, March). *Life circumstances and experiences in single-parent households: Data from a national survey.* Paper presented at the Society for Research in Child Development, New Orleans, LA.

Snarey, J. (1993). *How fathers care for the next generation: A four decade study.* Cambridge, MA: Harvard University Press.

The State of America's Children Yearbook. (1994). Washington, DC: Children's Defense Fund.

Steinberg, L. D. (1987). Single parents, stepparents, and the susceptibility of adolescents to antisocial peer pressure. *Child Development, 58*, 269–275.

Thiriot, T. L., & Buckner, E. T. (1991). Multiple predictors of satisfactory post-divorce adjustment of single custodial parents. *Journal of Divorce and Remarriage, 17*, 27–48.

Turner, P. H., Scadden, L., & Harris, M. B. (1990). Parenting in gay and lesbian families. *Journal of Gay and Lesbian Psychotherapy, 1*, 55–66.

U.S. Bureau of the Census. (1991). Child support and alimony: 1989. *Current Population Reports* (Series P60, No. 173). Washington, DC: U.S. Government Printing Office.

U.S. Bureau of the Census. (1992). Households, families, and children: A 30 year perspective. *Current Population Reports* (Series P23, No. 181). Washington, DC: U.S. Government Printing Office.

Vuchinich, S., Hetherington, E., Vuchinich, R., & Clingempeel, W. (1991). Parent–child interaction and gender differences in early adolescents' adaption to stepfamilies. *Developmental Psychology, 27*, 618–626.

Wallerstein, J. S., Corbin, S. B., & Lewis, J. M. (1988). Children of divorce: A ten-year study. In E. M. Hetherington & J. D. Arasteh (Eds.), *Impact of divorce, single-parenting, and stepparenting on children* (pp. 198–214). Hillsdale, NJ: Lawrence Erlbaum Associates.

Wasserman, G. A., Rauh, V. A., Brunelli, S. A., Garcia-Castro, M., & Necos, B. (1990). Psychosocial attributes and life experiences of minority mothers: Age and ethnic variations. *Child Development, 61*, 566–580.

Weinraub, M. (1978). Fatherhood: The myth of the second-class parent. In J. H. Stevens, Jr. & M. Matthews (Eds.), *Mother/child father/child relationships* (pp. 109–133). Washington, DC: National Association for the Education of Young Children.

Weinraub, M. (1986, August). Growing up in single parent families: Effects on child development. *Invited Fellows Symposium: Psychology of Women—Current Issues and Research.* Paper presented at meetings of the American Psychological Association, Washington, DC.

Weinraub, M., & Wolf, B. (1983). Effects of stress and social supports on mother–child interactions in single and two-parent families. *Child Development, 54*, 1297–1311.

Weinraub, M., & Wolf, B. (1987). Stressful life events, social supports, and parent-child interactions: Similarities and differences in single-parent and two-parent families. In Z. Boukydis (Ed.), *Research on support for parents and infants in the postnatal period* (pp. 114–135). Norwood, NJ: Ablex.

Weisner, T. S., & Garnier, H. (1992). Nonconventional family life-styles and school achievement: A 12-year longitudinal study. *American Education Research Journal, 29*, 605–632.

Weiss, R. S. (1979). *Going it alone: The family life and social situation of the single parent.* New York: Basic Books.

Whitehead, B. D. (1993). Dan Quayle was right. *The Atlantic, 271*, 47–84.

Williams, M. (1992). *The single-parent family: In search of my father* [Television Film]. Conjure Films.

Wolf, B. M. (1987). Stress and social supports: Impact on parenting and child development in single-parent and two-parent families (Doctoral dissertation, Temple University, 1987). *Dissertation Abstracts International, 48,* 1171–1172B.

Zimiles, H., & Lee, V. (1991). Adolescent family structure and educational progress. *Developmental Psychology, 27,* 314–320.

4

Grandparenthood

Peter K. Smith
University of Sheffield

INTRODUCTION

Grandparenting can provide a fascinating topic for investigation. It is possibly both easier, and more difficult, than the study of parenting. Easier, insofar as the social science stance of disinterested study and objective analysis may be more readily forthcoming in a domain where emotions and relationships are not quite so intense and therefore perhaps more transparent and honest than that between parent and child. More difficult certainly, in that there are more varieties of grandparent than of parent, and one is studying three generations rather than two with the additional varied perspectives that entails. The study of grandparenthood is also challenging, in that the grandparent–parent–grandchild set of relationships confronts us squarely with the processes of socialization, intergenerational transmission, and change over historical periods.

A majority of middle-age and older people will become grandparents; some 70 percent in the United States, according to Tinsley and Parke (1984). They quoted the average age of becoming a grandparent as approximately 50 years for women, and a couple of years older for men. On this reasoning, many people will remain grandparents for some 25 years or about a third of their life span. A more exact calculation of the frequency of grandparenthood in the United States comes from the study by Rossi and Rossi (1990) of some 2,000 respondents in the Boston area. They found that the mean generational gap was 28 years. With high death rates in the late 70s (especially men) and 80s (especially women), this means that children will typically grow up with both sets of grandparents, but lose perhaps grandfathers when they are in adolescence, and grandmothers as young adults. Their findings suggest that not so many adults have living grandparents—the proportion falls from 62 percent in the 20s to 27 percent by the 30s. Great-grandparenthood is correspondingly rare; typically, as adults go through their 50s, their parents die and their grandchildren are born.

Rossi and Rossi's (1990) findings do "demythologize" the idea of common or extensive four-generation families; in their sample, only 1.3 percent of Bostonians have any living great-grandparents (whereas one in four have at least one living grandparent, and one in four have a grandchild). Equally, the figures confirm that grandparenting is a common experience. Rossi and Rossi describe the three-generation family as modal; it can be considered normative for children up to early adulthood to have grandparents, and for people in their late 50s onwards to have grandchildren.

Grandparenthood is thus an important part of the life cycle for most people, both as a personal experience and for its impact on others. Terms such as grandparent, parent, child, and grandchild are relative; someone may be both a parent and a child, for example. Many researchers use generational labels such as G1, G2, and G3 to avoid this ambiguity. However, this device has its own difficulties, as if G1 refers to a grandparental generation then there is no appropriate label for any great-grand-parents. In this chapter, I take grandchildren as the reference point, and refer to their parents, grandparents, and great-grandparents.

The majority of the research literature on grandparenting is relatively recent, and the chapter starts by examining historical considerations, and then the classical research in this area. Following a review of theories bearing on the study of grandparenthood, the central issues covered by research are outlined in some detail. Two particularly interesting issues—the kinds of influence that grandparents have on grandchildren, and the transmission of attitudes and behaviors across three generations—each have their own major section. Some practical issues of grandparenting are then considered, and finally future directions for research are indicated.

HISTORICAL ISSUES IN THE STUDY OF GRANDPARENTING

A life-span perspective on development necessitates taking account of history. Development takes place in an historical context, and cross-sectional studies of development thus confound age effects with cohort effects (Baltes, Reese, & Lipsitt, 1980). The cohort of contemporary grandparents in their 70s, for example, as well as being older than parents and grandchildren, will also have experienced much less formal schooling. As Rossi and Rossi (1990) put it, a life-span perspective allows for the interplay of aging, historical, and cohort factors. Bengtson (1987) similarly distinguished period effects (historical period), cohort effects (when you were born while living in an historical period), and lineage effects (different generations within a family structure). Bengtson's emphasis on lineage rather than age is appropriate for this chapter, where we are primarily looking at the generational relationship of grandparenthood. Grandparents can of course vary in age a great deal, whereas lineage remains constant. Age then becomes one mediating factor (among many others) to be considered as affecting grandparental relations.

Almost all our evidence on grandparenthood comes from modern urban, industrial societies, particularly the United States and to a lesser extent Western Europe. As LeVine and White (1987) pointed out, generational relations would have been (and still are) very different in agrarian societies. They were embedded in a system with strong kinship ties and strong expectations of reciprocity. Parents tended to have many children, mortality was relatively high, and parents expected children to support them in old age. The urban-industrial revolution reduced the salience of kinship and parentage; and the concept of childrearing changed from one of lifelong reciprocity to one of launching children into an autonomous maturity in which their future relationship with parents was optional.

The last few centuries in urban-industrial societies have seen numerous changes, partially linked but proceeding at different rates in different countries such as England, France, Germany, Scandina-via, and the United States (LeVine & White, 1987). These include the demographic transition to lower birth and death rates, and longer life-span expectancy; rise of technology; mass public schooling; greater public interest and concern in children (LeVine & White, 1987); and greater parental involvement in children, although with some reduction in parental (especially paternal) control over matters such as marriage and career (see also Vinovskis, 1987). More recently, there has been the increase in divorce rates and in numbers of reconstituted families and stepkin (Hetherington & Stanely-Hagan, in this *Handbook*); greater health and financial security in older generations; and with this some greater ambiguity in the role of the grandparental lineage (Rossi & Rossi, 1990).

These factors need to be borne in mind when considering the nature and role of grandparenthood, but some recent changes may have also influenced the extent to which grandparenting has been an object of social scientific and psychological research. The topic was relatively neglected until recently. An analysis of original publications mentioning grandparents or grandchildren via bibliographic sources revealed only 5 publications prior to 1950, 5 in the 1950s, 4 in the 1960s, 17 in the 1970s, increasing to 33 for 1980–1984, and to 62 for 1985–1989 (P. K. Smith, 1991).

The neglect of grandparents by researchers in child development prior to the 1980s was commented on by Tinsley and Parke (1984). They suggested four reasons. One was the demographic change resulting in substantial increases in life expectancy, with more people becoming grandparents. Second was the tendency to view the family as a nuclear one, comprised of only parents and children; although psychologists started looking beyond the mother to the father and siblings in the 1970s, it is only even more recently that this "wider social network" has extended to grandparents (Cochran & Niego, in this *Handbook*). Third, consideration of grandparent–grandchild relationships forces investigators to think in a life-span framework, and consider processes of intergenerational influence. But the life-span perspective in developmental and child psychology only become influential in the 1980s; prior to that, developmental psychology and child development were often seen as virtually synonymous, in practice if not in theory; and this narrowed vision of developmental processes more or less ceasing at adulthood or "maturity" would not encourage thinking about grandparents. Fourth, Tinsley and Park pointed to some methodological difficulties associated with working with grandparents. Older subjects may be ill or in some ways less suitable research subjects, and theoretical and statistical models need to be more complex to cope with the often triadic or polyadic relationships and patterns of direct and indirect influence likely to be encountered in analyzing grandparent–grandchild influence and interaction.

P. K. Smith (1991) suggested that there may also be a cohort effect in the pool of researchers interested in working on the topic. Due to university policies of expansion (in the 1960s and early 1970s), a large proportion of university staff were appointed then in their 20s and 30s, a time of life when perhaps they were not especially interested in the topic of grandparenting; 15 to 20 years later, when these people were reaching their 40s or 50s and would soon (if not already) be grandparents, the topic might become more attractive.

CLASSICAL RESEARCH

The first articles about grandparents appeared in the 1930s and 1940s (P. K. Smith, 1991). These tended to be written by psychiatrists or clinicians, and to have a quite negative view of grandparental influence. Thus an article by Vollmer (1937) entitled "The Grandmother: A Problem in Child Rearing" and another by Strauss (1943) entitled "Grandma Made Johnny Delinquent" both berate the adverse influence of grandmothers who interfere with the mother's childrearing in old-fashioned and didactic ways. Vollmer ended by stating that, "The practical conclusion is that the grandmother is not a suitable custodian of the care and rearing of her grandchild: She is a disturbing factor against which we are obliged to protect the child according to the best of our ability" (p. 382).

Staples (1952) started to present a more balanced view, at the same time emphasizing problems of grandparents being coresident with children and grandchildren. She concluded that "the well-liked grandmother ... keeps up with the times ... can easily make the transition from a position of responsibility in the family to one of rendering interested, helpful services. The disliked grandmother is unable to adjust to change and is unpleasantly aggressive in her contacts with her family" (p. 340). Staples and Smith (1954) interviewed 87 grandmother–mother pairs and found the grandmothers to have stricter and more authoritarian views than the mothers, on every subscale. Views of grandmothers (and of mothers) were particularly strict when both lived in the same three-generation household (48 percent of her sample), and when they had had fewer years of formal education.

From the 1960s, grandparents started to be presented much more favorably. P. K. Smith (1991) suggested that this development reflects some actual changes in grandparental attitudes and roles; although the early studies are probably unrepresentative in terms of sampling, there is some evidence that more grandparents were coresident, and had a more authoritative attitude, earlier in the century. But by the 1960s certainly, many grandparents accepted a "formal" or "fun-seeking" role, clearly demarcating grandparental and parental roles. In Neugarten and Weinstein's study (1964), only a very small proportion of grandparents saw themselves as "reservoirs of family wisdom." This decrease in formality and authority probably allowed more indulgent and warm relationships between grandparents and other family members (Apple, 1956).

Studies by Kahana and Kahana (1970) and Robertson (1976, 1977) of the perception of grandparenthood gave a more positive picture, and set a trend for much subsequent research. Kornhaber and Woodward (1981) described the "vital connection" of grandparents and grandchildren, although worried by now that some grandparents were becoming remote and detached. Tinsley and Parke (1984) reviewed the importance of grandparents as support and socialization agents.

Bengtson and Robertson (1985) provided a clear compilation of the more positive research and views of grandparenthood that had accumulated over the previous decade. Cherlin and Furstenberg (1986) gave a thorough account of "the new American grandparent." Mangen, Bengtson, and Landry (1988) provided a comprehensive review of methodological issues in studying intergenerational relationships. P. K. Smith (1991) gave a selection of studies of grandparenthood from different industrialized countries, helping to balance the great bulk of research from the United States.

THEORETICAL PERSPECTIVES APPLICABLE TO GRANDPARENTHOOD

Several theoretical perspectives can be used to structure research and interpret data on grandparenting. These include evolutionary biology and sociobiology, psychoanalysis, family sociology and family systems theory, life-span development, and gerontology.

Evolutionary Biology and Sociobiology

The broadest or most "distal" theoretical framework that might be applied to grandparenthood is that of evolutionary biology. Remote as it might seem, this theory has application in several areas.

First, it is relevant to the evolution of features of the human life span such as the menopause and senescence. In nonhuman primates there does not seem to be a clear menopause—reproductive senescence does not proceed more rapidly or earlier than senescence in other systems (Altmann, 1987). Evolutionary theories of senescence generally predict the maximum life span being set at the point at which the probability of further reproduction is zero (Leek & Smith, 1991; Turke, 1988; Williams, 1957). But in humans, the menopause at 45–55 years clearly precedes likely mortality by some 20, 30, or even 40 years. Turke argued that this atypical primate pattern suggests that older humans (especially older women, who have a menopause) were able to help children and grandchildren effectively, and enhance their own reproductive success more by this than by having yet further children themselves. On this line of reasoning, it is perhaps no accident that the age of menopause is not greatly different from the likely age of becoming a grandparent.

Besides perhaps explaining the advent of the menopause, this approach leads to the prediction that grandparents could and often would provide support for children and grandchildren. Many studies confirm this (and Turke, 1988, found the same on the Micronesian atoll community of Ifaluk). Degree of relatedness should be a predictor of helping; again confirmed by many studies. As Rossi and Rossi (1990) put it for relationships generally, "what mattered most for obligation level was not a specific *type* of kinperson, but the degree of relatedness of ego to the various kintypes" (p. 491). The greater risk of stepgrandchildren for abuse (Margolin, 1992) would also be predicted.

M. S. Smith (1991) explained the standard differences in grandparental involvement and invest-ment (maternal grandmother > maternal grandfather = paternal grandmother > paternal grandfather) in terms of certainty of (genetic) relatedness; whereas mothers are certain of relatedness to their children, fathers are not so certain. The relatedness to maternal grandmother is definitely one fourth (of genes shared by common descent), whereas for paternal grandfather it is on average somewhere between one fourth and zero, with both links (grandfather–son; son–grandson) potentially uncertain. (For maternal grandfather and paternal grandmother there is one potentially uncertain link.)

Following genetic similarity theory (Rushton, Russell, & Wells, 1984), Leek and Smith (1991) suggested that grandparents might use indicators of phenotypic similarity as cues for relatedness, such that perceived similarity between grandparent and grandchild would also predict involvement or investment. They looked at both perceived similarity in physical appearance and perceived similarity in personality. Similarity in physical appearance did not yield any significant correlations, but perceived personality similarity did correlate with perceived value of help given to children and grandchildren.

There is scope for predictions of when conflict should arise among grandparents, their children, and grandchildren. Parent–offspring conflict theory (Trivers, 1974) has been extended to three generations (Fagen, 1976; Partridge & Nunney, 1977). Thus, grandparents might be expected to encourage more cooperation among their grandchildren (who are cousins to each other) than the grandchildren themselves might wish.

More work deserves to be done on these sociobiological predictions. Some findings are suggestive, but not all hypotheses are confirmed, and some that are may have alternative explanations. However evolutionary and sociobiological theories have a role to play in our understanding of grandparenthood, and can and should be integrated with more proximal, and cultural, explanations of relevant data, rather than seen as antithetical to them.

Psychoanalysis

Psychoanalytic views of grandparent–grandchild relationships were prominent in earlier reports, especially by clinicians. These have used psychoanalytic ideas such as the "Oedipus complex" (in which an infant boy represses sexual desire for his mother and murderous wishes to his father), and "transference" (in which someone may, for a period, transfer powerful but repressed emotional feelings for someone on to a substitute, as is regularly thought to happen in therapy). For example, Strauss (1943) explained the delinquency of a child called "Johnny" in terms of the Oedipal complex between the grandmother and Johnny's father, and the hostility to Johnny's mother that was then transferred to Johnny when his mother died. More recently, Battistelli and Farneti (1991) used ideas concerning the Oedipus complex, and the transference of a child's feeling from parent to grandparent, to throw light on the kinds of associations and dreams that children had about grandparents, as well as developmental trends in these. They argued that grandparents may have a "transitional object role" toward the adolescent grandchild.

The influence of psychoanalysis in developmental psychology waned after the 1960s; but some psychoanalytic ideas have had a revival via the recent developments in attachment theory and the rapprochement among developmental psychologists, systems theorists, and psychoanalysts in this area, pioneered by Bowlby but since taken up by other investigators. It is possible that psychoanalytic ways of describing and explaining complex emotional dynamics (such as rivalry, jealousy, and projection)—seen clearly in case studies such as those of Cohler and Grunebaum (1981) who draw on psychoanalytic concepts in this way—may be reworked in the future in productive ways more compatible with mainstream developmental ideas.

Family Sociology and Family Systems Theory

Concepts from family sociology have been employed extensively in describing aspects of grandpa-rental relationships. Thus, key concepts have been cohesion or solidarity, refined into associational, affectual, consensual, functional, normative, and goal components; and measures of intergenerational family structure (McChesney & Bengtson, 1988).

Sociological studies such as those by Cunningham-Burley (1984, 1985) and Cotterill (1992) draw attention to how grandparents perceive their role, and possible contradictions between such roles and wider familial or societal expectations. The in-depth, qualitative nature of these studies yields findings that are not appropriate for statistical generalization, but that do give a rounded picture of behavior in real-life situations.

Family systems theory (Minuchin, 1988) would have potential in elaborating the nature of three-generation family structure further; and it could be used in complementary fashion to some of the psychoanalytic concepts to explore more complex issues such as scapegoating, marginalizing, coalitions, and exclusions in larger family groups. As yet, however, it has not been used much in studies of grandparents.

Life-Span Development and Gerontology

An important theoretical framework currently is life-span development. This is an obvious way of viewing intergenerational influences, and the life-span concepts of Baltes et al. (1980) can be used as a framework for the impact of nonnormative life events—for example, how grandparents play a buffering role for children in divorcing families, or for how historical changes have affected grandparental roles. Authors such as Bengtson (1987) have emphasized the importance of cohort and period effects. The life-span perspective can also be seen as lying behind the distinction between direct and indirect influences of grandparents to grandchildren, as elaborated by Tinsley and Parke (1984), as well as the understanding of bidirectional effects in development (Bengtson, 1987).

Aging and gerontology provide another perspective for studying grandparenthood. Even though many grandparents are not "aged" in the conventional sense, they may experience negative stereotypes of aging. A significant proportion of grandparents will indeed be in old age, or suffer from particular infirmities of age such as senile dementia (Creasey, Myers, Epperson, & Taylor, 1989). More positively, aging can be seen as leading to more mature concepts of morality, and greater wisdom (Clayton & Birren, 1980). In some traditional agricultural societies, grandparenthood can be a precondition for achieving the status of respected elder in the community (Sangree, 1992). In general, theories from gerontology could be integrated with a life-span perspective to give insights into grandparenting insofar as it inevitably involves aging.

CENTRAL ISSUES IN STUDYING GRANDPARENTHOOD

The research carried out in the last decade or so has defined a number of issues central to the study of grandparenthood in contemporary society. Main topics discussed here are the frequency of contacts between grandparents and grandchildren; the mediating role of proximity; the nature of grandparent–grandchild contacts; varying characteristics of grandparents, such as sex, lineage, age, health of grandparent, age of grandchild; great-grandparents; styles of grandparents; perceived roles of grandparents; the impact of divorce; stepgrandparents; on-time and off-time grandparenthood; stereotypes of grandparents; perceptions of different generations; and the nature of African-American grandparenting. Later sections consider indirect and direct patterns of grandparent–grandchild influence, including acting as a surrogate parent, and sexual abuse; and intergenerational transmission.

Contacts Between Grandparents and Grandchildren:
How Frequent and How Satisfying?

A considerable number of studies have investigated how often contemporary grandparents and grandchildren see each other, and whether the relationship is close and satisfying, or conflictual. The consensus has been that contacts are usually (though not invariably) reasonably frequent and reasonably satisfying.

Frequent and *satisfying* are somewhat relative terms, and how one sees the typical grandparent–grandchild relationship may depend on one's expectations. Some studies have suggested that the links are infrequent and of little importance. Kornhaber (1985) reported that only 15 percent of over 1,000 grandparents interviewed reported "a close emotional bond between grandparent and grandchild" (pp. 159–160). He argued that many grandparents in the United States have adopted a "new social contract"—giving up emotional attachments to grandchildren—and as a result "have sheared apart the three-generational family and weakening the emotional underpinnings of the nuclear family" (pp. 159–160). Similarly, Gutmann (1985) argued that American grandparents have become new hedonists, adopting an ethic of self-sufficiency and independence. Both these authors regretted such changes, which have clearly become more possible as the grandparent generations have become more healthy and financially secure. Kivett (1985), surveying 99 grandfathers with grandchildren aged 2–43 years, reported that the data showed the grandfather role to be of little relative importance as seen through low levels of interaction and low priority as a role.

Other studies have pointed to negative aspects of grandparent–grandchild relationships. In a study of 200 people aged 75–84 years in Finland, Ruoppila (1991) found that 10 percent reported difficulties in relationships with grandchildren, and for 20 percent the relationship did not have special meaning. Also, not all grandchildren get on with their grandparents. In a study in Poland by Tyszkowa (1991), accounts of grandparents were obtained from 142 Polish students aged 15–23. One reported that "I don't like my grandmother; she's sloppy and disagreable ... I don't like visiting her"; and another "she's always running about, grumbling, nagging and shouting" (p. 56).

The wider nature of family relationships involving grandparents can be very complex, as is well brought out in case studies. Cohler and Grunebaum (1981) reported four detailed studies of three-generation Italian-American families. In one, Mrs. Scardoni, aged 53, is the mother of Mrs. Russo, aged 27, and grandmother of Charlotte. Mrs. Scardoni experienced violence from her own father and later her husband (with whom she had 11 children). Her ambivalence comes out in jealousy and continual criticism of her son-in-law, Mr. Russo, and overworrying about her grandchildren. Mrs. Russo is strongly influenced by her mother, talks to her on the telephone at least once a day, but is torn between loyalty to her and to her husband. By 6 years, Charlotte appeared well-behaved, but subdued and compliant "suggesting that Charlotte may have joined her mother and grandmother in the continuation of family conflicts into the third generation" (p. 350).

But, is the picture generally as gloomy as this? Kivett's (1985) actual data on grandfathers showed that 82 percent of them were visited by grandchildren, and 37 percent had visits once a week or more; 26 percent also attended church several times a month with grandchildren, and 88 percent of grandfathers said they felt very close to the grandchild with whom they had most contact. These data are not out of line with many other studies in the United States. The grandfathers in Kivett's study tended to rank grandfatherhood as the third most important role in their life, after being a spouse or parent. This seems realistic. Being a grandparent does not rank as high as being a husband (or wife) or being a parent; and it is true that some grandparents see some grandchildren seldom, if ever. But the modal tendency is for grandparents to see grandchildren often enough to share a quite close and satisfying relationship.

A group of studies in the United States has reported on the perceptions that college students or young adults have of their grandparents. Robertson (1976) questioned 86 grandchildren aged 18–26. She reported that they "espouse a series of very favourable attitudes towards grandparents" (p. 138); for example, 92 percent agreed that "a child would miss much if there were no grandparents when he was growing up," and two thirds felt some obligation to help grandparents. Hoffman (1979) surveyed 269 female undergraduates aged 17–23. He found considerable variability in contact and emotional closeness, but most grandchildren saw grandparents every month or so, and felt quite close to them (averaging around 4 on a 5-point scale of emotional closeness).

Hartshorne and Manaster (1982) interviewed 178 undergraduates, median age 21 years. Grandchildren generally visited grandparents several times a year, with more contacts by letter or telephone. Many felt they would like more contact than this. Virtually all the grandchildren rated the relationship as "important" or "very important" for them, and most as "very important" for the grandparents themselves (4 and 5 on 5-point scales). They concluded that "grandparents remain a significant factor in the lives of young adults" (p. 243).

Eisenberg (1988) gave questionnaires to 120 undergraduates, aged 18–23. On average grandchildren had contact with grandparents around once or twice a month, and rated the relationship as "close" (3 on a 5-point scale). Creasey and Koblewski (1991) surveyed 142 college students, mean age 19 years. Again, most managed to visit grandparents once a month or so, and telephoned more often. Although grandparents were not seen as major targets for intimacy, nor for help, relationships were generally good; on 5-point scales, grandparents rated high on continuity (4.1) and affection (4.0), mutual respect (3.9) and satisfaction (3.5), and low on power (1.7) and conflict (1.6). The authors concluded that "it is clear that most grandparents continue to play a relatively active role within their adolescent grandchildren's social networks" (p. 384).

Hodgson (1992) reported results from a national telephone survey, which obtained data from 208 grandchildren, mostly aged 18–40 years, who averaged one or two living grandparents. They were asked about the relationship with their closest grandparent. The majority were in some contact with the grandparent several times a month, 40 percent weekly (although 13 percent interacted only once a year or less). On a 4-point scale of closeness, the mean response was 3 ("quite close"). Overall, Hodgson concluded that despite variability, "the grandchild/grandparent bond continues with surprising strength into adulthood" (p. 222).

There are similar findings in other industrial societies. In Finland, Ruoppila's (1991) study found that about 70 percent of grandparents, even when quite elderly, saw their grandchildren at least once a week; and most saw the relationship in positive terms. Sticker (1991) reported on several studies in Germany; generally, grandparents see grandchildren weekly or, in the case of grandchildren who are of preschool age, more often. About three fourths of grandparent–grandchild dyads were characterised by "high" or "very high" emotional closeness. A majority of the Polish students in Tyszkowa's (1991) study visited grandparents at least once a month, and the emotional tone of the relationship was generally positive.

In summary, most grandparents see many grandchildren at least once a month, sometimes much more often; and generally the relationship is seen as positive, and important, by both generations. However this general picture should not be allowed to hide the very great variation in contact and satisfaction in grandparent–grandchild relationships.

The Mediating Role of Proximity

What leads to variations in contact and closeness between grandparents and grandchildren? One major factor is proximity. For example, in Hodgson's (1992) sample nearly one half of grandparents lived within 25 miles of grandchildren; but a fourth lived more than 500 miles away. This variation in proximity was the strongest factor she found predicting frequency of contact. Kivett (1985) found that in 93 percent of cases the grandchild whom a grandfather had most contact with was also the closest geographically. These findings fit into a larger literature on the importance of geographic distance for kin contact. Frankel and DeWit (1989) looked most specifically at contacts between the older people and their adult children, and found distance to be the most important predictor of all forms of contact. Litwak and Kulis (1987) examined the relationship of geographic distance to various kinds of contact, service, and exchange between kin. They found that face-to-face contact fell off steeply in frequency once someone lived more than one block away, but frequency of telephone contact increased with distance up to being two to five blocks away, before falling steeply as someone lived perhaps an hour or so away. What they call "normal" kin services, such as checking on someone daily, comforting, giving small gifts, providing meals, only fell off sharply when someone lived more than 30 minutes away.

In a study of intergenerational interaction in Finnish families with 12-year-old grandchildren, Hurme (1988) found that most had some grandparents within 60 kilometers, and a third had a maternal grandmother in the same town (only 1.5 percent in the same house). She found a sharp decline in frequency for contact, even after 20 kilometers; but little change in the perceived importance of the relationship, up to 60 kilometers.

The Nature of Contacts Between Grandparents and Grandchildren

The range of activities that grandparents and grandchildren engage in is wide, and obviously varies greatly with age; the particular role of surrogate parenting is discussed later. Robertson (1976) felt that the role was limited largely to emotional gratification, gift giving, and acting as bearers of family history. These are certainly important, and common findings. With younger children, giving gifts and treats is commonly reported. Also, grandparents will often know more about family history than anyone else, and can provide a sense of continuity in family traditions, which may be of considerable interest to grandchildren as they get older. Grandparents can pass on national history (Tyszkowa, 1991, reported that 20 percent of her grandchildren reported that grandparents had told them about episodes such as World War II). However, most studies suggest a wider range of activities than Robertson highlighted. For example, Eisenberg (1988) found a majority of her grandchildren reported having done the following with grandparents: having treats, giving a sense of family, imparting family history, taking part in family events, playing games, going on trips, babysitting, making you feel good, giving emergency help, giving personal advice, being someone to talk to, joining in religious activity, and giving advice on school.

Tyszkowa (1991) reported "conversations" as being prominent in activities reported by her Polish grandchildren. "When we go fishing with Grandpa, we talk. We tell each other about ourselves"; "with Grandma I can talk about my problems" (p. 20). This is echoed by some of the German grandchildren in Sticker's (1991) study: "... we talk about everything, also about confidences which concern our family as a whole," "if I don't like anything, I can say it, whatever it is ... I'm not afraid ... sometimes I also tell Grandma a secret" (p. 37). Because they are close but do not have a parental authority role, grandparents can sometimes act as confidants in situations where an older child might not wish to confide in a parent.

Varying Characteristics of Grandparents

Although external factors such as proximity of residence will affect grandparent–grandchild contacts and activities, so too will such factors as the sex, lineage, age, and health of the grandparent; and age of grandchild.

Sex and lineage. Mothers are more often the closer parent to children (Barnard & Martell, in this *Handbook*). Similarly many studies find that grandmothers are more involved with grandchildren than grandfathers. Also, grandparents through the mother's side—maternal grandmother and maternal grandfather—are more involved than those through the father's side—paternal grandmother and paternal grandfather. Thus, sex and lineage of grandparent may interact as influences, with the maternal grandmother often appearing as having the most contact and closest relationship with grandchildren. For example, Hoffman (1979) found maternal grandmother to be perceived as closest and seen most often by U.S. grandchildren, followed by maternal grandfather, and then the paternal grandparents. Eisenberg (1988) and Hodgson (1992) reported very similar results, as did Kahana and Kahana (1970) and Shea (1988); (who also pointed out interactions with sex of grandchild). Outside the United States, Battistelli and Farneti (1991) in Italy, M. S. Smith (1991) in Canada, and Tyszkowa (1991) in Poland reported a similar pattern. The general trend is maternal grandmother > maternal grandfather > paternal grandmother > or = paternal grandfather. Age of grandparent can be an interacting factor here; because on average women marry slightly older men, maternal grandmothers are often the youngest of all four grandparents. However the main explanation probably lies in the strength of mother–daughter bonds, reinforced by societal expectations and perhaps in a more distal causal sense by certainty of relatedness as indicated by considerations from evolutionary biology (M. S. Smith, 1991).

The implicit recognition of the greater influence of grandmothers is reflected in the larger number of studies that have specifically focused on them; for example, Staples and Smith (1954); Johnson (1983); Stevens (1984); Blackwelder and Passman (1986); Myers, Jarvis, and Creasey (1987); Gladstone (1989); Pearson, Hunter, Ensminger, and Kellam (1990); Hill-Lubin (1991); Wakschlag, Chase-Lansdale, and Brooks-Gunn (1993); and Musick (1994). A smaller number of studies have focused on grandfathers, for example, Goodwin, Cormier, and Owen (1983); Kivett (1985); and Radin, Oyserman, and Benn (1991).

Age and health of grandparent.   As noted earlier, age of grandparent will interact with other factors, notably health, age of grandchildren, cohort effects, and the image of grandparents as older persons. For example, Johnson (1983) found that grandparents over 65 years of age had less favorable attitudes to cohabitation (probably a cohort effect), were less family oriented and more friend oriented (probably reflecting older age and greater independence of grandchildren), and had less contact with grandchildren.

Thomas (1986) compared grandparents aged 45–60, 61–69, and 70–90; ages of grandchildren averaged 7–17; in this entirely White sample, no grandparents shared a household with grandchildren but 63 percent lived within 30 minutes travel of at least one grandchild. Thomas found no age differences in satisfaction with the role of grandparent, or in the amount of helping grandchildren. However, the two younger groups expressed greater responsibility for grandchildren's discipline and for giving childrearing advice. This latter finding probably reflects an age-of-grandchild effect (the oldest group mostly had adolescent grandchildren, the younger groups mostly preadolescents), although it could reflect either age of grandparent or cohort effects.

Kennedy (1991) looked at reasons given by college students for closeness to their most-close grandparent. Younger grandparents (50–60 years) received more reasons to do with love and appreciation, intimacy and shared activities; older grandparents, especially those over 75 years, received more reasons to do with caring for the grandparent.

Older grandparents are of course less likely to be in good health, and this can affect the relationship. Mild health problems may not decrease relationship satisfaction, and may indeed elicit caring from grandparents (Cherlin & Furstenberg, 1985; Troll, 1985). Creasey et al. (1989) compared grandparent–grandchild relationships when grandparents in their 60s and 70s did or did not have senile dementia of the Alzheimer's type. In both groups, grandchildren saw the grandparents about once a week; but, not surprisingly, grandchildren had poorer relationships with grandparents with Alzheimer's, perceiving lower companionship, intimacy, and affection (although not differing in nurturance).

Age of grandchild.   Some studies have reported on age of grandchild as a factor in relationships with grandparents. There could be similar possible confounds in the interpretation of these results, although given the rapid developmental changes of childhood, attribution of findings to age (rather than historical period or age of grandparent) may be more plausible. Kahana and Kahana (1970) gave interviews and questionnaires to children aged 4–5, 8–9, and 11–12 about their grandparents. The two older groups had more contact with grandparents, especially paternal grandparents. The youngest group saw paternal grandparents least, perhaps because they were most dependent on family (and mother's) arrangements; the older grandchildren had greater independent mobility, and also were more likely to verbalize a desire to treat all grandparents equally: "you have to love all your grandparents the same"; "I love them all the same" (p. 102). In terms of describing the relationship, the youngest children often referred to indulgent grandparents who gave them gifts or treats—"ego-centric" responses; the 8- to 9-year-olds gave reasons based more on mutuality and fun-sharing activities, and the 11- to 12-year-olds were generally more diverse in their reasons.

Summary

Several types of single-parent families exist, and differing circumstances characterize each family type. Although single-parent fathers and single-parent mothers may be different from each other in a variety of ways, divorced custodial fathers and divorced custodial mothers both face similar problems after the breakup of their marriage. For divorced families, disruption of the family members' lives and their household is a major challenge. How the divorced parent negotiates these challenges has important implications for the child's temporary coping and long-term adjustment. For adolescent mothers, negotiating the multiple challenges of personal identity, preparation for adulthood, and parenthood itself poses significant risks for the adolescent and her child, especially because the adolescent is often coming from a situation of economic and educational disadvantage. Finally, unmarried couples by choice, single mothers by choice, and solo mothers may also face different life circumstances. The degree of social support and the frequency of daily life stresses in these parents' lives may hold the keys for predicting whether or not single parenthood will affect children's development.

FUTURE RESEARCH DIRECTIONS

Appreciating the heterogeneity among single-parent families requires that researchers be more specific in describing samples of single-parent families. It also affords numerous opportunities to compare functioning within specific types of single-parent families to help understand why and how children in single-parent families are at risk.

A prime example of this approach to research is a study by Acock and Demo (1994) in which adjustment and academic performance among adolescents living in five prevalent family structures were examined. Children from two-parent family units, divorced, single-parent families, stepfamilies, and never-married noncohabiting families were found to vary dramatically on measures of family functioning and adolescent behavior. Compared to the other family types, divorced and stepparent families reported the most mother–child conflict and the lowest levels of parental control and parent–child interaction. As a result, it was not surprising that children in these families experienced more personal and emotional adjustment problems and had more difficulties with school performance. Although striking socioeconomic differences were observed, with never-married mothers singularly disadvantaged, it was not economic differences across families but differences in mother–child interaction that were most predictive of child outcome.

Studies comparing different types of single-parent families have yielded some useful information about the role of fathers in child development. Research on children of remarried single-parent families (e.g., Acock & Demo, 1994; Amato & Keith, 1991b; Steinberg, 1987; Vuchinich, Hetherington, Vuchinich, & Clingempeel, 1991; Zimiles & Lee, 1991), showing that children whose mothers have remarried do not necessarily show better psychological adjustment than children whose mothers have not remarried, suggests that the presence of a male figure in the home may not be the critical variable responsible for the at-risk status of single-parent families. Similarly, studies of two-adult households where one parent is not a father figure (e.g., Kellam, Ensminger, & Turner, 1977; Patterson, 1992) indicate that children reared in these households may not differ substantially from those in households in which there is a father, suggesting further that it may not be the father's "genderness" that is responsible for his important contribution to the family so much as it is his role as a "second," though not second-class parent. The importance of father's contributions may derive more from his serving as one of two involved, accepting, warm, nurturing caregivers who support each other emotionally and financially more than it derives from the uniqueness of his male gender (Weinraub, 1978).

Studies of large samples of single parents can also help tease out specific contextual and psychological features that contribute to the single parents at-risk status when these factors overlap. Father absence, economic deprivation, increased stressful life events, decreased social and instrumental supports, diminished parental role models, parental involvement, and lax child supervision

Kahana and Kahana (1970) interpreted some of these findings within a Piagetian developmental framework, as did Schultz (1980). He asked 4-, 9-, and 19-year-olds to give descriptions of their grandparents. Older children used many more abstract descriptors, and were also able to differentiate different grandparents more clearly.

Battistelli and Farneti (1991) gave a questionnaire on grandparents to children aged 8–9, 12–13, and 16–17. The youngest group more often described playing with grandparents. Older grandchildren, however, even if they saw grandparents as somewhat less important, also saw them as more patient and understanding than parents, with adolescents being much less likely to argue with grandparents than with parents. Consistent with Kahana and Kahana's findings, perhaps, these Italian children grew toward a more homogenized evaluation of different grandparents, the maternal grandparents (who received more positive evaluation in younger children) being evaluated equally with the paternal grandparents by adolescence.

Great-Grandparents

Not much has been written on great-grandparenthood. Wentowski (1985) interviewed 19 great-grand-mothers, aged 66 to 92. Proximity was a very strong influence on contact. Ninety-two-year-old Mrs. Smith saw some local great-grandchildren weekly with her daughter and granddaughter, but had never seen some nonlocal great-grandchildren. Although the role of great-grandmother was seen as similar to that of grandmother, the relationship did not seem to have the same intensity. As Mrs. Smith commented: "When you're a grandparent, you love 'em, you're glad to have them come, you fix 'em food, do things for 'em because they're precious to you. When you're a great-grandparent, you're older and you can't do as much. It's different." But even the youngest and healthiest great-grand-mothers (aged 66 and 71) were not so involved with great-grandchildren as with grandchildren: "Other people take care of this now" (p. 594). Similarly, Ruoppila (1991) found that elderly Finnish people saw great-grandchildren much less frequently than grandchildren; this was especially true for men. Nevertheless, most saw great-grandchildren at least monthly.

Burton and Bengtson (1985), in a study of young grandmothers, interviewed a number of great-grandmothers aged 46–73 and regarded those aged under 58 as "early" in the role; they also interviewed seven great-great-grandmothers and one great-great-great-grandmother! Generally, as is discussed later, these "early" grandmothers and great-grandmothers do not like being seen in this role, due to their own conflicting life concerns and also what they perceive as an association of (great)grandparenthood with aging and its associated negative stereotypes.

Styles of Grandparenting

Variations in grandparent–grandchild relationships can clearly be influenced by a multitude of factors, as well as purely individual differences of temperament, needs, and personality. In describing these variations, a number of researchers have come up with typologies of grandparenting, or different styles of grandparenting. The earliest, and one that has remained influential, is that of Neugarten and Weinstein (1964). Based on interviews with 70 sets of grandparents, they delineated five major styles: *formal* (following prescribed roles with a clear demarcation between parenting and grandparenting responsibilities); *fun seeker* (seeing grandchildren as fun and a source of self-indulgence or mutuality of satisfaction); *surrogate parent* (taking actual caregiving responsibility); *reservoir of family wisdom* (dispensing special skills or resources, with authority); and *distant* (only infrequent contacts with grandchildren on ritual occasions). They found the formal role to be more frequent in grandparents over 65, whereas the fun-seeker and distant styles were more frequent in younger grandparents.

This typology has been used in several other studies. For example McCready (1985) compared different U.S. ethnic groups in this way; Sticker (1991) summarized results from several studies, including a number of studies in Germany, which point to the fun-seeking style predominating with younger grandchildren, and the formal style increasing with older grandchildren.

The Neugarten and Weinstein (1964) roles are in fact a mixture of intrinsically age-related roles (especially "surrogate parent") with styles that may be overlapping rather than discrete (thus, McCready combined the formal and distant types). Inclusive, discrete typologies were produced by Robertson (1977) and Cherlin and Furstenberg (1985). Robertson assessed the personal meanings (meeting individual needs) and the social role meanings (meeting social norms) grandparents used to describe relationships with grandchildren; this yielded four styles, *apportioned* (high on both), *remote* (low on both), *individualized* (high on personal only), and *symbolic* (high on social only). Cherlin and Furstenberg distinguished two main aspects of grandparent–grandchild relationships, measured by scales of several items: those relating to exchange of services (giving and receiving help), and those relating to exerting parental-type influence (disciplining, advising on problems). Also, they took account of infrequent (less than once a month) or more frequent contact. This gave them a five-fold typology that was clearly defined. *Detached* grandparents were low on both scales and had infrequent contact. *Passive* grandparents were low on both scales and had more frequent contact. *Supportive* grandparents were high on exchange of services; *authoritative* grandparents were high on parentlike influence; whereas those high on both scales were *influential*. More African-American grandparents (especially grandmothers) were authoritative or influential (see later discussion).

Mangen and McChesney (1988), as part of a larger study investigating methodology of describing three-generation families in a sample of over 2,000 respondents (Mangen et al., 1988), described 14 types of grandparent role based on heirarchical cluster analysis of a large number of different measures of cohesion. The types vary in terms of amounts of contact and exchange, degree of reciprocity, emotional closeness, and geographical distance.

Perceived Roles of Grandparents

However social scientists describe grandparent roles, it is another matter whether the variety of roles or styles means that grandparents themselves have a clear idea of their own role, or whether instead it reflects a lack of societal consensus on what the grandparental role is. Clavan (1978) characterized grandparenthood as a "roleless role," meaning that it does not have the same clear rights and obligations as the parental role, and Wood (1982) called it an "ambiguous role."

There have in fact been clear changes through this century in the extent to which grandparents have been expected to have "authoritative" parental-type duties or just be "supportive," and this may be reflected in uncertainty especially at certain historical periods—a theme taken up by Kornhaber and Woodward (1981). Johnson (1983) found that U.S. grandmothers had not often consciously conceptualized the role, and thus could mold it to their own lifestyle and that of their families. However, individual grandmothers were quite able to give a list of rules that they used to regulate their behavior with their grandchildren. The "shoulds" typically included being an advocate, mediator, support, and source of enjoyment; the "should nots" involved not being too intrusive, overprotective, or parental—too "old-fashioned," in fact. Here, many of these 1980s grandmothers seem to be taking a "supportive" role and rejecting an "authoritative" role more common a generation or so before.

Divorce and Stepgrandparenthood

Divorce.   Interestingly, one of the clearest roles for grandparents seems to be manifest in times of family discord, and specifically when parents divorce. This is to act as a source of stability and continuity through a period when their grandchildren may be experiencing uncertainty and distress in their relations with parents (Hetherington & Stanley-Hagen, in this *Handbook*). Johnson (1983) interviewed 48 grandmothers whose children had divorced around 2 years previously. Most grandmothers, especially those under 65, saw grandchildren at least weekly; and after the divorce, the tendency was for this rate of contact to go up, not down. One grandmother described how she filled a gap between parents: "I pick them up on Friday after work. We go to the Pizza Hut for dinner—then home to watch TV. I keep lots of goodies around for them. They fight, I shush them. Then they zonk out. The next morning, I fix breakfast—they watch TV. Then I take them to their dad's and dump them. It's kinda nice" (pp. 553–554). This finding of enhanced contact of younger grandmothers with grandchildren of divorced parents was confirmed by Aldous (1985).

Sometimes, the paternal grandmother, for example, can maintain contacts with grandchildren when the father finds it difficult to do so. However, paternal grandparents may have to "tread carefully" if the mother has child custody, and may have problems in access to their grandchildren. In the longer term, marital discord was found by Rossi and Rossi (1990) to affect all grandparent–grandchild relationships negatively except that of maternal grandmother–granddaughter. Gladstone (1989) described how adult children can facilitate, or prevent, contact between grandparents and grandchildren after marriage breakdown and remarriage.

Stepgrandparenthood.   Johnson and Barer (1987) pointed out the complexity of three-generation family relationships that can ensue after divorce. A grandchild could have three types of stepgrandparent, resulting from a parent remarrying (the most usual), a grandparent remarrying, or even from the parent of a stepparent remarrying! Sanders and Trygstad (1989) compared U.S. college student grandchildren perceptions of grandparents and stepgrandparents. They found that grandparent–grandchild relationships were closer, in terms of more frequent contact, greater emotional involvement, and role expectations, than stepgrandparent–grandchild relationships. Nevertheless, about half their grandchild sample saw the stepgrandparent relationship as important. The differences appeared to be partly, but not completely, a product of the length of time for which they had known the (step)grandparent. Henry, Ceglian, and Matthews (1992) obtained the views of 62 mothers on grandparent relations with grandchildren and stepgrandchildren; the relationships were perceived as different, with more step-relationships described as "remote" in Robertson's (1977) typology.

On-Time and Off-Time Grandparents

For most people, becoming a grandparent is described as a positive experience. But this can depend on the age at which it happens, and be influenced by societal images of grandparents as elderly persons. Johnson (1983) reported that some grandmothers disassociated themselves from the role, saying "I'm too young to be a grandmother" or "I'm just not the grandmother type—I travel, take courses, I have my own interests" (p. 554). Such feelings can be especially strong if grandparenthood comes early. Burton and Bengtson (1985) interviewed African-American grandmothers, and described those who experienced the transition between 42 and 57 years as being "on-time," within the normal range of variation. But those women who became grandmothers "early," between 25 and 37 years, were discontented, feeling obligations placed on them which they were not ready for. "I'm really a grandmother in name only. I don't have time to do what I would like to do as a grandmother. I work everyday. I have young children. Right now I'm just too busy." They also felt that the grandmother label implied an undesirable image: "I am just too young to be a grandmother. That's something for old folks, not for me" (p. 68). Similar sentiments were voiced by a recent 29-year-old U.K. grandmother who advocated "more advice and sex education at schools. If I'd had better advice, I wouldn't be a granny now" ("Grandmother Aged 29," 1992, p. 7).

Timberlake and Chipungu (1992) compared the perceived value of grandchildren to African-American grandmothers, who became grandmothers either between the ages of 30 and 41, or between the ages of 45 and 60. The latter had a significantly higher evaluation of what their grandchildren meant to them.

By contrast, Burton and Bengtson (1985) found that those grandparents who experienced the transition "late," for example in their 70s, were likely to be disappointed that they would have relatively little time left to enjoy their grandchildren, and would be less likely to be sufficiently well and physically active to make the most of the grandparental role. In general, it appears that "off-time" grandparents, whether early or late, are likely to experience more difficulties in the role than are on-time grandparents.

Stereotypes of Grandparenthood

Many early grandparents, in their comments, show awareness of a stereotype of grandparents as aged, fussy, domesticated, and sedentary, probably with infirmities. This, unfortunately, is in line with the way grandparents are often portrayed in children's books, and on TV commercials. Janelli (1988) surveyed 42 North American children's books, published between 1961 and 1983; she found that 55 percent of grandmothers had white or grey hair, 31 percent wore glasses and 31 percent had aprons; 39 percent of grandfathers had bald heads, and 36 percent had both white hair and glasses. Many U.K. children's books show grandparents in a similar way (P. K. Smith, 1991).

This stereotype is out of step with demographic realities. Most grandchildren who read children's books will have grandparents in their 40s, 50s, and 60s. As Hagestad (1985) similarly pointed out for TV commercials, "Often, the grandmother presented on the screen should be a great-grandmother. The woman who has small, golden-haired grandchildren is not likely to have silver hair in a bun, serve lemonade on the porch, or worry about slipping dentures and 'irregularity.' She would more realistically be portrayed dressed in a jogging suit on her way to aerobic dancing, or in a suit coming home from work" (pp. 35–36).

The association of grandparenthood with old age also leads to an association of grandparenthood with the negative stereotypes associated with aging; for example, in a study of drawings of young and old people by 10- to 11-year-olds in Scotland, Falchikov (1990) reported that the content of the drawings of older people showed glasses, rocking chairs, walking frames, and smaller figures—generally, aging as a degenerative biological process. Nevertheless, Marcoen (1979) found that children's drawings of their own grandparents were more realistic, and less influenced by these negative stereotypes.

Another image of grandparents is of someone who spoils grandchildren, being overlenient or overindulgent. As one U.K. song puts it, "Granny spoils us, oh what fun, Have some sweets and a sticky bun, Don't tell mum you were up till ten, I want to come and babysit again" (Miller, 1989, p. 8). This image of spoiling may have some basis in reality. In an interview study of older people in the United Kingdom, 155 of whom had grandchildren, Townsend (1957) reported that "the grandparents were notably lenient towards grandchildren" (p. 106). This leniency and image of spoiling may have been a reaction, both real and perceived, against the strict and authoritarian role of grandparents which was, by the 1950s, being rejected. As one of Townsend's informants put it, "I used to slosh my children. But I don't like to see my grandchildren walloped," and another said "the grandmother can be free and easy. She [her daughter] has to be fairly strict with them" (pp. 106–107).

Perceptions of Different Generations

Although three generations are involved in grandparent–grandchild relationships, most studies have focused on the viewpoint of only one generation, via interviews or questionnaires. Sometimes, the views of grandparents have been elicited; more often, the perspective of the grandchild. However, the differing perceptions of differing generations may be important information. The few studies that have obtained multiple perspectives regularly report some incongruence. For example, Hurme (1988) found that 38 percent of her Finnish grandmothers rated their relationship with the grandchild as "very important," whereas only 27 percent of mothers so rated it. Mangen and Miller (1988) reported that correlations across generations for amount of contact, seemingly an objective fact, varied betwen .41 and .75. Disagreements here often signified relationship difficulties; one father claimed to visit the children's grandmother once a month, but the grandmother complained that he hardly ever came and that "I do not see my son's children enough to know their middle names" (p. 121). Landry and Martin (1988) found reasonable levels of agreement across generations about attitudes, but with the grandparent generation underestimating the grandparent–parent difference and the grandchild generation overestimating differences with their parents. These differing perceptions deserve more attention in future, both for their theoretical interest and possible practical benefits that might ensue if misunderstandings can be avoided.

African-American Grandparents

Several studies have documented the particular importance of grandparents, especially the maternal grandmother, in many African-American families. About one half of African-American children live in single-parent female-headed households, about three times the figure for White families; also, the generation gap tends to be shorter (Burton & Dilworth-Anderson, 1991; Tolson & Wilson, 1990). There is thus more opportunity in African-American families for younger grandparents to be involved with and support their grandchildren.

Historically, African-American grandmothers were important figures of support and continuity (Hill-Lubin, 1991), and often acted as supplementary and/or surrogate parents (Burton & Dilworth-Anderson, 1991). Pearson et al. (1990) studied a predominantly African-American community in Chicago, and found that 10 percent of households with target 6- to 8-year-old children had coresident grandmothers. The grandmothers had substantial childrearing roles in these families, in control, support, and punishment. They were about half as active as the mothers in these areas, and considerably more active than fathers (if present) and grandfathers. Timberlake and Chipungu (1992) found that active help with grandchildren was associated with more positive evaluation of the grandparental role in a sample of 100 African-American grandmothers.

Stevens (1984) found that grandmothers were supportive of teenage daughters with young grandchildren (13–30 months); they seemed to pass on useful information about norms of development, and they modeled a more responsive and less punitive interaction style with the infants. Tolson and Wilson (1990) compared African-American families with one or two parents and with or without a grandmother resident; their results (limited by small sample size) mainly suggest the influence of number of caregivers rather than who the extra caregiver is (usually, father, or grandmother).

DIRECT AND INDIRECT INFLUENCES

What influence do grandparents have on the development of grandchildren? Tinsley and Parke (1984) distinguished between direct influences, resulting from contact and face-to-face interaction, and indirect influences, mediated by other means such as parental behavior.

We have already seen examples of direct influence, including babysitting, giving gifts, being a companion and confidant, acting as an emotional support or "buffer" at times of family stress, passing on family history or national traditions, acting as a role model for aging; these varying in importance with age of grandchild. These are the reasons often given by grandchildren for feeling close to grandparents. Acting as a surrogate parent, discussed next, is a particularly strong direct influence when the child is young. Normally very positive, this can occasionally provide opportunities for sexual abuse.

Acting as a Surrogate Parent

Kennedy and Keeney (1988) reviewed 1970 U.S. census data, which indicate that in parent-absent families grandparents are the most common source of care, especially for preschool children. Grandparents also provide essential help in many single-parent families including many African-American families (Burton & Dilworth-Anderson, 1991; Kennedy, 1991).

Observational studies have shown that grandparents can act as a source of secure attachment for young children. Security of attachment is often assessed by a laboratory technique known as the "strange situation" (Ainsworth, Blehar, Waters, & Wall, 1978), which has seven brief episodes involving separation and reunion between infant, caregiver, and a stranger. Myers et al. (1987) extended this strange situation procedure to 13 episodes, including an observational assessment of grandmother–infant as well as mother–infant attachment. Similarly, Tomlin and Passman (1989) observed the behavior of 2-year-olds in a novel environment, with either their mother or grandmother present. In both studies, the more contact grandmothers had with grandchildren, the more they functioned like mothers in providing a secure base for attachment and exploration.

Radin et al. (1991) and Oyserman, Radin, and Benn (1993) examined 64 families where teen mothers of children under 2 were assisted by grandparents. They found that in this situation the grandmother had little effect on the child's development, but that involved grandfathers did have a positive influence, probably by modeling a male role of nurturance and cooperation. These were father-absent families, so perhaps the grandparents had a well-marked role to play. The relationship of grandmothers with adolescent mothers or mothers-to-be can be emotionally charged and rivalrous or conflictual as well as supportive (Musick, 1994).

A survey of Chinese children by Falbo (1991) found that grandparental preschool care was associated with somewhat better school performance than parental care; there are possible confounds in this finding (such as socioeconomic status), but frequency of grandparental contact, plus grandparental educational attainment, did predict positivly to language and mathematics scores in first- and fifth-grade children.

Surrogate parenting can later lead to very close grandparent–grandchild relationships, as reported by Hodgson (1992) "My grandmother took me in for five years. You can get pretty close in five years of living together" (p. 219). It can be a very positive role in African-American families (Timberlake & Chipungu, 1992). However, as noted by Cotterill (1992), some grandmothers, especially paternal grandmothers, may be reluctant to provide long-term support of this kind for working mothers: "One thing I've always said, even with my own daughter, I would never look after grandchildren on the same basis during the day whilst they go to work. I don't agree with that. I've brought up my own children and I don't want to be tied down every day looking after grandchildren" (p. 614).

Sexual Abuse by Grandparents

As with some parents, close contact with grandchildren via supplementary or surrogate parenting also gives grandparents opportunities for abuse. Although rare, some 10 percent of all reported cases of intrafamilial childhood sexual abuse involve grandfathers and granddaughters (Goodwin et al., 1983). Margolin (1992) also reported this to be the most common form of grandparent–grandchild sexual abuse, and both reports concur that such abuse is *not* gentle or benign. Margolin found the risk of abuse to be significantly higher for stepgrandchildren.

Indirect Sources of Influence

One source of indirect influence of grandparents is via financial support. For example, Dickemann (1979) argued that in traditional societies, dowry can be seen as maternal grandparents investing resources to place a daughter in an advantageous position on the marriage market, thus enhancing the reproductive success of their grandchildren.

Rather more studies have focused on how grandparents, by acting as parents themselves, will have influenced the way in which their children act as parents to the grandparents' grandchildren. Here, we are looking at intergenerational transmission of parenting.

INTERGENERATIONAL TRANSMISSION

A currently vigorous research area is looking at the transmission of attitudes and behaviors across three (or more) generations—the intergenerational transmission of parenting (see also Heinicke, in this *Handbook*). One area of growing interest has been the transmission of attachment or internal working models of relationships. Main, Kaplan, and Cassidy (1985) described internal working models as being internalized representations acquired in infancy and childhood, which reflect aspects such as trust or ambivalence learned in primary relationships and assessed in infancy in the "strange situation"; the latter leads to classifications of secure, avoidant, and ambivalent attachment with mother or caregiver. They also described the Adult Attachment Interview (AAI) as a means of assessing an adult's model of their relationships with their parents. These developments have started to generate studies of intergenerational transmission of attachment. For example, Ainsworth and Eichberg (1991) related attachment type of infants aged 12–18 months, to mothers' scores on the AAI for relationships with *their* mothers. They used a threefold classification scheme for the AAI: autonomous attachment (recalling earlier attachment-related experiences objectively and openly, even if these were not favorable), dismissive attachment (earlier attachment-related experiences seen as of little concern, value, or influence), and preoccupied attachment (still dependent on parents and actively struggling to please them). In general, adult autonomous attachment predicted to secure infants, adult dismissive attachment to avoidant infants, and adult preoccupied attachment to ambivalent infants; there was concordance for 37 pairs and disagreement for only 8 pairs. This finding would be predicted on the basis of intergenerational transmission, with the mother's internal working model of relationships having been acquired from her own early experiences, and now being passed on to her children. However, the theory does allow for adults to work through or resolve unsatisfactory relations with their parents and modify their internal working models, either through self-reflection or with the aid of therapy or counseling.

Other studies have been less tied to attachment theory, but have looked at transmission of more general qualities such as warmth, autonomy, and aggression. Wakschlag et al. (1993) found modest relations between mother–grandmother interactions, and mother–child interactions; in particular, mothers who were autonomous with grandmothers were more flexible, warm, and supportive with their children. Ruoppila (1991) found significant correlations between grandparental and parental childrearing attitudes and practices in his Finnish sample. These were most marked for grandmothers and their daughters; but there also appeared to be important influences from grandfathers to their sons, in terms of attitudes to child care.

Rossi and Rossi (1990) linked indices of marital relationship, cohesion, and attitudes across generations. They found that "the quality of G1 parents' marriage was echoed in the marital happiness of G2 adult children" and "a significant tendency for parents to transmit the same skills their own parents had taught them to their own children" (p. 358). Family cohesion tended to be stable across generations, and especially for women; attitudes, too, showed more influence from mothers than from fathers.

Vermulst, de Brock, and van Zutphen (1991) utilized Belsky's (1984) model of parental functioning, in a sample of 55 Dutch grandmother–mother dyads (grandchildren aged 8–12 years). They operationalized the model into social class (educational level), personality characteristics (psychological well-being, conformity), contextual characteristics (perceived support), parenting behavior (restriction, affection), and child characteristics (behavioral style). They first applied it separately to grandmothers and to mothers, and then made a combined model across the generations. The authors noted overall differences between generations, with mothers scoring higher than grandmothers on educational level, affection, perceived support, but lower on conformity and restriction. However they were more interested in the variations within each generation and how they connected—whether, for example, more educated grandmothers had more educated mothers, even if the overall level of education for the grandmothers was lower. They found that there were strong grandmother–mother links for educational level, and also for affection, and conformity; and also from grandmother affection to mother's psychological well-being. About one third of the variation found in mother's parental functioning could be explained in terms of earlier parental functioning of the grandmother.

Research on children's antisocial behavior has also pointed to intergenerational influences. Lefkowitz, Eron, Walder, and Huesmann (1977) linked the use of physically aggressive and punitive techniques in the grandparent–parent generation, to similar behavior in the parent–grandchild generation and to antisocial behavior in the grandchildren. Caspi and Elder (1988) found a reinforcing dynamic between problem behavior and unstable ties in the family across four generations of women in their Berkeley guidance study. Stein, Newcomb, and Bentler (1993) documented relations between both grandparent and maternal drug abuse and behavioral/developmental problems in (grand)children aged 2–8 years, especially for boys.

TWO PRACTICAL ASPECTS OF GRANDPARENTING

The increased recognition of the practical importance of grandparenthood is shown by two developments in modern industrial societies. One is the advent of courses for effective grandparenting, and of foster grandparent programs. The other is the growing pressure for grandparents to have visitation rights in cases of family separation and divorce.

Grandparents in Society

In the United States, there are now courses for grandparents. Strom and Strom (1989) offered an educational program for grandparents to help strengthen families including components on: sharing feelings and ideas with peers, listening to the views of younger people, learning about life-span development, improving family communication skills, and focusing self-evaluation. An evaluation (Strom & Strom, 1990) was positive. Kennedy and Keeney (1988) described the running of a psychotherapy group for grandparents who were the primary caregivers for children receiving mental health treatment. More generally, there are intergenerational programs such as the Three Generation Project (Hansen & Jacob, 1992) which aim to help both new parents and grandparents cope with shifts in family relationships that the transition to (grand)parenthood brings. Ingersoll-Dayton and Neal (1991) described an evaluation of bringing grandparents into family therapy sessions.

There are also foster grandparent programs. Werner (1991) described how these give "elders with low income the opportunity to provide companionship and caring for a variety of high-risk children and youths in return for a tax-exempt stipend" (p. 78). These take place in hospitals, residential institutions, day-care programs, and family shelters. The evaluation of these programs appears to be positive.

Visitation Rights

An important and growing issue for grandparents is what access and visitation rights they have with grandchildren of a noncustodial parent. Thompson, Tinsley, Scalora, and Parke (1989) review the legal situation in the United States; in recent years, statutes granting grandparents legal standing to petition for legally enforceable visitation with their grandchildren, even over parental objections, have been passed in all 50 states. In Britain, the 1989 Children Act, which highlights the interests of children, also allows grandparents to request access to grandchildren after divorce.

A study by Wilks and Melville (1990) of custody/access cases referred to a family court clinic in Toronto, Canada, found that two thirds of the cases had grandparental involvement. Grandparents generally had positive relationships with their grandchildren, and in most cases their involvement was seen as helpful.

FUTURE DIRECTIONS FOR THEORY AND RESEARCH

Despite a productive decade or so of research, there are some clear limitations to research on grandparenting to date. These include a somewhat limited use of methods of obtaining data, a narrow cultural range, and a lack of strong theoretical guidance.

Methods of Obtaining Data

A wider range of methodologies might be usefully employed. Most studies of grandparenthood have employed interviews, or else structured or semistructured questionnaires. These are straightforward ways of getting someone's perceptions of a role or relationship, but may not always be reliable indices of behavior. A few studies of grandparental relationships have used direct observation of behavior in standard situations (Myers et al., 1987; Tomlin & Passman, 1989). Radin et al. (1991) and Tinsley and Parke (1987) recorded grandparent behavior with infants in the home, finding them often to be involved in play and nurturing activities, though perhaps less competently than parents. More naturalistic home observations of grandparent–grandchild interaction might well be worthwhile in checking results based on attitude and perception against behavioral reality.

Other kinds of methodologies could be used more to elicit more complex, emotional, or unconscious feelings toward grandparents. These could be more projective or open-ended methods, for example, writing essays about grandparents (Ponzetti & Folkrod, 1989; Tyszkowa, 1991) or analyzing drawings that grandchildren draw of grandfathers and grandmothers (Marcoen, 1979). Case studies (Cohler & Grunebaum, 1981) and more qualitative approaches (Cunningham-Burley, 1984, 1985; Musick, 1994) can add important insights and complement more quantitative results.

Wider Cultural Comparisons

With a handful of exceptions (e.g., P. K. Smith, 1991) research on grandparenthood has been carried out in the United States. This has included description of subcultural variations, not only African American families but other ethnic groups (e.g., McCready, 1985; Schmidt & Padilla, 1983; Werner, 1991). Nevertheless, comparable studies of grandparenthood in different cultures, including Eastern as well as Western, nonindustrial as well as urban, will give a greater picture of variety (e. g., Sangree, 1992). This in turn will provide a better testing ground for integrated biocultural theories, which could attempt to account for both the differences between cultures and the commonalties across cultures.

The Need for Theory

A primary requirement is for greater theoretical underpinning to research in grandparenthood. Mancini and Blieszner (1989) wrote of intergenerational relationships that "relatively little research appears to be guided a priori by theories or conceptual frameworks. Most of the work is concerned with addressing a defined problem. Although research driven by problem solving is not without merit, when it is devoid of a theoretical context the understanding of the larger picture is stunted" (p. 283). This is rather true of research on grandparenthood, where many articles simply describe the amounts and kind of contact between grandparents and grandchildren, the influence of such factors as type of grandparent, age of grandchild, proximity, and so forth. It is important to get this descriptive information, but now there are surely sufficient data to look for a wider theoretical framework in which to interpret them.

We have seen that there are several relevant theoretical traditions. Rather than seeing all these as necessarily opposed, it will be helpful to work toward some expansion and integration. Hagestad (1987) made this kind of plea. She argued the need to move beyond the dyad and the need to reconcile what she called the alpha and omega traditions, the developmental studies of infancy and childhood, and the sociological and gerontological studies of older persons. To this, I would add the need to integrate biological theories with developmental and sociocultural ones (see also Rossi & Rossi, 1990). For example, biological theories about genetic relatedness and willingness to help others need to be linked to developmental theories of attachment, and to be able to take account of sociocultural differences. Research on grandparenthood has spanned a number of different disciplines; this has been part of its interest, but it also presents us with a challenge for future integration.

CONCLUSIONS

Grandparenthood is a fascinating area of research that has been relatively neglected until the last two decades. Yet, demographic tendencies in modern industrialized societies mean that it is an important part of the life span for most people. In understanding grandparenthood, theoretical perspectives can be brought to bear from evolutionary biology, psychoanalysis, family sociology, life-span development, and gerontology.

Being a grandparent does not usually have as much significance as being a parent; but relationships with grandchildren are usually seen as being positive and satisfying. Typically, grandparents may see grandchildren once or a few times a month. However the frequency and nature of contacts vary considerably. Living close to grandchildren, being a grandmother (especially maternal grandmother), being relatively younger and healthy, all predict to greater contact. In addition there are individual and cultural differences in style and role perceptions. Among African Americans the maternal grandmother tends to have a particularly influential role.

Grandparents engage in a variety of activities with grandchildren; particularly notable are acting as family historian, as a confidant, and as a support in times of family discord. Some grandparents become particularly close to young grandchildren by acting as a surrogate parent.

Grandparents can be on-time or off-time depending on when they first become a grandparent; generally, on-time grandparents experience the most satisfaction in the role. Greatgrandparents, and stepgrandparents, tend to have less contact and lower satisfaction.

Grandparents can influence their grandchildren's development in many ways. Some are direct, via contact. Some are indirect, via support of parents and intergenerational transmission of parenting skills. Generally, the influence of grandparents can be very positive. On occasions it can be less so, if they conflict with parents on childrearing values, or even abuse grandchildren.

Some issues connected to grandparenthood have direct societal implications. For example, there are courses for grandparents, and foster grandparent programs. Grandparents are getting more rights of access to grandchildren separated from them by their parent's divorce.

Research on grandparenthood is growing in strength and relevance; future directions may usefully see a broadening in methodology, studies in a greater variety of different cultures, and a more thorough application of theory to data collection and interpretation.

REFERENCES

Ainsworth, M. D. S., Blehar, M. C., Waters, E., & Wall, S. (1978). *Patterns of attachment: A psychological study of the strange situation.* Hillsdale, NJ: Lawrence Erlbaum Associates.

Ainsworth, M. D. S., & Eichberg, C. (1991). Effects on infant–mother attachment of mother's unresolved loss of an attachment figure, or other traumatic experience. In C. M. Parkes, J. Stevenson-Hinde, & P. Marris (Eds.), *Attachment across the life cycle* (pp. 160–183). London: Routledge.

Aldous, J. (1985). Parent–adult child relations as affected by the grandparent status. In V. L. Bengtson & J. F. Robertson (Eds.), *Grandparenthood* (pp. 117–132). Beverly Hills, CA: Sage.

Altmann, J. (1987). Life span aspect of reproduction and parental care in anthropoid primates. In J. B. Lancaster, J. Altmann, A. S. Rossi, & L. R. Sherrod (Eds.), *Parenting across the life span: Biosocial dimensions* (pp. 15–29). New York: Aldine de Gruyter.

Apple, D. (1956). The social structure of grandparenthood. *American Anthropologist, 58,* 56–63.

Baltes, P. B., Reese, H. W., & Lipsitt, L. P. (1980). Life-span developmental psychology. *Annual Review of Psychology, 31,* 65–110.

Battistelli, P., & Farneti, A. (1991). Grandchildren's images of their grandparents: A psychodynamic perspective. In P. K. Smith (Ed.), *The psychology of grandparenthood: An international perspective* (pp. 143–156). London: Routledge.

Belsky, J. (1984). The determinants of parenting: A process model. *Child Development, 55,* 83–96.

Bengtson, V. L. (1987). Parenting, grandparenting, and intergenerational continuity. In J. B. Lancaster, J. Altmann, A. S. Rossi, & L. R. Sherrod (Eds.), *Parenting across the life span: Biosocial dimensions* (pp. 435–456). New York: Aldine de Gruyter.

Bengtson, V. L., & Robertson, J. F. (Eds.). (1985). *Grandparenthood.* Beverly Hills, CA: Sage.

Blackwelder, D. E., & Passman, R. H. (1986). Grandmothers' and mothers' disciplining in three-generational families: The role of social responsibility in rewarding and punishing children. *Journal of Personality and Social Psychology, 50,* 80–86.

Burton, L. M., & Bengtson, V. L. (1985). Black grandmothers: Issues of timing and continuity of roles. In V. L. Bengtson & J. F. Robertson (Eds.), *Grandparenthood* (pp. 61–77). Beverly Hills, CA: Sage.

Burton, L. M., & Dilworth-Anderson, P. (1991). The intergenerational family roles of aged Black Americans. In S. K. Pfelfer & M. B. Sussman (Eds.), *Families: Intergenerational and generational connections* (pp. 311–330). Binghamton, NY: Haworth.

Caspi, A., & Elder, G. H. (1988). Emergent family patterns: The intergenerational construction of problem behaviour and relationships. In R. A. Hinde & J. Stevenson-Hinde (Eds.), *Relationships within families: Mutual influences* (pp. 218–260). Oxford, England: Oxford University Press.

Cherlin, A., & Furstenberg, F. F. (1985). Styles and strategies of grandparenting. In V. L. Bengtson & J. F. Robertson (Eds.), *Grandparenthood* (pp. 97–116). Beverly Hills, CA: Sage.

Cherlin, A., & Furstenberg, F. F. (1986). *The new American grandparent.* New York: Basic Books.

Clavan, S. (1978, October). The impact of social class and social trends on the role of the grandparent. *The Family Coordinator,* pp. 351–357.

Clayton, V., & Birren, J. E. (1980). The development of wisdom across the life span. In P. B. Baltes & O. G. Brim, Jr. (Eds.), *Life-span development and behavior* (Vol. 3, pp. 103–135). New York: Academic Press.

Cohler, B. J., & Grunebaum, H. U. (1981). *Mothers, grandmothers, and daughters: Personality and childcare in three-generation families.* New York: Wiley.

Cotterill, P. (1992). "But for freedom, you see, not to be a babyminder": Women's attitudes towards grandmother care. *Sociology, 26,* 603–618.

Creasey, G. L., & Koblewski, P. J. (1991). Adolescent grandchildren's relationships with maternal and paternal grandmothers and grandfathers. *Journal of Adolescence, 14,* 373–387.

Creasey, G. L., Myers, B. J., Epperson, M. J., & Taylor, J. (1989). Grandchildren of grandparents with Alzheimer's disease: Perceptions of grandparent, family environment, and the elderly. *Merrill–Palmer Quarterly, 35,* 227–237.

Cunningham-Burley, S. (1984). "We don't talk about it ...": Issues of gender and method in the portrayal of grandfatherhood. *Sociology, 19,* 421–436.

Cunningham-Burley, S. (1985). Constructing grandparenthood: Anticipating appropriate action. *Sociology, 19,* 421–436.

Dickemann, M. (1979). The ecology of mating systems in hypergynous dowry societies. *Social Science Information, 18,* 163–195.

Eisenberg, A. R. (1988). Grandchildrens' perspectives on relationships with grandparents: The influence of gender across generations. *Sex Roles, 19,* 205–217.

Fagen, R. M. (1976). Three-generation family conflict. *Animal Behaviour, 24,* 874–879.

Falbo, T. (1991). The impact of grandparents on childen's outcomes in China. *Marriage and Family Review, 16,* 369–376.

Falchikov, N. (1990). Youthful ideas about old age: An analysis of children's drawings. *International Journal of Aging and Human Development, 31,* 79–99.

Frankel, B. G., & DeWit, D. (1989). Geographic distance and intergenerational contact: An empirical examination of the relationship. *Journal of Aging Studies, 3,* 139–162.

Gladstone, J. W. (1989). Grandmother–grandchild contact: The mediating influence of the middle generation following marriage breakdown and remarriage. *Canadian Journal on Aging, 8,* 355–365.

Goodwin, J., Cormier, L., & Owen, J. (1983). Grandfather–granddaughter incest: A trigenerational view. *Child Abuse & Neglect, 7,* 163–170.

Grandmother aged 29 calls for more sex education in schools. (1992, July 14). *Guardian,* p. 7.

Gutmann, D. L. (1985). Deculturation and the American grandparent. In V. L. Bengtson & J. F. Robertson (Eds.), *Grandparenthood* (pp. 173–181). Beverly Hills, CA: Sage.

Hagestad, G. O. (1985). Continuity and connectedness. In V. L. Bengtson & J. F. Robertson (Eds.), *Grandparenthood* (pp. 31–48). Beverly Hills, CA: Sage.

Hagestad, G. O. (1987). Parent–child relations in later life: Trends and gaps in past research. In J. B. Lancaster, J. Altmann, A. S. Rossi, & L. R. Sherrod (Eds.), *Parenting across the life span: Biosocial dimensions* (pp. 405–433). New York: Aldine de Gruyter.

Hansen, L. B., & Jacob, E. (1992). Intergenerational support during the transition to parenthood: Issues for new parents and grandparents. *Families in Society: The Journal of Contemporary Human Services, October,* 471–479.

Hartshorne, T. S., & Manaster, G. J. (1982). The relationship with grandparents: Contact, importance, role conception. *International Journal of Aging and Human Development, 15,* 233–245.

Henry, C. S., Ceglian, C. P., & Matthews, D. W. (1992). The role behaviors, role meanings, and grandmothering styles of grandmothers and stepgrandmothers: Perceptions of the middle generation. *Journal of Divorce and Remarriage, 17,* 1–22.

Hill-Lubin, M. A. (1991). The African-American grandmother in autobiographical works by Frederick Douglass, Langston Hughes, and Maya Angelou. *International Journal of Aging and Human Development, 33,* 173–185.

Hodgson, L. G. (1992). Adult grandchildren and their grandparents: The enduring bond. *International Journal of Aging and Human Development, 34,* 209–225.

Hoffman, E. (1979). Young adults' relations with their grandparents: An exploratory study. *International Journal of Aging and Human Development, 10,* 299–310.

Hurme, H. (1988). *Child, mother and grandmother: Intergenerational interaction in Finnish families.* Jyvaskyla, Finland: University of Jyvaskyla Press.

Ingersoll-Dayton, B., & Neal, M. B. (1991). Grandparents in family therapy: A clinical research study. *Family Relations, 40,* 264–271.

Janelli, L. M. (1988). Depictions of grandparents in children's literature. *Educational Gerontology, 14,* 193–202.

Johnson, C. L. (1983). A cultural analysis of the grandmother. *Research on Aging, 5,* 547–567.

Johnson, C. L., & Barer, B. M. (1987). Marital instability and the changing kinship networks of grandparents. *The Gerontologist, 27,* 330–335.

Kahana, B., & Kahana, E. (1970). Grandparenthood from the perspective of the developing grandchild. *Developmental Psychology, 3,* 98–105.

Kennedy, G. E. (1991). Grandchildren's reasons for closeness with grandparents. *Journal of Social Behavior and Personality, 6,* 697–712.

Kennedy, G. E., & Keeney, V. T. (1988). The extended family revisited: Grandparents rearing grandchildren. *Child Psychiatry and Human Development, 19,* 26–35.

Kivett, V. R. (1985). Grandfathers and grandchildren: Patterns of association, helping, and psychological closeness. *Family Relations, 34,* 565–571.

Kornhaber, A. (1985). Grandparenthood and the "new social contract." In V. L. Bengtson & J. F. Robertson (Eds.), *Grandparenthood* (pp. 159–171). Beverly Hills, CA: Sage.

Kornhaber, A., & Woodward, K. (1981). *Grandparents/grandchildren: The vital connection.* Garden City, NY: Doubleday.

Landry, P. H., Jr., & Martin, M. E. (1988). Measuring intergenerational consensus. In D. J. Mangen, V. L. Bengtson, & P. H. Landry, Jr. (Eds.), *Measurement of intergenerational relations* (pp. 126–155). Newbury Park, CA: Sage.

Leek, M., & Smith, P. K. (1991). Cooperation and conflict in three-generation families. In P. K. Smith (Ed.), *The psychology of grandparenthood: An international perspective* (pp. 177–194). London: Routledge.

Lefkowitz, M. M., Eron, L. D., Walder, L. O., & Huesmann, L. R. (1977). *Growing up to be violent.* New York: Pergamon.

LeVine, R. A., & White, M. (1987). Parenthood in social transformation. In J. B. Lancaster, J. Altmann, A. S. Rossi, & L. R. Sherrod (Eds.), *Parenting across the life span: Biosocial dimensions* (pp. 271–293). New York: Aldine de Gruyter.

Litwak, E., & Kulis, S. (1987). Technology, proximity, and measures of kin support. *Journal of Marriage and the Family, 49,* 649–661.

Main, M., Kaplan, N., & Cassidy, J. (1985). Security in infancy, childhood, and adulthood: A move to the level of representation. In I. Bretherton & E. Waters (Eds.), *Growing points of attachment and research* (pp. 66–104). Chicago: University of Chicago Press.

Mancini, J. A., & Blieszner, R. (1989). Aging parents and adult children: Research themes in intergenerational relations. *Journal of Marriage and the Family, 51,* 275–290.

Mangen, D. J., Bengtson, V. L., & Landry, P. H., Jr. (Eds.). (1988). *Measurement of intergenerational relations.* Newbury Park, CA: Sage.

Mangen, D. J., & McChesney, K. Y. (1988). Intergenerational cohesion: A comparison of linear and nonlinear analytical approaches. In D. J. Mangen, V. L. Bengtson, & P. H. Landry, Jr. (Eds.), *Measurement of intergenerational relations* (pp. 208–221). Newbury Park, CA: Sage.

Mangen, D. J., & Miller, R. B. (1988). Measuring intergenerational contact in the family. In D. J. Mangen, V. L. Bengtson, & P. H. Landry, Jr. (Eds.), *Measurement of intergenerational relations* (pp. 98–125). Newbury Park, CA: Sage.

Marcoen, A. (1979). Children's perception of aged persons and grandparents. *International Journal of Behavioral Development, 2,* 87–105.

Margolin, L. (1992). Sexual abuse by grandparents. *Child Abuse & Neglect, 16,* 735–741.

McChesney, K. Y., & Bengtson, V. L. (1988). Solidarity, integration and cohesion in families: Concepts and theories. In D. J. Mangen, V. L. Bengtson, & P. H. Landry, Jr. (Eds.), *Measurement of intergenerational relations* (pp. 15–30). Newbury Park, CA: Sage.

McCready, W. C. (1985). Styles of grandparenting among White ethnics. In V. L. Bengtson & J. F. Robertson (Eds.), *Grandparenthood* (pp. 49–60). Beverly Hills, CA: Sage.

Miller, J. (1989). *Myself.* Christchurch, Dorset, England: Golden Apple Productions.

Minuchin, P. (1988). Relationships within the family: A systems perspective on development. In R. A. Hinde & J. Stevenson-Hinde (Eds.), *Relationships within families: Mutual influences* (pp. 7–26). Oxford, England: Oxford University Press.

Musick, J. S. (1994). Grandmothers, and grandmothers-to-be: Effects on adolescent mothers and adolescent mothering. *Infants and Young Children, 6,* 1–9.

Myers, B. J., Jarvis, P. A., & Creasey, G. L. (1987). Infants' behavior with their mothers and grandmothers. *Infant Behavior and Development, 10,* 245–259.

Neugarten, B. L., & Weinstein, K. K. (1964). The changing American grandparent. *Journal of Marriage and the Family, 26,* 199–204.

Oyserman, D., Radin, N., & Benn, R. (1993). Dynamics in a three-generation family: Teens, grandparents, and babies. *Developmental Psychology, 29,* 564–572.

Partridge, L., & Nunney, L. (1977). Three-generation family conflict. *Animal Behaviour, 25,* 785–786.

Pearson, J. L., Hunter, A. G., Ensminger, M. E., & Kellam. S. G. (1990). Black grandmothers in multigenerational households: Diversity in family structure and parenting involvement in the Woodlawn community. *Child Development, 61,* 434–442.

Ponzetti, J. J. Jr., & Folkrod, A. W. (1989). Grandchildren's perceptions of their relationships with their grandparents. *Child Study Journal, 19,* 41–50.

Radin, N., Oyserman, D., & Benn, R. (1991). Grandfathers, teen mothers and children under two. In P. K. Smith (Ed.), *The psychology of grandparenthood: An international perspective* (pp. 85–99). London: Routledge.

Robertson, J. F. (1976). Significance of grandparents: Perceptions of young adult grandchildren. *The Gerontologist, 16,* 137–140.

Robertson, J. F. (1977). Grandmotherhood: A study of role conceptions. *Journal of Marriage and the Family, 39,* 165–174.

Rossi, A. S., & Rossi, P. H. (1990). *Of human bonding: Parent–child relations across the life course.* New York: Aldine de Gruyter.

Ruoppila, I. (1991). The significance of grandparents for the formation of family relations. In P. K. Smith (Ed.), *The psychology of grandparenthood: An international perspective* (pp. 123–139). London: Routledge.

Rushton, J. P., Russell, R. J. H., & Wells, P. A. (1984). Genetic similarity theory: Beyond kin selection. *Behaviour Genetics, 14,* 179–193.

Sanders, G. F., & Trygstad, D. W. (1989). Stepgrandparents and grandparents: The view from young adults. *Family Relations, 38,* 71–75.

Sangree, W. H. (1992). Grandparenthood and modernization: The changing status of male and female elders in Tiriki, Kenya, and Irigwe, Nigeria. *Journal of Cross-Cultural Gerontology, 7,* 331–361.

Schmidt, A., & Padilla, A. M. (1983). Grandparent–grandchild interaction in a Mexican American group. *Hispanic Journal of Behavioral Sciences, 5,* 181–198.

Schultz, N. W. (1980). A cognitive-developmental study of the grandchild–grandparent bond. *Child Study Journal, 10,* 7–26.

Shea, L. P. (1988). Grandparent–adolescent relationships as mediated by lineage and gender (Doctoral dissertation, Virginia Polytechnic Institute and State University, 1987) *Dissertation Abstracts International, 49,* 351-A.

Smith, M. S. (1991). An evolutionary perspective on grandparent–grandchild relationships. In P. K. Smith (Ed.), *The psychology of grandparenthood: An international perspective* (pp. 157–176). London: Routledge.

Smith, P. K. (1991). Introduction: The study of grandparenthood. In P. K. Smith (Ed.), *The psychology of grandparenthood: An international perspective* (pp. 1–16). London: Routledge.

Staples, R. (1952). Appreciations and dislikes regarding grandmothers as expressed by granddaughters. *Journal of Home Economics, 44,* 340–343.

Staples, R., & Smith, J. W. (1954). Attitudes of grandmothers and mothers toward child rearing practices. *Child Development, 25,* 91–97.

Stein, J. A., Newcomb, M. D., & Bentler, P. M. (1993). Differential effects of parent and grandparent drug use on behavior problems of male and female children. *Developmental Psychology, 29,* 31–43.

Stevens, J. H., Jr. (1984). Black grandmothers' and Black adolescent mothers' knowledge about parenting. *Developmental Psychology, 20,* 1017–1025.

Sticker, E. J. (1991). The importance of grandparenthood during the life cycle in Germany. In P. K. Smith (Ed.), *The psychology of grandparenthood: An international perspective* (pp. 32–49). London: Routledge.

Strauss, C. A. (1943). Grandma made Johnny delinquent. *American Journal of Orthopsychiatry, 13,* 343–347.

Strom, R., & Strom, S. (1989). Grandparents and learning. *International Journal of Aging and Human Development, 29,* 163–169.

Strom, R., & Strom, S. (1990). Raising expectations for grandparents: A three generational study. *International Journal of Aging and Human Development, 31,* 161–167.

Thomas, J. L. (1986). Age and sex differences in perceptions of grandparenting. *Journal of Gerontology, 41,* 417–423.

Thompson, R. A., Tinsley, B. R., Scalora, M. J., & Parke, R. D. (1989). Grandparents visitation rights: Legalizing the ties that bind. *American Psychologist, 44,* 1217–1222.

Timberlake, E. M., & Chipungu, S. S. (1992). Grandmotherhood: Contemporary meaning among African American middle-class grandmothers. *Social Work, 37,* 216–221.

Tinsley, B. J., & Parke, R. D. (1984). Grandparents as support and socialization agents. In M. Lewis (Ed.), *Beyond the dyad* (pp. 161–194). New York: Plenum.

Tinsley, B. J., & Parke, R. D. (1987). Grandparents as interactive and social support agents for families with young infants. *International Journal of Aging and Human Development, 25,* 259–277.

Tolson, T. J. F., & Wilson, M. N. (1990). The impact of two- and three-generational Black family structure on perceived family climate. *Child Development, 61,* 416–428.

Tomlin, A. M., & Passman, R. H. (1989). Grandmothers' responsibility in raising two-year-olds facilitates their grandchildren's adaptive behavior: A preliminary intrafamilial investigation of mothers' and maternal grandmothers' effects. *Psychology and Aging, 4,* 119–121.

Townsend, P. (1957). *The family life of old people.* London: Routledge & Kegan Paul.

Trivers, R. L. (1974). Parent-offspring conflict. *American Zoologist, 14,* 249–264.

Troll, L. E. (1985). The contingencies of grandparenting. In V. L. Bengtson & J. F. Robertson (Eds.), *Grandparenthood* (pp. 135–149). Beverly Hills, CA: Sage.

Turke, P. W. (1988). Helpers at the nest: Childcare networks on Ifaluk. In L. Betzig, M. Borgerhoff Mulder, & P. Turke (Eds.), *Human reproductive behavior: A Darwinian perspective* (pp. 173–188). Cambridge, England: Cambridge University Press.

Tyszkowa, M. (1991). The role of grandparents in the development of grandchildren as perceived by adolescents and young adults in Poland. In P. K. Smith (Ed.), *The psychology of grandparenthood: An international perspective* (pp. 50–67). London: Routledge.

Vermulst, A. A., de Brock, A. J. L. L., & van Zutphen, R. A. H. (1991). Transmission of parenting across generations. In P. K. Smith (Ed.), *The psychology of grandparenthood: An international perspective* (pp. 100–122). London: Routledge.

Vinovskis, M. A. (1987). Historical perspectives on the development of the family and parent–child interactions. In J. B. Lancaster, J. Altmann, A. S. Rossi, & L. R. Sherrod (Eds.), *Parenting across the life span: Biosocial dimensions* (pp. 295–312). New York: Aldine de Gruyter.

Vollmer, H. (1937). The grandmother: A problem in child rearing. *American Journal of Orthopsychiatry, 7,* 378–382.

Wakschlag, L., Chase-Lansdale, P. L., & Brooks-Gunn, J. (1993). *Not just "ghosts in the nursery": Contemporaneous intergenerational relationships and parenting in young African-American families.* Manuscript submitted for publication.

Wentowski, G. J. (1985). Older women's perceptions of great-grandmotherhood: A research note. *Gerontologist, 25,* 593–596.

Werner, E. E. (1991). Grandparent–grandchild relationships amongst U.S.A. ethnic groups. In P. K. Smith (Ed.), *The psychology of grandparenthood: An international perspective* (pp. 68–82). London: Routledge.

Wilks, C., & Melville, C. (1990). Grandparents in custody and access disputes. *Journal of Divorce, 13,* 1–14.

Williams, G. C. (1957). Pleitropy, natural selection, and the evolution of senescence. *Evolution, 11,* 32–39.

Wood, V. (1982, Winter). Grandparenthood: An ambiguous role. *Generations: Journal of the Western Gerontological Society,* 18–24.

5

Adolescent Parenthood

Jeanne Brooks-Gunn
Teachers College, Columbia University
P. Lindsay Chase-Lansdale
University of Chicago

INTRODUCTION

Teenage pregnancy and parenthood have always existed. However, they received little attention or comment in the United States until the last quarter of this century. In brief, the rapid rise in the number of younger adolescents having intercourse, in their birth rate, and in babies born to single teenage mothers have all contributed to concern about early parenthood (Brooks-Gunn & Furstenberg, 1989; Furstenberg, Brooks-Gunn, & Chase-Lansdale, 1989; Hayes, 1987; Hofferth & Hayes, 1987; Moore et al., 1993; Vinovskis, 1988). By the mid 1980s, three fourths of African-American and almost one half of White girls had had intercourse by age 18. About four out of five girls and boys have had intercourse before they turn 20 (Moore, Nord, & Peterson, 1989; Sonenstein, Pleck, & Ku, 1989). Sexual intercourse is also becoming increasingly common earlier in adolescence (Brooks-Gunn & Paikoff, 1993).

Given irregular contraceptive use by boys and girls, many teenage girls become pregnant. For example, in 1984, 41 percent of African-American girls and 19 percent of White girls became pregnant by the age of 18 (Moore, 1985). Although adolescent males report using condoms more frequently today than a decade ago (a response in part to concerns about HIV and AIDS; Brooks-Gunn & Furstenberg, 1990; Sonenstein et al., 1989), most boys and girls do not use contraceptives each time they have intercourse. Unprotected sexual intercourse, then, is common.

It comes as no surprise that about one fourth of all girls become pregnant during their adolescent years (by the end of the 19th year; Hayes, 1987; Moore et al., 1993). Almost half of the teenage pregnancies are terminated voluntarily (Petchesky, 1984; U.S. Bureau of Census, 1988). Even so, in 1988, one fourth of African-American females had a first birth by 18.2 years, one fourth of Hispanic-American girls by 19.6 years, and one fourth of White girls by 22.1 years.

The situation is quite different in other countries. The United States has the highest teenage pregnancy rate of all of the Western countries. At the same time the rates of sexual activity are quite similar across nations (Jones et al., 1985; Jones, Forrest, Henshaw, Silverman, & Torres, 1988). The disparity in teenage birth rates between the United States and other Western nations is largely due to patterns of contraceptive use. Adolescents in Western Europe receive more information about sexuality and the practice of safe sex, have more access to contraceptives, and see public health campaigns promoting use of contraceptives. More generally, urging teenagers to practice safe sex is accepted by the public, and factious debates about the role of families and societal institutions (school, media) in controlling adolescent sexuality or in aiding adolescents manage sexuality are not part of the political landscape as they are in the United States (Brooks-Gunn & Paikoff, 1993; Jones et al., 1988).

Of those girls who carry their babies to term, the majority are not married (66 percent in 1987): 92 percent of births to African-American teenagers and 54 percent of births to White teenagers were out of wedlock (Furstenberg, 1991; these percentages being even higher for teenage mothers 17 years of age and younger; Moore, Simms, & Betsey, 1986; National Center for Health Statistics, 1988). Correspondingly, the number of teenage girls who are married by the age of 19 has dropped precipitously, from 40 percent in 1960 to 15 percent in 1986 (U.S. Bureau of Census, 1987). These trends continue through the 1990s. Childbearing outside the context of marriage has become normative for the teenage mother, just as has sexual intercourse. Never-married single parenthood also has become more common across the reproductive years. In 1990, 28 percent of all births were to unmarried women (Hernandez, 1993; U.S. Bureau of Census, 1991).

The increased concern about early parenthood is due to the changed context in which it occurs. Today, teenage parenthood is almost synonymous with single parenthood. Teenage mothers are disproportionately represented on welfare rolls and as high school dropouts. Policies and programs have been developed to prevent the number of teenage births as well as to provide services to young mothers and their children. The declining age of intercourse, the increasing rate of out-of-wedlock births, and the disappearance of teenage marriage mean that the young parent finds herself in a different situation today than previously (Mott & Maxwell, 1981). Additionally, she is able to stay in school today (pregnancy meant certain dismissal from high school a quarter of a century ago).

The vast majority of teenage pregnancies are unplanned (Zelnik & Kantner, 1980). The decision to continue a pregnancy is associated with school plans and aspirations, academic standing, perceptions of family support, number of friends who are already parents, religiosity, and attitudes toward abortion (Eisen, Zellman, Leibowitz, Chow, & Evans, 1983; Fox, 1982; Furstenberg et al., 1989; Hofferth & Hayes, 1987; Ooms, 1981; Zelnik, Kantner, & Ford, 1981). Little is known about the male role in the girl's decision to continue a pregnancy (Elster & Lamb, 1986).

Typically, teenage girls do not have educational or job skills making it difficult to be financially independent. In addition, because so few marry and their male partners, even though typically a few years older, also are not in positions to be self-supporting, teenage mothers turn to family for help, shelter, and child care. This is true whether or not a girl receives welfare supplements (Furstenberg & Crawford, 1978; Kellam, Adams, Brown, & Ensminger, 1982; Ooms, 1981). Coresidence with parents enables many teenagers to finish high school and obtain child care. Indeed, African-American females are more likely to complete high school after becoming mothers than are Whites, perhaps because of help from families and lower marriage rates (Marsiglio & Mott, 1986). However, a large proportion of teenage mothers do not complete high school. Mothers who live with their families for several years after the birth are more likely to complete high school than mothers who do not. These outcomes affect ultimate economic self-sufficiency throughout the life course (Brooks-Gunn & Furstenberg, 1986; Furstenberg, Brooks-Gunn, & Morgan, 1987).

We emphasize the importance of such contextual features of teenage parenthood throughout this chapter, as we stress the importance of developmental issues. Not only does the teenage parent face a number of developmental challenges, but so do her family members (Chase-Landsdale, Brooks-Gunn, & Paikoff, 1991). Our focus is on the offspring of the teenage mother as well as the teenage mother's family, specifically the kin involved in child care. Literature on the father of the child is not reviewed extensively, because the family system in which the teenage mother of today lives is her family of origin. Twenty years ago more attention would have been paid to the father, because so many teenage mothers got married; the lack of attention to the father, or, more accurately, the low attachment of teenage fathers to their children in many families with single teenage parents is addressed elsewhere (see Chase-Lansdale & Vinovskis, in press-b; Furstenberg et al., 1989; Furstenberg & Harris, 1989; Parke & Neville, 1987; Sullivan, 1990).

The chapter is organized around themes central to understanding adolescent parenthood. The concept of timing of transitions (in this case the timing of adolescent parenthood) is the organizing feature of much of the work on this topic. As it is so relevant to a developmental perspective, we first present a brief discussion of this concept. Next, we turn to the more specific conceptual frameworks that have been invoked when describing the effects of teenage parenthood upon various family members. Then, the life course of the teenage mother is reviewed from two perspectives—the consequences of adolescent parenthood for the young mother vis-à-vis work, education, and family, as well as the psychological response to becoming a mother. The life course of the children of teenage mothers is discussed next. The impact of the birth of a child upon the adolescent's family is reviewed, with a focus on the female kin who often participate in child care and who coparent. The chapter concludes with a brief discussion of policy implications of these findings.

ADOLESCENT PARENTHOOD AS A DEVELOPMENTAL TRANSITION

Timing is a feature of all role transitions; one that has been studied extensively is parenthood. Sociologists have distinguished individual, family, and historical time: (1) individual time refers to each family member's life course; (2) family time connotes the interweaving of individual members' life courses; and (3) historical time suggests the timing patterns in a societal and historical context (Elder, 1977; Hagestad, 1986; Hareven, 1977). Adolescent parenthood is defined as off-time or early today, even though in earlier historical epochs girls married and became mothers as teenagers. In part, the rise in age of childbearing is due to lower fertility and infant mortality rates as well as higher rates of employment and high school graduation by women (Modell, Furstenberg, & Hershberg, 1976). First-time parenthood has been extended in timing to the middle 30s and 40s, so that variability is quite great.

However, it is important to remember that, even within a society, subgroups may perceive timing norms quite differently: Teenage parenthood is much more common in neighborhoods characterized by poverty, high rates of unemployment, and low rates of college attendance (Brooks-Gunn, Duncan, Klebanov, & Sealand, 1993; Crane, 1991). Consequently, characterizations of teenage parenthood as being early or off-time may be less true in contexts in which a relatively large proportion of individuals are becoming mothers at a young age. Without making any casual attributions among these factors, it is true that girls in such neighborhoods not only know more peers who are mothers but give a lower age at which they could themselves become mothers (Furstenberg, Levine, & Brooks-Gunn, 1990).

The three timing dimensions are not always in synchrony. Individual timing of transitions must be considered in light of the life-course decisions of other family members as well as the family as a whole. To complicate matters further, each individual has multiple roles within the family, making the timing of transitions in each relevant. Therefore, the timing of high school graduation and entrance into the work force may be influenced by becoming a teenage mother, and they also are affected by the other family members' life-course trajectories. If the teenager's mother is in the work force and not near retirement, her ability to help the teenager with child care in order to encourage high school completion may be hampered. If the teenager's mother is elderly and not well, child care may be more difficult (anecdotal evidence from multigenerational studies of young mothers, grandmothers, and toddlers show that grandmothers with arthritis or sore backs find it quite uncomfortable to move the toddler around or feel that they could no longer care for the child given his or her weight; Chase-Lansdale, Brooks-Gunn, & Zamsky, 1994). If a grandmother has young children (her own or other grandchildren) in the household, child care may be shared among adult relatives; however, if the grandmother is the sole caregiver, an additional grandchild may be a burden. Clearly, the timing of transitions around the family members needs to be considered.

An interesting new line of research has emerged that conceptualizes timing somewhat differently from what has been discussed here. Geronimus (1987; Geronimus & Bound, 1990) suggested that early childbearing may not be disadvantageous for health outcomes for poor African-American young women. Her thesis is based on the fact that, because of poverty and discrimination, African Americans are likely to have increased rates of morbidity and mortality at earlier ages than are Whites. Termed the "weathering hypothesis," Geronimus provided evidence for a number of illnesses. She then went on to argue that early childbearing may be advantageous; her arguments are based on health outcomes of babies born to teenage mothers being no different from those born to older mothers (or even better). Literature does suggest few adverse effects and possible positive effects of early motherhood on neonatal health if prenatal care is obtained (Baldwin & Cain, 1980; McCarthy & Hardy, 1993). In an extension of this work, Geronimus and Korenman (1992) went on to argue that early childbearing also has fewer economic and social consequences for African Americans than the current literature would indicate. They are conducting work comparing sisters who do and do not become adolescent mothers, arguing that within-family designs control much better for selection factors than across-family, cross-sectional studies. Analyses based on such a design reduce the differences in outcomes between teenage mothers and their relatives who delayed childbearing, but do not eliminate them (Analyses of the Panel Study of Income Dynamics [PSID] and National Longitudinal Study of Youth [NLSY]; Hoffman, Foster, & Furstenberg, 1993; Moore et al., 1993).

FRAMEWORKS USED IN THE STUDY OF ADOLESCENT PARENTHOOD

Research focusing on adolescent parenthood appears in several separate lines of inquiry. The major thematic thrusts include the following. One line defines the transition into parenthood as a normative life challenge. The role changes that accompany parenthood, including the psychological preparation for parenthood, the realignment of relationships with one's own parents and spouse (or boyfriend), the negotiation of child-care responsibilities within the family, and the possible redefinition of one's identity (including motherhood into one's identity), are all aspects of the transition to parenthood (Belsky, 1984; Cowan & Cowan, 1992; Deutsch, Ruble, Fleming, Brooks-Gunn, & Stangor 1988; Parke, 1988; Ruble, Fleming, Hackel, & Stangor, 1988). Interestingly, research focusing on teenage parents does not use transition frameworks very often. We review research on psychological adaptation to motherhood, and attempt to link this tradition with what is known about teenage parenthood.

A second and perhaps the most well-known approach to understanding teenage parenthood does not focus on parenting explicitly, but on the consequences of early parenthood upon the mother herself. This approach is not psychologically driven, nor does it consider the meaning of parenthood or relational realignments of parenthood. Instead, the life course of teenage mothers is explored from a sociological and demographic viewpoint. Life-course transitions are of interest, of course, but not from a psychological perspective, or from a developmental viewpoint (i.e., the competing developmental demands of adolescence and parenthood are not studied, nor is parenthood in the context of the particular life stage in which it occurs).

A third body of work takes the life-course perspective as its starting point and incorporates a more family-oriented approach to the study of young parents. The effects of early parenthood upon the offspring as well as the parents of young mothers are studied. Interest in the intersection of lives has led to a consideration of how young mothers' life decisions and situations unfold in the lives of their own children. The linking of lives within families is a major contribution of the teenage parenthood literature to developmental theory more generally (Chase-Lansdale & Brooks-Gunn, 1994).

Direct observation of the parenting behavior of young mothers has been a response to the belief that the offspring of adolescent mothers on the average fare more poorly than the offspring of older mothers. This research tradition borrows directly from the research on parenting behavior and mother–child interaction during the infancy and preschool years. It focuses on the socialization practices of young mothers, in the traditions described by Maccoby and Martin (1983). However, it is rather static in that longitudinal work is rare, comparisons with samples of older mothers who are from the same social and economic background are not always made, within-group analyses are not conducted to unveil the mechanisms underlying adequate or poor parenting practices, contextually detailed observations are not included, and the complexity of family life for young mothers and their children is not acknowledged (Chase-Landsdale, Brooks-Gunn, & Paikoff, 1991).

An even more finely detailed family-oriented approach is emerging in the study of young mothers. So-called family systems approaches are focusing on effects of young parenthood not only on individual family members but on the family as a whole (Chase-Lansdale et al., in press). The formation of multigenerational households for the care of the young mother and her offspring is one impetus for this line of research.

Research using these five frameworks is reviewed in this chapter. All five not only have heuristic value, but describe somewhat different aspects of the experiences of teenage mothers and their families.

THE LIFE COURSE OF ADOLESCENT MOTHERS

Effects of Adolescent Parenthood upon Work and Family Trajectories

The life course of adolescent mothers has been described in great detail, with much of this excellent work coming from sociological and demographical approaches (Bachrach & Carver, 1992; Baldwin, 1993; Baldwin & Cain, 1980; Hofferth, 1987). We know about adolescent mothers' eventual marital, fertility, work, education, and living situations (Furstenberg et al., 1987; Hayes, 1987; Miller & Moore, 1990). Studies have either included appropriate comparison groups or have charted developmental courses within samples of teenage mothers. A few studies now look at the life courses of teenage mothers and their sisters who did not become teenage mothers in an effort to control for a variety of familial factors correlated with young motherhood (Geronimous, 1991; Geronimus & Korenman, 1992; Hoffman, Foster, & Furstenberg, 1993). A less well-developed literature exists on the educational and work lives of young fathers (Marsiglio, 1986).

To give a face to teenage mothers, three examples of the educational, work, and family lives over a 17-year period are presented. These are taken from the Baltimore Study of Teenage Motherhood. Over 300 primarily low-income African-American families have been followed for almost 20 years. The three case histories are taken from the book *Adolescent Mothers in Later Life* (Furstenberg et al., 1987).

The first woman, whom we shall call Doris, was 34 at the time of the interview. In many respects she resembles the popular stereotype of a teenage mother. Doris was unmarried and a school dropout when she became pregnant in 1966 at the age of 16. She went on welfare immediately and continued to receive public assistance for the next 17 years, even during the period of her brief marriage, which lasted for only 3 years. Doris had three children by three different men, none of whom was her husband. She had been employed periodically but never for more than a few years at a time and never yielding enough income to lift her off the welfare rolls. During her late twenties, she had a lengthy relationship with Harris, who fathered her third child. But in 1980, Harris left the household, and Doris has been living alone with her three children, and her grandchild, the 2-year-old son of Dalia, Doris's second oldest child. By the end of this chapter, we will know how many women in our sample resemble Doris.

Other Baltimore mothers may be more like Iris. Iris became pregnant at 16 and waited to marry the baby's father until finishing high school, the year after her child was born. Her marriage lasted about 10 years, during which time she had a second child. Except for the period right after her children were born, Iris has always worked. After her marriage broke up, she received public assistance for 2 years; she began a new relationship with a man named Lester, which was brief. When it dissolved, Iris moved in with her mother for a year as an alternative to going back on welfare. As soon as she could afford it, she moved out and is now living with her two children as a single parent. For the past 5 years, Iris has been steadily employed as a business administrator for the Baltimore School District.

Iris has managed reasonably well with the occasional assistance of her family and supportive services from the government. Her best financial years were when she was married and working at the same time. But most of her adult life, she has been economically hard pressed, relying primarily on her own income to support her children.

Helena's life history is different still. At her parents' insistence, Helena delayed her marriage to Nelson, the father of her child, until she had completed her schooling and had a secure job. She and Nelson were married in 1971 around her 20th birthday. They have been married continuously for nearly 14 years. During most of this period, both Helena and Nelson have been steadily employed. They now live in a comfortable garden apartment on the outskirts of Baltimore with their two children.

These three case histories, though unique in some sense, were selected to represent prototypes of varying adaptations to early childbearing. Despite efforts to find employment and settle into a stable relationship, Doris has not managed to achieve domestic or economic security. Iris has done somewhat better though she, too, has struggled to maintain economic independence and has barely scraped by as a single mother for the past 5 years. Both would envy Helena's marital and economic career, which since her early twenties has been progressively secure and stable. (pp. 23–25)

Comparisons with Older Mothers

In general, the life course of teenage mothers looks different from age-mates who do not become mothers early. The former are less likely to complete high school and to go on the postsecondary education, to marry, to avoid welfare, to be employed, to be stably employed, to earn other than minimum-wage incomes, and if married, to avoid divorce. Of utmost concern from a policy perspective is that, if girls leave school before or just after becoming mothers, their chances of completing high school are reduced (Upchurch & McCarthy, 1990). In contrast, young mothers who stay in school are more likely to finish high school (these trends are most pronounced for those youngsters who have not failed a grade). Special school programs have been started throughout the United States for pregnant teenagers; the existence of such services in part may explain the relatively high rates of high school completion for girls who are "on track" academically at the time of the pregnancy. Of interest from a two-generational perspective are those programs that offer child care and parenting classes, given that child care is one of the unmet needs for many young mothers (Cherlin, in press; Clewell, Brooks-Gunn, & Benasich, 1989; Seitz, Apfel, & Rosenbaum, in press; Wilson, Ellwood, & Brooks-Gunn, in press).

Context and Selection

These negative consequences of early parenthood are due to multiple factors. Teenage mothers are unable to afford child care and have difficulty locating child care, given their low earning power (similar to other poor mothers). Additionally, the Family Support Act of 1988 requires that young mothers stay in school, so that income cannot be earned (even if low-paying jobs were available; Chase-Lansdale, Brooks-Gunn, & Paikoff, 1994; Chase-Landsdale & Vinovskis, 1992). Child care is typically provided by relatives, so that the young mother is dependent on her family for support; other family members also work, so that child care is often comprised of makeshift arrangements (Cherlin, in press). Juggling child care, education, work, and leisure is difficult for all mothers. But teenage mothers may have special problems, given their low education, poor earning ability, and reliance on others for support. Problems are compounded if young mothers have more children (Hayes, 1987). Not all studies find teenage mothers to have more children than older childbearers from the same educational, economic, and racial strata. However, teenage mothers may be more likely to have their children more closely spaced. Having more than one child while still a teenager is a major risk factor for eventual economic dependency (Furstenberg et al., 1987).

An additional point needs to be made vis-à-vis the factors that place a teenager at risk for becoming a mother. Living in a poor neighborhood, attending low-quality schools, residing in a family where the parents have low education and are poor, school failure, low aspirations—all are associated with teenage parenthood (Furstenberg et al., 1989; Hayes, 1987; Miller & Moore, 1990). These so-called contextual precursors do not disappear after the birth of a child, but continue, further exacerbating the trends away from self-sufficiency. Research suggests that these factors explain much of the deleterious effects of teenage motherhood upon subsequent life course, but being a young mother in and of itself seems to influence later experiences as well (although research often cannot totally separate selection effects based on background variables from effects of young parenthood; Bachrach, Clogg, & Carver, 1993; Chase-Lansdale, Brooks-Gunn, & Paikoff, 1991; Miller, 1992, 1993).

Another selection factor has to do with being a single mother. There is a nearly universal link between teenage motherhood and single motherhood for African Americans and the strong link for Whites. Recently, Astone (1993) looked at the amount of variance in household income in the 5 years following the birth of a child that can be accounted for by single motherhood, as opposed to teenage motherhood (using the PSID national data set; Hill, 1992). Single motherhood is highly predictive of low subsequent family incomes, but it does not totally explain differences between women who give birth in their teenage years and those who give birth in their 20s. At the same time, both groups look more disadvantaged than those mothers who delay childbearing until the mid-20s. Astone questioned the usefulness of distinguishing between childbearing in the teenage years and in the early adult years vis-à-vis income (even though she acknowledged the possibility of parenting or psychological differences between these two groups).

Delaying childbirth until age 25 or later is associated with higher family incomes for Whites, but not for African Americans. These findings suggest that delayed childbirth may not confer as many benefits to African-American women, a thesis put forth by Geronimus and colleagues (Geronimus & Korenman, 1992), and debated by Hoffman and colleagues (1993) and Moore and colleagues (1993).

Moore and her colleagues (1993) also presented analyses relevant to the issue of selection (see Bachrach et al., 1993; Baldwin, 1993). Using the National Longitudinal Study of Youth (NLSY; Center for Human Resource Research, 1988; see Brooks-Gunn, Phelps, & Elder, 1991; Chase-Lansdale, Brooks-Gunn, & Paikoff, 1991, for a brief discussion of the national data sets), these authors considered the effect of age at first birth on income at age 27, finding effects for three ethnic/race groups—Whites, African Americans, and Hispanic Americans. The authors were interested in seeing how early childbearing might influence subsequent income, specifically poverty. Factors differed by ethnic group. For African Americans (for whom the age of birth effect was the weakest), the only mediator was number of children born before age 27. For Whites, timing of marriage, family size and employment/earnings mediated the link between age at first birth and income at age 27 (Moore et al., 1993). Astone (1993) also reported that marriage (specifically current marital status) is an important predictor of family income for Whites but not for African Americans.

Both of these analyses present a new trend in the literature on early childbearing, in that they go beyond documenting ill effects on subsequent well-being (in this case defined by income) and document the pathways through which teenage parenthood may exert effects on employment and school completion. A complementary approach involves separating the effects of high school dropout and teenage parenthood. It has been assumed that the major reason for girls' dropping out of school is pregnancy (Ekstrom, Goertz, Pollack, & Rock, 1986). Teenage childbearing is clearly and strongly associated with reduced schooling (Furstenberg, 1976; Hofferth & Hayes, 1987; Upchurch & McCarthy, 1989), but how the two interrelate is open to question (Hofferth, 1984; Upchurch & McCarthy, 1990). Using a transitions framework that focuses on the timing and sequencing of events occurring in early adulthood (Hogan & Astone, 1986), with NLSY data, Upchurch (1993) compared groups of teenage girls with respect to the timing of high school dropout and teenage parenthood. Not surprisingly, the young women who dropped out of school, became mothers, or both, came from more impoverished backgrounds than adolescents who did neither. Teenage mothers who do not drop out of school come from less disadvantaged families than those young mothers who drop out of school or those young women who drop out of school. The teenage mother high school graduates are disadvantaged vis-à-vis their family background relative to high school graduates who are not mothers. They also are less likely to go on for postsecondary schooling (generally, models need to look at the predictors of high school graduation and postsecondary schooling separately; Brooks-Gunn, Guo, & Furstenberg, 1993; Haveman, Wolfe, & Spaulding, 1991; Mare, 1980). This line of research uses a more detailed framework for looking at teenage mothers (timing and sequencing framework), considers possible selection factors (in this case, an examination of the backgrounds from which the different groups come), highlights the variability of outcomes, and argues for more contextually based research (see Brooks-Gunn, Duncan et al., 1993, for a discussion of the effects of neighborhood residence on teenage motherhood and high school dropout).

Predictors of Long-Term Outcomes

A final line of work focuses on long-term outcomes, taking a within-group perspective, rather than the across-group comparisons just reviewed. Long-term follow-ups suggest that teenage mothers continue to do less well in the employment and educational realm as they enter middle age. However, one of the surprising results of follow-up studies is the diversity in outcomes of teenage mothers. The findings from the Baltimore Study of Teenage Motherhood are illustrative. Similar findings are reported from a long-range study of New Haven teenage mothers (Horwitz, Klerman, Kuo, & Jekel, 1991).

The Baltimore and New Haven studies only address the long-term trajectories of African-American families (White girls were included in the Baltimore Study, but the sample was too small to analyze). Additionally, both studies focus on urban families in the Northeast. Rates of teenage parenthood are also high in other regions of the country. A lack of information about teenage parenthood in the context of rural poverty is notable. Both the Baltimore and New Haven studies would have benefited from more psychologically oriented measures. For example, information on self-efficacy, depressive affect, cognitive test scores, and coping strategies all would further our understanding of the life courses of teenage mothers.

Many of the young women continued to make efforts to improve their life options in both studies. In Baltimore, for example, many continued their schooling through the 17 years following the birth of the child. About one third had completed high school (of those who had not completed it earlier), and almost one third had received some postsecondary schooling. Many more were in the work force than might have been anticipated, given results from shorter term studies. About three fourths were working in 1983–1984, when the 17-year follow-up was conducted. And only one fourth were on welfare. In terms of fertility, the Baltimore Study mothers had on average a little over two children, similar to samples of older childbearers. Spacing and number of children were highly predictive of later success. This sample differs from more recent samples in that many were married at the time of the birth or within the first year after their child was born. However, the majority of these marriages did not last (only one fourth were still married). Only 16 percent of the first-born children were living with their father in 1983–1984 (Furstenberg et al., 1987).

What factors predicted positive outcomes for teenage mothers? Positive outcomes were defined as family annual income of $25,000 or more, no receipt of welfare in the last year, and having less than three children. The most potent influences involved the educational experience—being on grade level at the time of the pregnancy, having parents with more education (more than 10th grade), attending a special school for pregnant youngsters in Baltimore, and having high aspirations at the time of the birth. All of these were net of one another and a host of other factors. Other significant predictors included finishing high school within 4–5 years of the birth of the first child, limiting subsequent childbearing, and growing up in a family that did not receive welfare. Another factor promoting economic well-being was continuing in an early marriage. However, marriage might be considered a risky strategy for ensuring later success, in that so many of these marriages did not last. Mothers who got married early were less likely to complete their schooling, leaving those divorced mothers in a particularly bad situation vis-à-vis the job market (Brooks-Gunn & Chase-Lansdale, 1991; Brooks-Gunn & Furstenberg, 1987).

DEVELOPMENTAL ISSUES AND THE TRANSITION TO MOTHERHOOD

The birth of a first child, a major period of transition in the life of a woman, is marked by dramatic changes in self-related information seeking, self-definitions, and roles (Belsky, 1984; Cowan & Cowan, 1992; Deutsch et al., 1988). It also may herald alterations in adjustment, as inferred through postpartum increases in depressive affect, psychiatric illness, and marriage difficulties (Belsky, 1984; Hopkins, Marcus, & Campbell, 1984; Kumar, Robson, & Smith, 1984; Ruble et al., 1988). Antecedents of postpartum adjustment, such as the mental health of the mother, satisfaction with the motherhood role, and actual parenting behavior, are beginning to be studied as are the consequences of women's attitudes, self-definitions, and adjustment vis-à-vis parenting behaviors and relationships (Belsky, 1984; Cowan & Cowan, 1988, 1992; Feldman & Nash, 1984; Parke, 1988).

This literature does not focus on mothers who are young (i.e., teenagers), living without a partner, or from backgrounds other than the middle class. However, the approaches used to explain the transition to motherhood in the so-called "traditional" family may provide insights into how this transition is experienced in other family structures and by other ethnic groups. Here we consider the applicability of four research traditions on the transition to motherhood for teenage mothers: (1) intrapsychic, (2) self-definitional, (3) coping and stressful life events, and (4) adaptation to life changes framework.

Intrapsychic Perspectives on Becoming a Mother

Intrapsychically oriented models focus on adjustment to becoming a mother. They often stress that role definitions occur through identification with significant others—in the case of motherhood, typically identification with the pregnant woman's own mother. Indeed, positive relationships with one's mother are associated with self-confidence and perceived positive mothering characteristics in pregnant women. These associations are *not* due to self-esteem, information seeking, relationship with husband, and other factors (Deutsch et al., 1988). Frequency of maternal contact (both emotional support and physical sharing of child care) may also predict a sense of maternal competence (Abernathy, 1973).

In the case of the adolescent parent, her relationship with her mother may assume an even greater importance than for older mothers. There are several reasons for this conjecture. First, adolescent girls are more likely than older women to be redefining their relationships with their mothers (Blos, 1967; Brooks-Gunn & Zahaykevich, 1989; Grotevant & Cooper, 1984; Hauser, Borman, Powers, Jacobson, & Noam, 1990; Osofsky, Hann, & Peebles, 1993). This process not only takes several years but may be truncated by an early pregnancy in that the adolescent may have to reinterpret what separation from the mother means. She is, on the one hand, dependent on her mother for financial resources (teenage mothers typically do not have the resources to move out of their family's home). On the other hand, she is individuated from the mother in that her actions have created a new and separate human being. Her struggles with autonomy may render the maternal relationship more salient, although not necessarily more conflict-free.

Second, the adolescent girl may become reliant on the mother for information about parenthood, especially if few of her friends have become pregnant, if school dropout narrows her circle of friends, and if, like many women (young and old alike), she does not receive much information about pregnancy from doctors and other health professionals. In older White middle-class women, reading material is the primary source of pregnancy and parenthood information (Deutsch et al., 1988). The teenage mother is very likely to have been a poorer student than an older mother (Furstenberg et al., 1989; Hofferth & Hayes, 1987; Moore et al., 1993), making it likely that she will not turn to books readily.

Third, the adolescent girl may be less likely to have a male figure available for emotional support than are older women (Furstenberg et al., 1987). Recent studies suggest that for some adolescent mothers, boyfriends are perceived to provide emotional support, which is related to positive adaptation (it is unclear whether this association is due to actual male support or only to perceptions). Additionally, in larger families, child care by older siblings, especially sisters, may still be commonplace (Burton & Bengston, 1985). Finally, even in the United States earlier in this century and in the last century, when childbearing was much longer, families often included young children and older adolescents and experience with caregiving by teenagers was probably frequent (Hareven, 1977; Modell & Goodman, 1990; Modell et al., 1976).

Finally, the adolescent's mother may be more emotionally involved in her young daughter's pregnancy. Because mothers often find the separation process difficult (as do their teenage daughters; Brooks-Gunn & Zahaykevich, 1989; Paikoff & Brooks-Gunn, 1991; Smetana, 1988), the pregnant adolescent's mother may be preparing to become a mother of a young child again, in that she expects to take care of the new child, or at least to take a major role in caregiving (Burton, 1990). Given that a majority of teenage mothers live with their mothers in the first years after the birth, these expectations may be quite realistic (Hernandez, 1993).

Other intrapsychically oriented approaches have focused on constructs such as ego strength and maturity, both of which are associated with responsivity and reciprocity directed toward infants in middle-class mothers (Brunnquell, Crichton, & Egeland, 1981; Cowan & Cowan, 1992; Feldman & Nash, 1984). Teenage mothers are believed to have lower levels of ego strength and to be less mature socially and emotionally due to the necessity of negotiating the developmental tasks of adolescence (Hamburg, 1980, 1986). However, few studies have directly tested this hypothesis (Brooks-Gunn & Furstenberg, 1986). Early case studies tended to report difficulties in psychoanalytic terms (teenage pregnancies represent "hysterical disassociation states," Kasanin & Handschin, 1941; "object losses," Greenberg, Loesch, & Lakin, 1959; "passive dependencies," Barglow, Bornstein, Exum, Wright, & Visotsky, 1968). However, little verification exists in the developmental literature (Brooks-Gunn & Furstenberg, 1986).

Lack of maturity may be inferred from indicators of self-orientation during pregnancy. In middle-class married samples, women who are preoccupied with themselves, as measured by physical and sexual concerns, seem to show less effective parenting patterns in the postpartum year (Grossman et al., 1980). Directed inward, these mothers may not be especially sensitive to their children's needs (Cowan & Cowan, 1992). Whether this would be more true of teenage mothers than older mothers is not known, although it is plausible given the former's lower scores of many measures of maturity (see study by Osofsky et al., 1993, reporting more identity diffusion for teenage than older childbearers).

Another possible intrapsychic construct has been identified by Boyce, Schaefer, and Uitti (1985) who suggested that adjustment generally, and specifically as linked to social support, may be influenced by a sense of stability and permanence, the "belief or perception that certain central, valued elements of life experience are stable and enduring" (p. 1281). Included in the construct are "an awareness of the self as consistent, of relationships as stable, of places as special referent points, of routines as predictable, and of universal order" (p. 1282). Perceived social support in a small sample of teenage girls who were pregnant was associated with high levels of permanence. Interestingly, both social support and a sense of permanence were related to birth outcomes (as determined by medical records) as well as maternal positive affect (as determined by self-report). The authors speculate that a sense of permanence may influence the effects of social support and stress upon adaptation to early parenthood. Whether a sense of permanence is more likely in older than younger childbearers is not known.

Social and intrapsychic constructs may interact with cognitive competence. Research suggests that cognitive complexity increases during the adolescent years (Keating, 1990). By the middle of adolescence, however, cognitive skills are similar to those of young adults. At the same time, specific aspects of reasoning and social cognition might distinguish adolescents and young adults (Case, 1985; Keating, 1990). A relevant construct that might properly be considered social cognition is the Concepts of Development Questionnaire (CODQ), developed by Sameroff and colleagues (Gutierrez & Sameroff, 1990; Sameroff & Feil, 1985; Sameroff, Seifer, Barocas, Zax, & Greenspan, 1987). It conceptualizes beliefs about parenting in a four-stage sequence, ranging from fairly concrete and single-cause notions about parenting to more multicausal, reciprocal, and complex beliefs. More complex stages of reasoning are associated with better child outcomes, both higher intelligence test scores and lower behavior problems (Benasich & Brooks-Gunn, in press; Liaw & Brooks-Gunn, 1994; Sameroff et al., 1987; Sameroff, Seifer, Baldwin, & Baldwin, 1993). Teenage mothers may have less complex and multilevel beliefs about parenting, as recent analyses of a multisite study of over 800 mothers suggests (Benasich & Brooks-Gunn, in press). Another study using the CODQ did not focus on teenage mothers, but on children, adolescents, and young adults (Pratt, Hunsberger, Pancer, Roth, & Santolupo, 1993). In this small, nonrepresentative sample, adolescents had lower scores than young adults (i.e., less multicausal beliefs). The scores on the CODQ were associated with an integrative complexity score as well as a Piagetian task. Teenagers may have difficulty in conceptualizing parenthood as a complex, multifaceted task that involves reciprocal interactions with the child than adults. Such a stance toward parenting might explain, in part, the differences between younger and older mothers in actual parenting behavior.

Self-Definitional Approaches to Becoming a Mother

Cognitive-developmentalists argue that when important life changes occur individuals become motivated to examine and modify self-conceptions to fit the changing circumstances (e.g., Kohlberg, 1966; Ruble, 1983). For example, pregnancy has been described as "anticipatory parenthood" (Jessner, Weigert, & Fay, 1970), because at this time a sense of self as a mother seems to emerge (Ballou, 1978; Leifer, 1980). Pregnant women begin to visualize themselves as mothers, which is associated with postpartum adjustment and greater satisfaction with the mothering role (Oakley, 1980; Shereshefsky & Yarrow, 1973). Late pregnancy self-definitions as a mother are also associated with self-confidence as a mother and the perception of oneself as possessing mothering characteristics, both concurrently and several months postpartum (Deutsch et al., 1988).

Women also (1) actively seek information in anticipation of a first birth, (2) use this information to construct identities incorporating motherhood, and (3) seek more information as the event becomes closer (i.e., information seeking about labor is greatest in the second and third trimester, information about child care in the third trimester). Such information is a primary determinant of self-definitions of motherhood in primarily middle-class White women living with a male partner (Deutsch et al., 1988; Ruble, Brooks-Gunn, Fleming, Fitzmorris, Stangor, & Deutsch, 1990). It is unclear whether young mothers would as actively construct a self-definition of motherhood as do older mothers, given that the former are still constructing their self-definitions as independent and sexually mature women. Additionally, if information seeking about the pregnancy is more passive for young mothers (given the possible reliance on mothers' and friends' advice, rather than actively seeking out reading material or seeing health personnel), then their self-definitions may be less developed than that of older women. Because self-definitions in pregnancy are associated with subsequent satisfaction with mothering, and possibly with responsivity to the infant (Ruble et al., 1988), teenage mother's difficulty forming a maternal self-definition may be detrimental to her early childrearing experience. In turn, this difficulty in maternal self-definition may set the stage for future interactional difficulties, as has been found in some samples of teenage mothers who have been observed interacting with their young children (Field, 1980, 1982; McAnarney, Lawrence, Ricciuti, Polley, & Szilagyi, 1986; Osofsky et al., 1993; Sandler, Vietze, & O'Connor, 1981).

Maternal self-definitions are influenced by direct experience with children. These associations are more pronounced after the birth of the child; indeed, the basis of self-definition seems to shift from primarily indirect (outside the self) prenatally to primarily direct (experience with child care) postnatally, as one might expect (Deutsch et al., 1988). Teenage mothers, being children themselves, may not have had as much direct caregiving experience as older women, at least in the role of caregiver rather than occasional baby-sitter. In other cultures, caregiving by teenagers and prepubertal girls is common, and may act as a preparatory experience for the motherhood role (Whiting, 1981; Whiting & Edwards, 1988). In societies that require girls to go to school, this anticipatory training may be less likely to occur. Ethnographic studies of multigenerational households, particularly African-American families, report extensive sibling care as well (Burton, 1992; Jarrett, 1990). How frequently sibling care occurs in teenage mother-headed families is not known.

Characteristics of the child also influence parenting patterns and self-definitions (Bell, 1968; Belsky, 1984). For example, mothers who reported having temperamentally "easy" babies considered themselves better mothers than did mothers who reported having "difficult" babies (Deutsch et al., 1988). Having an easy baby, one perceived as being relatively happy, predictable, soothable, and sociable, may enhance a mother's feelings that she is an efficacious, good, and competent mother. It may also influence actual interactions with the child (see studies of mother–infant interaction and temperament with at-risk children for related findings; Brooks-Gunn & Lewis, 1984; Field, 1980). If teenage mothers have had little previous experience with infants (and thus little information with which to compare their baby's behavior), they may perceive them to be more difficult or be less aware of developmental milestones (Benasich & Brooks-Gunn, in press; de Lissovey, 1973; Field, 1981; Frodi, 1983; Osofsky, Eberhart-Wright, et al., 1992, 1993). At the same time, teenage mothers may be less skilled at handling a difficult baby (see studies on the problems that mothers have in modulating their interactions with low-birthweight babies; Field, 1980, 1982; Goldberg & DiVitto, in this *Handbook;* as well as work with teenage mothers; Hann, Castino, Jarosinski, & Britton, 1991; Hann, Robinson, Osofsky, & Little, 1991; Osofsky et al., 1993; Pope, Casey, Bradley, & Brooks-Gunn, 1993). Reasons for the lack of skill include teenage mothers' lack of experience, concern with other developmental issues, possible lack of a well-formed maternal self-definition, and sharing of child care with their own mothers (leading to less "experience" with their own child).

Finally, possible interactional difficulties or low maternal self-definitions may be exacerbated by any of several events that can co-occur with becoming a young mother; these would include having a low-birthweight or preterm infant, having a sick infant, becoming depressed during the pregnancy or after the birth, changing residence or school attendance patterns, or constricting one's social network. In a study of the transition to parenthood, the Cowans (1992) documented the difficulties that middle-class women (and men) in relatively stable relationships and with fairly good social networks have in managing the multiple events that co-occur with the birth of a child. Teenage mothers may not have a realistic idea of infant developmental progressions, in part because of their lack of caregiving experience and lowered information seeking. Some, but not all, studies find younger mothers to overestimate or underestimate their children's attainment of developmental milestones, as compared to older mothers (Benasich & Brooks-Gunn, in press; de Lissovey, 1973; Epstein, 1979; Field, 1981; Frodi, 1983). Teenage mothers may expect too little, too late in the areas of cognition and language, which is possibly related to the lower rates of vocalization seen in teenage mothers (Field, 1981; Osofsky & Osofsky, 1970; Sandler et al., 1981).

Adjustment to parenting, and the specific challenges of teenage parenthood, may be mediated by social support other than that provided by the mother. Perceived social support provided by the father of the child is quite important to teenager mothers (Colletta, 1981; Crnic, Greenberg, Ragozin, Robinson, & Basham, 1983; Crockenberg, 1987; Unger & Wandersman, 1985). Whether these effects are long term remains to be determined, especially because so many of the boyfriends of teenage mothers do not remain very involved in the rearing of their children, as measured by frequency of contact and support provided several years after the birth of the baby (Furstenberg et al., 1987;

Furstenberg & Harris, 1989). Unger and Wandersman made the important point that social support from the father of the baby or the girl's own mother may influence teenage mothers' behavior.

Coping Frameworks

Teenage motherhood as a crisis. How women manage crises and stressful life events and whether transitional events constitute a crisis are questions addressed using coping frameworks. Those who see pregnancy and childbirth as a crisis (e.g., Dyer, 1963; LeMasters, 1957) might hypothesize that pregnancy is more of a crisis for the younger than the older woman, as the former in all likelihood did not plan her pregnancy and was indeed quite surprised when it occurred (Brooks-Gunn & Furstenberg, 1989; Hofferth & Hayes, 1987; McCormick et al., 1987). However, there is little evidence that teenage pregnancy is perceived as a crisis, because the period of active upset is quite short (Crockenberg, 1987; Furstenberg, 1976). Having a child as a single mother does not seem to be met with universal community disapproval today as earlier (Furstenberg, 1976; see chapter by Kyu-taik Sung, 1992, for a description of the community sanctions on out-of-wedlock childbearing in Korea; the description is similar to what was reported in the United States 25 years ago.) Indeed, most family members, although acknowledging the difficulties inherent in having to rear a young infant, particularly in terms of juggling school, child care, work, and leisure activities, respond positively to the birth. (This research is focused on African-American families; it is presumed that family members greet the new baby positively in other ethnic groups as well.) In addition, responses at the time of the birth are not associated with later maternal or child outcomes (Furstenberg et al., 1987). However, very little information exists on possible factors that might increase the likelihood that a teenage pregnancy may be seen as a crisis (i.e., emotional state). Most studies to date have been more sociologically oriented, so that psychological evidence for early acceptance or emotional upset is sparse.

Teenage mothers have been found to be more depressed than older mothers in two studies conducted by Osofsky—the Topeka, Kansas and the New Orleans, Louisiana studies (Carter, Osofsky, & Hann, 1991; Hann, Robinson, et al., 1991; Osofsky & Eberhart-Wright, 1988). And, levels of depression and self-esteem were found to be associated with more behavior problems in the toddler period in the Topeka study (Osofsky, Culp, Eberhart-Wright, Ware, & Hann, 1988).

Anecdotal evidence from a study of teenage mothers in Newark, New Jersey suggests that many teenage mothers have very subdued affect and seem to have difficulty managing everyday tasks (Brooks-Gunn, Berlin, & Aber, 1993). It is not known whether these behaviors are indicative of depressive tendencies or the cumulative stress of being a mother, a teenager, and a poor person simultaneously. Depressed mood states and anxiety during pregnancy are associated with less effective parenting behavior in the year following the birth of a child in middle-class married samples (Feldman & Nash, 1985; Grossman et al., 1980; Ruble et al., 1988). Whether such associations would be found in teenage samples has not been tested, although we suspect that such links would be.

That most young mothers seem to accept an unplanned pregnancy (after a brief period of upset) may be explained by distinguishing between life crises and life changes (Stewart, Sokol, Healy, & Chester, 1986). Crises may be defined as "acute, short-term, and intense"; the period in which the young girl learns that she is pregnant and tells her family may be characterized in terms of a crisis model. For other crises, this period seems to be a time of increased risk for emotional problems (Klerman, 1974; Pearlin, 1975). After a crisis, individuals tend to return to their precrisis level of emotional functioning. Becoming a mother, then, might be conceptualized as a role transition, necessitating the changes in self-definitions and behaviors described earlier (Cowan & Cowan, 1992; Oakley, 1980) or as an event that heralds multiple stressors, given the requirement for changes in many aspects of life (Cohen & Lazarus, 1977). Much literature considers the possible negative effects of multiple stressors, including decrements in mental and physical health. These have been documented for the maternal transition in middle-class married samples (Oakley, 1980; Shereshefsy & Yarrow, 1973).

Stressors that the teenage mother often confronts include poverty and family mandates for early childbearing. First, stability and change in socioeconomic conditions are proposed mechanisms that set the stage for the type of socialization that occurs within the family and neighborhood (Featherman & Spenner, 1988). Exemplars exist in the research on the very disadvantaged (Wilson, 1987). In neighborhoods with persistent, concentrated poverty, such as many large inner cities, rates of unemployment for African-American teenage and young adult males have reached alarming proportions. This has co-occurred with early childbearing (although no causal links have been demonstrated for male unemployment and single parenthood; Jencks, 1988). However, if a community is characterized as (1) having few job opportunities, (2) providing little demonstrable evidence within a particular neighborhood that completing school will alter substantially one's life chances, and (3) perceiving out-of-wedlock childbearing as normative, then a form of implicit socialization for early parenthood may exist (Brooks-Gunn, Duncan, et al., 1993; Klebanov, Brooks-Gunn, & Duncan, 1994). In such a context, the transition to motherhood may not be very stressful, particularly if other changes do not co-occur with the child's birth. The fact that the vast majority of teenage mothers today do not marry, and most stay with their own mothers, might lessen the possibility of stress.

Second, family mandates also may exist for early childbearing, as Burton and Dilworth-Anderson (1991) suggested on the basis of a 3-year ethnographic investigation of families in a rural community and in a small city. Such mandates seem to "require" that teenage girls have babies in order to allow their mothers to parent. In these families, direct responsibility for parenting (at least in the last two generations) typically occurred when a woman became a grandmother. Child-care responsibility was given by the teenager to her mother with the expectation that her daughter would do the same for her (see Ward, 1986, for similar findings). At the same time, the teenage mother was expected to care for her grandmother as her own mother was busy with her child. As Burton (1992) suggested, teenage mothers in this community experienced stress because they were responsible for an elderly grandmother or for multiple generations rather than for their own young child.

In brief, teenage motherhood may be perceived as a crisis given that it is often unplanned and often requires family realignments. Teenage motherhood often signals changes in requests for help within the family. It often occurs in the context of persistent family poverty and/or neighborhood poverty; poverty in and of itself renders coping with everyday tasks difficult. Becoming a young mother in the context of poverty is likely to be stressful.

Teenage motherhood as a challenge.   More positive aspects of coping are emphasized in some approaches, such as that of Lazarus and Folkman (1984) who considered the ways in which life events may be seen as challenges. These challenges may be growth enhancing as well as restricting, given the situations in which they occur and the characteristics of the individual. Indeed, the great diversity seen in the outcomes of the teenage mothers in the Baltimore Study suggests that many young mothers manage to overcome the inherent difficulties of having a child while school, job, and male relationships are being sorted out. Clearly, some women manage to cope well with this challenge whereas others do not. Individual and environmental factors predict successful or unsuccessful adaptation, or, in the terminology of Lazarus and Folkman, how and in what circumstances the developmental challenge of early motherhood became growth enhancing (Furstenberg et al., 1987; Osofsky et al., in press). However, little research addresses the positive aspects of teenage parenthood.

Adaptation to Life Changes

Adaptation to life changes has been conceptualized as a sequence of emotional responses, with the work of Freud and Erikson providing the well-spring (Stewart, 1982; Stewart et al., 1986). Any change is hypothesized to induce a heightened state of awareness of the environment, which is both exciting and confusing. Four phases are hypothesized in an individual's response to life changes. In an effort to create meaning and understanding of a new set of circumstances, Stewart postulated that the sense of self is diminished, autonomy is reduced, and dependency feelings are enhanced in the first phase.

This receptive, dependent phase is gradually replaced by more autonomous functioning as the individual masters new aspects of the environment. The third phase is characterized by more assertion as the individual begins to take more initiative. The final phase is a more integrated one than the second or third, in that autonomous functioning is coupled with an understanding of roles and feelings of others. Life changes such as pregnancy may result in a temporary, possibly adaptive, dependency phase; an individual may need to be less active and efficacious while learning and observing what is expected and needed to interact successfully in a new situation. Stewart and her colleagues showed that new mothers go through a more dependent phase following the birth of a child. This is replaced with more autonomous functioning after several years, at least for those mothers who did not experienced multiple life events (such as illness or death of a relative, marital changes, work or residence changes) following the birth of the child. That is, the mothers who had other changes with which to cope were less able to progress to a more independent emotional stance (Stewart et al., 1986).

These findings have clear implications for understanding teenage mothers. The younger mother may be less likely to progress from a more dependent to a more autonomous emotional stance than older mothers. First, the teenage girl, prior to becoming pregnant, is experiencing a number of role and life changes (separation from the mother, formation of other intimate relationships, entrance into sexual relationships, etc.), making it likely that she is less mature than older mothers. Second, the advent of the birth of a child is likely to precipitate other changes in school, job, living arrangements, and male relationships. In all probability, a young mother will have experienced multiple life changes simultaneously. Research on adolescents who are not mothers suggests that the experience of multiple life events has deleterious effects on school achievement, peer relationships, and mental health (Brooks-Gunn, 1991; Brooks-Gunn & Petersen, 1991; Simmons & Blyth, 1987). The teenage mother is also likely to have experienced other events such as marital and school disruptions that are considered risky, and may contribute to poor outcomes in work and mental health vis-à-vis the pathways suggested by those who study cumulative risks in families (Brooks-Gunn, Klebanov, Liaw, & Duncan, 1994; Liaw & Brooks-Gunn, 1994; Sameroff et al., 1987, 1993). Future research needs to address how many teenage mothers reach more autonomous and integrated emotional phases, when this occurs, and what individual and environmental conditions facilitate this process (Chase-Landsdale, Wakschlag, & Brooks-Gunn, in press; Paikoff & Brooks-Gunn, 1991).

THE LIFE COURSE OF THE OFFSPRING OF ADOLESCENT MOTHERS

It is commonly presumed that early childbearing affects children adversely. Only a limited amount of evidence has been marshaled to demonstrate this seemingly obvious proposition, and almost all of this literature is confined to the period of infancy and early childhood (Baldwin & Cain, 1980; Brooks-Gunn & Furstenberg, 1986; Hofferth & Hayes, 1987; Osofsky et al., 1993).

In the first year or two of life, few differences are seen between infants born to teenage mothers and those born to older mothers. This is true for measures of cognitive development (*Bayley Scales of Development;* Coll, Vohr, Hoffman, & Oh, 1986) as well as for measures of social development (with secure attachment being studied most intensively; Benn & Saltz, 1989; Hann, Osofsky, Stringer, & Carter, 1988; Ward, Carlson, Plunkett, & Kessler, 1988). By the preschool years, small but consistent differences in cognitive functioning and psychosocial problems between offspring of early and later childbearers appear in preschool and continue into elementary school (Broman, 1981; Marecek, 1979, 1987). Such cognitive and psychosocial differences may set the stage for later school and social difficulties. By adolescence, school achievement among the offspring of teenage mothers is markedly lower and misbehavior, juvenile conduct disorders, and other school problems markedly higher (Brooks-Gunn & Furstenberg, 1986). For example, in the Baltimore Study of Teenage Motherhood, about one half of the adolescents of the teenage mothers had failed a grade, compared to about one in five from an appropriate comparison group from the National Study of Children

(Furstenberg et al., 1987; Furstenberg, Hughes, & Brooks-Gunn, 1992; see also Horwitz et al., 1991, for similar results in the New Haven study). Adolescent offspring of teenage mothers are also more likely to become teenage parents, as seen in the NLSY (Furstenberg et al., 1990).

The question still remains as to what factors account for these differences. Precise causal links between early childbearing and the well-being of children have not been well delineated especially if parenting goes well (Chase-Landsdale & Brooks-Gunn, 1994). Several factors may be operating, including the adverse social and economic effects associated with early parenthood, emotional immaturity associated with teenage motherhood, and/or less experienced and/or less adequate mothering by the young parent. The risks associated with becoming a teenage mother also operate later to affect the mother and her offspring. Living in poor families, as most of the offspring of teenage mothers do, affects children profoundly (Brooks-Gunn, in press-a; Brooks-Gunn, Klebanov, & Duncan, 1994; Chase-Lansdale, Brooks-Gunn, & Paikoff, 1991; Duncan, 1991; Huston, 1991; McLoyd, 1990; Parker, Greer, & Zuckerman, 1988). Residing in poor neighborhoods also exacts a toll on children and youth (Brooks-Gunn, Duncan et al., 1993; Duncan, Klebanov, & Brooks-Gunn, in press).

EFFECTS OF THE LIVES OF TEENAGE MOTHERS ON THEIR CHILDREN

Children's lives are influenced by the choices made by and the situations of their mothers. The Baltimore Study of Teenage Motherhood follows the tradition of Elder (1974) in *Children of the Great Depression* and Werner's (1982) study of the children of Kauai by looking at the intersection between the lives of mothers and their children. We found that characteristics of the teenage mothers' lives had large effects on their children's outcomes, as measured by low preschool readiness scores and behavior problems during the preschool years and grade retention, high school dropout, low literacy, early sexual intercourse, teenage parenthood, and behavior problems in the adolescent years. At each time period, maternal characteristics such as welfare receipt, low education, large family size, and single parenthood were associated with poorer child and adolescent outcomes (Baydar, Brooks-Gunn, & Furstenberg, 1993; Brooks-Gunn, Berlin, & Aber, 1993; Furstenberg et al., 1987, 1990, 1992).

Of more interest is the fact that the maternal characteristics were linked with the various indices of child success and failure somewhat differently as a function of age and outcome. Marital status was not predictive of preschool outcomes to any great extent, but was more important for adolescent outcomes, especially those concerned with sexuality and behavior problems. The presence of a father figure might be important in terms of supervision of girls, or support of the mother in the supervision of girls, during the transition to sexual maturity. The birth of additional children was more important for preschool than adolescent outcomes, perhaps indicating the importance of adult time available to spend with preschoolers (Baydar, Brooks-Gunn, & Senior, 1995). Further, maternal circumstances influence child outcomes when those circumstances change. For example, if a mother went off welfare between her child's preschool and adolescent years, the likelihood of grade failure was reduced during the elementary and middle school years. This was true even though preschool readiness scores predicted school-related problems in adolescence, and welfare receipt in the preschool years was highly associated with low school readiness scores. Taking into account these relations, going off welfare status decreases the child's chances of repeating a grade.

These findings are relevant for current policy debates about the possible benefits of helping mothers move off of welfare and into the work force (Chase-Lansdale, Brooks-Gunn, & Paikoff, 1991; Wilson et al., in press). Additionally, such analyses are the heart of developmental research, speaking to continuity and change, both in outcomes and in process or mediators (Bornstein & Krasnegor, 1989).

DEVELOPMENTAL ISSUES IN ADOLESCENT MOTHERS' PARENTING

Much research has focused specifically on the actual parenting behavior of adolescent parents. Most of this work considers the teenage mother and her infant. The first wave of research, as reviewed by Baldwin and Cain (1980) and Brooks-Gunn and Furstenberg (1986), suggested that mothers differed primarily in terms of verbal responsivity to children's cues (see also recent review by Osofsky et al., in press). Young mothers also perceive their infants to be more difficult and have unrealistic expectations for their developmental courses (Field, 1980; Frodi, 1983; Osofsky, Peebles, Fick, & Hann, 1992). Generally, teenage mothers seem to be as warm as older mothers toward their children. The recent work (reviewed by Chase-Landsdale & Brooks-Gunn, 1994; Osofsky et al., 1993) has replicated the early findings, as teenage mothers seem to provide a less stimulating and verbal environment for their young children and may also be more restrictive (Coll et al., 1986; Crockenberg, 1987; Culp, Appelbaum, Osofsky, & Levy, 1988; Culp, Culp, Osofsky, & Osofsky, 1991; Parks & Arndt, 1990). The environment of teenage mothers' homes seems to be less geared toward learning as well (Coll et al., 1986; Wasserman, Brunelli, Rauh, & Alvarado, 1994), as measured by the HOME (Caldwell & Bradley, 1984). Using national data sets such as the Children of the NLSY (Chase-Landsdale, Mott et al., 1991) confirms the findings on home environment from the smaller scale studies (Luster & Dubow, 1990; Moore & Synder, 1991).

Another line of research on teenage mothers' parenting was conducted by Osofsky and colleagues (1988, 1993). Using a risk and vulnerability model adapted from the field of developmental psychopathology, Osofsky looked at the links between parenting and child outcome, with a particular focus on maternal affect regulation and parent–child interaction as they feed into the child's own affect regulation and emotional development. Arguing that many young mothers have difficulty regulating their own emotional states, as evidenced by high rates of depression and possibly emotional lability, Osofsky studied how such regulatory disturbances might influence parent–child interaction. She cited literature showing how depressed mothers have difficulty responding to their children's cues and the resulting impact on the children (Downey & Coyne, 1990; Field, Healy, Goldstein, & Guthertz, 1990; Zahn-Waxler, Kochanska, Krupnick, & McKnew, 1990). Her own work with adolescents suggests problems in affect regulation, not just difficulties in responsivity, in many teenage mothers (Carter et al., 1991; Hann, Castino, et al., 1991; see also Leadbeater & Linares, 1992).

Osofsky also raised the critical issue of emotional availability of the teenage mother to the child (Osofsky et al., 1993; Sameroff & Emde, 1992). Her work in Topeka and New Orleans suggests that young mothers are less available to their children, both in the infancy and the toddler periods (Hann, Castino, et al., 1991; Hann, Robinson, et al., 1991; Osofksy et al., 1993). These patterns of parenting may play a role in the more frequent observation of insecure attachment and disorganized attachment in infants of teenage mothers as compared to older mothers (Hann, Castino, et al., 1991a; Hann, Robinson, et al., 1991; Lamb, Hopps, & Elster, 1987). However, research has not directly addressed the link between maternal availability and attachment.

Of particular concern in this line of work is the use of comparison groups. Even if ethnicity and neighborhood are comparable across groups (a requirement that not all studies meet), some studies use as their comparison older married mothers, thus confounding age and marital status. A more profitable approach is to compare teenage mothers with older mothers who are also single as well as those who are married, in order to investigate the effects of being a single parent versus being a young mother (research has shown moderate effects of single parenthood in the context of divorce and childbearing outside of marriage upon children's outcomes; Brooks-Gunn, in press-b; Cherlin et al., 1991; Garfinkel & McLanahan, 1986; Hetherington, 1993; McLanahan, Astone, & Marks, 1991; McLanahan & Sandefur, 1994; Thomson & McLanahan, 1993; Thomson, McLanahan, & Curtin, 1992).

Recent research includes some of the controls missing in earlier work. For example, the Baltimore Multigenerational Family Study compares young women who became mothers in their teenage years with those who become mothers in their early 20s. The study's design allowed for observation of mothers and grandmothers separately with preschoolers. Mothers' age at first birth ranged from 13 to 25 years, with a mean of about 18 years. Parenting behaviors were coded from a problem-solving task (a semistructured puzzle task adapted by Goldberg & Easterbrooks, 1984, from a tool task developed by Matas, Arend, & Sroufe, 1978). Both mothers and grandmothers were observed interacting with the toddlers. Parental affect, parenting disciplinary style (disengaged, authoritative, authoritarian), and problem-solving style (quality of assistance, supportive presence) were coded (see Baumrind, 1989; Chase-Lansdale et al., 1994; Hetherington & Clingempeel, 1992). Age at first birth is not related to parenting behavior in free play and problem-solving tasks with preschool-age children (Chase-Landsdale et al., 1994). It is important to note that education, Aid to Families with Dependent Children (AFDC) participation, marital status, and verbal ability are controlled, in order to see the effects of age. Mothers who become mothers early are quite different from young women who postpone motherhood.

Also, research has not looked at parenting practices vis-à-vis harshness and disciplinary styles. Nor has much work considered links between parenting behaviors and child outcomes after the infancy period. Consistency and change in parenting behaviors over time have not been a topic of investigation. A particularly provocative issue is whether teenage mothers become more adequate parents, or alter their behavior to become more responsive and less harsh, as they become older and possibly less centered on themselves (Chase-Landsdale & Brooks-Gunn, 1994).

The interpretation of findings from this work merits a cautionary note. This research relies on measures of parent–child interaction derived from work with primarily middle-class, married, older mothers. For example, most studies of teenage mothers have focused on the following constructs— maternal warmth, maternal responsivity or sensitivity, verbal interchanges, harsh parenting, and combinations of warmth and control (as in the dimensions originally identified by Baumrind, 1989; Maccoby & Martin, 1983; Matas et al., 1978). Many of the differences seem to be focused on verbal interchanges. Given that teenage mothers are on average likely to have lower verbal ability scores as well as less education, even when controlling for other demographic characteristics (Miller & Moore, 1990), it may not be surprising that differences might exist in the verbal arena.

Other aspects of parenting remain somewhat untapped. For example, the Baltimore Multi-generational Family Study shows teenage mothers playing more with toys on their own in free play situations than do grandmothers. Sometimes young mothers engage in what looks like parallel play—they play with some toys while their preschool children play with others. This is a type of behavior that we have not seen in work on older mothers. The same observation has been made in the Teenage Parent Demonstration, a sample of teenage mothers from Newark (Brooks-Gunn et al., 1993). Measures of parallel play might be developed and added to protocols involving teenage mothers.

Another problem with the current literature on parenting behavior of teenage mothers involves the transportation of coding systems from nonminority to minority households (Doucette-Gates, Brooks-Gunn, & Chase-Lansdale, in press). This issue transcends the teenage mother literature, being relevant for all studies of minority children and their parents (McLoyd, 1990; McLoyd & Steinberg, in press). It arises in the teenage parenthood literature because so many of the studies have focused on African-American multigenerational families. Multigenerational households are a common response to young single parenthood across ethnic groups, but are typically studied in only African-American families.

Important exceptions include work on Hispanic-American young mothers. Wasserman and her colleagues (Wasserman, Brunelli, & Rauh, 1990; Wasserman, Rauh, Brunelli, & Garcia-Castro, 1990; Wasserman et al., 1994) conducted an important study focusing on parenting behavior and attitudes as well as social support as they are associated with toddlers' outcome in Hispanic-American adolescent and adult mothers. Two groups of Hispanic-American immigrants residing in New York City were included—mothers from the Dominican Republic and from Puerto Rico as well as a sample of African-American mothers. Teenage mothers from all groups were less likely to be married than older mothers, and marriage was least likely in the African-American teenage mother sample. Teenage mothers were more likely to be depressed than adult mothers, although differences among ethnic groups were not found. Teenage mothers also had lower HOME scores than the adults, lived in more crowded households, and did less child care than older mothers. However, teenage and adult mothers had similar childrearing attitudes, although ethnic differences appeared. African-American mothers reported that they had more social support than the Hispanic-American mothers, and Puerto Rican mothers perceived that they had more support than mothers from the Dominican Republic. Hispanic-American mothers had more strict childrearing attitudes than African-American mothers across age; mothers from the Dominican Republic had stricter attitudes than mothers from Puerto Rico.

Garcia Coll has focused on Hispanic-American young mothers; her work has included samples of island Puerto Ricans, mainland African Americans, and mainland Whites (Garcia Coll, 1989; Lester, Garcia Coll, & Sepkoski, 1983). Garcia Coll looked at culture-specific patterns of pregnancy timing, marriage, and social support from the family as possible explanations for these differences (see also Leadbeater & Linares, 1992).

Field and her colleagues (Field & Widmayer, 1981) looked at young mothers (not all of which were teenage mothers) in interaction with their 4-month-olds. Groups included mainland Puerto Rican and Cuban families residing in Miami. Interactions were more positive in the mainland Puerto Rican mothers than the Cuban mothers. Both groups exhibited more positive behavior than the sample of African-American mothers from Miami. Little is known about the cultural context of childrearing in the Puerto Rican and Cuban communities in Miami, information necessary to understand the origin and meaning of such differences.

All of these research groups have discussed the possible influence of recency of immigration on household structure, childrearing attitudes and child-care patterns, support of different family members, and parenting behavior. All make the important point that in large part their samples are poor, and that cultural practices and beliefs must be interpreted in the context of poverty as well as ethnicity.

Little work has focused on possible constructs of relevance for subgroups (e.g., cultural or minority groups). Ethnographic observations have suggested that authoritarian parenting may be adaptive in some situations, particularly those involving minority families living in dangerous neighborhoods (Jarrett, in press; Steinberg, 1990). Whether the codes for control in the authoritarian style really represent what has been observed by ethnographers needs to be studied. Based on our work with low-income African-American families, we suspect that what is adaptive is not harsh control (which is often seen in White parents across income groups scoring high on authoritarian parenting), but a style of interaction that is very directive. That is, being quite directive may be adaptive in dangerous neighborhoods, because parents need to impress upon their children the necessity of following rules. Harsh parental control may not be an aspect of this adaptive response to ecological conditions. The current coding systems based on the original Baumrind framework may not distinguish among these two types of control adequately (although no research has tested our admittedly speculative proposition) (Baumrind, 1973). In summary, the research on parenting behavior would benefit from an expansion to other ethnic groups, a consideration of the applicability of current coding systems for young and minority mothers, and more analyses focusing on subgroups of teenage mothers (such as those who have and have not finished high school, who are or are not residing with their mothers).

FAMILY SYSTEMS APPROACHES: MULTIGENERATIONAL EFFECTS

The advent of teenage motherhood has effects on several members of the family, not just the teenage mother. In addition, a family system approach focuses not just on multiple family members, but on the family as a whole (Hinde & Stevenson-Hinde, 1988; Reiss, 1981). Because young mothers are highly likely to spend the first years after the birth of a child in a multigenerational household, the study of family systems is critical (Chase-Lansdale et al., 1991). Unmarried teenage mothers are unable to rely on male partners for support in those cases where they have not married. Even though a high proportion of fathers provide support a year after the child's birth, the amount of money provided is typically not enough to maintain a separate household and rear a child (Sullivan, 1990,

1993). Research is beginning to focus on multiple family members as well as on family climate and/or emotional quality.

The parents of a teenager are often unhappy about the impending birth, but they typically provide support to their daughter during the pregnancy and to the daughter and baby during the first few years after delivery (as studied in African-American families, Chase-Lansdale & Brooks-Gunn, in press; Furstenberg, 1976). This support often includes coresidence, which is particularly common among African-American families (Boyd-Franklin, 1989; Hill & Duncan, 1987; Hofferth, 1984; Hogan, Hao, & Parish, 1990; McAdoo, 1988; Wilson, 1986). Coresidence is about twice as likely among African-American than White single mothers (Hernandez, 1993; Paikoff, Brooks-Gunn, & Baydar, 1993). Little research describes the prevalence of grandmother involvement in teenage mothers' lives. It is clear that multigenerational residence is more likely when the mother is young, as assessed in the Children of the NLSY, a national study (Hogan et al., 1990; Paikoff et al., 1994). Another line of research, using the National Study of Families and Households, examined grandmothers' involvement with grandchildren. Baydar and Brooks-Gunn (1991) derived a profile of grandmothers in the United States. Approximately 12 percent resided with a grandchild. Differences appeared vis-à-vis ethnicity, such that 30 percent of African-American, 27 percent of Hispanic-American, and 9 percent of White grandmothers were currently living with a grandchild (the numbers ever living with a grandchild will presumably be much higher). Approximately half provide child care currently. Cluster analyses identified five groups of grandmothers. Of interest to us here are the two groups in which at least one half were providing child care. The first was composed of primarily White, older, married women who provided care but did not coreside. The second was comprised of primarily African-American, young, single women who were coresiding with their grandchildren. This second group, given their age, is likely to have teenage daughters who are mothers. It is the group upon which almost all of the research on multigenerational households focuses (Burton, 1990; Burton & Bengtson, 1985; Chase-Lansdale, Mott et al., 1991). In the Baltimore Multigenerational Family Study, for example, about one third of the adolescent mothers identified in the late 1960s lived with their mothers when their children were young. In the next generation of teenage mothers (based on data from the firstborn children of the original mothers), about three fifths are living with their mothers (Furstenberg et al., 1990). Historical changes in living arrangements, if they have occurred as the Baltimore Study data suggest, may have implications for interactions among generations. We address this topic here.

How does extended and often intensive support influence the family with regard to parenting behaviors exhibited across generations? Several lines of evidence point to both benefits and disadvantages of such support. We review research in four areas—grandmothers as parental role models, formation of multigenerational households, shared caregiving of grandmothers and mothers, and the relationship between teenage mothers and their mothers.

Grandmothers as Parental Role Models

One potential benefit of coresidence with the grandmother is the provision of a role model for young mothers to emulate with respect to their parenting behavior. Consequently, continuity across generations in parenting behavior might be predicted. Most research exploring continuity has considered parents' experiences when they were children to ascertain whether early parenting experiences influence subsequent parenting behavior (Rutter, 1989). Usually the early parenting experience is assessed retrospectively. Such studies suggest some continuity, especially in terms of harsh and negative parenting (Egeland, Jacobvitz, & Sroufe, 1988; Main & Goldwyn, 1984; Quinton & Rutter, 1988; Simmons, Whitbeck, Conger, & Chyi-in, 1991; see also Caspi & Elder, 1988, for a prospective study of continuity).

In the case of teenage mothers and their own mothers, continuity may be examined concurrently because both generations interact and care for the teenager's young child. We explored issues centering on continuity by examining low-income African-American families in the Baltimore Multigenerational Family Study (Chase-Landsale et al., 1994). Generally, concordance between mother and grandmother parenting was seen only for negative dimensions of parenting and only for younger mothers and grandmothers. Other research suggests that punitive, negative ways of interacting with children are more likely to be modeled than positive interactive styles (Patterson, 1986; Simmons et al., 1991). More positive aspects of parenting were associated across generations in only one instance—when the mother and grandmother were not living together and when the mother was older.

Formation of Multigenerational Households

Studies conducted in the late 1960s and early 1970s indicated that coresidence benefited the offspring of teenage mothers, compared to residing in a single-parent household (Furstenberg, 1976; Horwitz et al., 1991; Kellam, Ensminger, & Turner, 1977). These studies typically focused on relatively young mothers who resided in multigenerational households. It is important to note that the authors of these early studies pointed out that benefits might be timelimited: Coresidence might be a good solution when the offspring and mothers are young, but may be less beneficial as family members age. In the Baltimore Study of Teenage Mothers, for example, long-term residence in the mother's household predicted long-term welfare dependency in the daughters (Furstenberg et al., 1987).

Current studies are not all documenting positive effects of coresidence upon children. Using the Children of the NLSY, Paikoff and colleagues (1993) find that multigenerational coresidence in the first years of life is negatively associated with reading achievement scores at ages 5 and 6 in White children, controlling for a host of social and demographic characteristics. Both teenage mothers and mothers in their early 20s were included in this sample. Two other studies have reported the home environment of multigenerational households (as measured by the HOME: Caldwell & Bradley, 1984) is not superior to (and perhaps lower than) that of families who do not include three generations (Speiker, 1991; Wasserman, Brunelli, & Rauh, 1990). Among African-American young mothers residing in Newark, New Jersey, half of whom participated in a jobs-, skills-, and education-training program predicated on the federal JOBS program, coresidence was associated with lower verbal ability scores when the children (third generation) were between 3 and 5 years of age (Aber, Brooks-Gunn, & Maynard, 1995). Coresidence was beneficial in a sample of low-birthweight children residing in eight sites across the country and receiving medical surveillance in medical centers in these eight sites. Pope and her colleagues (1993) reported that coresidence of teenage mothers was associated with higher children's intelligence test scores at age 3.

These possible differential effects of multigenerational households upon children would be played out in family interactions. Of particular interest are the parenting styles and quality exhibited by young mothers and their mothers. Coresidence could influence either the mother, the grandmother, or both. Four hypotheses represent possible influences of coresidence on the parenting of young mothers and their mothers: Hypothesis 1, called "modeling and support," draws upon work initiated a generation ago that suggests that grandmothers' presence provides economic and emotional support and examples of good parenting to young mothers. The prediction in coresident households would be positive effects on mothers' parenting with no effect on grandmothers' parenting. Hypothesis 2, called "conflict," poses that living together and sharing childrearing are difficult, and that conflict between mothers and grandmothers would negatively affect both mothers' and grandmothers' parenting, as can occur in mother–father families (e.g., Emery, 1982). Hypothesis 3, called "mutual support," suggests that coresidence is an adaptive response to scarce resources, and that mothers' and grandmothers' mutual support would have positive effects on both individuals' parenting quality (e.g., Hogan et al., 1990; Stack, 1974). Finally, Hypothesis 4, "burden on grandmother," poses that coresidence is difficult for grandmothers and drains their resources. Grandmothers' parenting would be negatively affected, whereas mothers' parenting would be positive or neutrally affected (e.g., Burton, 1990; Hofferth, 1984).

Findings from the Baltimore Multigenerational Family Study suggest that coresidence with grandmothers has negative consequences for the parenting of both mother and grandmother (Chase-

Landsdale et al., 1994). It appears that multigenerational living arrangements are often stressful for young mothers and young grandmothers—the conflict hypothesis seems to fit these data. Living together may be difficult for both generations—the young mother who is balancing needs for autonomy and needs for child care simultaneously and the grandmother who is balancing the demands of adult midlife (work, relationships, parenting) with unanticipated child-care demands (Burton, 1990). Add to this equation the fact that these households are struggling with the demands of poverty, and intergenerational strain is not surprising.

Multigenerational residence may not be as beneficial today as in the past in part because of the deteriorating economic environment, the rise in single-parent childbearing, and the increase in neighborhoods with large numbers of poor people (Hogan et al., 1990; Wilson, 1987). These conditions make it more difficult to provide a supportive household environment. They may also render multigenerational residences more common, although little evidence exists on this topic. One exception is the work of Hernandez (1993) of the Census Bureau, who reported on multigenerational residence: About 11 percent to 14 percent of children in mother-only families had a grandparent in the home in the 1970s (the proportion of children in mother-only families living with a grandparent *decreased* from 20 percent to 27 percent in the 1940s to 1960s to the midteens in the 1970s). In 1980, when the last data are available, 22 percent of mothers who have never married were coresiding with their parent(s), and 10 percent of mothers who were ever married were in multigenerational households. Percentages are even higher for infants. The percentages of infants (first year of life) in 1980 who resided with grandparents in the home were 42 percent for never-married mothers and 25 percent for ever-married mothers (Hernandez, 1993).

In part as a response to the conflicting findings from the studies of the 1960s and 1970s and the recent studies, we hypothesized that coresidence might have different effects depending on the age of the young mother. Coresidence might be a more positive experience when the second-generation mother is younger. Shared parenting might be accepted by the teenage mother, who is uncertain of her own parenting skills and who, still negotiating many of the normative challenges of adolescence, invests less in parenthood. The young mother may welcome the help of her own mother, who, by taking on parental responsibility, allows the teenager to engage in adolescent activities (going out with friends, dating, etc., without arranging alternative child-care arrangements). In contrast, as the young women make the transition toward early adulthood, they may be less tolerant of sharing parenting decisions and of maternal monitoring.

Indeed, coresidence influenced both mothers' and grandmothers' parenting, depending on the age of the young mother. For those families in which the mother was very young (16 and under at first birth), coresiding mothers and grandmothers exhibited more positive and less harsh parenting than those who did not live together. In contrast, for those families in which the mother was older at the birth of the first child, coresidence had negative ramifications (Chase-Landsdale et al., 1994).

Shared Caregiving

A feature of multigenerational households is that parenting is often shared by members of two generations. Burton (1990, 1992) described various configurations of support and shared caregiving seen in three-generation families. She made the point that support does not always flow from the older to the younger generations, and often involves one generation supporting and caring for other generations.

Other investigators have focused more specifically on how multiple generations share in the care of young children. Four modes of caregiving were identified by Apfel and Seitz (1991) in a study of low-income African-American adolescent mothers, their mothers, and their 18-month-old children. Intensive interviews of the women allowed for a characterization of daily household activities and responsibilities, as well as time spent in caregiving and play, by all members of the household. The first mode of joint caregiving involves the replacement of the young mother by the grandmother as the primary caregiver. Contrary to popular opinion, this caregiving mode was relatively rare (10 percent of the sample). The next mode, labeled *parental supplement* by the authors, was the most common (50 percent of the sample). Young mothers shared childrearing tasks with their own mothers and other kin. Sharing was sometimes seen by task or by time of day. The third mode involved the grandmother acting as a role model to her daughter. It appeared that the grandmothers were engaged in training their daughter for eventual self-sufficiency. Although low frequency (10 percent of the sample), this mode of shared caregiving might be expected to result in shorter lengths of coresidence and, ultimately, greater maturity and more adequate parenting on the part of the young mother. Indeed, findings from the Baltimore Multigenerational Family Study tend to support this view, in that the young women who did not coreside with their own mothers during their 20s (i.e., those who had been able to move out) exhibited the most positive parenting styles, as did their own mothers. The last mode in the Apfel and Seitz study was labeled the *supported primary parent*. In these families, the grandmothers provided some caregiving help, but were definitely not coparents. Grandmother support existed, but was not high. In the Baltimore Multigenerational Family Study, these families might be best represented by the teenage mothers who did not coreside with their mothers. This group of teenagers left home very early; even though these young woman had contact with their mothers, primary support and caregiving were not typically provided.

Apfel and Seitz (in press) also interviewed their multigenerational families when the child was about age 6. They reported that family placement among the four groups changed. The mode in which the young mother (now in her 20s) is the primary support with some but fairly low caregiving was now characteristic of 50 percent of the families. Role modeling had withered away. Parental replacement was seen in 16 percent of the families, similar to what was seen earlier. And about 30 percent of families practiced parental supplement (down from 50 percent). Movement among caregiving arrangements was seen too. The two arrangements most likely to result in self-sufficiency, or sufficiency in the context of limited but appropriate support from other family members, were the role model and the parental supplement styles. In both cases grandmothers offered help, but did not either "take over" the child (the replacement mode) or ignore the child (the supported primary parent mode).

The authors suggest that either extreme on the shared caregiving and support continuum may be detrimental for the eventual well-being of young mothers vis-à-vis their ability to move toward a primary parenting role. In essence, the two groups in which grandmothers played an important but not primary role in the rearing of the grandchild may have helped balance the young mother's need to emerge as an independent young women with her need for reliance on others for child care and support.

Relationship of the Young Mother and Grandmother

The complexity of caregiving roles and responsibilities in multigenerational families may play out in the ways in which young mothers parent and move toward independence. The quality of mother–daughter relationships in the context of multigenerational childrearing might be affected by the ways in which caregiving and living arrangements are managed. Indeed, the quality of these relationships may be the mechanism underlying the effects of coresidence and age upon parenting behavior and child outcomes. However, little is known about the interactions between young mothers and their own mothers, because the relatively few investigations to date have focused on interactions with the children of young mothers and the phenomenon of shared caregiving itself.

In the Baltimore Multigenerational Family Study, we assessed the quality of the mother–grandmother relationship based on discussions of current disagreements (as defined by the mother and grandmother). We asked the mother and grandmother each to identify an area in which they disagreed. They were given 5–8 minutes to discuss each disagreement. The Scale of Intergenerational Relationship Quality (SIRQ; Wakschlag, Chase-Lansdale, & Brooks-Gunn, in press) was developed for this sample. It integrates concepts from developmental and family research with those derived from more culturally specific studies of the African-American family. Four factors were identified from the items on this scale—emotional closeness (emotional context of the relationship), dyadic positive affect (engaged, animated), grandmother affirmative parenting style (grandmother expresses herself in a firm, positive, and self-confident manner), and mother autonomy (young mother's ability to communicate clearly and to maintain her separateness while maintaining an atmosphere of mutuality). Mother autonomy within the context of the relationship with the grandmother was a strong predictor of mothers' parenting (and neither mother autonomy nor parenting were associated with maternal age). Mothers who had mature, flexible, and autonomous interactions with their own mothers were likely to be emotionally supportive, positive affectively, facilitative of children's puzzle-solving attempts, and authoritative. Surprisingly, emotional closeness and dyadic positive affect were not associated with young mothers' parenting. These findings highlight the role of autonomy for young women who are combining the transition to young adulthood with parenthood. Women who had high scores on autonomy were able to disagree with their mothers while, at the same time, listening to their mothers' point of view. The women with low scores seemed sullen, withdrawn, or uncommunicative with their mothers (Wakschlag et al., in press).

Autonomy was more tightly linked with parenting behavior in the two living situations that we previously identified as disadvantageous—not living with one's mother while being a teenage mother, and coresidence with one's mother while being an older mother. That is, autonomy played more of a protective function in these families vis-à-vis parenting behavior.

These qualities of the mother–daughter relationship played less of a role in the expression of the grandmothers' parenting. However, emotional closeness was higher in families where the grandmother and mother did not coreside. Perhaps grandmothers' parenting style is influenced more by previous events and contextual factors (e.g., coresidence; Wakschlag et al., in press). Alternatively, their parenting may be more linked to other current life-stage concerns, such as other caregiving responsibilities, work commitments, male relationships, and so on (Burton, 1990).

Another research tradition focuses on the possible indirect effects of grandmothers' parenting on children vis-à-vis effects upon adolescent mothers' behavior (Crockenberg, 1981; McNair, 1991). Nurturance and responsivity of the grandparent to the young mother have been identified as critical in these two studies. One study reported a more positive effect of grandfather nurturance upon teenage parenting behavior than grandmother nurturance (in one of the few studies of primarily White teenage mothers coresiding with their parents; Oyserman, Radin, & Benn, 1993). In brief, the emotional stances taken by the teenage mother and grandmother may influence the child, especially in terms of emotional relationships and the process of separation and individuation that occurs during the toddler and early childhood years (Bowlby, 1960; Mahler, Pine, & Bergman, 1975; Sroufe, 1979). A mother who is not emotionally integrated may find it difficult to promote autonomy in her young child. Having a grandmother who may perform the functions of an autonomous and integrated mother may buffer the young child from the less developed emotional functioning of the mother.

These studies are welcome additions to the field. They show the family-oriented approach, sensitivity to reciprocal and indirect effects within the family, and consideration of the links between parenting and other salient aspects of lives. Of particular importance is the focus on individual differences in how family members share child care and interact with one another. More information is needed on the ways in which families negotiate disagreements and the effects of family conflict upon the children.

CONCLUSIONS

Policy Implications of Research Findings

The study of adolescent parents has direct relevance to public policy. Indeed, much of the debate about how to structure welfare programs centers on young parents. The reason is that single young mothers are the group of parents most likely to be poor, and to remain poor, for many years. Over one half of all adolescent mothers, and about three fourths of all single adolescent mothers, join the welfare rolls in the 4 years after the birth of the child (Bane & Ellwood, 1986; Ellwood, 1988; Moore et al., 1993; U.S. House of Representatives, 1989). And teenage mothers account for a disproportionate amount of the funds spent on welfare, in part because they spend more time on welfare than older mothers.

This state of affairs, and concerns about the difficulty that young mothers have in completing high school and in entering the work force, have resulted in specific policy recommendations being written for them in the Family Support Act of 1988 (Chase-Lansdale & Brooks-Gunn, in press; Chase-Lansdale & Vinovskis, in press). Young women who become mothers as teenagers are required to stay in high school in order to receive welfare benefits. The policy may have unintended effects on the family system. For all practical purposes, young women cannot stay in school unless they have child care, and unless someone is supporting them (welfare benefits in most states would not enable young women to set up their own households given rental prices and to purchase child care given the cost of care; Brooks-Gunn et al., in press; Cherlin, in press). Consequently, the Family Support Act implicitly sets up a situation where the young mother's family in most cases will have to help with child care as well as household arrangements. Child support by noncustodial fathers of never-married mothers is very low (Furstenberg, in press; Garfinkel & McLanahan, in press.) The research that we have reviewed suggests that coresidence is not always a positive experience for the young mother, the grandmother, or the child.

Many programs for teenage mothers recognize the need for child care. School-based services often provide child care for young mothers. A few of the school-based endeavors have been evaluated (Benasich, Brooks-Gunn, & Clewell, 1992; Clewell et al., 1989). However, not enough school-based child-care services exist for all teenage mothers who have not completed high school. Fewer programs have focused on the grandmother explicitly. A review by Marx, Bailey, and Francis in 1988 suggests that many programs focusing on teenagers do provide services to others in the household, or at least recognize the need for such services. No evaluations have been conducted, nor has much attention been placed on the type of services that multigenerational families might need.

Another major thrust of the Family Support Act's provisions for women on welfare has to do with the movement of women from welfare toward self-sufficiency, or toward less dependency on federal support. These programs, under the JOBS title, offer employment, training, and educational services to mothers of all ages (Wilson et al., in press). However, several demonstration programs have targeted young mothers, given that they have the most difficulty in making the transition toward work. The Teenage Parent Demonstration program, the Young Single Women Demonstration Program, Project Redirection, and Project MATCH are exemplars (Halpern, 1993; Aber, Brooks-Gunn, & Maynard, in press; Polit, 1989). Most report that intensive job-training programs reduce teenage mothers' dependency on welfare. At the same time, great variability exists vis-à-vis mothers' responses to these programs. For example, many mothers are more likely to enter the workplace if they are first given job training rather than remedial education. Perhaps school-oriented programs are too similar to the arena in which so many young mothers have already failed. Mothers often do not see the payoff in such programs. In contrast, bringing home a paycheck, or working in a very low-paying job, highlights the importance of further education as a way to increase earning power (Halpern, 1993).

Teenage mother programs also offer child care referral as well as parenting classes, speaking to the recognition of the need for the former and the lack of experience and skill in the latter. Most have not conducted the developmentally oriented studies needed to demonstrate efficacy. Additionally, most programs offer parenting modules of low intensity; research from early childhood education would suggest that such approaches might not alter parenting behavior directly (Benasich et al., 1992; Bronfenbrenner, 1979; Brooks-Gunn, 1990; Ramey et al., 1992). However, they might influence parenting indirectly. Young mothers who enter the work force may have increased levels of self-efficacy and psychological well-being more generally, which might influence their parenting behavior (Wilson et al., in press; Zill, Moore, Smith, Stief, & Coiro, in press). For example, in a follow-up of young mothers who participated in Project Redirection, home environment scores were higher as were children's verbal ability scores, even though few differences in maternal outcomes were found between families who participated in the project and those who did not (Polit, 1989). Several current work-welfare demonstration projects collect information on parenting behavior and actual observations of parent–child interactions to understand what aspects of parenting might be influenced, and whether effects are direct or indirect (Teenage Parent Demonstration; New Chance Demonstration, JOBS Demonstration; Maynard et al., in press; Smith, in press-a, in press-b). These projects are a much-needed blend of developmental approaches to studying teenage mothers and their families, and programs developed to help teenage mothers overcome the disadvantages inherent in early single parenthood.

Research Recommendations

The study of adolescent parenthood has come a long way since Cambell's now-famous quote about life scripts of early childbearers. Not only are researchers stressing variability in outcomes, but they are now focusing on subgroups of teenage mothers and prospective mothers, in order to understand the life courses within specific groups of teenage mothers (Baldwin, 1993).

Recent work is considering how outcomes for teenage mothers are linked rather than considering them separately. The best example is the work considering school leaving and teenage births simultaneously (Upchurch, 1993). Measures of competency, mental health, and life satisfaction need to be considered over and above the well-studied (and important) outcomes involving school, fertility, marriage, and occupation. However, the range of outcomes studied needs to be broadened.

Work is commencing on intrafamilial differences, as well as the effects of timing of events within families (Geronimus, 1991; Geronimus & Korenman, 1992; Hoffman et al., 1993). The within-family level analyses have, to date, focused on mean comparisons, rather than explanations for differences within families. The field is posed to take the intrafamilial methodology to a more process-oriented analysis. A developmental perspective demands that we look at how experiences in different life epochs contribute to an individual's life choices and emotional states. As Elder (1974) demonstrated, experience of events such as parental job loss influences children and adolescents quite differently, which has implications for long-term adaptation.

Timing of events must be studied more explicitly. Spacing of children made a difference in the life-course trajectories of the teenage mothers in the Baltimore Study of Teenage Motherhood. It also made a difference in how the firstborn children fared: Births while the firstborn was still a preschooler had negative effects whereas births later on did not. The divorce literature suggests differential effects on children and adolescents, depending on the timing of the divorce (Booth & Dunn, 1995; Brooks-Gunn, 1995; Chase-Lansdale & Hetherington, 1990).

Intergenerational approaches are emerging as reviewed in this chapter. Looking at mothers, grandmothers, and other adult kin allows for a better understanding as to how families provide a context in which teenage childbearing is encouraged or discouraged.

A few scholars have considered cohort effects. Given changes in the demographics of teenage parenthood (in particular the rise in out-of-wedlock childbearing and to a lesser extent the rise in number of teenage mothers completing high school/GED [general equivalency diploma]), it is important to place each study in its historical context. For example, the comparison of teenage mothers in the Baltimore Study with their firstborn girls who also became teenage mothers illustrates a few differences that are cohort driven. These differences have vast implications for the life courses of these two cohorts (with mostly negative implications for the current generation of teenage mothers; Furstenberg et al., 1992).

A limitation of current research is that race and ethnicity are treated quite differently across studies, making it difficult to make cross-study comparisons for race/ethnicity. A few studies look at the different patterns of associations for ethnic groups separately (Wasserman et al., 1995). Clearly, given different housing, immigration, job patterns, as well as other pervasive effects of discrimination, the ways in which family support or schooling influence the outcomes of teenage mothers on their children might differ for Whites, African Americans, and Hispanic Americans.

The adolescent experience is missing from much of the work. We need to look at the role of arousal and the difficulty youth have in managing these feelings. We need to understand how youth negotiate sexual decisions between boys and girls (Brooks-Gunn & Furstenberg, 1989; Brooks-Gunn & Paikoff, 1993). Little is known about whether, and in what ways, teenage mothers manage autonomy and identity development differently than teenagers who are not mothers.

Research designs often do not focus on change. More attention must be paid to looking at change in various circumstances, which influence family members (teenage mother, teenage father, child, grandmother). In the Baltimore Study, moving off welfare after the preschool years reduced the likelihood of school failure and early sexuality. In order to conduct longitudinal, process-oriented studies, attention must be paid to family, peer, neighborhood, school, and individual processes (Bronfenbrenner & Weiss, 1983).

ACKNOWLEDGMENTS

This chapter was written with funding from the NICHD Child and Family Well-Being Research Network. Research by the authors was supported by the Commonwealth Fund, the Robert Wood Johnson Foundation, NICHD, the Office of Adolescent Pregnancy (DHHS), the Ford Foundation, and the Russell Sage Foundation. Portions of the chapter were presented at a conference sponsored by NICHD entitled "Outcomes of Early Childbearing: An Appraisal of Recent Evidence," May 1992, Bethesda, Maryland. We wish to thank W. Baldwin, C. Bachrach, L. Burton, K. Moore, L. Klerner, J. Osofsky, and D. Reiss for comments and guidance. We also acknowledge the support of the Chapin Hall School, University of Chicago, and the Division of Educational Policy Research, Educational Testing Service.

REFERENCES

Aber, J. L., Brooks-Gunn, J., & Maynard, R. (in press). The effects of welfare reform on teenage parents and their children. *The Future of Children.*

Abernathy, V. (1973). Social network and response to the maternal role. *International Journal of Sociology of the Family, 3,* 86–96.

Apfel, N. H., & Seitz, V. (1991). Four models of adolescent mother–grandmother relationships in Black inner-city families. *Family Relations, 40*(4), 421–429.

Apfel, N. H., & Seitz, V. (in press). *African-American mothers, their families, and their daughters: A longitudinal perspective over 12 years.* In B. J. Leadbeater and N. Way (Eds.), Urban Adolescent Girls: Resisting Stereotypes. New York: New York University Press.

Astone, N. M. (1993). Are adolescent mothers just single mothers? *Journal of Research on Adolescence, 3*(4), 353–373.

Bachrach, C. A., & Carver, K. (1992, May). *Outcomes of early childbearing: An appraisal of recent evidence.* Summary of a conference convened by the NICHD, Bethesda, MD.

Bachrach, C. A., Clogg, C. C., & Carver, K. (1993). Outcomes of early childbearing: Summary of a conference. *Journal of Research on Adolescence, 3*(4), 337–349.

Baldwin, W. (1993). The consequences of early childbearing: A perspective. *Journal of Research on Adolescence, 3*(4), 349–353.

Baldwin, W., & Cain, V. S. (1980). The children of teenage parents. *Family Planning Perspectives, 12*(1), 34–43.

Ballou, J. W. (1978). *The psychology of pregnancy: Reconciliation and resolution.* Lexington, MA: Heath.

Bane, M. J., & Ellwood, D. T. (1986). Slipping into and out of poverty: The dynamics of spells. *Journal of Human Resources, 21*(Winter), 1–23.

Barglow, P., Bornstein, M., Exum, D. B., Wright, M. K., & Visotsky, H. M. (1968). Some psychiatric aspects of illegitimate pregnancy in early adolescence. *American Journal of Orthopsychiatry, 38,* 672–678.

Baruch, G., & Brooks-Gunn, J. (Eds.). (1984). *Women in midlife.* New York: Plenum.

Baumrind, D. (1973). The development of instrumental competence through socialization. In A Pick (Ed.), Minnesota symposium on child psychology (Vol. 7). Minneapolis: Univeristy of Minnesota Press.

Baumrind, D. (1989). Rearing competent children. In W. Damon (Ed.), *Child development today and tomorrow* (pp. 349–378). San Francisco: Jossey-Bass.

Baydar, N., & Brooks-Gunn, J. (1994). The dynamics of child support and its consequences for children. In I. Garfinkel, S. McLanahan, & P. Robins (Eds.), *Child support reform and child well-being* (pp. 257–284). Washington, DC: Urban Institute Press.

Baydar, N., & Brooks-Gunn, J. (1991). *Profiles of America's grandmothers: Those who provide care for their grandchildren and those who do not.* Manuscript submitted for publication.

Baydar, N., Brooks-Gunn, J., & Furstenberg, F. F., Jr. (1993). Early warning signs of functional illiteracy: Predictors in childhood and adolescence. *Child Development, 64*(3), 815, 829.

Baydar, N., Brooks-Gunn, J., & Senior, A. M. (1995). How do living arrangements affect the development of Black infants? *Family Relations.*

Bell, R. Q. (1968). A reinterpretation of the direction of effects in studies of socialization. *Psychological Review, 75*(2), 81–95.

Belsky, J. (1984). The determinants of parenting: A process model. *Child Development, 55*(1), 83–96.

Benasich, A. A., & Brooks-Gunn, J. (in press). Enhancing maternal knowledge and child-rearing concepts: Results from an early intervention program. *Child Development.*

Benasich, A. A., Brooks-Gunn, J., & Clewell, B. C. (1992). How do mothers benefit from early intervention programs? *Journal of Applied Developmental Psychology, 13,* 311–362.

Benn, R., & Saltz, E. (1989). *The effects of grandmother support on teen parenting and infant attachment patterns within the family.* Paper presented at the meeting of the Society for Research in Child Development, Kansas City, MO.

Blos, P. (1967). The second individuation process of adolescence. In *The psychoanalytic study of the child (Vol. 22, pp. 172–186). New York: International Universities Press.*

Blos, P. (1979). The second individuation process. In P. Blos (Ed.), *The adolescent passage: Developmental issues at adolescence* (pp. 141–170). New York: International Universities Press.

Booth, A., & Dunn, J. (Eds.). (in press). *Stepparent families with children: Who benefits and who does not?* Hillsdale, NJ: Lawrence Erlbaum Associates.

Bornstein, M. H., & Krasnegor, N. E. (Eds.). (1989). *Stability and continuity in mental development: Behavioral and biological perspectives.* Hillsdale, NJ: Lawrence Erlbaum Associates.

Bowlby, J. (1960). Separation anxiety: A critical review of the literature. *Child Psychology and Psychiatry, 1,* 251–269.

Boyce, T., Schaefer, C., & Uitti, C. (1985). Permanence and change: Psychosocial factors in the outcome of adolescent pregnancy. *Social Science Medicine, 21*(11), 1279–1287.

Boyd-Franklin, N. (1989). *Black families in therapy: A multisystems approach.* New York: Guilford.

Broman, S. H. (1981). Longterm development of children born to teenagers. In K. Scott, T. Field, & E. Robertson (Eds.), *Teenage parents and their offspring* (pp. 195–224). New York: Grune & Sratton.

Bronfenbrenner, U. (1979). *The ecology of human development: Experiments by nature and design.* Cambridge, MA: Harvard University Press.

Bronfenbrenner, U., & Weiss, H. (1983). Beyond policies without people: An ecological perspective on child and family policy. In E. F. Zigler, S. L. Kagan, & E. Klugman (Eds.), *Children, families, and government: Perspectives on American social policy* (pp. 393–414). Cambridge, England: Cambridge University Press.

Brooks-Gunn, J. (1990). Promoting healthy development in young children: What educational interventions work? In D. E. Rogers & E. Ginzberg (Eds.), *Improving the life chances of children at risk* (pp. 125–145). Boulder, CO: Westview Press.

Brooks-Gunn, J. (1991). How stressful is the transition to adolescence in girls? In M. E. Colten & S. Gore (Eds.), *Adolescent stress: Causes and consequences* (pp. 131–149). Hawthorne, NY: Aldine de Gruyter.

Brooks-Gunn, J. (1995). Research on step-parenting families: Integrating discipline approaches and informing policy. In A. Booth & J. Dunn (Eds.), *Stepparent families with children: Who benefits and who does not?* Hillsdale, NJ: Lawrence Erlbaum Associates.

Brooks-Gunn, J. (in press-a). Growing up poor: Context, risk and continuity in the Bronfenbrenner tradition. In P. Moen, G. H. Elder, & K. Lusher (Eds.), *Linking lives and contexts: Perspective on the ecology of human development.* Washington, DC: American Psychological Association Press.

Brooks-Gunn, J. (in press-b). Opportunities for change: Effects of intervention programs on mothers and children. In P. L. Chase-Lansdale & J. Brooks-Gunn (Eds.), *Escape from poverty: What makes a difference for children?* New York: Cambridge University Press.

Brooks-Gunn, J., Berlin, L. J., & Aber, J. L. (1993, November). *A consideration of self sufficiency and parenting in the context of the Teenage Parent Demonstration Program.* Paper presented at the second National Head Start research conference, Washington, DC.

Brooks-Gunn, J., & Chase-Lansdale, P. L. (1991). Children having children: Effects on the family system. *Pediatric Annals, 20*(9), 467–481.

Brooks-Gunn, J., Duncan, G. J., Klebanov, P. K., & Sealand, N. (1993). Do neighborhoods influence child and adolescent development? *American Journal of Sociology, 99*(2), 353–395.

Brooks-Gunn, J., & Furstenberg, F. F., Jr. (1986). Antecedents and consequences of parenting: The case of adolescent motherhood. In A. Fogel & G. Melson (Eds.), *Origins of nurturance: Developmental, biological and cultural perspectives on caregiving* (pp. 233–258). Hillsdale, NJ: Lawrence Erlbaum Associates.

Brooks-Gunn, J., & Furstenberg, F. F., Jr. (1987). Continuity and change in the context of poverty: Adolescent mothers and their children. In J. J. Gallagher & C. T. Ramey (Eds.), *The malleability of children* (pp. 171–188). Baltimore: Brookes.

Brooks-Gunn, J., & Furstenberg, F. F., Jr. (1989). Adolescent sexual behavior. *American Psychologist, 44*(2), 249–257.

Brooks-Gunn, J., & Furstenberg, F. F., Jr. (1990). Coming of age in the era of AIDS: Sexual and contraceptive decisions. *Milbank Quarterly, 68,* 59–84.

Brooks-Gunn, J., Guo, G., & Furstenberg, F. F., Jr. (1993). Who drops out of and who continues beyond high school?: A 20-year follow-up of Black urban youth. *Journal of Research on Adolescence, 3*(3), 271–294.

Brooks-Gunn, J., Klebanov, P. K., & Duncan, G. (in press). Ethnic differences in children's intelligence test scores: Role of economic deprivation, home environment, and maternal characteristics. *Child Development.*

Brooks-Gunn, J., Klebanov, P. K., & Liaw, F. (1994). The learning, physical and emotional environment of the home in the context of poverty: The infant health and development program. *Children and Youth Services Review, 17,* 251.

Brooks-Gunn, J., Klebanov, P. K., Liaw, F., & Duncan, G. (in press). Toward an understanding of the effects of poverty upon children. In H. E. Fitzgerald, B. M. Leister, & B. Zuckerman (Eds.), *Children of poverty: Research, health care, and policy issues.* New York: Garland Press.

Brooks-Gunn, J., & Lewis, M. (1984). Maternal responsivity in interactions with handicapped infants. *Child Development, 55*(3), 782–793.

Brooks-Gunn, J., & Paikoff, R. L. (1993). "Sex is a gamble, kissing is a game": Adolescent sexuality, contraception, and pregnancy. In S. P. Millstein, A. C. Petersen, & E. O. Nightingale (Eds.), *Promoting the health of adolescents: New directions for the twenty-first century* (pp. 180–208). New York: Oxford University Press.

Brooks-Gunn, J., & Petersen, A. C. (1991). Studying the emergence of depression and depressive symptoms during adolescence. *Journal of Youth and Adolescence, 20*(2), 115–119.

Brooks-Gunn, J., Phelps, E., & Elder, G. H., Jr. (1991). Studying lives through time: Secondary data analysis in developmental psychology. *Developmental Psychology, 27* (6), 899–910.

Brooks-Gunn, J., & Zahaykevich, M. (1989). Parent–daughter relationships in early adolescence: A developmental perspective. In K. Kreppner & R. M. Lerner (Eds.), *Family systems and life-span development,* (pp. 223–246). Hillsdale, NJ: Lawrence Erlbaum Associates.

Brunnquell, D., Crichton, L., & Egeland, B. (1981). Maternal personality and attitude in disturbances of child rearing. *American Journal of Orthopsychiatry, 51*(4), 680–691.

Burton, L. M. (1990). Teenage childbearing as an alternative life-course strategy in multigeneration Black families. *Human Nature, 1*(2), 123–143.

Burton, L. M. (1992, May). *Intergenerational patterns of providing care in African-American families with adolescent childbearers.* Paper presented at the National Institute of Child Health and Development conference, Bethesda, MD.

Burton, L. M., & Bengston, V. L. (1985). Black grandmothers: Issues of time and continuity of roles. In V. L. Bengtson & J. Robertson (Eds.), *Grandparenthood* (pp. 61–77). Beverly Hills, CA: Sage.

Burton, L. M., & Dilworth-Anderson, P. (1991). The intergenerational family roles of aged Black Americans. *Marriage and Family Review, 16*(3 & 4), 311–330.

Caldwell, B. M., & Bradley, R. H. (1984). *Home observation for measurement of the environment.* Little Rock, AR: Authors.

Carter, S. L., Osofsky, J. D., & Hann, D. M. (1991). Speaking for the baby: A therapeutic intervention with adolescent mothers and their infants. *Infant Mental Health Journal, 12*(4), 291–301.

Case, R. (1985). *Intellectual development: Birth to adulthood.* New York: Academic Press.

Caspi, A., & Elder, G. (1988). Emergent family patterns: The intergenerational construction of problem behavior and relationships. In R. Hinde & J. Stevenson-Hinde (Eds.), *Relationships within the family: Mutual influences* (pp. 218–240). Oxford, England: Clarendon.

Center for Human Resource Research. (1988). *NLS Handbook 1988.* Columbus: Ohio State University Press.

Chase-Lansdale, P. L., & Brooks-Gunn, J. (1994). Correlates of adolescent pregnancy. In C. B. Fisher & R. M. Lerner (Eds.), *Applied Developmental Psychology.* Acmbridge, MA: McGraw-Hill.

Chase-Lansdale, P. L., & Brooks-Gunn, J. (Eds.). (in press). *Escape from poverty: What makes a difference for children?* New York: Cambridge University Press.

Chase-Lansdale, P. L., Brooks-Gunn, J., & Paikoff, R. L. (1991). Research and programs for adolescent mothers: Missing links and future promises. *Family Relations, 40*(4), 396–404.

Chase-Lansdale, P. L., Brooks-Gunn, J., & Zamsky, E. S. (1994). Young African-American multigenerational families in poverty: Quality of mothering and grandmothering. *Child Development, 65*(2), 373–393.

Chase-Lansdale, P. L., & Hetherington, E. M. (1990). The impact of divorce on life-span development: Short and longterm effects. In P. B. Baltes, D. L. Featherman, & R. M. Lerner (Eds.), *Life span development and behavior* (Vol. 10, pp. 107–151). Hillsdale, NJ: Lawrence Erlbaum Associates.

Chase-Lansdale, P. L., Mott, F. L., Brooks-Gunn, J., & Phillips, D. (1991). Children of the NLSY: A unique research opportunity. *Developmental Psychology, 27*(6), 918–931.

Chase-Lansdale, P. L., & Vinovskis, M. A. (1992). Adolescent pregnancy and child support. In R. Wollons (Ed.), *Children at risk in America: History, concept, & public policy* (pp. 202–229). Albany: State University of New York Press.

Chase-Lansdale, P. L., & Vinovskis, M. A. (in press). Whose responsibility? An historical analysis of the changing roles of mothers, fathers, and society. In P. L. Chase-Lansdale & J. Brooks-Gunn (Eds.), *Escape from poverty: What makes a difference for children?* New York: Cambridge University Press.

Chase-Lansdale, P. L., Wakschlag, L. S., & Brooks-Gunn, J. (in press). A psychological perspective on the development of caring in children and youth: The role of the family. *Journal of Adolescence.*

Cherlin, A. J. (in press). Child care for poor children: Policy issues. In P. L. Chase-Lansdale & J. Brooks-Gunn (Eds.), *Escape from poverty: What makes a difference for poor children?* New York: Cambridge University Press.

Cherlin, A. J., Furstenberg, F. F., Chase-Lansdale, P. L., Kiernan, K. E., Robins, P. K., Morrison, D. R., & Teitler, J. O. (1991). Longitudinal studies of effects of divorce on children in Great Britain and the United States. *Science, 252,* 1386–1389.

Clewell, B. C., Brooks-Gunn, J., & Benasich, A. A. (1989). Evaluating child-related outcomes of teenage parenting programs. *Family Relations, 38,* 201–209.

Cohen, J. B., & Lazarus, R. S. (1977). *Social Support Questionnaire.* Berkeley: University of California Press.

Colletta, N. D., Hadler, S., & Gregg, C. H. (1981, Fall). How adolescents cope with the problems of early motherhood. *Adolescence, 63,* 499–512.

Coll, C. G., Vohr, B. R., Hoffman, J., & Oh, W. (1986). Maternal and environmental factors affecting developmental outcomes of infants of adolescent mothers. *Developmental and Behavioral Pediatrics, 7,* 230–236.

Cowan, C. P., & Cowan, P. A. (1988). Who does what when partners become parents: Implications for men, women, and marriage. *Marriage and Family Review, 12*(3 & 4), 105–131.

Cowan, C. P., & Cowan, P. A. (1992). *When partners become parents: The big life change for couples.* New York: Basic Books.

Crane, J. (1991). The epidemic theory of ghettos and neighborhood effects on dropping out and teenage childbearing. *American Journal of Sociology, 96*(5), 1226–1259.

Crnic, K. A., Greenberg, M. T., Ragozin, A. S., Robinson, N. M., & Basham, R. B. (1983). Effects of stress and social support on mothers and premature and full term infants. *Child Development, 54,* 209–217.

Crockenberg, S. (1981). Infant irritability responsiveness, and social support influences on the security of infant–mother attachment. *Child Development, 52*(3), 857–865.

Crockenberg, S. (1987). Predictors and correlates of anger toward and punitive control of toddlers by adolescent mothers. *Child Development, 58*(4), 964–975.

Culp, R. E., Appelbaum, M. I., Osofsky, J. D., & Levy, J. A. (1988). Adolescent and older mothers: Comparison between prenatal maternal variables and newborn interaction measures. *Infant Behavior and Development, 11*(3), 353–362.

Culp, R. E., Culp, A. M., Osofsky, J. D., & Osofsky, H. J. (1991). Adolescent and toddler mothers' interaction patterns with their six-month-old infants. *Journal of Adolescence, 14*(2), 195–200.

de Lissovey, V. (1973). Child care by adolescent parents. *Children Today,* pp. 22–25.

Deutsch, F. M., Ruble, D. N., Fleming, A., Brooks-Gunn, J., & Stangor, C. (1988). Information-seeking and self-definition during the transition to motherhood. *Journal of Personality and Social Psychology, 55*(3), 420–431.

Doucette-Gates, A., Brooks-Gunn, J., & Chase-Lansdale, P. L. (in press). Adolescent research: The role of bias and equivalence. In V. McLoyd & L. Steinberg (Eds), *Studying minority adolescents.* Hillsdale, NJ: Lawrence Erlbaum Associates.

Downey, G., & Coyne, J. C. (1990). Children of depressed parents: An integrative review. *Psychological Bulletin, 108*(1), 50–76.

Duncan, G. J. (1991). The economic environment of childhood. In A. C. Huston (Ed.), *Children in poverty* (pp. 23–50). New York: Cambridge University Press.

Duncan, G. J., Brooks-Gunn, J., & Klebanov, P. K. (in press). Economic deprivation and early-childhood development. *Child Development, 65*(2), 296–318.

Dyer, E. D. (1963). Parenthood as crisis: A restudy. *Marriage and Family Living, 25,* 196–201.

Egeland, B., Jacobvitz, D., & Sroufe, L. A. (1988). Breaking the cycle of abuse. *Child Development, 59*(4), 1080–1088.

Eisen, M., Zellman, G. L., Leibowitz, A., Chow, W. K., & Evans, J. R. (1983). Factors discriminating pregnancy resolution decisions of unmarried adolescents. *Genetic Psychology Monographs, 108,* 69–95.

Ekstrom, R. B., Goertz, M. E., Pollack, J. M., & Rock, D. A. (1986). Who drops out of high school and why? Findings from a national study. *Teachers College Record, 87,* 356–373.

Elder, G. H. (1974). *Children of the great depression: Social change in life experience.* Chicago: University of Chicago Press.

Elder, G. H., Jr. (1977). *Children of the great depression.* Chicago: University of Chicago.

Ellwood, D. T. (1988). *Poor support: Poverty in the American family.* New York: Basic Books.

Elster, A. B., & Lamb, M. E. (1986). *Adolescent fatherhood.* Hillsdale, NJ: Lawrence Erlbaum Associates.

Emery, R. E. (1982). Interparental conflict and the children of discord and divorce. *Psychological Bulletin, 92*(2), 310–330.

Epstein, S. (1979). The stability of behavior: I. On predicting most of the people much of the time. *Journal of Personality and Social Psychology, 37,* 1097–1126.

Featherman, D. L., & Spenner, K. I. (1988). Class and the socialization of children: Constancy, change or irrelevance? In E. M. Hetherington, R. M. Lerner, & M. Perlmutter (Eds.), *Child development in life-span perspective* (pp. 67–90). Hillsdale, NJ: Lawrence Erlbaum Associates.

Feldman, S. S., & Nash, S. C. (1984). The transition from expectancy to parenthood: Impact of the first-born child on men and women. *Sex Roles, 11,* 61–78.

Feldman, S. S., & Nash, S. C. (1985). Antecedents of early parenting. In A. Fogel & G. F. Melson (Eds.), *Origins of nurturance: Developmental, biological and cultural perspectives on caregiving* (pp. 209–232). Hillsdale, NJ: Lawrence Erlbaum Associates.

Field, T. (1980). Interactions of high risk infants: Quantitative and qualitative differences. In D. B. Sawin, R. C. Hawkins, L. D. Walker, & J. H. Penticull (Eds.), *The exceptional infant* (Vol. 4, pp. 120–143). New York: Brunner/Mazel.

Field, T. (1981). Infant arousal, attention, and affect during early interactions. In L. Lipsitt & C. K. Rovee-Collier (Eds.), *Advances in infancy research* (Vol. 1, pp. 58–100). Norwood, NJ:Ablex.

Field, T. (1982). Affective displays of high-risk infants during early interactions. In T. M. Field & A. Fogel (Eds.), *Emotion and early interactions* (pp. 101–125). Hillsdale, NJ: Lawrence Erlbaum Associates.

Field, T. M., Healy, B., Goldstein, S., & Guthertz, M. (1990). Behavior-state matching and synchrony in mother–infant interactions of nondepressed versus depressed dyads. *Developmental Psychology, 26,* 7–14.

Field, T. M., & Widmayer, S. M. (1981). Mother–infant interaction among lower SES Black, Cuban, Puerto Rican and South American immigrants. In T. M. Field, A. M. Sostek, P. Vietze, & P. H. Liederman (Eds.), *Culture and early interactions* (pp. 41–62). Hillsdale, NJ: Lawrence Erlbaum Associates.

Field, T., Widmayer, S. M., Stringer, S., & Ignatoff, E. (1980). Teenage, lower-class, Black mothers and their preterm infants: An intervention and developmental follow-up. *Child Development, 51,* 426–436.

Fox, G. L. (1982). *The childbearing decision: Fertility attitudes and behavior.* Beverly Hills, CA: Sage.

Frodi, A. (1983). Attachment behavior and sociability with strangers in premature and full-term infants. *Infant Mental Health Journal, 4,* 13–22.

Furstenberg, F. F., Jr. (1976). *Unplanned parenthood: The social consequences of teenage childbearing.* New York: The Free Press.

Furstenberg, F. F., Jr. (1991). As the pendulum swings: Teenage childbearing and social concern. *Family Relations, 40*(2), 127–138.

Furstenberg, F. F., Jr. (in press). Dealing with dads: The changing roles of fathers. In P. L. Chase-Lansdale & J. Brooks-Gunn (Eds.), *Escape for poverty: What makes a difference for children?* New York: Cambridge University Press.

Furstenberg, F. F., Jr., Brooks-Gunn, J., & Chase-Lansdale, P. L. (1989). Adolescent fertility and public policy. *American Psychologist, 44*(2), 313–320.

Furstenberg, F. F., Jr., Brooks-Gunn, J., & Morgan, P. (1987). *Adolescent mothers in later life.* New York: Cambridge University Press.

Furstenberg, F. F., Jr., & Crawford, A. G. (1978). Family support: Helping teenage mothers to cope. *Family Planning Perspectives, 10*(6), 322–333.

Furstenberg, F. F., Jr., & Harris, K. M. (1989, April). *When fathers matter/why fathers matter: The impact of paternal involvement on the offspring of adolescent mothers.* Paper presented at the Adolescent Pregnancy Conference, Stanford University, Stanford, CA.

Furstenberg, F. F., Jr., Hughes, M. E., & Brooks-Gunn, J. (1992). The next generation: Children of teenage mothers grow up. In M. K. Rosenheim & M. F. Testa (Eds.), *Early parenthood* (pp. 113–135). New Brunswick, NJ: Rutgers University Press.

Furstenberg, F. F., Jr., Levine, J. A., & Brooks-Gunn, J. (1990). The daughters of teenage mothers: Patterns of early childbearing in two generations. *Family Planning Perspectives, 22*(2), 54–61.

Garcia Coll, C. T. (1989). The consequences of teenage childbearing in traditional Puerto Rican culture. In J. K. Nugent, B. Lester, & T. B. Brazelton (Eds.), *The cultural context of infancy: Biology, culture, and infant development* (Vol. 1, pp. 111–132). Norwood, NJ: Ablex.

Garfinkel, I., & McLanahan, S. (1986). *Single mothers and their children: A new American dilemma.* Washington, DC: Urban Institute Press.

Garfinkel, I., & McLanahan, S. (in press). The effects of child support reform on child well-being. In P. L. Chase-Lansdale & J. Brooks-Gunn (Eds.), *Escape from poverty: What makes a difference for poor children?* New York: Cambridge University Press.

Geronimus, A. (1987). On teenage childbearing and neonatal mortality in the United States. *Population and Development Review, 13*(2), 245–280.

Geronimus, A. (1991). Teenage childbearing and social and reproductive disadvantage: The evolution of complex questions and the demise of simple answers. *Family Relations, 40*(4), 463–471.

Geronimus, A. T., & Bound, J. (1990). Black/White differences in women's reproductive-related health status: Evidence from vital statistics. *Demography, 27*(3), 457–466.

Geronimus, A., & Korenman, S. (1992). The socioeconomic consequences of teen childbearing reconsidered. *Quarterly Journal of Economics, 107,* 1187–1214.

Goldberg, W. A., & Easterbrooks, M. A. (1984). Toddler development in the family: Impact of father involvement and parenting characteristics. *Child Development, 55*(3), 740–752.

Greenberg, N. H., Loesch, J. G., & Lakin, M. (1959). Life situations associated with the onset of pregnancy. *Psychosomatic Medicine, 21,* 296–310.

Grossman, F. K., Eichler, L. S., Winickoff, S. A., Anzalone, M. K., Gofseyeff, M. H., & Sargent, S. P. (1980). *Pregnancy, birth, and parenthood.* San Francisco: Jossey-Bass.

Grotevant, H., & Cooper, C. (Eds.). (1984). *New directions for child development: Adolescent development in the family.* San Francisco: Jossey-Bass.

Gutierrez, J., & Sameroff, A. (1990). Determinants of complexity in Mexican-American and Anglo-American mother's conceptions of child development. *Child Development, 61,* 384–394.

Hagestad, G. O. (1986). Dimensions of time and the family. *American Behavioral Scientist, 29*(6), 679–694.

Halpern, R. (1993). Poverty and infant development. In C. Zeanah (Ed.), *Handbook of infant mental health* (pp. 73–86). New York: Guilford.

Hamburg, B. A. (1980). Developmental issues in school-age pregnancy. In E. Purcell (Ed.), *Aspects of psychiatric problems of childhood and adolescence* (pp. 299–325). New York: Macy Foundation.

Hamburg, B. A. (1986). Subsets of adolescent mothers: Developmental, biomedical, and psychosocial issues. In J. B. Lancaster & B. A. Hamburg (Eds.), *School-age pregnancy and parenthood: Biosocial dimensions* (pp. 115–145). New York: Aldine de Gruyter.

Hann, D. M., Castino, R. J., Jarosinski, J., & Britton, H. (1991, April). Relating mother–toddler negotiation patterns to infant attachment and maternal depression with an adolescent mother sample. In J. D. Osofsky & L. Hubbs-Tait (Chairs), *Consequences of adolescent parenting: Predicting behavior problems in toddlers and preschoolers.* Symposium conducted at the biennial meeting of the Society for Research in Child Development, Seattle.

Hann, D. M., Osofsky, J. D., Stringer, S. S., & Carter, S. S. (1988, April) *Affective contributions of adolescent mothers and infants to the quality of attachment.* Paper presented at the International Conference on Infant Studies, Washington, DC.

Hann, D. M., Robinson, J. L., Osofsky, J. D., & Little, C. (1991, April). *Emotional availability in two caregiving environments: Low-risk adult mothers and socially at-risk adolescent mothers.* Paper presented at the biennial meeting of the Society for Research in Child Development, Seattle.

Hareven, T. K. (1977). Family time and historical time. *Daedalus, 106,* 57–70.

Hauser, S. T., Borman, E. H., Powers, S. I., Jacobson, A. M., & Noam, G. G. (1990). Paths of adolescent ego development: Links with family life and individual adjustment. *Psychiatric Clinics of North America, 13*(3), 489–510.

Haveman, R., Wolfe, B., & Spaulding, J. (1991). Childhood events and circumstances influencing high school completion. *Demography, 28*(1), 133–157.

Hayes, C. D. (Ed.). (1987). *Risking the future: Adolescent sexuality, pregnancy, and childbearing* (Vol. 1). Washington, DC: National Academy of Sciences Press.

Hernandez, D. J., & Myers, D. E. (1993). *America's children: Resources from family, government, and the economy.* New York: Russell Sage Foundation.

Hetherington, E. M. (1993). An overview of the Virginia longitudinal study of divorce and remarriage: A focus on early adolescence. *Journal of Family Psychology, 7,* 39–56.

Hetherington, E. M., & Clingempeel, W. G. (1992). Coping with marital transitions: A family systems perspective. *Monographs of the Society for Research in Child Development, 57*(2–3, Serial No. 227).

Hill, M. S. (1992). *The Panel Study of Income Dynamics: A user's guide.* Beverly Hills, CA: Sage.

Hill, M. S., & Duncan, G. J. (1987). Parental family income and the socioeconomic attainment of children. *Social Science Research, 16,* 39–73.

Hinde, R., & Stevenson-Hinde, J. (1988). *Relationships within families: Mutual influences.* Oxford, England: Clarendon.

Hofferth, S. L. (1984). Kin networks, race and family structure. *Journal of Marriage and the Family, 46,* 791–806.

Hofferth, S. L. (1987). The effects of programs and policies on adolescent pregnancy and childbearing. In S. L. Hofferth & C. D. Hayes (Eds.), *Risking the future: Adolescent sexuality, pregnancy, and childbearing* (Vol. 2, pp. 207–263). Washington, DC: National Academy of Sciences Press.

Hofferth, S. L., & Hayes, C. D. (Eds.). (1987). *Risking the future: Adolescent sexuality, pregnancy, and childbearing* (Vol. 2). Washington, DC: National Academy of Sciences Press.

Hoffman, S. D., Foster, E. M., & Furstenberg, F. F., Jr. (1993). Reevaluating the costs of teenage childbearing. *Demography, 30*(1), 1–14.

Hogan, D. P., & Astone, N. M. (1986). The transition to adulthood. *Annual Review of Sociology, 12,* 109–130.

Hogan, D. P., Hao, L. X., & Parish, W. L. (1990). Race, kin networks and assistance to mother-headed families. *Social Forces, 68,* 797–812.

Hopkins, J., Marcus, M., & Campbell, S. B. (1984). Postpartum depression: A critical review. *Psychological Bulletin, 95*(3), 498–515.

Horwitz, S. M., Klerman, L. V., Kuo, H. S., & Jekel, J. F. (1991). School-age mothers: Predictors of long-term educational and economic outcomes. *Pediatrics, 87*(6), 862–867.

Huston, A. C. (Ed.). (1991). *Children in poverty: Child development and public policy.* New York: Cambridge University Press.

Jarrett, R. L. (1990). *A comparative examination of socialization patterns among low-income African-Americans, Chicanos, Puerto-Ricans, and Whites: A review of the ethnographic literature.* New York: Social Science Research Council.

Jarrett, R. L. (in press). Community context, intrafamilial processes, and social mobility outcomes: Ethnographic contributions to the study of African-American families and children in poverty. In M. B. Spencer & G. K. Brookins (Eds.), *Ethnicity and diversity*. Hillsdale, NJ: Lawrence Erlbaum Associates.

Jencks, C. (1988, June). Deadly neighborhoods. *The New Republic,* pp. 24–32.

Jessner, L., Weigert, E., & Fay, J. L. (1970). The development of parental attitudes during pregnancy. In E. J. Anthony & T. Benedek (Eds.), *Parenthood: Its psychology and psychopathology* (pp. 209–244). Boston: Little, Brown.

Jones, E. F., Forrest, J. D., Goldman, N., Henshaw, S., Lincoln, R., Rosoff, J., Westoff, C., & Wulf, D. (1985). Teenage pregnancy in developed countries: Determinants and policy implications. *Family Planning Perspectives, 17*(2), 53–63.

Jones, E., Forrest, J. D., Henshaw, S. K., Silverman, J., & Torres, A. (1988). Unintended pregnancy, contraceptive practice and family planning services in developed countries. *Family Planning Perspectives, 20*(2), 53–67.

Kasanin, J., & Handschin, S. (1941). Psychodynamic factors in illegitimacy. *American Journal of Orthopsychiatry, 11,* 66–84.

Keating, D. P. (1990). Adolescent thinking. In S. S. Feldman & G. R. Elliott (Eds.), *At the threshold: The developing adolescent* (pp. 54–91). Cambridge, MA: Harvard University Press.

Kellam, S. G., Adams, R., Brown, C. H., & Ensminger, M. (1982). The long-term evolution of the family structure of teenage and older mothers. *Journal of Marriage and the Family, 44,* 539–554.

Kellam, S. G., Ensminger, M. E., & Turner, R. J. (1977). Family structure and the mental health of children: Concurrent and longitudinal community-wide studies. *Archives of General Psychiatry, 34,* 1012–1022.

Klebanov, P. K., Brooks-Gunn, J., & Duncan, G. J. (1994). Does neighborhood and family affect mothers' parenting, mental health, and social support? *Journal of Marriage and the Family 56*(2), 441–455.

Klerman, G. L. (1974). Depression and adaptation. In R. C. Friedman & M. M. Katz (Eds.), *The psychology of depression* (pp. 127–146) . Washington, DC: Winston.

Kohlberg, L. (1966). A cognitive-developmental analysis of children's sex-role concepts and attitudes. In E. E. Maccoby (Ed.), *The development of sex differences* (pp. 82–173). Stanford, CA: Stanford University Press.

Kumar, R., Robson, K. M., & Smith A. M. (1984). Development of a self-administered questionnaire to measure maternal adjustment and maternal attitudes during pregnancy and after delivery. *Journal of Psychosomatic Research, 28*(1), 43–51.

Lamb, M. E., Hopps, K., & Elster, A. B. (1987). Strange situation behavior of infants with adolescent mothers. *Infant Behavior and Development, 10,* 39–48.

Lazarus, R. S., & Folkman, S. (1984). *Stress appraisal and coping.* New York: Springer-Verlag.

Leadbeater, B. J., & Linares, O. (1992). Depressive symptoms in Black and Puerto Rican adolescent mothers in the first three years postpartum. *Development and Psychopathology, 4*(3), 451–468.

Leifer, M. (1980). *Psychological aspects of motherhood: A study of first pregnancy.* New York: Praeger.

LeMasters, E. E. (1957). Parenthood as crisis. *Marriage and Family Living, 19,* 352–353.

Lester, B., Garcia Coll, C. T., & Sepkoski, C. (1983). A cross-cultural study of teenage pregnancy and neonatal behavior. In T. M. Field & A. Sostek (Eds.), *Infants born at risk: Physiological, perceptual, and cognitive processes* (pp. 147–169). New York: Grune & Stratton.

Liaw, F., & Brooks-Gunn, J. (1994). Cumulative familial risks and low-birthweight children's cognitive and behavioral development. *Journal of Clinical Child Psychology 23*(4), 360–372.

Luster, T., & Dubow, E. (1990). Predictors of the quality of the home environment that adolescent mothers provide for their school-aged children. *Journal of Youth and Adolescence, 19*(5), 475–495.

Maccoby, E. E., & Martin, J. A. (1983). Socialization in the context of the family: Parent–child interaction. In P. H. Mussen (Series Ed.) & E. M. Hetherington (Vol. Ed.), *Handbook of child psychology: Vol 4. Socialization, personality, and social development* (4th ed., pp. 755–911). New York: Wiley.

Mahler, M. S., Pine, F., & Bergman, A. (1975). *Psychological birth of the human infant: Symbiosis and individuation.* New York: Basic Books.

Main, M., & Goldwyn, R. (1984). Predicting rejection of her infant from mother's representation of her own experience: Implications for the abused–abusing intergenerational cycle. *International Journal of Child Abuse and Neglect, 8,* 203–217.

Mare, R. D. (1980). Social background and school continuation decisions. *Journal of the American Statistical Association, 75,* 295–305.

Marecek, J. (1979). *Economic, social, and psychological consequences of adolescent childbearing: An analysis of data from the Philadelphia Collaborative Perinatal Project* (Final report to the National Institute of Child Health and Human Development). Swathmore, PA: Swathmore College.

Marecek, J. (1987). Counseling adolescents with problem pregnancies. *American Psychologist, 42*(1), 89–93.

Marsiglio, W. (1986). Teenage fatherhood: High school completion and educational attainment. In A. B. Elster & M. E. Lamb (Eds.), *Adolescent fatherhood* (pp. 67–88). Hillsdale, NJ: Lawrence Erlbaum Associates.

Marsiglio, W., & Mott, F. (1986). The impact of sex education on sexual activity, contraception use and premarital pregnancy among American teenagers. *Family Planning Perspectives, 18*(4), 151–162.

Marx, F., Bailey, S., & Francis, J. (1988). *Child care for the children of adolescent parents: Findings from a national survey and case studies* (Working paper No. 184). Wellesley College, Center for Research on Women, Wellesley, MA.

Matas, L., Arend, R., & Sroufe, A. L. (1978). Continuity of adaptation in the second year: The relationship between quality of attachment and competence. *Child Development, 49,* 547–556.

McAdoo, H.P. (Ed.). (1988). *Black families* (2nd ed.). Newbury Park, CA: Sage.

McAnarney, E. R., Lawrence, R. A., Ricciuti, H. N., Polley, J., & Szilagyi, M. (1986). Interactions of adolescent mothers and their one-year-old children. *Pediatrics, 78*(4), 588–590.

McCarthy, J., & Hardy, J. (1993). Age at first birth and birth outcomes. *Journal of Research on Adolescence, 3*(4), 373–392.

McCormick, M. C., Brooks-Gunn, J., Shorter, T., Wallace, C. Y., Holmes, J. H., & Heagarty, M. C. (1987). The planning of pregnancy among low-income women in central Harlem. *American Journal of Obstetrics and Gynecology, 156*(1), 145–149.

McLanahan, S., Astone, N. M., & Marks, N. F. (1991). The role of mother-only families in reducing poverty. In A. C. Huston (Ed.), *Children in poverty: Child development and public policy* (pp. 51–78). Cambridge, MA: Cambridge University Press.

McLanahan, S., & Sandefur, G. (1994). *Growing up with a single parent: What hurts, what helps.* Cambridge, MA: Harvard University Press.

McLoyd, V. C. (1990). The impact of economic hardship on Black families and children: Psychological distress, parenting, socioemotional development. *Child Development, 61,* 311–346.

McLoyd, V. C., & Steinberg, L. (Eds.). (in press). *Studying minority adolescence.* Hillsdale, NJ: Lawrence Erlbaum Associates.

McNair, S. (1991, April). *Gender difference in nurturance and restrictiveness in grandparents of young children of teen mothers.* Paper presented at the biennial meeting of the Society for Research in Child Development, Seattle.

Miller, B. C. (1992). Adolescent parenthood, economic issues, and social policies. *Journal of Family and Economic Issues, 13*(4), 467–475.

Miller, B. C. (1993). Families, science, and values: Alternative views of parenting effects and adolescent pregnancy. *Journal of Marriage and the Family, 55,* 7–21.

Miller, B. C., & Moore, K. A. (1990). Adolescent sexual behavior, pregnancy, and parenting: Research through the 1980s. *Journal of Marriage and the Family, 52*(4), 1025–1044.

Modell, J., Furstenberg, F., & Hershberg, T. (1976). Social change and transitions to adulthood in historical perspective. *Journal of Family History, 1,* 7–32.

Modell, J., & Goodman, M. (1990). Historical perspectives. In S. S. Feldman & G. R. Elliott (Eds.), *At the threshold: The developing adolescent* (pp. 93–123). Cambridge, MA: Harvard University Press.

Moore, K. A. (1985). *Facts at a glance.* Unpublished manuscript, Child Trends, Inc., Washington, DC.

Moore, K. A., Myers, D. E., Morrison, D. R., Nord, C. W., Brown, B., & Edmonston, B. (1993). Age at first childbirth and later poverty. *Journal of Research on Adolescence, 3*(4), 393–422.

Moore, K. A., Nord, C. W., & Peterson, J. L. (1989). Nonvoluntary sexual activity among adolescents. *Family Planning Perspectives, 21,* 110–114.

Moore, K. A., Simms, M. C., & Betsey, C. L. (1986). *Choice and circumstance: Racial differences in adolescent sexuality and fertility.* New Brunswick, NJ: Transaction Books.

Moore, K. A., & Snyder, N. O. (1991). Cognitive attainment among firstborn children of adolescent mothers. *American Sociological Review, 56* (5), 612–624.

Mott, F. L., & Maxwell, N. L. (1981). School-age mothers: 1968–1979. *Family Planning Perspectives, 13*(6), 287–292.

National Center for Health Statistics. (1988). *Advanced report of final natality statistics; 1986* (Monthly Vital Statistics Report No. 37:3) (Supplement). Hyattsville, MD: Public Health Services.

Oakley, A. (1980). *Women confined: Towards a sociology of childbirth.* New York: Schochen Books.

Ooms, T. (Ed.). (1981). *Teenage pregnancy in a family context: Implications for policy.* Philadelphia: Temple University Press.

Osofsky, H. J., & Osofsky, J. D. (1970). Adolescents as mothers: Results of a program for low-income pregnant teenagers with some emphasis upon infants' development. *American Journal of Orthopsychiatry, 40*(5), 825–834.

Osofsky, J. D., Barnard, K. B., Beckwith, L., Appelbaum, M., Morrisett, C., Hann, D. M., & Osofsky, J. D. (1993, March). *Early emotional development: Results of collaborative intervention project.* Paper presented at biennial meeting of Society for Research in Child Development, New Orleans.

Osofsky, J. D., Culp, A. W., Eberhart-Wright, A., Ware, L. M., & Hann, D. M. (1988). *Intervention program for adolescent mothers and their infants* (Final report to Kenworthy Foundation, Meninger Clinic, Topeka, Kansas, and Louisiana State University, New Orleans). New Orleans: Louisiana State University.

Osofsky, J. D., & Eberhart-Wright, A. (1988). Affective exchanges between high risk mothers and infants. *International Journal of Psychoanalysis, 69,* 221–231.

Osofsky, J. D., Eberhart-Wright, A., & Ware, L. M. (1992). Children of adolescent mothers: A group at risk for psychopathology. *Infant Mental Health Journal, 13*(2), 119–131.

Osofsky, J. D., Hann, D. M., & Peebles, C. (1993). Adolescent parenthood: Risks and opportunities for parents and infants. In C. H. Zeanah Jr. (Ed.), *Handbook of infant mental health.* New York: Guilford.

Osofsky, J. D., Peebles, C., Fick, A., & Hann, D. M. (1992). *Relationships between personality development and affective development in African-American adolescent mothers and their infants.* Manuscript submitted for publication.

Oyserman, D., Radin, N., & Benn, R. (1993). Dynamics in a three-generational family: Teens, grandparents, and babies. *Developmental Psychology, 29*(3), 564–572.

Paikoff, R., & Brooks-Gunn, J. (1991). Do parent–child relationships change during puberty? *Psychological Bulletin, 110*(1), 47–66.

Paikoff, R. L., Brooks-Gunn, J., & Baydar, N. (1993, March). *Multigenerational co-residence in a sample of 6–7 year-olds, NLSY.* Paper presented at the biennial meeting of the Society for Research on Child Development, New Orleans.

Parke, R. D. (1988). Families in life-span perspective: A multilevel developmental approach. In E. M. Hetherington, R. M. Lerner, & M. Perlmutter (Eds.), *Child development in life-span perspective* (pp. 159–190). Hillsdale, NJ: Lawrence Erlbaum Associates.

Parke, R. D., & Neville, B. (1987). Teenage fatherhood. In S. L. Hofferth & C. D. Hayes (Eds.), *Risking the future: Adolescent sexuality, pregnancy, and childbearing* (pp. 145–173). Washington DC: Urban Institute Press.

Parker, S., Greer, S., & Zuckerman, B. (1988). Double jeopardy: The impact of poverty on early child development. *Pediatric Clinics of North America, 35*(6), 1227–1240.

Parks, P. L., & Arndt, E. K. (1990). Differences between adolescents and adult mothers of infants. *Journal of Adolescent Health Care, 11*(3), 248–253.

Patterson, G. (1986). Performance models for antisocial boys. *American Psychologist, 41*(4), 432–444.

Pearlin, L. (1975). Sex roles and depression. In N. Datan & L. Ginsberg (Eds.), *Life-span developmental psychology: Normative life crises* (pp. 198–208). New York: Academic Press.

Petchesky, R. P. (1984). *Abortion and woman's choice: The state, sexuality, and the conditions of reproductive freedom.* New York: Longman.

Phipps-Yonas, S. (1980). Teenage pregnancy and motherhood: A review of the literature. *American Journal of Orthopsychiatry, 50*(3), 403–431.

Polit, D. F. (1989). Effects of a comprehensive program for teenage parents: Five years after project redirection. *Family Planning Perspectives, 21*(4), 164–169.

Pope, S., Casey, P., Bradley, R., & Brooks-Gunn, J. (1993). The effect of intergenerational factors on the development of low birth weight infants born to adolescent mothers. *Journal of the American Medical Association, 269*(11), 1396–1400.

Pratt, M. W., Hunsberger, B., Pancer, S. M., Roth, D., & Santolupo, S. (1993). Thinking about parenting: Reasoning about developmental issues across the lifespan. *Developmental Psychology, 29*(3), 585–595.

Quinton, D., & Rutter, M. (1988). *Parenting breakdown: The making and breaking of intergenerational links.* Aldershot, England: Avebury.

Ramey, C. T., Bryant, D. M., Wasik, B. H., Sparling, J. J., Fendt, K. H., & LaVange, L. M. (1992). The Infant Health and Development Program: Program elements, family participation, and child intelligence. *Pediatrics, 89*(3), 454–465.

Reiss, D. (1981). *The family's construction of reality.* Cambridge, MA: Harvard University Press.

Ruble, D. N. (1983). The development of social-comparison processes and their role in achievement-related self-socialization. In E. T. Higgins, D. N. Ruble, & W. W. Hartup (Eds.), *Social cognition and social development: A sociocultural perspective* (pp. 134–157). New York: Cambridge University Press.

Ruble, D. N., Brooks-Gunn, J., Fleming, A. S., Fitzmaurice, G., Stangor, C., & Deutsch, F. (1990). Transition to motherhood and the self: Measurement, stability, and change. *Journal of Personality and Social Psychology, 58*(3), 450–463.

Ruble, D. N., Fleming, A. S., Hackel, L. S., & Stangor, C. (1988). Changes in the marital relationship during the transition to first-time motherhood: Effects of violated expectations concerning division of household labor. *Journal of Personality and Social Psychology, 55*(1), 78–87.

Rutter, M. (1989). Pathways from childhood to adult life. *Journal of Child Psychiatry and Psychology and Applied Disciplines, 30,* 23–51.

Sameroff, A. J., & Emde, R. N. (Eds.). (1992). *Relationship disturbances in early childhood: A developmental approach.* New York: Basic Books.

Sameroff, A., & Feil, L. (1985). Parental conceptions of development. In I. E. Sigel (Ed.), *Parental belief systems: The psychological consequences for children* (pp. 83–105). Hillsdale, NJ: Lawrence Erlbaum Associates.

Sameroff, A. J., Seifer, R., Baldwin, A., & Baldwin, C. (1993). Stability of intelligence from preschool to adolescence: The influence of social and family risk factors. *Child Development, 64*(1), 80–97.

Sameroff, A., Seifer, R., Barocas, R., Zax, M., & Greenspan, S. (1987). IQ scores of 4–year-old children: Social-environmental risk factors. *Pediatrics, 79*(3), 343–350.

Sandler, H. M., Vietze, P., & O'Connor, S. (1981). Obstetric and neonatal outcomes following intervention with pregnant teenagers. In K. G. Scott, T. Field, & E. G. Robertson (Eds.), *Teenage parents and their offspring* (pp. 249–263). New York: Grune & Stratton.

Seitz, V., Apfel, N. H., & Rosenbaum, L. K. (in press). Effects of an intervention program for pregnant adolescents: Educational outcomes at 2 years postpartum. *American Journal of Community Psychology.*

Shereshefsky, P. M., & Yarrow, L. J. (1973). *Psychological aspects of a first pregnancy and early postnatal adaptation.* New York: Raven Press.

Simmons, R. G., & Blyth, D. A. (1987). *Moving into adolescence: The impact of pubertal change and school context.* New York: Aldine de Gruyter.

Simmons, R. L., Whitbeck, L. B., Conger, R. D., & Chyi-in, W. (1991). Intergenerational transmission of harsh parenting. *Developmental Psychology, 27*(1), 159–171.

Smetana, J. G. (1988). Concepts of self and social convention: Adolescents' and parents' reasoning about hypothetical and actual family conflicts. In M. R. Gunnar & W. A. Collins (Ed.), *Development during transition to adolescence: Minnesota symposia on child psychology* (Vol. 21, pp. 79–122). Hillsdale, NJ: Lawrence Erlbaum Associates.

Smith, S. (1995). *Two-generation programs for families in poverty.* Norwood, NJ: Ablex.

Smith, S. (in press). Two-generational program models: A new strategy and direction for future research. In P. L. Chase-Lansdale & J. Brooks-Gunn (Eds.), *Escape from poverty: What makes a difference for children?* New York: Cambridge University Press.

Sonenstein, F. L., Pleck, J. H., & Ku, L. C. (1989). Sexual activity, condom use, and AIDS awareness among adolescent males. *Family Planning Perspectives, 21*(4), 152–158.

Speiker, S. J. (1991, April). *Mothers in adolescence: Factors related to infant attachment and disorganization.* Paper presented at the biennial meeting of the Society for Research in Child Development, Seattle.

Sroufe, A. L. (1979). The coherence of individual development. *American Psychologist, 34*(10), 834–841.

Stack, C. B. (1974). *All our kin: Strategies for survival in a Black community.* New York: Harper & Row.

Steinberg, L. (1990). Autonomy, conflict, and harmony in the family relationship. In S. S. Feldman & G. R. Elliott (Eds.), *At the threshold: The developing adolescent* (pp. 255–276). Cambridge, MA: Harvard University Press.

Stewart, A. J. (1982). The course of individual adaptation to life changes. *Journal of Personality and Social Psychology, 42,* 1100–1113.

Stewart, A. J., Sokol, M., Healy, J. M., & Chester, N. L. (1986). Longitudinal studies of psychological consequences of life changes in children and adults. *Journal of Personality and Social Psychology, 50,* 143–151.

Sullivan, M. L. (1990). *The male role in teenage pregnancy and parenting: New directions for public policy.* New York: Vera Institute of Justice, Inc.

Sullivan, M. L. (1993). Culture and class as determinants of out-of-wedlock childbearing and poverty during late adolescence. *Journal of research on Adolescence, 3*(3), 295–317.

Sung, K. (1992). Teenage pregnancy and premarital childbirth in Korea: Issues and concerns. In M. K. Rosenheim & M. F. Testa (Eds.), *Early parenthood and coming of age in the 1990s* (pp. 173–183). New Brunswick, NJ: Rutgers University Press.

Thomson, E., & McLanahan, S. (1993, August). *Family structure and child well-being: Economic resource versus parental behavior.* Paper presented at the annual meeting of the American Sociological Association, Washington, DC.

Thomson, E., McLanahan, S. S., & Curtin, R. B. (1992). Family structure, gender, and parental socialization. *Journal of Marriage and the Family, 54,* 368–378.

Unger, D. G., & Wandersman, L. P. (1985). Social support and adolescent mothers: Action research contributions to theory and application. *Journal of Social Issues, 41*(1), 29–45.

Upchurch, D. M. (1993). Early schooling and childbearing experiences: Implications for postsecondary school attendance. *Journal of Research on Adolescence, 3*(4), 423–445.

Upchurch, D. M., & McCarthy, J. (1989). Adolescent childbearing and high school completion in the 1980s: Have things changed? *Family Planning Perspectives, 21*(5), 199–202.

Upchurch, D. M., & McCarthy, J. (1990). The timing of first birth and high school completion. *American Sociological Review, 55*(2), 224–234.

U.S. Bureau of Census. (1987). Marital status and living arrangements: March, 1986. In *Current Population Reports* (Series P-20, No. 418). Washington, DC: U.S. Government Printing Office.

U.S. Bureau of Census. (1988). *Statistical abstract of the United States* (108th ed.). Washington, DC: U.S. Government Printing Office.

U.S. Bureau of Census. (1991). Late expectations: Childbearing patterns of American women for the 1990's. In *Studies in American fertility, current population reports* (Series P-23, No. 176). Washington, DC: U.S. Government Printing Office.

U.S. House of Representatives, Committee on Ways and Means. (1989). *Background material and data on programs within the jurisdiction of the Committee on Ways and Means.* Washington, DC: U.S. Government Printing Office.

Vinovskis, M. A. (1988). Teenage pregnancy and the underclass. *The Public Interest, 93,* 87–96.

Wakschlag, L. S., Chase-Lansdale, P. L., & Brooks-Gunn, J. (in press). Not just ghosts in the nursery: The influence of current intergenerational processes on parenting and young African-American families. *Child Development.*

Ward, M. K. (1986). *Them children: A study in language learning.* New York: Waveland Press.

Ward, M. J., Carlson, E., Plunkett, S. W., & Kessler, D. B. (1988, March). Adolescent mother–infant attachment: Interactions, relationships, and adolescent development. In *Adolescents as mothers: Family processes and child outcomes.* Symposium conducted at the biennial meeting of the Society for Research on Adolescence, Alexandria, VA.

Wasserman, G. A., Brunelli, S. A., & Rauh, V. A. (1990). Social support and living arrangements of adolescent and adult mothers. *Journal of Adolescent Research, 5*(1), 54–66.

Wasserman, G. A., Brunelli, S. A., Rauh, V. A., & Alvarado, L. E. (1994). The cultural context of adolescent childrearing in three groups of urban minority mothers. In G. Lamberty & C. Garcia Coll (Eds.), *Puerto Rican woman and children: Issues in health, growth, and development.* New York: Plenum.

Wasserman, G. A., Rauh, V. A., Brunelli, S. A., Garcia-Castro, M., & Necos, B. (1990). Psychosocial attributes and life experiences of disadvantaged minority mothers: Age and ethnic variations. *Child Development, 61,* 566–580.

Werner, E. E., & Smith, R. S. (1982). *Vulnerable but invincible: A longitudinal study of resilient children and youth.* New York: McGraw-Hill.

Whiting, B. (1981). Environmental constraints on infant care practices. In R. H. Munroe, R. L. Munroe, & B. B. Whiting (Eds.), *Handbook of cross-cultural human development* (pp. 155–179). New York: Garland Press.

Whiting, B. B., & Edwards, C. P. (1988). *Children of different worlds: The formation of social behavior.* Cambridge, MA: Harvard University Press.

Wilson, J. B., Ellwood, D. T., & Brooks-Gunn, J. (in press). Welfare to work through the eyes of children: The impact on parenting of movement from AFDC to employment. In P. L. Chase-Lansdale & J. Brooks-Gunn (Eds.), *Escape from poverty: What makes a difference for children?* New York: Cambridge University Press.

Wilson, M. N. (1986). The Black extended family: An analytical consideration. *Developmental Psychology, 22*(2), 246–258.

Wilson, W. (1987). *The truly disadvantaged.* Chicago: University of Chicago Press.

Zahn-Waxler, C., Kochanska, G., Krupnick, J., & McKnew, D. (1990). Patterns of guilt in children of depressed and well mothers. *Developmental Psychology, 26* (1), 51–59.

Zelnik, M., & Kantner, J. F. (1980). Sexual activity, contraceptive use and pregnancy among metropolitan-area teenagers:1971–1979. *Family Planning Perspectives, 12*(5), 230–237.

Zelnik, M., Kantner, J. F. & Ford, K. (1981). *Sex and pregnancy in adolescence* (Sage Library of Social Research, Vol. 133). Beverly Hills, CA: Sage.

Zill, N., Moore, K. A., Smith, E. W., Stief, T., & Coiro, M. J. (in press). The life circumstances and development of children in welfare families: A profile based on national survey data. In P. L. Chase-Lansdale & J. Brooks-Gunn (Eds.), *Escape from poverty: What makes a difference for children?* New York: Cambridge University Press.

6

Nonparental Caregiving

K. Alison Clarke-Stewart
Virginia D. Allhusen
Darlene C. Clements
University of California, Irvine

INTRODUCTION

The past quarter century has seen dramatic changes in family life. One of the most notable of these changes is the trend toward greater labor force participation by mothers, coupled with greater involvement of caregivers other than parents in the care of young children. In 1970, only 30 percent of the mothers of children under 6 years of age in the United States were employed; this number has now doubled, and is expected to reach 70 percent by the year 2000. Some families have relatives (grandparents, aunts, older siblings) available to care for young children while the mother works. The trend observed in all Western societies toward smaller, more geographically spread out families, however, has clearly increased parents' need to find child care outside the family. Currently more than two thirds of preschool children in the United States receive care and education on a regular basis from persons other than their parents (National Center for Education Statistics, 1993).

The issue of the effects of nonparental care, often even non*familial* care, on young children's social and cognitive development has raised many questions among child development researchers. What is the significance of children's daily separations from their mothers? What is the nature of the attention children receive from their day-care providers? What are the effects of having multiple caregivers? What does it mean if these caregivers are unrelated to the family and if their styles of interacting with the child are different from the parents' and from each other's? Will children who spend several hours each day with other children be more dependent on their peers? Will they be more aggressive toward other children? Can children in day-care facilities with large groups of children and few caregivers be given enough stimulation to ensure their intellectual growth? Are day-care providers as committed as parents to fostering children's intellectual development? Questions such as these have engendered research and controversy among developmental psychologists.

In this chapter, we review the theories and studies bearing on these questions. We summarize the history of day care as it has developed in the United States and describe its current forms. The roles

---

Order of second and third authors is alphabetical.

of nonparental caregivers and the factors that influence caregivers' behavior are discussed. We cover the research comparing children with and without nonparental child-care experience and those enrolled in care of varying quality. Finally we look at the joint influences of family and child care and the direction of future research aimed at further understanding the effects of nonparental care in the context of the child's complete world.

THEORIES OF NONPARENTAL CARE

Several theories in developmental psychology have been applied to the topic of nonparental care, particularly in the first few years of a child's life. We discuss the three most significant of these theories in this section.

Attachment Theory

Early attachment theorists Bowlby (1969) and Ainsworth (Ainsworth, Blehar, Waters, & Wall, 1978) first emphasized the importance of the infant's relationship with an adult attachment figure as a prerequisite for the child's subsequent psychological development. Based on the quality of the attachment relationship formed during the first year of life, they suggested, the infant constructs an "internal working model" of the attachment figure—a set of expectations concerning that person's availability and a complementary view of the self as worthy or unworthy of such care. These working models contribute to the quality or level of "felt security" the infant experiences in the relationship with the adult and permit the child to venture forth to explore the world with confidence (Ainsworth et al., 1978; Bretherton, 1985).

Bowlby and Ainsworth's focus was almost exclusively upon the mother as the primary attachment figure. A large body of empirical work supported the idea that the quality of the infant's attachment to the mother is of central importance to the child's social development (see review by Lamb, Thompson, Gardner, & Charnov, 1985). However, many of these studies were conducted at a time when the vast majority of infants in the countries in which the studies were done were being cared for primarily by their mothers. As a result, attachment theorists developed their notions about the unique importance of the mother–infant relationship within the social and cultural context of the traditional maternal role—at home raising children.

As more mothers began to participate in the work force when their children were young, attachment theory adapted to the changing social context. A number of attachment theorists (e.g., Sroufe, 1983) acknowledged that children form attachments to several people during early childhood, including fathers and other caregivers. However, the mother–infant relationship was assumed to be at the base of a hierarchy of relationships; the mother was still viewed as the adult with whom the child forms the first and most influential attachment relationship, thereby setting the stage for the formation of subsequent relationships with a wider circle of partners (Ainsworth, 1982). Any internal working models formed from other adult–child attachments would be "colored" or influenced by the working models formed originally within the mother–child bond.

Now, when the majority of mothers of infants are in the work force and their infants are cared for by several adults during the infant's first year of life, the view of mother as primary attachment figure may need further change. All of these caregiving adults provide experiences upon which the infant may build distinct working models. Theoretically, these simultaneously formed models should be specific to particular infant–adult dyads (Howes, Rodning, Galluzzo, & Myers, 1988; Main & Weston, 1981; van IJzendoorn & Tavecchio, 1987). Moreover, each of these attachments should influence later relationships (Howes et al., 1988; Oppenheim, Sagi, & Lamb, 1988).

Nevertheless, some developmental psychologists (e.g., Barglow, Vaughn, & Molitor, 1987; Belsky, 1988) have argued that separation of the infant from the mother during the first year of life is a risk factor for emotional maladjustment. When the child spends much time every day away from the mother, starting at an early age, the argument goes, development of a secure relationship is threatened because the mother has less opportunity to get to know the child's signals and the child has less opportunity to experience the mother as consistently available to respond sensitively and appropriately to his or her needs.

This view, which is based on the norm of mothers at home rearing their children in splendid isolation, may underestimate the positive, buffering effects of attachment to alternative caregivers. Both Howes et al. (1988) and Oppenheim et al. (1988) demonstrated that children's social competence with peers, a combination of social and cognitive components, is more strongly predicted from their early attachment relationships with alternate caregivers than from their attachment relationships with their mothers. Moreover, when we look at child care around the world, one of the most striking features is the prevalence of nonparental caregiving and multiple caregivers provided to children in many cultures. In most nonindustrial, rural countries, where traditions of family and community life have persisted for many centuries, fathers and mothers are out of the home tending to business, while siblings or extended family—grandparents or other relatives who are too frail to be in the fields—care for infants and young children (see Smith, in this *Handbook,* and Whiting & Whiting, 1981). In most industrialized countries other than the United States, children are cared for in government-supported day care facilities (Melhuish & Moss, 1991). Thus, the vast majority of children in the world today do receive care from more than one caregiver.

Perhaps the detrimental effects of nonparental care on infants are not as marked as has been suggested by monomatric attachment theorists. Later in the chapter we evaluate the empirical data on this issue.

Sociobiological Theories

In recent years theories emphasizing biological influences on social behavior have gained prominence. Their relevance to the issue of nonparental caregiving lies in their argument that people demonstrate favoritism and protective behavior toward genetically similar others (Hamilton, 1964; Rushton, Russell, & Wells, 1984).

Favoritism toward one's close relatives has been demonstrated in a variety of studies. Segal (1984) observed more cooperation and altruism on joint tasks in monozygotic than dizygotic twins in middle childhood. Freedman (1979) found that biological relatives expressed stronger feelings of family ties than did nonbiological relatives. Barash (1979) demonstrated that parents prefer to raise their own children rather than adoptive children. In fact, resistance to adoption is not an uncommon experience among childless couples who hope to have children (see Brodzinsky, Lang, and Smith, in this *Handbook*). Moreover, several researchers have found an elevated risk of child abuse associated with stepparenting (Lightcap, Kurland, & Burgess, 1982; Wilson, Daly, & Weghorst, 1980; and see Hetherington & Stanley-Hagan, in this *Handbook*). These studies and others suggest that degree of genetic relatedness influences one's level of positive feelings, expectations, and behaviors toward a child.

From a sociobiological perspective, we might expect that the closer the genetic relation of a caregiver to a child, the greater will be the caregiver's investment in providing the best quality care for that child. An implication of this theory is that biological relatives, particularly parents and to a lesser extent grandparents, aunts, and uncles, are most invested in providing the best quality care for their children. On the other hand, it does not automatically follow that parents or other relatives are equipped to offer the best care. "Professional" caregivers often have more training and experience in child development than do parents. In addition, parents, being more invested in their child's future, are not always objective about the child's behavior. These tendencies may balance or outweigh the advantages of parental or familial child care. We also consider the empirical data bearing on this issue later in the chapter.

Cognitive and Social Stimulation Theories

The third set of theories of relevance to the issue of nonparental caregiving consists of those focused on the stimulation of children's cognitive and social development. It has long been believed that providing young children with toys and lessons and verbal interactions with a responsive adult will promote their cognitive development, whereas the absence of such stimulating opportunities will delay or depress development (Dennis, 1973; Hunt, 1961). The preschool intervention movement of the 1960s and 1970s, including Project Head Start, was premised on this cognitive stimulation theory (e.g., Schweinhart, Weikart, & Larner, 1986); that is, on the belief that children from "deprived" environments could be offered stimulation in preschool programs that would "compensate" for their lack of educational experience at home. Proponents of day care have suggested that a high-quality day-care setting offers the young child the same kinds of stimulation as a cognitively oriented preschool program (e.g., Caldwell, 1970; Scarr & Weinberg, 1986). The day-care setting provided by a professional day-care home provider or a center, like that of a preschool or Head Start program, is designed to be a stimulating environment for young children. The room setup and materials are geared to the size and developmental level of the child. The primary goal of the caregiver is to provide appropriate interaction for the well-being of the children in care. In contrast, the mother at home with her child must divide her time among multiple tasks, only one of which is child care.

There are limits, however, to the stimulation that can be provided in a day-care setting. In a group setting in which the adult's attention is spread thin because of the large number of children in care, even a professional caregiver will not be able to provide a steady diet of stimulating experiences for each child. The fear has been expressed that children in day care will suffer the same deprivation that has been observed for children growing up in residential institutions. On the basis of cognitive stimulation theory (e.g., Wachs & Gruen, 1982), it would be expected that children who receive nonparental care in a materially and verbally stimulating day-care environment with a moderate number of children would have advanced cognitive development and an easier transition into elementary school, whereas the development of children in an unstimulating or overcrowded child-care environment could be impaired.

In addition to the possibility of cognitive enrichment or deprivation, child-care arrangements outside the family typically provide young children with their first regular experience with peers. This social stimulation, too, can contribute—positively or negatively—to children's development. On the negative side, fears have been expressed that early rearing in a peer-oriented environment will deter the development of children's individuality and individualism, fantasy and creativity, that in a peer culture children become dependent on peers rather than on adult authority and will be less likely to conform to standards for socially acceptable behavior, such as courtesy and cooperation (Suransky, 1982).

On the positive side, it has been suggested that experience playing with peers at an early age fosters the development of children's social competence. Howes (1988) presented one model for the development of social competence with peers for children who are in day care. Although children who are not in day care may "catch up" or go through the developmental stages quickly to reach their age appropriate form of social competence when placed in group care, at age 4, children who entered care as infants are advanced in the frequency and quality of their play with both familiar and unfamiliar peers, because they have had more time to practice and perfect their social skills (Howes, 1991). There may even be something about the absence of the mother that encourages a positive orientation toward peers. Infants and young children in parent cooperative arrangements have been found to be more sociable and socially skilled and less aggressive with peers when their own mother is out of the room than when she is present (Field, 1979; Smith & Howes, 1993). When the mother is present, children focus their attention on her rather than participating in the peer group. According to Howes' model, children who never spend time away from the mother may have difficulty with the initial step toward social competence with peers, that is, with developing enough interest to attempt interaction.

Empirical data bearing on the questions of whether children in day care have advanced or delayed cognitive and social development and, if so, in what kinds of programs and settings, are discussed later in the chapter.

Theoretical Predictions Summarized

From the perspectives of these different theories, predictions about the effects of nonparental care on children's development are mixed. Traditional attachment theorists would predict that early separation from the mother creates a "risk" of later emotional difficulties for the child. This risk would be heightened if the alternate care were of poor quality. Sociobiologists would argue for the merits of child care provided by a biological relative and for the special advantage of parents because they are the child's closest relatives. Cognitive and social stimulation theorists, in contrast, would predict positive outcomes for the child from the enrichment provided by an alternate care arrangement that is of high quality, with a responsive caregiver and a balance of stimulating experiences with adults, peers, and materials. In fact, such an enriched environment should produce greater cognitive and social development than an unstimulating home environment. There is not a single theoretical position that predicts the effects of nonparental care, but several, with quite different outcomes.

HISTORY OF DAY CARE

The use of nonparental caregivers for young children is not a new phenomenon, even in this country. Only its prevalence has changed. What was once a service for a minority of families—the affluent, with their nannies, and the urban poor, whose children were in day nurseries—has become the norm for the majority of American families today.

As a formal service, the history of day care in this country goes back well into the last century, when day nurseries were established in response to the flood of immigration that brought more than 5 million foreign families to the United States between 1815 and 1860, and to the industrialization and urbanization that took women from their homes to factories during this period. Young children were left to fend for themselves—locked up at home, allowed to roam the streets, or put under the casual supervision of a neighbor or relative. The situation was ripe for philanthropic intervention, and wealthy women and well-meaning service organizations, appalled by this neglect, organized day nurseries to provide care for these children. The first American day nursery was opened in Boston in 1838 to provide care for the children of seamen's working wives and widows. By 1898 about 175 day nurseries were operating in various parts of the country, enough to justify the creation of a National Federation of Day Nurseries.

Over the next decade, expansion of day care continued. Day nurseries were most often set up in converted homes. They were open 6 days a week, 12 hours a day. Most were simply custodial, run by overworked matrons with one or two assistants, who had to do the laundry, cooking, and cleaning as well as looking after the children. They did not have the benefit of public support, monetary or ideological; the day nursery was considered a last resort for children who could not be cared for at home.

A few day nurseries with more energetic directors offered not only clean, safe places to keep children but something of interest to occupy their time. Beginning in the 1890s, some of the better day nurseries also began to offer a modest educational program, by hiring kindergarten teachers to come in and teach the children for several hours a day. They also offered services to working mothers beyond a place to leave their children: classes in sewing, cooking, English, and child care, access to job training and opportunities, and help with practical family problems. In the 1920s these mothers were also given help with family-centered psychological problems.

In 1933, to alleviate effects of the Great Depression, President Roosevelt initiated the Federal Economic Recovery Act and the Work Projects Administration. Public funds for the expansion of day care became available for the first time, in order to supply jobs for unemployed teachers, nurses, cooks, and janitors. By 1937 these programs had set up 1,900 day nurseries, caring for 40,000 children. Then, with World War II, and the massive mobilization of women into war-related industries, a further surge in day care occurred. By 1945, more than a million and a half children were in day care. With the end of the war and the withdrawal of federal funds in 1946, this day-care boom ended as precipitously as it had begun. Nearly 3,000 centers closed, and by 1950, only 18,000 children were in day-care centers. From 1950 to 1965, day care again became a marginal service for the poor, with an emphasis on social work and problem families. Unexpectedly, however, although the centers closed, women continued to work, and those who were not poor enough to qualify for publicly supported day care used the few available private day-care centers or made other arrangements for child care with relatives, neighbors, or housekeepers. Only in the mid-1960s did attitudes toward day care begin to become more positive as it was recognized that mothers were already working and as it seemed that provision of day care would allow more women to get off welfare. Federal support for day care became available once more, though still only for poor families.

This change in attitude and legislation was influenced also by what was happening in early childhood education. People were focusing their attention on the preschool years as a critical period for stimulating intellectual development, hoping for later benefits in scientific program and national achievement. For 1967 to 1970, enrollment in nursery schools and kindergartens increased markedly (from one fourth to one half of all eligible 3- to 5-year-olds), and enrollment in licensed day-care centers doubled.

By the beginning of the 1970s, then, daycare was on many people's minds, and efforts to support more and better services were becoming stronger. But with President Nixon's veto of the Comprehensive Child Development Act in 1972, hopes of further federal support for child care were dashed. In the ensuing years, day-care enrollment has grown because private enterprise took up the burden of day-care provision. At present, day care is a hodgepodge of arrangements, varying from state to state and family to family. The three most common types of care used today in the United States are described in the next section.

FORMS OF DAY CARE

Table 6.1 shows the distribution of the major types of child-care arrangements currently being used by working mothers of preschool children (U.S. Bureau of the Census, 1990). About one fourth of the families in which mothers work manage to cover child care by juggling the parents' schedules or by taking the child along to work. Another fourth rely on other relatives (e.g., aunts, grandmothers, older siblings) to provide child care. Over half of all children under 5 years of age whose mothers are employed, however, are cared for by a nonfamilial adult, either in the child's home or, more typically, in the adult's home or a day-care center. A small number of the families who use a nonrelated caregiver are able to afford a caregiver who comes to or lives in their home. About one fourth of families with working mothers employ a caregiver who looks after a number of children, perhaps including her own, in her home. This "day-care home" arrangement is the most common type of nonfamilial care for 1- and 2-year-olds whose mothers work full time. Day-care centers are used less frequently for infants and toddlers; they are much more commonly used for the care of 3- and 4-year-olds, with one third of all 3- and 4-year-olds whose mothers work being cared for in centers.

In Child's Home

Care in the child's own home is most commonly provided by a relative, either the father or another relative. The caregiver is usually untrained, unlicensed, and unmonitored. Except when the caregiver is the father, in-home caregivers tend to be older women (over 40). If the in-home caregiver is related to the child, this is the most economical and stable of all day-care arrangements; if the caregiver is not a relative, this form of care is the least stable. If the caregiver is trained in child development—a

TABLE 6.1
Primary Child-Care Arrangements Used by Working Parents for Children Under 5 Years

Type of Care	Infants	Preschool and Toddlers	Preschool Children
Familial Care			
Parents themselves	25%	23%	24%
Another relative	27%	21%	24%
Nonfamilial Care			
In child's home	7%	5%	6%
Day-care home	26%	18%	22%
Day-care center	16%	33%	24%

Note. Statistics based on the most recent data available (U.S. Bureau of the Census, 1990).

professional nanny—in-home care is the most expensive kind of care. Educational or group activities with peers are uncommon in in-home care.

Day-Care Home

A family day-care home is a care arrangement in which a woman cares for a small group of children in her own home. A recent national survey (Kisker, Hofferth, Phillips, & Farquhar, 1991) reveals some descriptive facts about family day care. Most day-care homes have no more than three children (aged 18–36 months) and one care provider present at one time. The typical day-care home provider is a young married woman with young children of her own. She is a high school graduate with 6 years of child-care experience, but she is likely to be untrained and unlicensed. She provides child care because she is fond of children and she wants to provide playmates for her own child while at the same time supplementing the family income. Most day-care home providers see their role as caring for children's physical needs and to be "like a mother" to the children. They spend about half of their time interacting with the children, and the rest of the time on housework or personal activities (Stallings, 1980). They are unlikely to offer organized educational games or structured activities; rather, children in day-care homes spend most of their day in free play (Eheart & Leavitt, 1989; Pence & Goelman, 1987b). In short, the main goal of most family day-care providers is to provide a warm "homelike" atmosphere for the children.

Day-Care Center

A day-care center is the most visible and easily identified child-care arrangement. The average day-care center provides care for 60 children. Children are usually divided into classes according to their age. The average group size is 7 infants, 10 toddlers, or 14 preschoolers (Kisker et al., 1991), but these sizes can vary enormously. Most children in day-care centers are 3 or 4 years old. Teachers in the centers tend to be women (97 percent[1]) under 40 years of age. Most have attended college (Whitebook, Howes, & Phillips, 1990). Day-care centers usually have some staff with training in child development and are likely to offer children educational opportunities and the chance to play with other children in a child-oriented, safe environment that is rich in materials and equipment. These qualities of staff training and a child-development-oriented program are especially likely in nonprofit, government-supported centers (Kagan, 1991; Whitebook et al., 1990).

As Table 6.1 suggests, working parents are only slightly more likely to choose familial (as opposed to nonfamilial) care for their infants than for their preschool-age children. However, they are somewhat more likely to choose more informal home like arrangements (i.e., care in the child's own

---

[1]Given the preponderance of female caregivers in homes and centers, we use the feminine pronouns (*she, her*) in our discussion.

home or in a day-care home) for their infants, and the more "school like" day-care center settings for their preschool-age children.

Many studies have attempted to detail differences in the "ecology" of center-based and family day care (Cochran, 1977a; Golden et al., 1978; Prescott, 1973). On the average, physical conditions (space, ventilation, light, toilets, cleanliness, toys, safety, nutrition, and immunization) are better in day-care centers, whereas day-care homes rank higher in social-personal conditions (fewer children per adult, more interaction with the caregiver, more conversation, more socialization attempts, more emotional input, and more sensitive approaches to the child by the caregiver). Kisker et al. (1991) found that children in day-care centers spent most of their time in free-choice activities, adult-directed creative activities, physical exercise and instruction, whereas children in home day care spent somewhat more than half the day in free-choice activities and physical exercise, and less than one third of their time in adult-directed creative activities and instruction.

Less is known about the differences between center or home day care and care in the child's own home. In contrast to center and home day care, care in the child's own home has not been studied very extensively, perhaps because of the "private" nature of this form of care. Our review of the empirical data on children's experiences in nonparental care thus focuses primarily on day-care homes and centers. In the next section we profile the adults who care for children in nonparental care and the roles they play in children's lives.

THE ROLES OF NONPARENTAL CAREGIVERS

The nonfamilial care provider is an important figure in the social networks of children who spend a significant portion of every day in nonparental care. The caregiver serves as a teacher and disciplinarian, a nurturer and playmate, and she may occupy a place in the child's hierarchy of attachment figures.

Teachers

Whether they do so formally and deliberately or not, nonfamilial caregivers teach children many things. Caregivers in day-care centers are more likely than caregivers in family day-care settings to think of themselves as teachers (Pence & Goelman, 1987b) and to use more academic teaching methods. They spend a major proportion of their time in curriculum planning and implementation (Phillips & Whitebook, 1990); they plan educational activities and pepper the children with questions. Teaching in family day care is more informal. Children learn through free exploration and in the context of "real-life" tasks and situations.

Caregivers in homes and in centers may also teach children social rules. In groups of children, where there is a higher probability that children will at least occasionally find themselves in conflict with peers, teaching social rules becomes quite important (Finkelstein, 1982). Children benefit from positive caregiver interventions in mediating peer conflicts; if left alone, children will most likely resort to aggression to resolve conflicts. Caregivers are more likely to intervene in negative toddler peer interactions (either spontaneously or after a child requests it) than in positive interactions. Interventions are most commonly verbal, and they often include explanations for the intervention; that is, caregivers use the negative peer interaction to teach a social rule to the children involved. Unfortunately, by ignoring positive peer encounters, caregivers miss opportunities to reinforce such behavior (Russon, Waite, & Rochester, 1990).

Disciplinarians

Caregivers also serve as disciplinarians. This may be especially important in a setting populated by a large group of children who are close in age. Praise is one way caregivers try to discipline or manage children. Praise can be used effectively to manipulate children's behavior in the day-care setting. If children are consistently praised for it, researchers have demonstrated, they will stay close to the caregiver and interact with her. They will play with a child they would ordinarily ignore if the teacher praises them for it. They will be more cooperative or more competitive, depending on which the caregiver praises. They will play with dolls rather than trucks if the caregiver rewards them for doing so (Serbin, Connor, & Denier, 1978). They will persist longer at tasks if they have been praised for working (Fagot, 1973). When caregivers do not expect children to behave in particular ways (e.g., cooperative, assertive, persistent, quiet, polite) and do not consistently encourage them to act in these ways and praise them for doing so, children are unlikely to learn these behaviors.

Nurturers and Attachment Figures

Day-care providers in both center-based and family day-care settings often describe their main goal as providing children with love and affection in a warm, loving environment (Eheart & Leavitt, 1989; Kisker et al., 1991; Nelson, 1990). In several studies, day-care providers in high-quality child-care settings have been shown to be sensitive and responsive to children, and to engage them in positive social and physical interactions (Allhusen, 1992; Anderson, Nagle, Roberts, & Smith, 1981; Howes, 1983). These types of interactions are generally thought of as being associated with optimal development (Belsky, 1984). However, one study suggests that caregivers and parents view physical contact between children and their day-care providers as less appropriate than contact between children and their parents (Hyson, Whitehead, & Prudhoe, 1988). A second study shows that the cognitive development of children in day care is less advanced when their caregivers hold and hug them more (Clarke-Stewart, Gruber, & Fitzgerald, 1994).

Because day-care providers spend significant portions of each day involved in caregiving and nurturant interactions with children, they are natural candidates for attachment figures in the hierarchy of children's attachment networks (Howes, Hamilton, & Allhusen, in preparation). A growing body of research suggests that not only do children in day care form attachment relationships with their caregivers (Goossens & van IJzendoorn, 1990; Howes & Hamilton, 1992), but that this has positive implications for children's development. Children who are rated as securely attached with their caregivers are more competent in their interactions with peers (Howes, Phillips, & Whitebook, 1992) and with adults (Howes et al., 1988). In the latter study, children who were insecure with both their mothers and their caregivers were rated lower in social competence than children who had at least one secure relationship, suggesting that a secure attachment with a day-care provider can play a compensatory role for an insecure relationship with the mother. Studies have consistently shown, however, that although children form attachments to their child-care providers, they prefer their mothers over these other caregivers (Farran & Ramey, 1977; Fox, 1977; Kagan, Kearsley, & Zelazo, 1978; Ricciuti, 1974; Sagi et al., 1985).

Caregivers Versus Mothers

Day-care settings are different from most children's homes because of the large number of other children who are present. Caregivers must make certain adjustments to adapt to the unique dynamics of caring for these children, who are often very close in age. There are likely to be more competing demands made on the caregiver and more conflicts between children that the caregiver must help to resolve. Although caregivers fill many of the same roles as mothers, differences between these settings require that they behave differently from one another in some ways. Interactions with the adult are less frequent in group-care settings than they are in the child's home; in day care, the peer group becomes more important (Cochran, 1977a; Hayes et al., 1983; Prescott, 1973; Rubenstein & Howes, 1979, 1983; Siegel-Gorelick, Ambron, & Everson, 1981b; Sylva, Roy, & Painter, 1980; Tizard,

Carmichael, Hughes, & Pinkerton, 1980). The larger the peer group and the more their competing demands, the less stimulating and responsive are caregivers (Stith & Davis, 1984).

Mothers also are often more emotionally invested in the child than are nonfamilial caregivers, just by virtue of their relationship to the child. As a result, mother–child interactions are more emotionally charged and affectionate than caregiver–child interactions (Clarke-Stewart et al., 1994; Rubenstein, Pedersen, & Yarrow, 1977; Siegel-Gorelick, Ambron, & Everson, 1981a; Stith & Davis, 1984). This supports the sociobiological argument presented earlier.

As to whether mothers or caregivers are more sensitive, or appropriately responsive, toward the child, the data are not completely consistent. In two studies, mothers were found to be more stimulating and sensitive with their infants than were the infants' caregivers (Caruso, 1989; Stith & Davis, 1984). However, Goossens and van IJzendoorn (1990) found that caregivers were more sensitive than either mothers or fathers in their interactions with the same child.

In terms of disciplinary styles, caregivers in day-care centers and nursery schools have been observed to be less directive and authoritarian, less critical and restrictive, and more likely to help, suggest activities, make tasks into games, respond to children's initiation of play, and mediate interactions with other children than mothers (Cochran, 1977a; Hess, Price, Dickson, & Conroy, 1981; Howes & Rubenstein, 1981; Prescott, 1973; Rubenstein & Howes, 1979, 1983; Tizard et al., 1980). Children also see their mother's role as being distinct from their caregiver's role: Mothers are perceived to be more involved in the children's physical care, whereas preschool teachers are seen more as providing play and stimulation (Smith, Ballard, & Barnham, 1989).

Even when the day-care setting is a home, differences between mothers and caregivers are found. Family day-care providers differ from both day-care center teachers and mothers in their interactions with children. Compared to teachers, home care providers interact more with each child individually, especially when there are only one or two children in the care arrangement, and they may be more positive and sensitive in their approach to children. They also do more supervisory disciplining. Compared to mothers, family day-care providers are more emotionally distant; they engage in less positive physical contact with the child (kissing, caressing), and they are less playful and stimulating (Stallings, 1980).

Nonparental Caregivers in Brief

Taken together, these last two sections suggest that not only do nonparental child-care arrangements fall into two general categories of physical settings (homes and centers), but in fact the adults in these different types of settings define their roles somewhat differently. That is, although there is some overlap in the roles that home and center caregivers fill, caregivers in home settings think and act more like "substitute mothers" toward the children, whereas caregivers in center-based settings behave more like teachers.

But a description of the general types of day care available in the United States today and the roles that caregivers play in those settings provides only part of the picture of children's experiences with nonparental caregivers. The crucial piece to fill in, of course, is the issue of the effects of nonparental care experiences on children's development. This issue is addressed in the next section.

DEVELOPMENTAL OUTCOMES FOR CHILDREN WITH AND WITHOUT NONPARENTAL CHILD-CARE EXPERIENCES

The earliest research to address the question of the effects of nonparental care on children's development focused primarily on the cognitive and social development of children with and without nonparental (or more often, nonmaternal) child-care experience. We review this body of literature in this section. Because the needs of preschoolers are dramatically different from those of infants, it is likely that nonfamilial care experiences have different meanings depending on the age of the child. We therefore review the findings separately for these two age groups.

Effects on Preschoolers

We begin our review with the research on preschool-age children, for two reasons. First, studies of this age group are considerably more numerous than studies of infants; and second, researchers are more clearly in agreement about what the effects of day care are for this age.

Cognitive development.   Children with experience in day care during the preschool years have advanced cognitive and language development relative to children who are at home (Andersson, 1989; Burchinal, Lee, & Ramey, 1989; Clarke-Stewart et al., 1994; Garber & Hodge, 1989; Larsen & Robinson, 1989, for boys; Osborn & Millbank, 1987; Robinson & Corley, 1989; Thornburg, Pearl, Crompton, & Ispa, 1990, for African-American children; see also reviews by Belsky, 1984; Clarke-Stewart & Fein, 1983; Hayes, Palmer, & Zaslow, 1990). This difference is not always found (e.g., Ackerman-Ross & Khanna, 1989; Cochran, 1977b; Thornburg et al., 1990, for White children; Vandell & Corasaniti, 1990), but there is a substantial body of research suggesting that the intellectual development of children who attend relatively high-quality day-care centers, nursery schools, or early childhood programs in the preschool years is advanced over the development of children from comparable family backgrounds who do not. Thus it seems that experience in center-based child care, even part time, can have at least temporary benefits for children's intellectual development.

This acceleration in cognitive development has not usually been observed for children in day-care homes or with in-home caregivers. Although in some studies no significant differences between children in home day care and day-care centers have been found, when there is a difference in intellectual development, it favors children in center-based care. On various measures of intellectual development, children in family day care or in-home care perform at levels similar to children at home with their mothers, whereas children in day-care centers may do better (Andersson, 1989; Clarke-Stewart, 1987; Cochran, 1977a, 1977b; Golden et al., 1978). In the New York City Infant Day Care Study, children in centers and family day-care homes had similar scores on standard intelligence tests when they started care at 6–12 months of age. They stayed at the same level through their second year, but by 3 years of age the scores of children in day-care homes had dropped to a significantly lower level than those of children in centers, and were at the same level as those of children who were at home with parents (Golden et al., 1978).

In the Chicago Study of Child Care and Development, a clear difference was found between children in home care (with parents, in-home caregiver, or day-care home provider) and center care (in nursery school, day-care center, or combined center and sitter arrangement), favoring the children attending centers, on a variety of measures of intellectual competence (Clarke-Stewart, 1984; Clarke-Stewart et al., 1994). The children in centers were, on the average, 6–9 months advanced over children cared for at home by their mothers or babysitters or in day-care homes. The differences appeared for children of all family backgrounds, for both boys and girls, after as little as 6 months in day care.

However, not all children will necessarily benefit from day-care experiences. The day-care centers in these studies, although not all "exceptional," were all of relatively good quality; poor-quality centers would not be expected to produce positive outcomes for children's cognitive development. Children from lower income families are more likely than children from middle-income families to benefit from high-quality day-care centers. Furthermore, the quality of care appears to be more important than the type of care (i.e., centers vs. family day care): Differences between children in day-care centers and day-care homes are less when the day-care homes are of high quality. For example, in one study, although the language competence of children in unlicensed day-care homes was inferior to that of children in centers, the language competence of children in regulated homes was equivalent (Goelman & Pence, 1987a). More telling, in another study, when care in day-care homes was enriched by the experimental addition of an educational curriculum, the intellectual performance of the children was observed to improve to the level of children in day-care centers

(Goodman & Andrews, 1981). The effects of variations in day-care quality on children's development is described more fully in a later section.

Social development.   Children who attend day-care programs have also been shown to be different from children without nonfamilial care experience in their social behavior. Compared with children without nonfamilial care experience, children with such experience are more self-confident, outgoing, assertive, verbally expressive, self-sufficient, and comfortable, and less distressed, timid, and fearful in new situations (Cochran, 1977b; Fowler, 1978; Kagan et al., 1978; Lally & Honig, 1977; Moskowitz, Schwarz, & Corsini, 1977; Schwarz, Krolick, & Strickland, 1973). They are more independent of their mothers in such situations; they go farther away and spend more time away and out of the mother's sight (Wynn, 1979). They exhibit more social skills and initiate more interaction in play with unfamiliar peers (Herwig, 1989; Wille & Jacobson, 1984; Wynn, 1979). They know more about social rules (Siegal & Storey, 1985). Like the differences in intellectual competence, differences in social competence appear frequently, although not invariably (e.g., Golden et al., 1978; Lamb, Hwang, Broberg, & Bookstein, 1988; Schenk & Grusec, 1987; Winnett, Fuchs, Moffatt, & Nerviano, 1977). Paralleling the results for cognitive development, children in centers have been found to be more socially competent (with unfamiliar adults and peers) than children in day-care homes or with in-home caregivers (Clarke-Stewart et al., 1994).

Researchers have also found that, in addition to being more independent and outgoing, children in day care are sometimes less polite, agreeable, and compliant with their mother's or caregiver's requests; louder and more boisterous, more irritable and rebellious, more likely to swear and have temper tantrums, and more likely to have behavior problems than children who are not or who have not been in day care (Fowler, 1978; Rabinovich, Zaslow, Berman, & Heyman, 1987; Robinson & Corley, 1989; Rubenstein & Howes, 1983; Rubenstein, Howes, & Boyle, 1981; Thornburg et al., 1990). With peers, day-care children have been observed to be more aggressive and to engage in more negative interactions (Bates et al., 1991; Haskins, 1985; Thornburg et al., 1990; Wille & Jacobson, 1984)—although this finding, too, is not inevitable (e.g., Hegland & Rix, 1990).

An argument has been made that the reason for this mixed bag of results is that participation in a stimulating day-care program fosters children's social development—social competence and independence—as it promotes their intellectual performance, but that because few programs focus on teaching children social rules—that is, teaching them effective ways of solving social problems—the consequence is that children express their competence and independence in less than polite ways with parents, peers, and other people (Clarke-Stewart, 1992). An alternative argument is that these aggressive children are acting out the emotional maladjustment they have suffered as a consequence of having formed an insecure attachment to their mothers earlier on (Belsky, 1988, 1992). This argument brings us to the next area of research: research on the effects of day care on infants.

Effects on Infants

Most studies show that for preschool children, day-care experience has few if any negative effects, and can have positive effects on children's cognitive and social development. The effects of nonfamilial care on infants, however, is more controversial. In particular, researchers have grappled with the question of whether or not early, extensive nonparental care leads to emotional insecurity and social maladjustment (Belsky, 1988, 1992; Clarke-Stewart, 1989, 1992). As already mentioned, research has consistently shown that infants of working mothers form attachment relationships with them and prefer their mothers to their day-care providers (see reviews by Clarke-Stewart & Fein, 1983; Rutter, 1982). Some have argued, however, that a review of the data on children's attachment security shows that the quality of the mother–child relationship is less secure for children of employed mothers than for children of nonemployed mothers (Belsky, 1988, 1992).

This position is not without its critics. Clarke-Stewart (1989, 1992) pointed out a number of problems with the conclusion that nonmaternal care results in heightened risk of insecure attachments.

First, a tabulation of the security classifications of 1,200 children in 16 studies shows that there is only a slightly higher chance of children in day care being rated as insecurely attached with their mothers (36 percent of children in full time day care were rated as insecure, compared with 29 percent of children who were not in full-time day care). A second problem is that the method of assessing attachment used in these studies, the Strange Situation (Ainsworth et al., 1978), has been validated only on children whose primary caregivers are their mothers. The Strange Situation is a 20-minute laboratory procedure in which the quality of the child's interactions with the mother, particularly upon her return after a brief separation, are assumed to reveal the nature of the child's attachment relationship with her. In developing the Strange Situation procedure, Ainsworth and her colleagues chose brief separation from the mother as a moderately stressful stimulus that should universally activate children's attachment behaviors. However, the Strange Situation may not be an appropriate method for assessing the attachment relationships of day-care children, who are quite accustomed to and therefore less alarmed by separations from their mothers. We do not know if the avoidant behavior observed in some of these children is truly reflective of insecurity or if it represents an adaptation by day-care infants toward greater independence and ease with infant–mother separation. Alternative methods of assessing attachment that do not involve separation should be fruitful in answering these questions. One such method, which involves rating children's behavior with their mothers at home after observing a substantial period of unstructured, natural interaction (Waters & Deane, 1985), has not revealed significant differences between children with extensive, early day-care experience and those without (Howes et al., 1988; Strayer, Moss, & Blicharski, 1989; Weinraub, Jaeger, & Hoffman, 1988).

The results of the studies reviewed in the last section suggest that preschool-age children are likely to benefit from nonfamilial care, but more caution is needed in considering the effects of different forms of day care for infants. The jury is still out on the effects of nonfamilial care for infants. However, as Scarr, Phillips, and McCartney (1989) pointed out, it is illogical to try to evaluate whether day care is universally harmful to children's development; rather, this question must be answered by taking into account the quality of the specific caregiving arrangements experienced by the individual child as well as other influential environmental factors in the child's ecology. In the next section, we review research that examines variations in caregiving quality and their effects on children's social and cognitive development.

VARIATIONS IN THE QUALITY OF NONPARENTAL CAREGIVING AND THEIR OUTCOMES FOR CHILDREN'S DEVELOPMENT

Studies comparing developmental outcomes for children who have experienced day care with the development of those who have not are limited in their ability to explain within-group differences. Not all children who attend day-care programs show advances in cognitive development or exhibit aggression on the playground. This is because, just as not all families are created equal, not all day-care environments are created equal. Nonparental care, whether in day-care centers, family day-care homes, or with a caregiver in the child's own home, ranges from custodial to excellent in quality (Zigler & Freedman, 1990). In this section, we take a closer look at how children's development is related to the quality of nonparental care.

A number of investigations have documented significant associations between global measures of day-care quality and children's cognitive development as assessed by tests of intelligence and language ability (Howes, 1988; Phillips, McCartney, & Scarr, 1987; Phillips, Scarr, & McCartney, 1987; Schlieker, White, & Jacobs, 1991; Whitebook et al., 1990) and social development as assessed by ratings of sociability, considerateness, compliance, and self-regulation (Howes, 1990; Howes & Olenick, 1986; Howes & Stewart, 1987; Phillips, McCartney, & Scarr, 1987; Phillips, Scarr & McCartney, 1987; Vandell, Henderson, & Wilson, 1988). Included in these measures of overall quality are the amount or appropriateness of attention the child receives, the safety and stimulation in the physical setting, the educational curriculum that is followed, the size of the class and the classroom—factors that day-care "experts" agree indicate high-quality care. But global indexes of quality are not helpful for uncovering connections between children's development and specific kinds of day-care experience. More useful are those studies in which researchers have examined the predictability of separate components of the day-care environment for separate developmental outcomes. We focus, therefore, on the results of these studies, and more specifically on studies of those aspects of day care that relate to the caregiver herself—her behavior or the factors that influence her behavior.

Caregivers' Behaviors

Not surprisingly, studies of day care show quite consistently that caregivers' behaviors predict the performance and development of the children in their care. Children whose teachers talk to them more are advanced in communication and language skills, and they score higher on intelligence tests (Carew, 1980; Phillips, McCartney, & Scarr, 1987; Phillips, Scarr, & McCartney, 1987; Rubenstein & Howes, 1983; Ruopp, Travers, Glantz, & Coelen, 1979; Whitebook et al., 1990). Even more closely related to children's performance and development is the quality of the attention the caregiver offers. Children whose caregivers are stimulating, educational, and respectful, and who offer the children "intellectually valuable" experiences, especially language mastery experiences, have more advanced social and intellectual skills (Carew, 1980; Clarke-Stewart et al., 1994; Golden et al., 1978; McCartney, 1984; Phillips, Scarr, & McCartney, 1987). Children spend more time working on a task, play at more complex levels, and perform better on tests of intelligence and achievement when their teachers are more positive and responsive to their questions, less physically affectionate, critical, and directive, and use positive rather than negative reinforcement (Clarke-Stewart et al., 1994; Fagot, 1973; Miller, Bugbee, & Hybertson, 1985; Rubenstein & Howes, 1979; and see Phyfe-Perkins, 1981). Children are more socially competent if teachers encourage their self-direction and independence, cooperation and knowledge, self-expression and social interaction (Miller & Dyer, 1975; Schweinhart et al., 1986). Children are more likely to develop secure attachments with their nonfamilial caregivers when care is sensitive and children's bids are answered consistently and appropriately (Allhusen, 1992; Galluzzo, 1990; Howes et al., 1992).

Studies such as these clearly indicate that the caregiver's behavior toward the child is a central mediator of the child's experience in nonfamilial care and, therefore, of the effects of nonfamilial care on the child's development. Certain characteristics of the caregiver (e.g., education and training, experience, stability and consistency, commitment to the child, and gender) may each play a role in the way the caregiver interacts with the child. We discuss the research on these characteristics next.

Caregivers' Characteristics

Education and training.   Many researchers have demonstrated a link between the level of education and/or training that a caregiver has received and her behavior with the children in her care. With more training in child development, day-care providers are more knowledgeable, and they are also more interactive, helpful, talkative, playful, positive, affectionate, involved, and didactic, and less authoritarian toward the children in their care (Berk, 1985; Fosburg et al., 1980; Kinney, 1988; Tyler & Dittman, 1980). In turn, the children in their care are more involved, cooperative, persistent, and learn more (Arnett, 1989; Clarke-Stewart, 1987; Howes, 1983; Klinzing & Klinzing, 1974; Lazar, Darlington, Murray, Royce, & Snipper, 1982; Ruopp et al., 1979; Whitebook et al., 1990). Center caregivers who have completed bachelor's degrees in early childhood education provide more appropriate caregiving and are more sensitive and less detached than teachers with vocational or high school-level training (Whitebook et al., 1990).

Center caregivers who have more training are more likely to rely on professional resources for information and to belong to professional child-care organizations; thus it may be that one way in which training leads to provision of high-quality care is via the increased reliance of more highly trained caregivers on professional sources to gauge and improve their own performance (Powell & Stremmel, 1989). Use of professional resources by family day-care providers has also been linked to provision of better quality care: Day-care home providers who consider themselves child-care professionals, read books on child care or child development, attend meetings, and take classes in child development are more likely to talk, help, teach, and play with the children and to provide a physical environment with more music, dancing, books, and nutritious meals (Stallings, 1980). Caregivers who provide family day care only because no better job is available, or as an informal agreement with friends, neighbors, or relatives are less interactive and stimulating and spend more time on housework.

However, teachers with very high levels of training in child development may develop an academic orientation, emphasizing school activities (reading, counting, lessons, learning) to the exclusion of activities that promote children's social or emotional development. In the Chicago study, children whose caregivers had more formal training in child development were advanced intellectually but were significantly less competent in interactions with an unfamiliar peer; children whose caregivers had a moderate level of training were more competent in both social and cognitive realms (Clarke-Stewart, 1987).

Experience. Another factor that predicts caregivers' behavior is their previous experience. With fewer than 2 or 3 years of experience in child care, there is a tendency for day-care providers simply to go along with children and not initiate educational activities. With more professional child-care experience, caregivers are likely to be more stimulating, responsive, accepting, and positive (Clarke-Stewart et al., 1994; Howes, 1983; Kontos & Fiene, 1987). This relation is not always found, however. For example, in the National Day Care Study (Ruopp et al., 1979), teachers with more extensive experience were observed to provide less stimulating and educational interaction than caregivers with less experience. In the National Day Care Home Study (Fosburg et al., 1980; Stallings, 1980), caregivers with more experience were not markedly different from caregivers with less experience. With more than 10 years of experience, there is a tendency for teachers and caregivers to be less stimulating, stricter, and more controlling (Kontos & Fiene, 1987; Phillips, Scarr, & McCartney, 1987; Ruopp et al., 1979). Thus, a moderate amount of experience appears to be most clearly related to higher quality caregiving and to more positive outcomes for children's development.

Stability and consistency. Another factor that influences the quality of care that providers offer is the length of time they have been in the particular day-care setting with a particular child. In stable child-care settings, the caregiver has more opportunity to get to know the child, read his or her signals more accurately, and respond appropriately. The more time children spend in a day-care setting, the more likely they are to form close relationships with their caregivers (Cummings, 1980; Howes et al., 1988; Smith, 1980). Children who experience many changes in their child-care arrangements (either because of caregiver turnover or because the parents change the care arrangement) have been shown to perform poorly on intelligence tests (Whitebook et al., 1990), to be more insecure in their attachments with their mothers (Vaughn, Gove, & Egeland, 1980), and to be less competent in their play with adults and peers (Howes & Stewart, 1987). However, there may be a ceiling on the positive effects of caregiver stability: Beyond 3 or 4 years, there is no evidence that staying longer improves the quality of care (Clarke-Stewart et al., 1994). Caregiver stability is important not only because it is facilitates the formation of close relationships between children and their day-care providers, but also because stability is an indicator of good working conditions, adequate wages, and high staff morale. Caregivers provide higher quality care when they are satisfied with their jobs (Whitebook et al., 1990).

Commitment to the child. Another characteristic that may affect the caregiver's behavior with the child is the degree of her commitment to or emotional investment in the child. Caregivers who are less committed or emotionally invested are likely to keep an emotional distance from the children they care for; this in turn decreases the likelihood that the child will form a secure attachment relationship with the caregiver (Smith, 1980). Although it is intuitively reasonable to suspect that nonfamilial caregivers may be less emotionally committed to the children they care for and that children would be more likely to develop secure attachments with relatives than with nonfamilial caregivers, there are no data to bolster this view. In fact, in one study, children whose security scores with their day-care providers were very low were more likely to be cared for by a relative than in center-based or family day care (Howes et al., in preparation).

Gender.   Does the sex of the caregiver make a difference in children's experiences in child care? Very little research is available to help answer this question, primarily because, as mentioned earlier, the overwhelming majority of child-care providers are women. The few studies that have been done of teachers in day-care centers suggest that men and women differ in their teaching styles and behaviors. For instance, although both male and female teachers are likely to encourage what might be considered more feminine behavior (sitting quietly, reading, painting, working on puzzles) in both boys and girls in day care, male teachers are less likely to do so. For boys, this has a positive effect on academic achievement.

Some have argued that adults treat boys and girls differently because the children behave differently (e.g., Ainsworth, 1973; Bowlby, 1969), but others have found that differences in adults' treatment of male and female infants has less to do with actual differences in the infants' characteristics or behaviors than in the adults' sex-stereotyped beliefs about boys and girls (Sidorowicz & Lunney, 1980; and see Fagot, in this *Handbook*). In one study where adults were led to believe that an infant was male or female, women in particular were more likely to seek help for a crying infant sooner when they thought it was a girl than when they thought it was a boy (Condry, Condry, & Pogatshnik, 1978). The authors suggested, however, that adults may be more likely to resort to sex-stereotyped treatment of an infant when the infant is unfamiliar to them. Research with parents shows that both mothers and fathers tend to interact more with same-sex than with opposite-sex infants (Parke & Sawin, 1980). If this is true for nonparental caregivers as well, then it may be that girls in day-care settings receive more attention than boys, given that most caregivers in day care are female. Two recent studies appear to support this conjecture: Female caregivers were less affectionate (Botkin & Twardosz, 1988), sensitive, responsive, and stimulating (Allhusen & Cochran, 1991) with boys than with girls. Studies that compare male and female caregivers are needed to answer the question of whether the caregiver's sex, the child's sex, or both influence the quality of care that nonparental caregivers provide.

Caregivers: The Key to Quality

Clearly, as the results of research discussed in this section have shown, the caregiver herself plays a crucial role in determining the quality of the child's experience in nonparental care. As we discussed, the caregiver's behavior and personal characteristics (e.g., education and training, experience, stability and consistency, commitment to the child, and sex) have been consistently related to various social and cognitive outcomes for the children in her care. However, caregiving does not take place in a vacuum; certain characteristics of the day-care setting itself also impinge on the quality of care that the nonparental caregiver provides. These setting characteristics are reviewed in the next section.

FACTORS THAT INFLUENCE CAREGIVER BEHAVIOR
AND THAT ARE MEDIATED BY THE CAREGIVER

Structural aspects of the caregiving environment such as adult–child ratios, group size, and certain aspects of the physical environment, and the inclusion of an educational curriculum in the program have been repeatedly shown to be important indicators of day-care quality (Clarke-Stewart, 1992; Howes et al., 1992; Phillips & Howes, 1987). In this section, we consider the ways in which each of these factors affects the caregiver's behavior or is mediated by her. As in the last section, these factors indirectly affect children's development by influencing the quality of nonfamilial care that the child receives.

Adult–Child Ratio and Group Size

The ratio of adults to children and the total number of children in the group are the two indicators of day-care quality most likely to have a direct effect on caregiver–child interaction (Howes, 1990). These factors have a substantial range from one setting to another. The government-approved staff–child ratio for infants, for instance, ranges from 1:3 (in Maryland, Massachusetts, and Kansas) to 1:12 (in Idaho); for 4-year-olds, ratios in different states range from 1:5 to 1:20. Significant associations showing the detrimental effect of low adult–child ratios and high class sizes for children's behavior and development have been found in a substantial number of studies (Holloway & Reichhart-Erickson, 1988; Howes, 1983, 1987; Howes & Rubenstein, 1985; Howes et al., 1988; Lamb, Sternberg, Knuth, Hwang, & Broberg, 1991; Phillips, McCartney, & Scarr, 1987; Phillips, Scarr, & McCartney, 1987; Ruopp et al., 1979; Smith & Connolly, 1980; Sylva et al., 1980; Whitebook et al., 1990). When researchers have experimentally reduced the adult–child ratio from 1:4 to 1:10 or 1:12 (Asher & Erickson, 1979; Smith & Connolly, 1980), children have been observed to have less contact with the caregiver, to have fewer of their questions answered, to engage in shorter conversations, and to be subject to more prohibitions. Correlational studies, similarly, have shown that with less favorable ratios and larger groups, caregivers interact less with the children, are less responsive and less positive in affect, spend less time stimulating children cognitively or socially, provide fewer activities, and are more likely to be restrictive and negative (Howes, 1983; Whitebook et al., 1990). In turn, children who are cared for in large groups or with many children per adult are less competent and more hostile with their peers; they are less cooperative and have more conflicts; they are less likely to be securely attached with their nonfamilial caregivers; and they spend more time in aimless activity (Howes et al., 1992; Ruopp et al., 1979; Smith & Connolly, 1980; Sylva et al., 1980). Group size exerts an effect on caregiving quality independent of the adult–child ratio. That is, even when the ratio of caregivers to children is kept small by adding caregivers to the class, the higher noise level and confusion of a larger class make it more difficult for caregivers to notice and attend to individual children's needs (Allhusen, 1992).

Not only does a large total group size or a high child–adult ratio decrease the chance that a child will receive individualized care and attention from the caregivers, it also increases the time that the child spends interacting with peers. Unlike the detrimental effect of diminished adult attention that occurs in large classes, the time a child spends interacting with another child or children in day care is not necessarily negatively related to the child's social and intellectual competence (McCartney, 1984). It may be positively related to the child's level of play (Rubenstein & Howes, 1979). This is especially likely if the other child is older: Children have been observed to play more maturely with older children in day care (Siegel-Gorelick et al., 1981b). There is some suggestion that children in classes with a heterogeneous age mix behave more competently than those in homogeneous groups. In mixed-age preschool classes, children have been observed to exhibit fewer dominance activities (hitting, kicking, demanding objects), more language (asking questions, conversing, imitating), more cooperation (offering objects) (Logue, 1989), more altruism (Bizman, Yinon, Mivtzari, & Shavit, 1978), and to increase in persistence, flexibility, intelligence, and positive response to a stranger (Beller, 1974).

Physical Environment

Several studies have revealed that children's behavior and development are linked to aspects of the physical environment of the day-care setting such as division of the classroom into interest areas (Holloway & Reichhart-Erickson, 1988) and availability of varied, age-appropriate, and educational toys, materials, and equipment (Connolly & Smith, 1978; Goelman & Pence, 1987a; Holloway &

Reichhart-Erickson, 1988; Howes & Rubenstein, 1985), much as these aspects of the home environment are related to children's development (see Bradley, in this *Handbook*). Simply adding novel materials to preschool classrooms or having more varied materials accessible, however, does not necessarily lead to cognitive gains; toys alone were not a direct promoter of development in two studies (Golden et al., 1978; Rubenstein & Howes, 1979). It is in combination with teachers' more stimulating behavior that aspects of the physical environment have an impact on children's development (Holloway & Reichhart-Erickson, 1988; Ruopp et al., 1979).

Educational Program

Studies of day care have also shown that children in more educationally oriented day-care programs (those including prescribed educational activities such as lessons, guided play sessions, story reading, teaching of specific content, and more direct teacher instruction) differ from those in less educationally oriented programs. In these educational programs, children have been observed to spend more time in constructive and complex play with materials and with peers and to score higher on intelligence and achievement tests (Ferri, 1980; Fowler, 1978; Goelman & Pence, 1987a; Goodman & Andrews, 1981; Johnson, Ershler, & Bell, 1980; Lazar, Hubbell, Murray, Rosche, & Royce, 1977; McCartney, 1984; Miller & Dyer, 1975; Sylva et al., 1980; Tizard, Philips, & Plewis, 1976; Winnett et al., 1977). When children spend their time in the day-care center just playing around with other children, they experience less "rich" play and are less competent in social and cognitive ways (McCartney, 1984; Phillips, McCartney, & Scarr, 1987; Phillips, Scarr, & McCartney, 1987; Sylva et al., 1980). On the other hand, having too much structured activity, too much academic pressure, also may predict less advanced social and cognitive development (Hirsh-Pasek, Hyson, & Rescorla, 1990; Miller & Dyer, 1975; Sylva et al., 1980).

Mediating Factors

The body of research that we have reviewed in this section clearly shows that factors such as adult–child ratios, group size, physical setting, and an educational program all play important mediating roles in determining children's development in nonparental care. As we suggested in the last section, however, the caregiver remains perhaps the most influential factor in the equation; the day-care setting factors that we discuss in this section merely influence her behavior or are mediated by her. However, the story of nonparental care is still not complete. The effects of child care on children's development are determined not only by their experiences within nonparental care settings, but also by their experiences at home. Familial factors are considered in the next section.

FAMILY AND CHILD-CARE INFLUENCES JOINTLY CONSIDERED

In our discussion of the relevance of attachment theory to research on nonparental caregiving, and again in the section on the effects of day care on infants, we discussed the widely held belief about the primacy of the mother in the young child's life and the concern expressed by some researchers that children's development may be at risk if they enter nonparental care in the first year(s) of life. It is interesting to note, however, that until very recently, family factors had not been taken into consideration in studying the effects of nonparental care on children's development. Yet if (as most would agree) the child's family, and particularly the mother, plays such a central influential role in the child's development, then it seems clear that family factors must also be entered into the equation in determining what effects nonparental care experiences have on children's development.

To explore the issue of how family and day-care experiences *together* contribute to children's development, researchers have begun to include assessments of family variables in studies of day-care children, that is, to consider both day-care and family predictors in a more integrated way. From these studies we are beginning to form a picture of how family and day-care variables interrelate and how both day-care and family variables together predict children's development.

Some researchers who have included both family and day-care variables in their studies have tried to compare the relative predictiveness of the two sets of variables. A number have found that family variables are more closely related to children's development than are day-care variables: Family variables were more predictive of children's cognitive, language, and social development than whether or not the child attended day care, the type of day care attended, or the quality of the day-care program (Bates et al., 1991; Broberg, Hwang, Lamb, & Bookstein, 1990; Desai, Chase-Lansdale, & Michael, 1989; Goelman & Pence, 1987b; Howes, 1988; Melhuish, Lloyd, Martin, & Mooney, 1990; Wadsworth, 1986). In several other studies, however, day-care attendance or quality was as highly predictive of children's development as family variables (Lamb et al., 1991; Phillips, Scarr, & McCartney, 1987; Vandell & Corasaniti, 1990; Wasik, Ramey, Bryant, & Sparling, 1990).

A few researchers have explored the issue of combined effects of home and day-care environments on development. Using regression or path analyses, they have found that the level of predictability of children's development is greater when both sets of variables are included—optimal development is supported when children receive high-quality care, stimulation, and encouragement in both home and day-care settings (Clarke-Stewart et al., 1994; Goelman & Pence, 1987b; Holloway & Reichhart-Erickson, 1989; Laosa, 1982; Sternberg et al., 1991). The positive effects of full-time high-quality day care were greatest for children whose home environments were least advantageous (Jarvis, 1987; Scarr, Lande, & McCartney, 1988; Schlieker et al., 1991; Tizard et al., 1976), and it is hypothesized that the negative effects of poor-quality care would be greater for children from more advantaged families (Long, Peters, & Garduque, 1985). Being in day care does not reduce or eliminate the influence of the family; family variables and day care both make separate and significant contributions to children's development (Clarke-Stewart et al., 1994). But this kind of research is just beginning. We have a long way to go before we will fully appreciate the significance of nonparental caregivers relative to parents.

FUTURE DIRECTIONS

Nonparental caregivers play an important role in the lives of a majority of young children in the United States today. There is wide variation in the quality of care that nonparental caregivers provide, and children's development is affected by the quality of that care. However, as we have pointed out, day care is only part of the picture: Children not only attend day-care programs of different kinds and qualities, they also live in families of different kinds and qualities. In order to understand the complex picture of the effects of nonfamilial caregiving experiences on children's development, it will be necessary to study not just variations in the quality of care that children experience in those settings, but also the additive, complementary, or compensatory effects of their experiences at home.

In the next 10 years, we may learn more about the effects of nonparental and parental care on children's development from several large-scale studies that have begun recently. In the NICHD Study of Early Child Care, a cohort of children has been identified and these children are being studied from birth through their first 3 years (and possibly longer). They are observed periodically at home and in any regular day-care arrangements in which they spend at least 10 hours per week. Their experiences at home and in day care will then be related to their cognitive, social, and emotional development, assessed using a variety of standard and original instruments. Twelve hundred infants, from a wide range of family backgrounds, in 10 different sites across the country, are being studied. In the Child and Family Study, being conducted by ChildTrends and the Manpower Demonstration Research Corporation, the effects of 1 year of day care on children whose welfare mothers are randomly assigned to the JOBS (Job Opportunity and Basic Skills Training) program are being studied. The cognitive, physical, emotional, and social development of 2,500 3- to 5-year-olds is being studied over a 5-year period. In a third study, the Expanded Childcare Options (ECCO) demonstration project funded by the Rockefeller Foundation, the development of 1,800 children is being assessed, beginning in early childhood and extending into young adulthood. The purpose of this study is to compare the effects of basic day care (1 year), extended day care (lasting until first grade), and extended enhanced day care (high-quality care lasting until first grade). Welfare mothers with children under 3 years of age are randomly assigned to one of these conditions.

Because of their scope and design, these studies promise to yield important data on the effects of nonparental care on children's behavior and development. They are the most significant and substantial studies of day care ever undertaken. They will tell us about a broader range of care than has ever been studied and will demonstrate the full range of day-care effects. They include more detailed assessments of how well children are doing and more detailed observations of the quality of their care than has ever been possible before. They will answer specific questions about what kinds of care are acceptable and about what kinds of day-care arrangements are optimal. When the results of these studies are in we will have a much fuller picture of the effects—great and small—of nonparental caregiving on the lives and development of young children.

CONCLUSIONS

The organization of our discussion of the effects of nonparental care on children's development has roughly paralleled the historical development of this body of research. One is reminded of Bronfenbrenner's (1979) concentric circles of the child's world from microsystem to macrosystem. The first attempts at characterizing the effects of day care on development consisted primarily of comparisons between day-care and home-reared children. Next, researchers began to look more closely at variations *within* day care and to link these variations to differences in child outcomes. As a third step, researchers began to construct their findings as flow charts, with some characteristics of the day-care setting having a direct influence on the child and others having indirect effects via other day-care characteristics. In the most recent (and most complex) set of studies, researchers have begun to insert familial influences into the diagram, finally recognizing that day-care factors alone cannot paint the complete picture of the effects of nonparental caregiving experiences on children's development.

The data we have reviewed suggest that theory, too, must take this broad perspective on the multiple determinants of developmental outcomes for children in nonparental care. Traditional attachment theory and sociobiological theory place mothers and other biologically related individuals at the center of influence on children's development. Although no one would disagree that mothers fill a very important role in young children's lives, the controversy begins when we assume that children who spend less than full-time at home with their mothers are at risk. In contrast to these theories, cognitive and social stimulation theories suggest that nonparental care that is of high quality is associated with developmental gains. What is left for the future is the development of theory that will integrate these diverse views of development, and that will go beyond a focus on either parental care or nonparental care to illuminate the larger and more complex ecology of contemporary children's lives.

REFERENCES

Ackerman-Ross, S., & Khanna, P. (1989). The relationship of high quality day care to middle-class 3–year-olds' language performance. *Early Childhood Research Quarterly, 4,* 97–116.

Ainsworth, M. D. S. (1973). The development of infant–mother attachment. In B. Caldwell & H. N. Ricciuti (Eds.), *Review of child development research* (Vol. 3, pp. 1–94). Chicago: University of Chicago Press.

Ainsworth, M. D. S. (1982). Attachment: Retrospect and prospect. In C. M. Parkes & J. Stevenson-Hinde (Eds.), *The place of attachment in human behavior* (pp. 3–30). New York: Basic Books.

Ainsworth, M. D. S., Blehar, M., Waters, E., & Wall, S. (1978). *Patterns of attachment: Observations in the Strange Situation and at home.* Hillsdale, NJ: Lawrence Erlbaum Associates.

Allhusen, V. D. (1992, May). *Caregiving quality and infant attachment in day care contexts of varying quality.* Poster presented at the Eighth International Conference on Infant Studies, Miami, FL.

Allhusen, V. D., & Cochran, M. M. (1991, April). *Infants' attachment behaviors with their day care providers.* Poster presented at the biennial meetings of the Society for Research in Child Development, Seattle.

Anderson, C. W., Nagle, R. J., Roberts, W. A., & Smith, J. W. (1981). Attachment to substitute caregivers as a function of center quality and caregiver involvement. *Child Development, 52,* 53–61.

Andersson, B.-E. (1989). Effects of public day care: A longitudinal study. *Child Development, 60,* 857–866.

Arnett, J. (1989). Caregivers in day-care centers: Does training matter? *Journal of Applied Developmental Psychology, 10,* 541–552.

Asher, K. N., & Erickson, M. T. (1979). Effects of varying child–teacher ratio and group size on day care children's and teachers' behavior. *American Journal of Orthopsychiatry, 49,* 518–521.

Barash, D. (1979). *The whisperings within.* New York: Harper & Row.

Barglow, P., Vaughn, B. E., & Molitor, N. (1987). Effects of maternal absence due to employment on the quality of infant–other attachment in a low-risk sample. *Child Development, 58,* 945–954.

Bates, J. E., Marvinney, D., Bennett, D. S., Dodge, K. A., Kelly, T., & Pettit, G. S. (1991, April). *Children's day-care history and kindergarten adjustment.* Paper presented at the biennial meetings of the Society for Research in Child Development, Seattle.

Beller, E. K. (1974). *Infant day care: A longitudinal study* Washington, DC: U.S. Government Printing Office.

Belsky, J. (1984). Two waves of day care research: Developmental effects and conditions of quality. In R. C. Ainslie (Ed.), *The child and the day care setting* (pp. 1–34). New York: Praeger.

Belsky, J. (1988). The "effects" of infant day care reconsidered. *Early Childhood Research Quarterly, 3,* 235–272.

Belsky, J. (1992). Consequences of child care for children's development: A deconstructionist view. In A. Booth (Ed.), *Child care in the 1990s: Trends and consequences* (pp. 83–94). Hillsdale, NJ: Lawrence Erlbaum Associates.

Berk, L. (1985). Relationship of educational attainment, child oriented attitude, job satisfaction, and career commitment to caregiver behavior toward children. *Child Care Quarterly, 14,* 103–129.

Bizman, A., Yinon, Y., Mivtzari, E., & Shavit, R. (1978). Effects of the age structure of the kindergarten on altruistic behavior. *Journal of School Psychology, 16,* 154–160.

Botkin, D., & Twardosz, S. (1988). Early childhood teachers' affectionate behavior: Differential expression to female children, male children, and groups of children. *Early Childhood Research Quarterly, 3,* 167–177.

Bowlby, J. (1969). *Attachment and loss: Vol. 1. Attachment.* New York: Basic Books.

Bretherton, I. (1985). Attachment theory: Retrospect and prospect. In I. Bretherton & E. Waters (Eds.), *Growing points of attachment theory and research* (pp. 3–38). *Monographs of the Society for Research in Child Development, 50*(1–2, Serial No. 209).

Broberg, A. G., Hwang, C.-P., Lamb M. E., & Bookstein, F. L. (1990). Factors related to verbal abilities in Swedish preschoolers. *British Journal of Developmental Psychology, 8,* 335–349.

Bronfenbrenner, U. (1979). *The ecology of human development: Experiments by nature and design.* Cambridge, MA: Harvard University Press.

Burchinal, M., Lee, M., & Ramey, C. (1989). Type of day care and preschool intellectual development in disadvantaged children. *Child Development, 60,* 128–137.

Caldwell, B. (1970). The rationale for early intervention. *Exceptional Children, 36,* 717–726.

Carew, J. (1980). Experience and the development of intelligence in young children. *Monographs of the Society for Research in Child Development, 45*(6–7, Serial No. 187).

Caruso, D. (1989). Quality of day care and home-reared infants' interaction patterns with mothers and day care providers. *Child & Youth Care Quarterly, 18,* 177–191.

Clarke-Stewart, K. A. (1984). Day care: A new context for research and development. In M. Perlmutter (Ed.), *Parent–child interaction and parent–child relations in child development. The Minnesota Symposia on Child Psychology* (Vol. 17, pp. 61–100). Hillsdale, NJ: Lawrence Erlbaum Associates.

Clarke-Stewart, K. A. (1987). Predicting child development from day-care forms and features: The Chicago study. In D. A. Phillips (Ed.), *Quality in child care: What does research tell us? Research Monographs of the National Association for the Education of Young Children* (Vol. 1, pp. 21–42). Washington, DC: National Association for the Education of Young Children.

Clarke-Stewart, K. A. (1989). Infant day care: Maligned or malignant? *American Psychologist, 44,* 266–273.

Clarke-Stewart, K. A. (1992). Consequences of child care for children's development. In A. Booth (Ed.), *Child care in the 1990s: Trends and consequences* (pp. 63–82). Hillsdale, NJ: Lawrence Erlbaum Associates.

Clarke-Stewart, K. A., & Fein, G. G. (1983). Early childhood programs. In P. H. Mussen, M. Haith, & J. Campos (Eds.), *Handbook of child psychology* (Vol. 2, pp. 917–1000). New York: Wiley.

Clarke-Stewart, K. A., Gruber, C. P., & Fitzgerald, L. M. (1994). *Children at home and in day care.* Hillsdale, NJ: Lawrence Erlbaum Associates.

Cochran, M. M. (1977a). A comparison of group day and family child-rearing patterns in Sweden. *Child Development, 48,* 702–707.

Cochran, M. M. (1977b). *Group day care and family childrearing patterns in Sweden.* Unpublished report to the Foundation for Child Development, Cornell University, Ithaca, NY.

Condry, J., Condry, S., & Pogatshnik, L. W. (1978, August). *Sex differences: A study of the ear of the beholder.* Paper presented at the meeting of the American Psychological Association, Toronto.

Connolly, K. J., & Smith, P. K. (1978). Experimental studies of the preschool environment. *International Journal of Early Childhood, 10,* 86–95.

Cummings, E. M. (1980). Caregiver stability and day care. *Developmental Psychology, 16,* 31–37.

Dennis, W. (1973). *Children of the creche.* New York: Appleton–Century–Crofts.

Desai, S., Chase-Lansdale, P. L., & Michael, R. T. (1989). Mother or market? Effects of maternal employment on the intellectual ability of four-year-old children. *Demography, 26,* 545–561.

Eheart, B. K., & Leavitt, R. L. (1989). Family day care: Discrepancies between intended and observed caregiving practices. *Early Childhood Research Quarterly, 4,* 145–162.

Fagot, B. E. (1973). Influence of teacher behavior in the preschool. *Developmental Psychology, 9,* 198–206.

Farran, D. C., & Ramey, C. T. (1977). Infant day care and attachment behaviors toward mothers and teachers. *Child Development, 48,* 1112–1116.

Ferri, E. (1980). Combined nursery centres. *Concern,* National Children's Bureau, No. 37.

Field, T. M. (1979). Infant behaviors directed toward peers and adults in the presence and absence of mother. *Infant Behavior and Development, 2,* 47–54.

Finkelstein, N. W. (1982). Aggression: Is it stimulated by day care? *Young Children, 37,* 3–12.

Fosburg, S., Hawkins, P. D., Singer, J. D., Goodson, B. D., Smith, J. M., & Brush, L. R. (1980). *National Day Care Home Study.* Cambridge, MA: Abt Associates.

Fowler, W. (1978). *Day care and its effects on early development: A study of group and home care in multi-ethnic, working-class families.* Toronto: Ontario Institute for Studies in Education.

Fox, N. (1977). Attachment of kibbutz infants to mother and metapelet. *Child Development, 48,* 1228–1239.

Freedman, D. G. (1979). *Human sociobiology.* New York: The Free Press.

Galluzzo, D. C. (1990, April). *Caregiver sensitivity and infant–caregiver attachment in child care.* Poster presented at the Seventh International Conference on Infant Studies, Montréal.

Garber, H. L., & Hodge, J. D. (1989). Risk for deceleration in the rate of mental development. *Developmental Review, 9,* 259–300.

Goelman, H., & Pence, A. R. (1987a). Effects of child care, family, and individual characteristics on children's language development: The Victoria Day Care Research Project. In D. A. Phillips (Ed.), *Quality in child care: What does research tell us?* (pp. 89–104). Washington, DC: National Association for the Education of Young Children.

Goelman, H., & Pence, A. R. (1987b). Some aspects of the relationship between family structure and child language in three types of day care. In I. E. Sigel, D. L. Peters, & S. Kontos (Eds.), *Annual advances in applied developmental psychology* (Vol. 2, pp. 129–149). Norwood, NJ: Ablex.

Golden, M., Rosenbluth, L., Grossi, M. T., Policare, H. J., Freeman, H., & Brownlee, E. M. (1978). *The New York City Infant Day Care Study.* New York: Medical & Health Research Association of New York City.

Goodman, N., & Andrews, J. (1981). Cognitive development of children in family and group day care. *American Journal of Orthopsychiatry, 51,* 271–284.

Goossens, F. A., & van IJzendoorn, M. H. (1990). Quality of infants' attachments to professional caregivers: Relation to infant–parent attachment and day-care characteristics. *Child Development, 61,* 832–837.

Hamilton, W. D. (1964). The genetical evolution of social behavior I. *Journal of Theoretical Biology, 7,* 1–16.

Haskins, R. (1985). Public school aggression among children with varying day-care experience. *Child Development, 56,* 689–703.

Hayes, C. D., Palmer, J. L., & Zaslow, M. J. (1990). *Who cares for America's children?* Washington, DC: National Academy Press.

Hayes, W. A., Massey, G. C., Thomas, E. A. C., David, J., Milbrath, C., Buchanan, A., & Lieberman, A. (1983). *Analytical and technical report of the National Infant Care Study.* San Mateo, CA: The Urban Institute for Human Services.

Hegland, S. M., & Rix, M. K. (1990). Aggression and assertiveness in kindergarten children differing in day care experiences. *Early Childhood Research Quarterly, 5,* 105–116.

Herwig, J. E. (1989, April). *Longitudinal effects of preschool experience on social and cognitive play behaviors of preschoolers.* Paper presented at the biennial meeting of the Society for Research in Child Development, Kansas City, MO.

Hess, R. D., Price, G. G., Dickson, W. P., & Conroy, M. (1981). Different roles for mothers and teachers: Contrasting styles of child care. In S. Kilmer (Ed.), *Advances in early education and day care* (Vol. 2, pp. 1–28). Greenwich, CT: JAI.

Hirsh-Pasek, K., Hyson, M. C., & Rescorla, L. (1990). Academic environments in preschool: Do they pressure or challenge young children? *Early Education and Development, 1,* 401–423.

Holloway, S. D., & Reichhart-Erickson, M. (1988). The relationship of day care quality to children's free-play behavior and social problem-solving skills. *Early Childhood Research Quarterly, 3,* 39–53.

Holloway, S. D., & Reichhart-Erickson, M. (1989). Child care quality, family structure, and maternal expectations: Relationship to preschool children's peer relations. *Journal of Applied Developmental Psychology, 10,* 281–298.

Howes, C. (1983). Caregiver behavior in centers and family day care. *Journal of Applied Developmental Psychology, 4,* 99–107.

Howes, C. (1987). Social competency with peers: Contributions from child care. *Early Childhood Research Quarterly, 2,* 155–167.

Howes, C. (1988). Peer interaction of young children. *Monographs of the Society for Research in Child Development, 53*(Serial No. 217).

Howes, C. (1990). Current research on early day care. In S. S. Chehrazi (Ed.), *Psychosocial issues in day care* (pp. 21–35). Washington, DC: American Psychiatric Press.

Howes, C. (1991). A comparison of preschool behaviors with peers when children enroll in child care as infants or older children. *Journal of Reproductive and Infant Psychology, 9,* 105–115.

Howes, C., & Hamilton, C. E. (1992). Children's relationships with caregivers: Mothers and child care teachers. *Child Development, 63,* 859–866.

Howes, C., Hamilton, C., & Allhusen, V. D. (in preparation). *Using the Attachment Q-set to describe non-familial attachments.* Unpublished manuscript.

Howes, C., & Olenick, M. (1986). Family and child care influences on toddler's compliance. *Child Development, 57,* 202–216.

Howes, C., Phillips, D. A., & Whitebook, M. (1992). Thresholds of quality: Implications for the social development of children in center-based child care. *Child Development, 63,* 449–460.

Howes, C., Rodning, C., Galluzzo, D. C., & Myers, L. (1988). Attachment and child care: Relationships with mother and caregiver. *Early Childhood Research Quarterly, 3,* 403–416.

Howes, C., & Rubenstein, J. L. (1981). Toddler peer behavior in two types of day care. *Infant Behavior and Development, 4,* 387–394.

Howes, C., & Rubenstein, J. L. (1985). Determinants of toddlers' experience in day care: Age of entry and quality of setting. *Child Care Quarterly, 14,* 140–151.

Howes, C., & Stewart, P. (1987). Child's play with adults, toys, and peers: An examination of family and child-care influences. *Developmental Psychology, 23,* 423–430.

Hunt, J. M. (1961). *Intelligence and experience.* New York: Ronald Press.

Hyson, M. C., Whitehead, L. C., & Prudhoe, C. M. (1988). Influences on attitudes toward physical affection between adults and children. *Early Childhood Research Quarterly, 3,* 55–75.

Jarvis, C. H. (1987, August). *Kindergarten days: Too much, too soon?* Paper presented at the meeting of the American Psychological Association, New York.

Johnson, J. E., Ershler, J., & Bell, C. (1980). Play behavior in a discovery-based and a formal-education program. *Child Development, 51,* 271–274.

Kagan, J., Kearsley, R. B., & Zelazo, P. R. (1978). *Infancy: Its place in human development.* Cambridge, MA: Harvard University Press.

Kagan, S. L. (1991). Examining profit and nonprofit child care: An odyssey of quality and auspices. *Journal of Social Issues, 47,* 87–104.

Kinney, P. F. (1988). *Antecedents of caregiver involvement with infants and toddlers in group care.* Unpublished doctoral dissertation, University of Maryland, College Park.

Kisker, E. E., Hofferth, S. L., Phillips, D. A., & Farquhar, E. (1991). *A profile of child care settings: Early education and care in 1990* (Report prepared for the U.S. Department of Education, Contract No. LC88090001). Princeton, NJ: Mathematica.

Klinzing, D. G., & Klinzing, D. R. (1974). An examination of the verbal behavior, knowledge, and attitudes of day care teachers. *Education, 95,* 65–71.

Kontos, S., & Fiene, R. (1987). Child care quality, compliance with regulations, and children's development: The Pennsylvania study. In D. A. Phillips (Ed.), *Quality in child care: What does research tell us?* (pp. 57–80). Washington, DC: National Association for the Education of Young Children.

Lally, J. R., & Honig, A. S. (1977). *The Family Development Research Program* (Final Report No. OCD-CB-100). Syracuse, NY: Syracuse University.

Lamb, M. E., Hwang, C-P., Broberg, A., & Bookstein, F. L. (1988). The effects of out-of-home care on the development of social competence in Sweden: A longitudinal study. *Early Childhood Research Quarterly, 3,* 379–402.

Lamb, M. E., Sternberg, K. J., Knuth, N., Hwang, C. P., & Broberg, A. G. (1991). In H. Goelman (Ed.), *Play and child care* (pp. 37–52). Albany: State University of New York Press.

Lamb, M. E., Thompson, R. A., Gardner, W., & Charnov, E. L. (1985). *Infant–mother attachment: The origins and developmental significance of individual differences in Strange Situation behavior.* Hillsdale, NJ: Lawrence Erlbaum Associates.

Laosa, L. M. (1982). Families as facilitators of children's intellectual development at 3 years of age: A causal analysis. In L. M. Laosa & I. E. Sigel (Eds.), *Families as learning environments for children* (pp. 1–46). New York: Plenum.

Larsen, J. M., & Robinson, C. C. (1989). Later effects of preschool on low-risk children. *Early Childhood Research Quarterly, 4,* 133–144.

Lazar, I., Darlington, R. B., Murray, H., Royce, J., & Snipper, A. (1982). Lasting effects of early education. *Monographs of the Society for Research in Child Development, 47*(2–3, Serial No. 195).

Lazar, I., Hubbell, R., Murray, H., Rosche, M., & Royce, J. (1977). *The persistence of preschool effects: A long-term follow-up of fourteen infant and preschool experiments* (Final Report to Office of Human Development Services, Grant No. 18-76-07843). Ithaca, NY: Cornell University.

Lightcap, J. L., Kurland, J. A., & Burgess, R. L. (1982). Child abuse: A test of some predictions from evolutionary theory. *Ethology and Sociobiology, 3,* 61–67.

Logue, M. E. (1989, April). *Social behavior of toddlers and preschoolers in same-age and multi-age day-care settings.* Paper presented at the biennial meetings of the Society for Research in Child Development, Kansas City, MO.

Long, F., Peters, D. L., & Garduque, L. (1985). Continuity between home and day care: A model for defining relevant dimensions of child care. In I. E. Sigel (Ed.), *Advances in applied developmental psychology* (pp. 131–170). Norwood, NJ: Ablex.

Main, M., & Weston, D. R. (1981). The quality of the toddler's relationship to mother and to father: Related to conflict behavior and the readiness to establish new relationships. *Child Development, 52,* 932–940.

McCartney, K. (1984). Effect of quality of day care environment on children's language development. *Developmental Psychology, 20,* 244–260.

Melhuish, E. (1991). Research on day care for young children in the United Kingdom. In E. C. Melhuish & P. Moss (Eds.), *Day care for young children: International perspectives* (pp. 142–160). London: Tavistock/Routledge.

Melhuish, E. C., Lloyd, E., Martin, S., & Mooney, A. (1990). Type of child care at 18 months: II. Relations with cognitive and language development. *Journal of Child Psychology and Psychiatry, 31,* 861–870.

Melhuish, E. C., & Moss, P. (Eds.). (1991). *Day care for young children: International perspectives.* London: Tavistock/Routledge.

Miller, L. B., Bugbee, M. R., & Hybertson, D. W. (1985). Dimensions of preschool: The effects of individual experience. In I. E. Sigel (Ed.), *Advances in applied developmental psychology* (Vol. 1, pp. 25–90). Norwood, NJ: Ablex.

Miller, L. B., & Dyer, J. L. (1975). Four preschool programs: Their dimensions and effects. *Monographs of the Society for Research in Child Development, 40*(5–6, Serial No. 162).

Moskowitz, D. W., Schwarz, J. C., & Corsini, D. A. (1977). Initiating day care at three years of age: Effects on attachment. *Child Development, 48,* 1271–1276.

National Center for Education Statistics. (1993). *Profile of preschool children's child care and early education program participation.* Washington, DC: U.S. Department of Education.

Nelson, M. K. (1990). *Negotiated care: The experience of family day care providers.* Philadelphia: Temple University Press.

Oppenheim, D., Sagi, A., & Lamb, M. E. (1988). Infant–adult attachments on the kibbutz and their relation to socioemotional development 4 years later. *Developmental Psychology, 24,* 427–433.

Osborn, A. F., & Milbank, J. E. (1987). *The effects of early education.* Oxford, England: Clarendon.

Parke, R. D., & Sawin, D. B. (1980). The family in early infancy: Social interactional and attitudinal analysis. In F. A. Pedersen (Ed.), *The father–infant relationship: Observational studies in the family setting* (pp. 44–70). New York: Praeger.

Pence, A. R., & Goelman, H. (1987a). Silent partners: Parents of children in three types of day care. *Early Childhood Research Quarterly, 2,* 103–118.

Pence, A. R., & Goelman, H. (1987b). Who cares for the child in day care? An examination of caregivers from three types of care. *Early Childhood Research Quarterly, 2,* 315–334.

Phillips, D. A., & Howes, C. (1987). Indicators of quality in child care: Review of research. In D. A. Phillips (Ed.), *Quality in child care: What does the research tell us?* (pp. 1–19). Washington, DC: National Association for the Education of Young Children.

Phillips, D. A., McCartney, K., & Scarr, S. (1987). Child-care quality and children's social development. *Developmental Psychology, 23,* 537–543.

Phillips, D. A., Scarr, S., & McCartney, K. (1987). Dimensions and effects of child care quality: The Bermuda study. In D. A. Phillips (Ed.), *Quality in child care: What does research tell us?* (pp. 43–56). Washington, DC: National Association for the Education of Young Children.

Phillips, D. A., & Whitebook, M. (1990). The child care provider: Pivotal player in the child's world. In S. S. Chehrazi (Ed.), *Psychosocial issues in day care* (pp. 129–146). Washington, DC: American Psychiatric Press.

Phyfe-Perkins, E. (1981). *Effects of teacher behavior on preschool children: Review of research.* Washington, DC: National Institute of Education. (ERIC Document Reproduction Service No. ED 211 176)

Powell, D. R., & Stremmel, A. J. (1989). The relation of early childhood training and experience to the professional development of child care workers. *Early Childhood Research Quarterly, 4,* 339–355.

Prescott, E. (1973). *A comparison of three types of day care and nursery school-home care.* Washington, DC: National Institute of Education. (ERIC Document Reproduction Service No. ED 078 910)

Rabinovich, B. A., Zaslow, M. J., Berman, P. W., & Heyman, R. (1987, April). *Employed and homemaker mothers' perceptions of their toddlers' compliance behavior in the home.* Paper presented at the biennial meeting of the Society for Research in Child Development, Baltimore.

Ricciuti, H. N. (1974). Fear and the development of social attachments in the first year of life. In M. Lewis & L. A. Rosenblum (Eds.), *The origins of fear* (pp. 73–106). New York: Wiley.

Robinson, J., & Corley, R. (1989, April). *The effects of day care participation: Sex differences in early and middle childhood.* Paper presented at the biennial meeting of the Society for Research in Child Development, Kansas City, MO.

Rubenstein, J. L., & Howes, C. (1979). Caregiving and infant behavior in day care and in homes. *Developmental Psychology, 15,* 1–24.

Rubenstein, J. L., & Howes, C. (1983). Social-emotional development of toddlers in day care: The role of peers and of individual differences. In S. Kilmer (Ed.), *Advances in early education and day care* (Vol. 3, pp. 13–45). Greenwich, CT: JAI.

Rubenstein, J. L., Howes, C., & Boyle, P. (1981). A two-year follow-up of infants in community based infant day care. *Journal of Child Psychology and Psychiatry, 22,* 209–218.

Rubenstein, J. L., Pedersen, F. A., & Yarrow, L. J. (1977). What happens when mother is away: A comparison of mothers and substitute caregivers. *Developmental Psychology, 13,* 529–530.

Ruopp, R., Travers, J., Glantz, F., & Coelen, C. (1979). *Children at the center.* Cambridge, MA: Abt Associates.

Rushton, J. P., Russell, R. J. H., & Wells, P. A. (1984). Genetic similarity theory: Beyond kin selection. *Behavior Genetics, 14,* 179–193.

Russon, A. E., Waite, B. E., & Rochester, M J. (1990). Direct caregiver intervention in infant peer social encounters. *American Journal of Orthopsychiatry, 60,* 428–439.

Rutter, M. (1982). Social-emotional effects of day care for preschool children. In E. Zigler & E. W. Gordon (Eds.), *Day care: Scientific and social policy issues* (pp. 3–32). Boston: Auburn House.

Sagi, A., Lamb, M. E., Lewkowicz, K. S., Shoham, R., Dvir, R., & Estes, D. (1985). Security of infant–mother, –father, and –metapelet attachments among kibbutz-reared Israeli children. In I. Bretherton & E. Waters (Eds.), *Growing points of attachment theory and research* (pp. 257–275). *Monographs of the Society for Research in Child Development, 50*(1–2, Serial No. 209).

Scarr, S., Lande, J., & McCartney, K. (1988). Child care and the family: Complements and interactions. In J. Lande, S. Scarr, & N. Gunzenhauser (Eds.), *Caring for children: Challenge to America* (pp. 1–21). Hillsdale, NJ: Lawrence Erlbaum Associates.

Scarr, S., Phillips, D., & McCartney, K. (1989). Working mothers and their families. *American Psychologist, 44,* 1402–1409.

Scarr, S., & Weinberg, R. A. (1986). The early childhood enterprise. *American Psychologist, 41,* 1140–1146.

Schenk, V. M., & Grusec, J. E. (1987). A comparison of prosocial behavior of children with and without day care experience. *Merrill–Palmer Quarterly, 33,* 231–240.

Schlieker, E., White, D. R., & Jacobs, E. (1991). The role of day care quality in the prediction of children's vocabulary. *Canadian Journal of Behavioural Science, 23,* 12–24.

Schwarz, J. C., Krolick, G., & Strickland, R. G. (1973). Effects of early day care experience on adjustment to a new environment. *American Journal of Orthopsychiatry, 43,* 340–346.

Schweinhart, L. J., Weikart, D. P., & Larner, M. D. (1986). Consequences of three preschool curriculum models through age 15. *Early Childhood Research Quarterly, 1,* 15–45.

Segal, N. L. (1984). Cooperation, competition, and altruism within twin sets: A reappraisal. *Ethology and Sociobiology, 5,* 163–177.

Serbin, L. A., Connor, J. M., & Denier, C. (1978). *Modification of sex typed activity and interactive play patterns in the preschool classroom: A replication and extension.* Paper presented at the annual meeting of the Association for the Advancement of Behavior Therapy, Chicago.

Sidorowicz, L. S., & Lunney, G. S. (1980). Baby X revisited. *Sex Roles, 6,* 67–73.

Siegal, M., & Storey, R. M. (1985). Day care and children's conceptions of moral and social rules. *Child Development, 56,* 1001–1008.

Siegel-Gorelick, B., Ambron, S. R., & Everson, M. D. (1981a, April). *Day care as a learning environment: The relation between environmental characteristics and social development in family day care.* Paper presented at the annual convention of the American Educational Research Association, Los Angeles.

Siegel-Gorelick, B., Ambron, S. R., & Everson, M. D. (1981b, April). *Direction of influence and intensity of affect in caregiver-child interactions in day care and at home.* Paper presented at the biennial meeting of the Society for Research in Child Development, Boston.

Smith, A. B., Ballard, K. D., & Barham, L. J. (1989). Preschool children's perceptions of parent and teacher roles. *Early Childhood Research Quarterly, 4,* 523–532.

Smith, E. W., & Howes, C. (1993). *The effect of parents' presence on children's social interactions in preschool.* Manuscript submitted for review.

Smith, P. K. (1980). Shared care of young children: Alternative models to monotropism. *Merrill–Palmer Quarterly, 26,* 371–389.

Smith, P. K., & Connolly, K. J. (1980). *The ecology of preschool behaviour.* Cambridge, England: Cambridge University Press.

Sroufe, L. A. (1983). Infant–caregiver attachment and patterns of adaptation in preschool: The roots of maladaptation and competence. In M. Perlmutter (Ed.), *Minnesota symposium in child psychology* (Vol. 16, pp. 41–83). Hillsdale, NJ: Lawrence Erlbaum Associates.

Stallings, J. A. (1980). An observation study of family day care. In J. C. Colberg (Ed.), *Home day care: A perspective* (pp. 25–47). Chicago: Roosevelt University.

Sternberg, K. J., Lamb, M. E., Hwang, C.-P., Broberg, A., Ketterlinus, R. D., & Bookstein, F. L. (1991). Does out-of-home care affect compliance in preschoolers? *International Journal of Behavioral Development, 14,* 45–65.

Stith, S. M., & Davis, A. J. (1984). Employed mothers and family day-care substitute caregivers: A comparative analysis of infant care. *Child Development, 55,* 1340–1348.

Strayer, F. F., Moss, E., & Blicharski, T. (1989). Biosocial bases of representational activity during early childhood. In L. T. Winegar (Ed.), *Social interaction and the development of children's understanding* (pp. 21–44). Norwood, NJ: Ablex.

Suransky, V. P. (1982). *The erosion of childhood.* Chicago: University of Chicago Press.

Sylva, K., Roy, C., & Painter, M. (1980). *Child watching at playgroup and nursery school.* London: Grant McIntyre.

Thornburg, K. R., Pearl, P., Crompton, D., & Ispa, J. M. (1990). Development of kindergarten children based on child care arrangements. *Early Childhood Research Quarterly, 5,* 27–42.

Tizard, B., Carmichael, H., Hughes, M., & Pinkerton, B. (1980). Four-year-olds talking to mothers and teachers. In L. A. Hersov & M. Berger (Eds.), *Language and language disorders in childhood* (pp. 49–77). London: Pergamon.

Tizard, B., Philips, J., & Plewis, I. (1976). Play in preschool centres: II. Effects on play of the child's social class and of the educational orientation of the centre. *Journal of Child Psychology and Psychiatry, 17,* 265–274.

Tyler, B., & Dittman, L. (1980). Meeting the toddler more than halfway: The behavior of toddlers and their caregivers. *Young Child, 35,* 39–46.

U.S. Bureau of the Census. (1990). Who's minding the kids? Child care arrangements, 1986–87. In *Current Population Reports* (Series P-70, No. 20). Washington, DC: U.S. Government Printing Office.

van IJzendoorn, M. H. & Tavecchio, L. W. C. (Eds.). (1987). *Attachment in social networks: Contributions to the Bowlby–Ainsworth attachment theory.* Amsterdam: North-Holland.

Vandell, D. L., & Corasaniti, M. A. (1990). Variations in early child care: Do they predict subsequent social, emotional, and cognitive differences? *Early Childhood Research Quarterly, 5,* 555–572.

Vandell, D. L., Henderson, V. K., & Wilson, K. S. (1988). A longitudinal study of children with day-care experiences of varying quality. *Child Development, 59,* 1286–1292.

Vaughn, B. E., Gove, F. L., & Egeland, B. (1980). The relationship between out-of-home care and the quality of infant–mother attachment in an economically disadvantaged population. *Child Development, 51,* 1203–1214.

Wachs, T. D., & Gruen, G. E. (1982). *Early experience and human development.* New York: Plenum.

Wadsworth, M. E. J. (1986). Effects of parenting style and preschool experience on children's verbal attainment: Results of a British longitudinal study. *Early Childhood Research Quarterly, 1,* 237–248.

Wasik, B. H., Ramey, C. T., Bryant, D. M., & Sparling, J. J. (1990). A longitudinal study of two early intervention strategies: Project CARE. *Child Development, 61,* 1682–1696.

Waters, E., & Deane, K. E. (1985). Defining and assessing individual differences in attachment relationships: Q-methodology and the organization of behavior in infancy and early childhood. In I. Bretherton & E. Waters (Eds.), *Growing points of attachment theory and research* (pp. 42–65). *Monographs of the Society for Research in Child Development, 50*(1–2, Serial No. 209).

Weinraub, M., Jaeger, E., & Hoffman, L. W. (1988). Predicting infant outcomes in families of employed and non-employed mothers. *Early Childhood Research Quarterly, 3,* 361–378.

Whitebook, M., Howes, C., & Phillips, D. (1990). *Who cares? Child care teachers and the quality of care in America. Final Report. National Child Care Staffing Study.* Oakland, CA: Child Care Employee Project.

Whiting, B. B., & Whiting, J. W. M. (1981). *Children of six cultures: A psycho-cultural analysis.* Cambridge, MA: Harvard University Press.

Wille, D. E., & Jacobson, J. L. (1984, April). *The influence of maternal employment, attachment pattern, extrafamilial child care, and previous experience with peers on early peer interaction.* Paper presented at the International Conference on Infancy Studies, Beverly Hills, CA.

Wilson, M. I., Daly, M., & Weghorst, S. J. (1980). Household composition and the risk of child abuse and neglect. *Journal of Biosocial Science, 12,* 333–340.

Winnett, R. A., Fuchs, W. L., Moffatt, S., & Nerviano, V. J. (1977). A cross-sectional study of children and their families in different child care environments. *Journal of Community Psychology, 5,* 149–159.

Wynn, R. L. (1979, March). *The effect of a playmate on day-care and home-reared toddlers in a strange situation.* Paper presented at the biennial meeting of the Society for Research in Child Development, San Francisco.

Zigler, E. F., & Freedman, J. (1990). Psychological-developmental implications of current patterns of early child care. In S. S. Chehrazi (Ed.), *Psychosocial issues in day care* (pp. 3–20). Washington, DC: American Psychiatric Press.

7

Sibling Caregiving

Patricia Zukow-Goldring
University of California, Irvine

INTRODUCTION

Next to the courtyard fence in a shady spot six children, ages 2 to 10, engage in very elaborate imaginative play in the small farming community of Santa Ana y Lobos at the southeastern edge of Guanajuata in Central Mexico. Amidst countless interruptions including urgent requests for food or drink, elimination accidents, breakage of highly prized miniature jarras (clay pots), teasing by older brothers and male cousins hanging over the fence, and tending to infants less than 2, Sara aged 10 and Cristina aged 7 still managed to organize an enactment of tortilla making.

The sisters, with the elder firmly guiding the others, call out directions and revisions to each other as they all simultaneously and continuously constitute and negotiate the emerging event. Sara and Cristina must chide Lalo aged 3 for his incessant requests for more water and temporarily banish Juana aged 2 for carelessly smashing a clay jar. Despite many distractions, these sisters demonstrate in play a complex subsequence required to attain competence in the most basic, yet the most difficult, achievement of Mexico's culinary arts. They gather implements, grind corn (dirt), mix the result with water to make masa (dough), shape balls of masa, pat them out to form tortillas, and cook them on a comal (round cookstone).

Twenty to 30 feet away, adults and adolescent siblings at work or at rest after long hours in the fields share checking out details of care only when something may be amiss. They call out only when a child elsewhere needs tending or when Juana shamed by being sent away goes to her father who with an older brother teases her gently. Using a younger male cousin as the carrot, first Sara, then Cristina ask Juana to rejoin them. Juana refuses Sara's invitation. A few moments later Juana walks to the infant now held by Cristina, then sweetly chucks him under the chin, murmuring niño = niño = niño/little boy = little boy = little boy accepting the second face-saving bid to go back to the group activity. Soon Sara seats her among the others and encourages her several times saying, ¡echa una tortillita!/pat out a little tortilla!. With little urging, Juana awkwardly and enthusiasticly takes a ball of masa prepared by her sisters and pats it into the proper flattened shape.

—Zukow (AMR, 3/3/82)

This segment of interaction, embedded in the most mundane daily activities of a Mexican family living in a rural, agrarian community of 700 people, illustrates the multifaceted role of sibling caregiving. Functional and adaptable, sibling care helps the family in its maintenance and survival. Siblings assist in the socializing of cultural ways of perceiving and knowing. Sibling caregivers select and promote detection of cultural practices within nested levels of care. Age and gender affect who plays or works together. These activities, whether involving groups or an individual, co-occur in the courtyard. Family members consider conflict and cooperation to be unavoidable *and* beneficial, both contributing to the socializing of members of the culture. Within this milieux, the social setting meets, shapes, and is shaped by the child. The primary question is not whether the social setting has or has not met the needs of the individual child, but whether the child assists the family in meeting its needs.

What roles do sibling caregivers play in the development of their younger sisters and brothers? How does giving care affect the development of older siblings? Answers to these questions reflect a dichotomy between findings arising from research conducted in urban-technological societies and those in rural-agrarian societies. In small, non-Western agrarian societies the mother's workload correlates significantly with children's assistance in household work (Harkness & Super, in this *Handbook;* Whiting & Edwards, 1988; Whiting & Whiting, 1975). Older siblings are highly valued caregivers of younger family members in agrarian societies whose assistance frees the mother to engage in economically more productive work (Rogoff, Sellers, Piorrata, Fox, & White, 1975; Weisner & Gallimore, 1977; Werner, 1979; Whiting & Edwards, 1988; Whiting & Whiting, 1975). A family's survival depends on the socializing and emergence of caregiving practices, which in turn mark the older sibling as developing into a competent and appreciated member of society (Weisner, 1987). Not surprisingly sibling caregiving is taken for granted in cultures that depend on the involvement of older brothers and sisters on a daily basis.

Yet most adults in Western technological cultures do not acknowledge the important function of sibling caregiving (Bank & Kahn, 1982; Lamb & Sutton-Smith, 1982; Zukow, 1989b). Even under circumstances of great hardship, members of technological societies have often ignored siblings as a resource for families, even among those with handicapped children (Weisner, 1993a), or judged such care as neglect, bad parenting, or worse when economics force all adult members of a family to work outside the home. Only recently have investigators in painstaking naturalistic observation grounded in ethological studies and ethnographies of daily life concluded that young siblings display sophisticated knowledge of the social world (Dunn, 1988; Dunn & Kendrick, 1982a). In similar studies, other researchers have documented that older siblings function as competent socializing agents of younger children in the family, not merely as monitors of the young child's most basic biological needs (Martini, 1994; Watson-Gegeo & Gegeo, 1989; Zukow, 1989c).

Disciplinary, theoretical, cultural, economic, historical, and generational forces all contribute to the assumptions held by members of technological societies regarding sibling caregivers. Unexamined presuppositions held by researchers in technological societies may bias "facts" that emerge from empirical studies. Interpretation, influenced by disciplinary bias, can cloud further the questions scholars need to ask about sibling caregiving around the world.

This chapter first examines existing biases that may prevent members of technological societies from appreciating the value of sibling caregiving. Subsequently, the chapter defines parenting goals, discusses their realizations within agrarian and technological societies, and considers the functions and contributions of sibling caregiving within this framework. The chapter next addresses the empirical research that documents the range of activities in which sibling caregivers engage including who gives and gets care, how siblings achieve the prerequisites for competent sibling caregiving, who socializes sibling caregivers and how, authority versus conflict, novice–expert roles, and the effective socializing of cultural practices manifested in the domains of cognition, play, and language. Finally, the chapter looks at future directions for research on sibling caregiving and what sibling research offers theories of child development and social policy.

THE STUDY OF SIBLING CAREGIVING: BIASES AND OPPORTUNITIES

Sibling caregiving is very widespread, yet it is understudied, even unseen. Why have theorists and researchers overlooked siblings as an important resource in the process of socializing younger children? Examining certain biases provides answers to this question. Theoretical approaches informing the study of siblings cluster at two ends of a continuum. Some theoretical perspectives and research flowing from psychology focus nearly exclusively on the individual child's development or individual differences among or between groups in culturally limited settings, whereas other views informed by anthropology, psychology, and sociology look at the child "coming of age" within his or her particular culture. Before discussing the benefits that both offer, this section addresses unexamined assumptions characteristic of each. These assumptions as well as historical and generational influences have impeded research on sibling caregiving and its implications for theory.

Biases

Western researchers perceive how children become competent members of their cultures and view children as individuals who can recognize, participate in, and communicate about ongoing events in a variety of ways. Investigation of these processes has been pursued within a near "crazy quilt" of theoretical approaches, including attachment, behavioral genetics, eco-cultural, ecological, exchange, family systems, general systems, hermeneutics, language socialization, organismic, personality (birth order, individual differences), Piagetian, psychodynamic, sociobiological, Vygotskian, and more. Theories, however, are ways of knowing that focus as well as limit what adherents notice and interpret. Much like the elephant described by the three blind men, the lens of a powerful *zeitgeist* can make some relationships prominent and others nearly invisible, ultimately distorting what is understood about the whole.

The notion that older siblings play an important role in their younger sisters' and brothers' development has gained prominence only since the publication of perceptive work by Dunn and Kendrick (1982a), Hartup (1979), Lamb (1982), Sutton-Smith (1982), and Weisner and Gallimore (1977) less than 20 years ago. Within psychology three biases in particular have contributed to overlooking and underestimating the significant contribution of siblings to each others' development. First, members of Western technological societies often assume that the nuclear family is the norm (Weisner & Gallimore, 1977), oblivious to influences from extended family members, such as relatives near in age (cousins, aunts, and uncles). Second, psychological theories reflect cultural values and beliefs that hold individual achievement in particularly high esteem and may ignore achievements arising from interdependence (LeVine, 1980). Third, psychodynamic theories of personality or psychological development did not include siblings as important socializing agents (Lamb, 1982), but focused instead on the conflict and competitiveness presumed to follow from assumed sibling rivalry for maternal love and affection (Dunn, 1988; Dunn & Kendrick, 1982a, 1982b; Nuckolls, 1993a). In harmony with these views, researchers concentrated their focus almost exclusively on the mother's role in her child's development rather than on any other family member (Dunn & Kendrick, 1982b; Lamb, 1976).

Shared caregiving among nonhuman primates. Human and infrahuman childrearing practices presumably irrelevant to Freudian theory went unnoticed, as if part of prehistory. Recently, historical overviews of childrearing practices draw a dramatically different picture. Exclusive maternal care of offspring is rarely the rule in primate development. Speculating from data documenting surrogate care among some Old World monkeys, McKenna (1987) suggested that allo-mothering has adaptive significance. Younger females assisting in infant care would release the mother to forage more efficiently. Under those circumstances, infant caregivers would establish and strengthen bonds among themselves. If a mother should die, a female who had previously handled the infant might adopt that infant.

Paralleling McKenna (1987), Lamb and Sternberg (1992) argued persuasively on the basis of the interplay between biological and economic necessity that exclusive maternal care of infants and children has rarely occurred throughout human history. Documentation of childcare in eighteenth- and nineteenth-century England and the United States describes women's work as requiring a system of shared caregiving including sibling caregiving. Even within the last few hundred years, death during childbirth, maternal employment outside the home, or the overseeing of large families and heavy workloads within the home were common experiences (Getis & Vinovskis, 1992; Hareven, 1989; Melhuish & Moss, 1992). In these situations, elder sisters often held caregiving responsibilities and became surrogate parents if one or both parents died (Hareven, 1989).

Shared caregiving among humans.   Based on this and other evidence, Lamb and Sternberg (1992) asserted that it is a myth to assume that maternal care is somehow normal, natural, or traditional. Problems arise when an elite, dominant group holds with this view. They may then judge deviations from this standard as alarming and disadvantageous. Because such ethnocentrism affects members of every cultural group, many scholars unwittingly blind themselves to the functions, advantages, disadvantages, and routine practice of sibling care.

Generational exclusion.   Membership in a particular generation can exclude an individual from participating in the activities of another cohort. Siblings commonly "educate" each other by sharing cultural practicies. Most adults cannot observe these activities because adults have no access to many day-to-day interactions among siblings (Zukow, 1989a). What is hidden from easy view is unlikely to be investigated, although researchers should not so readily accept such a limited perspective.

Studies of lineage.   In contrast to those psychologists who concentrated on child development and socialization within the nuclear family, anthropologists studied the whole range of family forms and also how individuals in agrarian societies governed each other within kin-based societies. For example, anthropologists have examined descent, the tracing of an individual's lineage or ancestry, and its relation to social solidarity in patrilineal societies without governments. Within this area of study, being a sibling merely marked group membership and was not considered functionally relevant to considerations of rank and position within the larger group. Because siblings are located at the same genealogical level, the analysis of antecedents may have concealed from investigators the importance of siblinghood (Nuckolls, 1993a). As interest has shifted away from investigating patriarchal lines of power and authority exclusively, the personnel and settings in which the socializing of new members takes place has gained more prominence.

Summary.   Powerful theories of social organization and human development arising in the last century and a quarter combined with the limiting lenses of adult status may have influenced scholars to overlook the importance of sibling caregiving until very recently. These theories directed research- ers away from siblings altogether or toward sibling discord and investigations of the nuclear family, individual achievement, the mother's role in child development, and the lineage of power and authority. Those same theories turned researchers away from the positive potential of sibling caregiving.

Opportunities

A number of researchers who have straddled more than one intellectual and cultural world have achieved some success in combining "rigorous" quantitative and "authentic" ethnographic (qualita- tive) methods (Cole, Hood, & McDermott, 1978; Price-Williams, 1975; Rogoff, Mistry, Göncü, & Mosier, 1993; Scribner & Cole, 1981). Further, integrating these perspectives has born fruit in the form of theories or thought-provoking essays that acknowledge that the sociocultural context is the matrix in which the novice-child member develops (LCHC, 1986; Rogoff, 1990; Super & Harkness, 1986; Watson-Gegeo & Gegeo, 1989, 1992; Weisner, 1989a; Whiting & Edwards, 1988; Whiting & Whiting, 1975).

Research grounded in Western psychological theory also contributes to the understanding of sibling caregiving, especially those informed by Piaget and Vygotsky. Studies grounded in Piagetian theorems as well as those inspired by information-processing models usually investigate the development of the individual child actively and independently exploring his or her rather passive environment. In contrast, research derived from Vygotsky or from the notion of "scaffolding" (Wood, Bruner, & Ross, 1976; Wood & Middleton, 1975) focuses on both an active child and an active environment, especially on the role of the expert while she or he assists the novice to know the world during social interaction.

Most of the research reviewed in this chapter was inspired by eco-cultural, social interactive, or cognitive theories along with a sprinkling from the other theories mentioned earlier. All contribute to understanding sibling caregiving, but so far no theory of child development encompasses what is known about sibling caregiving. In everyday life, however, there is little debate over the usefulness of sibling caregiving. The majority of the world's parents assume their children will become competent caregivers and depend on their assistance in socializing younger sisters and brothers.

THE FOUNDATION FOR SIBLINGS EMBODYING PARENTAL PRACTICES

Ethnographers work from the hypothesis that members' daily practices embody the beliefs and values of a culture. The most mundane activities of daily life can reveal coherent cultural themes as members interpret each other within these frames of meaning. To understand sibling caregiving, socializing practices must be considered so that the function and accomplishments of children in different societies can be appreciated (e.g., see Demuth, 1984; Martini, 1994; Ochs, 1988; Schieffelin, 1990; Watson-Gegeo & Gegeo, 1989).

Universal parenting goals

LeVine (1977) proposed that parents first seek to ensure the survival (health and safety) of their offspring, then provide the means for the child to learn economic self-sufficiency, and finally inculcate cultural values. Achievement at each level is a prerequisite for and interdependent with that which follows. How these achievements relate to each other depends on both the demands of daily life and the developmental level of the individuals. For instance, a neonate must survive the perils of infancy and develop motorically, perceptually, and intellectually during the intervening years in order to engage in chores that contribute to the welfare of the family. After meeting basic subsistence needs, time and energy can be devoted to the fulfillment of an individual child's culturally defined aesthetic, spiritual, self-actualizing activities. These "native" practices, then, presumably instantiate parental guidance regarding prestige, wealth, intellectual achievement, ethical conduct, and so forth. (See also Weisner, 1987; Whiting & Edwards, 1988.)

Parents' investment of time, attention, and economic resources, of course, depends on local conditions (LeVine, 1977, 1980, 1988; Weisner, 1987, 1989b; Whiting & Edwards, 1988). What is optimal in a rural agrarian society will not be optimal in one that is urban-technological. In an agrarian setting, parents value highly children's relatively unskilled assistance in food and artifact production and especially their assistance in tending younger siblings. Shared caregiving frees more mature individuals in these societies to engage in higher yield economic work that requires more complex abilities, helping to ensure the family's survival. Children have such value that in some Pacific Island societies children belong to the community, not to the biological parents (Martini & Kirkpatrick, 1992).

Sources of variation

The methods for achieving parental goals as well as the characteristics parents encourage their children to display varies among agrarian and technological cultures. In agrarian societies, a more sociocentric self embodies a more interdependent system of status and role (Nuckolls, 1993a; Shweder, 1990). A we-ness is fostered across the life span through practices that encourage solidarity along with emotional and economic exchanges. It is not surprising, then, that interdependence is a central goal of socialization in agrarian societies (LeVine, 1980; Mundy-Castle, 1974; Weisner, 1989b). According to Harrison, Wilson, Pine, Chan, and Buriel (1990), the socialization of ethnic minority children in the United States occurs within an extended family rooted in a similar collectivist world view that emphasizes interdependence as well. In contrast, technological societies typically encourage innovation and change (LeVine, 1980; Weisner, 1989b). In technological cultures the definition of self is more egocentric and autonomous. This view leads both to less intense family bonds as family members change and grow and to an emphasis on the individual's future, tangible achievements (Borstelmann, 1977). Independence and individual difference highlight the socializing aims within urban-technological societies (LeVine, 1980; Weisner, 1989b).

LeVine (1980) discussed concepts in psychological research that reflect the implications of these cultural assumptions. The Western ideal of self-reliance and self-confidence is set within a frame of egalitarian ideology. Parents greet these characteristics with elaborate displays of praise and reinforcement. Consequently, at the slightest accomplishment a child may draw excessive attention to him- or herself. In contrast, in agrarian societies such behaviors would undermine the ideal cooperative network of interrelationships. Children are often scolded or teased for "showing off or putting on airs" (Martini & Kirkpatrick, 1992; Schieffelin, 1990). In South India a new baby is not viewed as someone exceptional to cherish but another person who requires a particular kind of care (Seymour, 1993). Showering the baby with attention might result in the other children vying for attention themselves. Family members encourage children to experience their acts as contributions to work, providing intrinsic satisfaction according to the degree it helps the group as a whole (LeVine, 1988).

Summary

The core of parenting goals is universal but the particulars are realized quite differently depending on the particular setting. Preparing a child to become a competent member of an agrarian culture requires a different set of priorities than those needed for full membership in a technological one. Interdependence is crucial to the survival of the entire family in agrarian societies, whereas independence is prized in technological ones. The degree to which children participate in parenting younger sisters and brothers directly reflects the importance of shared caregiving to the economic welfare of the family. However, wherever cultures lie on the continuum between small-scale, rural agrarian societies and very complex, urban technological ones, siblings must pay attention to these goals, implicit or explicit, to be able to assist in socializing younger family members.

BEING AND BECOMING A SIBLING CAREGIVER

The process of socializing sibling caregivers entails who gives the care and who gets it. A child's own level of development affects his or her becoming a caregiver, because adults require and value particular prerequisites before entrusting the child with caring for a younger sibling. A range of family members using a variety of practices socialize child caregivers, conveying where, when, and how to engage in activities during the course of the day. The preponderance of studies that explicitly document the work of sibling caregivers comes from cross-cultural investigations of agrarian and foraging groups who recognize this contribution to daily life as valuable. With the exception of the Efe foragers, many nomadic and seminomadic hunter/gatherers lack surrogate caregivers and surplus food. Because shared caregiving is probably not routine, infants are taken along on excursions to find food (Draper & Harpending, 1987).

This chapter describes central tendencies as well as variations in sibling care. Differences in the form and function of sibling caregiving occur around the world as do intracultural variations in practice. This diversity relates to workload, cultural models and norms, availability of other adult caregivers, local demography, gender balance, child temperament, and more (Harkness & Super, 1992; Weisner, 1982; Weisner & Gallimore, 1977).

Extensiveness of sibling caregiving in agrarian societies. The Whitings and the those who collaborated with them have produced a body of work that provides the most comprehensive picture of sibling caregiving (Whiting, 1963; Whiting & Edwards et al., 1988; Whiting & Whiting, 1975). Their work spans 40 years of successive studies. The Six Cultures studies sampled behavior in small villages or towns in Mexico, India, the Philippines, Kenya, Okinawa (Japan), and the United States. A "new" sample added Peru, Guatemala, Liberia, several more groups in Kenya and India, and an upper middle-class suburban community in the United States. These investigations documented the quality, quantity, and pervasiveness of sibling care in agrarian cultures.

Since their germinal work, numerous investigations have supplemented and expanded these studies including Weisner and Gallimore's classic review (1977) and more recent investigations of agrarian communities located in Africa among the Gussii of Kenya (LeVine & LeVine, 1988), the Cameroons, West Africa (Nsamenang, 1992), the Kipsigis of Kenya (Harkness & Super, 1992), the Abaluyia of Kenya (Weisner, 1987, 1989b), Mandinka of Senegal (Whittemore & Beverly, 1989), Efe foragers and the Lese in Zaire (Morelli & Tronick, 1991), Wolof of Senegal, and West Africans in France (Rabain-Jamin & Wornham, 1993; Zempleni-Rabain, 1973); in the Pacific Islands among the Kwara'ae of the Solomon Islands (Watson-Gegeo & Gegeo, 1989), native Hawaiians (Gallimore, Boggs, & Jordan, 1974; Weisner, 1989a; Weisner, Gallimore, & Jordan, 1988), in the Outer Fiji Islands (West, 1988), in Samoa (Ochs, 1988), in the Marquesas (Martini, 1994; Martini & Kirkpatrick, 1992); in Latin America among the Maya of Guatemala (Howrigan, 1988; Rogoff et al., 1993), in the traditional culture of Central Mexico (Zukow, 1989a); in South Asia/India (Beals & Eason, 1993; Rogoff et al., 1993; Seymour, 1993), and in Turkey (Rogoff et al., 1993).

Under-estimation of sibling caregiving in technological societies.

Engaging in cross-cultural studies reveals implicit assumptions (Rogoff, Gauvain, & Ellis, 1984). That is, when familiar activities are organized differently (or absent in another culture) that strangeness draws attention to the activity and the structure of events becomes visible (Garfinkel, 1977–1978). The foregrounding of sibling caregiving in many cultures sharply contrasts with its invisibility in technological societies. Investigators have not documented the extent to which sibling caregiving occurs in technological societies. Future research may reveal more frequent sibling care than expected, especially in rural settings (Rogoff et al., 1984) and among ethnic minorities. Much needed ethnographies of sibling activities in the United States and other technological societies can fill this void (cf. Whiting & Whiting, 1975).

Given the paucity of sibling caregiving studies conducted in technological settings, gleaning information about such caregiving activities involves making inferences from studies of social, emotional, and cognitive development of the individual child. Consonant with the prizing of autonomy within technological culture, existing studies of siblings primarily investigate how the experience of receiving and giving care brings an individual child to his or her "personal" best rather than how assisting with caregiving is helpful to the family.

Who Becomes a Sibling Caregiver?

Summarizing the many studies acknowledged in the last section, most siblings engage in caregiving from the age of 5 to their 10th year. Where the mothers have very high workloads, children of 2 years may infrequently assist minding a younger infant. Girls fill this role far more often than boys and begin a year or two earlier than boys. Most frequently, the mother assigns caregiving responsibilities to the eldest daughter. However, Ochs (1988) did not observe more girls than boys acting as sibling caregivers in Samoa. All school-age children attended class regularly and each was kept home to assist in caregiving in an apparent rotating system. In agrarian societies, boys commonly serve as caregivers in the absence of an available elder sister, but rarely engage in caregiving after 7 years of age.

Sources of variation in technological settings.   Weisner (1987) stressed that common stages in the life course differ across cultures. In middle-class North America the sequence relating to child care usually consists of getting married, setting up a household, and then child care. Non-Western societies have a different pattern. Child care occurs first, and much later in life comes marriage and a new household. Given the sequence among the middle class, few studies have directly documented sibling care in technological societies with the exception of the Whitings and their colleagues' studies on families of normally developing children in a small New England town (Fischer & Fischer, 1963; Whiting & Edwards, 1988; Whiting & Whiting, 1975), as there may be far less to record. The few intraethnic investigations available are ethnographies by Ward (1971) among African-American working-class children in Louisiana and by Heath (1983) in South Carolina. In these families, the ubiquity of older girls (referred to by Stack in Weisner, 1987, as "boss girls") organizing and maintaining the sibling play group may reflect the pressures arising from caring for numerous children in the extended family, when mothers often work outside the home. Mirroring the basis for sibling caregiving in agrarian societies, the mother's workload, agrarian roots, a collectivist attitude, and a clear hierarchy among household work assignments in the family also influence the frequency of sibling caregiving in African-American families. Similar dynamics hold for Latino families living in working-class neighborhoods in Los Angeles (Zukow-Goldring, fieldnotes, 1989–1994). In families with delayed, physically disabled, or mentally-ill siblings, older *and* younger nonhandicapped brothers and sisters often provide essential caregiving assistance. These studies attest to the importance, benefits, and appreciation of sibling care in families with special needs (*Journal of the California Alliance for the Mentally Ill,* 1992; Lobato, 1990; McHale & Crouter, in press; McHale & Pawletko, 1992; Stoneman & Berman, 1993).

Sibling caregiving: Resource rather than neglect.   In the main, school occupies much of school-age children's day, segregating them in age-graded groups tended by adults (Rogoff et al., 1993). With the increase of dual-wage-earner families, parents who can afford afterschool care further decrease siblings' time together. For those who cannot, the number of "latch-key" siblings whose afterschool activities at home and in the neighborhood are unsupervised until parents return from work grow in number. However, siblings do spend many hours together in early morning, late afternoon, evenings, weekends, holidays, and vacation. In Los Angeles, for instance, children attend school only 180 days a year.

What occurs during the time these siblings spend together? Ethnographic studies designed to describe what siblings do after school might provide the basis for a large social policy benefit. The functional and adaptive values of deploying sibling caregivers to assist while parents work has an unexplored potential in technological settings. Organizing programs to encourage and take advantage of supervised sibling caregiving by grandparents and/or young single mothers would provide employment for the unemployed and turn what has been termed "neglect" or bad parenting from risk into benefit.

Who Gives and Who Gets Care?

This section examines the age range of siblings who receive care, the age of the siblings who give the care, and the variety of ages found in sibling groups. Most sibling groupings in high-fertility, low mortality, child-sharing communities are composed of a mixture of sisters and brothers.

The sibling group.   The structure of living arrangements and the distribution of work organizes the population of children receiving care. The sibling group includes siblings, half-siblings in polygynous societies, cousins or "classificatory siblings," and young aunts and uncles (Nuckolls, 1993a; Seymour, 1993; Watson-Gegeo & Gegeo, 1989; Whiting & Edwards, 1988; Zukow, 1989a). In the Solomon Islands the children of one's mother's sisters and father's brothers are classified as siblings and have the same obligations throughout the life span (Watson-Gegeo & Gegeo, 1989); whereas in southern India only the children of a father's brothers are included in this category (Nuckolls, 1993a; Seymour, 1993). Nuckolls noted that Westerners assigned the term *classificatory* to designate this basic kinship category as if such siblings were somehow less real or significant than "true" biological siblings.

Whiting and Edwards (1988) classified children in sibling groups by age based on Margaret Mead's system (1935). Children from about 0 to 1 are called *lap children*, those from 2 to 3 are *knee children*, from 4 to 5 *yard children*, and from 6 to 10 *community/school children*. Yard and community/school children usually care for lap and knee children. However, children appreciate from very early in development that they are embedded within nested levels of care (Ochs, 1988; Weisner, 1982). As members of the household move through daily work schedules, a particular child may be in charge of a smaller infant and simultaneously be deferring to and receiving guidance from a still older sibling.

Siblings who give care.   Girls usually have the responsibility of lap children and are observed more often in their company. Knee children receive more varied care. In one community in Kenya, Nyansango, the 2- to 3-year-olds preferred to be with the boys herding cattle, whereas in one small Indian village children of this age were not left with older siblings. Young children customarily play alone in this community. Girls far more frequently tend children of 5–7 years than do boys. Seymour's Indian sample demonstrates differences across castes. Among the lower caste families, most mothers had employment that took them outside the home. Girls tended siblings six times as often as girls in middle- and upper class families. Lower status boys cared for siblings twice as frequently as middle-class boys. Upper class boys never engaged in such behavior. Whiting and Edwards (1988) summarized these observations succinctly: "girls work while boys play" (p. 125).

Implications of shared work.   Many people share in the care of a younger child. Shared caregiving affords a multiplicity of sources of affection as well as possible strife (Martini & Kirkpatrick, 1992). The resulting lack of competition for care appears to reduce rivalry (Seymour, 1993). Further, if the children giving and getting care encounter some incompatibility, finding an alternative among several available caregivers resolves the conflict (Draper & Harpending, 1987). The fostering of children illustrates this common practice in Africa (Goody, 1982; Nsamenang, 1992). Parents loan or foster children out of their natal homes for many reasons, including learning a trade, strengthening social bonds, and disciplining recalcitrant children by those less emotionally attached than the immediate family. In Central Mexico, a difficult child might be sent to live in the compound of another family member nearby (Zukow, field notes, 1981–1982).

Technological settings.   Studies conducted in technological societies support cross-cultural findings that girls engage in more infant care. Kreppner, Paulsen, and Schuetze's (1982) research documenting that more girls fulfill the "parenting" role may be directly related to Kramer and Noorman's (1993) findings that plans to involve the elder child in infant care affected daughters most frequently. However, "going it alone" or "making it on your own" starts early in the United States. Whiting and Edwards (1988) noted that parents leave children alone far more of the time in the United States than parents do in other cultures, and assign them by far the fewest chores. Mothers and fathers in the United States do not perceive children of 5–9 years as competent to care for others, preferring those of 12 or more. Baby-sitting by preadolescent and adolescents may not be explicitly acknowledged as sibling care. Indeed, rather than contributing to the family's economic welfare, children in the same family receive payment to tend one another in middle-class families.

Turning from who gives and receives care, the next section addresses the bases for selecting sibling caregivers.

Prerequisites for Sibling Caregiving

Although very young children of even 2 years of age may assist with tending a baby, given the mother has a burdensome workload, sibling caregivers typically range in age from 7 to 13 or 14 years (Whiting & Edwards, 1988). Mothers prefer ages 7 or 8 to 10 (Rogoff et al., 1975; Whiting & Edwards, 1988).

Sources of the age 5–7 preference.   Why does this preference exist? Adults do not consider the younger siblings fully competent. Some adolescent siblings are unavailable because they have married, have been fostered, have other economic tasks to perform, or may be serving an apprenticeship in another locale (Weisner, 1987, 1989b). Under these circumstances, cultural beliefs regarding children's emerging abilities support an increase in the assignment of caregiving responsibilities at ages 5–7 (Rogoff et al., 1975). Adults regard a child of this age teachable, and as having "reason," common sense, and a stable personality.

Cognitive achievements.   Weisner (1987, in press) reviewed cultural pressures underlying this preference and developmental milestones related to the shift that occurs at ages 5–7. Rogoff and her colleagues (1975) provided findings that permit piecing this relation together. They argued that household chores provide the foundation for learning more general practices. Within the domestic setting two naturally occurring abilities that develop during middle childhood relate to the cognitive skills necessary for competently caring for others (Nerlove, Roberts, Klein, Yarbrough, & Habicht, 1974). The first, *self-managed sequencing* of activities, refers to the child's ability to carry out a sequence of acts in an exact order without supervision, such as preparing corn for masa: removing the dried kernels from the cobs, preparing the lime-laced water, soaking the kernels in that water, removing the husks from the kernels, judging the proper texture of the kernels for grinding, and so forth. If anything goes wrong during the sequence, the child must have enough flexibility to find alternative solutions. The second, *voluntary social activities,* entails knowing the goals and rules of everyday life, such as the appropriate ways of acting toward each member of the family in accord with their place in the kinship hierarchy. At least a minimal attainment of these two cultural practices appears to underlie assignment of caregiving responsibilities to siblings during middle childhood.

Social and emotional achievements.   Although these cognitive achievements are clearly important to caregiving, some qualitative descriptions by Whiting and Edwards (1988) make it dramatically evident that dynamic social and emotional abilities play a part as well. Sibling caregivers of 3–5 years and those older caregivers who are overburdened tend to overstimulate an infant and to become quite upset themselves when they cannot soothe a fussy baby. The inability to assess the internal state of another (the crying baby is not cranky, but sleepy), to foresee the implications of one's acts in relation to another person's response (more bouncing will not satisfy a hungry baby), to find alternative solutions (bouncing a cranky baby who continues to cry, rather than walking with or singing to the baby), and to control one's own impulses (not slapping the baby in frustration) illustrate missing competence. The following segments of interaction contrasting sibling caregivers of 5 and 8 in Central Mexico illustrate some aspects of the discrepancy. Note that the boys are from different levels within the poorest socioeconomic group known as *marginados* who live on the outskirts of Mexico City (Lomnitz, 1975). Mario who is 5 years old belongs to the very poorest level composed mainly of recent immigrants living without the basic utilities, whereas Jaime who is 8 lives with his extended family in a home with running water, gas, and electricity. Mario's mother came from a very "rustic" region in the mountains in the state of Puebla and her workload was very high. Because Mario was not old enough to attend school and his mother expected him to assist her on a daily basis, his responsibilities for caregiving his younger sisters were much closer to that of the traditional rural culture than Jaime's. Jaime's mother who was born in Mexico City expected him to attend school regularly and look after his brother in the afternoons if none of the older girls in the family were available. There were 6 children under 10 years of age in both households (Zukow, fieldnotes, 1981–1982).

Mario, 5, lives with his family in a semirural section of Mexico City a short walk from the pit in which his parents make bricks by hand. Mario has carried Irene, 21 months, to see their father working in the 20-foot-deep pit. He points at his father who is at least 50 feet away saying ¡*Mira, allí está papi!/Look, there's Daddy!* His younger sister does not respond but glances about vaguely. Mario repeats the same gesture and the variations on the same verbal message a dozen or more times as he attempts quite unsuccessfully to refocus her attention. He does not walk closer taking the pathway down into the pit or pick up a rock or shard of pottery to toss to the place his father is standing. His mother in a similar situation had revised her message by eventually throwing a rock at the place she wanted Irene to notice (Zukow, 1990). Mario's responses were inflexible and displayed an insensitivity regarding the perceptual information that might have redirected his sister's attention to her father (Zukow, IGS, 4/29/82).

In contrast, Jaime, nearly 8, who lives in a nearby *colonia popular,* working-class neighborhood, resolves ambiguity for Juan, 21 months, by guiding his gaze from the corner of his eye to the target of attention when his younger brother does not understand his message. Their aunt beats egg whites for a very special treat, *chiles rellenos.* The children of the family crowd into the small kitchen to watch in delight as some of the egg white spatters on their sister Beti's dress. Jaime points across the room to her as everyone laughs. Noticing that Juan does not understand what is funny, Jaime uses his index finger to trace the trajectory of vision for Juan from the corner of his eye as he walks all the way across the room to touch the egg white on Beti's dress. Juan then walks to his sister, reaches up to touch the egg white, and explores this unfamiliar experience by feeling its texture between his fingers. Clearly, Jaime revised his message on the basis of what his brother needed to perceive, quickly providing a re-viewing of the event that effectively guided Juan's knowing (Zukow, JLA, 7/9/82).

Nascent social understanding.   Although this older sibling of nearly 8 was more skilled than his 5-year-old counterpart in assisting his younger brother to perceive what he had just said, "younger" older siblings exhibit considerable understanding of infants. According to Dunn and Kendrick (1982a) and Wolfe (1984) young children in their second and third years in England and the United States may not know what others perceive, but what they do know can be seen in their actions and speech. In action they display that they understand the consequences of their own acts and what another might feel. These abilities emerge very early in development. Young children express the same sensitivity to others in rural settings in Central Mexico as well.

Lilia, 17 months, lived in a small farming *ejido,* cooperative, about 175 miles northwest of Mexico City in the state of Guanajuato. She behaved quite possessively about a small green rush-bottomed chair. While playing together, Ana, a courtyard cousin closer to 3 years of age, took the chair quite deliberately. Ana, quite sturdily built, set the chair down carefully a short distance away. She bent forward elaborately and slowly lifted her bottom up and back in order to sit squarely on the tiny chair. As she began to lower herself, without hesitation Lilia moved into the gap between "up and back" and "down." She efficiently walked behind her cousin and smoothly lifted the seat away at the exact instant that seat and bottom were meant to meet. A look of quiet satisfaction met Ana's loud protestations. (Zukow, MGMF, 5/5/82).

Was this a rare event or is there more supportive evidence that very young children understand the feelings and needs of others? Evidence comes not from the child alone but from the interplay between the changing cognitive, perceptual, and social abilities displayed by the child, and the continual adjustment of the social environment to the developing child. Some findings from the study of early sibling relationships in England suggest a resolution to part of this enigma.

In their studies of the development of social understanding, Dunn and her colleagues (Dunn, 1988; Dunn & Kendrick, 1982a, 1982b) have demonstrated that during interaction siblings reveal a remarkable understanding of each other. Dunn and her co-workers reasoned that children would display far more advanced behavior at home in a familiar setting going about the most mundane routines of daily life. Their three longitudinal studies conducted in Cambridge, England, followed 52 families for some subset of the second child's second and third years of life. Their observations of everyday life tapped ordinary daily activities, play, conversations, and narratives. To become a "person," Dunn and her colleagues emphasized that the child must be able to recognize and share emotional states, anticipate and interpret how others will respond, understand relationships between important other people, know which behaviors are appropriate and which are sanctioned, and comprehend that punishments follow violations. Dunn and her co-workers viewed the infant as rather wise, using social understanding achieved through careful observation of people and events to gain her or his own special interests. Dunn and Kendrick (1982a) provided many vivid examples of young siblings of less than 2 years of age knowing how to provoke their siblings by playing on their fears and preferences. Dunn (1989) described what happened after an 18-month-old overheard his mother telling the observer that his older sister detested a particularly fearsome toy spider: "Mother to observer: 'Anny [sibling] is really frightened of spiders. In fact there's a particular toy spider we've got that she just hates.' Child runs to next room, searches in toy box, finds toy spider, runs back to front room, pushes it at sibling—sibling cries" (p. 107). However, siblings at this age know how to soothe as well as torment their siblings.

Early expressions of comfort.   Siblings observed in the home comfort each other as early as the second year of life. In contrast to Whiting and Edwards' speculations (1988) that 3- to 5-year-olds may be unable to assess the internal states of others, Dunn and her colleagues (Dunn, 1988; Dunn & Kendrick, 1982a, 1982b) provided evidence that children of even 3 years have a nascent or "practical" understanding of the feelings of others. For example, the responses of siblings of 2 and 3 years to the distress of a younger sibling change as the children develop. The youngest 2-year-olds were clearly upset by the other's distress. By the second half of the second year rather awkward, formulaic attempts were made to comfort the other with kissing, patting, and going to the mother for help. Finally, during the third year siblings tailored comfort more exactly to the infant's needs. Children of 2 and 3 years also display an understanding of the connection between their own actions and other family members' fury, pleasure, or joy.

The relation of age to expressions of care continues according to related work conducted in the home by Gottlieb and Mendelson (1990). These researchers reported that older sisters of 38–57 months behave with greater affection toward a newborn sister or brother and can comfort with more sensitivity, than those of 28–37 months. Studies by Stewart and his colleagues (Stewart, 1983a, 1983b; Stewart & Marvin, 1984) demonstrated that children under 5 sometimes comfort younger siblings. These researchers linked perspective-taking skills among older siblings of 3–5 with their expression of empathy toward a distressed younger sibling during observations in a modified "Strange Situation" in the laboratory. The greater degree of comfort expressed in the familiar home setting observed by Dunn and her colleagues (Dunn, 1988; Dunn & Kendrick, 1982a, 1982b) suggests that the strangeness of the laboratory setting and the procedure itself may have inhibited how often siblings comforted one another. In a shortened and less aversive, modified Strange Situation, Howe and Ross (1990) found that comfort expressed by elder siblings of 36–58 months to their 14-month-old siblings was directly related to the intensity of the younger sibling's distress, not to perspective taking. These authors suggested that comforting another may arise simply from recognizing affective cues or from gratifying self-interest by eliminating aversive crying.

Self-interest as the core of conflict.   Although sibling caregivers must be able to comfort a younger sibling, competent caregiving requires more than this newfound sensitivity. Clearly the elder siblings in Dunn's studies did not manifest one of the other prerequisites for caregiving suggested by Whiting and Edwards. Putting the needs of another before those of the self is not found at 3. To the contrary, the self-interest of one sibling is often at odds with that of the other. At this age, threats to the child's self-interest are the core of conflict (Dunn, 1988). Further, in related work (Dunn & Shatz, 1989; Slomkowski & Dunn, 1992) younger siblings of 33 months successfully turned the topic of talk during arguments from others to the self. In a similar vein, in the Strange Situation less securely attached elder siblings of 2–7 "threatened" by the mother's leaving are less likely to comfort younger siblings of 1–2 than those siblings who are securely attached (Teti & Ablard, 1989). In more extreme situations, when younger siblings express very high levels of distress, even less securely attached elder siblings overcome their reticence and do comfort their younger siblings. Because the securely attached child does not need comfort in this setting, this child can attend more easily to the needs of her or his sibling. Investigating parental behaviors that might contribute to consoling another, Murphy (1992) found a relation between contingent responding by adults to the elder child's needs and that child's empathic responses to the younger brother or sister. If the elder sibling feels frightened, upset, and in need of comfort, he or she may find it quite difficult to comfort someone else. Although the expression of care involves increasing levels of social understanding and secure attachment, the role of elder sibling itself also plays a part in the quality of sibling interaction.

Pelletier-Stiefel, Pepler, Crozier, Stanhope, Corter, and Abramovitch (1986) observed more prosocial behavior in elder children of 3–4½, 4½–6, 6–7½ than in their siblings who were 1½ years younger. However, the relative proportion of prosocial behaviors did not change with age. Apparently, the key to prosocial acts is having someone to nurture rather than being cognitively more advanced. Little wonder that children in agrarian societies display comfort and nurturance earlier as their apprenticeship begins at 2 years of age and is more pervasive due to the sheer number of young children continuously available in the sibling group (Whiting & Edwards, 1988). Although there is considerable evidence that young children can and do comfort each other when their own needs have been met, how do they come to put their own concerns aside in the face of another's distress?

Overcoming self-interest. Murphy's (1992) investigation of sibling-infant relationships among school-age children of 5–11 provides a means to understand how siblings overcome self-interest as well as achieve the other prerequisites for competent sibling caregiving suggested by Whiting and Edwards (1988). A competent sibling caregiver can modulate the intensity of interaction depending on the response of the younger sibling and display flexibility in finding alternative solutions for comforting an unhappy baby. Some of Murphy's findings relate to the emergence of these abilities. Future research can extend her findings by determining how characteristics of sibling mutuality relate to competent sibling caregiving. Areas with potential for study include the relation between parents who respond contingently to the elder child's needs and who, in turn, responds contingently to her or his younger brother or sister, those parents who educate the elder to pick up perceptual information relating to the feelings and needs expressed by the infant, and parents who do not encourage the elder to interact when he or she is cranky.

Summary. Competent sibling caregivers understand the emotional states of younger sisters and brothers, know how to comfort a child in distress, can see more than one way to resolve a problem, and can put another's needs before their own. Children of 2 and 3 can display the rudiments of social understanding, but tailoring care to the particular needs of a younger sibling and putting self-interest aside does not usually occur until sometime between 5 and 7 years of age. However, the experiences that precipitate the transition to more sophisticated levels of social understanding require further investigation. Obviously, even if siblings display these social and cognitive skills, sibling caregiving does not occur unless the organization and structure of the culture and the family foster this role (Weisner, 1987, in press).

Socializing Sibling Caregivers

Whiting and Edwards (1988) saw economic and cultural forces manifested in the organization and structure of daily life as causing socialization rather than assuming that developmental changes prompt different socialization pressures from caregivers. A child becoming a caregiver receives "on the job training" during "apprenticeship experiences" in which the child learns by doing and by observing (Weisner, 1987). What sibling caregivers learn depends on "activity settings" (Weisner, 1989a) within the "cultural place" (Weisner, 1993a): where they are, whom they are with, and what others are doing (Whiting & Edwards, 1988). Children are not separated or excluded from the ebb and flow of daily life, but are immersed in the social and economic details to a greater degree in agrarian societies than in technological ones (Mundy-Castle, 1974). In the latter, separation of home, workplace, and social activities of adults prevents children from observing many aspects of adult economic and social life.

Maternal socializing practices.   Whiting and Edwards (1988) asserted that children learn through imitating a model, by trial and error followed by successful repetition, and direct tuition. The mother often remains in the vicinity when she assigns caregiving to a novice caregiver. She models and teaches appropriate behavior. Mothers most frequently use demonstration as their method of instruction. Weisner (1989b) noted that the Abaluyia of Kenya express most of these messages nonverbally. Research investigating mothers' messages to daughters learning cultural practices in a different domain confirm the widespread use of nonverbal messages in agrarian societies. Greenfield and her colleague (Childs & Greenfield, 1980; Greenfield, 1984) contrasted informal and formal teaching methods. The informal style is characterized by nonverbal guidance that rarely permitted any failure among the Zinacatecan Mayans in Southern Mexico who were teaching their daughters to weave. The formal, verbal style is common among highly educated caregivers in technological societies.

Interaction as a training ground for nurturance.   In agrarian societies, interacting with lap and very young knee children of 0–18 months affords a training ground for nurturance. Whiting and Edwards (1988) argued that infants come into the world with natural abilities to elicit and maintain involvement. Papoušek and Papoušek (in this *Handbook*) elaborate the related notion of "intuitive parenting." However, what is learned and what is "natural" is unclear (Dent, 1990; Zukow, 1990). Caregivers adjust an infant's posture, facing them toward others for interacting and communicating as early as 4 months (Ochs, 1988; Schieffelin, 1990). From a Vygotskian or various ecological perspectives, interaction may be the teacher precipitating cycles of contingent responding that benefit the infant receiving care and the child who is giving it (Whiting & Edwards, 1988; Zukow, 1989a, 1990). Soothing the infant gives immediate feedback to the older sibling, clearly attesting to the caregiver's competence. However, while teaching the sibling caregiver how to calm the infant, more competent caregivers may also embed the practices within a cultural framework. In the Marquesas, crying displays a dispreferred preoccupation with internal states (Martini & Kirkpatrick, 1992). Preschool caregivers are guided to jostle the infant to return him or her to social life, not just to relieve immediate distress. These Marquesan novice caregivers also learn a baby's likes, dislikes, and habits.

Harder lessons require that young elder siblings of 2–6 learn to put aside their own wants and needs and, instead, to attend to those of others. Sibling "nurses" begin by offering food and soothing fussy infants. However, natural generosity is not the source of such actions, but gentle prodding. "Personal trainers" reside in all cultures:

> For example, in a small farming community of 700 inhabitants in Guanajuato, Mexico, Lilia, a 15 month old, energetically and wholly focused on taking a sucker from Beto, her 9 month-old cousin, was patiently guided for a full 25 minutes to first enjoy some of the sweet herself, then to share it with the still disinterested infant, and finally to to smile and coo at the baby when he tasted the sucker. After 5 more months of encouragement and immersion in continuously occurring daily sharing, Lilia often shared food on request (Zukow, MGMF, 3/26/82.)

In Senegal, Wolof caregivers encouraged a recently weaned child to share his food with other siblings *and* the younger sibling who had taken his place at their mother's breast (Zempleni-Rabain, 1973).

Among the Kahluli in New Guinea, mothers use a "feeling sorry voice" to teach caring for younger siblings (Schieffelin, 1990). Requests for food in this plaintive voice function by telling the older sibling what to do from the content as well as how to feel from the form of the message. The younger sibling learns to appeal for help and/or compassion, whereas the older one learns to assist others and feel compassion for someone dependent or helpless. Summarizing the developmental course of sharing and caring for other's needs, Watson-Gegeo and Gegeo (1989) noted that Solomon Islanders begin instructing an infant to share at 6 months of age. By 18 months the child shares without hesitation, by 3 years shares automatically, and by 6 years may give her or his portion to a younger sibling if there is insufficient food for everyone.

Confirming that children of 3 or more share without guidance, children of 3 or more socialize each other to share food. Zempleni-Rabain (1973) described siblings of 3–8 working out the sharing of food without adult assistance, enacting the Wolof's "law of brothers and equals." In the Marquesas, Martini and Kirkpatrick (1992) documented similar exchanges among siblings of 3–5. Siblings also share objects and protect younger siblings from being hurt by others. This attention to sharing resources reflects its critical significance for group survival. According to Rabain-Jamain (in press), the Wolof consider nonsharing to be the most antisocial act.

The 6- to 8-year-olds who serve as child nurses in most nonindustrialized countries receive clear training messages. Most of the instructions at this age directed the children to attend to chores and other socially useful activities. Praising children for their achievements is rare indeed as being over proud (of individual accomplishments) works against interdependence (Martini & Kirkpatrick, 1992; Weisner, 1987; Whiting & Edwards, 1988).

"Practice makes perfect." According to Whiting and Edwards (1988), girls are assigned caregiving more often than boys. In addition, girls interact more with young children and are in the company of their mothers' modeling behavior toward younger siblings. In a reflexive cycle, girls receive more practice and become more adept at empathic and nurturant actions. Whiting and Edwards argued that practice relates to greater nurturing. Supporting their position, boys who act as caregivers nurture others outside of the caregiving role itself more than boys who do not (Ember, 1973). Given this broad foundation, girls have more confidence in these abilities and find the experience pleasurable.

Effects of status on sibling caregiving: Guidance or observation? Most research implicitly assumes that the practices gained in interaction move unidirectionally from adult to child and are "finely tuned" to the developmental level of the child. In contrast, Ochs and Schieffelin (1984; see also Ochs, 1988; Schieffelin, 1990) suggested that the higher status of adults in hierarchical societies, such as Samoa and the Kaluli of New Guinea, has powerful effects on socialization. The constraints of stratification lead members of those cultures to expect younger, lower status children to adapt to anyone with relatively higher status rather than the reverse. In harmony with this view, people avoid using any training strategy that includes guessing what children might need or mean when communicating, as middle-class parents in technological societies constantly do. Caregivers do not simplify the speech that they direct to children. Children must figure out what others expect them to do; they must "notice and attend." In the same vein, Heath (1983) emphasized children "coming up" rather than being "raised" in her study of an African-American community in the southern United States. Rogoff (1990) suggested that children "appropriate" cultural practices for current purposes rather than receive it predigested. This strong emphasis on children taking an active part in their own cultural development gives balance to implicit biases that cultural information flows unidirectionally from parent to child as if filling up an empty vessel.

These biases presuppose that adults closely guide the flow of information, rather than children picking out what they want to know. Given this possibility, what evidence supports the idea that children actively monitor what is going on around them without adult guidance? Rogoff and her co-workers (1993) noted that Guatemalan, Indian, and Turkish 12- to 24-month-old infants are "keen observers" who can monitor more than one event at a time or alternate between events more successfully than children reared in industrialized settings. The Guatemalan and Indian samples were living in rural settings, whereas the Turkish middle-class sample resided in a large urban center. However, the Turkish families had made a relatively recent shift from country to city. In closely related findings, Samoan children by age 4–5 can do several tasks at the same time (Ochs, 1988). In accord with the implications of status, in many nonindustrialized countries and within intraethnic groups in technological societies children are not *talked with,* considered "conversational partners" (Heath, 1983; Ochs, 1988; Ochs & Schieffelin, 1984; Schieffelin, 1990).

Not all hierarchical societies manifest similar caregiving styles. In some, children are *talked to.* When children "don't get it" in some agrarian cultures, caregivers work to make them understand. Although the Kwara'ae of the Solomon Islands belong to a society based on stratification, parents take a very active role in shaping their children's conduct. Parents discuss their children's responsibilities in nightly counseling sessions, *fa'amanata'anga* (Watson-Gegeo & Gegeo, 1989). Zukow-Goldring's (Zukow, 1989c, 1991; Zukow-Goldring, in press) work with families from the traditional Mexican culture in both Central Mexico and the United States suggests that caregivers continuously monitor whether children understand them. Negotiating a consensus for all "practical purposes," so work can continue, occurs frequently. When communication breaks down, these Mexican and Latino caregivers reduce ambiguity and "educate attention" by providing perceptual (nonverbal) information that marks the relation between what is said and what is happening. Weisner (1987, 1989b) also noted that adults very often guide novice caregivers nonverbally. In addition, studies of "informal teaching" of weaving among the Tzotzil-speaking Maya of Mexico documents that mothers demonstrate far more often than they verbally correct their daughters when teaching them weaving techniques (Childs & Greenfield, 1980; Greenfield, 1984). Given these somewhat contradictory results, do parents and more competent members finely tune their messages to young caregivers, or don't they?

The contradictions regarding whether cultural practices are given or taken may be related to methods of data collection. When data are audio transcriptions of interactions, nonverbal instruction by caregivers cannot be heard or seen. The nonverbal guidance or fine-tuning of children's behavior may have been overlooked in some studies if the collection net was not designed to gather such information. Other research has not focused on children actively seeking information. Important future research can assess how people make nonverbal, perceptual information prominent to each other. That is, how does one person mark perceptual information picked out for the other to notice and how does the targeted recipient pick up the information? How is "consensus for all practical purposes" communicated so interaction can proceed? Do expert and novice members of different cultures use different perceptual modalities to select and detect the cultural practices conveyed during socializing (Dent, 1990; Dent-Read & Zukow-Goldring, in press; Zukow-Goldring, in press).

Niche picks or niche-picking?   Another twist on the arguments over who is socializing whom relates to the degree to which children pick learning environments compatible with their own individual characteristics. Although behavioral geneticists and others argue forcefully that genetic endowments in the form of behavioral predispositions guide much of development (Dunn, 1985; Dunn & Plomin, 1990; Scarr, 1992; Scarr & McCartney, 1983), a particular social milieux and exposure to members of the culture are necessary before someone "can learn what s/he was born to be" (Draper & Harpending, 1987, p. 212). The following description of socialization among the Kwara'ae of the Solomon Islands suggests that the "niche" picks the child rather than the reverse (Watson-Gegeo & Gegeo, 1989; see also K. A. Watson-Gegeo & D. W. Gegeo, personal communication, March 9 and June, 1994):

> From the earliest observations of Susuli at 9 months she was sensitive, easily upset, and sometimes selfish. At the same time, she was quick to learn and perceptive towards the social relations around her. At 3 and 6 years old she was usually very responsible and skilled in performing work tasks in the home and garden, including caregiving of younger siblings. On the other hand, at times she threw temper tantrums and was

moody and stubborn. These bouts of ill-temper interfered with her being a good model for her younger siblings, from her parents' point of view. By age 9 Susuli had become more stubborn, was taking advantage of her younger sister, and was not doing well in school. She carried out her work at home less and less willingly. Because the Kwara'ae believe that it is unhealthy for a person to be emotionally labile, Susuli's mood swings were disruptive to the family. Further, an important cultural value held by the Kwara'ae is that the needs of the group come before those of the individual. Susuli's parents felt that she was too focused instead on herself.

Two years later Susuli seemed transformed: relaxed, calm, happy, gentle, nurturing toward her siblings, and showing a high level of responsibility. In the 2 intervening years, Susuli had received intensive *fa'amanata'anga,* from her parents, her father's sister, and her grandfather. Despite initial resistance from Susuli, these adults had gently, patiently, and unremittingly insisted through counseling sessions that she change. The transformed Susuli was poised, self-confident, and had willingly taken the role in the family that her family wanted her to take. She was highly valued within her family and by others in the village. (K. A. Watson-Gegeo & D. W. Gegeo, personal communication, March 9 and June, 1994)

As this summary of field notes from the Solomon Islands illustrates, ultimately, culture strongly affects how individual behaviors are played out (Weisner, 1993b). Further, culture and parental discipline constrains the range of conduct that different siblings can express.

Effects of a new baby on family practices.   And academic discipline apparently constrains what each studies. The themes of interdependence and individual development are quite striking when considering the research regarding adjustment to the new baby. Rather than making the assumption that older siblings will welcome the new infant and gradually take on caregiving responsibilities that will contribute to the overall well-being of the family group, research on socialization of elder siblings in technological cultures appears to focus nearly exclusively on what negative effects the baby's arrival will have on the firstborn and/or how to avoid disruptions to him or her (Dunn & Kendrick, 1982a; Kreppner, 1988; Kreppner et al., 1982; Stewart, 1990; Sutton-Smith & Rosenberg, 1970). As noted, the notion of sibling rivalry from psychodynamic theory has been a strong influence on the direction of this research. Rather than presupposing a limitation of resources, another approach may be the allocation of bountiful resources. In settings where shared caregiving is common the mother is not the exclusive source of nurturance. When the mother is not available, others fill in for her. Thus, receiving less from the mother may be less traumatic where surrogate care is the norm rather than where it is not, that is, in the nuclear family. Supporting this notion is evidence that the involvement of the father ameliorates the level of stress within the Western family during the infant's first 2 years of life (Kreppner et al., 1982; Kreppner, 1988).

Dunn and her colleagues (Dunn, 1988; Dunn & Kendrick, 1982a) speculated that having a younger sibling precipitates noticing the characteristics of self and other. The mother's comments regarding the baby as a person with desires, preferences, and intentions affect the pattern of interaction between the siblings. In a case study of his own children, Mendelson (1990) confirmed much of Dunn's theorizing. He described in detail the methods he and his wife used to prepare their 4-year-old son for the arrival of his new sibling and to guide him in becoming a sibling himself. Mendelson summarized the highlights as including ceaseless changes in infant and sibling that continuously elicited and shaped the behavior to come. In addition, the parents informally "taught" the eldest about his infant brother as they chatted about his care, emotions, and growing abilities. They also took care to sustain their relationship with their firstborn son. These parents also recognized that their elder son's negative behavior was often simply clumsiness or intrusiveness in the service of curiosity. They kept stern correction to a minimum.

How might the experience of having a sibling precipitate expressions of comfort? Perhaps the raw emotions perceived and felt provide a ground for detecting an intersubjectivity or invariances of experience across persons. The other cries and, although the elder child may not be crying now, she or he has cried on other occasions. The experience of crying provides a means to understand that the other is both like the self who has cried in the past and unlike the self who is not crying now. Parents often tell an older child that the younger sibling's state "is just like" what you used to do, still do, or is more or less intense. In the future, researchers may find that caregivers who guide children to notice the similarity of or difference in experience have provided the basis for accurate detection of the state of another.

Extending and confirming many of Dunn and Mendelson's findings, researchers have investigated the experiences of siblings of 3–11 who express and enact warmth and care to their younger siblings (Howe & Ross, 1990; Kramer & Noorman, 1993; Murphy, 1992, 1993). Because prior research primarily investigated firstborn elder siblings and their second-born brothers and sisters, Murphy (1993) extended this work by including some elder siblings who were later born children themselves. Conditions that contribute to sibling mutuality include an initial interest in the infant as proposed by Whiting and Edwards (1988; see also section entitled Prerequisites for Sibling Caregiving), many uninterrupted opportunities to interact that are accompanied by very little correction, contingent responses to the needs of the elder sibling by the parents, parents who include and share responsibility of the infant with the elder, parents who focus the elder's attention on the cues used to read the infant's needs and feelings, and parents who do not press the elder to interact when she or he is tired or fussy. Of these, Murphy (1993) speculated that the accessibility of and responsibility for the infant are most critical to the elder's becoming a caregiver during the first 18 months of the new baby's life.

Summary.   Although elder siblings have many opportunities to observe and imitate other more competent caregivers interact with younger children in the family, their caregivers ceaselessly monitor their children's cultural understanding of caregiving in many agrarian societies. Siblings can and do imitate and observe each other's emotional state. However, caregivers constantly refine young children's interpretations of the "here and now" and also embed what siblings perceive and know about others in a web of interrelated cultural practices. With seemingly infinite patience seasoned with cajoling, correcting, threatening, and teasing, caregivers guide older siblings as they learn to tend fussy, hungry, angry, sleepy younger siblings. Framed by vivid and predictable affect, the children themselves apparently detect what produces annoyance and provoke it with little assistance. Guidance from more competent members provides siblings with a flexible repertoire of responses to their younger siblings. Finally, by distracting, pushing, and prodding, more mature caregivers help older siblings to overcome self-interest so that they automatically tend to the needs of others before their own. Although this pattern has not been documented to the same degree among parents in technological societies, clearly learning the potential benefits of sibling caregiving from traditional societies might assist overburdened dual-wage earners of today.

Sibling Conflict: Authority or Rivalry?

Permitting children to socialize each other may be necessary and intrinsic to the development and smooth functioning of hierarchical sibling relations (Seymour, 1993). The conflict associated with sibling care need not be interpreted negatively. Traditional societies, instead, interpret conflict in terms of how it might serve continuity and cohesion as related to the group's survival. In contrast, since Cain and Abel, Western culture has highlighted the injurious effects to individual brothers and sisters of sibling rivalry arising from limited resources. More recently, investigators' studies in technological cultures have considered the positive effects of sibling discord, especially how conflict relates to practices that promote the needs or achievements of the individual.

The interplay of cooperation and conflict.   In many societies, such as those in the Pacific Islands, Africa, South Asia, group survival depends on shared resources and cooperation. Because the sibling relationship has greater importance economically and socially across the life span, these relationships are more differentiated than those of parents and children or of spouses (Nuckolls, 1993a, 1993b; Weisner, 1993b; see also B. B. Schieffelin, personal communication, Fall, 1979). In these cultures, sibling relationships have important functions throughout the course of their lives including economic (exchange/sharing, inheritance, and marriage payments), protection/defense, and ceremonial (age, initiation) obligations (Nuckolls, 1993a, 1993b; Watson-Gegeo & Gegeo, 1989; Weisner, 1987; Zempleni-Rabain, 1973; see also B. B. Schieffelin, personal communication, Fall, 1979).

In fact, in South Asia the great epics and legends extol the relationships among mythic siblings. The literary, mythological, and scriptural texts of South Asia that depict sibling relations include the *Ramayana,* the *Mahabharata,* and the *Mitakshara* (Beals & Eason, 1993; Nuckolls, 1993a, 1993b; Seymour, 1993). People frequently refer to these models of ideal conduct to resolve immediate problems and to socialize children (Beals & Eason, 1993; Nuckolls, 1993a). To ground these findings, Nuckolls (1993a) contrasted the perspectives of anthropologists informed by theories of symbolic interaction with those of developmental psychologists and psychological anthropologists. The former view systems of meaning (ideologies, conceptual systems, unconscious processes, symbolic frameworks) as the phenomena that form behavior. The latter study the processes that promote the development of abilities that permit survival within any particular culture.

Beals and Eason (1993) challenged the reader with the notion that a competitive society forces Western children to "repress" humanity's natural preference for harmony. Thomas (as cited in Martini, 1994, p. 99) referred to a "cooperation deficit." However, although siblings continually monitor and adjust to each other's needs (Nuckolls, 1993a), scholars do not paint a picture of life in agrarian societies as a Rousseau-like utopian paradise without dissension (Beals & Eason, 1993; Nuckolls, 1993a; Ochs, 1988; Schieffelin, 1990; Seymour, 1993; Weisner, 1987, 1989b; Whiting & Edwards, 1988; Whittemore & Beverly, 1989). Members of agrarian cultures continuously attempt to gain benefits from or maintain advantages over one another as adults, often struggling over all manner of assets including power, emotional well-being, spiritual practices, and material goods. Even with these exigencies of everyday life, within hierarchical societies cooperation keeps the system running smoothly, whereas too much conflict endangers the delicate balance. Enhancing cooperation and muting conflict need not suggest that these qualities are two ends of a continuum, but may be manifestations of separate dimensions that interact. Researchers regard conflict as a natural outgrowth and support of the organization and structure of these societies.

Authority embodying interdependence.   Whiting and Edwards (1988) and others (Ochs, 1988; Schieffelin, 1990) contended that in stratified societies prosocial dominance follows from variations in status. Older siblings have legitimate power when caring for younger children that embodies their lifetime relationship. Elder siblings learn to exercise this authority as they socialize one another, whereas younger siblings get used to another's will (Whittemore & Beverly, 1989). In this unequal relation, the elder has and wields power, whereas the younger negotiates for possessions and status (Nuckolls, 1993a; Zempleni-Rabain, 1973). The giver gains respect and self-esteem "by renouncing the doubtful advantage of possessing something" (Zempleni-Rabain, 1973, p. 229). Within this framework, no one gains and much can be lost if younger siblings express rivalry (Beals & Eason, 1993).

In everyday expressions of their authority, elder siblings use simple commands and coercive techniques to persuade their charges to behave appropriately and not hurt themselves (Whiting & Edwards, 1988). Sibling caregivers find caring for toddlers of 2 and 3 years more difficult and may chide them a great deal. Because adults consider the tantrums, rages, and expressions of hostility of younger children as normal, squabbling among children close in age receives little attention. Adults and older children greet these behaviors with teasing at most and usually simply ignore them. On occasion an older sibling's self-centered behavior negatively affects that of a younger child or results in actually hurting someone. The elder child who has overextended the authority granted to him or her will eventually be punished, especially if the conflict interferes with adult work. The younger sibling who does not heed the guidance of elder siblings risks collective shaming involving everyone nearby (Ochs, 1988). Siblings soon learn not to let problems get to older persons (Ochs, 1988), but, instead, monitor and criticize each other constantly (Martini, 1994; Watson-Gegeo & Gegeo, 1986).

Conflict promoting individual development. In contrast to conflict as it relates to the group, most researchers in technological societies study conflict in terms of the individual's course of development. Research conducted under the sway of psychodynamic theory focused on the negative effects of siblings' rivalrous feelings and actions arising from a continuous tug-of-war over the affectional resources of the mother (Lamb, 1976; Sutton-Smith & Rosenberg, 1970). Offering a different interpretation, Dunn (1988) argued that conflict within the family has beneficial effects. Sibling conflict is the emotional crucible that drives the emergence of a "practical" understanding of other people's feelings and intentions. Day in and day out, teasing and provoking are directly experienced as annoying and upsetting to the self and one's sibling (Dunn & Munn, 1985). However, these conflicts are resolved and discussed. Dunn and her colleagues (Dunn, 1988, 1991; Dunn & Kendrick, 1982a) emphasized the many positive effects of conflict, especially the importance of the mother's elaborating of the general moral tenets underlying the particulars of family rules and regulations. Eventually children invoke social rules to justify their behavior. Ross and her colleagues concur, based on their findings showing that middle-class parents actively intervene in more than half of the conflicts arising between siblings of 2-4 years of age (Ross, Filyer, Lollis, Perlman, & Martin, in press). They caution, however, that current models of parent intervention do not predict which rules siblings adopt and which they do not. In addition, Shantz and Hobart (1989) emphasized that paradoxically conflict demonstrates connectedness through providing practice in negotiating mutual consensus.

Summary. Across cultures sibling discord provides children with a means to explore the nuances and limits of their social world and to evaluate and calibrate emotional reactions.

Sibling Novices and Experts in Technological Cultures

By imitating and responding to sibling guidance and seeking information from them, younger siblings display that they notice and gather information while interacting with their older brothers and sisters. First, numerous investigations report that preschoolers and school-age siblings imitate their elder siblings far more frequently than they are imitated (Abramovitch, Corter, & Lando, 1979; Abramovitch, Corter, Pepler, & Stanhope, 1986; Berndt & Bulleit, 1985; Dunn & Kendrick, 1982a; Stoneman, Brody, & MacKinnon, 1984). Summers, Summers, and Ascione (1993) found far greater imitation of older siblings in single-parent families, pointing to their importance as role models. Second, studies document that younger siblings comply with the instructions of older siblings (Abramovitch et al., 1986) and play the part of the learner during games (Brody, Stoneman, & MacKinnon, 1982; Stoneman et al., 1984). Third, younger siblings ask older siblings for suggestions, demonstrating that they view them as having important cultural practices to impart (Azmitia & Hesser, 1993; Handel, 1986). In broad terms, younger siblings pay attention to what their older siblings do, repeat it, and in structured activities follow their directions.

Imitation's potential theoretical role. Piaget's theory (1962) and approaches informed by child language studies (Bloom, Hood, & Lightbown, 1974; Greenfield & Smith, 1976; Nelson, Carskaddon, & Bonvillian, 1973; Snow, 1981) propose that children imitate actions just coming into their repertoires. These findings imply, at the very least, that older siblings indirectly affect the younger child's development. Normally, younger children can imitate immediately or slightly after observing the activities of older siblings that are within their range of actions. A Vygotskian interpretation (Vygotsky, 1978; Wertsch, 1985) focuses on guidance provided during social interaction as the matrix within which more competent persons transmit cultural knowledge to others less fully informed. Although robust evidence demonstrates that younger siblings witness new activities while interacting with older siblings and enact them autonomously only after some delay, these findings from studies of imitation do not differentiate between the theoretical views. In the analysis of play and language this puzzle is taken up again.

Giving and taking directions. Besides serving as witting or unwitting models, in the manager role older siblings produce many more directives across a range of activities than the younger sibling (Tomasello & Mannle, 1985) and more than the mother when forbidding actions or guiding the younger child's play (Dunn & Kendrick, 1982a). These specific studies and those of Brody and Stoneman (Brody et al., 1982; Stoneman et al., 1984) do not assess the effectiveness of these directives, simply that older siblings try to direct the interactions. However, investigations of teaching and tutoring show that older sibling *do* guide the activities of the younger sibling (Cicirelli, 1972; Ellis & Rogoff, 1982; Koester & Johnson, 1984; Stewart, 1983b; Vandell, Minnett, & Santrock, 1988). When parents are not familiar with schoolwork, siblings help with homework, conveying the "tricks of the trade" (Pérez, Barajas, Domínguez, Goldberg, Juarez, Saab, Vergara, & Callanan, 1994; Snow, Barnes, Chandler, Goodman, & Hemphill, 1991). The degree of success depends on the task, the ages of the siblings, and the presence of adults.

Coregulation of sibling interactions. Azmitia and Hesser (1993) very carefully examined the roles of 9-year-old sibling and peer teachers and 7-year-old sibling learners. Confirming a variety of prior findings, the authors found that younger children looked at siblings' models more than at peers', imitated siblings more often, directed more questions and requests for help to siblings. The siblings provided more spontaneous teaching than peers. Girls taught more than boys. Their most important finding highlights the role of the younger child. The younger siblings elicited many more explanations from their older siblings than from the peer, signaling a "privileged" teaching status to their brothers and sisters. Further, the younger siblings blocked the older sibling from taking over the task and took more responsibility themselves when with a sibling. This study draws attention to the need to consider how "novice" and "expert" coregulate interactions.

Interactional bases for emerging intersubjectivity. Younger siblings pay a great deal of attention to older siblings (Dunn & Kendrick, 1982a; Martini & Kirkpatrick, 1992; Zukow, 1989a), often imitating their actions. Aside from learning new affordances for action with people, animals, and objects, imitation of siblings may be the source for a practical intersubjectivity or sharing of feeling, perceiving, and knowing during ongoing events. These speculations come from recent research documenting that imitation of other children occurs quite early and reliably in development. Dunn and her co-workers (Dunn, 1988; Dunn & Kendrick, 1982a) proposed that early play routines among siblings, such as tag, give-and-take, and mimicking, that entail variation, elaborations, accelerating affect, and role reversals, provide an arena for understanding another person is "like me." Novice peers of 14–18 months imitate object manipulation modeled by expert peers despite delays of up to 48 hours and changes in the context of the original action and personnel (Hanna & Meltzoff, 1993). Bouts of imitation among peers in which both initiator of the action and the introduction of variations in action switch back and forth occur robustly between 16 and 28 months of age (Eckerman, 1993). Although imitation may be a building block for treating others as "like the self" (Dunn & Kendrick, 1982; Meltzoff & Gopnik, 1993) how the content and organization of countless sequences of imitation among siblings evolve over time and affect development remain unexamined. These interactions no doubt contribute uniquely to siblings coming to know what other people feel, perceive, and know. In addition, having a sibling apparently contributes to knowing what others don't know. Siblings from larger families, independent of birth order, could predict that actions of a falsely informed story character more accurately than siblings from smaller families (Perner, Ruffman, & Leekam, 1994).

Several researchers note that older siblings imitate "regressive" activities, such as the way infants of 8 months or less act with bottles and blankets (Dunn & Kendrick, 1982a; Stewart, Mobley, van Tuyl, & Salvador, 1987). Dunn cautioned about making premature negative interpretation of these actions, because these same behaviors correlate with warm and affectionate future relationships between the siblings. Stewart and his co-workers interptreted this mimicry of the new baby as bids for attention from the parents. I suggest that there is a more positive interpretation of enacting "babyish" behavior. Through these actions the older sibling renews knowing what a baby experiences.

If so, those "regressive" imitations may serve the very important function of providing access to the infant sibling's state, a basis for intersubjectivity, "theory of mind," and/or perspective taking.

Summary.   A review of results from technological societies indicates that older siblings act and are treated as experts, whereas younger siblings embody the novice role most often. Imitation may provide the interactional basis through perception and action for knowing that the other is like the self and for coming to know what the other knows. The effectiveness and function of this relation require clarification beyond detecting that your sibling experiences a similar range of emotional states. For that analysis, studies of play and language provide evidence that interaction with siblings creates an environment in which children supply unique information to each other using methods rather different from those of adults.

Play

Vygotsky (1978) asserted that play is the setting within which cultural knowing emerges. In this view, children engage in cultural activities earlier and more frequently during interaction with more competent members of their culture and only manifest this knowing on their own at a later time. From a Piagetian perspective, the younger sibling seeks information. Without guidance, the child purportedly can absorb what she or he requires at any particular level of development through observation alone. This view interprets guidance as interferring at best (Piaget, 1962; Zukow, 1984, 1989a). Rather than life as a cafeteria from which the child selects whatever she or he considers a nutritious developmental diet, perhaps, life is a catered affair.

Unique and effective role of older siblings in agrarian settings.   In agrarian societies and among working-class African-Americans, the play of young children occurs almost exclusively among siblings (Martini, 1994; Ward, 1971; Watson-Gegeo & Gegeo, 1989; Zukow, 1989a). Zukow (1984b, 1986) documented that play with adult and sibling caregivers *is* more advanced than unguided play. Further, she demonstrated that play with siblings was significantly more advanced than play with adult caregivers. Older siblings of 4–11 often succeeded in enticing younger siblings of 12–27 months to leave less challenging and self-involved play with objects for more elaborate enactments of scenes from everyday life. In the segment that opened this chapter Juana was repeatedly invited to refrain from taking apart and putting together a plastic egg in favor of joining in the tortilla-making scenario by sisters of 7 and 10, guiding her from the *level of actual development* to the *level of potential development.* However, how "finely tuned" sibling guidance might be to the younger sibling's level of development cannot be determined from this one study. Zukow-Goldring and co-workers (Zukow, 1989a, 1990; Zukow-Goldring, in press; Zukow-Goldring, Romo, & Duncan, 1994) has argued that caregivers who dissambiguate their messages and actions by making perceptual information prominent and available assist children in achieving consensus about ongoing events. Studies examining whether younger siblings benefit more from such guidance can contribute to building more comprehensive theories of the emergence of cultural practices.

In other situations when the younger sibling responded inadequately (Zukow, 1989), older siblings with eagerness and impatience displayed their own competence by enacting requested actions. For instance, Marta, the mother of 21-month-old Irene, asked her to wash a doll in a basin of water by saying *Báñala/Bathe her.* Irene did not immediately douse the doll with water. After a brief pause, 3½-year-old Maximina chimed in with *¡YO lo hago!/I'LL do it!.* She washed the doll, providing a clear perceptual model of "appropriate" conduct which Irene promptly imitated. Sometimes the older child is blunt and critical. For instance, 4-year-old Victoria told 26-month-old Lucha with great disdain *¡Mira, tu no sabes!/Look, you don't know how!* while showing apprehensive Lucha how to hold a wriggling rabbit by its ears. Children of 3–5 need not take another's perspective, guess what the other needs to know, and/or scaffold carefully to promote a younger sibling's development as adult caregivers in Central Mexico often do. By displaying their own competence, slightly older siblings make their own definition of adequate behavior quite available. Younger older siblings do not mince words in stark contrast to adults' usual gentle adjustments. Being told and shown you are doing it wrong "may be quite as informative as gradually getting it right" (Zukow, 1989, p. 98). Perez and Callanan (1993) in the United States provided some confirmation from an unexpected source. In a sorting task, these reasearchers found that older siblings of 5–8 corrected far more than mothers, pointed to correct choices more often, or did the task for the younger siblings of 3–5. The younger siblings categorized more accurately during the "explicit teaching" session with their siblings than in those with their mothers who were more easygoing about placing puzzling items.

Returning to an agrarian site and to the study of play, Martini's (1994) ethnography of play in a sibling group numbering 13 in the Marquesas describes how children learn stratified roles, such as peripheral toddler, initiate, noisy leader, and quiet leader. These roles parallel the hierarchical interrelationships of the larger society. Two- to 5-year-olds learn self-reliance and emotional control as they negotiate dominance, consensus, and adherence to social rules with little or no adult assistance. Marquesans value the "sacredness of the individual and of personal plans" as long as they do not intrude on the interests of others. However, in the play group leaders quickly make evident the limits of "going your own way." One day all the children save one initiate, Rora, pretended to load water on an imaginary out-rigger canoe. As Rora washed the deck, Justin, a "noisy" leader, knocked the water out of his hands. The initiate swung at the older child who hit him roughly, causing him to cry. Soon afterwards Justin patted Rora on the head and handed him a container of water to load, quietly letting him know what he ought to do. In this stratified environment, the older siblings teach their younger brothers and sisters to pay attention to the group purpose, deal with frustration appropriately, and make light of an attack.

Methodological inconsistencies in technological settings. In contrast to agrarian societies, parents in technological societies do play with their children. Parents play at a more advanced level with a son or daughter of 12–18 months than older siblings who are from 1–6 years older (Stevenson, Leavitt, Thompson, & Roach, 1988; Teti, Bond, & Gibbs, 1988). Although Hartup and Laursen (1991) described the role of the play group as vague, pretend play occurs almost exclusively with siblings and peers (Dunn, 1988; Dunn & Kendrick, 1982a; Stevenson et al., 1988; White & Woollett, 1992).

Dunn (1983) suggested that play with parents provides the impetus for developmental change, whereas play with siblings serves to consolidate those modifications, especially in pretend play. In technological societies this observation may hold, but clearly, "cultural place" plays a part. In many agrarian societies siblings introduce each other to the layout of the rural setting, daily practices, and preferred behavior. Methodological inconsistencies, especially the effect of violating ecological validity, may account for some of these contradictory results (Cole et al., 1978; Malpass, 1977; Mischel, 1977). The unfamiliar laboratory setting, parents remaining in the room while the siblings play, and novel toys contribute to mistaking "stimulus" equivalence for "functional" equivalence. Further, interpreting the "directiveness" of older siblings as negative, rather than recognizing the unique and powerful advantage that explicit correction can make, may obscure the benefits of sibling interaction.

Summary. During play children learn about the organization and structure of everyday events, the affordances of objects, social roles and practices, and the degree of inter- or independence preferred in particular cultures. Findings from current studies of play, both in agrarian and techno-logical settings, favor a Vygotskian interpretation. These studies highlight the importance of social interaction as the source of knowing.

Language

Effective and unique role of older siblings in agrarian settings. Although comprehension of speech pervasively precedes speech production, most child language research focuses on the child's speech production. For the most part investigations of sibling speech do not depart from this pattern.

However, how caregivers treat the unintelligible utterances of language learning children and prompt them to talk does not explicate how children learn the relation between words and world in the first place. In Central Mexico and in the United States among Euro-American and Latino caregivers, those who interact with children do revise their own miscomprehended utterances, so that children can re-view how words relate to ongoing events. Siblings do too. Zukow and her co-workers research demonstrates that caregivers carefully educate attention, providing perceptual information that marks the relation between what they are saying and what is happening (Zukow, 1989a, 1990; Zukow & Ferko, 1994; Zukow-Goldring, in press) and can articulate what should be done when a child miscomprehends speech (Zukow, 1991). These practices disambiguate speech and correlate significantly with the child's later production:

> For instance, Jaime, almost 8, and Juan, his younger brother of 22 months, play in the bedroom with a toy monkey. At the time Juan could neither comprehend nor express location. Jaime asks him to place the monkey halfway across the room, pointing and saying *¡Páralo allí!/Stand it up there!*. When Juan repeats *¿Eh?/Hm?* several times, Jaime catches his gaze, walks to the place, and bends over. He carefully coordinates saying *¡Aquí, páralo!/Here, stand it up!* and point-touching the place on the floor. (Zukow, 1989a)

In this segment, Jaime provided a tangible, perceptual translation of his verbal message to assist his younger brother in comprehending what he had just said. Just as siblings carefully adjust problematic aspects of their messages to assist in their younger siblings' lexical growth, they also play a role in the emergence of other aspects of language.

In the Pacific Islands and in Africa, triadic conversations with infant, older sibling, and mother provide settings in which much language socialization takes place (Ochs, 1988; Rabain-Jamin, in press; Schieffelin, 1990; Watson-Gegeo & Gegeo, 1989). Although these authors described the role of siblings as important for the learning of lexical items and the rules and uses of language, they provided little specific detail. In contrast, Demuth (1984, in press) argued that among the Basotho of Lesotho in southern Africa siblings learn to use advanced linguistic forms, in particular relative clauses, during interaction with the sibling group. Utterances, such as *bring that thing that you found,* occur far more frequently when younger siblings of 25–55 months play with older siblings of 5–10 years than when interacting with adults. Mothers concur that children who interact frequently with other children speak earlier and better than those who stay with their mothers. Even though Zeisler and Demuth (1995) provided evidence that even siblings of 5-years of age appropriately use a special simplified speech register when talking to younger siblings, Demuth (personal communication, January 1995) speculated that older siblings sometimes do not attend as carefully as adults might to what a younger sibling is saying and doing. This proposed variability in attentiveness may forve the younger child to work harder at making himself or herself understood. Aware of the valuable role of sibling caregiving, researchers conducting studies in agrarian societies have looked for and found that siblings perform an important function in the language development of their younger brothers and sisters. Confirming that role in technological settings has been more of an uphill battle.

Illuminating the positive role of older siblings in technological settings.   Much research in the 1970s and 1980s emphasized that certain characteristics of caregiver speech observed in Euro-American, middle-class mothers, such as finely tuning utterances to the child's level of development and disentangling the meaning of the child's unintelligible speech, facilitate language learning (Barnes, Gutfreund, Satterly, & Wells, 1983; Cross, 1977; Ryan, 1974; Snow, 1977; Snow, Perlmann, & Nathan, 1987). Pervasive, unexamined assumptions regarding the superior achievement

---

[1]A reevaluation of this interpretation asserts that lower socioeconomic status and larger family size better account for differences observed than birth order (Ernst & Angst, 1983; Hoff-Ginsberg & Krueger, 1991).

[2]This brief review obscures the complexity of the questions, methodological inconsistencies or rigor, nuance, and directions of influence marking this growing area of research.

of firstborn children (Ernst & Angst, 1983)[1] plus the benefits attributed to speech especially adapted to language-learning children naturally led to speculations regarding the probable deleterious language environment of later born siblings. Indeed, the ways that mothers talk to an individual child differ markedly from 3- to 5-year-old siblings' speech to infants of 12–23 months of age or speech during triadic infant-sibling-mother conversations (Dunn & Kendrick, 1982a; Jones & Adamson, 1987; Tomasello & Mannle, 1985; Woollett, 1986).

Nonetheless, these researchers and those that followed focused mostly on the potential benefits of learning language in a richer social environment that includes mothers and siblings (Barton & Tomasello, 1991, 1992; Dunn & Shatz, 1989; Hoff-Ginsberg, 1993; Hoff-Ginsberg & Krueger, 1991; Jones & Adamson, 1987; Mannle, Barton, & Tomasello, 1992).[2] Why? Despite variations in language environment, children learn how to talk. Findings from some of the Pacific Islands document that adult caregivers in these settings do not finely tune speech to children, scaffold, and usually ignore children's poorly formed early speech (Ochs, 1988; Schieffelin, 1990). This research influenced researchers in technological settings to revise received opinions regarding the sibling speech environment.

In harmony with this larger perspective, later born children gain many pragmatic abilities that assist them in participating as conversational partners. Triadic conversations consist of far less scaffolded speech to the infant and far more complex speech than that usually directed to younger children in dyadic interactions (Dunn & Shatz, 1989; Hoff-Ginsberg & Krueger, 1991; Mannle et al., 1992). Even so, younger siblings consistently display that they can comprehend much of ongoing speech in these settings by participating actively and appropriately (Barton & Tomasello, 1991; Dunn & Shatz, 1989). Because preschool siblings do not adjust speech as much for younger siblings, this situation may precipitate the younger to work harder at expressing her or himself (Demuth, 1984; Dunn & Shatz, 1989; Jones & Adamson, 1987; Mannle et al., 1992; Woollett, 1986). Further, as several researchers speculated (Dunn & Kendrick, 1982a; Dunn & Shatz, 1989; Oshima-Takane, 1988; Woollett, 1986), being exposed to references to the self and others in "overheard" rather than "child-directed" speech disambiguates the usage of personal pronouns. Oshima-Takane, Goodz, and Derevensky (1993) confirmed that later born children at 21 and 24 months displayed a more advanced understanding and use of personal pronouns than did firstborn siblings.

Recent studies do not support the earlier opinions that firstborns learn language earlier and better nor that all sibling utterances are dramatically different from those of mothers. Especially when socioeconomic status is taken into consideration (Hoff-Ginsberg, 1993), later borns do not lag far behind firstborns in lexical growth (Hoff-Ginsberg & Krueger, 1991; Pine, 1993). Further, in the language game, although for "starters" children must have the lexical "building blocks," the rules for combining lexical "pieces" and strategies for communicating make a player competent. Firstborns of 18–26 months may have the lead for some aspects of syntax, whereas later born siblings have the edge in the area of pragmatics (Hoff-Ginsberg, 1993). Hoff-Ginsberg and Krueger (1991) demonstrated that 7- to 8-year-old siblings' speech to younger siblings of 18–36 months provides far more of the characteristics of mother's speech than that of 4- to 5-year-old siblings. These authors noted much of the "dismal" early evaluation of sibling speech may be due to choosing to study preschoolers, rather than 7- to 8-year-olds whose age is similar to that of sibling caregivers in agrarian societies. Finally, in a provocative twist regarding the assumed benefits of adult caregiver speech to infants, Trehub and her colleagues (Trehub, Unyk, & Henderson, 1994) speculated that older caregivers appropriated the child-like characteristics of "motherese" from the vocal and singing patters of siblings. Perhaps, older caregivers noticed how the higher pitch, exaggerated speech contours, slower tempo, and shorter utterances of young siblinlgs enhance gathering attention during interaction (Zukow-Goldring, in press). Clearly, the study of siblings' contribution to each other's language development in all cultures is only in its infancy.

CONCLUSIONS: BROADEN THE STUDY OF SIBLING CAREGIVING AND BRING COHERENCE TO THEORIES OF CHILD DEVELOPMENT

Sibling caregiving has many guises across cultures. Whether explicit or implicit, whether labeled caregiving or not, the impact of siblings is ubiquitous and universal as they teach each other about life during the most mundane daily activities of their cultures. In agrarian societies, sibling caregivers do more than attending to immediate biological needs and keeping younger children amused. Siblings are "culture-brokers," introducing their sisters and brothers to ways of acting and knowing through unique styles of interaction. Only in the last decade and a half have researchers in technological settings discovered the positive effect of sibling caregiving, better known as "interaction," in studies of play, cognitive, and language development of the individual child.

Although not perceived as "prerequisites" to sibling caregiving in technological societies, a very similar pattern of social, emotional, perceptual, and cognitive milestones underlie being a competent elder sibling anywhere on this planet. The older sibling's shifts from overwhelming self-interest related to the most basic necessities to the display of competence in cultural tasks to putting the needs of others before the self mirrors LeVine's (1980) description of parental goals. Parents and other caregivers apparently do successfully socialize their children for self-survival, inculcate cultural practices that will lead to economic self-sufficiency, and, finally, provide a lens through which to see the self appreciated through cultural practices embodied in the care of others.

Two ends may be coming toward the middle. As agrarian people move to urban settings and as schooling becomes available in rural areas, sibling caregiving is quietly "falling apart" (Broberg & Hwang, 1992; Harkness & Super, 1992; Lamb & Sternberg, 1992; Nsamenang, 1992). In technological settings, two-wage-earner families who cannot provide afterschool care for their children leave the sibling caregiving potential go begging. Urgent social policy questions for the future entail how each group can learn from the other. Ethnographies of actual patterns of care and need in all settings can inform resolution of these global problems.

Paraphrasing John Kennedy's famous words, Mace (1977) called for his colleagues to "ask not what's in your head, but what your head's inside of" (p. 43). Although Mace was addressing a different set of problems, that play on words points to one way to examine the cornucopia or cacophony of theoretical voices within sibling caregiving research. From the bewildering array of theories influencing more recent empirical research, a more coherent pattern can emerge. Findings from cross-cultural studies based on eco-cultural models highlight sibling caregiving and its variations, challenging more insular theories to be more inclusive. Close empirical contact with cross-cultural studies can benefit theories arising from Western psychological approaches by getting them to ask new questions and be less ethno- and egocentric. In the same vein, theories and research explaining and investigating social, emotional, perceptual, and language development broaden and contribute to understanding sibling caregiving. A coherent theory of child development will weave the many into one.

ACKNOWLEDGMENTS

The author's research conducted in Mexico was supported by NIMH Postdoctoral Fellowship No. 5 F32 MH 07996-02 and by a Spencer Foundation Grant awarded to Patricia Greenfield. The studies conducted in the United States with Latino and Euro-American families were funded by a grant to the author by the Spencer Foundation and by the Michelle F. Elkind Foundation. I wish to express my gratitude to Tom Weisner for perceptive comments and, especially, for his generosity during his reading of this manuscript. Special thanks go to Karen Watson-Gegeo, Cathy Dent-Read, Ann MacDonald, and to Marc Bornstein for their extremely careful readings.

REFERENCES

Abramovitch, R., Corter, C., & Lando, B. (1979). Sibling interaction in the home. *Child Development, 50,* 997–1003.

Abramovitch, R., Corter, C., Pepler, D. J., & Stanhope, L. (1986). Sibling and peer interaction: A final follow-up and a comparison. *Child Development, 57,* 217–229.

Azmitia, M., & Hesser, J. (1993). Why siblings are important agents of cognitive development: A comparison of siblings and peers. *Child Development, 64,* 430–444.

Bank, P. B., & Kahn, M. D. (Eds.). (1982). *The sibling bond.* New York: Basic Books.

Barnes, S., Gutfreund, H., Satterly, D., & Wells, G. (1983). Characteristics of adult speech which predict children's language development. *Journal of Child Language, 10,* 65–84.

Barton, M. E., & Tomasello, M. (1991). Joint attention and conversation in mother-infant-sibling triads. *Child Development, 62,* 517–529.

Barton, M. E., & Tomasello, M. (1992). The rest of the family: The role of fathers and siblings in early language development. In B. Richards & C. Gallway (Eds.), *Language addressed to children* (pp. 109–134). London: Cambridge University Press.

Beals, A. R., & Eason, M. A. (1993). Siblings in North America and South Asia. In C. W. Nuckolls (Ed.), *Siblings in South Asia: Brothers and sisters in cultural context* (pp. 71–101). New York: Guilford.

Berndt, T. J., & Bulleit, T. N. (1985). Effects of sibling relationships on preschoolers' behavior at home and at school. *Developmental Psychology, 56,* 761–767.

Borstelmann, L. J. (1977). Child rearing in the United States (1620–1970). *International encyclopedia of psychiatry, psychology, psychoanalysis, and neurology* (pp. 143–146). Aesculapius.

Broberg, A. G., & Hwang, C. P. (1992). The shaping of child-care policies. In M. E. Lamb, K. J. Sternberg, C. P. Hwang, & A. G. Broberg (Eds.), *Child care in context: Cross-cultural perspectives* (pp. 509–521). Hillsdale, NJ: Lawrence Erlbaum Associates.

Brody, G. H., Stoneman, Z., & MacKinnon, C. (1982). Role asymmetries among school-age children, their younger siblings, and their friends. *Child Development, 53,* 1364–1370.

Childs, C. P., & Greenfield, P. M. (1980). Informal modes of learning and teaching: The case of Zinacanteco weaving. In N. Warren (Ed.), *Studies in cross-cultural psychology* (Vol. 2, pp. 269–316). London: Academic Press.

Cicirelli, V. G. (1972). The effect of sibling relationships on concept learning of young children taught by child teachers. *Child Development, 43,* 282–287.

Cole, M., Hood, L., & McDermott, R. P. (1978). Concepts of ecological validity: Their differing implications for comparative cognitive research. *The Quarterly Newsletter of the Laboratory of Comparative Human Cognition, 2,* 34–37.

Cross, T. (1977). Mother's speech adjustments: The contribution of selected child listener variables. In C. Snow & C. Ferguson (Eds.), *Talking to children* (pp. 151–188). London: Wiley.

Demuth, K. A. (1984). *Aspects of Sesotho language acquisition.* Bloomington: Indiana University Linguistics Club.

Demuth, K. A. (in press). Collecting spontaneous production data. In D. McDaniel, C. McKee, & H. S. Cairns (Eds.), *Methods for assessing children's syntax.* Cambridge, MA: MIT Press.

Dent, C. (1990). An ecological approach to language development: An alternative functionalism. In C. Dent & P. G. Zukow (Eds.), *The idea of innateness: Effects on language and communication research* [Special issue]. *Developmental Psychobiology, 23,* 679–704.

Dent-Read, C., & Zukow-Goldring, P. G. (in press). *Changing ecological approaches to development: Organism-environment mutualities.* Washington, DC: American Psychological Association.

Draper, P., & Harpending, H. (1987). Parent investment and the child's environment. In J. B. Lancaster, J. Altmann, A. S. Rossi, & L. R. Sherrod (Eds.), *Parenting across the life span: Biosocial dimensions* (pp. 207–235). New York: Aldine de Gruyter.

Dunn, J. (1983). Sibling relationships in early childhood. *Child Development, 54,* 787–811.

Dunn, J. (1988). *The beginnings of social understanding.* Cambridge, MA: Harvard University Press.

Dunn, J. (1989). Siblings and the development of social understanding in early childhood. In P. G. Zukow (Ed.), *Sibling interaction across cultures: Theoretical and methodological issues* (pp. 106–116). New York: Springer-Verlag.

Dunn, J. F. (1991). Sibling influences. In M. Lewis & S. Feinman (Eds.), *Social influences and socialization in infancy* (pp. 97–109). New York: Plenum.

Dunn, J., & Kendrick, C. (1982a). *Siblings: Love, envy, and understanding.* Cambridge, MA: Harvard University Press.

Dunn, J., & Kendrick, C. (1982b). The speech of two- and three-year olds to infant siblings: "Baby talk" and the context of communication. *Journal of Child Language, 9,* 579–597.

Dunn, J., & Munn, P. (1985). Becoming a family member: Family conflict and the development of social understanding. *Child Development, 56,* 480–492.

Dunn, J., & Plomin, R. (1990). *Separate lives: Why siblings are so different.* New York: Basic Books.

Dunn, J., & Shatz, M. (1989). Becoming a conversationalist despite (or because of) having an older sibling. *Child Development, 60,* 399–410.

Eckerman, C. O. (1993). Toddlers' achievement of coordinated action with conspecifics: A dynamic systems perspective. In L. B. Smith & E. Thelen (Eds.), *A dynamic systems approach to development* (pp. 333–357). Cambridge, MA: MIT Press.

Ellis, S., & Rogoff, B. (1982). The strategies and efficacy of child versus adult teachers. *Child Development, 43,* 730–735.

Ember, C. (1973). Feminine task assignment and the social behavior of boys. *Ethos, 1,* 424–439.

Ernst, C., & Angst, J. (1983). *Birth order: Its influence on personality.* Berlin: Springer-Verlag.

Fischer, J. L., & Fischer, A. (1963). The New Englanders of Orchard Town, U.S.A. In B. B. Whiting (Ed.), *Six cultures: Studies of child rearing.* New York: Wiley. (Reprinted as a separate volume, 1966)

Gallimore, R., Boggs, J., & Jordan, C. (1974). *Culture, behavior, and education: A study of Hawaiian-Americans.* Beverly Hills, CA: Sage.

Garfinkel, H. (1978–1979). *Lectures.* University of California, Los Angeles.

Getis, V. L., & Vinovskis, M. A. (1992). History of child care in the United States before 1950. In M. E. Lamb, K. J. Sternberg, C. P. Hwang, & A. G. Broberg (Eds.), *Child care in context: Cross-cultural perspectives* (pp. 463–476). Hillsdale, NJ: Lawrence Erlbaum Associates.

Goody, E. N. (1982). *Parenthood and social reproduction: Fostering and occupational roles in West Africa.* Cambridge, England: Cambridge University Press.

Gottlieb, L. N., & Mendelson, M. J. (1990). Parental support and firstborn girls' adaptation to the birth of a sibling. *Journal of Applied Development Psychology, 11,* 29–48.

Greenfield, P. M. (1984). A theory of the teacher in the learning activities of everyday life. In B. Rogoff & J. Lave (Eds.), *Everyday cognition: Its development in social context* (pp. 117–138). Cambridge, MA: Harvard University Press.

Greenfield, P. M., & Smith, J. H. (1976). *The structure of communication in early language development.* New York: Academic Press.

Handel, G. (1986). Beyond sibling rivalry: An empirically grounded theory of sibling relationships. In P. A. Adler & P. Adler (Eds.), *Sociological studies of child development* (pp. 105–122). Greenwich, CT: JAI.

Hanna, E., & Meltzoff, A. N. (1993). Peer imitation by toddlers in laboratory, home, and day-care contexts: Implications for social learning and memory. *Developmental Psychology, 29,* 701–710.

Hareven, T. K. (1989). Historical changes in children's networks in the family and community. In D. Belle (Ed.), *Children's social networks and social supports* (pp. 15–36). New York: Wiley.

Harkness, S., & Super, C. M. (1992). Shared child care in East Africa: Sociocultural origins and developmental consequences. In M. E. Lamb, K. J. Sternberg, C. P. Hwang, & A. G. Broberg (Eds.), *Child care in context: Cross-cultural perspectives* (pp. 441–459). Hillsdale, NJ: Lawrence Erlbaum Associates.

Harrison, A. O., Wilson, M. N., Pine, C. J., Chan, S. Q., & Buriel, R. (1990). Family ecologies of ethnic minority children. *Child Development, 61,* 363–383.

Hartup, W. W. (1979). The social world of children. *American Psychologist, 34,* 944–950.

Hartup, W. W. & Laursen, B. (1991). Relationships as developmental contexts. In R. Cohen & A. W. Siegel (Eds.), *Context and development* (pp. 253–279). Hillsdale, NJ: Lawrence Erlbaum Associates.

Heath, S. B. (1983). *Way with words: Language, life, and work in communities and classrooms.* Cambridge, MA: Cambridge University Press.

Hoff-Ginsberg, E. (1993, July). *Differences in early language development associated with socioeconomic status and birth order.* Paper presented at the International Congress for the Study of Child Language, Trieste, Italy.

Hoff-Ginsberg, E., & Krueger, W. M. (1991). Older siblings as conversational partners. *Merrill–Palmer Quarterly, 37,* 465–482.

Howe, N., & Ross, H. S. (1990). Socialization, perspective-taking, and the sibling relationship. *Developmental Psychology, 26,* 160–165.

Howrigan, G. A. (1988). Fertility, infant feeding, and change in Yucatan. In R. A. LeVine, P. M. Miller, & M. M. West (Eds.), *Parental behavior in diverse societies* (pp. 3–12). San Francisco: Jossey-Bass.

Jones, C. P., & Adamson, L. B. (1987). Language use in mother–child and mother-child-sibling interactions. *Child Development, 58,* 356–366.

The Journal of the California Alliance for the Mentally Ill. Siblings [Special Issue]. (1992). *3.*

Koester, L. S. & Johnson, J. E. (1984). Children's instructional strategies: A comparison of sibling and peer tutoring. *Acta Paedologica, 1,* 23–32.

Kramer, L., & Noorman, S. (1993, March). *Maternal expectations and children's adaptation to becoming a sibling.* Poster presented at the meeting of the Society for Research in Child Development, New Orleans.

Kreppner, K. (1988). Changes in dyadic relationships within a family after the arrival of a second child. In R. A. Hinde & J. Stevenson-Hinde (Eds.), *Relationships within families: Mutual influences* (pp. 143–167). Oxford, England: Clarendon.

Kreppner, K., Paulsen, S., & Schuetze, Y. (1982). Infant and family development: from triands to tetrads. *Human Development, 25,* 373–391.

Laboratory of Comparative Human Cognition. (1986). Contribution of cross-cultural research to educational practices. *American Psychologist, 41,* 1049–1058.

Lamb, M. E. (1976). *The role of the father in child development.* New York: Wiley.

Lamb, M. E. (1982). Sibling relationships across the lifespan: An overview and introduction. In M. E. Lamb & B. Sutton-Smith (Eds.), *Sibling relationships* (pp. 1–11). Hillsdale, NJ: Lawrence Erlbaum Associates.

Lamb, M. E., & Sternberg, K. (1992). Sociocultural perspectives on nonparental child care. In M. E. Lamb, K. J. Sternberg, C. P. Hwang, & A. G. Broberg (Eds.), *Child care in context: Cross-cultural perspectives* (pp. 1–23). Hillsdale, NJ: Lawrence Erlbaum Associates.

Lamb, M. E., & Sutton-Smith, B. (1982). *Sibling relationships.* Hillsdale, NJ: Lawrence Erlbaum Associates.

LeVine, R. A. (1977). Child rearing as cultural adaptation. In P. H. Leiderman, S. R. Tulkin, & A. Rosenfeld (Eds.), *Culture and infancy: Variations in the human experience* (pp. 15–27). New York: Academic Press.

LeVine, R. A. (1980). Anthropology and child development. In C. M. Super & S. Harkness (Eds.), *Anthropological perspectives on child development* (pp. 71–86). San Francisco: Jossey-Bass.

LeVine, R. A. (1988). Human parental care: Universal goals, cultural strategies, individual behavior. In R. A. LeVine, P. M. Miller, & M. M. West (Eds.), *Parental behavior in diverse societies* (pp. 3–12). San Francisco: Jossey-Bass.

LeVine, R. A., & LeVine, S. E. (1988). Parental strategies among the Gusii of Kenya. In R. A. LeVine, P. M. Miller, & M. M. West (Eds.), *Parental behavior in diverse societies* (pp. 27–35). San Francisco: Jossey-Bass.

Lobato, D. J. (1990). *Brothers, sisters, and special needs.* Baltimore: Paul H. Brookes.

Lomnitz, L. (1975). *Como sobrviven los marginados.* Mexico, D.F.: Siglo Veinti-uno Editores.

Mace, W. (1977). Ask not what's in your head, but what your head's inside of. R. E. Shaw & J. Bransford (Eds.), *Perceiving, acting, and knowing* (pp. 43–65). Hillsdale, NJ: Lawrence Erlbaum Associates.

Mannle, S., Bartob, M., & Tomasello, M. (1992) Two-year-olds' conversations with their mothers and preschool-aged siblings. *First Language, 12,* 57–71.

Malpass, R. S. (1977). Theory and method in cross-cultural research. *American Psychologist, 32,* 1069–1079.

Martini, M. (1994). Peer interactions in Polynesia: A view from the Marquesas. In J. P. Roopnarine, J. E. Johnson, & F. H. Hooper (Eds.), *Children's play in diverse cultures* (pp. 73–103). Albany: State University of New York Press.

Martini, M., & Kirkpatrick, J. (1992). Parenting in Polynesia: A view from the Marquesas. In J. L. Roopnarine & D. B. Carter (Eds.), *Parent–child socialization in diverse cultures* (pp. 199–223). Norwood, NJ: Ablex.

McHale, S. M., & Crouter, A. C. (in press). The family contexts of children's sibling relationships. In G. Brody (Ed.), *Sibling relationships: Their causes and consequences.* Norwood, NJ: Ablex.

McHale, S. M., & Pawletko, T. M. (1992). Differential treatment of siblings in two family contexts. *Child Development, 63,* 68–81.

McKenna, J. J. (1987). Parental supplements and surrogates among primates: Cross-species and cross-cultural comparisons. In J. B. Lancaster, J. Altmann, A. S. Rossi, & L. R. Sherrod (Eds.) *Parenting across the life span: Biosocial dimensions* (pp. 143–184). New York: Aldine de Gruyter.

Mead, M. (1935). *Sex and temperament in three primitive societies.* New York: Morrow.

Melhuish, E., & Moss, P. (1992). Day care in the United Kingdom in historical perspective. In M. E. Lamb, K. J. Sternberg, C.-P. Hwang, & A. G. Broberg (Eds.), *Child care in context: Cross-cultural perspectives* (pp. 157–183). Hillsdale, NJ: Lawrence Erlbaum Associates.

Meltzoff, A., & Gopnik, A. (1993). The role of imitation in understanding persons and developing a theory of mind. In S. Baron-Cohen, H. Tager-Flusberg, & D. J. Cohen (Eds.), *Understanding other minds* (pp. 335–366). New York: Oxford University Press.

Mendelson, M. J. (1990). *Becoming a brother: A child learns about life, family, and self.* Cambridge, MA: MIT Press.

Mischel, W. (1977). On the future of personality measurement. *American Psychologist, 32,* 246–254.

Morelli, G. A., & Tronick, E. Z. (1991). Parenting and child development in the Efe foragers and Lese farmers of Zaïre. In M. H. Bornstein (Ed.), *Cultural approaches to parenting* (pp. 91–113). Hillsdale, NJ: Lawrence Erlbaum Associates.

Mundy-Castle, A. C. (1974). Social and technological intelligence in Western and non-Western cultures. *Universitas, 4,* 46–52.

Murphy, S. O. (1992). Using multiple forms of family data: Identifying pattern and meaning in sibling-infant relationships. In J. F. Gilgum, K. Daly, & G. Handel (Eds.), *Qualitative methods in family research* (pp. 146–171). Newbury Park, CA: Sage.

Murphy, S. (1993, March). Parent strategies and the transition to siblinghood. In D. Teti (Chair), *Becoming a sibling: Family-contextual factors and the transition to siblinghood.* Symposium conducted at the meeting of the Society for Research in Child Development, New Orleans.

Nelson, K. E., Carskaddon, G., & Bonvillian, J. (1973). Syntax acquisition: Impact of experimental variation in adult verbal interaction with the child. *Child Development, 44,* 497–504.

Nerlove, S. B., Roberts, J. M., & Klein, R. E., Yarbrough, C.,& Habicht, J. P. (1974). Natural indicators of cognitive development: An observational study of rural Guatemalan children. *Ethos, 2,* 265–295.

Nsamenang, B. A. (1992). Early childhood care and education in Cameroon. In M. E. Lamb, K. J. Sternberg, C. P. Hwang, & A. G. Broberg (Eds.), *Child care in context: Cross-cultural perspectives.* Hillsdale, NJ: Lawrence Erlbaum Associates.

Nuckolls, C. W. (1993a). An introduction to the cross-cultural study of sibling relations. In C. W. Nuckolls (Ed.), *Siblings in South Asia: Brothers and sisters in cultural context* (pp. 19–41). New York: Guilford.

Nuckolls, C. W. (1993b). Sibling myths in a South Indian fishing village: A case study in sociological ambivalence. In C. W. Nuckolls (Ed.), *Siblings in South Asia: Brothers and sisters in cultural context* (pp. 191–217). New York: Guilford.

Ochs, E. (1988). *Culture and language development: Language acquisition and socialization in a Samoan village.* Cambridge, MA: Cambridge University Press.

Ochs, E., & Schieffelin, B. B. (1984). Language acquisition and socialization: Three developmental stories and their implications. In R. Shweder & R. LeVine (Eds.), *Culture theory: Essays on mind, self, and emotion* (pp. 276–320). Cambridge, MA: Cambridge University Press.

Oshima-Takane, Y. (1988). Children learn from speech not addressed to them: The case of personal pronouns. *Child Language, 15,* 95–108.

Oshima-Takane, Y., Goodz, E., & Derevensky, J. L. (1993). *Birth order effects on early language development: Do secondborn children learn from overheard speech?* Unpublished manuscript under review.

Pelletier-Stiefel, J., Pepler, D., Crozier, K., Stanhope, L., Corter, C., & Abramovitch, R. (1986). Nurturance in the home: A longitudinal study of sibling interaction. In A. Fogel & G. F. Melson (Eds.), *Origins of nurturance: Developmental, biological and cultural perspectives on caregiving* (pp. 1–24). Hillsdale, NJ: Lawrence Erlbaum Associates.

Pérez, D., Barajas, N., Domínguez, M., Goldberg, J., Juarez, ???, Saab, M., Vergara, F., & Callanan, M. (1994). Siblings providing one another with opportunities to learn. *Focus on Diversity, 5,* 1–5.

Perez, D. R., & Callanan, M. (1994). *Conversations with mothers and siblings: Young children's semantic and conceptual development.* Unpublished manuscript.

Perner, J., Ruffman, T., & Leekam, S. R. (1994). Theory of mind is contagious: You catch it from your sibs. *Child Development, 65,* 1228–1238.

Piaget, J. (1962). *Play, dreams, and imitation in childhood.* New York: Norton.

Pine, J. (1993). *Variation in vocabulary development as a function of birth order.* Manuscript submitted for publication.

Rabain-Jamin, J. (1994). Language and socialization of the child in African families living in France. In. P. M. Greenfield & R. Cocking (Eds.), *Cross-cultural roots of minority child development.* Edison, NJ: Lawrence Erlbaum Associates.

Rabain-Jamin, J., & Wornham, W. L. (1993). Practices and representations of child care and motor development among West Africans in Paris. *Early Development and Parenting, 2,* 107–119.

Rogoff, B. (1990). *Apprenticeship in thinking: Cognitive development in social context.* New York: Oxford University Press.

Rogoff, B., Gauvain, M., & Ellis, S. (1984). Development viewed in its cultural context. In M. Bornstein & M. Lamb (Eds.), *Developmental psychology: An advanced textbook* (pp. 533–571). Hillsdale, NJ: Lawrence Erlbaum Associates.

Rogoff, B., Mistry, J., Göncü, A., & Mosier, C. (1993). Guided participation in cultural activity by toddlers and caregivers. *Monographs of the Society for Research in Child Development, 58*(8, Serial No. 236).

Rogoff, B., Sellers, M. J., Piorrata, S., Fox, N., & White, S. (1975). Age of assignment of roles and responsibilities to children: A cross-cultural survey. *Human Development, 18,* 353–369.

Ross, H., Filyer, R., Lollis, S., Perlman, M., & Martin, J. (in press). Administering justice in the family. *Journal of Family Psychology.*

Ryan, J. (1974). Early language development: Towards a communicative analysis. In M. P. M. Richards (Ed.), *The integration of the child into the social world* (pp. 185–213). Cambridge, MA: Cambridge University Press.

Scarr, S. (1992). Developmental theories for the 1990's: Development and individual differences. *Child Development, 63,* 1–19.

Scarr, S., & McCartney, K. (1983). How people make their own environment: A theory of genotype environment effects. *Child Development, 54,* 424–435.

Schieffelin, B. B. (1990). *The give and take of everyday life: Language socialization of Kaluli children.* Cambridge, MA: Cambridge University Press.

Scribner, S., & Cole, M. (1981). *The psychology of literacy.* Cambridge, MA: Harvard University Press.

Seymour, S. (1993). Sociocultural contests: Examining sibling roles in South Asia. In C. W. Nuckolls (Ed.), *Siblings in South Asia: Brothers and sisters in cultural context* (pp. 45–69). New York: Guilford.

Shantz, C. U., & Hobart, C. J. (1989). Social conflict and development: Peers and siblings. In T. H. Berndt & G. W. Ladd (Eds.), *Peer relationships in child development* (pp. 71–94). New York: Wiley.

Shweder, R. A. (1991). *Thinking through culture.* Cambridge, MA: Harvard University Press.

Slomkowski, C. L., & Dunn, J. (1992). Arguments and relationships within the family: Differences in young children's disputes with mother and sibling. *Developmental Psychology, 28,* 919–924.

Snow, C. E. (1977). The development of conversation between mothers and babies. *Journal of Child Language, 4,* 1–11.

Snow, C. E. (1981). The uses of imitation. *Journal of Child Language, 8,* 205–212.

Snow, C. E., Barnes, W. S., Chandler, J., Goodman, I. F., & Hemphill, L. (1991). *Unfulfilled expectations: Home and school influences on literacy.* Cambridge, MA: Harvard University Press.

Snow, C. E., Perlmann, R., & Nathan, D. (1987). Why routines are different: Toward a multiple-factor model of the relation between input and language acquisition. In K. E. Nelson & A. van Kleeck (Eds.), *Children's language* (Vol. 6, pp. 65–97). Hillsdale, NJ: Lawrence Erlbaum Associates.

Stevenson, M. B., Leavitt, L. A., Thompson, R. H., & Roach, M. A. (1988). A social relations model analysis of parent and child play. *Developmental Psychology, 24,* 101–108.

Stewart, R. B. (1983a). Sibling attachment relationships: Child-infant interactions in the strange situation. *Developmental Psychology, 19,* 192–199.

Stewart, R. B. (1983b). Sibling interaction: The role of the older child as teacher for the younger. *Merrill–Palmer Quarterly, 29*, 47–68.

Stewart, R. B., Jr. (1990). *The second child: Family transition and adjustment.* Newbury Park, CA: Sage.

Stewart, R. B., & Marvin, R. S. (1984). Sibling relations: The role of conceptual perspective-taking in the ontogeny of sibling caregiving. *Child Development, 55,* 1322–1332.

Stewart, R. B., Mobley, L. A., Van Tuyl, S. S., & Salvador, M. A. (1987). The firstborn's adjustment to the birth of a sibling: A longitudinal assessment. *Child Development, 58,* 341–355.

Stoneman, Z., & Berman, P. (Eds.). (1993). *The effects of mental retardation, disability, and illness on sibling relationships: Research issues and challenges.* Baltimore: Paul H. Brookes.

Stoneman, Z., Brody, G. H., & MacKinnon, C. (1984). Naturalistic observations of children's activities and roles while playing with their siblings and friends. *Child Development, 55,* 617–627.

Summers, M., Summers, C. R., & Ascione, F. R. (1993). *A comparison of sibling interaction in intact and single-parent families.* Unpublished manuscript.

Super, C. M., & Harkness, S. (1986). The developmental niche: A conceptualization at the interface of child and culture. *International Journal of Behavioral Development, 9,* 1–25.

Sutton-Smith, B. (1982). Epilogue: Framing the problem. In M. E. Lamb & B. Sutton-Smith (Eds.), *Sibling relationships* (pp. 383–386). Hillsdale, NJ: Lawrence Erlbaum Associates.

Sutton-Smith, B., & Rosenberg, B. G. (1970). *The Sibling.* New York: Holt, Rinehart & Winston.

Teti, D., & Ablard, K. E. (1989). Security of attachment and infant-sibling relationships: A laboratory study. *Child Development, 60,* 1519–1528.

Teti, D. M., Bond, L. A., & Gibbs, E. D. (1988). Mothers, fathers, and siblings: A comparison of play styles and their influence upon infant cognitive level. *International Journal of Behavioral Development, 11,* 415–432.

Tomasello, M., & Mannle, S. (1985). Pragmatics of sibling speech to one-year-olds. *Child Development, 56,* 911–917.

Trehub, S. E., Unyk, A. M., & Henderson, J. L. (1994). Children's songs to infant siblings: Parallels with speech. *Journal of Child Language, 21,* 735–744.

Vandell, D. L., Minnett, A. M., & Santrock, J. W. (1987). Age differences in sibling relationships during middle childhood. *Journal of Applied Developmental Psychology, 8,* 247–257.

Vygotsky, L.S. (1978). Play and its role in the mental development of the child. In M. Cole, V. John-Steiner, S. Scribner, & E. Souberman (Eds.), *Mind in society* (pp. 92–104). Cambridge, MA: Harvard University Press.

Ward, M. C. (1971). Them children: A study in language learning. New York: Holt, Rinehart & Winston.

Watson-Gegeo, K. A., & Gegeo, D. W. (1989). The role of sibling interaction in child socialization. In P. G. Zukow (Ed.), *Sibling interactions across cultures: Theoretical and methodological issues* (pp. 54–76). New York: Springer-Verlag.

Watson-Gegeo, K. A., & Gegeo, D. W. (1992). Schooling, knowledge, and power: Social transformation in the Solomon Islands. *Anthropology and Education Quarterly, 23,* 10–29.

Weisner, T. S. (1982). Sibling interdependence and child caretaking: A cross-cultural view. In M. Lamb & B. Sutton-Smith (Eds.), *Sibling relationships: Their nature and significance across the lifespan* (305–327). Hillsdale, NJ: Lawrence Erlbaum Associates.

Weisner, T. S. (1987). Socialization for parenthood in sibling caretaking societies. In J. B. Lancaster, J. Altmann, A. S. Rossi, & L. R. Sherrod (Eds.), *Parenting across the life span: Biosocial dimensions* (pp. 237–270). New York: Aldine de Gruyter.

Weisner, T. S. (1989a). Comparing sibling relationships across cultures. In P. G. Zukow (Ed.), *Sibling interactions across cultures: Theoretical and methodological issues* (pp. 11– 25). New York: Springer-Verlag.

Weisner, T. S. (1989b). Cultural and universal aspects of social support for children: Evidence from Abaluyia of Kenya. In D. Belle (Ed.), *Children's social networks and social supports* (pp. 70–90). New York: Wiley.

Weisner, T. S. (1993a). Ethnographic and ecocultural perspectives on sibling relationships. In Z. Stoneman & P. W. Berman (Eds.), *The effects of mental retardation, disability and illness on sibling relationships: Research issues and challenges* (pp. 51–83). Baltimore: Paul H. Brookes.

Weisner, T. S. (1993b). Overview: Sibling similarity and difference in different cultures. In C. W. Nuckolls (Ed.), *Siblings in South Asia: Brothers and sisters in cultural context* (pp.1–17). New York: Guilford.

Weisner, T. S. (in press). Cultural adaptations and the 5–7 transition: Caretaking and socially distributed support. In A. Sameroff & M. Haith (Eds.), *Reason and responsibility: The passage through childhood.* Chicago: Chicago University Press.

Weisner, T. S., & Gallimore, R. (1977). My brother's keeper: Child and sibling caretaking. *Current Anthropology, 18,* 169–190.

Weisner, T. S., Gallimore, R., & Jordan, C. (1988). Unpackaging cultural effects on classroom learning: Hawaiian peer assistance and child-generated activity. *Anthropology and Education Quarterly, 19,* 327–353.

Werner, E. E. (1979). *Cross-cultural child development: A view from planet Earth.* Monterey, CA: Brooks/Cole.

Wertsch, J. (1985). *Vygotsky and the social formation of mind.* Cambridge, MA: Harvard University Press.

West, M. M. (1988). Parental values and behavior in the Outer Fiji Islands. In R. A. LeVine, P. M. Miller, & M. M. West (Eds.), *Parental behavior in diverse societies* (pp. 12–25). San Francisco: Jossey-Bass.

White, D., & Woollett, A. (1992). *Families: A context for development.* London: Falmer Press.

Whiting, B. B. (Ed.). (1963). *Six cultures: Studies of child rearing.* New York: Wiley.

Whiting, B. B., & Edwards, C. P. (1988). *Children of different worlds: The formation of social behavior.* Cambridge, MA: Harvard University Press.

Whiting, B., & Whiting, J. W. (1975). *Children of six cultures.* Cambridge, MA: Harvard University Press.

Whittemore, R. D., & Beverly, E. (1989). Trust in the Mandinka way: The cultural context of sibling care. In P. G. Zukow (Ed.), *Sibling interactions across cultures: Theoretical and methodological issues* (pp. 26–53). New York: Springer-Verlag.

Wolf, D. P., Rygh, J., & Altshuler, J. (1984). Agency and experience: Actions and states in play narratives. In I. Bretherton (Ed.), *Symbolic play: The development of social understanding* (pp. 195–218). Orlando, FL: Academic Press.

Wood, D., Bruner, J. S., & Ross, G. (1976). The role of tutoring in problem solving. *Journal of Child Psychology and Psychiatry, 17,* 89–100.

Wood, D., & Middleton, D. A. (1975). A study of assisted problem-solving. *British Journal of Psychology, 66,* 181–191.

Woollett, A. (1986). The influence of older siblings on the language environment of young children. In M. Barrett & M. Harris (Eds.), Language and cognition in early social interaction [Special issue]. *British Journal of Developmental Psychology, 4,* 235–246.

Zeisler, Y. L., & Demuth, D. (1995). Noun class prefixes in Sesotho child-directed speech. In E. Clark (Ed.), *Proceedings of the 26th Annual Child Language Research Forum* (pp. 1–10). Stanford, CT: CLSI.

Zempleni-Rabain, J. (1973). Food and the strategy involved in learning fraternal exchange among Wolof children. In P. Alexandre (Ed.), *French perspectives in African studies* (pp. 221–233). London: Oxford University Press.

Zukow, P. G. (1984a). Criteria for the emergence of symbolic conduct: When words refer and play is symbolic. In L. Feagans, C. Garvey, & R. Golinkoff (Eds.), *The origins and growth of communication* (pp. 162–175). Norwood, NJ: Ablex.

Zukow, P. G. (1984b, November). *The relative contribution of sibling and adult caregivers to the emergence of play in Central Mexico.* Paper presented at the American Anthropological Association meeting, Denver. (ERIC Document Reproduction Service No. ED 23154)

Zukow, P. G. (1986). The relationship between interaction with the caregiver and the emergence of play activities during the one-word period. *British Journal of Developmental Psychology, 4,* 223–234.

Zukow, P. G. (1989a). Communicating across disciplines: On integrating psychological and ethnographic approaches. In P. G. Zukow (Ed.), *Sibling interactions across cultures: Theoretical and methodological issues* (pp. 1–8). New York: Springer-Verlag.

Zukow, P. G. (Ed.). (1989b). *Sibling interactions across cultures: Theoretical and methodological issues.* New York: Springer-Verlag.

Zukow, P. G. (1989c). Siblings as effective socializing agents: Evidence from Central Mexico. In P. G. Zukow (Ed.), *Sibling interactions across cultures: Theoretical and methodological issues* (pp. 79–105). New York: Springer-Verlag.

Zukow, P. G. (1990). Socio-perceptual bases for the emergence of language: An alternative to innatist approaches. In C. Dent & P. G. Zukow (Eds.), The idea of innateness: Effects on language and communication research [Special issue]. *Developmental Psychobiology, 23,* 679–704.

Zukow, P. G. (1991). A socio-perceptual/ecological approach to lexicaldevelopment: Affordances of the communicative context. *Anales de Psicologia, 7,* 151–163.

Zukow-Goldring, P. (in press). Educating attention: An ecological approach to acheiving concensus. In C. Dent-Read & P. Zukow-Goldring (Eds.), *Changing ecological approaches to development: Organism-environment mutualities.* Washington, DC: American Psychological Association.

Zukow-Goldring, P. G., & Ferko, R. (1994). Socializing attention: A socio-perceptual/ecological approach to the emergence of the lexicon. In V. John-Steiner, C. Panofsky, & L. Smith (Eds.), *Sociocultural approaches to language and literacy: An interactionist perspective* (pp. 170–190). New York: Cambridge University Press.

Zukow-Goldring, P. G., Romo, L., & Duncan, K. (1994). The relation of cultural heritage to the repair of communicative breakdowns in early educational settings. In A. Alvarez & P. del Rio (Eds.), *Education as cultural construction* (pp. 227–238) Madrid: Fundacion Infancia y Aprendizaje.

8

Parenting Adopted Children

David M. Brodzinsky
Rutgers University
Robin Lang
CPC Behavioral Healthcare, Red Bank, NJ
Daniel W. Smith
Medical University of South Carolina

INTRODUCTION

The practice of adoption has been an integral part of society from the beginning of recorded history. Nearly all the early major societies—Egyptian, Chinese, Indian, Greek, Roman—practiced some form of adoption. The oldest written laws setting forth the conditions of adoption are found in the Babylonian Code of Hammurabi (2800 BC).

Historically, the practice of adoption served quite different purposes than it does today (Benet, 1976). In the past, adoption was viewed as a legitimate means of meeting specific needs of adults (e.g., to ensure inheritance lines, for religious purposes, to meet requirements for holding public office, to secure additional labor for the family, to ensure one's maintenance and care in old age), as well as societal needs (e.g., to strengthen alliances between separate, and potentially rival, social groups). In contemporary society, the philosophy underlying adoption has changed dramatically. Although adoption is still seen by some as a means of meeting the needs of adults, especially infertile couples, today the primary focus of this social service practice is the "best interests of the child" (Goldstein, Freud, & Solnit, 1973). In this context, adoption is viewed as a vehicle for providing a permanent and nurturing home for children whose biological parents could not, or would not, care for them.

As a means of ensuring the physical and emotional well-being of children, adoption has proven to be an unqualified success. Adopted children fare significantly better than children reared in institutional environments or in foster care (Bohman, 1970; Bohman & Sigvardsson, 1990; Triseliotis & Hill, 1990). Furthermore, they show better long-term adjustment than children living with biological parents who are ambivalent about rearing them, or in fact, do not want them (Bohman, 1970).

For all the benefits associated with adoption, other professionals have pointed out the additional challenges and problems that this form of family life brings to its members (Kirk, 1964). Over the past four decades, a sizable empirical, clinical, and theoretical literature has emerged documenting the complexities of adoptive family life and the heightened psychological risk associated with this family status (Brodzinsky, 1993; Brodzinsky & Schechter, 1990; Wierzbicki, 1993). In this chapter, we explore some of the issues in parenting adopted children, with particular focus on the relation between parenting and family factors, and children's adjustment to adoption. We begin with a discussion of the rapidly changing nature of contemporary adoption practice, followed by an examination of family life-cycle issues in rearing infant-placed adopted children. An overview of children's adjustment to adoption then is presented, followed by discussions of the unique parenting issues, and adjustment outcomes, associated with special needs adoptions, transracial and intercountry adoptions, and open adoptions. Because this chapter focuses on *parenting* adopted children, a comprehensive review of research and theory on adoption adjustment is not presented. Readers interested in these topics are referred to Brodzinsky and Schechter (1990), Brodzinsky (1993), and Wierzbicki (1993).

CURRENT TRENDS IN ADOPTION PRACTICE

It is believed that approximately 2 percent to 4 percent of children in the United States are adopted (Bachrach, 1986; Stolley, 1993). Of these, a slight majority involve related adoptions—that is, children who are adopted by biological family members or stepparents (Hetherington & Stanley-Hagan, in this *Handbook*). The remaining children are youngsters adopted by individuals with whom they share no biological connection. It is this latter group of adoptees, and their families, that has received most of the attention in the psychological literature, and that is the focus of attention in this chapter.

The demographics of children being placed for adoption have changed significantly over the past few decades (Cole & Donley, 1990; Stolley, 1993). Traditionally, most children were healthy, White infants, adopted within a few days or weeks of birth. However, changes in social and sexual mores beginning in the 1960s and 1970s resulted in greater acceptance of single parenthood and opened the door for a growing number of unmarried mothers to keep their babies (Weinraub & Gringlas, in this *Handbook*). These changes, along with the legalization of abortion and the ready availability of contraception, led to a dramatic decrease in the number of healthy infants available for adoption. For example, prior to 1973, nearly 9 percent of all premarital births resulted in an adoption, whereas currently the figure is closer to 2 percent (Bachrach, Stolley, & London, 1992). The decline in adoption placement is primarily the result of fewer White women surrendering their babies for adoption (19.3 percent for 1952–1973 vs. 3.2 percent for 1982–1988); African-American women, in contrast, have consistently shown a low incidence of infant adoption placement (1.5 percent for 1952–1973 vs. 1.1 percent for 1982–1988).

With fewer healthy White babies available for adoption in the United States, many couples wishing to adopt children have had to consider other options. In some cases, couples adopt children of a different race. Typically, this practice involves White parents adopting non-White children. Domestic transracial adoption has declined, however, because of opposition from the African-American community, especially the National Association of Black Social Workers, as well as opposition from the Native-American community which pushed for the passage of the Indian Child Welfare Act of 1978, the goal of which was to discourage adoption of Native-American children by non-Native-American individuals.

Couples seeking to adopt children also began looking to foreign sources. Although intercountry adoption emerged after World War II, it escalated dramatically following the Korean War and the Vietnam War. In fiscal year 1991, for example, there were 9,008 foreign adoptions in the United

States, the majority of the children coming from countries such as Korea, Rumania, Colombia, Peru, India, and the Phillipines (U.S. Immigration and Naturalization Service, 1991). Most of these children were infants and toddlers; many, however, were somewhat older children.

In the United States, another source of adoptable children emerged with the passage of the Adoption Assistance and Child Welfare Act of 1980 (Public Law 96-272). This federal legislation encouraged the adoption of children traditionally considered to be hard to place. These "special needs" children included older youngsters lingering in foster care, minority children, members of sibling groups, children with medical problems, and children with physical, mental, and/or emotional handicaps.

In addition to the changes in characteristics of adopted children, dramatic changes have taken place in the characteristics of adoptive parents. Traditionally, most individuals seeking to adopt children were middle- and upper middle-class White couples. Although this group still accounts for the majority of individuals adopting healthy infants, the range of individuals adopting children has greatly increased. The elimination of income criteria for adoptive parents by public agencies, and the establishment of financial subsidies for special needs children, has allowed working-class and low-income families to adopt children, especially those who otherwise might not find permanent homes. Many agencies have also eliminated age and marital status criteria, thereby allowing older individuals and single adults to adopt children. A growing number of gay and lesbian individuals also have successfully adopted children (Patterson, in this *Handbook*). Finally, elimination of previous policy guidelines preventing or, at least, discouraging foster parents from seeking to adopt the children in their care has dramatically increased the number of foster parent adoptions (Derdeyn, 1990).

Another dramatic change in adoption that is radically affecting the way adopted children are being parented, is the emergence of open adoption (Baran & Pannor, 1993; Berry, 1993). Since the establishment of licensed adoption agencies early in this century, most adoptions have been confidential, closed placements—that is, birthparents and adoptive parents did not know one another's identity, and there was no direct contact between the parties either prior to the placement or in the postplacement period. In the 1970s, however, some agencies began to offer clients the option of open placements, where birthparents and adoptive parents could meet and share information, including the possibility of full disclosure of identity and the development of plans for ongoing contact after the adoption placement.

In short, adoption today is a much more complex social service practice than it once was. This fact alone makes it difficult to make generalizations about the challenges of parenting adopted children, as well as the possible outcome for these youngsters.

ADOPTIVE FAMILY LIFE CYCLE

Families have often been described as progressing through an orderly sequence of developmental changes that take place over time (Carter & McGoldrick, 1980; Duvall, 1977). Known as the family life cycle, this process involves the emergence of unique patterns of family structure, as well as stage-specific functional tasks that serve as the focal point for family interaction, contributing to the growth and development of family members.

Adoptive families also progress through a life cycle characterized by varying developmental tasks (Brodzinsky, 1987; Hajal & Rosenberg, 1991). Most of these tasks are similar to those experienced by nonadoptive families, whereas other tasks are unique to this particular form of family life. At each stage of the adoptive family life cycle, parents and children confront adoption-related issues that interact with, and complicate, the way in which family members cope with, and resolve, the more universal tasks of family life. Among the many adoption-related tasks experienced by parents over the family life cycle are those associated with the transition to adoptive parenthood, discussing adoption with their child, supporting the child's curiosity about the birth family, helping their child cope with adoption-related loss, supporting a positive self-image and identity in their child in relation to adoption, and in some cases, as the adoptee moves into late adolescence and adulthood, coping with plans to search for the birth family.

Transition to Adoptive Parenthood

It is widely recognized that the transition to parenthood presents significant challenges to new parents and is often accompanied by a decrease in overall marital satisfaction (Heinicke, in this *Handbook;* Wilson & Gottman, in this *Handbook*). Several factors have been suggested to underlie this decline: increased fatigue, decreased sexual activity, diminished social involvement, strained financial resources, and increased difficulty in managing conflict between family and work roles. In addition, parents possess prior hopes and expectations about parenthood, many of which are incongruent with their actual postnatal experiences. Violation of expectations, in conjunction with decreased marital satisfaction, is associated with problems in parent–child and family interactions (Belsky, Ward, & Rovine, 1986; Isabella & Belsky, 1985).

Adoptive parents face not only the usual normative stresses in their transition to parenthood, but also a number of unique challenges that may complicate the formation of a healthy family environment (Brodzinsky, 1987; Brodzinsky & Huffman, 1988; Kirk, 1964). One important stressor, for a sizable percentage of adoptive parents, is the experience of infertility, which is associated with a variety of psychological problems for both the individual and couple (Shapiro, 1988), including low self-esteem, distorted body image, anxiety, depression, disrupted marital communication, decreased sexual activity, and increased resentment toward one's spouse. When adoptive parents fail to cope effectively with these problems, intrafamilial trust, security, and unity may be threatened (Kirk, 1964; Schechter, 1970).

A second complication in the transition to adoptive parenthood is the uncertain time line that characterizes this process. Unlike pregnancy, the duration of the adoption process is highly variable. In private or independent adoptions, couples may wait only a few months to a year; in agency-based adoptions, particularly if the couple is adamant about adopting a healthy, White infant, the wait may well be several years. The lack of a clear timetable is often experienced by adoptive parents as anxiety arousing, and may inhibit effective planning for the child's arrival.

In addition to the indeterminate waiting period, most adoptive parents must also submit to an in-depth evaluation—called the "homestudy"—in order to prove their fitness to be parents. Although this process is intended to educate people about adoption and to empower them (Cole & Donley, 1990), it is often experienced as intrusive and demeaning for prospective parents, which, in turn, can heighten their anxiety about their ability to rear a child—particularly another woman's child.

Adoption also is associated with social stigma in our society (Kirk, 1964). It is viewed as a "second best" route to parenthood. As a result, when announcing their intention to adopt a child, couples are less likely to receive unqualified support from extended family and friends, especially when the adoption crosses racial or ethnic lines (Singer, Brodzinsky, Ramsay, Steir, & Waters, 1985). Thus, unlike biological parents, whose impending parental status typically is a source of celebration, adoptive parents frequently must justify to others their particular parenting decision. This experience, in turn, may well increase parental resentment and accentuate feelings of "differentness."

Because only a small percentage of the adult population chooses adoption as a means of achieving parenthood, there are relatively few individuals to whom the adoptive couple can turn for information and support regarding adoption-related issues. Consequently, individuals are more likely to have difficulty developing realistic expectations concerning the transition to adoptive parenthood. In turn, unrealistic or disconfirmed expectations can make this process even more stressful than it need be (Belsky et al., 1986).

Another factor that may impinge on the ability of adoptive parents to fully commit to their child and to develop healthy parent–child emotional bonds is the lack of security in their parental status at the time of the adoption placement (Levy-Shiff, Goldschmidt, & Har-Even, 1991). In most adoptions, there is a probationary period that precedes legal finalization of the parent–child relationship. During this period, the child's birthparents may have the right to revoke their consent for adoption—as seen in a number of highly publicized court cases in the 1980s and 1990s—or the adoption agency, which is monitoring the placement, may remove the child from the adoptive home if the placement is deemed to be unsatisfactory for some reason. The knowledge that a placement can be disrupted by circumstances beyond their control may prevent some adoptive parents from forming emotional connections as quickly or deeply as they otherwise might have.

Two child-related characteristics can also complicate the transition to adoptive parenthood. The first relates to the child's age at the time of placement. Unlike young infants, who enter the adoptive family with virtually no postnatal history that impacts immediately on their family adjustment, children who are placed for adoption later in infancy, or at older ages, bring with them a host of life experiences that often complicates parent–child relationships and family functioning (Rosenthal, 1993).

The second child-related factor that can affect the transition to adoptive parenthood is the increased biological risk associated with adoption. Research suggests that adopted children may be more likely to be born to adults who manifest psychological problems thought to have some genetic component (Cadoret, 1990; Loehlin, Willerman, & Horn, 1982). Furthermore, adopted children typically are the product of stressful and unsupported pregnancies, and more often experience prenatal and birth complications than their nonadopted counterparts (Bohman, 1970; Hoopes, 1982). Such biological vulnerabilities can produce more difficult temperament patterns and developmental delays that, in turn, could adversely affect parent–child relationships through the process of violated expectations.

Potentially offsetting these problems are a number of factors that are thought to buffer the couple from the unique stresses in the transition to parenthood (Brodzinsky & Huffman, 1988). For example, compared with biological parents, adoptive parents are older when the child first arrives, and therefore, more likely to be settled in their careers and to have greater financial security. In addition, they are likely to have developed more effective coping skills to handle the various stresses associated with family life, in general, and parenthood, in particular. They also have been married longer than first-time biological parents, which may foster greater marital sensitivity and communication. Finally, in response to the extended period of frustration and emotional pain associated with infertility, the adoptive couple is likely to feel a powerful sense of fulfillment with the arrival of a child, which in turn, may buffer them from the unique stresses associated with the early phase of adoptive family life.

Despite the many potential complications encountered in the transition to adoptive parenthood, both research and clinical experience suggest that most individuals and couples cope with this early phase of adoptive family life quite well (Brodzinsky & Huffman, 1988). No differences have been found between adoptive and nonadoptive families on observational and self-report measures of home environment, as well as infant mental and motor development, when the target children were 1 and 2 years old (Plomin & DeFries, 1985). Quality of mother–infant attachment also appears not to be adversely affected by the unique transitional problems experienced by adoptive parents (Singer et al., 1985). Finally, Levy-Shiff and her colleagues recently reported data from a longitudinal study of the transition to parenthood among Israeli couples (Levy-Shiff, Bar, & Har-Even, 1990; Levy-Shiff et al., 1991). At the expectancy phase (prebirth or preadoption), no differences on measures of ego strength or coping style were found between pregnant couples and those individuals anticipating an adoption placement. Pregnant mothers reported more depression than expectant adoptive mothers and had lower scores in some domains of self-concept. Adoptive parents-to-be also expressed more marital satisfaction and perceived greater social support from community agencies (i.e., social service agencies) than did biological parents-to-be. In addition, they had more positive expectations about the effects of having a child on their individual and family lives; these positive expectations were also associated with greater perceived loss due to infertility. At the 4-month postnatal/adoption assessment, adoptive parents reported better coping with the physical demands of parenthood and more satisfaction with their parental role compared with nonadoptive parents. Levy-Shiff and her colleagues concluded that adoptive parenthood, at least in its early stages, and when it involves the adoption of a young infant, is generally a positive experience for the majority of couples. These researchers cautioned, however, that the positive adjustment pattern among adoptive couples observed at this early stage of the family life cycle may reflect a "honeymoon" period (Schechter, 1970), prior to the onset of more serious challenges. If this is so, we would expect adjustment problems to emerge as the family moves beyond this initial transition period.

Parenting the Preschool Adopted Child

Most children in the preschool years are developing a sense of autonomy and initiative, and are beginning to explore the world beyond the family. This process is facilitated by developmental achievements in language and representational thought, as well as the establishment of reasonably secure emotional bonds with parents. Most parents recognize the importance of this early phase of separation and individuation, and support the child's developmental progress, even though they may experience some ambivalence about the child moving beyond the sphere of their protection.

In adoptive families, this normative stage of the family life cycle is complicated by a very important adoption-related task; namely, telling the child about his or her adoption. Most families begin this process relatively early in the child's life, usually between 2 and 4 years of age (Mech, 1973). For parents, the telling process is often accompanied by confusion and heightened anxiety. Adoptive parents are frequently unsure about what information to share with the child, and when. They worry about the child's reaction to the information. Will the child's feelings about the parents change? Will family relationships, and the child's sense of security and self-esteem, be undermined?

Parental stress regarding adoption revelation is tied, at least in part, to the recognition that this process creates psychological distance between parents and the child, which can never be fully closed again. "Telling acknowledges openly to all family members that one of the most basic links between parents and children, the biological link, is absent in their particular family" (Brodzinsky, 1987, p. 33). Thus, no matter how much adoptive parents may wish to pretend that the relationship with their child is exactly the same as that between parents and their biological children, they can no longer continue to do so once the child's adoption status is revealed (Kirk, 1964). In short, the telling process brings to the forefront of family life the reality that adopted children are inextricably bound to two sets of parents. Moreover, adoptive parents must now begin to face more fully the reality of having to share a place in their child's mental and emotional life with the birth family. At a time when the child's separation and individuation are already experienced with some ambivalence, these realizations are likely to create considerable anxiety in adoptive parents, and may undermine their sense of entitlement to the child.

Complicating the matter even more for parents is the fact that adoption professionals are somewhat divided on the best time for beginning the telling process. Whereas the majority of social service personnel and mental health professionals advocate beginning the telling process in the toddler and preschool years, traditional psychodynamic theorists urge that parents withhold adoption information until the child is 6 or 7 years old (Schechter, 1960; Wieder, 1977). The concern among these latter professionals is that the younger child, who is still in the midst of the Oedipal conflict, may not be sufficiently mature to cope with the idea of having two sets of parents with whom to identify. They also suggest that early telling may lead to an overreliance on the splitting defense, in which one set of parents is seen as "good" and the other as "bad." For some parents, the conflicting messages from the professional community accentuates the anxiety already associated with the telling process.

Because most parents begin discussing adoption with their children in the preschool years, it has been difficult to resolve empirically issues related to the timing of the telling process. Brodzinsky (1983; Brodzinsky, Schechter, & Brodzinsky, 1986) found that variation in the timing of adoption revelation, *within the toddler and preschool years,* was unrelated to psychological adjustment of adoptees, or to their adoption knowledge. Clinical and anecdotal evidence, however, suggests that when parents withhold adoption information too long, the child is more likely to find out about his or her family status in an unsupportive, and potentially damaging, way (e.g., overhearing family members talking about it, finding documents that reveal it, being told about it in anger during a family conflict), which could undermine family relationships (Kirk, 1964; Lifton, 1979; Sorosky, Baran, &

Pannor, 1978). Moreover, accounts by adult adoptees who were never told of their adoption and only found out about the "family secret" inadvertently in later childhood, adolescence, or adulthood have indicated significant anger toward, and feelings of betrayal by, their adoptive parents (Lifton, 1979).

Although disclosing adoption information during the preschool years does not appear to undermine children's psychological adjustment, as some psychodynamic theorists have warned, it also does not lead to much understanding about adoption—which can be somewhat confusing to parents, who tend to overestimate their children's adoption knowledge (Brodzinsky, 1983). Brodzinsky, Singer, and Braff (1984) reported that although preschool-age adopted children often label themselves as adopted, and occasionally can relate to others their "adoption story," they actually understand very little about their family status. In fact, it is not until the school-age years that most youngsters are able to clearly differentiate between birth and adoption as alternative ways of entering a family. As Brodzinsky (1987, 1990, 1993; Brodzinsky et al., 1986; Brodzinsky, Schechter, & Henig, 1992; Brodzinsky, Singer, & Braff, 1984) noted, the child's growing awareness of the meaning, and implications, of being adopted sets the stage for the emergence of adoption-related adjustment problems.

Parenting the School-Age Adopted Child

As children enter the elementary school years, several developmental changes occur that have a profound influence on adoptive family life. The development of more mature problem-solving skills and the emergence of logical thought, for example, provide a foundation for a more complex, and realistic, assessment of adoption on the part of the child (Brodzinsky et al. 1986; Brodzinsky, Singer, & Braff, 1984). This a time when children begin to express greater curiosity about their origins. Where did I come from? What did my birthmother and birthfather look like? What are their names? Why did they place me for adoption? Can they come back and get me? These are some of the questions that emerge when children begin to comprehend adoption more deeply. School-age children also begin to examine the dilemma faced by birthparents regarding the relinquishment decision, and question whether other options might have been chosen. They may ask: "If she didn't know how to be a mother, why didn't someone teach her? If she didn't have enough money to take care of me, why didn't she get a job?" For some children, the explanations offered by adoptive parents regarding the basis for the relinquishment are no longer as easily accepted as they once were.

The child's developing understanding of what constitutes a family also brings about new awareness of adoption-related issues. In the preschool years, children define a family primarily in terms of criteria such as coresidence of individuals and shared affection, whereas during the middle childhood years, there is increasing awareness of biology as a defining feature of family relationships (Newman, Roberts, & Syre, 1993). This change often leads to confusion among school-age children regarding the nature of their connection to the two families in their life—one of which they know, love, and live with, but are unrelated to biologically; the other of which they know little and do not live with, but that is the link to their biological heritage.

Another developmental achievement of this period having significant implications for adopted children and their parents is the child's understanding of logical reciprocity. With the emergence of this aspect of logical thought comes a profound insight in relation to adoption; namely, to be adopted, one first must be relinquished or surrendered. This awareness sensitizes children, perhaps for the first time, to the fact that being adopted means not only gaining a family, but *losing* one as well. According to Brodzinsky (1987, 1990, 1993), it is the experience of loss that ultimately leads to a sense of ambivalence about being adopted, as well as to the emergence of adoption adjustment problems.

The many changes that children are going through regarding adoption during this period can be confusing and pose significant challenges for parents. To begin with, parents must recognize that the growing ambivalence about being adopted experienced by their child is perfectly normal. It represents neither a failure of parenting, nor an indication of psychopathology on the part of the child. Rather, the child's sense of ambivalence is part of a grief reaction that emerges when he or she begins to focus on the inherent loss associated with adoption. As Brodzinsky (1987) noted, adoption-related loss is often subtle, but nevertheless quite pervasive. It involves the loss of birthparents, extended birth family, and often birth siblings. In addition, school-age children commonly experience status loss associated with the stigma of being adopted, whereas in adolescence and adulthood, loss of genealogical, racial, and/or ethnic continuity, as well as loss of part of their identity, are often felt. The challenge for adoptive parents during this period is to create a caregiving environment that supports their children's growing curiosity regarding their origins, reinforces a positive view of their heritage, maintains open communication about adoption issues, and supports their children's efforts to "work through" or cope with the grief associated with adoption-related loss. Parents must guard against forming a rigid, impermeable psychological barrier between the biological and adoptive families, which can present the child with a dilemma of divided loyalties (Butler, 1989). Although most parents appear quite successful in handling these parenting tasks, some are not. It is in the latter case that we begin to see more serious problems in children's adoption adjustment.

Parenting the Adopted Adolescent

Entrance into adolescence brings with it a host of developmental changes: rapid physical growth and sexual maturation, the development of abstract thought, exploration of identity, individuation and separation from family, and so forth. Many of these changes are tied to adjustment issues faced by adopted teenagers and their parents.

During this period, many adolescent adoptees become preoccupied with the lack of physical resemblance between themselves and family members. For these youngsters, the inability to look into the faces of their adoptive parents and siblings and see reflections of themselves—something that is typically taken for granted in biological families—is often experienced as disconcerting. Raynor (1980) reported that both adoptees and their parents were more satisfied with the adoptive experience when they were able to perceive, or imagine, physical resemblance between them.

The adolescent's sexual development also poses unique issues for adoptees and their parents. Easson (1973) questioned whether the renewed Oedipal feelings that are part of the parent–adolescent relationship are suppressed or repressed as easily in adoptive families compared to biological families. Other psychodynamic theorists have suggested that adolescent female adoptees may have more struggles with their sexual identity because of the conflict regarding identification with an infertile adoptive mother versus a sexually precocious, but perhaps irresponsible, biological mother (Schechter & Bertocci, 1990).

Perhaps the most significant issue facing adolescent adoptees is one of identity development (Hoopes, 1990; Stein & Hoopes, 1985). Integrating the past into the present, and developing a stable and unified sense of self, is thought to be more complex for adoptees because they have been cut off from their origins, and consequently, from part of themselves. Writing from a psychodynamic perspective, Sorosky, Baran, and Pannor (1975) suggested that difficulties in resolving a sense of ego identity among adopted teenagers is tied to four fundamental psychological issues: (1) disturbances in the development of early object (i.e., interpersonal) relations, which undermine trust and security; (2) problems in resolving Oedipal feelings toward parents and siblings with whom one shares no biological connection; (3) difficulties in resolving the family romance fantasy (Freud, 1909/1959), which involves learning to cope with ambivalent feelings toward parental figures, without excessive use of the splitting defense whereby the roles of "good parents" and "bad parents" are assigned to adoptive and biological parents in a rigid and/or arbitrary way; and (4) confusion and uncertainty regarding genealogical continuity—termed genealogical bewilderment by Sants (1964)—which is tied to the lack of knowledge about one's ancestors. According to Sants, the lack of "biological mutuality" among adoptive family members—that is, shared biologically based characteristics, including appearance, intellectual skills, personality traits, and so forth—impedes the teenager's ability to identify with adoptive parents. Moreover, Frisk (1964) argued that in the absence of sufficient information about one's biological background, adolescent adoptees are likely to create a "hereditary ghost," which becomes incorporated into a confused, unstable, and distorted sense of self.

In rearing adopted youth, parents must be aware of these many complexities, and provide their teenagers with the support they need to cope with various adoption-related tasks. They must recognize that the search for origins, which began earlier in the form of questions about the birth family and the reasons for the relinquishment, is likely to continue in one form or another in the adolescent years. For some adolescents, the search may include developing plans for gaining more information about one's origins, visiting one's place of birth, and even making contact with birth parents and/or birth siblings. The need for information and/or contact with birth family is highly variable among adopted adolescents and adults (Schechter & Bertocci, 1990). What is important for parents to recognize is that such an interest is a normal part of the adoption adjustment process. It does not usually reflect psychopathology on the youngster's part. On the other hand, whether adoptive parents decide to support an active search at this time for additional information and/or birth family must be a decision based on a thoughtful consideration of their child's motivation to search, emotional maturity, outcome expectations, and so forth. Unfortunately, the adoption literature provides little guidance on the outcome for searching in the teenage years, although Schechter and Bertocci indicated generally favorable outcomes—in terms of feelings of satisfaction—among adopted adults.

Finally, in preparing to launch their teenagers into the world, and supporting the ongoing process of individuation, adoptive parents must recognize the problems faced by adopted youth in their struggle to differentiate from their family of origin. Unlike adolescents who live with their biological family, adoptees must struggle to differentiate themselves from two families of origin—their rearing family and their biological one. The problem is that it is virtually impossible to successfully differentiate oneself from the biological family when it is largely unknown. It is like trying to push against a vacuum. The lack of resistance makes it impossible to gain distance and create appropriate separation. For many adoptees, the only resolution to their dilemma is greater knowledge about their origins, which may include an active search for birth family. Once again, the task for adoptive parents is to understand the normality of the process and to provide emotional, and perhaps practical, support for their adolescent and young adult children.

The numerous adoption-related issues faced by children and their parents across the family life cycle have raised questions among mental health professionals about the psychological outcome associated with adoption. The clinical literature has been quite consistent in viewing adoptees and their families as at increased risk for adjustment problems compared to their nonadopted counterparts (Easson, 1973; Frisk, 1964; Sorosky et al., 1975). In contrast, empirical research has provided a more equivocal view of the adoption adjustment process.

PSYCHOLOGICAL OUTCOME IN ADOPTION

Over the years, there has been a great deal of interest in the long-term psychological outcome of children placed for adoption. This interest can be traced to the work of Schechter (1960) and Kirk (1964), who were among the first researchers to point out that adoption, although a reasonable option to consider when children need out-of-home placement, is itself associated with increased risk for adjustment problems. Three sources of data address this issue of risk: (1) epidemiological studies on the incidence and prevalence of adoptees in mental health settings and special education classifications, (2) presenting symptomatology of clinical samples of adopted and nonadopted children, and (3) behavioral and personality characteristics, and adjustment patterns, of nonclinical samples of adopted and nonadopted children.

Epidemiological Studies

Research has consistently shown that adopted children are overrepresented in various types of mental health settings and special education settings (Wierzbicki, 1993). For example, although nonrelated adoptees constitute approximately 2 percent of the population of children in the United States (Zill, 1985), they represent nearly 5 percent of the children in outpatient mental health facilities (Mech, 1973), between 10 percent and 15 percent of youngsters in inpatient psychiatric settings (Piersma, 1987; Rogeness, Hoppe, Macedo, Fisher, & Harris, 1988), and between 6 percent and 9 percent of school children educationally classified as perceptually impaired, neurologically impaired, or emotionally disturbed (Brodzinsky & Steiger, 1991).

Although these data strongly suggest that adopted children manifest a disproportionate rate of adjustment problems compared to nonadopted children, it is possible that this pattern may represent, at least in part, differential use of mental health services by adoptive parents. A recent study by Warren (1992) supports this position. Drawing on data from a national health survey of 12- to 17-year-old adolescents, Warren found that, although adopted teenagers were more likely to be characterized by behavioral problems compared with nonadopted adolescents, their parents exercised a lower threshold for making psychiatric and psychological referral decisions. In other words, adopted children were more likely to be referred for clinical services than nonadopted youth when the problems manifested were relatively minor. Warren offered three possible explanations for this referral pattern. First, adoptive parents may make quicker referrals of their children for clinical services simply because they have grown accustomed to working with social service professionals, as well as the mental health community, in the process of adopting their children. Second, parents may be characterized by a negative attributional bias, in which adoption inherently is associated with increased problems. Thus, because their children are adopted, these parents may be primed to identify problems and to utilize mental health services at the first sign of unusual behavior. Finally, earlier utilization of mental health services could occur because the child's problems are viewed as a more serious threat to the identity and unity of the family system. In other words, more tenuous family relationships and the social stigma associated with adoption could result in parents becoming more reactive to their children's problems, leading to quicker psychiatric and psychological referral. In concluding, Warren noted that the results of her research "do not support the belief that adoptees appear more often in psychiatric settings *purely* [emphasis added] because they are more troubled" (p. 512).

Clinical Studies

Much of the research on the adjustment of adopted children has focused on clinical populations, with the goal of identifying symptoms most often presented by these individuals at the time of referral. A common pattern has emerged in the literature: Adopted children and youth who manifest adjustment difficulties generally are characterized by externalizing symptomatology, including increased aggression, oppositional and defiant behaviors, lying, stealing, running away, substance abuse, and other antisocial tendencies (Cohen, Coyne, & Duvall, 1993; Fullerton, Goodrich, & Berman, 1986; Kotsopoulos et al., 1988; Kotsopoulos, Walker, Copping, Cote, & Stavrakaki, 1993; Schechter, Carlson, Simmons, & Work, 1964). A higher rate of learning disabilities (Silver, 1989) and attention deficit hyperactivity disorder (Deutsch et al., 1982) also has been documented among adopted children and youth. In contrast, little difference has been found in adoptees compared to nonadoptees for internalizing disorders such as depression and anxiety (Kotsopoulos et al., 1988, 1993; Rogeness et al., 1988) or for psychotic disorders (Fullerton et al., 1986; Schechter et al., 1964).

To date, most of the research on clinical samples of adoptees has focused on the characteristics of the children, leaving unanswered whether the families of these youngsters differ in any significant way from the families of nonadopted children manifesting similar adjustment problems. One difference between families, noted previously, is that adoptive parents tend to refer their children for clinical services more quickly than do nonadoptive parents, especially when behavioral and emotional problems are still relatively minor (Warren, 1992). Other research by Cohen et al. (1993) has provided further insight into the characteristics of adoptive and nonadoptive families whose children have been referred for treatment. These researchers noted that the problems of adopted children are less likely to be associated with general marital and family dysfunction than the problems of nonadopted children. Adoptive parents also tend to have greater psychosocial resources than their nonadoptive counterparts. In addition, an interesting pattern emerged in the explanations parents endorsed regarding the basis for the child's problems. Adoptive parents were more likely than nonadoptive parents to endorse biological and early experience factors, and less likely to endorse family factors, as explanations for problems. They also were more likely to consider removing the child from the home as a solution to the problems. From a clinical perspective, these findings raise concerns about the way in which adoptive parents view their own role in the emergence of problems in their children. If these findings are reliable, they suggest that when adopted children develop adjustment difficulties, parents may be more prone to scapegoating the child, as well as others in the child's past, and less likely to see the role they may play themselves in the child's and family's problems.

Nonclinical Studies

Because of inherent problems in generalizing findings from clinical research, investigators often examine whether adopted children from community samples differ in behavioral and personality characteristics, and adjustment patterns, from their nonadopted peers. This literature is more equivocal than clinical research regarding the question of psychological risk associated with adoption—that is, some studies find no differences between the groups, whereas other studies show adoptees to be more maladjusted.

Research focusing on infants, toddlers, and preschoolers generally has failed to find any significant differences between these groups in such areas as attachment (Singer et al., 1985), temperament (Carey, Lipton, & Myers, 1974), mental and motor functioning (Plomin & DeFries, 1985), and communication development (Thompson & Plomin, 1988). Some studies focusing on older children also have failed to find evidence of increased psychological problems among adoptees compared to nonadoptees (Marquis & Detweiler, 1985; Norvell & Guy, 1977; Stein & Hoopes, 1985). In contrast, a sizable body of research has reported that elementary-school-age adopted children are rated by parents, teachers, and often by themselves, as doing less well emotionally, socially, and academically than their nonadopted peers (Bohman, 1970; Brodzinsky, Hitt, & Smith, 1993; Brodzinsky, Radice, Huffman, & Merkler, 1987; Brodzinsky, Schechter, Braff, & Singer, 1984; Hoopes, 1982; Lambert & Streather, 1980; Lindholm & Touliatos, 1980). In several longitudinal studies, however, the differences observed between the groups during middle childhood were no longer significant, or were substantially reduced, by the time the youngsters reached adolescence (Bohman & Sigvardsson, 1990; Maughan & Pickles, 1990; Stein & Hoopes, 1985). Other cross-sectional studies, however, do report greater adjustment problems among adopted adolescents (Loehlin, Willerman, & Horn, 1985; Zill, 1985).

Factors Associated With Adoption Adjustment

Although adopted children and youth are believed to be at increased risk for adjustment problems, there certainly is substantial variability in their patterns of adjustment. To date, relatively little research has explored the sources of this outcome variability.

As noted previously, age appears to be correlated with adjustment. In reviewing the literature, Brodzinsky (1993) noted that increased problems among infant-placed adoptees do not begin to emerge until 5–7 years of age, when their growing awareness of the meaning of adoption leads them to experience, for the first time, adoption-related loss. It is the experience of loss, according to Brodzinsky, that gives rise to the wide array of adjustment problems (Brodzinsky, 1990; Brodzinsky et al., 1992; Smith & Brodzinsky, 1994).

A number of family variables have been examined in relation to children's adjustment to adoption. One set of variables focuses on family structure. Researchers and clinicians have speculated that the presence of both biological and adopted children in the family may place adoptees at increased risk for problems because the family composition is likely to give rise more often to sibling comparisons that lead to feelings of jealously or envy regarding family status. Although some studies have reported greater maladjustment among adoptees when there is a biological child in the family (Hoopes, 1982; Kraus, 1978), other studies have failed to find such differences (Brodzinsky & Brodzinsky, 1992; Kaye, 1990). Nor has there been any consistent finding regarding the child's ordinal position in the family—that is, whether the child is the first youngster to be adopted, or whether he or she is adopted after others have been placed in the family (Brodzinsky & Brodzinsky, 1992; Kraus, 1978). It would appear that, although the order of being adopted, as well as the presence of both adopted and biological children in the family can complicate the dynamics of adoptive family life, these factors generally pose no serious problems for children's adjustment.

Several investigators have examined the types of communication patterns found in adoptive families in relation to adjustment outcome. Most of this work derives from the theoretical writings of Kirk (1964, 1981), who argued that an open, nondefensive, "acknowledgment-of-difference" approach to adoption issues is more conducive to healthy adjustment among family members than a closed, rigid, defensive, "rejection-of-difference" communication style. In support of this position, Stein and Hoopes (1985) found that adolescent adoptees who manifest fewer identity problems more often come from families with an open as opposed to closed style of communication regarding adoption issues. On the other hand, Kaye (1990) reported that families characterized by high levels of distinguishing between adoptive and biological relationships had teenagers with lower self-esteem and more family problems. Although this finding appears to contradict Kirk, it is in line with the notion that extreme styles of adoption-related communication at either end of the continuum are detrimental to the child's and family's adjustment. In other words, families that strenuously deny the differences between adoptive and nonadoptive family life, as well as those who are characterized by a negative attributional bias regarding adoption—what Brodzinsky (1987) called an "insistence-of-difference" pattern—are more likely to foster adjustment problems in family members. In keeping with this position, Brodzinsky and Reeves (1987) reported that parents who manifested an insistence-of-difference coping style viewed their children as having more adjustment problems than parents who tended to deny the differences of adoptive family life or parents who displayed a more moderate acknowledgment of difference coping style. Parents characterized by the insistence-of-difference pattern were also more likely to view the child's biological heritage as the primary determinant of his or her behavior, whereas parents who manifested either an acknowledgement-of-difference pattern or a rejection-of-difference pattern were more likely to see the caregiving environment as the primary factor influencing the child's life. These results suggest that when parents are experiencing highly conflicted relationships with their adopted youngsters, they may not only emphasize the differences between adoptive and biological family relationships, but project most of the blame for current family problems on to the "defective" biological heritage of the child.

Finally, other researchers have examined parental style, parental expectations, and emotional adjustment in parents as factors associated with adoption outcome. In summarizing this research, Kadushin (1980) reported that parental satisfaction with adoptive parenthood, coupled with a warm and accepting attitude toward the child, was associated with more positive adoption outcome than was parental coolness and rejection toward the child, or dissatisfaction with adoptive parenthood. In addition, research also has shown that more adverse adoption outcome is associated with the presence of psychopathology in adoptive parents, as well as a history of parental death or divorce in the family (Brodzinsky et al., 1993; Cadoret, 1990; Rosenthal, Schmidt, & Conner, 1988).

SPECIAL NEEDS ADOPTIONS

Adoption policy and practice changed dramatically in the 1980s. The Adoption Assistance and Child Welfare Act of 1980, which emphasized the principle of "permanency planning," mandated public adoption agencies to take prompt and decisive action to maintain children in their own homes or place them permanently with other families. The result of this legislation was a dramatic increase in so-called "special needs" adoptions; that is, adoptions involving children manifesting characteristics that, in the past, delayed or impeded adoption placement. These characteristics include older age (usually beyond 4 years), serious emotional or behavioral problems, developmental disabilities or serious medical conditions, minority status, sibling group membership, and foster care status. In 1986, 26.5 percent of unrelated domestic adoptions in the United States involved children with special needs (National Committee for Adoption, 1989). With the growth of these adoptions has come increased concern regarding the placement outcome for children and families. In this section, we examine adjustment patterns in special needs adoptions, as well as the unique challenges confronting individuals and couples who parent these children.

Disruption Rates and Adjustment Patterns

With the rise in special needs adoptions has come an increase in the number of adoption disruptions— that is, the removal of a child from a home prior to legal finalization of the parent–child relationship (Festinger, 1990; Rosenthal, 1993). The disruption rates for the majority of samples of special needs children fall between 10 percent and 20 percent. Older age at the time of placement and/or the presence of emotional and behavioral problems, such as aggressiveness, sexual acting out, fire setting, suicidal behavior, stealing, and serious eating disorders, are the most frequent child behavior correlates of adoption disruption (Barth & Berry, 1988; Festinger, 1990; Groze, 1986; Partridge, Hornby, & McDonald, 1986; Rosenthal, 1993; Rosenthal et al., 1988). Other researchers have noted that adoption disruption, as well as adjustment problems in children in intact special needs placements, are frequently tied to early environmental adversity such as neglect, physical and sexual abuse, and multiple foster placements (Festinger, 1986, 1990; McDonald, Lieberman, Partridge, & Hornby, 1991). In fact, Verhulst, Althans, and Versluis-Den Biemen (1992) concluded that it is this history of early environmental adversity, especially physical and sexual abuse, and not age at placement per se, that increases the child's risk for later adjustment problems.

In contrast to emotional and behavioral problems, physical and developmental disabilities, such as mental retardation, spina bifida, cerebral palsy, and Down syndrome, for the most part, have not been found to be associated with increased risk for disruption (Rosenthal, 1993). In a similar vein, the majority of studies of intact families adopting children with developmental or physical disabilities cite good outcomes in terms of parental satisfaction and family adjustment (Glidden, 1991; Rosenthal, 1993). In fact, when compared with a group of birth families of children with developmental disabilities, adoptive parents of developmentally disabled children reported less stress in parent, family, and child functioning (Glidden, 1991).

Despite higher disruption rates, as well as greater emotional and behavioral problems, it must be emphasized that the large majority of special needs adoptions are "successful," as measured by family intactness, parents' and children's reports of satisfaction with the adoption, and caseworkers' evaluations of placements (Rosenthal, 1993). Even children who experience a disrupted adoption often eventually go on to a successful adoption placement (Festinger, 1990; Rosenthal, 1993). In the past, many of the children in these special needs placements would never have been given the chance for a permanent adoptive home.

Parenting the Special Needs Adopted Child

A crucial question, then, is what constitutes a favorable home environment for a special needs child? Special needs children clearly present unique parenting challenges. What type of adults are likely to adopt these youngsters, and what type of parenting issues are associated with variability in adoption outcome? Regarding the latter question, five key areas have been identified: (1) integrating the child into the family, (2) forming attachments and supporting the grief process, (3) maintaining realistic expectations, (4) handling troublesome behavior, and (5) utilizing supports and services.

Characteristics of special needs adoptive parents. Today, foster parents, individuals over 40, single men and women, gay and lesbian individuals, people with limited financial means, adults who are relatively uneducated, disabled adults, and couples already rearing large families are all being considered and approved for adoptive parenthood (Nelson, 1985; Sandmaier, 1988). In the majority of cases, these individuals are adopting special needs children rather than young healthy children. The emphasis now in the placement process is on the prospective parents' degree of commitment, experience, and expectations, and ideally, on matching their strengths to a specific child's needs rather than using arbitrary restrictive criteria such as age, education, income, marital status, and sexual orientation as factors in selecting adoptive parents.

Studies that have examined placements with nontraditional adoptive parents have, on balance, demonstrated positive outcomes (Rosenthal, 1993). Minority status, lower income and education levels, older age of parents, and single-parent status, in general, do not increase the risk for disruption; in fact, these characteristics may actually be associated with greater parental satisfaction (Rosenthal, 1993). In the cases of single and older parents, the lack of difference in placement outcome compared with two parent families and younger parents is quite impressive because the former groups are more likely to adopt older, more troubled children (Barth & Berry, 1988; Groze, 1991).

A particularly robust result in the literature is the success of foster parent adoption, a practice that became increasingly possible in the 1970s as large numbers of children in foster care began being freed for adoption (Derdeyn, 1990). This was a controversial practice, with the major objection being that the goal of adoption conflicted with one of the major goals of foster care—namely, the child's reunification with his or her birth family. The concern was that foster parents, who hoped to adopt the children in their care, would not work toward reunification. Another objection was that foster parents are not screened as carefully prior to placement for compatibility with the child. Despite such objections, foster parent adoptions seem to have proven themselves by their consistently lower rates of disruption.

Although there is considerable variability in the characteristics of individuals and couples adopting special needs children, all share similar challenges in rearing these types of youngsters. How they handle these unique parenting issues will largely determine the success of adoption placement.

Integrating the child into the family system.   Any time a child enters a family, the family system must modify its patterns of functioning in order to integrate the new member. Parents assume new roles and responsibilities, children's roles are transformed as their ordinal positions in the family change, and established family routines are disrupted and revised. When a child is born into a family, the integration process is gradual and facilitated by readily available role models. However, when a child enters a family at an older age through adoption, the transition is usually less predictable and more difficult. In describing the dilemma faced by parents adopting an older child, Katz (1986) noted that:

> [M]ost children placed in middle childhood are neither gratifying to care for nor do they know how to enter into the intense mutuality that comes naturally to the newborn. Instead of a cycle of gratifying the child and feeling gratified themselves, the parents suffer the narcissistic blow of seeing the child's pain and being unable to be the ones who can relieve it. (p. 572)

It is during this early phase of the adoption that an adoptive father's involvement seems to be crucial; both parents need to be able to offer support and respite to each other during times when little gratification is coming from their interactions with the child.

The adopted child has a history of living in family systems that did not work and may resist attempts to become incorporated into the new family. Integration is facilitated by helping the child identify the daily routines, family traditions and family patterns from former placements that give him or her comfort, and incorporating those into the life of the new family. Integration can also be assisted through identifying similarities between the child and family members, rather than focusing only on differences, and by acquainting the child with the current family's history, traditions, and rituals. Other ways of integrating the child into the family include considering a nickname or a new middle name that ties the child to the family's history, incorporating pictures of the child with family members in the family album, and circulating the pictures among extended family members (Bourguignon & Watson, 1988). Finally, new family rituals that focus on the adopted child, such as celebrating the day the child entered the family, can be created. These efforts can be useful, not only in helping the child to feel integrated into the family, but in facilitating emotional bonds between the child and family members.

Forming attachments and supporting the grief process. One of the most important tasks faced by special needs adoptive families is forming parent–child attachments, which can be complicated by the impact of disrupted relationships from earlier periods of the child's life, as well as by heightened parental anxiety or a mismatch between parental expectations and the child's characteristics and behavior. Children placed for adoption within the first 6 months of life tend not to differ from nonadopted infants in developing secure attachment relationships with the adoptive parents (Singer et al., 1985). Children placed beyond 6–12 months may be at risk for attachment problems and developmental difficulties (Bowlby, 1973; Yarrow & Goodwin, 1973; Yarrow, Goodwin, Manheimer, & Milowe, 1973). These children are likely to experience acute separation distress due to the severing of previous attachment relationships. Furthermore, in cases where children have experienced multiple placements, or have suffered early maltreatment, the formation of secure attachments in the adoptive family may be compromised because these youngsters were never given the opportunity, prior to placement, to experience a stable, nurturing relationship.

Although many adoption professionals emphasize the importance of attachment in the emotional well-being of special needs adopted children, there is still little research on this issue (Johnson & Fein, 1991). One longitudinal study of children who spent the first 2½ years in an institution found that these youngsters were able to form close attachments to their adoptive parents (Hodges, 1989; Hodges & Tizard, 1989). Interestingly, close attachments were less likely to develop in children who were subsequently restored to their birth parents. The author attributed this finding to the adoptive parents' more active involvement with their child, and greater tolerance of the child's dependent behavior. Birth parents, in contrast, expected more independence from the child, spent less time in shared activities, felt ambivalent toward the child, and guilty about the time the child spent in care (Hodges, 1989).

Another study examining quality of parent–child relationships in special needs adoptions was reported by Barth and Berry (1988). Ratings of parent and child behaviors associated with relationship dimensions of reciprocity, exploration, and secure attachment were collected from parents. Results indicated that adoption disruption was more likely to occur when children were less able to have their needs for attention met by parents, manifested less spontaneous affection with family members, displayed less caring about the parents' approval, and manifested less curiosity in family interactions.

The implications of attachment theory for the study of adoption are profound. Application of newer, cognitively based attachment models (Main, Kaplan, & Cassidy, 1985) to the study of older child placements holds great promise for unraveling the complexities in family relationships, and adjustment outcomes, in these types of adoptions (Johnson & Fein, 1991).

Related to the the issue of attachment is the experience of separation and loss. Parents of special needs adoptees usually have to help their children grieve the loss of earlier attachment figures, including birth parents, birth siblings, extended birth family, foster family members, and so forth. It is believed by many adoption professionals that learning to cope with these losses is critical for the development of healthy attachments in the adoptive family. For many adoptive parents, the existence of these previous attachment figures is experienced as a threat to the integrity and stability of the family. Consequently, they tend to minimize the importance of these figures in the child's life, and provide little opportunity for the youngster to discuss his or her feelings about these individuals. In such cases, the chances of coping effectively with adoption-related loss is compromised, leading to increased risk for problems in the adoptive family (Brodzinsky, 1987, 1990; Brodzinsky et al., 1992; Nickman, 1985; Reitz & Watson, 1992).

Maintaining realistic expectations.   The parents' ability to develop and maintain realistic expectations regarding the child's potential, their own ability to help the child overcome previous problems, and the time frame for integrating the child into the family is perhaps the single most important factor in successfully parenting special needs adopted children. Research indicates that adoptions are more likely to disrupt if a child is considerably different from what parents had desired or expected (Barth, 1988; Valentine, Conway, & Randolph, 1988) and more likely to remain intact if parents are able to choose a child based on preferred child characteristics (Partridge et al., 1986) or get to know the child prior to beginning the adoption process (Barth, 1988).

The literature on adoption of children with chronic medical conditions, as well as those with significant developmental disabilities, further illustrates the importance of realistic parental expectations. As noted previously, these types of adoptions do not disrupt at high rates, and most studies cite good outcome in terms of parental satisfaction and family adjustment. Moreover, when compared with a group of birth families of children with developmental disabilities, adoptive parents of developmentally disabled children reported less stress in parent, family, and child functioning (Glidden, 1991). One explanation for such results is that adoptive parents of developmentally disabled children are likely to have more realistic expectations, and a greater sense of control, in their transition to parenthood than nonadoptive parents. The former *chose* to adopt a developmentally disabled child and are able to prepare for the entrance of the child into the family with the assistance of a readily available resource—the adoption agency. In contrast, when a developmentally disabled child is born into a family, there is often shock among family members. Parents must quickly adjust their expectations regarding the child and the parenting experience. They must also grieve the loss of their "ideal" child, and begin to learn about the special caregiving needs of their youngster and the resources available to assist them (Glidden, Valliere, & Herbert, 1988; Hodapp, in this *Handbook*). In this regard, adoptive parents of developmentally disabled children are often a step ahead of their nonadoptive counterparts.

For parents to enter into an adoption with realistic expectations, they must be provided with accurate child-specific background information prior to placement. Unfortunately, many parents do not feel sufficiently prepared by adoption agencies to rear their special needs child (Barth & Berry, 1988; Nelson, 1985). In a follow-up study of 927 older child adoptions, provision of insufficient or inaccurate (usually overly optimistic) information about a child was associated with "low-risk" placements that disrupted, whereas placements considered "high-risk" were less likely to disrupt when parents were given a complete and realistic assessment of the child's history and current behavior (Barth & Berry, 1988).

Finally, parents must also appreciate that their perceptions of a child's need for close and nurturing family ties may not match the child's readiness to accept such closeness. For parents who are looking to satisfy their own needs through close parent–child relationships, the experience of adopting older and special needs children can be particularly frustrating, especially as children begin to manifest troublesome behavior.

Handling troublesome behaviors.   Even if a child is able to form attachments to new parents, difficulties in interpersonal functioning may persist for the special needs child, often in the form of externalizing behaviors that can be particularly detrimental to placements. Behavior problems are the "single largest source of stress for families who adopt older and special needs children" (Rosenthal, 1993, p. 84). Children who are older when adopted may enter the new family with expectations about relationships that are based on a perception of the world as a dangerous, unpredictable place. They may also be characterized by patterns of interpersonal functioning that were adaptive in previous placements but that differ substantially from the adoptive family's style. Furthermore, they may be extremely reluctant to relinquish the "survival behaviors" previously acquired. For example, they may withdraw from relationships because they have learned that it is not safe to interact with adults. They may be aggressive because they have learned that the world is a place where adults hurt children. They may be constantly "testing" their new parents with acting-out behavior—in effect asking "Do you really love me? Will you leave me, too?" They may display inappropriate sexual behavior because that is how they received attention from adults in the past. They may demonstrate excessive self-reliant behavior, rejecting attempts by parents to nurture them, because they have learned to take care of themselves in previous physically and emotionally neglectful environments.

Parenting a child with these "survival behaviors" requires special skills. Caregivers often find that parenting techniques that were effective with other children may not work with these youngsters. Among the characteristics of adoptive parents often cited as contributing to successful special needs placements are tolerance for ambivalent and negative feelings, a sense of entitlement to care for the child, ability to find happiness in small increments of improvement, flexible expectations, good coping skills, tolerance for rejection, ability to delay parental gratification, good listening skills, a sense of humor, flexible family roles, strong support network, and availability of postplacement social and mental health services (Elbow, 1986; Katz, 1986; Rosenthal, 1993).

Research supports the importance of a number of these characteristics for successful special needs placements. As noted previously, realistic parental expectations has been consistently linked to more positive adoption outcome (Barth, 1988; Glidden, 1991). Satisfaction with special needs adoption also has been linked to the parents' capacity to handle troublesome child behavior, including emotional withdrawal and lack of responsivity, as well as acting-out behavior (Rosenthal et al., 1988). In addition, flexible parenting styles and less rigid role models have been associated with lower rates of disruption (Festinger, 1986; Kagan & Reid, 1986). Flexibility of adoptive fathers, in particular, as assessed by their sense of humor and creative discipline strategies, has been linked to more stable placement outcomes. Indeed, the role of the adoptive father seems to be an especially critical component of special needs placements. When both adoptive parents are equally committed to the adopted child, special needs placements are more likely to succeed (Partridge et al., 1986). In addition, Westhues and Cohen (1990) found that the affective, supportive, and active involvement of the adoptive father correlated with lower disruption rates.

Ongoing services and support.   The use of support services, such as extended family, neighbors, friends, other adoptive families, therapists, previous case workers, former foster families, and birth families, is an important component in successful special needs placements. Barth and Berry (1988) found that disrupters had fewer relatives within visiting distance and less contact with them when compared with sustainers. Rosenthal and Groze (1990) found that approval of adoption and support from family and friends positively affected placement outcome. Involvement with other adoptive parents and families is also cited by parents as important for success in special needs adoptions (Groze & Rosenthal, 1991). The benefits of such contact include: normalization of feelings; alleviation of a sense of isolation and alienation; fostering a sense of belonging in the adopted child; empowerment of adoptive parents; sharing of advice, information, and skills; and increasing the likelihood of seeking professional help when needed.

Financial subsidies are another critical factor in special needs adoptions. They have been essential in making adoption accessible to minority, low-income, and foster families—groups that typically adopt older and special needs children. Without these subsidies, many youngsters with special needs would never be adopted. Rather, they would linger in foster care or end up in institutional environments. Financial subsidies also appear to mitigate against disruption in high-risk placements (Barth & Berry, 1988).

Other service needs that have been identified as being important for successful special needs placements include: advocacy for specialized and individualized educational services, individual and family therapy, specialized training of mental health professionals regarding the dynamics of special needs adoptions, parenting skills classes emphasizing behavior management, identification of community resources, respite care, life planning for developmentally disabled children, intensive family preservation services, and availability of services over the life of the family (McKenzie, 1993; Rosenthal, 1993).

In summary, rearing adopted children with special needs presents individuals and couples with a number of unique parenting challenges. When these children are of a different race than adoptive parents, or come from quite different cultural backgrounds, the challenges can be magnified.

INTERNATIONAL AND TRANSRACIAL ADOPTION

Like children with special needs, foreign-born children are being adopted in growing numbers. With the reduced domestic availability of infants for adoption, more prospective parents are looking beyond the borders of the United States. According to data collected by the U.S. Immigration and Naturalization Service, the number of immigrant children admitted to the United States for adoption has recently doubled, from almost 5,000 in 1981 to more than 10,000 in 1987 (Bachrach, Adams, Sambrano, & London, 1989), accounting for 16.4 percent of all unrelated adoptions in 1987 (National Committee for Adoption, 1989).

About 3,000 to 5,000 of international adoptions in 1987 involved transracial placements (Silverman & Feigelman, 1990). International transracial adoptions largely began as a response to the ravages of war: Americans adopted children from Japan and China after World War II, from Korea following the Korean War, and from Southeast Asia as a result of the Vietnam War. Areas of more recent strife are reflected in international adoption statistics of the past few years, including a growing number of Hispanic children from Central and South America (Silverman & Feigelman, 1990).

In contrast, by the end of the 1970s, the number of domestic transracial adoptions had sharply declined, due in large part to opposition by minority ethnic groups. Currently, an estimated 1,000 to 2,000 African-American/White domestic adoptions occur annually, with the majority of these involving children with special needs (Silverman & Feigelman, 1990).

In transracial placements, the children, in general, are psychologically well adjusted, have close and mutually satisfying relationships with their adoptive parents, and have a positive sense of their racial identities (Silverman, 1993; Silverman & Feigelman, 1990; Tizard, 1991). Adoptive parents' attitudes and behaviors appear to have a significant impact on the child's adjustment and racial/ethnic identifications (McRoy & Zurcher, 1983; Silverman & Feigelman, 1990). Silverman and Feigelman concluded that "children whose parents deemphasized their racial identification and who isolated themselves and their families from the black community, often raised children who accepted, at least in part, some of the negative stereotypes about black people in American society" (p. 197).

Research on domestic transracial adoptions involving non-African-American children is sparse. Fanshel (1972) concluded from his study of Native American children adopted by White families that most of the youngsters were generally well-adjusted and secure. A study comparing Mexican-American children adopted by White and Mexican-American families reported findings similar to those for African-American/White adoptions: Although no significant differences existed between groups in self-esteem scores, the adoptive parents' attitudes and behavior played a major role in the development of the child's ethnic identity (Andujo, 1988).

International transracial adoptees in the United States may encounter more difficulty with their racial and ethnic identities than African-American children adopted by Whites. Feigelman and Silverman (1983) found that, compared with 70 percent of African American children living with White parents, only 57 percent of Korean children and 50 percent of Colombian children living with White parents expressed pride in their racial origins, with one fifth of the Korean children feeling ashamed of their origins and one fourth uncomfortable with their appearance. As compared with 67 percent of the African-American transracial adoptees, only 9 percent of the Korean children attended schools with many others from their racial group. Tizard (1991) suggested that "despite the anti-black racism in the U.S., the black children were able to identify with black people and culture in a way not available to Koreans, who remained different from both black and white groups" (p. 754).

Parents adopting from other countries, or across racial lines, face a number of parenting challenges. In many cases children have experienced serious malnutrition and inadequate health care prior to their placement in the adoptive family. They may also have experienced severe psychological trauma, especially children coming from war zones. In addition, there are often initial communication difficulties due to language barriers, and a lack of information about the child's experiences before emigration. For older children, learning to accommodate to the enormous differences in the physical and cultural environment proves to be particularly stressful. In transracial adoptions, whether domestic or international, parents must learn about the child's racial and ethnic heritage in preparation for fostering a positive self-image in their child. They must also prepare their child for the bigotry and prejudice that is part of society in the United States. Opponents of transracial adoption fear that this is an impossible task to accomplish for a nonminority parent.

Despite these challenges, most children and their families appear to adjust to the initial placement relatively quickly and continue to show good progress throughout the family life cycle (Silverman, 1993; Tizard, 1991). The adjustment process appears easier, however, when transracially or trans-culturally adopted children are exposed to others of the same racial or ethnic background in schools and communities and when adoptive parents actively help foster a sense of ethnic and racial pride in children.

OPEN ADOPTION

When adoption laws were first enacted in the United States in the late 1800s and early 1900s, there was great concern about protecting birth parents and adoptive parents from the unwelcomed curiosity of others, as well as protecting children from the social stigma of illegitimacy. Consequently, state adoption statutes emphasized the need for confidentiality in the adoption process, including sealing the child's original birth certificate and identifying adoption records.

The practice of confidential adoption continued unchallenged until the early 1970s, when adoption professionals began writing about the problems associated with this practice (Baran, Sorosky, & Pannor, 1974; Sorosky, Baran, & Pannor, 1976). At the same time, professionals began to advocate for unsealing adoption records, and the creation of open adoption placements (Amadio & Deutsch, 1983; Baran, Pannor, & Sorosky, 1976; Sachdev, 1989; Sorosky et al., 1978). Since then, there has been a growing movement within the adoption field toward creating greater openness in adoption.

Open adoption is defined as "the sharing of information and/or contacts between the adoptive and biological parents of an adopted child, before and/or after the placement of the child, and perhaps continuing for the life of the child" (Berry, 1993, p. 126). For some families, this involves relatively little contact and/or information about one another; for others, it involves frequent face-to-face meetings. Ideally, each open adoption is tailored to the specific needs of the parties, with the recognition that those needs may change with time, leading to either greater or lesser amounts of contact.

Relatively little is known about the actual impact of open placements on children and families. In summarizing this literature, Berry (1993) noted that proponents of this practice emphasize as possible benefits of open adoption the elimination of secrecy, the increase in control over the adoption process, the increase in knowledge about the child's heritage, the reduction of the child's sense of loss, the reduction in identity confusion for the adoptee, and the elimination of the need to search for one's origins. Open adoption is also thought to diminish the birth mother's sense of grief regarding the relinquishment of her child. Opponents of open adoption, on the other hand, emphasize the possibility that this type of placement may undermine the security and sense of entitlement on the part of adoptive parents. They also suggest that open placement may confuse children and interfere with their emotional attachments to adoptive parents. Finally, critics of open adoption worry that the grief of birthparents will be prolonged, and that they will develop overly dependent relationships with the adoptive parents.

To date, little empirical research has been conducted on open adoption. What has been done suggests the following. Birthmothers appear more willing to relinquish a child when they can receive information about the adoptive parents and maintain some degree of contact following the placement (Barth, 1987; Sandven & Resnick, 1990). Birthmothers also show better adjustment in the initial postplacement period when they are more satisfied with the degree of openness they have experienced in their child's placement (Brodzinsky, 1992). The relation between openness and birthparent grief, however, is still unclear. Whereas Blanton and Deschner (1990) found that openness led to prolonged grief following infant relinquishment, Brodzinsky (1992) found that greater openness in adoption was negatively correlated with postplacement grief and depression.

Adoptive parents tend to choose open placement because they believe it is in the best interests of their child (McRoy, Grotevant, & White, 1988). Furthermore, when adoptive parents have more contact with birthparents, they are more understanding and empathic of them, feel greater entitlement to, and are more empathic toward their child, communicate more with the child about adoption, are more secure in knowing about the child's heritage, and are less fearful that birth parents might try to reclaim the child (Berry, 1991; Grotevant, McRoy, Elde, & Fravel, in press; McRoy et al., 1988; Meezan & Shireman, 1985). A drawback of open placements for some adoptive parents, however, is that they do experience the birthparents as overly dependent (Berry, 1991). In addition, when adoptive parents feel less control over the contact between their children and birthparents, or former foster parents, they are less satisfied with the open arrangement and see it as less helpful to their family (Barth & Berry, 1988; Berry, 1991). Finally, in one of the few empirical studies on open adoption that collected data on children, Berry found that open adoption placements were associated with fewer behavior problems in children, as rated by parents, compared to closed adoption placements.

No firm conclusions concerning the outcome associated with open adoption can be drawn, as yet. There is far too much rhetoric and far too few empirical data on the benefits and drawbacks of this form of family life. It is clear, however, that open adoption will certainly pose unique challenges for parents and children. Whether it reduces the psychological risks associated with traditional, confidential adoption remains to be seen. At the very least, open adoption appears to represent a viable option for members of the adoption triad. Like most things in life, it will probably work well for some people, but not for others. The question for the future is the basis for variability in adoption outcome in relation to varying degrees of openness experienced by the parties.

CONCLUSIONS

The practice of adoption has changed dramatically over the past few decades, resulting in considerable variation in family structure among adoptive families. In turn, the task of parenting adopted children has grown extremely complex.

Although adoption is associated with increased risk for psychological problems, especially in school-age children, it should be emphasized that most adoptees and their families, including those involving special needs placements and transracial placements, do very well in terms of various adjustment criteria.

The key to parenting success is good preparation, realistic expectations, effective parenting skills, and adequate supports. Parenting adopted children is a different experience from rearing a biological child (Kirk, 1964). Acknowledging the inherent differences of adoptive family life, creating a rearing environment that is conducive to open and supportive dialogue about these differences, and supporting the child's search for self (Brodzinsky et al., 1992; Schechter & Bertocci, 1990) are critical tasks faced by adoptive parents. When adoptive parents are successful in meeting the challenges of these tasks, as most are, they find the experience of rearing adopted children to be personally rewarding and successful in terms of their children's adjustment.

REFERENCES

Amadio, C., & Deutsch, S. L. (1983). Open adoption: Allowing adopted children to stay in touch with blood relatives. *Journal of Family Law, 22,* 59-93.

Andujo, E. (1988). Ethnic identity of transethnically adopted Hispanic adolescents. *Social Work, 33,* 531-535.

Bachrach, C. A. (1986). Adoptive plans, adopted children, and adoptive mothers. *Journal of Marriage and the Family, 46,* 43-53.

Bachrach, C. A., Adams, P. F., Sambrano, S., & London, K. A. (1989). *Advance data: Adoption in the 1980s* (From Vital and Health Statistics No. 181). Hyattsville, MD: National Center for Health Statistics.

Bachrach, C. A., Stolley, K. S., & London, K. A. (1992). Relinquishment of premarital births: Evidence from national survey data. *Family Planning Perspectives, 24,* 27-32,48.

Baran, A., & Pannor, R. (1993). Perspectives on open adoption. *The Future of Children, 3,* 119-124.

Baran, A., Pannor, R., & Sorosky, A. D. (1976). Open adoption. *Social Work, 22,* 97-100.

Baran, A., Sorosky, A. D., & Pannor, R. (1974). Adoptive parents and the sealed records controversy. *Social Casework, 55,* 531-536.

Barth, R. P. (1987). Adolescent mothers' beliefs about open adoption. *Social Casework, 68,* 323-331.

Barth, R. P. (1988). Disruption in older child adoptions. *Public Welfare, 46,* 23-29.

Barth, R. P., & Berry, M. (1988). *Adoption and disruption.* New York: Aldine de Gruyter.

Belsky, J., Ward, M. J., & Rovine, M. (1986). Prenatal expectations, postnatal experiences, and the transition to parenthood. In R. Ashmore & D. Brodzinsky (Eds.), *Thinking about the family: Views of parents and children* (pp. 119-145). Hillsdale, NJ: Lawrence Erlbaum Associates.

Benet, M. K. (1976). *The politics of adoption.* New York: The Free Press.

Berry, M. (1991). The practice of open adoption: Findings from a study of 1,396 adoptive families. *Children and Youth Services Review, 13,* 379-395.

Berry, M. (1993). Risks and benefits of open adoption. *The Future of Children, 3,* 125-138.

Blanton, T. L., & Deschner, J. (1990). Biological mothers' grief: The postadoptive experience in open versus confidential adoption. *Child Welfare, 69,* 525-535.

Bohman, M. (1970). *Adopted children and their families: A follow-up study of adopted children, their background environment, and adjustment.* Stockholm: Proprius.

Bohman, M., & Sigvardsson, S. (1990). Outcome in adoption: Lessons from longitudinal studies. In D. Brodzinsky & M. Schechter (Eds.), *The psychology of adoption* (pp. 93-106). New York: Oxford University Press.

Bourguignon, J. P. & Watson, K. W. (1988). Areas of difficulty in adoption. In L. Coleman, K. Tilbor, H. Hornby, & C. Boggis (Eds.), *Working with older adoptees* (pp. 7-16). Portland: University of Southern Maine Press.

Bowlby, J. (1973). *Attachment and loss: Vol. 2. Separation.* New York: Basic Books.

Brodzinsky, A. (1992). *The relation of learned helplessness, social support, and avoidance to grief and depression in women who have surrendered an infant for adoption.* Unpublished doctoral dissertation, New York University, New York.

Brodzinsky, D. M. (1983). *Adjustment factors in adoption* (Rep. No. MH34549). Washington, DC: National Institute of Mental Health.

Brodzinsky, D. M. (1987). Adjustment to adoption: A psychosocial perspective. *Clinical Psychology Review, 7,* 25-47.

Brodzinsky, D. M. (1990). A stress and coping model of adoption adjustment. In D. Brodzinsky & M. Schechter (Eds.), *The psychology of adoption* (pp. 3-24). New York: Oxford University Press.

Brodzinsky, D. M. (1993). Long-term outcomes in adoption. *The Future of Children, 3,* 153-166.

Brodzinsky, D. M., & Brodzinsky, A. B. (1992). The impact of family structure on the adjustment of adopted children. *Child Welfare, 71,* 69-75.

Brodzinsky, D. M., Hitt, J. C., & Smith, D. (1993). Impact of parental separation and divorce on adopted and nonadopted children. *American Journal of Orthopsychiatry, 63,* 451-461.

Brodzinsky, D. M., & Huffman, L. (1988). Transition to adoptive parenthood. *Marriage and Family Review, 6,* 267-286.

Brodzinsky, D. M., Radice, C., Huffman, L., & Merkler, K. (1987). Prevalence of clinically significant symptomatology in a nonclinical sample of adopted and nonadopted children. *Journal of Clinical Child Psychology, 16,* 350-356.

Brodzinsky, D. M., & Reeves, L. (1987). *The relationship between parental coping strategies anad children's adjustment to adoption.* Unpublished manuscript.

Brodzinsky, D. M., Schechter, D. E., Braff, A. M., & Singer, L. M. (1984). Psychological and academic adjustment in adopted children. *Journal of Consulting and Clinical Psychology, 52,* 582-590.

Brodzinsky, D. M., Schechter, D. E., & Brodzinsky, A. B. (1986). Children's knowledge of adoption: Developmental changes and implications for adjustment. In R. Ashmore & D. Brodzinsky (Eds.), *Thinking about the family: Views of parents and children* (pp. 205-232). Hillsdale, NJ: Lawrence Erlbaum Associates.

Brodzinsky, D. M., & Schechter, M. D. (Eds.). (1990). *The psychology of adoption.* New York: Oxford University Press.

Brodzinsky, D. M., Schechter, M. D., & Henig, R. M. (1992). *Being adopted: The lifelong search for self.* New York: Doubleday.

Brodzinsky, D. M., Singer, L. M., & Braff, A. M. (1984). Children's understanding of adoption. *Child Development, 55,* 869-878.

Brodzinsky, D. M., & Steiger, C. (1991). Prevalence of adoptees among special education populations. *Journal of Learning Disabilities, 24,* 484-489.

Butler, I. C. (1989). Adopted children, adoptive families: Recognizing differences. In L. Combrinck-Graham (Ed.), *Children in family contexts* (pp. 161-186). New York: Guilford.

Cadoret, R. J. (1990). Biologic perspectives of adoptee adjustment. In D. Brodzinsky & M. Schechter (Eds.), *The psychology of adoption* (pp. 25-41). New York: Oxford University Press.

Carey, W. B., Lipton, W. L., & Myers, R. A. (1974). Temperament in adopted and foster babies. *Child Welfare, 53,* 352-359.

Carter, E. A., & McGoldrick, M. (Eds.). (1980). *The family life cycle.* New York: Gardner Press.

Cohen, N. J., Coyne, J., & Duvall, J. (1993). Adopted and biological children in the clinic: Family, parental, and child characteristics. *Journal of Child Psychology and Psychiatry, 34,* 545-562.

Cole, E. S., & Donley, K. S. (1990). History, values, and placement policy issues in adoption. In D. Brodzinsky & M. Schechter (Eds.), *The psychology of adoption* (pp. 273-294). New York: Oxford University Press.

Derdeyn, A. P. (1990). Foster parent adoption: The legal framework. In D. Brodzinsky & M. Schechter (Eds.), *The psychology of adoption* (pp. 332-347). New York: Oxford University Press.

Deutsch, D. K., Swanson, J. M., Bruell, J. H., Cantwell, D. P., Weinberg, F., & Baren, M. (1982). Overrepresentation of adoptees in children with attention deficit disorder. *Behavior Genetics, 12,* 231-238.

Duvall, E. (1977). *Marriage and family development* (5th ed.). Philadelphia: Lippincott.

Easson, W. (1973, July). Special sexual problems of the adopted adolescent. *Medical Aspects of Human Sexuality, 92-105.*

Elbow, M. (1986). From caregiving to parenting: Family formation with adopted older children. *Social Work, 31,* 366-370.

Fanshel, D. (1972). *Far from the reservation.* Metuchen, NJ: Scarecrow Press.

Feigelman, W., & Silverman, A. R. (1983). *Chosen children: New patterns of adoptive relationships.* New York: Praeger.

Festinger, T. (1986). *Necessary risk: A study of adoptions and disrupted adoptive placements.* Washington, DC: Child Welfare League of America.

Festinger, T. (1990). Adoption disruption: Rates and correlates. In D. Brodzinsky & M. Schechter (Eds.), *The psychology of adoption* (pp. 201-220). New York: Oxford University Press.

Freud, S. (1959). Family romances. In J. Strachey (Ed. and Trans.), *The standard edition of the complete psychological works of Sigmund Freud* (Vol. 9). London: Hogarth Press. (Original work published 1909)

Frisk, M. (1964). Identity problems and confused conceptions of the genetic ego in adopted children during adolescence. *Acta Paedo Psychiatrica, 31,* 6-12.

Fullerton, C. S., Goodrich, W., & Berman, L. B. (1986). Adoption predicts psychiatric treatment resistances in hospitalized adolescents. *Journal of the American Academy of Child and Adolescent Psychiatry, 25,* 542-551.

Glidden, L. M. (1991). Adopted children with developmental disabilities: Post-adoptive family functioning. *Children and Youth Services Review, 13,* 363-378.

Glidden, L. M., Valliere, V. N., & Herbert, S. L. (1988). Adopted children with mental retardation: Positive family impact. *Mental Retardation, 26,* 119-125.

Goldstein, J., Freud, A., & Solnit, A. (1973). *Beyond the best interests of the child.* New York: The Free Press.

Grotevant, H. D., McRoy, R. G., Elde, C. L., & Fravel, D. L. (in press). Adoptive family system dynamics: Variations by level of openness in the adoption. *Family Process.*

Groze, V. (1986). Special-needs adoption. *Children and Youth Services Review, 8,* 363-373.

Groze, V. (1991). Adoption and single parents: A review. *Child Welfare, 70,* 321-332.

Groze, V., & Rosenthal, J. (1991). A structural analysis of families adopting children with special needs. *Families in Society, 72,* 469-481.

Hajal, F., & Rosenberg, E. B. (1991). The family life cycle in adoptive families. *American Journal of Orthopsychiatry, 61,* 78-85.

Hodges, J. (1989). Aspects of the relationship to self and objects in early maternal deprivation and adoption. *Bulletin of the Anna Freud Centre, 12,* 5-27.

Hodges, J., & Tizard, B. (1989). Social and family relationships of ex-institutional adolescents. *Journal of Child Psychology and Psychiatry, 30,* 77-97.

Hoopes, J. L. (1982). *Prediction in child development: A longitudinal study of adoptive and nonadoptive families.* New York: Child Welfare League of America.

Hoopes, J. L. (1990). Adoption and identity formation. In D. Brodzinsky & M. Schechter (Eds.), *The psychology of adoption* (pp. 144-166). New York: Oxford University Press.

Isabella, R. A., & Belsky, J. (1985). Marital change during the transition to parenthood and security of infant–parent attachment. *Journal of Family Issues, 6,* 505-522.

Johnson, F., & Fein, E. (1991). The concept of attachment: Applications to adoption. *Child and Youth Services Review, 13,* 397-412.

Kadushin, A. (1980). *Child welfare services* (3rd ed.). New York: Macmillan.

Kagan, R. M., & Reid, W. J. (1986). Critical factors in the adoption of emotionally disturbed youths. *Child Welfare, 65,* 63-73.

Katz, L. (1986). Parental stress and factors for success in older child adoption. *Child Welfare, 65,* 569-578.

Kaye, K. (1990). Acknowledgment or rejection of differences? In D. Brodzinsky & M. Schechter (Eds.), *The psychology of adoption* (pp. 121-143). New York: Oxford University Press.

Kirk, H. D. (1964). *Shared fate.* New York: The Free Press.

Kirk, H. D. (1981). *Adoptive kinship—A modern institution in need of reform.* Toronto: Butterworth.

Kotsopoulos, S., Cote, A., Joseph, L., Pentland, N., Stavrakaki, C., Sheahan, M., & Oke, L. (1988). Psychiatric disorders in adopted children. *American Journal of Orthopsychiatry, 58,* 608-612.

Kotsopoulos, S., Walker, S., Copping, W., Cote, A., & Stavrakaki, C. (1993). A psychiatric follow-up study of adoptees. *Canadian Journal of Psychiatry, 38,* 391-396.

Kraus, J. (1978). Family structure as a factor in the adjustment of adopted children. *British Journal of Social Work, 8,* 327-337.

Lambert, L., & Streather, J. (1980). *Children in changing families.* London: National Children's Bureau.

Levy-Shiff, R., Bar, O., & Har-Even, D. (1990). Psychological adjustment of adoptive parents-to-be. *American Journal of Orthopsychiatry, 60,* 258-267.

Levy-Shiff, R., Goldschmidt, I., & Har-Even, D. (1991). Transition to parenthood in adoptive families. *Developmental Psychology, 27,* 131-140.

Lifton, B. J. (1979). *Lost and found.* New York: Dial Press.

Lindholm, B. W., & Touliatos, J. (1980). Psychological adjustment of adopted and nonadopted children. *Psychological Reports, 46,* 307-310.

Loehlin, L. C., Willerman, L., & Horn, J. M. (1982). Personality resemblances between unwed mothers and their adopted-away offspring. *Journal of Personality and Social Psychology, 42,* 1089-1099.

Loehlin, L. C., Willerman, L., & Horn, J. M. (1985). Personality resemblances in adoptive families when the children are late-adolescent or adult. *Journal of Personality and Social Psychology, 48,* 376-392.

Main, M., Kaplan, N., & Cassidy, J. (1985). Security in infancy, childhood, and adulthood: A move to the level of representation. In T. Bretherton & E. Waters (Eds.), *Growing points in attachment theory and research. Monographs of the Society for Research in Child Development, 50*(Serial No. 209), 66-104.

Marquis, K. S., & Detweiler, R. A. (1985). Does adoption mean different? An attributional analysis. *Journal of Personality and Social Psychology, 48,* 1054-1066.

Maughan, B., & Pickles, A. (1990). Adopted and illegitimate children growing up. In L. Robins & M. Rutter (Eds.), *Straight and devious pathways from childhood to adulthood* (pp. 36-61). New York: Cambridge University Press.

McDonald, T. P., Lieberman, A. A., Partridge, S., & Hornby, H. (1991). Assessing the role of agency services in reducing adoption disruptions. *Children and Youth Services Review, 13,* 425-438.

McKenzie, J. K. (1993). Adoption of children with special needs. *The Future of Children, 3,* 62-76.

McRoy, R. G., Grotevant, H. D., & White, K. L. (1988). *Openness in adoption: New practices, new issues.* New York: Praeger.

McRoy, R. G., & Zurcher, L. A. (1983). *Transracial and inracial adoptees.* Springfield, IL: Thomas.

Mech, E. V. (1973). Adoption: A policy perspective. In B. Caldwell & H.N. Ricciuti (Eds.), *Review of child development research* (Vol. 3, pp. 467-507). Chicago: University of Chicago Press.

National Committee for Adoption. (1989). *1989 adoption factbook.* Washington, DC: Author.

Nelson, K. A. (1985). *On the frontier of adoption: A study of special-needs adoptive families.* New York: Child Welfare League of America.

Newman, J. L., Roberts, L. R., & Syre, C. R. (1993). Concepts of family among children and adolescents: Effect of cognitive level, gender, and family structure. *Developmental Psychology, 29,* 951-962.

Nickman, S. L. (1985). Losses in adoption: The need for dialogue. *Psychoanalytic Study of the Child, 40,* 365-398.

Norvell, M. , & Guy, R. F. (1977). A comparison of self-concept in adopted and nonadopted adolescencts. *Adolescence, 12,* 443-448.

Partridge, S., Hornby, H., & McDonald, T. (1986). *Legacies of loss—visions of gain: An inside look at adoption disruption.* Portland: University of Southern Maine Press.

Piersma, H. L. (1987). Adopted children and inpatient psychiatric treatment: A retrospective study. *The Psychiatric Hospital, 18,* 153-158.

Plomin, R., & DeFries, J. (1985). *Origins of individual differences in infancy: The Colorado adoption project.* Orlando, FL: Academic Press.

Raynor, L. (1980). *The adopted child comes of age.* London: George Allen and Unwin.

Reitz, M., & Watson, K. W. (1992). *Adoption and the family system.* New York: Guilford.

Rogeness, G. A., Hoppe, S. K., Macedo, C. A., Fisher, C., & Harris, W. (1988). Psychopathology in hospitalized adopted children. *Journal of the American Academy of Child and Adolescent Psychiatry, 27,* 628-631.

Rosenthal, J. A. (1993). Outcomes of adoption of children with special needs. *The Future of Children, 3,* 77-88.

Rosenthal, J. A., & Groze, V. K. (1990). Special-needs adoptions: A study of intact families. *Social Service Review, 64,* 475-505.

Rosenthal, J. A., Schmidt, D. & Conner, J. (1988). Predictors of special needs adoption disruption: An exploratory study. *Children and Youth Services, 10,* 101-117.

Sachdev, P. (1989). *Unlocking the adoption files.* Lexington, MA: Lexington.

Sandmaier, M. (1988). *When love is not enough.* Washington, DC: Child Welfare League of America.

Sandven, K., & Resnick, M. D. (1990). Informal adoption among Black adolescent mothers. *American Journal of Orthopsychiatry, 60,* 210-224.

Sants, H. J. (1964). Genealogical bewilderment in children with substitute parents. *British Journal of Medical Psychology, 37,* 133-141.

Schechter, M. D. (1960). Observations on adopted children. *Archives of General Psychiatry, 3,* 21-32.

Schechter, M. D. (1970). About adoptive parents. In E. J. Anthony & T. Benedek (Eds.), *Parenthood: Its psychology and psychopathology* (pp. 105-121). Boston: Little, Brown.

Schechter, M. D., & Bertocci, D. (1990). The meaning of the search. In D. Brodzinsky & M. Schechter (Eds.), *The psychology of adoption* (pp. 62-92). New York: Oxford University Press.

Schechter, M. D., Carlson, P., Simmons, J., & Work, H. (1964). Emotional problems in the adoptee. *Archives of General Psychiatry, 10,* 37-46.

Shapiro, C. H. (1988). *Infertility and pregnancy loss.* San Francisco: Jossey-Bass.

Silver, L. B. (1989). Frequency of adoption in children and adolescents with learning disabilities. *Journal of Learning Disabilities, 22,* 325-328.

Silverman, A. R. (1993). Outcomes of transracial adoption. *The Future of Children, 3,* 104-118.

Silverman, A. R., & Feigelman, W. (1990). Adjustment in interracial adoptees: An overview. In D. Brodzinsky & M. Schechter (Eds.), *The psychology of adoption* (pp. 187-200). New York: Oxford University Press.

Singer, L. M., Brodzinsky, D. M., Ramsay, D., Steir, M., & Waters, E. (1985). Mother–infant attachment in adoptive families. *Child Development, 56,* 1543-1551.

Smith, D., & Brodzinsky, D. M. (1994). Stress and coping in adoption: A developmental study. *Journal of Clinical Child Psychology, 23,* 91-99.

Sorosky, A. D., Baran, A., & Pannor, R. (1975). Identity conflicts in adoptees. *American Journal of Orthopsychiatry, 45,* 18-27.

Sorosky, A. D., Baran, A., & Pannor, R. (1976). The effects of the sealed record in adoption. *American Journal of Psychiatry, 133,* 900-904.

Sorosky, A. D., Baran, A., & Pannor, R. (1978). *The adoption triangle.* New York: Doubleday.

Stein, L. M., & Hoopes, J. L. (1985). *Identity formation in the adopted adolescent.* New York: Child Welfare League of America.

Stolley, K. S. (1993). Statistics on adoption in the United States. *The Future of Children, 3,* 26-42.

Thompson, L. A., & Plomin, R. (1988). The sequenced inventory of communication development: An adoption study of two- and three-year-olds. *International Journal of Behavioral Development, 11,* 219-231.

Tizard, B. (1991). Intercountry adoption: A review of the evidence. *Journal of Child Psychology and Psychiatry, 32,* 743-756.

Triseliotis, J., & Hill, M. (1990). Contrasting adoption, foster care, and residential rearing. In D. Brodzinsky & M. Schechter (Eds.), *The psychology of adoption* (pp. 107-120). New York: Oxford University Press.

U.S. Immigration and Naturalization Service. (1991). *Statistical yearbook of the Immigration and Naturalization Service.* Washington, DC: U.S. Government Printing Office.

Valentine, D., Conway, P., & Randolph, J. (1988). Placement disruptions: Perspectives of adoptive parents. *Journal of Social Work and Human Sexuality, 6,* 133-153.

Verhulst, F. C., Althaus, M., & Versluis-Den Bieman, H. J. (1992). Damaging backgrounds: Later adjustment of international adoptees. *Journal of the American Academy of Child and Adolescent Psychiatry, 31,* 518-524.

Warren, S. B. (1992). Lower threshold for referral for psychiatric treatment for adopted adolescents. *Journal of the American Academy of Child and Adolescent Psychiatry, 31,* 512-517.

Westhues, A., & Cohen, J. S. (1990). Preventing disruptions of special-needs adoptions. *Child Welfare, 69,* 141-155.

Wieder, H. (1977). On being told of adoption. *Psychoanalytic Quarterly, 46,* 1-22.

Wierzbicki, M. (1993). Psychological adjustment of adoptees: A meta-analysis. *Journal of Clinical Child Psychology, 22,* 447-454.

Yarrow, L. J., & Goodwin, M. S. (1973). The immediate impact of separation: Reactions of infants to a change in mother figure. In L. J. Stone, H. T. Smith, & L. T. Murphy (Eds.), *The competent infant* (pp. 1032-1040). New York: Basic Books.

Yarrow, L. J., Goodwin, M. S., Manheimer, H., & Milowe, I. D. (1973). Infancy experiences and cognitive and personality development at 10 years. In L. J. Stone, H. T. Smith, & L. T. Murphy (Eds.), *The competent infant* (pp. 1274-1281). New York: Basic Books.

Zill, N. (1985, April). *Behavior and learning problems among adopted children: Findings from a U.S. national survey of child health.* Paper presented at the meeting of the Society for Research in Child Development, Toronto.

9

Parenting in Divorced and Remarried Families

E. Mavis Hetherington
University of Virginia
Margaret M. Stanley-Hagan
University of North Carolina, Charlotte

INTRODUCTION

After a period of rapid increase during the late 1960s and 1970s, both divorce and remarriage rates have remained relatively stable during the past decade. Still, approximately 48 percent of all couples in first marriages divorce (U.S. Bureau of the Census, 1992), and an additional 17 percent separate but do not divorce (Castro-Martin & Bumpass, 1989). Most divorced adults remarry, and today almost half of all new marriages are remarriages (U.S. Bureau of the Census, 1992). African-American couples have a divorce rate even higher than Whites, are more likely to separate but not go through a legal divorce, have a more prolonged separation before divorce, and are less likely to remarry (Castro- Martin & Bumpass, 1989). To put the figures in perspective, approximately 28 percent of all families are divorced single-parent families and 14 percent of two-parent families are actually stepfamilies. It has been estimated that between 40 percent and 50 percent of all children in the United States will spend time in a single-parent home (Glick & Lin, 1986), and most of these children will also experience life in a stepfamily. Thus, divorce and remarriage are non-normative events only when one considers that parents and children are coping with repeated family reorganizations in a social ecology that has just begun to establish norms and provide supports for families in transition; that is, families that differ from the *traditional* nuclear model.

As the numbers of single-parent and remarried families increased dramatically through the late 1960s and 1970s understandably so did interest in the adjustment of family members, especially children, within these families. Researchers initially approached the study of divorced and remarried families with the expectation that most parents and children were doomed to troubled lives marked by deviant behavior and psychopathology. This pathogenic or deficit model was sustained by evidence that individual adjustment and family relationships in divorced and remarried families often differ from those observed in nondivorced families and with evidence that children from "broken homes" are overrepresented in antisocial and delinquent populations. Many of the early studies, however, were methodologically limited. Cross-sectional studies on small nonrepresentative and clinical samples were common. Often, critical factors such as the developmental statuses of parents and children, time since transition, the availability of extended family and extrafamilial supports, and preexisting pathology were not examined. Even with such limitations, early work revealed not only great diversity in the adjustment of both parents and children from divorced and remarried families, but great diversity in the complex interacting factors that facilitate or impede coping and adjustment.

Contemporary research has begun to focus on these variations in adjustment and the life experiences and family processes that contribute to this diversity (Bray, 1992; Hetherington, 1988, 1991). Moreover, investigators have all but abandoned the pathogenic model in favor of developmental, family systems, and ecological models. From a developmental perspective family members are aging and confronting changing normative developmental tasks. Family members may be more sensitive to the stresses associated with a marital transition when a transition occurs concurrently with a normative developmental transition such as entry into adolescence. In addition, certain developmental changes such as those associated with adolescence may trigger latent delayed effects of divorce and remarriage. However, the most marked disruptions in personal adjustment and family process and reported distress are found in the first few years following a marital transition with the gradual establishment of new roles and relationships and a new family homeostasis emerging over time (Bray, 1992; Hetherington, 1991, 1993; Kitson & Holmes, 1992). At the center of the family-systems perspective is the view of the family as an interdependent dynamic system wherein changes in family structure or in any family member or family subsystem prompts changes throughout the system. Thus, this perspective has led to an examination of relationships and adjustments within and between marital, parent–child, and sibling subsystems as well as less frequently to an appraisal of family functioning at the level of the whole family system (Bray & Berger, 1993). The ecological perspective provides a framework for assessing the roles of contextual and extrafamilial factors (e.g., the peer group, educational institutions, employment, extended family and extrafamilial supports, legal and social norms) in explaining individual adjustment and family process differences. Although divorce and remarriage may confront parents and children with new stresses and challenges, in many families it also offers an escape from lonely, unsatisfying, or conflictual family relationships and an opportunity for more fulfilling family relationships and personal growth. Multidimensional models combining aspects of developmental, family systems, and ecological models can provide a framework more appropriate for identifying complex circumstances that influence and predict diverse individual and family outcomes.

Most children experience emotional and behavioral problems in the months immediately following parental divorce that can reemerge or intensify following parental remarriage (see Allison & Furstenberg, 1989; Camara & Resnick, 1988; Forehand et al., 1991; Guidubaldi, Perry, & Nastasi, 1987; Hetherington, Clingempeel et al., 1992; Hetherington, Cox, & Cox, 1982, 1985; Wallerstein & Kelly, 1980). Although these problems diminish with time, children from divorced and remarried families on the average exhibit more behavior problems and are less academically, socially, and psychologically well adjusted than those in nondivorced families (Amato & Keith, 1991a, 1991b; Hetherington et al., 1992). Furthermore, in adolescence and young adulthood problems in adjustment, family relations, and the formation of stable intimate relationships can emerge or intensify (Amato & Keith, 1991b; Bray & Berger, 1993; Hetherington, 1993; Hetherington, Clingempeel et al., 1992; Zill, Morrison, & Coiro, 1993). It is important to note that although severe psychological and behavioral problems are two to three times more prevalent in children from divorced and remarried families than from nondivorced families, the vast majority of children (70 percent to 80 percent) in the long run do not show severe or enduring problems in response to their parents' marital transitions and emerge as reasonably competent and well-adjusted individuals (Hetherington, 1993; Zill et al., 1993).

Just as in nondivorced homes, children's adjustment in divorced, single-parent, and remarried households is associated with the quality of the parenting environment regardless of the number of family reorganizations or the time since each transition (Baumrind, 1991; Fine & Kurdek, 1992;

Forgatch, Patterson, & Ray, in press; Hetherington, 1991, 1993; Hetherington et al., 1992). Parenting quality not only affects children directly, but modifies the impact of many ecological stressors associated with family transitions (Forgatch, Patterson, & Ray, in press; Hetherington et al., 1992; Lempers, Clark-Lempers, & Simons, 1989; Patterson, 1991). Children adjust best when the custodial parent is authoritative. An authoritative parent is warm, supportive, responsive to the child's needs, open in communication, monitors the children's activities, and exerts firm, consistent control (Hetherington et al., 1992; Steinberg, Mounts, Lamborn, & Dornbusch, 1991). Uniquely important to the adjustment of children in divorced and remarried homes is the degree to which divorced mothers and fathers are able to establish and maintain cooperative, shared parenting relationships and the quality of children's relationships with stepparents.

This chapter examines the parenting of divorced and remarried mothers and fathers and stepparents. Of special interest are: (1) parenting during the critical months immediately following marital transitions, (2) changes in parenting that occur as families restabilize over time, and (3) the importance and possibility of maintaining cooperative parenting relationships between exspouses. Special attention is given to the variations found in both parenting skills and the complex individual, family, and ecological factors that affect parenting.

It should be noted that following divorce, 86 percent of mothers retain physical custody of their children (U. S. Bureau of the Census, 1992). Only 14 percent of the children live with their fathers. It follows then that most remarried families (85 percent) are mother-custody, stepfather families. Not surprisingly, researchers have focused most of their attention on mother-custody divorced families and stepfather families and thus, comparatively little is known about parent–child relationships in father-custody divorced families or stepmother families. The discussion presented here reflects this balance. An overview of the empirical results of studies of parenting in divorced families is presented first with separate emphases given to parenting of custodial mothers and fathers, parenting of noncustodial mothers and fathers, and the qualities and impacts of different types of coparenting relationships. Parenting in remarried families is presented next including discussions of parenting of custodial and noncustodial parents and stepparents and the interdependence between the marital and parent–child relationships. The final section includes a discussion of individual, family, and contextual factors that contribute to the diversity found in parenting skills and parent–child relationships.

PARENTING IN DIVORCED FAMILIES

For all families, separation and divorce set in motion a series of changes that are potentially stressful for family members. In the months immediately following divorce, families are frequently faced with radically changed financial circumstances that can result in shifts in residences and new or second jobs or increased work hours. House and childcare tasks previously performed by two adults are now the responsibility of the single custodial parent. Family environments are often chaotic as household routines and roles break down. Children may express their confusion, anger, and resentment at the changes in the family by being demanding, noncompliant, withdrawn, and aggressive.

The stresses associated with these changes place both parents at risk for psychological and physical disorders that may interfere with their ability to be competent parents (Chase-Lansdale & Hetherington, 1990; Hetherington et al., 1982; Kitson & Holmes, 1992; Wallerstein & Kelly, 1980). During and after marital dissolution, adults often suffer anger, anxiety, and depression and exhibit impulsive and antisocial behavior. It is not unusual for custodial parents to report feeling optimistic about their abilities to manage single-parent demands one moment only to doubt their competence the next. Moreover, psychological stress can be exacerbated by reoccurring health problems. There is evidence that the stresses associated with marital disruption can lead to an altered immune system that in turn makes the divorced parent more susceptible to chronic and acute medical problems (Kiecolt-Glaser et al., 1987).

Despite the disequilibrium characteristic of the period before and immediately after divorce, families do attain a new homeostasis and usually do so within 2 years. However, divorced adults may continue to feel more depressed and more anxious than their nondivorced counterparts, and some custodial parents may continue to find single parenting stressful (Hetherington, 1993). In spite of this, most restabilized single-parent families function reasonably well provided they are not faced with sustained or new adversities.

Custodial Mothers

A sense of positive well-being is a strong predictor of the postdivorce adjustment of single, custodial mothers (Thiriot & Buckner, 1991). However, this sense of well-being depends on their sense of financial security and employment satisfaction, neutral if not positive relationships with their exspouses, a perception that their parenting skills are positive and effective, and most notably on the formation of a new, intimate support relationship (Hetherington et al., 1982; Kitson & Holmes, 1992; Thiriot & Buckner, 1991). Unfortunately, for most new single mothers, stressful disruptions in their financial and employment statuses as well as in their relation ships with their exspouses and children are common and loneliness is a common complaint of both divorced custodial mothers and fathers.

In contrast to noncustodial fathers who retain 90 percent of their predivorce income, custodial mothers retain only 67 percent (McLanahan & Booth, 1989). Moreover, the financial status of single-mothers is deteriorating rather than improving (Rowe, 1991), and remarriage is the most frequent route out of economic need for divorced women. Only 63 percent of custodial mothers with children under age 21 are awarded child support, and of these only half receive full or regular payments (U.S. Bureau of the Census, 1992). Adding to the stress of a significant drop in spendable income is job instability. Compared to parents in two-parent households, single custodial mothers are three times more likely to be unemployed during the first critical years following divorce, and those who are employed are more likely to experience changes in employment (Garfinkel & McLanahan, 1986). The drop in spendable income and lack of financial support from the children's father combined with job instability create feelings of financial distress that may be associated with inept parenting (Forgatch et al., in press).

Concerns about financial settlements and child support can also fuel ongoing conflict between exspouses. Disagreements about finances and childrearing practices are common, and many divorcing adults report that the conflict evident before and during the divorce is maintained or escalates after the divorce (Hetherington et al., 1982; Maccoby, Depner, & Mnookin, 1990; Tschann, Johnston, Kline, & Wallerstein, 1991). Thus, a positive or even neutral relationship between former spouses is attained by few. When conflict between mothers and fathers is high, fathers are more likely to disengage from parenting and to stop paying child support leaving mothers with total parenting plus financial responsibilities (Seltzer, 1991).

Parenting is a challenge when there are two involved parents. The problems in parenting may be exacerbated when custodial mothers suddenly find themselves alone as they juggle financial, housework, and childcare responsibilities (Hetherington et al., 1982). When emotionally and physically stressed mothers face children who are angry, depressed, noncompliant, and demanding, parenting is particularly difficult. Thus, it is common for the mothers to experience an initial period of diminished parenting characterized by irritability, unresponsiveness, poor monitoring and control, and erratic and sometimes punitive discipline (Camara & Resnick, 1988; Hetherington et al., 1982; Wallerstein, Corbin, & Lewis, 1988). Moreover, mother–child relationships are often conflicted and escalating, mutually coercive interchanges are common, particularly with sons (Hetherington et al., 1982).

Even when divorced households have restabilized they may still confront more negative life events and be more chaotic than nondivorced households, and many mothers report that the term *task overload* continues to be an accurate description of their lives (Hetherington et al., 1982; Stolberg, Camplair, Currier, & Wells, 1987). However, by 2 years following divorce three fourths of divorced women report that they are happier in their new situation than in the last year of their marriage, and most, in spite of the stresses, find rearing children alone easier than with a disengaged, undermining, or acrimonious spouse (Hetherington, 1993). Furthermore, in addition to perceiving themselves as more able parents than mothers in conflictual, unsatisfying marriages, divorced women on the average are less depressed, show less state anxiety, drink less, and have fewer health problems than those in unhappy, acrimonious, or emotionally disengaged marriages.

Many divorced women comment on the independence, self-fulfillment, and new competencies they developed in response to the challenges of divorce and being a single parent (Hetherington, 1993). These changes are reflected in improvements in mother–daughter relationships with divorced mothers and their preadolescent daughters often developing close, harmonious, companionate relationships (Hetherington 1989, 1991). As daughters enter adolescence, however, conflict between divorced mothers and daughters may reemerge especially if the daughter becomes sexually active or becomes involved in antisocial activities. Divorced mothers who earlier have granted their children considerable autonomy may attempt ineffectually to increase the monitoring and control of their adolescent daughters' behaviors (Hetherington, 1993; Hetherington, Clingempeel et al., 1992). In contrast, the poor monitoring and control and coercive interactions characteristic of early mother–son interactions may endure and eventually lead to mutual mother–son distancing in adolescence (Hetherington, 1993; Hetherington et al., 1992). About one third of adolescents in divorced and remarried families disengage and maintain physical and emotional distance from their families. Sometimes these adolescents form a close relationship with a friend's family, teacher, coach, or other relative such as an aunt or grandparent and this may be a successful solution to a difficult conflictual family environment. However, adolescents, especially boys, who do disengage from their families and have no close relationship with a caring adult are more susceptible to the influences of delinquent peers (Hetherington, 1991; Steinberg, 1987).

Even after the family has attained a new equilibrium, custodial mothers, especially mothers of sons, on the average report more childrearing stress than those in nondivorced families (Colletta, 1981; Hetherington, 1993). The most sustained problems for them appear to be in the areas of monitoring and control, and these problems are to some extent associated with the precocious autonomy and greater power of children in divorced families (Bank, Forgatch, Patterson, & Fetrow, 1991; Hetherington, 1991, 1993; Hetherington, Clingempeel et al., 1992; Hetherington et al., 1982, 1985; Maccoby & Mnookin, 1992).

Weiss (1979) commented on the fact that children in divorced families grow up faster. Girls are assigned more household and childcare tasks and responsibilities, and boys receive significantly less adult supervision (Hetherington, 1991). The assignment of responsibilities is sometimes associated with unusual social competence in daughters. However, if the task demands are age inappropriate or beyond the capabilities of the child, it also may be associated with low self-esteem, anxiety, and depression. In addition, children in divorced families have more power in family decision making, and are less compliant and responsive to their mothers' commands (Hetherington, 1988). This accelerated independence often makes the challenges associated with normative family realignments and autonomy seeking in early adolescence or the move into a stepfamily difficult.

Custodial Fathers

Since the mid-1970s, many states have changed custody laws to eliminate gender biases in custody decisions and to encourage if not mandate joint custody. Despite these changes and despite evidence that fathers are no less competent parents than mothers (Warshak, 1986) and that they can play a positive role in the postdivorce adjustment of their children, few fathers (13 percent) are awarded physical custody of their children at the time of divorce (Emery, 1988). A distinction must be made between joint legal custody, wherein both parents are held responsible for the welfare of their children regardless of residency arrangements, and joint physical custody, wherein the children alternately reside with both parents. Although both joint legal and physical custody have become more common over the past decade, even when joint physical custody is awarded, most children reside almost full-time with their mothers (Hetherington & Stanley-Hagan, 1986; Maccoby & Mnookin, 1992;

Shrier, Simring, Shapiro, Grief, & Lindenthal, 1991). The implication is that many physical custody decisions are made by the divorcing parents, not the courts, and there is evidence that these decisions may reflect concerns fathers themselves have about assuming full-time parenting (Maccoby & Mnookin, 1992). Many fathers report that they would like sole or joint physical custody of their children but choose not to pursue it because: (1) They believe their children would benefit more from the closer relationship children are perceived to have with their mothers, (2) fathers' job responsibilities are not flexible enough to accommodate the time demands of single parenthood, and (3) fathers' want to avoid exposing their children to prolonged negative custody battles (Hetherington & Stanley-Hagan, 1986; Maccoby, Buchanan, Mnookin, & Dornbusch, 1993).

As might be expected given their numbers, relatively little is known about the quality of the relationships those fathers who are awarded physical custody have with their children. On the one hand, newly divorced custodial fathers and mothers appear to share many of the same stresses and concerns. Fathers report feeling overloaded and socially isolated and worried about their parenting competence (Hetherington & Stanley-Hagan, 1986). On the other hand, custodial fathers have more economic resources and more extensive support systems than custodial mothers and once their families have restabilized, custodial fathers report better relations and fewer problems with their children (Furstenberg, 1988).

Researchers have found differences between the parenting of custodial fathers and that of custodial mothers. For example, fathers are more likely to assign household responsibilities to children than are mothers (Chase-Lansdale & Hetherington, 1990). In addition, in contrast to custodial mothers, custodial fathers do not have similar problems in control and discipline, although they have been found to be less competent monitors of their children's activities (Buchanan, Maccoby, & Dornbusch, 1992). The poorer monitoring may help to explain recent evidence that adolescents living with divorced fathers are more involved in delinquent activities than those living with divorced mothers (Buchanan et al., 1992; Maccoby & Mnookin, 1992).

How well custodial fathers actually fare with single parenthood appears to depend on whether they sought custody originally or assumed custody because the mother was incompetent or unwilling to parent (Hanson, 1988; Mendes, 1976a, 1976b). Custody seekers have been found to be more involved and able parents. However, fathers who seek custody tend to have had close relationships with their children prior to divorce, and the quality of this relationship may carry over into the new family unit (Parke & Tinsley, 1984). Moreover, custody seekers usually have more available resources and supports, and are more likely to be parenting older children and adolescents (Hetherington & Stanley-Hagan, 1986).

One focus of research has been whether or not a child adjusts better when in the custody of a parent of the same sex (Peterson & Zill, 1986; Warshak, 1986; Zaslow, 1988). Compared to daughters who live with their mothers following divorce, daughters in father- custody seem to have more adjustment problems, and fathers report more difficulty in dealing with adolescent daughters than adolescent sons (Camara & Resnick, 1988; Lee, Burkam, Zimilies, & Ladewski, 1994; Maccoby et al., 1993; Peterson & Zill, 1986; Santrock & Warshak, 1979). In contrast, the coercive cycles characteristic of mother–son interactions are rare between custodial fathers and sons. School-age boys in father custody appear to have higher self-esteems, to be more socially competent, and to have fewer behavior problems. However, these boys have been found to lack an openness in communication and expression of emotions that may be associated with lack of contact with a female role model (Santrock & Warshak, 1979). Although both sons and daughters report feeling close to their custodial parent regardless of whether that parent is the mother or the father (Hetherington, Clingempeel et al., 1992; Maccoby et al., 1993; White, Brinkerhoff, & Booth, 1985), recent evidence indicates that the adolescents' adjustment is more predictable from the parenting of a custodial parent of the same than of the opposite sex (Gunnoe, 1993). This suggestion of greater salience of a custodial parent of the same sex warrants further investigation. However, regardless of custody arrangements, children benefit from living with an authoritative parent in a family environment devoid of interparental conflict.

Noncustodial Parents

Although custodial parents are more salient than noncustodial parents in the adjustment of children, noncustodial parents who remain involved can contribute to their children's development.

Noncustodial fathers. Most noncustodial fathers become increasingly uninvolved over time (Furstenberg, 1988; Hetherington et al., 1982). Only 25 percent of children see their fathers once a week or more, and over 33 percent do not see their fathers at all or see them only a few times a year (Seltzer, 1991). For those noncustodial fathers who remain involved, a pattern of intermittent and infrequent visitations appears to affect the type of relationship they have with their children. They are more likely to be permissive than authoritative parents and to assume more of a recreational, companionate role than the role of teacher or disciplinarian (Furstenberg & Cherlin, 1991).

Recognizing the important roles fathers can play particularly if they can establish an authoritative relationship with their child and a cooperative coparenting relationship with their exspouse, researchers have tried to identify the factors associated with continued involvement. Fathers are more likely to remain involved with sons than daughters and with older children and adolescents than with younger children (Hetherington, 1989). Fathers are likely to reduce contact if they remarry or if they or their former wives relocate geographically (Gunnoe, 1993). Interestingly, although the levels of predivorce involvement with children have been found to predict whether or not a father will initially seek custody, predivorce involvement has been found to be associated with postdivorce involvement for custodial fathers but not for noncustodial fathers (Furstenberg, 1988; Hetherington, Stanley-Hagan, & Anderson, 1989). Some noncustodial fathers who are active parents prior to divorce find the lack of daily contact and the strain of intermittent visits painful and eventually disengage. Others who are less involved prior to divorce may be jolted by the fear of losing their children and become active, involved parents.

Regardless of child age or gender, geographic proximity, and the quality of predivorce relationships with their children, the best predictor of continued paternal involvement appears to be the father's relationship with his exspouse and his perceived control in decisions about the child's activities and well-being (Braver et al., 1993). Fathers are more likely to report being dissatisfied with parenting and to disengage when the legal wranglings with their exwives at the time of divorce were stressful (Buehler, Hogan, Robinson, & Levy, 1985), when interparental conflict remains high, when these conflicts center around disagreements over childrearing practices, and when they believe they have little say in their children's upbringing.

There is some evidence that suggests that noncustodial fathers may not be dropping out as much as they have in the past. Maccoby and her colleagues (1993) proposed that the recent changes in custody laws and changing gender norms are not only encouraging continued paternal contact and involvement but are beginning to make such involvement easier. More divorcing fathers are searching for ways to remain an active part of their children's lives.

Noncustodial mothers. Even less is known about the behavior of noncustodial mothers than of noncustodial fathers. What information there is indicates that noncustodial mothers have about twice as much contact with their children as do noncustodial fathers (Furstenberg, Nord, Peterson, & Zill, 1985; Zill, 1988) and that this contact seems to decline less over time or following the remarriage of the custodial father (Furstenberg & Nord, 1987; Gunnoe, 1993; Santrock, Sitterle, & Warshak, 1988; Santrock & Warshak, 1979). Although the research is not entirely consistent in this regard, increasing evidence indicates that mothers like fathers are more apt to maintain contact with sons than daughters (Gunnoe, 1993; Hetherington et al., 1982).

In contrast to noncustodial fathers, noncustodial mothers also maintain more of a parental role and are more likely to arrange their living situations to facilitate visits from their children (Furstenberg & Nord, 1987). Although notably poorer at monitoring and controlling their children's behaviors than nondivorced mothers, noncustodial mothers show greater monitoring and control than do noncustodial fathers (Gunnoe, 1993). They also are more sensitive to their children's emotional needs, communicate better, are more supportive in times of stress, and are more knowledgeable about and interested in their children's activities (Furstenberg & Nord, 1987; Gunnoe, 1993). Furthermore, compared to the impact contact with noncustodial fathers has on children's adjustment, contact with noncustodial mothers has been more strongly and consistently found to be positively associated with the adjustment of children, especially that of daughters (Brand, Clingempeel, & Bowen-Woodward, 1988; Gunnoe, 1993; Zill, 1988).

Shared Parenting

The move toward joint custody and facilitating visitation is based on the assumptions that continued contact with both parents is desirable and that parents can attain some modicum of cooperative, constructive parenting that puts the well-being of the child before their own feeling of acrimony or resentment (Camara & Resnick, 1988; Bray & Berger, 1993; Furstenberg, 1990; Maccoby et al., 1990). The superiority of such joint arrangements over sole physical custody measured in terms of positive child adjustment and parental satisfaction has not been clearly demonstrated (Camara & Resnick, 1988; Debner & Bray, 1993; Furstenberg, 1990; Maccoby et al., 1990). Children who alternate between mother and father residences fare better when the parents live in close geographic proximity so that the children's school and peer group memberships remain stable and when in the absence of a cooperative relationship, parents are not acrimonious (Hetherington & Stanley-Hagan, 1986).

Parents who report being satisfied with shared physical custody also report that: (1) They had positive relationships with their former spouses, particularly over parenting issues, prior to divorce; (2) there is congruence between their childrearing practices; (3) neither residence is considered to be the children's *primary* residence and the schedule for the children's shifts in residence is formalized; and (4) there was little conflict prior to the divorce and low to moderate conflict since (Benjamin & Irving, 1990). Dissatisfied parents share few if any of these characteristics and are likely to believe that they were coerced into the arrangement by the courts or the other parent. Mothers may have acquiesced out of guilt at denying their children access to their fathers or out of fear of loss of their children in a custody battle, and some parents are likely to have believed that a shared parenting relationship that necessitates continued contact might lead to a reconciliation.

Contemporary researchers are extending the definition of shared or coparenting to include the degree to which parents remain involved and work together to provide mutual parenting support and a more stable parenting environment for their children regardless of physical custody arrangements. Maccoby and her colleagues (1990, 1993) identified three parenting patterns that can be used to describe shared parenting in sole or joint custody families. *Cooperative parents* talk with each other about their children, avoid arguments, and support rather than undermine each other's parenting efforts. *Conflicted parents* talk with each other about their children but with criticism, acrimony, defensiveness, and attempts to undermine each other's parenting. *Disengaged parents* are both involved with their children but adopt what Furstenberg (1990) termed a *parallel parenting* model. Each parent adopts his or her own style and does not interfere with the other's parenting. Communication with each other is avoided except perhaps through their children. This reduces the likelihood of direct conflict but also reduces cooperation.

Cooperative coparenting is most satisfying to parents and children. When the biological parents are cooperative coparents, their children adjust better to the divorce and adjust more easily to one or both parents' remarriages, and the children's relationships with their stepparents are more positive (Bray & Berger, 1993; Crosbie-Burnett, 1991). Parents are more likely to be cooperative when there are a small number of children who are of school age, when there was little conflict at the time of divorce or since, and when both parents express an ongoing concern about the children's well-being (Maccoby et al., 1993).

Unfortunately, feelings of anger and resentment are difficult if not impossible for many divorced parents to control, and even 2 years after divorce about one fourth of divorced parents are involved in conflicted parenting (Maccoby & Mnookin, 1992). The adverse effects on children of exposure to ongoing parental conflict have been well documented (Camara & Resnick, 1988; Hetherington et al., 1982). However, mere exposure may not be as detrimental as experiencing loyalty conflicts by being caught in the middle of parental conflict (Buchanan, Maccoby, & Dornbusch, 1991; Hetherington, 1993). Children forced to serve as go-betweens may learn to exploit their parents and to play one off against the other, and when older, escape careful monitoring of their activities (Hetherington, Law, & O'Connor, 1992). Even when conflict is encapsulated and children are neither directly exposed nor caught in the middle, the impact of ongoing parental conflict may be felt through changes in parental support and monitoring (Patterson, 1991).

Although cooperative coparenting is associated with positive adjustment, in cases where both parents remain involved, the disengaged or parallel style of shared parenting is most common (Camara & Resnick, 1988; Bray & Berger, 1993; Furstenberg, 1990; Maccoby et al., 1990; Maccoby & Mnookin, 1992). Parents of young children are more likely to be conflicted initially. Over time, however, conflicted parenting decreases and disengaged parenting increases as the children move into adolescence (Maccoby & Mnookin, 1992). Moreover, even initially cooperative parents are likely to become conflicted or disengaged when one or both parents become involved in new relationships. Although a disengaged style is not the ideal, children have been found to adjust well provided their parents do not interfere with each other's parenting, conflict is low, and the children are not asked to act as go-betweens.

Summary

The family disequilibrium that accompanies the divorce transition is stressful for all family members. However, many divorced mothers report that they eventually gain greater self-confidence and self-fulfillment as a result of escape from an unsatisfying marriage and coping with the challenges faced as they work toward a new family equilibrium. Critical to the adjustment of children is the presence of an authoritative custodial parent, but whether or not parents are able to establish or maintain an authoritative approach to parenting depends on the degree to which they must cope with concurrent adversities. When custodial parents are faced with ongoing financial strain or with the full house and childcare responsibilities in the absence of close personal relationships and support from extended or extrafamilial sources, the psychological and physical well-being of parents and parenting quality often suffer.

Recent research indicates that neither mothers nor fathers are superior custodial parents, although there is some evidence that children may adapt better in the custody of parents of the same sex and that parents of the same sex as the child, whether custodial or noncustodial, may have more influence on their child's development. However, children function well in the custody of either parent provided that the parent can maintain a relatively authoritative approach and provided that the family is not faced with new or continuing adversities. There is a growing emphasis on shared parenting. However, even if the courts may mandate shared legal responsibility or even shared physical custody, courts cannot mandate a cooperative, consensual shared parenting relationship. Being caught in the middle of acrimonious parental relationships can have deleterious effects on children's development. Children adjust better to the loss of contact with the noncustodial parent than to continued exposure and involvement in parental conflict (Hetherington, 1991).

PARENTING IN REMARRIED FAMILIES

Remarried families occur in diverse sizes and organizations. The custodial and noncustodial parents and stepparent all may have been married and divorced, often more than once. These parents may have residential or nonresidential children from previous marriages and a large network of grandparents and other relatives may remain involved in the children's lives. Regardless of form and size, however, all newly reconstituted families face tasks unique to their status. The couple must define and strengthen their marriage while simultaneously renegotiating the biological parent–child relationships and establishing stepparent–stepchild and stepsibling relationships. The family must establish roles and relationships with the stepparent who has not participated in the shared family history and whose entry upsets the relationships established in the single-parent household. Extrafamilial relationships, especially those with the noncustodial parents will influence and will be changed by the remarriage. This complex network of new and old extended family relationships must be altered and integrated in the absence of clear guiding norms.

How successful families are in accomplishing these tasks depends in part on their beliefs and expectations at the outset. Clinicians have suggested that when remarried families believe that the traditional nuclear model is the ideal against which they should measure themselves, problems are virtually inevitable (Burchardt, 1990; Visher & Visher, 1990). In contrast to what many families expect or hope, adjustment is likely to be slow (Hetherington, Clingempeel, et al., 1992). Affection between the stepparent and stepchildren may develop slowly if at all, and the role of a disciplinarian may never be adopted. Newly remarried families are families in transition and the remarriage is but one in a series of transitions. There is some evidence that multiple transitions are more difficult to negotiate especially if the transitions are widely spaced and a new homeostasis has been established in the previous family form (Montgomery, Anderson, Hetherington, & Clingempeel, 1992). Thus, the reorganization is likely to take longer than did the reorganization following the initial divorce, and once a new equilibrium has been achieved family relationships and processes in a stepfamily are likely to look different from those found in nondivorced families (Hetherington, 1993; Hetherington, Clingempeel et al., 1992).

Remarried Mothers

Despite the various possible forms a stepfamily may take, 82 percent of remarried households are stepfather families, formed when a divorced, custodial mother remarries and children of the stepfather's first marriage are usually nonresidential (U.S. Bureau of the Census, 1992). For these mothers and their children, remarriage can signal a significant improvement in the quality of family life. The remarriage typically results in a positive change in their financial status and provides the custodial parent with emotional support and help with household and childcare responsibilities. However, even if more positive life events are found in stepfamilies than in single-parent families, more negative life changes than are found in nondivorced families also occur as the challenges of integrating a new member into the existing family system are confronted (Hetherington, 1993). Moreover, when families are faced with sharing financial resources with the stepfather's family from his first marriage and stepfather–stepchild relationships are troubled initially, high expectations are likely to fall.

As a result of the stresses associated with integrating a new member into the family and their concern about the marital relationship, many newly remarried mothers experience a temporary decline in their monitoring and control. Moreover, when remarriage occurs when children are preadolescents, monitoring and control problems are accompanied by an increase in conflictual mother–child exchanges. Remarried mothers are more likely to be poorer monitors of sons' behaviors, but conflict is likely to be higher with daughters. The early monitoring problems may represent a continuation of the poor monitoring found in divorced single mothers but mother–daughter conflict appears in response to the remarriage. In contrast to the mutually coercive relationships of divorced mothers and sons, daughters often have close, confiding, compassionate relationships with their divorced mothers during their time in a single-parent household. Once remarried, the mother's attention, time, and affection are shared with her new husband. Thus, the entry of the stepfather marks a significant change in the daughter's status in the family, which can lead to resentment and conflict with both the mother and the stepfather (Hetherington, Clingempeel, et al., 1992; Hetherington et al., 1989).

The age of the child at the time of the mother's remarriage has been found to be a factor in the long-term adjustment of the mother–child relationship. When children are preadolescents at the time of the remarriage, maternal monitoring and control problems improve by about 2 years after the remarriage but often reemerge when the children reach adolescence (Hetherington, 1993). On the other hand, when children are early adolescents at the time of remarriage, the improvement in maternal monitoring and control appears to remain stable. There is little evidence of enduring differences in the parenting of remarried and nondivorced mothers even though the early adolescents' behavior toward their remarried mothers remains more negative than that in nondivorced families (Bray, 1987; Hetherington, 1993). Despite this evidence, most remarried mothers' relationships with their children are renegotiated and tend to restabilize in a pattern fairly similar to that of nondivorced mothers (Gunnoe, 1993; Hetherington, Clingempeel et al., 1992; Pink & Wampler, 1985).

Stepfathers

For new stepfathers, a primary source of stress is the lack of clear stepparent roles (Peck, Bell, Waldren, & Sorrell, 1988). Although a few states have recently passed laws that require stepparents to contribute to the financial support of their stepchildren, stepparents have virtually no legal parenting rights or responsibilities. The lack of legal guidelines reflects a comparable lack of social norms. Stepfathers often report feeling poorly prepared for the task of integrating themselves into a preexisting family (Santrock et al., 1988). Many question the natural mother's ability to adequately control and monitor the children's activities (Hetherington, Clingempeel et al., 1992) and thus believe that they should provide discipline the children may need (Santrock et al., 1988). However, stepfathers often are unsure about what authority they should exert with their stepchildren or even how to show affection (Santrock et al., 1988), and these feelings can be exacerbated if they receive ambiguous or contradictory messages about their roles from their new wives and stepchildren. Whether or not stepfathers are able to assume a full parental role may depend on the ages of their stepchildren. Younger children are more likely than adolescents eventually to accept a stepfather as a parent. However, even with preadolescents, their precocious independence and power in the family makes a stepfather's assertion of authority and control problematic (Hetherington & Anderson, 1987; Hetherington, Clingempeel et al., 1992; Hetherington et al., 1989; Santrock et al., 1988).

A growing number of remarried mothers expect their new husbands to take an active role in discipline (Santrock et al., 1988). In families where mothers welcome such involvement and stepfathers are able to establish authoritative relationships with their stepchildren, the children, particularly preadolescent boys, manifest fewer adjustment problems. Unfortunately, efforts to adopt such a parental role too soon are often met with resentment and resistance from preadolescent stepchildren (Hetherington, 1988, 1989; Santrock et al., 1988). Furthermore, there is accumulating evidence that over time, the aversive, negative behavior of children may be more influential in increasing negativity and disengagement in the stepfather than the stepfather is in shaping stepchildren's behavior (Hetherington, 1993; Hetherington, Clingempeel et al., 1992). With younger children, the most successful strategy for stepfathers appears to be to build a warm, involved relationship with the children initially and to support the discipline of the mother (Hetherington, 1988, 1989). The move toward authoritative parenting should be gradual and in some families should not occur at all (Hetherington, 1988). With adolescents, immediate adoption of an authoritative parenting style appears to be advantageous (Hetherington, Clingempeel et al., 1992).

As a result of confused role definitions and family expectations as well as family experiences (e.g., age of children, time since divorce), great diversity has been found in the parenting of stepfathers, particularly when compared to that of natural fathers in nondivorced homes (Hetherington et al., 1982; Santrock et al., 1988). Over time, about one third of stepfathers, particularly those with young children, in contrast to over one half of nondivorced fathers, become active and involved authoritative parents (Hetherington, 1993; Hetherington, Clingempeel et al., 1992). However, most stepfathers remain or become disengaged but to varying degrees. Some who disengage do so completely. They are inattentive to their stepchildren and unsupportive of the mothers' parenting (Santrock et al., 1988). Others disengage only from an active disciplinarian role but develop affectively close relationships with their stepchildren and are supportive of the mothers' discipline and control efforts. Research to date suggests that when full authoritative involvement is not possible, an indirect engagement style may be best for children. Children have been found to adjust well when their natural mother is authoritative and retains full responsibility for discipline whereas their stepfather is warm and supportive towards them and involves himself indirectly in discipline through his support of the mother (Bray & Berger, 1993; Hetherington, 1988).

Stepmothers

Compared to stepfathers, residential stepmothers appear to have a more difficult time fitting themselves in to the family system (Brand et al., 1988; Clingempeel, Brand, & Ievoli, 1984; Salwen, 1990; Whitsett & Land, 1992). Their difficulties may be attributed to the greater role strain they experience (Whitsett & Land, 1992), a strain created when stepmothers attempt to adhere to existing gender norms in the absence of clear stepparent norms. It is not uncommon for custodial fathers to assume that their new wives will develop an instantaneous rapport with their children and take on the bulk of the day-to-day childcare responsibilities. However, stepmothers have many of the same initial concerns expressed by stepfathers. They worry that they will not be able to be as nurturant with stepchildren as the children's biological mother or to control and discipline the children as well as their natural father (Salwen, 1990). When stepmothers suppress their concerns and become active in childcare, the result is likely to be similar to that found in stepfather families, conflict with their stepchildren, particularly stepdaughters (Brand et al., 1988). Unfortunately, gender norms make it difficult if not impossible for stepmothers to assume a parental role gradually or to disengage when faced with resistant, noncompliant stepchildren. That stepmothers have more positive relationships with nonresidential than residential stepchildren (Ambert, 1986) lends further support to the conclusion that assumption of the dominant, disciplinarian role on the part of stepparents can lead to problems in interactions with stepchildren.

Noncustodial Parents

Early investigations of remarried families paid little attention to the complex relationships between residential and nonresidential family members, particularly natural parents. However, as use of the family-systems perspective and interest in postdivorce shared parenting relationships have grown, researchers have begun to assess the impact that continued involvement of the noncustodial parent has on the remarried family. For example, investigators have proposed that the problems residential stepmothers have in establishing positive, effective relationships with their stepchildren is exacerbated by the fact that the children's natural mother is likely to visit frequently and to be actively involved with the children (Brand et al., 1988). It is interesting to note, however, that continued involvement of noncustodial fathers has not been found to have a similar impact on stepfather–child relationships (Brand et al., 1988; Furstenberg, 1988). This seeming discrepancy may be because of the greater disengagement of stepfathers or the more companionable role of noncustodial fathers. In one report from a study based on a national sample, Gunnoe (1993) indicated that noncustodial mothers' monitoring, aggression, and positivity, and daughters' feelings of being caught between noncustodial mothers and stepmothers, are associated with girls' conduct problems, depression, and social responsibility. Noncustodial fathers' monitoring served as a deterrent to sons' conduct problems and depression. Thus, residential stepmothers who adopt a disciplinarian role are in competition with involved noncustodial mothers a situation exacerbated by the fact that children feel much closer to their noncustodial mothers (Ambert, 1986). If residential stepfathers establish an affectionate bond with the children and do not adopt a disciplinarian role, they are not in competition with the noncustodial fathers who remain actively involved in parenting. On the other hand, the noncustodial father who is permissive and who plays a less instrumental role is less likely to be competing with an authoritative stepfather. Thus, it is not contact with the noncustodial parent per se but the quality of the parent–child relationship that is important in children's adjustment and these relationships vary with the gender of the noncustodial parent and child.

Relations Between Marital and Parent–Child Subsystems in Remarried Families

A close marital relationship is often viewed as a firm foundation for positive family functioning, a foundation that promotes both responsive, competent parenting and the psychological well-being of children. Although the associations between the marital and parent–child subsystems and their impact on child adjustment in nondivorced families have been well documented, relatively little is known about these associations in remarried families. What little evidence is available suggests that the interactions among subsystems in remarried families may differ from those typical in nondivorced families (Bray & Berger, 1993; Hetherington, 1993; Hetherington, Clingempeel et al., 1992) and may vary as a function of family type. In stepmother families, higher marital quality has been found to be associated with more positive stepmother–stepson relationships and better stepson adjustment, but with less positive stepmother–stepdaughter relationships and poorer stepdaughter adjustment (Brand & Clingempeel, 1987). In stepfather families, stepfathers with close satisfying conjugal relationships are more positive toward stepchildren of both sexes (Brand & Clingempeel, 1987; Brand et al., 1988; Bray, 1988; Bray & Berger, 1993; Hetherington, Clingempeel et al., 1992). However, the quality and extent of the association between the marital relationship and stepfathers' and stepchildren's behavior toward each other may differ and may be related to the age of the child at the time of remarriage, the time since the remarriage, and the stepfathers' involvement in parenting.

In the months immediately following remarriage, stepfathers report higher marital satisfaction if they are not expected to either bond with or discipline their stepchildren immediately (Bray, 1988). Extending this line of investigation in long-term follow-ups of adjustment in a sample of stepfather families, Bray and Berger (1993) found that as remarried families begin to adjust, the marital satisfaction of both partners remains higher if stepfathers establish close emotional bonds with their stepchildren but support the mothers' discipline efforts rather than getting directly involved themselves. Interestingly, once the families had restabilized after 5 years, little evidence of a relationship between the marital relationship and parenting was found, a result that supports the findings of other researchers who have observed marital satisfaction and parenting to be less closely related in remarried than in nondivorced families (Hetherington, 1991, 1993).

The association of the quality of the marital relationship with children's behavior toward the stepfather varies with the age of the child. In newly remarried families with preadolescent children, especially with daughters, a close marital relationship is associated with high levels of negative, resistant behavior from children toward both the mother and stepfather. This relation is not significant for preadolescent boys after 2 years of remarriage but is sustained for girls (Hetherington, 1993). Furthermore, with preadolescent children, even in the longer remarried families, a close satisfying marital relationship is associated with both internalizing and acting out behavior in stepdaughters but with lower externalizing with stepsons (Hetherington, 1993). A satisfying marital relationship may be seen as more of a threat to continuation of close relationships between preadolescent daughters and their divorced mothers than it was to the frequently conflictual relations found between divorced mothers and sons.

In contrast to the findings with younger children when remarriages occur when children are early adolescents, both stepsons and stepdaughters are better adjusted and exhibit more positive, less conflictual parent–child relationships if parents have a close satisfying marital relationship (Hetherington, 1993; Hetherington, Clingempeel et al., 1992). Why should there be these differences in the correlates of marital satisfaction and the behavior of stepdaughters in preadolescent and early adolescent children? At this time, marked physical changes are occurring in children and they are becoming sensitive to issues of intimate relationships and sexuality. Many nondivorced fathers are disconcerted by their adolescent daughters' burgeoning sexuality (Hill, Holmbeck, Marlow, Green, & Lynch, 1985a, 1985b) and are concerned about the proper expression of physical affection at this time. Concerns about affection and sexuality may be more severe in the case of stepfathers and stepdaughters. A close marital relationship may be seen by adolescent daughters and their parents as a buffer against the threat of inappropriate intimacy between stepfathers and stepdaughters (Hetherington, 1993).

Further investigations on the linkages among family subsystems, how they change over time, and how they affect child adjustment are needed. Most critically needed, however, are longitudinal studies that will permit some disentangling of direction of effects among systems and between parents and children's behavior. Although it has been customary to think of parents influencing children's behavior it is apparent that in adapting to divorce and remarriage children play an important role in modifying the behavior of parents and stepparents (Hetherington, Clingempeel et al., 1992).

Summary

The challenges of establishing constructive, functional relationships within the family and with extended family members contribute to the risk of problems following remarriage. However, over time many remarried families appear able to achieve a workable integration of marital, parent– and stepparent–child, and sibling subsystems. In stepfather families, the remarriage can have a beneficial effect on the mother's parenting and on the adjustment of preadolescent boys. Even when the stepfather involves himself in parenting only indirectly through his support of the mother's efforts particularly with respect to discipline, mothers typically find parenting less stressful and the effects on their parenting more positive.

More research is needed on less typical remarried family structures. Results from the few studies that have been conducted on stepmother families and blended families in which both spouses bring children from an earlier marriage suggest that the adjustment processes in these families differ significantly from those observed in stepfather families. For example, relatively little is known about indirect effects in stepmother families. Compared to stepfathers, residential stepmothers are more likely to be involved in discipline. Thus, any benefits a custodial father may gain when a stepmother takes over childrearing tasks may be offset by the increase in family conflict that stems from her involvement or perhaps with less active involvement of the custodial father. With respect to blended families with two sets of children, disengagement by either parent figure is less possible and loyalty conflicts may be a particularly salient issue.

DIVERSITY IN DIVORCED AND REMARRIED FAMILIES

The diversity evident in the responses of both parents and children to divorce and remarriage can be attributed to complex interactions among many factors including: (1) parent and child gender, (2) the child's developmental status, (3) parent and child temperaments and personalities, and (4) the availability of both informal and formal supports. What follows is a brief summary of what is known about how these factors affect the immediate and long-term adjustment of parents and children.

Parent and Child Gender

Although gender effects were commonly found in early studies of divorce, they are less frequently found in more recent studies (Amato & Keith, 1991b). Furthermore, whether or not gender is a factor in children's adjustment following marital transitions depends on the age of the child at the time of the family transition and at the time of assessment. Gender differences have been found in the adjustment of younger children to divorce and remarriage but are rarely found with adolescents in divorced families. Regardless of the custody arrangement following divorce, younger boys act out more than do girls in divorced families or children in nondivorced families (Allison & Furstenberg, 1989; Hetherington & Camara, 1984; Hetherington et al., 1985; Zeiss, Zeiss, & Johnson, 1980; see also Fagot, in this *Handbook*). Children in divorced families are more likely to exhibit more behavioral, emotional, social, and learning problems than children in intact families, and these problems are more marked and enduring for young boys than girls (Guidubaldi et al., 1987; Hetherington et al., 1985; Zaslow, 1988).

In adolescence (Hetherington, 1972, 1993) and in young adulthood (Zill et al., 1993) as girls are becoming more involved in heterosexual relationships, delayed effects may occur in previously well-adjusted daughters of divorced mothers in the form of early sexuality, teenage pregnancy, and unstable intimate relationships. Problems in precocious sexuality and substance abuse are especially likely to occur in early physical maturing girls who associate with older peers and have a nonauthoritative mother who is overtly sexually active with multiple partners (Hetherington, 1993). Furthermore, both the absence of the biological father because of divorce, and the presence of a stepfather stimulate earlier menarche (Hetherington, 1993). Thus, more girls in divorced mother custody and stepfather families are likely to mature early, and their early maturity interacts with other factors to put them at risk for precocious sexual behavior (Hetherington, 1993).

The pattern of gender differences following remarriage of the custodial parent differs from that of divorce. Young girls in both stepfather and stepmother families have more trouble adjusting to the entry of the stepparent than do boys (Brand et al., 1988; Hetherington et al., 1992). Although both boys and girls may be initially upset and resistant to the new stepparent, preadolescent boys appear to adapt more quickly and benefit from the presence of an authoritative stepfather, and even in adolescence the presence of a stepfather protects boys against school dropout (Hetherington, 1991; Hetherington, Clingempeel et al., 1992; Zill et al., 1993).

The gender differences found in the adjustment of younger children and in the qualities of interactions of the divorced parent and child may result from complex reciprocal interactions between adults and children. On the one hand, the gender differences found in young children in divorced families may be attributed to differences in how parents treat boys versus girls. For example, in divorcing families, sons are more likely than daughters to be exposed to parental conflict and to be exposed for longer periods of time (Hetherington et al., 1982; Hetherington, 1989). They may even have been exposed to more conflict before the divorce because parents with sons are more likely to stay together than are parents with daughters (Hetherington et al., 1982). Given that boys interpret family disagreements less positively than do girls (Epstein, Finnegan, & Gythall, 1979) and are less able to express their feelings in constructive ways or to solicit support from others when stressed, coping with such family conflict may be more difficult for boys than girls (Hetherington, 1989). Congruently, because preadolescent boys tend to be more noncompliant and aggressive than girls, their behavior may exacerbate the problems of the already stressed divorced mother.

In remarried families, differences in how nondivorced parents and stepparents act toward boys versus girls may be a reaction to the different behaviors exhibited by the children. For example, in one recent longitudinal study of adjustment in nondivorced, divorced-single mother, and stepfather families, Hetherington and her colleagues (1992) found evidence that parenting of early adolescents in stepfather families may be more reactive than proactive. Earlier child externalizing was associated with increased subsequent negativity on the part of stepfathers. In addition, warm, supportive parenting by the remarried mother and stepfather was more likely to be evident in response to the children's earlier social competence. In remarried families, it is not surprising that stepparent–stepdaughter relationships are usually characterized as conflictual given that stepdaughters tend to be more resistant and combative than stepsons toward entering stepfathers or stepmothers (Bray & Berger, 1993; Clingempeel et al., 1984; Hetherington, Clingempeel et al., 1992; Santrock, Warshak, Lindberg, & Meadows, 1982).

Children's Developmental Status

Researchers and practitioners alike have expressed concerns about how the timing of a divorce or remarriage relative to a child's developmental status affects the parent–child relationship and child adjustment. Unfortunately, studies of the effects of age at divorce or remarriage on children's adjustment to family transitions have produced inconsistent results. Some researchers have found that preschoolers who are unable to understand the reasons for the family disruption or to seek out extrafamilial supports are more adversely affected by their parents' divorce than are older children or adolescents (Allison & Furstenberg, 1989; Zill et al., 1993) and that these effects of timing of divorce extend into young adulthood (Zill et al., 1993). Others have found evidence that adolescents are as adversely affected as young children (Frost & Pakiz, 1990; Needle, Su, & Doherty, 1990).

Although less work has been done on the timing of remarriage, there are indications that early adolescence may be an especially difficult time in which to have a remarriage occur. Younger children, especially boys, may eventually adapt to and directly benefit from the presence of a warm, involved stepfather and may benefit indirectly from improvements in the custodial mother's parenting associated with the support of a new spouse (Hetherington et al., 1985). Furthermore, older adolescents and young adults feel some relief from the responsibility of economic, emotional, and social support of their divorced mother when a remarriage occurs. However, similar benefits have not been found when the remarriage occurs in early adolescence. At this time dealing with the stresses associated with family formation may exacerbate problems in trying to cope with the pubertal transition particularly those associated with autonomy and sexuality (Hetherington, 1991, 1993). Moreover, even in restabilized divorced mother-headed and remarried families, in early adolescence family relationships may be disrupted, family cohesion decline and behavior problems emerge in previously well-adjusted children (Bray, 1990; Hetherington, 1989, 1991, 1993; Hetherington, Clingempeel et al., 1992).

Preexisting Problems, Temperament, and Personality

It has long been assumed that postdivorce and postremarriage problems observed in parent–child relationships and individual adjustment are caused by the stresses associated with family reorganization. However, this assumption can be attributed in part to the fact that most research has measured adjustment only after the marital transition occurred. Thus, the degree to which preexisting conditions contribute to an initial divorce or to problems in subsequent marriages has rarely been examined. There is evidence, however, that for some children and their parents, greater emotional, behavioral, and academic problems and poorer parenting skills may be present before the divorce (Block, Block, & Gjerde, 1989; Bray & Berger, 1993; Capaldi & Patterson, 1991; Cherlin et al., 1991).

Parents who are depressed or have antisocial personalities are more likely to divorce, to go through multiple marital transitions, to be unskilled parents, and to be less adaptable in the face of stresses associated with marital transitions (Block et al., 1989; Capaldi & Patterson, 1991). Antisocial or depressed parents may find it particularly difficult to deal with the emotional, acting out behavior in children associated with divorce or remarriage. These difficulties are likely to be exacerbated if the parent relies on distancing or escape/avoidance coping strategies (Holloway & Machida, 1991). On the other hand, parents who normally rely on more active behavioral and cognitive coping strategies in stressful life circumstance are more likely to feel they are in control in childrearing situations and are more capable of maintaining an authoritative parenting style.

It has also been found that children whose parents will later divorce exhibit more behavior problems prior to divorce than do children in nondivorced families (Block et al., 1989; Capaldi & Patterson, 1991; Cherlin et al., 1991). It could be argued that the children who are troubled prior to the divorce are simply responding to family problems, conflict, and inept parenting already evident. However, it also may be that having to deal with difficult children strains troubled marriages to the breaking point (Hetherington & Mekos, 1992). Difficult children are more likely than temperamentally easy children to elicit and receive their parents' criticism and displaced anger and anxiety especially when parents are stressed and they are less able to cope with erratic parenting and adverse life circumstances when they occur (Rutter, 1987; Werner, 1988). Furthermore, children with difficult temperaments are more likely to have preexisting emotional and behavioral problems that are exacerbated by the stresses of family disruption and reorganization (Block et al., 1989; Hetherington, 1989, 1991; Patterson & Dishion, 1988).

SUPPORT SYSTEMS

Perceived availability and use of both informal supports (e.g., friends, extended family members) and formal supports (e.g., divorce mediation, shared parenting classes) can do much to ameliorate the negative impact of adverse life events including the stresses associated with marital transitions (Cochran & Niego, in this *Handbook*). To date, however, most of the research on the associations between supports and family transition adjustment has been limited to studies of divorced families. The impact on remarried family adjustment has been largely unexplored.

Informal Support Systems

Support from friends and extended family members can help divorcing parents maintain a positive attitude about themselves and thus facilitate their parenting. Between 25 percent and 33 percent of newly divorced custodial mothers reside with relatives, usually their parents, following divorce (Hernandez, 1988). Grandparents can help with economic resources and child care, and grandfathers can be positive role models for boys. For children whose home environments are changing and whose parents are temporarily unresponsive, support can come from outside the home. For example, day-care centers and schools that offer warm, structured, and stable environments can provide the stability children lack at home. Responsive adults such as teachers, coaches, or parents of friends can help children maintain feelings of self-worth, competence, and self-control (Guidubaldi et al., 1987; Hetherington, 1993; Hetherington et al., 1982, 1985, 1988; Rutter, 1987). As children get older and move into adolescence, siblings and peers can be important sources of support, and children in divorced and remarried families are especially susceptible to peer pressure (Hetherington, 1991).

Divorce Mediation

In an effort to reduce the conflict that often erupts and escalates when divorcing couples disagree about child custody or visitation arrangements, many states have instituted divorce mediation programs. Participation is recommended in some states, required in others, and the content and quality of divorce mediation programs are as diverse as the families they are designed to assist. The primary goal of most mediation programs, however, is to provide the opportunity for couples to reach decisions about child custody and visitation in an environment less acrimonious and adversarial than a court setting. Decisions about disputed assets and financial support typically are resolved through court litigation.

Generally, couples who resolve custody and visitation disputes through mediation rather than more adversarial court litigation are less likely to need or pursue further court hearings, reach resolutions more quickly, and are more likely to comply with agreements (Emery et al., 1991). Early studies of the impact of divorce mediation on parents' satisfaction with the resolution process also suggested that parents are more satisfied with the resolution process when disputes are mediated rather than litigated (Emery et al., 1991). However, the results of more recent work indicate that beliefs about the fairness of the resolution process and satisfaction with agreements differ for fathers and mothers (Emery et al., 1991; Emery & Wyer, 1987). Despite the legal emphasis on gender-neutral custody decisions, many courts still interpret the "best interests of the child" as mother custody. Thus, when custody disputes are litigated in the court rather than mediated in a less adversarial setting, fathers are still more likely to lose the custody battle. When arrangements are worked out through mediation, however, joint legal custody is the more likely outcome (Emery et al., 1991; Emery & Wyer, 1987). Not surprisingly, compared to fathers who go through litigation, fathers who go through mediation are more likely to report that their interests and rights have been protected and that they are satisfied with the agreements. For mothers, the picture is less clear. Although both mothers who go through mediation and mothers who go through litigation report that their rights have been protected, litigating mothers who are more likely to receive sole custody are more satisfied with the resultant agreements (Emery et al., 1991; Emery & Wyer, 1987).

Shared Parenting Programs

Divorce mediation programs rarely address coparenting after the legal divorce. Instead, evidence that a cooperative, consensual coparenting arrangement is in the best interests of the child has fostered a rapid growth in shared parenting programs. Many use cognitive therapy and family-systems principles to help divorced couples learn shared parenting skills (see Kramer & Washo, 1993; Leek, 1992) with the goals of improving communication between the parents and helping them develop a pattern of functioning that is adaptive for each family member. In order to work, the programs frequently must help couples come to terms with their own preexisting problems and recognize that their problems are between them and involving their children is likely to prove detrimental to their children's adjustment. Shared parenting programs are promising, but it might be expected that unless court mandated only exceptionally concerned child-oriented parents would become involved in such programs.

The past decade has seen a rapid rise in interventions and support programs such as divorce mediation, shared parenting classes, changes in custody laws, and even coping skills training programs for children and their parents. Such programs indicate an increasing awareness of the need to address those factors that are most likely to ameliorate or exacerbate problems in divorced homes, but more longitudinal evaluative research needs to be conducted before firm conclusions are reached about their effectiveness (Grych & Fincham, 1992; Patterson, 1992). With growing recognition of the number of children living in remarried families, more policies and more programs designed to meet the special needs of these families are to be expected. At present, however, there is little empirical evidence to guide such efforts (Maccoby et al., 1993).

CONCLUSIONS

Each marital transition is characterized by an initial period of disequilibrium followed by reorganization and eventual restabilization. The patterns of equilibrium attained, however, are likely to differ from either the patterns that existed before the transition or the patterns observed in many nondivorced families. These differences may be due to the stresses during and following transition, and they may reflect adaptive changes in interaction processes rather than the presence of problems within the families (Bray & Berger, 1993).

In the past two decades, a substantial body of research knowledge has been gathered on the functioning of divorced families and the adjustment of children in mother-headed households. Less is known about the family system, family processes, and the development of children in father-custody or remarried families. What is notable is the great diversity in children's responses to their parents' marital transitions and the central role that involved, responsive parenting plays in the resiliency and adaptability of children in all families.

Research findings indicate that children are more resilient than was once thought. Studies of children's adjustment to divorce and remarriage have shown that relatively few children and adolescents experience enduring problems (Amato & Keith, 1991b; Clingempeel & Segal, 1986; Hetherington, 1991, 1993; Hetherington, Clingempeel et al., 1992; Santrock et al., 1982; Wallerstein & Blakeslee, 1989). Rather than concluding that parental divorce and remarriage are preludes to serious or pervasive adjustment problems in most children, it would be more accurate to conclude that family transitions place children at risk. Whether or not they experience severe problems is likely to be determined by complex interactions among many factors. Some of the important factors appear to be those associated with adjustment problems in any family; the presence of concurrent stressors such as continued financial distress in the household, household disorganization, disrupted parenting practices; children's involvement in parental conflict, and lack of effective support systems. However, although all of these variables are important the presence of an involved, caring, responsive authoritative adult plays a critical role in protecting children from the possible adverse effects of divorce and remarriage and in promoting children's psychological well- being when they are coping with the changes and challenges associated with marital transitions.

REFERENCES

Allison, P. D., & Furstenberg, F. F. (1989). How marital dissolution affects children: Variations by age and sex. *Developmental Psychology, 25,* 540–549.

Amato, P. R., & Keith, B. (1991a). Parental divorce and adult well-being: A meta-analysis. *Journal of Marriage and the Family, 53,* 43–58.

Amato, P. R., & Keith, B. (1991b). Parental divorce and the well-being of children: A meta-analysis. *Psychological Bulletin, 110,* 26–46.

Ambert, A. M. (1986). Being a stepparent: Live-in and visiting stepchildren. *Journal of Marriage and the Family, 48,* 795–804.

Bank, L., Forgatch, M. S., Patterson, G. R., & Fetrow, R. A. (1991). *Parenting practices: Mediators of negative contextual factors in divorce.* Unpublished manuscript.

Baumrind, D. (1991). Effective parenting during the early adolescent transition. In P. A. Cowan & E. M. Hetherington (Eds.), *Family transitions* (pp. 111–163). Hillsdale, NJ: Lawrence Erlbaum Associates.

Benjamin, M., & Irving, H. H. (1990). Comparison of the experience of satisfied and dissatisfied shared parents. *Journal of Divorce and Remarriage, 14,* 43–61.

Block, J., Block, J. H., & Gjerde, P. F. (1989). Parental functioning and the home environment in families of divorce: Prospective and concurrent analyses. *Annual Progress in Child Psychiatry and Child Development,* 192–207.

Brand, E., & Clingempeel, W. G. (1987). Interdependence of marital and stepparent–stepchild relationships and children's psychological adjustment: Research findings and clinical implications. *Family Relations Journal of Applied Family and Child Studies, 36,* 140–145.

Brand, E., Clingempeel, W. G., & Bowen-Woodward, K. (1988). Family relationships and children's psychosocial adjustment in stepmother and stepfather families. In E. M. Hetherington & J. D. Arasteh (Eds.), *Impact of divorce, single-parenting, and stepparenting on children* (pp. 299–324). Hillsdale, NJ: Lawrence Erlbaum Associates.

Braver, S. L., Wolchik, S. A., Sandler, I. N., Sheets, V. L., Fogas, B., & Bay, R. C. (1993). A longitudinal study of noncustodial parents: Parents without children. *Journal of Family Psychology, 7,* 1–16.

Bray, J. H. (1987, August). *Becoming a stepfamily.* Symposium presented at the meeting of the American Psychological Association, New York.

Bray, J. H. (1988). Children's development in early remarriage. In E. M. Hetherington & J. D. Arasteh (Eds.), *The impact of divorce, single-parenting, and stepparenting on children* (pp. 279–298). Hillsdale, NJ: Lawrence Erlbaum Associates.

Bray, J. H. (1990). Impact of divorce on the family. In R. E. Rakel (Ed.), *Textbook of family practice* (4th ed., pp. 111–122). Philadelphia: Saunders.

Bray, J. H. (1992). Family relationships and children's adjustment in clinical and nonclinical stepfather families. *Journal of Family Psychology, 6,* 60–68.

Bray, J. H., & Berger, S. H. (1993). Developmental issues in stepfamilies research project: Family relationships and parent–child interactions. *Journal of Family Psychology, 7,* 1–17.

Buchanan, C. M., Maccoby, E. E., & Dornbusch, S. M. (1991). Caught between parents: Adolescents' experience in divorced homes. *Child Development, 62,* 1008–1029.

Buchanan, C. M., Maccoby, E. E., & Dornbusch, S. M. (1992). Adolescents and their families after divorce: Three residential arrangements compared. *Journal of Research on Adolescence, 2,* 261–291.

Buehler, C. A., Hogan, M. J., Robinson, B. E., & Levy, R. J. (1985). The parental divorce transition: Divorce-related stressors and well-being. *Journal of Divorce, 9,* 61–81.

Burchardt, N. (1990). Stepchildren's memories: Myth, understanding, and forgiveness. In R. Samual & P. Thompson (Eds.), *The myths we live by* (pp. 239–251). London: Routledge.

Camara, K. A., & Resnick, G. (1988). Interparental conflict and cooperation: Factor moderating children's post-divorce adjustment. In E. M. Hetherington & J. D. Arasteh (Eds.), *Impact of divorce, single-parenting, and stepparenting on children* (pp. 169–195). Hillsdale, NJ: Lawrence Erlbaum Associates.

Capaldi, D. M., & Patterson, G. R. (1991). Relation of parental transitions to boys' adjustment problems: I. A linear hypothesis. II. Mothers at risk for transitions and unskilled parenting. *Developmental Psychology, 27,* 489–504.

Castro-Martin, T., & Bumpass, L. (1989). Recent trends and differentials in marital disruption. *Demography, 26,* 37–51.

Chase-Lansdale, P. L., & Hetherington, E. M. (1990). The impact of divorce on life-span development: Short and long term effects. In P. B. Baltes, D. L. Featherman, & R. M. Lerner (Eds.), *Life-span development and behavior* (Vol. 10, pp. 105–150). Hillsdale, NJ: Lawrence Erlbaum Associates.

Cherlin, A. J., Furstenberg, F. F., Chase-Lansdale, P. L., Kiernan, K. E., Robins, P. K., Morrison, D. R., & Teitler, J. O. (1991). Longitudinal studies of the effects of divorce on children in Great Britain and the United States. *Science, 252,* 1386–1389.

Clingempeel, G. W., Brand, E., & Ievoli, R. (19 84). Stepparent–stepchild relationships in stepmother and stepfather families: A multimethod study. *Family Relations, 33,* 465–473.

Clingempeel, G. W., & Segal, S. (1986). Stepparent–stepchild relationships and the psychological adjustment of children in stepmother and stepfather families. *Child Development, 57,* 474–484.

Colletta, N. D. (1981). Social support and risk of maternal rejection by adolescent mothers. *Journal of Psychology, 109,* 191–197.

Crosbie-Burnett, M. (1991). Impact of joint versus sole custody and quality of co-parental relationship on adjustment of adolescents in remarried families. *Behavioral Sciences and the Law, 9,* 439–449.

Emery, R. E. (1988). *Marriage, divorce, and children's adjustment.* Newbury Park, CA: Sage.

Emery, R. E., Matthews, S . G., & Wyer, M. M. (1991). Child custody mediation and litigation: Further evidence on the differing views of mothers and fathers. *Journal of Consulting and Clinical Psychology, 59,* 410–418.

Emery, R. E., & Wyer, M. M. (1987). Child custody mediation and litigation: An experimental evaluation of the experience of parents. *Journal of Consulting and Clinical Psychology, 55,* 179–186.

Epstein, N., Finnegan, D., & Gythall, D. (1979). Irrational beliefs and perceptions of marital conflict. *Journal of Consulting and Clinical Psychology, 67,* 608–609.

Fine, M. A., & Kurdek, L. A. (1992). Adjustment of adolescents in stepfather and stepmother families. *Journal of Marriage and the Family, 54,* 725–736.

Forehand, R., Wierson, M., Thomas, A. M., Fauber, R., Armistead, L., Kemptom, T., & Long, N. (1991). A short-term longitudinal examination of young adolescent functioning following divorce: The role of family factors. *Journal of Abnormal Child Psychology, 19,* 97–111.

Forgatch, M. S., Patterson, G. R., & Ray, J. A. (in press). Divorce and boys' adjustment problems: Two paths with a single model. In E. M. Hetherington (Ed.), *Stress, coping, and resiliency in children and the family.* Hillsdale, NJ: Lawrence Erlbaum Associates.

Frost, A. K., & Pakiz, B. (1990). The effects of marital disruption on adolescents: Time as a dynamic. *American Journal of Orthopsychiatry, 60,* 544–555.

Furstenberg, F. F. (1988). Child care after divorce and remarriage. In E. M. Hetherington & J. Arasteh (Eds.), *Impact of divorce, single-parenting, and stepparenting on children* (pp. 245– 261). Hillsdale, NJ: Lawrence Erlbaum Associates.

Furstenberg, F. F. (1990). Divorce and the American family. *Annual Review of Sociology, 16,* 379–403.

Furstenberg, F. F., & Cherlin, A. (1991). *Divided families: What happens to children when parents part.* Cambridge, MA: Harvard University Press.

Furstenberg, F. F., & Nord, C. W. (1987). Parenting apart: Patterns of childrearing after marital disruption. *Journal of Marriage and the Family, 47,* 893–904.

Garfinkel, I., & McLanahan, S. (1986). *Single mothers and their children: New American dilemma.* Washington, DC: Urban Institute.

Glick, P. C., & Lin, S. (1986). Recent changes in divorce and remarriage. *Journal of Marriage and the Family, 48,* 737–747.

Grych, J. H., & Fincham, F. D. (1992) . Marital conflict and children's adjustment: A cognitive-contextual framework. *Psychological Bulletin, 108*(2), 267–290.

Guidubaldi, J., Perry, J. D., & Nastasi, B. K. (1987). Growing up in a divorced family: Initial and long-term perspectives on children's adjustment. *Applied Social Psychology Annual, 7,* 202–237.

Gunnoe, M. L. (1993). *Noncustodial mothers' and fathers' contributions to the adjustment of adolescent stepchildren.* Unpublished doctoral dissertation, University of Virginia, Charlottesville.

Hanson, S. M. H. (1988). Single custodial fathers and the parent–child relationship. *Nursing Research, 30,* 202–204.

Hernandez, D. J. (1988). Demographic trends and the living arrangements of children. In E. M. Hetherington & J. D. Arasteh (Eds.), *Impact of divorce, single-parenting, and stepparenting on children* (pp. 3–22). Hillsdale, NJ: Lawrence Erlbaum Associates.

Hetherington, E. M. (1972). Effects of father absence on personality development in adolescent daughters. *Developmental Psychology, 7*(3), 313–326.

Hetherington, E. M. (1988). Parents, children, and siblings six years after divorce. In R. Hinde & J. Stevenson-Hinde (Eds.), *Relationships within families* (pp. 311–331). Cambridge, MA: Cambridge University Press.

Hetherington, E. M. (1989). Coping with family transitions: Winners, losers, and survivors. *Child Development, 60,* 1–14.

Hetherington, E. M. (1991). Families, lies, and videotapes. *Journal of Research on Adolescence, 1,* 323–348.

Hetherington, E. M. (1993). An overview of the Virginia longitudinal study of divorce and remarriage with a focus on early adolescence. *Journal of Family Psychology, 7,* 1–18.

Hetherington, E. M., & Anderson, E. R. (1987). The effects of divorce and remarriage on early adolescents and their families. In M. D. Levine & E. R. McAnarney (Eds.), *Early adolescent transitions* (pp. 49–67). Lexington, MA: Heath.

Hetherington, E. M., & Camara, K. A. (1984). Families in transition: The process of dissolution and reconstitution. In R. D. Parke (Ed.), *Review of child development research* (pp. 398–439). Chicago: University of Chicago Press.

Hetherington, E. M., Clingempeel, W. G., Anderson, E. R., Deal, J. E., Stanley-Hagan, M., Hollier, E. A., & Lindner, M. S (1992). Coping with marital transitions: A family systems perspective. *Monographs of the Society for Research in Child Development, 57*(2–3, Serial No. 227).

Hetherington, E. M., Cox, M., & Cox, R. (1982). Effects of divorce on parents and children. In M. E. Lamb (Ed.), *Nontraditional families* (pp. 233–288). Hillsdale, NJ: Lawrence Erlbaum Associates.

Hetherington, E. M., Cox, M., & Cox, R. (1985). Long-term effects of divorce and remarriage on the adjustment of children. *Journal of the American Academy of Child Psychiatry, 24,* 518–530.

Hetherington, E. M., Law, T. C., & O'Connor, T. G. (1992). Divorce: Challenges, changes, and new chances. In F. Walsh (Ed.), *Normal family processes* (2nd ed., pp. 208–234). New York: Guilford.

Hetherington, E. M., & Mekos, D. (in press). Alterations in family life following divorce: Effects on children and adolescence. In N. Alessi (Ed.), *Handbook of child and adolescent psychiatry.*

Hetherington, E. M., & Stanley-Hagan, M. (1986). Divorced fathers: Stress, coping, and adjustment. In M. E. Lamb (Ed.), *The father's role: Applied perspectives* (pp. 103–134). New York: Wiley.

Hetherington, E. M., Stanley-Hagan, M., Anderson, E. R., (1989). Marital transitions: A child's perspective. Social Issue: Children and their development: Knowledge base, research agenda, and social policy application. *American Psychologist, 44,* 303–312.

Hill, J., Holmbeck, G., Marlow, L., Green, T., & Lynch, M. (1985a). Menarcheal status and parent–child relations in families with seventh grade girls. *Journal of Youth and Adolescence, 14,* 301–316.

Hill, J., Holmbeck, G., Marlow, L., Green, T., & Lynch, M. (198 5b). Pubertal status and parent–child relations in families of seventh grade boys. *Journal of Early Adolescence, 5,* 31–44.

Holloway, S. D., & Machida, S. (1991). Child-rearing effectiveness of divorced mothers: Relationship to coping strategies and social support. Special Issue: Women and divorce/men and divorce. *Journal of Divorce and Remarriage, 14,* 179–201.

Kiecolt-Glaser, J. K., Fisher, L. D., Ogrocki, P., Stout, J. C., Speicher, C. E., & Glaser, R. (1987). Marital quality, marital disruption, and immune function. *Psychosomatic Medicine, 49,* 13–34.

Kitson, G. C., & Holmes, W. M. (1992). *Portrait of divorce: Adjustment to marital breakdown.* New York: Guilford.

Kramer, L. & Washo, C. A. (1993). Evaluation of a court mandated prevention program for divorcing parents: The Children First Program. *Family Relations, 42,* 179–186.

Lee, V. E., Burkham, D. T., Zimiles, H., & Ladewski, x. (994). Family structure and its effect on behavioral and emotional problems in young adolescents. *Journal of Research on Adolescence, 4,* 405–437.

Leek, D. F. (1992). Shared parenting support program. *American Journal of Forensic Psychology, 10,* 49–64.

Lempers, J. D., Clark-Lempers, D., & Simons, R. (1989). Economic hardship, parenting and distress in adolescence. *Child Development, 60,* 25–39.

Maccoby, E. E., Buchanan, C. M., Mnookin, R. H., & Dornbusch, S. M. (1993). Post-divorce roles of mothers and fathers in the lives of their children. *Journal of Family Psychology, 7,* 1–15.

Maccoby, E. E., Depner, C. E., & Mnookin, R. H. (1990). Co-parenting in the second year after divorce. *Journal of Marriage and the Family, 52,* 141–155.

Maccoby, E. E., & Mnookin, R. H. (1992). *Dividing the child: Social and legal dilemmas of custody.* Cambridge, MA: Harvard University Press.

McLanahan, S., & Booth, K. (1989). Mother-only families: Problems, prospects, and politics. *Journal of Marriage and the Family, 51,* 557–580.

Mendes, H. A. (1976a). Single-fatherhood. *Social Work, 21,* 308– 312.

Mendes, H. A. (1976b). Single fathers. *Family Coordinator, 25,* 439–444.

Montgomery, M. J., Anderson, E. R., Hetherington, E. M., & Clingempeel, W. G. (1992). Patterns of courtship for remarriage: Implications for child adjustment and parent–child relationships. *Journal of Marriage and the Family, 54,* 686–698.

Needle, R. H., Su, S. S., & Doherty, W. J. (1990). Divorce, remarriage and adolescent substance abuse: A prospective longitudinal study. *Journal of Marriage and the Family, 52,* 157–169.

Parke, R. D., & Tinsley, B. R. (1984). Historical and contemporary perspectives on fathering. In K. A. McCluskey & H. W. Reese (Eds.), *Life-span developmental psychology: Historical and generational effects in life-span human development* (pp. xx–xx). New York: Academic Press.

Patterson, G. R. (1991, April). *Interaction of stress and family structure and their relation to child adjustment.* Paper presented at the biennial meeting of the Society for Research on Child Development, Seattle.

Patterson, G. R. (1992). Developmental changes in antisocial behavior. In R. D. Peters, R. J. McMahon, V. L. Quinsey (Eds.), *Aggression and violence throughout the life span* (pp. 52–82). Newbury Park, CA: Sage.

Patterson, G. R., & Dishion, T. J. (1988). Multilevel family process models: Traits, interactions and relationships. In R. A. Hinde & J. Stevenson-Hinde (Eds.), *Relationships within families* (pp. 283–310). London: Clarendon.

Peck, C., Bell, N., Waldren, T., & Sorrell, G. (1988). Patterns of functioning in families of remarried and first-married couples. *Journal of Marriage and the Family, 50,* 699–708.

Peterson, J. L., & Zill, N. (1986). Marital disruption, parent–child relationships, and behavior problems in children. *Journal of Marriage and the Family, 48,* 295–307.

Pink, J., & Wampler, K. (1985). Problem areas in stepfamilies: Cohesion, adaptability and the stepparent–adolescent relationship. *Family Relations, 34,* 327–335.

Rowe, B. R. (1991). The economics of divorce: Findings from seven states. *Journal of Divorce and Remarriage, 16,* 5–17.

Rutter, M. (1987). Psychosocial resilience and protective mechanisms. *American Journal of Orthopsychiatry, 57,* 316–331.

Salwen, L. V. (1990). The myth of the wicked stepmother [Special issue: Motherhood: A feminist perspective]. *Women and Therapy, 10,* 117–125.

Santrock, J. W., Sitterle, K. A., & Warshak, R. A. (1988). Parent–child relationships in stepfather families. In P. Bronstein & C. P. Cowan (Eds.), *Fatherhood today: Men's changing roles in the family* (pp. 144–165). New York: Wiley.

Santrock, J. W., & Warshak, R. A. (1979). Father custody and social development in boys and girls. *Journal of Social Issues, 35*(4), 112–125.

Santrock, J. W., Warshak, R. A., Lindberg, C., & Meadows, L. (1982). Children's and parent's observed social behavior in stepfather families. *Child Development, 53,* 472–480.

Seltzer, J. A. (1991). Relationships between father and children who live apart: The father's role after separation. *Journal of Marriage and the Family, 53,* 79–101.

Shrier, D. K., Simring, S. K., Shapiro, E. T., Grief, J. B., & Lindenthal, J. J. (1991). Level of satisfaction of fathers and mothers with joint or sole custody arrangements. *Journal of Divorce and Remarriage, 16,* 163–169.

Steinberg, L. (1987). Single parents, stepparents, and the susceptibility of adolescents to antisocial peer pressure. *Child Development, 58,* 269–275.

Steinberg, L., Mounts, N. S., Lamborn, S. D., & Dornbusch, S. M. (1991). Authoritative parenting and adolescent adjustment across varied ecological niches. *Journal of Research on Adolescence, 1,* 19–36.

Stolberg, A. L., Camplair, C. W., Currier, K., & Wells, M. J. (1987). Individual, familial, and environmental determinants of children's post-divorce adjustment and maladjustment. *Journal of Divorce, 11,* 51–70.

Thiriot, T. L., & Buckner, E. T. (1991). Multiple predictors of satisfactory post-divorce adjustment of single custodial parents. *Journal of Divorce and Remarriage, 17,* 27–48.

Tschann, J. M., Johnston, J. R., Kline, M., & Wallerstein, J. S. (1991). Conflict, loss, change, and parent–child relationships: Predicting children's adjustment during divorce. *Journal of Divorce, 13,* 1–22.

U.S. Bureau of the Census (1992). Studies in marriage a nd the family: Married couple families with children. In *Current population reports* (Series P-23, No. 162). Washington, DC: U.S. Government Printing Office.

Visher, E. B., & Visher, J. S. (1990). Dynamics of successful stepfamilies. *Journal of Divorce and Remarriage, 14,* 3–12.

Wallerstein, J. S., & Blakeslee, S. (1989). *Second chances: Men, women, and children a decade after divorce.* New York: Ticknor and Fields.

Wallerstein, J. S., Corbin, S. B., & Lewis, J. M. (1988). Children of divorce: A ten-year study. In E. M. Hetherington & J. D. Arasteh (Eds.), *Impact of divorce, single-parenting, and stepparenting on children* (pp. 198–214). Hillsdale, NJ: Lawrence Erlbaum Associates.

Wallerstein, J., & Kelly, J. (1980). *Surviving the breakup.* New York: Basic Books.

Warshak, R. A. (1986). Father custody and child development: A review and analysis of psychological research. *Behavioral Sciences and the Law, 4,* 185–202.

Weiss, R. S. (1979). Growing up a little faster: The experience of growing up in a single-parent household. *Journal of Social Issues, 35,* 97–111.

Werner, E. E. (1988). Individual differences, universal needs: A 30–year study of resilient high risk infants. *Zero to Three Bulletin of National Center for Clinical Infant Programs, 8,* 1–5.

White, L. K., Brinkerhoff, D. B., & Booth, A. (1985). The effect of marital disruption on child's attachment to parents. *Journal of Family Issues, 6,* 5–22.

Whitsett, D. P., & Land, H. M. (1992). Role strain, coping, and marital satisfaction of stepparents. *Families in Society, 73,* 79–92.

Zaslow, M. J. (1988). Sex differences in children's responses to parental divorce: I. Research methodology and post-divorce family forms. *American Journal of Orthopsychiatry, 58,* 355–378.

Zeiss, A. M., Zeiss, R. A., & Johnson, S. M. (1980). Sex differences in initiation of and adjustment to divorce. *Journal of Divorce, 4,* 21–33.

Zill, N. (1988). Behavior, achievement, and health problems among children in stepfamilies: Findings from a national survey of child health. In E. M. Hetherington & J. D. Arasteh (Eds.), *Impact of divorce, single parenting, and stepparenting on children* (pp. 325–368). Hillsdale, NJ: Lawrence Erlbaum Associates.

Zill, N., Morrison, D. R., & Coiro, M. J. (1993). Long-term effects of parental divorce on parent–child relationships, adjustment, and achievement in young adulthood. *Journal of Family Psychology, 7,* 1–13.

10

Lesbian and Gay Parenthood

Charlotte J. Patterson
University of Virginia

INTRODUCTION

The central heterosexist assumption that everyone is or ought to be heterosexual is nowhere more prevalent than in the area of parent–child relationships. Not only are children usually assumed to be heterosexual in their orientation, but mothers and fathers are also generally expected to exemplify heterosexuality in their attitudes, values, and behavior. From such a perspective, children with lesbian and gay parents seem not to exist; for many, the idea of lesbian or gay parenthood may be difficult even to imagine. In contrast to such expectations, however, many lesbian women and gay men are parents.

In this chapter, I first review the historical context in which lesbian and gay parenting has emerged. I then provide an overview of lesbian and gay parenthood today, including information about the prevalence and diversity of lesbian and gay parenting, and about the legal contexts in which lesbian and gay families currently live. I then describe the results of research on lesbian and gay parents and their children, and discuss some implications of the research findings for theories of psychological development and for the politics of family life. Next, I describe services that have been developed specifically for lesbian and gay families. The chapter concludes with a discussion of future directions for research, service, and advocacy relevant to the needs of lesbian mothers, gay fathers, and their children.

HISTORICAL CONTEXT

The emergence of large numbers of openly self-identified lesbian women and gay men is an historical phenomenon of relatively recent vintage (Boswell, 1980; D'Emilio, 1983; Faderman, 1981, 1991). Although the origins of homophile organizations date to the 1950s and even earlier (D'Emilio, 1983; Faderman, 1991), the origins of contemporary gay liberation movements are generally traced to police raids on the Stonewall bar in the Greenwich Village neighborhood of New York City in 1969, and to resistance shown by gay men and lesbian women to these attacks (Adam, 1987; D'Emilio, 1983). In the years since that time, more and more gay men and lesbian women have abandoned secrecy, declared their identities, and begun to work actively for lesbian and gay rights (Blumenfeld & Raymond, 1988).

With greater openness among lesbian and gay adults, a number of family forms are becoming more and more visible in which one or more of a child's parents identify as lesbian or gay. Many such families involve children from a previous marriage. Others involve children born or adopted after the parents have identified themselves as lesbian or gay. In the last 10 to 20 years, such families have been the subject of increasing attention in the media and in the popular press (Goleman, 1992; Gross, 1991; Martin, 1993; Rafkin, 1990; Schulenberg, 1985).

Although it is widely believed that family environments exert important influences on children who grow up in them, authoritative scholarly reviews of such matters have generally failed to consider children growing up in families with lesbian and/or gay parents (e.g., Jacob, 1987; Lamb, 1982; Parke, 1984). Given the multiplicity of new lesbian and gay families, and in view of their apparent vitality, scientists today are faced with remarkable opportunities to study the formation, growth, and impact of new family forms.

To the extent that parental influences are seen as critical in psychosocial development, and to the extent that lesbians and/or gay men may provide different kinds of influences than heterosexual parents, then the children of gay men and lesbians can been expected to develop in ways that are different from children of heterosexual parents. Whether any such differences are expected to be beneficial, detrimental, or nonexistent depends, of course, on the viewpoint from which the phenomena are observed. Lesbian and gay families with children thus present an unusual opportunity to test basic assumptions that many scientists have long taken for granted.

LESBIAN AND GAY PARENTHOOD TODAY

How many lesbian and gay families with children are there in the United States today? What are the important sources of diversity among them? And what is the nature of the legal context within which lesbian and gay families are living? In this section, I discuss each of these questions in turn.

Prevalence of Lesbian and Gay Parenthood

For many reasons, no accurate count of the numbers of lesbian and gay families with children is available. First, the numbers of lesbian and gay adults in the United States today cannot be estimated with confidence. Because of fear of discrimination, many take pains to conceal their sexual orientation (Blumenfeld & Raymond, 1988). It is especially difficult to locate lesbian and gay parents. Concerned that they might lose child custody and/or visitation rights if their sexual orientation were to be known, many lesbian and gay parents attempt to conceal their gay or lesbian identities (Pagelow, 1980), sometimes even from their own children (Dunne, 1987).

Despite acknowledged difficulties, estimates of the numbers of lesbian and gay families with children in the United States have been offered. Estimates of the number of lesbian mothers generally run from about 1 million to 5 million, and those for gay fathers from 1 million to 3 million (Gottman, 1990). Estimates of the numbers of children of lesbian or gay parents range from 6 million to 14 million (Editors of the *Harvard Law Review,* 1990). The accuracy of these numbers is not known.

One approach to making estimates of this kind is to extrapolate from what is known or believed about base rates in the population. For example, there are over 250 million people in the United States today (U.S. Bureau of the Census, 1992). According to one estimate drawn from Kinsey, Pomeroy, and Martin (1948), approximately 10 percent of the population can be considered lesbian or gay. Using these figures, one might estimate that there are about 25 million gay men and lesbians in the United States today. According to some large-scale survey studies (e.g., Bell & Weinberg, 1978; Blumstein & Schwartz, 1983), about 10 percent of gay men and about 20 percent of lesbians are parents, most of whom have children from a heterosexual marriage that ended in divorce. Calculations using these figures suggest that there may be about 3 million to 4 million lesbian or gay parents in the United States today. If, on average, each parent has two children, that would place the number of children of lesbians and gay men at about 6 million to 8 million.

The accuracy of such estimates is, of course, no better than that of the figures on which they are based. Results of recent surveys (e.g., Fay, Turner, Klassen, & Gagnon, 1989; Rogers & Turner, 1991) suggest that the 10 percent figure from Kinsey and his associates may be too high. Other work (e.g., Bradford & Ryan, 1988) suggests that greater proportions of lesbian and gay adults may be parents. Although the exact numbers will probably never be known with certainty, it does seem clear that substantial numbers of people are involved.

In addition to lesbians and gay men who became parents in the context of heterosexual marriages before coming out, growing numbers of lesbians and gay men become parents after coming out. One recent estimate holds that 5,000 to 10,000 lesbians have borne children after coming out (Seligmann, 1990). The number of lesbians who are bearing children is also believed to be increasing (Patterson, 1994a). Additional avenues to parenthood, such as foster care, adoption, coparenting, and multiple parenting, are also being explored increasingly both by lesbians and by gay men (Patterson, 1994b; Ricketts, 1991). In one recent study, over half of gay men who were not fathers said that they would like to rear a child (Sbordone, 1993). Estimates like the aforementioned may therefore minimize the actual figures, and there may be a shift among openly lesbian and gay adults toward considering parenthood as an option.

Diversity Among Lesbian Mothers, Gay Fathers, and Their Children

The numbers of lesbian and gay families with children would thus appear to be sizeable. In considering the numbers, however, it is important not to overlook the many sources of diversity among these families. In an effort to begin to characterize the diversity that characterizes lesbian and gay families with children, some of the differences among such families are examined next.

As suggested previously, one important distinction among lesbian and gay families with children involves the sexual identity of parents at the time of a child's birth or adoption. Probably the largest group of children with lesbian and gay parents today are those who were born in the context of heterosexual relationships between the biological parents, and whose parent or parents subsequently identified as lesbian or gay. These include families in which the parents divorced when the husband came out as gay, families in which the parents divorced when the wife came out as lesbian, families in which the parents divorced when both parents came out, and families in which one or both of the parents came out and the parents decided not to divorce. Lesbian or gay parents may be single, or they may have same-sex partners. A lesbian or gay parent's same-sex partner may or may not assume stepparenting relationships with the children. If the partner has also had children, the youngsters may or may not also assume stepsibling relationships with one another. In other words, lesbian and gay families with children born in the context of heterosexual relationships are themselves a relatively diverse group.

In addition to children born in the context of heterosexual relationships between parents, lesbians and gay men are believed increasingly to be choosing parenthood (Patterson, 1994a, 1994b; Pies, 1985, 1990). The majority of such children are probably conceived by means of donor insemination (DI). Lesbians who wish to bear children may choose a friend, relative, or acquaintance to be the sperm donor, or may choose instead to use sperm from an unknown donor. When sperm donors are known, they may take parental or avuncular roles relative to children conceived via DI, or they may not (Patterson, 1994a, 1994b; Pies, 1985, 1990). Gay men may also become biological parents of children whom they intend to parent, whether with a single woman (who may be lesbian or heterosexual), with a lesbian couple, or with a gay male partner. Options pursued by gay men and lesbians also include both adoption and foster care (Ricketts, 1991). Thus, children are today being brought up in a diverse array of lesbian and gay families.

In addition to differences in parents' sexual identities at the time of a child's birth, another set of distinctions concerns the extent to which family members are related biologically to one another (Pollack & Vaughn, 1987; Riley, 1988; Weston, 1991). Although biological relatedness of family members to one another is taken for granted less and less as heterosexual stepfamilies proliferate, it is often even more prominent as an issue in lesbian and gay than in heterosexual families. When children are born via DI into lesbian families, they are generally related biologically only to the birthmother, not to her partner. Similarly, when children are born via surrogacy to a gay couple, only the father who served as a sperm donor is likely to be biologically related to the child. In adoption and foster care, of course, the child will probably have no biological relation to any adoptive or foster parent.

Another issue of particular importance for lesbian and gay families concerns custodial arrangements for minor children. As in heterosexual families, children may live with one or both biological parents, or they may spend part of their time in one parent's household, and part of their time in another's. Many lesbian mothers and gay fathers have, however, lost custody of their children to heterosexual spouses following divorce, and the threat of custody litigation almost certainly looms larger in the lives of most divorced lesbian mothers than it does in the lives of divorced heterosexual ones (Lyons, 1983; Pagelow, 1980). Although no authoritative figures are available, it seems very likely that a greater proportion of lesbian and gay than of heterosexual parents has lost custody of children against their will. Probably for this reason, more lesbians and gay men seem to be noncustodial parents (i.e., do not have legal custody of their children) and nonresidential parents (i.e., do not live in the same household with their children) than might otherwise be expected.

Beyond these basic distinctions, many others can also be considered. Other important ways in which lesbian and gay families with children may differ from one another include income, education, race/ethnicity, gender, and culture. Difficulties and ambiguities in the definition of sexual orientation should also be acknowledged (Brown, 1995; Fox, 1995). Although such variability undoubtedly contributes to differences in the qualities of life, little research has yet been directed to understanding such differences among lesbian and gay families.

Legal and Public Policy Issues

When considering the environment within which lesbian and gay parenting takes place, it must be acknowledged that the legal system in the United States has long been hostile to lesbians and to gay men who are or who wish to become parents (Editors of the *Harvard Law Review,* 1990; Falk, 1989; Polikoff, 1990; Rivera, 1991). Lesbian mothers and gay fathers have often been denied custody and/or visitation with their children following divorce (Falk, 1989). Although some states now have laws stipulating that parental sexual orientation as such cannot be a factor in determining child custody following divorce, in other states lesbian or gay parents are presumed to be unfit as parents. Regulations governing foster care and adoption in many states have also made it difficult for lesbians and gay men to adopt or to serve as foster parents (Ricketts, 1991; Ricketts & Achtenberg, 1990).

One of the central issues underlying judicial decision making in custody litigation and in public policies governing foster care and adoption has been questions about the fitness of lesbians and gay men to be parents. Specifically, policies have sometimes been constructed and judicial decisions have often been made on the assumptions that lesbians and gay men are mentally ill and hence not fit to be parents, that lesbians are less maternal than heterosexual women and hence do not make good mothers, and that lesbians' and gay men's relationships with sexual partners leave little time for ongoing parent–child interactions (Editors of the *Harvard Law Review,* 1990; Falk, 1989). Because these assumptions have been important ones in denying or limiting lesbian and gay parental rights, and because they are open to empirical evaluation, they have guided much of the research on lesbian and gay parents that is discussed later.

In addition to judicial concerns about parents themselves, three principal kinds of fears about effects of lesbian and gay parents on children have also been reflected in judicial decision making about child custody and in public policies such as regulations governing foster care and adoption (Patterson, 1992). One of these concerns is that development of sexual identity among children of lesbian and gay parents will be impaired. For instance, judges may fear that children will themselves grow up to be lesbian or gay, an outcome that they generally view as negative. Another concern is that lesbian and gay parents will have adverse effects on other aspects of their children's personality development. For example, judges may fear that children in the custody of lesbian or gay parents will be more vulnerable to behavior problems or to mental breakdown. A third general concern is that these children will have difficulties in social relationships. For instance, judges may believe that children will be teased or stigmatized by peers because of their parent's sexual orientation. Because such concerns have often been explicit in judicial determinations when lesbian or gay parents' custody or visitation rights have been denied or curtailed (Editors of the *Harvard Law Review,* 1990; Falk, 1989; Polikoff, 1990; Rivera, 1991), and because these assumptions are open to empirical test, they have provided an important impetus to research.

RESEARCH ON LESBIAN MOTHERS AND GAY FATHERS

Case reports about lesbian mothers, gay fathers, and their children began to appear in the psychiatric literature in the early and mid-1970s (e.g., Osman, 1972; Weeks, Derdeyn, & Langman, 1975), but systematic research on these families is a more recent phenomenon. Despite the diversity of lesbian and gay parenting communities, research to date has with few exceptions been conducted with relatively homogeneous groups of participants. Samples of parents have been mainly White, well-educated, affluent, and living in major urban centers. Any studies that provide exceptions to this rule are specifically noted as such. In this section, research on those who became parents in the context of heterosexual relationships, before coming out as lesbian or gay, is presented first. Studies of lesbians who became parents after coming out are described next. For other reviews of research on lesbian and gay parents, see Barret and Robinson (1990), Falk (1989), and Patterson (1994c, 1995b).

Lesbians and Gay Men Who Became Parents in the Context of Heterosexual Relationships

One important impetus for research in this area has come from extrinsic sources, such as judicial concerns about the psychological health and well-being of lesbian as compared with heterosexual mothers. Other work has arisen from concerns that are more intrinsic to the families themselves, such as what and when children should be told about their parents' sexual orientation. In this section, I review first the research arising from extrinsic, then the work stemming from intrinsic concerns. Because studies tend to focus either on mothers or on fathers, I present first the research on mothers, then that on fathers. Although some of these parents may not have been married to the heterosexual partner with whom they had children, it is likely that most of the research participants were married. To avoid the use of more cumbersome labels, then, I refer to divorced lesbian mothers and to divorced gay fathers.

Divorced lesbian mothers.   Because the overall mental health of lesbian as compared to heterosexual mothers has often been raised as an issue by judges presiding over custody disputes (Falk, 1989), a number of studies have focused on this issue. Consistent with data on the mental health of lesbian women in general (Gonsiorek, 1991), research in this area has revealed that divorced lesbian mothers score at least as high as divorced heterosexual mothers on assessments of psychological health. For instance, studies have found no differences between lesbian and heterosexual mothers on self-concept, happiness, overall adjustment, or psychiatric status (Falk, 1989; Patterson, 1995b).

Another area of judicial concern has focused on maternal sex-role behavior, and its potential impact on children (Falk, 1989). Stereotypes cited by the courts suggest that lesbians might be overly masculine and/or that they might interact inappropriately with their children. In contrast to expectations based on the stereotypes, however, neither lesbian mothers' reports about their own sex-role behavior nor their self-described interest in childrearing have been found to differ from those of heterosexual mothers. Reports about responses to child behavior and ratings of warmth toward children have been found not to differ significantly between lesbian and heterosexual mothers (Kweskin & Cook, 1982; Mucklow & Phelan, 1979; Thompson, McCandless, & Strickland, 1971).

Some differences between lesbian and heterosexual mothers have also been found. Lyons (1983) and Pagelow (1980) reported that divorced lesbian mothers had more fears about loss of child custody than did divorced heterosexual mothers. Similarly, Green, Mandel, Hotvedt, Gray, and Smith (1986) reported that lesbian mothers were more likely than heterosexual mothers to be active in feminist organizations. Given the environments in which these lesbian mothers were living, findings like these are not surprising. How such differences may affect parenting behavior, if at all, is at present unknown.

A few other scattered differences seem more difficult to interpret. For instance, Miller, Jacobsen, and Bigner (1981) reported that lesbian mothers in their sample were more child centered than heterosexual mothers in their discipline techniques. In a sample of African-American lesbian mothers and African-American heterosexual mothers, Hill (1987) found that lesbian mothers reported being more flexible about rules, more relaxed about sex play and modesty, and more likely to have nontraditional expectations for their daughters.

Several studies have also examined the social circumstances and relationships of lesbian mothers. Divorced lesbian mothers have consistently been reported to be more likely than divorced heterosexual mothers to be living with a romantic partner (Harris & Turner, 1985–1986; Kirkpatrick, Smith, & Roy, 1981; Pagelow, 1980). Whether this represents a difference between lesbian and heterosexual mother-headed families, on the one hand, or reflects sampling biases of the research, on the other, cannot be determined on the basis of information in the published reports. Information is sparse about the impact of such relationships in lesbian mother families, but what has been published suggests that, like heterosexual stepparents, coresident lesbian partners of divorced lesbian mothers can be important sources of conflict as well as support in the family (Kirkpatrick, 1987).

Relationships with the fathers of children in lesbian mother homes have also been a topic of study. Few differences in the likelihood of paternal financial support have been found for lesbian and heterosexual families with children; Kirkpatrick and her colleagues (1981) reported, for example, that only about half of heterosexual and about half of lesbian mothers in their sample received any financial support from the fathers of their children. Findings about frequency of contact with fathers are mixed, with some (e.g., Kirkpatrick et al., 1981) reporting no differences in frequency of contact as a function of maternal sexual orientation and others (e.g., Golombok, Spencer, & Rutter, 1983) reporting more contact with fathers among lesbian than among heterosexual mothers.

Although most research to date has involved assessment of possible differences in personality and social behavior between lesbian and heterosexual mothers, a few studies have reported other types of comparisons. For instance, in a study of divorced lesbian mothers and divorced gay fathers, Harris and Turner (1985–1986) found that gay fathers were likely to report greater financial resources and to say that they encouraged more sex-typed toy play among their children whereas lesbian mothers were more likely to describe benefits such as increased empathy and tolerance for differences among their children as a result of having lesbian or gay parents. In comparisons of relationship satisfaction among lesbian couples who did or did not have children, Koepke, Hare, and Moran (1992) reported that couples with children scored higher on overall measures of relationship satisfaction and of the quality of their sexual relationship. These findings are intriguing, but much more research will be needed before their interpretation will be clear.

Another important set of questions, as yet little studied, concerns the conditions under which lesbian mothers experience enhanced feelings of well-being and support. Rand, Graham, and Rawlings (1982) reported that psychological health of lesbian mothers was associated with mothers' openness about their sexual orientation with employers, exhusbands, children, and friends, and with their degree of feminist activism. Kirkpatrick (1987) reported that lesbian mothers living with partners and children had greater economic and emotional resources than those living alone with their children. Much is still to be learned about determinants of individual differences in psychological well-being among lesbian mothers.

Many other issues that have arisen in the context of divorced lesbian mother families are also in need of study. For instance, when a mother is in the process of coming out as a lesbian to herself and to others, at what point in that process should she address the topic with her child, and in what ways should she do so—if at all? And what influence ought the child's age and circumstances to have in such a decision? Reports from research and clinical practice suggest that early adolescence may be a particularly difficult time for parents to initiate such conversations, and that disclosure may be less stressful at earlier points in a child's development (Patterson, 1992, 1994c), but systematic research on these issues is just beginning. Similarly, many issues remain to be addressed regarding stepfamily and blended family relationships that may emerge as a lesbian mother's household seeks new equilibrium following her separation or divorce from the child's father.

Divorced gay fathers.   Although considerable research has focused on the overall psychological adjustment of lesbian mothers as compared with that of heterosexual mothers, no published studies of gay fathers make such comparisons with heterosexual fathers. This fact may be attributable to the greater role of judicial decision making as an impetus for research on lesbian mothers. In jurisdictions where the law provides for biases in custody proceedings, these are likely to favor female and heterosexual parents. Perhaps because, other things being equal, gay fathers are extremely unlikely to win custody battles over their children after divorce, fewer such cases seem to have reached the courts. Consistent with expectations based on this view, only a small minority of divorced gay fathers have been reported to live in the same households with their children (Bigner & Bozett, 1990; Bozett, 1980, 1989).

Research on the parenting attitudes of gay versus heterosexual divorced fathers has, however, been reported (Barret & Robinson, 1990). Bigner and Jacobsen (1989a, 1989b) compared gay and heterosexual fathers, each of whom had at least two children. Results showed that, with one exception, there were no significant differences between gay and heterosexual fathers in their motives for parenthood. The single exception concerned the greater likelihood of gay than heterosexual fathers to cite the higher status accorded to parents as compared with nonparents in the dominant culture as a motivation for parenthood (Bigner & Jacobsen, 1989b).

Bigner and Jacobsen (1989a) also asked gay and heterosexual fathers in their sample to report on their own behavior with their children. Although no differences emerged in the fathers' reports of involvement or intimacy, gay fathers reported that their behavior was characterized by greater responsiveness, more reasoning, and more limit setting than did heterosexual fathers. These reports by gay fathers of greater warmth and responsiveness, on the one hand, and greater control and limit setting, on the other, are strongly reminiscent of findings from research with heterosexual families, and would seem to raise the possibility that gay fathers are more likely than their heterosexual counterparts to exhibit authoritative patterns of parenting behavior such as those described by Baumrind (1967; Baumrind & Black, 1967). Caution must be exercised, however, in the interpretation of results such as these, which stem entirely from paternal reports about their own behavior.

In addition to research comparing gay and heterosexual fathers, a few studies have made other comparisons. For instance, Robinson and Skeen (1982) compared sex-role orientations of gay fathers with those of gay men who were not fathers, and found no differences. Similarly, Skeen and Robinson (1985) found no evidence to suggest that gay men's retrospective reports about relationships with their own parents varied as a function of whether or not they were parents themselves. As noted earlier, Harris and Turner (1985–1986) compared gay fathers and lesbian mothers, reporting that, although gay fathers had higher incomes and were more likely to report encouraging their children to play with sex-typed toys, lesbian mothers were more likely to believe that their children received positive benefits such as increased tolerance for diversity from growing up with lesbian or gay parents. Studies like these begin to suggest a number of issues for research on gender, sexual orientation, and parenting behavior, and it is clear that there are many valuable directions that future work in this area could take.

A great deal of research in this area has arisen from concerns about the gay father identity and its transformations over time. Thus, work by Miller (1978, 1979) and Bozett (1980, 1981a, 1981b, 1987) has sought to provide a conceptualization of the processes through which a man who considers himself to be a heterosexual father may come to identify himself, both in public and in private, as a gay father. Based on extensive interviews with gay fathers both in the United States and in Canada, these authors have emphasized the centrality of identity disclosure and of the reactions to disclosure by significant people in a man's life. Miller (1978) suggested that, although a number of factors such as extent of occupational autonomy and amount of access to gay communities may affect how rapidly a gay man discloses his identity to others, the most important of these is likely to be the experience of falling in love with another man. It is this experience, more than any other, Miller argued, that leads a man to integrate the otherwise compartmentalized parts of his identity as a gay father. This hypothesis is very much open to empirical evaluation, but such research has not yet been reported.

Lesbians and Gay Men Choosing to Become Parents

Although for many years lesbian mothers and gay fathers were generally assumed to have become parents in the context of previous heterosexual relationships, both men and women are believed increasingly to be undertaking parenthood in the context of preexisting lesbian and gay identities (Crawford, 1987; Patterson, 1994a, 1994b). A substantial body of research addresses the transition to parenthood among heterosexuals (e.g., Cowan & Cowan, 1992; Heinicke, in this *Handbook*), but very little research has explored the transition to parenthood for gay men or lesbian women. Many issues that arise for heterosexuals also face lesbian women and gay men (e.g., concerns about how children will affect couple relationships, economic concerns about supporting children), but gay men and lesbian women must also cope with many additional issues because of their situation as members of stigmatized minorities. These issues are best understood when viewed against the backdrop of heterosexism and antigay prejudice.

Antigay prejudice is evident in institutions involved with health care, education, and employment that often fail to support, and in many cases, are openly hostile to lesbian and gay families (Casper, Schultz, & Wickens, 1992; Martin, 1993). Lesbian and gay parents may encounter antigay prejudice and bigotry even from members of their families of origin (Pollack & Vaughn, 1987). Many if not most of the special concerns of lesbian and gay parents and prospective parents stem from problems created by such hostility.

A number of interrelated issues are often faced in particular by lesbians and gay men who wish to become parents (Crawford, 1987; Martin, 1989, 1993; Patterson, 1994b). One of the first needs among prospective lesbian and gay parents is for accurate, up-to-date information on how lesbians and gay men can become parents, how their children are likely to develop, and what supports are available to assist them. In addition to such educational needs, lesbians and gay men who are seeking biological parenthood are also likely to encounter various health concerns, ranging from medical screening of prospective birthparents to assistance with DI techniques, prenatal care, and preparation for birth. As matters progress, a number of legal concerns about the rights and responsibilities of all parties are likely to emerge. Associated with all of these will generally be financial issues; in addition to the support of a child, auxiliary costs of medical and legal assistance may be considerable. Finally, social and emotional concerns of many different kinds are also likely to emerge (Patterson, 1994b; Pies, 1985, 1990; Pollack & Vaughn, 1987; Rohrbaugh, 1988).

As this brief outline of issues suggests, numerous questions are posed by the emergence of prospective lesbian and gay parents. What are the factors that influence lesbians' and gay men's inclinations to make parenthood a part of their lives? What effects does parenting have on lesbians or gay men who undertake it, and how do these effects compare with those experienced by heterosexuals? How effectively do special services such as support groups serve the needs of lesbian and gay parents and prospective parents for whom they were designed? What are the elements of a social climate that is supportive for lesbian and gay parents and their children? As yet, little research has addressed such questions.

The earliest studies of childbearing among lesbian couples were reported by McCandlish (1987) and by Steckel (1985, 1987). Both investigators reported research based on small samples of lesbian couples who had given birth to children by means of DI. Their focus was primarily on the children in such families, and neither investigator conducted systematic assessments of mothers. McCandlish did, however, highlight some events and issues that were significant among families in her sample. For instance, she noted that, regardless of their interest in parenting prior to birth of the first child, the nonbiological mothers in each couple unanimously reported an "unexpected and immediate attachment" (p. 28) to the child. Although both mothers took part in parenting, they reported shifting patterns of caregiving responsibilities over time, with the biological mother taking primary responsibility during the earliest months, and the nonbiological mother's role increasing in importance after the child was 12 or more months of age. Couples also reported changes in their own relationships following the birth of the child, notably a reduction or cessation in sexual intimacy. That lesbian couples reported less sexual activity after the birth of a child in the McCandlish study would seem to be at odds with the finding reported by Koepke and her colleagues (1992) that lesbian couples with children were more satisfied with their sexual relationship than were those without children. Further research will be needed to provide a definitive interpretation of these apparently contradictory results, and to clarify the associations of such variables with the qualities of actual behavior in parenting roles.

A recent study by Hand (1991) examined the ways in which 17 lesbian and 17 heterosexual couples with children under 2 years of age shared child care, household duties, and occupational roles. Her principal finding was that lesbian couples reported sharing parental duties more equally than did heterosexual couples. Lesbian nonbiological mothers were significantly more involved in child care than were heterosexual fathers. The lesbian nonbiological mothers also regarded their parental role as significantly more salient than did heterosexual fathers. Lesbian biological mothers viewed their maternal role as more salient than did any of the other mothers, whether lesbian or heterosexual. Fathers viewed their occupational roles as more salient than did any of the mothers, whether lesbian or heterosexual.

Another recent study (Osterweil, 1991) involved 30 lesbian couples with at least one child between 18 and 36 months of age. Consistent with Hand's (1991) results for parents of younger children, Osterweil reported that biological mothers viewed their maternal role as more salient than did nonbiological mothers. In addition, although household maintenance activities were shared about equally, biological mothers reported having more influence in family decisions and more involvement in childcare. Osterweil also reported that the couples in her study scored at about the mean for normative samples of heterosexual couples in overall relationship satisfaction. Taken together, results of the Hand and Osterweil studies thus suggest that lesbian couples who have chosen to bear children are likely to share household and child-care duties more equally than do heterosexual couples, and that lesbians are relatively satisfied with their couple relationships.

Patterson (1995a) studied 26 families headed by lesbian couples who had children between 4 and 9 years of age. Consistent with results of other investigators (Koepke et al., 1991; Osterweil, 1991), Patterson found that lesbian parents' relationship satisfaction was generally high, relative to norms for heterosexual couples. Although they reported sharing household tasks and decision making equally, couples in this study reported that biological mothers were more involved in childcare and that nonbiological mothers spent longer hours in paid employment. The differences reported by Patterson between lesbian parents' involvement in childcare were smaller by far, however, than those reported by Hand (1991) between heterosexual parents. Within this context, Patterson also found that children were better adjusted and parents were more satisfied in lesbian mother families when child care was shared more equally between parents.

Two studies of men who became fathers after identifying themselves as gay have also been reported. Sbordone (1993) studied 78 gay men who had become parents through adoption or through surrogacy arrangements, and compared them with 83 gay men who were not fathers. Consistent with Skeen and Robinson's (1985) findings with divorced gay fathers, there were no differences between fathers and nonfathers on reports about relationships with the men's own parents. Gay fathers did, however, report higher self-esteem and fewer negative attitudes about homosexuality than did gay men who were not fathers.

An interesting result of Sbordone's (1993) study was that 54 percent of the gay men who were not fathers indicated that they would like to rear a child. Those who said they wanted children were younger than those who said they did not, but the two groups did not otherwise differ (e.g., on income, education, race, self-esteem, or attitudes about homosexuality). Given that fathers had higher self-esteem and fewer negative attitudes about homosexuality than either group of nonfathers, Sbordone speculated that gay fathers' higher self-esteem might be a result rather than a cause of parenthood.

A study of gay couples choosing parenthood was conducted by McPherson (1993), who assessed division of labor, satisfaction with division of labor, and satisfaction with couple relationships among 28 gay and 27 heterosexual parenting couples. Consistent with evidence from lesbian parenting couples (Hand, 1991; Osterweil, 1991; Patterson, in press-a), McPherson found that gay couples reported a more even division of responsibilities for household maintenance and child care than did heterosexual couples. Gay parenting couples also reported greater satisfaction with their division of child-care tasks than did heterosexual couples. Finally, gay couples also reported greater satisfaction with their couple relationships, especially in the areas of cohesion and expression of affection.

As this brief discussion has revealed, research on lesbians and gay men who have chosen to become parents is as yet quite sparse. Most research has been conducted on a relatively small scale, and many important issues have yet to be addressed. Existing research suggests, however, that lesbian and gay parenting couples are more likely than heterosexual couples to share tasks involved in child care relatively evenly, and perhaps also to be more satisfied than heterosexual couples with their arrangements. Much remains to be learned about the determinants of lesbian and gay parenting, about its impact on lesbian and gay parents themselves, and about its place in contemporary communities. In the next section, I summarize what is known about the impact of parental sexual orientation on children.

RESEARCH ON CHILDREN OF LESBIAN AND GAY PARENTS

As with research on parents, an important impetus for studies of children with lesbian and gay parents has been the issues raised by the courts in the context of child custody hearings. Reflecting concerns that have been seen as relevant in the largest number of custody disputes, most of the research on children of lesbian and gay parents compares development of children with custodial lesbian mothers to that of children with custodial heterosexual mothers. Because many children living in lesbian mother-headed families have undergone the experience of parental separation and divorce, it has been widely believed that children of divorced but heterosexual mothers provide the best comparison group. Research has also focused mainly on age groups and topics relevant to the largest numbers of custody disputes. Thus, most research compares children of divorced custodial lesbian mothers with children of divorced custodial heterosexual mothers, and most studies focus on school-age children. Other reviews of this literature can be found in Gibbs (1988), Kleber, Howell, and Tibbits-Kleber (1986), Patterson (1992, 1995b), and Tasker and Golombok (1991).

One main area of concern discussed by judges in custody proceedings involves the development of sexual identity among children of lesbian and gay parents (Patterson, 1992). Studies of gender identity and of gender role behavior have, however, revealed few if any significant differences between children of lesbian or gay parents, on the one hand, and those of heterosexual parents, on the other. For instance, in one study (Gottman, 1990), 35 adult daughters of divorced lesbian mothers did not differ either from 35 adult daughters of divorced heterosexual mothers who had remarried or from 35 adult daughters of divorced heterosexual mothers who had not remarried on indexes of gender role preferences (see also Green, 1978; Hoeffer, 1981).

An area of perennial concern in the area of sexual identity is that of the development of sexual orientation. Are the offspring of lesbian and gay parents themselves more likely to become lesbian or gay? Research to date gives no evidence to support the view that having nonheterosexual parents predisposes a child to become lesbian or gay (Patterson, 1992). In Gottman's (1990) study, for example, the percentage of adult daughters who self-identified as lesbian did not differ as a function of mothers' sexual orientations.

Other concerns voiced by judges about lesbian mother homes include worries about other aspects of personal development, and about social relationships among the children (Patterson, 1992). Research relevant to these issues has, however, found no evidence to sustain any of these concerns. Children of lesbian mothers have proven to have no particular behavioral or emotional problems, no special difficulties with self-concept (Huggins, 1989), and no evidence of disruption in their social relationships with children or adults. For example, Golombok et al. (1983) compared school-age children of divorced lesbian mothers to same-age children of divorced heterosexual mothers on a wide array of assessments of behavioral problems, issues in peer relations, and relationships with adults. They found no differences, except that lesbian mothers reported that their children had more contact with their fathers than did heterosexual mothers. Children's contacts with fathers were also studied by Kirkpatrick et al. (1981), who reported no differences between children of divorced lesbian and divorced heterosexual mothers. Overall, then, the picture drawn by the existing research is one of great similarity between children of lesbian and heterosexual divorced mothers.

Some research has also been conducted to describe development among children born to or adopted by lesbian parents. The earliest studies in this area were those by McCandlish (1987) and Steckel (1985, 1987), both of whom reported similarities in overall patterns of development among young children born to lesbian and children born to heterosexual couples. This general pattern of findings has also been reported in recent studies by Patterson (1994a). Results of research on lesbian childrearing converge on the conclusion that children of lesbian mothers are developing in a normal fashion.

Despite the diversity evident within lesbian and gay communities, research on variations among lesbian and gay families with children is as yet quite sparse. Existing data suggest that children may fare better when mothers are in good psychological health and living with a lesbian partner. Patterson (in press-a) reported that children were described as more well-adjusted when their lesbian mothers reported sharing child-care duties more evenly. Existing data also suggest the value of a supportive milieu, in which parental sexual orientation is accepted by other significant adults, and in which children have contact with peers in similar circumstances. Research findings are still few in number, however, and much remains to be learned in this area.

SERVICES FOR LESBIAN AND GAY FAMILIES

In response to the varied special concerns of lesbian and gay families with children, many services and programs have been created. In this section, examples of programs and services that have arisen in three different contexts are described: parent groups, health care centers, and legal advocacy groups. For more detailed discussion of these issues, see Patterson (1994b).

Parent Groups

Lesbian and gay parents have formed many different kinds of support groups in localities in the United States and around the world. These include informal children's playgroups arranged by friends, regional associations that hold picnics, carnivals, and other community events, and international organizations that publish newsletters and sponsor conferences. In addition to addressing the needs of existing families, many groups also provide services and programs for lesbians and gay men who are considering parenthood.

The largest such group in North America is the Gay and Lesbian Parents' Coalition International (GLPCI). The GLPCI newsletter lists more than 40 chapters in cities around the world, is published quarterly, and is sent to readers in 55 countries. It contains news of national and chapter activities, interviews with lesbian and gay parents, reports of current legal issues, and notices about other matters of interest for lesbian and gay parents and prospective parents. The group also sponsors "Just for Us," an organization for children of lesbian and gay parents.

Through its central office and local chapters, GLPCI sponsors numerous activities for parents and prospective parents, including an annual convention. The national Alternative Parenting Resources project collects information regarding the policies of adoption agencies, sperm banks, and fertility programs; researches state laws as they pertain to adoption by openly lesbian families; creates lists of supportive gynecologists and fertility specialists in every state; and disseminates this information. The GLPCI central office has also compiled a lengthy bibliography on gay fathers, lesbian mothers, and their families.

Much of the support that GLPCI provides to prospective parents is made available through the efforts of local chapters that sponsor workshops and support groups for gay men and lesbians who are interested in parenthood. For example, at least one chapter sponsors a support group for individuals and couples who are in various stages of adoption and/or surrogacy arrangements. Through such activities, prospective lesbian and gay parents can learn more about local parenting opportunities, legal issues, and medical resources, as well as meet others in the lesbian and gay community who are interested in becoming parents (Patterson, 1994b).

Health Care Centers

Some medical clinics that focus on the health care needs of lesbian and gay communities also provide services for parents and prospective parents. Such clinics have generally not been formally affiliated with hospitals or medical schools but have been established as freestanding primary care centers for urban lesbian and/or gay communities. Two well-known examples are the Lyon-Martin Women's Health Services in San Francisco and the Whitman-Walker Clinic in Washington, DC.

Lyon-Martin Women's Health Services, founded in 1978, is a primary care community clinic specifically for women, with a primary focus on health care for lesbians and bisexual women. The clinic provides an array of medical and health-related services, including preventive and primary health care, HIV services, support services for mothers, and programs for sexual minority youth. It also sponsors the Lyon-Martin Lesbian/Gay Parenting Services (LGPS), which provides services for current and prospective lesbian and gay male parents.

Over the last several years, the LGPS has offered a broad array of programs for lesbian and gay families with children. These include an information and referral service, support groups for prospective parents, and workshops, forums, and special events for lesbian and gay families. Support groups are led by professional health educators and range from 8-week groups for lesbians considering parenthood to 6-week childbirth education classes. Many informational meetings and workshops on Considering Parenthood, Legal Issues, Adoption, Choices in Pregnancy and Birth, and Lesbians and Gay Men Parenting Together are also offered by the Lyon-Martin LGPS. Panel participants include professionals in health care, social services, and the law, all speaking from a lesbian- and gay-affirmative perspective.

In addition to educational programming, LGPS also sponsors a number of special events that are primarily social and recreational in character. Examples include a lesbian and gay family picnic and a parenting fair that provides access to information on a range of local parenting resources in a festive atmosphere. These kinds of community events offer valuable information, support, and recreational opportunities for lesbian and gay families.

Under the auspices of its Lesbian Choosing Children Project (LCCP), the Whitman-Walker Clinic also makes available services for lesbian and gay male parents and prospective parents. The LCCP was a cosponsor with GLPCI of Metropolitan Washington DC of a workshop on creating alternative families (described earlier). In addition, the LCCP has sponsored "Maybe Baby" groups for lesbians considering parenthood, and workshops on special topics such as "Options and Issues for Non-Biological Mothers." Similar programs are beginning to be available in other urban areas.

Legal Advocacy Groups

Legal advocacy groups within lesbian and gay communities also provide services to current and prospective lesbian parents. Especially prominent among such groups are the Lambda Legal Defense and Education Fund and the National Center for Lesbian Rights.

Lambda Legal Defense and Education Fund (LLDEF), founded in 1973 and based in New York City, works to advance the rights of sexual minorities through litigation and to provide education to the public, the legal profession, and the government about discrimination based on sexual orientation. The work of LLDEF covers a broad spectrum of issues including, " … discrimination in employment, in housing, in immigration, and in the military; AIDS and HIV-related issues; parenting and relationship issues; domestic partner benefits; and constitutional rights" (Perkins, 1992, p. 2). LLDEF filed amicus briefs in cases involving the rights of lesbian nonbiological parents in New Mexico, Minnesota, and Wisconsin (Perkins, 1992; Perkins & Romo-Carmona, 1991). For instance, an attorney for LLDEF represented the plaintiff in *Alison D. v. Virginia M.,* a well-known New York case in which a nonbiological mother sought visitation rights following the breakup of her relationship with her child's biological mother (Rubenstein, 1991). Work by LLDEF in this and related cases has been influential in legal advocacy for causes that are critical to lesbian and gay families with children.

The National Center for Lesbian Rights (NCLR), founded in 1977 and based in San Francisco, promotes awareness, respect, and recognition of lesbians and their rights (Chasnoff, 1992). The NCLR offers legal representation, *amicus* work, and technical assistance to cooperating counsel and other attorneys around the country. For example, NCLR has filed *amicus* briefs in cases involving the rights of nonbiological lesbian parents following the death of a biological parent and the breakup of a relationship between biological and nonbiological parents.

The NCLR has also been a pioneer in second-parent adoptions (Chasnoff, 1992; Ricketts & Achtenberg, 1990). Second-parent adoptions enable an unmarried parent to adopt a child without another parent of the same sex giving up his or her legal rights or responsibilities as a parent. Because they secure legal recognition of the relationship between nonbiological parents and their children, the availability of second-parent adoptions is of particular importance to lesbian and gay couples who wish to parent. Due in part to the efforts of NCLR attorneys, hundreds of second-parent adoptions have been granted to date in seven states and the District of Columbia (Chasnoff, 1992). In addition to representing nonbiological parents in second-parent adoption cases, NCLR provides technical assistance to parents and their attorneys who are seeking such adoptions, is developing a manual for use by attorneys in such cases, and provides training sessions for lawyers who handle second-parent adoption cases. NCLR has also drafted model statewide legislation in California that would change the existing stepparent adoption law to a second-parent adoption law. If enacted, this reform would streamline and simplify the process of seeking second-parent adoptions (Chasnoff, 1992).

An additional aspect of NCLR activities in support of lesbian and gay families with children is the NCLR publications program. They include a variety of materials relevant to lesbian and gay parenting, including "AIDS and Child Custody: A Guide to Advocacy," "Lesbians Choosing Motherhood: Legal Implications of Donor Insemination and Co-Parenting," and "A Lesbian and Gay Parent's Legal Guide to Child Custody." These publications can assist parents and prospective parents in their efforts to secure legal protection for their families.

DIRECTIONS FOR RESEARCH, SERVICE, AND ADVOCACY

Although some innovative programs and services are available for lesbian mothers, gay fathers, and their children, their availability is still extremely limited. In this section, directions for research, service, and advocacy relevant to lesbian and gay families with children are described.

Directions for Research

One of the important directions for research is to identify and to explore factors that influence lesbian and gay couples' and individuals' inclinations to make parenthood a part of their lives (Crawford, 1987). Having lived so long in the shadow of antigay prejudice, many lesbians and gay men do not consider parenthood as an option. What kinds of influences are important in this regard? Does the degree of an individual's or a couple's integration with different parts of gay/lesbian and/or heterosexual communities make a difference? What roles do personal, social, and economic variables play in such decisions? We need to know more about the factors that influence decisions about parenthood among lesbians and gay men.

A related direction for research is assessment of the climate for lesbian and gay parenting in various areas. What are the important criteria that should be used in such an assessment, and how do different locales measure up against them? One approach might be to use state-level indicators as rough indices. For example, a statewide lesbian/gay rights law would be a positive indicator with regard to the climate for lesbian and gay parenting, as would the accomplishment of second-parent adoptions in that state. On the other side, negative indicators would include the existence of sodomy laws and/or other adverse legal precedents. One might also review regulations pertaining to adoption and foster care placements. Ratings of this sort could be useful for couples and individuals seeking parenthood, parents considering relocation, and for activists and advocacy groups deciding how best to direct their activities.

The climates of local communities might also be assessed with the needs of lesbian and gay parents and their children in mind. For instance, one might ask whether or not there are lesbian and gay parent groups already in existence, whether or not any second-parent adoptions have been completed within this community, and whether or not relevant health care and medical resources are available to lesbian and gay families. Such assessments should be geared to specific locales, because communities that are located in geographical proximity to one another may vary tremendously in the climates they provide for lesbian and gay families with children.

Such efforts to examine and to describe the atmosphere for lesbian and gay family life also raise questions about what aspects of a community make it an attractive place for lesbian and gay parents and their children to live. Such characteristics might in some cases be similar to those for heterosexual families (e.g., safe streets, good schools), whereas in other cases they might vary even among lesbian and gay families as a function of the family's other identities, interests, or needs. For instance, multiracial families might value especially the opportunity to live in multiracial neighborhoods.

It would also be valuable to learn more about the effectiveness of existing services for lesbian and gay families. Although many new services and programs have emerged for prospective parents as well as for parents and their children, there have been few attempts to evaluate their effectiveness. How effectively do available services fill the needs that they are intended to address? What populations are targeted by existing programs, and with what success do programs and services reach the communities for which they are intended? What are the essential elements of effective programs? And how can existing programs be improved? All of these are critical questions for community-oriented research on lesbian and gay parenting services (see D'Augelli & Garnets, 1995).

Finally, the knowledge base relevant to lesbian and gay parenting is still very limited. Courts need accurate information about the impact, if any, of parental sexual orientation upon the development of children. Lesbians and gay men interested in parenting often want descriptive information about child and adolescent development among the offspring of lesbian and gay parents. Many lesbians and gay men considering parenthood also have questions about the ways in which parenthood can be expected to affect existing couple relationships in lesbian and gay families. Others are concerned about relationships with members of their families of origin as well as with friends, neighbors, and colleagues. Still others focus on family members' interactions with institutional contexts such as educational, legal, and medical settings. Scientists want to develop better understanding of the important variables in parenting, and this requires greater knowledge about parenting and about child development in lesbian and gay families. Such topics are open to empirical study, and the work has begun, but much remains to be accomplished.

Directions for Service

There are a number of ways in which efforts to provide improved services for lesbian and gay parents might be directed. In part because services for lesbian and gay parents are so new, and in part because of widespread discrimination, expanded services are needed at all levels. At the national level, an organization like GLPCI has the potential to develop lists of health care, legal, and other resources on a state-by-state basis, as well as to provide technical assistance to local groups. At regional and local levels, individual parent groups are mounting educational events and other programs in support of lesbian and gay parenting in local communities. Even in major urban areas, however, most such programs are in a nascent state, depend heavily on the efforts of volunteers, and reach mainly affluent, well-educated segments of lesbian and gay communities. In many smaller towns and rural areas, there are as yet no services at all.

One of the major needs, then, is for expansion of services. Programs and services should be developed by and for low-income and ethnic minority lesbian and gay individuals and couples who are parents or who wish to become parents. Of necessity, such work would involve identification of medical, legal, and other resources that are open to members of sexual minorities as well as to ethnic minorities and low-income communities. Services could also be developed for the children of lesbian and gay parents.

In seeking to expand services for sexual minority parenting communities, it will be important not to overlook important resources outside lesbian and gay communities themselves. For instance, building public library collections in areas relevant to lesbian and gay parenting can provide an important resource that is available to large numbers of people, regardless of sexual orientation. Educational institutions such as high schools, colleges, and universities can also provide important resources for prospective lesbian and gay parents by including accurate information in the curriculum, by providing speakers and other relevant programming, and by making available to students articles, books, and video materials that relate to parenting by individuals with sexual minority identities (Casper et al., 1992). Similarly, religious groups can offer meaningful support by providing special activities for lesbian and gay families with children, and by educating all members of congregations about lesbian and gay parenting (Kahn, 1991).

Another major aim of service to prospective lesbian and gay parents is to eliminate discrimination against lesbian and gay parents and their children. To the degree that this effort meets with success, many of the special needs of lesbian or gay parents and their children will decrease in significance. Although it is unlikely that antigay prejudice will be eliminated in the foreseeable future, work in this direction is nevertheless an item of great importance. Prevention efforts relevant to lesbian and gay parenting should be designed to counter unfavorable stereotypes of lesbians and gay men with accurate information about the realities of life in lesbian and gay families, and to provide an understanding of psychosocial processes underlying prejudice and discrimination.

Directions for Advocacy

Among the greatest current needs of lesbian and gay families with children is for activism to promote social and political change. Lesbian and gay parents and their children have issues in common with those of many other families, but they also have unique concerns that arise from prejudice against lesbian and gay families.

The basic issues of children and families in the United States are, in many cases, also the issues of lesbian and gay families with children. For instance, many families with children would benefit from enhanced neighborhood safety, better public schools, flexible working hours for parents, and better access to health care. Improved economic conditions and a more equal distribution of economic resources would benefit children in economically stressed lesbian and gay families, just as they would benefit children in other economically disadvantaged homes. In other words, a common stake is held by lesbian, gay, and heterosexual families in many issues of public policy relevant to families with children.

Even allowing for overlap with the needs of other families, though, lesbian and gay families with children also have a unique agenda. Lesbian and gay families with children are less likely than heterosexual families to enjoy legal recognition for their family relationships, equal access to medical care, or freedom from harassment, bigotry, and hate crimes. The quality of life for lesbian and gay parents would be greatly enhanced if they could be confident that their sexual orientation would not be held against them as they pursue parenthood, bring up their children, or seek custody of their children after a partner's death or the breakup of an intimate relationship between parents. Like the offspring of heterosexual parents, children of lesbian and gay parents would feel more secure if their relationships with parents were protected by law. Accomplishment of such aims is an important goal for advocacy efforts on behalf of lesbian and gay families with children (Polikoff, 1990; Rubinstein, 1991).

CONCLUSIONS

Research on lesbian mothers, gay fathers, and their children is still relatively new. Systematic study of lesbian and gay families with children began in the context of judicial challenges to the fitness of lesbian and gay parents. For this reason, much research has been designed to evaluate negative judicial presumptions about psychological health and well-being of parents and children in lesbian and gay families. Although much remains to be done to understand conditions that foster positive mental health among lesbian mothers, gay fathers, and their children, the results of early research are exceptionally clear. Findings of studies to date provide no reason under the prevailing "best interests of the child" standard to deny or curtail parental rights of lesbian or gay parents on the basis of their sexual orientation, nor do they provide any support for the belief that lesbians or gay men are less suitable than heterosexuals to serve as adoptive or foster parents.

With these conclusions in mind, researchers are now beginning also to turn their attention to areas of diversity among lesbian and gay families, and are starting to explore conditions that help lesbian and gay families to flourish. This transition, now well underway, appears to be gathering momentum, and it suggests that research on lesbian and gay families has reached a significant turning point (Patterson, 1992). Having addressed negative assumptions represented in psychological theory, judicial opinion, and popular prejudice, researchers are now in a position to explore a broader range of issues.

From a methodological viewpoint, a number of directions seem especially promising. Longitudinal research is needed to follow families over time and illuminate how changing life circumstances affect both parents and children. There is also a clear need for observational studies, and for work conducted with large samples. A greater focus on family interactions and processes as well as on structural variables is also likely to be valuable (Patterson, 1992).

From a substantive point of view, many issues relevant to lesbian and gay families are in need of study. First and most obvious is that studies representing the demographic diversity of lesbian and gay families are needed. With few exceptions (e.g., Hill, 1987), existing research has involved White, well-educated, middle-class families who live in urban areas of the United States. More work is needed to understand differences that are based on race and ethnicity, family economic circumstances, and cultural environments. Research of this kind should elucidate differences as well as commonalities among lesbian and gay families with children.

Future research should also, insofar as possible, encompass a larger number of levels of analysis. Existing research has most often focused on children or on their parents, considered as individuals. As valuable as this emphasis has been, it will also be important to consider couples and families as such. Assessments of dyadic adjustment or family climate could enhance understanding of individual level variables such as self-esteem. When families are considered at different levels of analysis, nested within the neighborhood, regional, and cultural contexts in which they live (Cochran & Niego, in this *Handbook*), a more comprehensive understanding of lesbian and gay families is likely to emerge.

In this effort, it will be valuable to devote attention to family process as well as to family structure. How do lesbian and gay families negotiate their interactions with institutional settings such as the school and the workplace (Casper et al., 1992)? How are family processes and interactions affected by economic, cultural, religious, and legal aspects of the contexts in which families live? How do climates of opinion that prevail in their communities affect lesbian and gay families, and how do families cope with prejudice and discrimination when these are encountered?

Gender is a matter deserving of special attention in this regard. Inasmuch as lesbian and gay relationships encourage the uncoupling of gender and behavioral roles, one might expect to find considerable variability among families in the ways in which they carry out essential family, household, and child-care tasks (Hand, 1991; McPherson, 1993; Osterweil, 1991; Patterson, 1995a). In what ways do nontraditional divisions of labor affect children who grow up in lesbian and gay homes? And in what ways does the performance of nontraditional tasks affect parents themselves? In general terms, it will be valuable to learn more about the relative importance of gender and behavioral roles in lesbian and gay families with children.

One additional issue that should be given special emphasis involves the conceptualization of parents' sexual identities. In research on lesbian and gay parenting, scant attention has been devoted to the fluidity of sexual identities over time, or to the implications of any such fluidity for children (Brown, 1995). For instance, many parents are probably bisexual to some degree, rather than exclusively heterosexual, gay, or lesbian, yet this has rarely been noted or studied directly in the existing research literature. Increasing numbers of adults seem to be identifying themselves as bisexual (Fox, 1995). Future research might benefit from closer attention to issues in assessment of parental sexual orientation.

Although research to date on lesbian mothers, gay fathers, and their children has been fruitful, there is yet much important work to be done. Having addressed many of the heterosexist concerns of jurists, theorists, and others, researchers are now poised to examine a broader range of issues raised by the emergence of different kinds of lesbian and gay families with children. Results of future work in this area have the potential to increase our knowledge about lesbian and gay parenthood, stimulate innovations in our theoretical understanding of human development, and inform legal rulings and public policies relevant to lesbian mothers, gay fathers, and their children.

ACKNOWLEDGMENTS

I wish to acknowledge support from the Society for Psychological Study of Social Issues for my own research on lesbian families with children, and to thank Marc Bornstein, Deborah Cohn, and Dan McPherson for their contributions to this chapter.

REFERENCES

Adam, B. D. (1987). *The rise of a gay and lesbian movement.* Boston: Twayne.

Barret, R. L., & Robinson, B. E. (1990). *Gay fathers.* Lexington, MA: Lexington.

Baumrind, D. (1967). Childcare practices anteceding three patterns of preschool behavior. *Genetic Psychology Monographs, 75*, 43–88.

Baumrind, D., & Black, A. E. (1967). Socialization practices associated with dimensions of competence in preschool boys and girls. *Child Development, 38*, 291–327.

Bell, A. P., & Weinberg, M. S. (1978). *Homosexualities: A study of diversity among men and women*. New York: Simon & Schuster.

Bigner, J. J., & Bozett, F. W. (1990). Parenting by gay fathers. In F. W. Bozett & M. B. Sussman (Eds.), *Homosexuality and family relations* (pp. 155–176). New York: Harrington Park Press.

Bigner, J. J., & Jacobsen, R. B. (1989a). Parenting behaviors of homosexual and heterosexual fathers. In F. W. Bozett (Ed.), *Homosexuality and the family* (pp. 173–186). New York: Harrington Park Press.

Bigner, J. J., & Jacobsen, R. B. (1989b). The value of children to gay and heterosexual fathers. In F. W. Bozett (Ed.), *Homosexuality and the family* (pp. 163–172). New York: Harrington Park Press.

Blumenfeld, W. J., & Raymond, D. (1988). *Looking at gay and lesbian life*. Boston: Beacon.

Blumstein, P., & Schwartz, P. (1983). *American couples*. New York: Morrow.

Boswell, J. (1980). *Christianity, social tolerance, and homosexuality: Gay people in Western Europe from the beginning of the Christian era to the fourteenth century*. Chicago: University of Chicago Press.

Bozett, F. W. (1980). Gay fathers: How and why they disclose their homosexuality to their children. *Family Relations, 29*, 173–179.

Bozett, F. W. (1981a). Gay fathers: Evolution of the gay-father identity. *American Journal of Orthopsychiatry, 51*, 552–559.

Bozett, F. W. (1981b). Gay fathers: Identity conflict resolution through integrative sanctioning. *Alternative Lifestyles, 4*, 90–107.

Bozett, F. W. (1987). Children of gay fathers. In F. W. Bozett (Ed.), *Gay and lesbian parents* (pp. 39–57). New York: Praeger.

Bozett, F. W. (1989). Gay fathers: A review of the literature. In F. W. Bozett (Ed.), *Homosexuality and the family* (pp. 137–162). New York: Harrington Park Press.

Bradford, J. B., & Ryan, C. (1988). *National lesbian health care survey: Final report*. Washington, DC: National Lesbian and Gay Health Foundation.

Brown, L. (1995). Lesbian identities: Conceptual issues. In A. R. D'Augelli & C. J. Patterson (Eds.), *Lesbian, gay and bisexual identities across the lifespan* (pp. 3–23). New York: Oxford University Press.

Casper, V., Schultz, S., & Wickens, E. (1992). Breaking the silences: Lesbian and gay parents and the schools. *Teachers College Record, 94*, 109–137.

Chasnoff, D. (1992, Spring). *Newsletter of the National Center for Lesbian Rights*. San Francisco: National Center for Lesbian Rights.

Cowan, C. P., & Cowan, P. A. (1992). *When partners become parents: The big life change for couples*. New York: Basic Books.

Crawford, S. (1987). Lesbian families: Psychosocial stress and the family-building process. In Boston Lesbian Psychologies Collective (Ed.), *Lesbian psychologies: Explorations and challenges* (pp. 195–214). Urbana: University of Illinois Press.

D'Augelli, A. R., & Garnets, L. (1995). Lesbian, gay and bisexual communities. In A. R. D'Augelli & C. J. Patterson (Eds.), *Lesbian, gay and bisexual identities across the lifespan* (pp. 293–320). New York: Oxford University Press.

D'Emilio, J. (1983). *Sexual politics, sexual communities: The makings of a homosexual minority in the United States, 1940–1970*. Chicago: University of Chicago Press.

Dunne, E. J. (1987). Helping gay fathers come out to their children. *Journal of Homosexuality, 13*, 213–222.

Editors of the *Harvard Law Review*. (1990). *Sexual orientation and the law*. Cambridge, MA: Harvard University Press.

Faderman, L. (1981). *Surpassing the love of men*. New York: Morrow.

Faderman, l. (1991). *Odd girls and twilight lovers: A history of lesbian life in twentieth century America*. New York: Columbia University Press.

Falk, P. J. (1989). Lesbian mothers: Psychosocial assumptions in family law. *American Psychologist, 44*, 941–947.

Fay, R. E., Turner, C. F., Klassen, A. D., & Gagnon, J. H. (1989). Prevalence and patterns of same-gender sexual contact among men. *Science, 243*, 338–348.

Fox, R. C. (1995). Bisexual identities. In A. R. D'Augelli & C. J. Patterson (Eds.), *Lesbian, gay and bisexual identities across the lifespan* (pp. 48–86). New York: Oxford University Press.

Gibbs, E. D. (1988). Psychosocial development of children raised by lesbian mothers: A review of research. *Women and Therapy, 8*, 55–75.

Goleman, D. (1992, December 2). Studies find no disadvantage to growing up in a gay home. *The New York Times*, p. C-14.

Golombok, S., Spencer, A., & Rutter, M. (1983). Children in lesbian and single-parent households: Psychosexual and psychiatric appraisal. *Journal of Child Psychology and Psychiatry, 24*, 551–572.

Gonsiorek, J. C. (1991). The empirical basis for the demise of the illness model of homosexuality. In J. C. Gonsiorek & J. D. Weinrich (Eds.), *Homosexuality: Research implications for public policy* (pp. 115–136). Beverly Hills, CA: Sage Publications.

Gottman, J. S. (1990). Children of gay and lesbian parents. In F. W. Bozett & M. B. Sussman (Eds.), *Homosexuality and family relations* (pp. 177–196). New York: Harrington Park Press.

Green, R. (1978). Sexual identity of 37 children raised by homosexual or transsexual parents. *American Journal of Psychiatry, 135*, 692–697.

Green, R., Mandel, J. B., Hotvedt, M. E., Gray, J., & Smith, L. (1986). Lesbian mothers and their children: A comparison with solo parent heterosexual mothers and their children. *Archives of Sexual Behavior, 7*, 175–181.

Gross, J. (1991, February 11). New challenge of youth: Growing up in a gay home. *The New York Times*, pp. A-1, B-7.

Hand, S. I. (1991). *The lesbian parenting couple.* Unpublished doctoral dissertation, The Professional School of Psychology, San Francisco.

Harris, M. B., & Turner, P. H. (1985–1986). Gay and lesbian parents. *Journal of Homosexuality, 12,* 101–113.

Hill, M. (1987). Child-rearing attitudes of Black lesbian mothers. In Boston Lesbian Psychologies Collective (Eds.), *Lesbian psychologies: Explorations and challenges* (pp. 215–226). Urbana: University of Illinois Press.

Hoeffer, B. (1981). Children's acquisition of sex-role behavior in lesbian-mother families. *American Journal of Orthopsychiatry, 5,* 536–544.

Huggins, S. L. (1989). A comparative study of self-esteem of adolescent children of divorced lesbian mothers and divorced heterosexual mothers. In F. W. Bozett (Ed.), *Homosexuality and the family* (pp. 123–135). New York: Harrington Park Press.

Jacob, T. (Ed.). (1987). *Family interaction and psychopathology: Theories, methods, and findings.* New York: Plenum.

Kahn, Y. H. (1991). Hannah, must you have a child? *Out/Look,* Spring 1991 (Issue 12), 39–43.

Kinsey, A. C., Pomeroy, W. B., & Martin, C. E. (1948). *Sexual behavior in the human male.* Philadelphia: Saunders.

Kirkpatrick, M. (1987). Clinical implications of lesbian mother studies. *Journal of Homosexuality, 13,* 201–211.

Kirkpatrick, M., Smith, C., & Roy, R. (1981). Lesbian mothers and their children: A comparative survey. *American Journal of Orthopsychiatry, 51,* 545–551.

Kleber, D. J., Howell, R. J., & Tibbits-Kleber, A. L. (1986). The impact of parental homosexuality in child custody cases: A review of the literature. *Bulletin of the American Academy of Psychiatry and Law, 14,* 81–87.

Koepke, L., Hare, J., & Moran, P. B. (1992). Relationship quality in a sample of lesbian couples with children and child-free lesbian couples. *Family Relations, 41,* 224–229.

Kweskin, S. L., & Cook, A. S. (1982). Heterosexual and homosexual mothers' self-described sex-role behavior and ideal sex-role behavior in children. *Sex Roles, 8,* 967–975.

Lamb, M. E. (Ed.) (1982). *Nontraditional families: Parenting and child development.* Hillsdale, NJ: Lawrence Erlbaum Associates.

Lyons, T. A. (1983). Lesbian mothers' custody fears. *Women and Therapy, 2,* 231–240.

Martin, A. (1989). The planned lesbian and gay family: Parenthood and children. *Newsletter of the Society for the Psychological Study of Lesbian and Gay Issues, 5,* 6, 16–17.

Martin, A. (1993). *The lesbian and gay parenting handbook: Creating and raising our families.* New York: HarperCollins.

McCandlish, B. (1987). Against all odds: Lesbian mother family dynamics. In F. Bozett (Ed.), *Gay and lesbian parents* (pp. 23–38). New York: Praeger.

McPherson, D. (1993). *Gay parenting couples: Parenting arrangements, arrangement satisfaction, and relationship satisfaction.* Unpublished doctoral dissertation, Pacific Graduate School of Psychology, Palo Alto, CA.

Miller, B. (1978). Adult sexual resocialization: Adjustments toward a stigmatized identity. *Alternative Lifestyles, 1,* 207–234.

Miller, B. (1979). Gay fathers and their children. *Family Coordinator, 28,* 544–552.

Miller, J. A., Jacobsen, R. B., & Bigner, J. J. (1981). The child's home environment for lesbian versus heterosexual mothers: A neglected area of research. *Journal of Homosexuality, 7,* 49–56.

Mucklow, B. M., & Phelan, G. K. (1979). Lesbian and traditional mothers' responses to adult responses to child behavior and self concept. *Psychological Reports, 44,* 880–882.

Osman, S. (1972). My stepfather is a she. *Family Process, 11,* 209–218.

Osterweil, D. A. (1991). *Correlates of relationship satisfaction in lesbian couples who are parenting their first child together.* Unpublished doctoral dissertation, California School of Professional Psychology, Berkeley/Alameda.

Pagelow, M. D. (1980). Heterosexual and lesbian single mothers: A comparison of problems, coping and solutions. *Journal of Homosexuality, 5,* 198–204.

Parke, R. D. (Ed.). (1984). *Review of child development research: Vol. 7. The family.* Chicago: University of Chicago Press.

Patterson, C. J. (1992). Children of lesbian and gay parents. *Child Development, 63,* 1025–1042.

Patterson, C. J. (1994a). Children of the lesbian baby boom: Behavioral adjustment, self-concepts, and sex-role identity. In B. Greene & G. Herek (Eds.), *Contemporary perspectives on lesbian and gay psychology: Theory, research, and applications* (pp. 156–175). Beverly Hills, CA: Sage.

Patterson, C. J. (1994b). Lesbian and gay couples considering parenthood: An agenda for research, service, and advocacy. *Journal of Gay and Lesbian Social Services, 1,* 33–55.

Patterson, C. J. (1994c). Lesbian and gay families. *Current Directions in Psychological Science, 3,* 62–64.

Patterson, C. J. (1995a). Families of the lesbian baby boom: Parents' division of labor and children's adjustment. *Developmental Psychology, 31,* 115–123 .

Patterson, C. J. (1995b). Lesbian mothers, gay fathers, and their children. In A. R. D'Augelli & C. J. Patterson (Eds.), *Lesbian, gay and bisexual identities across the lifespan* (pp. 262–290). New York: Oxford University Press.

Perkins, P. (Ed.). (1992). *The Lambda update* (Vol. 9, No. 1). New York: Lambda Legal Defense and Education Fund.

Perkins, P., & Romo-Carmona, M. (1991). *The Lambda update* (Vol. 8, No. 1). New York: Lambda Legal Defense and Education Fund.

Pies, C. (1985). *Considering parenthood.* San Francisco: Spinsters/Aunt Lute.

Pies, C. (1990). Lesbians and the choice to parent. In F. W. Bozett & M. B. Sussman (Eds.), *Homosexuality and family relations* (pp. 137–154). New York: Harrington Park Press.

Polikoff, N. (1990). This child does have two mothers: Redefining parenthood to meet the needs of children in lesbian mother and other nontraditional families. *The Georgetown Law Review, 78,* 459–575.

Pollack, S., & Vaughn, J. (Eds.). (1987). *Politics of the heart: A lesbian parenting anthology.* Ithaca, NY: Firebrand Books.

Rafkin, L. (Ed.). (1990). *Different mothers: Sons and daughters of lesbians talk about their lives.* Pittsburgh: Cleis Press.

Rand, C., Graham, D. L. R., & Rawlings, E. I. (1982). Psychological health and factors the court seeks to control in lesbian mother custody trials. *Journal of Homosexuality, 8,* 27–39.

Ricketts, W. (1991). Lesbians and gay men as foster parents. Portland, ME: National Child Welfare Resource Center for Management and Administration.

Ricketts, W., & Achtenberg, R. (1990). Adoption and foster parenting for lesbians and gay men: Creating new traditions in family. In F. W. Bozett & M. B. Sussman (Eds.), *Homosexuality and family relations* (pp. 83–118). New York: Harrington Park Press.

Riley, C. (1988). American kinship: A lesbian account. *Feminist Issues, 8,* 75–94.

Rivera, R. (1991). Sexual orientation and the law. In J. C. Gonsiorek & J. D. Weinrich (Eds.), *Homosexuality: Research implications for public policy* (pp. 81–100). Newbury Park, CA: Sage.

Robinson, B. E., & Skeen, P. (1982). Sex-role orientation of gay fathers versus gay nonfathers. *Perceptual and Motor Skills, 55,* 1055–1059.

Rogers, S. M., & Turner, C. F. (1991). Male-male sexual contact in the U.S.A.: Findings from five sample surveys, 1970–1990. *Journal of Sex Research, 28,* 491–519.

Rohrbaugh, J. B. (1988). Choosing children: Psychological issues in lesbian parenting. *Women and Therapy, 8,* 51–63.

Rubenstein, W. B. (1991). We are family: A reflection on the search for legal recognition of lesbian and gay relationships. *The Journal of Law and Politics, 8,* 89–105.

Sbordone, A. J. (1993). *Gay men choosing fatherhood.* Unpublished doctoral dissertation, City University of New York, New York.

Schulenberg, J. (1985). *Gay parenting: A complete guide for gay men and lesbians with children.* New York: Anchor.

Seligmann, J. (1990, Winter/Spring). Variations on a theme. *Newsweek* (Special ed.: The 21st Century Family), pp. 38–46.

Skeen, P., & Robinson, B. (1985). Gay fathers' and gay nonfathers' relationships with their parents. *Journal of Sex Research, 21,* 86–91.

Steckel, A. (1985). *Separation-individuation in children of lesbian and heterosexual couples.* Unpublished doctoral dissertation, The Wright Institute Graduate School, Berkeley, CA.

Steckel, A. (1987). Psychosocial development of children of lesbian mothers. In F. W. Bozett (Ed.), *Gay and lesbian parents* (pp. 75–85). New York: Praeger.

Tasker, F. L., & Golombok, S. (1991). Children raised by lesbian mothers: The empirical evidence. *Family Law, 21,* 184–187.

Thompson, N., McCandless, B., & Strickland, B. (1971). Personal adjustment of male and female homosexuals and heterosexuals. *Journal of Abnormal Psychology, 78,* 237–240.

U.S. Bureau of the Census. (1992). *Statistical abstract of the United States, 1991.* Washington, DC: U.S. Department of Commerce.

Weeks, R. B., Derdeyn, A. P., & Langman, M. (1975). Two cases of children of homosexuals. *Child Psychiatry and Human Development, 6,* 26–32.

Weston, K. (1991). *Families we choose: Lesbians, gays, kinship.* New York: Columbia University Press.

PART II

SOCIAL CONDITIONS
OF PARENTING

11

Determinants of the Transition to Parenting

Christoph M. Heinicke
University of California, Los Angeles

INTRODUCTION

The transition to becoming a parent represents a major life change. Interest in this developmental change is universal. Professionals writing in the 1940s through the 1960s stressed the adjustments necessary to deal with the arrival and care of the infant. Global descriptions of the essence of these adjustments differed. Some authors concluded that the birth of the infant represented a crucial positive fulfillment of the developmental and psychic needs of the woman (Deutsch, 1945). Other writers characterized pregnancy and the transition to parenthood as a period of crisis (Bibring, Dwyer, Huntington, & Valenstein, 1961; Hill, 1949). Shereshefsky and Yarrow (1973) saw this developmental disequilibrium as an opportunity to facilitate positive change through intervention. They systematically assessed the impact of counseling on the adjustment to pregnancy and early infancy. One of their most important findings was that the clarity and confidence in visualizing themselves as future parents was found to anticipate a more adequate postnatal adjustment.

Other pioneer longitudinal studies (Grossman, Eichler, & Winikoff, 1980) stimulated detailed description of the transition to parenting and to delineation of those aspects of the family system likely to influence family development. Both for its own sake and as a guide to more effective intervention, investigators recognized the need for more specific information about the determinants of parenting.

Within a family system framework this chapter examines the impact of prebirth parent personality and relationship functioning on key areas of parent and child development. According to the general hypothesis, the personality characteristics of the parents as well as their relationship support systems (partner and extended family) to a significant extent define future parenting transactions with their child. Within this hypothesis, more specific statements will be made and supported with research findings. For example, couples who are characterized by *prebirth* and *continuing positive mutuality* continue their optimal parenting in the first years, and have children who are secure and autonomous in preschool, are less aggressive, and score higher on achievement tests at the end of kindergarten.

Certain concepts will be used throughout the chapter to summarize and integrate the knowledge on the prebirth determinants of parenting and child development. At the risk of oversimplifying, they are briefly defined here. *Adaptation-competence* of the parent is the efficient nonanxious flexible approach to problem solving. The *capacity for sustained positive relationships* refers to empathy and positive mutuality in an ongoing relationship. The *positive self-development* of the parent is characterized by a sense of autonomy and confidence, as opposed to insecurity. Two primary contexts in which these personality characteristics will be studied are the relationship to the partner, and past and present extended family and social networks.

Parallel to the three adult characteristics are the descriptions of three components of the child's developing self. The *competent self* is associated with being an agent, task persistence, and self-regulation; the *secure self* is associated with expecting care from a relationship (attachment) and feeling worthy; and the growing *separate self* is seen in the awareness of the self and others as well as a sense of autonomy.

Three parent–infant transactions provide a conceptual link between the adult and child development. Parental exposure of the child to new cognitive experiences as well as teaching them transacts with the developing competent self. They influence each other. Similarly, parental responsiveness to need enhances and is enhanced by the developing security in the child. Parental preparation for and encouragement of autonomy interacts with that quality in the child.

The previous concepts provide a means for integrating findings from various projects. A further context for current research is to review the theoretical frameworks and supporting data that provide the immediate historical background.

This chapter outlines three theoretical frameworks initially formulated in the early 1980s. The first of these addresses the transition to parenthood (C. P. Cowan, P. A. Cowan, L. Coie, & J. D. Coie, 1978) and thus lends itself to describing *normative changes* that occur as "partners become parents." The second and third (Belsky, 1984; Heinicke, 1984) conceptualize and summarize previous research on the "determinants of parenting": How do pre-birth characteristics influence *individual variation* in parenting?

These reviews in turn provide the background for defining the central issues as well as the essential propositions of the chapter. The first proposition states that parent personality and marital functioning is relatively stable in the transition to parenthood. Parents functioning more adequately than other parents before the birth of their child also tend to function more adequately after the birth. Given this potential for a relatively consistent impact, it is next proposed that differences in the quality of the pre-birth parent personality and experienced support are linked to differences in parent-child and child functioning. Finally, given the conclusion that prebirth characteristics are stable and impact parenting and child development, it then follows that intervention must include addressing those parent characteristics within a family system context. Three frameworks are used to organize research in the 1980s, and the following studies are summarized: C. P. Cowan et al. (1978), Belsky (1984), and Heinicke (1984).

CONCEPTUALIZATION AND SUMMARY OF RESEARCH FROM THE 1970S TO THE MID-1980S

The Transition to Parenthood: The Five-Domain Structural Model of Marital and Family Adaptation

Starting with the examination of early concepts that had dominated the study of family formation— namely, that the arrival of the first child represents a "crisis" in the lives of couples (Hobbs & Coles, 1976)—P. A. Cowan and C. P. Cowan (1988) noted that many studies of the transition to parenthood do indicate a significant, but not large, decline in marital satisfaction (Belsky & Pensky, 1988). However, they also stressed that the concept of crisis and other aspects of the transition needed to be redefined by focusing on the structural connections among five domains. Using data from the study of 72 couples expecting their first child, and 24 couples not yet decided about having children, the authors described changes that were found in couples welcoming their first child. The following five domains of family functioning are used to organize these findings.

The characteristics of each individual: Self-esteem and the sense of self. Using the Adjective Check List (Gough & Heilbrun, 1980), the authors found remarkable stability over 21 months in self-esteem for all subsamples (C. P. Cowan et al., 1985). As indicated previously, stability refers to the fact that the placement (or rank) of a family within a group of families remains the same from one time point to another.

By contrast, description of the salient life roles showed significant changes from prebirth to 6 months. At each point, each parent was asked to indicate the importance of each aspect of themselves by dividing a "pie" into sections. The parent aspect of self increased markedly from pregnancy to 6 months postpartum, especially for women, but the size of the "partner" or "lover" aspect of self declined sharply. Whereas "worker" or "student" aspects of the self remained stable for men, women described marked declines in their involvement in work outside the family.

Marital interaction: Roles and communication. P. A. Cowan and C. P. Cowan (1988) stressed that partners' role arrangements and communication styles are the primary contributors to marital satisfaction. Information on mutual role arrangements was derived from the *"Who Does What?"* questionnaire. Childless couples described more equal sharing of household tasks than parents did at all assessment times, and these assessments remained stable. New parents began to assume more traditional, gender-specialized arrangements of family tasks—more than nonparents, more than they had established before childbirth, and more than they had expected. And, whereas childless partners' satisfaction with their role arrangements as a couple remained stable over time, role satisfaction declined for the partners who became parents (Cowan et al., 1985). The association between the mutual role arrangements and marital satisfaction is also documented (P. A. Cowan & C. P. Cowan, 1988). At both 6 and 18 months postpartum, satisfaction with the division of household and childcare tasks was consistently correlated with marital satisfaction for both men (r values ranging from .47 to .64) and women (r values ranging from .47 to .62). That is, even more important for the marriage than the fact of sharing tasks was each partner's feelings about how the tasks were divided.

Marital communication refers to the overt and covert patterns of communication in which partners exchange information and expectations in order to share tasks, convey feelings, make decisions, resolve conflicts, and show their caring. All of these communication and problem-solving skills were brought to bear in the manner in which expectant couples made their decision to have a first child. Variations in this process were associated both with their postnatal marital satisfaction and the more general ability to confront and resolve the problems between them (C. P. Cowan & P. A. Cowan, 1992). Parents were classified as (1) planners, (2) those who easily accepted the fate of being pregnant, (3) those who were ambivalent (positive and negative), and (4) those who had strong unresolved conflict about becoming pregnant (Yes–No). The ambivalent parents showed lower levels of marital satisfaction from pregnancy to child age 18 months. Yes–No parents declined dramatically in their marital satisfaction from pregnancy to 18 months, and had significantly greater difficulty resolving other problems that arose between them. In most instances, the father had reluctantly given in to the pregnancy and all seven of these couples eventually divorced.

Study of the total sample revealed that parents and childless spouses differed in their total marital conflict and disagreement ratings, with conflict declining for childless spouses and increasing for new parents from pregnancy to 18 months postpartum. At each assessment, "who does what" was at the top of partners' lists of issues leading to conflict and disagreement. Despite reports of increased dissension in new parent couples, men and women tended to agree about the amount of conflict that they were experiencing as they moved from couple to family life; this aspect of communication was one in which new parent's views did not diverge (C. P. Cowan et al., 1985).

By contrast, in descriptions of change in their sexual relationships, there were gender differences in both parent and nonparent couples. Wives reported increasingly positive changes in their sexual relationships, whereas their husbands reported fewer positive changes. In other words, regardless of parenthood status, men and women became more discrepant in their perceptions of this intimate aspect of couple communication (C. P. Cowan et al., 1985).

Parent–child relationship.   In regard to this domain, P. A. Cowan and C. P. Cowan (1988) stressed the transactional influence of positive marital and parent–child relationships. This is documented further in later parts of this chapter.

The three-generational perspective.   This domain focuses on the influence of men's and women's relationships with their own parents on their adaptation to pregnancy and parenthood. P. A. Cowan and C. P. Cowan (1988) cited the finding by Shereshefsky and Yarrow (1973) that women who reported more positive relationships with their mothers were rated by observers as more confident in their maternal role, and as having better functioning marriages and more individuated infants. Similarly, P. A. Cowan and C. P. Cowan (1988) found that men who described their families of origin as more cohesive, more expressive, and lower in conflict on the Family Environment Scale (Moos, 1974) tended to become more involved in the care of their 18-month-old children, to experience lower parenting stress, and to decline less in their marital satisfaction (C. P. Cowan & P. A. Cowan, 1992).

To assess men's and women's memories of their early relationships with *each* parent and the parent's relationship with each other, the Becoming a Family Project (C. P. Cowan et al., 1985) also administered the Family Relationship Questionnaire (adapted from Grossman et al., 1980). Correlations between positive relationships with parents and marital satisfaction showed much stronger cross-gender than same-gender effects. The more positively women described their relationship with their fathers ($r = .47$), the greater was their own marital satisfaction when their babies were 6 months old. Contrary to the finding by Shereshefsky and Yarrow (1973), there was no significant correlation between marital satisfaction and women's description of the past relationship with their mothers. The more positively men described their past relationship with their mothers, the greater was their own marital satisfaction when their babies were 18 months old ($r = .36$). There was no systematic link between men's marital happiness and their descriptions of their relationships with their fathers.

Life stress–social support balance.   In this domain, P. A. Cowan and C. P. Cowan (1988) discussed the possibility that individuals' social support may protect them from the negative effects of life stress events—including childbirth. They suggested that the impact of social support varies with the category of the people in the support network (family, friends who are parents, friends who are not parents), the kind of support (socializing, emotional, encouragement, cognitive guidance), and the gender of the recipient. Using a measure of life stress events adapted from Horowitz and his colleagues (Horowitz, Schaefer, Hiroto, Wilner, & Levin, 1977), C. P. Cowan et al. (1985) found no statistically significant changes in the level of general life stress from pregnancy to 18 months postpartum. In general, new parents reported no more and no fewer life stressors during the family formation period than the childless couples. They recognized that both the type of stress and its relation to the type of support needs further study.

The aforementioned summary focussed on the expectable changes in couples' transition to parenthood. Two 1984 reviews provided a theoretical integration of research findings focusing on how variations in prebirth parent personality and support characteristics influence variations in future parenting. Belsky (1984) provided a general framework integrating the determinants of parenting, and Heinicke (1984) focused on the prebirth determinants of parent–infant transactions. Because of the value of the conceptual schema, and the research data used to support it, the Belsky (1984) review is summarized in some detail. Heinicke's argument is outlined very briefly and then expanded to provide a framework for presenting a contemporary set of statements regarding the "prebirth determinants of parenting."

The Determinants of Parenting: A Process Model

Belsky (1984) focused his review around a model presuming that parenting is directly influenced by forces emanating from within the individual parent (personality), within the individual child (child characteristics of individuality), and from the broader social context in which the parent–child relationship is embedded (marital relations, social network, and the occupational experiences of parents). Furthermore, the model assumes that parents' developmental histories, marital relations, social networks, and jobs influence individual personality and general psychological well-being of parents and, thereby, parental and child development.

Consistent with the goal of this chapter, this section focuses on those aspects of Belsky's review that document the impact of "the enduring characteristics of the individual" (parent) on what Belsky (1984, p. 85) designated as his major outcome variable: "Parent's sensitive attunement to children's capabilities and to the developmental tasks they face." Indeed, Belsky cited evidence that supports the hypothesis that personal maturity, psychological well-being, and growth-facilitating parenting co-vary with each other. Thus, if age is conceived as a marker for maturity, then the observation that primiparous mothers interact with their young infants in a more positively affectionate, stimulating, and sensitive manner the older they are (Ragozin, Basham, Crnic, Greenberg, & Robinson, 1982) provides one piece of evidence for the hypothesized relation between personality and parental functioning. So, too, do data on teenage mothers, who are presumably less psychologically mature than other mothers. Belsky (1984) referred to research showing that such young mothers express less desirable childrearing attitudes and have less realistic expectations for infant development than do older mothers (Field, Widmayer, Stringer, & Ignatoff, 1980), that they tend to be less responsive to their newborns (Jones, Green, & Krauss, 1980), and are less inclined to engage infants in verbal interaction (J. J. Osofsky & J. D. Osofsky, 1970). Belsky also cited a study by Mondell and Tyler (1981) providing direct support for a personality–parenting linkage. They reported data linking internal locus of control, high levels of interpersonal trust, and an active coping style on the part of parents to high levels of observed warmth, acceptance, and helpfulness and to low levels of disapproval when interacting with their young children.

Belsky (1984) reviewed investigations of psychologically disturbed adults to show the influence of personal psychological attributes on parental functioning (e.g., A. L. Baldwin, Cole, & E. P. Baldwin, 1982; Rutter, 1966). He concluded that the disturbance in parental psychological functioning that has received the most attention in this regard is depression (Fabian & Donahue, 1956; Pollitt, 1965), with Weissman providing one of the most extensive and informative studies (Orraschel, Weissman, & Kidd, 1980; Weissman & Paykel, 1974). Depressed mothers offer a disruptive, hostile, rejecting home environment to their children, which, not surprisingly, undermines child functioning.

Having provided support for the personality–parenting linkage, Belsky (1984) went on to provide research support for the generalization that the linkages between parents' psychological well-being and their parental functioning may be traced back, at least to some extent, to the experiences parents had while they were growing up. Belsky used three sets of data to document a relation between the parent's own developmental history and the quality of their parenting of their own child. Literature on child abuse furnished the first set by underscoring an association between experience of mistreatment in one's own childhood and mistreatment of one's own children (Belsky, 1978, 1980; Parke & Collmer, 1975). Studies of depression provided a second set of data linking developmental history and parenting. This research indicates that the stressful separation from their own parents as a child is not only a risk factor in the etiology of this affective disturbance (Brown & Harris, 1978), but also relates to difficulties in caring for young children (Frommer & O'Shea, 1973a, 1973b) and, probably as a consequence, to less than optimal functioning on the part of the child (Hall, Pawlby, & Wolkind, 1980). A third set of research findings linking their own experiences of parenting to becoming a parent focused on the father (Belsky, Crnic, & Gable, 1993).

Belsky (1984) summarized the previous presentation with the following general hypothesis: "Supportive developmental experiences give rise to a mature healthy personality, that is then capable of providing sensitive parental care which fosters optimal child development" (p. 86). We cannot do justice to Belsky's consideration of the two other major domains of influence on parenting: the influence of the child and the contextual sources of stress–support. In terms of the child's contribution, he suggested that it is not the child's characteristics per se but the "goodness-of-fit" between parent and child that determines the development of parent–child relationships. Three sources of support (or stress) are considered as possible determinants of parenting: the marital relationship, social networks, and the work opportunities. Belsky reviewed evidence linking positive forms of these support systems to positive parental competence.

Having reviewed research documentation of the importance of three major domains as determinants of parenting—personality/psychological well-being, the characteristics of the child, and contextual sources of stress and support—Belsky then explored their interrelation. Within the concept that strength in one area can buffer against stresses from the other two sources, he asked which domain is likely to be of greatest importance in determining parental competence. He first explored the relative importance within sources of support. Two studies are cited to provide evidence in relation to the hypothesis that the marital system, when compared with social network and work support, is likely to be of greater relative importance in enhancing potential competence. Thus, in Colletta and Gregg's (1981) investigation of 50 adolescent mothers, the emotional assistance received from family of origin (i.e., social network) predicted maternal attitudes and affectionate behavior, and support received from boyfriend or spouse was next in order of importance, followed finally by friendship support. In another investigation, studying 105 mothers and their term and preterm 4-month-olds, "intimate support [from spouse] proved to have the most general positive effects, although community and friendship support appear[ed] valuable to maternal attitudes as well" (Crnic, Greenberg, Ragozin, Robinson, & Basham, 1983, p. 215).

Continuing his exploration of interrelations among the three major determinants of parenting, Belsky suggested that the personality/psychological well-being of the parent is likely to have the greatest potential for buffering because of its direct effect on parental competence, and also because individual psychological characteristics affect not only selection of a spouse, the establishment of friendships, and the job one obtains, but the quality of the relationships one maintains with a spouse, friends, relatives and neighbors, and co-workers. Belsky acknowledged that studies are needed to document the greater relative role of personality characteristics in determining parenting. He cited considerable evidence to indicate that child risk characteristics can be overcome (buffered) where both personal resources and support systems function effectively (Sameroff & Chandler, 1975). One approach to evaluating the relative importance of personality and support characteristics on later parenting is to assess these qualities before the birth of the first child, and thus before the child impacts the parent characteristics. Heinicke's review (1984) followed this direction.

Impact of Prebirth Parent Personality and Marital Functioning on Family Development

As part of the general task of reviewing research linking pre-birth personality and marital characteristics to later family development, Heinicke (1984) began by delineating a larger framework of significant influences on parent and infant development. These influences were organized in terms of four constructs:

(1) *Personality* refers to those stabilized behaviors activated in a variety of situations and can include, for example, the tendency to be nurturant in a relationship.
(2) Constructs of *social interaction* focus on the behavior patterns seen in relation to specific persons like the husband, friends, and relatives.
(3) *Role* is that prescription of behavior defined by the self but also by the social and cultural value context in which the person exists.
(4) The *ecology* of the family describes the larger context of events likely to make a significant impact on family functioning.

Within this framework, the focus of the review fell on delineating associations between personality and social interaction phenomena. In order to substantiate the impact of prebirth parent personality and marital interaction on postnatal family development, the review provided evidence for two conclusions. First, both parent personality and marital functioning tend to be relatively stable in the transition to parenthood. Changes do occur, but the relative position of a couple within a population is very similar before and after the arrival of the child. This means the potential influence on the expanding family system is consistent, and the postnatal transactions and family developments cannot simply be accounted for by variations in child functioning. Second, variation in prebirth parent personality and marital functioning anticipated variation in postnatal family development. Support for the previous two conclusions are summarized in the remainder of the chapter.

PREBIRTH DETERMINANTS, PARENTING, AND THE CHILD'S DEVELOPMENT: A CONCEPTUAL FRAMEWORK

In further pursuing the goals of this chapter, we focus on a limited number of *parent and child personality* and *social interaction* variables defined here. Citations are given for the operational definition of these concepts. Characterization of the mother's and father's personality has scrutinized their *adaptation-competence,* their *capacity for positive sustained relationships,* and their *self-development.* Consideration of their supportive relationships focuses on their *partners* (including marital) and their *extended family.*

Characterization of parenting was defined by three parent–infant transactions (social interaction variables) and the associated components of the child's emerging self (personality variables). It is recognized that even if one limits oneself to tracing interconnections between personality and social interaction variables across the transition to family formation, the number of potential mutual influences and levels of abstraction is great. In organizing this chapter, we confine ourselves to those interconnections that have actually been studied and specified.

Turning to the definition of the parent personality concepts, *adaptation-competence* refers to the efficient, nonanxious, persistent, and flexible approach to problem solving. It has been operationally specified as ego strength (Barron, 1953), adaptation-competence (Heinicke, Diskin, Ramsey-Klee, & Given, 1983)—and, more recently, as maternal competence (Teti, Gelfand, & Pompa, 1990)—and the absence of task-related anger (Heinicke, 1993).

The *capacity for positive sustained relationships* refers to empathy and positive mutuality expressed by the parent in an ongoing relationship. It has been operationally specified in relation to parenting by the mother's and father's coherent, objective, and balanced account of their childhood relationship experiences (Fonagy, H. Steele, & M. Steele, 1991; Main & Goldwyn, 1991), and by the parent's recall of their own parenting as loving (Main & Goldwyn, 1991), low in conflict (P. A. Cowan, C. P. Cowan, Schulz, & Heming, 1993), and generally positive (Heinicke & Guthrie, 1992). It is also defined by sensitivity to other's needs (Brunnquell, Crichton, & Egeland, 1981), trusting as opposed to being skeptical of interpersonal relationships (Pianta, Egeland, & Erickson, 1989), and warmth (Heinicke, Diskin, Ramsey-Klee, & Oates, 1986).

Definition of the *parent's self-development* has involved their experienced autonomy and confidence as opposed to insecurity. It has been operationally specified in relation to parenting as the clarity and confidence in visualizing self as a parent (Heinicke et al., 1983; Shereshefsky and Yarrow, 1973). C. P. Cowan et al. (1985) assessed both the parent's self-esteem and which life roles are most important to them: partner, lover, worker, and so on. Diamond, Heinicke, and Mintz (1994) operationally defined the autonomy of each parent using concepts of individuation-separation. The link of self-development to past and current relationships is stressed by examining the relation to the family of origin, self-directed autonomous activities, and mutuality with and differentiation from the current partner.

The parent's *positive experience of their partnerships* (including marriage) is also central to our summary of research. Specific definitions have focused on different aspects of this experience. P. A.

Cowan and C. P. Cowan (1988) stressed the importance of the partner's consensus on their mutual role arrangements (who does what) and the openness of their communication. Both inventories (P. A. Cowan & C. P. Cowan, 1988; Belsky et al., 1989) and interviews (Heinicke et al., 1983) have been used to define the expressed satisfaction with the partner. Direct observations of the quality of the marital interaction of parents underline the importance of both expressing negative affects and yet remaining on the task of resolving conflicts (Balaguer & Markham, 1991; Heinicke & Guthrie, 1994; Pratt, Kevig, P. A. Cowan, & C. P. Cowan, 1988).

In defining the likely link of the prebirth parent characteristics to postnatal family development, it is most meaningful to focus on those qualities of parenting that are not only likely to link to prebirth parent characteristics but are in turn a part of significant transactions defined by both parenting and child qualities. Thus, we highlight certain qualities of parenting by relating them to the development of the child's self. The key forms of parenting are teaching and exposing the child to new cognitive experiences, responding to the needs of the infant, and promoting the autonomy of the child. (For operational definition of these parent–infant transactions, see Ainsworth, Blehar, Waters, & Wall, 1978; Bornstein & Tamis-Le Monda, 1989; Heinicke & Guthrie, 1992).

Consistent with Sroufe's (1989) discussion of relationships, self, and individual adaptation, components of the self are defined as emerging from the interaction of early infant characteristics and the constellation of parent characteristics and parenting relationship potentials. Self as an organization integrates the infant's adaptation and accompanying feelings and thoughts. The development of the components of the self can be related to the quality and goals of these relationships (Sroufe, 1989).

The "Competent Self" is associated with a sense of being an agent (Stern, 1985), goal orientation, attention (Heinicke, 1980), and self-regulation. It emerges out of and continues in the context of the type of parental responsiveness that teaches and exposes the child to new cognitive experiences (Bornstein & Tamis-LeMonda, 1989). The emphasis on adaptive capacities includes early modes of self-regulation or defense such as suppression, turning the passive into active, avoidance, and control. The "Secure Self" (Ainsworth et al., 1978) and the closely associated "Expectation of Being Cared for" (Heinicke & Guthrie, 1992), "Sense of Self as Worthy" (Sroufe, 1989), and "Modulation of Aggression" (Heinicke et al., 1986) emerge out of and continue in a relationship characterized by parents' responsiveness to the needs of the infant (Bornstein & Tamis-LeMonda, 1989). The "Separate Self," subjective awareness of the self and other (Stern, 1985), begins in the second half of the first year of life and is seen as emerging out of and continuing in a relationship that prepares for and promotes autonomy as well as providing control (limits) for that expansion (Heinicke & Guthrie, 1992).

The profile of variables has guided our integration of the research findings, but it is important to note that the definition and measurement of the variables are clarified in each study reviewed. Before examining whether the relative standing of couples on various prebirth parent qualities within a sample remain *stable* from the pre- to postbirth period, and then formulating specific statements linking these parent qualities to parent and parent–child *variations* in development, we give a narrative description of one family. The concepts used are illustrated and the findings to be presented are anticipated.

THE DEVELOPMENT OF LAURIE'S FAMILY FROM PREGNANCY TO 4 YEARS OF AGE

The father, Mark, and the mother, Gina, had been married for 11 years. They were respectively 39 and 32 years old as they expected their first child. Their prebirth adaptation, capacity for relationship, and their mutuality, as well as sense of autonomy were, by comparison with the other couples in the research sample, at the highest level (Heinicke & Guthrie, 1992). Moreover, their level of role differentiation and capacity to resolve conflictual issues was sustained throughout their daughter's first 4 years. Three important events impacted this positive stability and represented a challenge: The mother's return to full-time work, a recurrence of the father's chronic illness when the daughter, Laurie, was 1 year old, and the mother becoming pregnant with her second child when Laurie was 17 months old.

Prebirth Assessments

Review of the prebirth interview, psychological testing, home visits, and marital interaction data by three different clinicians before the birth of Laurie led to the following summary and predictions:

This is a very attractive couple in the sense of being competent and giving. Their relationship is mutually satisfying and supportive. They communicate clearly and especially what they expect of each other. They have dealt with changes in a flexible manner, and the expectation is that they will make the adjustments to include their infant in a "very close" dyad. They recognize that a sense of control which they now have over their lives and being together will be seriously changed. They are able to resolve this by talking about a sanctuary both in terms of being alone and having time to themselves. This issue is raised in the following recorded marital interaction, and different perspectives are given in the context of positive regard:

Mother: . . . We should probably really keep in mind to make time for us to just be by ourselves not necessarily get a babysitter when we're going out with somebody else but to have time for ourselves to do things cause we really need that.

Father: I just guess I don't quite believe that it takes as much time as people say it does. Cause I just feel like we'll have time for each other but—

Mother: Well it will probably take more time than we think but I feel like we shouldn't assume that one hundred percent of our time from the time the baby is born has to be directed toward the baby. I think that it'd be good if there are times when we could sort of let the baby play by itself. You know, some people never do that. They're always involved with the baby. They never give the baby any time to itself. Maybe that's something we should remember and it'll help us have a little more time. There are times when the baby can play quietly.

Father: But you never know. I mean, we might be really pulled toward the baby too you know, and away from each other. . . .

Mother: Yeah, which I think we should be careful of . . . cause otherwise we'll be faced with getting to know each other again. When the baby starts to be old enough so that it needs to be independent it can; I think babies need to be independent at a very early age. I mean, maybe have some time by themselves.

Their enthusiasm for the birth, their confidence as future parents, as well as their warmth, individuality, and competence lead to the expectation that they would be responsive to the needs of their infant and promote the learning and autonomy of their child.

The clinicians reviewing their prebirth material also articulated that there would be two particular challenges to this positive adjustment: the possible deterioration in the father's health, and the mother's return to work at a very early date. It was anticipated that because of financial pressures and the mother's wish to pursue her work, she would be less flexible in this question. It was also anticipated that this might be partially resolved by the father sharing in the caretaking.

After a lengthy labor, Laurie was delivered by Caesarian-section. Both parents were thrilled with their baby girl. The hospital observer described her as a very beautiful, nicely formed, large baby with pink skin and light brown hair. There were no obstetrical complications (Littman & Parmalee, 1974).

Summary comments from the Brazelton Behavior Assessment Scale (Brazelton, 1973) were: "Laurie is a very pretty baby. She aroused to the alert state quickly. She was very responsive to stimulation (animate), and was mature in several of her responses."

After several efforts, the mother successfully nursed her new infant on the fourth day. She continued the nursing more than the prescribed time: "It made no sense to pull her off the breast just because the clock said a certain time." The mother stroked her back and neck and spoke softly to her in soothing tones when she was awake. She mentioned that she thought the baby liked her and liked being held closely. This pleased her immensely because as she said: "I love to hold her." Thus, a responsive mother and responsive infant formed a positive relationship in the first few days: "I just can't believe it, here she is and she's so perfect. I can't believe she's really mine." She talked in the same positive tone about her husband and then became concerned that she might have to go back to work for financial reasons.

Observations in the home revealed that by 1 month the bodily closeness to the infant included the father. He enjoyed Laurie deeply, was beaming with pride, and was often tempted to pick her up even when he knew he shouldn't. The baby was responsive to voices, and made good eye contact. The mother was pleased with her increasing ability to read Laurie's signals. She often stroked her hair and would lean forward to kiss her. Laurie responded to this loving care by lengthening her nighttime sleep periods and continuing to be easy to nurse. As the mother's attachment grew, she became increasingly conflicted about returning to work. Yet the financial pressures to do so were considerable. It was also clear that the cries of a dependent infant taxed her need to control her life. In her first contact with the mother–infant group when Laurie was 5 weeks old, Nancy recounted how terrible the first few weeks had been, and that now during Laurie's fussy times (between 10 p.m. and 1 a.m.) she often finds herself crying along with the baby.

In the next two mother–infant group sessions, the group leader noted that Gina "enjoys her baby and within their tight closeness has a very nice, gentle way with her." When the mother removed her wet diaper, Laurie responded to her freedom with gurgling, movement, and visual contact. Gina told the other mothers that she was surprised at how reluctant she had become to leave her infant and go to work again. Having to replace her initial sitter again activated her doubts.

As the return to work actually occurred, Laurie adjusted well. Observations in the home at 3 months emphasized that the mutual responsiveness of mother, father, and infant was continuing. Being with the baby-sitter had encouraged Laurie to experiment more and move into the environment more. By contrast, mother was less able in the evening to put her down and have her be apart: "I haven't been with her all day."

Family Development at 6 Months

At 6, 12, 24, and 48 months, the parents and infant were assessed through interviews, testing, and observations in the home.

From both the interview and observation in the home at 6 months, it became clear that Laurie had been successfully integrated into her parent's positive mutuality. Mother's intense affection continued to be expressed through holding, kissing, and nursing her in the morning and evening. But by this age, the mother was also encouraging exploration, helped her to "stand up," and let her "roam" on the floor.

The father–daughter relationship was by now one of obvious infatuation. As the father played various games with her on the floor, he would often spontaneously hug and kiss her. Laurie would make everyone laugh with her happy vocalizations and noises.

During the Bayley Scale Assessment, Laurie showed above-average goal directedness, attention, and endurance. Both the mental and motor development were above average; the mental development index was 129 and the motor development index was 112. The examiner made the following observations: "Mother and infant share a calm and deliberate physical space reflecting a relaxed, secure relationship. Laurie's primary orientation is toward the social, but she also examined each stimulus with interest. The mother encouraged this with a moderate amount of exposing and teaching."

As part of the Bayley assessment, the infant's reaction to a brief separation is tested (Heinicke, Recchia, James, Berlin, & James, 1993). Initially vigilant, Laurie soon cried and pushed away from the examiner. Upon reunion, Laurie immediately visually engaged and cuddled her mother and then reengaged the examiner visually and vocally. This reaction to separation was scored as demonstrating low anxiety with positive reunion.

Global ratings have been used to summarize the home observations (Heinicke et al., 1993). Table 11.1 presents the ratings for each month.

As shown in the table, the 6-month global ratings indicate a positive family development. In terms of the major transactions that are the focus of this chapter, all ratings are high (i.e., 4 or 5): (1) The child's expectation of being cared for (an index of the secure self) interacting with mother responsiveness to need; (2) the child's sense of separate self interacting with mother encourages autonomy; and (3) the child's adaptation-competence interacting with mother stimulates cognitive experiences. The global parent–child ratings for the father were very similar to those on the mother. Changes in these indices of family development did occur. The reasons for these changes are discussed later.

Family Development at 12 Months

Whereas the various assessments of development had been uniformly positive up to 6 months, at 12 months some indications confirmed the continuing positive development whereas others showed signs of stress. Gina and Frank had further pursued their careers and continued to be close not only with each other, but with Laurie. In her more intimate interview with her social worker, Gina's depression concerning her husband's illness was evident. This was not evident in her interaction with Laurie at home or in the laboratory test situation. In the test situation the mother offered appropriate demonstrations and affectionate approval. Anticipating Laurie's frustration on a particular task, she gave her a hug, and this allowed Laurie to reengage. The observation in the home pictured a very alert, energetic, interested child who made numerous forays into every corner of the room, bringing out all her favorite toys. When tired, Laurie would allow herself to be picked up, caressed, and then would again "read a book" or experiment with a toy. The mother could mostly sit back, name or point to things when invited, and was no longer as driven to pick her up. She was clearly comfortable in her mothering, and especially so since a very affectionate daily in-house caregiver had been with them in the last 6 months. Ratings done by the home observer at 12 months reflected a very positive parent–child and child development (see Table 11.1).

TABLE 11.1
Global Child and Mother–Child Ratings at Four Assessment Points
5-Point Scales: Five Is High

Ratings	Months			
	6	12	24	48
Global Child				
Expectation of being cared for	5	5	4	3
Sense of separate self	4	5	5	4
Sense of positive self	5	5	4	3
Adaptation-competence	5	5	4	3
Global Mother–Child				
Mother affection	5	5	4	3
Mother responsive to need	4	5	5	4
Mother encourages autonomy	4	4	5	4
Mother stimulates cognitive experience	4	5	4	3

The test examiner also concluded that "Laurie shows a secure attachment to a responsive mother." However, Laurie was noticeably less social than at 6 months, and while making eye contact with and reaching for her mother during the reunion after a brief separation, there was an absence of any obvious feeling. A muted and even defensive response was suggested. Taken together with the decline in her general social responsiveness, this momentary defensiveness did raise the question about whether some insecurity in the child was enhanced by the mother's daily absence and/or the concern about the father's illness.

Family Development at 24 Months

At this point in Laurie's life, her mother was 7 months pregnant. Although tired, the mother still had a soft, gentle way with her daughter. Laurie's extensive vocabulary allowed her to communicate her needs, which the mother responded to with sensitivity. The mother avoided control battles with Laurie and instead facilitated her daughter's involvement with activities of her own choosing.

The excellent communication, role differentiation, and positive mutuality between the parents came into play as Gina had concluded that she was missing too much of her daughter's development. She and Mark agreed that she would take care of Laurie in the mornings and he would be home in the afternoon.

In the Bayley testing situation both mother and daughter displayed a mutually accepting, quiet, and reflective manner. Laurie was cooperative, attentive, and goal directed. This task persistence was clearly associated with a Mental Development Index of 121 (above average), and a Motor Development Index of 131 (superior). Within this positive context of family development, the Bayley assessment situation also suggested signs of distress in the mother–daughter relationship. The examiner noted a lack of exuberance, both in the daughter and the mother. There were next to no playful interactions. When separated from her mother, she reassured herself with "Mommy right back," pointed to the door, and turned to the examiner for comfort. But, despite an affectionate invitation from the mother at reunion, she was unresponsive, did not return her mother's hug, and turned instead to her own play. The examiner inferred that her daughter's actual and anticipated lack of attention from her pregnant mother could be accentuating both anger and unresponsiveness.

The observations of the family made shortly after the birth of the baby brother, Tim, are best summarized by the phrase "a lovely family," and this is reflected in the ratings shown in Table 11. 1. A quiet enthusiasm was associated with various family activities. The parents reported that Laurie "socializes easily" with other children, likes to read books, but as she says "likes to talk too." During the visit she played on her own, but also became involved in family tasks. There were no problems around control or aggression. The parents were responsive to their children and to each other. They expressed some concern about Laurie's nail biting and that she does not like to be left. As if this last quality was somehow negative, they quickly added that she does not get that upset or have a fit. This report of her reaction to being left was consistent with what had been observed during the separation from the mother in the test situation. Yet the predominant picture emerging from the total assessment was that both individually and in their interactions, this family was continuing to develop in a very positive direction.

Family Development at 48 Months

As at previous assessment points, observations were made in the home, the mother was interviewed, and Laurie was tested (the Weschler Preschool Test of Intelligence). The observer, the parents, and the preschool teacher also filled out the California Child Q-Sort (J. Block & J. H. Block, 1980). One hundred descriptions of child functioning were judged as most versus least characteristic of Laurie.

Both the positive communication between the parents and the acceptance by both of them of their respective roles had further insured an overall positive family development. The mother had decided to quit her job and be at home full time; it was clear from her behavior and answers to the interview questions that she had never been so happy. The father's increasing business success had brought greater financial security, and thus in part made this possible.

The parents were also clearly enchanted with their 2-year-old son. As the observer described it: "He has that cherubic kind of glow about him that you just want to pick him up and play with him." Not surprisingly, Laurie had difficulty with a rival that would so easily receive positive attention. At times she would get impatient and interrupt. Though not openly aggressive, her interaction was often controlling. On one occasion she grabbed his shirt and said, "Wait a minute, big boy."

Another adaptation to the newcomer was to be boyish and very active. She greeted the observer in a Superman outfit. "Oh," said the observer, "you are Superwoman." "No, no," she said, "I am Superman," and proceeded to jump all over the couch. The mother added that when her daughter is in doubt she becomes a Superhero.

But clearly the most difficult for the parents was Laurie's reaction to separation. She just didn't like her mother to drop her off at the play group: "Don't go Mommy." Yet, the mother added, she reacts fairly quietly and does not throw a fit. The difficulty in being away from her mother interfered with her IQ test performance. She had to check on her mother in the adjoining room and had difficulty completing the subtest. Thus her verbal IQ of 115 was probably an underestimate. On the performance IQ she scored 123. She had an excellent fund of information, a good vocabulary, and a good number concept.

Moreover, her overall capacity for engagement in the IQ test was reflected in the Q-sort items that teacher, parents, and observer agreed were most characteristic: is attentive and able to concentrate; is curious and exploring, eager to learn, and open to new experiences; and is persistent in activities. Several items reflected her autonomy and independence: is self assertive; and seeks to be independent and autonomous. There was also agreement on her pride: tends to be pleased with her products and accomplishments. Her energy level was seen as very characteristic: is vital, energetic, lively; is agile and well coordinated; and has a rapid personal tempo. Other items agreed on were: responds to humor; is creative in perception, thought, work, or play; and does not tease children or her sibling.

In regard to social interaction, after a difficult period following the birth of her brother, she did at this time play with him and had some playmates. In preschool, she tended to avoid the rough boys and was often by herself. The observer noted in the home that she was not easy to engage and at times seemed like an unhappy child. The father commented that he loves to talk to her, but that the "sweetness" is not always there; sometimes she is difficult to reach and seeks attention in a boisterous way.

The global ratings for the 48-month points when compared with the 6-month points reveal a decline in the expectation of being cared for, the sense of positive self, and her adaptation-competence. By contrast, the sense of separate self remained the same. Declines are also seen in the mother stimulating Laurie's cognitive experiences, and especially in affection. Although there was therefore less affectionate involvement, the mother's response to her daughter's needs and the encouragement of autonomy did not decline.

Summary of Family Development

Longitudinal observation of Gina, Mark, Tim, and Laurie illustrates the major findings of this chapter. Prebirth characteristics of the couple and of each individual partner anticipate qualities of their parenting, and especially their responsiveness to need and encouragement of autonomy. Their capacity for efficient adaptation, their positive mutuality, and evolving security in their role could be linked to the development of security, autonomy, and competent cognitive functioning in their child. This was especially evident in the first 2 years of life. Crucial to the family functioning was the parent's ability to confront difficult problems, express their feelings, and come to some resolution. This was seen in relation to protecting their need for alone time as a couple in the prebirth marital interaction, and was evidenced postnatally in the way in which the parents resolved the issue of how much, if at all, the mother should work.

Within this picture of positive adjustment, the increasing charm and security of 2-year-old Tim had threatened the security of his 4-year-old sister. Her boisterous, attention-seeking, and anxious/defensive reaction to separation from her mother irritated the other members of the family. However, her task motivation, independence, and learning was not impaired. Given the resources of the parents and the continuing response to Laurie's needs and encouragment of autonomy, it was anticipated that this issue would be resolved in a positive direction.

We turn now to a summary of the research findings documenting both the stability of parental characteristics and how differences in those characteristics influence differences in family development.

THE STABILITY OF PARENT PERSONALITY AND MARITAL CHARACTERISTICS

Review of the research literature suggests a striking consensus that a considerable number of parent personality and marital characteristics are stable across the transition to parenthood and thus are likely to exert a continuing and generally consistent influence on postnatal family development. Grossman et al. (1980) showed that the mother's emotional well-being, marital adjustment, and level of anxiety and depression during pregnancy and at 2 months postpartum correlated significantly with measures of those same qualities as assessed at 12 months postpartum. Similarly, these authors demonstrated that measures of the father's marital adjustment and level of anxiety as assessed during pregnancy and at 2 months postpartum anticipated assessment of that same quality at the 12-month postpartum point.

Although they delineated change in certain domains of couple functioning, P. A. Cowan and C. P. Cowan (1988) documented the relative stability of the following characteristics by citing the correlation between prebirth and 18-month assessments as follows: Marital satisfaction ranges from .50 to .70; role satisfaction is .56 for men and .62 for women; self-esteem is .75 for men and .76 for women. Similarly, Wolkind and Zajidek (1981) found that assessments of the mother's self-esteem at 4 and 14 months after the birth of her child tended to be highly consistent. Huston and McHale (1983) compared the marital relationship of samples of families who had a child during approximately the first year after their marriage with those who did not. Couples who had children shared more joint activities (almost exclusively in childcare) and also moved toward more traditional sex roles in terms of instrumental activities. Having a child did not, however, differentially affect involvement with kin and friends or the overall evaluation of and the expression of affection within the marriage. Although these last two indexes of the marriage declined, the magnitude of the change in evaluation of the marriage was not great. Consistent with these findings, Cox and Owen (1993) found that prenatal and 3-month assessments of marital discord were significantly correlated.

Findings from two longitudinal studies (Heinicke & Guthrie, 1992) also support the hypothesis that measures of both personality functioning and marital quality significantly correlate even when the time interval extends from prebirth to the child's fourth birthday. Factor scores describing the mother's positive experience of the marriage based on ratings of recorded interviews with her during pregnancy and at 1, 6, 12, 24, 36, and 48 months of age were significantly correlated. With the exception of the correlation between the pre-birth and 6 month assessments, all intercorrelations were statistically significant.

As cited earlier, P. A. Cowan and C. P. Cowan (1988) also reported the consistency in marital functioning, but noted that there is a lower correlation between pregnancy and 6 months than pregnancy and 18 months. This exception suggests the possible impact of the transition to parenthood. Indeed, there is variation in the patterns of *change* in marital patterns (Heinicke & Guthrie, 1992). However, the relative position of each couple within a group of families remains relatively stable from prebirth to 48 months. Indices of the mother's adaptation-competence and warmth are also significantly intercorrelated in the period from prebirth to 48 months (Heinicke & Lampl, 1988). Schaeffer, Edgerton, and Hunter (1983) found similar levels of association between pregnancy and postpartum measures of a quality closely linked to adaptation-competence, namely, maternal locus of control.

In summary, the previous findings suggest considerable stability in global indexes of marital quality and personality functioning when prebirth and postnatal assessments are compared. This stable and consistent impact on postnatal family development of both personality and marital characteristics, begs the question of which of these characteristics link to emerging parent transactions with the infant, and thus influence infant development?

THE IMPACT OF PREBIRTH PARENT CHARACTERISTICS ON POSTNATAL FAMILY DEVELOPMENT

Maternal Prebirth Functioning, Mother's Responsiveness, and the Security of Her Child

The mother's prebirth adaptive competence and capacity to sustain positive relationships (especially those with her partner) anticipate her responsiveness to the needs of her infant in the period from 1 month to 4 years of age. Moreover, these same prebirth characteristics anticipate the development of security in her child. The previous two statements can be rephrased as follows: If before the birth of her child, the mother copes well with various life issues, has the capacity to form positive, trusting relationships, and has a mutually positive relationship with her partner, then she is more likely to be responsive to her child's needs, and her child will develop greater security in the first 4 years of life. The research support for these statements is presented here. This reflects the fact that the transaction of parent responsiveness to need and the child's security are intercorrelated. Moreover, this transactional association is reflected in the first set of findings. Based on the review of research summarized (Belsky, 1984; Heinicke, 1984), a hypothesized path analysis can be tested and was reported in Heinicke, Diskin, Ramsey-Klee, and Oates (1986).

Focusing on statistically significant associations relevant to the development of security, it was found that husband–wife adaptation, maternal adaptation-competence, and maternal warmth all have a direct and independent impact on variations in parent responsiveness to need at 1 month that impacts infant fretting at 3 months. Three-month infant fretting in turn anticipates child modulation of aggression and parent responsiveness at 2 years. Modulation of aggression is here being used as an index of the child's security (Heinicke et al., 1986; Heinicke & Guthrie, 1992). The previous two research reports document the potential chain of effects from prebirth to 1 month, to 3 month, and then to 2 years. Suggesting the continuing influence of stable parent characteristics is the direct association (path) from prebirth husband–wife adaptation, maternal adaptation-competence, and maternal warmth to 2-year modulation of aggression.

A number of prospective longitudinal studies starting with assessments of the parents before the birth of their first child have reported findings consistent with the aforementioned model. Belsky and Isabella (1986) found that mothers who scored poorly before the birth of their first child on both ego strength and interpersonal affection were likely to experience the most negative change in their marriage. In addition these two personality characteristics, as well as the quality of the postnatal marital experience, and the perception of their child as becoming less adaptable, all contributed to the development of an insecure infant–mother relationship at 12 months as measured by the child's reaction to separation from and reunion with the mother. Findings by Grossman et al. (1980) are also consistent with the hypotheses outlined in that parent responsiveness and infant soothability at 2 months are anticipated by prenatal indexes of maternal adaptation, anxiety, and marital style in the case of the firstborn child. Moreover, with respect to maternal personality aspects, Moss (1967) demonstrated that accepting the prebirth nurturant role, and viewing the care of a baby as gratifying rather than burdensome, are associated with each other; both these factors anticipate the mother's actual responsiveness to her baby as observed at 3 weeks and 3 months.

Results from the Minnesota Mother–Child Interaction project reported by Egeland and his colleagues (Brunnquell et al., 1981; Egeland & Farber, 1984; Pianta et al., 1989) also support the power of prebirth measures of the mother's emotional stability as predictors of maternal responsive caregiving and a secure infant attachment. Thus, in this poverty at-risk sample, mothers who scored significantly higher on a prebirth factor entitled "Level of Personality Integration" (Brunnquell et al., 1981) met the physical and emotional needs of their children at 3 months and their children were at 12 months more frequently classified as secure (Egeland & Farber, 1984). Level of Personality Integration is "composed of an amalgam of affective and intellectual elements, each of which contributes to the overall conception of the mother's recognition of her own psychological needs and processes, her ability to perceive those needs and processes in others, and her ability to integrate the two sets of needs and processes." Among the measures related to this construct are IQ, Locus of Control, the feeling of being able to control what happens to oneself, and the Cohler scales—such as encouragement versus discouragement of reciprocity, appropriate versus inappropriate control of the child's aggression, and acceptance versus denial of emotional complexity in childcare. Further analyses of these data revealed that prebirth maternal characteristics were also associated with whether or not the mother anticipated and in fact found her child "difficult" as opposed to "easy" at 3 and 6 months (Vaughn, Deinard, & Egeland, 1980; Vaughn, Taraldson, Chrichten, & Egeland, 1981). The importance of the contribution of the mother's adaptation-competence and capacity for relationships to her future caregiving is supported by the fact that the best discriminator of the maltreating and inadequate caring mothers as followed up in this sample at child age 64 months is the emotional and stability scale of the 16PF Personality test also administered at this time. Pianta et al. (1989) discussed two concepts in relation to this scale: emotional instability (impulsiveness) and being skeptical of interpersonal relationships.

In a recent study, Isabella and Gable (1993) found that in bivariate analyses, mothers' prenatal reports of personal sympathy were predictive of both sensitive responsivity and rejection at three postnatal measurement periods. Mothers who had described themselves as compassionate, empathic, and sensitive to the needs of others were likely to exhibit sensitively responsive and nonrejecting behaviors at 1, 4, and 9 months, whereas insensitivity and rejection were most likely observed in mothers who had described themselves as inconsiderate and slow to recognize the needs of others. Measures of the type of social support and marital quality were also associated with maternal interactive behavior. Women who reported higher levels of prenatal family support were likely to exhibit more sensitively responsive behaviors at 4 months, and less rejecting behaviors at both 4 and 9 months. Linking marital quality to mothering revealed that mothers who were more satisfied with their marriages prenatally were likely to exhibit higher levels of sensitivity at 9 months. In additional analyses, Isabella and Gable (1993) found that the association between prenatal maternal sympathy and 1-month sensitivity was no longer significant when the impact of the child's social responsiveness was considered. However, prenatal sympathy did anticipate the *change* in the mother's sensitivity from 1 to 4 months. Again by contrast, the change in maternal sensitivity from 4 to 9 months was not predicted by any variable. The authors suggest that this may be due to the high correlation between the 4- and 9-month maternal behavior—that is, there is little change. In summary, these authors suggested that in the first month the focus is on immediate mutual mother–infant adjustment, that in the next 3 months (1 to 4 months) changes in maternal responsiveness are to a great extent governed by aspects of her personality, but because of the considerable stability in her sensitivity during the 4- to 9-month period, this sensitivity is no longer subject to prenatally assessed personality influences.

The complexity of intercorrelations between pre-birth parent characteristics, parenting, and infant characteristics is underlined by the fact that contrary to the previous findings, Heinicke and Lampl (1986) found that 1-month parent responsiveness to the infant's needs was anticipated by the mother's prebirth adaptation-competence and positive marital adjustment, even when 1-month infant social responsiveness was taken into account. Indeed, the influence of the prebirth marital adaptation on parent responsiveness and child security was seen throughout the first 4 years of life.

One study has specifically addressed the issue of the relative contribution of parent, parent–infant, and infant characteristics to the development of a secure attachment at 1 year of age. Del Carmen, Pedersen, Huffman, and Bryan (1993) studied the relative power of prebirth maternal anxiety, postbirth 3-month maternal response to distress, and the infant characteristic of negative affect as predictors of security of attachment at 1 year of age. The results indicate that 3-month distress management and prenatal maternal anxiety are the strongest predictors in classifying security of attachment. The authors' interpretation of these findings is consistent with the emphasis of this chapter on the importance of regulating affect. Mothers who cannot manage their own affect (distress) will have difficulty managing the distress (affect) of their 3-month-old infant.

What other evidence is there that the parental adaptation-competence, as well as their relationship capacity, are likely to influence variation in the child's development of security? Main and Goldwyn (1991) showed that the classification from the Adult Attachment Interview stressing the mother's coherent, objective, and balanced account of her childhood is significantly associated with the development of security in her infant's attachment. Very relevant to predicting the transaction of parental responsiveness to the needs and security of the child are the findings of Ward and Carlson (1991) linking the classification derived from the Adult Attachment Interview to maternal sensitivity and security of attachment in children at 15 months. Mothers classified as autonomous—as opposed to dismissing, preoccupied, or unresolved—showed higher levels of sensitivity at 3 and 9 months, and their infants were more frequently classified as secure at 15 months. Ward and Carlson (1991) stressed that the mothers placed in the autonomous attachment classification have achieved a coherent view of their current and past relationships.

As the experience of classifying the responses to the attachment interview suggests, the categories being used seem to speak as much to the issues of adaptation-competence or current ego functioning as they do to the capacity to form an empathic trusting relationship (Main & Goldwyn, 1991). A prospective study by Fonagy, H. Steele, and M. Steele (1991) linking the prebirth Parental Attachment Interview classifications to the developing security of the 1-year-old permits further discussion of this question. The Adult Attachment Interview was administered to 100 mothers expecting their first child and, at 1-year follow-ups, 96 mothers again were seen with their infants in the Strange Situation to assess the quality of their child's attachment. Maternal representations of attachment (autonomous vs. dismissing or preoccupied) predicted subsequent infant-mother attachment patterns (secure vs. insecure) 75 percent of the time. In addition to deriving these major classifications, each interview was also rated on eight 9-point scales describing the adult's probable childhood experience of having been parented, the current state of mind with respect to attachment, and the overall coherence of the interview. Both anxious resistant and secure, as opposed to avoidant, children had mothers who recalled their relationship with their mothers as significantly more loving and less rejecting, whereas coherence was highest among mothers of securely attached infants. So, both the parent's specific positive remembrance of their own parenting and an index of ego integration (i.e., coherence) anticipate the development of a secure child attachment. The question then arises of whether alternate measures of the mother's organizational functioning not necessarily tied to questions about her relationship history would predict her child's secure attachment. Fonagy, M. Steele, H. Steele, Moran, and Higgitt (1991) studied this issue in terms of the capacity of the mother to reflect on her mental functioning. All recorded Adult Attachment Interviews were rated on the absence or presence of reflective functions. Strong evidence of self-reflection was seen in statements indicating the subject's ability to understand psychological states, including conscious and unconscious motivations underlying their own reactions and those of others. Relating this measure of the mother's functioning to the ratings of the attachment interview and the security of the child, it was found that the mother's self-reflection was highly correlated (.73) with the previous ratings of quality of recall and coherence; that as already noted, the coherence of the mother's interview predicted a secure child attachment; and when reflective self-function was controlled for, coherence no longer related significantly to infant security. This suggests that self-reflection is an essential component of the mother's ability to organize her relationship experiences.

Related to further search for those maternal adaptive functions that predict secure attachment and parent sensitivity to the child's need (Ainsworth et al., 1978), Teti et al. (1990) found that this sensitivity correlated with the availability and adequacy of attachment figures, marital harmony, major negative life events, daily hassles, infant difficulty, and maternal depression, but all these significant relations became nonsignificant when controlled for by maternal self-efficacy in dealing with the child. It would seem that both maternal self-reflection and self-efficacy are adaptive functions that enhance the development of a secure mother–child attachment and thus warrant further study.

Both our initial summary statement and the supporting research findings have focused on the association of the mother's prebirth characteristics and her responsiveness to the needs of her infant. Several other studies either focus on the father or include both mother and father.

Paternal Prebirth Functioning, and Father's Positive Relationship to His Child

The father's prebirth adaptive competence and capacity to sustain positive relationships (especially those with his partner) anticipate a positive relationship with his child during the first year of life. Research evidence supporting this statement is limited but consistent. Grossman et al. (1980) found that an interview measure of paternal adaptation at 2 months postpartum is anticipated by the following first trimester measures: the father's tendency to identify positively with his own mother and good marital adjustment. Similarly, Feldman, Nash, and Aschenbrenner (1983) showed that the father's caregiving and playfulness with his 6-month-old infant and his satisfaction with fatherhood are anticipated by prebirth indices of general adjustment and marital happiness as reported by the husband and/or wife. For example, satisfaction with fatherhood was predicted by the father's empathy with his wife, few if any problems in the marriage, a match between the desired and actual sex of the baby, and a self-description low in characteristics like gullible and childlike.

In a series of reports, Cox and her colleagues showed how prebirth measures of father *and* mother functioning anticipate postnatal parent responsiveness and child security. The first report (Cox, Owen, Lewis, & Henderson, 1989) used both an interview based 3-month parent attitude as well as observations of sensitive parental behavior as outcome measures. Mothers had a more positive attitude toward their 3-month-old infant if that infant was a son and if their own prebirth psychological assessment (adaptation-competence) was adequate. Both this adequate adjustment and the positive quality of their marriage anticipated the sensitive behavioral responding to their infant. Similarly, but also slightly different, both an adequate prebirth adjustment and positive marriage anticipated the father's positive attitude toward his 3-month-old child. The father was likely to respond warmly if his own adjustment was adequate and his infant was a son. A second report (Cox, Owen, Henderson, & Margaund, 1992) showed that an expanded version of the previous 3-month parent attitudinal and observational variables predicted the 12-month secure attachment continuum. Twelve-month infant–mother security was anticipated by the mother's positive and sensitive interaction with her infant, by her physical affection, and by the total amount of time spent with her infant, but not by her attitude toward her infant. Infant–father security at 12 months was anticipated by all of the aforementioned 3-month variables. However, the association between time spent and infant–father security was negative. Although not easy to interpret, this last finding points to the importance of considering these variables in a total family context. Cox and Owen (1993) reported that prebirth measures of marital discord and psychological adjustment anticipated both 3-month parent positive interaction/attitude and 12-month infant security. Infant–father attachment security at 12 months was anticipated directly by the father's positive interaction/attitude toward his 3-month-old child and by prebirth marital discord (negatively). The father's prebirth psychological adjustment also had a significant impact on his child's security, but indirectly so, via marital discord and father positive interaction/attitude (Cox & Owen, 1993). The comprehensive analysis of the same variables predicting to infant–mother security was not significant. However, significant correlations emerged when the association of variables was evaluated separately by gender. For boys, security of 12-month attachment was significantly associated with the mother's 3-month parenting, but was not related to marital discord or mother's adjustment. For girls, the prebirth marital relations predicted 12-month security.

In summary, in the previous two sections, it has been shown that, if the mother copes well with various life issues, has the capacity to form positive and trusting relationships, and has a mutually positive relationship with her partner before the birth of her child, she is more likely to be responsive to her child's needs, and her child will develop greater security in the first 4 years of life. There is some evidence to suggest that similar statements also apply to the father and/or other partners. However, there is less support for such conclusions, and all models outlined so far suggest the need for further studies of the father's role in a couple and family systems context, and that the gender of the child must be considered in such studies.

Prebirth Couple Functioning and Child Security and Autonomy in the First 4 Years

Couples characterized by positive mutuality, partner autonomy, and the ability to confront problems and regulate negative affect are responsive to the needs of their infants, promote their autonomy, and have more secure and autonomous children, as seen throughout the first 4 years of life. This statement and its documentation clearly overlap with the previous discussion of individual prebirth determinants of responsive parenting. The evidence cited here stresses the impact of the prebirth couple (partner) interaction on the parent's promotion of the child's secure, separate, and positive self.

That the prebirth marital relationship and particularly the quality of their interaction predict postnatal family development has been documented widely. Applying path analysis models to the same representative sample discussed earlier and extending it to child age 48 months revealed that of the various prebirth parent characteristics, only the overall quality of the husband–wife adaptation still had a direct impact on the transaction of the child's security and parent responsiveness to need at 48 months (Heinicke & Lampl, 1988). This led us to analyze differentiations of this global marital adjustment using two cohorts of 46 families each. Thus, within the overall impact of the marital quality, six different patterns of postnatal marital development were defined on a larger sample ($N = 92$), and three positive patterns were shown to be associated with the development of those parent–child interactions (responsiveness to need and promotion of autonomy) that enhance a secure and separate self in the first 2 years of life (Heinicke & Guthrie, 1992). Moreover, the more positive marital patterns were anticipated by ratings of the parent's open discussion and remembrance in the prebirth period of their own positive parenting experience, and by indices of maternal adaptation-competence derived from pre-birth videotaped interviews with the mother and by her Minnesota Multiphasic Personality Inventory (MMPI) responses.

Evidence from the Pennsylvania State Family Development Project links a declining postnatal marital pattern to the development of an insecure attachment at 1 year of age. Belsky, Youngblade, Rovine, and Volling (1991) showed the association between these declining marital patterns and observations of fathers and mothers interacting with their 3-year-olds in a free-play and teaching task situation. Relevant to the parent facilitating the autonomy of the child was the finding that in declining marital relationships fathers were more intrusive and aversive as opposed to positive and facilitative.

In tracing the link between prebirth measures of partner personality and marital functioning to the child's academic achievement and social competence in kindergarten, P. A. Cowan et al. (1993) proceed in two longitudinal steps. The first related prebirth, 6-month, and 18-month measures of relationship functioning to observations of marital interaction and the parent's interaction with their child when the child is in preschool (or 3½ years). A second step linked this marital interaction and parent–child interaction with measures of the child's academic achievement and social competence in late kindergarten. The first set of findings involves a self-report measure of marital satisfaction (Locke & Wallace, 1959) in pregnancy and at 18 months. The decline in marital satisfaction during this period is associated with the observed angry, cold, and competitive as opposed to warm, responsive, and cooperative marital interaction when the child is 3½ years. This conflictual marital interaction is in turn associated with both the father and mother being less warm with their child and the father communicating less well and not being able to present the assigned tasks in a manner that helped their preschool child to manage the task. Pratt et al. (1988) showed that parents who are warm and structuring also tend to provide scaffolding for their children—to move in at the appropriate level when their children are having difficulty and back off when their children are succeeding on their own. Another prebirth measure, the Family Environment Scale (Moos, 1974) was linked to marital stress at 6 months, to the decline in marital quality (prebirth to 18 months) and to marital and parent–child interaction at 3½ years. Parents who during pregnancy remember the atmosphere in the families they grew up as high in conflict and experienced more stress at 6 months were more conflicted in their marital interaction when their child was 3½. Further analyses showed that high levels of stress at 6 months linked directly to less adequate parenting styles and indirectly via the decline in marital satisfaction from prebirth to 18 months. As already reported, this decline anticipated conflicted marital interaction and less responsive parenting styles when the child was age 3½ years old.

Summarizing, the findings reported in these three sections support the general statement that pre-birth measures of the parent's adaptation-competence and capacity for relationships, as well as their marital relationship anticipate certain postnatal family transactions including parent responsiveness to need interacting with child security, and parent encouragement of autonomy interacting with child sense of separate self.

Prebirth Marital Interaction and the Child's Security and Autonomy

Because the aforementioned results are based on prebirth parent responses to self inventories and interviews, the question arises as to whether indices of the quality of the husband–wife relationship derived from direct observation of their prebirth marital interaction also anticipate variation in postnatal family development. Studies by Markman, Howes, and their colleagues (Howes & Markman, 1991), and Heinicke and Guthrie (1994) are relevant to this question. The couples of our second cohort ($N = 46$) were, in the prebirth period, asked to discuss and resolve differences on three important issues (Heinicke & Guthrie, 1993). Systematic coding resulted in classifications contrasting those who could realistically confront the tasks and express negative feelings while maintaining a context of positive mutuality from those who could not. Those who could not resolve issues were either consistently low or decreased in their postnatal marital adjustment. As already documented, the positive patterns of postnatal marital changes were associated with the development of a secure attachment in the first child and their capacity to promote autonomy when that child was 2 years old. Similarly, Markman and his colleagues (Belaguer & Markman, 1991; Howes & Markman, 1991) documented an association between premarital and prebirth marital interaction measures and the development of attachment and self-concepts in the child. Thus, premarital relationship problem discussions were coded and related to measures of attachment (the Waters Q-sort) when the first child was between 1 and 3 years of age. Correlational results indicated that avoidance of conflict and emotional invalidation in the parents' premarital relationship predicted less secure attachment relationships between mothers and their firstborns. Codes describing women as facilitating the resolution of conflict during premarital discussions predicted more secure attachment relationships between fathers and their firstborns. Howes and Markman (1991) summarized these as well as other findings by concluding that "abilities in regulating negative affect by acknowledging and addressing differences appears to be critical to both spousal and parent–child relationships" (p. 10). Similarly, Belaguer and Markman (1991) found an association between the quality of marital interaction both before marriage and before the birth of the first child and measures of the child's self-concept at ages 4 to 7. A mother's support of her future husband, and both partners support of each other, in problem-solving marital interactions before the birth of their first child anticipate the child's experience of the self as part of positive family interaction. They stressed the importance to the child of not being exposed to destructive conflict. The additional finding that negative escalation as seen in both father and mother during prebirth interactions anticipates lower levels of the child's experience of positive self affect is consistent with this emphasis.

In a subsequent study of the same sample (Renick & Odell, 1993), it was shown that codes of family interaction videotaped when the child was 4 to 7 years old were associated with both the child's concurrent positive self-ratings and the couple's premarital negative escalation. That is, those families who could cooperate in a game and showed positive as opposed to negative affect, and who had children with a positive self-esteem, avoided negative escalation during a premarital interaction session.

Summarizing this section, it has been found that the parent's ability to confront conflictual issues, regulate their negative effect, and resolve their differences is associated with a setting in which their children develop greater security and autonomy. These results, based on observed interaction, are consistent with those based on inventory and interview data.

Couple Functioning and Preschool and Kindergarten Family Development

Couples characterized by prebirth and continuing positive mutuality continue their optimal parenting of their children whose development is characterized as follows: They are secure, autonomous, and task oriented in preschool; are less aggressive and shy in early kindergarten; and score higher on achievement tests at the end of kindergarten. The primary documentation for this statement comes from the Becoming a Family Project (P. A. Cowan et al., 1993). In the previous section, we reported the influence of positive marital quality on spouse's warmth and cooperation with one another, and their greater warmth and structuring with their preschool child in a task situation. P. A. Cowan et al. (1993) also documented the association between these preschool variables and children's kindergarten assessments. The kindergarten children who scored lower on the Peabody Individual Achievement Test (reading recognition, reading comprehension, spelling, mathematics, and general information) had parents who were more conflicted in their interaction with each other and less warm and encouraging of the autonomy of their preschool child. For this outcome variable (i.e. academic achievement), the prebirth to 18 months quality of relationship variables had an indirect effect via the preschool status; there were no direct links from prebirth to kindergarten.

Variation in the preschool parent and parent–child interaction also anticipated variation in the kindergarten child's shyness and aggression. Parents who were competitive and hostile in their marital interaction and did not work cooperatively in front of their preschooler tended to have children who showed more aggressive interactions or who were shy and withdrawn with their classmates 2 years later. Further findings were that low levels of father and mother warmth and responsiveness at $3\frac{1}{2}$ linked to high levels of classroom aggressiveness. However, different levels of parent structuring did not predict levels of aggression.

In contrast to the prediction of academic achievement, there were direct as well as indirect links from the prebirth family relationship to the kindergarten child's level of shyness and aggressiveness. Thus, parents who during pregnancy remembered the atmosphere in the families they grew up in as high in conflict tended to have children who were rated shy and/or aggressive.

Path analysis diagrams (Figures 11.1 and 11.2) best summarize our own findings on the antecedents of 4-year-old task orientation and modulation of aggression. Consistent with the emphasis of Cowan et al. (1993) that the prebirth and continuing positive quality of the husband–wife adaptation is central to family adaptation, Figures 11.1 and 11.2 show that this prebirth quality is the only direct link to both aggression modulation and task orientation. Also consistent with the results reported by Cowan et al. (1993) is the finding that, even when all previous influences are allowed for, both child indices are still correlated with their respective preschool transactional counterparts: Parent responsiveness to infant needs correlates with "child modulates aggression" (.75), and child task orientation correlates with parent stimulates the child's cognitive and verbal experiences (.34).

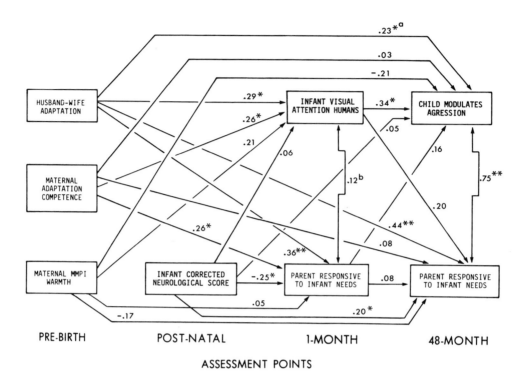

FIGURE 11.1. Path analysis diagram for two indices of 48-month positive parent–child mutuality: Child aggression modulation and parent responsiveness to need ($N = 44$). *$p < .05$. [a]Beta weights placed by across time paths.**$p < .01$ [b]Vertical lines indicate cross-sectional correlations

These same diagrams also show the indirect influence on aggression modulation of variations in early child and prebirth maternal characteristics. Thus, prebirth husband–wife adaptation and maternal adaptation-competence influence the 1-month infant's visual attention to humans, and variation in this quality anticipate variations in aggression modulation (see Figure 11.1).

Another early infant characteristic, postnatal neurological adaptation, affects the parent responsive to need aspect of the transaction being discussed. At 1 and 48 months, the parent's response to the needs of their infant is influenced not only by their prebirth marital adaptation, but by the adaptive (neurological) characteristics of their infant. At 1 month there is a negative association. The more difficult the infant, the more responsive the parent. A form of compensation is suggested. By 48 months there is a positive link between infants who show an optimal response right after birth and optimal parent responsiveness. We assume that the compensatory behavior is not maintained and the infant's initial status has some prevailing impact on the parent–infant mutuality.

In a similar way, 48-month task orientation is directly anticipated by husband–wife adaptation and prior 24-month child verbal expressiveness and parent stimulates cognitive and verbal experiences (see Figure 11.2). Each of these parts of a correlated transaction (child verbal expressiveness and parent stimulation) is anticipated by prebirth maternal adaptation competence and maternal verbal IQ. Given all of the previous significant influences, we concluded (as did P. A. Cowan et al., 1993) that task orientation is influenced both by a social-emotional network here represented by the parent's marital quality and by intellectual and adaptive antecedents such as maternal adaptation and verbal IQ.

In summary, available research suggests that couples characterized by continuing positive mutuality also provide continuing optimal parenting and have children who are secure, autonomous, task motivated, less aggressive, and score higher on kindergarten achievement tests.

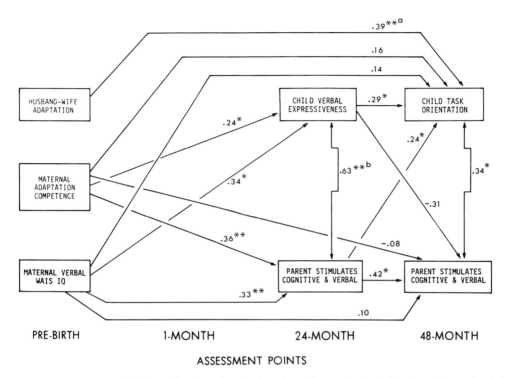

FIGURE 11.2. Path analysis diagram for 48-moth task orientation and parental stimulation of cognitive and verbal: Cognitive antecedents ($N = 44$). $*p < .05$. [a]Beta weights by across time paths. $**p < .01$. [b]Vertical lines indicate cross-sectional correlations.

CONCLUSIONS AND PRACTICAL IMPLICATIONS

The research on the prebirth determinants of parenting permits several general conclusions. Parents capable of efficient, nonanxious, flexible problem solving; able to sustain a positive mutuality, especially with their partner; and also able to maintain their autonomy and self-esteem are more likely to provide an optimal parenting environment. In the context of the studies reviewed, this optimal parenting includes responsiveness to need, encouragement of autonomy, and exposure to cognitive experiences. It is shown that variations in these qualities of parenting are of central significance in the family interactions enhancing security, autonomy, and task motivation in the child. These developments in turn are associated with higher academic achievement and less disruptive aggression in kindergarten. That is, motivation to learn and modulation of aggression, which are crucial to later academic and social development, are influenced by parent and marital characteristics that are present before birth and tend to have a consistent influence in the emerging family interactions. If supported by further research, these conclusions have important practical implications. Within a family systems context, preventative intervention would focus on parent adaptation, relationship, and partner (marital) functioning as well as parenting–infant interactions and infant development (C. P. Cowan & P. A. Cowan, 1992; Heinicke, 1991); on those child functions—the development of security, autonomy, and task orientation—that are linked to the aforementioned and more likely to respond to a sociobehavioral intervention; and on those developmental moments when the family system is both motivated and amenable to intervention (Heinicke, 1990).

In regard to the timing of intervention, the conclusions of this review stressing the stability and ongoing influence of family system characteristics argue for "the earlier the better." But variation in the amenability and/or access qualify this conclusion. Markham, Floyd, Stanley, and Storaasli (1988) intervened during the couples engagement period. The intervention emphasized communication and problem-solving skills, clarifying and sharing expectations, and sensual/sexual enhancement. The point at which the couple is trying to decide about whether to have a child may well be another moment of accessibility. Intervention initiated both during pregnancy and shortly after birth has been found to be effective. See Heinicke (1991) for a summary of results.

Although the previous framework, conclusions, and implications are likely to be confirmed by further research, generalizations must be viewed with some caution. The conclusion that prebirth parent characteristics have a significant impact on parenting and child development is based on the prebirth measurement and proven stability of these characteristics. These prebirth assessments reflect family system characteristics that continue, and are influenced by but not exclusively determined by, the characteristics of the child. However, it may be possible that other influences, such as a profile of genetic determinants, could affect both pre- and postbirth developments. For example, we have hypothesized that the 2-year-olds' sustained attention and the mother's capacity to stimulate her child are both related to prebirth measures of her IQ (Heinicke et al., 1986).

Other limitations of the previous conclusions relate to those aspects of the total model that have not been studied. The pre- to postbirth studies of the father's functioning, the quality of family support, and the stress conditions are very limited in number. As reviewed here, several studies link marital and maternal pre- to postbirth developments in the first 2 years of life. However, very few have studied the continuity of development from prebirth to kindergarten. Although the model of research used in this review stresses the influence of stable parent characteristics and functioning as assessed before the birth of the child impacts that functioning, much further research is needed to establish how and which early infant characteristics (temperament) do also impact the parent functioning. Because change as well as stability characterizes that transaction, measurement must occur frequently enough to permit assessment of change.

Further questions must be raised concerning the specific transactions involved in accounting for global associations that have been documented in this chapter. Particularly promising in this regard is the longitudinal study of the couple's (partner's) capacity to resolve conflict. The predictive power of the pre-birth variations in couple's ability to confront problems and to handle the negative feelings generated by efforts to solve them poses the question as to whether couples characterized by continuing positive mutuality also continue to resolve their conflicts. Several recent studies indeed support such an assumption (Cox & Owen, 1993; Lindahl & Markman, 1993).

The search for ways of breaking the cycle of generational transmission of parent characteristics that do not enhance family development is not a new one. The evidence provided here provides a view of this process and has already influenced the design of effective early family intervention.

ACKNOWLEDGMENTS

We are grateful to Phillip and Carolyn Cowan for their critique of earlier versions of this chapter, and especially want to acknowledge the supportive and constructive readings of our work by our editor, Marc Bornstein. Amy Sherman has been most helpful in the editing and processing of this chapter. This research was supported by the Ahmanson Foundation of Los Angeles; the Lita Annenberg Hazen Charitable Trust, New York; the National Institute of Child Health and Human Development, Grant No. HD 13186; and the National Institute of Mental Health, Grant No. MH 45722.

REFERENCES

Ainsworth, M. D. S., Blehar, M. D., Waters, E., & Wall, S. (1978). *Patterns of attachment: A psychological study of the strange situation*. Hillsdale, NJ: Lawrence Erlbaum Associates.

Balaguer, A., & Markman, H. J. (1991). *The effects of marital communication and conflict management on child self-concept: A longitudinal perspective*. Unpublished manuscript.

Baldwin, A. L., Cole, R. E., & Baldwin, E. P. (1982). Parent pathology, family interaction, and the competence of the child in school. *Monographs of the Society for Research in Child Development, 47*(5, Serial No. 197).

Barron, F. (1953). An ego-strength scale which predicts response to psychotherapy. *Journal of Consulting Psychology, 17,* 327–333.

Belsky, J. (1978). Three theoretical models of child abuse: A critical review. *International Journal of Child Abuse and Neglect, 2,* 37–49.

Belsky, J. (1980). Child maltreatment: An ecological integration. *American Psychologist, 35,* 320–335.

Belsky, J. (1984). The determinants of parenting: A process model. *Child Development, 55,* 83–96.

Belsky, J., Crnic, K., & Gable, S. (1993). Coparenting of toddlers: A descriptive, developmental and explanatory analysis. *Abstracts of the Biannual Meeting of the Society for Research in Child Development, 9,* 26.

Belsky, J., & Isabella, R. (1986). Maternal, infant, and social-contextual determinants of attachment security. In J. Belsky & R. Isabella (Eds.), *Clinical implications of attachment* (pp. 41–94). Hillsdale, NJ: Lawrence Erlbaum Associates.

Belsky, J., & Pensky, E. (1988). Marital change across the transition to parenthood. *Marriage and Family Review, 12,* 133–156.

Belsky, J., Rovine, M., & Fish, M. (1989). The developing family system. In M. Ganner & E. Thelen (Eds.), *Systems and development.* Minnesota Symposium on Child Psychology. Vol. 22 (pp. 119–166). Hillsdale, NJ: Lawrence Erlbaum Associates.

Belsky, J., Youngblade, L., Rovine, M., & Volling, B. (1991). Patterns of marital change and parent–child interaction. *Journal of Marriage and the Family, 53,* 487–498.

Bibring, C. S., Dwyer, T. F., Huntington, D. S., & Valenstein, A. F. (1961). A study of the psychological processes in pregnancy and the earliest mother–child relationship. In *The psychoanalytic study of the child* (Vol. 16, pp. 9–72). New York: International Universities Press.

Block, J., & Block, J. H. (1980). *The California Child Q-set.* Palo Alto, CA: Consulting Psychologists Press.

Bornstein, M. H., & Tamis-LeMonda, C. S. (1989). Maternal responsiveness and cognitive development in children. In M. H. Bornstein (Ed.), *Maternal responsiveness: Characteristics and consequences* (pp. 49–61). San Francisco: Jossey-Bass.

Brazelton, T. B. (1973). *Neonatal Behavior Assessment Scale* (Clinics in Development Medicine No. 50). Philadelphia: Lippincott.

Brown, G. W., & Harris, T. (1978) *Social origins of depression: A study of psychiatric disorder in women.* New York: Free Press.

Brunnquell, D., Crichton, L., & Egeland, B. (1981). Maternal personality and attitude in disturbances of child-rearing. *Journal of Orthopsychiatry, 51,* 680–691.

Colletta, N. D., & Gregg, C. H. (1981). Adolescent mothers' vulnerability to stress. *Journal of Nervous and Mental Disease, 169,* 50–54.

Cowan, C. P., & Cowan, P. A. (1992). *When partners become parents.* New York: Basic Books.

Cowan, C. P., Cowan, P. A., Heming, G., Garrett, E., Coysh, W. S., Curtis-Boles, H., & Boles, A. J. (1985). Transitions to parenthood: His, hers, and theirs. *Journal of Family Issues, 6,* 451–481.

Cowan, C. P., Cowan, P. A., Coie, L., & Coie, J. D. (1978). Becoming a family: The impact of a first child's birth on the couple's relationship. In W. B. Miller & L. F. Newman (Eds.), *The first child and family formation* (pp. 296–324). Chapel Hill: University of North Carolina.

Cowan, P. A., & Cowan, C. P. (1988). Changes in marriage during the transition to parenthood: Must we blame the baby? In G. Michaels & W. A. Goldberg (Eds.), *The transition to parenthood: Current theory and research* (pp. 114–154). Cambridge, England: Cambridge University Press.

Cowan, P. A., Cowan, C. P., Schulz, M., & Heming, G. (1993). Pre-birth to preschool family factors in children's adaptation to kindergarten. In R. Parke & S. Kellam, (Eds.), Exploring family relationships with other social contexts. *Advances in Family Research* (Vol. 4, pp. 1–65). Hillsdale, NJ: Lawrence Erlbaum Associates.

Cox, M. J., & Owen, M. T. (1993). Marital conflict and conflict negotiation. *Abstracts of the Biannual Meeting of the Society for Research in Child Development, 9.*

Cox, M. J., Owen, M. T., Henderson, V. K., & Margaud, N. A. (1992). Prediction of infant–father and infant–mother attachment. *Developmental Psychology, 28,* 474–483.

Cox, M. J., Owen, M. T., Lewis, J. M., & Henderson, V. K. (1989). Marriage, adult adjustment, and early parenting. *Child Development, 60,* 1015–1024.

Crnic, K. A., Greenberg, M. T., Ragozin, A. S., Robinson, N. M, & Basham, R. (1983). Effects of stress and social support on mothers and premature and full-term infants. *Child Development, 54,* 209–217.

Del Carmen, R., Pedersen, F. A., Huffman, L. C., & Bryan, Y. E. (1993). Dyadic distress management predicts subsequent security of attachment. *Infant Behavior and Development, 16,* 131–147.

Deutsch, H. (1945). *The psychology of women: Motherhood* (Vol. 2). New York: Grune & Stratton.

Diamond, D., Heinicke, C. M., & Mintz, J. (1994). *Separation-individuation as a family transactional process in the transition to parenthood.* Manuscript submitted for publication.

Egeland, B., & Farber, E. A. (1984). Infant–mother attachment: Factors related to its development and changes over time. *Child Development, 55,* 753–771.

Fabian, A. A., & Donahue, J. F. (1956). Maternal depression: A challenging child guidance problem. *American Journal of Orthopsychiatry, 26,* 400–405.

Feldman, S. S., Nash, S. C., & Aschenbrenner, R. B. (1983). Antecedents of fathering. *Child Development, 54,* 1628–1636.

Field, T. M., Widmayer, S. M., Stringer, S., & Ignatoff, E. (1980). Teenage, lower-class, Black mothers and their preterm infants: An intervention and developmental follow-up. *Child Development, 51,* 426–436.

Fonagy, P., Steele, H., & Steele, M. (1991). Maternal representations of attachment during pregnancy predict the organization of infant–mother attachment at one year of age. *Child Development, 62,* 891–905.

Fonagy, P., Steele, M., Steele, H., Moran, G. S., & Higgitt, A. C. (1991). The capacity for understanding mental states: The reflective self in parent and child and its significance for security of attachment. *Infant Mental Health Journal, 13,* 200–216.

Frommer, E., & O'Shea, G. (1973a). Antenatal identification of women liable to have problems in managing their infants. *British Journal of Psychiatry, 123,* 157–160.

Frommer, E., & O'Shea, G. (1973b). The importance of childhood experiences in relation to problems of marriage and family building. *British Journal of Psychiatry, 123,* 157–160.

Gough, G., & Heilbrun, A. B., Jr. (1980). *The adjective check list manual.* Palo Alto, CA: Consulting Psychologist Press.

Grossman, F. K., Eichler, L. W., & Winikoff, S. A. (1980). *Pregnancy, birth and parenthood.* San Francisco: Jossey-Bass.

Hall, F., Pawlby, S., & Wolkind, S. (1980). Early life experience and later mothering behavior: A study of mothers and their 20-week-old babies. In D. Shaffer & J. Dunn (Eds.), *The first year of life* (pp. 153–174). New York: Wiley.

Heinicke, C. M. (1980). Continuity and discontinuity of task orientation. *Journal of the American Academy of Child Psychiatry, 19,* 637–653.

Heinicke, C. M. (1984). Impact of pre-birth parent personality and marital functioning on family development: A framework and suggestions for further study. *Developmental Psychology, 20,* 1044–1053.

Heinicke, C. M. (1990). Towards generic principles of treating parents and children: Integrating psychotherapy with the school-aged child and early family intervention. *Journal of Consulting and Clinical Psychology, 58,* 713–719.

Heinicke, C. M. (1991). Early family intervention: Focussing on the mother's adaptation-competence and quality of the partnership. In D. G. Unger & D. R. Powell (Eds.), *Families as nurturing systems: Support across the life span* (pp. 127–142). New York: Haworth.

Heinicke, C. M. (1993). Maternal personality, involvement in interaction, and family development. *Abstracts of the Biannual Meeting of the Society for Research in Child Development, 9,* 116.

Heinicke, C. M., Diskin, S., Ramsey-Klee, D., & Given, K. (1983). Pre-birth parent characteristics and family development in the first year of life. *Child Development, 54,* 194–208.

Heinicke, C. M., Diskin, S. D., Ramsey-Klee, D. M., & Oates, D. S. (1986). Pre and post-birth antecedents of two-year-old attention, capacity for relationships, and verbal expressiveness. *Developmental Psychology, 22,* 777–787.

Heinicke, C. M., & Guthrie, D. (1992). Stability and change in husband–wife adaptation, and the development of the positive parent–child relationship. *Infant Behavior and Development, 15,* 109–127.

Heinicke, C. M., & Guthrie, D. (1993). *Pre-birth marital interactions and post-birth marital development.* Manuscript submitted for publication.

Heinicke, C. M., & Lampl, E. (1988). Pre- and post-birth antecedents of 3- and 4-year-old attention, IQ, verbal expressiveness, task orientation, and capacity for relationships. *Infant Behavior and Development, 2,* 381–410.

Heinicke, C. M., Recchia, S., James, C., & Berlin, P. (1993). *Manual for coding global child and parent-child ratings.* Unpublished manuscript.

Hill, R. (1949). *Families under stress.* New York: Harper.

Hobbs, D., & Coles, S. (1976). Transition to parenthood: A decade replication. *Journal of Marriage and the Family, 38,* 723–731.

Horowitz, M., Schafer, C., Hiroto, D., Wilner, N., & Levin, B. (1977). Life Event Questionnaire for measuring presumptive stress. *Psychosomatic Medicine, 39,* 413–31.

Howes, P. W., & Markman, H. J. (1991). Longitudinal relations between premarital and prebirth adult interaction and subsequent parent-child attachment. *Abstracts of the Biannual Meeting of the Society for Research in Child Development, 8.*

Huston, J. L., & McHale, S. M. (1983). Changes in the topography of marriage following the birth of the first child. *Abstracts of the Biannual Meeting of the Society for Research in Child Development, 4.*

Isabella, R. A., & Gable, S. (1993). *The determinants of maternal behavior across the first year: An ecological consideration.* Unpublished manuscript.

Jones, F. A., Green, V., & Krauss, D. R. (1980). Maternal responsiveness of primiparous mothers during the postpartum period: Age differences. *Pediatrics, 65,* 579–583.

Lindahl, K. M., & Markman, H. J. (1993). Managing negative affect in the family: Implications for marital and parent–child relationships. *Abstracts of the Biannual Meeting of the Society for Research in Child Development, 9.*

Littman, B., & Parmalee, A. H., Jr. (1974). *Manual for obstetrical complications.* Los Angeles, University of California, Marion Davie's Children's Center.

Locke, H., & Wallace, K. (1959). Short marital adjustment and prediction tests: Their reliability and validity. *Marriage and Family Living, 21,* 251–255.

Main, M., & Goldwyn, R. (1991). Interview-based adult attachment classifications: related to infant–mother and infant–father attachment. *Developmental Psychology.*

Markman, H. J., Floyd, F. J., Stanley, S. M., & Storaasli, R. D. (1988). Prevention of marital distress: A longitudinal investigation. *Journal of Consulting and Clinical Psychology, 56,* 210–217.

Mondell, S., & Tyler, F. (1981). Parental competence and styles of problem solving/play behavior with children. *Developmental Psychology, 17,* 73–78.

Moos, R. H. (1974). *Family Environment Scale.* Palo Alto, CA: Consulting Psychologists Press.

Moss, H. (1967). Sex, age, and state as determinants of mother-infant interaction. *Merrill–Palmer Quarterly, 13,* 19–36.

Orraschel, H., Weissman, M. M., & Kidd, K. K. (1980). Children and depression: The children of depressed parents; the children of depressed patients; depression in children. *Journal of Affective Disorders, 2,* 1–16.

Osofsky, J. J., & Osofsky, J. D. (1970). Adolescents as mothers. *American Journal of Orthopsychiatry, 40,* 825.

Parke, R., & Collmer, C. (1975). Child abuse: An interdisciplinary review. In E. M. Hetherington (Ed.), *Review of child development research* (Vol. 5, pp. 509–590). Chicago: University of Chicago Press.

Pianta, R., Egeland, B., & Erickson, M. F. (1989). The antecedents of maltreatment: Results of the Mother–Child Interaction Research Project. In D. Cichetti & V. Carlson (Eds.), *Child maltreatment: Theory and research on the causes and consequences of child abuse and neglect* (pp. 203–253). New York: Cambridge University Press.

Pollitt, J. (1965). *Depression and its treatment.* London: Heinemann.

Pratt, M. W., Kerig, P. K., Cowan, P. A., & Cowan, C. P. (1988). Mothers and fathers teaching 3-year-olds: Authoritative parenting and adults' use of the zone of proximal development. *Developmental Psychology, 24,* 832–839.

Ragozin, A. S., Basham, R. B., Crnic, K. A., Greenberg, M. T., & Robinson, N. M. (1982). Effects of maternal age on parenting role. *Developmental Psychology, 18,* 627–634.

Renick, M. J., & Odell, S. (1993). Premarital communication, family interaction, and children's self esteem. *Abstracts of the Biannual Meeting of the Society for Research in Child Development, 9,* 564.

Rutter, M. (1966). *Children of sick patients: An environmental and psychiatric study* (Institute of Psychiatry, Maudsley Monographs No. 16). London: Oxford University Press.

Sameroff, A., & Chandler, M. J. (1975). Reproductive risk and the continuum of caretaking casualty. In F. D. Horowitz (Ed.), *Review of child development research* (Vol. 4, pp. 187–244). Chicago: University of Chicago Press.

Schaefer, F. S., Edgerton, M., & Hunter, M. (1983, August). *Childbearing and child development correlates of maternal locus of control.* Paper presented at the meeting of the American Psychological Association, Los Angeles.

Shereshefsky, P. M., & Yarrow, L. J. (1973). *Psychological aspects of a first pregnancy and early postnatal adaptation.* New York: Raven.

Sroufe, L. A. (1989). Relationships and Relationship disturbances. In A. J. Sameroff & R. N. Emde (Eds.), *Relationship disturbances in early childhood* (pp. 97–124). New York: Basic Books.

Stern, D. N. (1985). *The interpersonal world of the infant.* New York: Basic Books.

Teti, D. M., Gelfand, D. M., & Pompa, J. (1990). Depressed mothers' behavioral competence with their infants: Demographic and psychosocial correlates. *Development and Psychopathology, 2,* 259–270.

Vaughn, B., Deinard, A., & Egeland, B. (1980). Measuring temperament in pediatric practice. *Journal of Pediatrics, 96,* 510–514.

Vaughn, B., Taraldson, B., Crichton, L., & Egeland, B. (1981). The assessment of infant temperament: A critique of the Carey infant temperament questionnaire. *Infant Behavior and Development, 4,* 1–17.

Ward, M. J., & Carlson, E. A. (1991). The predictive validity of the Adult Attachment Interview for Adolescent Mothers. *Abstracts of the Biannual Meeting of the Society for Research in Child Development, 8.*

Weissman, M. M., & Paykel, E. S. (1974). *The depressed woman: A study of social relations.* Chicago: University of Chicago Press.

Wolkind, S., & Zajicek, E. (1981). *Pregnancy: A psychological and social study.* London: Academic Press.

12

Parents' Knowledge and Expectations

Jacqueline J. Goodnow
Macquarie University

INTRODUCTION

This chapter is about cognitive aspects of parenting, a topic covering the ways in which parents notice some events and not others, interpret what they observe, anticipate change in what their children can do, attribute characteristics to themselves or others, seek or reject advice, remember or reconstruct the past.

These questions reflect a field of research with both theoretical and practical goals. No one expects that attention to parents' ways of thinking will account for the whole of parenting, or that changing parents' ideas (often a goal in "parent education") will automatically alter parents' actions, parents' moods, and the way children develop, although that often may be the case. The hope, however, is that the analysis of ideas will advance our understanding of the way parents act, feel, and respond to advice, and will provide one way of specifying the social context in which development occurs.

Within this chapter I focus on cognitive aspects that are contained within the phrase: "knowledge and expectations." The emphasis is on ideas that are (1) about the present and the future (expectations rather than reconstructions of the past) and (2) related to information or evidence of some kind. These ideas may be regarded as some kind of knowledge rather than as dreams, unfounded hopes, general feelings, or wishful thinking.

To sharpen this general focus, I adopt an approach marked by three features. First, I concentrate on a particular set of questions. By and large, analyses of parents' ideas contain three sets of questions: sets that take as their focus the nature of parents' ideas, their consequences, or their bases (the conditions that influence parent's ideas). Influences are the focus of this chapter. The questions emphasized then take the form: How are parents' ideas established or revised? What are the connections, for instance, to personal experience with children or to the accepted wisdom of the cultural group? Some material on the nature of parents' ideas—on ways to describe their content and structure—emerge in the course of pursuing those questions about influence. In general, however, analyses of this issue are better sought in Holden and Edwards (1989), in Goodnow and Collins (1990) and, within this *Handbook,* in the chapters by Holden and by McGillicuddy-De Lisi and Sigel.

Second, I take a different approach to the issue of consequences than do Holden (in this *Handbook*) or McGillicuddy-De Lisi and Sigel (in this *Handbook*). They consider a variety of consequences, covering the impact of parents' ideas on both parents' actions and on several aspects of child development. I single out one particular consequence: the extent to which children's ideas match those of their parents. This is a consequence that has again a particular relevance to understanding the influence, on one person's ideas, of the ideas that others present to them.

Third, I adopt a particular perspective. Like Holden (in this *Handbook*) I see a need to link research on the cognitive aspects of parenting to general research on adult social cognition. The research in both cases is about the way people form and revise ideas about themselves and about others. Moreover, researchers working on the cognitive aspects of parenting have often been involved in some degree of blending. They have come to the topic either by starting with parenting and then feeling the need to know more about cognition in general, or by starting from a general interest in cognition and then becoming aware of parenting as an area that offered both challenges and promise.

At the same time, it is not obvious how the two areas might best be linked or how their overlaps can best be brought out. Nor is it clear what parts of the general material on cognition are likely to be the most profitable to turn to. I turn to two main lines of theory and research. Both, I propose, can enrich the study of parents' ideas, prompting an awareness of gaps and pointing to models and methods that can guide research.

The first of these lines of theory and research looks to conditions within the individual and is to be found under the label of experimental social psychology. It is here that one finds, for instance, analyses of content in terms of schemas or attributions, and analyses of influences in terms of social comparisons or disconfirming information. Some applications of this kind of material to parents' ideas are to be found in Goodnow (1988) and in Holden (in this Handbook); the present chapter adds to these.

The second line of theory and research looks to conditions outside the individual. It is here that one finds, for instance, an interest in questions about the extent to which ideas are widely shared in a social group or about the extent to which there are competing views about the nature of childhood and parenting (e.g., views of children as an undeclinable gift from God or as a parent's choice). It is here also that one finds questions about influences in terms of the state of the information that parents may encounter, the degree of social pressure that comes with particular definitions of "being a good parent," or the messages signaled by routine arrangements (e.g., the lukewarm reception often given to fathers in settings designed for "women and children").

This second line of research and theory is less well known to psychologists than is an emphasis upon conditions within the individual, and a brief note in is order. Some of this material is to be found in developmental psychology. Several developmentalists, for instance, have argued for the need to compare parents' ideas across cultures and to consider the way ideas are absorbed from other adults as well as from a parent's direct experience with children (work by Ninio, 1978, is an early example; work by Pomerleau, Malcuit, & Sabatier, 1991, a more recent one). In addition, Sameroff has consistently argued that what parents know is partly a function of the quality of what experts are prepared to tell them or can tell them (e.g., Sameroff & Feil, 1985). More is to be found in social psychology under the label of *social representations theory* (e.g., Moscovici, 1984; Mugny & Carugati, 1985). The term *social* in this case is a way of underlining ideas that are shared by members of a social group, and that are acquired along with membership in a group. I take on certain ideas and expectations, for instance, because I am now a parent; my direct experience with a child is by no means all that matters. Finally, a lively interest in the social conditions that influence "the acquisition of knowledge" is to found in sociology and anthropology (Goodnow, 1990, provided a partial review). Particularly for the question—What kinds of information about children and parenting do parents encounter?—material from scholars such as Bourdieu (1979) and Foucault (1980) provides a background that psychologists may well find novel and useful.

A few general points about the history of interest in the cognitive aspects of parenting are worth noting at the start. They constitute the first section of this chapter. The sections that follow then deal with (1) the way parents seek information about children and parenting, (2) the nature of the information available or encountered, and (3) the use of new or disconfirming information: information that is unexpected or that upsets ideas already in place. In each of these sections, I combine material from studies of parents' ideas with material from the broader literature. That blend applies also to the final section. It takes up a set of four issues that challenge any assumption that information or evidence is all that matters and that highlight the need to consider the interrelationship of ideas, actions, and feelings.

A BRIEF HISTORY

In broad terms, attention to parents' ideas is sparked by the wish to understand the conditions that influence development, and if possible to improve them. These conditions must include the nature of parenting. "The nature of parenting," however, goes well beyond its cognitive aspects and, as a topic, predates serious attention to cognitive aspects. Interest in cognitive aspects, in fact, has long been embedded within an interest in parents' attitudes (see Holden, in this *Handbook*). In part, the singling out of cognition came from a general sense that the components of attitudes (cognitive, affective, behavioral) needed to be dissected out from one another (e.g., Eagley & Chaiken, 1993). It came also, within developmental psychology, from a reaction against exclusively behavioral accounts of parenting. To take a description from Parke (1978), psychologists tended to account for mother–infant interactions entirely in terms of contingencies between the mother's actions and the child's actions. This approach, Parke pointed out, granted the mother the same level of cognitive complexity as the child was allowed, a position that could be corrected by adding attention to the mother's interpretations of the child's behavior.

The research has since expanded to cover all phases of parenting. It ranges, for instance, from ideas about an infant's temperament, formed during pregnancy, to ideas about the household rules that adolescents or young adults should follow. The research has also appeared under a variety of conceptual labels (parents' beliefs, ideas, theories, schemas, paradigms, working models) and has attracted several reviews (Goodnow, 1985; Goodnow & Collins, 1990; Holden & Edwards, 1989; Miller, 1988; Murphey, 1992; Sigel, 1985; Sigel, McGillicuddy-De Lisi, & Goodnow, 1992).

Over time, a number of changes have occurred. To start with, three questions have emerged:

(1) How are we to describe the content and the quality of the ideas that parents hold?
(2) What are the sources of these ideas? How are they established or changed?
(3) What are the consequences of parents' ideas for parents (their actions and feelings) and for children?

These three questions, once neatly separate, have come to be recognized as interrelated. One may be singled out for emphasis, but the others cannot be set completely aside. I give particular attention, for instance, to the extent to which parents' ideas are easy or difficult to change. That topic clearly belongs under the second question. It could also, however, be regarded as part of the description of the quality of parents' ideas. It may also be regarded as part of the consequences to particular ideas. As I note at several points, expectations can invite disappointment, and avoiding disappointment can be one of the reasons for holding on to an idea, ignoring the evidence that runs counter to it. In effect, the affective consequence can also be part of the sources that maintain a particular viewpoint.

Over time, three other changes relevant to the particular focus of this chapter have also occurred. The sources of interest have widened. So also have the views taken of the possible bases for various cognitive aspects, and of the kinds of theory that might offer a useful conceptual backing. Each of these changes has brought with it research of a particular kind.

Change in the sources of interest in parents' ideas.   To the interest in correcting or ex-panding behavioral accounts there has been added an interest in questions of adult development, with ideas about parenting regarded as an area in which one might observe, among adults, changes in the content of thought or in expertise (e.g., Goodnow, 1985; Holden, 1988). That source of interest has sparked, for instance, attention to the specific ways in which experience with children alters the kinds of explanations that adults consider when an infant cries, together with the kinds and the number of questions they ask in order to decide on the cause (Holden & Klingner, in press).

Interest in parents' ideas about children and parenting has also arisen as part of a search for effective ways to describe the social or cultural context of children's development. "Social context," everyone agrees, is an important factor in development. Describing context, however, is not an easy next step. Descriptions in terms of the views of people responsible for children offer an attractive way forward, one that may offer as well a way of describing cultural differences in context. That proposal is illustrated by Super and Harkness' (1986) concept of a "developmental niche," with niche referring to the settings in which children are likely to be found, the activities in which they engage, and the "psychology of the caregivers." It is from this direction of interest that there emerge studies comparing the expectations of parents in one cultural group with those in another (e.g., Goodnow, Cashmore, Cotton, & Knight, 1984; Hess, Kashigawi, Azuma, Price, & Dickson, 1980; Ninio, 1978; Pomerleau et al., 1991): studies now sizeable enough to warrant a volume entitled *Parents' Cultural Belief Systems* (Harkness & Super, in press).

Change in ideas about the possible sources of parents' views.   For psychologists, the source of ideas that comes most readily to mind consists of a parent's direct experience with children and the information it provides. That line of thought leads quickly to questions about the accuracy of parents' perceptions (e.g., Miller, in press) and to the comparison of parents with nonparents, mothers with fathers, or parents of one child with parents of more than one, on the assumption that different degrees of exposure to children would or should bring changes in the views held (Goodnow, 1985, provided a summary of these studies).

Complicating the assumption that experience and exposure matter, however, was the recognition that differential exposure often involved as well differential responsibility. The need to hold a particular view—as a parent or as a caregiver in a day-care center—could be as important as the degree of exposure or experience (Hess, Price, Dickson, & Conroy, 1984). "Maternal thinking," to use a phrase from Ruddick (1982) that was intended to cover both parents, might stem less from experience of the child than from an increased awareness of the tension between the responsibility involved and the vulnerability of a child, between the wish to keep one's children safe—all their lives—and the recognition of an unsafe world. More empirically, a difference in responsibility could account for why the staff at day-care centers differ from parents in their ideas about the age at which children should acquire certain skills (Hess et al., 1984), and for why the explanations for a child's poor performance in school are likely to be different among teachers from what they are among parents (Mugny & Carugati, 1985).

Enriching the picture of sources still further was the proposal that the views parents held about children and parenting might be more "cultural constructions" than they are the result of direct personal experience with children (Goodnow & Collins, 1990, have provided an overview). From this perspective, parents encounter—both before and after they become parents—the prevailing views of their social group. Parents' ideas may then reflect more a process of taking these prevailing ideas over in ready made fashion ("appropriating" them) than they reflect a process of constructing one's own ideas on the basis of direct observation (Goodnow, 1985; Mugny & Carugati, 1985).

This type of possibility gives a new twist to what may be thought of as covered by a term such as *information.* If one follows this view, what I encounter as a parent is not so much the raw material of children's actions or of my own successes and failures but a set of ideas that are presented to me as describing the way children "are," what I should expect of myself as a mother or father, and how I should define success or failure. These ideas may be expressed to me by way of the language of my group (by the terms, e.g., that divide *babies* from *toddlers* and *preschoolers,* or *children* from *adolescents),* by way of the advice that others give me, by way of everyday arrangements (e.g., the presence or the lack of provisions for fathers to be present at the birth of a child), or—as Chombart de Lauwe (1984) in particular pointed out—by way of a society's stories for and about children.

This type of possibility also directs attention to research on the nature of parents' encounters with the prevailing views of a social group. How do these come to be known or to be accepted as one's own? It directs attention as well to the degree to which there is consensus or variability among parents (e.g., Reid & Valsiner, 1986) and to the conditions that give rise to one "cultural construction" rather than another: the economic conditions, for instance, that promote an acceptance of mothers in paid work or an insistence that the child needs her full-time care at home (e.g., Gergen, Gloger-Tippelt, & Berkowitz, 1990), or the physical conditions that promote varying degrees of priority to a child's physical survival or emotional well-being (e.g., LeVine, 1988).

Change in the concern with placing research on parents' ideas.   One last comment on history completes this brief summary. It has to do with an increasing concern with the conceptual grounding of research and theory related to parents' views and with the implications of any particular grounding. The present chapter, for instance, and the one by Holden, both argue for turning first to the methods and models psychologists use for the general analysis of ideas, schemas, or attitudes. That is an extremely reasonable turn to take: one that can well benefit from being explored systematically (Goodnow, 1988).

The use of frameworks from psychologists' studies of social cognition, however, calls for two provisos. One of these is the need to recognize that this field has itself a changing history. The other is the need to recognize that these frameworks may need supplementing.

The changing history can be briefly described. Within the field known as "adult social cognition" or "experimental social cognition," one of the early moves was an exploration of the extent to which people could be described as "everyday scientists": alert to evidence, changing as counterevidence emerged, always ready to entertain an alternative view, constructing their viewpoints largely on the basis of their own direct experience rather than taking over others' ideas without reflection (an idealized picture of the way science proceeds but nonetheless one model of how thinking might proceed). There soon developed the recognition that people often use short-cuts or "heuristics" in their thinking, that mood and emotion can have major effects on the way people process information, that evidence is often ignored, and that the appropriate description might be less in terms of "everyday scientist" than in terms of "motivated cognition" (Showers & Cantor, 1985) or of attachment to "old-shoe" beliefs (Abelson, 1986). With ample evidence now at hand of the ways in which people ignore, discount, or resist information that runs counter to their established ideas, the more positive question has begun to acquire prominence: Under what conditions *are* people open to new information or flexible in their ideas? The concern is again with a variety of conditions, covering the degree of affect, the nature of the goal (e.g., accuracy as against comfort or a need for closure), and shifts in the popularity and status of particular ideas. The aim, however, is to acccount for flexibility in ideas rather than inertia or resistance.

At the same time, there has emerged among some psychologists the sense that the frameworks usually supplied by psychologists may not be sufficient (e.g., Glick, 1985; Goodnow, 1990; Mugny & Carugati, 1985; Sameroff & Feil, 1985). If we are to understand parents' knowledge and expectations, for instance, it will not be enough to consider only how people process information. At the least, one needs also to ask about the availability of the information and about its quality (Goodnow, 1990). Do "experts" in fact have the information you need? How easy is it to get hold of the information needed, without being made to feel incompetent or pushy? And once people (e.g., teachers or physicians) agree to share information with you, how useable or understandable is the information they provide? For questions such as these, psychology itself may not be the best source. The researcher interested in parents' ideas may instead discover a stronger conceptual base in discussions by anthropologists and sociologists of the acquisition of knowledge, especially those concerned with issues of access and control (e.g., Bourdieu, 1979; Foucault, 1980).

Does this increasing enrichment or complexity mean that the field now displays no particular coherence or direction? My argument would be that this is not the case. We have certainly come to be careful about simple assumptions. We would no longer expect, for instance, that providing parents with new information will readily lead to the establishment and acceptance of new ideas. It also means that, as researchers, we are less likely to proceed blithely to comparisons of parents with nonparents, and mothers with fathers, on the assumption that these groups differ mainly in the extent of their exposure to children and the information this provides. We are certainly now far more aware than earlier that parents' expectations stem from a mixture of experience, advice, cultural norms, mood, and parents' own needs: what they need to think, for instance, in order to stay on the job of parenting, to avoid more regret than is comfortable, or to feel at one with other members of their social group.

More specifically, my argument is that the greater richness now produces a more interesting story when one asks—as I proceed to do in this chapter—the following questions:

(1) What do we know about the seeking of information? When do parents seek it? What kind of information do they seek or prefer? Whom do they turn to?

(2) What kind of information do they encounter? Is it freely available? Is it useful or does it come in pat phrases such as "don't worry, it's just a stage?"

(3) How do parents respond when information becomes available? In particular, what do they do when faced with information that runs counter to their own ideas? Do they revise their ideas? Temporarily or for good? Create an exception? Ignore the new evidence? Develop a reason for why it should be regarded as less than reliable? When are these several alternatives likely to occur?

These three sets of questions provide the bases for the next three sections of the chapter. The final section, as I noted earlier, takes up the issue: Is information all that matters? Here I consider briefly four topics that are particularly relevant to our understanding of the way information is related to parents' actions and feelings, and to the ideas that children in their turn acquire. The first of these four topics concerns the assumption that more information is always better than less (a frequent assumption in parent education programs). That assumption may not be warranted. Information can itself be a source of stress and unhappiness. The second has to do with the issue of cross-generation agreement: a topic that involves questions about the information parents provide, the accuracy with which it is perceived, and the warmth of the relationship. The third involves the need to consider any information provided in the light of a particular quality of ideas. This is the extent to which ideas are differentially accessible, differentially likely to rise quickly to the surface: a difference related to the extent to which information is processed in automatic or more conscious fashion. The fourth involves the proposal that we study the impact of "practices" or everyday routines upon the ideas that parents hold. Parents' actions may well stem from or reflect parents' ideas. It is also likely, although less often considered, that actions shape ideas. Routine actions express in concrete fashion and maintain the ideas parents are expected to acquire and to keep. (The differential involvement of most mothers and fathers in the daily care of children, for example, signals what is usually expected of parents; the age at which children enter primary school signals what is usually expected of children by this age). Each of these four topics tells a story of links among ideas, actions, and emotions that is again more complex than expected but again also more interesting.

SEEKING INFORMATION

We know that parents often seek information. Mothers feel their stomachs to see if the baby has begun to "move." Parents read school reports; they ask their children where they have been; they ask friends, relatives, friendly pharmacists, nurses, or physicians for comments on a rash, a temperature, or a child's change of mood. They may go to classes for parents; they may also buy books and may read them (or parts of them).

At the same time, we know that parents do not always seek information, even when it is easily available or offered. Parents facing the birth of a first child, for instance, do not always want to know the sex of the child, even when prenatal testing may make that information available (Rothman, 1986). And many a parent will avoid conferences with teachers or, after the first child, frequent visits to a clinic for checks on a baby's weight and state.

The interesting questions have come to be: (1) What kind of information do parents seek? (2) Who is most likely to seek information? (3) When is information sought? (4) What determines the nature of the search? What determines, for instance, the extent to which the search for information is public or private? For each of these questions, I draw material both from studies of parenting and from general studies of social cognition.

What kind of information is sought?   From studies of parenting, I take as an example a study of pregnant women. To determine the state of the baby, women may turn toward the information given by what they can feel or from what they can see in externalized form. In West Germany, for instance, ultrasounds are a routine part of prenatal care, making it possible for Gloger-Tippelt (1991) to ask mothers whether they prefer the knowledge gained from "tactile" or "visual" sources. The preference for ultrasound information, she found, was correlated with anxiety and was the strongest predictor of the mother's observed responsiveness to the child at 4–6 months after birth. (The preference for ultrasound information was associated with lesser responsiveness.) The sample is small in this study, but it is a nice example of what it may mean to seek and to rely upon one kind of information rather than another.

From studies of adult social cognition, a useful general proposal takes the form: Attention to the qualities of another person will be greatest when the outcome of one's project—the reaching of one's goals—depends on the contributions or the nature of the other (e.g., Erber & Fiske, 1984). That kind of hypothesis suggests one reason for variations in a parent's alertness to the qualities of a partner or of a child. The more I need to know what they are like in order to reach my goals, the more alert I will be to what they are like. The proposal is as well a useful background against which to set Dix's (1991, 1992) proposal that parental goals organize the attention parents give to various facets of a child's behavior, and his distinction between parents who take the child's happiness as their primary goal and parents who give priority to their own state of mind.

Who is most likely to seek information?   It is possible to describe the determinants of search in terms of some general qualities of parents. A parent's years of schooling, for instance, makes a difference to the extent to which they seek information about how well a child is doing in school or why a child is repeating first grade (Alexander & Entwisle, 1988). Why education should have an effect, however, is still an open question. One intriguing possibility is that education influences the extent to which parents see the school bureaucracy as "a monolithic structure," alien to them, rather than as made up of individuals who vary in their approachability (Alexander & Entwisle, 1988, p. 155). These perceptions, rather than years of education per se, then change the likelihood of a parent's asking questions.

From the general literature on social cognition, there is evidence also that the extent to which adults seek information varies with the extent to which, in various situations, they seek accuracy (e.g., Neuberg & Fiske, 1987), as against structure (e.g., Jamieson & Zanna, 1989) or closure (e.g., Kruglanski, Peri, & Zakai, 1991). These differences in goal are of particular relevance to the study of parental ideas. It is easy to take a view of parents as always interested in holding accurate ideas. That is by no means always the case. In fact, one of the challenging pieces of data in research on parents' ideas has to do with the ease and the speed with which parents make judgments, with very little information, about a baby's temperament. Mothers make these judgments while the baby is in utero (Broussard & Hartner, 1971; Gloger-Tippelt, 1991; Zeaman & Anders, 1987) or shortly after birth (Fischer & Fischer, 1963; Meares, Penman, Milgrim-Friedman, & Baker, 1982).

One possible basis for these speedy judgments, it has been suggested, is that Western parents need to "divine the child's potential" in order to provide the right environment (Fischer & Fischer, 1963). But nurses, who have no such responsibility, also make quick judgments about the personality and the ability of newborns (Bennett, 1971). For both sets of adults, the wide range of possibilities opened up by the prospect of individual differences may need to be quickly narrowed down to a smaller set of alternatives, to a manageable number of "types" or possible story lines. The effect may perhaps not appear in cultures with less emphasis upon individualism. In these, Fischer and Fischer suggested, "babies" and "children" are defined more in terms of their roles than in terms of their qualities as individuals. They are accordingly more likely to be seen as generally similar to one another rather than as potentially offering an unlimited array of possibilities. Whatever the basis, it is abundantly clear that accurate ideas are not always a parent's primary concern, especially if the price of accuracy is delay in forming opinions.

When is information most likely to be sought?   This question has a strong base in both parental material and in the general study of social cognition. Parents seek information when they are close to taking actions for which the information will be relevant. Parents-to-be, for instance, seek information about pregnancy when they are in the early stages of pregnancy, about birth in the later stages, and about life with a baby as they get close to that point (Deutsch, Ruble, Fleming, Brooks-Gunn, & Stangor, 1988; Gloger-Tippelt, 1991; Maccoby, Romney, Adams, & Maccoby, 1959). Pregnant mothers also seek information first about the baby's physical shape (is everything there?) and later—still while the baby is in utero—about potential temperament (is it likely to be placid or active? an easy sleeper or restless?) (Gloger-Tippelt, 1991).

Ruble (in press) combined data of this kind with data from general cognition to argue for an account of information seeking that is closely tied to the phase of any transition. In essence, her argument is that any transition involves three phases in the life of a schema: construction, consolidation, and integration. The first phase, construction, occurs at the point where the individual is about to enter, or has just entered, a new state: one in which the old categories and expectations may not apply. At this point, the individual is maximally open to new information and seeks it. The consolidation phase brings a drop in the breadth of interest in new information. The information sought is now more focused, designed to fill gaps in a picture that has already acquired some shape. At this point also, the established picture is expected to exert a strong effect upon the way new information is perceived or remembered. The search for information moves toward a state that has been called "schema-driven" (Fiske & Taylor, 1991), and inconsistent information may well be ignored or forgotten. In the third stage that Ruble proposed (integration), the ideas established in phase two are seen as becoming elaborated and linked both to other ideas and to concepts of identity. The ideas come to display an "application to self-regulatory … behaviors" (Ruble, in press), specifying goals and actions (this is what *I* should do). It is at this point that new information may be most actively avoided or resisted in order to maintain a course of action or a particular sense of identity.

Ruble's (in press) proposals are based on several kinds of data: data related to mothers' transitions during pregnancy, children's transitions through school grades, and experimental studies that build a schema from new material. For parenting, the implication is that each new transition, from birth to life with teenagers to an "empty nest," involves a return to a construction phase. The model is as yet provisional. As Ruble noted, we know least at this point about the initial construction phase and about the shift from open to more focused information seeking. Nonetheless, the proposal clearly offers a conceptual base that can link the nature of parents' searches for information to a more general theory about the development of schemas.

There is, however, one aspect of parenting that may not be completely easy to fit into Ruble's (in press) useful picture. This aspect has to do with what Rothman (1986) termed "the tentative pregnancy." In contemporary times, pregnant women may choose to have an ultrasound and/or an amniocentesis or chorionic villi sampling. Under these conditions, Rothman reported, women may delay making a commitment to the pregnancy until a decision has been made about these procedures or, if the decision is made to seek this kind of evidence, until the results are clear. Many of the women in Rothman's sample, for instance, reported no experienced movement of the fetus until after the amniocentesis results were available and clear (some weeks after the norm for such experience). Such results suggest that the quality of commitment to a particular view of oneself or of one's child may be a thread that runs through all phases of a transition, affecting all aspects of a search for information and its use.

How does a search proceed?   Sameroff and Feil (1985) suggested that parents are unlikely to spend much time looking for explanations of a child's behavior or health as long as things are going well, unless they happen to be parents who believe that things could always be better, that "a still better way" of facilitating development or achievement might be found. For a parent without such beliefs, a satisfactory state of affairs confirms whatever hypothesis the parent holds about the child's development: hypotheses that may range from the importance of "good genes" to the power of chicken soup. The sense of a satisfactory state of affairs also contributes to a mood state (no dissonance, low to moderate affect) that in experimental studies is associated with no active search for alternative explanations (Zanna & Cooper, 1978)and a fairly ready acceptance of the information that comes one's way, with few checks on the validity of that information (Isen, Means, Patrick, & Nowicki, 1982).

Such effects from mood are clearly relevant to parenting. Relevant also—but far less often considered in experimental studies—are factors related to the extent to which a search for information may be public or private. In everyday life, for instance, it is widely acceptable to ask, "how old is your baby?" The answer is recognized as often allowing a rapid comparison with one's own child or grandchild, but it is seldom objected to. In contrast, questions about how well someone else's child is doing at school are, at least in Western culture, not readily made or accepted. Even children, in the early grades of school, learn to be indirect in their search for information about how well other children are doing (Frey & Ruble, 1985).

I emphasize the social aspects of search because it is easy to forget that parenting is often a public performance: visible to others and open to judgments by others. Decisions about what to ask and whom to ask are not solely a reflection of an individual parent's need for closure or accuracy. In everyday life, these decisions reflect as well the acceptability to oneself and others of appearing ignorant. In laboratory-based studies, the public nature of ignorance may not be a significant factor. It is, however, an essential factor to include in any account of the way parents seek information and must be part of what determines the advice parents seek from friends, nurses, physicians, or teachers.

There seems, unfortunately, to be relatively little data on this score. Barsch (1968), however, noted that particular difficulties occur for the parent of a child with a handicap. This parent has to walk a fine line: "If he questions too much, he has a 'reaction formation' and may be oversolicitous. If he questions too little, he is branded as disinterested and insensitive" (p. 8). The sharpest example that I know comes from an English study of working-class parents whose children were in grammar schools that allowed progression to university (Jackson & Marsden, 1966). These parents often avoided asking teachers about the prerequisites for entry to various universities (often with sad consequences) because they did not wish to appear ignorant in the eyes of the teachers. The teachers, for their part, assumed that any parent would know or would ask. The parents turned instead to friendship or occupational networks, where asking carried little social cost but was not always productive.

In summary, several questions arise when one starts to consider the approaches that people make to gaining information about children and parenting: questions that have to do with the kind of information sought, who is most likely to start asking questions, when this is most likely to occur, and how a search proceeds. Our knowledge in relation to these issues is far from complete. What we do know, however, eliminates any easy assumption that parents will always be seeking the information that experts on parenting may hold. Eliminated also is any assumption by researchers or parent educators that the issues are purely cognitive. Mood, for instance, makes a difference. So also does the significance to oneself and to others of needing to ask.

Seeking information, however, is only part of a parent's becoming well informed. A critical part is the focus of the next section: What kind of information or knowledge is available?

WHAT KIND OF INFORMATION IS AVAILABLE?

Up to now, the focus has been on parents—on their interests, moods, or confidence, on the state of development of their ideas. We cannot stop, however, with a parent asking questions, seeking information. We need also to ask about the nature of the information available or likely to be encountered. Even the most highly motivated of parents, for instance, will have difficulty making sense of reports, from a teacher or a physician, to the effect that a child is "making satisfactory progress" or is "doing as well as could be expected."

The state of the information available is the topic for this section. The first part describes a number of ways in which the information available may depart from a perfect state. The second outlines some views on the acquisition of knowledge that start with the assumption of an imperfect world. These views come predominantly from sociology and anthropology rather than cognitive psychology, a discipline inclined to describe the individual as operating in a "free market" where the only barriers to knowledge lie in the capacity, energy, and interests of the individual.

Limits to a Perfect World

In everyday life, the situations that parents encounter often depart from the ideal state that may apply in laboratory studies. Instead, parents are likely to encounter situations where:

Little information is available.   Parents of children who do not fit the conventional norm seem especially likely to encounter this difficulty. Compared with parents whose children fit the norm, they face a shortage of readily available material on the progressions or difficulties to expect. Even without a departure from the norm, however, the supply of information may be better in some areas than in others. An example is provided by Rubin, Mills, and Krasnor (1992). Mothers of 4-year-olds were given two stories describing acts of aggression and two describing acts of shyness, and were asked how they would feel and what they would do if their child acted in this way. Nine possible emotions were offered for rating. Acts of aggression elicited mainly ratings of concern, anger, and disappointment. Acts of withdrawal elicited mainly ratings of concern, puzzlement, and surprise. For acts of withdrawal, mothers also reported themselves as more likely to use lower power strategies and more likely to seek information than they would for acts of aggression. Aggression, Rubin et al. proposed, is a topic often commented on in the media, with the result that parents feel no great need for new information. Withdrawal, in contrast, has been slow to emerge in the public forum as an acknowledged problem (one that may be expected to occur among children), with the result that parents experience its occurrence as more puzzling.

The available information is poorly explained.   Parents, Sameroff and Feil (1985) commented, do not always encounter information expressed in useable form. It is difficult, for instance, to make effective use of advice in the form of "it's just a stage," "it's nothing to worry about," or "they all grow out of it, sooner or later." In similar fashion, it takes some skill (and some experience with a school system) to decode report cards that say a child "could do better" or "is very sociable in class" (Evans, Barber, Gadsden, Paris, & Park, 1989).

The information comes with overtones that undermine confidence.   Schlossman (1976, 1978) argued that, historically, the parent education movement has been based on the assumption that low-income parents are incompetent. Clarke-Stewart (1978) extended this type of comment to all parents. Within North American "primers for parents," she noted, the dominant image of all parents, regardless of class, is of people who lack competence and are in need of expert guidance.

Negative overtones may come also from the very phrases used to describe adults and children. "The day-care child" and "the working mother," for instance, suggest an aberrant state by the very way they add a qualifier to norms that are generally used without one. That type of effect may seem subtle. Consider, however, the use of terms such as "a young grandmother," "a lady jockey," or "a male nurse." In each such case, we signal by the qualifier that we are referring to an unusual state of affairs. The lack of a qualifier signals the norm. So also, Thorne (1987) pointed out, does the everyday joining of terms. "Women and children," for instance, suggests a normative unit. These are people, it is implied, who belong together and may perhaps be thought of as like one another. Women without children or men with children then come to be perceived as possibly "strange" and certainly "different."

The information exists but is restricted.   I began with the possibility that there is little information available. It might simply not exist, or be hard to find. Information may also be in short supply, however, because the people with the information restrict parents' access to it. This might be on the grounds of their inability to understand, or their lack of a "right to know." This kind of phenomenon is relatively familiar to scholars interested in the sociology of knowledge. Bok's (1982) analysis of secrecy provides a range of examples, often based on the way restricted access maintains the status of experts.

There is no reason to expect that parents in their search for information will be exempt from encounters with closed doors or experts who use distance as a way of maintaining their status. Few studies, however, appear to detail parents' encounters with restricted information. The closest example—and an especially interesting one—seems to be Joffe's (1977) analysis of a preschool center where the staff struggled to maintain their "trained" status in the face of two undercutting factors. One was the structure of this particular center. It was established as "parent-run" (parents hired "trained" teachers to be "in charge of the center" but the initiators and the advisory board were parents). The result was that parents felt they had implicit constitutional rights to come into the center at times of their choice and to express opinions about the way things were being done. The second factor would apply to any preschool setting. People are in general reluctant to grant the status of experts to those who look after small children. Such staff are still viewed largely as "carers," essentially doing what "every good mother" would do. Parents then are not simply passive in the hands of "experts." On the contrary, they play an active part both in granting the status of expert to others and in resisting some claims to expertise. The field is very much in need of analyses that would bring out more fully the nature of this two-way process.

The information is not consistent.   A provocative example comes from Frankel and Roer-Bornstein (1982). For events such as miscarriage or difficulties in a child's development, young Yemenite mothers in Israel encounter two incompatible types of information. Their own mothers are likely to offer "animist" explanations (spirits, the ill-will of others). The Israeli health services offer explanations with a physical base. The result, Frankel and Roer-Bornstein reported, is that these young mothers end with no coherent ways of accounting for states of health or illness. Their ideas, to use a term from Palacios and his colleagues, are "paradoxical" (Palacios, 1990; Palacios, Gonzalez, & Moreno, 1992), with some expressing one perspective on parenting and others expressing a quite different perspective. A paradoxical state of affairs, Palacios proposed, is especially likely to occur when people are in transitional states: when they move, for example, from a village with its coherent traditionalism to a town and to school systems that, for those who are fully immersed in them, also offer a coherent set of ideas, a set united by a "modern" or "progressive" perspective.

The concept of paradox is provocative, not only for the way it may fit states of migration or mobility but also for the way it raises the question: How coherent, how single-minded, is any social setting? Is it not possible that a certain degree of paradox or contradiction is part of every social setting? If so, what are the processes by which parents emerge with a coherent picture or with a degree of looseness and inconsistency in their ideas that strikes both parents and observers as "normal?" How are we to begin thinking about such questions? To do so, we need a conceptual base. Let us consider then some possible conceptual pictures.

Some Possible Conceptual Pictures

From material related to parenting, I have drawn attention to several examples of information that is less than free or perfect. Are there some general theoretical pictures to which such observations may be related? As Glick (1985) and Goodnow (1990) pointed out, cognitive psychology is not the best source for this issue. Both developmental and general studies tend to start from the assumption that information is available and sufficient. The restrictions upon understanding or knowledge then come from the state of the individual.

One source of alternative viewpoints may be found in the work of psychologists who emphasize that our views of children and of parenting are social or cultural "constructions" (e.g., Kessen, 1979). They vary from one cultural group to another and from one historical period to another, with the changes often reflecting social or economic conditions rather than any change in what children or parents are "really" like. The image of a vulnerable child in need of close monitoring by an ever-present parent, for instance, is especially prominent in times of little need for women in the paid work force (Gloger-Tippelt & Tippelt, 1986; Kessen, 1979). Rosenkrantz (1978) provided a particularly telling example. She documented historically the way in which changes in English child labor laws (along with the argument that child labor was not "good for children") followed, in various parts of the country, declines in the need for child labor. This does not mean that no one argued against child labor at earlier times. These voices, however, were not widely heard, and their views did not become a majority view or embodied in law until economic conditions made their message more attractive. At the least, arguments and evidence of this kind make one aware that the information we encounter about parenting and child development is often not neutral. Some particular viewpoints are promoted or endorsed rather than others.

Sociology and anthropology provide a second source of alternative assumptions about the state of information parents encounter. Particularly relevant are the writings of Bourdieu and Foucault. In these, there is an explicit recognition that knowledge is a commodity, often claimed as a monopoly by some, dispensed only to a chosen few, or delivered with so little detail about how to proceed that the expert retains the appearance of "wizardry" (e.g., Bourdieu, 1979). There is as well the explicit recognition that part of what needs to be learned in the course of becoming knowledgeable are the forms of discourse regarded as appropriate for asking a question or stating a problem: forms of discourse that in themselves reflect relationships of power (e.g., Foucault, 1980). For psychologists, these materials are not always easy reading. (For a partial introduction without explicit reference to the state of parents, see Goodnow, 1990.) The assumptions of restriction, imperfection, and bias in information, however, are an essential correction to the view that information is available and is neutral in its quality, with the traits, the capacities, and the state of the individual's schemas then accounting for all the variance in the ideas that people come to hold.

Sociology and anthropology are a source also for an alternative to what cognitive psychologists often label as "inconsistent" information and leave unexamined (or regard as simply a source of "noise": a nuisance in the study of how people come to understand the way the world works). In essence, the alternative says that the presence of more than one way of looking at the world is a normal state of affairs in any culture. Rather than regard this pluralism or heterogeneity as a nuisance, one should proceed to ask: How are these several views related to one another? And how do people respond to the presence of alternatives?

Let me make these rather abstract notions more concrete and more relevant to parenting. I have already mentioned the Yemenite mothers observed by Frankel and Roer-Bornstein (1982). They encounter both the views of their own mothers, emphasizing spirits and the evil eye as explanations for children's ill-health, and the views of the Israeli health system: a system emphasizing physical causes. These two views coexist. One, however, is regarded as the more official, the more "correct";

it is also the more widely held. Moreover, the holders of the official view are likely to look with some scorn upon what they regard as a "primitive" view of children's health. The Yemenite mothers are then faced with several alternatives. They can choose one view or the other. If they choose the unofficial view, they may need to disguise their beliefs: to take their views underground. They may aim instead at creating some kind of blend between the two sets of ideas. Or they may come to hold both, going back and forth between one and the other as circumstances change.

Foucault (1980) is a prominent example of a sociologist who argues that pluralism or heterogeneity is the normal state of affairs. Contemporary Western society, he has pointed out, contains both "formal" and "alternative" proposals for education and for health care. The popularity of each varies from one time to another. Alternative medicine and alternative education, for instance, flourish when people are dissatisfied with standard approaches to the treatment of their bodies or their children.

How does this way of thinking affect our understanding of parent's ideas? First of all, it helps us gain a better understanding of the position of parents. They face a world that contains more than one viewpoint and that greets the parent's own viewpoint with varying degrees of respect or scorn.

In addition, an emphasis upon heterogeneity as a normal state of affairs helps us gain a different perspective upon the issue of what is often called the "consistency" or the "ambivalence" of parents' ideas (Holden, in this *Handbook*). Take, for instance, parents who hold ideas that to an outsider are contradictory. They describe themselves, for instance, as agreeing both with the statement "children's household jobs and money should be kept quite separate from one another," and with the statement, "if they're getting money, they should be doing something in return" (Goodnow & Warton, 1992). Both views—family jobs should be labors of love, and "nothing for nothing"—exist in contemporary Western culture. Western parents (Australian parents at least) hold both. The majority see no contradiction. (A purist 10 percent or so insist that there are no circumstances under which money can be connected to children's household jobs.) The majority might be regarded as easing the contradiction by developing two categories of household jobs. One set is labeled *regular* jobs. These should not be done for money. The other set is labeled *extra* jobs. These may sometimes be paid for. The division allows these parents to act out both a "no money" and a "money" principle. They do so, however, with no sense of the contradiction that the more single-minded are determined to avoid.

An emphasis upon heterogeneity in viewpoints also helps us take a second look at changes in parents' ideas: rapid changes especially. Any parent is familiar with the way one's perception of parenting and of a child may shift almost from moment to moment. There are times when parenting is felt to be an undiluted joy, and times when it seems a heavy burden. There are times when we see children as vulnerable, and times when we see them as resilient. There are times when we feel willing to "do everything" for our children, and times when we feel that they might do more for themselves. These rapid shifts, it has been proposed, are made possible by our already holding both viewpoints. We have not held only one and then suddenly constructed the other. The interesting question then becomes, as Quinn and Holland (1987) have pointed out for alternative views in general: When do we *not* shift easily from one viewpoint to another? To take one of their examples, we may vary from time to time in our assessment of marriage as a rewarding or a constraining arrangement. We vary less, however, in our view that marriage is an arrangement that takes work and is not easy to walk away from. The same point may readily be applied to parents' views of parenting.

Two last points on these alternate perspectives: perspectives that emphasize the way parents may encounter information that is far from neutral ("this is what you should believe"), far from generously available ("let me make those decisions for you"), and far from containing a single position that leads only to questions about various degrees of acceptance or "internalization."

First, I have presented these alternative perspectives as coming predominantly from sociology and anthropology. In these fields, they are a strong voice. The same perspectives, however, are to be found in psychology, mainly under the label of ideas as "social representations" (e.g., Moscovici, 1984; Mugny & Carugati, 1985). Mugny and Carugati, in fact, provided a strong demonstration of the way most parents hold a view of intelligence as both inherited and as open to influence, as referring both to abstract or academic skills and to social adaptability. The same study also illustrates the way parents change in the degree to which they endorse one viewpoint or another as they become swept up in the school system or as they find themselves in a position of double responsibility (some are both mothers and school teachers). In effect, although most of the conceptual work is not expressed in terms of parents' ideas, the application to parents' ideas has begun and looks extremely promising.

Second, that promise by no means implies that we should now ignore the characteristics of parents. The two sets of characteristics—those of the informational world "out there" and those of the parent—need to be brought together. We do not yet have much in the way of research that does so, but it should be possible to develop, in time, a transactional view similar to that proposed for the way that the characteristics of the parent and the characteristics of the child influence one another (e.g., Bornstein, Tal, & Tamis-LeMonda, 1991; Bugental, 1992; Sameroff, 1983). In a domain where information is easily available and easily understood, for instance, we should not expect to find much difference between the views held by parents with varying degrees of education or assertiveness. All may believe, for example, that children benefit from immunization shots. They will then vary only in their knowledge as to where such shots are available and in their ability to cover the cost. It is when information is not readily available or easily understood that we should expect individual differences to appear. It is then that the kind of picture that Alexander and Entwisle (1988) described should be the one that emerges. The parent who gets to know what is happening to a child in the school system is the one whose own experience of schooling has led to confidence about asking, plus a knowledge of who to ask and how to interpret what is said.

THE USE OF NEW OR DISCONFIRMING INFORMATION

Parenting is one encounter after another with demands to revise or update one's ideas. Children change, in themselves and in the groups to which they belong. Many a parent, for instance, may be unaware that a child sings flat or has "two left feet" until kindergarten forces a new set of social comparisons (Entwisle & Hayduk, 1978). Parents also change, both in their level of energy and in their estimates of how well they are managing the job of being a parent (e.g., confidence postpartum, is not correlated with confidence in oneself at the toddler phase: Williams et al., in press.) And the times change, often bringing a shift in the standards of parenting. No longer is it enough, for instance, for a father to be "a good provider," for a mother to be "a kind soul," or for either to be a "good enough" parent. In contemporary times, mothers seem to be more and more regarded as the source of all problems (more often than they are the gainers of credit when their children do well); the demands for all-round perfection on their part seem always to be escalating.

What do we know about the way parents revise or update their ideas? And what concepts can we bring to bear upon this issue? To answer these questions, I begin by noting briefly some proposals from general experimental studies of cognitive change. The material that follows asks how these proposals fit with what is known about change in parents' ideas.

General Proposals About Revision and Disconfirming Information

At the heart of many experimental studies of social cognition and of persuasion lies an interest in the extent to which new information fits with what a person already knows. What happens, psychologists often ask, when what one hears or reads "disconfirms" or is "incongruent" with the ideas that a person already holds? The ideal person—the ideal machine perhaps—might easily and rationally update the old idea. In fact, however, we often hold on to the old idea as long as possible, dragging our feet and creating "exceptions" to explain away the new data. In Abelson's (1986) vivid phrase, we act as if our ideas are possessions we have come to live comfortably with and are loathe to give away. As such human ways of thinking have come to be recognized, the questions that have come to attract particular attention take the form: Under what circumstances are the old ideas revised? What are the steps to revision or the means by which revision is delayed or resisted?

As a start, one may note that the discussions, as Showers and Cantor (1985) have pointed out, take two directions. One direction concentrates on the difficulties involved in attempts at persuasion or in therapies aimed at changing people's ideas of themselves or others. The overall theme is one of resistance to change. The other direction is more positive. It emphasizes the presence of flexible revision when the goals are important, the mood is positive, and the individual has some level of expertise to use as a base.

Research on disconfirming information has also brought out several suggestions dealing with how revision may proceed (the steps along the way) and what the factors are that contribute to easy change or to resistance. Weber and Crocker (1983), for instance, outlined three possible routes to revision. In one of these (a "bookkeeping model"), each new piece of evidence brings a corresponding change in the original idea. In the second (a "subtyping" model), new categories (e.g., a category of "exceptions") are created to take care of the new material but leave the original notions intact. In the third ("conversion" model), the original idea undergoes a radical change, usually in response to dramatic new evidence.

The factors currently proposed as important for the occurrence and the nature of revision are even more varied. Broadly speaking, these factors cover the quality of the new information (e.g., the dramatic properties that make it difficult to ignore), the characteristics of the person (e.g., the extent to which they monitor themselves for consistency), the social circumstances (e.g., the extent to which one's opinions are open to scrutiny by others), and the source of the disconfirming information (e.g., the extent to which it comes from a person whom one admires or identifies with).

That list contains a mixture of "cognitive" factors (e.g., the individual's sense of ambiguity or uncertainty) with more "social" factors (e.g., the extent to which one's ideas are open to inspection by others or are part of one's identity). The cognitive factors have claimed the larger share of research attention. The social factors, however, may in the long run be the more relevant to analyses of parenting. There is, for instance, an intuitive relevance to Turner's (1985) proposal that people hold on to ideas that are part of their membership in a social group. Revising these ideas could mean, for instance, that one can no longer regard oneself, or be regarded, as "a true Christian" or "a good parent." Attractive also is Abelson's (1986) discussion of ideas as like possessions. Like pieces of furniture or clothing, one acquires ideas that fit comfortably with one another and with one's sense of place or identity. Attempts by others to question or to impose new ideas may be reacted to "as though one's appearance, taste, or judgment had been called into question" (Abelson, 1986, p. 23). Discarding is uncomfortable, and new ideas—like new clothes or new furniture—may be resisted or quietly dropped when, for all their attractiveness in themselves, they do not "fit the style" of the ideas already present.

Do these several proposals from general analyses of disconfirming information fit with analyses of parents' ideas? They are relevant to material on (1) the rate of revision, (2) steps in revision, and (3) factors in revision.

The Rate of Revision

There is certainly evidence that parents' ideas may lag behind changes in their children. To take one example, the parents of children receiving clinical help for behavior problems may often report no change in a child's behavior even though clinical staff—and in some studies teachers—report a change (Griest & Wells, 1983). To take another, parents' views of what their children are like or what their children think may lag behind the changes that occur in children during adolescence (Collins, in press). Lag, however, is not the only possibility. Some parents, Collins pointed out, may leap ahead rather than lag behind, raising their expectations, for instance, at the first sign of a child's move into physical adolescence.

We need to ask not only whether parents vary in the likelihood of holding ideas that lag behind changes in their children but also in the changes they watch for. One approach to this question is nicely illustrated by research on children's changing performance in school. In the Baltimore studies conducted by Entwisle and her colleagues, African-American parents were less responsive than were Euro-American parents to the details of the child's school performance in the first grades of school (Alexander & Entwisle, 1988). On the one hand, this meant that their expectations remained high. On the other, these parents were especially disturbed by a child's having to repeat Grade 1. The

Euro-American parents often responded to a child's repeating by paying close attention to grades over the course of the repeated year, giving particular importance to marks in the fourth quarter. These are the marks most likely to predict placement in the next school year and to yield evidence of a child's catching up. For the African-American parents, in contrast, the occurrence of repeating a grade in itself "appears to take a heavy toll, while specific performance levels are discounted" (Alexander & Entwisle, 1988, p. 113). The effect, it is proposed, reflects the greater marginality of African Americans in relation to the school system, contributed to both by their own years of schooling and their current social position vis-à-vis the school.

A second example comes again from the area of school performance. More specifically, it comes from a comparison of mothers in Beijing and in Chicago. The study, by Chen and Uttal (1988), is one of a series directed toward understanding why children's achievement levels in mathematics vary so greatly between the United States and China or Japan (cf. Stevenson et al., 1985). The two sets of mothers in the Chen and Uttal study did not differ in the levels of performance that they expected for their first-, third-, and fifth-grade children. They did differ, however, in the extent to which they were satisfied with their child's performance (the Chinese mothers were less so) and, of particular interest, when they would become concerned if their child's performance was below the average for the class. Mothers of fifth-grade children in the two cultural groups were alike. Both would become concerned if their children fell slightly below the mean. Concern in first grade yielded a different picture. The mothers in Chicago described themselves as becoming concerned if a child's performance was well below average (1 standard deviation below). The mothers in Beijing allowed for less leeway. As in the higher grade, they would become concerned as soon as performance fell even slightly below the average. Success in school may be of greater importance to the Beijing than to the Chicago mothers, although both expressed equal ambition. There appears as well, however, to be a difference in the importance attached to an early sign of how one's child compares with others. U.S. mothers, one suspects, may be more tolerant of a slow start in first grade, and perhaps more accustomed to thinking in terms of "late bloomers."

The final example relates alertness to change to parents' values and tolerance for diversity or variation. These are the factors that Worthman (in press) argued for in her analyses of the closeness with which parents in various African groups monitor physical changes in a child. In some, the monitoring is close. Clitoridectomy and circumcision, for instance, are tightly linked to a girl's breast development (a good predictor for the onset of menarche) and a boy's first seminal emissions. In other African groups, the links to physical change are less tight. The variations, Worthman proposed, reflect the extent to which sexual maturity and early pregnancy are of importance, with either positive or negative value attached. More generally, she argued, variations in parental alertness and response to physical change of any kind will need to consider the nature of the change (e.g., its visibility, its timing), the interpretations attached, and the options open in terms of action.

Steps in Revision

Noted earlier was the observation, in general studies of social cognition, that revision may follow a bookkeeping, a subtyping, or a conversion model. Studies of parents' thinking have little to say on bookkeeping, with its incremental revisions of ideas keeping pace with each new piece of information.

Subtyping (the making of exceptions that allow one's current ideas to stand) is certainly displayed by parents. To take one example, parents may comment that a particular method of discipline (e.g., always giving reasons) "is a good idea, but it wouldn't work with my child" (Grusec & Goodnow, 1994). To take another, North American couples about to have their first child expect that they will share the extra work after the child is born. Reminded that this seems not to happen as a rule, their response is that their relationship will be "different" (Ruble, Fleming, Hackel, & Stangor, 1988).

Making an exception appears to be particularly important when a parent seeks to maintain a particular view of a child or of a relationship. What appears to be at work is not some simple "inertia" but the need to maintain a "factful deception" (Backett, 1982, p. 95), especially one that keeps at bay an unwelcome view of events. A child's antisocial actions, for instance, may for some time be regarded as something that the child will grow out of. The explanation starts to falter, and the parent to feel distressed, as the child grows older and the behavior can no longer be written off as just a stage (Dix, Ruble, Grusec, & Nixon, 1986). In similar fashion, a child's untidiness may be written off as "normal, messy behavior," a parent's as "not seeing what needs to be done." A variety of explanations will in fact be held for low participation in the work of the household—"doesn't see," "doesn't know how," "would be willing if I asked"—rather than considering the presence of unwillingness or evasion: alternatives that run counter to a view of "happy families" in which people care for one another (Backett, 1982; Goodnow, in press-a).

Ideally, one would hope for longitudinal evidence of the steps that occur during the course of revision in a parent's ideas. That kind of data does not seem available. There is, however, a detailed step-wise proposal for changes in the way parents view a severely handicapped child. In the first phase, Farber (1983) proposed, the parent seeks to minimize the child's difficulty, often by the use of labels. The child is, for instance, "a little clumsy" or "a little breathless" rather than having clear difficulty in actions or speech. In the second phase, the parent takes more note of the child's development in relation to others, but still attempts to place the child somewhere within the normal range. The problem is acknowledged but its severity still dampened. Only when this "fiction of normality" (p. 114) fails to work, Farber proposed, does the parent move to a radically revised view of the child's state and of the need for a change in family patterns or childcare. (The fiction of normality apparently extends to what the mother or the family can do—the usual pattern will simply be stretched rather than altered—as well as to perceptions of the child.) Until this radical change occurs, however, Farber suggested that revisions are likely to be small, successive, and made only with reluctance.

Factors in Revision

For parents' ideas, one would expect to find relevant the range of factors identified in general studies of cognition: the nature and the source of the new information, the extent to which a schema is being constructed or is established, the needs of the individual to hold onto a particular point of view in order to persist with a task, maintain a relationship, or preserve self-esteem. We have, in fact, already noted a number of these factors at work.

The study of parents' ideas, however, draws attention to additional factors that are less likely to surface in laboratory studies. The two I single out have to do with changes in the parent's social position, and changes in the fashionableness of particular ideas.

Mugny and Carugati (1985) have provided an example of the effect of changes in a parent's social position. They noted that European culture contains at least two definitions of intelligence: intelligence as social skill and adaptability, and intelligence as the ability to solve abstract problems, with problems in logic and mathematics as prime examples. Before their children enter school, Swiss and Italian parents favor social definitions. Entry into school, however, brings an increase in the extent to which problem-solving definitions are endorsed. The shift, Mugny and Carugati argued, is not only in the exposure to the definitions advocated by schools. A shift has also occurred in the social group to which a parent now belongs. The parent is now "the parent of a school child" and expected to take on the views that go with this social position. People who become teachers are even more likely to adopt a school-based definition, again because these views are part of their membership in the social group, "teachers." If people did not hold these views, they would presumably either not enter or not continue with teaching as a profession, unless perhaps some position on its margins (entertaining ideas that are "far out" but not completely beyond the group's range) can be found.

The impact of changes in fashionableness or style is less easy to document by way of clear data. It is not difficult to observe, however, that ideas about children and parenting go out of fashion, become "politically incorrect," or acquire the connotation of being held only by people who are a little "backward," "quaint," or "not with it." Such variations in style have been amply demonstrated by Bourdieu (1979) for European ideas about the "ideal body" and the "right kind of food." Parents' ideas about the ideal parent, the ideal child, or the "good enough" parent are surely responsive to similar changes in what Bourdieu labels as "taste."

The fact of the matter is that we are often far from understanding what gives rise to variations in parents' ideas, either over time or across subpopulations. I return to the Baltimore studies for examples. These have to do with variations across groups, but they point up as well the difficulties faced in accounting for changes across time.

The first example consists of variations in parents' school expectations in relation to the method of delivery at birth. In Entwisle and Alexander's (1987) sample, parents whose children had been delivered by Cesarean section "believed that their children had higher ability to do schoolwork than did parents of other children, irrespective of the child's tested status. The effect ... was substantial—as large or larger than the effects of objective test scores on those beliefs. These beliefs were maintained despite the fact that by second grade over half of the parents had seen the school folders that contained their children's CAT scores" (Entwisle & Alexander, 1987, p. 681: CAT refers to achievement tests that assess a child's standing in comparison with national scores on tests of reading and arithmetic). Entwisle and Alexander commented that the result might stem from "cognitive dissonance" (the stress of a Cesarean delivery is offset by placing a higher value on the child) or from the more positive mood that may arise in households where fathers tend to become more involved in childcare (a further correlate of Cesarean delivery). The possible explanations are clearly multiple.

The second example has to do with the effects of household composition. In the Baltimore sample, "parents in mother-father households hold higher expectations for their child's reading performance than do parents in one-parent homes. This pattern holds for black children ... and for white children. Furthermore, the household effects ... are not accounted for by [the child's] entry level performance or parents' general performance expectations" (Thompson, Alexander, & Entwisle, 1988, pp. 437–438). The effect is specific to reading expectations. Moreover, it occurs also—within the African-American sample—in households that contain a mother plus a member of the extended family. It is then the presence of another involved adult that raises expectations. Solo parents, it is suggested, may make a more "realistic assessment of limited resources and reading material in the home" (Thompson et al., 1988, p. 446). The fact of the matter is that we do not as yet have, within material related to parenting, clear evidence as to how such "realistic" revisions come about.

Where then do we stand overall with regard to what determines whether parents will revise their ideas about children or parenting in the face of information that does not fit with the ideas they hold? Parenting, I noted at the start, is an occupation in which this state of affairs is frequent, if only because children change so often. We should not, I have proposed, expect that parents will simply and easily update or revise their ideas when children change or when experts advise them that their ideas need to change. Instead, we should look carefully at studies with parents for evidence as to when ideas change, who is most open to change, how revision proceeds, and what factors increase or decrease the likelihood of change. Profitable also will be a turn toward discussions of cognitive change outside the field of parenting. Some of these discussions take the form of sociological analyses of the way some ideas become fashionable whereas others come to be seen as "dated." Others are to be found within the area known as experimental social cognition, an area that is particularly concerned with the impact of "disconfirming" information and with resistance to change. Both types of discussion yield ideas as to whether and when parents are likely to alter their ideas in the face of information that does not fit with their existing ideas.

ACTIONS AND EMOTIONS IN PARENTS' IDEAS

In the previous three sections, I have concentrated on the nature and use of information of various kinds: a focus that goes hand in hand with the question—How do parents' ideas come into being and change? In these final comments, I focus on the question: Is information all that matters? I have already indicated a number of ways in which the study of parents' knowledge and expectations needs to go beyond attention to the nature and the use of information or evidence. I now argue explicitly that what needs especially to be added is a concern with the several ways in which actions and emotions are intertwined with parents' ideas. To bring out the need to consider these interconnections, I consider four topics that are not adequately covered by the material in the previous sections. The topics have to do with (1) information as a source of negative affect, (2) cross-generation agreement, (3) concepts of accessibility, and (4) actions as a source of ideas. Each represents an area that warrants both additional research and theory.

Information as a Source of Negative Affect

It is easy to assume that more information is always better, just as it is easy to assume that parents who are accurate in their assessments of themselves and their children will be happier and will produce more competent children. Neither assumption may hold.

Miller (in press) dissected assumptions about accuracy. I concentrate on the assumption that more information is always better. For an example, I return to studies of children with a handicap. It is not surprising to read that parents of handicapped children often resist programs designed to teach them about their child's probable course of development or to teach them how to "work" with their children. In many ways, this change of activity may be seen as raising issues of identity, as not in keeping with what "parents" do, as distinct from "trainers." Programs designed to offer social support and reduce isolation would appear to be less threatening and more likely to lower stress. That, however, is also not always the case.

The results that raise a doubt come from a study by Granger of mothers of handicapped children (reported in Wright, Granger, & Sameroff, 1984). For some of these mothers, the provision of social support—the provision of people who could supply information if needed, help with child care, or be available to talk—lowered stress. For others, the level of stress was heightened. The distinguishing feature was the initial complexity of the mother's ideas about the child. The mothers who derived benefit were those who, in Sameroff and Feil's (1985) classification, were "perspectivistic" in their views. They already held a complex, multifactorial view of events, and encounters with others' viewpoints could be accommodated into this. The mothers who did not benefit, and were often made more anxious, were those who held single factor or "categorical" explanations of the child's state. For them, encounters with new viewpoints threatened the simplicity of the schemas they had come to live with.

Cross-Generation Agreement

In the course of this chapter, I have deliberately avoided questions about the extent to which, and the processes by which, parents' ideas are related to a child's cognitive or social performance. Such questions are certainly to be found in research on parents' ideas (Murphey, 1992, provided a review; see also Holden, in this *Handbook;* McGillicuddy-De Lisi & Sigel, in this *Handbook*). Questions about consequences are not unrelated to issues of information or evidence. As Alexander and Entwisle (1988) suggested, children are less likely to be influenced by parents' expectations for them in school when these expectations move too far away from what is possible and parents lose credibility.

The topic of consequences, however, is a very large topic in itself. I limit this discussion of it to an aspect that brings out issues of information and affect and that provides an extension to a question already considered: how parents come to hold the ideas they do or come to change them. That aspect has to do with the extent to which the ideas of one generation are congruent with those of their parents or diverge from them (usually referred to as cross-generation agreement). That aspect is chosen because, in time, the frameworks we use to understand how children come to hold their views of the world should overlap conceptually with the frameworks we use to understand how parents come to hold their ideas: come, for instance, to agree or to disagree with the views of their social group.

Cross-generation agreement is a topic with a considerable history, surfacing whenever scholars begin to ask about the transmission or the reproduction of values. It is also a topic that, as Furstenberg

(1971) pointed out, has contained a discrepancy between the expectation that the warmth of the relationship between parent and child would predict the occurrence of agreement, and research results pointing to connections that were at best weak and often not present. Furstenberg suggested that, over and above warmth, attention needed to be given to the child's perception of a parent's position. A warm relationship but inaccurate perception, for instance, could yield a lack of congruence between the positions of parent and child.

Furstenberg's (1971) hypothesis is one that had also occurred to Cashmore and Goodnow (1985), who proceeded to elaborate and test it. Their "two-process" model of agreement proposes two steps. The first is the child's perception of a parent's position. That step is seen as primarily influenced by cognitive factors: by the nature of the information that parents provide (e.g., its clarity or its redundancy) and by the child's capacity to process or decode the information provided. The second step is the child's acceptance or rejection of the view that the parent is thought to hold. That step is regarded as likely to be affected more strongly by the warmth of the relationship. The Cashmore and Goodnow study was directed primarily toward confirming the first step. When parents agreed with one another, or when the topic was one on which parents were likely to have been explicit (e.g., the importance of being neat), adolescents were accurate in their perceptions of where their parents stood. (Accuracy means that the adolescents filled out ratings for their parents that agreed closely with the ratings that parents themselves gave.) Whether the child's own position was close to that perceived for parents, however, depended on the child's vested interests. The importance to a parent of a child's being neat, or obedient, for instance, was accurately perceived by a child, but the child's own position diverged from that of parents.

That type of result directs our attention to the further question: What kind of information do parents provide to children? Just as they themselves do not always encounter information that is freely given and easy to understand, so also do their children. The information that parents provide to their children may be poorly explained, inconsistent, restricted ("you'll learn about that when you're older"), laden with negative overtones ("nice children don't ask questions like that"), or—like the reports given to parents by teachers or physicians—difficult to decode. Parents say to children, for instance, "what's the magic word?" when what they want the child to do is to say "please." They ask, "Were you born in a tent?" when they want the child to close the door after coming in or going out. Or they say, "curiosity killed the cat," when they want a child not to ask questions (Becker & Goodnow, 1992). It is not clear how parents come to use such indirect statements, or why. One possibility, however, is that indirect statements convey a parent's irritation without provoking a direct confrontation, and may well model the expected family style when one is irritated. A further possibility is that indirect statements tell the child that something is expected, and that it is the child's responsibility to work out what that something is. That type of possibility could apply also to parents. When parents are in the situation of novices—learning their expected position in relation to teachers, nurses, or physicians—it seems possible that the elliptical statements they are given also indicate to parents the work they are expected to put into discovering what they are supposed to do.

Finally, the type of hypothesis presented by Cashmore and Goodnow (1985) raises the question: How important is it to parents that their children adopt positions similar to those of their parents? Analyses of parenting often appear to assume that similarity across generations is the goal of parenting. Often, however, a parent may hope that a child will not repeat the errors of a parent's views of the world and what life might offer, that the child will exceed the parent's vision of what is possible. What we need to know are the content areas where agreement matters or does not matter, why some areas matter and others do not, and what repair steps parents take when they come to recognize that a child does not agree in an area that matters (Goodnow, 1992, in press-b; Goodnow, Knight, & Cashmore, 1985; Grusec & Goodnow, 1994; Smetana, 1988). We need also to know more about the family interactions that bring a parent to the realization that there is in fact a divergence of opinion or values: a realization that may occur only when parents encounter some dramatic event (e.g., a child's violation of a sacred family rule or an illegal act that comes to the attention of others) (Alessandri & Wozniak, 1987). These are again aspects of agreement and divergence that hold promise as further ways of gaining insights into the way two generations may come to hold different views of each other or of the nature of family life.

Accessibility and Automatic Processing

This topic goes back to a question noted in the Introduction: What is the nature of parents' ideas? How are we to describe their content or their quality? The most frequent descriptions of content are in terms of categories, scripts, propositions, or rules, usually differentiated from one another in terms of such qualities as the extent to which ideas are firmly held, are expressed in black-and-white or in shaded terms, or are more likely to be expressed by one group than another (e.g., by mothers or by fathers) (Goodnow & Collins, 1990, provided an overview).

If we are to understand connections among ideas, actions, and affect, however, it seems advisable to add a further property: one often emphasized in general studies of social cognition. The property in this case is "accessibility" or "relative accessibility" (e.g., Higgins, King, & Mavin, 1982). In any situation, some ideas come more quickly to the surface than do others, requiring less prompting or priming. And some come quickly to the surface in almost every situation. The child who sees hostility in every ambiguous situation provides one example. The paranoid adult provides another. In the language of social psychologists, these are cases of "chronic accessibility."

Differences in accessibility are of interest first of all because they may be used to characterize the difference between one idea and another, or—a possibility of particular relevance to parenting—between two possible interpretations of the same event, both entertained by the one individual. Parents may, for instance, perceive children in more than one way. Children may be perceived essentially as property. In this view, they belong to parents who may dispose of them as parents decide. Children may also be regarded as having rights of their own. Both ideas may be held by the one parent, but one of the two may well be more accessible than the other.

In turn, differences in accessibility bring with them differences in the kind of processing that occurs. Highly accessible ideas are likely to be processed "automatically" rather than given the "conscious processing" that we normally think of information as being given (Bargh, 1982, 1990). In times of parental stress, for instance, the concept of children as property may be the one to come more quickly to the surface, to be processed automatically, to require some effort at inhibition, and to be the source of action. This may also be the view of children that, when threatened, is particularly associated with affect.

This type of possibility has been of particular interest to Bugental and her colleagues, in a series of studies designed to allow analogues of what may underlie abuse (Bugental, 1992; Bugental et al., in press; Bugental, Blue, & Cruzcosa, 1989; Bugental & Shennum, 1984). In these experimental studies, parents are categorized as attributing control in their interactions with children to the parent or to the child. They are then paired with children who simulate, in a game type situation, being responsive or unresponsive to the adult's advice or directions. Parents with high perceived adult control experience little difference in the stress these encounters bring about. They cope well with both responsive and unresponsive children. Parents with low perceived control, however, feel threatened by the unresponsive child. (Their sense of threat and disadvantage may be termed "chronically accessible.") They then engage in actions designed to reduce the threat (e.g., actions of ingratiation or dominance) and they feel more affectively aroused (the measures of affect are both physiological and self-report). These arousal effects, for the group of parents with low perceived control, are more pronounced when parents are under time pressure than when there is ample time to inhibit the sense of threat and disadvantage brought on by a child who does not affirm the adult's sense of power and control.

I give this possibility particular attention not only because it provides a challenging way of looking at the contents of parents' ideas and their links with affect. It offers as well a challenging possibility with regard to intervention programs for abusive parents. These parents may acquire a second layer of ideas about children and parenting in the course of a program. In the heat of the moment, however, the old ideas are likely to be the ones accessed and acted upon. What abusive parents may then need is not only information but also training at the level of action: practice, for instance, in pausing before action (counting to 10 etc.), with that interval allowing a drop in affect and a chance for more conscious processing and interpretation to occur (Bugental, 1989).

Actions as a Source of Ideas

Analyses of parents' ideas are often concerned with the direction of effects. Is emotion, for instance, the source or the consequence of ideas? We now recognize that the connections may go in both directions. Affect shapes ideas in a variety of ways (Hoffman, 1986, provided an effective overview for effects in general; Dix, 1991, 1992, took up the issues in the context of parenting). Affect stems also from the outcomes of one's ideas, from expectations being met or violated: a point made with regard to parenting by Belsky (1985), by Dix et al. (1986), and by Ruble et al. (1988).

The same bidirectionality applies to parents' actions (Goodnow, 1988; Miller, 1988). Ideas may shape or give rise to actions. In a reverse direction, ideas may also follow actions: that is, we begin with actions and from these our ideas emerge. This second kind of proposal (actions come first) is the less well known within the study of parents' ideas. It deserves particular attention, however, because of its relevance not only to analyses of how parents' ideas come into being, but also to analyses of how one might change the ideas that parents hold.

To make the argument more familiar, consider the title of an article by West and Zimmerman (1987): "Doing Gender." As children or adults, the argument runs, we are engaged in (or "recruited" into) a set of everyday routines or activities that express a difference in gender. As males and females, we are assigned to different spaces, are involved in different activities, are spoken to in different ways. In a word, we are constantly "doing gender." In the process, we learn how to identify ourselves to others as male or female. More subtly, Frye (1983) argued, "We ... become what we practice being" (p. 34) and we may not be able to change our sense of identity, or the identity others ascribe to us, unless our practices change. To use an example from West and Zimmerman, the usual divisions of labor in households are practices that express both differences in gender and in status. Without a change in these everyday practices, the usual ways in which we think about being male or female may not alter.

The impact of practices upon schemas is a concept more prominent within anthropology (e.g., Goodnow, in press-a; Ortner, 1985) than within psychology. Within psychology, the concept has gained attention mainly with reference to children and to some particular content areas: areas dealing with children's acquisition of gender schemas (e.g., Duveen & Lloyd, 1991) and of schemas related to family relationships, expressed in the routines related to divisions of labor (e.g., Goodnow, in press-a; Goodnow & Warton, 1991), or in the "family rituals" related to mealtimes, bedtimes, or parents' stories of their childhood (e.g., Sameroff & Fiese, 1992).

It seems reasonable, however, to propose that the study of parents' ideas may also benefit from the concept of practices as a basis for the ideas that parents come to hold. From this point of view, particular views of children or parenting emerge from and are learned in the course of routine activities. The differential roles of mothers and fathers, for instance, need not be expressed for us in what anyone says. They are, instead, expressed in the degree to which fathers are welcomed into prenatal classes and delivery rooms, are expected to appear at conferences with teachers or physicians, or are greeted with looks of surprise, anxiety, or pleasure when they are seen, in public places, as in sole charge of a young child.

Overall, where would an interest in the links among ideas, actions and feelings lead us? As a start, we might well ask: (1) What are the actions or routines by which we come to know the conventional definitions of mother or father? (2) What are the actions by which we signal to others that I am "the parent" of this child: not its babysitter or its "minder" but its parent, in fact its "good parent?" (3) What are the specific cues we use to identify various relationships between adults and children? (4)

Do people experience the same sense of ambiguity and concern when they cannot identify the relationship between an adult and a young child that many tend to feel when they cannot identify whether a child or an adult is male or female? (5) Is it possible to change ideas about parenting, mothering, or fathering unless we also change everyday practices that express or embody these ideas? When would it be best to initiate a move towards change by beginning with a change in the practice rather than with other information related to a parent's ideas? These several qeustions would all acknowledge the variety of ways in which parents' ideas, actions, and feelings are interwoven.

CONCLUSIONS

This chapter has been concerned with a question that has both conceptual and practical implications: What conditions shape the ideas that parents hold about children and parenting? The conceptual implications have to do with our understanding of the bases to parents' ideas and their openness to change. The practical implications have to do with the need for this understanding in any attempt to devise or evaluate advice and information directed toward parents.

The position taken is that this question is best met by combining analyses of parents' ideas with concepts and research from general analyses of adult cognition. It is possible to utilize as well concepts drawn from theories of cognitive development among children. Children, for instance, are known to develop from positions that take only one factor into account to positions that consider and coordinate several factors. That general feature of change has been used to good effect as a way of differentiating among parents in terms of the one-dimensional versus multidimensional quality of the ideas they hold (Newberger, 1980; Sameroff, 1983). From theories that concentrate upon child development, it is also possible to take an emphasis upon one particular influence: namely, the challenges that experience with children present to the expectations or schemas that parents already hold. Analyses of adult cognition, however, offer a broader account of the ways in which ideas may differ from one another (e.g., there is more attention to the structure of ideas, to their interrelationships with one another). They also offer—a point of particular relevance to this chapter—a broader account of influences than do theories of change in children's ideas, perhaps because a lack of concern with adults' logical capacity leaves more room for attention to factors such as mood, degree of interest in accuracy, attachment to old ideas, or resistance to the new.

Two lines of research and theory have in fact been drawn upon for the present chapter. One has to do with conditions inside the individual. The concern here is with conditions such as the state of development of an idea (early stages or wellestablished) and the nature of the individual's goals, mood, level of experience, degree of responsibility, or degree of need to hold some ideas rather than others. Most of this research has developed under the umbrella label of experimental social cognition. The other line of research and theory has to do with conditions outside the individual: in particular, the nature of the information encountered by the individual—the extent to which it is accessible to parents (or restricted to those with formal expertise), easily understood, neutral rather than biased, in favor of one view of children and parenting or allowing several views to be held. To consider only conditions within or external to the individual, this chapter has argued, is insufficient. The challenge is to consider both and, eventually, to find ways of analyzing and predicting the particular effects of various combinations.

In this chapter, an interest in considering both kinds of conditions gives rise to a set of questions about whether and when parents seek information, not only in the form of turning to experts outside the family but also in the form of asking questions of themselves, each other, their children, their friends, their own parents. They are most likely to do so, it appears, shortly before they need the information, when they are in the early stages of developing their ideas, when their mood is positive, when the goal is one of accuracy rather than a "quick fix," and when asking questions does not expose them to negative judgments by others. The impact of factors such as goal, mood, or timing warns us not to assume that parents will always be interested in advice or information. The impact of possible judgments by others warns us not to assume that information seeking is a purely private matter, influenced only by conditions inside the individual.

What are those outside conditions likely to be where parents' ideas are concerned? The focus in this chapter has been on the state of the information that is likely to be encountered. Experimental studies of adult cognition might lead us to expect that information is always perfect. The study of parents' ideas—and several proposals from sociology and anthropology—underline instead the presence of several forms of information. What parents encounter may be a closed door, an incomplete or unusable explanation, a biased view, or an inconsistent account.

Worth particular attention, I have proposed, is the nature of "inconsistency." It is easy to regard double messages in a negative light and to see progress as a movement toward a single truth. The analysis of parents' ideas could benefit, however, from an alternate view: one that regards the presence of several positions as the normal state of affairs in the world. In a sense, there is always a formal and an alternative view of education, medicine, childrearing, good parenting. This state of affairs can be regarded both as regularly occurring and as having positive features for both parents and researchers. Parents, for instance, may now be seen as in a position of choice or active blending. Researchers may look upon the acquisition of ideas as the acquisition of several viewpoints, rather than as the internalization of one. Researchers may also now take a different view of what might otherwise seem perplexing: the extent to which parents can show rapid changes in their ideas, for instance, or—a phenomenon noted by Holden (in this *Handbook*)—display "ambivalence" in their ideas about themselves and their children. Shifts, ambivalence, and inconsistency all appear in a different light when one considers that any culture, and any parent, may look upon parenting and childhood in more than one way. One way may be more salient or receive stronger endorsement than the other at particular times, but the alternate view is not likely to be completely absent. Advisors to parents, and parents themselves, might well benefit from the recognition that double endorsements, varying in their strength but nonetheless double, are more likely to be the case than not.

Advisors in particular might well take note also of what is emerging with regard to one particular kind of encounter for parents: encounters with information that is out of line with—that disconfirms— ideas already established. This is the kind of encounter most likely to be involved in any attempt at education or persuasion. Once again, experimental social psychology is a useful source. This field has long contained an interest in the nature of persuasion and the impact of "propaganda" or "reeducation" programs. That interest has swung from optimism to an awareness of the need to understand resistance and, more recently, to a focus on the conditions associated with people taking account of information that runs counter to their usual ideas. For anyone concerned with parents' ideas, the implications of these general experimental studies are that we should anticipate more than one route to revision. We should also expect that revision will be most likely to occur when the revision is in line with a parent's social position or sense of identity. Revisions that carry a loss of self-esteem, are out of line with what most parents in a particular role are expected by others to believe, or that call for actions that a parent will find difficult to sustain—these have the lesser chance of success.

What else might advisors or researchers take into account? Throughout the chapter, and especially in the final section, I have noted the need to consider the several ways in which ideas are linked to emotions and to actions. To pull out one of those connections, we need to recognize that the ideas we hold may arise from the actions we take and may be difficult to change unless we change the actions that express them and support them. A view of oneself as an adult with rights, for instance, may be difficult to sustain when one's routine actions are of a sacrificial kind. A view of children as people with rights and skills is difficult to sustain when one's routine actions leave few decisions for children to make. A change in ideas then may need to start with a change in actions.

In sum, attention to the conditions that shape parents' ideas about children and parenting can both benefit from theory and research related to adult cognition in general, and can enrich general theory and research. To bring the two together, and to consider the combination in terms of both conceptual and practical implications, is a challenge that is both major and likely to be rewarding.

ACKNOWLEDGMENTS

This chapter has been written independently but builds upon collaborative work with others—people I am happy to acknowledge as the source of much stimulation: in particular, and in alphabetical order, Jennifer Bowes, Judith Cashmore, Andy Collins, Joan Grusec, and Pamela Warton. Financial support came from Macquarie University's Research Committee.

REFERENCES

Abelson, R. P. (1986). Beliefs are like possessions. *Journal for the Theory of Social Behavior, 16,* 223–250.

Alessandri, S. M., & Wozniak, R. H. (1987). The child's awareness of parental beliefs concerning the child: A developmental study. *Child Development, 58,* 316–323.

Alexander, K. L., & Entwisle, D. R. (1988). Achievement in the first two years of school: Patterns and processes. *Monographs of the Society for Research in Child Development, 53*(2, Serial No. 218).

Backett, K. C. (1982). *Mothers and fathers: The development and negotiation of parental behaviour.* London: Macmillan.

Bargh, J. A. (1982). Automatic and conscious processing of social information. In R. S. Wyer Jr., & T. K. Srull (Eds.), *Handbook of social cognition* (Vol. 3, pp. 1–43). Hillsdale, NJ: Lawrence Erlbaum Associates.

Bargh, J. A. (1990). Auto-motives: Preconscious determinants of social interaction. In E. T. Higgins & R. M. Sorrentino (Eds.), *Handbook of motivation and cognition* (Vol. 2, 93–130). Hillsdale, NJ: Lawrence Erlbaum Associates.

Barsch, R. (1968). *The parent of the handicapped child.* Springfield, IL: Thomas.

Becker, J. A, & Goodnow, J. J. (1992). "What's the magic word"? "Were you born in a tent"?—The challenge of accounting for parents' indirect use of speech with children. *Newsletter of Laboratory of Comparative Human Development, 50,* 517–522.

Belsky, J. (1985). Exploring individual differences in marital change across the transition to parenthood: The role of violated expectations. *Journal of Marriage and the Family, 47,* 1037–1044.

Bennett, S. (1971). Infant–caretaker interaction. *Journal of the American Academy of Child Psychiatry, 10,* 321–325.

Bok, S. (1982). *Secrets: On the ethics of concealment and revelation.* New York: Pantheon.

Bornstein, M. H., Tal, J., & Tamis-LeMonda, C. S. (1991). Parenting in cross-cultural perspective: The United States, France, and Japan. In M. H. Bornstein (Ed.), *Cultural approaches to parenting* (pp. 69–90). Hillsdale, NJ: Lawrence Erlbaum Associates.

Bourdieu, P. (1979). *Distinction: A social critique of the judgment of taste.* London: Routledge & Kegan Paul.

Bugental, D. B. (1989, April). *Caregiver cognitions as moderators of affect in abusive families.* Paper presented at meeting of the Society for Research in Child Development, Kansas City, MO.

Bugental, D. B. (1992). Affective and cognitive processes within threat-oriented family systems. In I. Sigel, A. McGillicuddy-De Lisi, & J. J. Goodnow (Eds.), *Parental belief systems* (pp. 219–248). Hillsdale, NJ: Lawrence Erlbaum Associates.

Bugental, D. B., Blue, J., Cortez, V., Fleck, K., Kopeikin, H., Clayton-Lewis, J., & Lyon, J. (in press). Social cognitions as organizers of autonomic and affective responses to social challenge. *Journal of Personality and Social Psychology.*

Bugental, D. B., Blue, J., & Cruzcosa, M. (1989). Perceived control over caregiving outcomes: Implications for child abuse. *Developmental Psychology, 25,* 532–539.

Bugental, D. B., & Shennum, W. (1984). "Difficult" children as elicitors and targets of adult comuication patterns: An attributional-behavioral transactional analysis. *Monographs of the Society for Research in Child Development, 49*(1, Serial No. 205).

Cashmore, J. A., & Goodnow, J. J. (1985). Agreement between generations: A two-process approach. *Child Development, 56,* 493–501.

Chen, C., & Uttal, D. H. (1988). Cultural values, parents' beliefs, and children's achievement in the United States and China. *Human Development, 31,* 351–358.

Chombart de Lauwe, M-J. (1984). Changes in the representation of the child in the course of social transmission. In R. M. Farr & S. Moscovici (Eds.), *Social representations* (pp. 185–210). Cambridge: Cambridge University Press.

Clarke-Stewart, K. A. (1978). Popular primers for parents. *American Psychologist, 33,* 359–369.

Collins, W. A. (in press). Resolving discrepancies in parents' judgments of adolescents. In J. Smetana (Ed.), *Socio-cognitive models of parenting.* San Francisco: Jossey-Bass.

Deutsch, F. M., Ruble, D. N., Fleming, A., Brooks-Gunn, J., & Stangor, C. S. (1988). Information seeking and maternal self-definition during the transition to motherhood. *Journal of Personality and Social Psychology, 5,* 420–431.

Dix, T. (1991). The affective organization of parenting: Adaptive and maladaptive processes. *Psychological Bulletin, 110,* 3–25.

Dix, T. (1992). Parenting on behalf of the child: Empathic goals in the regualation of responsive parenting. In I. E. Sigel, A. V. McGillicuddy-De Lisi, & J. J. Goodnow (Eds.), *Parental belief systems* (2nd ed., pp. 319–348). Hillsdale, NJ: Lawrence Erlbaum Associates.

Dix, T., Ruble, D. N., Grusec, J. E., & Nixon, S. (1986). Social cognition in parents: Inferential and affective reactions to children of three age levels. *Child Development, 57,* 879–894.

Duveen, G., & Lloyd, B. (1991). An ethnographic approach to social representations. In G. Breakwill & D. Cantor (Eds.), *Empirical approaches to the study of representations* (pp. 90–108). Oxford, England: Oxford University Press.

Eagley, A. H., & Chaiken, S. (1993). *The psychology of attitudes.* New York: Harcourt Brace.

Entwisle, D. R., & Alexander, K. L. (1987). Long-term effects of Caesarean delivery on parents' beliefs and children's schooling. *Developmental Psychology, 23,* 676–682.

Entwisle, D. R., & Hayduk, L. A. (1978). *Too great expectations: The academic outlook of young children.* Baltimore: Johns Hopkins University Press.

Erber, R. T., & Fiske, S. T. (1984). Outcome dependency and attention to inconsistent information. *Journal of Personality and Social Psychology, 47,* 709–726.

Evans, M., Barber, B. L., Gadsden, V. C., Paris, S. G., & Park, S. H. (1989, April). *What knowledge do parents have about educational assessment tasks?* Paper presented at meeting of the Society for Research in Child Development, Kansas City, MO.

Farber, B. (1983). Perceptions of crisis and related variables in the impact of a retarded child on the mother. *Journal of Health and Human Behavior, 1,* 108–118.

Fischer, J. L., & Fischer, A. (1963). The New Englanders of Orchardtown, U.S.A. In B. B. Whiting (Ed.), *Six cultures: Studies of child rearing* (Vol. 5, pp. 869–1010). New York: Wiley.

Fiske, S. T., & Taylor, S. E. (1991). *Social cognition.* New York: McGraw-Hill.

Foucault, M. (1980). *Power-knowledge: Selected interviews and other writings.* London: Brighton & Harvester Press.

Frankel, D. G., & Roer-Bornstein, D. (1982). Traditional and modern contributions to changing infant-rearing ideologies of two ethnic communities. *Monographs of the Society for Research in Child Development, 47*(4, Serial No. 196).

Frey, D., & Ruble, D. N. (1985). What children say when the teacher is not around: Conflicting goals in social comparison and performance assessment in the classroom. *Journal of Personality and Social Psychology, 48,* 550–562.

Frye, M. (1983). *The politics of reality: Essays in feminist theory.* Trumansberg, NY: Crossing Press.

Furstenberg, F. F., Jr. (1971). The transmission of mobility orientation in the family. *Social Forces, 49,* 595–603.

Gergen, K. J., Gloger-Tippelt, G., & Berkowitz, P. (1990). The cultural construction of the developing child. In G. R. Semin & R. J. Gergen (Eds.), *Everyday understanding: Social and scientific implications* (pp. 108–129). Beverly Hills, CA: Sage.

Glick, J. (1985). Culture and cognition revisited. In E. Neimark, R. Delisi, & J. L. Newman (Eds.), *Moderators of competence* (pp. 99–116). Hillsdale, NJ: Lawrence Erlbaum Associates.

Gloger-Tippelt, G. (1991, July). *Mothers' conceptions of their first child during pregnancy and their effects on sensitive maternal behavior.* Paper presented at the biennial meeting of International Society for the Study of Behavioral Development, Minneapolis.

Gloger-Tippelt, G., & Tippelt, R. (1986). Kindheit und kindliche entwicklung als soziale konstructionen. *Bildung und Erziehung, 2,* 149–164.

Goodnow, J. J. (1985). Parents' ideas about parenting and development: A review of issues and recent work. In M. Lamb, A. Brown, & B. Rogoff (Eds.), *Advances in developmental psychology* (Vol. 4, pp. 193–242). Hillsdale, NJ: Lawrence Erlbaum Associates.

Goodnow, J. J. (1988). Parents' ideas, actions and feelings: Models and methods from developmental and social psychology. *Child Development, 59,* 286–320.

Goodnow, J. J. (1990). Using sociology to extend psychological accounts of cognitive development. *Human Development, 33,* 81–197.

Goodnow, J. J. (1992). Parents' ideas, children's ideas: Correspondnce and divergence. In I. Sigel, A. McGillicuddy-De Lisi, & J. J. Goodnow (Eds.), *Parental belief systems* (2nd ed., 293–318). Hillsdale, NJ: Lawrence Erlbaum Associates.

Goodnow, J. J. (in press-a). From household practices to parents' ideas about work and interpersonal relationships. In S. Harkness & C. Super (Eds.), *Parents' cultural belief systems.* New York: Guilford.

Goodnow, J. J. (in press-b). Parenting: Acceptable disagreement across generations. In J. Smetana (Ed.), *Socio-cognitive models of parenting.* San Francisco: Jossey-Bass.

Goodnow, J. J., Cashmore, J., Cotton, S., & Knight, R. (1984). Mothers' developmental timetables in two cultural groups. *International Journal of Psychology, 9,* 193–205.

Goodnow, J. J., & Collins, W. A. (1990). *Development according to parents: The nature, sources, and consequences of parents' ideas.* Hillsdale, NJ: Lawrence Erlbaum Associates.

Goodnow, J. J., Knight, R., & Cashmore, J. (1985). Adult social cognition: Implications of parents' ideas for approaches to development. In M. Perlmutter (Ed.), *Social cognition: Minnesota symposia on child development* (Vol. 18, 287–324). Hillsdale, NJ: Lawrence Erlbaum Associates.

Goodnow, J. J., & Warton, P. M. (1991). The social basis of social cognition: Interactions about work and lessons about relationships. *Merrill–Palmer Quarterly, 37,* 27–58.

Goodnow, J. J., & Warton, P. M. (1992). Contexts and cognitions: Taking a pluralist view. In P. Light & G. Butterworth (Eds.), *Context and cogniton* (pp. 85–112). London: Harvester Wheatsheaf.

Griest, D. L., & Wells, K. C. (1983). Behavioral family therapy with conduct disorders in children. *Behavior Therapy, 14,* 37–53.

Grusec, J. E., & Goodnow, J. J. (1994). The impact of parental discipline methods on the child's internalization of values: A reconceptualization of current points of view. *Developmental Psychology, 30,* 4–19.

Harkness, S., & Super, C. (Eds.). (in press). *Parents' cultural belief systems.* New York: Guilford.

Hess, R. D., Kashigawi, H., Azuma, G. R., Price, G. R., & Dickson, W. P. (1980). Maternal expectations for mastery of developmental tasks in Japan and in the United States. *International Journal of Psychology, 15,* 259–271.

Hess, R. D., Price, G. G., Dickson, W. P., & Conroy, M. (1984). Different roles for mothers and teachers: Contrasting styles of child care. In S. Kilmer (Ed.), *Advances in early education and day care* (Vol. 3, pp. 1–28). Greenwich, CT: Johnson.

Higgins, E. T., King, G., & Mavin, G. H. (1982). Individual construct accessibility and subjective impressions and recall. *Journal of Personality and Social Psychology, 43,* 35–47.

Hoffman, M. L. (1986). Affect, cognition, and motivation. In R.M. Sorrentino & E.T. Higgins (Eds.), *Handbook of motivation and cognition* (pp. 242–280). New York: Guilford.

Holden, G. W. (1988). Adults' thinking about a child-rearing problem: Effects of experience, parental status, and gender. *Child Development, 59,* 1623–1632.

Holden, G. W., & Edwards, L. A. (1989). Parental attitudes towards child rearing: Instruments, issues, and implications. *Psychological Bulletin, 106,* 29–58.

Holden, G. W., & Klingner, A. (in press). Learning through experience: Differences in how expert and novice nurses diagnose why an infant is crying. *Journal of Nursing Education.*

Isen, M. A., Means, B., Patrick, R., & Nowicki, G. (1982). Some factors influencing decision-making strategy and risk-taking. In M. S. Clark & S. T. Fiske (Eds.), *Affect and cognition: The 17th annual Carnegie symposium on cognition* (pp. 243–262). Hillsdale, NJ: Lawrence Erlbaum Associates.

Jackson, B., & Marsden, D. (1966). *Education and the working class.* Harmondsworth, England: Penguin.

Jamieson, D. W., & Zanna, M. P. (1989). Need for structure in attitude formation and expression. In A. R. Pratkanis, S. J. Breckler, & A. G. Greenwald (Eds.), *Attitude structure and function* (pp. 383–406). Hillsdale, NJ: Lawrence Erlbaum Associates.

Joffe, C. (1977). *Friendly intruders: Childcare professionals and family life.* Berkeley: University of California Press.

Kessen, W. (1979). The American child and other cultural inventions. *American Psychologist, 34,* 815–820.

Kruglanski, A. W., Peri, N., & Zakai, D. (1991). Interactive effects of need for closure and initial confidence on social information seeking. *Social Cognition, 9,* 127–148.

LeVine, R. A. (1988). Human parental care: Universal goals, cultural strategies, individual behavior. In R. A. LeVine, P. M. Miller, & M. M. West (Eds.), *Parental behavior in diverse societies* (pp. 3–12). San Francisco: Jossey-Bass.

Maccoby, N., Romney, A. K., Adams, J. S., & Maccoby, E. E. (1959). "Critical periods" in seeking and accepting information. *American Psychologist, 14,* 358.

Meares, R., Penman, R., Milgrom-Friedman, J., & Baker, K. (1982). Some origins of the "difficult" child: The Brazelton scale and the mother's view of her new-born's character. *British Journal of Medical Psychology, 55,* 77–86.

Miller, S. A. (1988). Parents' beliefs about children's cognitive development. *Child Development, 59,* 259–285.

Miller, S. A. (in press). Parental beliefs, parental accuracy, and children's cognitive performance: A search for causal relations. *Developmental Psychology.*

Moscovici, S. (1984). The phenomenon of social representations. In R. M. Farr & S. Moscovici (Eds.), *Social representations* (pp. 3–70). Cambridge, England: Cambridge University Press.

Mugny, G., & Carugati, F. (1985). *L'intelligence au pluriel: les représentations sociales de l'intelligence et de son développement.* Cousset, France: Editions Delval. (Reprinted in 1989 in English as *Social representations of intelligence* by Cambridge University Press)

Murphey, D. (1992). Constructing the child: Relations between parents' beliefs and child outcomes. *Developmental Review, 12,* 199–232.

Neuberg, S. L., & Fiske, S. T. (1987). Motivational influences on impression formation: Outcome dependency, accuracy-driven attention, and individuating processes. *Journal of Personality and Social Psychology, 53,* 431–440.

Newberger, C. M. (1980). The cognitive structure of parenthood: Designing a descriptive measure. In R. L. Selman & R. Yando (Eds.), *Clinical-developmental psychology* (Vol. 7, pp. 45–68). San Francisco: Jossey-Bass.

Ninio, A. (1978). The naive theory of the infant and other maternal attitudes in two subgroups in Israel. *Child Development, 50,* 976–980.

Ortner, S. (1985). Theory in anthropology since the sixties. *Comparative Studies in Society and History, 26,* 126–166.

Palacios, J. (1990). Parents' ideas about the development and education of their children: Answers to some questions. *International Journal of Behavioral Development, 13,* 137–155.

Palacios, J., Gonzaléz, M-M., & Moreno, M-C. (1992). Stimulating the child in the realm of cognitive development. In I. E. Sigel, A. V. McGillicuddy-De Lisi, & J. J. Goodnow (Eds.), *Parental belief systems* (2nd ed., pp. 71–94). Hillsdale, NJ: Lawrence Erlbaum Associates.

Parke, R. D. (1978). Parent–infant interaction: Progress, paradigms and problems. In G. P. Sackett (Ed.), *Observing behavior* (Vol. 1, pp. 69–94). Baltimore: University Park Press.

Pomerleau, A., Malcuit, G., & Sabatier, C. (1991). Child-rearing practices and parental beliefs in three cultural groups of Montreal: Quebecois, Vietnamese, Haitian. In M. H. Bornstein (Ed.), *Cultural approaches to parenting* (pp. 45–68). Hillsdale, NJ: Lawrence Erlbaum Associates.

Quinn, N., & Holland, D. (1987). Culture and cognition. In D. Holland & N. Quinn (Eds.), *Cultural models in language and thought* (pp. 3–42). Cambridge, England: Cambridge University Press.

Reid, B. W., & Valsiner, J. (1986). Consistency, praise, and love: Folk theories of American parents. *Ethos, 124,* 1–25.

Rosenkrantz, B. G. (1978). Reflections on 19th century conceptions of childhood. In E. M. R. Lomax, J. Kagan, & B. G. Rosenkrantz (Eds.), *Science and patterns of child care* (pp. 1–18). San Francisco: Freeman.

Rothman, B. K. (1986). *The tentative pregnancy: Prenatal diagnosis and the future of motherhood.* London: Pandora.

Rubin, K. H., & Mills, R. S. L. (1992). Parents' thoughts about children's socially adaptive and maladaptive behaviours: Stability, change, and individual differences. In I. E. Sigel, A. V. McGillicuddy-De Lisi, & J. J. Goodnow (Eds.), *Parental belief systems* (2nd ed., pp. 41–70). Hillsdale, NJ: Lawrence Erlbaum Associates.

Ruble, D. N. (in press). A phase model of transitions: Cognitive and motivational consequences. In M. Zanna (Ed.), *Advances in experimental social psychology.* New York: Academic Press.

Ruble, D. N., Fleming, A. C., Hackel, L. S., & Stangor, C. (1988). Changes in the marital relationship during the transition to motherhood: Effects of violated expectations concerning divisions of household labor. *Journal of Personality and Social Psychology, 55,* 78–87.

Ruddick, S. (1982). Maternal thinking. In V. Thorne & M. Yalom (Eds.), *Rethinking the family* (pp. 76–94). New York: Longmans.

Sameroff, A. J. (1983). Developmental systems: Contexts and evolution. In W. Kessen (Ed.), *Handbook of child psychology* (Vol. 1, 237–294). New York: Wiley.

Sameroff, A. J., & Feil, L. A. (1985). Parental concepts of development. In I. E. Sigel (Ed.), *Parental belief systems* (pp. 83–105). Hillsdale, NJ: Lawrence Erlbaum Associates.

Sameroff, A. J. & Fiese, B. H. (1992). Family representations of development. In I. E. Sigel, A. V. McGillicuddy-De Lisi, & J. J. Goodnow (Eds.), *Parental belief systems* (2nd ed., pp. 347–372). Hillsdale, NJ: Lawrence Erlbaum Associates.

Schlossman, S. L. (1976). Before home start: Notes toward a history of parent education in America, 1897–1929. *Harvard Educational Review, 46,* 436–467.

Schlossman, S. L. (1978). The parent education game: The politics of child psychology in the 1970's. *Teachers College Record, 79,* 788–808.

Showers, G. C., & Cantor, V. (1985). Social cognition: A look at motivated strategies. *Annual Review of Psychology, 36,* 275–305.

Sigel, I. E. (Ed.) (1985). *Parental belief systems.* Hillsdale, NJ: Lawrence Erlbaum Associates.

Sigel, I. E., McGillicuddy-De Lisi, A. V., & Goodnow, J. J. (Eds.), (1992). *Parental belief systems* (2nd ed.). Hillsdale, NJ: Lawrence Erlbaum Associates.

Stevenson, H. W., Stigler, J. W., Lee, S. Y., Lucker, G. W., Kitamura, S., & Hsu, C. C. (1985). Cognitive performance and academic achievement of Japanese, Chinese, and American children. *Child Development, 56,* 718–734.

Super, C., & Harkness, S. (1986). The developmental niche: A conceptualization of the interface of child and culture. *International Journal of Behavioral Development, 9,* 546–569.

Thompson, M. S., Alexander, C. L., & Entwisle, D. R. (1988). Household composition, parental expectations, and school achievement. *Social Forces, 67,* 424–451.

Thorne, B. (1987). Re-visioning women and social change: Where are the children? *Gender and Society, 1,* 85–109.

Turner, J. C. (1985). Social categorization and the self-concept: A social cognitive theory of group behavior. In E. J. Lawler (Ed.), *Advances in group processes* (Vol. 2, pp. 77–122). Greenwich, CT: JAI.

Weber, R., & Crocker, J. (1983). Cognitive processes in the revision of stereotypic beliefs. *Journal of Personality and Social Psychology, 45,* 961–977.

West, C., & Zimmerman, D. H. (1987). Doing gender. *Gender and Society, 1,* 125–151.

Williams, T. M., Joy, L. A., Travis, L., Gotowiec, A., Blum-Steele, M., Alken, L. S., Painter, S. L., & Davidson, S. M. (in press). Transition to motherhood: A longitudinal study. *Infant Mental Health Journal.*

Worthman, C. M. (in press). Biocultural interactions in human development. In M. E. Perieira & L. A. Fairbanks (Eds.), *Juvenile primates: Life history, development, and behavior.* Oxford, England: Oxford University Press.

Wright, J. D., Granger, R. D., & Sameroff, A. J. (1984). Parental acceptance and developmental handicap. In J. Blacher (Ed.), *Severely handicapped children and their families* (pp. 51–90). New York: Academic Press.

Zanna, M. P., & Cooper, J. (1976). Dissonance and the attribution process. In J. Harvey, W. J. Ickes, & R. F. Kidd (Eds.), *New directions in attribution research* (Vol. 1, pp. 199–217). Hillsdale, NJ: Lawrence Erlbaum Associates.

Zeaman, C. H., & Anders, T. F. (1987). Subjectivity in parent–infant relationships: A discussion of internal working models. *Infant Mental Health Journal, 8,* 237–250.

13

Parental Beliefs

Ann V. McGillicuddy-De Lisi
Lafayette College
Irving E. Sigel
Educational Testing Service

INTRODUCTION

This chapter concerns parental beliefs as sources of influence on the developing child, on the parents, and on the parent–child relationship. Psychological investigations of parental beliefs have largely been derived from assumptions that implicit and explicit beliefs guide parental actions with children (Ashmore & Brodzinsky, 1986). This chapter is dedicated to the argument that beliefs permeate parents' actions, not only with their children, but also with the larger environment. Beliefs organize the world for individuals, enabling them to cope with everyday life without being overwhelmed by information and decision-making demands. In addition, beliefs provide a means for generating behaviors, that may then affect the child's development, in response to parenting demands. Finally, beliefs can provide adults with a means to preserve their self-esteem, creating a standard against which to assess fulfillment of the parent role and setting both limits and weights to different aspects of parental role responsibilities.

A short history of the interest in beliefs and belief systems is presented first to create a context for this exposition. Current theory and research are linked to a long tradition of concern with parenting and ideas about the nature of the child. These historical notes serve as an entre to a presentation of the current evolving body of literature in which investigators, although using different conceptual models and different research paradigms, continue to study parental beliefs as determinants of both parental behavior and children's social and cognitive development. After summarizing recent empirical research we turn our attention to some of the critical issues that research must address in order to develop a coherent framework concerning the role that beliefs play in children's and in parents' development. A belief complex, which represents an initial attempt to integrate various approaches and definitions of parental beliefs, is described in the course of this discussion.

The review of more recent theoretical formulations and empirical work is restricted for the most part to articles published since 1985, rather than serving as an exhaustive review. It focuses on programmatic research efforts and several studies that have significantly advanced the nature of this work on beliefs. Many of these investigations have used different terms for the construct of belief, and labels such as parental perceptions, ideas, attributions, attitudes, values, expectations, and knowledge are often used interchangeably. Belief constructs can be differentiated from attitudes and values in that beliefs consist of knowledge or ideas that are accepted as true (Sigel, 1985). Attitudes and values may include a cognitive component, but these are not seen as facts or truth. For example, attitudes include an evaluative aspect that is an integral component of the parent's cognitive orientation, as in a "positive" or "negative attitude" (Holden, in this *Handbook*). Values, another form of adult social cognition, refer to longstanding goals that the parent holds for child, rather than truths (Kohn, 1969). In the course of describing the belief complex, beliefs are further differentiated from these other constructs through the discussion of the centrality of the cognitive component of beliefs.

Several reviews predate the present effort. For example, Miller (1988) analyzed studies of the nature and origin of beliefs, relations of beliefs to parenting practices, as well as their relation to children's cognitive development. Murphey (1992) also reviewed the literature regarding the relation between parental beliefs and child outcomes. Sigel (1986, 1992) discussed the connection between beliefs and behaviors at length. Goodnow and Collins (1990) analyzed the consequences of parents' ideas for both parents and children, as well as their relation to affect and the sociohistorical context of social representations of children. In addition, Goodnow (1992) and Simons, Beaman, Conger, and Chao (1992) examined intergenerational trends in beliefs. Most recently, Okagaki and Divecha (1993) discussed the literature on sources of parental beliefs as well as the belief-behavior relationship. Work discussed within these reviews is summarized briefly and serves as a basis for further examination of current efforts to explore the origin and function of beliefs in the context of the developing family.

HISTORICAL BACKGROUND

Three Histories of Beliefs About Children

Goodnow and Collins (1990) asserted that adults have held and presented ideas about children and about the nature of children's development throughout the history of humanity. Parental beliefs are a domain of knowledge and study that goes back to the time when families first existed. In order to understand current psychological research on parental beliefs, it is useful to conceptualize it as an outgrowth of at least three histories that have both shaped and limited the focus, the underlying assumptions, and the content of parental beliefs. These three histories are: (1) the history of Western philosophical thought as it has been applied to the meaning of life, human's place in the world, and the nature of development; (2) the history that is shared by peoples within a culture as they seek to explain the nature of the child and optimize child outcomes; and (3) the history of social science theory and method, which has influenced the course of formal articulated conceptions of human nature, behavior, and development. Each of these histories has contributed to current conceptualizations concerning the nature of beliefs about children.

We do not intend to document these various perspectives in detail. A brief acknowledgment of the three different types of perspectives on the child is offered to place the examination of parent beliefs in its historical context. Current theoretical social science perspectives are linked to their intellectual forbearers as we move toward an increasingly sophisticated understanding of the intricate forces that influence children's intellectual, social, and emotional development.

Western philosophical thought.   Philosophers, religious teachers, and educators from the early days of the Greeks and Romans presented formal views about the nature of the child and about what our purpose is as individuals, as peoples, and as parents. These philosophical positions have had an impact on current conceptualizations of child development.

For example, Aristotle, Plato, and Socrates offered suggestions about the nature of human development and how rearers of children should behave that have influenced the course of thinking about children ever since the articulation of these views. The actions that were suggested for parents and teachers stemmed from their particular conception of the developing child, and were often related to larger conceptions of the nature of the world and the individual's place in that world.

Aristotelian and Platonic realism, for example, have affected many of the assumptions that people have made about the nature of knowledge and subsequently the nature of knowledge acquisition, that is, children's development. The ancient theory that universals exist and are independent of instances in which they are observed can be viewed as the basis for beliefs that there is a structure to human nature that is real and can be discovered. Educational movements that emphasize content learning (as opposed to process) and external determinants of human behavior are derived from these philosophical arguments. These and other ancient and modern western philosophical views have established ways of looking at the world in general and at children in particular that influenced formal psychological theory and assumptions about development that form the basis of theories and research questions in modern times (Cairns, 1983).

Ethnotheories.   In addition to these articulated philosophical views of the child and of development in general, folk theories and ethnotheories evolved within particular societies or cultures, at times independently of philosophical analyses, and at times in tandem with such reflections. These folk perspectives of the nature of children and of parental roles in child development are less formal and less fully articulated, but are nonetheless characteristic of the approaches to children by members of a particular society or culture (Reid & Valsiner, 1986). These are sometimes referred to as ethnotheories, especially when the focus is on how beliefs are presented as particular childrearing practices that characterize groups of peoples within a shared culture (Harkness & Super, 1992). For example, Pomerleau, Malcuit, and Sabatier (1991) studied maternal beliefs about infant development and parenting practices among Québécois, Vietnamese, and Haitian mothers. The ethnic groups differed in their beliefs and practices in a manner that was consistent with the sociocultural history of the group. Québécois mothers, for example, saw children as unique competent individuals and viewed the mother's role as important in stimulating the infant. Pomerleau et al. linked these beliefs and values to cultural origins and to mothers' encouragement of exploratory behavior and early presentation of stimulating toys and activities. These beliefs differed from those of the Vietnamese immigrants to Québec, whose emphasis on formal learning situations was viewed as derived from their culture of origin.

Although there may be variability in the particular content of such beliefs across societies or cultures, it is assumed that all members of all societies use childrearing methods that are derived from an underlying belief structure regarding the nature of child growth and development (LeVine, 1988). The aim of such parental cognition has historically been to optimize opportunities for children to become functioning members of the society, but the goals of *current* folk theorizing have been broadened to include an understanding of the role that beliefs play in the parent's own life as well as in maximizing outcomes for children that are valued by the culture (Goodnow & Collins, 1990).

These everyday customs, vis-à-vis the child, also provide important contexts for understanding the nature of beliefs about children. Each theorist and each approach to beliefs cannot be separated from the cultural milieu in which the notions of the child and the parent's role in relation to child development were formed. In essence, we deny the existence of a singular "olympian universal" cultural perspective on children but contend that what is universal is that every society has a culture and every culture is in part instantiated in the parent beliefs about the nature of childhood. In effect, beliefs are not products of our culture, but are, in fact, our culture. The study of beliefs perforce must be tied to an ecological context. Related to this assertion is the conviction that what may be universal are the categories of beliefs, for example, beliefs about the origins of childhood and causes of development. The cultural instantiations, however, are in the content of the categories, for instance, the particular explanation of origins of development, birth, the role of heredity, the sources of growth (Stigler, Shweder, & Herdt, 1990).

Recent history in psychology.   The third historical context for beliefs about children and the nature of development are the scientific theories and methods of social science, but this history is not independent from either the Western philosophical thought from which psychology was born or from the ethnotheories held by individuals prior to the formalization of ideas about children and childrearing into early developmental theories. In addition, the field of psychology has its own more recent history, that is not limited to perspectives on children, childrearing, and development, but includes more general theories of behavior and paradigms for the study of behavior. This recent history in psychology has influenced the approaches to parental beliefs that are characteristic of current research.

As "scientific" theories and methods developed, they were applied to the study of beliefs about children both directly and indirectly as children became the objects of study. For example, the salience of inherited characteristics in children's development was emphasized with advances in genetic theory and research. Biological underpinnings of development were intrinsic to the beliefs of many developmentalists, and this belief continues to prevail among researchers and parents alike (e.g., Gesell, 1946).

Later, with the advent of behaviorism and concomitant use of psychological methods, a shift in point of view came about. Learning theorists, deriving some of their assumptions from Watson (1928) as well as Pavlov (1927), attributed changes in development to the conditioning that parents used as they socialized their children. Prescriptive recommendations were made as to how to rear children. This belief that children could be trained through properly implemented learning strategies continued for some time into the 1930s and reflected views that children were malleable, in contrast to the more genetic and evolutionary models of development (Bergeman & Plomin, 1989). These differences become polarized as the nature-nurture controversy—an ongoing issue among parents as well as behavioral scientists (Scarr & Ricciuti, 1991).

An outgrowth of the nature-nurture controversy was increased interest in identification and assessment of environmental features as sources of influence. It was in this context, along with the application of psychoanalytic theory and attitude research, that parents' attitudes became the focus of such research (Holden & Edwards, 1989). Developmental psychologists began to address attitudinal questions, adopting techniques from attitude research conducted by the social psychologists (e.g., Allport, 1950; Holden, in this *Handbook*). Interest in the affective nature of the mother–child relationship derived from psychoanalytic theory also provided a venue for assessing parents' attitudes (e.g., Sears, Maccoby, & Levin, 1957).

During the 1950s, there was a polarization of ideologies of learning theorists who emphasized parents' behaviors, in contrast to those who focused on attitudes, feelings, and beliefs—a mentalistic emphasis. Many "how to" books became popular after the success of Dr. Benjamin Spock, reflecting one or the other of these positions (Spock, 1946). Parents were sometimes trained to use learning techniques for managing children's "problem" behaviors at home, whereas attitude research continued, struggling to show the importance of feelings and attitudes for children's development (Powell, 1988). In spite of much research on parent attitudes during this period, lack of consistency between expressed attitudes and observed parental behaviors was found. Nevertheless, research activity is still flourishing regarding parents' attitudes as a way to evaluate developmental outcomes for children (Holden, in this *Handbook*), and a general reinvigoration of attitude research (Eagly, 1992), is in part sustained by the historical, philosophical, and folk assumptions that parental ideas influence child outcomes.

In the past 30 years, new interest in cognitive psychology has begun to grow with changing conceptualizations of significant determinants of behaviors. Children and adults have come to be viewed as naive theorists or active information processors (Baldwin, 1965; Heider, 1958). At this point, at least three different domains of study of parent cognitions coexisted, and each of these became a self-sustaining conceptualization applied to the study of parents' ideas about children. These approaches began to emerge during the late 1960s and the 1970s and continue to be a major source of current research on parental beliefs. The first of these is a new look at parent attitudes, which are generally viewed as consisting of three components: an affective component, a cognitive component, and a behavioral component. Holden (in this *Handbook*) addresses the body of research that has been based on this perspective of parent's ideas. The second is the domain of parental expectations—what parents think that children should be able to do and the age at which these behaviors should occur

(Goodnow, in this *Handbook;* Winterbottom, 1958). Some have expressed interest in the accuracy of these expectations as well (Goodnow, 1985, in this *Handbook;* Miller, 1986). The third area is the focus of the remainder of this chapter—the study of parental beliefs.

The present day conceptualizations of beliefs do not derive from a single definition or perspective, but rather range from everyday and common usage of the "belief" term to quasi-philosophical conceptualizations (McGillicuddy-De Lisi, 1982a; Sigel, 1985, 1986). For these reasons, the definitions and the research conducted on parental beliefs vary from study to study and from investigator to investigator. In the next section, current research is presented with the aim of providing an overview of diverse approaches to beliefs and, in so doing, demonstrates how the belief construct or its analog might be identified. Empirical methods and findings from selected research programs and individual studies are summarized to illustrate the types of approaches used to investigate beliefs as well as to organize current knowledge in terms of both consistencies and contradictions in understanding of how beliefs influence children and mothers and fathers. In the final sections, a model of the belief complex is proposed as a means for defining and connecting the study of parental beliefs from a variety of different perspectives.

CURRENT CONCEPTUALIZATIONS AND RESEARCH

Interest in adult cognition has resulted in a reconceptualization of human behavior in general, and childrearing in particular, as influenced by cognition. Parents' cognitions can take many forms, however, and the study of beliefs is not driven by a single theoretical account of the formation and functioning of beliefs. As a result, current conceptualizations of beliefs vary considerably, and empirical research on beliefs can range from inclusion of several interview probes concerning beliefs about the importance of homework to children's knowledge acquisition to in-depth interviews concerning the nature of children and development in moral, social, cognitive, and personality domains.

In some instances, different labels for adult cognitions are used both within and between studies. The terms *belief, attitude, cognition, attribution, perception, idea,* and the like may be used interchangeably. There is also diversity in the specificity of the definitions, which can range from everyday use in reference to an opinion or idea to structural considerations, including notions of automatic versus controlled cognitions. Similarly, there is variability in the conceptualizations of the origin and function of beliefs relative to the parent who holds them, and about how these beliefs relate to other cognitions of the parent or to parents' affective states.

Some authors prefer to be inclusive and specify that a variety of types of cognitions are to be included and should not be further specified (Goodnow & Collins, 1990). In such cases, the tie that binds these terms together is the underlying premise of adult social cognition; that is, these are notions of reality held by parents about children (e.g., Goodnow, 1988; Miller, 1988). Other researchers are very specific in their definitions of beliefs, often separating affect or values from the central cognitive component, or delineating the theoretical basis as in the case of attributions or personal constructs (Dix, Ruble, & Zambarano, 1989; McGillicuddy-De Lisi, 1982a).

For the most part, however, the belief label is used but undefined in empirical studies. Assessments of knowledge about what a child can do, about developmental processes responsible for change in children's cognitive development or social competence, of attributions for success and failure on particular tasks, of parents' role in their children's lives, of educational goals, of typical or preferred ways of teaching or disciplining the child, of the nature of people in general and children in particular, are each studied as beliefs. There is typically little elaboration of why these ideas are called beliefs. The reason for this state of affairs is that the literature does not yield a generally acceptable term for belief, nor is there any agreed-upon taxonomy for differentiating among the various cognitive constructs that are included under the rubric of beliefs (Pajares, 1992; Sigel, 1985).

The range of cognitions assessed as beliefs necessitates an examination of either the theoretical basis or an explanation of the functioning of beliefs if we wish to understand how beliefs function for, within, and between persons. Beliefs become one set of constructs embedded in a larger model of the parenting process. Some reviews have categorized empirical studies topically (see Luster & Okagaki, 1993; Miller, 1988). The studies included in this chapter are organized on the basis of the researcher's theoretical perspective because it is from this vantage that investigators frame their theoretical conceptualization of beliefs and methodological strategies.

As social and behavioral scientists, we come to the study of any problem of interest with a commitment to some implicit or explicit theory of behavior and method of study. The topic of parent belief systems is no exception. Behaviorism, information processing, transactional approaches, constructivism, and psychoanalytic frameworks are among the major theoretical perspectives that reflect the orientation of researchers who seek to understand the forces that guide the course of a child's development. Because these are powerful ideas that guide the development of theory and method for studying parent beliefs, we organized our review of the empirical studies within each theoretical perspective. As we see, then, it is not the definition of belief that creates apparent discrepancies, but rather the model or theoretical framework in which it is embedded.[1]

We have identified four psychological conceptualizations in which the belief construct or its analog is embedded. The first of these is based on *attribution* theory. The second is based on *information-processing* models of cognition. The third approach can be summarized as a *constructivist* perspective, and the fourth as a *transactional* approach. General findings that are representative of current research within each perspective are summarized in the following section. The studies presented as exemplars of each of the categories are somewhat arbitrary because investigators often do not explicate their conceptual orientation and are sometimes eclectic in approach. Nevertheless, for our purposes, we believe that the four major perspectives listed here include most of the major theoretical orientations that have provided a framework for the study of parental beliefs.

Four conceptualizations of beliefs

Attribution approaches.   Many investigators assume that the parent, like any adult, is actively cognitive, making sense out of the world through causal attributions. The parent's attributions about causes of the child's (and perhaps her or his own) behavior either mediate or moderate the parent's behaviors (Weiner, 1985). In mediational models, the parent observes some event, makes an attribution about the event, and then responds to the event. In such cases the parent's cognition links the stimulus to the response. As a mediator, the attribution is a conduit to the behavior and operates similarly across individuals. Attributions function as moderators when the parent's cognitions affect the nature of the response in terms of degree and content of the response, transforming the effect of the stimulus by its operation. When attributions function as moderators, the parents' responses are differentially affected by the type of attribution or some aspect of the attribution. Origins of attributions are likely to be experiences with the child and the parent's own personal history that may predispose him or her toward particular types of attributions (e.g., internal/external, stable/unstable).

Dix and his colleagues (Dix & Grusec, 1985; Dix, Ruble, Grusec, & Nixon, 1986; Dix et al., 1989) have conducted several studies that examined mothers' causal attributions of children's misbehavior. Their results suggest that mothers form theories of discipline that take the child's age and ability into account. These attributions about causes of the child's behavior are related to the type of discipline strategies mothers report they would use to handle misbehavior. These authors suggested that when mothers think the child is capable and responsible for his or her own behavior, their choice of discipline strategies is more severe. Mothers' moods similarly appear to influence self-reported behaviors. Attributions are often viewed as mediating variables between the child's behavior as stimulus and the types of behaviors parents report during a interactions with their child.

---

[1]The shared meanings may only be on a surface level, but tacit meanings may not be shared. Thus constructions may function at two levels, a phenotypic and a genotypic one. The latter may be private and not necessarily shared (Polanyi, 1958; Sigel & Holmgren, 1983).

Several other investigators have examined individual differences in parents' causal attributions about children's school performance. For example, Parsons, Adler, and Kaczala (1982) and Holloway and Hess (1985) asked parents to indicate degrees of effort and ability that are responsible for children's school achievement. Parents' attributions, especially about mathematics achievement, tend to disfavor girls in that success is more likely to be attributed to effort than to ability (Eccles, 1987). Parental attributions are related to the child's self-concept and attributions of his or her own ability and likely future success.

Mothers' attributions about children's social and personality characteristics as well as their attributions about school achievements have been studied. Gretarsson and Gelfand (1988) reported that mothers' perceptions of their children showed a positive bias that was similar to findings of attributions about school performance and ability in the sense that parents think their own children are more capable, secure, and generally more mature than independent assessments indicate. These authors suggested that the mother's self-worth may be enhanced by this bias in appraising the child. In this case, the content of the attributions may help mothers feel capable as parents and in control of childrearing.

The literature on attributions generally suggests a mediational role for adult cognitions. Child behavior is appraised and childrearing practices depend on the outcomes of that appraisal (Dix & Grusec, 1985). There is considerable variability in causal attributions, which vary with culture (Hess & McDevitt, 1986), the child's gender (Parsons et al., 1982), the child's age and the parents' mood (Dix et al., 1986). Mothers (and occasionally fathers) of children ranging from preschool through high school have been studied, usually in a questionnaire format (but occasionally by interview). Attributions are presumed to influence children because they influence discipline and affective-motivational behaviors of parents, and may benefit parents through protection of self-esteem and provide some sense of coherence to others' behaviors (Dix & Grusec, 1985; Holloway & Machida, 1992).

Information-processing models.   A second framework is provided by information-processing (I-P) models of cognition. Within these models, parental cognitions are most likely to be conceptualized as mediating factors that filter experiences with the child into strategies for parental practices. Particular aspects of the child's behavior have more salience, for example, and are therefore likely to be attended to as the parent processes information and makes evaluations of the child. These evaluations then guide behavioral responses. The parent is seen as an active processor of information within this theoretical framework. Affective processes may or may not be included as additional mediators of responses in an I-P model. Cognitive-mediational models are sometimes viewed as specific examples of information-processing approaches to cognition.

Rubin and Mills (Mills & Rubin, 1990; Rubin & Mills, 1992; Rubin, Mills, & Rose-Krasnor, 1989) described an information-processing model of parental beliefs in relation to children's social competence. Within this model, parents set socialization goals for their children that guide their socialization strategies. These are known as proactive behaviors. When the child fails to meet those goals, reactive behavior strategies are employed. The parent's behavior is not only influenced by socioecological and personal-social setting factors (such as socioeconomic status and age), but parents make appraisals about the child's personality, about the quality of the parent–child relationship, about why the child might be off-time, and which strategy they think is most effective given the problem behavior. Affective responses to children's behaviors appear to moderate the belief-strategy connection. The parental response derived from the belief will be influenced by how strongly the parent feels about the child's behavior/skill. Child behaviors that are viewed as more negatively or as problems will most likely receive more rapid and extreme behavioral responses from the parent.

The research by Rubin and Mills and their collaborators differs from that of others who also take an information-processing perspective in that their focus is on children's social competence rather than on intellectual development, academic achievement, or problem solving. Rubin and Mills' research program also includes longitudinal investigations of mothers' beliefs on a sample of 45 parents of children in a narrow age range (4–6 years over the period of the follow-up). Beliefs remained stable over the 2-year period. Changes that were observed included a decrease in the mothers' need to seek out more information, a lower likelihood of explaining behavior through age-related factors, and a belief that maladaptive behavior would be handled directly by the mother rather than be ignored. In the follow-up study, mothers advocated strategies that relied on the child's own observational learning rather than on direct instruction from adults more often. The parent may view the older child as less in need of direct adult tutelage except when there is a behavior problem. These findings suggest that even if parents' beliefs are relatively stable over time, some aspects of beliefs appear open to change as a result of the child's developing capabilities or as a result of increasing experience with the particular child.

Rubin and Mills (1992) suggested that many of the changes in mothers' beliefs result from increased knowledge of their own child's characteristic patterns and abilities. As a result, the mother may be less compelled to seek additional information. Her behavior may, in fact, stem more from her beliefs at this point as they are based on much information gleaned over the child's early years. This is in agreement with Holloway and Hess' (1985) finding that mothers rely on historical information to make attributions about their children's behavior and performance in school as well.

The I-P model has also been applied by researchers who are interested in how beliefs direct attention, whether or not beliefs make some information more salient than others, and how memories that are influenced by beliefs influence the interpretation of presently observed behaviors and the generation of strategies in relation to children's development in other domains as well. For example, Goodnow, Cashmore, Cotton, and Knight (1984) studied parent ideas about household tasks and developmental timetables from such an information-processing approach. Holden's (1988) finding that nonparents required more information to solve a childrearing problem than parents suggests that adult cognitive processing about child states and behaviors is affected by learning and experience in a manner that is consistent with information-processing accounts of problem-solving behavior (also see Holden & Zambarano, 1992).

Information-processing studies of maternal behaviors in general suggest that the content and reliance on specific types of information may change as the child develops, but that the general processing functions, and many of the beliefs themselves, evidence stability over time. There is some indication that, with increasing experience as a parent in general and with experience with a particular child, information necessary prior to making decisions or solve problems in childrearing decreases. Processing becomes more efficient and less reliant on specific information.

The role of beliefs within information-processing models is similar to that of cognition in attribution models in that the beliefs mediate between external events (e.g., the child's behavior or a socioecological setting) and parenting strategies. Affect plays a role in some of the attribution and some of the information-processing models. Most of the studies conducted within an information-processing approach rely on questionnaires, although some interview data and some creative paradigms examining decision-making processes have been employed (e.g. Holden, 1988). Mothers of preschool children serve as subjects most often, but parents of infants and of young school-age children have also participated. With the exception of the longitudinal data reported by Rubin and Mills (1992), comparisons of beliefs of parents of children in different age groups have not been a focus of research conducted within the information-processing framework. Finally, most attribution models include some reference to information-processing mechanisms (e.g., attention, memory), and most information-processing models include causal attributions as one step in the mental processing that leads to a particular behavior. Thus, there is considerable overlap in the constructs researchers refer to as they describe the role of beliefs within either attribution or information-processing models.

Constructivist perspectives. The third conception of parental beliefs—constructivist perspectives—differs from attribution and information-processing models in that the parents' cognitions are not viewed as mediators between environmental factors and parenting strategies, but as the starting point for all experiences the parent has with the child. Beliefs are the guides to action, having been constructed in the course of experiencing interaction with children and adults throughout life.

Beliefs about children are viewed as analogous to Kelly's (1955) personal constructs, derived from experience and used to predict others' behaviors and guide one's own behaviors (Applegate, Burke, Burleson, Delia, & Kline, 1985; Applegate, Burleson, & Delia, 1992; Johnson & Martin, 1985; McGillicuddy-De Lisi, 1982b; Sigel, 1985). Throughout life, each individual has been creating an idea of what a child is, how children change, and what causes development at the same time that other beliefs about the nature of humanity, the nature of the universe, ideas about God and religion, values, and the like, are constructed. These are not necessarily adopted from the teaching of others, although the parent may interpret and transform beliefs about children from a variety of experiences, including expert advice, observation of other parents, and observation of children other than their own (McGillicuddy-De Lisi, 1980; Okagaki & Divecha, 1993). Beliefs are created from an internal organization of experience into a coherent system.

This process will also involve the individual coming to develop shared meanings that evolve through social dialogue and exposure to culturally based ethnotheories. To the extent that meanings are shared, we communicate and function in a social contexts. To the extent that meanings are not shared, there may be cultural and/or social-psychological gaps between people or individuals (see Footnote 1).

Experiences in everyday interactions with others serve to confirm some beliefs and challenge others. Particular parenting strategies are presumed to derive from the system of beliefs of the parent. For example, parents who believe that children are empty vessels waiting to be filled with knowledge will be more likely to instruct their children verbally when teaching rather than encouraging self-discovery through questioning or demonstrations (McGillicuddy-De Lisi, 1982a).

Research within this perspective has demonstrated a low but significant relation between number of children and beliefs, providing support (in addition to that derived from research conducted within an I-P model) for the notion that parenting experience is related to beliefs, although this relation could exist for a variety of reasons other than construction of beliefs through experience with children. Moderate relations have been found between the ways that parents communicate with their children within studies generated under communication and under distancing theory (Applegate et al., 1985, 1992; McGillicuddy-De Lisi, 1982a; Sigel, 1982).

There is some factor analytic support for the notion that these beliefs are mentally organized into a coherent system that is somewhat similar for mothers and for fathers. This appears to be true for beliefs concerning processes responsible for both children's cognitive development (McGillicuddy-De Lisi, 1982a) and for children's personal-social development (McGillicuddy-De Lisi, 1992). Sigel, Stinson, and Flaugher's (1991) factor analyses of an interview assessing different types of knowledge revealed three groups of ideas about development: sociomoral, physical, and intrapersonal. Parents' beliefs about how children learned in each of these domains varied, as did parents' instructional behaviors during interactions with their children (Sigel, Stinson, & Kim, 1993).

Although many studies of parents' beliefs have focused on mothers, a series of studies that included mothers and fathers (McGillicuddy-De Lisi, 1985, 1992; Sigel, 1992) suggests that mothers and fathers hold different constructs of developmental processes to be responsible for children's cognitive development to differing degrees. Fathers are more likely than mothers to refer to constructs such as readiness, innate characteristics, and positive and negative feedback than mothers. In studies of processes responsible for social-personality development, mothers endorsed nearly every type of developmental construct more than fathers did (McGillicuddy-De Lisi, 1992). It was suggested that mothers have been socialized into the parenting role more intensely than fathers, which may have led to more reflection and acceptance of alternative explanations of development on the part of mothers.

Parents' beliefs have also been found to differ with the gender of their children. Simons et al. (1992) reported that adolescent children come to know their parents' beliefs about children and about childrearing from the parents' practices over time. These relations between occurrence and knowledge of parental beliefs were somewhat stronger for girls than for boys. Different socialization experiences in which girls are encouraged to devote more thought to children and to childrearing, and perhaps to be more invested in the outcomes, were considered as a possible source of significant gender differences among the adolescents. These gender differences may be a precursor to those observed when beliefs of mothers and fathers are compared. Furthermore, the relation of beliefs to behaviors has been shown to vary for mothers and fathers. In more than one study, fathers beliefs were shown to relate more strongly to observed teaching behaviors than mothers' beliefs (McGillicuddy-De Lisi, 1982b; Sigel, McGillicuddy-De Lisi, Flaugher, & Rock, 1983).

In summary, the review of samples studied within the constructivist perspective reveals that mothers and fathers of preschool and school-age children are studied most often, but there have been several studies of adolescents as well (Simons et al., 1992; Youniss, DeSantis, & Henderson, 1992). Data collection procedures include both questionnaires and interviews, but interview procedures appear to be preferred by investigators using a constructivist perspective because they provide an opportunity to assess parents' beliefs in more depth and detail (Miller, 1988; Sigel, 1986).

Transactional perspectives.   Within transactional models, the parent brings particular cognitions and behaviors to social exchanges and interactions with others. In some models, beliefs are created through the transaction between culture/society and the individual, whereas in other models, beliefs are created through the course of social interchanges between individuals. In the case of coconstructivism and some Vygotskian models, the cognitive outcomes of interactions may be attributable to similar processes, although some coconstructivist models link collective cultures (e.g., traditional), and personal (individual) cultures through such a process (Okagaki & Divecha, 1993). We have included several approaches to beliefs under the rubric of transactional perspectives because they have their basis in social interactions. There are important differences in approaches that are based on transactions between individual and society and those based on transactions among individuals, however, and subsequent work may make it necessary to consider the differences so salient that these should no longer be grouped together.

Studies conducted by Lightfoot and Valsiner (1992), Valsiner (1989), Palacios (1990), and Palacios, Gonzalez, and Moreno (1992) are consistent with transactional perspective because beliefs are viewed as existing within the culture, but they are then constructed by the individual through the person's interaction with that culture. Palacios explained that the cultural and individual experiential basis of these constructions may be weighted differently for different parents, given their particular place in the developing society. Palacios identified traditional (rural, low education, pessimistic expectations, innatist beliefs), modern (urban, high education, beliefs include aspects of nature and nurture in interaction, parents can influence development), and paradoxical (low-medium education, belief in environmental determinism, not view parent as major influence on developmental outcomes) types of parents that result from the parent's own life organization. Each parent then creates a life organization that affects the child's development. Palacios provided data that support the assumption that parental constructs of ideas are interwoven with the culture and representations of the child are constructed through transactions with that culture.

Sameroff and Feil (1985), Sameroff and Fiese (1992), Dekovi and Gerris (1992), Dekovi (1992), and Dekovi, Gerris, and Janssens (1991) studied the complexity of parents' concepts of development from a somewhat different transactional perspective. This work centers on definition of the parent–child interactions utilizing a bidirectional model of effects in interpersonal relationships. The work conducted by Dekovi and her colleagues is similar to that of Sameroff and his colleagues in that both focus on levels of reasoning that represent different ways a parent can understand their relationship with the child. Dekovi employed the construct of "parental reasoning complexity." Four levels of reasoning range from a self-centered, self-orientation of the parent to a process orientation, which represents a mutual interactive relationship. Higher parental reasoning complexity levels were related to authoritative parenting, whereas lower level reasoning complexity was related to authoritarian practices. Further, the parenting practices associated with lower reasoning complexity were also related to negative outcomes in terms of children's self-esteem and popularity among peers.

Sameroff and Feil (1985) maintained that levels of reasoning complexity function through a connectedness with many other dimensions of the caregiving environment to have an impact on children. These levels are derived from a system analogous to Piagetian cognitive stages. Levels range from nonreflective views of children's development to a perspective where the parent can take the point of view of the child. Parents' understanding of children's development becomes increasingly complex with each level. In addition to focusing on parents' levels of reasoning, Sameroff and Fiese (1992) acknowledged the need to offer a more comprehensive array of social and familial factors that serve to regulate the interactions between parents and children. Their model includes culture as a regulatory context. Other regulatory codes are expressed in family paradigms, which are beliefs about the social world, and family myths, which influence family processes. Family narratives and rituals complete the family cultural code that regulates transactions among family members. For these authors, parent beliefs serve a central regulatory function within the family code.

Bugental and her colleagues (Bugental, 1992; Bugental, Blue, & Cruzcosa, 1989; Bugental & Shennum, 1984) and Iverson and Segal (1992) also presented beliefs as originating out of interpersonal interactions, but they did not focus on stageslike levels of adult reasoning. Cognitions are classified as two types: automatic and conscious or intentional: (1) *Automatic cognitions* are caregiving schema that may not be subject to conscious awareness; these are triggered by the child's behavior acting as an eliciting stimulus. (2) *Conscious* or *intentional cognitions* are reflective and deliberate. Within the models proposed by both Bugental and her colleagues and by Iverson and Segal, what the parent and child each brings to the situation affects the parents' behaviors. Beliefs are important because the mothers' cognitions moderate the transactional process. A critical aspect of maternal cognitions that has been repeatedly identified in Bugental's work with children at risk for abuse is the mothers' sense of control.

Simons, Whitbeck, Conger, and Melby (1990) conducted a study that included beliefs as one determinant of mothers' and fathers' parenting behavior. Hypotheses were presented in terms of social learning and exchange theory. However, the explanation of beliefs as derived simultaneously from the nature of the parent–child and the mother-father relationships, as well as hypotheses that the degree of perceived control is salient in determining parental practices, is consistent with Bugental's framework and reflects a transactional approach as well, and for these reasons it is included within the transactional category. Simons et al. reported that factors such as beliefs about parenting efficacy, beliefs about the degree of impact of parenting on child outcomes, views of the marital relationship, beliefs of the spouse, perceptions of the child, level of depression, marital satisfaction, education, and degree of financial distress are each related to parenting behaviors. As was the case in comparisons of the belief-behavior relation conducted within the constructivist perspective, the relation of parenting behavior to beliefs varied with gender. For example, the belief that parenting has important effects on child development was significantly related to the behavior of fathers, but not to the behavior of mothers. Marital satisfaction, on the other hand, was related to mothers' behaviors with the child, but not to fathers' behaviors.

As these studies indicate, there are two general approaches to the study of parental beliefs within the transactional perspective. The first focuses on how interactions with the culture provide representations of children. There are elements of coconstructivism in some of these analyses, creating some overlap with constructivist perspectives in assumptions and in the types of questions addressed empirically and theoretically (e.g., Lightfoot & Valsiner, 1992). In addition, some investigators include elements of a dialectic adopted from Vygotsky's writings (Palacios et al., 1992; Valsiner & Van der Veer, 1993). Unlike most of the research conducted within the attribution and information-processing approach, the primary target of interest is the parent and the nature of his or her thinking, although some investigators link those beliefs to child outcomes. As a result of the transactional perspective focus on the parent's place in the society or culture, however, the age of the child seems less important and children are sometimes not even included as participants in these studies.

The second type of transactional approach focuses upon the relationship and mutual exchanges that exist between parent and child, as was the case in research conducted by collaborators of Sameroff, of Dekovi, and of Bugental. Within each of these approaches, the parent and the child come to the interaction with some history that affects their relationship and the cognitions that moderate their interactions. There is emphasis on infancy across many of these studies, although parents of preschool and school-age children have also been studied from a transactional perspective. Simons et al. (1990) focused on parents of children in early adolescence and viewed the interaction as a function of the values and beliefs about proper parenting that are brought to the interaction by the adolescent as well as those brought by the parent (although adolescent beliefs were not examined). Finally, the children studied within the transactional perspective are more often from an at-risk or abused/neglected population in these studies. Bugental, Sameroff, and Iverson and Segal have each studied families of abused, neglected, or at-risk infants and Simons et al. focused on constructive versus destructive parenting practices.

The transactional approach is quite different from the attribution and information-processing approaches in that transactional approaches rely heavily on social context and interactions in the description of beliefs. The transactional and the constructivist views are consistent with one another in their assumptions that adults are active processors of information, but the potential for change in beliefs for the individual parent is different under the two perspectives. Within the transactional perspective, the individual adopts practices and views of the child that predominate and are assumed to be true in the larger community and by those generations who have reared children before. These ideas are somewhat more static, less open to change, and are relatively stable over time. For the constructing adult who is creating his or her own reality on the basis of experiences, forming predictions, testing, reorganizing on the basis of discrepant information, beliefs about children may change at any point in the individual's life. In fact they are likely to change during adulthood as the child passes through childhood and creates discrepancies for the parent. Both the constructivist and the transactional approaches to beliefs differ from other perspectives in the ways that beliefs may change. The constructivist and transactional model each suggests an ongoing dynamic between parents' internal cognitions and the outer world in which they behave that is more reciprocal than information-processing and attribution models. Within both the transactional and constructivist positions, beliefs are not a result of accumulation, or adoption from another person or society. Nor are beliefs molded or created through isolated self-reflection. Beliefs, at every point in time, hold the potential to be transformed, created, and reorganized with every experience.

Conclusions Concerning Conceptualizations of Beliefs

These four major conceptualizations of parental beliefs have many features in common. These include a view of cognition at the core of beliefs, of parents as mentally active in their consideration of children, of experiences with children as important in the formation of those beliefs, and of beliefs as an important determinant of parental practices. The review of empirical findings within the four perspectives revealed evidence of some convergent validity in reports of similar findings across studies conducted within different perspectives.

On the other hand, differences in the four theoretical approaches to beliefs have led to variability in how beliefs are defined, what domains of beliefs are investigated, what types of samples are studied, what types of assessments are used, the types of functions and effects of beliefs that are examined, and the place of parent beliefs in the family context. The differences in definitions, theoretical underpinnings, and approaches are important because they influence the selection of the content of beliefs to be studied and they influence views of how these beliefs are related to other cognitions, to affect, and the implications for change in beliefs as the adult develops as a parent. This diversity of perspective and of methods is positive in many respects, increasing the breadth of cognitions that are studied and providing some convergent validity information.

The study of beliefs has moved forward in the past 15 years in part because beliefs have been amenable to investigation from this variety of perspectives, and in part because beliefs provide a useful way to conceptualize intersections among family members, development as a result of reciprocal interactions, and the ways in which parenting is embedded within cultures. Nevertheless, it is distressing that the same issues (e.g., belief-behavior relations, the role of affect, the origins of beliefs, the effects of beliefs, the structure of beliefs) are examined and reexamined in isolation within each perspective; that consideration of gender, social class, race, ethnic, and cultural differences are not incorporated into the whole range of research programs; that self-report data predominate almost to the exclusion of other methods; that the primary statistical tool is some type of correlational analysis that allows for minimal inferences as to the nature of observed statistical relationships without addressing the source of the commonality; that beliefs of parents of school-age and adolescent children are seldom studied; and that conceptualization of beliefs is surprisingly adevelopmental from both the perspective of developing parents and developing children (Fincham & Bradbury, 1987). The diversity of perspectives has led to ambiguous and vague definitions of the belief construct that has hindered shared meaning within and across specialties and theoretical orientations. It is our contention that each aspect of adult cognition that has been studied under the four major theoretical perspectives is indeed an aspect of beliefs, but these different cognitions are not isomorphic with one another. They are, in our view, each an indicator of a complex of beliefs. Because beliefs have great potential impact on parents and children through the functions of organizing perceptions and ideas, providing a source of parenting strategies, affecting the individual's appraisal of their own parenting, and influencing the cognitive, social, and personality development of children, the more we can elaborate the components of this complex, the more we will come to understand the nature of the influence of beliefs. An initial attempt to describe the belief complex is presented, followed by suggestions for its use in research.

THE BELIEF COMPLEX

Rationale and Preliminary Definition

In the foregoing model, described as the belief complex, we build on the research derived from the four current conceptualizations of beliefs, incorporating the various components into a single unit with interrelated parts. It is hoped that the belief complex will provide a means for locating research that utilizes some definition of belief in relation to other studies and definitions. A clarification of the multiple but overlapping aspects of beliefs that exist in the literature should result in a more coherent view of the functioning of beliefs. In addition, the interrelations among definitions and findings can become more readily accessible to investigators working from diverse theoretical perspectives, and yet each component can maintain its integrity. In this manner, both the breadth and depth of investigations that are a strong point of research in this area can be preserved.

We refer to this model as the belief complex because each component is connected to the other components through a core cognitive component. A single core cognitive component is not presumed to be shared by all aspects of the belief complex. Rather, each component is related to a presumed underlying cognitive aspect of beliefs. For example, attributions and constructions are each presumed to be cognitions, but the nature of the cognitions differs and therefore their applications differ. The belief complex accommodates both attributions and constructions, however. The thinking parent may make attributions about the causes of children's behavior and may construct beliefs about developmental processes responsible for concept formation. These two aspects are each connected to the core cognitive component, but the connection differs for constructions and for attributions. Attributions are inferences about an observed behavior. They are more singular and connected to a preceding external event than a construction about the nature of the child, which is a result of an internal organization of experiences with children. The belief complex is an interdependent and interactive system of components that in their totality impact parents' practices and policies regarding development, not only in the home, but also in the broader social context—school, church, neighborhood, and family network.

There are those who argue that to engage in this task of exploring the nature of beliefs is an exercise in articulating a folk psychology and that beliefs are not truly suitable subjects for scientific study.

For example, Stich (1983) rejected the usefulness of beliefs altogether when he asserted that " … the concept of belief … ought not to play a significant role in a science aimed at explaining human cognition and behavior" (p. 5). Bruner (1990), on the other hand, justified the use of "beliefs, intentions and desires" as legitimate objects of scientific study. He wrote:

> … folk psychology, though it changes, does not get displaced by scientific paradigms. For it deals with the nature, causes, and consequences of those intentional states—beliefs, desires, intentions, commitments—that most scientific psychology dismisses in its effort to explain human action from a point of view that is outside human subjectivity. … Antimentalist fury about folk-psychology simply misses the point. The idea of jettisoning it in the interest of getting rid of mental states in our everyday explanations of human behavior is tantamount to throwing away the very phenomena that psychology needs to explain. It is in terms of folk-psychological categories that we experience ourselves and others. It is through folk psychology that people anticipate and judge one another, draw conclusions about the worthwhileness of their lives, and so on. (pp. 14–15)

The point of this discussion is to place parental beliefs into the legitimate context of empirical study and to untangle some of the complexity regarding the relationships between parents and children in the context of the family. The elaboration of the belief complex is guided and encouraged by Bruner's admonition that ignoring the relevance of beliefs, intentions, and desires ignores phenomena that move people in everyday life.

In order to understand the structure of beliefs and how they function, it is necessary to deconstruct the complex and determine the nature of the components and how they interact. We believe that conceptualization of beliefs as deconstruction with identified entities results in a model that can encompass and accommodate the constructivist view of developmental processes, beliefs about the parent's role in children's development, attributions about the causes of children's behavior and abilities, and how perceived experiences are organized and interpreted within the information-processing system of the parent.

This approach differs from the current literature on beliefs in two ways. First, previous studies of parent beliefs use the term belief in its everyday sense with no explicit definition, referring to different aspects of the belief complex as if these aspects are not different from one another in a salient way. Such vagueness allows readers of those studies to infer any meaning they wish. If one intends to pursue the study of the beliefs in terms of function, development, stability, and change, it is necessary to elucidate a conceptual model of beliefs as a first step. Second, there is generally little coherence to the body of findings on beliefs. Because it is not clear what constitutes consistent or contradictory findings, there is no way to connect one body of research to another. Some initial ways to connect approaches and findings across theoretical perspectives are attempted.[2]

Components of the Belief Complex

The components of the complex are *cognitive content, structure, source, function, and relation to affect, intention, and value.* We are indebted to the work of many social psychologists, most notably Ajzen and Fishbein (Ajzen & Fishbein, 1980; Fishbein & Azjen, 1975), who provided a means of organizing aspects of adult social cognition. These components of the belief complex encompass the relevant features that enable the identification of aspects of beliefs that influence the parents' development qua parent. In addition, we should be able to assess relations between parents' beliefs and behaviors, and the relation between parent beliefs and children's developmental outcomes.

---

[2]We have attempted to put aside our own belief in constructivist approaches to advocate a model in which several cognitive orientations can be understood in relation (and at time, juxtaposition) to one another. The reader should understand, however, that our Western, technological, constructivist origins frame our approach to issues even as we struggle to coordinate multiple perspectives.

Cognition.   Beliefs are cognitions. Beliefs must be defined first in terms of cognition because— "the term 'cognition' refers to all the processes by which the sensory input [our concept of experience] is transformed, reduced, elaborated, stored, recovered, and used" (Neisser, 1966, p. 4). Cognition can be employed in reference to engagement with any particular object, event, or experience. This definition is *not* synonymous with attributions, perceptions, or perspectives. These labels share the notion that each of these concepts *reflects* a cognitive process, but our argument is that these constructs refer to different aspects of cognition and are therefore not interchangeable. Attributions are derived from such beliefs. Perceptions are inferences that are based on such beliefs in conjunction with elements of the information inherent in the information to be processed. Perspectives result from a consolidation or activation of interrelated beliefs.

The distinctive conceptual feature of beliefs is that they are knowledge based, derived from experience with objects, events, or persons, and are accepted as truth. Belief has been defined previously as " ... knowledge in the sense that the individual knows that what he (or she) espouses is true or probably true, and evidence may or may not be deemed necessary; or if evidence is used, it forms a basis for the belief but is not the belief itself" (Sigel, 1985, p. 348). Knowledge is the major cognitive dimension of beliefs. At issue here is that the individual knows about any of a number of child development factors: knowledge of child development states, knowledge concerning the nature of the child, knowledge of developmental processes, and confidence or certainty in one's own knowledge. The knowledge may or may not be veridical. The important point is that the individual presumes the knowledge and its consequence—its truth value. Knowledge is the base from which subsequent dimensions flow. It is therefore a conception of reality.

The content of beliefs in the context of parenting is therefore to know some aspect of the child and development. From this knowledge is derived a system of causal attributions regarding the child's behaviors; from this knowledge, attention is directed toward assimilation of some relevant information and disregard of contradictory or irrelevant information, given the knowledge; reflection on such knowledge will lead to controlled cognitions and planful behavior; knowledge that is deeply processed and routinized, easily activated, will be automatized; knowledge derived across many customs of childrearing will be organized into categories or ethnotheories that shape attention and interpretation of parental roles vis-à-vis the child (Bornstein, 1991). Thus, the content of beliefs is knowledge, accepted as truth by the parent. All other "ideas" (types of beliefs) flow into or out of this most basic component of the belief complex.

Beliefs as a structure.   The knowledges that are beliefs are organized in domains. Beliefs vary with domains of knowledge of the exogenous and endogenous environments. These translate into knowledge about the environment including the history of one's culture. Beliefs are organized schemas, bounded and coherent. If this is the case, identification of the contents and boundaries of belief schemas have to be addressed. For example, we have found that some parents believe children learn about the physical world through exploration and experimentation. Others believe that children acquire such knowledge through didactic instruction. The *content* of beliefs in children's physical knowledge domain as defined by the parent will vary from parent to parent, in terms of the parents' beliefs. However, both parents believe that children learn about moral-social concepts through didactic instruction. Thus the content and the relation among the different domains (i.e., the *boundaries* of the beliefs) varied for these two parents (Sigel, 1992).

The relation among such schema will vary among cultures as well as among individuals within the culture. For example, in a theocratic environment there may be no separation among religion, science, politics, leisure activities, or education. Beliefs regarding the nature of the child will be integrally related to those dealing with moral principles. In a secular society the relation between religion and daily life may be quite separate with rules of behavior varying among families and persons.

The boundaries may also vary in permeability, depending on commitment the parent has to that belief and the content of the domain (knowledge) and the interconnections among the domains. The nature of the boundaries is the aspect of beliefs that is assessed when attention is focused on the parents' confidence in their beliefs and when interrelatedness of beliefs is examined and within many cross-cultural or comparative studies of beliefs. Many of the studies conducted within the four psychological perspectives—information processing, attribution, constructivist, and transactional— are consistent with such a structural definition. For example, the attribution studies delineated some aspects of the boundaries of beliefs when the mother's moods and the child's intentionality were found to influence the content of beliefs activated to drive behavioral responses (Dix, 1992). When relations among beliefs pertaining to development of moral, physical, and intrapersonal knowledge were investigated within the constructivist perspective, boundaries of beliefs were the target of analysis (Sigel et al., 1991). The focus of analysis depends on the purpose of the research and the theoretical approach to a great degree. Nevertheless, the cognitive organization of beliefs is relevant within each of the four perspectives. Acknowledgement of the boundaries of beliefs (vs. a focus on content, e.g.) clarifies both the nature of the research and the meaningfulness of the findings. Further, the degree of openness of the boundaries may depend on the affective strength of those boundaries. We have more to say about this when we address the role of affect in the belief complex.

In addition, beliefs are organized on some categorical dimension, because they are in fact concepts or cognitions. At one level these can be traditional categories that are labeled by the culture: beliefs about children, beliefs about families, beliefs about politics, beliefs about spirituality, and so forth. These categories may form a system that provides some coherence relative to one's view of the world and one's place in it. Differences among beliefs may produce conflict, with the potential for growth and greater understanding through resolution of the differences, or may have deleterious effects if contradictions are not dealt with constructively. In the former case, the individual may have achieved a certain harmony among beliefs, whereas in the latter there is reason to expect tension and disharmony, precluding a coherent and even satisfying sense of parenting. This definition of belief and its structure are applicable to any belief organization including those of parents.

The source of beliefs.   We have argued that beliefs are constructed from experience, broadly defined, and are held as absolute or probabilistic truth. This constructivist perspective is unlikely to be adopted by researchers using some of the other approaches. Yet, attention should be devoted to sources of beliefs because developmental issues with respect to parental cognition will not be addressed otherwise. There are some general characteristics of the origins of beliefs that are consistent within a variety of approaches to the belief complex. For example, within each perspective, beliefs emerge from social exchanges of some kind—with children, other parents, peers, societal institutions, word media. In fact, in our modern culture, there is a host of events that provides the grist for the constructivist mill of the individual at every age and in every setting. Such experiences are among the sources of information processed within the information-processing system, and reflect opportunities for transactions with others or coconstructions, and orient us toward particular causal attributions. The knowledge that comprises beliefs can be viewed as internalizations or imitations that are acquired, stored, and used within the information-processing system, for example. Research conducted within each theoretical perspective must address issues regarding how such knowledge is acquired and stored. How do processing/perceptual inference/decision making change with new or discrepant experiences? Do controlled cognitions become automatic? If so, through what mechanism? In their review of sources of influence on parents' beliefs, Okagaki and Divecha (1993) concluded that future research must examine influences on both acquisition and developmental change in beliefs. An understanding of both structure and function requires that each perspective address the issue of where beliefs come from.

The acquisition of beliefs is a developmental process where development refers to the acquisition and transformation of knowledge over time and place. The child develops beliefs constrained by range of experience and intellectual competence. The parent as a mature adult has already developed a set of beliefs about many aspects of the world. The child's and the parent's acquisition of new knowledge is therefore a function of already established beliefs. The development of beliefs can be thought of as a spiral that evolves with each set of experiences assimilated into the ongoing complex of beliefs. The way these experiences are processed in part depends on the individuals' emotional receptivity to experience and level of comprehension of meaning of events and actions. Within constructivist and transactional perspectives, this process of knowledge acquisition is not additive. Beliefs are constructed, leading to internal organizations of experiences. Some of these cognitive organizations are shared among members of a society, and others are unique to the individual. Idiosyncratic beliefs are the products of particular personal experiences. The salience of shared social beliefs may also vary from individual to individual, because the incorporation of new experiences into existing schema will depend on a number of factors such as cognition, affect, and value within the belief complex.

In terms of Bronfenbrenner's (1979) ecosystem approach, it is apparent that some important sources of beliefs for all individuals reside in the individual's microsystem. Personal experiences, especially social exchanges and observations of events involving children, as well as experience as a child, contribute to knowledge about children's and parents' roles and responsibilities in relation to child development. These experiences must be, at minimum, consistent with the culture because they are embedded and were created within the macroculture. For some experiences, little internal organization or transformation may be necessary in the process of belief formation. Such knowledges are akin to automatic cognitions for information-processing theorists (Bugental, 1992), praxis beliefs for constructivists (Sigel, 1986), co-constructed realities for transactional approaches (Lightfoot & Valsiner, 1992), and modeled attribution styles for attribution approaches (Kelley, 1971; Weiner, 1985).

In addition, beliefs are probabilistic. In the course of acquiring beliefs, the individual learns that knowledge is not necessarily fixed and immutable, nor are the derived beliefs necessarily fixed. The degree to which an individual holds a proposition to be true can vary in strength or confidence. In quantitative terms, the range can be from 100 percent (such as, "I believe that when one lets go of an object on earth, the chances are 100 percent that it will fall, depending on certain conditions") to 0 percent (such as "I believe that I can run a 2-minute mile, although I have not trained"). The qualifications indicate that some truths are not absolute, but the certainty depends on the conditions, such as setting, material, or oxygen level. Some beliefs may be held as absolute and are not subject to change even with contradictory evidence (e.g., "God exists"). Scientific beliefs (e.g., "black holes exist") are often held as probability statements and the probability may shift with new or additional information or experiences.

Functions of beliefs.   Beliefs serve comparable functions for everyone, irrespective of culture, although the particular content of beliefs may vary with particular historical or present aspects of the culture (LeVine, 1988). Our contention is that beliefs serve a primary adaptive function enabling the individual to meet sociocultural requirements and cognitive demands. Beliefs enable adults to organize their world in a psychologically consistent manner, make predictions, perceive similarities, and relate new experiences to past ones (Kelly, 1955). In addition, beliefs provide parents with a means for setting parenting priorities, evaluating success in parenting as well as a means of preserving self-efficacy (Goodnow & Collins, 1990). Beliefs can serve as a source of parental teaching and management behaviors, influencing the child's intellectual and personal-social development. To the extent that these parenting strategies reflect beliefs that can be inferred by the child, the parent's behavior also becomes more predictable and understandable to the child, decreasing stress and providing a model for interpreting everyday events (McGillicuddy-De Lisi, 1985).

Within the functional perspective of beliefs espoused here, beliefs are necessary conditions for adaptation to life as a parent. Beliefs organize our world, providing a sense of certainty about what will happen. It is because we all believe the sun will rise tomorrow that we do not go to sleep anxious about the world surviving. We believe that we can understand the world to some extent, we can make decisions, we can engage in life activities, we can act. All beliefs may not be held with the same degree of certainty. In the context of childrearing these probabilistic variations may temper the degree to which beliefs are consistently connected to action.

Although the functions of beliefs are basically to make life easier for the cognizing parent, beliefs can be seen to have different effects, some for the parent and some the child. For example, the parent may be uncomfortable when contradictions arise between beliefs that are held as truths and contrary beliefs espoused by others. Discomfort and doubt may arise when contradictions in the content of beliefs makes it difficult to organize them into a structure. On the other hand, beliefs may be a source of comfort when problems are attributed to factors not under parental influence, or when attributions of a job well done follow successes in parenting. In addition, beliefs are a source of parenting practices. This may be conscious, in the sense that parents may reflect on the goals that they wish to accomplish in handling a specific situation and may select one strategy over another or even create a new way to handle the situation. On the other hand, the belief-behavior may be automatic or unconscious, as when practices are reflections of deep-seated assumptions about the child promulgated by the culture.

And last, there are many outcomes for the child. The child's environment, both interpersonal and physical, will be created within the context of the content of the parent's beliefs. These experiences will influence the child in the specific sense of exerting an influence over cognitive and personal-social development, and in a general sense in that the child will find that the parent's behavior is more organized and coherent across contexts, and cognitive demands on the child are therefore reduced. The child's world is more predictable, for example, when the parent's behaviors reflect the organization of some beliefs. Finally, the child may perceive and understand that these beliefs exist, perhaps even adopting them as his or her own.

Relation of beliefs to affect.   Goodnow (1988) proposed that there are two general positions regarding the relation between parents' ideas about children and parents' feelings: (1) that affect shapes thinking or (2) that ideas shape affect. Other researchers who have explored the relation between cognition and affect add three other approaches that can apply to current research on parental beliefs. These are that: (3) Affect and cognitions exert reciprocal influences on one another, (4) ideas and emotions form two separate but parallel systems, and (5) cognition and affect are fused and indissociable (see Sigel, 1986). Each of these positions has its advocates in the literature. No single perspective covers all the exigencies in the complex interplay of affect and beliefs, and the relation between affect and cognition can best be conceptualized as a changing one, dependent on many situational factors, regardless of the research model undertaken. However, all ideas have a degree of appeal and are somewhat pleasant or unpleasant. This may occur because there always some degree of affect, however minimal, in the social contexts in which beliefs emerge. We prefer to think of affect as entwined with cognition, regardless of whether affect precedes or derives from cognition.

The indissociability of cognition and affect can be approached in terms of a figure-ground metaphor. The figure will vary from time to time to the degree that cognitive or affective features are highlighted. In the course of solving an emotional problem, affective features of the situation may be pronounced with the cognitive aspects in a background position. Affect may facilitate cognitive processing, or it may interfere with cognitive processing. In solving a mathematics problem, cognitive strategies may be viewed as the figure, directing attention, planning strategy, and applying recalled algorithms. Affect plays a more moderate role during the solution process, perhaps influencing feelings of confidence or pride, but it is a background factor as rationality, logic, and reasoning direct behavior.

Under other circumstances, or in another person who has similar knowledge, the figure-ground relation between knowledge and affect can shift to produce a quite different relation between affect and cognition. Affect may take the position of figure and knowledge become the ground in our figure-ground metaphor. Knowledge will then provide a vague backdrop to the mathematics problem solution ("I know that I know this! Why can't I do it?") when anxiety is high. Action can be determined more by the affective dimension than the knowledge dimension in such a context. The demands of the situation as judged by the individual serve as sources of arousal to action. It is this process of filtering experience and ongoing perceptions that instigates actions.

Previous experiences may influence when and how an individual will be moved to action. The predisposition to act is a function of what the affective dimension arouses. Affect is not only directed at the external set of events but also at internal reality as assessed by the individual. Inherent in this affect is the strength of feeling that is in part related to the strength of the belief.

Relation of beliefs to intentionality.   There are two interrelated aspects of intentionality that are components of the belief complex. The first of these is the parent's desires or goals of parenting, both long-term ("I want my child to be successful") and short-term ("I want my child to understand this idea"). The second aspect is the parent's intent to act in purposeful manner. These two aspects are related to one another because the intention to act presupposes some type of goal regardless of how planful the action is.

Intentionality, then, is inherently related to volitional control, and will be involved whenever beliefs are expressed as overt actions that have an effect on the external world. The method of action and the timing in which a belief will be instantiated is, by implication, a choice of the parent. For example, a mother who believes that children should be obedient in public might find herself with a child who is resistent to compliance with her wishes. The mother desires to instill obedience as a long-term goal and believes that the child should be punished to accomplish this goal. She fully intends to implement punishment. But she refrains from doing so in a public place. She chooses the timing and the setting. It is this type of relation between belief and intentionality that contributes to difficulties in drawing the connections between beliefs and practices. The intention to act is influenced by time and place as well as the parent's beliefs.

The expression of a belief in a behavior varies in degree of intentionality. This apparent contradiction can be understood through the example of the mother who states her belief in and her intention to breastfeed her infant. When asked why she prefers to breastfeed she may or may not have an answer. In some cases, it may be the consequence of accepting social customs that are instantiations of a belief, but without conscious reflection (see Harkness & Super, 1992). The choice may be derived from tacit belief about health and nutrition of which the mother is not conscious. Or it may be the case that this is a purely volitional action and the mother is conscious of the action. Intentionality then refers to volitional behavior, where automatization will refer to actions that are automatic and nonvolitional. In the end, the parent's knowledge may be fixed and unchanging, established as given, but intentionality will influence how that knowledge is translated into a goal and into a plan of action. Investigations of parents' expectations, childrearing goals, childrearing orientation, and beliefs about childrearing strategies are closely related to the parents' intentionality for action.

Relation to values.   The final component of the belief complex as it is currently conceptualized is parental values. Values have been defined in terms of what parents would like to see embodied in their children (Kohn, 1969). For example, some parents may value conformity, whereas others may value their child's autonomy. Value consists of the importance that is assigned to a particular behavior or the worth of a characteristic. How important is it for my child to achieve in school? Very important. Even if it causes a little unhappiness? How much unhappiness? The value of the knowledge, our feelings about it, and the worth are all part of the belief complex.

With respect to parental beliefs, values concerning the parent's own behavior in reference to the child, as well as values relative to outcomes in the child, must be included in the complex. The parent in the breastfeeding example reveals her value of that action on her part. It is not a value to be inculcated in the child. Within our definition of the belief complex, value refers to what the parent considers an important outcome either in the child, in their relationship, or in the parent's own life. If the parent values the child's independence the parent becomes more likely to place a value on actions that are believed to foster such autonomy. But if the parent is anxious in the face of that autonomy and values physical safety for the child and contact with the child, those behaviors that foster autonomy in the child become less likely to occur. Once again, we see that the belief-behavior relation will be affected by noncognitive components in the belief complex.

In summary, then, the expression of a belief is influenced by the parent's ideas (knowledge or beliefs about what is true), by the feelings that are attached to those ideas, by the parents' desires (intentions), and by the value assigned to particular behaviors, child outcomes, or events.

Conclusions.   The belief complex consists of many components, a few of which have been described in an initial attempt to draw some of the recurring issues in the study of beliefs into a framework in which these different approaches and definitions can be studied and understood in relation to one another. It should be clear that the time is not ripe for any grand theory of beliefs. As our review of the literature suggests, investigators have defined beliefs within their own perspectives and, although aware of the work of others, the relations are tenuous. Thus, future research in this area will continue to be directed at particular questions within each of the conceptual frameworks, and this is healthy and productive.

To that end, we propose that one aspect of the belief complex be considered as the core. The core of the belief complex is the central knowledge that serves as an influence on the processes by which we seek out, store, and interpret relevant information. Indeed, without prior knowledge and corresponding preconceptions, our understanding of everyday experience would demand considerably more time and effort and would in all likelihood result in greatly diminished understanding and knowledge of our world. These core beliefs may be in consciousness/awareness, with the result that beliefs about how children grow and develop may also be conscious. Core beliefs may also be tacit. Degree of reflection and specific stimulation to examine one's beliefs about children and development (in terms of all four components) may influence the degree of awareness. In either conscious or unconscious form, these beliefs are basic and their content is defined as truth or knowledge. The belief complex also consists of other types of cognitions that are both derived from and feed into these core beliefs. That is, beliefs include intentionality, affect, and value components. Affect, desire (intention), and value are intertwined with these knowledges, cannot be separated from them, and are important factors in the instantiations of beliefs (Rokeach, 1980). These components are more closely related to overt behavior.

The actions derived from beliefs vary depending on a number of intervening and constraining factors. Suffice for the moment to assert that the ways of action stemming from such beliefs may not appear consistent with the avowed core belief as verbalized by the informant. The contradiction maybe in the eyes of the beholder. For example, one believes the young child needs adult guidance to learn, and further that adults are the best source of such knowledge. This "knowledge" is represented in a core belief. The effect of this belief on the parent's teaching of the child or setting up situations for the child to learn based the praxis beliefs. The parent has a number of options within the core belief, but the degrees of freedom may be limited because the parent also holds that the adult is a necessary ingredient to learning. Thus, this parental perspective may lead to a didactic supervised authoritative teaching mode. Another parent may believe that the young child learns through exploration and experimentation. One praxis belief that may follow is providing opportunities for the child to explore and regulate his own learning. In effect, the core belief is the same for the two parents, but they differ in how they are executed.

RESEARCH AGENDA

The research agenda that can be derived from such a conceptualization leads us directly into issues currently being addressed by researchers for a variety of problems. For example, Miller (1988) wrote that: "The link between beliefs and behavior remains the most often discussed and least often studied topic in the parental beliefs literature" (p. 282). As developmental psychologists, why have we so seldom asked what events generate change? The converse is also important; what are the features that maintain beliefs? How do intentionality, affect, and values influence these processes?

These concerns should produce various research procedures because the link to the definition of beliefs is made. However, what is not clear is the mode in which the inquiry should proceed. It is not only the method (e.g., self-report methods like interviews, questionnaires, etc.), but the structure of the items that is relevant. This is an area that has received little attention (Sigel, 1992). The approach to this question requires clarification of the construct and the logical derivation of item structure. For example, stems of sentences might vary as a function of whether an item is clearly a knowledge item, "I know that. …" as opposed to an assessment of the value attached to a belief, "It is important that. …" In addition, more experimental work and more behavioral measures (vs. self-report measures) are needed, focusing on particular aspects of the belief complex.

Much of the current research is unidirectional and correlational in spite of disclaimers and caveats. Interest in the development of adults as parents can improve this situation as researchers ask what do beliefs do for the parent? Where do they come from and why? What, if anything, influences their content and structure? How do the components of the belief complex come together in different individuals, especially those with different experiences (cultural, racial, ethnic, social class, and gender groups)? How do the contents of intentionality, affect, and value exert different effects within such groups? (See Goodnow & Collins, 1990, for a detailed discussion of consequences of beliefs.)

The range of outcomes of beliefs for both parent and child can and should be specified. We have seen that beliefs relate to children's social development as well as to their cognitive development and academic achievement. What exactly is it about beliefs that are responsible for such relations? Is it the content (knowledge)? The affect? The relation between the two? And so on, through the various components of the belief complex.

Families are developmental organizations, one of the few social groups in which the members grow together and where the roles of power, control, relative ability, and authority shift over time. Few studies have assessed change and stability over time, in the family structure and in the sociohistorical milieu. There are some exceptions, for example, a few short-term longitudinal studies (Baldwin, Baldwin, Sameroff, & Seifer, 1989; Rubin & Mills, 1992; Sigel et al., 1993), comparisons of families that differ in number of children (McGillicuddy-DeLisi & Sigel, 1991), and a tracking of representations of children through periods in a society (Lightfoot & Valsiner, 1992; Siegel & White, 1982; Young, 1990). These are not issues that are systematically addressed, however, nor has there been consideration that other aspects of the belief complex, besides the particular content, might be factors that underlie developmental change. In addition, these studies have focused on parents of infants and preschoolers. It is unclear what happens to the parents' beliefs, to the affect, to the value, as children enter the middle years. What are developmental effects as children enter adulthood? How do aspects of the belief complex change when society has changed or when the parent role has changed and parents become grandparents (Smith, in this *Handbook*)? There is a serious need to study the changing complex of beliefs both from the individual family point of view as well as the societal (Vygotsky, 1962; Wertsch, 1991).

Although the focus has been on parents' beliefs regarding child development, we realize that these sets of beliefs are embedded in a large world view—beliefs about politics, religion, education, social change, and the like. The question of the interrelationships among these beliefs remains an open one. For example, is there a coherent system that supports and reinforces the parents' childrearing beliefs? Are these sets of beliefs encapsulated and highly differentiated? Do these beliefs form a coherent system? Would changes in any one domain (e.g., religious beliefs) carry over to childrearing beliefs and/or practices? The field is wide open for the study of these questions.

A final set of questions that arises in reviews of research on beliefs revolves around data analysis issues as we struggle to utilize strategies that reflect some of the complexities of ideas about the role of beliefs in the life of the parent engaged in a multitude of functions within the family, influenced and influencing all aspects of the environment. Issues of structural analytic techniques, panel analyses, covariates, decisions about quantitative versus qualitative analyses, reliability and validity, and so forth, do not concern us as much as the nature of the questions chosen for study and the way aspects of the belief complex are conceptualized in relation to one another. However, in our search for understanding of this complex set of relationships, serious attention must be directed toward our research paradigms. There continues to be considerable controversy regarding the appropriateness of a physicalist model for the study of these social and behavioral issues (Baker, 1987). It may well be that the complex questions we are asking require such alternatives ranging from personal narratives and scripts to complex computer models. Perhaps the biggest challenge is to create new models of data collection and analyses that include various multiple perspectives of parents at different time points, without losing sight of the whole parent in relation with other adults, their own history, and the larger sociocultural historical milieu at any point in time.

CONCLUSIONS

An overview of several empirical approaches and a perspective for the study of parent beliefs have been presented. Controversy concerning the research on beliefs continues, ranging from the position that the study of beliefs is a nonscience that is not a suitable target of social scientists to the position that the study of everyday ideas has merits on its own. One can argue that to study how and why beliefs are important requires a more detailed functional analysis of beliefs. This argument reveals that beliefs are perceived as important guides for parents' actions influencing interactions with their children. It is evident from the history of thought about children as well as from current empirical analyses that humans in a variety of social contexts have expressed their beliefs through childrearing. From the point of view of psychologists interested in parenting, it is imperative to understand why people hold beliefs, what functions they serve, and their effects on parents, children, and families (Okagaki & Sternberg, 1991).

The literature reveals that there are multiple concurrent avenues of research on parental beliefs. It is our position that this is a strength, in spite of the ambiguity of definitions and often fragmented research questions regarding the role of beliefs in the lives of parents and children. Our aim in describing the belief complex was to take those aspects of adult cognition that appear to be general to many different approaches and fuse them with findings that are characteristic of research in parenting to date. We do not advocate that each investigator should use the identical concepts, but that the belief construct must be articulated clearly and in relation to the components of the belief complex so that there are intimate relations among the belief construct, its measurement, and the outcome. To use the word *belief* without specification of its characteristics (cognitive component, structure, source, and development, functions, and its relation to affect, intentionality, and values) does not help clarify the research questions, the instruments, or the findings from the research.

Let it be made clear that we do not hold that the definition of belief is synonymous with any singular approach, including our own constructivist approach. The belief complex can apply to all belief systems, in addition to that of parents. Beliefs about the universe, God, the human-environment relationship, can all be examined within the framework of the belief complex. Thus, it is general. At the same time, belief constructs used by different researchers who come to the study of beliefs from different theoretical perspectives can be related to one another through these components of the belief complex.

A grand theory of beliefs is out of reach, premature, and would be harmful to the development of full understanding of parent cognitions. Shared meanings and findings among investigators from different fields within the social sciences has begun (e.g., Harkness & Super, 1992). Potential benefits will be realized only if the breadth of questions, approaches, and paradigms that are applied to parents' thinking about their children and their role in child development are accessible to a diversity of perspectives that extends even beyond those offered here.

REFERENCES

Ajzen, I., & Fishbein, M. (1980). *Understanding attitudes and predicting social behavior.* Engelwood Cliffs, NJ: Prentice-Hall.
Allport, G. W. (1950). Attitudes. In *Nature of personality: Selected papers* (pp. 1–47). Cambridge, MA: Addison-Wesley. (Original work published 1935)
Applegate, J. L., Burke, J. A., Burleson, B. R., Delia, J. G., & Kline, S. L. (1985). Reflection-enhancing parental communication. In I. E. Sigel (Ed.), *Parental belief systems: The psychological consequences for children* (pp. 107–142). Hillsdale, NJ: Lawrence Erlbaum Associates.

Applegate, J. L., Burleson, B. R., & Delia, J. G. (1992). Reflection-enhancing parenting as an antecedent to children's social-cognitive and communicative development. In I. E. Sigel, A. V. McGillicuddy-De Lisi, & J. J. Goodnow (Eds.), *Parental belief systems: The psychological consequences for children* (2nd ed., pp. 3–39). Hillsdale, NJ: Lawrence Erlbaum Associates.

Ashmore, R. D., & Brodzinsky, D. M. (Eds.). (1986). *Thinking about the family: Views of parents and children.* Hillsdale, NJ: Lawrence Erlbaum Associates.

Baker, L. R. (1987). *Saving belief: A critique of physicalism.* Princeton, NJ: Princeton University Press.

Baldwin, A. (1965). A is happy—B is not. *Child Development, 36,* 583–600.

Baldwin, A. L., Baldwin, C., Sameroff, A. J., & Seifer, R. (1989, April). *Protective factors in adolescent development.* Paper presented at the biennial meeting of the Society for Research in Child Development, Kansas City, MO.

Bergeman, C. S., & Plomin, R. (1989). Genotype-environmental interaction. In M. H. Bornstein & J. S. Bruner (Eds.), *Interaction in human development* (pp. 157–171). Hillsdale, NJ: Lawrence Erlbaum Associates.

Bornstein, M. H. (1991). Approaches to parenting in culture. In M. H. Bornstein (Ed.), *Cultural approaches to parenting* (pp. 3–19). Hillsdale, NJ: Lawrence Erlbaum Associates.

Bronfenbrenner, U. (1979). *The ecology of human development: Experiments by nature and design.* Cambridge, MA: Harvard University Press.

Bruner, J. (1990). *Acts of meaning.* Cambridge, MA: Harvard University Press.

Bugental, D. B. (1992). Affective and cognitive processes within threat-oriented family systems. In I. E. Sigel, A. V. McGillicuddy-De Lisi, & J. J. Goodnow (Eds.), *Parental belief systems: The psychological consequences for children* (2nd ed., pp. 219–248). Hillsdale, NJ: Lawrence Erlbaum Associates.

Bugental, D. B., Blue, J., & Cruzcosa, M. (1989). Perceived control over caregiving outcomes: Implications for child abuse. *Developmental Psychology, 25,* 532–539.

Bugental, D. B., & Shennum, W. A. (1984). "Difficult" children as elicitors and targets of adults communication patterns: An attributional-behavioral transactional analysis. *Monographs of the Society for Research in Child Development, 49*(1, Serial No. 205).

Cairns, R. B. (1983). The emergence of developmental psychology. In P. H. Mussen (Ed.), *Handbook of child psychology* (4th ed., Vol. 1, pp. 41–102). New York: Wiley.

Dekovi, M. (1992). *The role of parents in the development of child's peer acceptance.* Assen, The Netherlands: Van Gorcum.

Dekovi, M., & Gerris, J. R. M. (1992). Parental reasoning complexity, social class, and child-rearing behaviors. *Journal of Marriage and the Family, 54,* 675–685.

Dekovi, M., Gerris, J. R. M., & Janssens, M. A. M. (1991). Parental cognitions, parental behavior, and the child's understanding of the parent–child relationships. *Merrill–Palmer Quarterly, 37,* 523–541.

Dix, T. H. (1992). Parenting on behalf of the child: Emphatic goals in the regulation of responsive parenting. In I. E. Sigel, A. V. McGillicuddy-De Lisi, & J. J. Goodnow (Eds.), *Parental belief systems: The psychological consequences for children* (2nd ed., pp. 319–346). Hillsdale, NJ: Lawrence Erlbaum Associates.

Dix, T. H., & Grusec, J. E. (1985). Parent attribution processes in the socialization of children. In I. E. Sigel (Ed.), *Parental belief systems: The psychological consequences for children* (pp. 201–233). Hillsdale, NJ: Lawrence Erlbaum Associates.

Dix, T. H., Ruble, D. N., Grusec, J. E., & Nixon, S. (1986). Social cognition in parents: Inferential and affective reactions to children of three age levels. *Child Development, 57,* 879–894.

Dix, T. H., Ruble, D. N., & Zambarano, R. J. (1989). Mothers' implicit theories of discipline: Child effects, parent effects, and the attribution process. *Child Development, 60,* 1373–1391.

Eagly, A. H. (1992). Uneven progress: Social psychology and the study of attitudes. *Journal of Personality and Social Psychology, 63,* 693–710.

Eccles, J. S. (1987). Gender roles and achievement patterns: An expectancy value perspective. In J. M. Reinisch, L. A. Rosenblum, & S. A. Sanders (Eds.), *Masculinity/femininity* (pp. 240–280). New York: Oxford University Press.

Fincham, F., & Bradbury, T. (1987). The impact of attributions in marriage: A longitudinal analysis. *Journal of Personality and Social Psychology, 53,* 510–517.

Fishbein, M., & Ajzen, I. (1975). *Belief, attitude, intentions and behavior: An introduction to theory and research.* Boston: Addison-Wesley.

Gesell, A. (1946). The ontogenesis of infant behavior. In L. Carmichael (Ed.), *Manual of child psychology* (pp. 295–331). New York: Wiley.

Goodnow, J. J. (1985). Change and variation in ideas about childhood and parenting. In I. E. Sigel (Ed.), *Parental belief systems: The psychological consequences for children* (pp. 235–271). Hillsdale, NJ: Lawrence Erlbaum Associates.

Goodnow, J. J. (1988). Parents' ideas, actions, and feelings: Models and methods from developmental and social psychology. *Child Development, 59,* 289–320.

Goodnow, J. J. (1992). Parents' ideas, children's ideas: Correspondence and divergence. In I. E. Sigel, A. V. McGillicuddy-De Lisi, & J. J. Goodnow (Eds.), *Parental belief systems: The psychological consequences for children* (2nd ed., pp. 293–317). Hillsdale, NJ: Lawrence Erlbaum Associates.

Goodnow, J. J., Cashmore, J., Cotton, S., & Knight, R. (1984). Mothers' developmental timetables in two cultural groups. *International Journal of Psychology, 19,* 193–205.

Goodnow, J. J., & Collins, W. A. (1990). *Development according to parents: The nature, sources, and consequences of parents' ideas*. Hillsdale, NJ: Lawrence Erlbaum Associates.

Gretarsson, S. J., & Gelfand, D. M. (1988). Mothers' attributions regarding their children's social behavior and personality characteristics. *Developmental Psychology, 24,* 264–269.

Harkness, S., & Super, C. (1992). Parental ethnotheories in action. In I. E. Sigel, A. V. McGillicuddy-De Lisi, & J. J. Goodnow (Eds.), *Parental belief systems: The psychological consequences for children* (2nd ed., pp. 373–391). Hillsdale, NJ: Lawrence Erlbaum Associates.

Heider, F. (1958). *The psychology of interpersonal relations*. New York: Wiley.

Hess, R. D., & McDevitt, T. M. (1986). Some antecedents of maternal attributions about children's performance in mathematics. In R. D. Ashmore & D. M. Brodzinsky (Eds.), *Thinking about the family: Views of parents and children* (pp. 95–118). Hillsdale, NJ: Lawrence Erlbaum Associates.

Holden, G. W. (1988). Adults' thinking about a child-rearing problem: Effects of experience, parental status, and gender. *Child Development, 59,* 1623–1632.

Holden, G. W., & Edwards, L. A. (1989). Parental attitudes toward child rearing: Instruments, issues, and implications. *Psychological Bulletin, 106,* 29–58.

Holden, G. W., & Zambarano, R. J. (1992). Passing the rod: Similarities between parents and their young children in orientations toward physical punishment. In I. E. Sigel, A. V. McGillicuddy-De Lisi, & J. J. Goodnow (Eds.), *Parental belief systems: The psychological consequences for children* (2nd ed., pp 143–172). Hillsdale, NJ: Lawrence Erlbaum Associates.

Holloway, S. D., & Hess, R. D. (1985). Mothers' and teachers' attributions about children's mathematics performance. In I. E. Sigel (Ed.), *Parental belief systems: The psychological consequences for children* (pp. 177–199). Hillsdale, NJ: Lawrence Erlbaum Associates.

Holloway, S. D., & Machida, S. (1992). Maternal child-rearing beliefs and coping strategies: Consequences for divorced mothers and their children. In I. E. Sigel, A. V. McGillicuddy-De Lisi, & J. J. Goodnow (Eds.), *Parental belief systems: The psychological consequences for children* (2nd ed., pp. 249–265). Hillsdale, NJ: Lawrence Erlbaum Associates.

Iverson, T. J., & Segal, M. (1992). Social behavior of maltreated children: Exploring links to parent behavior and beliefs. In I. E. Sigel, A. V. McGillicuddy-De Lisi, & J. J. Goodnow (Eds.) *Parental belief systems: The psychological consequences for children* (2nd ed., pp. 267–289). Hillsdale, NJ: Lawrence Erlbaum Associates.

Johnson, J. E., & Martin, C. (1985). Parents' beliefs and home learning environments: Effects on cognitive development. In I. E. Sigel (Ed.), *Parental belief systems: The psychological consequences for children* (pp. 25–50). Hillsdale, NJ: Lawrence Erlbaum Associates.

Kelley, H. H. (1971). Casual schemata and the attribution process. In E. E. Jones, D. E. Kanouse, H. H. Kelley, R. E. Nisbett, S. Valins, & B. Weiner (Eds.), *Attribution: Perceiving the causes of behavior* (pp. 151–174). Morristown, NJ: General Learning Press.

Kelly, G. A. (1955). *The psychology of personal constructs* (2 vols.). New York: Norton.

Kohn, M. L. (1969). *Class and conformity: A study in values*. Homewood, IL: Dorsey.

LeVine, R. A. (1988). Human parental care: Universal goals, cultural strategies, individual behavior. In W. Damon (Series Ed.) & R. A. LeVine, P. M. Miller, & M. M. West (Vol. Eds.), *New directions for child development: Parental behavior in diverse societies* (Vol. 40, pp. 3–11). San Francisco: Jossey-Bass.

Lightfoot, C., & Valsiner, J. (1992). Parental belief systems under the influence: Social guidance of the construction of personal cultures. In I. E. Sigel, A. V. McGillicuddy-De Lisi, & J. Goodnow (Eds.), *Parental belief systems: The psychological consequences for children* (2nd ed., pp. 393–414). Hillsdale, NJ: Lawrence Erlbaum Associates.

Luster, T., & Okagaki, L. (1993). Multiple influences on parenting: Ecological and life-course perspectives. In T. Luster & L. Okagaki (Eds.), *Parenting: An ecological perspective* (pp. 227–251). Hillsdale, NJ: Lawrence Erlbaum Associates.

McGillicuddy-De Lisi, A. V. (1980). The role of beliefs in the family as a system of mutual influences. *Family Relations, 29,* 317–323.

McGillicuddy-De Lisi, A. V. (1982a). Parental beliefs about developmental processes. *Human Development, 25,* 192–200.

McGillicuddy-De Lisi, A. V. (1982b). The relationship between parents' beliefs about development and family constellation, socioeconomic status, and parents' teaching strategies. In L. M. Laosa & I. E. Sigel (Eds.), *Families as learning environments for children* (pp. 261–299). New York: Plenum.

McGillicuddy-De Lisi, A. V. (1985). The relationship between parental beliefs and children's cognitive level. In I. E. Sigel (Ed.), *Belief systems: The psychological consequences for children* (pp. 7–24). Hillsdale, NJ: Lawrence Erlbaum Associates.

McGillicuddy-De Lisi, A. V. (1992). Parents' beliefs and children's personal-social development. In I. E. Sigel, A. V. McGillicuddy-De Lisi, & J. J. Goodnow (Eds.), *Parental belief systems: The psychological consequences for children* (2nd ed., pp. 115–142). Hillsdale, NJ: Lawrence Erlbaum Associates.

McGillicuddy-DeLisi, A. V., & Sigel, I. E. (1991). Family environment and children's representational thinking. In S. Silvern (Ed.), *Development of literacy* (Vol. 5, pp. 63–90). Greenwich, CT: JAI.

Miller, S. A. (1986). Parents' beliefs about their children's cognitive abilities. *Developmental Psychology, 22,* 276–284.

Miller, S. A. (1988). Parents' beliefs about children's cognitive development. *Child Development, 59,* 259–285.

Mills, R. S. L., & Rubin, K. H. (1990). Parental beliefs about social behaviors in early childhood. *Child Development, 61,* 138–151.

Murphey, D. A. (1992). Constructing the child: Relations between parents' beliefs and child outcomes. *Developmental Review, 12,* 199–232.

Neisser, U. (1966). *Cognitive psychology.* New York: Appleton–Century–Crofts.

Okagaki, L., & Divecha, D. J. (1993). Development of parental beliefs. In T. Luster & L. Okagaki (Eds.), *Parenting: An ecological perspective* (pp. 35–67). Hillsdale, NJ: Lawrence Erlbaum Associates.

Okagaki, L., & Sternberg, R. J. (1991). Cultural and parental influences on cognitive development. In L. Okagaki, & R. J. Sternberg (Eds.), *Directors of development: Influences on the development of children's thinking* (pp. 101–120). Hillsdale, NJ: Lawrence Erlbaum Associates.

Pajares, M. F. (1992). Teachers' beliefs and educational research: Cleaning up a messy construct. *Review of Educational Research, 62,* 307–332.

Palacios, J. (1990). Parents' ideas about the development and education of their children: Answers to some questions. *International Journal of Behavioral Development, 13,* 137–155.

Palacios, J., Gonzalez, M.-M., & Moreno, M.-C. (1992). Stimulating the child in the Zone of Proximal Development: The role of parents' ideas. In I. E. Sigel, A. V. McGillicuddy-De Lisi, & J. J. Goodnow (Eds.), *Parental belief systems: The psychological consequences for children* (2nd ed., pp. 71–94). Hillsdale, NJ: Lawrence Erlbaum Associates.

Parsons, J. E., Adler, T. F., & Kaczala, C. M. (1982). Socialization of achievement attitudes and beliefs: Parental influences. *Child Development, 53,* 310–321.

Pavlov, I. P. (1927). *Conditioned reflexes: An investigation of the physiological activity of the cerebral cortex.* London: Oxford University Press.

Polanyi, M. (1958). *Personal knowledge: Toward a post-critical philosophy.* Chicago: University of Chicago Press.

Pomerleau, A., Malcuit, G., & Sabatier, C. (1991). In M. H. Bornstein (Ed.), *Cultural approaches to parenting* (pp. 45–68). Hillsdale, NJ: Lawrence Erlbaum Associates.

Powell, D. R. (Ed.). (1988). *Advances in applied developmental psychology: Vol. 3. Parent education as early childhood intervention: Emerging directions in theory, research, and practice.* Norwood, NJ: Ablex.

Reid, B. B., & Valsiner, J. (1986). Consistency, praise and love: Folk theories of American parents. *Ethos, 14,* 976–980.

Rokeach, M. (1980). Some unresolved issues in theories of beliefs, attitudes, and values. In H. E. Howe, Jr., & M. M. Page (Eds.), *Nebraska symposium on motivation, 1979* (pp. 261–304). Lincoln: University of Nebraska Press.

Rubin, K. H., & Mills, R. S. L. (1992). Parents' thoughts about children's socially adaptive and maladaptive behaviors: Stability, change, and individual differences. In I. E. Sigel, A. V. McGillicuddy-De Lisi, & J. J. Goodnow (Eds.), *Parental belief systems: The psychological consequences for children* (2nd ed., pp. 41–69). Hillsdale, NJ: Lawrence Erlbaum Associates.

Rubin, K. H., Mills, R. S. L., & Rose-Krasnor, L. (1989). Maternal beliefs and children's social competence. In B. Schneider, G. Attili, J. Nadel-Brulfert, & R. Weissberg (Eds.), *Social competence in developmental perspective* (pp. 313–331). The Netherlands: Kluwer.

Sameroff, A., & Feil, L. A. (1985). Parental concepts of development. In I. E. Sigel (Ed.), *Parental belief systems: The psychological consequences for children* (pp. 83–105). Hillsdale, NJ: Lawrence Erlbaum Associates.

Sameroff, A. J., & Fiese, B. H. (1992). Family representations of development. In I. E. Sigel, A. V. McGillicuddy-De Lisi, & J. J. Goodnow (Eds.), *Parental belief systems: The psychological consequences for children* (2nd ed., pp. 347–369). Hillsdale, NJ: Lawrence Erlbaum Associates.

Scarr, S., & Ricciuti, A. (1991). What effects do parents have on their children? In L. Okagaki & R. J. Sternberg (Eds.), *Directors of development: Influences on the development of children's thinking* (pp. 3–23). Hillsdale, NJ: Lawrence Erlbaum Associates.

Sears, R. R., Maccoby, E. E., & Levin, H. (1957). *Patterns of child rearing.* Evanston, IL: Row, Peterson.

Siegel, A. W., & White, S. H. (1982). The child study movement: Early growth and development of the symbolized child. In H. W. Reese (Ed.). *Advances in child development and behavior* (Vol. 17, pp. 233–285). New York: Academic Press.

Sigel, I. E. (1982). The relationship between parents' distancing strategies and the child's cognitive behavior. In L. M. Laosa & I. E. Sigel (Eds.), *Families as learning environments for children* (pp. 47–86). New York: Plenum.

Sigel, I. E. (1985). A conceptual analysis of beliefs. In I. E. Sigel (Ed.), *Parental Belief systems: The psychological consequences for children* (pp. 345–371). Hillsdale, NJ: Lawrence Erlbaum Associates.

Sigel, I. E. (1986). Reflections on the belief-behavior connection: Lessons learned from a research program on parental belief systems and teaching strategies. In R. D. Ashmore & D. M. Brodzinsky (Eds.), *Thinking about the family: Views of parents and children* (pp. 35–65). Hillsdale, NJ: Lawrence Erlbaum Associates.

Sigel, I. E. (1992). The belief-behavior connection: A resolvable dilemma? In I. E. Sigel, A. V. McGillicuddy-De Lisi, & J. J. Goodnow (Eds.) *Parental belief systems: The psychological consequences for children* (2nd ed., pp. 433–456). Hillsdale, NJ: Lawrence Erlbaum Associates.

Sigel, I. E., & Holmgren, A. (1983). A constructivist dialectic view of the development of the person: An update. In J. Adams-Webber & J. C. Mancuso (Eds.), *Applications of personal construct theory* (pp. 55–71). New York: Academic Press.

Sigel, I. E., McGillicuddy-De Lisi, A. V., Flaugher, J., & Rock, D. A. (1983). *Parents as teachers of their own learning disabled children* (ETS Report No. RR 83–21). Princeton, NJ: Educational Testing Service.

Sigel, I. E., Stinson, E. T., & Flaugher, J. (1991). Socialization of representational competence in the family: The distancing paradigm. In L. Okagaki & R. J. Sternberg (Eds.), *Directors of development: Influences on the development of children's thinking* (pp. 121–144). Hillsdale, NJ: Lawrence Erlbaum Associates.

Sigel, I. E., Stinson, E. T., & Kim, M.-I. (1993). Socialization of cognition: The distancing model. In R. Wozniak & K. W. Fischer (Eds.), *Development in context: Acting and thinking in specific environments* (pp. 211–224). Hillsdale, NJ: Lawrence Erlbaum Associates.

Simons, R. L., Beaman, J., Conger, R. D., & Chao, W. (1992). Gender differences in the intergenerational transmission of parenting beliefs. *Journal of Marriage and the Family, 54,* 823–836.

Simons, R. L., Whitbeck, L. B., Conger, R. D. & Melby, J. N. (1990). Husband and wife differences in determinants of parenting: A social learning/exchange model of parental behavior. *Journal of Marriage and the Family, 52,* 375–392.

Spock, B. M. (1946). *The common sense book of baby and child care.* New York: Duell, Sloan & Pearce.

Stich, S. (1983). *From folk psychology to cognitive science: The case against belief.* Boston: MIT Press.

Stigler, J. W., Schweder, R. A., & Herdt, G. (Eds.). (1990). *Cultural psychology: Essays on comparative human development.* New York: Cambridge University Press.

Valsiner, J. (1989). *Culture and human development.* Lexington, MA: Heath.

Valsiner, J., & Van der Veer, R. (1993). The encoding of distance: The concept of the Zone of Proximal Development and its interpretations. In R. C. Cocking & K. A. Renninger (Eds.), *The development and meaning of psychological distance* (pp. 35–62). Hillsdale, NJ: Lawrence Erlbaum Associates.

Vygotsky, L. S. (1962). *Thought and language* (E. Hanfmann & G. Vakar, Trans.). Cambridge, MA: MIT Press.

Watson, J. B. (1928). *Psychological care of infant and child.* New York: Norton.

Weiner, B. (1985). An attributional theory of achievement motivation and emotion. *Psychological Review, 92,* 548–573.

Wertsch, J. V. (1991). *Voices of the mind: A sociocultural approach to mediated action.* Cambridge, MA: Harvard University Press.

Winterbottom, M. R. (1958). The relation of need for achievement to learning experience in independence and mastery. In J. W. Atkinson (Ed.), *Motives in fantasy, action, and society* (pp. 453–478). Princeton, NJ: Van Nostrand.

Young, K. T. (190). American conceptions of infant development from 1955 to 1984: What the experts are telling parents. *Child Development, 61,* 17–28.

Youniss, J., DeSantis, J. P., & Henderson, S. H. (1992). Parents' cognitions and developmental changes in relationships during adolescence. In I. E. Sigel, A. V. McGillicuddy-De Lisi, & J. J. Goodnow (Eds.), *Parental belief systems: The psychological consequences for children* (2nd ed., pp. 199–216). Hillsdale, NJ: Lawrence Erlbaum Associates.

14

Parental Attitudes Toward Childrearing

George W. Holden
University of Texas, Austin

INTRODUCTION

In the study of parent–child relationships, no psychological construct has held as much promise, maintained a similar level of interest and popularity, or achieved such prominence as parental attitudes toward childrearing. The eager reception given to the construct of parental attitudes has resulted in a wide variety of attitudes being studied and concerted efforts to link childrearing attitudes with both parent and child outcomes. However, the negative side of the enthusiasm has been a naïve and uncritical acceptance of childrearing attitudes as being more than they are, and it has retarded the systematic study of parental social cognition. Only of late has there been a rapprochement between the promise and the reality, as this chapter describes.

The early proponents of the study of parents' childrearing attitudes pledged that merely by uncovering childrearing attitudes the mysteries of children's development would be revealed. For example, one early advocate recognized that although attitudes were "impalpable and intangible" they were also of key importance for "fashioning the lives of our children" (Glueck, 1927, pp. 3–4). Attitudes began to be considered of key importance for revealing the "destiny" of children. Psychiatrists wrote about the "common parental attitudes that do a great deal of damage in the way of warping the development of children" (Richards, 1926, p. 226) and warned that "How successfully a given individual will traverse the path from the asocial and amoral state of infancy to an adequately socialized adulthood … will depend more on the character and wisdom and attitudes of his parents than on anything else" (Glueck, 1928, p. 741). Before long, attitudes ascended into first place among determinants of children's development. "Parental attitudes must be of paramount importance because the very young child is exposed to them continually, and the attitudes themselves are relatively fixed and constant" (Pearson, 1931, p. 290). By 1940, it could be written: "We recognize more and more that we are dealing with problem environments and problem parents rather than problem children. … The parents' experiences, their attitudes and behavior, influence the character and behavior of the children, who in turn carry over these attitudes into their later lives, their marital adjustments and in relation to their own families. Thus a vicious circle is created" (Field, 1940, p. 293).

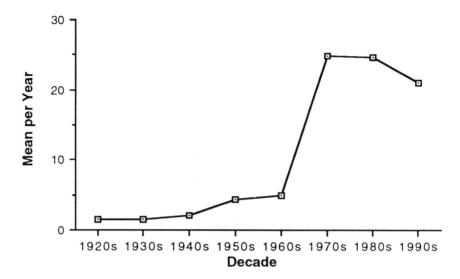

FIGURE 14.1. Mean number of childrearing attitude articles published per decade as referenced in *Psychological Abstracts.*

By the late 1950s, the significance of parental attitudes was so well accepted that the following statement was made: "The importance of parental attitudes in the development of personal and social behavior is one of the *basic tenets* in the fields of child development and parent education" (Burchinal, Hawkes, & Gardner, 1957, p. 65, italics added). Given these and other pronouncements about the importance of parental attitudes, researchers with wide-ranging interests have studied childrearing attitudes. Investigations into clinical, community, counseling, cross-cultural, educational, personality, school, and social psychology have all adopted parental attitudes as a fundamental construct. Childrearing attitudes have been used both as independent and dependent variables to: quantify the social environment, study interindividual family differences, identify differences between groups of individuals, screen individuals at risk for maladaptive parenting, assess the effects of intervention programs, examine parental correlates of child pathology, as well as address a wide range of other research questions.

With such a broad spectrum of interest, it has not been difficult for the study of parental childrearing attitudes to maintain a high level of popularity and interest. Many of the classic studies of parent–child relationships included assessment of parental attitudes as a central focus (e.g., Baldwin, Kalhorn, & Breese, 1945; Baumrind, 1971; Sears, Maccoby, & Levin, 1957). Thousands of studies have been conducted based on more than 100 different attitude assessment instruments. And the production of new attitude studies continues at a prodigious rate. As an index of the frequency of these publications, yearly citations for childrearing attitudes were counted in *Psychological Abstracts* from 1927 to 1991. The average number of published articles per year was then computed for each decade, and these averages are depicted in Figure 14.1. The average ranges from 1.6 for the last 3 years of the 1920s and the 1930s to a high of 24.9 in the 1970s. The dramatic increase in the average from the 1960s to the 1970s is in part real but in part an artifact of new indexing procedures at *Psychological Abstracts;* many more journals were included beginning in 1970. Nevertheless, the 21.0 average per year for the first 2 years included in the 1990s, indicates that there continues to be a high rate of publication of parental attitude studies.

This chapter is intended to provide a current appraisal of the construct of parental childrearing attitudes. A brief history of research into childrearing attitudes is presented next, followed by a discussion of the assessment of parental attitudes. The childrearing attitude literature is then summarized. Next, the central methodological and theoretical concerns in the use of parental attitudes are discussed. The final section of the chapter consists of a discussion of the key directions for future research.

A BRIEF HISTORY OF RESEARCH INTO PARENTAL ATTITUDES

The study of parental attitudes emerged as the confluence of interest from psychologists and psychiatrists. According to Gordon Allport's (1935) history of attitude research, Herbert Spencer was the first psychologist to use the term *attitude* in his writing in 1862. The construct rapidly gained popularity and became incorporated into the work of such American theorists as James Mark Baldwin, John Dewey, William James, and George Herbert Mead. Experimental psychologists in Germany (the Wurzburg school) pioneered the study attitudes in the laboratory by using reaction time measurements. By the 1920s, social and experimental psychologists in the United States were investigating a wide variety of attitudes.

Investigations into parental childrearing attitudes were present almost at the beginning of American psychology. Charles Sears (1899), in collaboration with G. Stanley Hall, developed a questionnaire to assess 486 adults' opinions about punishment for children. Questions concerned topics such as the purpose of punishment, punishable and nonpunishable offenses, and opinions about "breaking the will." The results consisted of lists of responses and some quotes from parents; no descriptive statistics were included. For example, Sears reported that attitudes toward misbehaviors regarded as most punishable were those perceived as intentional, persistent, or due to repeated carelessness.

In all likelihood, the first systematic study of parents published in North America focused on assessing parental attitudes. In her Columbia University dissertation, Laws (1927) recruited 50 mothers enrolled in a parent education class. Each mother filled out four different "tests" concerning their childrearing attitudes. A total of 346 questions assessed attitudes toward particular childrearing practices (e.g., spank, nag, breastfeed), attitudes toward interacting with their children (e.g., affectionate, calm, critical), perceptions of their children's current behavior (e.g., sleeps quietly at night, teases playmates), and attitudes toward 56 nouns or verbs associated with parenting (e.g., authority, cooperation, noise, coddling). Among the descriptive results, she found that most of the mothers thought that they should never ridicule (90 percent) or humiliate (82 percent) the child, nor should they keep the child "tied to apron strings" (78 percent) or "throw cold water" on the child's enthusiasms (80 percent). Laws recognized a number of limitations with the approach (e.g., multiple interpretation of items, inclusion of abstract concepts, multiple determinants of attitudes) but nevertheless concluded that "It is practicable to develop relatively objective means of rating the attitudes and practices of parents ..." (p. 32).

The 1930s was a decade of rapid growth in the assessment of parental childrearing attitudes. Stogdill was a major player, as he developed four parent attitude questionnaires designed to assess parents' attitudes toward undesirable child behavior, parental control, and the effect of parental practices on children (Stogdill, 1931, 1934, 1936a, 1936b). A number of other investigators focused on various other childrearing attitudes as well. Studies assessed attitudes toward pregnancy (Despres, 1937), sex education (Ackerley, 1935), self-reliance in children (Ojemann, 1935), and independence in children (Koch, Dentler, Dysart, & Streit, 1934). These investigators poured the foundation for childrearing attitudes to be a basic paradigm in the study of parent–child relationships.

Besides the psychological research, the other major source of interest in attitudes came from Freud's psychoanalytic theory. Freud saw attitudes, stemming from the unconscious, as the source of love, rejection, and many other proclivities toward children. Although Freud devoted few words to parents' attitudes and their effects on children (e.g., Freud, 1936), his disciples such as Jones (1923), Horney (1933), and Ribble (1943) each gave prominent attention to parental attitudes.

The major legacy of the psychoanalytic theory to parental childrearing attitudes has been in the area of parental overprotection. The basic premise was that the normal attitude of the parent is one of affection. However, if the parents' emotional needs had not been met at some point in their development, then parents would carry these unresolved needs into their childrearing behavior. These

FIGURE 14.2. The implicit model of the relations between parental attitudes, behavior, and child outcome.

needs were then thought to appear in the form of overprotection or rejection of the child, according to the psychiatrist Levy (1931, 1943):

> It is generally accepted that the most potent of all influences on social behavior is derived from the primary social experience with the mother. If a mother maintains toward the child a consistent attitude of, let us say, indifference and hostility, the assumption is made that the child's personality is greatly affected thereby. His outlook on life, his attitude toward people, his entire psychic well-being, and his destiny are presumed to be altered by the maternal attitude. ... If human behavior is influenced so markedly by maternal attitudes, then surely the most important study of man as a social being is a study of his mother's influence on his early life. (Levy, 1943, p. 3)

The study of maternal overprotection—defined as the prolonging of infantile care through excessive control—was thought to be caused by one of several different possible causes—such as rejection from one's own parents. Subsequently the concept of overprotection was dropped in favor of the conceptually simpler constructs of acceptance and rejection. Interest in the causes and consequences of parental acceptance or rejection has continued steadily since the 1930s; there are now over 800 studies that have been published on the topic (Rohner, 1986).

The study of overprotection and rejection led the way for a variety of other childrearing attitudinal "excesses" to be investigated. Childrearing attitudes of anxiety, authority, indulgence, perfectionism, permissiveness, responsibility, solicitude, and strictness all began to receive attention in the 1930s (see reviews by Bakwin & Bakwin, 1942; Symonds, 1949). This work resulted in a new clinical orientation for parents called "attitude therapy," designed to modify errant parental attitudes (Garrett, 1936).

The model of parental childrearing attitudes shared by the psychologists and psychiatrists was simplistic yet held a powerful appeal. Once you understood the core philosophy that guides a parent's childrearing you could then understand both parental behavior and the child's development. The unidirectional, deterministic relation is diagrammed in Figure 14.2.

Admittedly, not all of the early psychologists accepted such a simple model of development. Some researchers recognized that parental attitudes did not necessarily reflect behavior but could be better conceived of as filters that indirectly affected parental behavior. Nevertheless, parental attitudes were often considered to be a useful proxy of a child's home environment (e.g., Francis & Fillmore, 1934; Updegraff, 1939). Whatever way someone chose to view parental attitudes, the common denominator was the great importance attached to the construct. Consequently, the assessment of a wide variety of childrearing attitudes became the popular focus of parenting research.

THE ASSESSMENT OF ATTITUDES

What is a childrearing attitude? Although the term *attitude* has been used in many ways (Symonds, 1927), and there continues to be some disagreement over exactly how attitude should be defined (Tesser & Shaffer, 1990), the classic definition was established by Allport. His definition was: "An attitude is a mental and neural state of readiness, organized through experience, exerting a directive or dynamic influence upon the individual's response to all objects and situations with which it is related" (Allport, 1935, p. 810). This definition is still used today (Rajecki, 1990), although a recent revision reduces it to: "a psychological tendency that is expressed by evaluating a particular entity with some degree of favor or disfavor" (Eagly, 1992, p. 693). With regard to childrearing, a particular entity, or what is commonly labeled an *attitude object* in the psychological lexicon, might be using physical punishment, expressing warmth, or promoting academic achievement.

Parental attitudes toward childrearing reflect a subjective psychological state. This state can be assessed either indirectly or directly. Indirect assessments of attitudes could come from either inferences based on observed behavior or others' perceptions of the parents' attitudes. But only a few investigators have taken the indirect assessment route—such as by collecting children's perceptions of their parents' attitudes (e.g., Spence & Helmreich, 1978). Other than those few exceptions, virtually all of the research into parental attitudes has consisted of direct assessments of those attitudes as obtained through self-reports on interviews or questionnaires.

Interview Assessments

Interview studies of parents' attitudes toward childrearing were prominent in the 1950s and 1960s. For instance, in 1957 one of the most extensive interview studies of mothers was conducted by Sears et al. A total of 379 mothers of 5-year-old children were asked 72 open-ended questions with more than 100 additional probes. The questions ranged from attitudes about obedience, spoiling, children doing chores, and "sex play" to reports about behavioral practices (e.g., "How often do you spank"; "When did you start bowel training"). The interview data were subsequently reduced to 188 scales for each mother, and statistical analyses were performed on those scales. The results appeared in the classic book entitled *Patterns of Child Rearing*. Based on the interviews, the researchers concluded that childrearing attitudes varied widely, but it was possible to identify some underlying childrearing global traits such as permissiveness versus strictness, general family adjustment, and orientations toward aggression and punishment.

A variety of other interview studies has been conducted to assess childrearing attitudes. The largest studies were by Miller and Swanson in the United States and the Newsons in England. Miller and Swanson (1958) studied 582 mothers in Detroit and among their conclusions, determined that maternal attitudes were a function, in part, of the age of the child. The Newsons conducted two interview studies of hundreds of English mothers of 4- and 7-year-old children (Newson & Newson, 1968, 1976) and discovered considerable attitudinal differences across social groups. For example, upper socioeconomic status parents were more democratic and believed in using reasons when disciplining, in contrast to the lower socioeconomic status parents who were authoritarian and threatened their children into obedience (Newson & Newson, 1976).

In contrast to those massive interview studies, many more modest interview studies of parental attitudes have been conducted. For example, Radke (1946) conducted one of the first interview studies of attitudes in an effort to identify parents' orientations toward authority. In the late 1960s, Stolz (1967) published a pioneering investigation into the determinants of mothers' and fathers' behavior, based on interviews that focused on attitudes. Yarrow, Campbell, and Burton (1968) also conducted an interview study of mothers of preschoolers in an effort to replicate the findings of Sears and his colleagues concerning dependency, aggression, and conscience development. Finally, Baumrind developed her influential categorization of parents into authoritarian, authoritative, and permissive types based, at least in part, on interviews assessing parental attitudes and practices (Baumrind, 1971; Baumrind & Black, 1967).

Questionnaire Assessments

Despite those noteworthy studies, and other examples of interviews used to assess parental attitudes (e.g., Cox, Owen, Lewis, & Henderson, 1989; Frodi et al., 1982), the vast majority of the parent attitude studies have relied on questionnaire assessments of childrearing attitudes. Today well over 90 different parental childrearing attitude questionnaires (PCRAs) have been developed; a detailed review of the first 83 attitude instruments can be found in Holden and Edwards (1989). To understand what is known about parental childrearing attitudes, one must be familiar with how attitudes are assessed. Therefore, what follows next is a description of the purposes, structure, and content of childrearing attitude questionnaires.

Purpose.   Childrearing attitude surveys have been developed with one of four major purposes in mind. These purposes were descriptive, theoretical, clinical, or methodological. Most instruments were developed simply to describe or quantify one or more parental attitudes. The descriptive goals range from assessing individual differences in a group of mothers or fathers (Nichols, 1962; Palkovitz, 1984) to identifying cross-cultural attitudinal differences (Holtzman, Diaz-Guerrero, & Swartz, 1975). A second purpose was to create an instrument that could test a theory about development—such as psychoanalytic theory (Cohler, Weiss, & Grunebaum, 1970) or family systems (Roehling & Robin, 1986). Such theoretically driven instruments appear infrequently. Still less common was the goal of developing an attitude questionnaire to serve as a clinical tool. Surveys have been developed in an effort to identify those holding attitudes at risk for child abuse (Gaines, Sandgrund, Green, & Power, 1978) or at risk for rejecting their children (Hurley, 1965). Finally, a few instruments have been designed as methodological improvements on previous instruments—such as attempting to avoid the "social desirability bias" (Pumroy, 1966). This refers to the tendency of respondents to give the answer they think is the most socially correct, whether or not that response corresponds with their own attitude.

Structure.   Questionnaires contain four basic structural components: the format of the question, the number and phrasing of the items, and the response scale. A variety of format approaches has been tried, such as word associations, paired comparisons, fill in the blanks, and short vignettes. Most surveys adopt the simplest approach—using single-sentence phrases depicting an attitude object. The length of surveys has varied greatly, with the number of items ranging from 10 to 491 (median = 50 items). With regard to how the items were phrased, there has been more consistency. Before the 1950s, numerous approaches to the phrasing of items was tried. However, after the publication of an influential monograph by Shoben (1949), many subsequent developers of surveys were swayed by the argument that short statements in the third-person format (i.e., "Mothers very often feel that they can't stand their children a moment longer") were best because they would avoid potential bias due to parents' feeling of making a "confession" if they filled out an item in the first-person format (i.e., "I often feel angry with my child"). About three fourths of the instruments have been written in the third person. As is discussed in a later section of this chapter, such wording leads to interpretation problems.

Shoben (1979) made a second fateful decision about the phrasing of items. Rather than describing specific situations, which he feared would result in the data becoming "stimulus bound" and therefore losing the power of generalizability, Shoben decided to utilize three types of items. Items were written in the form of clichés ("A child should be seen and not heard"), rationalizations ("A child should have strict discipline in order to develop a fine, strong character"), or truisms ("Children should have lots of parental supervision"). Most PCRAs have items reflecting this level of generality.

The fourth structural component of an attitude questionnaire is its response scale. Although a variety of potential formats exists, such as multiple choice, ranking, fill in the blanks, and forced choice, most developers of parental attitude questionnaires have opted for the Likert-type response scale. Typically this means that an item is followed by an agreement/disagreement scale with 5 points on it (strongly disagree to strongly agree) though the number of points has ranged from 3 to 11. Likert-type scales are the most popular because of the ease of development, administration, and analysis (Converse & Presser, 1986). However, at least some of the items presented with Likert-type response scales are thought to be susceptible to what is called the social desirability bias.

To guard against this bias, an alternative approach called the Q-sort has been used. First used in parent attitude questionnaires by Block (1965), this approach involves sorting cards, imprinted with relatively neutral attitude objects, into a series of piles that range from least to most descriptive of the parent. Despite the increased difficulty as well as time needed for respondents to use this technique and the added problems encountered in data reduction, it is likely that this approach does indeed reduce the likelihood of social desirability bias in responses. Consequently, other attitude instruments using the Q-sort format have been developed (e.g., Lawton et al., 1983; Sameroff & Feil, 1985).

Content.   There are two types of content in attitude scales: the content (or type) of subscale and the content of the items. Most instruments were designed to assess more than one attitude as indicated by the number of subscales they include. The median number of subscales is 3; one instrument contains 27. Over 140 childrearing attitudes or related attitudes have been sampled by parental attitude scales (Holden & Edwards, 1989). About 80 percent of the subscales concern parental orientations toward, thoughts about, or views as to the consequences of particular childrearing practices. Most commonly these subscales concerned views about controlling a child—such as parental orientations to discipline and punishment. Other subscales focus on the more general parenting style such as authoritarian or rejecting orientations. Another 17 percent of subscales address parents' views about their own children or children in general (e.g., dependency, emotional health, fearfulness). The final category of subscales represents about 3 percent of the scales and focuses on different issues associated with marital relations. Examples of commonly assessed childrearing attitudes can be found in Table 14.1.

Examination of the content of the items shows that the label of attitude is nominal at best. Although many items do indeed attempt to assess childrearing attitudes (e.g., whether one agrees with the use of a particular parenting practice), a substantial number of items focus on other aspects of social cognition. Not only are there items that are directed at attitudes, but questions also are commonly directed at parental beliefs, parents' perceptions of their children, parents' childrearing behavior, and parents' feelings about themselves.

Historically, attitude researchers have thought of attitudes as a construct that can be divided into three components: an evaluative component, a cognitive or belief component, and a behavioral intention component (Ajzen & Fishbein, 1980). Although there is now some disagreement about the scientific merits of the tripartite division (see Tesser & Shaffer, 1990), the distinctions help to reveal the conceptual confusion associated with parental attitudes. The evaluative component—or judgments about the goodness or favorableness of an attitude object—are typically what is thought of when the term attitude is used. But that evaluation is commonly a reaction to the supposed facts about an object or situation. Thus, attitudes are a function of underlying beliefs.

TABLE 14.1
Examples of Frequently Studied Parental Attitudes Toward Childrearing

Attitudes Related to Discipline and Control

Authoritarian control	Democratic vs. autocratic
Permissiveness vs. restrictiveness	Punitiveness
Firm	Restrictiveness
Physical punishment	

Attitudes Related to Affection

Acceptance	Approval
Hostility or rejection	Warmth

Other Parental Attitudes

Consistency of parenting	Role in educating/teaching child
Encouragement of independence vs. dependence	Overinvolvement
Toilet training	Worries about childrearing

Attitudes Related to Views About Child or Child Characteristics

Assertiveness of child	Approval of child
Conformity/deviance of child	Emotional health of child
Fears of child	Health of child
Judgments about child behaviors	Sex-role expectations of child
Sex behavior of child	Verbal output of child
Achievement of child	

The belief component refers to the knowledge or ideas that are accepted as true (Sigel, 1985; McGillicuddy-De Lisi & Sigel, in this *Handbook*). Beliefs are sometimes called *ideas, knowledge, judgments,* or *conceptions.* As Stolz (1967) pointed out, parents have descriptive beliefs about childrearing—such as beliefs about how children develop or how parents affect children—and instrumental beliefs—the ways in which a parent can achieve particular goals. For example, the statement "Most children are toilet trained by 15 months of age" reflects a different type of belief than "I believe physical punishment to be the best way to discipline." Stolz identified nearly 5,000 beliefs based on her interview study of 78 parents.

The behavioral component of attitudes consists of *behavioral intentions* or the intention to behave in a particular manner. These types of items may assess general orientations toward behavioral practices, or contingencies to act in certain ways, or the willingness to act in harmony with one's beliefs. Although some instruments purportedly assess "practices," most actually assess behavioral intentions (e.g., "I let my child make many decisions for himself"). Only a few parenting instruments have been explicitly designed only to assess childrearing practices. These instruments focus on specific behaviors and ask how often the parent behaves in certain ways such as "Require your child to put away his or her clothes" (Crase, Clark, & Pease, 1979).

Besides the three major components of attitudes, some attitude questionnaires also include values, perceptions, and self-perceptions. Values, though sometimes used synonymously with attitudes, are actually a superordinate category that reflect abstract goals (e.g., to raise a happy child) or a coherent set of attitudes (e.g., respect one's parents). Perceptions refer to items assessing parents' views or reactions to their children (e.g., views about how difficult the child is). Self-perceptions form the final category of items sometimes found on attitude scales. These items consist of parents' own reactions or feelings about their parenting ability or views about their relationships with their children (e.g., "I find some of my greatest satisfactions in my child").

Typically one finds that a majority of the items in an attitude questionnaire do not address attitudes per se, but rather descriptive and instrumental beliefs. Attitudes and self-perceptions appear next most often, followed by values, behavioral intentions, and perceptions of the child. However some instruments focus on one domain or another, such as scales assessing unrealistic parental beliefs (Roehling & Robin, 1986) or values (Segal, 1985). To provide examples of how attitudes are assessed, the three most popular PCRAs developed to date are described next.

Three Prominent Surveys

Of the more than 90 attitude questionnaires that have been developed, 3 stand out in terms of their popularity and longevity. The first such instrument to achieve that status was the Parental Attitude Research Instrument (PARI), developed by Schaefer and Bell (1958). The questionnaire utilizes the popular Likert-type response scales, has a large number of subscales (23), and achieved popularity so rapidly that a review of studies using the instrument was published only 7 years later (Becker & Krug, 1965). Although some investigators accept the subscales developed and identified by the authors, other investigators use the dimensions based on factor analysis studies. Three major factors have been identified on the PARI: (1) Authoritarianism-Control, (2) Hostility-Rejection, and (3) Democracy or Egalitarianism (Radin & Glasser, 1972; Zuckerman, Oltean, & Monashkin, 1958). Despite the outdated or outmoded nature of some of the items (e.g., "breaking the will," "sex criminal," "stunting a personality"), it continues to be used with some regularity today—more than 35 years after it was published.

The second prominent questionnaire that is currently among the most commonly used attitude instruments is Block's (1965) Child Rearing Practices Report (CRPR). Its popularity is based on two features: its multiple subscales and its use of the Q-sort method for eliciting responses. Different investigators have used the CRPR in different ways. It was originally designed to have 21 factors, but factor analyses have indicated from 28 to 33 factors (Block, 1965). Investigators have reduced the piles of items in a variety of ways, such as 16 "broad categories" (Durrett, O'Bryant, &

Pennebaker, 1975) or 22 "item clusters" (Roberts, Block, & Block, 1984), although some clusters have been found to have low internal consistency (McNally, Eisenberg, & Harris, 1991).

The third member of the "big three" instruments was developed by Cohler and his colleagues (Cohler et al., 1970). The Maternal Attitude Scale (MAS) is a Likert-type instrument that distinguishes itself from the others by assessing different types of attitudes than are commonly measured. Attitudes that focus on the quality of relationship are assessed including "encouragement of reciprocity" and interpersonal conflicts such as "appropriate or inappropriate closeness." It is intended to differentiate those mothers who have a more mature understanding of the mother–infant relationship, such as acknowledging that they hold mixed feelings about motherhood and being able to recognize that their child has needs separate from their own. Some of the characteristics of each of these three instruments are listed in Table 14.2. Throughout the chapter, all of the unattributed examples of attitude items come from these big three attitude questionnaires.

RESEARCH FINDINGS

Given the promise of parental attitudes, and the large investment of time and effort in assessing parents' childrearing attitudes, what is there to show for it? This section of the chapter provides a summary of some of the representative findings concerning what has been learned about parental childrearing attitudes and their role in development. These findings can be organized around four topics: (1) childrearing attitudes as determinants of parental behavior, (2) childrearing attitudes and maternal functioning, (3) childrearing attitudes and children's outcomes, and (4) miscellaneous studies of parents' attitudes.

Childrearing Attitudes as Determinants of Parental Behavior

Parental attitudes have often been assessed as a key determinant of parental behavior. To date, most of the research into attitudinal determinants has been in five areas: social class differences, ethnic and cross-cultural differences, sex-typed behavior, intergenerational transmission, and father involvement.

Social class differences.   Relating parenting attitudes to differences in socioeconomic status (SES) has long been a topic of interest. One of the first studies to identify such differences found that lower socioeconomic status mothers had strict attitudes toward discipline, were less certain about their childrearing abilities, and felt less responsible for their children's problem behaviors than middle or upper socioeconomic class mothers (Gildea, Glidewell, & Kantor, 1961). Subsequently Tulkin and Cohler (1973) discovered that middle-class mothers differed from working-class mothers on four of

TABLE 14.2
Three Prominent Parent Childrearing Attitude Questionnaires

Name	Number of Items	Response Scale	Number & Examples of Subscales
Parent Attitude Research Instrument (PARI; Schaefer & Bell, 1958)	115	4-pt agree	23; strictness, breaking the will; suppression of sexuality
Child Rearing Practices Report (CRPR; Block, 1965)	91	7 pile Q-Sort	21; authoritarian control; expression of affect; worry
Maternal Attitude Scale (MAS; Cohler et al., 1970)	233	6-pt agree	13; encouragement of reciprocity; appropriate vs. inappropriate closeness; acceptance vs. denial of emotional complexity

the five attitude subscales from the MAS. Middle SES mothers reported they were more moderate in controlling aggressive impulses, more encouraging of reciprocity, more accepting of the emotional complexities in childrearing, and believed in providing greater comfort for their child's needs than did lower SES mothers. Moss and Jones (1977) found reliable SES differences in the attitudes of pregnant women on two childrearing attitudes. Soon-to-be mothers from a higher SES were more interested in affectionate contact and social interaction with the infant than mothers from a lower SES group. And a final recent example is the work by Segal (1985), who found that higher SES parents held more positive attitudes toward independence and responsibility of their children than lower SES parents who favored more obedience.

The relation between parents' childrearing attitudes and SES has also been the focus of one of the most successful attempts of a theoretical explanation of a determinant of parenting. Kohn (1963) proposed that parents from divergent social classes differ in the characteristics that they value most in their children. He hypothesized that parents from working-class backgrounds would be more likely to value conformity to external rules and be more likely to emphasize obedience, good manners, and to impose constraints on their offspring. Kohn proposed that these values stem directly from the requirements associated with their work. For typical working-class occupations, the essential job requirements are to conform to superiors and to be able to follow instructions. However, the higher the parents' occupational status, the more likely it is that the type of work they perform requires self-direction, initiation, and creativity. Thus, parents from higher occupational levels should value self-direction, self-control, and be more supportive of independence in their children. Kohn's model of the relation of social class to values to parental behavior is depicted in Figure 14.3.

In a series of studies, Kohn found substantial support for his theory (Kohn, 1969, 1979). Even more impressive is that his theory has been confirmed in studies in different countries (Kohn, Naoi, Schenbach, Schooler, & Slomczynski, 1990) and by other investigators in the United States (Luster, Rhoades, & Haas, 1989).

Ethnic and cross-cultural studies.   Parental attitudes have also been used to identify cultural determinants of parenting. A few investigators have explored childrearing attitudes held by members of different ethnic groups in the United States. For example, in a study of the childrearing attitudes (on the CRPR) of Mexican-American, African-American, and White mothers it was found that Mexican-American mothers were less authoritative but more protective than the African-American or White mothers (Durrett et al., 1975). In a more recent study comparing African-American mothers with Hispanic-American mothers (Wasserman, Rauh, Brunelli, Garcia-Castro, & Necos, 1990), an ethnic group difference emerged on one of four attitude subscales. Hispanic-American mothers endorsed stricter disciplinary attitudes than African-American mothers. When the Hispanic-American group was divided further, it was found that mothers originally from the Dominican Republic had childrearing attitudes reflecting greater strictness and aggravation with their children than mothers from Puerto Rico.

More common than ethnic studies are cross-cultural investigations of parental attitude differences. Kitano (1964) published one of the first such studies, comparing childrearing attitudes of two generations of Japanese women and Japanese-American women. Although he did not find cross-cultural differences on their attitudes assessed with the PARI, he did find evidence for generational

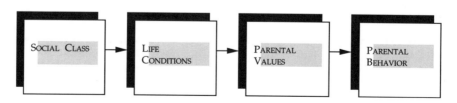

FIGURE 14. 3. Kohn's model of the relations between social class and parental behavior.

differences: older Japanese and older Japanese-American women held more restrictive childrearing attitudes than the younger women. A number of other studies have taken a similar approach by examining how acculturation affects maternal attitudes. The work by Lambert provides a good illustration. Lambert and his colleagues (Lambert, 1987; Lambert, Hamers, & Frasure-Smith, 1979) examined childrearing attitudes among four immigrant groups in Canada. Among their findings was that parents who were born in Italy and immigrated to Canada showed a persistence of certain attitudes learned from their country of origin (e.g., they were reluctant to encourage independence in their children) along with some attitudinal change in the direction of the normative attitudes of their new country (e.g., concerning their sex-role expectations for their children).

Chui (1987) also compared parenting attitudes of mothers from different backgrounds. He found that Chinese mothers from Taiwan, in comparison to Chinese-American immigrants and White-American mothers, held the most restrictive attitudes on the PARI and the Anglo-Americans held the least restrictive of the three groups. In a similar study, using a shortened version of the CRPR that was modified into a Likert-scale instrument (Lin & Fu, 1990), it was found that Chinese and immigrant Chinese parents had higher ratings on control, emphasis on achievement, and unexpectedly on encouragement of independence than White parents. A final example comes from Israel. Orr, Assor, and Priel (1989) used the PARI to find several significant differences between the childrearing attitudes of kibbutz mothers and those of mothers residing in urban settings.

Sex-typed behavior.   Parental attitudes have frequently been studied as they relate to their own sex-typed behavior. With only a few exceptions, studies of parental attitudes and gender role have assessed parents' attitudes toward gender roles or gender stereotypes rather than attitudes toward socializing children into specific gender roles. Using instruments such as "attitudes toward women" (Spence & Helmreich, 1978), some studies have found that parental attitudes toward gender roles predict parent behavior, although others have not. For example, McHale and Huston (1984) discovered that mothers' sex-role attitudes did indeed relate to the types of child-care activities they performed. In Australia, Antill (1987) found that egalitarian attitudes toward sex roles were associated with the encouragement of opposite-sex traits in their children. And recently, Fagot and her colleagues reported that mothers who had more traditional sex-role attitudes were more sex typed in their play with young children (Fagot, Leinbach, & O'Boyle, 1992; see also Fagot, in this *Handbook*). However, a number of other efforts designed to link sex-role attitudes with behavior have not been successful (see Huston, 1983).

Intergenerational transmission of parenting.   Since the late 1940s investigators have looked at the intergenerational transmission of attitudes as a determinant of parenting behavior (e.g., Radke, 1946). Despite the fact that this topic is fraught with methodological problems, and the best method—that of conducting a long-term longitudinal study—has yet to be conducted, useful data are being collected. Typically studies have mothers (Generation #2) of young children fill out attitude questionnaires and have their mothers (Generation #1) do so at about the same time (Cohler & Grunebaum, 1981; Staples & Smith, 1954). Alternative approaches have been to use nonparents (i.e., undergraduate students) and their mothers (Ho & Kang, 1984) or to use only children's self-reports and reports of their parents' attitudes (Spence & Helmreich, 1978). This last approach is not as problematic as it sounds for Goodnow (1992) argued that transmission is determined by a two-process model. The first part of her model involves individuals' subjective perception of their parents' attitudes. Part two of the model consists of whether individuals then accept or reject the perceived parental attitudes. Consequently, Goodnow argued that the perceived attitudes are more important than the actual attitudes held by the parents.

More than a dozen studies have examined the relation between childrearing attitudes of one generation and their parents (see Holden & Zambarano, 1992; van IJzendoorn, 1992). These "cross-sectional" studies of transmission find evidence of continuity with correlations of childrearing attitudes typically in the range of .16 to .37 (Hanson & Mullis, 1986; Itkin, 1952). Among the attitudes that have received the most attention are parents' attitudes toward discipline in general and attitudes toward physical punishment in particular. For example, Simons and his colleagues (Simons, Whitbeck, Conger, & Chyi-In, 1991) found that parents' attitudes toward harsh parenting (physical punishment and yelling) correlated with their reports of their own parents' harsh parenting. Evidence for the early transmission of attitudes toward spanking has also been found. Holden and Zambarano discovered a trend between mothers' attitudes toward physical punishment and their 8-year-old children's intentions to spank ($r(20) = .36, p < .10$).

Fathers' involvement in childrearing. Although mothers' attitudes are most commonly assessed, at least since 1943 fathers' childrearing attitudes have sometimes been studied (Gardner, 1943; Nichols, 1962). Much of the work has been descriptive, such as relating personality characteristics to childrearing attitudes (Block, 1955), comparing fathers' and mothers' childrearing attitudes (Frodi et al., 1982), or linking fathers' childrearing attitudes to their concerns about work and other adult issues (De Luccie & Davis, 1991). Many of the recent paternal attitude studies have been directed at understanding the determinants of fathers' involvement in childrearing. Bigner (1977) found a modest but positive correlation between fathers' child-oriented attitudes and the degree of fathers' involvement with their children. The work by Palkovitz (1984) and others (e.g., McHale & Huston, 1984) has shown that fathers' attitudes toward childrearing, in conjunction with mothers' attitudes, determine the fathers' level of involvement in childrearing.

Functioning of Mothers

Childrearing attitudes have also been used to assess how well mothers function as parents. These studies can be sorted into four categories: adjustment to motherhood, adolescent mothers, maternal employment, and the effects of parent education.

Adjustment to motherhood. Given the psychoanalytic origins of parent attitude research, it should come as no surprise that many studies have looked at the relation of maternal attitudes during pregnancy or shortly thereafter and adaptation to mothering (Clifford, 1962; Despres, 1937; Heinicke, in this *Handbook*). Davids and Holden (1970) found that mothers' prenatal PARI scores were subsequently associated with certain personality attributes. For example, a hostile childrearing attitude was associated with anxiety and depression in mothers when their infants were 8 months old. Similarly, Crockenberg and McCluskey (1986) reported some predictive utility of a childrearing attitude: mothers' prenatal attitude toward responsiveness correlated with observed responsivity to their 12-month-old infants.

It is also clear that prior maternal attitudes are not the only determinants of maternal adjustment. Conger and his colleagues (Conger, McCarty, Yang, Laney, & Kropp, 1984) discovered current maternal authoritarian attitudes were negatively related to positive parenting behavior and affect but positively correlated with negative behavior. In a large study of 267 high-risk mothers in which attitudes (on the MAS) and personality variables were assessed, the investigators did not find any single attitude or set of attitudes that differentiated high-functioning mothers from inadequate ones. Rather, the best discriminator was a factor comprised of both childrearing attitudes and personality variables. The authors described that factor as the "level of personal integration" that successfully differentiated the quality of care the infants received (Brunnquell, Crichton, & Egeland, 1981). Rickel, Williams, and Loigman (1988) also identified several personality characteristics that related to childrearing attitudes on the CRPR. Mothers who were depressed or anxious had less nurturant but more restrictive attitudes. Finally, some investigators have assessed other childrearing attitudes (such as negative concept of child) in an effort to detect individuals who are at risk for maladaptive or abusive parenting (Avison, Turner, & Noh, 1986; Milner & Chilamkurti, 1991; Rauh, Wasserman, & Brunelli, 1990).

Other variables besides maternal personality have been linked to maternal adjustment. As Belsky's (1984) model of the determinants of parenting indicates, other key influences on parenting include such variables as social support, work, and child behavior. The presence or absence of social support for the mothers can have a potent impact on maternal attitudes and adjustment (Cochran & Brassard, 1979; see also Cochran & Niego, in this *Handbook*). Crnic and his colleagues (Crnic, Greenberg, Ragozin, Robinson, & Basham, 1983; see also Crnic & Acevedo, in this *Handbook*) found that stress and social support both predicted maternal attitudes toward satisfaction with parenting. Greater stress was associated with more negative attitudes in mothers of 1-month-old infants, whereas social support was correlated with more positive attitudes. Mothers' attitudes toward their own effectiveness as mothers has been found by Cutrona and Troutman (1986) to be positively related to social support but negatively related to infant difficulty and maternal depression. It follows that Crockenberg (1987) found young mothers holding angry, punitive parenting attitudes experienced little social support and had memories of being rejected by their own parents.

In studies that adopt more of a family-systems approach, childrearing attitudes have also been linked to marital adjustment. Mothers in happy marriages, compared with those experiencing unhappy marital relations, reported attitudes of greater warmth and more encouragement of independence toward their toddler while feeling less aggravation with the children (Goldberg & Easterbrooks, 1984). Similarly, other investigators reported that mothers in close, confiding marriages are warmer and more sensitive to their children and their husbands hold more positive childrearing attitudes than parents in less happy relationships (Cox et al., 1989). A third study also reported significant relations between childrearing attitudes and marital adjustment. Maternal attitudes toward anticipated enjoyment of child care were predicted by the quality of the marital relationship as well as the mother's physical condition (i.e., fatigue), and her prior caregiving experience (Fleming, Ruble, Flett, & Shaul, 1988). At 1 month postdelivery, the mother's enjoyment of child care was still predicted by the marital relationship (along with her physical condition and mood).

Adolescent mothers.   A number of investigators have employed attitude scales to assess reactions to pregnancy, anticipation of parenting, and the subsequent quality of mothering provided by adolescent or unwed mothers (Brooks-Gunn & Chase-Lansdale, in this *Handbook*). Clifford (1962) used an attitude questionnaire to compare unwed mothers with mothers expecting their first or second child. He found that unwed mothers held more negative attitudes toward the pregnancy and motherhood than the married women. Similarly, in a study of 400 pregnant teenagers, Furstenberg (1976) found that 20 percent reported they were "happy" at becoming pregnant and 75 percent said they wished they had not become pregnant. Their attitudes toward the pregnancy remained consistent—women who were initially unhappy continued to report low interest in their children 4 years later. However, at least one other study came to a very different conclusion: Camp and Morgan (1984) found that in their sample of adolescent mothers, positive attitudes toward the pregnancy and the infant were more common than negative ones.

With regard to the childrearing attitudes of adolescent mothers, the results have also been mixed. For example, one study reported that low-income adolescent mothers held dysfunctional childrearing attitudes (McKenry, Kotch, & Browne, 1991). In contrast, a study of pregnant teenagers in a health care program reported the adolescents had parenting attitudes that were more negative than adult norms but more positive than adolescent norms (Fox, Baisch, Goldberg, & Hochmuth, 1987). Other studies have found no differences in childrearing attitudes between adolescent and older mothers (Baranowski, Schilmoeller, & Higgins, 1990; Roosa, 1983; Wasserman et al., 1990) or pregnant and nonpregnant adolescents (Roosa, 1983). These conflicting results indicate that there is no uniform association between adolescent pregnancy and childrearing attitudes, but that the results depend on such variables as sample characteristics and the type of questionnaire being used.

Maternal employment.   The role of maternal attitudes toward childrearing and work have been utilized to measure maternal adjustment regarding employment (Gottfried, Gottfried, & Bathurst, in this *Handbook*). Some work has been done investigating whether maternal attitudes toward childrearing are systematically related to maternal employment status. Typically, few if any relations are found; when they are identified, such differences tend to be of modest magnitude (Goldberg & Easterbrooks, 1988).

More successful are the studies that look at maternal attitudes toward the dual roles of childrearing and employment. Hock and her colleagues (e.g., Hock, McBride, & Gnezda, 1989) have developed several different attitude instruments to measure mothers' attitudes and related thoughts toward parenting and employment outside the home. For example, the Maternal Separation Anxiety Scale is a 35-item questionnaire that yields three subscales: the value of exclusive maternal care (e.g., "Only a mother just naturally knows how to comfort her distressed child"); perception of separation effects on the child (e.g., "Exposure to many different people is good for my child"); and employment-related separation concerns (e.g., "I would not regret postponing my career in order to stay home with my child"). Hock and her colleagues have shown that mothers' attitudes toward work versus parenthood mediate their mood and functioning. For example, mothers who preferred to work but remained at home have higher levels of depression (Hock & DeMeis, 1990).

Effects of parent education. Childrearing attitudes have sometimes been used to gauge how parent education can affect maternal adjustment. A number of studies have reported changes in childrearing attitudes and beliefs as a consequence of parent education (Bronner, 1936; Wulf & Bartenstein, 1980). A representative study was conducted by Radin and Glasser (1972) who used the PARI to chart how low-income mothers' attitudes moved in the direction of normative childrearing attitudes as a result of attending intervention programs.

Children's Adjustment and Outcomes

A large number of investigators, following the pronouncements of parent attitude advocates, have tested relations between parental attitudes and children's behavior or behavior problems. Some investigations have indeed found links in the areas of (1) children's behavioral outcomes, (2) the effect on children of the concordance between parents' attitudes, (3) gender identity, and (4) children's intelligence and achievement.

Children's behavioral outcomes. Shoben's (1949) monograph, showing that his childrearing attitude scale could differentiate mothers of problem versus nonproblem children, stimulated considerable interest in using parenting attitudes for identifying and discriminating the source of children's behavior problems. One of the first domains examined by a number of researchers was the link between maternal attitudes and childhood schizophrenia. Although an early report found a number of statistically significant differences between the childrearing attitudes of mothers of schizophrenic children and the attitudes of mothers of nonschizophrenics (Mark, 1953), subsequent attitude studies that controlled for other variables (e.g., mother's education) found few or no significant differences (Freeman & Grayson, 1955; Zuckerman et al., 1958).

Investigations that focused on less dramatic behavior problems have generally achieved more success at finding associations between childrearing attitudes and children's behavioral outcomes. Both mothers and fathers of children referred to a clinic were found to hold more autocratic attitudes and were less well adjusted and less sociable than a comparison group of parents (Peterson, Becker, Hellmer, Shoemaker, & Quay, 1959). In the case of boys who stuttered, their mothers were found to be more likely to hold rejecting attitudes than the mothers from a comparison group (Kinstler, 1961). With older children, Winder and Rau (1962) reported that parental attitudes of ambivalence and punitiveness in childrearing were most commonly related to problems of aggression, dependence, withdrawal, or depression in preadolescent boys, and Chorost (1962) discovered that authoritarian control was positively correlated with overt adolescent hostility. In the most recent evidence for the discriminant validity of maternal attitudes and child behavior problems, Rickard, Graziano, and

Forehand (1984) found that several scales of an instrument they developed to assess parental expectations, attitudes, and beliefs did indeed discriminate clinic-referred from nonclinic children.

Despite those positive findings, some of the studies failed to adequately control for differences in background characteristics (e.g., educational level) and a number of replication attempts have failed to find consistent differences between children's problem status and parental attitudes. For example, no relation was found between parental attitudes toward acceptance of their children and various child personality attributes (Burchinal et al., 1957), nor in a study of maternal attitudes toward responsibility, discipline, and rejection and children's behavior problems (Gildea et al., 1961). A third example was a study by Medinnus (1961) who had parents of 6-year-old children fill out the PARI. Teachers then differentiated the children into well- or poorly adjusted children. Only 4 of the 23 scales differentiated the groups based on the mothers' data; none did so for fathers' data. It should be kept in mind that when differences are found, they could reflect changes in attitudes in reaction to the child's problem behavior, rather that the pre-existing attitudes that caused the problem. In a review of studies reporting on the relation between parental attitudes, as assessed by the PARI, and child adjustment, Becker and Krug (1965) concluded that there was no consistent and reliable association between the two.

Childrearing attitudes have also been tested in relation to a popular domain for research in social development—that of security of attachment. At least two studies have been published that find relations between parental attitudes and children's security of attachment status. Easterbrooks and Goldberg (1984) discovered that maternal attitudes of strictness and paternal attitudes of aggravation with the child were related to less secure attachment in 20-month-old boys. Egeland and Farber (1984) also found an attitude-attachment link. Mothers of insecurely attached children were less likely to accept the emotional complexity of childrearing as assessed by the MAS than were mothers of securely attached children.

Attitude concordance between parents and child adjustment. A handful of investigators has taken a different approach to studying the link between childrearing attitudes and child adjustment. Rather than relating specific attitudes with behaviors, these investigators have looked at the degree of concordance between mothers' and fathers' childrearing attitudes and then related this agreement rate to children's behaviors. The first such study was conducted by Block and her colleagues (Block, Block, & Morrison, 1981) who found that 6-year-old boys of parents with concordant attitudes received higher intelligence test scores than boys of discordant parents. At the same time, it was found that girls from concordant parents had lower levels of impulse control and less concern for others as determined by personality ratings. In a subsequent assessment of the same children when they were adolescents, Vaughn, Block, and Block (1988) reported that parental agreement at age 3 years was positively associated with teenage boys' intellectual functioning and with teenage girls' competence and self-confidence. Gjerde (1988) also found a number of positive consequences for children who had concordant parents. When relating attitudes from the CRPR with observations of parent–child interactions, he found eight reliable relations. However five of them were limited to mother–son dyads: mothers from more concordant marriages were less authoritarian, less intrusive, but more resourceful, more indirect in communicating, and more permissive with their sons than mothers in discordant marital relationships. A fourth study (Deal, Halverson, & Wampler, 1989) also revealed positive effects for parents who share similar childrearing attitudes. Spouses with high levels of agreement were characterized having higher marital satisfaction, used more positive parenting, and generally had healthier families. In contrast to those studies, one replication study did not found positive effects from concordance. Using a Swedish sample of families, Lamb and his colleagues (Lamb, Hwang, & Broberg, 1989) failed to find any significant relations between the degree of parental agreement and children's intellectual development.

Gender identity. A number of studies have looked at the relation between parents' attitudes toward gender role orientation and their children's gender typed behavior and schemata (Fagot, in this *Handbook*). Lytton and Romney (1991), in a meta-analysis of literature on parents' differential socialization of boys and girls, found very few reliable differences. The single biggest sex-of-child effect in how parents socialize their children concerns the encouragement of sex-typed activities. Some of the studies that this finding was based on used childrearing attitudes (e.g., Lansky, 1967). Despite this differential encouragement, Huston (1983) concluded that research has shown parents' attitudes toward gender stereotypes are generally poor predictors of children's gender-typed behavior. However, those same parental attitudes occasionally do predict children's gender-role schemata such as stereotypes (Meyer, 1980). Similarly, Fagot et al. (1992) found that mothers who had more traditional sex-role attitudes had children who scored higher on a gender identity task and Weinraub et al. (1984) reported that fathers who held more conservative attitudes toward women had children who scored higher on the gender-labeling and gender identity tasks.

Children's intelligence and achievement.   A number of studies have investigated links between parents' attitudes and children's cognitive outcomes. In particular, intellectual functioning and school achievement have been repeatedly studied. At least one study found that maternal attitudes toward rejection and punishment were significantly correlated with intelligence test scores (Hurley, 1965), although the relation was not strong. Two studies have determined that positive relations exist between mothers' attitudes toward democratic childrearing on the PARI and IQ scores of toddlers (Ramey, Farran, & Campbell, 1979) and preschoolers (Radin & Glasser, 1972).

More studies have looked at relations between parental attitudes and children's achievement. However, the results are inconclusive. For example, in one study, mothers of high-achieving gifted and high-achieving average IQ junior high students were more authoritarian and restrictive than mothers of low-achieving students (Drews & Teahan, 1957). Almost the opposite results were found in a study conducted 22 years later. Banner (1979) reported that mothers of low-achieving elementary-school-age children scored higher on PARI scales of dominance, rigidity, and restrictiveness than mothers of average- or high-achieving children. The results appear to depend on a variety of variables, including the race and gender of the participant.

A different approach to the attitude-achievement connection was taken by Katkovsky, Preston, and Crandall (1964). They found that mothers' and fathers' attitudes toward their own achievement could be seen in differential behavior with their children; parents who valued intellectual achievement tended to participate more in their children's intellectual activities. More recently, Parsons, Adler, and Kaczala (1982) discovered that college-educated mothers' own attitudes toward math may be implicated in their daughters' lower expectations for math achievement; mothers were less interested in math and held a more negative view of their own mathematical abilities than their husbands did. It may be that their daughters adopt a similar attitude toward their own math abilities, however Parsons and her colleagues were unable to find supporting evidence.

Interest in the role of parental attitudes in children's achievement has seen renewed interest with a series of cross-cultural group studies conducted in America and Asia by Stevenson and other investigators (e.g., Stevenson, Azuma, & Hakuta, 1986). Stevenson and his colleagues have conducted a series of studies into the relations between parent's attitudes and their children's achievement in China, Japan, and the United States. Chen and Stevenson (1989) examined mothers' and fathers' attitudes toward their children's homework. One of their findings concerned mothers' attitudes: Most American mothers' (92 percent) believed they must intervene with their children to ensure that the homework was completed in contrast to just over 57 percent of the Japanese mothers and 68 percent of the Chinese mothers.

In another study, Lummis and Stevenson (1990) assessed mothers' attitudes toward their children's achievement in reading and mathematics. Mothers' beliefs about their children's abilities were similar across the three cultures, with the most striking finding being that mothers tended to think that girls were better readers than boys. This attitudinal bias occurred despite the fact that the boys' performance was similar to that of the girls'. A third study by Stevenson and his colleagues (Stevenson, Chen, & Uttal, 1990) focused on parental attitudes concerning their children's achievement in different ethnic groups in America. In a total sample of 968 mothers, they found that minority mothers (African-American and Hispanic-American) held positive attitudes toward education and in fact valued good grades more than did White mothers. However, both African-American and Hispanic-American mothers were less likely to expect their children to go on to college (63 percent and 43 percent, respectively) than White mothers (71 percent).

Miscellaneous Topics

Various other topics concerning childrearing attitudes have been addressed by researchers, ranging from attitudes toward having children to the expression of physical affection to children. A number of investigators have examined parents' or expectant parents' attitudes toward having and rearing children. Lott (1973), for example, identified several sex differences in nonparents' attitudes toward having children and Hoffman, Thornton, and Manis (1978) assessed adults' attitudes toward the value of children. Other investigators have examined societal changes regarding attitudes toward bearing and rearing children (Thornton, 1989; Veroff, Douvan, & Kulka, 1981).

Childrearing attitudes have also been examined to determine whether they are related to the development of prejudice in children. For instance, one study found that prejudiced children, aged 9 to 11 years, had mothers with more authoritarian and rigid childrearing attitudes than mothers of nonprejudiced children (Harris, Gough, & Martin, 1950). That finding was subsequently replicated with a younger sample of children (Mosher & Scodel, 1960).

A final example of another miscellaneous childrearing attitude investigation comes in the wake of the increasing awareness of the problem of sexual abuse. Hyson, Whitehead, and Prudhoe (1988) assessed adults' attitudes toward the expression of physical affection between adults and children. In an effort to get some initial normative information about these attitudes, they sampled male and female parents, nonparents, and early childhood professionals. Hyson and her colleagues report that women had more positive attitudes than men concerning displays of physical affection toward children and early childhood professionals held more positive attitudes toward physical affection toward children than either parents or nonparents.

Overview

This brief review of the parent childrearing attitude research, although far from exhaustive, is representative of the types of work and findings that have accrued to date. It is clear that parental attitudes have not provided the key for revealing the mysteries of development. On the other hand, the construct of parent childrearing attitudes has been useful for understanding determinants of parental behavior, influences on mothers' adjustment to parenthood, and some of the ingredients to the behavioral outcomes of child. The area continues to be an active domain of research with new findings generated frequently.

In comparing the more recent childrearing attitude research with the older studies, a few trends can be identified. One such trend is to focus on specific rather than global attitudes. Similarly, the types of questions asked or relations sought tend to be sharper and more context-specific than commonly found in the earlier work. More recent studies also tend to use multiple methods, rather than relying simply on one attitude questionnaire. These trends indicate progress toward improving the quality of studies concerning parental attitudes.

At the same time there continues to be a considerable amount of conflicting or nonreplicated results. In some cases the results are at odds with each other, such as with the attitudes of adolescent mothers. In many more cases, the magnitude of the correlations found is modest at best. And those correlations reflect the results of successful studies—there is no way of knowing how many similar studies were conducted but never published because they failed to find significant relations. Yet another problem is that all too many studies exist in a theoretical vacuum and do not build on the findings of previous work. The most serious and fundamental critique is that despite all the attention and countless studies devoted to the topic of childrearing attitudes, the approach remains surprisingly primitive and simplistic. This lack of sophistication gives rise to many concerns about the study of childrearing attitudes.

METHODOLOGICAL AND CONCEPTUAL CONCERNS ABOUT CHILDREARING ATTITUDES

Despite the popularity of parental attitudes for addressing a wide variety of issues, there have been continuing concerns about the quality of the research. Part of these concerns is accounted for by the inescapable reliance on self-report data: Using parents as informants of their own attitudes and behavior is a problem-laden methodology. If parents are providing reports about themselves and their children, then one has no way of judging the veridicality of the reports. A number of other concerns have also been identified. In fact, since the 1930s (Watson, 1933) problems with assessing attitudes in general, and parental childrearing attitudes in specific, have periodically appeared in the literature. The more forgiving critiques have recommended cleaning up the study of childrearing attitudes, whereas the harsher critiques have advocated abandoning the study of attitudes all together (Wicker, 1969). The concerns with parental attitudes that have been identified fall into two categories: methodological and conceptual.

Methodological Concerns

At the most basic level, there are critics who contend that self-report data are by definition fundamentally flawed and that this is even more the case with the psychological construct of attitude. However, such a knee-jerk reaction fails to appreciate that even when self-reports do not reflect behavior, valuable information can be learned from them. Childrearing attitudes represent a varied class of attitude "objects," ranging from global values to specific evaluations of particular childrearing practices. In some cases self-reports may reflect objective reports of parental attitudes, although in other instances the attitude may not be accessible to the parent for an impartial report (Bates & Bayles, 1984). Thus, a more reasoned position is that the quality of self-report data depends on such factors as what is being reported on and how it is being reported.

Methodological concerns focus on how attitudes are accessed. A number of methodological problems have been identified with attitude questionnaires. The major problems associated with questionnaires include concerns about: (1) item composition, (2) response scales, (3) reliability, and (4) validity.

Item composition. It is unfortunate that most developers of parent attitude scales did not do their homework. Apparently very few took the trouble, before they started composing their question-naires, to read the advice from one of the founding fathers of questionnaires. In 1932 Likert recommended that authors of surveys should: (1) word items as clear, concise, and straightforward statements, (2) omit "double-barreled" or dual questions, and (3) remember that "above all ... each statement must avoid every kind of ambiguity" (pp. 45–46). Although his recommendations are all too often neglected, his advice still holds (Converse & Presser, 1986).

Ambiguity of the items appears in two ways. First, vague terms are often used intentionally as a way to tap a global attitude. Statements like: "It is frequently necessary to drive the mischief out of a child before he will behave" are open to widely discrepant interpretations. Furthermore, if you ask a mother to respond to an item such as "A 7-month-old baby should be picked up when he (she) cries," she will begin by protesting that more information is needed about the specifics of the situation. Second, the majority of PCRAs have items phrased in the third-person format (e.g., "A good mother should protect her child from life's little difficulties") to avoid having mothers feel self-conscious (Shoben, 1949). The problem is that a parent does not know how to respond to such items. For example, to the "good mother" question, does a mother respond based on her own behavior, her beliefs about the ideal behavior, her observations of others, or her perceptions of professional opinion (Becker

& Krug, 1965)? Other problems with items include use of double-barreled items, inclusion of antiquated terms or concepts, confusing items with negatives, the social desirability bias, and questions that do not correspond with the parents' experiences (e.g., questions about bottlefeeding given to breastfeeding mothers). Table 14.3 lists many of the problems identified with attitude questionnaires and provides some additional examples.

Response scales.   There are a number of problems with most Likert-type response scales as well. Vague probability terms, such as "sometimes" or "occasionally," are included all too often. There is sometimes a mismatch between the item and the response scale making it unclear what it means to moderately agree with that item. For example, what does it mean to moderately agree with the item "I joke and play with my child"? This is a poor item not only because it is a double-barreled question, but it is unclear what it means to agree with it. Less common problems are the presence of unlabeled points (which respondents may interpret differently) and the potential of using "response sets" or the ways someone might respond that are independent of the item. Response sets include acquiescence set (agreeing with oppositely worded statements), the opposition set (disagreeing with all statements), or the extreme set (selecting extreme responses). Although there are ways of dealing with these response sets, such as reversing a certain percentage of items, such precautions are not commonly taken.

Reliability.   There are two types of reliability problems: The reliability of the instrument or subscale may not be tested, and the reliability of the instrument may be low. The two most commonly

TABLE 14.3
Chief Methodological Problems with Attitude Questionnaires

Problem	*Example(s) of Problem*
A. *Item Composition*	
1. Vague words	"I believe in early toilet training"
2. Phrased in third person	"Few men realize that a mothers needs some fun in life too"
3. Lack of specificity	Response depends on situation
4. Double barreled	"I joke and play with my child"
5. Antiquated terms	"Children who take part in sex play become sex criminals . . ."
6. Social desirability	The socially desirable response
7. Mix of questions	Attitudes, beliefs, behavior intentions, perceptions
8. Inappropriate question results in assessment of nonattitude	"It is upsetting to a mother when her infant leaves half the formula in his (her) bottle"
B. *Response Scale*	
1. Response sets	Acquiescence (agreeing with opposite items)
2. Vague probability terms	"Sometimes" may be someone else's "rarely"
3. Mismatch between item and ratings scale	Unclear what it means to moderately agree with the item "I joke and play with my child"
4. Difficult to differentiate	Some scales have unlabeled points
5. Confusing	Disagreeing with double negative statements
C. *Reliability*	
1. No information	Only 25% of surveys provide test–retest data.
2. Low levels of reliability	Average coefficient alpha is .74
D. *Validity*	
1. No information	Only 43% of surveys have any validity data.
2. Low validity	Of those with data, evidence is weak.

Note. Examples are from the PARI, CRPR, or MAS.

reported forms of reliability are the internal consistency and the test–retest reliability. Only 45 percent of the 83 attitude questionnaires reviewed had internal consistency data, and 25 percent had test–retest data (Holden & Edwards, 1989). The median internal consistency of instruments using Cronbach's coefficient alpha to compute consistency was .76; only six instruments attained the recommended .80 level for research purposes. On the instruments that did report test–retest reliability, the mean correlation was .76.

Validity. Almost half of the developers of childrearing attitude instruments include some type of validity data. A variety of validity data is reported, including three types of construct validity—convergent, discriminant, and population—and three types of criterion validity—criterion groups, behavioral assessments, and predictive validity (Messick, 1980). Nevertheless, often the evidence purportedly supporting the validity of an instrument is limited at best and sometimes of dubious quality. For instance, the most important type of validity data concerns behavioral validity. However, as discussed later, there are relatively few assessments of the behavior link. More information about the reliability and validity of parent attitude questionnaires can be found in Holden and Edwards (1989).

Conceptual and Theoretical Issues

In addition to the methodological concerns, several conceptual concerns or theoretical issues can be raised about childrearing attitudes. The first concern is the continuing lack of theoretical orientation. With only scarce exceptions, the research into parental childrearing attitudes has been atheoretical. Without using theories to test hypotheses, build upon previous findings, and make predictions, progress has been limited in constructing a comprehensive understanding of the role parental attitudes play in parenting behavior or children's development. What makes the atheoretical nature of the work all the more surprising is that much of the attitude research in social psychology is theory driven. Social psychologists have been developing and testing "consistency" theories about attitudes since the appearance of Heider's (1946) balance theory. But with rare exceptions, parent attitude research has ignored attitude theories.

Other concerns involve the assumptions that underlie much of the parental attitude research, including: (1) Childrearing attitudes are preexisting, (2) childrearing attitudes are stable, (3) childrearing attitudes are unidimensional, and (4) childrearing attitudes determine parenting behavior.

Childrearing attitudes are preexisting. The preexistence of childrearing attitudes has largely been taken for granted. It is presumed that parents develop and hold a wide range of childrearing attitudes. However, there are various reasons why parents may not have a preexisting evaluation about a childrearing topic. First, the parent may simply have not thought about the issue before. Perhaps the attitude object had not yet been experienced, was not experienced frequently enough, or was not adequately salient for the parent to arrive at an evaluation. For example, a parent may not have considered an issue before if it concerned a child behavior, characteristic, or family structural configuration different from their own experience—such as questions dealing with older children or items concerning sibling relations when the parent has only one child. The attitude responses then provided by the parent represent what social psychologists call "nonattitudes" (Converse, 1970). No attitude instrument has asked "Have you thought about this issue before" or "Do you have an opinion"; maybe they should. Parents can respond to attitude questions but it may be with transient "newly constructed beliefs" (Sigel, 1986; see also McGillicuddy-De Lisi & Sigel, in this *Handbook*). Alternatively, the parent may have experienced the attitude object before, but just not arrived at a single, coherent evaluation of it. This could be due to a lack of attention given to the object or to the fact the parent may be ambivalent about the topic and unable to evaluate it in a consistent way. For whatever reason, to assume that the assessed attitude was preexisting can be misleading.

Childrearing attitudes are stable. A second assumption commonly made is that childrearing attitudes are stable. It is generally assumed that if an attitude is going to have a consistent effect on the child, then the attitude must be stable. Although it is possible that a short-lived but potent attitude (e.g., rejection of the child) could result in a lasting effect, there are no empirical data to support such speculation. Rather, it is commonly believed that attitudes are stable as they are formed from previous experience (Allport, 1935). As an early advocate of the importance of childrearing attitudes wrote, "Attitudes are acquired and molded by a thousand subtle influences which begin to impinge upon the human individual from the moment of birth. And from the moment of birth, also, the tiny and helpless human infant becomes an energizer of attitudes in those about him" (Glueck, 1928, p. 724). But such a constructionist and bidirectional view of attitudes implies a certain amount of plasticity to attitudes. Indeed, some investigators have found that childrearing attitudes are modified by changes in the child (Coleman, Kris, & Provence, 1953) or may differ across children in the family (Symonds, 1949). The feedback given by children to their parents can also be a potent influence for attitude change. As Patterson and Reid (1984) recognized, " ... parents' attitudes, attributions, and the manner in which they combine and label the ongoing behavior of their children are continuously shaped by their day-to-day microsocial interchanges with their children" (p. 253).

Several researchers have collected empirical data concerning the stability of attitudes. Investigators report that childrearing attitudes change as a result of the birth of a child (Zemlick & Watson, 1953) or passage of time (Hurley & Hohn, 1971). On the other hand, various investigators report childrearing attitudes are stable over time. For example, Hock and Lindamood (1981) found a median correlation of about .64 on the subscales of the MAS over 41 months. The least amount of stability was found for acceptance of emotional complexity in childrearing ($r = .56$); in contrast the highest level of stability was appropriate closeness with the child ($r = .78$). Another study reported that maternal negative attitudes toward children remained stable; $r = .52$ over a 12-month period (Rauh et al., 1990). In a longer longitudinal study, Roberts and his colleagues (1984) found a moderate degree of stability over ages of 3–12 years and concluded "the overall picture that emerges is one of considerable continuity in the general attitudes, values, and goals of the parents across many areas but with some changes toward increasing emphasis on achievement and independent behavior and decreasing emphasis on the expression of physical affection between parent and child from early childhood to early adolescence" (p. 545). Most recently McNally and her colleagues (1991) reported stability across 8 years on eight clusters of the CRPR, ranging from a low of .31 (enjoyment of children) to a high of .73 (expression of affect), with the median correlation of .57. The results of these studies indicate that at least some attitudes and values are based on deep-seated views that show little change, but to assume that all attitudes are stable is unfounded. It remains an open question which attitudes are stable, which are most susceptible to change, and why.

Childrearing attitudes are unidimensional. It is commonly thought that attitudes are easily measured entities that have one dimension to them—the parent is either in favor or not of the attitude object. Based on such implicit reasoning, attitudes are reduced to scores of acceptance or rejection, warmth or hostility, strictness or permissiveness. However, attitudes concerning interpersonal relations are likely to be more complex and more differentiated, given the rich knowledge base a parent has concerning a child.

For a variety of reasons, it can be argued that parental attitudes are probably more multidimensional than unidimensional. It is likely that parents hold a series of interdependent attitudes about the same attitude object—mediated by a variety of variables. As Stolz (1967) concluded based on her analysis of her interviews concerning parental attitudes, "parents operate within a milieu of psychological pressures" (p. 278). The pressures may result from competing ideas of short- and long-term goals, conflicts between attitudes, or the competing needs of different individuals. But to try to reduce those psychological pressures into a unidimensional attitude score is problematic, at best.

Childrearing attitudes determine behavior. The single most important assumption underlying the parent attitude research is that attitudes determine behavior, or at least are related to behavior. Despite the importance of that question, there are fewer than 20 studies that have investigated the links between childrearing attitudes and parenting behavior. The PARI has been the most commonly used attitude survey for this purpose; five studies have attempted to relate it to behavioral observations. For example, Zunich (1962) correlated attitude scales and behavior in the laboratory. Only 12 of 272 correlations were significant—fewer than would be expected by chance! Similarly, Brody (1965) found that only 1 of the 23 PARI scales was correlated to observed behavior in the laboratory. A more successful effort was conducted by Radin and Glasser (1972) when they correlated the PARI with behavior in the home. They found the authoritarian-control factor was negatively associated with observed nurturant behavior and four out of the five other behaviors coded.

The use of other instruments has produced a similar pattern of mixed results. Tulkin and Cohler (1973) obtained some success when they correlated the MAS with maternal behavior in the home. Fifteen reliable correlations (out of 85) were found. For example, middle-class mothers with positive attitudes toward promoting interaction with their children were observed to engage in more face-to-face interactions, to hold their children more, and to put their infants in the playpen less often than mothers who did not hold that value. It is interesting to note that only four of the relations held with the working-class mothers. Tulkin and Cohler speculated that working-class mothers did not believe they could affect their children's development in the way the middle-class mothers did; therefore their behavior was less likely to correspond with their attitudes.

Iverson and Segal (1992) also achieved some success at linking attitudes with behavior when they observed parents interacting with their preschool children. They found that positive attitudes toward such goals as responsibility, independence, and creativity in their children (vs. obedience) were positively correlated with spending more time with children, asking more questions, and being less critical of their children. Some other investigations have also found significant relations between attitudes and behaviors (e.g., Baumrind, 1971; Easterbrooks & Goldberg, 1984; Egeland & Farber, 1984), however the number of significant correlations tends to be few and limited to one sex of parent or child.

Miller (1988), in a review of parents' beliefs, concluded that there is indeed evidence relating parental beliefs with actions but too little research has been done on the topic. There are a number of reasons why researchers have had only marginal success in relating childrearing attitudes to parental behavior. Given that behavior is multiply determined, it is unlikely that just childrearing attitudes (even if they were perfectly assessed) could be found to determine behavior. Goodnow (1984, 1988, in this *Handbook*) believes that researchers can do much better in finding links between parental social cognition and behavior. Part of the problem is that studies addressing the link have failed to assess behaviors that would reflect the attitudes studied, patterns of attitudes have not been considered, and maternal behaviors have not been aggregated across a range of childrearing situations. Furthermore, global attitudes cannot be expected to predict specific behaviors. She recommends that studies need to: (1) aim for a closer fit between attitudes and behavior, (2) ask for specific rather than general reports, (3) increase awareness to increase the correspondence, (4) use aggregated data, and (5) recognize that correspondence will be higher in some people than others, and under some conditions and actions than under others.

Sigel (1986) made several different but important points based on his research into parental beliefs and behavior. He found that decontextualized and global beliefs or attitudes do not map onto behavior. Although attitudes or beliefs can be guides for action, the realization of those abstract beliefs into behavior is mediated by specific and concrete beliefs. Furthermore, the behavioral expression of those specific beliefs can be mediated by the nature of the context. For example, a parent can have a positive attitude toward the use of physical punishment, but also have several more specific beliefs about when a spank is appropriate. In addition, if the context is not appropriate for spanking (e.g., others present), the parent may inhibit the behavior.

Researchers are beginning to conduct better studies to assess attitude-behavior links. Kochanska, Kucyznski, and Radke-Yarrow (1989) designed their study with some of the aforementioned comments in mind. It paid off as they found a reliable correspondence between mothers' childrearing attitudes (assessed with the CRPR) and observed behavior when the attitude items matched the content of the action and when aggregated data were used. However, the magnitude of the correlation was modest. A different approach was taken by Holden, Coleman, Schmidt, and O'Dell (1993) who focused on the relation of one specific attitude to reports of the corresponding behavior. Mothers reported, in daily telephone interviews, how they had responded to their 3-year-old children's misbehaviors. After 2 weeks, their reports of spanking were aggregated and then correlated with their attitudes toward physical punishment, as assessed by a 10-item questionnaire. Attitudes were reliably correlated with reported behavior, indicating that specific attitudes can indeed be significantly linked to specific behavior. Although this study does not demonstrate a causal link, presumably the preexisting maternal attitude helped to determine maternal behavior.

Summary

A number of methodological and conceptual concerns have been raised about parental childrearing attitudes. Each of these concerns can be addressed with appropriate research, although to date they have not been adequately studied. Despite these concerns, the construct of childrearing attitudes is too valuable to dispense with. At the same time, there is much work to be done to improve the quality of attitude assessments and the research. A number of interesting and important issues concerning parental attitudes merit investigation.

FUTURE DIRECTIONS

It is safe to predict that the study of childrearing attitudes will be popular for a long time to come. Childrearing attitudes are too entrenched, too appealing, and too easy to use. At the same time, as indicated in the previous review, parental attitudes have been useful and continue to hold much promise. But it would be a shame if they continued to be used in the primitive and relatively thoughtless way they appear all too frequently. Such efforts would be largely a waste of time. Instead, future work into parental attitudes might pursue four directions: (1) explicating the nature of parental attitudes, (2) studying the origins and modification of childrearing attitudes, (3) identifying the conditions when attitudes impact behavior, and (4) revealing the ways in which attitudes modify information processing.

The Nature of Attitudes

It is startling to realize that, despite all the attitude studies that have been published, very little is known about the nature of parents' attitudes. Typically, the only index of a childrearing attitude is a numerical score indicating the extent to which a parent agrees or disagrees with the attitude object. The only information this provides is that the parent reacted to particular questions in a particular way. There is a great deal of other meaningful data that could be collected but is commonly ignored. A full explication of parental attitudes would include differentiating attitudes from nonattitudes and identifying key characteristics of attitudes.

The first place to start in explicating attitudes is to determine whether the parent does indeed hold an attitude toward the attitude object. As discussed earlier, some childrearing attitude questions may be orthogonal to the parent's experience and thus the parent has not yet formed an opinion. If the parent does not hold an opinion, the measured attitude is actually a nonattitude and any subsequent finding would most likely be spurious.

A full assessment of the nature of childrearing attitudes should also involve characterizing attitudes on a variety of indices. Some morphological indices to capture the nature of attitudes are being developed by social psychologists (Abelson, 1988; Pratkanis, Breckler, & Greenwald, 1989; Schlegel & DiTecco, 1982). Among the indices that appear especially useful for measuring childrearing attitudes are the organization and differentiation, intensity and extremity, and complexity and degree of ambivalence of the attitudes.

The structure of childrearing attitudes, indexed by its organization and differentiation, needs to be examined. With the exception of some correlational and factor analysis studies, there have been no systematic efforts to explore the organization of parental attitudes. For instance, can a hierarchical organization be found, whereby some attitudes are indeed subordinate to broader values? It would be extremely useful to apply some of the concepts (e.g., networks, categorization) and methods used in cognitive development to chart the landscape of childrearing attitudes. Bacon and Ashmore (1986) presented one such model for doing this and illustrated the utility of looking at how parents categorize children's behavior (Bacon & Ashmore, 1985). Similarly, the intensity and extremity of childrearing attitudes are two other characteristics of attitudes that have been largely ignored. Instead of assuming that the strength of an attitude falls on a linear scale, the inclusion of indices of the intensity and extremity of attitudes would help to better reveal its nature.

There are ample indications that many of the attitudes parents hold can be characterized by varying degrees of complexity and ambivalence. For instance, there is anecdotal evidence that parents do indeed hold ambivalent attitudes. As the author Rich (1976) wrote, "My children cause me the most exquisite suffering of which I have any experience. It is the suffering of ambivalence: the murderous alternation between bitter resentment and raw-edged nerves, and blissful gratification and tenderness" (p. 21). Holden and Ritchie (1988) discussed the phenomenon of ambivalence in attitudes, though it sometimes appears under the guise of dilemmas, conflicts, or guilt. Ambivalence can be found in both "outer" conflicts—associated with sources external to the parent (e.g., professional advice, spouse, mother-in-law)—and inner conflicts. The inner ones are probably more pervasive and perturbing. Ambivalent attitudes are likely to be found in such domains as parental involvement in childrearing, dependency versus autonomy, and balancing the needs of the individuals in the family.

Hock and her co-workers (DeMeis, Hock, & McBride, 1986) recognized that ambivalence is a common attribute of maternal attitudes toward employment in our society. With regard to a number of issues, such as the level of involvement, the amount of choice given to a child, and the degree of protection from potential negative influences, parents must make various decisions. It is likely that the most effective and competent parents are the ones who do not hold rigid attitudes but rather are ambivalent and make adjustments in their behavior based on a variety of considerations (Holden & Ritchie, 1988). Other investigators have made similar arguments. Recall that Cohler's MAS questionnaire (Cohler et al., 1970) measures ambivalent feelings about the childrearing role and interprets that to be a healthy response; Egeland and Farber (1984) found empirical support for this as mothers of securely attached infants admitted to more ambivalent feelings about the childrearing role on the MAS than mothers of insecurely attached infants. Belsky (1984) and his colleagues also appeared to agree: "In summary, the most effective pattern of parenting for facilitating children's success at school as well as their general intellectual development seems to involve being nurturant without being too restrictive, responsive but not overly controlling, and stimulating but not too directive" (p. 66). If these investigators are right, then a great deal more attention needs to be devoted to balance and ambivalence in childrearing attitudes.

The Origins and Modification of Childrearing Attitudes

If researchers are to fully understand parental childrearing attitudes and their impact on behavior, systematic inquiries into their development are needed. To date, the origins of childrearing attitudes have been investigated exclusively through the approach of intergenerational transmission. But the observed correlations between generations are typically low—far lower than can be accounted for by measurement error. Evidently there are other important ingredients in the development of parenting attitudes. Efforts need to be directed at documenting how previous experiences with children, information from child-care advice books (Clarke-Stewart, 1978; Young, 1990), intervention or parent education classes (Radin & Glasser, 1972), and other sources of information and experience contribute to the development of particular attitudes.

Going hand in hand with the origins of attitude formation is attitude change. Although few studies have looked at how childrearing attitudes have changed over time, there needs to be more attention devoted to efforts to change parental attitudes. Social psychologists call the study of attitude change "persuasion" (e.g., Perloff, 1993). Studies explicitly focusing on persuading individuals to modify their childbearing and childrearing attitudes are needed in order to address contemporary social problems. Issues such as sex education, adolescent pregnancy, abortion, adoption, prenatal care, paternal involvement, breastfeeding, physical punishment, wife and child abuse, and child support payments are applied issues that can fit under the province of attitude research. Investigations looking into the way preexisting attitudes can be modified should be an important goal for attitude researchers.

The Attitude-Behavior Relation

The single most important question concerning childrearing attitudes is how do they relate to parenting behavior. And as indicated in the previous review, there are many unresolved questions in this area. For example, when is parental behavior guided by attitudes and philosophies and when is it more influenced by what is most convenient or expeditious? A great deal of work is needed in two areas: examining concurrent attitude-behavior relations and testing whether attitudes predict subsequent parenting behavior (or vice versa).

One good place to start is to borrow attitude-behavior models from social psychology. The well-known expectancy value model or the theory of reasoned action (Ajzen & Fishbein, 1980) has been useful in understanding behavioral choice by assessing not just attitudes but beliefs about the attitude object, beliefs about norms, motivation to comply to the norms, and a weighting of the attitudes and norms. In one of the few examples where a social psychological attitude model was applied to developmental issues, the theory of reasoned action was successfully applied in the prediction of whether mothers would bottle- or breastfeed their babies (Manstead, Proffitt, & Smart, 1983).

Of the alternative models to the attitude-behavior relation, such as the functional measurement methodology (Anderson, 1981), the most promising is Fazio's (1986) five-step Attitude Accessibility Model. The basic premise is that accessible attitudes—those activated more quickly—will be more powerful determinants of behavior than less accessible attitudes. In the first step, the attitude is activated by retrieving from memory one's evaluation of the attitude object. The activation step is critical: If the attitude is not activated, then it cannot guide information processing and behavior. Once activated, the attitude influences perception of the attitude object. That, in turn, helps to influence the interpretation of the situation. These perceptions influence subsequent behavior toward the object. Fazio identified the prime determinant of activation as the "associative strength" or the degree of association between the attitude object (e.g., spanking) and the evaluation of that attitude object (e.g., not effective). The strength then determines an attitude's chronic accessibility—the likelihood it will be activated upon exposure to the attitude object. One implication of this theory is that attitudes can affect behavior without any effort or intention in a spontaneous or automatic manner for well-learned associations.

This model as well as others can provide a useful avenue for making theoretical progress toward understanding the attitude-behavior link. That in turn will be useful for predicting parenting behavior. To date there are only a few studies that have reported that attitudes predict parental behavior. In one study, prenatal maternal attitudes toward responsiveness were positively correlated with maternal sensitivity in a behavioral assessment when their children were 12 months old (Crockenberg & McCluskey, 1986). Kochanska (1990) found that mothers who endorsed authoritative attitudes on the CRPR when the children were 2 years old avoided prohibitive interventions when the children were 5 years old.

Childrearing Attitudes and Social Cognition

Until recently, attitudes have been studied in a vacuum, independent of other aspects of parental social cognition or parental affect. Part of the reason for this is that childrearing attitudes have not been adequately differentiated, as discussed earlier. Attitude has been used synonymously with beliefs, values, and perceptions and attitude questionnaires have typically contained a mix of questions concerning instrumental and descriptive beliefs, values, perceptions, behavioral intentions, and expectations. Presumably, if the different components were kept separate, reflecting improved conceptual clarity, new and clearer findings would result (Goodnow, in this *Handbook*).

In general, childrearing attitudes must be renovated to reflect contemporary thinking about social cognition. Rather than the passive, global attitudes of old, parenting attitudes must be rebuilt to reflect what we know about how social cognition is used in everyday life. For example, a number of researchers in parenting have written about childrearing as being goal driven or goal regulated (Dix, 1991; Emmerich, 1969; Kuczynski, 1984; Maccoby & Martin, 1983). A parental goal might be to get a child to clean up a room, to keep a child quiet and compliant during a shopping trip, or to have fun with a child. How childrearing attitudes impact on or are influenced by the specific goals or contexts has never been studied. A more complex, context-specific understanding of the role of attitudes in social cognition is clearly warranted.

Besides understanding how attitudes relate to other aspects of social cognition, further understanding relations between attitudes and how they affect information processing is needed. There are at least three main ways in which childrearing attitudes can affect information processing: selective exposure, selective perception, and selective memory (Eagly, 1992). Festinger's (1957) theory of cognitive dissonance provides a well-known example of how attitudes can modify information processing. He found that individuals sought out information that supports their attitude and avoided information that challenges it. This has subsequently been labeled selective exposure and attention. Selective perception and judgment refers to evidence that prior attitudes affect what is perceived and how that information is evaluated. For instance, information that challenges attitudes will be unfavorably evaluated. However, information that is congruent with attitudes is more likely to be remembered—a phenomenon that has been recognized for many decades and labeled the "congeniality bias" (see Eagly, 1992). Selective memory refers to the effect that attitudes tend to bias us to remember some things but not others. The ways in which childrearing attitudes may be related to these three selective processes in parents merits research attention.

Perhaps the clearest evidence that childrearing attitudes are related to information processing appeared in a study by Dix, Ruble, and Zambarano (1989). They found that mothers who endorsed authoritarian attitudes on a questionnaire reported they would be more upset, more stern, and give longer time-outs than mothers who scored low on authoritarian attitudes. Those findings suggest a related area of research merits investigation—links between parenting attitudes and parent affect. As Dix (1991) theorized, parental emotion is closely linked to parental goals; it is likely that childrearing attitudes—especially those characterized by extremity, may well be associated with parental affect. Given the salience of affect in parenting, work at the interface of childrearing attitudes and emotion is needed.

Summary

These four areas will provide ample work for the near future. Each represents efforts to understand better the processes and mechanisms associated with parental attitudes. Studies relating parental attitudes to child outcomes will undoubtedly continue. It seems many investigators cannot resist the appeal of finding a significant correlation or two between parent and child variables. However, such correlations often go unreplicated and ultimately are not very useful in understanding development. An orientation toward understanding the processes associated with children's outcomes is what is needed for advancing knowledge in the field. As is evident in these prescriptions for future research, much more attention needs to be given to the work by social psychologists, as reviewers of parental social cognition research have already called for (Goodnow, 1988; Goodnow, in this *Handbook;* McGillicuddy-De Lisi & Sigel, in this *Handbook;* Miller, 1988; Sigel, 1986). Researchers into parental attitudes have almost completely ignored both the research and the theoretical models. Collaborative efforts between social and developmental researchers would undoubtedly be a fruitful relationship.

CONCLUSIONS

After more than 60 years of study and despite great popularity of the research paradigm, the promise of childrearing attitudes has yet to be realized. A balanced evaluation of the approach must conclude that it has been useful for addressing and understanding some of the questions associated with parenting. For example, the parenting attitudes have been especially useful for understanding the determinants of parental behavior and the functioning of mothers. To a lesser extent childrearing attitudes have been helpful in revealing correlates of children's adjustment and outcomes. But childrearing attitudes have been least successful at the very thing they were billed to do: revealing why children develop as they do. This is in part due to overselling of what attitudes could do and in part due to poor methodology and untested assumptions. The problems have been exasperated by the fact that many researchers have been superficial consumers of the paradigm. It is time to move beyond the first stage of childrearing attitude research—a stage characterized by descriptive and atheoretical investigations, simplistic models, weak methodology, and untested assumptions.

That having been said, it remains clear that childrearing attitudes represent a powerful construct of both theoretical and practical importance for understanding, predicting, and changing parental behavior. But the promise of the construct will never be realized without a more evolved conceptualization and greater methodological sophistication. It is time to carefully test the underlying assumptions and adopt theoretically rich approaches in order to build an accurate understanding of the role that childrearing attitudes play in both children's and their parents' functioning and development. Only by developing a more refined approach to conceptualizing and studying childrearing attitudes can one fully reap the benefits from it.

ACKNOWLEDGMENTS

I thank Mitchell Greene and Brandon Haga for library research and Pamela O'Dell for comments on a previous draft. The preparation of this chapter was supported, in part, by NICHD Grant 1 RO1 HD26574-01A1.

REFERENCES

Abelson, R. P. (1988). Conviction. *American Psychologist, 43*, 267–275.

Ackerley, L. A. (1935). The information and attitudes regarding child development possessed by parents of elementary school children. In G. D. Stoddard (Ed.), *University of Iowa studies: Studies in child welfare: Vol. 10. Researchers in parent education* (pp. 113–167). Iowa City: University of Iowa.

Ajzen, I., & Fishbein, M. (1980). *Understanding attitudes and predicting social behavior.* Engelwood Cliffs, NJ: Prentice-Hall.

Allport, G. (1935). Attitudes. In C. Murchison (Ed.), *A handbook of social psychology* (pp. 798–844). Worcester, MA: Clark University Press.

Anderson, N. H. (1981). *Foundations of information integration theory.* San Diego: Academic Press.

Antill, J. K. (1987). Parents' beliefs and values about sex roles, sex differences, and sexuality: Their sources and implications. In P. Shaver & C. Hendrick (Eds.), *Sex and gender: Review of personality and social psychology* (Vol. 7, pp. 294–328). Beverly Hills, CA: Sage.

Avison, W. R., Turner, R. J., & Noh, S. (1986). Screening for problem parenting: Preliminary evidence on a promising instrument. *Child Abuse & Neglect, 10,* 157–170.

Bacon, M. K., & Ashmore, R. D. (1985). How mothers and fathers categorize descriptions of social behavior attributed to daughters and sons. *Social Cognition, 3,* 193–217.

Bacon, M. K., & Ashmore, R. D. (1986). A consideration of the cognitive activities of parents and their role in the socialization process. In R. D. Ashmore & D. M. Brodzinsky (Eds.), *Thinking about the family: Views of parents and children* (pp. 3–33). Hillsdale, NJ: Lawrence Erlbaum Associates.

Bakwin, R. M., & Bakwin, H. (1942). *Psychologic care during infancy and childhood.* New York: Appleton–Century.

Baldwin, A. L., Kalhorn, J., & Breese, F. (1945). Patterns of parent behavior. *Psychological Monographs, 58*(3, Whole No. 268).

Banner, C. N. (1979). Child-rearing attitudes of mothers of under-, average-, and over-achieving children. *British Journal of Educational Psychology, 49,* 150–155.

Baranowski, M. D., Schilmoeller, G. L., & Higgins, B. S. (1990). Parenting attitudes of adolescent and older mothers. *Adolescence, 25,* 781–790.

Bates, J. E., & Bayles, K. (1984). Objective and subjective components in mothers' perceptions of their children from age 6 months to 3 years. *Merrill-Palmer Quarterly, 30,* 111–130.

Baumrind, D. (1971). Current patterns of parental authority. *Developmental Psychology Monographs, 4,* (No. 1, Pt. 2).

Baumrind, D., & Black, A. E. (1967). Socialization practices associated with dimensions of competence in preschool boys and girls. *Child Development, 38,* 291–327.

Becker, W. C., & Krug, R. S. (1965). The Parent Attitude Reseach Instrument—A research review. *Child Development, 36,* 329–365.

Belsky, J. (1984). The determinants of parenting: A process model. *Child Development, 55,* 83–96.

Bigner, J. J. (1977). Attitudes toward fathering and father–child activity. *Home Economics Research Journal, 6,* 98–106.

Block, J. (1955). Personality characteristics associated with fathers' attitudes toward child-rearing. *Child Development, 26,* 41–48.

Block, J. H. (1965). *The Child-Rearing Practice Report (CRPR): A set of Q items for the description of parental socialization attitudes and values.* Berkeley: University of California, Institute of Human Development.

Block, J. H., Block, J., & Morrison, A. (1981). Parental agreement-disagreement on child-rearing orientations and gender-related personality correlates in children. *Child Development, 52,* 965–974.

Brody, G. F. (1965). Relationship between maternal attitudes and behavior. *Journal of Personality and Social Psychology, 2,* 317–323.

Bronner, E. V. (1936). Can parents' attitudes toward their problem children be modified by child guidance treatment? *Smith College Studies in Social Work, 7,* 1–16.

Brunnquell, D., Crichton, L., & Egeland, B. (1981). Maternal personality and attitude in disturbances of child rearing. *American Journal of Orthopsychiatry, 51,* 680–691.

Burchinal, L. G., Hawkes, G. R., & Gardner, B. (1957). The relationship between parental acceptance and adjustment of children. *Child Development, 28,* 65–77.

Camp, B. W., & Morgan, L. J. (1984). Child-rearing attitudes and personality characteristics in adolescent mothers: Attitudes toward the infant. *Journal of Pediatric Psychology, 9,* 57–63.

Chen, C., & Stevenson, H. W. (1989). Homework: A cross-cultural examination. *Child Development, 60,* 551–561.

Chiu, L. H. (1987). Child-rearing attitudes of Chinese, Chinese-American, and Anglo-American mothers. *International Journal of Psychology, 22,* 409–419.

Chorost, S. B. (1962). Parental child-rearing attitudes and their correlates in adolescent hostility. *Genetic Psychology Monographs, 66,* 49–90.

Clarke-Stewart, A. (1978). Popular primers for parents. *American Psychologist, 33,* 359–369.

Clifford, E. (1962). Expressed attitudes in pregnancy of unwed women and married primigravida and multigravida. *Child Development, 33,* 945–951.

Cochran, M., & Brassard, J. (1979). Child development and personal social networks. *Child Development, 50,* 601–616.

Cohler, B. J., & Grunebaum, H. U. (1981). *Mothers, grandmothers, and daughters: Personality and childcare in three-gerneration families.* New York: Wiley.

Cohler, B. J., Weiss, J. L., & Grunebaum, H. U. (1970). Child care attitudes and emotional disturbance among mothers of young children. *Genetic Psychology Monographs, 82,* 3–47.

Coleman, R. W., Kris, E., & Provence, S. (1953). The study of variations of early parental attitudes. *The Psychoanalytic Study of the Child, 8,* 20–47.

Conger, R. D., McCarty, J. A., Yang, R. K., Laney, B. B., & Kropp, J. P. (1984). Perception of child, child-rearing values, and emotional distress as mediating links between environmental stressors and observed maternal behaviors. *Child Development, 55,* 22.

Converse, J. M., & Presser, S. (1986). *Survey questions: Handcrafting the standardized questionnaire.* Beverly Hills, CA: Sage.

Converse, P. E. (1970). Attitudes and non-attitudes: Continuation of a dialogue. In E. R. Tufte (Ed.), *The quantitative analysis of social problems* (pp. 168–189). Reading, MA: Addison-Wesley.

Cox, M. J., Owen, M. T., Lewis, J. M., & Henderson, V. K. (1989). Marriage, adult adjustment, and early parenting. *Child Development, 60,* 1015–1024.

Crase, S. J., Clark, S. G., & Pease, D. (1979). *Iowa parent behavior inventory manual.* Ames: Iowa State University.

Crnic, K. A., Greenberg, M. T., Ragozin, A., Robinson, N., & Basham, R. (1983). Effects of stress and social support on mothers and premature and full-term infants. *Child Development, 54,* 209–217.

Crockenberg, S. (1987). Predictors and correlates of anger toward and punitive control of toddlers by adolescent mothers. *Child Development, 58,* 964–975.

Crockenberg, S. B., & McCluskey, K. (1986). Change in maternal behavior during the baby's first year of life. *Child Development, 57,* 746–753.

Cutrona, C. W., & Troutman, B. R. (1986). Social support, infant temperament, and parenting self-efficacy: A mediational model of post-partum depression. *Child Development, 57,* 1507–1518.

Davids, A., & Holden, R. H. (1970). Consistency of maternal attitudes and personality from pregnancy to eight months following childbirth. *Developmental Psychology, 2,* 364–366.

Deal, J. E., Halverson, C. F., Jr., & Wampler, K. S. (1989). Parental agreement on child-rearing orientations: Relations to parental, marital, family, and child characteristics. *Child Development, 60,* 1025–1034.

De Luccie, M. F., & Davis, A. J. (1991). Do men's adult life concerns affect their fathering orientations. *Journal of Psychology, 125,* 175–188.

DeMeis, D. K., Hock, E., & McBride, S. L. (1986). The balance of employment and motherhood: Longitudinal study of mothers' feelings about separation from their first-born infants. *Developmental Psychology, 22,* 627–632.

Despres, M. A. (1937). Favorable and unfavorable attitudes toward pregnancy in primiparae. *Journal of Genetic Psychology, 51,* 241–254.

Dix, T. (1991). The affective organization of parenting: Adaptive and maladaptive processes. *Psychological Bulletin, 110,* 3–25.

Dix, T., Ruble, D. N., & Zambarano, R. J. (1989). Mothers' implicit theories of discipline: Child effects, parent effects, and the attribution process. *Child Development, 60,* 1373–1391.

Drews, E. M., & Teahan, J. E. (1957). Parental attitudes and academic achievement. *Journal of Clinical Psychology, 13,* 328–332.

Durrett, M. E., O'Bryant, S., & Pennebaker, J. W. (1975). Child-rearing reports of White, Black, and Mexican-American families. *Developmental Psychology, 11,* 871.

Eagly, A. H. (1992). Uneven progress: Social psychology and the study of attitudes. *Journal of Personality and Social Psychology, 63,* 693–710.

Easterbrooks, M. A., & Goldberg, W. A. (1984). Toddler development in the family: Impact of father involvement and parenting characteristics. *Child Development, 55,* 740–752.

Egeland, B., & Farber, E. A. (1984). Infant–mother attachment: Factors related to its development and changes over time. *Child Development, 55,* 753–771.

Emmerich, W. (1969). The parental role: A cognitive-functional approach. *Monographs of the Society for Research in Child Development, 34*(8, Serial No. 132).

Fagot, B. I., Leinbach, M. D., & O'Boyle, C. (1992). Gender labeling, gender stereotyping, and parenting behaviors. *Developmental Psychology, 28,* 225–230.

Fazio, R. H. (1986). How do attitudes guide behavior? In R. M. Sorrentino & E. T. Higgins (Eds.), *Handbook of motivation and cognition: Foundations of social behavior* (pp. 204–243). New York: Guilford.

Festinger, L. (1957). *A theory of cognitive dissonance.* Stanford, CA: Stanford University Press.

Field, M. (1940). Maternal attitudes found in twenty-five cases of children with behavior primary disorders. *American Journal of Orthopsychiatry, 10,* 293–311.

Fleming, A. S., Ruble, D. N., Flett, G. L., & Shaul, D. L. (1988). Postpartum adjustment in first-time mothers: Relations between mood, maternal attitudes, and mother–infant interactions. *Developmental Psychology, 24,* 71–81.

Fox, R. A., Baisch, M. J., Goldberg, B. D., & Hochmuth, M. C. (1987). Parenting attitudes of pregnant adolescents. *Psychological Reports, 61,* 403–406.

Francis, K. V., & Fillmore, E. A. (1934). The influence of environment upon the personality of children. *University of Iowa Studies in Child Welfare, 9,* 1–71.

Freeman, R. V., & Grayson, H. M. (1955). Maternal attitudes in schizophrenia. *Journal of Abnormal & Social Psychology, 50,* 45–52.

Freud, S. (1936). *The problem of anxiety.* New York: Norton.

Frodi, A. M., Lamb, M. E., Frodi, M., Hwang, C., Forsstrom, B., & Corry, T. (1982). Stability and change in parental attitudes following an infant's birth into traditional and nontraditional Swedish families. *Scandinavian Journal of Psychology, 23,* 53–62.

Furstenberg, F. F. J. (1976). *Unplanned parenthood: The social consequences of teenage childbearing.* New York: The Free Press.

Gaines, R., Sandgrund, A., Green, A. H., & Power, E. (1978). Etiological factors in child maltreatment: A multivariate study of abusing, neglecting, and normal mothers. *Journal of Abnormal Psychology, 87,* 531–540.

Gardner, L. P. (1943). A survey of the attitudes and activities of fathers. *Journal of Genetic Psychology, 63,* 15–53.

Garrett, A. (1936). Attitude therapy. In E. R. Groves & P. Blanchard (Eds.), *Readings in mental hygiene* (pp. 36–40). New York: Holt.

Gildea, M. C.-L., Glidewell, J. C., & Kantor, M. B. (1961). Maternal attitudes and general adjustment in school children. In J. C. Glidewell (Ed.), *Parental attitudes and behavior* (pp. 42–89). Springfield, IL: Thomas.

Gjerde, P. F. (1988). Parental concordance on child rearing and the interactive emphases of parents: Sex-differentiated relationships during the preschool years. *Developmental Psychology, 24,* 700–706.

Glueck, B. (1927). Concerning parental attitudes. *Child Study, 4,* 3–11.

Glueck, B. (1928). The significance of parental attitudes for the destiny of the individual. *Mental Hygiene, 12,* 722–741.

Goldberg, W. A., & Easterbrooks, M. A. (1984). Role of marital quality in toddler development. *Developmental Psychology, 20,* 504–514.

Goldberg, W. A., & Easterbrooks, M. A. (1988). Maternal employment when children are toddlers and kindergartners. In A. E. Gottfried & A. W. Gottfried (Eds.), *Maternal employment and children's development: Longitudinal research* (pp. 121–154). New York: Plenum.

Goodnow, J. J. (1984). Parents' ideas about parenting and development: A review of issues and recent work. In M. Lamb, A. Brown, & B. Rogoff (Eds.), *Advances in developmental psychology* (pp. 193–242). Hillsdale, NJ: Lawrence Erlbaum Associates.

Goodnow, J. J. (1988). Parents' ideas, actions, and feelings: Models and methods from developmental and social psychology. *Child Development, 59,* 286–320.

Goodnow, J. J. (1992). Parents' ideas, children's ideas: Correspondence and divergence. In I. E. Sigel, A. V. McGillicuddy-De Lisi, & J. J. Goodnow (Eds.), *Parental belief systems: The psychological consequences for children* (pp. 293–317). Hillsdale, NJ: Lawrence Erlbaum Associates.

Hanson, R. A., & Mullis, R. L. (1986). Intergenerational transfer of normative parental attitudes. *Psychological Reports, 59,* 711–714.

Harris, D. B., Gough, H. G., & Martin, W. E. (1950). Children's ethnic attitudes: Vol. 2. Relationship to parental beliefs concerning child rearing. *Child Development, 21,* 169–181.

Heider, F. (1946). Attitudes and cognitive organization. *Journal of Psychology, 21,* 107–112.

Ho, D. Y. F., & Kang, T. K. (1984). Intergenerational comparisons of child-rearing attitudes and practices in Hong Kong. *Developmental Psychology, 20,* 1004–1016.

Hock, E., & DeMeis, D. K. (1990). Depression in mothers of infants: The role of maternal employment. *Developmental Psychology, 26,* 285–291.

Hock, E., & Lindamood, E. (1981). Continuity of child-rearing attitudes in mothers of young children. *Journal of Genetic Psychology, 138,* 305–306.

Hock, E., McBride, S. L., & Gnezda, M. T. (1989). Maternal separation anxiety: Mother–infant separation from the maternal perspective. *Child Development, 60,* 793–802.

Hoffman, L. W., Thornton, A., & Manis, J. D. (1978). The value of children to parents in the United States. *Journal of Population, 1,* 91–131.

Holden, G. W., Coleman, S. D., Schmidt, K. L., & O'Dell, P. C. (1993, March). *Maternal use of physical punishment: Instrumental practices in the home.* Paper presented at the biennial meeting of the Society for Research in Child Development, New Orleans.

Holden, G. W., & Edwards, J. (1989). Parental attitudes toward child rearing: Instruments, issues, and implications. *Psychological Bulletin, 106,* 29–58.

Holden, G. W., & Ritchie, K. L. (1988). Child rearing and the dialectics of parental intelligence. In J. Valsiner (Ed.), *Child development within culturally structured environments: Vol. 1. Parent cognition and adult-child interaction* (pp. 30–59). Norwood, NJ: Ablex.

Holden, G. W., & Zambarano, R. J. (1992). Passing the rod: Similarities between parents and their young children in orientations toward physical punishment. In I. E. Sigel, A. V. McGillicuddy-De Lisi, & J. J. Goodnow (Eds.), *Parental belief systems: The psychological consequences for children* (2nd ed., pp. 143–172). Hillsdale, NJ: Lawrence Erlbaum Associates.

Holtzman, W. H., Diaz-Guerrero, R., & Swartz, J. D. (1975). *Personality development in two cultures.* Austin: University of Texas Press.

Horney, K. (1933). Maternal conflicts. *American Journal of Orthopsychiatry, 3,* 455–463.

Hurley, J. R. (1965). Parental acceptance-rejection and children's intelligence. *Merrill–Palmer Quarterly, 11,* 19–31.

Hurley, J. R., & Hohn, R. L. (1971). Shifts in child-rearing attitudes linked with parenthood and occupation. *Developmental Psychology, 4,* 324–328.

Huston, A. C. (1983). Sex typing. In E. M. Hetherington (Ed.), *Handbook of child psychology: Vol. 4. Socialization, personality, and social development* (pp. 387–467). New York: Wiley.

Hyson, M. C., Whitehead, L. C., & Prudhoe, C. M. (1988). Influences on attitudes toward physical affection between adults and children. *Early Childhood Research Quarterly, 3,* 55–75.

Itkin, W. (1952). Some relationships between intra-family attitudes and pre-parental attitudes toward children. *Journal of Genetic Psychology, 80,* 221–252.

Iverson, T. J., & Segal, M. (1992). Social behavior of maltreated children: Exploring links to parent behavior and beliefs. In I. E. Sigel, A. McGillicuddy-De Lisi, & J. J. Goodnow (Eds.), *Parent beliefs systems: The psychological consequences for children* (2nd ed., pp. 267–289). Hillsdale, NJ: Lawrence Erlbaum Associates.

Jones, E. (1923). The phantasy of the reversal of generations. *Papers on psycho-analysis* (pp. 674–679). New York: Wood.

Katkovsky, W., Preston, A., & Crandall, V. J. (1964). Parents' achievement attitudes and their behavior with their children in achievement situations. *Journal of Genetic Psychology, 104,* 105–121.

Kinstler, D. B. (1961). Covert and overt maternal rejection in stuttering. *Journal of Speech and Hearing Disorders, 26,* 145–155.

Kitano, H. H. L. (1964). Inter and intragenerational differences in maternal attitudes toward child rearing. *Journal of Social Psychology, 63,* 215–220.

Koch, H. L., Dentler, M., Dysart, B., & Streit, H. (1934). A scale for measuring attitude toward the question of children's freedom. *Child Development, 5,* 253–266.

Kochanska, G. (1990). Maternal beliefs as long-term predictors of mother–child interaction and report. *Child Development, 61,* 1934–1943.

Kochanska, G., Kuczynski, L., & Radke-Yarrow, M. (1989). Correspondence between mothers' self-reported and observed child-rearing practices. *Child Development, 60,* 56–63.

Kohn, M. L. (1963). Social class and parent–child relationships: An interpretation. *American Journal of Sociology, 68,* 471–480.

Kohn, M. L. (1969). *Class and conformity: A study in values.* Homewood, IL: Dorsey.

Kohn, M. L. (1979). The effects of social class on parental values and practices. In D. Reiss & H. Hoffman (Eds.), *The American family: Dying or developing* (pp. 45–68). New York: Plenum.

Kohn, M. L., Naoi, A., Shoenbach, C., Schooler, C., & Slomczynski, K. M. (1990). Position in the class structure and psychological functioning: A comparative analysis of the United States, Japan, and Poland. *American Journal of Sociology, 90,* 964–1008.

Kuczynski, L. (1984). Socialization goals and mother–child interaction: Strategies for long-term and short-term compliance. *Developmental Psychology, 20,* 1061–1073.

Lamb, M. E., Hwang, C.-P., & Broberg, A. (1989). Associations between parental agreement regarding child-rearing and the characteristics of families and children in Sweden. *International Journal of Behavioral Development, 12,* 115–129.

Lambert, W. (1987). The fate of Old-Country values in a new land: A cross-national study of child rearing. *Canadian Psychology, 28,* 9–20.

Lambert, W. E., Hamers, J. F., & Frasure-Smith, N. (1979). *Child-rearing values.* New York: Praeger.

Lansky, L. M. (1967). The family structure also affects the model: Sex-role attitudes in parents of preschool children. *Merrill–Palmer Quarterly, 13,* 139–150.

Laws, G. (1927). *Parent–child relationships.* New York: Columbia University Press.

Lawton, J., Coleman, M., Boger, R., Pease, D., Galejs, I., Poresky, R., & Looney, E. (1983). A Q-sort assessment of parents' beliefs about parenting in six midwestern states. *Infant Mental Health Journal, 4,* 344–351.

Levy, D. M. (1931). Maternal over-protection and rejection. *Journal of Nervous and Mental Diseases, 73,* 65–77.

Levy, D. (1943). *Maternal overprotection.* New York: Columbia University Press.

Likert, R. (1932). A technique for the measurement of attitudes. *Archives of Psychology, 22,* 5–22.

Lin, C.-Y. C., & Fu, V. R. (1990). A comparison of child-rearing practices among Chinese, immigrant Chinese, and White-American parents. *Child Development, 61,* 429–433.

Lott, B. E. (1973). Who wants the children? Some relationships among attitudes toward children, parents, and the liberation of women. *American Psychologist, 28,* 573–582.

Lummis, M. & Stevenson, H. W. (1990). Gender differences in beliefs and achievement: A cross-cultural study. *Developmental Psychology, 26,* 254–263.

Luster, T., Rhoades, K., & Haas, B. (1989). The relation between parental values and parenting behavior: A test of the Kohn hypothesis. *Journal of Marriage and the Family, 51,* 139–147.

Lytton, H., & Romney, D. M. (1991). Parents' differential socialization of boys and girls: A meta-analysis. *Psychological Bulletin, 109,* 267–296.

Maccoby, E. E., & Martin, J. A. (1983). Socialization in the context of the family: Parent–child interaction. In E. M. Hetherington (Ed.), *Handbook of child psychology: Vol. 4. Socialization, personality, and social development* (pp. 1–102). New York: Wiley.

Manstead, A. S. R., Proffitt, C., & Smart, J. L. (1983). Predicting and understanding mothers' infant-feeding intentions and behavior: Testing the theory of reasoned action. *Journal of Personality and Social Psychology, 44,* 657–671.

Mark, J. C. (1953). The attitudes of the mothers of male schizophrenics toward child behavior. *Journal of Abnormal and Social Psychology, 48,* 185–189.

McHale, S. M., & Huston, T. L. (1984). Men and women as parents: Sex role orientations, employment, and parental roles. *Child Development, 55,* 1349–1361.

McKenry, P. C., Kotch, J. B., & Browne, D. H. (1991). Correlates of dysfunctional parenting attitudes among low-income adolescent mothers. *Journal of Adolescent Research, 6,* 212–234.

McNally, S., Eisenberg, N., & Harris, J. D. (1991). Consistency and change in maternal child-rearing practices and values: A longitudinal study. *Child Development, 62,* 190–198.

Medinnus, G. R. (1961). The relation between several parent measures and the child's early adjustment to school. *Journal of Educational Psychology, 52,* 153–156.

Messick, S. (1980). Test validity and the ethics of assessment. *American Psychologist, 11,* 1012–1027.

Meyer, B. (1980). The development of girls' sex-role attitude. *Child Development, 51,* 508–514.

Miller, D. R., & Swanson, G. E. (1958). *The changing American parent: A study in the Detriot area.* New York: Wiley.

Miller, S. A. (1988). Parents' beliefs about children's cognitive development. *Child Development, 63,* 259–285.

Milner, J. S., & Chilamkurti, C. (1991). Physical child abuse perpetrator characteristics: A review of the literature. *Journal of Interpersonal Violence, 6,* 345–366.

Mosher, D. L., & Scodel, A. (1960). Relationships between ethnocentrism in children and the ethnocentrism and authoritarian rearing practices of their mothers. *Child Development, 31,* 369–376.

Moss, H. A. & Jones, S. J. (1977). Relations between maternal attitudes and maternal behavior as a function of social class. In P. H. Leiderman, S. R. Tulkin, & A. Rosenfeld (Eds.), *Culture and infancy: Variations in the human experience* (pp. 439–467). New York: Academic Press.

Newson, J., & Newson, E. (1968). *Four years old in an urban community.* London: Allen & Unwin.

Newson, J., & Newson, E. (1976). *Seven years old in the home environment.* New York: Wiley.

Nichols, R. C. (1962). A factor analysis of parental attitudes of fathers. *Child Development, 33,* 791–802.

Ojemann, R. H. (1935). The measurement of attitude toward self-reliance. In G. D. Stoddard (Ed.), *University of Iowa studies: Studies in child welfare: Vol. 10. Researchers in parent education* (pp. 101–111). Iowa City: University of Iowa Press.

Orr, E., Assor, A., Priel, B. P. (1989). Maternal attitudes and children's self-perceptions in three Israeli social contexts. *Genetic, Social, and General Psychology Monographs, 115,* 7–24.

Palkovitz, R. (1984). Parental attitudes and fathers' interactions with their 5–month-old infants. *Developmental Psychology, 20,* 1054–1060.

Parsons, J. E., Adler, T. F., & Kaczala, C. M. (1982). Socialization of achievement attitudes and beliefs: Parental influences. *Child Development, 53,* 310–321.

Patterson, G. R., & Reid, J. B. (1984). Social interaction processes within the family: The study of the moment-by-moment family transactions in which human social development is imbedded. *Journal of Applied Developmental Psychology, 5,* 237–262.

Pearson, G. H. J. (1931). Some early factors in the formation of personality. *American Journal of Orthopsychiatry, 1,* 284–291.

Perloff, R. M. (1993). *The dynamics of persuasion.* Hillsdale, NJ: Lawrence Erlbaum Associates.

Peterson, D. R., Becker, W. C., Hellmer, L. A., Shoemaker, D. J., & Quay, H. C. (1959). Parental attitudes and child adjustment. *Child Development, 30,* 119–130.

Pratkanis, A. R., Breckler, S. J., & Greenwald, A. G. (Eds.). (1989). *Attitude structure and function.* Hillsdale, NJ: Lawrence Erlbaum Associates.

Pumroy, D. (1966). Maryland Parent Attitude Survey: A research instrument with social desirability controlled. *Journal of Psychology, 64,* 73–78.

Radin, N., & Glasser, P. (1972). The utility of the Parental Attitude Research Instrument for intervention programs with low-income families. *Journal of Marriage and the Family, 34,* 448–458.

Radke, M. J. (1946). *The relation of parental authority to children's behavior and attitudes.* Minneapolis: University of Minnesota Press.

Rajecki, D. W. (1990). *Attitudes* (2nd ed.). Sunderland, MA: Sinauer Associates.

Ramey, C. T., Farran, D. C., & Campbell, F. A. (1979). Predicting IQ from mother–infant interactions. *Child Development, 50,* 804–814.

Rauh, V. A., Wasserman, G. A., & Brunelli, S. A. (1990). Determinants of maternal child-rearing attitudes. *Journal of American Academy of Child Adolescent Psychiatry, 29,* 375–381.

Ribble, M. A. (1943). *The rights of infants: Early psychological needs and their satisfaction.* New York: Columbia University Press.

Rich, A. (1976). *Of woman born: Motherhood as experience and institution.* New York: Norton.

Richards, E. L. (1926). Practical aspects of parental love. *Mental Hygiene, 10,* 225–241.

Rickard, K. M., Graziano, W., & Forehand, R. (1984). Parental expectations and childhood deviance in clinic-referred and non-clinic children. *Journal of Clinical Psychology, 13,* 179–186.

Rickel, A. U., Williams, D. L., & Loigman, G. A. (1988). Predictors of maternal child-rearing practices: Implications for intervention. *Journal of Community Psychology, 16,* 32–40.

Roberts, G. C., Block, J. H., & Block, J. (1984). Continuity and change in parents' child-rearing practices. *Child Development, 55,* 586–597.

Roehling, P. V., & Robin, A. L. (1986). Development and validation of the Family Beliefs Inventory: A measure of unrealistic beliefs among parents and adolescents. *Journal of Consulting and Clinical Psychology, 54,* 693–697.

Rohner, R. P. (1986). *The warmth dimension: Foundations of parental acceptance–rejection theory.* Beverly Hills, CA: Sage.

Roosa, M. W. (1983). A comparative study of pregnant teenagers' parenting attitudes and knowledge of sexuality and child development. *Journal of Youth and Adolescence, 12,* 213–223.

Sameroff, A. J., & Feil, L. A. (1985). Parental concepts of development. In I. E. Sigel (Ed.), *Parental belief systems: The psychological consequences for children* (pp. 83–105). Hillsdale, NJ: Lawrence Erlbaum Associates.

Schaefer, E. S., & Bell, R. Q. (1958). Development of a parental attitude research instrument. *Child Development, 29,* 339–361.

Schlegel, R. P., & DiTecco, D. (1982). Attitudinal structures and the attitude-behavior relation. In M. P. Zanna, E. T. Higgins, & C. P. Herman (Eds.), *Consistency in social behavior: The Ontario symposium* (Vol. 2, pp. 17–49). Hillsdale, NJ: Lawrence Erlbaum Associates.

Sears, C. H. (1899). Home and school punishments. *Pedagogic Seminary, 6,* 159–187.

Sears, R. R., Maccoby, E. E., & Levin, H. (1957). *Patterns of childrearing.* Evanston, IL: Row Peterson.

Segal, M. (1985). A study of maternal beliefs and values within the context of an intervention program. In I. E. Sigel (Ed.), *Parental belief systems: The psychological consequences for children* (pp. 271–286). Hillsdale, NJ: Lawrence Erlbaum Associates.

Shoben, E. J. (1949). The assessment of parental attitudes in relation to child adjustment. *Genetic Psychology Monographs, 39,* 101–148.

Sigel, I. E. (1985). A conceptual analysis of beliefs. In I. E. Sigel (Ed.), *Parental belief systems: The psychological consequences for children* (pp. 345–371). Hillsdale, NJ: Lawrence Erlbaum Associates.

Sigel, I. E. (1986). Reflections on the belief-behavior connection: Lessons learned from a research program on parental belief systems and teaching strategies. In R. D. Ashmore & D. M. Brodzinsky (Eds.), *Thinking about the family: Views of parents and children* (pp. 35–65). Hillsdale, NJ: Lawrence Erlbaum Associates.

Simons, R. L., Whitbeck, L. B., Conger, R. D., & Chyi-In, W. (1991). Intergenerational transmission of harsh parenting. *Developmental Psychology, 27,* 159–171.

Spence, J. T., & Helmreich, R. L. (1978). *Masculinity & feminity: Their psychological dimensions, correlates, and antecedents.* Austin: University of Texas Press.

Staples, R., & Smith, J. W. (1954). Attitudes of grandmothers and mothers toward child-rearing practices. *Child Development, 25,* 91–97.

Stevenson, H., Azuma, H., & Hakuta, K. (Eds.). (1986). *Child development and education in Japan.* New York: Freeman.

Stevenson, H. W., Chen, C., & Uttal, D. H. (1990). Beliefs and achievement: A study of Black, White, and Hispanic children. *Child Development, 61,* 508–523.

Stogdill, R. M. (1931). Parental attitudes and mental-hygiene standards. *Mental Hygiene, 15,* 813–827.

Stogdill, R. M. (1934). Attitudes of parents toward parental behavior. *Journal of Abnormal and Social Psychology, 29,* 293–297.

Stogdill, R. M. (1936a). Experiments in the measurement of attitudes toward children: 1899–1935. *Child Development, 7,* 31–36.

Stogdill, R. M. (1936b). The measurement of attitudes toward parental control and the social adjustments of children. *Journal of Applied Psychology, 20,* 359–367.

Stolz, L. M. (1967). *Influences on parental behavior.* Stanford, CA: Stanford University Press.

Symonds, P. M. (1927). What is an attitude? *Psychological Bulletin, 24,* 200–201.

Symonds, P. M. (1949). *The dynamics of parent–child relationships.* New York: Columbia University Press.

Tesser, A., & Shaffer, D. R. (1990). Attitudes and attitude change. *Annual Review of Psychology, 41,* 479–523.

Thornton, A. (1989). Changing attitudes and family issues in the United States. *Journal of Marriage and the Family, 51,* 873–893.

Tulkin, S. R., & Cohler, B. J. (1973). Childrearing attitudes and mother–child interaction in the first year of life. *Merrill–Palmer Quarterly, 19,* 95–106.

Updegraff, R. (1939). Recent approaches to the study of the preschool child: Vol. 3. Influence of parental attitudes upon child behavior. *Journal of Consulting Psychology, 3,* 34–36.

Van IJzendoorn, M. H. (1992). Intergenerational transmission of parenting: A review of studies in nonclinical populations. *Developmental Review, 12,* 76–99.

Vaughn, B. E., Block, J. H., & Block, J. (1988). Parental agreement on child rearing during early childhood and the psychological characteristics of adolescents. *Child Development, 59,* 1020–1033.

Veroff, J., Douvan, E., & Kulka, R. A. (1981). *The inner American: A self-portrait from 1957 to 1976.* New York: Basic Books.

Wasserman, G. A., Rauh, V. A., Brunelli, S. A., Garcia-Castro, M., & Necos, B. (1990). Psychosocial attributes and life experiences of disadvantaged minority mothers: Age and ethnic variations. *Child Development, 61,* 566–580.

Watson, G. (1933). A critical note on two attitude studies. *Mental Hygiene, 17,* 63–64.

Weinraub, M., Clemens, L. P., Sockloff, A., Ethridge, T., Gracely, E., & Myers, B. (1984). The development of sex role stereotypes in the third year: Relationships to gender labeling, gender identity, sex-typed toy preference, and family characteristics. *Child Development, 55,* 1493–1503.

Wicker, A. W. (1969). Attitudes versus actions: The relationship of verbal and overt behavioral responses to attitude objects. *Journal of Social Issues, 25,* 41–78.

Winder, C. L., & Rau, L. (1962). Parental attitudes associated with social deviance in preadolescent boys. *Journal of Abnormal and Social Psychology, 64,* 418–424.

Wulf, K. M., & Bartenstein, E. (1980). Changing mother attitudes toward child rearing. *School Psychology International, 1,* 7–9.

Yarrow, M. R., Campbell, J. D., & Burton, R. V. (1968). *Child rearing: An inquiry into research and methods.* San Francisco: Jossey-Bass.

Young, K. T. (1990). American conceptions of infant development from 1955 to 1984: What the experts are telling parents. *Child Development, 61,* 17–28.

Zemlick, M. J., & Watson, R. I. (1953). Maternal attitudes of acceptance and rejection during and after pregnancy. *American Journal of Orthopsychiatry, 23,* 570–584.

Zuckerman, M., Oltean, M., & Monashkin, I. (1958). The parental attitudes of mothers of schizophrenics. *Journal of Consulting Psychology, 22,* 307–310.

Zunich, M. (1962). Relationship between maternal behavior and attitudes toward children. *Journal of Genetic Psychology, 100,* 155–165.

15

Parenting and Social Networks

Moncrieff Cochran
Starr Niego
Cornell University

INTRODUCTION

Our purpose in this chapter is to examine the ways that parenting beliefs, attitudes, and behaviors are influenced by parents' networks of social relations. Of primary concern are the various kinds of support and assistance provided to parents, both in meeting everyday responsibilities and in promoting the optimal development of their children. We use social networks as a framework for charting the structure and content of parents' relations, as well as for tracing the lines of influence into the family from larger social systems and institutions. Guided by an ecological perspective, we consider how social relations serve different functions and carry different meanings for families with differing life circumstances, needs, expectations, and resources. Throughout the chapter, as in the *Handbook* as a whole, *parenting* is defined broadly: Grandparents, aunts and uncles, close friends, neighbors, day-care providers, and baby sitters all have relationships with children (other than their own) that include or require some parenting activities.

We begin by presenting brief sketches of parents' networks through case studies of Cathy Conrad and Lisa and Christopher Jefferson. These sketches are composites, constructed from actual interviews with mothers and fathers. The characters are fictitious, but the life circumstances depicted are representative of the kinds of situations described to us in our research. Drawing on these accounts, we offer a definition of the network and a strategy for its measurement. In the next part of the chapter connections are drawn between networks and parenting, first by considering the effects of network relations on adults as parents and then on their children. Our view broadens as we examine the ways that network-building opportunities are limited by parents' social position. Specifically, we review studies that illustrate the effects of culture, class, race, and family structure on the pool of potential network members available to parents. Then an overall framework is presented, and we consider some of the ways that networks may be strengthened through personal initiatives of parents as well as by policy and programmatic interventions. Finally, in the concluding section of the chapter, we suggest directions for future research.

Throughout the chapter we cite studies conducted for the Comparative Ecology of Human Development Project, a cross-national, longitudinal investigation of stresses and supports in families with young children (Cochran, Larner, Riley, Gunnarsson, & Henderson, 1990). We refer in particular to the U.S. segment of the investigation, which also incorporated a programmatic intervention. The Family Matters program provided home visitors, parent support clusters, or a combination of both types of support to 160 of the 225 families that participated in the longitudinal study. We look at the Family Matters data to consider whether and how participation in the program stimulated network-activity building by parents.

Cathy Conrad

Cathy Conrad, age 27, is a White, single mother with two children, Brandon (age 5 years) and Sally (age 2 years). She rents an apartment in a blue-collar neighborhood on the outskirts of a small city. During the day Cathy works as a secretary at a large insurance company. At night she attends classes at the nearby community college, where she is in training to become a nurse practitioner. The father of her children has moved to another state and pays no child support, and neither Cathy nor her children have any contact with his parents or his siblings.

Cathy's social network consists of six kinfolk and seven nonkin. She has remained close to her own mother and father, who live just four blocks away. Her sister and brother are also important to her, and her sister-in-law is sometimes helpful. She also stays in touch with a cousin of the same age, with whom she grew up.

Cathy includes three neighbors in her network. Mrs. Macomber, who lives downstairs and owns the duplex containing her apartment, is always nice to the children and hasn't hassled her when the rent check is a little late. Several times she has sat in with the children when Cathy had to run down to the store for milk or Pampers. Mrs. Jackson, who lives around the corner and down three blocks, is a family day-care provider who looks after both children while Cathy is at work. Sandy is a new friend whom Cathy met when their children were playing over at the local play park. She is also a solo parent, and her Sherri is the same age as Sally. Two other friends, Gerri and Donna, are also secretaries at the insurance company. Cathy has known them ever since she started working there 4 years ago. Her other two friends, Marcie and Patty, are also studying to be nurse practitioners. She met them within the last few months, when they began the training program together, but already they have become very important to her.

Cathy says that her network affects her parenting and the care of her children in a variety of ways, some helpful and others not so. Whenever she is worried about the behavior of one of the children she talks to her mother about it first. That is usually helpful, but at the same time the response is often "Then give him or her a good smack," and Cathy remembers hating it as a child when one of her parents hit her. Her sister Joan lives in another state, but calls often and is a great listener. Sandy has had some good ideas about the children when they talk over at the park, and she shares tips from the single-parent support group she attends. At work Gerri and Donna give Cathy "shoulders to cry on" when she is feeling down about the struggles of parenting, but they don't have children so can't help out with advice. Marcie and Patti are so helpful with schoolwork and so much fun to talk to about other things that Cathy doesn't want to "bore" them with parenting issues.

Cathy relies quite heavily on her network for child-care support and other surrogate parenting assistance. Mrs. Jackson has the children for a total of 43 hours each week, and Cathy feels lucky to have a reasonably priced day-care provider so nearby. At the same time, Mrs. Jackson looks after three other preschool children, and seems to rely pretty heavily on the TV to entertain them. On the three nights each week that Cathy has classes her mother comes over to the apartment to look after the children, but her dad has been grumbling more and more about how that disrupts his evenings, so it may not last much longer. Billy, her brother, has been great about taking the kids out to watch softball games at the local park and down to the lake front to splash in the water, but his wife Jan gets irritated easily by rambunctious little children. Cathy wants Billy to stay involved with the children because they need to know and trust good men, so she is looking for better ways to get them all together without hassling Jan.

All in all, Cathy can't imagine how she would manage to rear her children without the help of her relatives and friends.

Lisa and Christopher Jefferson

Lisa and Christopher Jefferson, both 28 years old and African American, have been married for 6 years. They live together with their 3-year-old daughter Betsy in a small Northeastern city. Two years ago, with financial assistance from Lisa's parents, the couple purchased their own home in a stable, working-class neighborhood where there are parks and playgrounds for Betsy to play. Close by live both sets of parents and other extended family members. Having grown up in large, tight-knit families, Lisa and Chris look forward to gatherings with their relatives throughout the year, from Christmas to summer barbecues.

Since graduating from high school, Lisa has held a number of secretarial jobs. Currently she is employed part-time, 25 hours each week, at a local elementary school. Chris, who is also a high school graduate, was recently laid off from a large manufacturing company where he had worked for several years. He and his brother have formed a partnership and are planning to set up their own electrical contracting firm. Meanwhile he has enrolled in an accounting class at the local community college to sharpen his business skills.

In separate interviews each parent was asked to name the individuals "who make a difference" in their lives. The network of people Lisa nominated includes 15 relatives: her parents, in-laws, aunts, uncles, and siblings and their children. Although Lisa feels close to many of these people, it is her parents and older sister who are described as "especially important." Her mother and father offered encouragement when Lisa decided to return to work after spending 2 years at home with Betsy. Now her mother helps out by picking up Betsy from the child-care center where she spends the morning and staying with her until Lisa returns from work. Even with just part-time enrollment at the center, Lisa and Chris find themselves struggling to pay the bills; they could not afford the additional expense of a babysitter. Lisa's sister Alice is a good source of advice and comfort when Lisa feels overwhelmed with her responsibilities as a wife, mother, and worker. Alice's three children are Betsy's favorite cousins.

Apart from kin, Lisa names nine additional network members. Four of these are neighbors, including Mr. and Mrs. Mulcahy, who live next door. When the Jefferson's car breaks down, Mr. Mulcahy can often repair it. Most of all Lisa enjoys casual conversations with this older couple as they work in their garden and Betsy plays outside, sometimes helping them collect vegetables or pull weeds. Peter, Beth, and Darleen are three people Lisa has met at work. Peter, a second-grade teacher, came to the school at the same time as Lisa, and his sense of humor cheered her during the first, uncertain days on the job. Beth and Darleen are secretaries who sit beside Lisa in the main office. Darleen has worked for the district for more than 20 years and has friends in all of the schools. She has promised to look out for a full-time position that Lisa might apply for.

Finally, Lisa names two friends she has known since childhood. As working mothers, Lisa, Maggie, and Christine regularly pitch in to care for one another's children. Occasionally, though, Lisa finds herself reluctant to answer the telephone when it rings early on Saturday mornings. After a full week, she would prefer not to have extra work during her "days off." Lisa wonders when was the last time that she, Maggie, and Christine spent a day together, without their spouses or children. Having more time alone with her friends is something she looks forward to as Betsy gets a little older and enters school.

Chris Jefferson describes a smaller social network than his wife, naming a total of 13 members. Included in his network are eight relatives: his parents and in-laws, Lisa's sister Alice, his own brother Ted, Ted's wife Joan, and their 8-year-old son Charles. Apart from these kin, who are all named in Lisa's network as well, Chris mentions few additional, independent social ties. He recognizes that people would be willing to assist him but explains that he generally prefers to rely on Lisa.

Before leaving his job, Chris had enjoyed spending time with some of his co-workers at the plant. Since the lay-off, though, he has lost touch. In his network he does include Mr. and Mrs. Mulcahy, both "generous and kind" neighbors. Mr. Mulcahy's help with car repairs has saved them a considerable amount of money over the past year. Three other people named are "actually Lisa's friends."

With fewer people to turn to, Chris relies on five primary relations—his parents, parents-in-law, and brother—for nearly all of the support he receives. They provide child care, childrearing advice, and support with practical and work-related concerns. When Chris and Lisa want to spend time together, they know they can ask his parents to watch Betsy. And he and Ted have grown particularly close as they've worked to establish their company. As partners, they complement each other. Ted talks easily, and has built up contacts and potential clients throughout he city. Quieter and more organized, Chris manages the paperwork and legal documents. Chris also admires the role Ted plays as a father to Charles—their own father was pretty distant from them when they were boys. Now that he's home most afternoons, Chris has been spending more time with Betsy, reading, playing, and talking to her. Lisa appreciates some time out from child care.

Even with his closest relations, Chris chooses not to discuss financial and emotional matters. In these two areas he recognizes that Lisa's support is especially important.

WHAT IS A SOCIAL NETWORK?

The individuals who "make a difference" in Cathy Conrad's and Lisa and Chris Jefferson's lives—relatives, co-workers, neighbors, and friends—comprise the membership of each parent's social network. In this chapter we use the term *social network* to refer to specific sets of linkages between defined sets of people (Mitchell, 1969). The linkage is operationalized through our principal question—"Who makes a difference in your life?"—and amplified by probing for the individuals whom parents "do things with" or "know and depend on." In response, parents speak about people they see with some regularity or exchange goods and services with.[1]

It is important to recognize that our sketches reveal only partial views of networks. Total networks, consisting of the web of relationships among all members of a society, are nearly impossible to map. The partial networks that we study are *personal* social networks, networks anchored to a specific individual and defined in response to specific questions and probes. Illustrated previously are the personal networks of three parents. Alternatively, we might look at the network relations of Lisa and Chris' daughter Betsy, for example, or aggregate all three of their personal networks into a Jefferson family network.

Cochran and Brassard (1979) defined personal social networks as consisting of "those people outside the household who engage in activities and exchanges of an affective and/or material nature with members of the immediate family" (p. 601). Two facets of this definition merit elaboration. First, applying the definition to the Jeffersons, we note that neither Chris nor Betsy would be included in Lisa Jefferson's personal network. Family members, as long as they live together in one household, are excluded from network membership. We and other investigators have found that relations with household members are qualitatively distinct from other social ties (Brassard, 1982; Crnic, Greenberg, Ragozin, Robinsin, & Basham, 1983). From a conceptual standpoint the important distinction is between the nuclear family and the personal network, a distinction well articulated by Bott (1957) in *Family and Social Network*. The study of nuclear families has a long tradition in sociology and anthropology, and the subdiscipline of family sociology has become well established during the past half-century. Family historians and other social researchers conceive of the family as an emotional entity resting on sentimental ties between husband and wife, and parents and children, and as a social unit with economic significance (Hareven, 1984). Thus, the nuclear family is a concept that has meaning in the real world and importance for the development of the individual, separate from the impacts of other kin, associates, and friends.

The second facet of our definition that requires elaboration is the nature of the links between the individual at the center of the network (the "anchor") and the members included within. Cochran and Brassard (1979) described these links as "activities and exchanges of an affective and/or material nature" (p. 601). Is this phrase a proxy for social support? As suggested earlier, there is a certain degree of affinity between the concepts of social support and social network, particularly because both have been applied to assess the impact of personal relationships on human development. Yet, in constructing social networks we aim to describe relations of broader range and structural complexity than usually incorporated in studies of social support.

---

[1]Milardo (1988) noted that other methodological techniques yield alternative pictures of parents' networks.

Most of the researchers using the social support concept refer to work of Cobb (1976), who defined such support as information that leads an individual to believe that he or she is cared for and loved, valued, and a member of a network of mutual obligation. More recently Crockenberg (1988) described social support as emotional, instrumental, or informational help that other people provide to an individual:

> With respect to families, emotional support refers to expressions of empathy and encouragement that convey to parents that they are understood and capable of working through difficulties in order to do a good job in that role. Instrumental support refers to concrete help that reduces the number of tasks or responsibilities a parent must perform, typically household and child care tasks. Informational support refers to advice or information concerning child care or parenting. (p. 141)

Thus, the concept of social support emphasizes the types of support provided (emotional, instrumental, informational) and the psychological state of the recipient ("cared for and loved, valued"). Those networks researchers who focus on support have tended to map the networks of their respondents with the use of probes that are explicitly oriented to support, like "Please give me the names of all the people who provide you with emotional support." Such a strategy leads to the identification of a partial network that excludes people in an individual's life not thought of primarily in terms of support.

The definition presented by Cochran and Brassard (1979), in contrast, suggests a wider view of social relations. The content of linkages between respondents and their network members ranges from information of various kinds (where to find work, how to rear a child, which day-care arrangement to choose) to emotional and material assistance and access to role models (Cochran & Brassard, 1979; Mitchell, 1969). As the range of possible exchanges is broadened, we find that naturally occurring social relations may influence parenting in ways that extend well beyond those included within the domain of social support. For Cathy Conrad, a working parent rearing two children on her own, having friends and relatives help with child care is one form of assistance that is particularly important. Having her brother as a role model to her children is a second. In Cathy's network there are also friendships in which she leaves aside for a while her concerns as a parent.

At the same time, we recognize that network relations, even supportive ones, may also be conflictual. Cathy and her mother sometimes express different attitudes toward childrearing, even as Cathy values and depends on her mother's assistance with child care on the nights she attends school. Additionally, network members' expectations for reciprocal care can burden parents who feel they have little left to give. From a study of low-income mothers with young children, Belle (1982) concluded that "one cannot receive support without also risking the costs of rejection, betrayal, burdensome dependence, and vicarious pain" (p. 143). Similarly, Wellman (1981) articulated various ways in which social support may oversimplify the nature of network relations:

> Its focus on a simple "support/nonsupport" dichotomy de-emphasizes the multi-faceted, often contradictory nature of social ties. Its assumption that supportive ties form a separate system isolates them from a person's overall network of interpersonal ties. Its assumption that all of these supportive ties are connected to each other in one integrated system goes against empirical reality and creates the dubious expectation that solidary systems are invariably more desirable. Its assumption that there are no conflicts of interest between "supporters" invokes the false premise of a common good. (p. 173)

A final point of departure from the social support model is networks researchers' emphasis on the characteristics of the "set of linkages" between network anchors and their members. By this we refer to structural dimensions of the network, including size, diversity of role relationships, diversity of sex, age, life stage, and density, or the extent to which network members know one another. Typically, these characteristics are used to transcend individual relationships and view networks as a whole. For instance, we might be interested in comparing the extent of kin versus nonkin membership in Cathy Conrad's and Lisa Jefferson's networks. Attention to network structure stems from a concern with the limits imposed by society on personal relationships, as well as to the content of those relationships, as described earlier. Beginning with the earliest studies conducted by British social anthropologists in the 1950s, there has been tension between individual choice and social-structural constraints in network models. We return to this issue later in the chapter.

HOW ARE SOCIAL NETWORKS MEASURED?

A variety of techniques exists for measuring and describing network relations. Surveys and question-naires have been used successfully to gather information with large samples. Face-to-face interviews permit researchers to offer follow-up prompts, amplify definitions, and elicit respondents' own perspectives of their naturally occurring relations. The strategy presented next, based on a semi-structured interview format, was designed for the Comparative Ecology of Human Development project, the international research mentioned in the Introduction (Cochran et al., 1990). The instru-ment was developed collaboratively, by social scientists from four Western industrialized countries. It has proved suitable for use with diverse populations, representing a range of cultural and educational backgrounds, family structures, and social environments. The four parts of the interview proceed as follows:

(1) Name generation. In the first part of the interview, the interviewer leads the respondent through a series of direct questions in order to elicit a network membership list. The interviewer begins by asking for the names of individuals outside of the immediate family "who are important to you in one way or another." The word *important* is clarified by a time frame ("people you have contact with from time to time") and by examples of the kinds of exchanges that might characterize the relationship ("I mean people whom you might turn to for general help or if you need a baby sitter. Or when you need to borrow something, or perhaps when a personal problem is on your mind.") The following role- and context-related prompts are used: neighbors, relatives, workmates, schoolmates, organiza-tions and agencies, and other friends.

(2) Characteristics of network members and their relationship to respondents. The interviewer then collects and records information about the location of each relationship in time and space, including geographic proximity, frequency of contact, and duration of contact. Information concern-ing the age, sex, and family life stage of network members is also gathered.

(3) Exchange content. A checklist procedure is employed to determine which network members engage in each of four kinds of social exchange with the respondent: child-related support, practical support, emotional support, and social activities.

(4) Intensity of relations. Finally, respondents are asked to name the individuals on their mem-bership list who are especially important to them. No limit is placed on the number of members who may be so designated.

Summarized in Table 15.1 are the questions and prompts included in the social networks interview, and dimensions of the network associated with them.

THE EFFECTS OF SOCIAL NETWORKS
ON ADULTS AS PARENTS

There are two main routes by which social networks affect childrearing, and thus parenting in the broadest sense. One route is through impacts on adults, who modify their parenting beliefs, attitudes, and behaviors as a result of network influences. The other route is not via the parents, but involves the direct impact of network members on children, by engaging with them in face-to-face interactions affecting their development. In this section of the chapter we are concerned with the first of these lines of influence transmission, the links between network influences and parents in their caregiving

TABLE 15.1
The Social Networks Interview

Questions	Network Dimensions
1. Name generation	
"Please give me the names of all of the people who are important to you in one way or another." "People in the neighborhood . . . " "Relatives of yours . . . " "People you see at work . . . " "People you know through school . . . " "People who you come in contact with at agencies or organizations . . . (e.g., Day Care Council, church)" "Other people who don't fit into any of these categories . . . "	Size Diversity of role relationships
2. Characteristics of network members and their relationship to respondents	
"Where does X live?" "How often do you see X?" "How long have you known X?" "Please check the name of all network members who are more than 20 years older than you are." "Is X male or female?" "Which members have children under age 10?"	Location in time and space (three dimensions) Diversity of age, sex, and life stage
3. Exchange content	
"Please check the names of people whom you turn to if you need a baby-sitter or if you want to discuss childrearing issues" " . . . people whom you turn to if you want to borrow something, if you need practical advice and information." " . . . people whom who feel you can turn to if you feel down or depressed, people you can talk to about everything." " . . . people whom you do things with on your leisure time, like sports, fishing, parties, movies."	Extent of child-related support Extent of practical support Extent of emotional support Extent of social activities
4. Intensity of relations	
"Please check the names of people who mean the most to you—who are especially important."	Primary network membership

roles. Four types of network exchange content are distinguished: instrumental assistance, emotional support, childrearing advice, and other informational support. We also address the question of network stress, and consider the causes and consequences of social isolation. Drawing on the work of Crockenberg (1988), we then suggest four processes through which the various forms of social support may influence parental behavior. Is there any empirical evidence linking parents' network resources to child-related outcomes? Answering affirmatively, we conclude the section by briefly reviewing studies of infants and school-age children.

Instrumental Assistance and Emotional Support

Studies of parents' social networks conducted during the 1980s indicate that assistance with child care, unconditional emotional support, and advice about how to maintain authoritative control over the child's behavior proved particularly helpful to young mothers, especially when the women are single, divorced, or separated (Weinraub & Gringlas, in this *Handbook*). Belle (1982) studied the costs and benefits of social ties identified as important by 43 low-income mothers with young children. Although working within the broader "social support and health outcomes" tradition of Cobb (1976), with particular interest in personal mastery and depression in adults, she was also interested in the quality of interaction between the mothers and their children. Belle found that it was not network size, proximity of membership, or frequency of contact that was associated with emotional well-being, but rather the number of people reported as engaged specifically in providing child care assistance and "someone to turn to."

Longfellow, Zelkowitz, Saunders, and Belle (1979) also considered social support in its relation to parent–child processes. Working with data from the Belle study, they found that availability of support in the area of child care (baby-sitting, discussions of childrearing problems) was positively related to the quality of mother–child interactions. Those women who reported access to child care support were less dominating, emotionally warmer, and more sensitive to the needs of their children than were mothers who did not report this type of network support. The authors were careful to warn against overgeneralization, pointing out that their sample was limited to low-income mothers. Colletta (1981) considered the significance of social supports for maternal functioning in several different studies. Working with 50 adolescent mothers, both White and African American, she found a link between emotional support and maternal affection. Colletta noted that "with high levels of emotional support adolescent mothers reported being less aggressive and rejecting; less likely to nag, scold, ridicule or threaten their children" (p. 193).

Brassard (1982) conducted a study of 20 single parents' personal social networks that included a comparison group made up of 20 married mothers, well matched with the divorced or separated women on occupation, educational level, family size, and religious background. One major advantage of the Brassard study was that it included assessment of mother– child interaction patterns, gathered through direct observation. All 40 families contained preschool children, divided equally by sex in each subgroup. Brassard found that network members contributed both support and stress to the lives of the mothers she interviewed, but that support outweighed stress in this sample of employed, lower middle-class, White women. The single mothers experienced more stress than did the women in two-parent homes, even when differences in working hours and income were controlled for. Emotional support from adults in the network was especially important for these single women. This support was related to increases in activities containing egalitarian power relationships, a more neutral stance toward children of both sexes, and a more inhibiting style with sons. Brassard suggested that:

> The network supports and guides the single mother in making this role shift toward assuming primary, daily responsibility for being an authoritative leader with her child. ...She needs help in sorting out a reasonable, consistent style of home discipline that maintains a workable family equilibrium. The single mother looks to her network for this guidance. (pp. 151–153)

Childrearing Advice

Riley (1990) broadened the discussion of networks and parenting to include men in the parenting role by capitalizing on one of very few data sets that includes information about the networks of fathers. The question he asked was "In what ways would a father use social ties in the service of his childrearing efforts?" One important way might be to turn to network members to discuss parenting concerns and to gather childrearing advice. Whom would fathers go to for such advice? Would they prefer advice from their own parents or siblings, or from other young parents? Are there fathers who report no one with whom they talk about childrearing? To answer these questions, Riley focused on the 70 married, employed fathers from two-parent households who participated in the larger study of parental supports and stresses referred to earlier (Cochran et al., 1990). Most fathers in the sample reported that they discussed childrearing concerns with several people they knew well. The average network included about five sources of childrearing advice. But there was great variation. Eleven of the 70 fathers reported 10 or more network members willing to give advice, whereas 12 fathers reported no such people.

Riley (1990) then related aspects of the fathers' networks to the men's level of involvement in rearing their 6-year-olds. In particular, he examined fathers' participation in routine child-care tasks and play. To understand patterns of variation in the sample, Riley looked more closely at the men's family circumstances and identified wives' employment status as a crucial factor. In the two-earner families, for example, fathers' participation in child care was influenced by the presence in their networks of nonkin allies and local female kin. Nonkin allies are those highly elective and supportive network members who provided fathers with three or more of the following six kinds of support: practical borrowing, financial assistance, work-related support, discussion of marital issues, emotional support, and social activities. Local female kin consisted of the number of adult female relatives (including in-laws) in the father's network who lived in the same section of town. Of these two sources of network support, the nonkin allies variable was a much stronger predictor of fathers' involvement than was the number of local female kin. Riley noted that the two sources were related; fathers with fewer local kinfolk had more nonkin allies. He suggested the intriguing possibility that today some men are substituting multiply supportive nonkin bonds for traditional bonds to members of the extended family.

In the case of the single-earner families, in contrast, the "male network" variable exerted a powerful influence on fathers' childrearing efforts. As the percentage of men in the network increased, the father's share of parent–child play declined. The existence of local female relatives also decreased the father's play involvement. Local female kin seemed to reduce the demand for the father's assistance in childrearing, and the male peer group maintained attitudes and activities in competition with the father's role at home.

Riley (1990) concluded that fathers are often pushed into childrearing involvement, or away from it, by situational demands related to their wives' employment status. The mother's work situation (exclusively inside or also outside the family) serves to distinguish two types of American families, each apparently responding to very different network influences. The existence of a local female kin network appeared to relieve the pressure on the father to participate in childrearing (or it may have competed with him if he wanted more responsibility for his children). At the same time, there was evidence that fathers may to some extent select or construct social environments that influence them in the future, given that the male peer group and nonkin allies are amenable to active construction by the individual. Chris Jefferson's recent change in employment status, for example, offered him the opportunity to reconsider his role as a father to Betsy. Instead of nonkin allies, however, it was his brother Ted who provided guidance and modeling as Chris engaged in new activities with Betsy.

Informational Support

Cotterell (1986) was interested in the independent and joint influences on childrearing of the mother's social network, the father's workplace, and the local community. Working with a sample of 96 married mothers living in rural towns of inland Australia, he compared the personal networks and childrearing milieus provided by those women whose husbands were present on a regular basis with those whose partners' jobs routinely required periods of absence from home. Aspects of the childrearing environment were measured with the Caldwell *HOME* inventory (Caldwell & Bradley, 1984), and the quality of maternal expectations and beliefs was assessed with the *Parent as a Teacher* (PAAT) inventory (Strom, 1982). Analysis of the network data indicated that mothers with absentee husbands relied more heavily on their neighbors than those whose husbands were at home. When the "quality of childrearing" variables were analyzed by father presence/absence and mother's amount of informational support from the network, the effects of support were statistically significant for six of seven childrearing measures. Cotterell concluded that network support, general character of the community, and father's work situation do not operate independently. He suggested that "the chain of influence of father's work is connected to maternal behavior via the patterns of social relationships established by the mother" (p. 371). His findings indicated that the wives of absentee husbands had smaller networks, and that these women had a more limited range of settings available for contacting network members.

Network Stress

Belle (1982), Brassard (1982), and Wellman (1981) all emphasized the importance of recognizing the stresses as well as the supports in network relations. Cochran and Henderson (1990) were interested in how single parents' perceptions of their children might be affected not only by those network members providing the parent with child-related assistance and emotional support, but also by members whom mothers may have identified as "making life difficult for them" in one way or another. The links of interest were between those network influences and the mother's free response to the question "Is your [3-year-old] child easy or difficult to raise?" Of the 48 White, single-parent families in a larger study of family stresses and supports, Cochran et al. (1990) focused on a subsample of 27 in which mothers were living with no other adults (either male partners or their own parents). Their findings indicated that perception of the child varied directly with the number of kinfolk mothers included in primary networks. That is, as the number of relatives defined as "especially important" increased, mothers' views of their children became more positive. But the strength of this positive relation was affected by the educational backgrounds of the women. It was strongest for the nine mothers with less than a high school education, followed by those with a high school diploma, and then by those with more than 12 years of school. The picture that emerged was one of women with differing needs, expectations, and resources, for whom close involvement with kinfolk appeared to mean different things.

The distinction between women with more or less education was dramatized by the network variable called "difficult kin," those relatives identified as "making things more difficult" in one way or another. These were not contacts included in the network *primarily* because of their difficult characteristics. Rather, mothers were told not to leave someone off the list because that individual was in some sense difficult. Once the network list was completed, respondents were asked whether there was anyone included whom they found difficult in one way or another. Thus, people identified as difficult also had other characteristics, some of which may have been very supportive. Reporting more of such people was linked to more positive perceptions by the least educated mothers, and less positive perceptions by those with the most education. Less educated mothers seemed willing to accept the stress associated with close kinship relations in order to benefit from the support also provided, but more educated women, perhaps with stronger and more independent personal identities, appeared to find certain kinds of relatives meddlesome and irritating. This study provided preliminary evidence that similar amounts and types of support and stress coming from network members may be perceived quite differently, and translated into different perceptions of the child, depending on past educational experiences and the aspirations the mother has for her own development.

Social Isolation

Another body of research focuses not on how parents are affected by network influences, but instead on the causes and consequences of social isolation. Interest in factors causing isolation stems from evidence linking the absence of constructive social ties with child abuse and neglect. Crockenberg (1988), in summarizing a number of findings, introduced the possibility that "characteristics of the mothers account both for their low support and their abusive parenting" (p. 160). One study that fits within this framework included a comparison of neglectful with nonneglectful mothers (Polansky, Gaudin, Ammons, & Davis, 1985). The researchers used a comparison group that was similar to the neglectful families not only in socioeconomic and family characteristics, but also regarding the geographic accessibility of relatives and proximity to the community where they grew up. One innovative feature of the study involved interviewing a neighbor of every neglectful and control family to determine their perceptions of the friendliness and helpfulness of neighbors, whether there were neighbors one could call on for help, and whether there were neighbors who needed help in rearing their children. The researchers found that neglectful mothers described their neighborhoods as less supportive and friendly than did parents in the control group or neighbors of the parents in either group. That is, they described a different *psychological* reality, although there was no evidence from the neighbors of *objective* differences in the supportive potential. Additional evidence suggested that neglectful parents were less helpful than control parents to others in the neighborhood, based on both their own reports and the reports of their neighbors. The researchers concluded from their data that "inadequacies of ability, and perhaps motivation, cut them off from helping networks dependent on mutuality. Related inadequacies lead to their being stigmatized and held at a distance socially" (p. 274).

Crittenden (1981, 1985a) conducted research that provides greater understanding of what the "inadequacies" referred to by Polansky et al. (1985) might consist of, as well as some indication of their origins. She proposed that adults possess internalized working models of social relationships that are developed from experiences in early childhood, and then modified over time based on the social relations experienced during later childhood and adolescence. Applying this conceptual orientation to network relations, Crittenden (1985b) suggested that "a mother may influence her relationship with her network, just as she appears to do in her relationship with her child, through the processes of generalization and repetition of ingrained patterns of behavior" (p. 1301). This idea received support from her comparison of the networks and parent-professional relationships of adequate mothers with those of neglectful and abusive/neglectful mothers. She found that mothers in the adequate group had far more supportive and satisfying network relationships than the mothers in either of the other two groups. This was true despite the fact that the adequate and maltreating mothers were often living in the same neighborhoods. The adequate mothers were also more cooperative in the parent-professional relationship, and less defensive or withdrawn. Crittenden (1985b) concluded that her data were "highly consistent with the notion that the mothers' approach to relationships of all kinds was reflected both in their relationships with their children and in their relationships with network members" (p. 1311). She argued that the interaction styles of these women—cooperative, defensive, withdrawn—reflect internalized working models of relationships, and result in greater or lesser openness to and capacity for the establishment and maintenance of satisfying and supportive network relations.

Conceptualizing How Social Support Affects Parental Behavior

Crockenberg (1988) provided a very useful review of the theories explaining how social support affects parental behavior. She identified four processes by which benefits might be conveyed. First, support can reduce the sheer number of stressful events. The instrumental assistance described earlier in this section probably operates largely in this manner. Baby-sitting, childrearing advice, and financial assistance simply provide relief from daily burdens that might otherwise accumulate to incapacitate the parent, or press her or him into inappropriate or even abusive behavior patterns.

It is possible that social support may not directly reduce the number of stressful events experienced by the parent, but instead serve as a buffer, preventing the parent from being adversely affected by a stressful event, like divorce or job loss, and enabling the parent to maintain satisfactory childrearing routines in difficult situations. This second process is probably not an alternative to sheer reduction of stressful events, but rather operates in addition to it. The effects of emotional support reported in several of the studies referenced earlier may operating in this buffering manner.

Crockenberg (1988) identified the construction of active coping strategies as the third process by which social supports may have beneficial effects on parents. For example, a mother's self-confidence may be bolstered by praise from a supportive and more experienced network member, and her childrearing skills may improve as a result of suggestions from this person. The result of this process may be greater willingness and ability to take positive initiatives in other situations involving the child (Cochran, 1988). Riley's (1990) "nonkin allies" and Cathy Conrad's friend Sandy probably provide coping strategies of this sort.

The fourth process identified by Crockenberg (1988) also involves the emotional support that emerged from several of the studies reviewed earlier as an important predictor of more effective parenting behaviors. She tied emotional support to the idea of "working models of relationships" outlined previously in relation to maltreating parents (Crittenden, 1985b), pointing out that "ongoing emotional support or nurturance may affirm this sense [of herself or himself as a person deserving of care and capable of caring for someone else] and in doing so encourage the individual's inclination to be nurturant to others" (p. 146).

The Personal Networks of Mothers and Child-Related Outcomes

Do the social resources available to parents actually have an impact on the development of their children? Three examples illustrate the link to child development. Crockenberg (1981) was interested in ways that social support might affect the nature of the emotional bond between mother and infant. She assessed infants' reactions to short periods of separation from their mothers and documented clear, consistent patterns within a middle- and working-class sample. Low social support was associated with resistant, avoidant, and anxious behavior when infants were reunited with their mothers. With irritable babies, the association was especially strong, leading Crockenberg to suggest that the "availability of social support is particularly critical when the family is under particular stress" (p. 862). The fact that the positive relationship between social support for the mother and the attachment behaviors of the child was obtained primarily in the case of irritable babies is important to note. An environmental demand, the irritable baby, appears to have created the conditions calling for mobilization of existing support.

Research by Tietjen (1985) yielded findings that suggest a connection between the social networks of mothers and those of their children, specifically their daughters. Her sample consisted of 72 Swedish mothers and their 8- to 9-year-old children. Mothers and children were interviewed separately. Tietjen found similarities between the networks of mothers and their daughters that were not apparent for mothers and sons. For instance, the greater the percentage of neighbors in the married mother's network, the greater the likelihood that the daughter would play with several friends together, rather than with a single friend. Among unmarried mothers in the sample, there was an association between involvement in instrumental exchange with network members and the number of friends whom daughters named, especially at school. Tietjen proposed modeling, teaching, and the provision of opportunities for interaction as the processes that might account for such commonalities.

Homel, Burns, and Goodnow (1987) interviewed the fathers, mothers, and 9- to 11-year-old children in 305 Australian families. These families were drawn from areas in Sydney defined as high, medium, and low according to the number of social risk indicators contained in each area. Information about the "family" network was gathered from one or the other parent (alternating), yielding data about the frequency, location, and dependability of relations with neighbors, friends, and relatives, as well as affiliation with community organizations. Data collected from the children included information about their happiness, negative emotions, social skills, friendship networks, and school adjustment. The authors reported that the child's happiness with the family, negative emotions, peer-related social skills, extensiveness and diversity of friendship networks, and school adjustment all related to the presence/absence or the number of dependable adult friends in the family network. Also important were local friendship networks and ties to community organizations. The family friends were nonkin, as distinguished from the kinfolk in the networks. One especially interesting detail in the larger array of findings pertains to the relation between the friendship networks of family and child, and complements Tietjen's (1985) results mentioned previously. Where the parents reported the presence of just one dependable friend, the child was likely to report friendship with one or two children or membership in a small clique. Children whose parents reported a number of dependable friends tended themselves to describe peer contact with a number of equally liked friends.

In this section we considered the ways that social network relations influence adults in their roles as parents. Now we turn to another line of influence, this one extending from parents' adult network members directly to children.

THE EFFECTS OF SOCIAL NETWORKS ON CHILDREN

Although many parents nominate children to their networks, we focus here on adult network members and the distinct roles they may play for a developing child. The potential for such influence arises when children engage in face-to-face interaction with adults known to their parents, whether or not their parents are present at the time. Cathy Conrad presented one example in describing the outings led by her brother Jim as an opportunity to introduce her children to positive male role models. Yet, despite the prevalence of such relations in daily life, only recently have researchers moved beyond the family to look at the developmental consequences for children of relationships with a broad range of people. Our discussion, then, is necessarily speculative.

It should be noted that the majority of data on which our ideas are based were gathered in studies that had as their central focus the personal networks of children. Lewis, Feiring, and Kotsonis (1984), for example, described the networks of children at two points in time, first when they were 3 years old, and again at age 6. In their analysis, these authors were able to identify important distinctions between adults and peers, and kin and nonkin contacts. But, readers may wonder, can we draw inferences from children's networks (even when reported by their mothers) about relationships with adults who are anchored to parents' social networks? Research by Tietjen (1985), as well as by Cochran and Riley (1988), sheds light on this issue. After conducting separate interviews with Swedish mothers and their 8- to 9-year-old children, Tietjen reported significant overlap of networks, especially with girls. With a sample of 225 U.S. mothers and their 6-year-old children, Cochran and Riley found that the degree of overlap varied from 46 percent, with nonkin adult network members in African-American, two-parent families, to 85 percent for adult kinfolk in White, two-parent families. From these studies we can conclude that some, and often many, of the adults included in children's networks are also named by parents to their own networks.

The Content of Adult–Child Relationships

From a developmental perspective, nonparental adults can be thought of as representing various kinds of interactive potential for the child, including parental role-related behaviors, such as child care, task-oriented activities, social outings to contexts beyond the home (e.g., parks, museums, libraries), and formal teaching directed toward cognitive and social stimulation. In Cochran et al. (1990) mothers were asked, "What kinds of things do [child] and [adult contact] usually do when they are together?" Responses to this open-ended question were organized into five categories of activity, as shown in Table 15.2. Few differences were found in the kinds of activities pursued with children by kin and nonkin adults.

The Impacts on Children of Adult–Child Interactions

In what ways might these activities influence children's development? We hypothesize that enhanced socioemotional functioning is one possible outcome. At the most basic level, an adult who interacts

TABLE 15.2
The Content of Relations Between Parents' Network Members and Children

Activity	Illustration
Parent role	Paid or unpaid child care
Task oriented	Washing car, gardening, marketing
Outings	Trips to park, library, nature area
Formal teaching	Paid lessons, YMCA activities
Social activities	All other adult–child activities

with a child in any of the ways described in Table 15.2 may demonstrate through words or actions that the child is loved, cared for, and valued. Responsiveness, support, and warmth foster the child's trust in adults and, by extension, the social world that he or she is beginning to explore. We predict that interactions that occur with some regularity, and in which both partners are actively engaged, would carry the greatest potential (Cochran & Brassard, 1979).

Time together is also likely to include the exchange of ideas and feelings that are a part of everyday conversation. With practice and encouragement, a child gains confidence and skill in expressing his or her own beliefs, as well as in listening to the views of others. Adults will encourage children to behave appropriately and follow instructions (talking quietly in museums and libraries, not wandering off in a park) to ensure that standards are met. From these social processes we identify the dimensions of "responsiveness" and "demandingness" described in Baumrind's (1980) model of authoritative parenting. In our view, the benefits of firm, warm, and flexible behavior with children transcend the biological relationship linking parent and child. Adult network members, too, through such "ordinary" activities as gardening or a visit to the park, may enhance the social and emotional well-being of children.

Evidence supporting this argument can be discerned from an investigation relating social networks to pro- and antisocial behavior among 92 16-year-old Norwegian boys (Cochran & Bø, 1989). One key finding of the study was that boys with more educated parents and larger numbers of nonkin adults in their networks showed better school performance, less absenteeism, and more positive social behavior. Negative behaviors such as alcohol use and illegal activities, in contrast, were associated with higher neighborhood risk and less time spent by the parents with their sons. In reviewing their findings, the authors called attention to the particular benefits of adult nonkin membership for the adolescent boys in their sample. They further suggested that social processes operating to prevent antisocial behavior may differ from those that contribute to the development of constructive behavior.

In addition, older children and adolescents may take advantage of activities with adults outside the family to explore attitudes and values different from those presented at home. Teenagers seeking to define an authentic identity for themselves enjoy probing others' ideas about such varied issues as morality, personal relationships, religion, and future plans (Erikson, 1968). More practically, parents' acquaintances may provide suggestions or direct links to possible employment for part-time, internship, or summer positions.

Interaction between children and adult network members can also foster gains in cognitive development. Here we draw on Cochran and his colleagues' (1990) findings to suggest that task-oriented activities may offer the greatest potential. Joint participation by children and adults challenges partners to cooperate toward constructing goals and performance standards and making decisions. For adults, a primary responsibility is to provide a "scaffold" for the child, giving enough support while challenging the individual toward further mastery. In this process the child can learn meta-cognitive problem-solving strategies, in time acquiring the skills necessary for independent performance. In other words, joint interaction is an excellent context for social influences on cognitive development—in particular, as conceived by Vygotskian theory (Cochran & Riley, 1988).

The ecological contrasts made possible by the design of the Comparative Ecology of Human Development studies enabled us to examine whether the benefits of joint-task participation would be equal for children growing up under differing social conditions. We predicted that measures of early school success would show the greatest gains among single-parent boys. Our expectation was based on the knowledge that (1) conditions for adequate childrearing were often in jeopardy, and (2) the benefits of social network resources would be greatest when the need was greatest. Analysis of the data revealed significant increases in the boys' academic achievement only when the adult accompanying the child was a relative, most often uncles or noncustodial fathers. Thus, although we previously noted that nonkin adults offered significant benefits to adolescent boys, we find that at younger ages boys appear to benefit most by interacting with their kinfolk.

It may also be possible that preexisting differences in the children are responsible both for their school grades and their network differences. We recognize that children who are brighter, especially as demonstrated by social competence, are likely to elicit more joint activities with adults and are also to likely perform better in school. Although the intellectual and social-emotional competencies of mother and child contribute strongly to their network-building skills, our ecological perspective leads us to believe that the networks constructed with these skills have different effects on children living in different social contexts.

Having looked at the content within social relationships, we step back now to consider how network members represent particular, partial views of the broader social world and the possible impact of such views for the child. Who children do and do not come in contact with, and the particular roles in which adults are seen, help to shape fundamental attitudes and beliefs regarding such issues as social diversity and sex roles. For example, Cross (1990) looked at the racial homogeneity of mothers' networks. He found significant differences in the images presented to White and African-American children, as well as in the content of commonplace activities and experiences. Cross found that African-American children are far more likely than their White peers to engage in bicultural experiences. We wonder about the developmental effects for White children who have little or no early experiences with people of color, or whose impressions must be based on occasional contact with a single individual representing another race.

Additionally, we believe that the role parents play in introducing network members to their children are related in part to parents' visions for the future of their children. Although African-American mothers in two-parent families retained strong ties to kinfolk, their children were typically involved with fewer relatives than were African-American children from single-parent households. This pattern recalls the earlier work of Stack (1974), who suggested that upward mobility of African-American families often requires a "breaking free" from the network of social ties to the past. Through a process of anticipatory socialization, the married African-American mothers in Cross' (1990) study may have been preparing their children for a future that would be different, even separate, from their own past and present. Similarly, after Lisa and Chris Jefferson moved to a predominantly White, working-class neighborhood, they understood that most of the children Betsy would meet at the day-care center, and later at school, would be White. They saw a sharp contrast between Betsy's experiences and their own, having spent much of their lives in African-American communities.

Much work remains to be done in documenting the impacts on children's development of their relationships with adult network members. Nevertheless, our glimpse at some of the ways adults outside the home "parent" children reinforces the broad definition of parenting underlying the chapter and, indeed, the *Handbook*. We have seen how adult network members provide psychological and material resources to children at the same time as they represent partial views of the wider social world. We look further at the ways in which networks may be limited in the following section of the chapter, in which we discuss constraints to the pool of members available to parents.

CONSTRAINTS ON PARENTS' ACCESS TO NETWORK MEMBERSHIP

The implicit assumptions underlying much of the research reviewed thus far are that all parents have equal access to deep reservoirs of social ties and that, if some parents are tied into more of those resources than others, it is because of the personal value they place in such relationships and the effort they exert to establish and maintain them. But Wellman (1981) warned us that:

> There are dangers in studying interpersonal networks in isolation, as if they are the only relevant social phenomena. We must also realize that such networks are really systems that transport resources to and from individuals, and that the structure of large-scale social systems largely determines the allocation of those resources. (p. 195)

There is now good evidence that the network resources available to parents vary substantially depending on parents' educational experience, income, occupation, the number of parents in the household, race, and even the culture in which they live. We refer to these circumstances as *constraint factors,* because the absence of certain characteristics and conditions considered advantageous by the dominant culture constrains or limits access to some kinds of network resources. In this section of the chapter we document what happens to their networks when parents are constrained by social class, as indicated by educational experiences, income, and occupational level, citizenship in societies with traditional beliefs about women's roles, single-parent status, or identification as African Americans.

Social Class

Family income, the educational level of parents, and the status and complexity of the occupations parents engage in are thought of by sociologists as defining the social class in which a family is located (Hoff-Ginsberg & Tardif, in this *Handbook*). Fischer (1982) was the first sociologist to provide empirical evidence for the relationships between dimensions of social class and network ties. Fischer's team interviewed a cross-section of people ($N = 1,000$) in a 20-county area around San Francisco about their personal social networks. Although some were parents, others were not. The sample reflected the diversity in educational, occupational, economic, gender, and life-cycle characteristics of that part of California. Of these background factors, Fischer found that educational level had the most consistent effect upon personal networks:

> Other things being equal, the more educational credentials respondents had, the more socially active they were, the larger their networks, the more companionship they reported, the more intimate their relations, and the wider the geographic range of their ties. In general, education by itself meant broader, deeper, and richer networks. (p. 252)

Fischer also found that household income made a sizeable difference in the networks reported, even with education held constant. People with more income included more nonkin in their networks, and were more likely to report adequate amounts of companionship and practical support than were the poor.

Fischer's (1982) work also provides insight into the impacts of life-cycle stage and gender on personal networks. Married people named more relatives and neighbors than did those who were unmarried, whereas single people were more involved with nonkin. Children restricted the social involvement of their parents, and especially of their mothers. "Women with children at home had fewer friends and associates, engaged in fewer social activities, had less reliable social support, and had more localized networks than did otherwise similar women without children" (Fischer, 1982, p. 253). An analysis by gender revealed that women tended to be more involved with kinfolk and to report more intimate ties than did men.

Culture and Class: Influences on Role and Identity

Cochran and Gunnarsson (1990) extended Fischer's (1982) general approach to a comparison of parents' networks across cultures (Sweden, United States, Wales, West Germany), social class (blue collar vs. white collar), and family structure (one- vs. two-parent families). The mothers in all four countries were White, and each had a 3-year-old child when first interviewed. These researchers confirmed Fischer's finding about the effects of social class on parents' networks, and extended it across cultures. They found in all four countries that mothers in white-collar families reported larger networks than did women in blue-collar households. Interestingly, the magnitude of the difference proved to be about the same in every country except the United States, where the class differences were larger. When they looked beyond network size to the functions performed by network members, again differences by class were readily apparent. Mothers in the white-collar families reported involvement with a higher number of network members in every category of social support. This difference was most visible for social and recreational activities. The data suggest, as an hypothesis, that mothers in white-collar families have more leisure time at their disposal (especially in Sweden and the United States), and spend some of that "extra" time in social and recreational activities with network members.

These comparisons also uncovered consistent network size differences by culture. The pattern was illustrated most dramatically by the contrast between Germany and the United States, in which the networks of young German mothers were about half the size of those reported by the mothers of young children in the United States. A closer examination of these size data distinguished two pairs of countries; German and Welsh mothers reported smaller total networks than mothers in either Sweden or the United States. Although the most dramatic cultural contrasts were seen in the social and recreational activities mentioned earlier, even in the area of emotional support Swedish mothers reported 50 percent, and white-collar Americans almost 100 percent, more network members whom they called upon for assistance (as compared to mothers in Wales and Germany).

In considering both cultural and class-bound differences in mothers' networks, Cochran and Gunnarsson (1990) suggested that the critical distinction involved both role and identity. Societies and social classes differ in terms of the roles women are permitted or encouraged to adopt (mother vs. worker, e.g.) and in the extent to which they can develop identities beyond those roles. From a developmental perspective, one can distinguish between development as a parent (parent role) and development as a person (personal identity). Network members can be thought of as contributing more or less to one or another of these developmental trajectories. It is reasonable to suggest, for instance, that kinfolk contribute heavily to definition and reinforcement of the parental role, whereas "other friends" are more likely to contribute to "development of self as person" or personal identity. The larger proportion of other friends engaged in social and recreational activities in the networks of white-collar women and of U.S. and Swedish mothers suggests greater involvement with personal development beyond the roles of wife and mother. This impression is reinforced by the data involving relatives and neighbors; German and Welsh mothers interacted more heavily around child-related and practical than social and recreational matters.

Cochran and Gunnarsson (1990) pointed out that the expectations in blue-collar families regarding the roles of men and women are somewhat more conservative than those found in white-collar families. This pattern was also reflected in their network data. Across cultures, blue-collar networks were somewhat smaller, more kin dominated, less geographically dispersed, and more child related and practical in content than their white-collar counterparts.

One-Parent Families

Gunnarsson and Cochran (1990) also examined whether solo parenting was associated with patterns of social relationship that differ from those maintained by parents in two-parent families. This led in the Family Matters Project to the oversampling of single-parent families by the Swedish and U.S. teams. Comparisons of these networks with those maintained by mothers in two-parent families showed that they were smaller, regardless of culture or class. A major factor accounting for the difference in total size was a smaller number of relatives in the networks of single mothers. In the U.S. sample there was an average difference of more than four relatives between single and married mothers, regardless of social class. In Sweden, where the networks of mothers in two-parent families were themselves smaller and less kin centered than in the United States, there was still an average of two more relatives in the networks of the coupled women than in those of the single mothers.

In the "other friends" sector, single mothers in white-collar families nominated more members than mothers in blue-collar families, both in Sweden and in the United States The average of eight nonkin friends in the networks of American white-collar single mothers outranked all the other subgroups of women by a substantial margin, and was nearly twice as large as in the case of U.S. blue-collar single mothers. Several circumstances surrounding single mothers in the United States help to explain this difference. It is important to understand that other friends are acquired relationships. Whereas ties to kin are ascribed by birth or marriage, individual initiative is necessary to develop and maintain friendships. Also required are access to people, interest, motivation, and the social and material resources with which to sustain the process. The white-collar single mothers in the U.S. sample were more likely to work outside the home than were the blue-collar single mothers, and thus had access to workmates. White-collar jobs are likely to provide more opportunities for socializing than is usual with blue-collar jobs. Training for white-collar jobs usually involves educational situations where opportunities to meet people are also present and social interaction and development of social skills are encouraged. Finally, financial and material resources are likely to be more available to the white-collar single mothers in the sample, by virtue of the fact that their jobs pay better.

It is interesting to note that in Sweden more than 70 percent of the neighbors included in the networks of single mothers were themselves mothers with young children. In the United States, in contrast, the corresponding figure was only 48 percent to 59 percent. This cultural difference was especially extreme for blue-collar single parents (86 percent vs. 48 percent). The difference may stem from the fact that in the United States such families are often forced by financial disadvantage to live in high-crime areas with substandard housing, where parents are suspicious of their neighbors and are afraid to allow their children to play outside, whereas in Sweden income redistribution has made it possible to ensure that all families can live in safe, relatively "child friendly" neighborhoods. Swedish single mothers tend to live in well-maintained public-housing areas containing safe play areas designed specially for young children.

Differences by Race and Ethnicity

Cross (1990) examined the personal networks of African-American single and married mothers, and compared the size and functioning of their networks with the social ties reported by White ethnic and nonethnic mothers from similar socioeconomic circumstances living in the same city. When he compared the networks of African-American single mothers ($N = 38$) with those of their counterparts in two-parent families ($N = 27$), Cross found that overall the networks of the latter were more than 25 percent larger than those of the single women (19.1 members vs. 14.3 members), a pattern similar to that found by Gunnarsson and Cochran (1990) for White mothers. At the same time, the absolute number of kinfolk in these networks was virtually identical for all African-American mothers, regardless of family structure. Thus the larger networks of African-American mothers in two-parent homes could be traced to the greater number of nonkin neighborhood and work-related contacts (workmates) included as members.

Cross (1990) then compared the networks of the 65 African-American women with those of 50 ethnic and 40 nonethnic White mothers, again distinguishing women in one-parent from those in two-parent families. He found that the networks of the ethnic White mothers were larger than those of either nonethnic White or African-American mothers, regardless of family structure. This difference in favor of ethnic White women was apparent both for kinfolk and for nonkin in their networks.

When he compared the networks of nonethnic White and African-American mothers, Cross (1990) found very few differences in the kin sector, and numbers of nonkin neighbors and work-mates were also similar. However, the White, nonethnic women reported many more ties with other friends, those nonkin who lived outside the neighborhood and were not work-mates (White two-parent = 5.0; White one-parent = 6.6; African-American two-parent = 2.9; African-American one-parent = 3.4).

Cross (1990) also examined the cross-race membership in the networks of these women, testing the likelihood that at least one opposite-race contact would appear at the functional level of the network. The results of this analysis revealed that 21 percent of the African-American mothers and 16 percent of the White mothers in one-parent families had at least one opposite-race friend. This modest disparity by race increased as family structure changed and socioeconomic level became higher; within the two-parent sample 41 percent of the African-American women but only 11 percent of the Whites named friends of the opposite race. Indeed, after moving to a largely White neighborhood and starting work at a local school, the majority of Lisa Jefferson's new friends were White. Lisa recognized that she was the first African-American friend some of these people ever had.

Cross (1990) postulated a relation between the relative lack of African Americans in the networks of White mothers and the smaller number of other friends reported by the African-American women.

On the one hand, he suggested that the exclusion of African Americans as potential friends would not have much of an effect on the overall size of White networks, because the large numbers of Whites in all sectors of everyday life provide numerous opportunities to meet and incorporate new White nonkin contacts. On the other hand, he noted, this is not the case for African-American people living in the same community. In the northeastern city where this study was conducted, only about 12 percent of the population was African American. Thus, the pool of potential same-race network members was much smaller for African-American than for White mothers, meaning that any cross-race avoidance that might have occurred would have placed the African-American women at a relative disadvantage.

In this section of the chapter we have presented evidence that structural factors operating at the levels of culture, class, education, race, ethnicity, and family structure constrain the network-building opportunities of some parents more than others. Such constraints yield a relatively smaller pool of "eligibles" from which network membership will be selected. African-American parents, nonethnic White parents, parents with relatively little education, and parents living in cultures shaped by beliefs that lead to narrow definitions of the woman's role, all have smaller pools of potential network membership available to them than do their more socioeconomically and socially advantaged counterparts. Constraints accumulate for single parents, who often have less access to relatives, further education, jobs paying a decent salary, and housing in neighborhoods that are supportive of neighboring activities.

PARENTING AND PERSONAL NETWORKS: A FRAMEWORK[2]

At the outset of the chapter we introduced case studies of Cathy Conrad and Lisa and Chris Jefferson to illustrate some of the ways that network members both support (and sometimes interfere with) adults in their parenting roles and also engage directly with the children of these adults in parentlike roles, relationships, and activities. In subsequent sections we reviewed empirical investigations of the nature and function of network relationships, as well as of the constraints parents face in building and maintaining social ties. We proceed now to integrate all that we have learned about parenting and social networks.

At the center of our framework we locate one or two parents and their children engaged with kin and nonkin contacts in relationships that provide more or less emotional support, instrumental assistance, and information.

Just as every network involves some combination of stress and support, so too do we find that each component relationship brings relatively greater or fewer demands. We have provided empirical evidence (where available) and informed speculation (where evidence is lacking) regarding the kinds of impacts—on parents, on parenting, and on child development—that accrue from these social processes.

But networking and parenting do not operate in a vacuum. Both processes are heavily influenced by the location of parents and network members in larger social and economic systems. We have documented the constraints imposed upon the pool of potential network membership that are associated with lower levels of education, lower income, less prestigious employment, racial characteristics deemed less desirable by American society, or even citizenship in a culture in which custom limits the roles available to women. Thus, as depicted in Figure 15.1, the pool of potential network members available to adults for assistance in their parenting roles varies quite dramatically, depending on a set of socioeconomic factors and personal characteristics, some of which are beyond their power to alter.

The term *potential* connotes the possibility and need for parents to take initiative in order to realize available opportunities. Cochran (1990) included *personal initiative* in a model of parental network development, as we have in Figure 15.1, to incorporate the actions required, first, in selecting as

---

[2]The reader is referred to Cochran, Riley, Larner, Gunnarsson, and Henderson (1990, chap. 14, 15, 16) and Cochran (1993) for elaboration of this model.

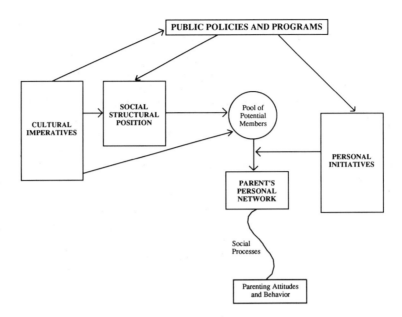

FIGURE 15.1. Parenting and personal networks: A framework.

members those people not already prescribed by kin relations and, second, to maintain relationships once established. Cochran identified nine possible factors contributing to the amount of initiative a parent might take in building and maintaining network ties: personality characteristics, human capacity, time and energy resources, stage of development, discrete life events (divorce, loss of family member, job loss), self-esteem, personal and group identity, educational experience, and social and cognitive skills. He further asserted that educational achievement beyond secondary school is so important for expanding the network *because* it enhances the achievement component of personal identity, raises self-esteem, and expands social and cognitive skills simultaneously. In summary, participation in higher education alters significantly the capacity and the motive of the parent to build new, highly functional social relationships and to phase out relationships that bring more stress than support to the parenting role.

It is very important to understand that the networks of parents are not static, even in those instances where those parents face severe socioeconomic and culturally defined constraints. Larner (1990), for instance, documented a 22 percent turnover in parent network membership over just 3 years. Only 9 percent of kinfolk were involved in these shifts, whereas 33 percent of all nonkin were included. Within our framework, change is linked to factors affecting both constraint and initiative. For instance, shortly after Cathy Conrad enrolled in the local community college for training as a nurse practitioner, she added Marcie and Patty to her network. Looking toward the future, we anticipate that more networking possibilities will open up to her as she continues her education and enters the nursing profession (reduced constraint). Experiences at college give Cathy increased self-confidence, new skills in social interaction and intellectual exchange, and a new personal and professional identity as a caring person and a member of a caring profession. All of these changes make her more willing and able to approach strangers and to establish new relationships (personal initiative), even though she considers herself a rather shy person.

Network change need not be brought about only by large-scale social and economic changes in the living conditions of classes or groups, or defined simply by developmental and life-cycle transitions. There is evidence that social programs initiated by local communities can effect positive changes in parents' networks. Network changes, in turn, can facilitate healthy child development. In the next section we review studies documenting such impacts.

PROGRAMMATIC AND POLICY EFFORTS
TO ENHANCE PARENTAL NETWORKS

Is there any evidence that community-level programs can have positive effects on the natural helping networks of parents? One of the earliest indicators of such potential was associated with an experimental intervention carried out in Chicago by Hess, Shipman, Brophy, and Bear (1968). The focus of this project was on helping mothers in low-income families stimulate the cognitive capacities of their young children more effectively. The authors noted in passing that the mothers receiving the intervention were more likely than those in a control group to have become involved in social activities outside the home (e.g., clubs, courses). Two implications were drawn from this finding: first, that a program focused on parent–child interaction might stimulate the mother to become involved with social activities outside the home and, second, that this outside social involvement might reinforce interest in parenting activities.

A more explicit emphasis on social networks was included in an intervention study carried out in a blue-collar Detroit neighborhood by Powell and his colleagues (Eisenstadt & Powell, 1987; Powell, 1979, 1987, 1988) with families containing children up to 6 months old. The Child and Family Neighborhood Program (CFNP) was designed to strengthen family supports by improving families' use of social networks and neighborhood resources for childrearing. Peer participants were identified as potential providers of informal support to parents in the program. The strategy of choice involved neighborhood group meetings, supported by home visits and health and social services.

Powell (1988) reported that parents' social networks first came into play during the recruitment phase of the program, in several different ways:

> There were instances where mothers routinely and frequently congregated with family and friends. One individual, for example, socialized with her own mother and sisters several times a week. The program, she reported, would be duplicative of these gatherings. It also seemed that significant members of one's social network had an influence on the decision about joining. It was not uncommon to learn that a person's husband or mother did not approve of the program. There were also cases of a mothers' relatives (especially her own mother) encouraging program participation but the mother not wanting to join. (p. 130)

Powell also found a relationship between parents' social networks and their decision to stop participating in the program. Those mothers who terminated involvement early had less extensive social networks than did mothers who remained in the program longer.

Cochran, Bronfenbrenner, and Cross designed an experimental family support initiative that had a number of features in common with Powell's Child and Family Neighborhood Program (Cochran, 1991). The Family Matters Program had five major goals, all related broadly to the parenting role: (1) to recognize parents as experts, (2) to exchange information with parents about children, the neighborhood, community services, schools, and work, (3) to reinforce and encourage parent–child activities, (4) to exchange informal resources such as baby-sitting, childrearing advice, and emotional support with neighbors and other friends, and (5) to facilitate concerted action by program participants on behalf of their children, where those parents deemed such action appropriate. The program was offered to 160 families, each containing a 3-year-old child, in 10 different urban neighborhoods. Two processes were used to involve families in activities related to their children: a home-visiting approach aimed at individual families and a cluster-building approach aimed at linking together all the Family Matters families in a given neighborhood. Families were involved with program activities for an average of 24 months. A comparison group of 128 families, living in eight other neighborhoods in the same city, was also included in the study.

The findings revealed that networks were affected positively by the program, and that networks-related changes were associated with attitudes, activities, or school performance among certain types of families.

Single Mothers

Unmarried mothers were especially responsive in network terms to program involvement. This responsivity was more evident with White women than with their African-American counterparts. By the end of the study, African-American, unmarried program mothers reported more nonrelatives in their networks, both overall and at the primary level. A closer look at the content of exchanges revealed involvement with larger numbers of people for borrowing and work-related and emotional support, always with nonkin. At the primary network level, change consisted primarily of the addition of nonrelatives who were not present in the network 3 years earlier. Overall, these women reported contact with somewhat fewer relatives at follow-up than had been the case at baseline. In terms of outcomes, these mothers' perceptions of themselves as parents emerged as a key determinant of their children's performance in school. More positive parental self-perceptions were also associated with increases in both the primary networks and the number of activities mothers reported engaging in with their children. There is evidence that the nonkin sector of the mothers' primary networks played an especially positive role in preparing their children for entry into school.

African-American unmarried mothers who participated in the program also added a significant amount of new nonkin membership to the primary portion of their networks. They were less likely, however, to report increases beyond the primary level, and the increase in new primary membership was about as likely to involve relatives as nonrelatives. This reflected a more general tendency among African-American women to rely upon kinship ties. In terms of outcome measures, increases in the number of relatives included in the mother's primary support network were associated with reports of more joint activity with the child. Joint activity involving household chores was linked in turn to children's higher performance in school. Expansion of nonkin membership in the primary networks of these mothers was also linked with school readiness outcomes (personal adjustment, interpersonal relations, relations with the teacher).

Married Mothers

Program effects were less pervasive with married women than was found with single mothers, and the effects that could be discerned were confined to relations with kin. White married mothers who participated in the program reported an overall decrease in network size in comparison with the appropriate controls. This decrease was found only among nonrelatives, and balanced at the primary level by an increase in kin. Closer examination showed that typically these kin had been present in the network 3 years earlier, but not defined as especially important at that time. Only one set of possible links to outcomes was discerned for these women, and only if they had additional schooling beyond high school. Under this condition, higher perception of self as parent, more mother–child activities, and better performance by the child in school were observed.

In the case of married African-American women there was an increase at follow-up in the number of relatives reported in the primary network, many of whom were new additions. Increased involvement with kin was related to greater amounts of mother–child activity. However, neither the increases in primary kin nor the greater parent–child activity appeared to be associated with better school performance.

One of the exciting aspects of social supports as program outcomes is their potential for further development of the individual into the future. Others have used the *convoy* analogy (House, 1980; Larner, 1990), and we also find it useful. Such an analogy clearly implies that network-related changes associated with an early childhood or family support program might be as strongly linked to subsequent developments in the child as they are to more immediate ones. The findings reported earlier begin to provide outlines for the forms of transport making up such convoys. One vehicle is likely to be composed of close friends and relatives committed to the welfare of both parent and child. This is the conveyance that was the central focus of the research by Powell (Eisenstadt & Powell, 1987; Powell, 1979, 1987, 1988) and by Cochran and his colleagues (1990). Another vehicle is parental self-confidence, which Cochran and his colleagues believed comes in part from the support of key network members, but is also necessary to stimulate network building or modification. A third vehicle, and perhaps the one heading the convoy, is the parent's level of formal education. Cochran (1990) suggests that schooling provides parents with both network-building skills and access to people outside the kinship circle.

Public education is itself an intervention into the childrearing process far more comprehensive than anything else undertaken by local communities. Taken as a whole, the network studies carried out by Cochran and his associates (1990) through the Family Matters Project provide compelling evidence for the argument that 40 percent to 50 percent of the support parents receive from their personal networks is strongly affected by their level of schooling. In this research the critical step appeared to involve access to postsecondary education: Those parents who had acquired such schooling were much richer in network resources than those who had not. College scholarships, student loans, and programs providing incentives to adolescents and young adults for continuation of schooling through high school and beyond would seem to be an especially good investment to society from this standpoint.

Policies that stimulate job creation and continuation might also deserve high priority from a "networks in context" perspective. The workplace proved to be an important context for network building for Family Matters families, and the economic returns associated with working provide some of the resources needed to sustain network relations.

The findings presented in this section have led us to conclude that public and private policies and programs must be included in our parenting and social networks framework because of their very real potential for altering the network resources of adults in their parenting roles. We close the chapter by identifying future directions for networks research. The results of such studies would fill in some of the major gaps in our understanding of why and how parents engage with network members around parenting issues, and just what impacts such activities have on their parenting attitudes and behaviors.

CONCLUSIONS

"It takes a whole village to rear a child," states an African proverb. Social networks represent one way of describing that village, a community defined not by geography but by relations and relationships. In this chapter we have offered a broad perspective on parenting. We showed how parents like Cathy Conrad and Lisa and Chris Jefferson turn to their network members for advice, emotional support, practical assistance, and help caring for their children. Yet, we demonstrated as well that parenting cannot be understood in isolation from the larger set of social and economic structures in which it is embedded. It is clear that poverty, unemployment, and lack of educational opportunity dramatically influence the networks of families, limiting their capacity to nurture and support parents and their children.

Although our society expects parents to accept full responsibility for rearing its future workers, citizens, and leaders, from the research reviewed in this chapter we discern the wisdom of an alternative view. In particular, the growing body of research linking social networks to parenting demonstrates that the actions of communities, states, and society as a whole are a decisive factor in determining whether parents have the resources necessary for fulfilling our expectations of them. Access to education, well-paying jobs, and secure housing enables parents like Cathy, Lisa, and Chris to build and maintain strong networks and to use those networks in support of their own development, as well as that of their children.

Strengthening parents' networks requires that we increase our knowledge of the ways in which networks develop, function, and change over time. Let us conclude, then, by identifying six key areas for future research.

To begin, we would like to see further study of the factors that encourage parents to initiate network-building activities, or that inhibit them from doing so. One obvious, but as yet unexploited area of inquiry involves the possible connection between parents' personality type (extroverted/introverted, shy/outgoing) and their willingness to initiate social relations with other parents, neighbors, or co-workers. Another approach would focus on context, by investigating whether parents with sustained involvement in particular settings (the workplace, the neighborhood, elementary school) or in settings organized in one or another particular way (e.g., workplaces with hierarchical or horizontal chains of command, neighborhoods with open spaces for play, arrangement of dwellings in a housing development) engage in more or less network building.

Further inquiry is also needed on the connections between personal ideologies or belief systems and parents' propensity to engage in network-building activities. It is quite possible that some people are reared within a strong ethic of self-sufficiency, whereas others experience interdependent exchanges of assistance and support through childhood and adolescence. We expect that new parents holding such different beliefs about the appropriate functions of social relations would respond quite differently to opportunities for parenting-related network building.

Cochran and his colleagues (1990) identified clusters of parents with similar patterns of variation along several dimensions of their networks: total size, proportion of kin versus nonkin membership, degree to which members served multiple roles, and the overlap between mothers' and fathers' membership. We are left to wonder whether there may be specific network typologies associated with particular beliefs, attitudes, and behaviors of parents toward their children. Investigating possible links between parenting and network typologies would add a strong ecological dimension to the already substantial literature on parenting styles.

In an earlier section we discussed the possible effects on children's development of interaction with adult members of parents' networks. Our broad understanding of parenting—extending well beyond biological relationships linking parents and their children—leads us to wonder about the many ways adults may promote social, emotional, and cognitive competence in children. In future studies we would like to see greater attention to the roles adults play in children's everyday lives—at day-care centers, schools, after-school programs, and in neighborhood and family gatherings. A networks perspective would enable researchers to perform fine-grained analyses in order to determine the nature and meaning of such relations, as well as the different outcomes for children associated with particular social conditions.

Changes in the nature and meaning of intrafamilial relations—between spouses and between parents and their children—have been associated with children's movement from infancy through adolescence and adulthood. As expectations and role relations are altered within the family, we would expect to find additional changes in family members' relations with individuals outside the household. Study of this issue would help us to better understand the dynamic properties of networks, as well as their capacity to promote and respond to the personal identity development of family members across the life course.

Finally, our review of the literature uncovered very few evaluations of early intervention, early childhood, or family support programs that included network change as a possible outcome. From a parenting perspective, we would particularly like to see such a focus in evaluations of the family support programs now burgeoning in the United States, many of which include "parent education" as a centerpiece. Network building is possible in *any* program that brings parents together, or that could do so; we encourage evaluators to include measures of network-related consequences as part of their overall assessment strategy.

REFERENCES

Baumrind, D. (1980). New directions in socialization research. *American Psychologist, 35,* 639–652.
Belle, D. (1982). Social ties and social support. In D. Belle (Ed.), *Lives in stress: Women and depression* (pp. 133–144). Beverly Hills, CA: Sage.
Bott, E. (1957). *Family and social networks.* London: Havistock.

Brassard, J. (1982). *Beyond family structure: Mother–child interaction and personal social networks.* Unpublished doctoral dissertation, Cornell University, Ithaca, New York.

Caldwell, B. M., & Bradley, R. H. (1984). *Home observation for measurement of the environment.* Little Rock: University of Arkansas at Little Rock/Center for Child.

Cobb, S. (1976). Social support as a moderator of life stress. *Psychosomatic Medicine, 38,* 300–314.

Cochran, M. (1988). Parental empowerment in Family Matters: Lessons learned from a research program. In D. Powell (Ed.), *Parent education as early childhood intervention: Emerging directions in theory, research and practice* (pp. 23–52). Norwood, NJ: Ablex.

Cochran, M. (1990). Factors influencing personal social initiative. In M. Cochran, M. Larner, D. Riley, L. Gunnarsson, & C. Henderson, Jr., *Extending families: The social networks of parents and their children* (pp. 297–306). London/New York: Cambridge University Press.

Cochran, M. (1991). Personal social networks as a focus of support. In D. Unger & D. Powell (Eds.), *Families as nurturing systems* (pp. 45–68). New York: Haworth.

Cochran, M. (1993). Parenting and personal social networks. In T. Luster & L. Okagaki (Eds.), Parenting: An ecological perspective (pp. 149–178). Hillsdale, NJ: Lawrence Erlbaum Associates.

Cochran, M., & Bø, I. (1989). The social networks, family involvement, and pro- and anti-social behavior of adolescent males in Norway. *Journal of Youth and Adolescence, 18*(4), 377–398.

Cochran, M., & Brassard, J. (1979). Child development and personal social networks. *Child Development, 50,* 609–615.

Cochran, M., & Gunnarsson, L., Grabe, S., & Lewis, J. (1990). The social networks of coupled mothers in four cultures. In M. Cochran, M. Larner, D. Riley, L. Gunnarsson, & C. Henderson, Jr., *Extending families: The social networks of parents and their children* (pp. 86–104). London/New York: Cambridge University Press.

Cochran, M., & Henderson, C. R., Jr. (1990). Network influences upon perception of the child: Solo parenting and social support. In M. Cochran, M. Larner, D. Riley, L. Gunnarsson, & C. Henderson, Jr., *Extending families: The social networks of parents and their children* (pp. 119–130). London: Cambridge University Press.

Cochran, M., Larner, M., Riley, D., Gunnarsson, L., & Henderson, C., Jr. (1990). *Extending families: The social networks of parents and their children.* London/New York: Cambridge University Press.

Cochran, M. M., & Riley, D. (1988). Mother reports of children's personal networks: Antecedents, concomitants, and consequences. In S. Salzinger, M. Hammer, & J. Antrobus (Eds.), *Social networks of children, youth and young adults* (pp. 113–147). Hillsdale, NJ: Lawrence Erlbaum Associates.

Colletta, N. (1981). Social support and the risk of maternal rejection by adolescent mothers. *Journal of Psychology, 109,* 191–197.

Cotterell, J. (1986). Work and community influences on the quality of childrearing. *Child Development, 57,* 362–374.

Crittenden, P. (1981). Abusing, neglecting, problematic, and adequate dyads: Differentiating by patterns of interaction. *Merrill–Palmer Quarterly, 27,* 1–18.

Crittenden, P. (1985a). Maltreated infants: Vulnerability and resistance. *Journal of Child Psychology and Psychiatry, 26,* 85–96.

Crittenden, P. (1985b). Social networks, quality of child-rearing, and child development. *Child Development, 56,* 1299–1313.

Crockenberg, S. (1981). Infant irritability, mother responsiveness, and social support influences on the security of infant-mother attachment. *Child Development, 52,* 857–865.

Crockenberg, S. (1988). Social support and parenting. In W. Fitzgerald, B. Lester, & M. Yogman (Eds.), *Research on support for parents and infants in the postnatal period* (pp. 67–92). New York: Ablex.

Cross, W. (1990). Race and ethnicity: Effects on social networks. In M. Cochran, M. Larner, D. Riley, L. Gunnarsson & C. Henderson, Jr., *Extending families: The social networks of parents and their children* (pp. 67–85). London/New York: Cambridge University Press.

Crnic, K., Greenberg, M., Ragozin, A., Robinsin, N., & Basham, R. (1983). Effects of stress and support on mothers and premature and full-term infants. *Child Development, 54,* 209–217.

Eisenstadt, J., & Powell, D. (1987). Processes of participation in mother–infant programs as modified by stress and impulse control. *Journal of Applied Developmental Psychology, 8,* 17–37.

Erikson, E. H. (1968). *Identity: Youth and crisis.* New York: Norton.

Fischer, C. (1982). *To dwell among friends: Personal networks in town and city.* Chicago: University of Chicago Press.

Gunnarsson, L., & Cochran, M. (1990). The social networks of single parents: Sweden and the United States. In M. Cochran, M. Larner, D. Riley, L. Gunnarsson, & C. Henderson, Jr., *Extending families: The social networks of parents and their children* (pp. 105–116). London/New York: Cambridge University Press.

Hareven, T. (1984). Themes in the historical development of the family. In R. D. Parke (Ed.), *Review of child development research* (Vol 7, pp. 137–178). Chicago: University of Chicago Press.

Hess, R., Shipman, V, Brophy, J., & Bear, R. (1968). *The cognitive environments of urban preschool children.* Unpublished manuscript, University of Chicago, Graduate School of Education, Chicago.

Homel, R., Burns, A., & Goodnow, J. (1987). Parental social networks and child development. *Journal of Social and Personal Relationships, 4,* 159–177.

House, J. (1980). *Work, stress, and social support.* Reading, MA: Addison-Wesley.

Larner, M. (1990). Change in network resources and relationships over time. In M. Cochran, M. Larner, D. Riley, L. Gunnarsson, & C. Henderson, Jr., *Extending families: The social networks of parents and their children* (pp. 181–204). London/New York: Cambridge University Press.

Lewis, M., Feiring, C., & Kotsonis, M. (1984). The social network of the young child: A developmental perspective. In M. Lewis (Ed.), *Beyond the dyad* (pp. 129–160). New York: Plenum.

Longfellow, C, Zelkowitz, P., Saunders, E., & Belle, D. (1979, March). *The role of support in moderating the effects of stress and depression.* Paper presented at the biennial meeting of the Society for Research in Child Development, San Francisco.

Milardo, R. (Ed). (1988). *Families and social networks.* Beverly Hills, CA: Sage.

Mitchell, J. C. (1969). The concept and use of social networks. In J. C. Mitchell (Ed.), *Social networks in urban situations* (pp. 1–50). Manchester, England: Manchester University Press.

Polansky, N., Gaudin, J., Ammons, P., & Davis, K. (1985). The psychological ecology of the neglectful mother. *Child Abuse & Neglect, 9,* 265–275.

Powell, D. (1979). Family environment relations and early childrearing: The role of social networks and neighborhood. *Journal of Research and Development in Education, 13,* 1–11.

Powell, D. (1987). A neighborhood approach to family support groups. *Journal of Community Psychology, 15,* 51–62.

Powell, D. (1988). Client characteristics and the design of community-based intervention programs. In A. Pence (Ed.), *Ecological research with children and families* (pp. 122–142). New York: Teachers College Press.

Riley, D. (1990). Network influences on father involvement in childrearing. In M. Cochran, M. Larner, D. Riley, L. Gunnarsson, & C. Henderson, Jr., *Extending families: The social networks of parents and their children* (pp. 131–153). London/New York: Cambridge University Press.

Stack, C. (1974). *All our kin: Strategies for survival in a Black community.* New York: Harper & Row.

Strom, R. D. (1982). *Parent as a Teacher inventory. Manual and instructions.* Bensenville, IL: Scholastic Testing Service, Inc.

Tietjen, A. (1985). Relationships between the social networks of Swedish mothers and their children. *International Journal of Behavioral Development, 8,* 195–216.

Wellman, B. (1981). Applying network analysis to the study of support. In B. H. Gottlieb (Ed.), *Social networks and social support* (pp. 171–200). Beverly Hills, CA: Sage.

16

Parenting and Public Policy

James Garbarino
Cornell University
Kathleen Kostelny
Erikson Institute for Advanced Study in Child Development

INTRODUCTION

The quality and character of parenting result in part from the social context in which families operate. One important feature of this social context is public policy. This chapter examines several public policy issues that affect parenting. It does so within an ecological framework that arises from efforts to understand the interaction of human biological and psychological systems with human social and cultural systems. The issues discussed include policies regarding family planning, state responsibility for children, the role of neighborhoods in family support, economic conditions affecting families, child safety, resiliency, and the allocation of economic and social resources to prevention, intervention, support, and empowerment programs.

Parents face different opportunities and risks in rearing their children because of parental and child mental and physical makeup *and* because of the social environment they inhabit as a family. Moreover, the social environment affects parenting through its impact on the very physical makeup of the child (and the parent). These influences constitute one important factor within the human ecology and form one of the root concepts in the ecological perspective, *social biology*.

In contrast to sociobiology, which emphasizes a genetic origin for social behavior, social biology concentrates on the social origins of biological phenomena including the impact of economic conditions and social policy on brain growth and physical development (e.g., environmental lead poisoning of children that leads to mental retardation and/or behavioral problems).

These social biological effects are often negative (e.g., the impact of poverty and famine on children that leads to mental retardation, or the effect of industrial carcinogens that have mutagenic consequences). But social biological effects may be positive as well: intrauterine surgery or nutritional therapy for a fetus with a genetic disorder. When these positive and negative social influences operate in psychological or sociological terms, we refer to them as sociocultural opportunities and risks, and they constitute an important force in shaping the parenting agenda.

Thus, when we refer to "opportunities for development" that affect parenting, we mean interpersonal and institutional relationships (with kith and kin, with professionals, with neighbors, with community authorities, etc.) in which parents find material, emotional, and social encouragement compatible with their needs and capacities as they exist at a specific point in their parenting career. For each parent (as for each child), the best fit must be worked out through experience, within some very broad guidelines of basic human needs, and then renegotiated as development proceeds and situations change.

This complex pattern of interactions has profound implications for understanding parenting. We can start from recent findings regarding the "accumulation of risk." For example, Sameroff, Barocas, Zax, and Greenspan (1987) reported that the average IQ scores of 4-year-old children are related to the number of familial and social risk factors present in their lives: a rigid and punitive childrearing style, parental substance abuse, parental educational attainment, father absence, poverty, and so forth. But this research reveals that the relation is not simply additive. Average IQ for children with zero, one, or two of the factors is above 115. With the addition of a third and fourth risk factor, the average IQ score drops precipitously to nearly 90, with relatively little further decrement as there is further accumulation of the fifth through eighth risk factors. As Dunst and Trivette's (1992) recent work reveals, understanding developmental opportunities helps to explain the variance in outcomes left unaccounted for in models that simply address risk. An ecological perspective on parenting makes good sense empirically, theoretically, and programmatically.

"Windows of opportunity" for intervention on behalf of parents appear repeatedly across the life course, and what may be a critical threat at one point may be benign or even developmentally enhancing at another. For example, Elder's analyses (1974) of the Great Depression (the economic crisis of the 1930s in the United States) reveal that the impact was mediated by parents: Children whose families were unaffected by unemployment and significant income loss showed little effect on their social, emotional, and vocational development. But when parents of *young* children were hit hard by the economic crisis, the development of those children suffered—in the form of problems with self-esteem, relationship formation, vocational aspirations, and academic achievement. In contrast, some adolescents—particularly daughters—benefited from the fact that *paternal* unemployment often meant special opportunities for enhanced responsibility and status in the family. As a result, these youth showed patterns of greater competence and achievement.

Analyzing research by Rutter and others, Bronfenbrenner (1986) confirmed that the stress of urban life associated with "family adversity" (Rutter's term) is most negative and potent for the development of *young* children (although such adversity may even stimulate some adolescents who have had a positive childhood). One important theme in current and future research seeking to illuminate the impact of public policy on parenting is to improve our understanding of the circumstances and conditions that constitute challenges and adversity that are growth inducing in contrast to those that are debilitating. A second important theme is to recognize that the "interests" of parents and children are not necessarily synonymous.

Risks to parenting can come both from direct threats and from the absence of normal, expectable opportunities. The experience of homelessness is one example of a sociocultural risk factor that has profound implications for parenting. "Home" implies permanence, a lack of contingency. You have a home when you have a place to go, no matter what. You have a home when there is a place with which you are connected permanently, that endures and represents *you*.

We might note here that it is only a small step from this concept of home to the analogous political concept of "homeland" in a sense that one is part of a nation, that one belongs somewhere politically. This essentially ideological phenomenon of having a political home may serve as a powerful force in parenting. For example, Punamaki (1987) reported that it sustains parenting under extremely stressful circumstances such as are found among Palestinians living in refugee camps in the midst of chronic political violence.

We need to study the hypothesis that both home and homeland may be important resources in identity formation in childhood and adolescence, and a childhood lack of either or both may lead to mental health problems associated with alienation, conduct disorder, rootlessness, violence, and depression in adolescence—problems that become intergenerational when they extend into adulthood. J. Gilligan (1991) explored just such an analysis in his study of the relations between shame (linked to negative personal and social identity) and violence. Individuals and groups who are ashamed of who they are (e.g., made to feel this way because of personal rejection or racism), are likely to express that negative self-definition in self- and socially destructive acts.

Understanding the experience of home may help sort out the divergent psychological impact and character of experiences that appear similar on the surface—such as being an "immigrant" and a "refugee" or having "moved" and being "displaced." With millions of families worldwide experiencing homelessness, this is a crucial issue for further study (see Garbarino, Kostelny, & Dubrow, 1991a). Before going further in our analysis, we should consider more explicitly the *ecological perspective* implicit in our approach to parenting.

AN ECOLOGICAL PERSPECTIVE ON PUBLIC POLICY

An ecological perspective is a systems approach to human development. It examines the environment at four levels beyond the individual organism—from the micro to the macro (Bronfenbrenner, 1979, 1986; Garbarino & Associates, 1992). Viewing parents only in terms of organismic and interpersonal dynamics precludes an understanding of the many other avenues of influence that might be open to us as helpers, or that might be topics of study for us as scientists. This message provides a crucial guide to research on intervention and program evaluation, and reflects the operation of systems of personality, family, community, economy, culture, and ideology. The starting point for this analysis are microsystems.

Microsystems

Microsystems are the immediate settings in which individuals develop. The shared experiences that occur in each setting provide a record of the microsystem and offer some clues to its future. Microsystems evolve and develop much as do individuals themselves from forces generated both within and without. The quality of a microsystem depends on its ability to sustain and enhance development, and to provide a context that is emotionally validating and developmentally challenging. This in turn depends on its capacity to operate in what Vygotsky (1986) called "the zone of proximal development," the distance between what the child can accomplish alone (the level of actual development) and what the child can do when helped (the level of potential development).

Children can handle (and need) more than infants. Adolescents can handle (and need) more than children. We measure the social richness of an individual's life by the availability of enduring, reciprocal, multifaceted relationships that emphasize playing, working, and loving. And we do that measuring over time, because microsystems, like individuals, change over time. Risk on the other hand, lies in patterns of abuse, neglect, resource deficiency, and stress that threaten the child and thwart development (Garbarino, Guttman, & Seeley, 1986).

The "same" day-care center is very different in June from what it was in September for the "same" infants who, of course, are themselves not the same as they were at the beginning of the year. The setting of the family, as the firstborn child experiences it, is different from that experienced by subsequent offspring. Naturally, children themselves change and develop, as do others in the setting. It is also important to remember that our definition speaks of the microsystem as a pattern *experienced* by the developing person. Individuals influence their microsystems and those microsystems influence them in turn. Each participant acts on the basis of an emergent social map—a phenomenological record and projection.

Mesosystems

Mesosystems are relationships *between* microsystems in which the individual experiences reality. These links themselves form a system. We measure the richness of a mesosystem in the number and quality of its connections. One example is the connection between an infant's day-care group and his or her home. Do staff visit the child at home? Do the child's parents know his or her friends at day care? Do parents of children at the center know each other?

A second example concerns the connection between the hospital and the home for a chronically ill child. What role do the parents play in the hospital regime? Do the same health care professionals who see the child in the hospital visit the home? Is the child the only one to participate in both? If he or she is the only "linkage," the mesosystem is weak and that weakness may place the child at risk. Research suggests that the strength of the mesosystem linking the setting in which an intervention is implemented with the settings in which the individual spends the most significant time is crucial to the long-term effectiveness of the intervention, and to the maintenance of its effects (Whittaker, Garbarino, & Associates, 1983).

Exosystems

Exosystems are settings that have a bearing on the development of children, but in which those children do not play a direct role. For most children, the key exosystems include the workplace of their parents and those centers of power such as school boards, church councils, and planning commissions that make decisions affecting children's day-to-day life. Note that the concept of an exosystem illustrates the projective nature of the ecological perspective, for the same setting that is an exosystem for a child may be a microsystem for the parent, and vice versa. Thus, one form of intervention may aim at transforming exosystems into microsystems, such as by initiating greater participation in important institutions for isolated, disenfranchised, and powerless clients—for example, by getting parents to visit the family day-care home or by creating on-site day care at the workplace.

In exosystem terms, both risk and opportunity come about in two ways. The first is when the parents or other significant adults in a child's life are treated in a way that impoverishes (risk) or enhances (opportunity) their behavior in the microsystems they share with children. Examples include elements of the parents' working experience that impoverish or enhance family life—such as unemployment, low pay, long or inflexible hours, traveling, or stress, on the one hand, in contrast to an adequate income, flexible scheduling, an understanding employer, or subsidies for child care, on the other (Bronfenbrenner & Crouter, 1983).

The second way risk and opportunity flow from the exosystem lies in the orientation and content of decisions made in those settings that affect the day-to-day experience of children and their families. For example, when the state legislature suspends funding for early intervention programs, it jeopardizes children's development. When public officials expand prenatal health services or initiate specialized day care in high-risk communities, they increase developmental opportunities for children (and may reduce infant mortality or morbidity).

Albee (1980) went so far as to identify powerlessness as the primary factor leading to impaired development and mental disability. Powerlessness plays a large role in determining the fate of groups of individuals via public policy and is important when considering individual cases—such as whether or not parents have the "pull" to get a medically vulnerable child enrolled in a special treatment program. In many cases, risk and opportunity at the exosystem level are essentially political matters.

One of the most useful aspects of the ecological approach is its ability to highlight situations in which the actions of people with whom the individual has no direct contact significantly affect their development. The following example illustrates the relationship between social policy and individual child development. Because of a leveraged corporate takeover, a board of directors decides to shift operations from one plant to another. Hundreds of families with young children are forced to move to new locations. Local services are underfunded in a period of escalating demand. Parents lose their jobs and thus their health insurance. The quality of prenatal and well-baby care declines and infant mortality increases. This is a classic illustration of an exosystem effect. It highlights the fact that exosystem events may establish much of the agenda for day-to-day early intervention on behalf of children at risk.

At this point, it is worth emphasizing that the ecological perspective forces us to consider the concept of risk beyond the narrow confines of individual personality and family dynamics. In the ecological approach, both are "causes" of the child's developmental patterns and "reflections" of broader sociocultural forces. We can make good use of the aphorism: "If the only tool you have is a hammer you tend to treat every problem as if it were a nail." Inflexible loyalty to a specific focus (e.g., the parents) is often a stumbling block to effective intervention. However, the obverse must also be considered: "If you define every problem as a nail, the only tool you will seek is a hammer." Viewing children at risk only in terms of organismic and interpersonal dynamics precludes an understanding of the many other avenues of influence that might be open to us as helpers, or that might be topics of study for us as scientists. This message provides a crucial guide to our discussions of early intervention and social policy affecting parenting.

Macrosystems

Meso- and exosystems are set within the broad ideological, demographic, and institutional patterns of a particular culture or subculture. These are the *macrosystems* that serve as the master "blueprints" for the ecology of human development. These blueprints reflect a people's shared assumptions about how things should be done, as well as the institutions that represent those assumptions. Macrosystems are ideology incarnate. Thus, we contrast societal blueprints that rest upon fundamental institutional expressions, such as a "collective versus individual orientation." Religion provides a classic example of the macrosystem concept because it involves both a definition of the world and a set of institutions reflecting that definition—both a theology and a set of roles, rules, buildings, and programs.

Macrosystems refer to the general organization of the world as it is and as it might be. Historical change demonstrates that the "might be" is quite real, and occurs either through evolution (many individual actions guided by a common reality) or revolution (dramatic change introduced by a small cadre of decision makers). The Iranian revolution of 1978–1979, for example, overturned a "modernizing" society and embodied a changed institutional and ideological landscape that shaped the most basic experiences of childhood. Current efforts to "modernize" in China include a massive shift from "collective reward" to "private initiative" as the dominating economic force. More directly relevant still is the "one child policy" that has altered the demography of the family, and appears to be altering the social fabric at each level of the human ecology (Schell, 1982).

In the United States, the increasing concentration of high-risk families in a geographically concentrated "underclass" (Lemann, 1986; Wilson, 1987) is exerting dramatic influences on the need and the prognosis for early interventions. Pockets of marked vulnerability show poverty and infant mortality rates many times the average found in unafflicted communities. For early intervention services to be plausible in such high-risk ecological niches they must target "ecological transformation" as the program goal (Garbarino & Kostelny, 1994).

For example, Chicago's Center for Successful Child Development ("The Beethoven Project") is an effort to prevent developmental delays among an entire birth cohort in a public housing project (i.e., all the children born in 1 year who live in the same kindergarten catchment area). The program employs home health visitors, early developmental screening, prenatal health care and parent education, job training for parents, infant day care, child abuse prevention programming, Head Start participation, and other transforming and supportive services (Barclay-McLaughlin, 1987). When such efforts are conducted in the context of thoughtful evaluation research they can serve as the kind of "transforming experiments" that advance an ecologically valid science of early intervention (Bronfenbrenner, 1979).

An ecological perspective has much to contribute to the process of formulating, evaluating, and understanding social policy. It gives us a kind of social map for navigating a path through the complexities of programming. It helps us see the relations (potential and actual) among programs—how, for example, some programs are complementary whereas others may be competitive. It aids us in seeing the full range of alternative conceptualizations of problems affecting children and points us in the direction of multiple strategies for intervention. It provides a framework to use in thinking about what is happening, and what to do when faced with developmental problems and social pathologies that afflict children. It does this by asking us always to consider the micro-, meso-, exo-, and macrosystem dimensions of developmental phenomena and interventions. It constantly suggests the possibility that context shapes causal relationships. It always tells us "it depends" and stimulates an attempt to find out "on what."

Consider the case of child abuse. We need to look to the community that establishes laws and policies about child abuse, as well as to the families that offer a powerful definition of reality for the next generation. We also should look to the culture that defines physical force as an appropriate form of discipline in early childhood. But we must also look within the individual, as a psychological system affected by conscious and changing roles, and unconscious needs and motives, to know why and how each individual adjusts in ways that generate conflict. In addition, we must also look "across" systems to see how the several systems involved (family, social services, social network, and economy) adjust to new conditions.

FAMILY PLANNING

The most fundamental way in which public policy affects parenting is, of course, through its influence on who is born in the first place. Public policies with respect to family planning take several forms. Some seek to stimulate nativity—typically through financial incentives (e.g., state-funded children's allowances or the paying of special bonuses for bearing large numbers of children). Others seek to limit the number of children born through some combination of incentives for small families and penalties for large ones. The Chinese one child policy is one such example.

The Chinese government in the 1970s limited population growth by enforcing a policy of one child per family. This policy was implemented through a combination of incentives and penalties. For example, in many communities families who made a public commitment to one child were given preferential treatment in social services and economic benefits programs. Conversely, those who gave birth to a second child received reduced benefits. In some cases, strong social pressures were brought to bear on women who conceived a second child and did not voluntarily seek an abortion. The government mounted massive public information ("propaganda") campaigns to support the policy.

The outcomes of this policy are difficult to determine given the secretiveness of Chinese society and the severe limitations on demographic data. It does seem, however, that the bias in favor of males led to many families refusing to "waste" their allocation on girls (Garbarino, 1992b). As a result, significant numbers of female children were either hidden or killed after birth. The impact of this on parenting is unknown, as is the changed composition of the population to include predominantly only children (and thus abolition of the roles of sibling, cousin, and uncle/aunt). The long-term "nucle-arization" of the Chinese family is clear; its impact on parenting remains largely unexplored. Loosening of the one child policy in recent years has diminished but not eliminated concern that the roles of sibling, cousin, and aunt-uncle will disappear.

More broadly, policies regarding abortion and contraception also have an impact on parenting. The clearest effect is to alter the number of "unwanted" and "unplanned" children born. That this is important is demonstrated generally by studies of the impact of acceptance and rejection on children. Unwanted children manifest impaired development that extends into adolescence. It seems that the effects are due to the adverse parenting practices of the mothers. We know from other research that rejection is a "psychological malignancy" (Garbarino et al., 1986; Rohner, 1980). A European study tracked the negative developmental outcomes for children whose mothers sought abortions but were denied them for policy reasons (David, Dytrych, Matejcek, & Schuller, 1988). This study provides an important resource in any discussion of the effects of abortion and family-planning policy on parenting.

Policy can affect nativity through the allocation or denial of resources to those who lack private means to seek abortion. For example, data from Michigan reveal a significant increase in births to young and poor mothers and in "high-risk offspring" in the years immediately following a termination of state funding for abortion in 1988. Examining the data for the period 1987–1990 indicates a 27 percent decrease in overall abortions, a 36 percent decrease in abortions to women under 20 years of age, a 15 percent increase in low-birthweight babies (under 2,500 grams), and a 457 percent increase in the number of infants born with congenital abnormalities.

It appears that in this case public policy has had a direct effect on the number of "medically fragile" children being born—mainly to low-income, young women. It seems fair to assume that this combination of high risk, coupled with the presumption that many of these children were unwanted, means a significant increase in the number of families facing very challenging parenting contexts.

PUBLIC RESPONSIBILITY FOR CHILDREN

The state plays an important role in setting the parameters for parental responsibility, and thus for the realms in which variation in parenting skills affects child development. For example, most state governments in the United States accept responsibility for providing the public with basic services such as potable water and waste disposal. Borrowing a term commonly used in injury control, this is *passive prevention* in the sense that it requires no action on the part of parents to protect their children. In contrast, immunization programs require more active efforts of parents—bringing the young child to a facility that provides the immunization (or at least permitting the child to be immunized as part of the program at a school or daycare center).

Passive prevention efforts in the form of community water and sewage systems absolve individual parents of the responsibility to provide clean water and to dispose of sewage. Thus, variations in child health due to cholera and other water- or sewage-born agents are absent. Requiring immunization as an entrance requirement for mandatory school enrollment reduces the role of parental initiative. Of course, the fact that less than 100 percent of young children are immunized is evidence of "costs" of anything less than fully passive prevention. Similarly, the deregulation of television programming aimed at children is a prime example of how public policy can affect the individual responsibility of parents (Carlsson-Paige & Levin, 1990). Deregulating television programming aimed at children has increased the individual responsibility of parents to monitor and regulate the television viewing of their children.

When government does not assume responsibility for passive prevention measures, we find significant variation in parental behavior linked to a series of predictable family variables—education of parents, social class, personal history of parents, and family system functioning. Thus, if government did not assume responsibility for providing potable water and for sewage treatment, we would expect to find substantial variation in child health due to differences in parental skill, motivation, and resources, as we do in the areas of childhood television viewing—and to a lesser degree immunization against childhood illnesses.

Variations in state responsibility for children penetrate into many aspects of parenting. For example, in an effort to prevent the international "kidnapping" of children by noncustodial parents, a number of governments now require written consent of both parents prior to issuing a visa for a minor. Australia and Mexico are two examples.

Perhaps the key issue of public responsibility emerges from the following personal account. When one of the authors moved to the State of Illinois in 1985, he brought with him a 3-year-old daughter and a 3-year-old automobile. The State of Illinois sent a clear message regarding its conception of responsibility. The state required that the car be registered. It further required that it be inspected on a regular basis and that the driver be licensed to operate it. And, Illinois required liability insurance to operate the automobile. The message was clear: Cars are a public matter. With respect to the daughter, however, no messages of public interest were given. She was invisible to the state (until she reached the age of 6 and was required to attend school).

POLICIES AFFECTING THE SAFETY OF SOCIAL
ENVIRONMENTS FOR PARENTS

Hundreds of thousands of American children face the developmental challenge of living amidst chronic community violence. There is evidence that this problem has been growing in recent years. For example, since 1974, the rate of serious assault (potentially lethal assaults with knives and guns) has increased 400 percent in Chicago (and other major metropolitan areas reveal similar patterns). Interviews with families living in public housing projects in Chicago revealed that virtually all the children had firsthand experiences with shooting by the time they were 5 years old (Garbarino, Dubrow, Kostelny, & Pardo, 1992).

Other surveys found that 30 percent of the children living in high-crime neighborhoods of Chicago have witnessed a homicide by the time they are 15 years old, and more than 70 percent have witnessed a serious assault (Bell, 1991). These figures derive in part from the fact that killings are more public now than they were in the past. For example, Chicago has seen a 50 percent increase in the likelihood that a homicide is committed "in public" versus "in private" in the 10-year period from 1982–1992. In 1982, 32 percent of homicides were committed in public, whereas in 1992 that figure was 49 percent. This means that more and more children witness violence (added to the fact that the number of homicides has also increased during that period).

By the age of 14 years, most children living in these environments have personal knowledge of someone who has been killed in an act of violence. These data bear a greater resemblance to the experience of children in the war zones around the world than they do to what we should expect for our own children living in "peace" (Garbarino, Kostelny, & Dubrow, 1991a, 1991b). However, outright community violence is not the whole, or even the primary issue facing parents, and with which public policy must contend. More broadly, there is the problem of geographic concentration of risk factors, and the challenges these risk factors present to parents.

Amidst such a setting, many parents are likely to confront children who experience the symptoms of posttraumatic stress disorder (PTSD), symptoms that include sleep disturbances, re-creating trauma in play, extreme startle responses, diminished expectations for the future, and even biochemical changes in the brain that impair social and academic functioning. Research reports that there is a significant correlation between witnessing violence and both PTSD and more general childhood problems (Achenbach, 1991) especially when children are exposed to violence in the family as well (Garbarino, Kostelny, & Grady, 1993; Richters & Martinez, 1993). There is also evidence that young children are more likely than adolescents to experience PTSD when confronted with traumatic events. In one study, 56 percent of the children 10 years and younger showed signs of PTSD versus 18 percent of those 11 years of age or older (Davidson & Smith, 1990).

What is more, one element that contributes to the problem of community crime and violence is the deterioration of the physical environment. The symbolic value of a deteriorating physical community is that it sends negative signals to residents, particularly to marginal members who are particularly prone to antisocial behavior. The cycle is recognized: Graffiti proliferates, trash accumulates, painting and other needed maintenance is delayed or foregone, vacant housing units increase, illicit drug sales and use escalate, and violence surges. Those responsible for the physical quality and security of the community's housing can play an important role in preventing or exacerbating this cycle, as is illustrated at a later point.

The experience of trauma can produce significant psychological problems that interfere with learning and appropriate social behavior in school and that interfere with normal parent–child relationships. It can also make children prime candidates for involvement in gangs, where the violent economy of the illicit drug trade offers a sense of belonging and solidarity as well as a cash income for kids who have few prosocial alternatives. It requires extraordinary parenting to overcome these forces.

Does public policy create or tolerate social environments in which the accumulation of risk factors exceeds the "average expectable competence" of parents? It takes an extraordinary parent to succeed in a "socially toxic" environment (Garbarino, 1995). No public policy can be considered humane if it requires extraordinary parenting. For example, there are many similarities between the experiences of children growing up in refugee and "displaced persons" camps in Thailand, Hong Kong, and the Middle East, and some low-income housing projects in Chicago and other American cities (Garbarino, Dubrow, Kostelny, & Pardo, 1992):

(1) In both the camps and the housing projects, there is a proliferation of weapons—a kind of "arms race"—which exacerbates the effects of conflict and violence. It is common for young people—particularly males—to be heavily armed and to be engaged in armed attacks and reprisals. Substantial numbers of "bystander" injuries are observed.

(2) In both the camps and the housing projects, representatives of "mainstream" society have only partial control over what happens. International relief workers typically leave the camps at the end of the working day, as do the social workers and educators in the public housing projects. Both the camps and the projects are under the control of the local gangs at night. Therefore, no action during the day can succeed unless it is acceptable to the gangs that rule the community at night. For example, there have been cases in housing projects in Chicago in which local gangs have established curfews on their own initiative and in which gangs make the decision about whether or not someone who commits a crime against residents will be identified and punished.

(3) In both the camps and the projects, women—particularly mothers—are in a desperate situation. They are under enormous stress, often are the target of domestic violence, and have few economic or educational resources and prospects. Men play a marginal role in the enduring life of families—being absent for reasons that include participating in the fighting, fleeing to escape enemies, being injured or killed, and (particularly in the case of the American public housing projects) being imprisoned. Largely as a result, there is a major problem of maternal depression. Studies in both settings have reported 50 percent of the women being seriously depressed.

(4) In both the camps and the projects, one consequence of maternal depression is the neglect of children. This connection is well established in research findings that neglect leads to elevated levels of "accidental injuries" to children. Only the most dedicated and highly motivated mothers can overcome the depressive effects of these high-crime, high-stress environments and rally to protect their children effectively. And even this effort becomes more difficult as children reach adolescence and become increasingly independent of maternal control and thereby potentially under the influence of gangs in the environment.

(5) In both the camps and the projects, children and youth have diminished prospects for the future. This lack of a positive future orientation produces depression, rage, and disregard for human life—their own and others'. In its most extreme form this disconnection from the future takes on the guise of "terminal thinking," the belief that the inevitable outcome of life in such an environment is early death. When asked, "What will you be when you are 30 years old?" some children respond, "Dead."

These environments are particularly relevant to our discussion of public policy issues affecting parenting, because these settings do not arise "naturally." Rather, they are the direct result of public policy decisions. They are deliberate social creations—even if their consequences and dynamics were not intentional or even anticipated. As a case example, one of the authors was involved as an expert witness in a case in California in which residents of a low-income housing project (owned by a group of private investors) sued the owners for liability because of deteriorating security conditions that produced an increase in violence resulting in traumatic stress for child residents. Tax policies and leniency toward white-collar crime permitted owners of this project to make money while neglecting their responsibility to the tenant residents. The report (Garbarino, 1992a) concluded:

(1) Significant numbers of the children residing in Kennedy Manor evidence signs of chronic stress and trauma related to the overall level of danger present and their first hand, specific encounters with threat

and violence. Reports from parents suggest children are manifesting signs of Post Traumatic Stress Disorder and more general indicators of anxiety and fear (including rashes, asthma, stomach pains, etc.). Young children are reported to evidence sleep disorders, fearfulness, clinging, and anger that they must live within the restrictions on their day-to-day lives imposed by their parents in an attempt to protect them from the high level of danger in the environment.

(2) Significant numbers of parents and other caregivers responsible for children in Kennedy Manor report serious distress related to the conditions of life, including the pervasive threat and demoralizing conditions. There are numerous reports of stress-related psychosomatic conditions and sleep disturbances, as well as depression, humiliation, and anger for the adults who care for children.

It is not necessary to have daily incidents of violence to create and sustain a social climate of fear and threat. For example, if shooting occurs regularly—several times per month—that is enough to create an atmosphere of imminent danger, affecting the behavior of parents and children. The probability of violence is sufficiently high in Kennedy Manor to produce such effects. The day-to-day life of children in Kennedy Manor reflects a generalized perception of chronic danger. Children and parents are aware of multiple incidents of violence and fully expect such incidents to recur unless a major change in the management of the community addresses security concerns.

The conditions described by residents and observers in the Kennedy Manor Apartments are quite consistent with conditions in situations of chronic community violence observed in other locations around the United States. Our best estimate is that these conditions of life present a serious threat to the development and psychological well-being of the children who live there. The threat includes specific conditions such as Post Traumatic Stress Disorder related to first-hand encounters with violence and more general problems of chronic fear, anxiety, and depression, with resulting adaptations that impair academic, emotional, and social development. Children who live in such an environment are particularly prone for recruitment into gang activity when they reach adolescence.

Furthermore, the management of the Kennedy Manor can exert significant influence over the social environment in the complex through policies and practices with respect to the quality of the physical environment (maintenance and rehabilitation of units and common areas), maintaining high standards for continued residence (by screening new tenants and proceeding with evictions as needed), and committing sufficient resources to on-site security to create a safer environment for residents (and as a result a greater sense of security for children). (pp. 10–13)

This analysis was successful: The insurance company representing the owners of Kennedy Manor settled the case with an out of court payment to the residents of nearly $3 million.

THE ECONOMICS OF PARENTHOOD

No study of parenting can be complete without an appreciation of economic issues. As noted by Bronfenbrenner (1986), correlations between measures of income or socioeconomic status and basic child outcomes are often higher in some societies than others. Why? Because in some societies parental income is the principal determinant of access to resources whereas others adopt policies designed to minimize this correlation.

For example, low income is a better predictor of developmental deficits in the United States than in other "modern" societies, presumably because American social policies tend to exaggerate rather than minimize the impact of family income on access to preventive and rehabilitative services (Bronfenbrenner, 1986). Thus, one important aspect of policy is income transfer payments and other efforts to "guarantee" income to parents (e.g., "child allowances" that are based on the child's existence rather than parental earning capacity). Another is the extent to which crucial supportive services such as home health visitors are available to everyone (perhaps with a sliding fee schedule) as opposed to on the basis of availability of special grants in response to some assessment of "risk."

The human significance of poverty for parenting has both "objective" and "subjective" dimensions. Among the objective dimensions are implications for illness (morbidity) and death (mortality).

Both are substantially—but differentially—correlated with poverty in most societies, but more or less so as a function of public policy. Among the important subjective concerns are the experience of deprivation, and its concomitant, shame and negative identity (both of which appear to be associated with violence and aggression) (Gilligan, 1991).

Beyond this concern with the developmental impact of poverty is a broader concern with the economic context of parents and parenthood. The economic "miracles" of the last four decades in nations around the world have raised expectations, and have led to more and more of daily life becoming part of the monetarized economy, i.e., having a dollar price (Giarini, 1980). This can have important implications for families; without the transition to a "sustainable society," parents (and thus children) will be ever more susceptible to the vagaries of the modern economic order (Garbarino, 1992b). Thus, families will be more vulnerable to the periodic recessions, employment dislocations, and overall polarization of the population into haves and have nots, as the rich really do get richer while the poor do indeed get poorer. Children cost too much when their caregivers cannot generate enough income to meet popular expectations for participating in the monetarized economy of day-to-day life.

Thus, children are increasingly an economic burden, directly because of what it costs to rear them and indirectly because of what they cost in lost parental income. Conventional economists tell us to assume that these costs are accounted for automatically in the market place and result in the general good—the "invisible hand" of capitalism. Sustainable economics challenges this glib assumption, arguing that "business as usual" can lead to social and economic, as well as environmental disaster. We must study this hypothesis in detail across a variety of cultural and political contexts to have a full appreciation for the economics of parenthood. As we do so, we are drawn to the study of neighborhoods as contexts in which social policy translates into concrete influences on parenting.

NEIGHBORHOOD-BASED PROGRAMMING AS PARENT SUPPORT

However we as a society define "neighborhood," we must struggle to understand the potential and actual impact of "neighborhood-based programming" on parenting (Garbarino & Kostelny, 1992, 1994a, 1994b; Garbarino, Stocking, & Associates, 1980). The defining characteristics of a neighborhood-based approach to parenting is premised on the notion that deliberately engineered social support, provided during a formative period in child and family development, can buffer the child and family from some of the psychological and social effects of poverty, promote personal development and psychological well-being, and stimulate healthy patterns of interaction both within the family and between the family and the broader environment (Weiss & Halpern, 1991). In starker terms, it may be argued that deliberately engineered social support can be potent enough to alter parenting capacities and styles acquired and reinforced through a lifetime of experience in a particular familial and social world. The role of social support systems in preventing child maltreatment lies in the linking of social nurturance *and* social control (Garbarino, 1987). Such support systems do more than simply offer nurturance. They also offer feedback, validate the individual, and serve a social control function (Caplan & Killilea, 1976).

When we look at social support as a strategy for enhancing parenting we can identify two corollary premises. The first premise is that the support provided can be internalized in some manner, and thus have an effect beyond the period during which it is provided. The second premise is that the support provided can strengthen childrearing enough to have a meaningful effect on child health and development (Weiss & Halpern, 1991).

These corollaries reverberate through all analyses of neighborhood-based parent support in the form of two recurrent questions: (1) Can parent support be a "treatment" or must it be a condition of life? (2) Can parent support succeed amidst conditions of high risk? Both call our attention to the limiting factors on neighborhood support: whether it is possible to "synthesize" neighborhood, and, whether neighborhood-based programming is feasible among the neediest families.

One of the origins of the social support "movement" for parents lies in the settlement houses that were created as part of liberal reform movements in the nineteenth century (e.g., Hull House in Chicago; see Halpern, 1990). These settlement houses sought to provide a neighborhood focus and to serve a wide range of needs—ameliorative, preventive, and enabling. Staff lived in the settlement house, and the overall theme was one of establishing a center for promoting the culture, values, and resources of middle-class America among the poor and immigrant populations.

A second origin of the social support approach lies in the early concept of the visiting nurse. By sending nurses into the community, and by defining their role as "holistic," the visiting nurse programs of the nineteenth and early twentieth centuries complemented the settlement house by incorporating the concept of "friendly visitors" and "mutual help" into day-to-day practice. Visiting nurses clearly bear a direct conceptual (and often historical) relation with contemporary approaches to parental social support, in which "community nursing" figures prominently (Froland, Pancoast, Chapman, & Kimboko, 1981; Kagan, Powell, Weissbourd, & Zigler, 1987). From the 1930s through the 1950s other neighborhood-based strategies emerged.

Current approaches include a wide and proliferating variety of programs and organizations designed to establish social support in the environment of parents. These efforts are often called "family support and education programs" (e.g., the "Family Focus Program" developed by Weissbourd and her colleagues), "social support networks" (Belle, 1989), "parent education projects" (e.g., the "New Parents as Teachers Program"—Pfannesntiel & Seltzer, 1989), or "home health visitor programs" (e.g., the Elmira, New York, project—Olds & Henderson, 1990; Olds, Henderson, Tatelbaum, & Chamberlain, 1986).

A study by Freudenburg and Jones (1991) of 23 communities experiencing rapid population growth found that all but 2 communities had a disproportionate increase in crime, and suggested that changes in a community's social structure that accompany rapid growth result in a breakdown of social control. As the "density of acquaintanceship" (i.e., the proportion of a community's residents who know each other) decreases, criminal activity increases. Another issue concerns out migration from neighborhoods beginning to "turn bad." Such out migration may have debilitating effects on social networks (Fitchen, 1981). What is more, the fact that out migration is not random means that those who choose to stay and those who have no choice may increasingly constitute a sample unrepresentative of the general population. This can confound any assessment—and therefore any intervention effort.

Beyond even these obvious selection factors, neighborhoods differ on the basis of "ethos." Some areas are more vital and coherent, even among middle-class families (Warren, 1978). There are common problems too. A survey in South Carolina (Melton, 1992) revealed that on a scale of 1–7—with 7 indicating high involvement—the average score for neighborhood residents was 2+ in response to the question "How involved are you in other people's children?"; and, the same survey revealed that most people could not name one human service agency that had been particularly helpful on behalf of children.

Social context is important to parenting and the impact of policy (as is self-selection and the content of "treatment"). For example, one recent study reported that youth whose families were relocated to subsidized housing in the suburbs were more than twice as likely to attend college (54 percent vs. 21 percent) and find employment (75 percent vs. 41 percent) as youth who were relocated to subsidized housing in inner-city areas (Rosenbaum & Kaufman, 1991). Assuming that there were no systematic differences in who relocated where, this result suggests a powerful social support effect on important life-course events (i.e., attending college and finding employment).

The role of neighborhood factors in parenting derives from an understanding of the link between low income and child maltreatment (Garbarino, 1987; National Center on Child Abuse and Neglect, 1981; Pelton, 1978, 1981, 1994). Poverty is associated with a significantly elevated risk of child maltreatment. From this observation flows a two-fold conception of risk as applied to neighborhoods and families (Garbarino & Crouter, 1978). The first refers to areas with a high absolute rate of child maltreatment (based on cases per unit of population). In this sense, concentrations of socioeconomically distressed families are most likely to be at high risk for child maltreatment. For example, in

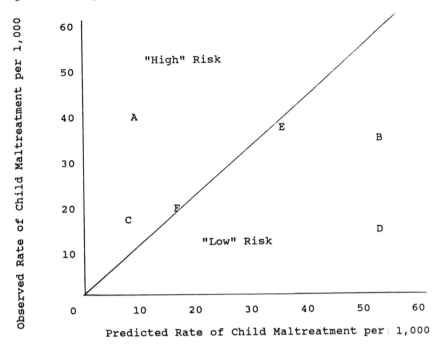

FIGURE 16.1. Two meanings of *Risk* in assessing community areas.

Omaha, Nebraska, socioeconomic status accounted for approximately 40 percent of the variation across neighborhoods in reported rates of child maltreatment. The magnitude of this correlation may reflect a social policy effect. It seems reasonable to hypothesize that in a society in which low income is not correlated with access to basic human services (e.g., maternal infant health care) this correlation would be smaller. In a society totally devoid of policies to ameliorate the impact of family-level differences in social class, it might be even larger.

It is the second meaning of high risk that is of greater relevance here, however. High risk can also mean that an area has a higher rate of child maltreatment *than would be predicted knowing its socioeconomic character.* Thus, two areas with similar socioeconomic profiles may have very different rates of child maltreatment. In this sense, one is high risk whereas the other is low risk, although both may have higher rates of child maltreatment than other, more affluent areas (see Figure 16.1).

In Figure 16.1, areas A and B have high observed rates of child maltreatment while areas C and D have lower observed rates. However, areas A and C have higher observed rates than predicted rates (10 per 1,000 predicted and 36 per 1,000 observed for A; 7 per 1,000 predicted and 16 per 1,000 observed for C), whereas areas B and D have lower observed than predicted rates (55 per 1,000 predicted and 34 per 1,000 observed for B; 54 per 1,000 predicted and 14 per 1,000 observed for D). In this sense, A and C are both high risk, and B and D are both low risk. Areas E and F evidence a close approximation between predicted and actual rates. This classification system provides the basis for identifying contrasting social environments. Unfortunately, this sort of community risk analysis is lacking in virtually all programatic efforts aimed at preventing child maltreatment (indeed, in all areas in which social support programs might be aimed at improved family functioning).

Perhaps the most comprehensive analysis of the human ecology of social pathology to date concerns Chicago neighborhoods (Garbarino & Kostelny, 1992a, 1993). It illustrates the challenges that must be faced in order to translate policy into parent support programs in the current context of extremely high levels of socioeconomic deprivation, geographic concentrations of poverty, and community violence. It further illuminates the negative social momentum characterizing many inner-city neighborhoods where child maltreatment is a disproportionately severe problem. Much of the variation among community rates of child maltreatment (using a composite measure that includes all forms, but is largely composed of physical abuse and neglect) is linked to variations in nine socioeconomic and demographic characteristics (with the multiple correlation being .89, thus accounting for 79 percent of the variation).

This is the statistical picture of the context in which prevention programs must operate. One specific piece of evidence communicates the urgency: child deaths due to maltreatment. Such child deaths are a particularly telling indicator of the bottom line in a community. Four Chicago neighborhoods in our statistical analysis reported a total of 19 such deaths during a 3-year period. Eight of these deaths (a rate of one death for each 2,541 children) occurred in a neighborhood identified as high risk. In an area that shared many problems but was identified in the statistical analysis as low risk, the rate was one death for each 5,571 children. The fact that deaths due to child maltreatment were twice as likely in the high-risk area than the low-risk area seems consistent with the overall findings of our statistical analyses and interviews. This is an environment in which there is truly an ecological conspiracy against parents *and* children (Garbarino & Kostelny, 1993a).

FACTORS LEADING TO RESILIENCY AND COPING

Convergent findings from several studies of life-course responses to stressful early experience suggest a series of ameliorating factors that lead to prosocial and healthy adaptability (Lösel & Bliesener, 1990): (1) actively trying to cope with stress (rather than just reacting), (2) cognitive competence (at least an average level of intelligence), (3) experiences of self-efficacy and a corresponding self-confidence and positive self-esteem, (4) temperamental characteristics that favor active coping attempts and positive relationships with others (e.g., activity, goal orientation, sociability) rather than passive withdrawal, (5) a stable emotional relationship with at least one parent or other reference person, (6) an open, supportive educational climate and parental model of behavior that encourages constructive coping with problems, and (7) social support from persons outside the family. These factors have been identified as important when the stresses involved are in the "normal" range found in the mainstream of modern industrial societies: poverty, family conflict, childhood physical disability, and parental involvement in substance abuse. They thus provide a starting point for efforts to understand the impact of policy on parenting—and ultimately on children.

Of the seven factors identified in the research on resilience and coping, several are particularly relevant to policy (and some of the others are indirectly relevant). We are particularly interested in the factors of "social support from persons outside the family," "an open, supportive educational climate and parental model of behavior that encourages constructive coping with problems," and "a stable emotional relationship with at least one parent or other reference person." In these three factors is the beginning of an agenda for policy initiatives to enhance parenting—particularly under conditions of high stress and threat.

The first factor is at the heart of our concern: social support from persons outside the family. It complements our ecological perspective, and exemplifies the role of meso- and exosystems. We see this as a generic affirmation of the validity of policies designed to promote parent support efforts. It tells us that the importance of social support increases inversely with the inner resources of the parent: The poorer *need* more help. Moreover, it is frequently the case that the more troubled and impoverished a parent, the less effective he or she will be in identifying, soliciting, and making effective use of resources *outside* the family.

This is the message of research on neglecting parents conducted by Guadin and Polansky (1985). Neglecting mothers are less ready, willing, and able to see and make use of social support in their neighborhoods and more in need of such support than other mothers. This vicious cycle is evident repeatedly in studies of child maltreatment (Garbarino, 1977).

The second resilience factor explicitly targets the community's institutions. Schools, religious institutions, civic organizations, and other social entities operationalize the concept of "an open, supportive educational climate." Programs and role models that teach and reward the reflective "processing" of experience are an essential feature of social support at the neighborhood and community level.

The third resilience factor is a stable emotional relationship with at least one parent or other reference person. How does this translate into policies affecting parenting? It does so through repeated findings that depth—as opposed to simply breadth—is an important feature of social support (and one often neglected in programatic approaches). In addition to having social support effectively available through friends, neighbors, co-workers, and professionals, parents need social support in its most intensive form: You need "someone who is absolutely crazy about you." This is clear from research on parenting (children must have someone in this role), but it is also important in the functioning and development of youth and adults, including those in parenting roles.

The implications of this ecological analysis are quite significant. For example, in his efforts to prevent child maltreatment among malfunctioning parent–child dyads, Wahler (1980) found that the effects of programatic intervention were negligible for mothers who had no close allies who supported revisions in their parenting styles and practices. Only by identifying and incorporating into the preventive intervention such a maternal ally was Wahler (1980) able to ensure that the preventive strategies he was teaching to mothers would endure. For poor mothers, this person is likely to be neighborhood based. This finding parallels other studies emphasizing the importance of social support for the goals of professional intervention (e.g., the congruence of residential treatment goals for youth in the postrelease social environment—see Whittaker & Garbarino, 1983).

Social support has at least two distinct dimensions: making the individual feel connected and promoting prosocial behavior (e.g., avoiding child maltreatment even under stressful conditions). This understanding of the dual nature of social support offers an explanation for the finding that under conditions of social stress parents whose only social network is kin are more likely to abuse children than families whose network includes nonkin (Gelles & Straus, 1988). Kin-only networks are more likely than more diverse networks to offer consensus support for an interpretation of child behavior and a corresponding rationale for parent behavior. Considering the structure of social support without regard to its value and cultural content is insufficient. We can see further evidence of this by explicitly focusing on socially maladaptive methods of coping.

CONCLUSIONS

Children in conditions of developmental risk (such as that associated with the conditions that produce child maltreatment) need relationships with adults—"teaching" relationships—to help them process their experiences in a way that prevents developmental harm. Vygotsky (1986) referred to this developmental space between what the child can do alone and what the child can do with the help of a teacher as the "zone of proximal development." Developmentalists have come to recognize that it is the dynamic relation between the child's competence alone and the child's competence in the company of a guiding "teacher" that leads to forward movement. Children who experience incapable or inaccessible parents are generally denied that processing within the family. Indeed, they receive just the opposite of what they need, particularly in conditions of social risk derived from the social environment outside the home. This is one reason why measures to enhance parenting in the context of high-stress/low-support social environments deserve the highest priority as a matter of social policy.

Mediation and processing are critical in the case of moral development where the child's moral teachers (be they adults or peers) lead the child toward higher order thinking by presenting positions that are one stage above the child's characteristic mode of responding to social events as moral issues. When all this happens in the context of a nurturant affective system—a warm family, for example— the result is ever-advancing moral development, the development of a principled ethic of caring (Gilligan, 1982). What is more, even if the parents create a rigid, noninteractive "authoritarian" family context (and thus block moral development), the larger community may compensate: " ... the child of authoritarian parents may function in a larger more democratic society whose varied patterns provide the requisite experiences for conceptualizing an egalitarian model of distributive justice" (Fields, 1987, p. 5).

If school teachers, neighbors, and other adult representatives of the community are unable or disinclined to model higher order moral reasoning, then the process of moral truncation that is "natural" to situations of family and community violence will proceed unimpeded. This may well be happening in many urban school systems in which teachers are demoralized, parents incapacitated, and students apathetic. The result is to permit the natural socialization of the depleted community to proceed, with its consequences in intergenerational aggression, neighborhood deterioration, and family malfunction (e.g., child maltreatment).

Families can provide the emotional context for the necessary cognitive processing of making positive moral sense of social experience outside the home. But to do so they must be functioning well themselves as systems within the ecology of the child. Thus, in cases of problematic parenting within families, neighbors and professionals in communities usually must carry things the next step, stimulating higher order moral development and compensatory socialization in children. They do this by presenting a supportive and democratic milieu (e.g., in schools, in churches, in neighborhood associations, and in local political parties). Without these efforts, the result is likely to be impaired social and moral development, particularly among boys who are more vulnerable to this consequence of living at risk as they are to most other risks (Werner, 1990).

The bottom line in our efforts to enhance parenting through social policy lies in the degree to which we are able to replace risk with opportunity in the lives of children (or at least *compensate* for risk by providing opportunities). The foundation for success in these efforts lies in an ecological perspective, in an appreciation for the role of social context in mediating relations between individuals and the larger society. This recognition that there are multiple systems between the individual and the society is fundamental to our ecological perspective. It focuses attention on the crucial role of policy in stimulating, guiding, and enhancing these intermediary systems (the meso- and exosystems) on behalf of more effective parenting. Social policy decisions influence child development through their effects on parenting. The need for understanding is great. The stakes are high.

REFERENCES

Achenbach, T. (1991). *Manual for the child behavior checklist/4–18 and 1991 profile.* Burlington: University of Vermont Department of Psychiatry.

Albee, G. (1980). Primary prevention and social problems. In G. Gerbner, C. Ross, & E. Zigler (Eds.), *Child abuse: An agenda for action* (pp. 106–117). New York: Oxford University Press.

Barclay-McLaughlin, G. (1987). *The center for successful child development.* Chicago: The Ounce of Prevention Fund.

Bell, C. (1991). Traumatic stress and children in danger. *Journal of Health Care for the Poor and Underserved, 2,* 175–188.

Belle, D. (Ed.). (1989). *Children's social networks and social supports.* New York: Wiley.

Bronfenbrenner, U. (1979). *The ecology of human development: Experiments by nature and design.* Cambridge, MA: Harvard University Press.

Bronfenbrenner, U. (1986). Ecology of family as a context for human development. *Developmental Psychology, 22,* 723–742.

Bronfenbrenner, U., & Crouter, A. (1983). The evolution of environmental models in developmental research. In P. Mussen (Ed.), *The handbook of child psychology* (pp. 357–414). New York: Wiley.

Caplan, G., & Killilea, M. (Eds.). (1976). *Support systems and mutual help: Multidisciplinary explorations.* New York: Grune & Stratton.

Carlsson-Paige, N., & Levin, D. (1990). *Who's calling the shots? How to respond effectively to children's fascination with war play and war toys.* Philadelphia: New Society Publishers.

David, H., Dytrych, Z., Matejcek, Z., & Schuller, V. (1988). *Born unwanted: Developmental effects of denied abortion.* New York: Springer.

Davidson, J., & Smith, R. (1990). Traumatic experiences of psychiatric outpatients. *Journal of Traumatic Stress Studies, 3,* 459–475.

Dunst, C. & Trivette, C. (1992). *Risk and opportunity factors influencing parent and child functioning.* Unpublished manuscript based on presentations made at the ninth annual Smoky Mountain Winter Institute, Asheville, NC.

Elder, G. (1974). *Children of the Great Depression: Social change in life experience*. Chicago: University of Chicago Press.

Fields, R. (1987, October). *Terrorized into terrorist: Sequelae of PTSD in young victims*. Paper presented at the meeting of the Society for Traumatic Stress Studies, New York.

Fitchen, J. (1981). *Poverty in rural America: A case study*. Boulder, CO: Westview Press.

Freudenburg, W., & Jones, R. (1991). Criminal behavior and rapid community growth: Examining the evidence. *Rural Sociology, 56*, 619–645.

Froland, C., Pancoast, D., Chapman, N. & Kimboko, P. (1981). *Helping networks and human services*. Beverly Hills, CA: Sage.

Garbarino, J. (1977). The human ecology of child maltreatment: A conceptual model for research. *Journal of Marriage and the Family, 39*, 721–736.

Garbarino, J. (1987). Family support and the prevention of child maltreatment. In S. Kagan, R. Powell, B. Weissbourd, & E. Zigler (Eds.), *America's family support programs: Perspectives and prospects* (pp. xx–xx). New Haven, CT: Yale University Press.

Garbarino, J. (1992a). *Childhood in Kentucky Manor Apartments: Developmental significance of living in chronic danger*. Chicago: Erikson Institute.

Garbarino, J. (1992b). *Towards a sustainable society: An economic, social and environmental agenda for our children's future*. Chicago: The Noble Press.

Garbarino, J. (1995). Raising children in a socially toxic environment. San Francisco: Jossey-Bass.

Garbarino, J., & Associates. (1992). *Children and families in the social environment* (2nd ed.). Hawthorne, NY: Aldine de Gruyter.

Garbarino, J., & Crouter, A. (1978). Defining the community context of parent-child relations. *Child Development, 49*, 604–616.

Garbarino, J., Dubrow, N., Kostelny, K., & Pardo, C. (1992). *Children in danger: Coping with the consequences of community violence*. San Francisco: Jossey-Bass.

Garbarino, J., Guttman, E., & Seeley, J. (1986). *The psychologically battered child: Strategies for identification, assessment, and intervention*. San Francisco: Jossey-Bass.

Garbarino, J., & Kostelny, K. (1992). Child maltreatment as a community problem. *International Journal of Child Abuse and Neglect, 16*(4), 455–464.

Garbarino, J., & Kostelny, K. (1993). Neighborhood and community influences on parenting. In T. Luster & L. Okagaki (Eds.), *Parenting: An ecological perspective* (pp. 203–226). Hillsdale, NJ: Lawrence Erlbaum Associates.

Garbarino, J. & Kostelny, K. (1994a). Family support and community development. In S. Kagan and B Weissbourd (Eds.), *Putting families first: America's family support movement and the challenge of change* (pp. 297–320). San Francisco: Jossey-Bass.

Garbarino, J., & Kostelny, K. (1994b). *Neighborhood-based programs* (Report prepared for the U.S. Advisory Board on Child Abuse and Neglect). Washington, DC: U.S. Advisory Board on Child Abuse and Neglect.

Garbarino, J., Kostelny, K., & Dubrow, N. (1991a). *No place to be a child: Growing up in a war zone*. Lexington, MA: Lexington.

Garbarino, J., Kostelny, K., & Dubrow, N. (1991b). What children can tell us about living in danger. *American Psychologist, 46*(4), 376–383.

Garbarino, J., Kostelny, K. & Grady, N. (1993). Children in dangerous environments: Child maltreatment in the context of community violence. In D. Cicchetti & S. Toth (Eds.), *Child abuse, child development, and social policy* (pp. 167–189). Norwood, NJ: Ablex.

Garbarino, J., Stocking, H., & Associates. (1980). *Protecting children from abuse and neglect: Developing and maintaining effective support systems for families*. San Francisco: Jossey-Bass.

Gaudin, J., & Polansky, N. (1985). Social distancing of the neglectful family: Sex, race, and social class influences. *Social Service Review, 58*, 245–253.

Gelles, J., & Straus, M. (1988). *Intimate violence: The definitive study of the causes and consequences of abuse in the American family*. New York: Simon and Schuster.

Giarini, O. (1980). *Dialogue on wealth and welfare*. New York: Pergamon.

Gilligan, C. (1982). *In a Different Voice*. Cambridge, MA: Harvard University Press.

Gilligan, J. (1991, May). *Shame and humiliation: The emotions of individual and collective violence*. Paper presented at the Erikson Lectures, Harvard University, Cambridge, MA.

Halpern, R. (1990). Parent support and education programs. *Children and Youth Services Review, 12*, 285–308.

Kagan, S., Powell, D., Weissbourd, B., & Zigler, E. (Eds.). (1987). *America's family support programs: Perspectives and prospects*. New Haven, CT: Yale University Press.

Lemann, N. (1986, June). The origins of the underclass. *Atlantic*, pp. 31–61.

Lösel, F., & Bliesener, T. (1990). Resilience in adolescence: A study on the generalizability of protective factors. In K. Hurrelmann & F. Lösel (Eds.), *Health hazards in adolescence* (pp. 29–320). Berlin: Walter de Gruyter.

Melton, G. (1992). It's time for neighborhood research and action. *Child Abuse and Neglect, 16*(6), 909–913.

National Center on Child Abuse and Neglect. (1981). *The national incidence study of child abuse and neglect: Report of findings.* Washington, DC: Author.

Olds, D., & Henderson, C. (1990). The prevention of maltreatment. In D. Cicchetti & V. Carlson (Eds.), *Child maltreatment* (pp. 722–763). New York: Cambridge University Press.

Olds, D., Henderson, C., Tatelbaum, R., & Chamberlain, R. (1986). Preventing child abuse and neglect: A randomized trial of nurse home visitation. *Pediatrics, 78,* 65–78.

Pelton, L. (1978). Child abuse and neglect: The myth of classlessness. *American Journal of Orthopsychiatry, 48,* 608–617.

Pelton, L. (1981). *The social context of child abuse and neglect.* New York: Human Sciences Press.

Pelton, L. (1994). *The role of material factors in child abuse and neglect.* Washington, DC: U.S. Advisory Board on Child Abuse and Neglect.

Pfannesntiel, J., & Seltzer, D. (1989). New parents as teachers: Evaluation of an early parent education program. *Early Childhood Research Quarterly, 4*(1), 1–18.

Punamaki, R. (1987). Psychological stress responses of Palestinian mothers and their children in conditions of military occupation and political violence. *The Quarterly Newsletter of the Laboratory of Comparative Human Cognition, 9*(2), 76–84.

Richters, J., & Martinez, P. (1993). The NIMH community violence project: I. Children as victims of and witnesses to violence. *Psychiatry, 56,* 7–21.

Rohner, R. (1980). Worldwide tests of parental acceptance-rejection theory: An overview. *Behavior Science Research, 15,* 1–21.

Rosenbaum, J., & Kaufman, J. (1991, August). *Educational and occupational achievements of low income Black youth in White suburbs.* Paper presented at the annual meetings of the American Sociological Association, Cincinnati, OH.

Sameroff, A., Seifer, R., Barocas, R., Zax, M., & Greenspan, S. (1987). Intelligence quotient scores of 4–year-old children: Social-environmental risk factors. *Pediatrics, 79,* 343–350.

Schell, J. (1982). *The fate of the earth.* New York: Knopf.

Vygotsky, L. (1986). *Thought and language.* Cambridge, MA: MIT Press.

Wahler, R. (1980). The insular mother: Her problems in parent–child treatment. *Journal of Applied Behavior Analysis, 13,* 207–219.

Warren, R. (1978). *The community in America.* Boston: Houghton Mifflin.

Weiss, H., & Halpern, R. (1991). *Community-based family support and education programs: Something old or new?* New York: Columbia University, National Center for Children in Poverty.

Werner, E. (1990). Protective factors and individual resilience. In R. Meisells & J. Shonkoff (Eds.), *Handbook of early childhood intervention* (pp. 97–116). Cambridge, England: Cambridge University Press.

Whittaker, J., Garbarino, J., & Associates. (1983). *Social support networks on informal helping in the human services.* Hawthorne, NY: Aldine de Gruyter.

Wilson, W. (1987). *The truly disadvantaged: The inner city, the underclass, and public policy.* Chicago: University of Chicago Press.

17

Parenting and the Law

Pauline M. Pagliocca
Tulane University
Gary B. Melton
University of South Carolina
Victoria Weisz
University of Nebraska, Lincoln
Phillip M. Lyons, Jr.
University of Nebraska, Lincoln

INTRODUCTION

Traditionally, American law has viewed relationships between parents and their children from the perspective of the parents. The law has emphasized parents' rights and interests, except when these might conflict with those of the state.[1] At the same time, however, the law frequently purports to act in the best interests of children. That which is in the best interests of parents may not be in the best interests of children. Obviously, it is difficult to ascertain what is in the best interests of children when the law views family matters from the perspective of parents. In considering the sometimes competing interests of parents, children, and the state, courts and legislatures have addressed questions concerning definitions, rights, and duties of parenthood.

A comprehensive review of all of the law affecting parenthood is clearly beyond the scope of this chapter. Although debates may rage as to when other aspects of parenthood begin, one thing is clear—legal regulation of parenthood begins *before* conception (e.g., reproductive rights) and touches upon matters ranging from transporting children (e.g., child safety restraint laws) to income taxation (e.g., deductions for dependents). The scope of regulation is no less than awesome.

Not only is there diversity of activities to which the law is directed, but also diversity of approach undertaken through these laws. Thus, the law may vary both from time to time and from jurisdiction

---

[1]The use of the term *state* in this chapter parallels its use in other legal contexts in that it refers to a sovereign government. The term is particularly confusing in the case of republics such as the United States because the federal sovereign is comprised of relatively independent individual state sovereigns. Consequently, the reader should construe the term generically unless the context clearly indicates that reference is being made to individual states.

to jurisdiction. This state of affairs renders it impossible to describe definitively and comprehensively what the "law of parenting" is. Instead, this chapter describes how the law approaches some of the more salient aspects of parenthood and family life.

In this chapter, we begin by examining legal concepts of parenthood and the family. We note the law's use in various contexts of both biological and psychological definitions of *parenthood* and both formal and functional definitions of *family*. Next, we discuss legal interpretations of the different parental roles of authority, provider, caregiver, and socializer.

WHO IS THE PARENT? LEGAL VIEWS OF PARENTS AND FAMILIES

Generally, the law defines parenthood in terms of a *relationship,* a woman's biological relationship to a child, a man's marital relationship to a child's natural mother, or a nonbiological relationship established by adoption or remarriage. Less commonly, the law may acknowledge an emotional or psychological relationship between people who are otherwise unrelated. Within these various definitions, both legal and social tradition stress the primacy of the nuclear family and the functions it fulfills in the lives of children.

One of the reasons for the complexities regarding the meaning of parent is that parents function in multiple ways in regard to their children. Parents biologically produce children. They provide the economic resources to sustain children. They prepare food for their children, do their laundry, transport them to activities, help them with homework, take care of them when they are ill, and obtain health care for them when needed. Parents form intense affectionate, highly interactive bonds with their children. Parents socialize their children; they inculcate the values of the majority culture as well as their own unique values, morals, and beliefs. Differing legal definitions of parenthood vary in the way these various aspects of parent–child relationships are taken into account.

Biological Parent

The biological nature of parenthood has legal importance in establishing financial obligations for child support and presumptive rights to custody or visitation. When biological parents are in dispute with nonparents for the custody of children, the traditional view has been that biology is paramount (Chambers, 1984). The biological parent *always* would prevail as long as the parent was considered "fit,"[2] and he or she had not abandoned the child previously. Individual states differ in how far they have drifted from the traditional view. A number of these states continue to maintain a strong presumption in favor of the biological parent (parental rights jurisdictions) (e.g., *In re Ackenhausen,* 1963). Such states give custody to biological parents as long as they are fit and they have not

---

[2]"Suitable or appropriate. Conformable to a duty. Adapted to, designed, prepared. Words 'fit' and 'proper' on issue of custody in divorce cases are usually interpreted as meaning moral fitness" (Black's Law Dictionary, 6th ed., 1990, p. 637, citations omitted).Definitions of "moral fitness," of course, may vary widely. In one (hopefully unrepresentative) early case (*Painter v. Bannister,* 1966), the Supreme Court of Iowa decided that custody of a child should be awarded to the child's grandparents because of the unfitness of the biological father. The court commented on the father's fitness as follows:

> Mr. Painter is either an agnostic or atheist and has no concern for formal religious training. He has read a lot of Zen Buddhism and "has been very much influenced by it." … He is a political liberal and got into difficulty in a job at the University of Washington for his support of the activities of the American Civil Liberties Union in the university news bulletin. … There were "two funerals" for his wife. One in the basement of his home in which he alone was present. He conducted the service and wrote her a long letter. The second at a church in Pullman was for the gratification of her friends. He attended in a sport shirt and sweater. (p. 166)

It is also worth noting that the definition of fitness may vary as functions of the legal issue involved and the legal interests of the parties. For example, because prospective adoptive parents have no vested constitutional interest in prospective adoptees (and because the demand for adopted children is high and the supply is low), the threshold for fitness may be quite high. In contrast, because biological parents do have a vested constitutional interest in their children, the threshold for fitness should be much lower. Similarly, as regards visitation, because the scope of responsibilities of noncustodial parents is narrower than the scope of responsibilities of custodial parents, the threshold for fitness in this context may be lower still.

abandoned the child (occasional birthday cards or gifts are evidence of nonabandonment). Such a presumption may apply, even when the court believes that taking the child from another home and placing him or her with the biological parents will be traumatic or harmful (Smith, 1978).

Intermediate jurisdictions—so called because they consider neither the child's interests nor the parents' interests to be dispositive—view the biological parent's interests as secondary to the child's interests, but they do consider parental interests to some degree (e.g., *Wallin v. Wallin,* 1971). Courts in these states weigh factors concerning the child's welfare, but also consider the reasons that the parent and child were separated in determining custody (Smith, 1978). Consequently, if a parent was separated from his or her child for socially valued reasons (e.g., military service), the court might be quite supportive of returning the child to the parent if at all possible.

Finally, a number of jurisdictions focus primarily on the child's interests (e.g., *Rhinehart v. Nowlin,* 1990). These states provide for award of custody to an individual who is not a biological parent if doing so is the best way to meet those needs. An Illinois court, for example, denied custody to a biological mother after her children's custodial father died, and instead awarded custody to their stepmother with whom they had been living (*Cebrzynski v. Cebrzynski,* 1978). This decision was reached despite the court's recognition of the biological mother's fitness.

The biological nature of parenthood also is considered in the law's approach to the rights of unwed fathers, particularly whether they can block adoption proceedings instituted by the mother. Although biological ties historically have been given enormous weight in consideration of parental rights, they commonly have been recognized only when the father was married to the mother at the time that the child was born. The marital presumption, which has been accepted uniformly, assumes that a child born to a woman living with her husband is the biological child of the husband (e.g., Uniform Parentage Act, 1973; Uniform Putative and Unknown Fathers Act, 1988; Zinman, 1992). Thus, fatherhood status is conferred via the marital relationship with the birthmother.

The strength of the marital presumption was evidenced by a 1985 case in New York (*Karin T. v. Michael T.*). In that case, Karin and Michael were married and Karin twice became pregnant through artificial insemination. The couple separated some 6 years later and Karin sought child support for the two children born during the marital union. Michael (who also was known as Marlene—but not to the clerk who issued the marriage license) disclaimed any responsibility by asserting that, because she was a woman, she could not be the parent of the children (i.e., because Karin was the mother and Michael was her husband, Michael would have to be the father, a biological impossibility). The court rejected Michael's argument and found both (1) that she was a woman and (2) that she was the parent (i.e., the father) of the child. Undoubtedly, the fact that such a finding was in the best interest of the children (i.e., because of the additional source of support) carried some weight. The fact that Michael, pursuant to the artificial insemination contract, had agreed to be the father also was persuasive.

Because legal fatherhood arises from the marital relationship with the birth mother, the traditional view has been that unwed fathers have no rights whatsoever regarding their offspring (e.g., *Michael H. v. Gerald D.,* 1989; *Shoecraft v. Catholic Social Services Bureau, Inc.,* 1986; *Stanley v. Illinois,* 1972). Before 1972, an unwed father could not stop the termination of his parental rights if the mother placed her child for adoption (Zinman, 1992). In *Stanley v. Illinois* (1972), however, the U.S. Supreme Court held that unwed fathers did have some parental rights protected by the due process clause of the Fourteenth Amendment. In that case, an unwed father who had participated in the care of his child was held to be entitled to a hearing to determine his parental fitness before his parental rights could be terminated. The biological relationship is not sufficient, however, to sustain parental rights of an unwed father. An unwed father has to show that he has had an actual parental relationship with the child in order to obtain legal recognition of his interest in the preservation of that relationship (Zinman, 1992).

This "biology plus" requirement obviously cannot be met by unwed fathers of babies who are given up for adoption at birth. Some jurisdictions are moving to give unwed fathers greater protections even when they do not have an existing relationship with their child. In 1990, a New York court (*In re Raquel Marie X*) held that an unwed father who is willing to assume custody of his infant and who demonstrates parental responsibility can veto a proposed adoption, whether or not he had lived with the child or the child's mother prior to the proposed adoption.

The law regarding unwed fathers' rights is still unsettled. The Supreme Court has not ruled yet on the scope of the parental rights of an unwed father and the steps that he can take to protect them. Some argue that unless unwed fathers are given temporary custody of their infants while their parental rights are adjudicated, a father's rights to rear his child likely will not be vindicated (Zinman, 1992). The initial placement of the child with prospective adoptive parents creates a situation where it generally will be in the child's best interest to remain with them rather than be placed with their fathers with whom they have had little, if any, contact.

Other unsettled areas of law regarding biological relationships between parents and children are artificial insemination and surrogate motherhood. According to the Uniform Parentage Act (1973), the donor of semen in artificial insemination of a married woman is not considered to be the biological father of the child. Rather, relying on the marital presumption, the husband of the mother is considered to be the father. Where there is no husband, however, the donor presumably would be the father.

Consequently, unmarried women who seek artificial insemination are having difficulty keeping the sperm donor from retaining parental rights and obligations (Bartlett, 1988). In one case, for example, (*Jhordan C. v. Mary K.,* 1986) a California statute provided that the donor of semen provided to a licensed physician for artificial insemination was not the father of the child. Jhordan C. (the donor/biological father), however, asserted paternal rights on the ground that the statute was not effective where, as in their case, the sperm was provided directly without the involvement of a physician (Mary K. was a nurse). Because the statute at issue severed an important constitutional right (i.e., the right to one's child), the court construed the statute strictly and found that it was not operative in the case because it had not been complied with fully.

Similar uncertainties regarding whether statutory and constitutional protections of parental rights can be waived before the birth of one's child cloud the law relating to surrogate motherhood. If such parental rights cannot be waived before birth, surrogacy contracts are unlikely to be enforceable.

Thus, although legal and social traditions are based on a presumption of biology in most determinations of parenthood, biotechnological advances have introduced perplexing questions for which the law still is developing answers. Courts soon may have to fashion a "presumption of maternity" as an analogue to the presumption of paternity. Is the mother the wife of the biological father (e.g., where a man provides his sperm to a surrogate mother)? Is the mother the donor of the egg (e.g., where a gestational surrogate mother is involved)? Or, is the mother the person from whom the child is delivered? As Hill (1991) asked, "Where various parties have made distinct contributions to the procreative process [i.e., coitus, conception, and gestation], who should be recognized as parents of the child?" (p. 355).

Psychological Parent

The concept of the psychological parent was articulated two decades ago by Goldstein, Freud, and Solnit (1973) as a means of shifting the focus of custody disputes away from the rights of the biological parents to the best interests of the child, as manifested by the child's need for stability and continuity with regard to relationships with significant others in the child's life. The psychological parent may be a biological parent but is not necessarily so. Rather, the psychological parent is the individual who has fulfilled the child's "psychological needs for a parent" (Goldstein et al. 1973, p. 98). Goldstein et al. argued that a child would suffer significant psychological harm from disruption of a relationship with the psychological parent.

Courts most commonly have raised the concept of the psychological parent when they were choosing between custodial arrangements offered by biological and nonbiological parents, particularly if they were attempting to justify refusal to award custody of a child to a biological parent. Some courts have awarded custody to a stepparent rather than a biological parent if the stepparent has had a prior strong relationship with the child and is seen as more likely to fulfill the child's need for stability and continuity.[3] In an analogous case, a court ordered the guardianship of a child with Down syndrome, who had been institutionalized for years and virtually was abandoned emotionally by his biological parents, to a couple who had provided familylike relationships for him through their involvement at the institution (*In re Phillip B.,* 1980). Thus, some jurisdictions place great value on supporting stable and long-lasting attachment relationships for the child, even if those relationships are not with biological parents.

Another area of law involving the concept of psychological parenthood concerns adoption (Brodzinsky, Lang, & Smith, in this *Handbook*). In California, the adoption consent statutes direct courts to consider the extent of bonding by the child with the adopters and the "potential to bond" with the biological parents when birth mothers try to withdraw their consent to the termination of their parental rights (California Family Code, 1994). The court then is required to decide whether the child's best interests would be served by a return to the birth mother or by remaining with the adoptive parents. Thus, courts in California and other child-focused jurisdictions are balancing psychological parenthood and biological ties in their decisions (Dickson, 1991).

Finally, the statutory establishment of grandparents' rights to petition for visitation with their grandchildren (that may have been prevented by parental divorce or death) reflects a recognition of the psychological value to children of maintaining relationships with their grandparents (Smith, in this *Handbook*). Legislators endorsed these statutes because the lawmakers believed that grandparental relationships were important not only to children but also to grandparents. Many also placed considerable significance on the value of intergenerational supports to children. However, the laws create some difficulties for courts that are required to determine whether psychological parenting relationships exist between particular grandparents and grandchildren, and whether it would be in the children's best interests to preserve such relationships (Thompson, Scalora, Castrianno, & Limber, 1992).

Formal Concepts of Family Life

In defining family relationships, courts generally have adopted a formal analysis in which they designate only members of nuclear families as *family, spouse,* or *parent* (see, e.g., *City of Ladue v. Horn,* 1986). Exceptions to this view arise when tradition (e.g., inclusion of extended family) or the language of specific legislation directs that alternative family compositions be considered (Note, 1991). Such a traditional view of family persists in the law, despite the extraordinary shifts in family demographics in the last generation.

This formal analysis focuses on the "automatic" ties created by biology (kinship), marriage, and adoption, rather than the question of whether these relationships *actually* meet society's expectations of the nuclear family. Jurisdictions that follow this approach require a finding that an individual meets a formal criterion for parenthood as a condition for recognition of a legitimate interest in any procedure affecting a child's welfare. Such recognition may occur even if the individual has not fulfilled any traditional parental roles, such as providing for the economic or emotional well-being of the child.

In most cases, legal parents are the same adults who fulfill society's—and the law's—expectations for the nuclear family. Generally, the law holds a presumption of competence regarding the parenting abilities of biological and other legal parents and refrains from interference in the day-to-day functioning of families. When such competence is questioned, however, or when family members are in dispute with one another, the conflict between legal and functional definitions of family may arise.

---

[3]The Supreme Court of Wisconsin (*In re Adoption of Tachick,* 1973) commented on the "separation trauma" associated with disruption of a child's environment as follows:

At one time, the courts paid less attention to the psychological trauma attendant upon disturbing the continuity of a child's environment than the courts do today. Some courts today have gone to the extreme and have held this factor to be controlling in adoption. It has been said by a noted psychiatrist that the stability of environment is far more crucial than its precise nature and content. (p. 872)

Functional Concepts

The functional view includes the traditional nuclear family, but also "legitimizes non-nuclear relationships that share the essential characteristics of traditional relationships" (Note, 1991, p. 1641). Rather than focusing on kinship and other legal ties, the functional view stresses the needs and functions that are fulfilled in determining family membership. Criteria include such functions as sharing of wealth, participation in domestic responsibilities, and provision of affection (e.g., *City of Ladue v. Horn*, 1986; *Desiato v. Abbott*, 1992). Under this view, parent status may be granted to a nonrelative who fulfills the roles traditionally met by legal parents. For example, a domestic partner—whether in a heterosexual or same-sex relationship—might be considered a parent for legal purposes in a jurisdiction adopting a functional view of the family.

Minow (1991) argued that a functional view is consistent with the child's best interests because family is defined from the child's perspective by highlighting the roles (rather than the legal ties) of parents. Utilizing the concept of the psychological parent (Goldstein et al., 1973), Minow described a parent as someone who "has taken care of the child on a daily basis, is known to the child as a parent, and has provided love and financial support" (p. 274). She argued that courts should focus their inquiry on questions of function in determining whether a group of people is a family: "[D]o they share affection and resources, think of one another as family members, and present themselves as such to neighbors and others?" (p. 270).

Although broader and more consistent with changing social structures, a functional definition of family presents potential pitfalls upon application. First, the functions by which families are judged are derived from examination of the traditional nuclear family; thus, true alternatives to such a prototype may not be recognized legally. As a practical matter, formal and functional definitions may differ little. Second, in making such comparisons, it is not clear which family features should be weighted most heavily. Third, because of an absence of authoritative guidelines, functional criteria must be established on a case-by-case basis. Such an inquiry necessarily invites intrusion into families' private lives (Note, 1991).

To be sure, legislatures, courts, and commentators from both the legal and social scientific communities have struggled and continue to struggle to define what constitutes a family relationship. As the preceding discussion makes clear, the issues are not merely academic; the particular conceptualization that is applicable to a specific situation may have a profound effect on the parties involved (e.g., to whom custody is awarded, who is entitled to visitation, etc.). In some instances deciding "who" is a "what" to "whom" ends the inquiry. In other cases, however, the law delves more deeply into the nature of the relationship by not only declaring who occupies a particular role vis-à-vis other prospective family members, but also by fleshing out the contours of that role.

LEGAL INTERPRETATIONS OF PARENTAL ROLES

Despite the difficulties in defining a parent, doing so is important because legal recognition as a parent determines who may claim both rights and duties under a variety of laws pertaining to parent–child relationships. Although rights and duties vary across legal questions, such legal entitlements and obligations typically can be categorized according to the various roles parents assume under both social and legal custom. Parents may be described as authorities, providers, caregivers, protectors, and socializers. Parental privileges and responsibilities do not necessarily hold equal status across or within each role, however. For example, rights may take precedence over duties when parents function in the role of authority, but the reverse may be true when they function as providers.

PARENT AS AUTHORITY

As with other domestic relationships (e.g., Wadlington, 1990), the laws controlling parent–child relationships are primarily matters of particular states rather than the federal government. In both legal and social realms, parents generally are recognized as having primary authority in all aspects of childrearing. Such authority is based on beliefs:

> that parents are in the best position to know and care about their children's needs, that giving parents authority encourages them to assume and discharge the responsibilities of parenthood and that diffusing authority over how children will be raised promotes cultural and social diversity. (Harris, Waldrop, & Waldrop, 1990, p. 700)

Accordingly, pursuant to the protection of liberty under the Fourteenth Amendment, parents generally possess a right to rear their children without interference. For example, the Supreme Court has ruled that, absent a contrary compelling state interest, parents have a right to guide their children's education (*Meyer v. Nebraska,* 1923; *Pierce v. Society of Sisters,* 1925; *Wisconsin v. Yoder,* 1972). Even when parents have been shown to be abusive or neglecting, the state bears a high burden in justifying coercive action (Rogosch, Cicchetti, Shields, & Toth, in this *Handbook*). In cases involving state attempts to terminate parental rights to their children, the Supreme Court has held that the state must provide notice and a hearing for parents (*Stanley v. Illinois,* 1972) and must present clear and convincing evidence of a parent's lack of fitness (*Santosky v. Kramer,* 1982).

PARENT AS PROVIDER

As a general matter, simply stated, parents have a legal duty to provide for their children. This duty is based in part on the presumption that most children cannot provide for themselves adequately during their own childhood. The law, of course, is neither general nor simple. Specific questions emerge and the law must answer them. Some of these questions include: (1) Which "parents" owe such a duty?, (2) To which "children" is such a duty owed?, (3) What should be done when the presumption fails and children never will be able to provide for themselves (e.g., children with certain disabilities)?, and (4) What should be done when children will be able to provide for themselves, but only after a period of continued dependency on their parents well into the children's legal adulthood (e.g., adult children attending college)? An overview of the law's answers to these questions follows.

Support for Minor[4] Children

Of course, parenthood brings duties as well as rights. The duty to provide financial support and other necessaries, such as food and shelter, for children is rooted in parental rights (French, in this *Handbook;* Harris et al., 1990). Historically, parents—especially fathers—have held rights to their children's custody, control, services, and earnings (Johnson, 1987). In return for such considerations, parents are expected to provide children with financial support in order to prevent the community from assuming the burden of financial maintenance (Harris et al., 1990): "The duty is … a legal and natural obligation, the consistent enforcement of which is equally essential to the well-being of the state, the morals of the community, and the development of the individual" (Johnson, 1987, p. 184). Although originally viewed as a moral rather than legal obligation based on the "voluntariness" of having given birth to a child (Schuele, 1988–1989), financial support of minor children now is regarded by all American jurisdictions as both a moral and legal responsibility of parents (Johnson,

---

[4]The term *minor* is used to refer to individuals who are not adults according to the particular jurisdiction whose laws are applicable. Although the precise ages vary from jurisdiction to jurisdiction, each jurisdiction has established an age—the age of majority—(usually around 18 years) at which individuals become legal adults. At that point the legal "disabilities of minority" (e.g., inability to contract, inability to vote, inability to purchase alcoholic beverages, etc.) are removed. The use of the term herein is somewhat oversimplified. Actually, each jurisdiction has established different ages of majority for different purposes. Thus, a person may be considered an adult at ages 16, 17, 18, and 21 years for the purposes of driving, criminal liability, purchase of cigarettes, and voting, respectively.

1987; Mnookin & Weisberg, 1989). Traditionally, this duty pertained only to fathers, with mothers assuming responsibility upon a father's death or refusal to pay. The current trend is to hold both parents responsible for financial support, and to apportion parents' responsibilities according to their ability to pay, although some states hold each parent equally responsible (Friedman, 1992; Mnookin & Weisberg, 1989).

Adhering to the principle of parental autonomy, government usually does not impose standards for parental support on intact families (Harris et al., 1990). Although refraining from determining specific types and amounts of support, courts usually have held parents responsible for providing food, clothing, shelter, education, and medical attention for minor and other children not capable of self-support (Johnson, 1987). However, when courts do intervene, mostly in cases of divorce, amounts typically are determined according to the financial and social status, as well as the age and health, of both parent and child, and usually extend beyond the provision of basic necessities alone, especially where parents can afford more (Hetherington & Stanley-Hagan, in this *Handbook;* Johnson, 1987). This approach requires case-by-case analysis and grants considerable discretion to the courts.

Parents' financial responsibility for their children is not without limits. Courts have sustained parental authority to set conditions under which parents may terminate support to their minor children (Friedman, 1992; Harris et al., 1990). For example, a New York court held that a parent could impose reasonable restrictions on the behavior of a child (requiring the daughter to live in a college dormitory rather than in an off-campus apartment) in exchange for continued financial support (*Roe v. Doe,* 1971).

Although allowing parents some discretion in establishing conditions for support, legislatures and courts have dealt harshly with parents who fail to provide support when they are financially capable. Failure to provide the basic necessities to children now is considered a criminal offense in all states. Some forms of neglect are treated as felonies (e.g., California Penal Code, 1988b—child endangerment), whereas other forms are treated as misdemeanors (e.g., California Penal Code, 1988a—simple neglect). Although child neglect statutes are frequently vague, common forms of neglect are related to the same fundamental responsibilities to "support the child, including providing the child with clothing, food, shelter, medical care, and education" (Texas Family Code Annotated, 1986a; see also Friedman, 1992).

Divorce is the most common circumstance for establishment of legal standards for child support. Divorce presents the potential for financial responsibilities to be assumed by or imposed on four different parties: custodial parents, noncustodial parents, stepparents, and the state. In general, custodial parents are viewed as having primary obligation for supporting minor children. Some statutes impose a support duty on custodial parents (Johnson, 1987). Most often, though, their status is comparable to that of parents in intact families. That is, the state usually does not intervene to impose specific financial duties on custodial parents (Harris et al., 1990).

The state's position of nonintervention in the case of custodial parents does not apply to noncustodial parents, however. In divorce, noncustodial parents usually are ordered to pay some level of child support, according to their financial ability and social status and the needs of the particular children. Although other debts may be considered by the court, they normally will not exempt a parent from meeting the child support obligation (e.g., *Kost v. Kost,* 1994; *Park v. Park,* 1981), and a noncustodial parent can anticipate an escalation in ordered amounts over time.

In requiring noncustodial parents to contribute to the financial support of their children, courts essentially break the traditional link between parental control and parental duty (Harris et al., 1990). Although they lose all or much of their control, noncustodial parents are not absolved of their duties as parents. In fact, their obligations may be specified more clearly than any control or rights they retain. In contrast, custodial parents retain their control rights whereas they remain relatively free of state-imposed standards for support. Thus, for them, the connection between their duty to support and their right to control remains intact.

Stepparents usually are not held legally responsible for the financial support of their stepchildren. Perhaps in recognition of a moral or social responsibility, however, some states have enacted statutes that impose a limited duty that applies with full force only while the stepparent is married to the child's natural parent (e.g., New Hampshire Revised Statutes Annotated, 1974; see also Friedman, 1992).

When biological parenthood is involved, marriage is not a prerequisite to financial responsibility. Under common law, mothers have held a duty to support their children born outside of marriage. Statutes now impose a duty on unwed fathers to contribute to the financial support of their children (e.g., Oregon Revised Statutes, 1993). This duty does not apply, though, to biological fathers of children born to women who are married to someone else, because the law presumes the woman's husband to be the father.

Support for Emancipated and Adult Children

The responsibility to provide for the support of a child does not persist in perpetuity. Another problem involves the determination of the point at which such responsibility ends. Although this transition typically occurs at the age of majority, it can occur earlier if the child is emancipated or later if the child is disabled.

The duty of parental support is based on a child's inability to support him- or herself. Because complete emancipation relieves a parent of financial obligations, courts and legislatures are generally conservative in determining emancipation of a minor child. Generally accepted criteria include marriage and enlistment in the military. Other circumstances are assessed on a case-by-case basis, but may include:

> … whether the child is living at home, whether the child is paying room and board if living at home, whether the parents are exercising disciplinary control over the minor, whether the child is independently employed, whether the child has been given the right to retain wages and spend them without parental restraints, whether the child is responsible for debts incurred and the extent of the parents' contributions toward the payment of outstanding bills, whether the child owns a major commodity such as a car, and whether the parent has listed the child as a dependent for tax purposes. Age, of course, is also a critical element. None of these factors, however, is conclusive. (Katz, Schroeder, & Sidman, 1973, p. 218)

There also is typically no bright line standard to determine whether parents have a financial obligation to their adult child, but such a duty generally applies where an adult child is incapable of self-support because of mental or physical disability. However, state statutes may set limitations on the duty or, in the absence of any statute, a parent may have no legal obligation, regardless of the adult child's ability to support himself or herself (Johnson, 1987).

One area in which the issue of parental obligation for support of a "capable" adult child may come before the court involves payment for postsecondary education. The general rule is that parents are not required to finance education and training for an adult child (e.g., *Blue v. Blue,* 1992; see also Friedman, 1992), but the trend is to view higher education as a necessary for which parents are responsible, considering their means and the aptitude of the particular child (Johnson, 1987). In divorce, statutes in some states require providing for a college education (e.g., *Childers v. Childers,* 1978; Missouri Annotated Statutes, 1994; Washington Revised Code, 1986), but others mandate support for minor children only, regardless of educational level (e.g., Illinois Revised Statutes, 1993). In the absence of statutory specificity regarding age limits, courts have been divided over financial responsibility for the education of adult children, with some courts finding a duty (e.g., *Newburgh v. Arrigo,* 1982) and others holding that none exists (e.g., *Nolfo v. Nolfo,* 1992) (see also Harris et al., 1990).

Inheritance

To some degree, parents continue as designated providers even after death. In every state, intestate laws provide for some share of a parent's estate to go to his or her children when that parent has failed to leave a will. In such situations, all siblings receive an equal share, regardless of age or other limitations on earning power. The "natural" distribution thus may be unfair to younger and disabled children, who might have longer need for parental support than older and more able children (Mnookin & Weisberg, 1989).

Although provision of support after the death of a parent may be expected by the law, such support generally is not a duty. When a parent has drawn a will, every state (except Louisiana; see *Succession of Terry*, 1993) allows parents to disinherit children, making no provision for them after the parent's death. No such mechanism for disinheritance exists for spouses, however, so that some level of protection may remain for children who are not listed as intended beneficiaries in the deceased parent's will.

PARENT AS CAREGIVER

Of course, children need more than financial support. The law supports and values the performance by parents of numerous caregiving activities on behalf of their children.

A controversial approach developed in West Virginia has used care for children as the standard for determination of child custody in divorce (Chambers, 1984; *Garska v. McCoy*, 1981; Neely, 1984; West Virginia Code, 1993). Neely argued that a presumption in favor of the person who has been the primary caregiver generally will protect mothers from bargaining away their financial settlement in order to retain custody, whereas such a presumption does not penalize fathers with a gender-based maternal preference.

West Virginia law defines the primary caretaker as the parent who takes primary responsibility for:

(1) preparing and planning of meals;
(2) bathing, grooming and dressing;
(3) purchasing, cleaning and care of clothes;
(4) medical care, including nursing and trips to physicians;
(5) arranging for social interaction among peers after school, i. e., transporting to friends' houses or, for example, to girl or boy scout meetings;
(6) arranging alternative care, i. e., babysitting, daycare, etc.;
(7) putting child to bed at night, attending to child in the middle of the night, waking child in the morning;
(8) disciplining, i. e., teaching general manners and toilet training;
(9) educating, i. e., religious, cultural, social, etc.; and
(10) teaching elementary skills, i. e., reading, writing and arithmetic. (*Garska v. McCoy*, 1981, p. 363)

The parent who performs the majority of these functions is defined as the primary caretaker and will be awarded custody in most cases. West Virginia's reliance on this test indicates both its interest in protecting the economic welfare of divorcing mothers and their children, and its recognition of the importance and value of the everyday care of children by their parents.

The area of law regarding children's health care is illustrative of the law's view of the importance of and limits to the caregiving function of parents. For example, in their role as caregivers of their child's basic needs, parents are given legal authority to make numerous decisions regarding their child's medical care. As noted earlier, the parental role of caregiver has been viewed to include obtaining and arranging medical care for the child (e.g., Tinsley & Lees, in this *Handbook*): "It is the right and duty of parents under the law of nature as well as the common law and the statutes of many states to protect their children, to care for them in sickness and in health. ..." (Johnson, 1987).

Parental Consent to Treatment

Parents' rights in executing their health caregiving authority are established in parental consent requirements for treatment. The general rule giving parents authority over their minor children's health care derives from the common law. Excepting specific contexts that are discussed later, parental consent is both a necessary and sufficient requirement for medical treatment of minors (Holder, 1985; Mnookin & Weisberg, 1989; Rozovsky, 1984).

Traditionally, the common law viewed minors as incapable of consenting to medical or surgical treatment. Consent, however, had to be given in order to protect the physician from a legal action for battery. Thus, the law looked to parents to provide the legal consent for treatment for their children.

Weithorn and McCabe (1988) listed several reasons for reliance on parental consent, rather than direct consent from minor children when health care is at issue. The historical reason is that children were viewed at common law as the property of their parents with no rights of their own (Rodham, 1973). Under current law, however, the Constitution protects parental authority through the doctrine of family privacy, which protects married couples from government intrusion into matters involving their families. That doctrine is based in part on the assumption that parents are best able to make decisions promoting their children's interests. Thus, allowing parents decision-making authority for health care is viewed as ultimately beneficial to minors.

Most directly, the law has viewed minors as inherently limited in their judgment and reasoning (e.g., Rozovsky, 1984; *Schall v. Martin,* 1984; *Stanford v. Kentucky,* 1989; *Thompson v. Oklahoma,* 1988). The corollary rejection of minors' autonomy typically is based on the assumption that incompetent people are prone to make such self-injurious decisions that the state has a compelling interest in preventing them from doing so. Some also regard incompetence as a factor negating personhood—membership in the moral community—and therefore making personal interests in autonomy meaningless.

Parental consent is required in most situations involving medical treatment and nonemergency treatments of children and such treatments that have not been authorized by parents have resulted in successful lawsuits. However, in the past 30 years there have been no successful lawsuits by parents for treatment of adolescents over 15 years of age, when the adolescent has provided informed consent (Holder, 1985).

Minors' Consent to Their Own Treatment

The failure of parents to prevail in lawsuits is not the only sign of lessening of the stringency of parental consent. As one court observed:

> The traditional common law approach to minors and consent to treatment has undergone a number of modifications. Medical emergencies have provided an inroad, permitting treatment without parental consent in certain situations. The "mature minor" and "emancipated minor" rules, in which certain children are considered capable of giving consent, have also gained recognition. (*Belcher v. Charleston Area Medical Center,* 1992, p. 835)

These gradual changes have increased adolescents' autonomy and privacy. Exceptions to the parental consent requirement have been made when minors appear to be able to care for themselves competently or when the treatment needs are such that it has been determined that there is a societal interest in the state's assumption of the role of caregiver from the parents.

The American Law Institute's (1934) Restatement of the Law of Torts stated the governing *mature minor rule* as follows: "If a child ... is capable of appreciating the nature, extent and consequences of the invasion (of his body) his assent prevents the invasion from creating liability, though the assent of the parent, guardian, or other person is not obtained or is expressly refused" (§ 59a).

Recognizing that the public health sometimes requires permitting minors to obtain confidential health care, most states have enacted laws authorizing the treatment of minors for sexually transmitted diseases and substance abuse without parental notification or consent (e.g., Virginia Code Annotated, 1993). The United States Supreme Court has recognized a constitutionally protected privacy interest of minors in access to contraception (*Carey v. Population Services International,* 1977) and abortion

(*City of Akron v. Akron Center for Reproductive Health, Inc.,* 1983; *Ohio v. Akron Center for Reproductive Health,* 1990), although the Court also has held that minors' privacy can be limited in ways that would be unconstitutional if applied to adult women. Specifically, the Court has upheld state laws requiring parental notification or consent when an alternative confidential opportunity to go before a judge is available (*Bellotti v. Baird,* 1979; *Hodgson v. Minnesota,* 1990; *Planned Parenthood of Southeastern Pennsylvania v. Casey,* 1992).

State-Ordered Treatment

States do intervene in specific situations regarding young children (as well as older children) when parents fail to provide necessary medical treatment to a minor child, even if the reason for the failure is the parents' religious beliefs. There is considerable legal authority for states to remove children from the custody of their parents in order to obtain necessary treatment (e.g., California Welfare & Institutional Code, 1984). Courts do so through their *parens patriae* power, the authority and duty to act in the place of the parent to protect the interests of the child.

Psychiatric Hospitalization

Another caregiving area in which the rights and interests of parents and their children may come into conflict involves psychiatric hospitalization. Historically, parents have held the right to seek hospital placement for minor children who exhibit a wide variety of disturbing behaviors. Such commitments, even when taking place over the objections of the children, have been considered "voluntary," because they are initiated and/or sanctioned by parents and regarded as falling within the scope of constitutionally protected rights of parental authority and family privacy.

Until the mid-1970s, parental commitment of children, accompanied by the concurring opinion of an admitting physician or institution director, but without any judicial hearing or other legal review, was permitted in over three fourths of the states (Brakel, 1985). Then, both state statutes and individual case decisions began to adopt procedural protections for minors facing psychiatric hospitalization. For example, the California Supreme Court, in a case of a 14-year-old committed by his mother for treatment (*In re Roger S.,* 1977), held that although minors' rights may be "less comprehensive" (p. 1288) than those of adults, "no interest of the state or of a parent sufficiently outweighs the liberty interest of a minor old enough to independently exercise his right of due process to permit the parent to deprive him of that right" (p. 1292). This is but one example of the trend in strengthening children's rights and due process protections through case law during that time.

Despite this trend at the state level, the United States Supreme Court reaffirmed parental authority in the psychiatric commitment of minor children and held that no formal due process hearing was required prior to a minor's admission to a psychiatric facility, although a postadmission review may be required (*Parham v. J. R.,* 1979). This holding was strikingly out of step with the course being pursued by individual states, as well as with the Supreme Court's own decisions relative to the constitutional rights of minors (e.g., *Carey v. Population Services International,* 1977; *In re Gault,* 1967; *Planned Parenthood of Central Missouri v. Danforth,* 1976; *Tinker v. Des Moines Independent School District,* 1969). Although cited as a "resounding victory for parental authority" (Wald, 1980, p. 18), *Parham* had little impact on actual practice; that is, rather than setting new guidelines, it merely provided constitutional approval for prevailing standards (Levine, Ewing, & Hager, 1987). In states that already had begun to establish more stringent criteria, the *Parham* decision did little to interrupt the legislative development of procedural protections for children involved in civil commitment (Burlingame & Amaya, 1985).

Currently, although few states provide legally for the *involuntary* commitment of minor children, the process for their commitment to public psychiatric hospitals typically remains essentially the same as that of adults. In some states, the distinction between voluntary and involuntary commitment is difficult to discern; included in voluntary statutes are those that require the consent of the child and/or a court hearing if he or she objects. Although current research suggests that adolescents are capable of participating competently in decision making regarding hospitalization (e.g., Weithorn, 1985), they "may perceive no real choice" (Melton, 1984, p. 156), given the stress of the situation and the potential outcomes of such direct conflict with their own parents.

Other statutes provide for an automatic court hearing, whether the child agrees or objects to hospitalization. Such laws are essentially the same as those governing the involuntary commitment of adults. A third category of statutes may come closer to a "true voluntary model" (Brakel, 1985, p. 46) of commitment. These statutes set specific age standards (usually between 12 and 18 years) above which a minor cannot be hospitalized solely upon the petition of parents. It should be noted, however, that many states still conduct such "voluntary" commitments, as permitted by *Parham v. J. R.* (1979).

The law is replete with contradiction and confusion regarding the psychiatric hospitalization of children—the blurred distinctions between voluntary and involuntary commitment, the differences between the Supreme Court's interpretations and the trend in statutory and case law, the range of statutory requirements and limitations, and the extent to which any of these is understood by clinical and legal professionals, as well as by parents and children involved in psychiatric commitment. As observed by Jackson-Beeck, Schwartz, and Rutherford (1987), "For teenagers [and children] admitted by their parents, hospitalization can be a legal twilight zone, inescapable without parental approval yet beyond legal control" (p. 164).

The "legal twilight zone" of confusion and contradiction parallels a societal twilight zone for children, particularly adolescents. It seems somehow perverse that an adolescent simultaneously could be considered (1) young enough to need parental consent for an aspirin and (2) old enough to be put to death for wrongdoing (e.g., *Thompson v. Oklahoma*, 1988). Moreover, social expectations change over time—not only for the individuals across their own development, but also for adolescents as a group historically. Because children's abilities to care for themselves are the flip side of the same coin as parental obligations for caregiving, both must evolve hand in hand. As they become increasingly capable of managing their own autonomy and independence, a transfer of authority from parents to adolescents themselves must occur if the latter are to be accorded the respect that is commensurate with the responsibilities that they are capable of undertaking.

PARENT AS SOCIALIZER

The concept of parenting is an elusive one. The confusion inherent in the concept is reflected in the laws pertaining to it. Thus, parental responsibilities for providing and caring for children, at times, are complex, confusing, and poorly defined. Conceptually, however, these responsibilities are somewhat more straightforward than are other parental obligations. The parental responsibility for socializing children—the topic turned to next—is one of these especially vague obligations. Although the contours are delineated imprecisely, the following sections address some of the issues that recur frequently in this context.

Parents' Educational Rights and Obligations

From the state's perspective, parents' responsibility to support and care for their children is rooted in the state's interest in the healthy socialization of children as citizens and workers. In performing this socializing function, most parents rarely come into direct contact with the legal system. Socialization of children occurs in the shadow of the law, however, and both parents and children are likely to find themselves under court jurisdiction when socialization is unsuccessful.

Perhaps the most obvious legal duty of parents in that regard is to ensure that children receive at least a minimal level of education (e.g., Connors & Epstein, in this *Handbook*). Every state requires children to participate in some type of schooling. Accordingly, parental authority over school-age children largely is limited as a practical matter to after-school hours, although parents do retain some authority for decisions about their children's education. The state may regulate the ages of mandatory school attendance, requirements for teacher certification, content of instruction, and the standards and procedures for student discipline.

Education is not a right protected by the U.S. Constitution (*San Antonio Independent School District v. Rodriguez,* 1973), although many state constitutions provide such a right. Thus the federal government has no *direct* constitutional power over education and schooling, but it has considerable direct involvement in education through "strings" on federal funds and indirect control through statutes and the Fourteenth Amendment that limit state discretion. For example, antidiscrimination laws regulate allocation of funding for school sports programs, and the religion clauses of the First Amendment limit religious exercise in public schools and government regulation of private schools.

Because of their right and obligation to direct and safeguard the upbringing of their children, parents generally are seen as sharing the same legal interests as their school-age children (Valente, 1985/1989). For example, the Supreme Court upheld an exception for Amish parents from the law requiring their high-school-age children to attend school (*Wisconsin v. Yoder,* 1972). The majority recognized the success that Amish parents typically have in socializing law-abiding children. In dissent, however, Chief Justice Douglas argued that the Court had missed the key interests: "the parents, absent dissent, normally speak for the entire family, the education of the child is a matter on which the child will often have decided views" (*Wisconsin v. Yoder,* 1972, p. 244).

Although *Yoder* was decided in favor of the parents' rights to free exercise of religion under the First Amendment, Justice Douglas' dissent pointed out that the court had "treated the religious interest of the child as a factor in the analysis" but should have sought actively the children's own religious views, rather than assuming them to be identical to those of the parents (*Wisconsin v. Yoder,* 1972, p. 242). Interestingly, the particular facts of the case may have rendered this impossible. Although the children of Amish parents are inculcated in Amish values, the custom is such that only adults can be Amish—and then, only after taking affirmative, decisive steps to join their ranks. Thus, whereas there are children of the Amish, there are no Amish children. This fact may have precluded the approach espoused by Justice Douglas in that the children could not have chosen to be Amish.

Even the First-Amendment-based exception to the state's authority to require school attendance is limited in *Yoder* to high-school-age children. Determination of whether parents may decide *whether* to educate their children does not end the inquiry, however. Parents also have an interest in determining *what* their children will be taught. Parents' rights to oversee the education of their children was recognized by the Supreme Court first in 1923 in a case that questioned the state's policy limiting the teaching of a foreign language to children who had completed eighth grade (*Meyer v. Nebraska,* 1923). Although the Court held that the constitutional protection of a parent's liberty to bring up children applied to the content of the school curriculum, it recognized that such parental rights sometimes must be limited in order to preserve state interests.

More recently, the issue of controlling educational content has focused on free speech and disciplinary practices, rather than directly on academic subject matter (Friedman, 1992). For example, in a Baltimore case, the court found that the introduction of sex education into the public school curriculum did not violate the constitutional prohibition against the establishment of religion, but instead, could be considered "quite simply as a public health measure" (*Cornwell v. State Board of Education,* 1969, p. 344).

Although parents are required to provide their children with an education, they are allowed some latitude in *where* that education is provided. The ability of parents to choose private, rather than public, schools for their children has long been settled (*Pierce v. Society of Sisters,* 1925), although questions remain in many states about the nature of "approved" private schools. The debate centers on home schooling (see Baker, 1988) and proposals to allow parents to use public funds (through school vouchers) to purchase education in the setting of their choice (see Tweedie, 1989).

Although the level of parental involvement that is permitted or required in curricular decisions about their children is unsettled as a general matter, the answer is clear in regard to special education (see Hodapp, in this *Handbook*). The Education for All Handicapped Children Act of 1975 (originally titled the Education of the Handicapped Act, 1970, and now known in modified form as the Individuals with Disabilities Education Act, 1990 [IDEA]) establishes elaborate procedures for parental involvement in establishment of individual educational plans (IEPs) for their children with disabilities and for parental appeals in cases of disputes with school authorities about the content of IEPs.

Appeals are infrequent (Clune & Van Pelt, 1985), however, and the legal structure for parental involvement often does not translate into actual involvement: "In most cases, parental rights in special education do not significantly change school officials' approaches to decision making. ... Parental rights 'work' only for the small number of children whose parents participate assertively and knowledgeably in IEP meetings and hearings" (Tweedie, 1989, pp. 414–415).

In short, in a professionalized, bureaucratized environment, planning and decision making are apt to take place with minimal parental involvement and little generalized change in ways of doing business. The history of IDEA suggests that this principle applies even when there is an elaborate, judicially affirmed statutory scheme for parental involvement, at least when allocation of public resources is affected.

Although parental rights often have been hollow in the enforcement of positive rights (entitlements to government services), the force of parental rights in the educational context may be greater in regard to negative rights (freedom from governmental intrusion). IDEA's statutory and regulatory structure for parental approval of pupil assessments and control of information generated in that process are mimicked by more general provisions in federal law for protection of student and family privacy (see, e.g., Family Educational Rights and Privacy Act, 1990, commonly known as the Buckley Amendment, and Hatch Amendment, 1990, thereto; *Merriken v. Cressman,* 1973).

Requirements for parental consent to testing and release of personal information probably are honored generally because they require little investment of resources and because they can be actualized in routine bureaucratic procedures (i.e., obtaining parents' signatures on forms). This fact should not be overgeneralized, though. Although some protection of negative rights is operational in education, compulsory school attendance by its nature involves massive (even if justified) restrictions on student and parental liberty and rampant opportunities to pierce the veil of family privacy. Essentially, compulsory attendance laws require parents to submit to state authority as their children are plucked from the family environment and parental influence and subjected to state-controlled indoctrination (or to forfeit their economic interests—if they can—to fund private education). To use a relatively benign example of intrusion into family privacy, consider the potential disclosures of private family matters when students are asked to write essays describing their summer vacations (see Melton, 1992).

The de facto limitations on parental authority in education are rendered stark when one remembers that school staff historically have been viewed as acting in the place of parents (*in loco parentis*) and thus temporarily assuming authority reserved for parents in other contexts. Thus, schools are free to exercise disciplinary practices disapproved by parents, as long as such practices are intended to protect an educational environment and not obviously arbitrarily applied (see, e.g., *Goss v. Lopez,* 1975). The Supreme Court has held that even corporal punishment is constitutionally permissible when it "is reasonably necessary for the proper education and discipline of the child" (*Ingraham v. Wright,* 1977, p. 670), even when parents have objected to the practice.

Parental Rights and Obligations to Discipline Children

Outside the public school context, parents have broad discretion in fulfilling their duty to provide guidance and discipline for their children. The law generally is not involved in parents' daily exercise of control over their children, but two separate but related types of "failures" can bring parents into direct confrontation with the legal system. Court jurisdiction can be invoked when parents fail to control either the public behavior of their children or their own behavior in the course of disciplining their children.

In considering *juvenile justice,* the legal system may become involved with families whose children misbehave even if that misbehavior does not constitute actual crime. Historically, the legal system rendered identical treatment to children whose behavior was considered "criminal" as it did to *status offenders* whose behavior was considered "illegal" only because of their age (Note, 1974). Minors whose only offense was staying out late, disobeying parents, running away, being truant from school, or being "incorrigible" were subjected to the same juvenile proceedings and subsequent treatment alternatives, including incarceration, as those who had been violent. Although the Juvenile Justice and Delinquency Prevention Act of 1974 limited the use of incarceration as a disposition in status offense cases, status offenders still typically are subject to the jurisdiction of juvenile and family courts.

It is noteworthy that parents themselves often are the complainants in status offense cases. In such instances, parents use the courts to provide additional authority to assist them in their efforts to socialize their children. In effect, parents and state unite against—although in the interests of—the child. The ability of courts to resolve such family problems is questionable, however, and some states have altered their status offense statutes to make use of such jurisdiction a last resort contingent on trials of other family services (e.g., New Jersey Revised Statutes, 1987, establishing a "juvenile-family crisis intervention" system).

When law violations (delinquent offenses) are alleged, the procedures used in juvenile courts are generally comparable to those in adult criminal cases. However, juveniles often lack some of the rights available to adult defendants (e.g., the right to a jury trial; see *McKeiver v. Pennsylvania*, 1971), and the role of parents results in some unusual considerations. For example, *Gault* (*In re Gault*, 1966) requires notice of the charge to the juvenile *and* his or her parents.

The significance of parental involvement becomes apparent in the juvenile process even at the initial points of investigation and interrogation. Although the Fourth Amendment applies to juveniles as well as adults, juveniles' dependent status raises questions about their authority to exercise control over property in school lockers (see *New Jersey v. T.L.O.*, 1985) and their parent-owned home. Weinreb (1974), for example, has commented:

> It does not startle us that a parent's consent to a search of the living room in the absence of his minor child is given effect; but we should not allow the police to rely on the consent of the child to bind the parent. The common sense of the matter is that the host or parent has not surrendered his privacy of place in the living room to the discretion of the guest or child; rather, the latter have privacy of place there in the discretion of the former. (p. 60)

After a suspect has been taken into custody, police generally question him or her about the alleged offense. Although the Supreme Court has held that validity of juvenile respondents' waiver of the right to silence must be seen in the light of the totality of the circumstances (*Fare v. Michael C.*, 1979), research has shown juveniles to be both more likely to waive their rights and less likely to do so competently than adults (Grisso, 1980, 1981). Responding to these facts, some courts have treated a juvenile's request to see a parent as tantamount to an adult defendant's request for legal counsel (see, e.g., *People v. Burton*, 1971) and thus as invoking the right to silence under *Miranda v. Arizona* (1966). Others have required or strongly encouraged the presence of a parent during interrogation of juveniles (see Grisso, 1981, pp. 164-165, and citations therein). Such a requirement may be hollow protection, however, in view of evidence that parents often encourage their children to confess and that waivers of rights by juveniles are no less frequent when their parents are present (Grisso, 1981).

Parents also may be de facto adversaries of their children in juvenile court in other ways. For example, juvenile respondents may be kept in detention prior to an adjudication hearing if parents are unwilling or unable to accept them back into the home. An extreme example occurred in one urban juvenile court in which the practice was to detain status offenders with bail set at $1, payable only by a parent.

Although such power is used infrequently, courts do have authority to hold parents responsible, at least in part, for the misbehavior of their children. Such authority to *prosecute parents* arises in four ways.

First, most juvenile codes give courts authority to order particular parental actions as part of the disposition of a juvenile case (e.g., Texas Family Code Annotated, 1986b). Parents can be held in contempt of court for failure to comply with such an order (e.g., to participate in counseling).

Second, most states permit prosecution of parents for contributing to the delinquency of a minor if their actions caused or tended to cause such misbehavior (e.g., Texas Family Code Annotated, 1986c). Such laws may be applied, for example, if parents involve their children in activities (e.g., gambling, consuming alcoholic beverages, prostitution) that are illegal, at least for minors.

Third, parents may be civilly liable for torts (civil wrongs) committed by their children (e.g., California Civil Code, 1988). Parental liability laws reverse the common-law presumption that children, rather than their parents, are liable for their own torts. The low maximum limits of compensation (sometimes as low as $250) in such statutes serve as evidence that parental liability laws are not intended primarily to provide restitution to the victims whose losses often far exceed such amounts. Instead, parental liability laws are intended to curb delinquency by holding parents responsible and to place the burden for any losses on the parents, rather than directly on the victims of crime (Geis & Binder, 1991). Despite the widespread existence of such laws, they are applied rarely, perhaps because the parents of many young offenders are no more capable than their children of compensating victims for losses.

Fourth, states are attempting to hold parents directly responsible for status and delinquent offenses committed by their children. Unlike civil parental liability laws whose remedies are confined to financial remuneration, the newer parental responsibility laws criminalize parents' failure to control the conduct of their children, thus subjecting parents to criminal sanction (e.g., Street Terrorism Enforcement and Prevention Act, 1994). "Parental responsibility laws rest on the common legal presumption that the child's delinquent behavior ... is a consequence of poor parenting" (Humm, 1991, p. 1133). In essence, such laws hold that if a child commits a crime, the parent has committed a crime (Geis & Binder, 1991).

Primarily through newspaper accounts, the general public is becoming aware of "statutes [that] do not punish parents *for* their children's acts but *because* of the acts" (Weinstein, 1991, p. 867). We read about parents being fined or incarcerated—or at least threatened with such sanctions—for their children's chronic truancy, unlawful use of a firearm, and participation in gang-related crimes. Reduction of economic benefits as a result of such behavior also has become a plank in some welfare reform platforms.

Unfortunately, although parental responsibility laws may highlight when a parent has *not* met society's parenting expectations, they do not delineate what a parent *should* do in carrying out the socializing functions of parenthood. Little recognition is given to the realities of controlling the behavior of children as they grow older and come under the influence of many sources, other than parents (Humm, 1991, p. 1160). Even in the absence of scholarly or research evidence for what constitutes "good parenting," courts may be treading on areas of family privacy and discretion and establishing standards for childrearing when heretofore they have been reluctant to do so.

Parental responsibility laws have been criticized on a variety of additional grounds, including vagueness (Humm, 1991; Parsley, 1991; Weinstein, 1991), imposition of harsher penalties on accessories (parents) than on principals (children) (Humm, 1991; Weinstein, 1991), and disregard for due process rights of parents (Weinstein, 1991). Humm attacked the basic premise of the statutes:

Parental responsibility laws symbolize the frustration of a nation which does not know how to cope with the problems of its youth. Unable to contain juvenile violence and crime, legislators have begun to fashion vaguely written laws which grant sweeping authority to police and prosecutors to intervene in the affairs of the family. (p. 1160)

In short, although the law still seldom punishes parents for their children's misdeeds, public discussion of such measures now is commonplace. In effect, juvenile misbehavior is being conceptualized as a family problem—the product of parental irresponsibility—rather than a societal one.

There are myriad factors that influence children's development and shape them into adults. The law accords parents a central role in the processes through which these factors are given force. Formal education figures prominently in the lives of most children. Therefore, it is unsurprising that parents retain considerable decision-making authority as regards their children's formal education. Informal education (i.e., education of children that occurs in less formal settings) also is important. Thus, parents possess considerable legal latitude in their efforts to rear their children in accordance with the parents' own values. Even when the state *must* intervene—as does the juvenile justice system—parents still occupy a role of relative centrality.

CONCLUSIONS

The state has a compelling interest in the welfare of its youngest citizens. The state is concerned about both the status of children qua children and the status of children qua future adults. Childhood experience affects directly not only the child but also the adult the child will become. Thus, the laws and policies relating to childhood are oriented at once both to the present and to the future.

As important as nurturing "citizens" is, the state cannot rear its children. To do so would intrude excessively into the lives of children and their families. Moreover, however successful such a practice might be in inculcating the values of society as a whole, the individual values and mores of particular families would be lost—and with them, much of the richness and diversity that make us who we are as a people. Consequently, the responsibility of parenting is left appropriately to parents. However, because the interests at stake are so stark, it is perhaps unsurprising that government regulates parenthood, childhood, and family life more generally.

Although reference has been made to parenthood, childhood, and family as if they were patently obvious constructs, the law does not leave these matters to chance. Thus, the law defines who are a family and prescribes the corollary rights and obligations that attach to the respective roles (e.g., unwed fathers, noncustodial parents). The law delineates not only who provides support, but also who may receive it (e.g., natural children, stepchildren), for how long (e.g., disabled adult offspring), and for what purpose (e.g., postsecondary education). These laws reflect the kind of variability that one would expect to find when canvassing the product of over 50 different sovereigns struggling with and seeking to balance complex, significant, and often competing interests.

Despite the varying permutations of legal interests and approaches thereto that dot the landscape of child and family law, some consistent themes emerge. It is in the interest of the state and arguably everyone involved that children be kept alive and healthy. Consequently, laws that ostensibly maximize the outcome of treatment decision making are in place (e.g., parental consent laws and minor consent laws), and other laws may be invoked when the former fail (e.g., statutes providing for removal from the home for medical neglect). These laws dovetail nicely with statutes that require more generalized care in the form of provision of food, shelter, and clothing.

The provision of education to children is another consistent theme across all jurisdictions. Education is regarded as essential not only to the cultivation of self-sufficient and productive citizens, but also to the promotion of respect for others and the law—all of which are acute concerns of the state and fellow citizens. As a result, governments mandate school attendance, but accord some respect to parental decisions regarding what, where, and how long students must learn. This is especially so where parents have demonstrated that alternative educational approaches are equally efficacious in furthering state interests (e.g., *Wisconsin v. Yoder,* 1972).

No educational strategy, however, is guaranteed to further the interests of the state or anyone else. Some individuals either do not learn or do not embrace the values of the larger society. As is the case with treatment decision making, the law has a backup—the juvenile justice system. When parents, for whatever reason, cannot regulate the conduct of their children within certain boundaries, the juvenile justice system stands ready to supplant parental authority with the state's police power and/or the state's own parental powers (i.e., *parens patriae*). And in some states the backup has a backup. If punitive sanctions against children fail, punitive sanctions may be imposed against parents (parental responsibility laws).

Regulation of childhood, parenthood, and family life, as the preceding discussion makes clear, is extensive, but the law is self-limiting to a considerable degree. Previously we mentioned governments' obligation to refrain from intruding excessively into the private lives of families. Government interests must be weighed against parental autonomy and privacy. The need for good citizens is pitted against "the right to be let alone" (*Olmstead v. U.S.*, 1928, p. 478; Brandeis, J., dissenting). What we call "parenting" hangs in the balance.

REFERENCES

American Law Institute. (1934). *Restatement of the law of torts.* St. Paul, MN: American Law Institute Publishers.

Baker, J. S. (1988). Parent-centered education. *Notre Dame Journal of Law, Ethics, and Public Policy, 3,* 535–561.

Bartlett, K. T. (1988). Re-expressing parenthood. *Yale Law Journal, 98,* 293–334.

Belcher v. Charleston Area Medical Center, 422 S.E.2d 827 (W.Va. 1992).

Bellotti v. Baird, 443 U.S. 622 (1979).

Blue v. Blue, 616 A.2d 628 (Pa. 1992).

Brakel, S. J. (1985). Involuntary institutionalization. In S. J. Brakel, J. Parry, & B. A. Weiner (Eds.), *The mentally disabled and the law* (3rd ed., pp. 21–176). Chicago: American Bar Foundation.

Burlingame, W. V., & Amaya, M. (1985). Psychiatric commitment of children and adolescents: Issues current practices, and clinical impact. In D. H. Schetky & E. P. Benedeek (Eds.), *Emerging issues in child psychiatry and the law* (pp. 229–249). New York: Brunner/Mazel.

Cal. Civ. Code § 1714.1 (West 1988).

Cal. Fam. Code § 8815(d) (West Supp. 1994).

Cal. Pen. Code § 270 (West 1988a).

Cal. Pen. Code § 273a(1) (West 1988b).

Cal. Welf. & Inst. Code § 300(b) (West 1984 & Supp. 1994).

Carey v. Population Services International, 431 U.S. 678 (1977).

Cebrzynski v. Cebrzynski, 379 N.E.2d 713 (1978).

Chambers, D. L. (1984). Rethinking the substantive rules for custody disputes in divorce. *Michigan Law Review, 83,* 477–569.

Childers v. Childers, 89 Wn.2d 592, 575 P.2d 201 (1978).

City of Akron v. Akron Center for Reproductive Health, Inc., 462 U.S. 416 (1983).

City of Ladue v. Horn, 720 S.W.2d 745 (Mo. App. 1986).

Clune, W. H., & Van Pelt, M. H. (1985). A political method of evaluating the Education for all Handicapped Children Act of 1975 and the several gaps of analysis. *Law and Contemporary Problems, 48*(1), 7–62.

Cornwell v. State Board of Education, 314 F.Supp 340 (D. Md. 1969).

Desiato v. Abbott, 617 A.2d 678 (N.J. Super. Ct. Ch. Div. 1992).

Dickson, J. H. (1991). The emerging rights of adoptive parents: Substance or specter? *UCLA Law Review, 38,* 917–990.

Education for All Handicapped Children Act of 1975, Pub. L. No. 94–142, 89 Stat. 773 (1975) (codified as amended at 20 U.S.C. §§ 1400–1485) (1988 & Supp. IV 1992).

Education of the Handicapped Act, Pub. L. No. 91–230, 84 Stat. 121 (1970) (codified as amended at 20 U.S.C. §§ 1400–1485) (1988 & Supp. IV 1992).

Family Educational Rights and Privacy Act, 20 U.S.C. § 1232g (1990 & Supp. 1991).

Fare v. Michael C., 442 U.S. 707 (1979).

Friedman, S. E. (1992). *The law of parent–child relationships: A handbook.* Chicago: American Bar Association.

Garska v. McCoy, 278 S.E.2d 357 (1981).

Geis, G., & Binder, A. (1991). Sins of their children: Parental responsibility for juvenile delinquency. *Notre Dame Journal of Law, Ethics, and Public Policy, 5*(2), 303–322.

Goldstein, J., Freud, A., & Solnit, A. J. (1973). *Beyond the best interests of the child.* New York: Macmillan.

Goss v. Lopez, 419 U.S. 565 (1975).

Grisso, T. (1980). Juveniles' capacities to waive *Miranda* rights: An empirical analysis. *California Law Review, 68,* 1135–1166.

Grisso, T. (1981). *Juveniles' waiver of rights: Legal and psychological competence.* New York: Plenum.

Harris, L. J., Waldrop, K., & Waldrop, L. R. (1990). Making and breaking connections between parents' duty to support and right to control their children. *Oregon Law Review, 69,* 689–739.

Hatch Amendment [to the Family Educational Rights and Privacy Act], 20 U.S.C. § 1232h (1990 & Supp. 1991).

Hill, J. H. (1991). What does it mean to be a "parent"? The claims of biology as the basis for parental rights. *New York University Law Review, 66,* 353–420.

Hodgson v. Minnesota, 497 U.S. 417 (1990).

Holder, A. R. (1985). *Legal issues in pediatric and adolescent medicine.* New Haven, CT: Yale University Press.

Humm, S. R. (1991). Criminalizing poor parenting skills as a means to contain violence by and against children. *University of Pennsylvania Law Review, 139,* 1123–1161.

Ill. Rev. Stat. ch. 750, ¶ 5/510(d) (1993 & Supp. 1994).

In re Ackenhausen, 244 La. 730 (La. 1963).

In re Adoption of Tachick, 210 N.W.2d 865 (Wis. 1973).

In re Gault, 387 U.S. 1 (1967).

In re Phillip B., 92 Cal.App.3d 796, *cert. denied sub nom.* 445 U.S. 949 (1980).

In re Raquel Marie X, 559 N.E.2d 418 (N.Y. 1990).

In re Roger S., 569 P.2d 1286 (Cal. 1977).

Individuals with Disabilities Education Act, Pub. L. No. 101-476, 104 Stat. 1141 (1990) (codified as amended at 20 U.S.C. §§ 1400-1485) (Supp. IV 1992).

Ingraham v. Wright, 430 U.S. 651 (1977).

Jackson-Beeck, M., Schwartz, I. M., & Rutherford, A (1987). Trends and issues in juvenile confinement for psychiatric and chemical dependency treatment. *International Journal of Law and Psychiatry, 10,* 153–165.

Jhordan C. v. Mary K., 224 Cal.Rptr. 530 (Cal. Ct. App. 1986).

Johnson, S. L. (1987). Parent and child. *American Jurisprudence (2nd), 59,* 129–279.

Juvenile Justice and Delinquency Prevention Act of 1974, 42 U.S.C. 5601-5640 (1983 & Supp. 1994).

Katz, S. N., Schroeder, W. A., & Sidman, L. R. (1973). Emancipating our children: Coming of legal age in America. *Family Law Quarterly, 7,* 211–241.

Kost v. Kost, 1994 WL 141062 (S.D. 1994).

Levine, M., Ewing, C. P., & Hager, R. (1987). Juvenile and family mental health law in sociohistorical context. *International Journal of Law and Psychiatry, 10,* 167–184.

McKeiver v. Pennsylvania, 403 U.S. 528 (1971).

Melton, G. B. (1984). Family and mental hospitals as myths: Civil commitment of minors. In N. D. Reppucci, L. A. Weithorn, E. P. Mulvey, & J. Monahan (Eds.), *Children, mental health, and the law* (pp. 151–167). Beverly Hills, CA: Sage.

Melton, G. B. (1992). Respecting boundaries: Minors, privacy, and behavioral research. In B. Stanley & J. E. Sieber (Eds.), *Social research on children and adolescents* (pp. 65–87). Newbury Park, CA: Sage.

Merriken v. Cressman, 364 F.Supp. 913 (E.D. Pa. 1973).

Meyer v. Nebraska, 262 U.S. 390 (1923).

Michael H. v. Gerald D., 491 U.S. 110 (1989).

Minow, M. (1991). Redefining families: Who's in and who's out? *Colorado Law Review, 62,* 269–285.

Miranda v. Arizona, 384 U.S. 436 (1966).

Mnookin, R. H., & Weisberg, D. K. (1989). *Child, family and state: Problems and materials on children and the law* (2nd ed.). Boston: Little, Brown.

Mo. Ann. Stat. § 452.340.5 (Supp. 1994).

Neely, R. (1984). The primary caretaker rule: Child custody and the dynamics of greed. *Yale Law and Policy Review, 3,* 168–186.

New Jersey v. T.L.O., 469 U.S. 325 (1985).

Newburgh v. Arrigo, 443 A.2d 1031 (N.J. 1982).

N.H. Rev. Stat. Ann. § 546–A:2 (1974).

N.J. Rev. Stat. §§ 2A:4A-76-2A:4A-87 (1987).

Nolfo v. Nolfo, 188 A.D.2d 451 (N.Y. App. Div. 1992).

Note. (1974). Ungovernability: The unjustifiable jurisdiction. *Yale Law Journal, 83*(7), 1383–1409.

Note. (1991). Looking for a family resemblance: The limits of the functional approach to the legal definition of family. *Harvard Law Review, 104,* 1640–1659.

Ohio v. Akron Center for Reproductive Health, 497 U.S. 502 (1990).

Olmstead v. U.S., 277 U.S. 438 (1928).

Or. Rev. Stat. § 109.103 (1993).

Painter v. Bannister, 140 N.W.2d 152 (Wis. 1966).

Parham v. J. R., 442 U.S. 584 (1979).

Park v. Park, 309 N.W.2d 827 (S.D. 1981).

Parsley, K. J. (1991). Constitutional limitations on state power to hold parents criminally liable for the delinquent acts of their children. *Vanderbilt Law Review, 44,* 441–472.

People v. Burton, 6 Cal.3d 375 (1971).

Pierce v. Society of Sisters, 268 U.S. 510 (1925).

Planned Parenthood of Central Missouri v. Danforth, 428 U.S. 52 (1976).

Planned Parenthood of Southeastern Pennsylvania v. Casey, 112 S.Ct. 2791 (1992).

Rhinehart v. Nowlin, 805 P.2d 88, 94 (N.M. Ct. App. 1990).

Rodham, H. (1973). Children under the law. *Harvard Education Review, 43,* 487–514.

Roe v. Doe, 29 N.Y.2d 188 (1971).

Rozovsky, F. A. (1984). *Consent to treatment: A practical guide.* Boston: Little, Brown.

San Antonio Independent School District v. Rodriguez, 411 U.S. 1 (1973).

Santosky v. Kramer, 455 U.S. 745 (1982).

Schall v. Martin, 467 U.S. 253 (1984).

Schuele, D. (1988–1989). Origins and development of the law of parental child support. *Journal of Family Law, 27,* 807–841.

Shoecraft v. Catholic Social Services Bureau, Inc., 385 N.W. 2d 448 (Neb. 1986).

Smith, S. H. (1978). Psychological parents versus biological parents: The courts' response to new directions in child custody dispute resolution. *Journal of Family Law, 17,* 545–576.

Stanford v. Kentucky, 492 U.S. 361 (1989).

Stanley v. Illinois, 405 U.S. 645 (1972).

Street Terrorism Enforcement and Prevention Act, Cal. Penal Code §§ 186.20-186.28 (West Supp 1994).

Succession of Terry, 624 So.2d 1201 (La. 1993).

Tex. Fam. Code Ann. § 12.04(3) (West 1986a).

Tex. Fam. Code Ann. § 54.041(a)(1)) (West 1986b).

Tex. Fam. Code Ann. § 72.002(a) (West 1986c).

Thompson, R. A., Scalora, M. J., Castrianno, L., & Limber, S. P. (1992). Grandparent visitation rights: Emergent psychological and psycholegal issues. In D. K. Kagehiro & D. S. Laufer (Eds.), *Handbook of psychology and law* (pp. 292–317). New York: Springer-Verlag.

Thompson v. Oklahoma, 487 U.S. 815 (1988).

Tinker v. DesMoines Independent School District, 393 U.S. 503 (1969).

Tweedie, J. (1989). Parental rights and accountability in public education: Special education and choice. *Yale Law and Policy Review, 7,* 396–418.

Uniform Parentage Act (1973), § 4, 9B U.L.A. 287, 298-299.

Uniform Putative and Unknown Fathers Act (1988), § 1, 9B U.L.A. 22 (Supp. 1990).

Va. Code Ann. § 54.1-2969D (Michie Supp. 1993).

Valente, W. D. (1985 & Supp. 1989). *Education and law: Public and private.* St. Paul, MN: West.

W. Va. Code § 48-2-15 (Supp. 1993).

Wadlington, W. (1990). *Cases and other materials on domestic relations.* Westbury, NY: Foundation Press.

Wald, P. (1980). Introduction to the juvenile justice process: The rights of children and the rites of passage. In D. H. Schetky & E. P. Benedek (Eds.), *Child psychiatry and the law* (pp. 9–20). New York: Brunner/Mazel.

Wallin v. Wallin, 187 N.W.2d 627, 630 (Minn. 1971).

Wash. Rev. Code § 26.09.100 (1986).

Weinreb, L. L. (1974). Generalities of the Fourth Amendment. *University of Chicago Law Review, 42,* 47–85.

Weinstein, T. (1991). Visiting the sins of the child on the parent: The legality of criminal parental liability statutes. *Southern California Law Review, 64,* 859–901.

Weithorn, L. A. (1985). Children's capacities for participation in treatment decision-making. In D. H. Schetky & E. P. Benedek (Eds.), *Emerging issues in child psychiatry and the law* (pp. 22–36). New York: Brunner/Mazel.

Weithorn, L. A., & McCabe, M. A. (1988). Legal and other problems in pediatric psychology. In D. K. Routh (Ed.), *Handbook of pediatric psychology* (pp. 567–606). New York: Guilford.

Wisconsin v. Yoder, 406 U.S. 205 (1972).

Zinman, D. C. (1992). Father knows best: The unwed father's right to raise his infant surrendered for adoption. *Fordham Law Review, 60,* 971–1001.

Author Index

Subject Index

About the Authors

VIRGINIA D. ALLHUSEN is a research associate in the Department of Psychology and Social Behavior, School of Social Ecology, at the University of California. She earned a BS at Duke University and an MA and PhD at Cornell University. She is site coordinator for the California site of the NICHD Study of Early Child Care. She is a member of the American Psychological Association, the Society for Research in Child Development, and the National Association for the Education of Young Children. Her research interests include children's attachment relationships with parents and other care providers, day-care quality and its effects on social development, and the social networks of young children and their families.

* * *

KATHRYN E. BARNARD is a professor of nursing and psychology and affiliate of the Child Development and Mental Retardation Center at the University of Washington. She received her BS in nursing at the University of Nebraska, her MSN at Boston University and her PhD in the ecology of early child development from the University of Washington. She is a fellow in the Institute of Medicine and the American Academy of Nursing. She is a member of the American Nurses Association, Society for Research in Child Development, American Public Health Association. She is on the board and past president of the Zero-to-Three: National Center for Clinical Infant Programs. She has been active in the World Association for Infant Mental Health. Her research efforts have been on parenting, high-risk conditions of children, both biological and environmental. She has been studying mother–infant interaction and has for the past 20 years been involved in research studies to evaluate early intervention and preventive efforts. She has received awards for her contributions to research from the American Nurses Association, American Public Health Association, Academy of Pediatrics, and Sigma Theta Tau. She is author of many research publications, and serves on the Advisory board of the *Infant Mental Health Journal* and *Nursing Scholarship*.

* * *

DAVID M. BRODZINSKY is associate professor of Clinical and Developmental Psychology at Rutgers University. He received his PhD from the State University of New York, Buffalo. Brodzinsky is a past vice president of the Jean Piaget Society. He is director of the Rutgers Foster Care Counseling Project and maintains a private practice in clinical psychology with a primary focus on children and families. His major research and professional interests include the psychology of adoption and foster care, stress and coping in children, developmental psychopathology, and the relation between psychology and the law. Brodzinsky is co-author of *Being Adopted: The Lifelong Search for Self* and *Lifespan Human Development*, and he is co-editor of *The Psychology of Adoption* and *Thinking About the Family: Views of Parents and Children*.

* * *

JEANNE BROOKS-GUNN is Virginia and Leonard Marx Professor in Child Development at Teachers College and Professor of Pediatrics at the College of Physicians & Surgeons, Columbia University. She is also director of the Center for Children and Families and the Adolescent Study Program at Columbia University. She received her PhD from the University of Pennsylvania, an EdM from Harvard University, and a BA from Connecticut College. Brooks-Gunn is president of the Society for Research in Adolescence and is a member of the National Academy of Sciences panel on Child Abuse and Neglect as well as the Panel of Defining Poverty. Her research focuses on transitions during childhood and adolescence, intergenerational transmission of parenting behavior and beliefs, policy research on poverty, and interventions including parents as well as children and/or adolescents. She co-edited *Depression in Adolescence, Transitions Through Adolescence: Interpersonal and Contextual Issues,* and *Escape From Poverty: What Makes a Difference for Children?*

* * *

P. LINDSAY CHASE-LANSDALE is assistant professor in the Irving B. Harris Graduate School of Public Policy Studies and faculty associate at the Center for the Study of Urban Inequality, the Chapin Hall Center for Children, and the Population Research Center at the University of Chicago. She received her BA from Harvard University and Radcliffe College and her PhD from the University of Michigan. Her research focuses on how societal condition affect the emotional and cognitive development of children and the well-being of families, including such topics as poverty, adolescent parenthood, community revitalization, divorce, and maternal employment. Chase-Lansdale serves on the board of the Foundation for Child Development, the Technical Review Panel for the National Longitudinal Surveys of Labor Market Experience, and on the governing council of the Society for Research on Adolescence. She recently edited *Escape From Poverty: What Makes a Difference for Children?*

* * *

K. ALISON CLARKE-STEWART is professor in the Department of Psychology and Social Behavior, School of Social Ecology, at the University of California, Irvine. She received her BA and MA at the University of British Columbia and PhD at Yale University. Clarke-Stewart was assistant professor at the University of Chicago's Department of Education and the Committee on Human Development. She is a fellow of the American Psychological Association and the American Psychological Society, and a member of the Society for Research in Child Development and the National Association for the Education of Young Children. Her research interests include the study of family interactions, day care, divorce and child custody, and children's eyewitness testimony. She is a principal investigator in the NICHD Study of Early Child Care. Clarke-Stewart is author of *Daycare* and *Children at Home and in Day Care.*

* * *

DARLENE C. CLEMENTS received her BA at Hofstra University in New York and MA and PhD at the University of California, Los Angeles. She is a member of the Society for Research in Child Development. Her research includes adult–child attachment, day care, and peer relationships and interaction. She was project coordinator for the California site of the NICHD Study of Early Child Care in 1992–1993.

* * *

MONCRIEFF COCHRAN is professor of human development and family studies in the College of Human Ecology at Cornell University. Cochran received his AB from Harvard College and MA and PhD from the University of Michigan. Cochran's research interests relate to environmental systems affecting parent and child development, and his program development activities involve empowerment-oriented family support programs based on that research. The content of his research and program development work includes child care, home–school relations, the social networks of parents and children, and the empowerment process. Cochran has co-authored *Extending Families: The Social Networks of Parents and their Children* and edited the *International Handbook of Child Care Policies and Programs.*

* * *

JAMES GARBARINO is president of the Erikson Institute for Advanced Study in Child Development. He earned his PhD in Human Development and Family Studies from Cornell University and his BA from St. Lawrence University. Awards he has won include the Brandt F. Steele Award from the Kempe National Center on Child Abuse and Neglect, the Society for Psychological Study of Social Issues prize for research on child abuse, the American Psychological Association's Award for Distinguished Professional Contributions to Public Service, and the American Humane's Association's Vincent De Francis Award for nationally significant contributions to child protection. He is the author of *Let's Talk About Living in a World with Violence*; *Children in Danger: Coping with the Consequences of Community Violence*; *Towards a Sustainable Society: An Economic, Social, and Environmental Agenda for our Children's Future*; *Children and Families in the Social Environment*; *No Place to Be a Child: Growing Up in a War Zone*; *What Children Can Tell Us*; *The Psychologically Battered Child*; *Troubled Youth, Troubled Families*; *Adolescent Development: An Ecological Perspective*; *Protecting Children From Abuse and Neglect*; and *Understanding Abusive Families*.

* * *

JACQUELINE JARRETT GOODNOW is a professorial research fellow at Macquarie University, Sydney, Australia. She obtained her BA from the University of Sydney and her PhD from Harvard. Previous positions were held at the University of Sydney, Harvard, Walter Reed Institute of Research, and George Washington University. Her work has consistently displayed a twin concern with cognition, broadly defined, and with the role of social context (familial or cultural). The cognitive emphasis is especially clear in research on studies of concept attainment by adults and drawings by children. The blending of both concerns is apparent in work with an increasingly familial emphasis: work dealing with the social issues that affect families and women and children's views of everyday life; and parents' views of parenting, child development, and family divisions of labor. The basic assumption throughout her work is that the analysis of any behavior—parenting being one of these—benefits from attention to the way people frame tasks, perceive options, and operate from some set of goals and principles. Even apparently bizarre behavior, Goodnow argues, displays an order when one comes to understand these cognitive aspects and to uncover the individual's viewpoint. Goodnow is co-author or co-editor of *A Study of Thinking*; *Children Drawing*; *Children and Families in Australia*; *Women, Social Science, and Social Policy*; *Home and School: Child's-Eye Views*; *Development According to Parents*; *Parental Belief Systems* (2nd edition); and *Men, Women, and Household Work*.

* * *

MARCY B. GRINGLAS is an instructor in the Department of Pediatrics at Thomas Jefferson University Hospital and a staff psychologist at the Children's Rehabilitation Hospital in Philadelphia. She received her BM from Indiana University in Bloomington, her MA from Columbia University, and her PhD from Temple University. Gringlas is a member of the American Psychological Association, the Society for Research in Child Development, and the National Center for Clinical Infant Programs.

* * *

CHRISTOPH M. HEINICKE is professor in the Department of Psychiatry and Biobehavioral Sciences and director of the Family Development Project at the University of California, Los Angeles. Heinicke received his PhD from Harvard University. His clinical training began at the Anna Freud Hampstead Clinic, London, where he collaborated with Bowlby in the study of the effects of mother–child separation. Heinicke has focused his career on using sociobehavioral methodology to test hypotheses shaped by clinical and family–child observations. He has studied child outcomes of psychotherapy; how casework combines with individualized day care to affect child development; prebirth parent personality and marital characteristics that impact early family development; and optimal conditions of home interventions to enhance family development of first-time mothers identified as being at risk for neglecting and abusing children. Heinicke's book *Brief Separation* was awarded the Lester Hoffheimer Prize for research in psychiatry.

* * *

E. MAVIS HETHERINGTON is James M. Page professor of psychology at the University of Virginia. She received her BA and MA from the University of British Columbia and her PhD from the University of California, Berkeley. After practicing as a clinical psychologist, Hetherington taught at Rutgers University and at the University of Wisconsin before coming to Virginia. Her research concerns personality and social development, childhood psychopathology, and stress and coping in children and families as well as divorce, one-parent families, and remarriage. Hetherington served as editor of *Child Development* and as president of Division 7 of the American Psychological Association (APA), the Society for Research in Child Development (SRCD), and the Society for Research in Adolescence (SRA). She has received the G. Stanley Hall Distinguished Scientist Award and the Distinguished Teaching in Psychology Award (APA), the University of Virginia's Thomas Jefferson Award, the Distinguished Scientist Award (SRA), and the William James Distinguished Scientist Award (American Psychological Society). Her recent books include *Advances in Family Research: Vol. 2. Family Transitions,* an SRCD monograph "Coping with Marital Transitions," and *Separate Social Worlds of Siblings.*

* * *

GEORGE W. HOLDEN is associate professor in the Department of Psychology at the University of Texas, Austin. Holden received his BA from Yale University and MA and PhD from the University of North Carolina, Chapel Hill. Since earning his degree in developmental psychology with a minor in social psychology, he has been on the faculty at the University of Texas. He has served on the editorial board of *Child Development.* Holden's research interests are int he area of social development with a focus on parent–child relations. He is especially interested in understanding the determinants of parental behavior, parental social cognition, and methodological issues related to the study of parents. Some of his recent research investigates how spousal violence affects parenting and children's development. His research has been supported by grants from the National Institute of Child Health and Human Development, the Guggenheim Foundation, and the Hogg Foundation for Mental Health. He is author of numerous scientific papers and chapters and he is currently completing a book on parent–child relationships.

* * *

KATHLEEN KOSTELNY is a research associate at the Erikson Institute for Advanced Study in Child Development. She received her PhD in child development from Erikson Institute/Loyola University, her MA from the University of Chicago, and her BA from Bethel College. She has worked as a research analyst at the National Committee for Prevention of Child Abuse and as a counselor for emotionally disturbed children at the University of Chicago's Orthogenic School. Kostelny has conducted research on children and families living in dangerous environments, including Cambodia, Nicaragua, Mozambique, Northern Ireland, the Israeli Occupied Territories, and inner-city Chicago. She is co-author of *Children in Danger: Coping with the Consequences of Community Violence* and *No Place to Be a Child: Growing up in a War Zone.*

* * *

ROBIN LANG is a staff psychologist at CPC Behavioral Healthcare in red Bank, New Jersey. She received her PsyD in clinical psychology from the Graduate School of Applied and Professional Psychology at Rutgers University. Her primary research and professional interests are related to adoption, foster care, and developmental psychopathology.

* * *

PHILLIP M. LYONS, JR. is assistant professor of criminal justice at Sam Houston State University. He has earned degrees from the University of Houston, Clear Lake (BS) and the University of Nebraska, Lincoln (JD, MA), where he is completing his PhD in forensic clinical psychology. Lyons was a patrol officer and a detective specializing in crimes involving children. He has written about the influence of physical attractiveness in legal decision making, children's perceptions of child abuse, and dilemmas in AIDS research. Other areas of his interests include mentally disordered sex offenders, community policing, child abuse, and freedom of thought and expression.

* * *

LOUISE K. MARTELL is assistant professor in the Department of Parent Child Nursing, at the University of Washington. She received a diploma in Nursing from the Massachusetts General Hospital School of Nursing, her BS from Northern Illinois University, her BSN from the Oregon Health Sciences University, MN from the University of Washington, and PhD from Oregon State University in human development and family science. She was previously affiliated with Oregon Health Sciences University and the Intercollegiate Center for Nursing Education in Spokane, Washington. She is a member of the National Council on Family Relations. Currently her research interests are health needs of childbearing families and the transition to parenthood.

* * *

ANN V. MCGILLICUDDY-DE LISI is associate professor in the Department of Psychology, Lafayette College. McGillicuddy-De Lisi received her PhD from the Catholic University of America. She was formerly a research associate at Educational Testing Service. Her research interests include the effects of the family environment on children's and parents' development, development of spatial concepts in males and females, gender and science, and the nature and influence of parental beliefs about children. She co-edited *Parental Belief Systems: The Psychological Consequences for Children* (2nd edition).

* * *

GARY B. MELTON is director of the Institute for Families in Society at the University of South Carolina, where he also is professor of neuropsychiatry, law, and psychology. He was educated at the University of Virginia (BA) and Boston University (PhD). He is a past president of the American Psychological Association (APA) Division of Child, Youth, and Family Services, and the American Psychology–Law Society and past vice-chair of the U.S. Advisory Board on Child Abuse and Neglect. Melton has received awards for distinguished contributions to the public interest from APA, the APA Division of Child, Youth, and Family Services, the APA Division of Psychologists in Public Service, Psi Chi, and the National Committee to Prevent Child Abuse. Melton's research and consultation extend to the various domains of law affecting children and families. His current work relates to service system development, the process of policymaking and implementation, child protection, violence prevention, and international developments, especially in children's rights. His work as been cited by a number of courts including the U.S. Supreme Court. Melton is the author or editor of numerous books and book chapters as well as articles that have appeared in both social science journals and law reviews.

* * *

STARR NIEGO received her PhD from the Department of Human Development and Family Studies at Cornell University in 1994. After completing a BA at Williams College, Niego worked for women's research, advocacy, and service organizations in New York, investigating such issues as child care and career advancement. At Cornell, Niego pursued research in the areas of families and social networks and female adolescent development. For her MA, she looked at the ways in which family networks serve as a system of support for parents rearing young children. Niego engaged in a collaborative investigation of identity and critical consciousness with high school girls. Linking her diverse projects is the goal of combining theory and practice to facilitate individual and social change.

* * *

PAULINE M. PAGLIOCCA is assistant professor of psychology at Tulane University. She received her PhD from the University of Virginia. Pagliocca completed a clinical internship and an advanced fellowship in psychological trauma at Cambridge Hospital/Harvard Medical School and then served as a postdoctoral research fellow at the Center on Children, Families and the Law at the University of Nebraska, Lincoln. Pagliocca was a public school teacher, teacher trainer, and educational administrator in the juvenile justice field. She is the co-founder and former director of the Community Crisis Response Team in Boston. Her general research interests relate to children and the law and psychological trauma, and she has conducted studies of delinquency diversion programs and decision making in juvenile courts.

* * *

ROSS D. PARKE is professor of psychology and director of the Center for Family Studies at the University of California, Riverside. Parke was educated at the universities of Toronto and Waterloo and previously was affiliated with the universities of Wisconsin and Illinois and the Fels Research Institute. His is a past president of Division 7, the Developmental Psychology Division of the American Psychological Association. He has been editor of *Developmental Psychology* and associate editor of *Child Development*. Parke is author of *Fathers* and co-author of *Child Psychology: A Comtemporary Viewpoint* (4th edition).

* * *

CHARLOTTE J. PATTERSON is associate professor of psychology at the University of Virginia. She received her PhD from Stanford University. Patterson has served on the editorial boards of *Child Development*, *Developmental Psychology, Merrill–Palmer Quarterly of Human Development*, and the *Journal of Social and Personal Relationships*. She studies social and personality development among children and adolescents. Her Bay Area Families Study is an ongoing investigation of psychosocial development among children who were born to or adopted by lesbian mothers. Patterson is co-editor of *Lesbian, Gay and Bisexual Identities across the Lifespan* (Oxford University Press, 1995), and she is also guest editor for a 1995 special issue of *Developmental Psychology* devoted to sexual orientation and human development.

* * *

IRVING E. SIGEL is distinguished research scientist (emeritus) at Educational Testing Service. Sigel received his BA from Clark University and PhD from the University of Chicago. His past positions were at Michigan State University, Wayne State University, The Merrill–Palmer Institute, and the State University of New York at Buffalo. Sigel was president of Division 7, APA and president of the Jean Piaget Society. His interests include cognition and social development in sociocultural contexts. He is editor of the *Journal of Applied Developmental Psychology* and of the *Advances in Applied Developmental Psychology*. Sigel co-authored *Cognitive Development from Childhood to Adolescence: A Constructivist Perspective*. He is editor of *Parental Belief Systems: The Psychological Consequences for Children* (1st edition), and co-editor of *Methods of Family Research* (volumes 1 and 2), *Changing Families*, and *Parental Belief Systems: The Psychological Consequences for Children* (2nd edition).

* * *

DANIEL SMITH is a postdoctoral fellow at the Crime Victims Center of the Medical University of South Carolina. He received his PhD from Rutgers University. His primary research and professional interests include adoption, foster care, child abuse, the psychology of trauma, and developmental psychopathology.

* * *

PETER K. SMITH is a professor at the Department of Psychology, University of Sheffield, England. He was educated at Oxford and Cambridge Universities, and obtained his PhD at Sheffield University. A fellow of the British Psychological Society, Smith is European editor of *Ethology and Sociobiology* and an associate editor of the *International Journal of Behavioural Development*. He has researched widely in children's development, especially using observational methods and ethological perspectives. He is co-author of *Understanding Children's Development* and *The Ecology of Children's Behaviour*. He edited *Play in Animals and Humans* and *Children's Play: Theoretical Perspectives and Practical Applications,* and co-edited *Practical Approaches to Bullying* and *School Bullying: Insights and Perspectives*. Smith also has interests in three-generation relationships and cooperation and conflict among grandparents, parents, and (grand)children, and he edited *The Psychology of Grantparenthood: An International Perspective.*

* * *

MARGARET M. STANLEY-HAGEN is an associate professor of psychology at the University of North Carolina, Charlotte. She completed her PhD at the University of Virginia. Her research focuses on individual differences in coping with life stresses and the personal, family, and community factors that facilitate or impede coping. She studies relationships and adjustment in families experiencing marital transitions and has published on family relationships within divorced and remarried families. Stanley-Hagen works with a Charlotte-based intervention program that coordinates community-based services to improve the family and community lives of poor preschool children who are at risk for school failure.

* * *

MARSHA WEINRAUB is a professor in the Department of Psychology, College of Arts and Sciences, at Temple University. She received her BA at Brandeis University and her PhD at the University of Michigan. She is a fellow of the American Psychological Association, the American Psychological Society, and a member of the Society for Research in Child Development. Weinraub has served on the editorial boards of *Child Development* and *Psychology of Women*. She has published several papers in the areas of infant attachment, family interactions, day care, and gender role development. Currently, she is a principal investigator in the NICHD Study of Early Child Care.

* * *

VICTORIA WEISZ is research assistant professor of psychology in the Center on Children, Families, and the Law at the University of Nebraska, Lincoln. Weisz was educated at the University of Rochester (BA), Washington University (PhD), and the University of Nebraska, Lincoln (master of legal studies). She currently has a private clinical psychology practice that includes the assessment and treatment of children, families, and adults. Weisz also conducts custody evaluations and other legal assessments that involve children. She currently is researching the psychosocial impact of bone marrow donation on children and adolescents, the psychosocial needs of traumatized refugee children, and the psycholegal issues involved in children's participation in custody decision making in divorce.

* * *

PATRICIA ZUKOW-GOLDRING is adjunct assistant professor in the School of Social Ecology, University of California, Irvine. She received her doctorate from the University of California, Los Angeles, obtained a 2-year National Institute of Mental Health postdoctorate to conduct fieldwork in Central Mexico, and held positions at the University of Southern California and the University of California, Los Angeles. Her research focuses on the emergence of play and language based on several longitudinal studies conducted in the United States among Latino and Euro-American families and in Central Mexico. Currently she is investigating the processes that guide perceiving, acting, and knowing both at home and at school. She is editor of *Sibling Interaction Across Cultures* and co-editor of *The Idea of Innateness: Effects on Language and Communication Research* and *Changing Ecological Approaches to Development: Organism–Environment Mutualities*.

* * *

A30-73